An Anthology of
# Canadian Literature
## in English

Third Edition

# An Anthology of
# Canadian Literature
# in English

Edited by

**Donna Bennett** and **Russell Brown**

## OXFORD
UNIVERSITY PRESS

# OXFORD
### UNIVERSITY PRESS

8 Sampson Mews, Suite 204, Don Mills, ON M3C 0H5
www.oupcanada.com

Oxford University Press is a department of the University of Oxford.
It furthers the University's objective of excellence in research, scholarship,
and education by publishing worldwide in

Oxford   New York

Auckland   Cape Town   Dar es Salaam   Hong Kong   Karachi
Kuala Lumpur   Madrid   Melbourne   Mexico City   Nairobi
New Delhi   Shanghai   Taipei   Toronto

With offices in

Argentina   Austria   Brazil   Chile   Czech Republic   France   Greece
Guatemala   Hungary   Italy   Japan   Poland   Portugal   Singapore
South Korea   Switzerland   Thailand   Turkey   Ukraine   Vietnam

Oxford is a trade mark of Oxford University Press
in the UK and in certain other countries

Published in Canada
by Oxford University Press

**Library and Archives Canada Cataloguing in Publication Data**

An anthology of Canadian literature in English / edited by Donna Bennett and Russell Brown.— 3rd ed.

Previous ed. published under title: A new anthology of Canadian literature in English.
Includes index.
ISBN 978-0-19-542781-3

1. Canadian literature (English).   I. Bennett, Donna, 1945–   .   II. Brown, Russell, 1942–   .
III. Title: Canadian literature in English.   IV. Title: New anthology of Canadian literature in English.

PS8233.A57 2010        C810.8        C2009-906155-4

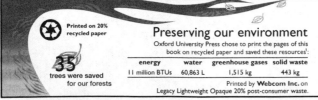

Printed on 20%
recycled paper

**35**

trees were saved
for our forests

### Preserving our environment

Oxford University Press chose to print the pages of this
book on recycled paper and saved these resources[1]:

| energy | water | greenhouse gases | solid waste |
| --- | --- | --- | --- |
| 11 million BTUs | 60,863 L | 1,515 kg | 443 kg |

Printed by **Webcom Inc.** on
Legacy Lightweight Opaque 20% post-consumer waste.

**FSC**

**Mixed Sources**
Product group from well-managed
forests, controlled sources and
recycled wood or fiber

Cert no. SW-COC-002358
www.fsc.org
© 1996 Forest Stewardship Council

[1]Estimates were made using the Environmental Defense Paper Calculator.

Oxford University Press is committed to our environment. The pages of this book have
been printed on paper which has been certified by the Forest Stewardship Council
(© 1996 FSC, Cert. no. SW-COC-002358), and which contains 20% post-consumer waste.

Printed and bound in Canada.

1 2 3 4 — 13 12 11 10

# Contents

PREFACE  xiii

INTRODUCTION  xvii

SAUKAMAPEE  1
[Life among the Peigans]  2

FRANCIS BROOKE  10
From *The History of Emily Montague*
    Letter 1  11
    Letter 10  12
    Letter 11  14
    Letter 49  19
    Letter 80  20
    Letter 123  22
    Letter 127  24
    Letter 131  24
    Letter 169  26

SAMUEL HEARNE  27
From *A Journey from Prince of Wales's Fort
    in Hudson's Bay to the Northern Ocean*  29

DAVID THOMPSON  37
From *Narrative of His Explorations in
    Western North America, 1784–1812*
    [Nahathaway Indians]  38
    [Life Among the Nahathaways]  42

OLIVER GOLDSMITH  50
The Rising Village  51

JOHN FRANKLIN AND
DR JOHN RICHARDSON  65
From *Narrative of a Journey to the Shores
    of the Polar Sea in the Years 1819, 20, 21
    and 22*  67

ANNA BROWNELL JAMESON  84
From *Winter Studies and Summer Rambles in
    Canada*  87

THOMAS CHANDLER HALIBURTON  94
The Trotting Horse  96
The Clockmaker  98

CATHARINE PARR TRAILL  101
From *The Backwoods of Canada*
    Letter IX  102
    Letter X  107

SUSANNA MOODIE  108
From *Roughing It in the Bush*
    Introduction to the Third Edition  110
    1. A Visit to Grosse Isle  112
    8. Uncle Joe and His Family  117
    9. Brian, The Still-Hunter  129
    22. The Fire  135
    25. Adieu to the Woods  139

CHARLES SANGSTER  140
From *The St Lawrence and the Saguenay*  142
From *Sonnets Written in the Orillia Woods*  145

ISABELLA VALANCY CRAWFORD  146
Malcolm's Katie: A Love Story  149
Esther  187
Canada to England  188
Said the Canoe  190

CHARLES G.D. ROBERTS  192
Tantramar Revisited  194
The Mowing  196
In an Old Barn  196
The Flight of the Geese  197
The Skater  197
Going Over  198
As Down the Woodland Ways  199
Under the Ice-Roof  200

**BLISS CARMAN** 206
The Eavesdropper 207
Low Tide on Grand Pré 208
Lord of My Heart's Elation 209
Morning in the Hills 210
The World Voice 211

**SARA JEANNETTE DUNCAN** 212
From *The Imperialist*
    Chapter II 214
    Chapter III 219

**E. PAULINE JOHNSON** 225
The Song My Paddle Sings 226
His Majesty the West Wind 228
A Cry from an Indian Wife 228
The Flight of the Crows 230
Silhouette 231
'Through Time and Bitter Distance' 232
The Lost Island 233

**ARCHIBALD LAMPMAN** 235
Heat 236
The Frogs 238
The Railway Station 240
In November 241
A Summer Dream 242
The City of the End of Things 243
Voices of Earth 245
Winter Evening 245
To a Millionaire 246
At the Long Sault: May, 1660 246

**DUNCAN CAMPBELL SCOTT** 249
At the Cedars 251
The Onondaga Madonna 253
Watkwenies 253
Night Hymns on Lake Nipigon 254
The Forsaken 255
The Battle of Lundy's Lane 258
The Height of Land 260
To a Canadian Aviator Who Died for
    His Country in France 265
Labrie's Wife 266

**JESSIE GEORGINA SIME** 276
Munitions! 278

**NELLIE McCLUNG** 283
The Elusive Vote: An Unvarnished Tale of
    September 21st, 1911 285

**STEPHEN LEACOCK** 293
The Marine Excursion of the Knights
    of Pythias 294

**L.M. MONTGOMERY** 307
How Betty Sherman Won a Husband 309

**FREDERICK PHILIP GROVE** 315
Snow (1922) 317
Snow (1932) 335

**E.J. PRATT** 341
The Shark 343
Newfoundland 344
Silences 346
The Prize Cat 348
Come Away, Death 349
The Truant 351
*Towards the Last Spike* 356

**MARJORIE PICKTHALL** 384
The Sleep-Seekers 385
The Bird in the Room 386
Made in His Image 387
The Third Generation 387

**ETHEL WILSON** 395
The Window 396

**F.R. SCOTT** 406
The Canadian Authors Meet 407
Trans Canada 408
Lakeshore 409
Poetry 411
W.L.M.K. 412
All the Spikes But the Last 413

**HARRY ROBINSON** 414
Coyote Challenges God 415
Indian Doctor 419

**A.J.M. SMITH** 425
The Lonely Land 427
Far West 428
Sea Cliff 429
Business as Usual: 1946 430
Fear as Normal: 1954 430
On Reading an Anthology of
    Popular Poetry 431
The Wisdom of Old Jelly Roll 432

MORLEY CALLAGHAN   432
Watching and Waiting   434

EARLE BIRNEY   439
Vancouver Lights   440
Anglosaxon Street   441
The Ebb Begins from Dream   443
Pacific Door   445
Bushed   446
Can. Lit.   447
El Greco: *Espolio*   448
Newfoundland   449

SINCLAIR ROSS   449
The Runaway   451

A.M. KLEIN   462
Reb Levi Yitschok Talks to God   464
Heirloom   446
The Rocking Chair   467
Political Meeting   468
Portrait of the Poet as Landscape   469
Autobiographical   475

SHEILA WATSON   478
And the Four Animals   480

DOROTHY LIVESAY   481
Green Rain   483
The Difference   483
Day and Night   484
Bartok and the Geranium   489
The Secret Doctrine of Women   490
The Artefacts: West Coast   492

ANNE WILKINSON   495
The Great Winds   496
Winter Sketch, Rockcliffe, Ottawa   497
Easter Sketches, Montreal   498
In June and Gentle Oven   500
Nature Be Damned   501

IRVING LAYTON   504
The Birth of Tragedy   506
The Cold Green Element   507
The Fertile Muck   508
Whatever Else Poetry Is Freedom   509
Keine Lazarovitch 1870–1959   511
Butterfly on Rock   512
A Tall Man Executes a Jig   512

P.K. PAGE   516
Stories of Snow   518
Photos of a Salt Mine   519
Cry Ararat!   521
Evening Dance of the Grey Flies   524
Arras   525
The Gold Sun   526
Poor Bird   527
Kaleidoscope   529
Unless the Eye Catch Fire   531

MARGARET AVISON   547
The Butterfly   548
Neverness   549
Perspective   551
Snow   552
Butterfly Bones; or Sonnet Against Sonnets   553
Tennis   553
The Swimmer's Moment   554
We the Poor Who Are Always with Us   554
Job: Word and Action   555
Poetry Is   565

AL PURDY   567
The Country North of Belleville   569
Trees at the Arctic Circle   571
Wilderness Gothic   573
Lament for the Dorsets   574
At the Quinte Hotel   576
Roblin's Mills (2)   578
Elegy for a Grandfather [1986]   580
For Steve McIntyre   581
On the Flood Plain   582
Grosse Isle   584
Say the Names   585

RAYMOND SOUSTER   587
The Penny Flute   588
At Split Rock Falls   589
Like the Last Patch of Snow   589
Get the Poem Outdoors   590
Queen Anne's Lace   590
Trying One on for Size   591

MAVIS GALLANT   593
Varieties of Exile   594

MARGARET LAURENCE   608
To Set Our House in Order   609

JAMES REANEY  620
The School Globe  622
The Lost Child  623
The Alphabet  624
Starling with a Split Tongue  626

PHYLLIS WEBB  628
Marvell's Garden  629
From *Naked Poems*
    Suite I  631
    Suite II  633
Spots of Blood  635
I Daniel  636
The Making of a Japanese Print  640

ROBERT KROETSCH  645
F.P. Grove: The Finding  647
Seed Catalogue  649

TIMOTHY FINDLEY  665
Dreams  667

ALICE MUNRO  681
The Progress of Love  683

MORDECAI RICHLER  702
Playing Ball on Hampstead Heath  704

ALDEN NOWLAN  712
Temptation  713
Country Full of Christmas  714
Canadian January Night  714
The Broadcaster's Poem  715
On the Barrens  716

LEONARD COHEN  718
You Have the Lovers  720
Suzanne  722
From *Book of Mercy*
    In the Eyes of Men  723
    It Is All Around Me  723
    Holy Is Your Name  724
Everybody Knows  724
Closing Time  726
Thousand Kisses Deep  727
'the truth of the line'  730
Looking Through My Dreams  731

RUDY WIEBE  732
Where Is the Voice Coming From?  734

GEORGE BOWERING  740
Grandfather  742
From *Kerrisdale Elegies*
    Elegy Two  744
The Great Local Poem  748
From 'Pictures'
    Prodigal (with Angela Bowering)  749

JOY KOGAWA  750
Obasan  752
Where There's a Wall  758
Road Building by Pick Axe  758
Minerals from Stone  761

CAROL SHIELDS  762
Hazel  764

ALISTAIR MacLEOD  776
As Birds Bring Forth the Sun  777

CLAIRE HARRIS  783
August  784
Black Sisyphus  785
Conception of Winter  786
To Dissipate Grief  787
No God Waits on Incense  789

JACK HODGINS  790
The Crossing  791

JOHN NEWLOVE  798
Four Small Scars  799
The Double-Headed Snake  800
Samuel Hearne in Wintertime  801
Ride Off Any Horizon  803
The Green Plain  807

MARGARET ATWOOD  810
This Is a Photograph of Me  814
Progressive Insanities of a Pioneer  815
From *The Journals of Susanna Moodie*
    Disembarking at Quebec  818
    Further Arrivals  819
    Death of a Young Son by Drowning  820
    Dream 2: Brian the Still-Hunter  821
    Thoughts from Underground  822
Tricks with Mirrors  823
Siren Song  826
Spelling  827
Orpheus (2)  828

The Line: Five Variations  829
The Age of Lead  832

PATRICK LANE  842
Because I Never Learned  844
Stigmata  844
The Long Coyote Line  845
CPR Station—Winnipeg  846
Weasel  847
From *Winter* 1990
    Winter 1  847
    Winter 4  848
    Winter 22  849
    Winter 33  849
    Winter 35  849
    Winter 40  850
    Winter 42  851
The Far Field  851
Cut-throat  853
The Spoon  853
For Gwendolyn MacEwen  854
The Sooke Potholes  855

DENNIS LEE  857
Sibelius Park  859
The Coat  861
When I Went Up to Rosedale  861
The Gods  863
Hunger  866
Hiatus  867
Desaparecidos  868
Wordly  868
Tale  869

FRED WAH  870
Waiting for Saskatchewan  871
From *Diamond Grill*  872

MARIA CAMPBELL  886
Jacob  887

GWENDOLYN MacEWEN  895
Icarus  896
Manzini: Escape Artist  898
The Portage  899
Dark Pines under Water  900
The Real Enemies  901
The Death of the Loch Ness Monster  902
Polaris  903

DON McKAY  904
Kestrels  906
Twinflower  907
Short Fat Flicks  908
To Danceland  910
Homing  911
Icarus  912
Astonished—  914
Petrified—  915
Pond  915
Varves  917
Gneiss  917
Some Last Requests  918

DAPHNE MARLATT  920
Imagine: a town  922
coming home  923
winter/ rice/ tea strain  923
listen  925
(is love enough?)  927

MICHAEL ONDAATJE  928
The Time Around Scars  930
Letters & Other Worlds  931
Pig Glass  934
Light  935
Sally Chisum/Last Words on Billy the Kid.
    4 A.M.  937
The Cinnamon Peeler  939
Lunch Conversation  940
To a Sad Daughter  943
The Medieval Coast  945
Wells  946

THOMAS KING  948
A Coyote Columbus Story  949

bpNICHOL  953
From *The Martyrology*
    From Book 1: 'The Sorrows of
    Saint Orm'  955
    From Book 3, Section VIII.  960
    From Book 5, Chain 8  966
landscape: I  969
lament  969

BRONWEN WALLACE  970
The Woman in this Poem  972
Joseph Macleod Daffodils  974
Testimonies  977

The Watermelon Incident 979
Songbirds and Hurtin' Songs 981
An Easy Life 982

ROBERT BRINGHURST 989
Essay on Adam 992
Leda and the Swan 992
These Poems, She Said 994
The Reader 995
Conversations with a Toad 996
Bone Flute Breathing 1002

LORNA CROZIER 1006
This One's for You 1007
Poem about Nothing 1008
Forms of Innocence 1010
Getting Pregnant 1011
On the Seventh Day 1012
The Old Order 1014
At the Millstone 1017
From A Saving Grace: The Collected Poems
    of Mrs. Bentley
    Two Eternal Things 1018
    Wilderness 1019
The Sacrifice of Abraham 1020
The Sacrifice of Isaac 1020
Ice-fog 1021
My Last Erotic Poem 1022

JANE URQUHART 1023
The Drawing Master 1024

ANNE CARSON 1027
Short Talk on Rectification 1029
Short Talk on Who You Are 1030
Book of Isaiah 1030
TV Men: Hektor 1036

BARBARA GOWDY 1045
Presbyterian Crosswalk 1046

M.G. VASSANJI 1057
Her Two Husbands 1059

GUY VANDERHAEGHE 1069
Man on Horseback 1070

ROHINTON MISTRY 1086
Swimming Lessons 1087

DIONNE BRAND 1103
From No Language Is Neutral
    hard against the soul 1105
I Have Been Losing Roads 1108
Land to Light On 1115
From thirsty:
    I 1118
    III 1119
    XXVIII 1119
    XXX 1120
    XXXIII 1120

ERIN MOURÉ 1121
Blindness 1123
Miss Chatelaine 1125
Seebe 1126
Dream of the Towns 1129
Amygdala 1130
14 Descriptions of Trees 1133
From Sheep's Vigil by a Fervent Person
    VII  From Garrison Creek I see the
        earth to the antipodes of the
        Universe . . . 1135
    XX  The Humber is pretty fabulous,
        really 1136
    XXXI  If at times I claim flowers smile
        and rivers sing 1136

JAN ZWICKY 1137
The New Room 1138
Bill Evans: 'Here's That Rainy Day' 1139
Transparence 1140
Driving Northwest 1143
String Practice 1143
Robinson's Crossing 1145
Study: North 1149

ANNE MICHAELS 1149
Lake of Two Rivers 1151
Flowers 1155
There Is No City That Does Not Dream 1155
Ice House 1156
Repairing the Octave 1159

GEORGE ELLIOT CLARKE 1164
From The Adoration of Shelley, Whylah Falls
    The Argument 1166
    The River Pilgrim: A Letter 1167
    Rose Vinegar 1168
    Bees' Wings 1168

Blank Sonnet  1169
The Wisdom of Shelley  1169
Each Moment Is Magnificent  1170
Primitivism  1171
From *Execution Poems*
The Killing  1172
Nu(is)ance  1173
George & Rue: Coda  1174
Mortality Sonnet  1176

LISA MOORE  1177
Craving  1178

CHRISTIAN BÖK  1182
Crystals  1184
From *Eunoia*
Chapter O  1186
Vowels  1192

MICHAEL REDHILL  1193
The Flesh Collectors  1194

EDEN ROBINSON  1206
Queen of the North  1207

KEN BABSTOCK  1223
In Brendan's Boat  1224
Montana Nocturne  1225
Marsh Theatre  1226
Regenerative  1227
To Willow  1228
Essentialist  1231
The World's Hub  1233
Compatibilist  1235

WADE COMPTON  1237
The Blue Road: A Fairy Tale  1240
The Reinventing Wheel  1255

MADELEINE THIEN  1267
Dispatch  1268

ACKNOWLEDGEMENTS  1277

INDEX  1282

# Preface

This is the fourth version of a Canadian literature anthology that had its origin in a 1979 class on English-Canadian poetry. Because the poems studied that day were filled with references unfamiliar to student readers, a great deal of class time had to be given over to explanation. After class, when a sales representative from Oxford University Press called to discuss text adoptions for the following year, we expressed our frustration at the lack of footnotes and critical headnotes in Canadian literature anthologies. That complaint led to our editing the first version of this anthology, published in two volumes in 1982–3. In 1990, assisted by Nathalie Cooke, we prepared a compact version of that text, adding authors who had emerged since 1983. In 2002, we undertook a more thorough revision and updating. This current edition represents another substantial revision.

Before Europeans arrived, individuals in the part of North America that became Canada passed on their experiences to others in the forms of oral stories, songs, and poetry. The first European explorers set down their perceptions of, and described their interactions with, the land and its peoples in written accounts intended for an absent audience. Most of their readers, like those in the settlement era that followed, lived in Europe and were unfamiliar with North American experience. Thus, the earliest beginnings of a written Canadian literature were effectively 'letters home', attempts to relate Canadian experience to a distant people. Such writing tends to be descriptive and indebted to the forms, conventions, and culture already familiar to the audience. Nineteenth-century Europe's interest in defining its separate states as having distinct national identities had an effect on settlement colonies such as Canada: they began to define themselves as branches of their home cultures, in which their experience of the landscape and the youth of their societies led their literary and other artistic efforts to diverge from their inherited traditions. Even before Confederation, attempts to identify an English-Canadian literature, through the gathering of poems into anthologies and through critical essays, began to appear. By the early twentieth century, extended critical studies were being devoted to the idea that a distinctive body of *Canadian* writing existed. These early critics focused on Canadian literature's sources and on how to define the nature of the literary tradition—which, from an early point, was conflated with the poetic tradition. Within a generation, arguments were made that a canon of English-Canadian poetry existed as well as a tradition. Although Albert Watson and Lorne Pierce's *Our Canadian Literature: Representative Prose and Verse* (1922) extended that canon beyond poetry (because theirs was the first anthology to include prose), the landmark anthology that followed, A.J.M. Smith's *The Book of Canadian Poetry* (1943)—notable as the book that first allowed the critic Northrop Frye to glimpse a wholeness in Canadian literature—continued to treat the Canadian canon as poetry-based.

As the second half of the twentieth century began, a cultural nationalism flourished that was given extra impetus during the 1960s by the Canadian Centennial and Expo 67. This nationalist view of English-Canadian culture argued that a unified English-Canadian literature existed and needed to be encouraged—in part as a bulwark against the incursion of the overwhelming wave of American cultural enterprises. The increased desire for a vital national literature produced new editing of, and intensified the critical attention being paid to, Canada's literature: new writers were celebrated and the work of earlier writers was made more available. One of the functions of anthologies during this period was to capture these assessments and reassessments of Canadian writing and to provide the material for critical narratives of the development of a Canadian literary tradition. No entirely fixed canon held sway—canons are always in flux, particularly when societies are rapidly growing and changing. Still, the fact that fifty-five writers who were in the first edition of this anthology reappear in this one and that forty-nine authors have been in all four versions does suggest that the Canadian canon, while changing and expanding over the last twenty-five years, now has a stable core.

The anthology you hold in your hands also attests to the changing nature of Canadian literature during the period since the first edition was published. The 1982–3 edition held the work of eighty-six authors—including two playwrights and several essayists. For reasons of space we dropped the plays and essays in the later one-volume editions, with the result that six authors have been omitted altogether in subsequent editions. The 1990 compact edition presented work by seventy-three authors. The 2002 edition—the only one to include a number of extracts from novelists—contained eighty-five. Though several authors present in previous editions are not retained in this current volume, it has the largest number yet: ninety-two authors, eleven of whom appear for the first time. This breadth shows twenty-first century Canadian literature continuing to be vital in a society that has not yet slowed in developing its literary culture.

As suggested already, formal changes have always affected anthologists' choices. When English-Canadian literature first became an object of serious study in universities, around the middle of the twentieth century, short fiction—from the early nineteenth-century sketches of Thomas Chandler Haliburton through the successful magazine fiction of Morley Callaghan to the finely-crafted tales of Ethel Wilson—had a place, but poetry was at the centre of the Canadian canon, its tradition defined by the Confederation poets and the modernism of E.J. Pratt, Earle Birney, Margaret Avison, and P.K. Page. In the 1960s and 1970s, the Canadian canon began to take in more fiction, in particular the short story—as a result of the outstanding accomplishments of writers such as Alice Munro, Alistair MacLeod, and Mavis Gallant. Since that time, a further shift is apparent: fine new short story writers continue to appear and poetry finds new ways to command attention, but the novel occupies the most prominent place in the contemporary canon. And the novel's length—like that of full-length drama—presents a challenge for anthologists. We decided, in this volume, not to offer excerpts from full-length fiction—with two exceptions. We continue to reprint some of the fictional letters from Frances Brooke's first novel, *The History of Emily Montague*, because of their value as the first example of English-language fiction dramatizing subjective responses to Canada's new landscape. And we have included two complementary chapters from *The Imperialist*, the classic novel by Sara Jeannette Duncan, because they can stand alone as sketches and because they show her place in the development of Canadian humour. We have, as well, reprinted Mordecai Richler's 'Playing Ball on Hampstead Heath', which appeared as a short story before Richler used it as a set piece in his novel *St. Urbain's Horseman*. Other novelists have a presence here because they also have written important short stories or poems, but readers should be aware that a number have been omitted entirely—including Hugh MacLennan, Robertson Davies, David Adams Richards, Wayne Johnston, Anne-Marie MacDonald, and Yann Martel—who ought to be read for a full appreciation of English-Canadian literature.

ii

In adding footnotes to the texts in this anthology, we have tried to find a judicious balance, seeking to expedite the informed reading of the selections but not to replace standard reference aids or to document every allusion. To minimize distraction, more than one item is sometimes glossed in a single footnote; in such cases, the superscript is usually appended to the first item and the additional words being glossed are repeated in the note. All quotations from the Bible are from the King James Version (also known as the Authorized Version) except where otherwise indicated. Two notes on colours use hex codes in reference to the recent advent of online colour charts. When more than one version of a text exists, we have chosen the author's most recent revision. We have silently corrected a few obvious typographical errors. The dates, appended on the left margins to the end of texts, are, if single, the date of first book publication. Where substantive changes were later made, then the date of the revision follows that date (e.g., '1962; rev. 1968') and the second date is that of the text used in the anthology. When two dates are provided without other indication (e.g., '1962, 1972'), the second date is that of first book publication and the first is the date of first journal publication, included because it significantly predates the work's inclusion in a book. When two dates are provided and the first is in brackets (e.g., '[1870], 1984'), the bracketed date indicates the composition of a work that was not published until a much later date. Where poets have appended dates at the end of their poems, we have retained those and placed them to the right.

As with any project of size and duration, our indebtedness is beyond counting. Over the years our students have been unfailingly helpful when asked questions about what needed explanation and notation. We have frequently been assisted by colleagues, friends, librarians, and researchers, and by the writers themselves. It is the extraordinary generosity of the literary and scholarly communities in Canada that makes projects like this a pleasure. In addition to those thanked in earlier editions, and to the many helpful comments and responses we received from colleagues and readers in preparing this edition, individuals we would like to single out for their help and advice include

MaryAnne Laurico, who provided us with extraordinary editorial assistance, Bert Almon, Andrew Dubois, Margaret Fulford, Robin Elliott, Dennis Patrick, Branko Gorjup, Colin Hill, Nick Mount, Ian Rae, Magdalene Redekop, and Jeff Rybak. We are indebted to the authors in this volume for having created a rich and diverse body of work, and specifically want to thank Patrick Lane for his willingness to comment on his elegy for Gwendolyn MacEwen, Ken Babstock for his comments on two of his poems, and Wayde Compton for answering questions about 'The Reinventing Wheel'. Looking back over the four versions we have now edited, we would like to thank again Fred McFarland of Norton who first discussed the need for an anthology of this kind in Canada and express our gratitude to Oxford University Press for their assistance over the years—which means William Toye in the first instance, without whose guidance we cannot imagine having gone forward, as well as Phyllis Wilson, whose patience has seemed unbounded. Our readers have always played an important role and can be expected to continue to do so. We invite those who have feedback on this newest edition to contact us at rbrown@chass.utoronto.ca.

*Donna Bennett*
*Russell Brown*
*Feb. 15, 2010*

# Introduction

There are many ways to approach the collection of Canadian writing contained in these pages. Readers might initially focus on a single time period or region. Or they might choose to study only poetry or short fiction. Some might seek out themes and topics that emerge in this body of work, such as pioneer and rural experience; the search for identity; the roles of women; or the experience of immigration and the mixing of cultures. Other readers might want to trace out the changes in techniques employed by writers and the ways those correspond to newer modes of understanding the relationship between reality and representation.

Many readers will want to start their study of English-Canadian literature by investigating the major figures in Canada's literary history—perhaps beginning with Susanna Moodie and Charles G.D. Roberts, and ranging through E.J. Pratt, Earl Birney, Irving Layton, and P.K. Page, to Al Purdy, Alice Munro, Margaret Atwood, and Michael Ondaatje. They might then want to locate these writers among their precursors, their contemporaries, and those they influenced. Readers who move widely through the entire collection will become intrigued by the many cross-connections that emerge (as, for example, when both Robert Bringhurst and Lorna Crozier rethink the story of Leda and the swan); they will enjoy seeing how later Canadian writers learn from, or are inspired by, earlier ones (as Archibald Lampman was inspired by Roberts, and Thomas King informed by reading Harry Robinson); and they will observe later writers entering into conversations with their precursors, as Robert Kroetsch does in his poem 'For F.P. Grove: The Finding' and as Atwood does in her Susanna Moodie poems.

Taken together, these chronologically arranged selections, along with our head-notes introducing them, provide a history of English-Canadian literature. It is important to remember that, before the first Europeans arrived in Canada, Aboriginal peoples had their own orature, oral tales that some of these early settlers heard and recorded. Although during the early period of European settlement, Natives had only limited access to print culture, which was mediated through transcriptions made by Europeans, Native voices made themselves heard; they have continued to do so and have come to occupy an important place in contemporary Canadian writing. Nonetheless, the greatest part of Canadian literature in English is the product of an immigrant–settlement culture.

One way of understanding the literary history found in these pages is to see it as moving through a series of stages producing English Canada's literary traditions.

(1) *The first stirrings of a literary culture before Confederation.* Pre-Confederation writers, often expressing an explorer's excitement of discovery or an immigrant's sense of loss and displacement, responded to new environments while looking

back to the places they had left behind. Writing home, they found themselves—as can be seen in the passages from Frances Brooke's early novel—searching for suitable language and appropriate forms of expression.

(2) *The emergence of a national literature.* The writers who flourished in the era immediately following Confederation, many of them born in Canada, were conscious of living in a time of nation-building. While these writers drew on the Romantic and post-Romantic heritage that came to them from the United Kingdom and the United States, they transformed it into something that spoke to their own milieu. Because they wanted to write not as colonials but as Canadians they took it as a goal to establish their own distinct national literature, one that would be indigenous, with its own sustaining tradition.

(3) *The emergence of regional literature.* While the second stage of English-Canadian literature continued into the early years of the twentieth century, as Eastern and Central Canada were coalescing into an established culture, the West was only beginning to be settled by families moving from the East and by new immigrants. Thus, settlement, rather than nationalism, shaped emerging writers in the West, who often preferred fiction to poetry. This cultural unevenness of development between East and West meant that concern for *nation* and for national culture was challenged by internal distinctions, most noticeably that of *region*.

(4) *The coming of literary Modernism.* The first decades of the twentieth century in Canada saw both a large influx of European immigrants and new challenges to nineteenth-century ways of writing. English-Canadian writers responded to the international influence of Modernist ideas, interpreting these through various colonial, national, or regional perspectives. In Ontario, Sara Jeannette Duncan blended an urbane, Jamesian realism with her own witty, often satirical, responses to small-town ways and her awareness of Central Canada's colonial condition. In Manitoba, Frederick Philip Grove, recording the experiences of an emerging settlement while finding his own way in a new language, identity, and culture, responded to the Modernist aesthetics he had encountered in Europe by employing a regional realism that tested the bounds of lingering Victorian propriety. As the century wore on, Canadian fiction writers and poets showed little interest in the more revolutionary aspects of 'International Modernism', with its desire to provoke and its tendency to break sharply with the past. Instead, they wrote about the new ways of seeing things that the young century had brought, while exploring Modernism's formal concerns, introducing innovations in language and in technique, and investigating voice and point of view.

(5) *Post-war nationalism and departures from Modernism.* The era following the Second World War saw a new wave of cultural nationalism that made it

look as if a unitary means of defining the characteristics of English-Canadian literary culture was at last possible. (Indeed, several critics undertook the task—though that attempt produced strong regional resistances.) Many factors encouraged this new sense of literary and cultural identity at a national level, including the federal government's support for the arts and media through the Canada Council and the CBC; the emergence of a stronger and more autonomous publishing industry; more accessible trans-Canadian travel; an increasingly urban populace; and the expansion of post-secondary education, coinciding with a postcolonial drive for national identity.

Whether this era marked a break with the past in terms of formal techniques is less clear. Some of the most important writing of those years—the fiction of Robertson Davies, Mavis Gallant, Margaret Laurence, David Adams Richards, and Alistair MacLeod; the poetry of Irving Layton and P.K. Page—remained largely within the conventions of Modernist aesthetics. Other writers, such as Alice Munro, only seemed to remain within the confines of Modernism while subverting its conventions in subtle ways. Writers such as Robert Kroetsch, Leonard Cohen, and George Bowering made definitive breaks with Modernism, producing radically experimental works. Poets like bpNichol also departed from Modernism in experiments with form and by testing the bounds of language, but many Canadian poets—following the direction taken by Al Purdy, who wrote in a more colloquial and accessible voice than that utilized by Modernist poets, or opted for the stripped diction of the West Coast *Tish* poets—created a plain-style poetry that did not fit easily into either Modern or postmodern classifications.

(6) *The fragmented aesthetics of the turn of the millennium.* The end of the twentieth century and the beginning of the twenty-first show new forces shaping Canadian literature. Neither in Canada nor elsewhere has this contemporary period been given a name, though its characteristics can be described. The first is an increasingly multicultural society, which in Canada has produced a newly diverse literature—one that, in stories like M.G. Vassanji's 'Her Two Husbands', responds both to local and global circumstances. A second characteristic is an awareness of ecological concerns, reflected in Canada in the renewed nature poetry written by individuals such as Don McKay. A third characteristic of the contemporary era is the continuing influence of 'language' writing that has led poets like Erin Mouré to destabilize texts in ways that present great challenges for readers expecting 'communication' as the chief function of language. During this period, many of Canada's leading novelists embraced a strongly lyrical style and created narratives that unfold the way a poem does, while other fiction writers have chosen the elliptical style of minimalism.

At the same time, the modes of artistic expression themselves are becoming less clearly defined, and the definitions of, and limits on, what is 'literary' are less clear.

(Our first anthology reflected this change in its inclusion of accounts of exploration and settlement: such accounts have since come to be viewed as part of a larger category called 'life writing' and the importance granted to such writing has increased.) There is more crossing of the boundaries that once delineated one form from another. The phenomenon in Canada of poet-novelists such as Margaret Atwood, Michael Ondaatje, Dionne Brand, and Anne Michaels is often remarked upon, but many other Canadian writers move freely across artistic forms. George Elliott Clarke leaps from poetry to drama to film scripts to opera libretto to personal and critical essays to the novel. A single book by Fred Wah—*Diamond Grill*—seems to partake of the novel, the memoir, the poem, and the essay. P.K. Page turned from expressing herself verbally in poetry and short fiction to visually in paintings—and back again. Ann Carson paints volcanoes and titles her poems 'essays', 'novels', and 'tangos', refusing to distinguish between her scholarly and her creative work. Wayde Compton takes this anthology full circle—back to the oral—in a poem that draws simultaneously on the histories of poetry and of hip hop, and that exists equally on the page, in live performances, and on the Internet.

Perhaps the literary anthology of the future will be a multimedia work. While we await that future, the literature gathered here is already richly varied—and endlessly fascinating.

*For Sophia Della Bitta,*
*and her parents Michael and Kathryn*

# Saukamapee

## c. 1700–1793

Saukamapee was a Nahathaway who left his own people and joined the Peigans to the west. By the time he met David Thompson (in the winter of 1787–8), he had become an elder chief of a Peigan band (The Nathaways and Peigans are members of the Algonkian-speaking First Nations.) He took great interest in telling the writer-explorer about his past experiences—prompting Thompson to provide a long description of Saukamapee in his journals and to transcribe the account he gave of North American life prior to and just after the first European contact.

Before Europeans arrived, First Nations tales and beliefs were transmitted chiefly in oral form—now sometimes referred to as *orature* (to contrast it to written literature). Because most transcriptions of these early oral materials are the product of European pens such as Thompson's, they have been regarded with suspicion by scholars of Native culture as unintentionally distorting, if not explicitly falsifying. More recently, scholars have begun to feel that such records, if used carefully, can provide valuable accounts that might otherwise be unavailable. Thompson's journals have proved especially important because, while not free of cultural biases—especially his feeling that Christianity provided a more enlightened view than Native religious perspectives—he made a conscious effort to record information objectively and sought out the elders of the tribes he visited, hoping that their knowledge of their cultures prior to European contact could be preserved.

Saukamapee is described by Thompson in the following way:

*he was full six feet in height, erect and of a frame that shewed strength and activity. . . . After a few days the old man spoke to me in the Nahathaway language and asked me if I understood it, and how*

*long since I had left my own country. I answered this is my fourth winter and the Nahathaways are the people we trade with, and I speak their tongue sufficient for common purposes. Upon which, with a smile, he said, I am not a Peigan of these plains I am a Nahathaway of the Pasquiau River (a River that joins the Kisiskatachewan about fifty miles below Cumberland House). . . . He said it is many winters since I last saw the ground where my parents lie. . . . Although erect and somewhat active, and in full possession of his faculties, yet from the events he related, and comparing them with the accounts of the French writers on the fur trade of Canada he must have been near ninety years of age, or more for his relation of affairs went back to near the year one thousand seven hundred. . . . He was fond of conversing in his native tongue, and recounting the events of his life, the number and positions of the different tribes of Indians, how they were allied, and the battles they had fought to gain the country of the Bow River. . . . Almost every evening for the time of four months I sat and listened to the old man, without being in the least tired, they were blended with the habits, customs, and manners, politics, and religion such as it was, anecdotes of the Indian Chiefs and the means of their gaining influence in war and peace, that I always found something to interest me.*

Since the war between the Blackfoot and the Snake Indians (the Shoshonean) took place around 1730, at which point Saukamapee was around sixteen, Thompson has overestimated Saukamapee's age here.

As well as being a unique source of the history of the Algonkian in the early eighteenth century (the events that Saukamapee recalls include the introduction of firearms and how it affected the mode of fighting around that time; the arrival of the horse on the plains; and the first smallpox epidemic), these tales have an immediacy that gives them continuing fascination.

# [Life among the Peigans]

\* \* \*

'The Peigans[1] were always the frontier Tribe, and upon whom the Snake Indians made their attacks, these latter were very numerous, even without their allies; and the Peigans had to send messengers among us to procure help. Two of them came to the camp of my father, and I was then about his age (pointing to a lad of about sixteen years); he promised to come and bring some of his people, the Nahathaways[2] with him, for I am myself of that people, and not of those with whom I am. My father brought about twenty warriors with him. There were a few guns amongst us, but very little ammunition, and they were left to hunt for the families; our weapons were a Lance, mostly pointed with iron, some few of stone, a Bow and quiver of Arrows; the Bows were of Larch, the length came to the chin; the quiver had about fifty arrows, of which ten had iron points, the others were headed with stone. He carried his knife on his breast and his axe in his belt. Such were my father's weapons, and those with him had much the same weapons. I had a Bow and Arrows and a knife, of which I was very proud. We came to the Peigans and their allies. They were camped in the Plains on the left bank of the River (the north side) and were a great many. We were feasted, a great War Tent was made, and a few days passed in speeches, feasting and dances. A war chief was elected by the chiefs, and we got ready to march. Our spies had been out and had seen a large camp of the Snake Indians on the Plains of the Eagle Hill, and we had to cross the River in canoes, and on rafts, which we carefully secured for our retreat. When we had crossed and numbered our men, we were about 350 warriors. They had their scouts out, and came to meet us. Both parties made a great show of their numbers, and I thought that they were more numerous than ourselves.

'After some singing and dancing, they sat down on the ground, and placed their large shields before them, which covered them: we did the same but our shields were not so many, and some of our shields had to shelter two men. Theirs were all placed touching each other; their Bows were not so long as ours, but of better wood, and the backs covered with the sinews of the Bisons which made them very elastic, and their arrows went a long way and whizzed about us as balls do from guns. They were all headed with a sharp, smooth, black stone (flint) which broke when it struck anything. Our iron headed arrows did not go through their shields, but stuck in them. On both

1  The Peigans (US: Piegans) are one of the three allied Algonkian tribes that make up the Blackfoot. They were much feared by trappers.
2  Thompson explains that 'Nahathaway' is a general name for the Natives who inhabit the area south of 'a people who call themselves "Dinnie"' (i.e., the Dene, who, Thompson tells us, were called 'by the Hudson Bay Traders "Northern Indians" and by their southern neighbours "Cheepawyans"'). He further explains that the Nahathaways were referred to by the French voyageurs as the Cree, a name he says they did not use for themselves, adding that the Nahathaways 'are separated into many tribes or extended families, under different names, but all speaking dialects of the same language, which extends over this stony region, and along the Atlantic coasts southward to the Delaware River in the United States . . . and by the Saskatchewan River westward, to the Rocky Mountains'.

sides several were wounded, but none lay on the ground; and night put an end to the battle, without a scalp being taken on either side, and in those days such were the results, unless one party was more numerous than the other. The great mischief of war then was, as now, by attacking and destroying small camps of ten to thirty tents, which are obliged to separate for hunting. I grew to be a man, became a skilful and fortunate hunter, and my relations procured me a Wife. She was young and handsome and we were fond of each other. We had passed a winter together, when Messengers came from our allies to claim assistance.

'By this time the affairs of both parties had much changed: we had more guns and iron headed arrows than before; but our enemies the Snake Indians and their allies had *Misstutim* (Big Dogs, that is Horses) on which they rode, swift as the Deer, on which they dashed at the Peigans, and with their stone *Pukamoggan*[3] knocked them on the head, and the Peigans thus lost several of their best men. This news we did not well comprehend and it alarmed us, for we had no idea of Horses and could not make out what they were. Only three of us went and I should not have gone, had not my wife's relations frequently intimated, that her father's medicine bag would be much honored by the scalp of a Snake Indian. When we came to our allies, the great War Tent was made, with speeches, feasting and dances as before; and when the War Chief had viewed us all it was found that between us and the Stone (Assiniboine) Indians we had ten guns and each of us about thirty balls, and powder for the war, and we were considered the strength of the battle. After a few days' march, our scouts brought us word that the enemy was near in a large war party, but had no Horses with them, for at that time they had very few of them. When we came to meet each other, as usual, each side displayed their numbers, weapons and shields, in all which they were superior to us, except for our guns which were not shown, but kept in their leathern cases, and if we had shown [them], they would have taken them for long clubs. For a long time they held us in suspense; a tall Chief was forming a strong party to make an attack on our centre, and the others were to enter into combat with those opposite to them. We prepared for the battle the best we could. Those of us who had guns stood in the front line, and each of us had two balls in his mouth, and a load of powder in his left hand to reload.

'We noticed they had a great many short stone clubs for close combat, which is a dangerous weapon, and had they made a bold attack on us, we must have been defeated as they were more numerous and better armed than we were, for we could have fired our guns no more than twice; and were at a loss what to do on the wide plain, and each Chief encouraged his men to stand firm. Our eyes were all on the tall Chief and his motions, which appeared to be contrary to the advice of several old Chiefs, all this time we were about the strong flight of an arrow from each other. At length the tall chief retired and they formed their long usual line by placing their shields on the ground to touch each other, the shield having a breadth of full three feet or more. We sat down opposite to them and most of us waited for the night to make a hasty retreat. The War Chief was close to us, anxious to see the effect of our guns.

3  (Also spelled 'pogamagan'): a club consisting of a stone wrapped in leather and fastened to a wooden handle.

The lines were too far asunder for us to make a sure shot, and we requested him to close the line to about sixty yards, which was gradually done, and lying flat on the ground behind the shields, we watched our opportunity when they drew their bows to shoot at us. Their bodies were then exposed and each of us, as opportunity offered, fired with deadly aim, and either killed, or severely wounded, every one we aimed at.

'The War Chief was highly pleased, and the Snake Indians finding so many killed and wounded kept themselves behind their shields; the War Chief then desired we would spread ourselves by two's throughout the line, which we did, and our shots caused consternation and dismay along their whole line. The battle had begun about Noon, and the Sun was not yet half down when we perceived some of them had crawled away from their shields, and were taking to flight. The War Chief seeing this went along the line and spoke to every Chief to keep his Men ready for a charge of the whole line of the enemy, of which he would give the signal. This was done by himself stepping in front with his Spear and calling on them to follow him as he rushed on their line. In an instant the whole of us followed him, the greater part of the enemy took to flight, but some fought bravely. We lost more than ten killed and many wounded. Part of us pursued and killed a few, but the chase had soon to be given over, for at the body of every Snake Indian killed, there were five or six of us trying to get his scalp, or part of his clothing, his weapons, or something as a trophy of the battle. As there were only three of us, and seven of our friends, the Stone Indians, we did not interfere, and got nothing.

'The next morning the War Chief made a speech, praising their bravery, and telling them to make a large War Tent to commemorate their victory, to which they directly set to work and by noon it was finished.

'The War Chief now called on all the other Chiefs to assemble their men and come to the Tent. In a short time they came, all those who had lost relations had their faces blackened; those who killed an enemy, or wished to be thought so, had their faces blackened with red streaks on the face, and those who had no pretensions to the one, or the other, had their faces red with ochre. We did not paint our faces until the War Chief told us to paint our foreheads and eyes black, and the rest of the face of dark red ochre, as having carried guns, and to distinguish us from all the rest. Those who had scalps now came forward with the scalps neatly stretched on a round willow with a handle to the frame; they appeared to be more than fifty, and excited loud shouts and the war whoop of victory. When this was over, the War Chief told them that if any one had a right to the scalp of an enemy as a war trophy it ought to be us, who with our guns had gained the victory, when from the numbers of our enemies we were anxious to leave the field of battle; and that ten scalps must be given to us; this was soon collected, and he gave to each of us a scalp. All those whose faces were blackened for the loss of relations, or friends, now came forward to claim the other scalps to be held in their hands for the benefit of their departed relations and friends; this occasioned a long conversation with those who had the scalps; at length they came forward to the War Chief, those who had taken the trophy from the head of the enemy they had killed, said the Souls of the enemy that each of us has slain, belong to us, and we have given them to our relations which are in the other world to be their slaves, and we are contented. Those who had scalps taken from the enemy that were found dead under the shields were at a loss what to say, as not one could declare he had actually slain the enemy whose scalp he held, and yet each wanted to send their Souls to be the slaves of their departed relations. This caused much discussion; and the old Chiefs decided it could not be done, and that no one could send the soul of an enemy to be a slave in the other world except the warrior who actually killed him. "The scalps you hold are trophies of the Battle, but they give you no right to the soul of the enemy from whom it is taken, he alone who kills an enemy has a right to the soul, and to give it to be a slave to whom he pleases." This decision did not please them, but they were obliged to abide by it. The old Chiefs then turned to us, and praising our conduct in the battle said, "Each of you have slain two enemies in battle, if not more, you will return to your own people, and as you are young men, consult with the old men to whom you shall give the souls of those you have slain; until which time let them wander about the other world." The Chiefs wished us to stay, and promised to each of us a handsome young wife, and to adopt us as their sons, but we told them we were anxious to see our relations and people, after which, perhaps we might come back. After all the war ceremonies were over, we pitched away in large camps with the women and children on the frontier of the Snake Indian country, hunting the Bison and Red Deer which were numerous, and we were anxious to see a horse of which we had heard so much. At last, as the leaves were falling we heard that one was killed by an arrow shot into his belly, but the Snake Indian that rode him got away; numbers of us went to see him, and we all admired him. He put us in mind of a Stag that had lost his horns; and we did not know what name to give him. But as he was a slave to Man, like the dog, which carried our things, he was named the Big Dog.

'We set off for our people, and on the fourth day came to a camp of Stone Indians, the relations of our companions, who received us well and we stayed a few days. The scalps were placed on poles, and the Men and Women danced round them, singing to the sound of Rattles, Tambours and Flutes. When night came, one of our party, in a low voice, repeated to the Chief the narrative of the battle, which he in a loud voice walking about the tents, repeated to the whole camp. After which, the Chiefs called those who followed them to a feast, and the battle was always the subject of the conversation and driving the Snake Indians to a great distance. There were now only three of us to proceed, and upon enquiry, we learned a camp of our people, the Nahathaways were a day's journey from us, and in the evening we came to them, and all our news had to be told, with the usual songs and dances. But my mind was wholly bent on making a grand appearance before my Wife and her Parents, and presenting to her father the scalp I had to ornament his Medicine Bag. Before we came to the camp we had dressed ourselves, and painted each other's faces to appear to the best advantage, and were proud of ourselves. On seeing some of my friends I got away and went to them, and by enquiries learned that my parents had gone to the low countries of the Lakes, and that before I was three Moons away my wife had given herself to another man, and that her father could not prevent her, and they were all to the northward there to pass the winter.

'At this unlooked for news I was quite disheartened; I said nothing, but my heart was swollen with anger and revenge, and I passed the night scheming mischief. In the morning my friends reasoned with me upon my vexation about a worthless woman, and that it was beneath a warrior's anger, there were no want of women to replace her, and a better wife could be got. Others said, that if I had stayed with my wife instead of running away to kill Snake Indians, nothing of this would have happened. My anger moderated, I gave my scalp to one of my friends to give to my father, and renouncing my people, I left them and came to the Peigans who gave me a hearty welcome. Upon my informing them of my intention to remain with them, the great Chief gave me his eldest daughter to be my wife. She is the sister of the present Chief and, as you see, now an old woman.

'The terror of that battle and of our guns has prevented any more general battles, and our wars have since been carried by ambuscade and surprise, of small camps, in which we have greatly the advantage, from the guns, arrows shod of iron, long knives, flat bayonets and axes from the Traders. While we have these weapons, the Snake Indians have none, but what few they sometimes take from one of our small camps which they have destroyed. They have no Traders among them. We thus continued to advance through the fine plains to the Stag River when death came over us all, and swept more than one-half of us by the small pox, of which we knew nothing until it brought death among us. We caught it from the Snake Indians. Our Scouts were out for our security, when some returned and informed us of a considerable camp which was too large to attack and something very suspicious about it; from a high knoll they had a good view of the camp, but saw none of the men hunting, or going about. There were a few Horses, but no one came to them; and a herd of Bisons were feeding close to the camp with other herds near. This somewhat alarmed us as a stratagem of War; and our Warriors thought this camp had a larger one not far off; so that if this camp was attacked, it was strong enough to offer a desperate resistance, and the other would come to their assistance and overpower us, as had been once before done by them, and in which we had lost many of our men.

'The council ordered the Scouts to return and go beyond this camp and be sure there was no other. In the mean time we advanced our camp. The scouts returned and said no other tents were near, and the camp appeared in the same state as before. Our Scouts, who had been going too much about their camp and may have been seen, expected what would follow, and all those that could walk, as soon as night came on, went away. Next morning at the dawn of day, we attacked the Tents, and with our sharp flat daggers and knives cut through the tents and entered for the fight; but our war whoop instantly stopped. Our eyes were appalled with terror; there was no one to fight with but the dead and the dying, each a mass of corruption. We did not touch them, but left the tents, and held a council on what was to be done. We all thought the Bad Spirit had made himself master of the camp and destroyed them. It was agreed to take some of the best of the tents, and any other plunder that was clean and good, which we did, and we also took away the few Horses they had, and returned to our camp.

'The second day after, this dreadful disease broke out in our camp, and spread from one tent to another as if the Bad Spirit carried it. We had no belief that one Man could give it to another, any more than a wounded Man could give his wound to another. We did not suffer so much as those that were near the river, into which they rushed and died. We had only a little brook, and about one third of us died, but in some of the other camps there were tents in which every one died. When at length it left us and we moved about to find our people, it was no longer with the song and the dance, but with tears, shrieks, and howlings of despair for those who would never return to us. War was no longer thought of, and we had enough to do to hunt and make provisions for our families, for in our sickness we had consumed all our dried provisions. The Bisons and Red Deer were also gone. We did not see one-half of what was before, and whither they had gone we could not tell. We believed the Good Spirit had forsaken us and allowed the Bad Spirit to become our Master. What little we could spare we offered to the Bad Spirit to let us alone and go to our enemies. To the Good Spirit we offered feathers, branches of trees, and sweet smelling grass. Our hearts were low and dejected, and we shall never be again the same people. To hunt for our families was our sole occupation and to kill Beavers, Wolves and Foxes to trade for our necessaries. We thought of War no more, and perhaps would have made peace with the Snake Indians for they had suffered dreadfully as well as us and had left all this fine country of the Bow River to us.

'We were quiet for about two or three winters, and although we several times saw their young men on the scout, we took no notice of them, as we all require young men to look about the country that our families may sleep in safety and that we may know where to hunt. But the Snake Indians are a bad people, even their allies the Saleesh and Kootanaes cannot trust them, and do not camp with them. No one believes what they say, and they are very treacherous; every one says they are rightly named Snake People, for their tongue is forked like that of a rattlesnake, from which they have their name. I think it was about the third falling of the leaves of the trees, when five of our tents were pitched away to the valleys in the Rocky Mountains, up a branch of the Bow River to hunt the Big Horn Mountain Sheep, as their horns make fine large bowls and are easily cleaned. They were to return on the first snow. All was quiet and we waited for them until the snow lay on the ground; then we got alarmed for their safety and about thirty warriors set off to seek them. It was only two days march, and in the evening they came to the camp. It had been destroyed by a large party of Snake Indians, who had left their marks of snakes' heads painted black on sticks they had set up. The bodies were all there with the Women and Children, but scalped and partly devoured by the Wolves and Dogs.

'Our party returned and related the fate of our people. Other camps, on hearing the news, came and joined us. A War Tent was made and the Chiefs and Warriors assembled. The red pipes were filled with Tobacco, but before being lighted an old Chief arose, and beckoning to the Man who had the fire to keep back, addressed us, saying, "I am an old man, my hair is white and I have seen much: formerly we were healthy and strong and many of us, now we are few to what we were, and the great sickness may come again. We were fond of War, even our Women flattered us to war, and nothing was thought of but scalps for singing and dancing. Now think of what has happened to us all, by destroying each other and doing the work of the Bad Spirit; the Great Spirit became angry with our making the ground red with blood: he called to the Bad Spirit to punish and destroy us, but in doing so, not to let one spot of the ground to be red with blood. And the Bad Spirit did it as we all know. Now we must revenge the death of our people and make the Snake Indians feel the effects of our guns, and other weapons; but the young women must all be saved, and if any has a babe at the breast, it must not be taken from her, nor hurt. All the Boys and Lads that have no weapons must not be killed, but brought to our camps, and be adopted amongst us, to be our people, and make us more numerous and stronger than we are. Thus the Great Spirit will see that when we make war we kill only those who are dangerous to us, and make no more ground red with blood than we can help, and the Bad Spirit will have no more power on us." Everyone signified his assent to the old Chief, and since that time, it has sometimes been acted on, but more with the Women than the Boys, and while it weakens our enemies it makes us stronger. A red pipe was now lighted and the same old Chief taking it, gave three whiffs to the Great Spirit praying him to be kind to them and not forsake them, then three whiffs to the Sun, the same to the Sky, the Earth and the four Winds. The Pipe was passed round, and other pipes lighted. The War Chief then arose, and said "Remember my friends that while we are smoking, the bodies of our friends and relations are being devoured by Wolves and Dogs, and their Souls are sent by the Snake Indians to be the slaves of their relations in the other world. We have made no war on them for more than three summers, and we had hoped to live quietly until our young men had grown up, for we are not many as we used to be; but the Snake Indians, that race of liars, whose tongues are like rattle snakes, have already made war on us, and we can no longer be quiet. The country where they now are is but little known to us, and if they did not feel themselves strong, they would not have dared to have come so far to destroy our people. We must be courageous and active, but also cautious; and my advice is, that three scout parties, each of about ten warriors with a Chief at their head, take three different directions, and cautiously view the country, and not go too far, for enough of our people are already devoured by wolves and our business is revenge, without losing our people."

'After five days, the scout parties returned without seeing the camp of an enemy, or any fresh traces of them. Our War Chief, Kootanae Appe, was now distressed. He had expected some camp would have been seen, and he concluded that the Snake Indians had gone to the southward to their allies, to show the scalps they had taken and make their songs and dances for the victory, and in his speech declared constant war on them until they were exterminated. Affairs were in this state when we arrived, and the narrative [of the] old man having given us the above information. He lighted his pipe; and smoking it out said, the Snake Indians are no match for us; they have no guns and are no match for us, but they have the power to vex us and make us afraid for the small hunting parties that hunt the small deer for dresses and the Big Horn for the same and for Bowls. They keep us always on our guard.

\*　　\*　　\*

The Chief soon collected his warriors and, having examined their arms, he saw that every one had two pairs of shoes, some dried provisions, and other necessaries. In the evening the principal War Chief addressed the Chief at the head of the party; reminding him that the warriors now accompanying him would steadily follow him, that they were sent to destroy their enemies, not to be killed themselves, and made the slaves of their enemies, and that he must be wise and cautious and bring back the Warriors entrusted to his care. Among them was the eldest son of the Old Man in whose tent we lived. They all marched off very quietly as if for hunting. After they were gone, the old man said it was not a war party, but one of those they frequently sent, under guidance of those who had showed courage and conduct in going to war, for we cannot afford to lose our people, we are too few, and these expeditions inure our men to long marches and to suffer hunger and thirst. At the end of about twenty days they returned with about thirty-five Horses in tolerable condition, and fifteen fine Mules, which they had brought away from a large camp of Snake Indians. The Old Man's son gave him a long account of the business. On the sixth evening the scouts ahead came and informed the Chief, that we must be near a camp, as they had seen horses feeding. Night came on, and we went aside to a wood of cotton and poplar trees on the edge of a brook. In the morning some of us climbed the trees and passed the day, but saw nothing. In the night we went higher up the brook and, as it was shoal, we walked in it for some distance, to another wood, and there lay down. Early the next morning, a few of us advanced through the wood, but we had not gone far, before we heard the women with their dogs come for wood for fuel. Some of us returned to the Chief, and the rest watched the women. It was near midday before they all went away. They had only stone axes and stone clubs to break the wood; they took only what was dry, and cut none down. Their number showed us the camp must be large, and sometimes some of them came so close to us that we were afraid of being discovered. The Chief now called us round him, and advised us to be very cautious, as it was plain we were in the vicinity of a large camp, and needed to manage our little provisions, for we must not expect to get any more until we retreated; if we fire a gun at the Deer it will be heard; and if we put an arrow in a deer and he gets away, and they see the deer, it will alarm them, and we shall not be able to get away. My intention is to have something to show our people, and when we retreat, take as many horses as we can with us, to accomplish which, we must have a fair opportunity, and in the mean time be hungry, which we can stand some time, as we have plenty of water to drink. We were getting tired, and our solace was of an evening to look at the horses and mules. At length he said to us to get ready, and pointing to the top of the Mountains, said "See the blue sky is gone and a heavy storm is there, which will soon reach us; and so it did: About sunset we proceeded through the wood, to the horses, and with the lines we carried, each helping the other, we soon had a horse or a mule to ride on. We wanted to drive some with us, but the Chief would not allow it; it was yet daylight when we left the wood, and entered the plains, but the Storm of Wind was very strong and on our backs, and at the gallop, or trot, so as not to tire our horses, we continued to midnight, when we came to a brook, with plenty of grass, and let them get a good feed. After which we held on to sun rising, when seeing a fine low ground, we stayed the rest of the day, keeping watch until night, when we continued our journey. The storm lasted two days and greatly helped us.

'The Old Man told his son, who, in his relation had intimated he did not think the Chief very brave; that it was very fortunate that he was under such a Chief, who had acted so wisely and cautiously; for had he acted otherwise not one of you would have returned. Some young men coming into the tent whom he supposed might have the same opinions as his son, he told them; 'that it required no great bravery for a War Party to attack a small camp, which they were sure to master; but that it required great courage and conduct, to be for several days in the face of a large camp undiscovered; and each of you to bring away a horse from the enemy, instead of leaving your own scalps.'

[1846–51], 1916 (modernized)

# Frances Brooke
## 1724–1789

### Early English-Language Publications in the Northern British Colonies of North America

In contrast to the oral expression of First Nations peoples, the first English-language writing in what became Canada consisted of communications about the experiences of an unfamiliar territory directed to readers who lived elsewhere—audiences who had never seen and might never see what was being described. Such texts exemplified the deep desire by those who had come from away to 'write home', to convey news of the New World to the Old World. The forms these communications took varied widely. Some books began as actual letters to family members or friends before finding a more general audience through publication; others were the journals of settlers or explorers; still others were reports prepared by travellers to communicate their experiences once they had returned to their homeland. Even literary writing was a kind of writing home, since the literary reading public remained in Europe.

Frances Brooke's *The History of Emily Montague* (1769) is doubly this kind of communication: not only is the novel aimed at an audience in England but, as an epistolary novel, it also dramatizes characters in the act of writing letters, many of which are directed to friends and family back in England.

### Frances Brooke

*The History of Emily Montague*, published in London, is often described as the first Canadian novel (and the first North American one). Its author was already well-established as a writer in England before she travelled to Quebec in 1763 to join her husband, the chaplain of the garrison there. Brooke had been part of a literary circle around Samuel Richardson (she adopted the epistolary form of her fiction from Richardson) and, before coming to Canada, she published a novel (*The History of Lady Julia Mandeville*, 1763), a book of poetry, and a play, and had served as editor of a weekly periodical called *The Old Maid*. In addition, she had translated Marie-Jeanne Riccoboni's popular French romance, *Letters from Juliet Lady Catesby, to her Friend Lady Henrietta Campley*, which speaks to an interest in French literature and culture that helped her respond to what had, until very recently, been New France. Except for one visit home, Brooke remained in Quebec until her return, with her husband, to England in 1768.

In *The History of Emily Montague*, Canada stands in relationship to England as do the enchanted woods to the everyday world in Shakespeare's comedies: a place for a pastoral interlude from which all the principals must eventually return to the orderly world of their origins, it allows for a temporary escape from the world of social conventions into romantic intrigues and the confusions of love. The novel's 228 letters are mostly by its young English lovers—Colonel Ed. Rivers, a half-pay officer who originally plans to settle in Canada but eventually returns to England; the beautiful Emily Montague, with whom he falls in love; and Emily's best friend, the coquettish Arabella Fermor.

*Emily Montague* met with a favourable reception in Europe: it was reprinted twice in its author's lifetime and was translated into French. The novel seems to have had little direct influence on later Canadian writers but, because it provides one of the earliest imaginative responses to the country, it is a valuable work for understanding the Canadian literary tradition. Brooke used her novel to depict the garrison-based society at Quebec and to describe the surrounding landscape and the climate, showing the effect these had on the individuals living there; she offers interesting observations about the co-existence of the French and English settlers; and she responds to the Native people and their culture. The experience of the immigrant in the New World receives one of its first literary treatments here and is used to comment on, and to give freshness to, the plot of an otherwise conventional romance—as when Rivers says that if only Emily loves him, 'I know in my own heart, that Canada will no longer be a place of exile' (Letter 83). As well, Brooke sees North American society as raising new questions about the roles of women; and she finds in the New World a need for new language, metaphors, and myths to deal with the radically new experiences she is encountering.

At the same time, Brooke's European background is evident. It is apparent in the way her perception of the Natives seems influenced by a reading of Rousseau, and in the way her reactions to the landscape are shaped by the eighteenth-century fascination with the sublime.

# From *The History of Emily Montague*

## LETTER I
To John Temple, ESQ; at Paris
[From Ed. Rivers]

Cowes, April 10, 1766

After spending two or three very agreeable days here, with a party of friends, in exploring the beauties of the Island, and dropping a tender tear at Carisbrook Castle on the memory of the unfortunate Charles the First,[1] I am just setting out for America, on a scheme I once hinted to you, of settling the lands to which I have a right as a lieutenant-colonel on half pay. On enquiry and mature deliberation, I prefer Canada to New-York for two reasons, that it is wilder, and that the women are handsomer: the first, perhaps, every body will not approve; the latter, I am sure, *you* will.

You may perhaps call my project romantic, but my active temper is ill suited to the lazy character of a reduc'd officer:[2] besides that I am too proud to narrow my circle of life, and not quite unfeeling enough to break in on the little estate which is scarce sufficient to support my mother and sister in the manner to which they have been accustom'd.

---

1 Charles I was incarcerated in Carisbrook Castle on the Isle of Wight before his execution in 1649. The sentiments expressed in this passage owe much to the Gothic sensibility of Brooke's period, with its fondness for indulging in the melancholy feelings inspired by ruined castles.
2 One discharged from active service and put on half pay, subject to recall.

What you call a sacrifice is none at all; I love England, but am not obstinately chain'd down to any spot of earth; nature has charms every where for a man willing to be pleased: at my time of life, the very change of place is amusing; love of variety, and the natural restlessness of man, would give me a relish for this voyage, even if I did not expect, what I really do, to become lord of a principality which will put our large-acred men in England out of countenance. My subjects indeed at present will be only bears and elks, but in time I hope to see the *human face divine* multiplying around me; and, in thus cultivating what is in the rudest state of nature, I shall taste one of the greatest of all pleasures, that of creation, and see order and beauty gradually rise from chaos.

The vessel is unmoor'd; the winds are fair; a gentle breeze agitates the bosom of the deep; all nature smiles: I go with all the eager hopes of a warm imagination; yet friendship casts a lingering look behind.

Our mutual loss, my dear Temple, will be great. I shall never cease to regret you, nor will you find it easy to replace the friend of your youth. You may find friends of equal merit; you may esteem them equally; but few connexions form'd after five and twenty strike root like that early sympathy, which united us almost from infancy, and has increas'd to the very hour of our separation.

What pleasure is there in the friendships of the spring of life, before the world, the mean unfeeling selfish world, breaks in on the gay mistakes of the just-expanding heart, which sees nothing but truth, and has nothing but happiness in prospect!

I am not surpriz'd the heathens rais'd altars to friendship: 'twas natural for untaught superstition to deify the source of every good; they worhsip'd friendship, which animates the moral world, on the same principle as they paid adoration to the sun, which gives life to the world of nature.

I am summon'd on board. Adieu!

*Ed. Rivers*

## LETTER 10
To Miss Rivers, Clarges Street
[From Arabella Fermor[1]]

Silleri, August 24

I have been a month arrived, my dear, without having seen your brother, who is at Montreal, but I am told is expected to-day. I have spent my time however very agreably. I know not what the winter may be, but I am enchanted with the beauty of this country in summer; bold, picturesque, romantic, nature reigns here in all her wanton luxuriance, adorned by a thousand wild graces which mock the cultivated beauties of Europe. The scenery about the town is infinitely lovely; the prospect extensive, and diversified by a variety of hills, woods, rivers, cascades, intermingled with smiling farms and cottages, and bounded by distant mountains which seem to scale the very Heavens.

1 Brooke borrowed this name from the woman to whom Alexander Pope dedicated *The Rape of the Lock* (1712) and who served as a model for its central character, Belinda—the epitome of a mannered coquette. Brooke may also have liked the name because its eighteenth-century pronunciation—'Farmer'—would have made it, like 'Rivers', appropriate to her rustic setting. This letter is addressed to Lucy Rivers, Ed. Rivers' sister, who remains in London.

The days are much hotter here than in England, but the heat is more supportable from the breezes which always spring up about noon; and the evenings are charming beyond expression. We have much thunder and lightening, but very few instances of their being fatal: the thunder is more magnificent and aweful than in Europe, and the lightening brighter and more beautiful; I have even seen it of a clear pale purple, resembling the gay tints of the morning.

The verdure is equal to that of England, and in the evening acquires an unspeakable beauty from the lucid splendor of the fire-flies sparkling like a thousand little stars on the trees and on the grass.

There are two very noble falls of water near Quebec, la Chaudiere and Montmorenci: the former is a prodigious sheet of water, rushing over the wildest rocks, and forming a scene grotesque, irregular, astonishing: the latter, less wild, less irregular, but more pleasing and more majestic, falls from an immense height, down the side of a romantic mountain into the river St Lawrence, opposite the most smiling part of the island of Orleans, to the cultivated charms of which it forms the most striking and agreable contrast.

The river of the same name, which supplies the cascade of Montmorenci, is the most lovely of all inanimate objects: but why do I call it inanimate? It almost breathes; I no longer wonder at the enthusiasm of Greece and Rome; 'twas from objects resembling this their mythology took its rise; it seems the residence of a thousand deities.

Paint to yourself a stupendous rock burst as it were in sunder by the hands of nature, to give passage to a small, but very deep and beautiful river; and forming on each side a regular and magnificent wall, crowned with the noblest woods that can be imagined; the sides of these romantic walls adorned with a variety of the gayest flowers, and in many places little streams of the purest water gushing through, and losing themselves in the river below: a thousand natural grottoes in the rock make you suppose yourself in the abode of the Nereids;[2] as a little island, covered with flowering shrubs, about a mile above the falls, where the river enlarges itself as to give it room, seems intended for the throne of the river goddess. Beyond this, the rapids, formed by the irregular projections of the rock, which in some places seem almost to meet, rival in beauty, as they excel in variety, the cascade itself, and close this little world of enchantment.

In short, the loveliness of this fairy scene alone more than pays the fatigues of my voyage; and, if I ever murmur at having crossed the Atlantic, remind me that I have seen the river Montmorenci.

I can give you a very imperfect account of the people here; I have only examined the landscape about Quebec, and have given very little attention to the figures; the French ladies are handsome, but as to the beaux, they appear to me not at all dangerous, and one might safely walk in a wood by moonlight with the most agreable Frenchman here. I am not surprized the Canadian ladies take such pains to seduce our men from us; but I think it a little hard we have no temptation to make reprisals.

2  Sea nymphs.

I am at present at an extreme pretty farm on the banks of the river St Lawrence; the house stands at the foot of a steep mountain covered with a variety of trees, forming a verdant sloping wall, which rises in a kind of regular confusion,

'Shade above shade, a woody theatre',[3]

and has in front this noble river, on which the ships continually passing present to the delighted eye the most charming moving picture imaginable: I never saw a place so formed to inspire that pleasing lassitude, that divine inclination to saunter, which may not improperly be called, the luxurious indolence of the country. I intend to build a temple here to the charming goddess of laziness.

A gentleman is just coming down the winding path on the side of the hill, whom by his air I take to be your brother. Adieu! I must receive him: my father is at Quebec. Yours,

*Arabella Fermor*

Your brother has given me a very pleasing piece of intelligence: my friend Emily Montague is at Montreal, and is going to be married to great advantage; I must write to her immediately, and insist on her making me a visit before she marries. She came to America two years ago, with her uncle Colonel Montague, who died here, and I imagined was gone back to England; she is however at Montreal with Mrs Melmoth, a distant relation of her mother's. Adieu! *ma tres chere!*

3  Milton, *Paradise Lost*: 'Cedar, and pine, and fir, and branching palm, / A sylvan scene, and, as the ranks ascend / Shade above shade, a woody theatre / of stateliest view' (IV, 139–42). Milton's depictions of Eden frequently inform Brooke's descriptions of the New World's landscapes.

## LETTER 11
To Miss Rivers, Clarges Street
[From Ed. Rivers]

Quebec, September 10

I find, my dear, that absence and amusement are the best remedies for a beginning passion; I have passed a fortnight at the Indian village of Lorette,[1] where the novelty of the scene, and the enquiries I have been led to make into their antient religion and manners, have been of a thousand times more service to me than all the reflection in the world would have been.

I will own to you that I staid too long at Montreal, or rather at Major Melmoth's; to be six weeks in the same house with one of the most amiable, most pleasing of women, was a trying situation to a heart full of sensibility, and of a sensibility which has been hitherto, from a variety of causes, a good deal restrained. I should have avoided the danger from the first, had it appeared to me what it really was; but I thought myself secure in the consideration of her engagements, a defence however which I found grow weaker every day.

1  More properly Jeune Lorette, where the Hurons settled in 1697, having previously taken refuge from the Iroquois at Lorette a generation earlier.

But to my savages: other nations talk of liberty, they possess it; nothing can be more astonishing than to see a little village of about thirty or forty families, the small remains of the Hurons, almost exterminated by long and continual war with the Iroquoise, preserve their independence in the midst of an European colony consisting of seventy thousand inhabitants; yet the fact is true of the savages of Lorette; they assert and they maintain that independence with a spirit truly noble. One of our company having said something which an Indian understood as a supposition that they had been *subjects* of France, his eyes struck fire, he stop'd him abruptly, contrary to their respectful and sensible custom of never interrupting the person who speaks. 'You mistake, brother,' said he; 'we are subject to no prince; a savage is free all over the world.' And he spoke only truth; they are not only free as a people, but every individual is perfectly so. Lord of himself, at once subject and master, a savage knows no superior, a circumstance which has a striking effect on his behaviour; unawed by rank or riches, distinctions unknown amongst his own nation, he would enter as unconcerned, would possess all his powers as freely in the palace of an oriental monarch, as in the cottage of the meanest peasant: 'tis the species, 'tis man, 'tis his equal he respects, without regarding the gaudy trappings, the accidental advantages, to which polished nations pay homage.

I have taken some pains to develop their present, as well as past, religious sentiments, because the Jesuit missionaries have boasted so much of their conversion; and find they have rather engrafted a few of the most plain and simple truths of Christianity on their ancient superstitions, than exchanged one faith for another; they are baptized, and even submit to what they themselves call the *yoke* of confession, and worship according to the outward forms of the Romish church, the drapery of which cannot but strike minds unused to splendor; but their belief is very little changed, except that the women seem to pay great reverence to the Virgin, perhaps because flattering to the sex. They anciently believed in one God, the ruler and creator of the universe, whom they called *the Great Spirit* and the *Master of Life*; in the sun as his image and representative; in a multitude of inferior sprits and demons; and in a future state of rewards and punishments, or, to use their own phrase, in *a country of souls*. They reverenced the spirits of their departed heroes, but it does not appear that they paid them any religious adoration. Their morals were more pure, their manners more simple, than those of polished nations, except in what regarded the intercourse of the sexes: the young women before marriage were indulged in great libertinism, hid however under the most reserved and decent exterior. They held adultery in abhorrence, and with the more reason as their marriages were dissolvable at pleasure. The missionaries are said to have found no difficulty so great in gaining them to Christianity, as that of persuading them to marry for life: they regarded the Christian system of marriage as contrary to the laws of nature and reason; and asserted that, as the *Great Spirit* formed us to be happy, it was opposing his will, to continue together when otherwise.

The sex we have so unjustly excluded from power in Europe have a great share in the Huron government; the chief is chose by the matrons from amongst the nearest male relations, by the female line, of him he is to succeed; and is generally an aunt's or sister's son; a custom which, if we examine strictly into the principle on which it is founded, seems a little to contradict what we are told of the extreme chastity of the married ladies.

The power of the chief is extremely limited; he seems rather to advise his people as a father than command them as a master: yet, as his commands are always reasonable, and for the general good, no prince in the world is so well obeyed. They have a supreme council of ancients, into which every man enters of course at an age fixed, and another of assistants to the chief on common occasions, the members of which are like him elected by the matrons: I am pleased with this last regulation, as women are, beyond all doubt, the best judges of the merit of men; and I should be extremely pleased to see it adopted in England: canvassing for elections would then be the most agreeable thing in the world, and I am sure the ladies would give their votes on much more generous principles than we do. In the true sense of the word *we* are the savages, who so impolitely deprive you of the common rights of citizenship, and leave you no power but that of which we cannot deprive you, the resistless power of your charms. By the way, I don't think you are obliged in conscience to obey laws you have had no share in making; your plea would certainly be at least as good as that of the Americans, about which we every day hear so much.

The Hurons have no positive laws; yet being a people not numerous, with a strong sense of honor, and in that state of equality which gives no food to the most tormenting passions of the human heart, and the council of ancients having a power to punish atrocious crimes, which power however they very seldom find occasion to use, they live together in a tranquillity and order which appears to us surprizing.

In more numerous Indian nations, I am told, every village has its chief and its councils, and is perfectly independent of the rest; but on great occasions summon a general council, to which every village sends deputies.

Their language is at once sublime and melodious; but, having much fewer ideas, it is impossible it can be so copious as those of Europe: the pronunciation of the men is guttural, but that of the women extremely soft and pleasing; without understanding one word of the language, the sound of it is very agreeable to me. Their style even in speaking French is bold and metaphorical: and I am told is on important occasions extremely sublime. Even in common conversation they speak in figures, of which I have this moment an instance. A savage woman was wounded lately in defending an English family from the drunken rage of one of her nation. I asked her after her wound; 'It is well,' said she; 'my sisters at Quebec (meaning the English ladies) have been kind to me; and piastres,[2] you know, are very healing.'

They have no idea of letters, no alphabet, nor is their language reducible to rules: 'tis by painting they preserve the memory of the only events which interest them, or that they think worth recording, the conquests gained over their enemies in war.

When I speak of their paintings, I should not omit that, though extremely rude, they have a strong resemblance to the Chinese, a circumstance which struck me the more, as it is not the stile of nature. Their dances also, the most lively pantomimes I ever saw, and especially the dance of peace, exhibit variety of attitudes resembling the figures on Chinese fans; nor have their features and complexion less likeness to the pictures we see of the Tartars, as their wandering manner of life, before they became Christians, was the same.

2 Coins.

If I thought it necessary to suppose they were not natives of the country, and that America was peopled later than the other quarters of the world, I should imagine them the descendants of Tartars; as nothing can be more easy than their passage from Asia, from which America is probably not divided; or, if it is, by a very narrow channel. But I leave this to those who are better informed, being a subject on which I honestly confess my ignorance.

I have already observed, that they retain most of their antient superstitions. I should particularize their belief in dreams, of which folly even repeated disappointments cannot cure them: they have also an unlimited faith in their *powawers*, or conjurers, of whom there is one in every Indian village, who is at once physician, orator, and divine, and who is consulted as an oracle on every occasion. As I happened to smile at the recital a savage was making of a prophetic dream, from which he assured us of the death of an English officer whom I knew to be alive, 'You Europeans', said he, 'are the most unreasonable people in the world; you laugh at our belief in dreams, and yet expect us to believe things a thousand times more incredible.'

Their general character is difficult to describe; made up of contrary and even contradictory qualities; they are indolent, tranquil, quiet, humane in peace; active, restless, cruel, ferocious in war: courteous, attentive, hospitable, and even polite, when kindly treated; haughty, stern, vindictive, when they are not; and their resentment is the more to be dreaded, as they hold it a point of honor to dissemble their sense of an injury[3] till they find an opportunity to revenge it.

They are patient of cold and heat, of hunger and thirst, even beyond all belief when necessity requires, passing whole days, and often three or four days together, without food, in the woods, when on the watch for an enemy, or even on their hunting parties; yet indulging themselves in their feasts even to the most brutal degree of intemperance. They despise death, and suffer the most excruciating tortures not only without a groan, but with an air of triumph; singing their death song, deriding their tormentors, and threatening them with the vengeance of their surviving friends: yet hold it honorable to fly before an enemy that appears the least superior in number or force.

Deprived by their extreme ignorance, and that indolence which nothing but their ardor for war can surmount, of all the conveniencies, as well as elegant refinements of polished life; strangers to the softer passions, love being with them on the same footing as amongst their fellow-tenants of the woods, their lives appear to me rather tranquil than happy: they have fewer cares, but they have also much fewer enjoyments, than fall to our share. I am told, however, that, though insensible to love, they are not without affections; are extremely awake to friendship, and passionately fond of their children.

They are of a copper color, which is rendered more unpleasing by a quantity of coarse red on their cheeks; but the children, when born, are of a pale silver white; perhaps their indelicate custom of greasing their bodies, and their being so much exposed to the air and sun even from infancy, may cause that total change of complexion, which I know not how otherwise to account for: their hair is black and shining, the women's very long, parted at the top, and combed back, tied behind, and often twisted with a

3 That is, to pretend not to be insulted.

thong of leather, which they think very ornamental: the dress of both sexes is a close jacket, reaching to their knees, with spatterdashes[4] all of coarse blue cloth, shoes of deer-skin, embroidered with porcupine quills, and sometimes with silver spangles; and a blan-ket thrown across their shoulders, and fastened before with a kind of bodkin,[5] with necklaces, and other ornaments of beads or shells.

They are in general tall, well made, and agile to the last degree; have a lively imag-ination, a strong memory; and, as far as their interests are concerned, are very dextrous politicians.

Their address is cold and reserved; but their treatment of strangers, and the unhappy, infinitely kind and hospitable. A very worthy priest, with whom I am acquainted at Quebec, was some years since shipwrecked in December on the island of Anticosti:[6] after a variety of distresses, not difficult to be imagined on an island without inhabitants, during the severity of a winter even colder than that of Canada; he, with the small remains of his companions who survived such complicated distress, early in the spring, reached the main land in their boat, and wandered to a cabbin of savages; the ancient of which, having heard his story, bid him enter, and liberally sup-plied their wants: 'Approach, brother,' said he; 'the unhappy have a right to our assis-tance; we are men, and cannot but feel for the distresses which happen to men;' a sentiment which has a strong resemblance to a celebrated one in a Greek tragedy.[7]

You will not expect more from me on this subject, as my residence here has been short, and I can only be said to catch a few marking[8] features flying. I am unable to give you a picture at full length.

Nothing astonishes me so much as to find their manners so little changed by their intercourse with the Europeans; they seem to have learnt nothing of us but excess in drinking.

The situation of the village is very fine, on an eminence, gently rising to a thick wood at some distance, a beautiful little serpentine river in front, on which are a bridge, a mill, and a small cascade, at such a distance as to be very pleasing objects from their houses; and a cultivated country, intermixed with little woods lying between them and Quebec, from which they are distant only nine very short miles.

What a letter have I written! I shall quit my post of historian to your friend Miss Fermor; the ladies love writing much better than we do; and I should perhaps be only just, if I said they write better.

Adieu!

*Ed. Rivers*

---

4 Leggings worn to protect the trousers or stockings from mud.
5 A small pointed instrument.
6 Ile d'Anticosti in the Gulf of St Lawrence
7 In fact this is a rather common sentiment in Greek tragedy; the resemblance Brooke has in mind may be to Theseus' first speech in Sophocles' *Oedipus at Colonus*:

> . . . *no wanderer shall come, as you do,*
> *And be denied my audience or aid.*
> *I know I am only a man; I have no more*
> *To hope for in the end than you have.*

8 Characteristic.

**LETTER 49**

To Miss Rivers, Clarges Street

[From Arabella Fermor]

Silleri, Jan. 1

It is with difficulty I breathe, my dear; the cold is so amazingly intense as almost totally to stop respiration. I have business, the business of pleasure, at Quebec; but have not the courage to stir from the stove.

We have had five days, the severity of which none of the natives remember to have ever seen equaled: 'tis said, the cold is beyond all the thermometers here, tho' intended for the climate.

The strongest wine freezes in a room which has a stove in it; even brandy is thickened to the consistence of oil: the largest wood fire, in a wide chimney, does not throw out its heat a quarter of a yard.

I must venture to Quebec to-morrow, or have company at home: amusements are here necessary to life; we must be jovial, or the blood will freeze in our veins.

I no longer wonder the elegant arts are unknown here; the rigour of the climate suspends the very powers of the understanding; what then must become of those of the imagination? Those who expect to see

'A new Athens rising near the pole',[1]

will find themselves extremely disappointed. Genius will never mount high, where the faculties of the mind are benumbed half the year.

'Tis sufficient employment for the most lively spirit here to contrive how to preserve an existence, of which there are moments that one is hardly conscious: the cold really sometimes brings on a sort of stupefaction.

We had a million of beaux here yesterday, notwithstanding the severe cold: 'tis the Canadian custom, calculated I suppose for the climate, to visit all the ladies on New-year's-day, who sit dressed in form to be kissed. I assure you, however, our kisses could not warm them; but we were obliged, to our eternal disgrace, to call in rasberry brandy as an auxiliary.

You would have died to see the men; they look just like so many bears in their open carrioles,[2] all wrapped in furs from head to foot; you see nothing of the human form appear, but the tip of a nose.

They have intire coats of beaver skin exactly like Friday's in Robinson Crusoe, and casques[3] on their heads like the old knights errant in romance; you never saw such tremendous figures; but without this kind of cloathing it would be impossible to stir out at present.

---

1 Adapted from a passage in Pope, 'Two Chorus's to the Tragedy of Brutus' (1717), about the Muses going into exile from ancient Greece to distant Britain, whereupon the island will:

*See arts her savage sons controul,*
*And* Athens *rising near the pole!*

2 A kind of sleigh, usually for one person.

3 Helmets. In Daniel Defoe's *Robinson Crusoe* (1719), Friday has a coat made of goatskin.

The ladies are equally covered up, tho' in a less unbecoming style; they have long cloth cloaks with loose hoods, like those worn by the market-women in the north of England. I have one in scarlet, the hood lined with sable, the prettiest ever seen here, in which I assure you I look amazingly handsome; the men think so, and call me the *Little red riding-hood*; a name which becomes me as well as the hood.

The Canadian ladies wear these cloaks in India silk in summer, which, fluttering in the wind, look really graceful on a fine woman.

Besides our riding-hoods, when we go out, we have a large buffaloe's skin under our feet, which turns up, and wraps round us almost to our shoulders; so that, upon the whole, we are pretty well guarded from the weather as well as the men.

Our covered carrioles too have not only canvas windows (we dare not have glass, because we often overturn), but cloth curtains to draw all around us; the extreme swiftness of these carriages also, which dart along like lightening, helps to keep one warm, by promoting the circulation of the blood.

I pity the Fitz;[4] no tiger was ever so hard-hearted as I am this weather: the little god[5] has taken his flight, like the swallows. I say nothing, but cruelty is no virtue in Canada; at least at this season.

I suppose Pygmalion's statue was some frozen Canadian gentlewoman, and a sudden warm day thawed her.[6] I love to expound ancient fables, and I think no exposition can be more natural than this.

Would you know what makes me chatter so this morning? Papa has made me take some excellent *liqueur*, 'tis the mode here; all the Canadian ladies take a little, which makes them so coquet and agreable. Certainly brandy makes a woman talk like an angel. Adieu!

Yours,

*A. Fermor*

4 Captain J. Fitzgerald, Arabella's suitor in Canada.
5 Cupid.
6 In Greek mythology Pygmalion was a sculptor who made a statue of such beauty that he fell in love with it. The goddess Aphrodite took pity on his plight and brought the statue to life.

## LETTER 80
To Miss Rivers, Clarges Street
[From Arabella Fermor]

Silleri, Feb. 25

Those who have heard no more of a Canadian winter than what regards the intenseness of its cold, must suppose it a very joyless season: 'tis, I assure you, quite otherwise; there are indeed some days here of the severity of which those who were never out of England can form no conception; but those days seldom exceed a dozen in a whole winter; nor do they come in succession, but at intermediate periods, as the winds set in from the North-West; which, coming some hundred leagues, from frozen lakes and rivers, over woods and mountains covered with snow, would be insupportable, were it not for the furs with which the country abounds, in such variety and plenty as to be within the reach of all its inhabitants.

Thus defended, the British belles set the winter of Canada at defiance; and the season of which you seem to entertain such terrible ideas, is that of the utmost chearfulness and festivity.

But what particularly pleases me is, there is no place where women are of such importance:[1] not one of the sex, who has the least share of attractions, is without a levee[2] of beaux interceding for the honor of attending her on some party, of which every day produces three or four.

I am just returned from one of the most agreable jaunts imagination can paint, to the island of Orleans, by the falls of Montmorenci; the latter is almost nine miles distant, across the great bason of Quebec; but as we are obliged to reach it in winter by the waving line, our direct road being intercepted by the inequalities of the ice, it is now perhaps a third more. You will possibly suppose a ride of this kind must want one of the greatest essentials to entertainment, that of variety, and imagine it only one dull whirl over an unvaried plain of snow; on the contrary, my dear, we pass hills and mountains of ice in the trifling space of these few miles. The bason of Quebec is formed by the conflux of the rivers St Charles and Montmorenci with the great river St Lawrence, the rapidity of whose flood tide, as these rivers are gradually seized by the frost, breaks up the ice, and drives it back in heaps, till it forms ridges of transparent rock to an height that is astonishing, and of a strength which bids defiance to the utmost rage of the most furiously rushing tide.

This circumstance makes this little journey more pleasing than you can possibly conceive: the serene blue sky above, the dazzling brightness of the sun, and the colors from the refraction of its rays on the transparent part of these ridges of ice, the winding course these oblige you to make, the sudden disappearing of a train of fifteen or twenty carrioles, as these ridges intervene, which again discover themselves on your rising to the top of the frozen mount, the tremendous appearance both of the ascent and descent, which however are not attended with the least danger; all together give a grandeur and variety to the scene, which almost rise to enchantment.

Your dull foggy climate affords nothing that can give you the least idea of our frost pieces in Canada; nor can you form any notion of our amusements, of the agreableness of a covered carriole, with a sprightly fellow, rendered more sprightly by the keen air and romantic scene about him; to say nothing of the fair lady at his side.

Even an overturning has nothing alarming in it; you are laid gently down on a soft bed of snow, without the least danger of any kind; and an accident of this sort only gives a pretty fellow occasion to vary the style of his civilities, and shew a greater degree of attention.

But it is almost time to come to Montmorenci; to avoid, however, fatiguing you or myself, I shall refer the rest of our tour to another letter, which will probably accompany this: my meaning is, that two moderate letters are vastly better than one long one; in which sentiment I know you agree with.

Yours,

*A. Fermor*

---

1 In Letter 6 Brooke had Ed. Rivers say almost the same thing of the women he encounters among the French farmers: they play a civilizing role and 'Their conversation is lively and amusing, all the little knowledge of Canada is confined to the [female] sex. . . .'

2 An assembly of visitors, especially but not necessarily in the morning.

## LETTER 123
To the Earl of ———
[From Captain Wm. Fermor[1]]

Silleri, April 14

England, however populous, is undoubtedly, my Lord, too small to afford very large supplies of people to her colonies: and her people are also too useful, and of too much value, to be suffered to emigrate, if they can be prevented, whilst there is sufficient employment for them at home.

It is not only our interest to have colonies; they are not only necessary to our commerce, and our greatest and surest source of wealth, but our very being as a powerful commercial nation depends on them: it is therefore an object of all others most worthy our attention, that they should be as flourishing and populous as possible.[2]

It is however equally our interest to support them at as little expence of our own inhabitants as possible: I therefore look on the acquisition of such a number of subjects as we found in Canada, to be a much superior advantage to that of gaining ten times the immense tract of land ceded to us, if uncultivated and destitute of inhabitants.

But it is not only contrary to our interest to spare many of our own people as settlers in America; it must also be considered, that, if we could spare them, the English are the worst settlers on new lands in the universe.

Their attachment to their native country, especially amongst the lower ranks of people, is so very strong, that few of the honest and industrious can be prevailed on to leave it; those therefore who go, are generally the dissolute and the idle, who are of no use any where.

The English are also, though industrious, active, and enterprizing, ill fitted to bear the hardships, and submit to the wants, which inevitably attend an infant settlement even on the most fruitful lands.

The Germans, on the contrary, with the same useful qualities, have a patience, a perseverance, and abstinence, which peculiarly fit them for the cultivation of new countries; too great encouragement therefore cannot be given to them to settle in our colonies: they make better settlers than our own people; and at the same time their numbers are an acquisition of real strength where they fix, without weakening the mother country.

It is long since the populousness of Europe has been the cause of her sending out colonies: a better policy prevails; mankind are enlightened; we are now convinced, both by reason and experience, that no industrious people can be too populous.

The northern swarms[3] were compelled to leave their respective countries, not because those countries were unable to support them, but because they were too idle to cultivate the ground: they were a ferocious, ignorant, barbarous people, averse to

---

1 Arabella's father. A Polonius-like character, he writes letters full of pompous statements and conventional wisdom. In Letter 135 he observes: 'People who have no ideas out of the common road are, I believe, generally the greatest talkers.'

2 Fermor's colonial attitude is expressed even more emphatically in Letter 133: 'Every advantage you give the North American trade centers at last in the mother country, they are the bees, who roam abroad for that honey which enriches the paternal hive.'

3 Fermor here refers to the medieval migration of barbarians out of northern Europe.

labor, attached to war, and, like our American savages, believing every employment not relative to this favorite object, beneath the dignity of man.

Their emigrations therefore were less owing to their populousness, than to their want of industry, and barbarous contempt of agriculture and every useful art.

It is with pain I am compelled to say, the late spirit of encouraging the monopoly of farms, which, from a narrow, short-sighted policy, prevails amongst our landed men at home, and the alarming growth of celibacy amongst the peasantry, which is its necessary consequence, to say nothing of the same ruinous increase of celibacy in higher ranks, threatens us with such a decrease of population, as will probably equal that caused by the ravages of those scourges of heaven, the sword, the famine, and the pestilence.[4]

If this selfish policy continues to extend itself, we shall in a few years be so far from being able to send emigrants to America, that we shall be reduced to solicit their return, and that of the posterity, to prevent England's becoming in its turn an uncultivated desert.

But to return to Canada; this large acquisition of people is an invaluable treasure, if managed, as I doubt not it will be, to the best advantage; if they are won by the gentle arts of persuasion, and the gradual progress of knowledge, to adopt so much of our manners as tends to make them happier in themselves, and more useful members of the society to which they belong: if with our language, which they should by every means be induced to learn, they acquire the mild genius of our religion and laws, and that spirit of industry, enterprize, and commerce, to which we owe all our greatness.

\* \* \*

Your Lordship enquires into the nature of this climate in respect to health. The air being uncommonly pure and serene, it is favorable to life beyond any I ever knew: the people live generally to a very advanced age; and are remarkably free from diseases of every kind, except consumptions, to which the younger part of the inhabitants are a good deal subject.

It is however a circumstance one cannot help observing, that they begin to look old much sooner than the people in Europe; on which my daughter observes, that it is not very pleasant for women to reside in a country where people have a short youth, and a long old age.

The diseases of cold countries are in general owing to want of perspiration; for which reason exercise, and even dissipation, are here the best medicines.

The Indians therefore shewed their good sense in advising the French, on their first arrival, to use dancing, mirth, chearfulness, and content, as the best remedies against the inconveniences of the climate.

I have already swelled this letter to such a length, that I must postpone to another time my account of the peculiar natural productions of Canada; only observing, that one would imagine heaven intended a social intercourse between the most distant

---

4 For much of the previous century, holdings of farmland in Britain had been becoming more and more concentrated among relatively few large landholders. The notion that the consequent displacement of farm families would result in a decline in fertility was a common—if unwarranted—fear of the time.

nations, by giving them productions of the earth so very different each from the other, and each more than sufficient for itself, that the exchange might be the means of spreading the bond of society and brotherhood over the whole globe.

In my opinion, the man who conveys, and causes to grow in any country, a grain, a fruit, or even a flower, it never possessed before, deserves more praise than a thousand heroes: he is a benefactor, he is in some degree a creator.

I have the honor to be,

My Lord,

Your Lordship's, &c.

*William Fermor*

## LETTER 127

To John Temple, ESQ; Pall Mall

[From Arabella Fermor]

Silleri, April 18

\* \* \*

Cruel creature! why did you give me the idea of flowers? I now envy your foggy climate: the earth with you at this moment covered with a thousand lovely children of the spring; with us, it is an universal plain of snow.

Our beaux are terribly at a loss for similies: you have lilies of the valley for comparisons; we nothing but what with the idea of whiteness gives that of coldness too.

This is all the quarrel I have with Canada: the summer is delicious, the winter pleasant with all its severities; but alas! the smiling spring is not here; we pass from winter to summer in an instant, and lose the sprightly season of the Loves.

A letter from the God of my idolatry[1]—I must answer it instantly.

Adieu! Yours, &c.

*A. Fermor*

1  Captain Fitzgerald.

## LETTER 131

To the Earl of ———

[From Wm. Fermor]

Silleri, April 20, Evening

We are returned, my Lord, from having seen an object as beautiful and magnificent in itself, as pleasing from the idea it gives of renewing once more our intercourse with Europe.

Before I saw the breaking up of the vast body of ice, which forms what is here called *the bridge,* from Quebec to Point Levi, I imagined there could be nothing in it worth attention; that the ice would pass away, or dissolve gradually, day after day, as the influence of the sun, and warmth of the air and earth increased; and that we should see the river open, without having observed by what degrees it became so.

But I found *the great river*, as the savages with much propriety call it, maintain its dignity in this instance as in all others, and assert its superiority over those petty streams which we honor with the names of rivers in England. Sublimity is the characteristic of this western world; the loftiness of the mountains, the grandeur of the lakes and rivers, the majesty of the rocks shaded with a picturesque variety of beautiful trees and shrubs, and crowned with the noblest of the offspring of the forest, which form the banks of the latter, are as much beyond the power of fancy as that of description: a landscape-painter might here expand his imagination, and find ideas which he will seek in vain in our comparatively little world.

The object of which I am speaking has all the American magnificence.

The ice before the town, or, to speak in the Canadian stile, *the bridge*, being of a thickness not less than five feet, a league in length, and more than a mile broad, resists for a long time the rapid tide that attempts to force it from the banks.

We are prepared by many circumstances to expect something extraordinary in this event, if I may so call it: every increase of heat in the weather for near a month before the ice leaves the banks; every warm day gives you terror for those you see venturing to pass it in carrioles; yet one frosty night makes it again so strong, that even the ladies, and the timid amongst them, still venture themselves over in parties of pleasure; though greatly alarmed at their return, if a few hours of uncommon warmth intervene.

But, during the last fortnight, the alarm grows indeed a very serious one: the eye can distinguish, even at a considerable distance, that the ice is softened and detached from the banks; and you dread every step being death to those who have still the temerity to pass it, which they will continue always to do till one or more pay their rashness with their lives.

From the time the ice is no longer a bridge on which you see crowds driving with such vivacity on business or pleasure, every one is looking eagerly for its breaking away, to remove the bar to the continually wished and expected event, of the arrival of ships from that world from whence we have seemed so long in a manner excluded.

The hour is come; I have been with a crowd of both sexes, and all ranks, hailing the propitious moment: our situation, on the top of Cape Diamond, gave us a prospect some leagues above and below the town; above Cape Diamond the river was open, it was so below Point Levi, the rapidity of the current having forced a passage for the water under the transparent bridge, which for more than a league continued firm.

We stood waiting with all the eagerness of expectation; the tide came rushing with an amazing impetuosity; the bridge seemed to shake, yet resisted the force of the waters; the tide recoiled, it made a pause, it stood still, it returned with redoubled fury, the immense mass of ice gave way.

A vast plain appeared in motion; it advanced with solemn and majestic pace: the points of land on the banks of the river for a few moments stopped its progress; but the immense weight of so prodigious a body, carried along by a rapid current, bore down all opposition with a force irresistible.

There is no describing how beautiful the opening river appears, every moment gaining on the sight, till, in a time less than can possibly be imagined, the ice passing Point Levi, is hid in one moment by the projecting land, and all is once more a clear plain before you; giving at once the pleasing, but unconnected, ideas of that direct intercourse with Europe from which we have been so many months excluded, and of the earth's again opening her fertile bosom, to feast our eyes and imagination with her various verdant and flowery productions.

I am afraid I have conveyed a very inadequate idea of the scene which has just passed before me; it however struck me so strongly, that it was impossible for me not to attempt it.

If my painting has the least resemblance to the original, your Lordship will agree with me, that the very vicissitudes of season here partake of the sublimity which so strongly characterizes the country.

The changes of season in England, being slow and gradual, are but faintly felt; but being here sudden, instant, violent, afford to the mind, with the lively pleasure arising from meer change, the very high additional one of its being accompanied with grandeur. I have the honor to be,

My Lord,

Your Lordship's, &c.

*William Fermor*

## LETTER 169
To Captain Fermor, at Silleri
[From Ed. Rivers[1]]

Aug. 6

I have been taking an exact survey of the house and estate with my mother, in order to determine on some future plan of life.

'Tis inconceivable what I felt on returning to a place so dear to me, and which I had not seen for many years; I ran hastily from one room to another; I traversed the garden with inexpressible eagerness: my eye devoured every object; there was not a tree, not a bush, which did not revive some pleasing, some soft idea.

I felt, to borrow a very pathetic expression of Thompson's,

'A thousand little tendernesses throb',[2]

on revisiting those dear scenes of infant happiness; which were increased by having with me that estimable, that affectionate mother, to whose indulgence all my happiness had been owing.

\* \* \*

The situation of the house is enchanting; and with all my passion for the savage luxuriance of America, I begin to find my taste return for the more mild and regular charms of my native country.

We have no Chaudieres, no Montmorencis, none of those magnificent scenes on which the Canadians have a right to pride themselves; but we excel them in the lovely,

1 After his return to England.
2 Actually 'Ten thousand little tendernesses throb': James Thomson, *Agamemnon. A Tragedy* (1738), I, iii, 8.

the smiling: in enameled meadows, in waving corn-fields, in gardens the boast of Europe; in every elegant art which adorns and softens human life; in all the riches and beauty which cultivation can give.

I begin to think I may be blest in the possession of my Emily, without betraying her into a state of want; we may, I begin to flatter myself, live with decency, in retirement; and, in my opinion, there are a thousand charms in retirement with those we love.

Upon the whole, I believe we shall be able to live, taking the word live in the sense of lovers, not of the *beau monde*, who will never allow a little country squire of four hundred pounds a year to *live*.[3]

Time may do more for us; at least, I am of an age and temper to encourage hope.

All here are perfectly yours.

Adieu! my dear friend,

Your affectionate

*Ed. Rivers*

1769

3　As in many works of the period that deal with marriage among the landed gentry on fixed incomes, the question of money plays an important role in the question of matrimony. The opposition in this passage between fashionable society (the *beau monde*) and a simple country life that embodies the pastoral ideal of moderation occurs several times in the book. Compare Letter 177: 'Upon the whole, I believe, the most agreable, as well as most free of all situations, to be that of a little country gentleman, who lives upon his income, and knows enough of the world not to envy his richer neighbours.' In the conclusion to the novel, however, Brooke places Ed. Rivers and his new wife beyond all financial constraints by having Emily turn out to be a lost heir.

# Samuel Hearne
## 1745–1792

### Exploration Narratives

A set of interrelated desires—to observe the environment closely, to map physical and relational space, to document the details of one's milieu, and to discover the sources of the present—has been evident in Canadian writing across historical eras and literary movements. This habit of mind, which may arise out of a need to make the new country comprehensible, first manifested itself in the early non-fiction of what became English Canada as a drive to record the objective details of experience. A particularly important form of this early communication was the exploration narrative. Even before

Britain took over France's North American colonies in the mid-eighteenth century, English-language explorers, land surveyors, and traders arrived as representatives of empire and agents of commercial enterprises, such as the fur-trading Hudson's Bay and North West companies, seeking information about Canadian seacoasts and the remoter parts of Canada. Their records became useful sources for more than just the institutions that sponsored their endeavours; published in England, these documents helped shape understanding of the new national territories that Britain had acquired.

Reworked from hasty field notes into finished and shapely stories, these exploration narratives are, as Germaine Warkentin observes in her preface to *Canadian Exploration Literature*, best understood as ' "incremental" texts', because they had passed through 'several stages of composition of which the daily log is only the first': some had 'additions by fellow explorers'; and most were 'revised by other hands before appearing as a grand quarto volume of "travels" to ornament a gentleman's library.' In an age when the British public was fascinated by the heroism of adventurers exploring the unknown, these tales of endurance and discovery were compelling reading that found a ready market.

The fact that these accounts were, in their published form, intended for a European audience played a role in what they described and how they were shaped. While close attention to detail and a desire to provide detached observation and useful scientific knowledge about the flora and fauna remained an important feature of the texts, they had to have a narrative meant to hold the reader's attention. The establishing of trade and the opening up of the land therefore became secondary to a focus on individual experience: to European readers the record of personal suffering and danger epitomized the exploration of a northern land such as Canada. These narratives of survival affirmed the ability of British men—accompanied by their helpful French-Canadian or Métis guides and assisted by the Native peoples they encountered—to overcome extreme conditions in distant outposts. In Canada in the twentieth century, such accounts began to play a different role: as cultural nationalism invited new investigations into the nation's origins, these early writings were viewed as an important source of Canadian cultural discourse and were given new editions by scholars and excerpted in anthologies.

## Samuel Hearne

The variety of goals that sent early wanderers out into the wilderness is eloquently attested to in the 'Orders and Instructions' given to Samuel Hearne by the Hudson's Bay Company in 1769. Instructed to explore 'the Northern Indians Country, &c.', Hearne was told to locate the Indian guide Matonabbee and, with him, to seek out 'a river represented by the Indians to abound with copper ore, animals of the furr kind, &c., and which is said to be so far to the Northward, that in the middle of the Summer the Sun does not set. . . . And if the said river be likely to be of any utility, take possession of it on behalf of the Hudson's Bay Company.' If this were not enough, a subsequent letter of instruction enjoins him also to undertake a 'quest of a North West Passage, Copper Mines, or any other thing that may be serviceable to the British Nation in general, or the Hudson's Bay Company in particular.'

Hearne, a Londoner, had already served in the Royal Navy for nearly ten years before joining the Hudson's Bay Company in 1766 at the age of twenty-one. After sailing for a time in Hudson Bay, he demonstrated his ability to travel on foot by making an overland trip along the west coast of the bay from Fort Prince of Wales (Churchill, Manitoba) to York Factory and back. The series of three journeys that Hearne eventually made in fulfillment of his 1769 commission took him into difficult territory. A line in the introduction to his journals gives a sense of how little was known of the area he entered: 'I drew a Map on a large skin of parchment . . . but left the interior parts blank, to be filled up during my Journey.' In 1771–2, he arrived at the Coppermine River; following it to its mouth, recording his travels as he went, he became the first European to reach the Arctic Ocean by travelling over land.

In 1774, Hearne founded Cumberland House, the Hudson's Bay Company's first inland post; the next year, he was made governor of Fort Prince of Wales. In 1782, he made a controversial surrender to a French expedition led by the Comte de Lapérouse. Lapérouse destroyed the fort but returned Hearne's journals to him after extracting a promise that Hearne would have them published. When the fort was rebuilt in 1783, Hearne returned as governor, remaining until 1787. He then retired to London, where he spent the rest of his life working on a final version of his journals, *A Journey from Prince of Wales's Fort in Hudson's Bay, to the northern ocean, undertaken by order of the Hudson's Bay Company, for the discovery of copper mines, a north west passage, &c. in the years 1769, 1770, 1771, & 1772.* Not published until three years after his death, this understated chronicle of stoic endeavour has become one of the classic exploration narratives. Its author's scrupulous concern for accuracy can be seen in the careful descriptions of the animals and plants of the North, which show Hearne as an excellent natural historian with exceptional powers of memory and observation. Hearne was also the first explorer known to have lived alone with the Natives, travelling with them in nomadic fashion and, like them, depending on the land for his sustenance. Although not free from cultural bias, his accounts avoided the earlier stereotypes that idealized North American Aboriginals or treated them as barbarous savages. Because Hearne depicts Native peoples more dispassionately than did earlier travellers, his work has been of value to later ethnographers.

# From *A Journey from Prince of Wales's Fort in Hudson's Bay to the Northern Ocean*

*[Between 6 November and 11 December 1769 Samuel Hearne made an abortive journey from Fort Prince of Wales through the Barren Lands in search of copper and the Coppermine River. Hardships were increased by the perfidy of his first Native guide, Chawchinahaw. In February 1770 he set out on a second attempt to find the Coppermine with a new guide, Conne-e-queese, who led him on a slow, uncertain trek during which Hearne became assimilated into the migratory life of the Natives.]*

## June 5th–23rd 1770

The snow was by this time so soft as to render walking in snow-shoes very laborious; and though the ground was bare in many places, yet at times, and in particular places, the snow-drifts were so deep, that we could not possibly do without them. By the sixth, however, the thaws were so general, and the snows so much melted, that as our snow-shoes were attended with more trouble than service, we all consented to throw them away. Till the tenth, our sledges proved serviceable, particularly in crossing lakes and ponds on the ice; but that mode of travelling now growing dangerous on account of the great thaws, we determined to throw away our sledges, and every one to take a load on his back.

This I found to be much harder work than the winter carriage, as my part of the luggage consisted of the following articles, viz. the quadrant[1] and its stand, a trunk containing books, papers, &c., a land-compass, and a large bag containing all my wearing apparel; also a hatchet, knives, files, &c. beside several small articles, intended for presents to the natives. The aukwardness of my load, added to its great weight, which was upward of sixty pounds, and the excessive heat of the weather, rendered walking the most laborious task I had ever encountered; and what considerably increased the hardship, was the badness of the road, and the coarseness of our lodging, being, on account of the want of proper tents, exposed to the utmost severity of the

---

1 An instrument used in navigation for measuring angles and taking bearings.

weather. The tent we had with us was not only too large, and unfit for barren ground service, where no poles were to be got, but we had been obliged to cut it up for shoes, and each person carried his own share. Indeed my guide behaved both negligently and ungenerously on this occasion; as he never made me, or my Southern Indians,[2] acquainted with the nature of pitching tents on the barren ground; which had he done, we could easily have procured a set of poles before we left the woods. He took care, however, to procure a set for himself and his wife; and when the tent was divided, though he made shift to get a piece large enough to serve him for a complete little tent, he never asked me or my Southern Indians to put our heads into it.

Beside the inconvenience of being exposed to the open air, night and day, in all weathers, we experienced real distress from the want of victuals. When provisions were procured, it often happened that we could not make a fire, so that we were obliged to eat the meat quite raw; which at first, in the article of fish particularly, was as little relished by my Southern companions as myself.

Notwithstanding these accumulated and complicated hardships, we continued in perfect health and good spirits; and my guide, though a perfect niggard of his provisions, especially in times of scarcity, gave us the strongest assurance of soon arriving at a plentiful country, which would not only afford us a certain supply of provisions, but where we should meet with other Indians, who probably would be willing to carry part of our luggage. This news naturally gave us great consolation; for at that time the weight of our constant loads was so great, that when Providence threw any thing in our way,[3] we could not carry above two days provisions with us, which indeed was the chief reason of our being so frequently in want.

From the twentieth to the twenty-third we walked every day near twenty miles, without any other subsistence than a pipe of tobacco, and a drink of water when we pleased: even partridges and gulls, which some time before were in great plenty, and easily procured, were now so scarce and shy, that we could rarely get one; and as to geese, ducks, &c. they had all flown to the Northward to breed and molt.

Early in the morning of the twenty-third, we set out as usual, but had not walked above seven or eight miles before we saw three musk-oxen grazing by the side of a small lake. The Indians immediately went in pursuit of them; and as some of them were expert hunters, they soon killed the whole of them. This was no doubt very fortunate; but, to our great mortification, before we could get one of them skinned, such a fall of rain came on, as to put it quite out of our power to make a fire; which, even in the finest weather, could only be made of moss, as we were near an hundred miles from any woods. This was poor comfort for people who had not broke their fast for four or five days. Necessity, however, has no law; and having been before initiated into the method of eating raw meat, we were the better prepared for this repast: but this was by no means so well relished, either by me or the Southern Indians, as either raw venison or raw fish had been: for the flesh of the musk-ox is not only coarse and tough, but smells and tastes so strong of musk as to make it very disagreeable when raw, though it is tolerable eating when properly cooked. The weather continued so remarkably bad,

2  The Cree or Chipewyan.
3  That is, when heaven provided game.

accompanied with constant heavy rain, snow, and sleet, and our necessities were so great by the time the weather permitted us to make a fire, that we had nearly eat to the amount of one buffalo quite raw.

Notwithstanding I mustered up all my philosophy on this occasion, yet I must confess that my spirits began to fail me. Indeed our other misfortunes were greatly aggravated by the inclemency of the weather, which was not only cold, but so very wet that for near three days and nights I had not one dry thread about me. When the fine weather returned, we made a fire, though it was only moss, as I have already observed; and having got my cloaths dry, all things seemed likely to go on in the old channel, though that was indifferent enough; but I endeavoured, like a sailor after a storm, to forget past misfortunes.

None of our natural wants, if we except thirst, are so distressing, or hard to endure, as hunger; and in wandering situations, like that which I now experienced, the hardship is greatly aggravated by the uncertainty with respect to its duration, and the means most proper to be used to remove it, as well as by the labour and fatigue we must necessarily undergo for that purpose, and the disappointments which too frequently frustrate our best concerted plans and most strenuous exertions: it not only enfeebles the body, but depresses the spirits, in spite of every effort to prevent it. Besides, for want of action, the stomach so far loses its digestive powers, that after long fasting it resumes its office with pain and reluctance. During this journey I have too frequently experienced the dreadful effects of this calamity, and more than once been reduced to so low a state by hunger and fatigue, that when Providence threw any thing in my way, my stomach has scarcely been able to retain more than two or three ounces, without producing the most oppressive pain. Another disagreeable circumstance of long fasting is, the extreme difficulty and pain attending the natural evacuations for the first time; and which is so dreadful, that of it none but those who have experienced can have an adequate idea.

To record in detail each day's fare since the commencement of this journey, would be little more than a dull repetition of the same occurrences. A sufficient idea of it may be given in a few words, by observing that it may justly be said to have been either all feasting, or all famine: sometimes we had too much, seldom just enough, frequently too little, and often none at all. It will be only necessary to say that we have fasted many times two whole days and nights; twice upwards of three days; and once, while at the She-than-nee,[4] near seven days, during which we tasted not a mouthful of any thing, except a few cranberries, water, scraps of old leather, and burnt bones. On those pressing occasions I have frequently seen the Indians examine their wardrobe, which consisted chiefly of skin-clothing, and consider what part could best be spared; sometimes a piece of an old, half-rotten deer skin, and at others a pair of old shoes, were sacrificed to alleviate extreme hunger. The relation of such uncommon hardships may perhaps gain little credit in Europe; while those who are conversant with the history of Hudson's Bay, and who are thoroughly acquainted with the distress which the natives of the country about it frequently endure, may consider them as no more than the common occurrences of an Indian life. . . .

---

4 A lake on the Seal River, not far from Fort Prince of Wales.

*[Hearne and Conne-e-queese eventually lost their way. His quadrant broken, Hearne turned back, arriving at the fort in November after nearly nine months of fruitless wandering—though on the last leg of this journey he met Matonabbee, the knowledgeable guide he had been searching for all along. Soon after his return, in December 1770, with Matonabbee and a company of Chipewyans, Hearne set out on his third and longest journey. Under Matonabbee's leadership they drew near to the Coppermine River over six months later.]*

## May 31st 1771

Though it was so late when we left the women, we walked about ten miles that night before we stopped. In our way we saw many deer; several of which the Indians killed. To talk of travelling and killing deer in the middle of the night, may at first view have the appearance of romance; but our wonder will speedily abate, when it is considered that we were then to the Northward of 64° of North latitude, and that, in consequence of it, though the Sun did not remain the whole night above the horizon, yet the time it remained below it was so short, and its depression even at midnight so small at this season of the year, that the light, in clear weather, was quite sufficient for the purpose both of walking, and hunting any kind of game.

It should have been observed, that during our stay at Clowey[5] a great number of Indians entered into a combination of those of my party to accompany us to the Copper-mine River; and with no other intent than to murder the Esquimaux, who are understood by the Copper Indians[6] to frequent that river in considerable number. This scheme, notwithstanding the trouble and fatigue, as well as danger, with which it must be obviously attended, was nevertheless so universally approved by those people, that for some time almost every man who joined us proposed to be of the party. Accordingly, each volunteer, as well as those who were properly of my party, prepared a target, or shield, before we left the woods of Clowey. Those targets were composed of thin boards, about three quarters of an inch thick, two feet broad, and three feet long; and were intended to ward off the arrows of the Esquimaux. Notwithstanding these preparations, when we came to leave the women and children, as has been already mentioned, only sixty volunteers would go with us; the rest, who were nearly as many more, though they had all prepared targets, reflecting that they had a great distance to walk, and that no advantage could be expected from the expedition, very prudently begged to be excused, saying, that they could not be spared for so long a time from the maintenance of their wives and families; and particularly, as they did not see any then in our company, who seemed willing to encumber themselves with such a charge. This seemed to be a mere evasion, for I am clearly of opinion that poverty on one side, and avarice on the other, were the only impediments to their joining our party; had they possessed as many European goods to squander away among their countrymen as Matonabbee and those of my party did, in all probability many might have been found who would have been glad to have accompanied us.

---

5  A small lake east of Great Slave Lake.
6  Also known as the Yellowknives; like the Chipewyan, they were an Athapaskan band. Formerly widespread and powerful, they had been driven north and west at the beginning of the eighteenth century, when the Hudson's Bay Company's practice of supplying guns to the Chipewyan upset the historic balance among the bands.

When I was acquainted with the intentions of my companions, and saw the war-like preparations that [they] were carrying on, I endeavoured as much as possible to persuade them from putting their inhuman design into execution; but so far were my intreaties from having the wished-for effect, that it was concluded I was actuated by cowardice; and they told me, with great marks of derision, that I was afraid of the Esquimaux. As I knew my personal safety depended in a great measure on the favourable opinion they entertained of me in this respect, I was obliged to change my tone, and replied, that I did not care if they rendered the name and race of the Esquimaux extinct; adding at the same time, that though I was no enemy to the Esquimaux, and did not see the necessity of attacking them without cause, yet if I should find it necessary to do it, for the protection of any one of my company, my own safety out of the question, so far from being afraid of a poor defenceless Esquimaux, whom I despised more than feared, nothing should be wanting on my part to protect all who were with me. This declaration was received with great satisfaction; and I never afterwards ventured to interfere with any of their war-plans. Indeed, when I came to consider seriously, I saw evidently that it was the highest folly for an individual like me, and in my situation, to attempt to turn the current of a national prejudice which had subsisted between those two nations from the earliest periods, or at least as long as they had been acquainted with the existence of each other.

\*   \*   \*

*[In July 1771 Hearne and his company at last 'arrived at that long wished-for spot, the Coppermine River', which turned out to be a much less impressive body of water than reports had led Hearne to expect. He began to map the river, though he quickly realized that it was not navigable.]*

## July 15th–17th 1771

Early in the morning of the fifteenth, we set out, when I immediately began my survey, which I continued about ten miles down the river, till heavy rain coming on we were obliged to put up; and the place where we lay that night was the end, or edge of the woods, the whole space between it and the sea being entirely barren hills and wide open marshes. In the course of this day's survey, I found the river as full of shoals as the part which I had seen before; and in many places it was so greatly diminished in its width, that in our way we passed by two more capital falls.

Early in the morning of the sixteenth, the weather being fine and pleasant, I again proceeded with my survey, and continued it for ten miles farther down the river; but still found it the same as before, being every where full of falls and shoals. At this time (it being about noon) the three men who had been sent as spies met us on their return, and informed my companions that five tents of Esquimaux were on the west side of the river. The situation, they said, was very convenient for surprising them; and, according to their account, I judged it to be about twelve miles from the place we met the spies. When the Indians received this intelligence, no farther attendance or attention was paid to my survey, but their whole thoughts were immediately engaged in planning the best method of attack, and how they might steal on the poor Esquimaux the ensuing night, and kill them all while asleep. To accomplish this bloody design more effectually, the Indians thought it necessary to cross the river as soon as possible; and, by the account of the spies, it appeared that no part was more convenient for the purpose than that where we had met them, it being there very smooth, and at a considerable distance from any fall. Accordingly, after the Indians had put all their guns, spears, targets, &c. in good order, we crossed the river, which took up some time.

When we arrived on the West side of the river, each painted the front of his target or shield; some with the figure of the Sun, others with that of the Moon, several with different kinds of birds and beasts of prey, and many with the images of imaginary beings, which, according to their silly notions, are the inhabitants of the different elements, Earth, Sea, Air, &c.

On enquiring the reason of their doing so, I learned that each man painted his shield with the image of that being on which he relied most for success in the intended engagement. Some were contented with a single representation; while others, doubtful, as I suppose, of the quality and power of any single being, had their shields covered to the very margin with a group of hieroglyphics quite unintelligible to every one except the painter. Indeed, from the hurry in which this business was necessarily done, the want of every colour but red and black, and the deficiency of skill in the artist, most of those paintings had more the appearance of a number of accidental blotches, than 'of any thing that is on the earth, or in the water under the earth';[7] and though some few of them conveyed a tolerable idea of the thing intended, yet even these were many degrees worse than our country sign-paintings in England.

When this piece of superstition was completed, we began to advance toward the Esquimaux tents; but were very careful to avoid crossing any hills, or talking loud, for fear of being seen or overheard by the inhabitants; by which means the distance was not only much greater than it otherwise would have been, but, for the sake of keeping in the lowest grounds, we were obliged to walk through entire swamps of still marly clay, sometimes up to the knees. Our course, however, on this occasion, though very serpentine, was not altogether so remote from the river as entirely to exclude me from view of it the whole way: on the contrary, several times (according to the situation of the ground) we advanced so near it, as to give me an opportunity of convincing myself that it was as unnavigable as it was in those parts which I had surveyed before, and which entirely corresponded with the accounts given of it by the spies.

It is perhaps worth remarking, that my crew, though an undisciplined rabble, and by no means accustomed to war or command, seemingly acted on this horrid occasion with the utmost uniformity of sentiment. There was not among them the least altercation or separate opinion; all were united in the general cause, and as ready to follow where Matonabbee led, as he appeared to be ready to lead, according to the advice of an old Copper Indian, who had joined us on our first arrival at the river where this bloody business was first proposed.

7 A loose paraphrase of Revelation 5:13: 'And every creature which is in heaven, and on the earth, and under the earth, and such as are in the sea . . .'

Never was reciprocity of interest more generally regarded among a number of people, than it was on the present occasion by my crew, for not one was a moment in want of any thing that another could spare; and if ever the spirit of disinterested friendship expanded the heart of a Northern Indian, it was here exhibited in the most extensive meaning of the word. Property of every kind that could be of general use now ceased to be private, and every one who had any thing which came under that description, seemed proud of an opportunity of giving it, or lending it to those who had none, or were most in want of it.

The number of my crew was so much greater than that which five tents could contain, and the warlike manner in which they were equipped so greatly superior to what could be expected of the poor Esquimaux, that no less than a total massacre of every one of them was likely to be the case, unless Providence should work a miracle for their deliverance.

The land was so situated that we walked under cover of the rocks and hills till we were within two hundred yards of the tents. There we lay in ambush for some time, watching the motions of the Esquimaux; and here the Indians would have advised me to stay till the fight was over, but to this I could by no means consent; for I considered that when the Esquimaux came to be surprised, they would try every way to escape, and if they found me alone, not knowing me from an enemy, they would probably proceed to violence against me when no person was near to assist. For this reason I determined to accompany them, telling them at the same time, that I would not have any hand in the murder they were about to commit, unless I found it necessary for my own safety. The Indians were not displeased at this proposal; one of them immediately fixed me a spear, and another lent me a broad bayonet for my protection, but at that time I could not be provided with a target, nor did I want to be encumbered with such an unnecessary piece of lumber.

While we lay in ambush, the Indians performed the last ceremonies which were thought necessary before the engagement. These chiefly consisted in painting their faces; some all black, some all red, and others with a mixture of the two; and to prevent their hair from blowing into their eyes, it was either tied before and behind, and on both sides, or else cut short all round. The next thing they considered was to make themselves as light as possible for running; which they did, by pulling off their stockings, and either cutting off the sleeves of their jackets, or rolling them up close to their arm-pits; and though the muskettoes at that time were so numerous as to surpass all credibility, yet some of the Indians actually pulled off their jackets and entered the lists quite naked, except their breech-cloths and shoes. Fearing I might have occasion to run with the rest, I thought it also advisable to pull off my stockings and cap, and to tie my hair as close up as possible.

By the time the Indians had made themselves thus completely frightful, it was near one o'clock in the morning of the seventeenth; when finding all the Esquimaux quiet in their tents, they rushed forth from their ambuscade, and fell on the poor unsuspecting creatures, unperceived till close at the very eves of their tents, when they soon began the bloody massacre, while I stood neuter in the rear.

In a few seconds the horrible scene commenced; it was shocking beyond description; the poor unhappy victims were surprised in the midst of their sleep, and had neither time nor power to make any resistance; men, women, and children, in all upward of twenty, ran out of their tents stark naked, and endeavoured to make their escape; but the Indians having possession of all the landside, to no place could they fly for shelter. One alternative only remained, that of jumping into the river; but, as none of them attempted it, they all fell a sacrifice to Indian barbarity!

The shrieks and groans of the poor expiring wretches were truly dreadful; and my horror was much increased at seeing a young girl, seemingly about eighteen years of age, killed so near me, that when the first spear was stuck into her side she fell down at my feet, and twisted round my legs, so that it was with difficulty that I could disengage myself from her dying grasps. As two Indian men pursued this unfortunate victim, I solicited very hard for her life; but the murderers made no reply till they had stuck both their spears through her body, and transfixed her to the ground. They then looked me sternly in the face, and began to ridicule me, by asking if I wanted an Esquimaux wife; and paid not the smallest regard to the shrieks and agony of the poor wretch, who was twining round their spears like an eel! Indeed, after receiving much abusive language from them on the occasion, I was at length obliged to desire that they would be more expeditious in dispatching their victim out of her misery, otherwise I should be obliged, out of pity, to assist in the friendly office of putting an end to the existence of a fellow-creature who was so cruelly wounded. On this request being made, one of the Indians hastily drew his spear from the place where it was first lodged, and pierced it through her breast near the heart. The love of life, however, even in this most miserable state, was so predominant, that though this might justly be called the most merciful act that could be done for the poor creature, it seemed to be unwelcome, for though much exhausted by pain and loss of blood, she made several effort to ward off the friendly blow. My situation and the terror of my mind at beholding this butchery, cannot easily be conceived, much less described; though I summed up all the fortitude I was master of on the occasion, it was with difficulty that I could refrain from tears; and I am confident that my features must have feelingly expressed how sincerely I was affected at the barbarous scene I then witnessed; even at this hour I cannot reflect on the transactions of that horrid day without shedding tears.

[Hearne reached the mouth of the Coppermine and found that the 'mine' he had heard about was a disappointment. His commission fulfilled, he turned back. During his final trek, the most difficult of all, several of the Natives accompanying him died of sickness and starvation. Hearne did not arrive back at Fort Prince of Wales until a year and a half after he had left it. His account of his explorations concludes with these words: 'Though my discoveries are not likely to prove of any material advantage to the Nation at large, or indeed to the Hudson's Bay Company, yet I have the pleasure to think that I have fully complied with the orders of my Masters, and that it has put a final end to all disputes concerning a North West Passage through Hudson's Bay.']

1795

# David Thompson

## 1770–1857

David Thompson was recruited from a London charity school at fourteen to become an apprentice clerk with the Hudson's Bay Company. Although he later wrote that when he arrived at Fort Prince of Wales (Churchill, Man.) in 1784, 'I bid a long and sad farewell to my . . . country, an exile for ever', Thompson seems to have been eager to learn what he could of the company's operations. Confined by a broken leg at nineteen, he spent almost a year at Cumberland House studying mathematics, astronomy, and field surveying, and made himself one of the best cartographers of his time. In twenty-eight years of exploring the Canadian west, he managed to survey and map nearly two million square miles with such accuracy that later maps at the beginning of this century were still based on his work. The explorer J.B. Tyrrell, who oversaw the first publication of Thompson's narrative, called him 'the greatest practical land geographer that the world had produced.'

In 1797 Thompson left the employ of the Hudson's Bay Company and went to the rival North West Company as a surveyor and mapmaker, instructed to determine the position of company posts in relation to the recently established boundary at the 49th parallel. Thompson travelled widely in the Canadian west and northwest in the years that followed. He married Charlotte Small, the daughter of an English fur trader and a Native mother. In 1815 Thompson and his wife retired to Williamstown, Upper Canada; however, he did not cease working. He served as astronomer and surveyor to the British Boundary Commission, establishing the United States–Canada boundary for Ontario and Quebec, and revised the maps he made on his trips of Western exploration. In 1846, he began to write a narrative account of his travels based on journals that he had begun in 1789 (they eventually ran to thirty-nine volumes). Thompson laboured on this project for the next five years, but blindness brought it to a halt before it was completed. *David Thompson's Narrative of his Explorations in Western North America 1784–1812*, edited by J.B. Tyrrell, was published in 1916.

When he first arrived at Fort Prince of Wales, Thompson served under Hearne and disliked the older man, both for his supposed cowardice in surrendering the fort to the French and for being a freethinker and follower of Voltaire. He may, however, have known Hearne's journals in manuscript; certainly in his narrative Thompson reveals the same strengths as the earlier writer-explorer. He was a keen observer and diligent recorder who provided accounts that are both factual and anecdotal; and he expressed himself in an unaffected style that gives his writing authority and immediacy. In particular, like Hearne, he was able to learn the languages of the Native peoples, and to understand and be accepted by those he visited. Beginning with the stories he gathered after travelling, at the age of seventeen, to the foothills of the Rockies to winter over with the Peigans in 1787–8 and to learn their language, through his later setting down of what he learned during the time he spent with the Nahathaways (he lived with them for three extended periods between 1792 and 1806), his journals are among the most valuable sources for the depiction of eighteenth-century Canada and its peoples.

All Thompson's activities were governed by an intensely inquiring mind. He was never intimidated by harsh conditions in his determined effort to study and understand his environment, as may be seen in his description of crossing the Rockies by way of the Athabasca Pass:

*The view now before us was an ascent of deep snow. . . . It was to me a most exhilarating sight, but to my uneducated men a dreadful sight. They had no scientific object in view, their feelings were of the place they were. . . . Many reflections came on my mind; a new world was in a manner before me.*

# From *Narrative of His Explorations in Western North America, 1784–1812*

## [NAHATHAWAY INDIANS]

\* \* \*

Of all the several distinct Tribes of Natives on the east side of the Rocky Mountains, the Nahathaway Indians appear to deserve the most consideration; under different names the great families of this race occupy a great extent of country, and however separated and unknown to each other, they have the same opinions on religion, on morals, and their customs and manners differ very little. They are the only Natives that have some remains of ancient times from tradition. In the following account I have carefully avoided as their national opinions all they have learned from white men; my knowledge was collected from old men, whom with my own age, extend backwards to upwards of one hundred years ago, and I must remark that, whatever other people may write as the creed of these natives, I have always found it very difficult to learn their real opinion on what may be termed religious subjects. Asking them questions on this head, is to no purpose; they will give the answer best adapted to avoid other questions, and please the enquirer. My knowledge has been gained when living and travelling with them and, in times of distress and danger, hearing their prayers to invisible powers and their view of a future state of themselves and others. Like most mankind, those in youth and in the prime of life think only of the present, but declining manhood and escapes from danger turn their thoughts on futurity.

After a weary day's march as we sat by a log fire, the bright Moon, with thousands of sparkling stars passing before us, we could not help enquiring who lived in those bright mansions; for I frequently conversed with them as one of themselves. The brilliancy of the planets always attracted their attention, and when their nature was explained to them, they concluded them to be the abodes of the spirits of those that had led a good life.

A Missionary has never been among them, and my knowledge of their language has not enabled me to do more than teach the unity of God and a future state of rewards and punishments; hell fire they do not believe, for they do not think it possible that any thing can resist the continued action of fire: It is doubtful if their language in its present simple state can clearly express the doctrines of Christianity in their full force. They believe in the existence of the Keeche Keeche Manito[1] (the Great, Great Spirit. They appear to derive their belief from tradition, and believe that the visible world, with all its inhabitants must have been made by some powerful being: they have not the same idea of his constant omnipresence, omniscience and omnipotence that we have, but think that he is so when he pleases. He is the master of life, and all things are at his disposal; he is always kind to the human race, and hates to see the blood of

---

1  Now usually spelled 'Manitou'.

mankind on the ground, and sends heavy rain to wash it away. He leaves the human race to their own conduct, but has placed all other living creatures under the care of Manitos (or inferior Angels) all of whom are responsible to Him; but all this belief is obscure and confused, especially on the Manitos, the guardians and guides of every genus of Birds and Beasts; each Manito has a separate command and care, as one has the Bison, another the Deer; and thus the whole animal creation is divided amongst them. On this account the Indians, as much as possible, neither say, nor do anything to offend them, and the religious hunter, at the death of each animal, says, or does, something, as thanks to the Manito of the species for being permitted to kill it. At the death of a Moose Deer, the hunter in a low voice cries 'wut, wut, wut', cuts a narrow strip of skin from off the throat, and hangs it up to the Manito. The bones of the head of a Bear are thrown into the water, and thus of other animals. If this acknowledgment was not made the Manito would drive away the animals from the hunter, although the Indians often doubt their power or existence. Yet like other invisible beings they are more feared than loved. They believe in ghosts but as very rarely seen, and those only of wicked men, or women; when this belief takes place, their opinion is that the spirit of the wicked person being in a miserable state comes back to the body and round where he used to hunt. To get rid of such a hateful visitor, they burn the body to ashes and the ghost then no longer haunts them. The dark Pine Forests have spirits, but there is only one of them which they dread, it is the *Pah Kok*, a tall hateful spirit. He frequents the depths of the Forest; his howlings are heard in the storm; he delights to add to its terrors; it is a misfortune to hear him, something ill will happen to the person; but when he approaches a Tent and howls, he announces the death of one of the inmates. Of all beings he is the most hateful and the most dreaded. The Sun and Moon are accounted Divinities and though they do not worship them. They always speak of them with great reverence. They appear to think of the Stars only as a great number of luminous points, perhaps also divinities, and mention them with respect. They have names for the brightest stars, as Sirius, Orion and others, and by them learn the change of the seasons, as the rising of Orion for winter, and the setting of the Pleiades for summer. The Earth is also a divinity, and is alive, but they cannot define what kind of life it is, but say, if it was not alive it could not give and continue life to other things and to animated creatures.

The Forests, the ledges and hills of Rock, the Lakes and Rivers have all something of the Manito about them, especially the Falls in the Rivers, and those to which the fish come to spawn. The Indians, when the season is over, frequently place their spears at the Manito stone, as an offering to the Spirit of the Fall, for the fish they have caught. These stones are rare, and sought after by the native to place at the edge of a water fall; they are the shape of a cobbler's lap stone, but much larger, and polished by the wash of the water. The 'Metchee Manito', or Evil Spirit, they believe to be evil, delighting in making men miserable, and bringing misfortune and sickness on them, and if he had the power would wholly destroy them. He is not the tempter: his whole power is for mischief to, and harrassing of, them. To avert all that they use many ceremonies and sacrifices of such things as they can spare. Sometimes a dog is painted and killed. Whatever is given to him is laid on the ground, frequently at the foot of a pine tree. They believe in the immortality of the soul, and that death is only a change of existence which takes place directly after death. The good find themselves in a happy country, where they rejoin their friends and relations, the Sun is always bright, and the animals plenty; and most of them carry this belief so far, that they believe whatever creatures the great Spirit has made must continue to exist somewhere, and under some form; But this fine belief is dark and uncertain; when danger was certain and it was doubtful if we saw the day, or if we saw it, whether we should live through it, and a future state appeared close to them, then their minds wavered: they wished to believe what they felt to be uncertain. All that I could do was to show them the immortality of the soul, as necessary to reward of the good and punishment of the wicked. But all this was the talk of man with man. It wanted the sure and sacred promise of the Heavenly Redeemer of mankind, who brought life and immortality to light.[2]

There is an important being, with whom the Natives appear better acquainted with than the others, whom they call 'Weesarkejauk' (the Flatterer). He is the hero of all their stories always promising them some good, or inciting them to some pleasure, and always deceiving them. They have some tradition of the Deluge, as may be seen from the following account related by the old men. After the Great Spirit made mankind, and all the animals, he told Weesarkejauk to take care of them and teach them how to live, and not to eat of bad roots; that would hurt and kill them; but he did not mind the Great Spirit; he became careless and incited them to pleasure; mankind and the animals all did as they pleased, quarelled and shed much blood, with which the Great Spirit was displeased. He threatened Weesarkejauk that if he did not keep the ground clean he would take everything from him and make him miserable, but he did not believe the Great Spirit and in a short time became more careless; and the quarrels of Men, and the animals made the ground red with blood, and so far from taking care of them he incited them to do and live badly. This made the Great Spirit very angry and he told Weesarkejauk that he would take every thing from him, and wash the ground clean. But still he did not believe; until the Rivers and Lakes rose very high and over flowed the ground for it was always raining; and the *Keeche Gahme* (the Sea) came on the land, and every man and animal were drowned, except one Otter, one Beaver and one Musk Rat. Weesarkejauk tried to stop the sea, but it was too strong for him, and as he sat on the water crying for his loss, the Otter, the Beaver and the Musk Rat rested their heads on one of his thighs.

When the rain ceased and the sea went away, he took courage, but did not dare to speak to the Great Spirit. After musing a long time upon his sad condition he thought if he could get a bit of the old ground he could make a little island of it, for he has the power of extending, but not of creating anything. He had not the power of diving under the water, but as he did not know the depth to the old ground he was at a loss what to do. Some say the Great Spirit took pity on him, and gave him the power to renovate everything, provided he made use of the old materials, all of which lay buried under water to an unknown depth. In this sad state, as he sat floating on the water he told the three animals that they must starve unless he could get a bit of the old ground

2   Because they have had the Christian revelation available to them, Thompson sees Europeans as having religious advantage over Native peoples.

from under the water of which he would make a fine Island for them. Then addressing himself to the Otter, and praising him for his courage, strength and activity and promising him plenty of fish to eat, he persuaded the Otter to dive, and bring up a bit of earth; the Otter came up without having reached the ground: by praises, he got the Otter to make two more attempts, but without success, and he was so much exhausted he could do no more. Weesarkejauk called him a coward of a weak heart, and said that the Beaver would put him to shame: then, speaking to the Beaver, he praised his strength and wisdom and promised to make him a good house for winter, and told him to dive straight down. The Beaver made two attempts without success, and came up so tired that Weesarkejauk had to let him repose a long time; then promising him a wife if he brought up a bit of earth, told him to try a third time; to obtain a wife, he boldly went down and stayed so long, that he came up almost lifeless. Weesarkejauk was now very sad, for what the active Otter and strong Beaver could not do, he had little hopes the Musk Rat could do; but this was his only resource. He now praised the Musk Rat and promised him plenty of roots to eat, with rushes and earth to make himself a house; the Otter and the Beaver he said were fools, and lost themselves, but he would find the ground, if he went straight down. Thus encouraged he dived, and came up, but brought nothing; after reposing, he went down a second time, and stayed a long time. On coming up Weesarkejauk examined his fore paws and found they had the smell of earth, and showing this to the Musk Rat, promised to make him a Wife, who should give him a great many children, and become more numerous than any other animal, and told him to have a strong heart and go direct down. The Musk Rat went down the third time and stayed so long that Weesarkejauk feared he was drowned. At length seeing some bubbles come up, he put down his long arm and brought up the Musk Rat, almost dead, but to his great joy with a piece of earth between his forepaws and his breast. This he seized, and in a short time extended it to a little island, on which they all reposed. Some say Weesarkejauk procured a bit of wood, from which he made the Trees, and from bones, he made the animals; but the greater number deny this, and say, the Great Spirit made the rivers take the water to the Keeche Gahma of bad water (the salt sea) and then renovated Mankind, the Animals, and the Trees; in proof of which, the Great spirit deprived him of all authority over Mankind and the Animals, and he has since had only the power to flatter and deceive. It has been already noticed that this visionary being is the hero of many stories, which the women relate to amuse away the evenings. They are all founded upon the tricks he plays upon, and the mischief he leads the animals into, by flattering and deceiving them, especially the Wolf and the Fox. But the recital of the best of these stories would be tameness itself to the splendid Language and gorgeous scenery of the tales of the oriental nations.[3]

The Nahathaway Indians have also another tradition relative to the Deluge to which no fable is attached. In the latter end of May 1806, at the Rocky Mountain House,[4] (where I passed the summer) the Rain continued the very unusual space of full three weeks, the Brooks and the River became swollen, and could not be forded, each

3  Thompson has earlier mentioned his nostalgic fondness for *The Arabian Nights*.
4  A Hudson's Bay fort on the North Saskatchewan River.

stream became a torrent, and there was much water on the ground: A band of these Indians were at the house, waiting for the Rain to cease and the streams to lower before they could proceed to hunting. All was anxiety, they smoked and made speeches to the Great Spirit for the Rain to cease, and at length became alarmed at the quantity of water on the ground; at length the rain ceased. I was standing at the door watching the breaking up of the clouds, when of a sudden the Indians gave a loud shout, and called out 'Oh, there is the mark of life, we shall yet live.' On looking to the eastward there was one of the widest and most splendid Rainbows I ever beheld; and joy was now in every face.

The name of the Rainbow is Peeshim Ecappeah (Sun lines). I had now been twenty two years among them, and never before heard the name of the mark of life given to the rainbow (Peemah tisoo nan oo Chegun) nor have I ever heard it since; upon enquiring of the old Men why they kept this name secret from me, they gave me the usual reply, 'You white men always laugh and treat with contempt what we have heard and learned from our fathers, and why should we expose ourselves to be laughed at'; I replied 'I have never done so, our books also call the Rainbow the mark of life[5]. . .'.

5  Thompson refers to the promise God makes Noah in Genesis 9, after the flood: 'And I will establish my covenant with you; neither shall all flesh be cut off any more by the waters of a flood; neither shall there any more be a flood to destroy the earth. . . . I do set my bow in the cloud, and it shall be for a token of a covenant between me and the earth. And it shall come to pass, when I bring a cloud over the earth, that the bow shall be seen in the cloud.'

## [LIFE AMONG THE NAHATHAWAYS]

\*　　\*　　\*

It may now be time to say something of myself, and of the character of the Natives and the French Canadians entertained of me: they were almost my only companions. My instruments for practical astronomy were a brass Sextant of ten inches radius; an achromatic Telescope[1] of high power for observing the Satellites of Jupiter and other phenomena; one of the same construction for common use; Parallel glasses and quicksilver horizon for double Altitudes; and Compass, Thermometer, and other requisite instruments, which I was in the constant practice of using in clear weather for observations on the Sun, Moon, Planets and Stars to determine the positions of the Rivers, Lakes, Mountains and other parts of the country I surveyed from Hudson Bay to the Pacific Ocean. Both Canadians and Indians often inquired of me why I observed the Sun, and sometimes the Moon, in the daytime, and passed whole nights with my instruments looking at the Moon and Stars. I told them it was to determine the distance and

1  An achromatic lens is one that does not introduce colour by breaking light into its constituent parts. In taking readings with his sextant, Thompson needed an artificial horizon since he could not, as mariners could, always see the true horizon; for this purpose mercury ('quicksilver') was carried in a flat rectangular tray, shielded from the wind by glass plates that had to have truly parallel faces so as not to introduce any distortion in the light passing through them (hence 'parallel glasses'). Position could then be calculated by taking the angle of an astronomical body, and of its reflection, in the horizontal surface of the mercury pool at rest (a 'double altitude').

direction from the place I observed to other places. Neither the Canadians nor the Indians believed me; for both argued that if what I said was truth, I ought to look to the ground and over it and not to the Stars. Their opinions were that I was looking into futurity and seeing everybody and what they were doing and that I knew how to raise the wind, but did not believe I could calm it. This they argued from seeing me obliged to wait the calming of the wind on the Great Lakes, to which the Indians added that I knew where the Deer were, and other superstitious opinions.

During my life I have always been careful not to pretend to any knowledge of futurity, and I said that I knew nothing beyond the present hour. Neither argument nor ridicule had any effect, and I had to leave them to their own opinions. Yet inadvertently on my part, several things happened to confirm their opinions. One fine evening in February two Indians came to the house to trade. The Moon rose bright and clear with the planet Jupiter a few degrees on its east side and the Canadians as usual predicted that Indians would come to trade in the direction of this star. To show them the folly of such predictions I told them the same bright star, the next night, would be as far from the Moon on its west side. This of course took place from the Moon's motion in her orbit and is the common occurence of almost every month, and yet all parties were persuaded I had done it by some occult power to falsify the predictions of the Canadians. Mankind is fond of the marvelous; it seems to heighten their character by relating they have seen such things.

I had always admired the tact of the Indian in being able to guide himself through the darkest pine forests to exactly the place he intended to go; his keen, constant attentions on everything, the removal of the smallest stone, the bent or broken twig, a slight mark on the ground, all spoke plain language to him. I was anxious to acquire this knowledge, and often being in company with them, sometimes for several months, I paid attention to what they pointed out to me and became almost equal to some of them, which became of great use to me. The North West Company of Furr Traders, from their Depot in Lake Superior sent off Brigades of Canoes loaded with about three Tons weight of Merchandise, Provisions and Baggage. Those for the most distant trading Posts are sent off first, with an allowance of two days' time between each Brigade to prevent incumbrances on the Carrying Places. I was, in my first year, in the third Brigade of six Canoes each and having nothing to do but sketch off my survey and make Observations. I was noticing how far we gained or lost ground on the Brigade before us by the fires they made, and other marks, as we were equally manned with five men to each canoe. In order to prevent the winter coming on us, before we reached our distant winter quarters, the Men had to work very hard from daylight to sunset, or later, and at night slept on the ground, constantly worried by mosquitoes, and had no time to look about them. I found we gained very little on them. At the end of fifteen days we had to arrive at Lake Winnipeg (that is a Sea Lake from its size) and for more than two days it had been blowing a northwest gale, which did not allow the Brigade before us to proceed. I told the Guide that early the next morning we should see them. These Guides have charge of conducting the march and are all proud of coming up to the canoes ahead of them, and by dawn of day we entered the Lake now calm, and as the day came on us saw the Brigade that were before us only one Mile ahead of us. The Guide and the men shouted with joy, and when we came up to them told them of my wonderful predictions, and that I had pointed out every place they had slept at, and all by looking at the Stars. One party seemed delighted in being credulous, the other in exageration; such are ignorant men, who never give themselves a moment's reflection.

\* \* \*

This section of the Stony Region is called the Musk Rat Country and contains an area of about 22,360 square miles, of which full two-fifths of this surface is Rivers and Lakes, having phenomena distinct from the dry, elevated, distant, interior countries. The Natives are Nahathaway Indians, whose fathers from time, beyond any tradition, have hunted in these Lands. In conversing with them on their origin they appear never to have turned their minds to this subject; and think that mankind and the animals are in a constant state of succession; and the time of their great grandfathers is the extent of their actual knowledge of times past. Their tradition of the Deluge and of the Rainbow I have already mentioned; yet their stories all refer to times when Men were much taller and stronger than at present, the animals more numerous, and many could converse with mankind, particularly, the Bear, Beaver, Lynx and Fox. Writers on the North American Indians always write comparing them with themselves, who are all men of education, and of course the Indians lose by comparison. This is not fair. Let them be compared with those who are uneducated in Europe; yet even in this comparison the Indian has the disadvantage in not having the light of Christianity. Of course his moral character has not the firmness of Christian morality, but in practice he is fully equal to those of his class in Europe; living without law, they are a law to themselves. The Indian is said to be a creature of apathy. When he appears to be so he is in an assumed character to conceal what is passing in his mind, as he has nothing of the almost infinite diversity of things which interest and amuse the civilised man. His passions, desires and affections are strong, however subdued they appear, and engage the whole man. The law of retaliation, which is fully allowed, makes the life of man respected; and in general he abhors the shedding of blood. And should sad necessity compel him to it, which is sometimes the case, he is held to be an unfortunate man. But he who has committed wilful murder is held in abhorrence, as one with whom the life of no person is in safety, and possessed with an evil spirit.

When Hudson Bay was discovered, and the first trading settlement made, the Natives were far more numerous than at present. In the year 1782 the small pox from Canada extended to them and more than one-half of them died; since which, although they had no enemies and their country is very healthy, yet their numbers increase very slowly. The Musk Rat country, of which I have given the area, may have ninety-two families, each of seven souls, giving to each family an area of two-hundred-and-forty-eight square miles of hunting grounds; or thirty-five square miles to each soul—a very thin population. A recent writer (Ballantyne)[2] talks of myriads of wild animals. Such

2 The Scottish writer R.M. Ballantyne (1825–94), who was employed by the Hudson's Bay Company from 1841 to 1847, began publishing his stories of life among Company fur traders around the time Thompson was writing his memoirs.

writers talk at random; they have never counted nor calculated. The animals are by no means numerous, and only in sufficient numbers to give a tolerable subsistence to the Natives, who are too often obliged to live on very little food and sometimes all but perish with hunger. Very few Beaver are to be found, the Bears are not many, and all the fur-bearing animals an Indian can kill can scarcely furnish himself and family with the bare necessaries of life.

A strange Idea prevails among these Natives, and also of all the Indians to the Rocky Mountains, though unknown to each other, that when they were numerous, before they were destroyed by the small pox, all the animals of every species were also very numerous and more so in comparison of the number of Natives than at present; and this was confirmed to me by old Scotchmen in the service of the Hudson's Bay Company, and by the Canadians from Canada. The knowledge of the latter extended over all the interior countries, yet no disorder was known among the animals; the fact was certain, and nothing they knew of could account for it. It might justly be supposed the destruction of Mankind would allow the animals to increase, even to become formidable to the few Natives who survived, but neither the Bison, the Deer, nor the carnivorous animals increased, and as I have already remarked, are no more than sufficient for the subsistence of the Natives and Traders. The trading Houses over the whole country are situated on the banks of lakes of at least twenty miles in length by two or three miles in width . . . as it is only large and deep Lakes that have Fish sufficient to maintain the Trader and his Men, for the Indians at best can only afford a Deer now and then.

\*   \*   \*

Formerly the Beavers were very numerous. The many Lakes and Rivers gave them ample space and the poor Indian had then only a pointed stick shaped and hardened in the fire, a stone Hatchet, Spear and Arrowheads of the same. Thus armed he was weak against the sagacious Beaver who, on the banks of a Lake, made itself a house of a foot thick or more, composed of earth and small flat stones, crossed and bound together with pieces of wood, upon which no impression could be made but by fire. But when the arrival of the White People had changed all their weapons from stone to iron and steel, and added the fatal Gun, every animal fell before the Indian. The Bear was no longer dreaded, and the Beaver became a desirable animal for food and clothing and the fur a valuable article of trade; and as the Beaver is a stationary animal, it could be attacked at any convenient time in all seasons, and thus their numbers soon became reduced. The old Indians, when speaking of their ancestors, wonder how they could live, as the Beaver was wiser and the Bear stronger than them, and confess that if they were deprived of the Gun they could not live by the Bow and Arrow and must soon perish.

The Beaver skin is the standard by which other Furs are traded; and London prices have very little influence on this value of barter, which is more a matter of expedience and convenience to the Trader and the Native than of real value. The only Bears of this country are the small Black Bear, with a chance Yellow Bear;[3] this latter has a fine fur and trades for three Beavers in barter when full grown. The Black Bear is common, and according to size passes for one or two Beavers. The young are often tamed by the Natives and are harmless and playful until near full grown, when they become troublesome and are killed or sent into the woods. While they can procure roots and berries they look for nothing else; but in the Spring, when they leave their winter dens, they can get neither the one nor the other. Then they prowl about, and go to the Rapids where the Carp are spawning. Here Bruin lives in plenty; but not content with what it can eat, amuses itself with tossing ashore ten times more than it can devour, each stroke of its forepaw sending a fish eight or ten yards according to its size. The fish thus thrown ashore attract the Eagle and the Raven. The sight of these birds flying about leads the Indian to the place and Bruin loses his life and his skin. The meat of the Bear feeding on the roots and berries becomes very fat and good, and in this condition it enters its den for the winter, at the end of which the meat is still good, and has some fat; but at the very first meal of fish the taste of the meat is changed for the worse, and soon becomes disagreeable. When a Mahmees Dog in the winter season has discovered a den, and the Natives go to kill the Bear, on uncovering the top of the den Bruin is found roused out of its dormant state and sitting ready to defend itself. The eldest man now makes a speech to it, reproaching the Bear and all its race with being the old enemies of Man, killing the children and women when it was large and strong, but now, since the Manito has made him small and weak to what he was before, he has all the will, though not the power, to be as bad as ever; that he is treacherous and cannot be trusted; that although he has sense he makes bad use of it and must therefore be killed. Parts of the speech have many repetitions to impress its truth on the Bear, who all the time is grinning and growling, willing to fight, but more willing to escape, until the axe descends on its head, or it is shot—the latter more frequently, as the den is often under the roots of fallen trees and protected by the branches of the roots.

When a Bear thus killed was hauled out of its den I enquired of the Indian who made the speech whether he really thought the Bear understood him. He replied, 'How can you doubt it? Did you not see how ashamed I made him, and how he held down his head?' 'He might well hold down his head when you were flourishing a heavy axe over it, with which you killed him.' On this animal they have several superstitions, and he acts a prominent part in many of their tales.

\*    \*    \*

What is called Mirage is common on all these Lakes, but frequently is simply an elevation of the woods and shores that bound horizon; yet at times draws attention to the change of scenery it exhibits, and on these Lakes it has often kept me watching it for many minutes; and I would have stayed longer if the cold had permitted. The first and most changeable Mirage is seen in the latter part of February and the month of March, when the weather is clear, the wind calm, or light; the Thermometer from ten above

3  Actually a colour phase of the black bear.

to twelve degrees below zero, the time about ten in the morning. On one occasion, going to an Isle where I had two traps for Foxes, when about one mile distant the ice between me and the Isle appeared of a concave form, which, if I entered, I should slide into its hollow; and although I was sensible of the illusion, it had the power to perplex me. I found my snow shoes on a level and advanced slowly, as afraid to slide into it; in about ten minutes this Mirage ceased, the ice became distinct and showed a level surface, and with confidence I walked to my traps, in one of which I found a red Fox. This sort of Mirage is not frequent. That most common elevates and depresses objects, and sometimes makes them appear to change places.[4]

In the latter end of February at the Reed Lake, at its west end, a Mirage took place in one of its boldest forms. About three miles from me was the extreme shore of the Bay; the Lake was near three miles in width, in which was a steep Isle of rock and another of tall Pines; on the other side a bold Point of steep rock. The Mirage began slowly to elevate all objects, then gently to lower them, until the Isles and the Point appeared like black spots on the ice, and no higher than its surface. The above bold Bay Shore was a dark black curved line on the ice. In the time of three minutes they all arose to their former height and became elevated to twice their height. Beyond the Bay the rising grounds, distant eight miles, with all their woods appeared, and remained somewhat steady for a few minutes; the Isles and Point again disappeared. The Bay Shore with the distant Forests came rolling forward with an undulating motion, as if in a dance; the distant Forests became so near to me I could see their branches, then with the same motion retired to half distance. The Bay Shore could not be distinguished; it was blended with the distant land, thus advancing and retiring with different elevations for about fifteen minutes when the distant Forests vanished, the Isles took their place, and the Lake shores their form. The wild scenery was a powerful illusion, too fleeting and changeful for any pencil.

This was one of the clearest and most distinct Mirages I had ever seen. There can be no doubt it is the effect of a cause which, perhaps, was waves of the atmosphere loaded with vapours, though not perceptible to the eye, between the beholder and the objects on which the Mirage acts, with the Sun in a certain position. When the objects were seen on the ridge of the wave, it gave them their elevation; when in the hollow of the wave, their greatest depression; and viewed obliquely to the direction of the wave, the objects appeared to change places. There may be a better theory to account for the Mirage.

While the Mirage is in full action, the scenery is so clear and vivid, the illusion so strong, as to perplex the Hunter and the Traveller. It appears more like the power of magic than the play of nature. When enquiring of the Natives what they thought of it, they said it was Manito Korso—the work of a Manito—and with this argument they account for everything that is uncommon.

Although the climate and country of which I am writing is far better than that of Hudson's Bay, yet the climate is severe in Winter, the Thermometer often from thirty

4 What Thompson accurately describes here is what began to be called, early in the nineteenth century, a *fata Morgana*, a distortion of light that results in the distortion or displacement of images because of a temperature inversion, common in very cold temperatures.

to forty degrees below Zero. The month of December is the coldest. The long absence of the Sun gives full effect to the action of the cold; the Snow increases in depth—it may be said to fall as dry as dust; the ice rapidly increases in thickness and the steady cold of the rest of winter adds but little to that of the end of the month. But its contraction by intense cold causes the ice to rend in many places with a loud rumbling noise, and through these rents water is often thrown out and flows over part of the ice, making bad walking. This month has very variable weather; sometimes a calm of several days, then Gales of wind with light snow, which from its lightness is driven about like dust. This dull month of long nights we wish to pass away. The country affords no tallow for candles nor fish oil for lamps; the light of the fire is what we have to work and read by. Christmas when it comes finds us glad to see it and pass; we have nothing to welcome it with.

In one of the calms of this month, Tapahpahtum, a good hunter, came to us for some provisions and fish hooks. He said his three wives and his children had had very little to eat for nearly a whole Moon, adding, 'You may be sure that we suffer hunger when I come to beg fish, and get hooks for my women to angle with.' He took away about thirty pounds of fish, which he had to carry about twenty miles to his tent. I felt for him, for nothing but sad necessity can compel a Nahathaway hunter to carry away fish, and angle for them; this is too mean for a hunter. Meat he carries with pleasure, but fish is degradation. The calm still continued, and two days after Tapahpahtum came in the evening. He looked somewhat wild; he was a powerful man of strong passions. As usual I gave him a bit of Tobacco. He sat down and smoked, inhaling the smoke as if he would have drawn the tobacco through the pipe stem; then saying, 'Now I have smoked, I may speak. I do not come to you for fish. I hope never to disgrace myself again. I now come for a wind which you must give me.' In the mood he was in, to argue with him was of no use, and I said, 'Why did you not bring one of your women with you? She would have taken some fish to the tent.' 'My women are too weak. They snare a hare, or two every day, barely enough to keep them alive. I am come for a wind which you must give me.' 'You know as well as I do that the Great Spirit alone is master of the Winds; you must apply to him and not to me.' 'Ah, that is always your way of talking to us. When you will not hear us, then you talk to us of the Great Spirit. I want a Wind. I must have it. Now think on it and dream how I am to get it.' I lent him an old Bison Robe to sleep on, which was all we could spare. The next day was calm. He sat on the floor in a despondent mood, at times smoking his pipe, and saying to me, 'Be kind to me, be kind to me, give me a Wind that we may live.' I told him the Good Spirit alone could cause the wind to blow. And my French Canadians were as foolish as the poor Indian, saying to one another, 'It would be a good thing, and well done, if he got a wind. We should get meat to eat.'

The night was very fine and clear. I passed most of it observing the Moon and Stars as usual. The small meteors were very numerous, which indicated a Gale of Wind. The morning rose fine, and before the appearance of the Sun, though calm with us, the tops of the tall Pines were waving, all foretelling a heavy gale, which usually follows a long calm. All this was plain to everyone. Very early Tapahpahtum said, 'Be kind and give me a strong wind.' Vexed with him, I told him to go and take care that the trees did not fall upon him. He shouted, 'I have got it', sprang from the floor, snatched his gun, whipped on his Snow Shoes, and dashed away at five miles an hour. The gale from North East came on as usual with snow and high drift and lasted three days. For the two first days we could not visit the nets, which sometimes happens; the third day the drift ceased, but the nets had been too long in the water without being washed, and we had to take them up. On this gale of wind, a common occurence, I learnt my men were more strangely foolish than the Indians. Something better than two months after this gale I sent three of the men with letters to another trading house and to bring some articles I wanted. Here these men related how I had raised a storm of wind for the Indian, but had made it so strong that for two days they got no fish from the nets, adding they thought I would take better care another time. In these distant solitudes, Men's minds seem to partake of the wildness of the country they live in. . . .

Wiskahoo was naturally a cheerful, good-natured, careless man, but hard times had changed him. He was a good Beaver worker and trapper, but an indifferent Moose Hunter, though now and then he killed one by chance. He had been twice so reduced by hunger as to be twice on the point of eating one of his children to save the others, when he was fortunately found and relieved by the other Natives. These sufferings had at times unhinged his mind, and made him dread being alone. He had for about a month been working Beaver and had now joined Tapahpahtum, and their Tents were together. He came to trade, and brought some meat the other had sent. It is usual when the Natives come to trade to give them a pint of grog, a liquor which I always used very sparingly. It was a bad custom, but could not be broken off. Wiskahoo, as soon as he got it, and while drinking it, used to say in a thoughtful mood, 'Nee weet to go' 'I must be a Man eater.' This word seemed to imply, 'I am possessed of an evil spirit to eat human flesh', 'Wee tee go'[5] is the evil Spirit that devours humankind. When he had said this a few times, one of the Men used to tie him slightly and he soon became quiet. These sad thoughts at times came upon him from the dreadful distress he had suffered; and at times took him in his tent, when he always allowed himself to be tied during this sad mood, which did not last long.

Three years afterwards this sad mood came upon him so often that the Natives got alarmed. They shot him and burnt his body to ashes to prevent his ghost remaining in this world.

[1846–51], 1916 (modernized)

---

5  Also spelled 'Windigo': a cannibalistic monster, formerly a man. Thompson's is one of the earliest records of this Native myth, which is thought to have functioned both as a prohibition of cannibalism and as a warning against the abuses of power—especially among shamans and other powerful leaders who needed to remember not to use their strength to consume the essence of their companions.

# Oliver Goldsmith
## 1794–1861

Oliver Goldsmith, the Canadian grandnephew and namesake of the British author of *The Vicar of Wakefield* and *She Stoops to Conquer*, published *The Rising Village: A Poem* in London in 1825 as a response to his great-uncle's long pastoral poem, *The Deserted Village* (1770). Where the earlier poem laments the rise of modernization that has led to the depopulation of the English countryside and to the vanishing rural life of the poet's childhood, *The Rising Village* counters this lament by suggesting that a Canadian agrarian village society is now emerging that will be a replacement for what Britain has lost.

In composing *The Rising Village*, Goldsmith the younger emphasized its continuities with his great-uncle's poem by retaining the form (rhyming couplets), the imagery, and even the diction of his more-than-five-decades-old model. His poem became the first volume of Canadian verse to receive serious critical attention, mostly from British reviewers; unfortunately, and to its author's dismay, many made unflattering comparisons with *The Deserted Village*. Discouraged, Goldsmith lost interest in poetry, though he did eventually revise the poem, shortening it by twenty-two lines; this revision was published in New Brunswick in 1834.

The son of a British army officer who settled in Canada after fighting in the American Revolutionary War, Goldsmith was born in 1794 in Saint Andrews, New Brunswick, and grew up in Halifax. At fifteen years of age, he found his permanent career with the Commissariat, the civilian supply branch of the British army, remaining with the military until his retirement in 1855. A lifelong bachelor, Goldsmith then moved to Liverpool to live with his sister. There, he composed his *Autobiography* (it remained unpublished until 1943), which records how he came to undertake his venture into poetry:

*the celebrated Author of the 'Deserted Village' had pathetically displayed the Anguish of his Countrymen, on being forced, from various causes, to quit their native plains, endeared to them by so many delightful recollections, and seek a Refuge at that time but little known. . . . In my humble poem I, therefore, endeavoured to describe the sufferings they experienced in a new and uncultivated Country, the Difficulties they surmounted, the Rise and progress of a Village, and the prospects which promised Happiness to its future possessors.*

Despite Goldsmith's description of his poem as being about progress and future happiness, there are features of *The Rising Village* that give it an ironic tension. The melodramatic story of Albert and Flora forms an uneasy centre for a pastoral poem; even before this episode, the poet occasionally adds, to apparently innocent passages, afterthoughts that make the pleasant aspects of village life seem ridiculous and the benevolent ones seem dangerous. Lines 131–52, with their move from the pleasures of a 'snug and safe' tavern to the vexations of an over-solicitous host whose questions exhaust and perplex his guests, provide a good example of the way light social satire creeps unexpectedly into the poem. And the description of the emerging professions in the Rising Village is rather sinister: there may be something good about the openness of a new society, since it enables a wandering peddler to become a prosperous merchant but, unfortunately, it also allows unqualified schoolteachers to become instructors. Still worse, a poorly trained doctor, who 'cures, by chance, or ends each human ill', can practise here without challenge. Though the poem ends with a rallying patriotic conclusion, invoking loyal homage to Britain, these discordant notes linger in the reader's mind.

# The Rising Village

Thou dear companion of my early years,[1]
Partner of all my boyish hopes and fears,
To whom I oft addressed the youthful strain,[2]
And sought no other praise than thine to gain;
Who oft hast bid me emulate his[3] fame
Whose genius formed the glory of our name;
Say, when thou canst, in manhood's ripened age,
With judgment scan the more aspiring page,
Wilt thou accept this tribute of my lay,
By far too small thy fondness to repay?                    10
Say, dearest Brother, wilt thou now excuse
This bolder flight of my adventurous muse?

    If, then, adown your cheek a tear should flow
For Auburn's Village,[4] and its speechless woe;
If, while you weep, you think the 'lowly train'[5]
Their early joys can never more regain,
Come, turn with me where happier prospects rise,
Beneath the sternness of Acadian skies.
And thou, dear spirit! whose harmonious lay
Didst lovely Auburn's piercing woes display,                20
Do thou to thy fond relative impart
Some portion of thy sweet poetic art;
Like thine, Oh! let my verse as gently flow,
While truth and virtue in my numbers glow:
And guide my pen with thy bewitching hand,
To paint the Rising Village of the land.

    How chaste and splendid are the scenes that lie
Beneath the circle of Britannia's sky!
What charming prospects there arrest the view,
How bright, how varied, and how boundless too!             30
Cities and plains extending far and wide,
The merchant's glory, and the farmer's pride.
Majestic palaces in pomp display

---

1  The poet's brother, Henry, to whom the poem is dedicated. The opening twelve lines of this poem, concluding
   with their mention of a muse, suggest epic or mock-epic intentions on Goldsmith's part. They recall the opening of Alexander Pope's *The Rape of the Lock* (1814), which begins with an address to a friend and with the command to 'say' rather than the conventional request for the muse to 'sing', as well as echoing the opening of
   Milton's invocations to his muse in his epic poem, *Paradise Lost* (1674). (In Book 1, Milton asks his muse for
   help with his 'adventrous song' aand in Book 3 he calls once more on the muse, now 'with bolder wing'.)
   Goldsmith's idealizations of the Acadian landscape in *The Rising Village* sometimes recall Milton's Eden.
2  Song; hence, any verse.
3  The elder Oliver Goldsmith.
4  The village of *The Deserted Village*.
5  Compare *The Deserted Village*, 251–2: 'Yes! let the rich deride, the proud disdain, / These simple blessings of the
   lowly train.' 'Train' here means a group or class of people.

The wealth and splendour of the regal sway;
While the low hamlet and the shepherd's cot,
In peace and freedom mark the peasant's lot.
There nature's vernal bloom adorns the field,
And Autumn's fruits their rich luxuriance yield.
There men, in busy crowds, with men combine,
That arts may flourish, and fair science shine;                40
And thence, to distant climes their labours send,
As o'er the world their widening views extend.
Compar'd with scenes like these, how lone and drear
Did once Acadia's woods and wilds appear;
Where wandering savages, and beasts of prey,
Displayed, by turns, the fury of their sway.
What noble courage must their hearts have fired,
How great the ardour which their souls inspired,
Who leaving far behind their native plain,
Have sought a home beyond the Western main;[6]                50
And braved the perils of the stormy seas,
In search of wealth, of freedom, and of ease!
Oh! none can tell but they who sadly share
The bosom's anguish, and its wild despair,
What dire distress awaits the hardy bands,
That venture first on bleak and desert lands.
How great the pain, the danger, and the toil,
Which mark the first rude culture of the soil.
When, looking round, the lonely settler sees
His home amid a wilderness of trees:                          60
How sinks his heart in those deep solitudes,
Where not a voice upon his ear intrudes;
Where solemn silence all the waste pervades,
Heightening the horror of its gloomy shades;
Save where the sturdy woodman's strokes resound,
That strew the fallen forest on the ground.
See! from their heights the lofty pines descend,
And crackling, down their pond'rous lengths extend.
Soon from their boughs the curling flames arise,
Mount into air, and redden all the skies;                     70
And where the forest once its foliage spread,
The golden corn triumphant waves its head.
    How blest, did nature's ruggedness appear
The only source of trouble or of fear;

---

6 In the last part of *The Deserted Village*, the poet imagines the displaced villagers—too proud to beg—seeking 'beyond the Western main' (the Atlantic) for the New World, where they would unfortunately meet 'the various terrors of that horrid shore' (337–84).

How happy, did no hardship meet his view,
No other care his anxious steps pursue;
But, while his labour gains a short repose,
And hope presents a solace for his woes,
New ills arise, new fears his peace annoy,
And other dangers all his hopes destroy.                            80
Behold the savage tribes in wildest strain,
Approach with death and terror in their train;
No longer silence o'er the forest reigns,
No longer stillness now her power retains;
But hideous yells announce the murderous band,
Whose bloody footsteps desolate the land;
He hears them oft in sternest mood maintain,
Their right to rule the mountain and the plain;
He hears them doom the *white man's* instant death,
Shrinks from the sentence, while he gasps for breath,                90
Then, rousing with one effort all his might,
Darts from his hut, and saves himself by flight.
Yet, what a refuge! Here a host of foes,
On every side, his trembling steps oppose;
Here savage beasts around his cottage howl,
As through the gloomy wood they nightly prowl,
Till morning comes, and then is heard no more
The shouts of man, or beast's appalling roar;
The wandering Indian turns another way,
And brutes avoid the first approach of day.[7]                     100
    Yet, tho' these threat'ning dangers round him roll,
Perplex his thoughts, and agitate his soul,
By patient firmness and industrious toil,
He still retains possession of the soil;
Around his dwelling scattered huts extend,
Whilst every hut affords another friend.
And now, behold! his bold aggressors fly,
To seek their prey beneath some other sky;
Resign the haunts they can maintain no more,
And safety in far distant wilds explore.                            110

7 With these lines about the terrors the first settlers found, compare *The Deserted Village*, 349–56, in which the
  New World settler is imagined encountering
  > *Those matted woods where birds forget to sing,*
  > *But silent bats in drowsy cluster cling,*
  > *Those poisonous fields with rank luxuriance crowned,*
  > *Where the dark scorpion gathers death around;*
  > *Where at each step the stranger fears to wake*
  > *The rattling terrors of the vengeful snake;*
  > *Where crouching tigers wait their hapless prey,*
  > *And savage men, more murderous still than they.*

His perils vanished, and his fears o'ercome,
Sweet hope portrays a happy peaceful home.
On every side fair prospects charm his eyes,
And future joys in every thought arise.
His humble cot, built from the neighbouring trees,
Affords protection from each chilling breeze;
His rising crops, with rich luxuriance crowned,
In waving softness shed their freshness round;
By nature nourished, by her bounty blest,
He looks to Heaven, and lulls his cares to rest.               120
    The arts of culture now extend their sway,
And many a charm of rural life display.
Where once the pine upreared its lofty head,
The settlers' humble cottages are spread;
Where the broad firs once sheltered from the storm,
By slow degrees a neighbourhood they form:
And, as it bounds, each circling year, increase
In social life, prosperity, and peace,
New prospects rise, new objects too appear,
To add more comfort to its lowly sphere.                        130
Where some rude sign or post the spot betrays,
The tavern first its useful front displays.
Here, oft the weary traveller at the close
Of evening, finds a snug and safe repose.
The passing stranger here, a welcome guest,
From all his toil enjoys a peaceful rest;
Unless the host, solicitous to please,
With care officious mar his hope of ease,
With flippant questions to no end confined,
Exhaust his patience, and perplex his mind.[8]                  140
    Yet, let no one condemn with thoughtless haste,
The hardy settler of the dreary waste,
Who, far removed from every busy throng,
And social pleasures that to life belong,
Whene'er a stranger comes within his reach,
Will sigh to learn whatever he can teach.
To this, must be ascribed in great degree,
That ceaseless, idle curiosity,
Which over all the Western world prevails,
And every breast, or more or less, assails;                     150

---

8  This description of the tavern contrasts with the more idealized description, in *The Deserted Village*, of the public
  house 'where nut-brown draughts inspired, / Where grey-beard mirth and smiling toil retired, / Where village
  statesmen talk'd with looks profound . . .' (220-36).

Till, by indulgence, so o'erpowering grown,
It seeks to know all business but its own.
Here, oft when winter's dreary terrors reign,
And cold, and snow, and storm, pervade the plain,
Around the birch-wood blaze the settlers draw,
'To tell of all they felt, and all they saw.'[9]
When, thus in peace are met a happy few,
Sweet are the social pleasures that ensue.
What lively joy each honest bosom feels,
As o'er the past events his memory steals,                       160
And to the listeners paints the dire distress,
That marked his progress in the wilderness;
The danger, trouble, hardship, toil, and strife,
Which chased each effort of his struggling life.

    In some lone spot of consecrated ground,
Whose silence spreads a holy gloom around,
The village church in unadorned array,
Now lifts its turret to the opening day.
How sweet to see the villagers repair
In groups to pay their adoration there;                          170
To view, in homespun dress, each sacred morn,
The old and young its hallowed seats adorn,
While, grateful for each blessing God has given,
In pious strains, they waft their thanks to Heaven.

    Oh, heaven-born faith! sure solace of our woes,
How lost is he who ne'er thy influence knows,
How cold the heart thy charity ne'er fires,
How dead the soul thy spirit ne'er inspires!
When troubles vex and agitate the mind,
By gracious Heaven for wisest ends designed,                     180
When dangers threaten, or when fears invade,
Man flies to thee for comfort and for aid;
The soul, impelled by thy all-powerful laws,
Seeks safety, only, in a Great First Cause![10]
If, then, amid the busy scene of life,
Its joy and pleasure, care, distrust, and strife;
Man, to his God for help and succour fly,
And on his mighty power to save, rely;
If, then, his thoughts can force him to confess
His errors, wants, and utter helplessness;                       190

---

9  The elder Goldsmith says that the loss of Auburn is a great personal loss because, deprived of returning to his
   village at the end of his life, he will not be able to enjoy a time when he will 'around my fire an evening group
   to draw, / And tell of all I felt, and all I saw' (91–2).
10  Original cause or creator of the universe: God.

How strong must be those feelings which impart
A sense of all his weakness to the heart,
Where not a friend in solitude is nigh,
His home the wild, his canopy the sky;
And, far removed from every human arm,
His God alone can shelter him from harm.
    While now the Rising Village claims a name,
Its limits still increase, and still its fame.
The wandering Pedlar, who undaunted traced
His lonely footsteps o'er the silent waste;           200
Who traversed once the cold and snow-clad plain,
Reckless of danger, trouble, or of pain,
To find a market for his little wares,
The source of all his hopes, and all his cares,
Established here, his settled home maintains,
And soon a merchant's higher title gains.
Around his store, on spacious shelves arrayed,
Behold his great and various stock in trade.
Here, nails and blankets, side by side, are seen,
There, horses' collars, and a large tureen;           210
Buttons and tumblers, fish-hooks, spoons and knives,
Shawls for young damsels, flannel for old wives;
Woolcards and stockings, hats for men and boys,
Mill-saws and fenders, silks, and children's toys;
All useful things, and joined with many more,
Compose the well-assorted country store.
    The half-bred[11] Doctor next then settles down,
And hopes the village soon will prove a town.
No rival here disputes his doubtful skill,
He cures, by chance, or ends each human ill;           220
By turns he physics,[12] or his patient bleeds,
Uncertain in what case each best succeeds.
And if, from friends untimely snatched away,
Some beauty fall a victim to decay;
If some fine youth, his parents' fond delight,
Be early hurried to the shades of night,
Death bears the blame, 'tis his envenomed dart
That strikes the suffering mortal to the heart.
    Beneath the shelter of a log-built shed
The country school-house next erects its head.         230

11 Half-educated.
12 To treat with medicine, especially with purgatives.

No 'man severe,' with learning's bright display,
Here leads the opening blossoms into day;[13]
No master here, in every art refined,
Through fields of science guides the aspiring mind;
But some poor wanderer of the human race,
Unequal to the task, supplies his place,
Whose greatest source of knowledge or of skill
Consists in reading, and in writing ill;
Whose efforts can no higher merit claim,
Than spreading Dilworth's great scholastic fame.                240
No modest youths surround his awful chair,
His frowns to deprecate, or smiles to share,[14]
But all the terrors of his lawful sway
The proud despise, the fearless disobey;
The rugged urchins spurn at all control,
Which cramps the movements of the free-born soul,
Till, in their own conceit so wise they've grown,
They think their knowledge far exceeds his own.[15]
  As thus the village each successive year
Presents new prospects, and extends its sphere,                250
While all around its smiling charms expand,
And rural beauties decorate the land.
The humble tenants, who were taught to know,
By years of suffering, all the weight of woe;
Who felt each hardship nature could endure,
Such pains as time alone could ease or cure,
Relieved from want, in sportive pleasures find
A balm to soften and relax the mind;
And now, forgetful of their former care,
Enjoy each sport, and every pastime share.                     260
Beneath some spreading tree's expanded shade
Here many a manly youth and gentle maid,
With festive dances or with sprightly song
The summer's evening hours in joy prolong,

13 The 'blossoms' are the young students, who ought to be opening into illumination when their schoolmaster
  brings them knowledge.
14 Thomas Dilworth was the author of several eighteenth-century school texts, including an arithmetic and a
  spelling book.
15 Compare the idealized portrait of the schoolmaster in *The Deserted Village* (195–216), which begins: 'There in
  his noisy mansion, skilled to rule, / The village master taught his little school; / A man severe he was, and stern
  to view,' and end by describing how his:
        *words of learned length and thundering sound*
        *Amazed the gazing rustics ranged around;*
        *And still they gazed, and still the wonder grew,*
        *That one small head could carry all he knew.*

And as the young their simple sports renew,
The aged witness, and approve them too.
And when the Summer's bloomy charms are fled,
When Autumn's fallen leaves around are spread,
When Winter rules the sad inverted year,
And ice and snow alternately appear, 270
Sports not less welcome lightly they essay,
To chase the long and tedious hours away.
Here, ranged in joyous groups around the fire,
Gambols and freaks[16] each honest heart inspire;
And if some venturous youth obtain a kiss,
The game's reward, and summit of its bliss,
Applauding shouts the victor's prize proclaim,
And every tongue augments his well-earned fame;
While all the modest fair one's blushes tell
Success had crowned his fondest hopes too well. 280
Dear humble sports, Oh! long may you impart
A guileless pleasure to the youthful heart,
Still may your joys from year to year increase,
And fill each breast with happiness and peace.
   Yet, tho' these simple pleasures crown the year,
Relieve its cares, and every bosom cheer,
As life's gay scenes in quick succession rise,
To lure the heart and captivate the eyes;
Soon vice steals on, in thoughtless pleasure's train,
And spreads her miseries o'er the village plain. 290
Her baneful arts some happy home invade,
Some bashful lover, or some tender maid;
Until, at length, repressed by no control,
They sink, debase, and overwhelm the soul.
How many aching breasts now live to know
The shame, the anguish, misery and woe,
That heedless passions, by no laws confined,
Entail forever on the human mind.
Oh, Virtue! that thy powerful charms could bind
Each rising impulse of the erring mind. 300
That every heart might own thy sovereign sway,
And every bosom fear to disobey;
No father's heart would then in anguish trace
The sad remembrance of a son's disgrace;
No mother's tears for some dear child undone
Would then in streams of poignant sorrow run,

16 Capers.

Nor could my verse the hapless story tell
Of one poor maid who loved—and loved too well.
　　Among the youths that graced their native plain,
Albert was foremost of the village train; 310
The hand of nature had profusely shed
Her choicest blessings on his youthful head;
His heart seemed generous, noble, kind, and free,
Just bursting into manhood's energy.
Flora was fair, and blooming as that flower
Which spreads its blossom to the April shower;
Her gentle manners and unstudied grace
Still added lustre to her beaming face,
While every look, by purity refined,
Displayed the lovelier beauties of her mind. 320
　　Sweet was the hour, and peaceful was the scene
When Albert first met Flora on the green;
Her modest looks, in youthful bloom displayed,
Then touched his heart, and there a conquest made
Nor long he sighed, by love and rapture fired,
He soon declared the passion she inspired.
In silence, blushing sweetly, Flora heard
His vows of love and constancy preferred;
And, as his soft and tender suit he pressed,
The maid, at length, a mutual flame confessed. 330
　　Love now had shed, with visions light as air,
His golden prospects on this happy pair;
Those moments soon rolled rapidly away,
Those hours of joy and bliss that gently play
Around young hearts, ere yet they learn to know
Life's care or trouble, or to feel its woe.
The day was fixed, the bridal dress was made,
And time alone their happiness delayed,
The anxious moment that, in joy begun,
Would join their fond and faithful hearts in one. 340
'Twas now at evening's hour, about the time
When in Acadia's cold and northern clime
The setting sun, with pale and cheerless glow,
Extends his beams o'er trackless fields of snow,
That Flora felt her throbbing heart oppressed
By thoughts, till then, a stranger to her breast.
Albert had promised that his bosom's pride
That very morning should become his bride;
Yet morn had come and passed; and not one vow
Of his had e'er been broken until now. 350

But, hark! a hurried step advances near,
'Tis Albert's breaks upon her listening ear;
Albert's, ah, no! a ruder footstep bore,
With eager haste, a letter to the door;
Flora received it, and could scarce conceal
Her rapture, as she kissed her lover's seal.
Yet, anxious tears were gathered in her eye,
As on the note it rested wistfully;
Her trembling hands unclosed the folded page,
That soon she hoped would every fear assuage,                    360
And while intently o'er the lines she ran,
In broken half breathed tones she thus began:
    'Dear Flora, I have left my native plain,
And fate forbids that we shall meet again:
'Twere vain to tell, nor can I now impart
The sudden motive to this change of heart.
The vows so oft repeated to thine ear
As tales of cruel falsehood must appear.
Forgive the hand that deals this treacherous blow,
Forget the heart that can afflict this woe;                      370
Farewell! and think no more of Albert's name,
His weakness pity, now involved in shame.'
    Ah! who can paint her features as, amazed,
In breathless agony, she stood and gazed!
Oh, Albert, cruel Albert! she exclaimed,
Albert was all her faltering accents named.
A deadly feeling seized upon her frame,
Her pulse throbb'd quick, her colour went and came;
A darting pain shot through her frenzied head,
And from that fatal hour her reason fled!                        380
    The sun had set; his lingering beams of light
From western hills had vanished into night.
The northern blast along the valley rolled,
Keen was that blast, and piercing was the cold,
When, urged by frenzy, and by love inspired,
For what but madness could her breast have fired!
Flora, with one slight mantle round her waved,
Forsook her home, and all the tempest braved.
Her lover's falsehood wrung her gentle breast,
His broken vows her tortured mind possessed;                    390
Heedless of danger, on she bent her way
Through drifts of snow, where Albert's dwelling lay,
With frantic haste her tottering steps pursued
Amid the long night's darkness unsubdued;

Until, benumbed, her fair and fragile form
Yielded beneath the fury of the storm;
Exhausted nature could no further go,
And, senseless, down she sank amid the snow.
   Now as the morn had streaked the eastern sky
With dawning light, a passing stranger's eye,       400
By chance directed, glanced upon the spot
Where lay the lovely sufferer: To his cot
The peasant bore her, and with anxious care
Tried every art, till hope became despair.
With kind solicitude his tender wife
Long vainly strove to call her back to life;
At length her gentle bosom throbs again,
Her torpid limbs their wonted power obtain;
The loitering current now begins to flow,
And hapless Flora wakes once more to woe:      410
But all their friendly efforts could not find
A balm to heal the anguish of her mind.
   Come hither, wretch, and see what thou hast done,
Behold the heart thou hast so falsely won,
Behold it, wounded, broken, crushed and riven,
By thy unmanly arts to ruin driven;
Hear Flora calling on thy much loved name,
Which, e'en in madness, she forbears to blame.
Not all thy sighs and tears can now restore
One hour of pleasure that she knew before;      420
Not all thy prayers can now remove the pain,
That floats and revels o'er her maddened brain.
Oh, shame of manhood! that could thus betray
A maiden's hopes, and lead her heart away;
Oh, shame of manhood! that could blast her joy,
And one so fair, so lovely, could destroy.
   Yet, think not oft such tales of real woe
Degrade the land, and round the village flow.
Here virtue's charms appear in bright array,
And all their pleasing influence display;      430
Here modest youths, impressed in beauty's train,
Or captive led by love's endearing chain,
And fairest girls whom vows have ne'er betrayed,
Vows that are broken oft as soon as made,
Unite their hopes, and join their lives in one,
In bliss pursue them, as at first begun.
Then, as life's current onward gently flows,
With scarce one fault to ruffle its repose,

With minds prepared, they sink in peace to rest,
To meet on high the spirits of the blest.                                440
    While time thus rolls his rapid years away,
The Village rises gently into day.
How sweet it is, at first approach of morn,
Before the silvery dew has left the lawn,
When warring winds are sleeping yet on high,
Or breathe as softly as the bosom's sigh,
To gain some easy hill's ascending height,
Where all the landscape brightens with delight,
And boundless prospects stretched on every side,
Proclaim the country's industry and pride.                               450
Here the broad marsh extends its open plain,
Until its limits touch the distant main;
There verdant meads along the uplands spring,
And grateful odours to the breezes fling;
Here crops of grain in rich luxuriance rise,
And wave their golden riches to the skies;
There smiling orchards interrupt the scene,
Or gardens bounded by some fence of green;
The farmer's cottage, bosomed 'mong the trees,
Whose spreading branches shelter from the breeze;                        460
The winding stream that turns the busy mill,
Whose clacking echos o'er the distant hill;
The neat white church, beside whose walls are spread
The grass-clad hillocks of the sacred dead,
Where rude cut stones or painted tablets tell,
In laboured verse, how youth and beauty fell;
How worth and hope were hurried to the grave,
And torn from those who had no power to save.
    Or, when the Summer's dry and sultry sun
Adown the West his fiery course has run;                                 470
When o'er the vale his parting rays of light
Just linger, ere they vanish into night,
How sweet to wander round the wood-bound lake,
Whose glassy stillness scarce the zephyrs wake;
How sweet to hear the murmuring of the rill,
As down it gurgles from the distant hill;
The note of Whip-poor-Will how sweet to hear,
When sadly slow it breaks upon the ear,
And tells each night, to all the silent vale,
The hopeless sorrows of its mournful tale.                               480
Dear lovely spot! Oh may such charms as these,
Sweet tranquil charms, that cannot fail to please,

Forever reign around thee, and impart
Joy, peace, and comfort to each native heart.
   Happy Acadia! though around thy shore
Is heard the stormy wind's terrific roar;
Though round thee Winter binds his icy chain,
And his rude tempests sweep along thy plain,
Still Summer comes, and decorates thy land
With fruits and flowers from her luxuriant hand;     490
Still Autumn's gifts repay the labourer's toil
With richest products from thy fertile soil;
With bounteous store his varied wants supply,
And scarce the plants of other suns deny.
How pleasing, and how glowing with delight
Are now thy budding hopes! How sweetly bright
They rise to view! How full of joy appear
The expectations of each future year!
Not fifty Summers yet have blessed thy clime,
How short a period in the page of time!     500
Since savage tribes, with terror in their train,
Rushed o'er thy fields, and ravaged all thy plain.
But some few years have rolled in haste away
Since, through thy vales, the fearless beast of prey,
With dismal yell and loud appalling cry,
Proclaimed his midnight reign of terror nigh.
And now how changed the scene! the first, afar,
Have fled to wilds beneath the northern star;
The last has learned to shun man's dreaded eye,
And, in his turn, to distant regions fly.     510
While the poor peasant, whose laborious care
Scarce from the soil could wring his scanty fare;
Now in the peaceful arts of culture skilled,
Sees his wide barn with ample treasures filled;
Now finds his dwelling, as the year goes round,
Beyond his hopes, with joy and plenty crowned.
   Nor culture's arts, a nation's noblest friend,
Alone o'er Scotia's fields their power extend;
From all her shores, with every gentle gale,
Commerce expands her free and swelling sail;     520
And all the land, luxuriant, rich, and gay,
Exulting owns the splendour of their sway.
These are thy blessings, Scotia, and for these,
For wealth, for freedom, happiness, and ease,
Thy grateful thanks to Britain's care are due,
Her power protects, her smiles past hopes renew,

Her valour guards thee, and her councils guide,
Then, may thy parent ever be thy pride!
   Happy Britannia! though thy history's page
In darkest ignorance shrouds thine infant age,      530
Though long thy childhood's years in error strayed,
And long in superstition's bands delayed;
Matur'd and strong, thou shin'st in manhood's prime,
The first and brightest star of Europe's clime.
The nurse of science, and the seat of arts,
The home of fairest forms and gentlest hearts;
The land of heroes, generous, free, and brave,
The noblest conquerors of the field and wave;
Thy flag, on every sea and shore unfurled,
Has spread thy glory, and thy thunder hurled.      540
When, o'er the earth, a tyrant[17] would have thrown
His iron chain, and called the world his own,
Thine arm preserved it, in its darkest hour,
Destroyed his hopes, and crushed his dreaded power,
To sinking nations life and freedom gave,
'Twas thine to conquer, as 'twas thine to save.
   Then blest Acadia! ever may thy name,
Like hers, be graven on the rolls of fame;
May all thy sons, like hers, be brave and free,
Possessors of her laws and liberty;      550
Heirs of her splendour, science, power, and skill,
And through succeeding years her children still.
And as the sun, with gentle dawning ray,
From night's dull bosom wakes, and leads the day,
His course majestic keeps, till in the height
He glows one blaze of pure exhaustless light;
So may thy years increase, thy glories rise,
To be the wonder of the Western skies;
And bliss and peace encircle all thy shore,
Till empires rise and sink, on earth, no more.      560

1825, rev. 1834

---

17 Napoleon Bonaparte, who was defeated at the Battle of Waterloo in 1815.

# John Franklin
## 1786–1847

# Dr John Richardson
## 1787–1865

### The Northwest Passage and the Search for Franklin

For more than three hundred years, Europeans searched for a Northwest Passage, a water route passing through Arctic sea lanes that would make possible travel to Asia and the Indies by way of North America. The most famous attempt to find this passage, the legendary Franklin expedition of 1845, was also the most ill-fated. After John Franklin and his crew disappeared, along with his two ships, the *Terror* and the *Erebus*, a search, begun in 1847, found a series of tantalizing clues—first, a few graves, then a cairn of discarded tins, stories among the Inuit, and a message left behind. They did not discover the final fate of the expedition until 1859. During the intervening twelve years, some thirty expeditions went out to look for the missing ships and men— in the process, contributing substantially to our knowledge of the Arctic—turning the search for Franklin into one of the most famous quests of the nineteenth century, one that acquired mythic dimensions and inspired a popular ballad.

The *Terror* and the *Erebus* are mentioned at the beginning of Joseph Conrad's *Heart of*

*Darkness*, and the search for Franklin is alluded to in Thoreau's *Walden*; however, the longest-lasting impressions of Franklin and his lost crew have been left on Canadian culture. In one of the chapters in *Strange Things: The Malevolent North in Canadian Literature* (1995), Margaret Atwood surveys some of the responses of Canada's writers—from E.J. Pratt (who considered, but did not pursue, an epic poem on the subject), through Gwendolyn MacEwen and Al Purdy, to Mordecai Richler and Rudy Wiebe. Atwood, who herself made the expedition's fate a central metaphor in her 1991 story 'The Age of Lead' (reprinted in this anthology), concludes the chapter by reproducing the song, 'Northwest Passage'—by the Canadian singer-songwriter Stan Rogers— which has for its chorus, 'Ah, for just one time, I would take the Northwest Passage / To find the hand of Franklin reaching for the Beaufort Sea / Tracing one warm line through a land so wild and savage / And make a Northwest Passage to the sea.'

### John Franklin

Born in Lincolnshire, England, John Franklin became the epitome of the nineteenth-century scientific adventurer. He joined the Royal Navy at the age of fourteen and saw action for the first time the following year. Two years after that, he survived a shipwreck, and he later took part in the Battle of Trafalgar in 1805 and in the War of 1812. He rose through the ranks to become a lieutenant and retired on half pay after the Napoleonic Wars ended. A few years later, he returned to service to join the Royal Navy's search for the Northwest Passage. (The quest for

the passage had not been actively pursued for some time. The decision to take it up again seems to have been stimulated by the need to employ the men and ships left idle after the defeat of Napoleon.)

After travelling as second in command on an abortive venture in 1818, Franklin was asked in 1819 to lead the first of what eventually became three Arctic expeditions under his command. The 1819–22 expedition was a near disaster, costing the lives of some ten men (most of them voyageurs and Natives who joined him after he reached North America). Despite—or because of—his difficulties, the book he published a year after his return, his *Narrative of a Journey to the Shores of the Polar Sea in the Years 1819, 20, 21 and 22*, was immensely popular and secured him an enduring reputation as a man of heroic stature. It was mostly based on Franklin's own journals, but it also incorporated excerpts from those of the three men who accompanied him. As well as being a chronicle of suffering and epic endurance, the book's extensive appendices on the flora and fauna of the area and on the crew's scientific observations of the aurora borealis and the actions of the compass near the North Pole showed that Franklin took a deep scientific interest in his voyage. He was elected a Fellow of the Royal Society soon after his return to England.

He exercised more caution on his next expedition, undertaken in 1825, and succeeded in mapping and gathering new information about the Arctic before turning back in 1827. He was knighted in 1829, and, after retiring once more from naval service, he was appointed lieutenant-governor of Van Diemen's Land (now Tasmania), a post he held from 1837 to 1843. In 1845, when he was 59 years old, Franklin, believing that developments in technology would help him overcome difficulties previously encountered, offered to lead another expedition into the North. He assumed the command of the *Erebus* and the *Terror*, which were sailing vessels, outfitted them with a propeller and steam engines, and clad their prows with sheets of iron to help them push their way through the ice. (John Ross, a friend of Franklin's, had previously experimented with a steam engine in his Arctic exploration of 1829, but his vessel got caught in an ice pack; Ross and his compatriots remained there for an unprecedented four years before being rescued.) Franklin's were massive steam engines, originally designed for railway locomotives, but they did not prevent him from becoming similarly icebound.

By 1867, Franklin's searchers were able to reconstruct the details of his fate: after he was trapped by ice, he had waited through the two following summers for a thaw. Franklin died in June 1847, not long after his supplies ran out and his next in command, Captain Francis Crozier, led the starving crew off the ships to attempt an overland trek back to civilization. They made it as far as Victory Point (now part of Nunavut); there they left a brief record of events but perished shortly after pushing on from there.

Neither the remains of the ships themselves nor the grave of Franklin has ever been found. The reasons for the lost expedition's failure continue to intrigue investigators. In the 1980s, a group of anthropologists found the bodies of three of Franklin's sailors buried in the frozen tundra and discovered that the men had suffered from severe lead poisoning. The food Franklin took along included eight thousand tins sealed with lead, which may have caused lead poisoning , leaving those who consumed it confused and debilitated and contributing to the failure of the expedition.

## Dr John Richardson

John Richardson, who took part in, and contributed sections to, Franklin's accounts of his first and second Arctic journeys, was born in Dumfries, Scotland. He studied medicine at the University of Edinburgh before becoming a surgeon in the Royal Navy. A naturalist as well as a physician, he, along with the midshipmen George Back and Robert Hood, was appointed by the Lords Commissioners of the Admiralty to join Franklin's first expedition; he also participated in the second Arctic expedition with Franklin in 1825, but did not join the expedition of 1845. (Richardson was knighted for his services to the state the year after it departed.) He did, however, decide to return to the Arctic in 1848 to join the search for Franklin, publishing a record of this unsuccessful trip, and went on to write other books about his adventures and explorations. The most important of Richardson's later works is *The Polar Regions* (1861), in which, as well as discussing the Canadian North in detail, he summarized what had been learned of Franklin and his men. Observing that Franklin's expedition had come within miles of reaching the known waters to the west, he wrote that they had 'forged the last link of the North-West Passage with their lives.'

## Stories of Northern Exploration

The excerpt reprinted here appears near the end of Franklin's first book, an account of an overland journey to the Coppermine River (some fifty years after Samuel Hearne first traversed the area) and Coronation Gulf, then eastward to Point Turnagain (Kent Peninsula) and back by the Hood River. Although Franklin derived great satisfaction in being the first European to map the area he passed through, as well as in naming its various features after friends and famous Englishmen, what most strikes readers are the grave hardships and constant suffering caused by the extremes of the cold and by the fact that food was in such short supply. These journals show the travellers preoccupied with the simple necessities for bare survival—not only food but, in land without trees, enough wood for a fire. Members of the expedition were sometimes driven to eat whatever they could find—even parts of their own garments—and to burn pieces of their shelters for warmth.

These tales of sheer endurance (Dr Richardson praises Robert Hood for 'the patience and fortitude with which he sustained . . . unparalleled bodily sufferings'), especially in extremes of climate, became a popular genre in their day: prompted by the example of Franklin's narrative, a number of Arctic and polar adventurers set out to prove their own mettle and to return, after enduring comparable adversity, to write their own bestselling accounts. And just as the popularity of American pulp westerns gave rise to the myth of the Old West, so, too, these books played a powerful role in shaping the expectations of, and even a myth of, the North and in that way contributed to the formation of a Canadian identity.

## From *Narrative of a Journey to the Shores of the Polar Sea in the Years 1819, 20, 21 and 22*

*[On his 1819 expedition to determine the exact position of the mouth of the Coppermine River and to map the shore of the Polar Sea to the east, Franklin was accompanied by three other officers, George Back, Robert Hood, and Dr John Richardson, along with two sailors, John Hepburn and Samuel Wilkes, and four Orkney boatmen. On 30 August 1819, the party arrived at York Factory, on the west coast of Hudson Bay (south of where Churchill, Manitoba, now stands). From there they began an overland journey north, following a chain of Hudson's Bay posts, to Lake Athabaska. On 29 July 1820, they arrived at the most northerly post of the North West Company, Fort Providence, at the western end of Great Slave Lake. Joined by a party that included Willard Wentzel (a trader at Fort Providence), Native guides, voyageurs, interpreters, and three women accompanying their husbands (with their three children), they now formed a group of thirty-one and made slow progress north, stopping in August 1820 at Winter Lake to construct a winter base camp, which they dubbed Fort Enterprise. They explored the area around their camp and made contact with a small band of Copper Indians; their leader, Akaitcho, assisted and advised Franklin.*

*Because they were beginning to run low on supplies, George Back set off with a small group on a winter journey to the outposts at Forts Providence, Resolution, and Chipewyan, before returning with supplies to the main party. His account of that trek concludes: 'on the 17th [of March 1821], at an early hour, we arrived at Fort Enterprise, having travelled about eighteen miles a-day. I had the pleasure of meeting my friends all in good health, after an absence of nearly five months, during which time I had travelled one thousand one hundred and four miles, on snow shoes, and had no other covering at night, in the woods, than a blanket and deer-skin, with the thermometer frequently at −40° and once at −57°; and sometimes passing two and three days without tasting food.'*

*In June 1821, the expedition travelled on to Point Lake and then, using two birchbark canoes, began their descent to the coast of the Arctic Ocean. On 14 July 1821, Dr Richardson climbed a hill at the mouth of the Coppermine River to become the fourth European to view the Arctic Ocean from the mainland of North America. The next day they met Inuit for the first time. Franklin recorded that nearby: 'Several human skulls which bore the marks of violence, and many bones were strewed about the ground. . . . [A]s the spot exactly answers the description given by Mr Hearne, of the place where the Chipewyans who accompanied him perpetrated the dreadful massacre on the Esquimaux, we had no doubt of this being the place. . . . We have, therefore, preserved the appellation of Bloody Fall, which he bestowed upon it.' On 18 August, they reached what became the most easterly point in their travels, a place on the Arctic coast that Franklin dubbed Point Turnagain. Inferring from the presence of whales that open sea lay ahead, he concluded, 'Our researches, as far as they have gone, seem to favour the opinion of those who contend for the practicability of a North-West Passage.' The extract that follows tells of their arduous return to Fort Enterprise across the Barren Grounds.]*

## CHAPTER XI

About noon Samandrè coming up, informed us that Crédit and Vaillant[1] could advance no further. Some willows being discovered in a valley near to us, I proposed to halt the party there, while Dr Richardson went back to visit them. I hoped too, that when the sufferers received the information of a fire being kindled at so short a distance, they would be cheered, and use their utmost efforts to reach it, but this proved a vain hope. The Doctor found Vaillant about a mile and a half in the rear, much exhausted with cold and fatigue. Having encouraged him to advance to the fire, after repeated solicitations he made the attempt, but fell down amongst the deep snow at every step. Leaving him in this situation, the Doctor went about half a mile farther back, to the spot where Crédit was said to have halted, and the track being nearly obliterated by the snow drift, it became unsafe for him to go further. Returning he passed Vaillant, who having moved only a few yards in his absence had fallen down, was unable to rise, and could scarcely answer his questions. Being unable to afford him any effectual assistance, he hastened on to inform us of his situation. . . . Mr Hood and Dr Richardson proposed to remain behind, with a single attendant, at the first place where sufficient wood and *tripe de roche*[2] should be found for ten days consumption;

1 François Samandrè, Crédit (the name given to Mathew Pelonquin), and Registe Vaillant, along with Joseph Peltier and Joseph Benoit (mentioned later in this extract), were among the 'Canadians' (i.e. voyageurs) who joined Franklin's expedition after its arrival in the North. (Samandrè, Pelonquin, and Peltier all died while with the expedition.)

2 Franklin has earlier explained *tripe de roche*: 'In the afternoon we got into a more hilly country, where the ground was strewed with large stones. The surface of these was covered with lichens of the genus gyrophora, which the Canadians term *tripe de roche*.' Also known as rock tripe, this lichen can be found on rocks in the northern parts of the United States and extends into the Far North. It forms broad, flat, leathery brown, grey-ish-black, or blackish expansions several inches wide. Its nutritional value is slight, and it is eaten only in cases of extreme need. Not long after the members of the expedition begin to make it a staple, Franklin comments on the difficulty they had digesting the plant: 'this unpalatable weed was now quite nauseous to the whole party, and in several it produced bowel complaints. Mr Hood was the greatest sufferer from this cause.'

and that I should proceed as expeditiously as possible with the men to the house, and thence send them immediate relief. . . .

At length we reached Fort Enterprise, and to our infinite disappointment and grief found it a perfectly desolate habitation. There was no deposit of provision, no trace of the Indians, no letter from Mr Wentzel to point out where the Indians might be found. It would be impossible for me to describe our sensations after entering the miserable abode, and discovering how we had been neglected: the whole party shed tears, not so much for our own fate, as for that of our friends in the rear, whose lives depended entirely on our sending immediate relief from this place. . . .

We now looked round for the means of subsistence, and were gratified to find several deer skins, which had been thrown away during our former residence. The bones were gathered from the heap of ashes, these with the skins, and the addition of *tripe de roche*, we considered would support us tolerably well for a time. . . . When I arose the following morning, my body and limbs were so swollen that I was unable to walk more than a few yards. Adam was in a still worse condition, being absolutely incapable of rising without assistance. My other companions fortunately experienced this inconvenience in a less degree, and went to collect bones, and some *Tripe de roche* which supplied us with two meals. The bones were quite acrid, and the soup extracted from them excoriated the mouth if taken alone, but it was somewhat milder when boiled with *tripe de roche*, and we even thought the mixture palatable, with the addition of salt, of which a cask had been fortunately left here in the spring. . . .

In making arrangements for our departure, Adam disclosed to me, for the first time, that he was affected with œdematous swellings[3] in some parts of the body, to such a degree as to preclude the slightest attempt at marching. . . . It now became necessary to abandon the original intention of proceeding with the whole party towards Fort Providence, and Peltier and Samandrè having volunteered to remain with Adam, I determined on setting out with Benoit and Augustus, intending to send them relief by the first party of Indians we should meet. My clothes were so much torn, as to be quite inadequate to screen me from the wind, and Peltier and Samandrè fearing that I might suffer on the journey in consequence, kindly exchanged with me parts of their dress, desiring me to send them skins in return by the Indians. Having patched up three pair of snow-shoes, and singed a considerable quantity of skin for the journey, we started on the morning of the 20th. Previous to my departure, I packed up the journals of the officers, the charts, and some other documents, together with a letter addressed to the Under-Secretary of State, detailing the occurrences of the Expedition up to this period, which package was given to Peltier and Samandrè, with direction that it should be brought away by the Indians who might come to them. I also instructed them to forward succour immediately on its arrival to our companions in the rear, which they solemnly promised to do, and I left a letter for my friends, Richardson and Hood, to be sent at the same time. I thought it necessary to admonish Peltier, Samandrè, and Adam, to eat two meals every day, in order to keep up their

---

3  Jean-Baptiste Adam travelled with the group as an interpreter; 'oedematous': resulting from oedema (now usually spelled 'edema'), i.e. swollen because of an accumulation of subdermal fluids—here as a result of prolonged exposure to severe cold.

strength, which they promised me they would do. No language that I can use could adequately describe the parting scene. I shall only say there was far more calmness and resignation for the Divine will evinced by every one than could have been expected. We were all cheered by the hope that the Indians would be found by the one party, and relief sent to the other. Those who remained entreated us to make all the haste we could, and expressed their hope of seeing the Indians in ten or twelve days.

At first starting we were so feeble as scarcely to be able to move forwards, and the descent of the bank of the river through the deep snow was a severe labour. When we came upon the ice, where the snow was less deep, we got on better, but after walking six hours we had only gained four miles, and were then compelled by fatigue to encamp on the borders of Round-Rock Lake. Augustus[4] tried for fish here, but without success, so that our fare was skin and tea. Composing ourselves to rest, we lay close to each other for warmth. We found the night bitterly cold, and the wind pierced through our famished frames.

The next morning was mild and pleasant for travelling, and we set out after breakfast. We had not, however, gone many yards before I had the misfortune to break my snow-shoes by falling between two rocks. This accident prevented me from keeping pace with Benoit and Augustus, and in the attempt I became quite exhausted. Being convinced that their being delayed on my account might prove of fatal consequence to the rest, I resolved on returning to the house, and letting them proceed alone in search of the Indians. I therefore halted them only whilst I wrote a note to Mr Back, stating the reason of my return, and requesting he would send meat from Rein-Deer Lake by these men, if St Germain should kill any animals there. If Benoit should miss Mr Back, I directed him to proceed to Fort Providence, and furnished him with a letter to the gentlemen in charge of it, requesting immediate supplies might be sent to us.

On my arrival at the house, I found Samandrè very dispirited, and too weak, as he said, to render any assistance to Peltier; upon whom the whole labour of getting wood and collecting the means of subsistence would have devolved. Conscious, too, that his strength would have been unequal to these tasks, they had determined upon taking only one meal each day; under these circumstances I considered my return as particularly fortunate, as I hoped to stimulate Samandrè to exertion, and at any rate I could contribute some help to Peltier. I undertook the office of cooking, and insisted they should eat twice a-day whenever food could be procured, but as I was too weak to pound the bones, Peltier agreed to do that in addition to his more fatiguing task of getting wood. We had a violent snow storm all the next day, and this gloomy weather contributed to the depression of spirits under which Adam and Samandrè were labouring. Neither of them would quit their beds, and they scarcely ceased from shedding tears all day; in vain did Peltier and myself endeavour to cheer them. We had even to use much entreaty before we prevailed upon them to take the meals we had prepared. Our situation was indeed distressing, but in comparison with that of our friends in the rear, we considered it happy. Their condition gave us unceasing solicitude, and was the principal subject of our conversation.

4 The name by which the expedition referred to Tattannoeuck, an Inuit guide who had joined the party.

Though the weather was stormy on the 26th, Samandrè assisted me to gather *tripe de roche*. Adam, who was very ill, and could not now be prevailed upon to eat this weed, subsisted principally on bones, though he also partook of the soup. The *tripe de roche* had hitherto afforded us our chief support, and we naturally felt great uneasiness at the prospect of being deprived of it, by its being so frozen as to render it impossible for us to gather it.

We perceived our strength decline every day, and every exertion began to be irksome; when we were once seated the greatest effort was necessary in order to rise, and we had frequently to lift each other from our seats; but even in this pitiable condition we conversed cheerfully, being sanguine as to the speedy arrival of the Indians. We calculated indeed that if they should be near the situation where they had remained last winter, our men would have reached them by this day. Having expended all the wood which we could procure from our present dwelling, without endangering its falling, Peltier began this day to pull down the partitions of the adjoining houses. Though these were only distant about twenty yards, yet the increase of labour in carrying the wood fatigued him so much, that by the evening he was exhausted. On the next day his weakness was such, especially in the arms, of which he chiefly complained, that he with difficulty lifted the hatchet: still he persevered, Samandrè and I assisting him in bringing in the wood, but our united strength could only collect sufficient to replenish the fire four times in the course of the day. As the insides of our mouths had become sore from eating the bone-soup, we relinquished the use of it, and now boiled our skin, which mode of dressing we found more palatable than frying it, as we had hitherto done.

On the 29th, Peltier felt his pains more severe, and could only cut a few pieces of wood. Samandrè, who was still almost as weak, relieved him a little time, and I assisted them in carrying in the wood. We endeavoured to pick some *tripe de roche*, but in vain, as it was entirely frozen. In turning up the snow, in searching for bones, I found several pieces of bark, which proved a valuable acquisition, as we were almost destitute of dry wood proper for kindling the fire. We saw a herd of rein-deer sporting on the river, about half a mile from the house; they remained there a considerable time, but none of the party felt themselves sufficiently strong to go after them, nor was there one of us who could have fired a gun without resting it.

Whilst we were seated round the fire this evening, discoursing about the anticipated relief, the conversation was suddenly interrupted by Peltier's exclaiming with joy, '*Ah! le monde!*' imagining that he heard the Indians in the other room; immediately afterwards, to his bitter disappointment, Dr Richardson and Hepburn entered, each carrying his bundle. Peltier, however, soon recovered himself enough to express his joy at their safe arrival, and his regret that their companions were not with them. When I saw them alone my own mind was instantly filled with apprehensions respecting my friend Hood, and our other companions, which were immediately confirmed by the Doctor's melancholy communication, that Mr Hood and Michel[5] were dead. Perrault and Fontano had neither reached the tent, nor been heard of by them. This intelligence

5  Michel Teroahauté, an Iroquois voyageur. Vincenza Antonio Fontano was an Italian national who, after serving in North America with a British regiment, remained and became a voyageur.

produced a melancholy despondency in the minds of my party, and on that account the particulars were deferred until another opportunity. We were all shocked at beholding the emaciated countenances of the Doctor and Hepburn, as they strongly evidenced their extremely debilitated state. The alteration in our appearance was equally distressing to them, for since the swellings had subsided we were little more than skin and bone. The Doctor particularly remarked the sepulchral tone of our voices, which he requested us to make more cheerful if possible, unconscious that his own partook of the same key.

Hepburn having shot a partridge, which was brought to the house, the Doctor tore out the feathers, and having held it to the fire a few minutes, divided it into seven portions. Each piece was ravenously devoured by my companions, as it was the first morsel of flesh any of us had tasted for thirty-one days, unless indeed the small gristly particles which we found occasionally adhering to the pounded bones may be termed flesh. Our spirits were revived by this small supply, and the Doctor endeavoured to raise them still higher by the prospect of Hepburn's being able to kill a deer next day, as they had seen, and even fired at, several near the house. He endeavoured, too, to rouse us to some attention to the comfort of our apartment, and particularly to roll up, in the day, our blankets which (expressly for the convenience of Adam and Samandrè,) we had been in the habit of leaving by the fire where we lay on them. The Doctor having brought his prayer-book and testament, some prayers and psalms, and portions of scripture, appropriate to our situation, were read, and we retired to bed.

Next morning the Doctor and Hepburn went out early in search of deer; but, though they saw several herds and fired some shots, they were not so fortunate as to kill any, being too weak to hold their guns steadily. The cold compelled the former to return soon, but Hepburn persisted until late in the evening.

My occupation was to search for skins under the snow, it being now our object immediately to get all that we could, but I had not strength to drag in more than two of those which were within twenty yards of the house until the Doctor came and assisted me. We made up our stock to twenty-six, but several of them were putrid, and scarcely eatable, even by men suffering the extremity of famine. Peltier and Samandrè continued very weak and dispirited, and they were unable to cut fire-wood. Hepburn had in consequence that laborious task to perform after he came back. The Doctor having scarified the swelled parts of Adam's body, a large quantity of water flowed out, and he obtained some ease, but still kept his bed.

After our usual supper of singed skin and bone soup, Dr Richardson acquainted me with the afflicting circumstances attending the death of Mr Hood and Michel, and detailed the occurrences subsequent to my departure from them, which I shall give from his journal, in his own words; but, I must here be permitted to express the heart-felt sorrow with which I was overwhelmed at the loss of so many companions; especially for that of my friend Mr Hood, to whose zealous and able co-operation I had been indebted for so much invaluable assistance during the Expedition, whilst the excellent qualities of his heart engaged my warmest regard. His scientific observations, together with his maps and drawings, evince a variety of talent, which, had his life been spared, must have rendered him a distinguished ornament to his profession, and which will cause his death to be felt as a loss to the service.

## DR RICHARDSON'S NARRATIVE

After Captain Franklin had bidden us farewell we remained seated by the fire-side as long as the willows, the men had cut for us before they departed, lasted. We had no *tripe de roche* that day, but drank an infusion of the country tea-plant,[6] which was grateful from its warmth, although it afforded no sustenance. We then retired to bed, where we remained all the next day, as the weather was stormy, and the snow-drift so heavy, as to destroy every prospect of success in our endeavours to light a fire with the green and frozen willows, which were our only fuel. Through the extreme kindness and fore-thought of a lady, the party, previous to leaving London, had been furnished with a small collection of religious books, of which we still retained two or three of the most portable, and they proved of incalculable benefit to us. We read portions of them to each other as we lay in bed, in addition to the morning and evening service, and found that they inspired us on each perusal with so strong a sense of the omnipresence of a beneficent God, that our situation, even in these wilds, appeared no longer destitute; and we conversed, not only with calmness, but with cheerfulness, detailing with un-restrained confidence the past events of our lives, and dwelling with hope on our future prospects. Had my poor friend been spared to revisit his native land, I should look back to this period with unalloyed delight.

On the morning of the 29th, the weather, although still cold, was clear, and I went out in quest of *tripe de roche*, leaving Hepburn to cut willows for a fire, and Mr Hood in bed. I had no success, as yesterday's snow-drift was so frozen on the surface of the rocks that I could not collect any of the weed; but, on my return to the tent, I found that Michel, the Iroquois, had come with a note from Mr Franklin, which stated, that this man, and Jean Baptiste Belanger being unable to proceed, were about to return to us, and that a mile beyond our present encampment there was a clump of pine trees, to which he recommended us to remove the tent. Michel informed us that he quitted Mr Franklin's party yesterday morning, but, that having missed his way, he had passed the night on the snow a mile or two to the northward of us. Belanger, he said, being impatient, had left the fire about two hours earlier, and, as he had not arrived, he sup-posed he had gone astray. It will be seen in the sequel, that we had more than suffi-cient reason to doubt the truth of this story.

Michel now produced a hare and a partridge which he had killed in the morning. This unexpected supply of provision was received by us with a deep sense of gratitude to the Almighty for his goodness, and we looked upon Michel as the instrument he had chosen to preserve all our lives. He complained of cold, and Mr Hood offered to share his buffalo robe with him at night: I gave him one of two shirts which I wore, whilst Hepburn, in the warmth of his heart, exclaimed, 'How I shall love this man if I find that he does not tell lies like the others.' Our meals being finished, we arranged that the greatest part of the things should be carried to the pines the next day; and, after read-ing the evening service, retired to bed full of hope.

---

6 Richardson probably refers to what Franklin elsewhere identifies as Labrador tea, a northern rhododendron that, in Arctic areas, grows as a dwarf, low and close to the ground. Its leaves, when crushed and brewed, produce an aromatic herbal tea, rich in vitamin C.

Early in the morning Hepburn, Michel, and myself, carried the ammunition, and most of the other heavy articles to the pines. Michel was our guide, and it did not occur to us at the time that his conducting us perfectly straight was incompatible with his story of having gone astray on his way to us. He now informed us that he had, on his way to the tent, left on the hill above the pines a gun and forty-eight balls, which Perrault had given to him when with the rest of Mr Franklin's party, he took leave of him. It will be seen, on a reference to Mr Franklin's journal, that Perrault carried his gun and ammunition with him when they parted from Michel and Belanger. After we had made a fire, and drank a little of the country tea, Hepburn and I returned to the tent, where we arrived in the evening, much exhausted with our journey. Michel preferred sleeping where he was, and requested us to leave him the hatchet, which we did, after he had promised to come early in the morning to assist us in carrying the tent and bedding. Mr Hood remained in bed all day. Seeing nothing of Belanger to-day, we gave him up for lost.

On the 11th, after waiting until late in the morning for Michel, who did not come, Hepburn and I loaded ourselves with the bedding, and, accompanied by Mr Hood, set out for the pines. Mr Hood was much affected with dimness of sight, giddiness, and other symptoms of extreme debility, which caused us to move very slow, and to make frequent halts. On arriving at the pines, we were much alarmed to find that Michel was absent. We feared that he had lost his way in coming to us in the morning, although it was not easy to conjecture how that could have happened, as our footsteps of yesterday were very distinct. Hepburn went back for the tent, and returned with it after dusk, completely worn out with the fatigue of the day. Michel too arrived at the same time, and relieved our anxiety on his account. He reported that he had been in chase of some deer which passed near his sleeping place in the morning, and although he did not come up with them, yet that he found a wolf which had been killed by the stroke of a deer's horn, and had brought a part of it. We implicitly believed this story then, but afterwards became convinced from circumstances, the detail of which may be spared, that it must have been a portion of the body of Belanger or Perrault. A question of moment here presents itself; namely, whether he actually murdered these men, or either of them, or whether he found the bodies on the snow. Captain Franklin, who is the best able to judge of this matter, from knowing their situation when he parted from them, suggested the former idea, and that both Belanger and Perrault had been sacrificed. When Perrault turned back, Captain Franklin watched him until he reached a small group of willows, which was immediately adjoining to the fire, and concealed it from view, and at this time the smoke of fresh fuel was distinctly visible. Captain Franklin conjectures, that Michel having already destroyed Belanger, completed his crime by Perrault's death, in order to screen himself from detection. Although this opinion is founded only on circumstances, and is unsupported by direct evidence, it has been judged proper to mention it, especially as the subsequent conduct of the man shewed that he was capable of committing such a deed. The circumstances are very strong. It is not easy to assign any other adequate motive for his concealing from us that Perrault had turned back, and his request overnight that we should leave him the hatchet; and his cumbering himself with it when he went out in the morning, unlike a hunter who makes use only of his knife when he kills a deer, seem to indicate that he took it for the purpose of cutting up something that he knew to be frozen. These opinions, however, are the result of subsequent consideration. We passed this night in the open air.

On the following morning the tent was pitched, and Michel went out early, refused my offer to accompany him, and remained out the whole day. He would not sleep in the tent at night, but chose to lie at the fire-side.

On the 13th there was a heavy gale of wind, and we passed the day by the fire. Next day, about two, p.m., the gale abating, Michel set out as he said to hunt, but returned unexpectedly in a very short time. This conduct surprised us, and his contradictory and evasory answers to our questions excited some suspicions, but they did not turn towards the truth.

*October* 15th.—In the course of this day Michel expressed much regret that he had stayed behind Mr Franklin's party, and declared that he would set out for the house at once if he knew the way. We endeavoured to soothe him, and to raise his hopes of the Indians speedily coming to our relief, but without success. He refused to assist us in cutting wood, but about noon, after much solicitation, he set out to hunt. Hepburn gathered a kettle of *tripe de roche*, but froze his fingers. Both Hepburn and I fatigued ourselves much to-day in pursuing a flock of partridges from one part to another of the group of willows, in which the hut was situated, but we were too weak to be able to approach them with sufficient caution. In the evening Michel returned, having met with no success.

Next day he refused either to hunt or cut wood, spoke in a very surly manner, and threatened to leave us. Under these circumstances, Mr Hood and I deemed it better to promise if he would hunt diligently for four days, that then we would give Hepburn a letter for Mr Franklin, a compass, inform him what course to pursue, and let them proceed together to the fort. The non-arrival of the Indians to our relief, now led us to fear that some accident had happened to Mr Franklin, and we placed no confidence in the exertions of the Canadians that accompanied him, but we had the fullest confidence in Hepburn's returning the moment he could obtain assistance.

On the 17th I went to conduct Michel to where Vaillant's blanket was left, and after walking about three miles, pointed out the hills to him at a distance, and returned to the hut, having gathered a bagful of *tripe de roche* on the way. It was easier to gather this weed on a march than at the tent, for the exercise of walking produced a glow of heat, which enabled us to withstand for a time the cold to which we were exposed in scraping the frozen surface of the rocks. On the contrary, when we left the fire, to collect it in the neighbourhood of the hut, we became chilled at once, and were obliged to return very quickly.

Michel proposed to remain out all night, and to hunt next day on his way back. He returned in the afternoon of the 18th, having found the blanket, together with a bag containing two pistols, and some other things which had been left beside it. We had some *tripe de roche* in the evening, but Mr Hood, from the constant griping[7] it produced, was unable to eat more than one or two spoonfuls. He was now so weak as

---

7 Sharp pains in the bowels.

to be scarcely able to sit up at the fire-side, and complained that the least breeze of wind seemed to blow through his frame. He also suffered much from cold during the night. We lay close to each other, but the heat of the body was no longer sufficient to thaw the frozen rime formed by our breaths on the blankets that covered him.

At this period we avoided as much as possible conversing upon the hopelessness of our situation, and generally endeavoured to lead the conversation towards our future prospects in life. The fact is, that with the decay of our strength, our minds decayed, and we were no longer able to bear the contemplation of the horrors that surrounded us. Each of us, if I may be allowed to judge from my own case, excused himself from so doing by a desire of not shocking the feelings of the others, for we were sensible of one another's weakness of intellect though blind to our own. Yet we were calm and resigned to our fate, not a murmur escaped us, and we were punctual and fervent in our addresses to the Supreme Being.

On the 19th Michel refused to hunt, or even to assist in carrying a log of wood to the fire, which was too heavy for Hepburn's strength and mine. Mr Hood endeavoured to point out to him the necessity and duty of exertion, and the cruelty of his quitting us without leaving something for our support; but the discourse far from producing any beneficial effect, seemed only to excite his anger, and amongst other expressions, he made use of the following remarkable one: 'It is no use hunting, there are no animals, you had better kill and eat me.' At length, however, he went out, but returned very soon, with a report that he had seen three deer, which he was unable to follow from having wet his foot in a small stream of water thinly covered with ice, and being consequently obliged to come to the fire. The day was rather mild and Hepburn and I gathered a large kettleful of *tripe de roche*; Michel slept in the tent this night.

*Sunday, October* 20.—In the morning we again urged Michel to go a hunting that he might if possible leave us some provision, to-morrow being the day appointed for his quitting us; but he shewed great unwillingness to go out, and lingered about the fire, under the pretence of cleaning his gun. After we had read the morning service I went about noon to gather some *tripe de roche*, leaving Mr Hood sitting before the tent at the fire-side, arguing with Michel; Hepburn was employed cutting down a tree at a short distance from the tent, being desirous of accumulating a quantity of fire wood before he left us. A short time after I went out I heard the report of a gun, and about ten minutes afterwards Hepburn called to me in a voice of great alarm, to come directly. When I arrived, I found poor Hood lying lifeless at the fire-side, a ball having apparently entered his forehead. I was at first horror-struck with the idea, that in a fit of despondency he had hurried himself into the presence of his Almighty Judge, by an act of his own hand; but the conduct of Michel soon gave rise to other thoughts, and excited suspicions which were confirmed, when upon examining the body, I discovered that the shot had entered the back part of the head, and passed out at the forehead, and that the muzzle of the gun had been applied so close as to set fire to the night-cap behind. The gun, which was of the longest kind supplied to the Indians, could not have been placed in a position to inflict such a wound, except by a second person. Upon inquiring of Michel how it happened, he replied, that Mr Hood had sent him into the tent for the short gun, and that during his absence the long gun had gone off, he did not know whether by accident or not. He held the short gun in his hand at the time he was speaking to me. Hepburn afterwards informed me that previous to the report of the gun Mr Hood and Michel were speaking to each other in an elevated angry tone; that Mr Hood being seated at the fire-side, was hid from him by intervening willows, but that on hearing the report he looked up, and saw Michel rising up from before the tent-door, or just behind where Mr Hood was seated, and then going into the tent. Thinking that the gun had been discharged for the purpose of cleaning it, he did not go to the fire at first; and when Michel called to him that Mr Hood was dead, a considerable time had elapsed. Although I dare not openly to evince any suspicion that I thought Michel guilty of the deed, yet he repeatedly protested that he was incapable of committing such an act, kept constantly on his guard, and carefully avoided leaving Hepburn and me together. He was evidently afraid of permitting us to converse in private, and whenever Hepburn spoke, he inquired if he accused him of the murder. It is to be remarked, that he understood English very imperfectly, yet sufficiently to render it unsafe for us to speak on the subject in his presence. We removed the body into a clump of willows behind the tent, and, returning to the fire, read the funeral service in addition to the evening prayers. The loss of a young officer, of such distinguished and varied talents and application, may be felt and duly appreciated by the eminent characters under whose command he had served; but the calmness with which he contemplated the probable termination of a life of uncommon promise; and the patience and fortitude with which he sustained, I may venture to say, unparalleled bodily sufferings, can only be known to the companions of his distresses. Owing to the effect that the *tripe de roche* invariably had, when he ventured to taste it, he undoubtedly suffered more than any of the survivors of the party. *Bickersteth's Scripture Help* was lying open beside the body, as if it had fallen from his hand, and it is probable that he was reading it at the instant of his death. We passed the night in the tent together without rest, every one being on his guard. Next day, having determined on going to the Fort, we began to patch and prepare our clothes for the journey. We singed the hair off a part of the buffalo robe that belonged to Mr Hood, and boiled and ate it. Michel tried to persuade me to go to the woods on the Copper-Mine River, and hunt for deer instead of going to the Fort. In the afternoon a flock of partridges coming near the tent, he killed several which he shared with us.

Thick snowy weather and a head wind prevented us from starting the following day, but on the morning of the 23d we set out, carrying with us the remainder of the singed robe. Hepburn and Michel had each a gun, and I carried a small pistol, which Hepburn had loaded for me. In the course of the march Michel alarmed us much by his gestures and conduct, was constantly muttering to himself, expressed an unwillingness to go to the Fort, and tried to persuade me to go to the southward to the woods, where he said he could maintain himself all the winter by killing deer. In consequence of this behaviour, and the expression of his countenance, I requested him to leave us and to go to the southward by himself. This proposal increased his ill-nature, he threw out some obscure hints of freeing himself from all restraint on the morrow; and I overheard him muttering threats against Hepburn, whom he openly accused of having told stories against him. He also, for the first time, assumed such a tone of superiority in addressing me, as evinced that he considered us to be completely in his power, and he gave vent to several expressions of hatred towards the white people, or as he termed us in the idiom of the voyagers, the French, some of whom, he said, had killed and eaten his uncle and two of his relations. In short, taking every circumstance of his conduct into consideration, I came to the conclusion, that he would attempt to destroy us on the first opportunity that offered, and that he had hitherto abstained from doing so from his ignorance of the way to the Fort, but that he would never suffer us to go thither in company with him. In the course of the day he had several times remarked that we were pursuing the same course that Mr Franklin was doing when he left him, and that by keeping towards the setting sun he could find his way himself. Hepburn and I were not in a condition to resist even an open attack, nor could we by any device escape from him. Our united strength was far inferior to his, and, beside his gun, he was armed with two pistols, an Indian bayonet, and a knife. In the afternoon, coming to a rock on which there was some *tripe de roche*, he halted, and said he would gather it whilst we went on, and that he would soon overtake us. Hepburn and I were now left together for the first time since Mr Hood's death, and he acquainted me with several material circumstances, which he had observed of Michel's behaviour, and which confirmed me in the opinion that there was no safety for us except in his death, and he offered to be the instrument of it. I determined, however, as I was thoroughly convinced of the necessity of such a dreadful act, to take the whole responsibility upon myself; and immediately upon Michel's coming up, I put an end to his life by shooting him through the head with a pistol. Had my own life alone been threatened, I would not have purchased it by such a measure; but I considered myself as intrusted also with the protection of Hepburn's, a man, who, by his humane attentions and devotedness, had so endeared himself to me, that I felt more anxiety for his safety than for my own. Michel had gathered no *tripe de roche*, and it was evident to us that he had halted for the purpose of putting his gun in order, with the intention of attacking us, perhaps, whilst we were in the act of encamping.

I have dwelt in the preceding part of the narrative upon many circumstances of Michel's conduct, not for the purpose of aggravating his crime, but to put the reader in possession of the reasons that influenced me in depriving a fellow-creature of life. Up to the period of his return to the tent, his conduct had been good and respectful to the officers, and in a conversation between Captain Franklin, Mr Hood, and myself, at Obstruction Rapid, it had been proposed to give him a reward upon our arrival at a post. His principles, however, unsupported by a belief in the divine truths of Christianity, were unable to withstand the pressure of severe distress. His countrymen, the Iroquois, are generally Christians, but he was totally uninstructed and ignorant of the duties inculcated by Christianity; and from his long residence in the Indian country, seems to have imbibed, or retained, the rules of conduct which the southern Indians prescribe to themselves. . . .

On the 26th, the weather being clear and extremely cold, we resumed our march, which was very painful from the depth of the snow, particularly on the margins of the small lakes that lay in our route. We frequently sunk under the load of our blankets, and were obliged to assist each other in getting up. After walking about three miles and a half, however, we were cheered by the sight of a large herd of rein-deer, and Hepburn went in pursuit of them; but his hand being unsteady through weakness he missed. He was so exhausted by this fruitless attempt that we were obliged to encamp upon the spot, although it was a very unfavourable one.

Next day we had fine and clear, but cold, weather. We set out early, and, in crossing a hill, found a considerable quantity of *tripe de roche*. About noon we fell upon Little Marten Lake, having walked about two miles. The sight of a place that we knew inspired us with fresh vigour, and there being comparatively little snow on the ice, we advanced at a pace to which we had lately been unaccustomed. In the afternoon we crossed a recent track of a wolverine, which, from a parallel mark in the snow, appeared to have been dragging something. Hepburn traced it, and upon the borders of the lake found the spine of a deer, that it had dropped. It was clean picked, and, at least, one season old; but we extracted the spinal marrow from it, which, even in its frozen state, was so acrid as to excoriate the lips. We encamped within sight of the Dog-rib Rock, and from the coldness of the night and the want of fuel, rested very ill.

On the 28th we rose at day-break, but from the want of the small fire, that we usually made in the mornings to warm our fingers, a very long time was spent in making up our bundles. This task fell to Hepburn's share, as I suffered so much from the cold as to be unable to take my hands out of my mittens. We kept a straight course for the Dog-rib Rock, but, owing to the depth of the snow in the valleys we had to cross, did not reach it until late in the afternoon. We would have encamped, but did not like to pass a second night without fire; and though scarcely able to drag our limbs after us, we pushed on to a clump of pines, about a mile to the southward of the rock, and arrived at them in the dusk of the evening. During the last few hundred yards of our march, our track lay over some large stones, amongst which I fell down upwards of twenty times, and became at length so exhausted that I was unable to stand. If Hepburn had not exerted himself far beyond his strength, and speedily made the encampment and kindled a fire, I must have perished on the spot. This night we had plenty of dry wood.

On the 29th we had clear and fine weather. We set out at sunrise, and hurried on in our anxiety to reach the house, but our progress was much impeded by the great depth of the snow in the valleys. Although every spot of ground over which we travelled to-day, had been repeatedly trodden by us, yet we got bewildered in a small lake. We took it for Marten Lake, which was three times its size, and fancied that we saw the rapid and the grounds about the fort, although they were still far distant. Our disappointment when this illusion was dispelled, by our reaching the end of the lake, so operated on our feeble minds as to exhaust our strength, and we decided upon encamping; but upon ascending a small eminence to look for a clump of wood, we caught a glimpse of the Big-Stone, a well known rock upon the summit of a hill opposite to the Fort, and determined upon proceeding. In the evening we saw several large herds of rein-deer, but Hepburn, who used to be considered a good marksman, was now unable to hold the gun straight, and although he got near them all his efforts proved fruitless. In passing through a small clump of pines we saw a flock of partridges, and he succeeded in killing one after firing several shots. We came in sight of the fort at dusk, and it is impossible to describe our sensations, when on attaining the eminence that overlooks it, we beheld the smoke issuing from one of the chimneys. From not having met with any footsteps in the snow, as we drew nigh our once cheerful residence, we had been agitated by many melancholy forebodings. Upon entering the now desolate building, we had the satisfaction of embracing Captain Franklin, but no words can convey an idea of the filth and wretchedness that met our eyes on looking around. Our own misery had stolen upon us by degrees, and we were accustomed to the contemplation of each other's emaciated figures, but the ghastly countenances, dilated eye-balls, and sepulchral voices of Mr Franklin and those with him were more than we could at first bear.

*Conclusion of Dr Richardson's Narrative.*

The morning of the 31st was very cold, the wind being strong from the north. Hepburn went again in quest of deer, and the Doctor endeavoured to kill some partridges: both were unsuccessful. A large herd of deer passed close to the house, the Doctor fired once at them, but was unable to pursue them. Adam was easier this day, and left his bed. Peltier and Samandrè were much weaker, and could not assist in the labours of the day. Both complained of soreness in the throat, and Samandrè suffered much from cramps in his fingers. The Doctor and Hepburn began this day to cut the wood, and also brought it to the house. Being too weak to aid in these laborious tasks, I was employed in searching for bones, and cooking, and attending to our more weakly companions.

In the evening Peltier, complaining much of cold, requested of me a portion of a blanket to repair his shirt and drawers. The mending of these articles occupied him and Samandrè until past one a.m., and their spirits were so much revived by the employment, that they conversed even cheerfully the whole time. Adam sat up with them. The Doctor, Hepburn, and myself, went to bed. We were afterwards agreeably surprised to see Peltier and Samandrè carry three or four logs of wood across the room to replenish the fire, which induced us to hope they still possessed more strength than we had supposed.

*November* 1.—This day was fine and mild. Hepburn went hunting, but was as usual unsuccessful. As his strength was rapidly declining, we advised him to desist from the pursuit of deer; and only to go out for a short time, and endeavour to kill a few partridges for Peltier and Samandrè. The Doctor obtained a little *tripe de roche*, but Peltier could not eat any of it, and Samandrè only a few spoonfuls, owing to the soreness of their throats. In the afternoon Peltier was so much exhausted, that he sat up with difficulty, and looked piteously; at length he slided from his stool upon his bed, as we supposed to sleep, and in this composed state he remained upwards of two hours, without our apprehending any danger. We were then alarmed by hearing a rattling in his throat, and on the Doctor's examining him, he was found to be speechless. He died in the course of the night. Samandrè sat up the greater part of the day, and even assisted in pounding some bones; but on witnessing the melancholy state of Peltier, he became very low, and began to complain of cold and stiffness of the joints. Being unable to keep up a sufficient fire to warm him, we laid him down and covered him with several blankets. He did not, however, appear to get better, and I deeply lament to add he also died before daylight. We removed the bodies of the deceased into the opposite part of the house, but our united strength was inadequate to the task of inter-ring them, or even carrying them down to the river.

It may be worthy of remark that poor Peltier, from the time of Benoit's departure, had fixed on the first of November as the time when he should cease to expect any relief from the Indians, and had repeatedly said that if they did not arrive by that day, he should not survive.

Peltier had endeared himself to each of us by his cheerfulness, his unceasing activ-ity, and affectionate care and attentions, ever since our arrival at this place. He had nursed Adam with the tenderest solicitude the whole time. Poor Samandrè was willing to have taken his share in the labours of the party, had he not been wholly incapaci-tated by his weakness and low spirits. The severe shock occasioned by the sudden dis-solution of our two companions rendered us very melancholy. Adam became low and despondent, a change which we lamented the more, as we had perceived he had been gaining strength and spirits for the two preceding days. I was particularly distressed by the thought that the labour of collecting wood must now devolve upon Dr Richardson and Hepburn, and that my debility would disable me from affording them any ma-terial assistance; indeed both of them most kindly urged me not to make the attempt. They were occupied the whole of the next day in tearing down the logs of which the store-house was built, but the mud plastered between them was so hard frozen that the labour of separation exceeded their strength, and they were completely exhausted by bringing in wood sufficient for less than twelve hours' consumption.

I found it necessary in their absence, to remain constantly near Adam, and to con-verse with him, in order to prevent his reflecting on our condition, and to keep up his spirits as far as possible. I also lay by his side at night.

On the 3d the weather was very cold, though the atmosphere was cloudy. This morning Hepburn was affected with swelling in his limbs, his strength as well as that of the Doctor, was rapidly declining; they continued, however, to be full of hope. Their utmost exertions could only supply wood, to renew the fire thrice, and on making it up the last time we went to bed. Adam was in rather better spirits, but he could not bear to be left alone. Our stock of bones was exhausted by a small quantity of soup we made this evening. The toil of separating the hair from the skins, which in fact were our chief support, had now become so wearisome as to prevent us from eating as much as we should otherwise have done.

*November* 4.—Calm and comparatively mild weather. The Doctor and Hepburn, exclusive of their usual occupation, gathered some *tripe de roche*. I went a few yards from the house in search of bones, and returned quite fatigued, having found but three. The Doctor again made incisions in Adam's leg, which discharged a considerable quantity of water, and gave him great relief. We read prayers and a portion of the New

Testament in the morning and evening, as had been our practice since Dr Richardson's arrival; and I may remark that the performance of these duties always afforded us the greatest consolation, serving to reanimate our hope in the mercy of the Omnipotent, who alone could save and deliver us.

On the 5th the breezes were light, with dark cloudy weather, and some snow. The Doctor and Hepburn were getting much weaker, and the limbs of the latter were now greatly swelled. They came into the house frequently in the course of the day to rest themselves, and when once seated, were unable to rise without the help of one another, or of a stick. Adam was for the most part in the same low state as yesterday, but sometimes he surprised us by getting up and walking with an appearance of increased strength. His looks were now wild and ghastly, and his conversation was often incoherent.

The next day was fine, but very cold. The swellings in Adam's limbs having subsided, he was free from pain, and arose this morning in much better spirits, and spoke of cleaning his gun ready for shooting partridges, or any animals that might appear near the house, but his tone entirely changed before the day was half over; he became again dejected, and could scarcely be prevailed upon to eat. The Doctor and Hepburn were almost exhausted. The cutting of one log of wood occupied the latter half an hour; and the other took as much time to drag it into the house, though the distance did not exceed thirty yards. I endeavoured to help the Doctor, but my assistance was very trifling. Yet it was evident that, in a day or two, if their strength should continue to decline at the same rate, I should be the strongest of the party.

I may here remark that owing to our loss of flesh, the hardness of the floor, from which we were only protected by a blanket, produced soreness over the body, and especially those parts on which the weight rested in lying, yet to turn ourselves for relief was a matter of toil and difficulty. However, during this period, and indeed all along after the acute pains of hunger, which lasted but three or four days, had subsided, we generally enjoyed the comfort of a few hours' sleep. The dreams which for the most part, but not always accompanied it, were usually (though not invariably,) of a pleasant character, being very often about the enjoyments of feasting. In the day-time we fell into the practice of conversing on common and light subjects, although we sometimes discussed with seriousness and earnestness topics connected with religion. We generally avoided speaking directly of our present sufferings, or even of the prospect of relief. I observed, that in proportion as our strength decayed, our minds exhibited symptoms of weakness, evinced by a kind of unreasonable pettishness with each other. Each of us thought the other weaker in intellect than himself, and more in need of advice and assistance. So trifling a circumstance as a change of place, recommended by one as being warmer and more comfortable, and refused by the other from a dread of motion, frequently called forth fretful expressions which were no sooner uttered than atoned for, to be repeated perhaps in the course of a few minutes. The same thing often occurred when we endeavoured to assist each other in carrying wood to the fire; none of us were willing to receive assistance, although the task was disproportioned to our strength. On one of these occasions Hepburn was so convinced of this waywardness that he exclaimed, 'Dear me, if we are spared to return to England, I wonder if we shall recover our understandings.'

*November 7.*—Adam had passed a restless night, being disquieted by gloomy apprehensions of approaching death, which we tried in vain to dispel. He was so low in the morning as to be scarcely able to speak. I remained in bed by his side to cheer him as much as possible. The Doctor and Hepburn went to cut wood. They had hardly begun their labour, when they were amazed at hearing the report of a musket. They could scarcely believe that there was really any one near, until they heard a shout, and immediately espied three Indians close to the house. Adam and I heard the latter noise, and I was fearful that a part of the house had fallen upon one of my companions, a disaster which had in fact been thought not unlikely. My alarm was only momentary; Dr Richardson came in to communicate the joyful intelligence that relief had arrived. He and myself immediately addressed thanksgiving to the throne of mercy for this deliverance, but poor Adam was in so low a state that he could scarcely comprehend the information. When the Indians entered, he attempted to rise but sank down again. But for this seasonable interposition of Providence, his existence must have terminated in a few hours, and that of the rest probably in not many days.

The Indians had left Akaitcho's encampment on the 5th November, having been sent by Mr Back with all possible expedition, after he had arrived at their tents. They brought but a small supply of provision that they might travel quickly. It consisted of dried deer's meat, some fat, and a few tongues. Dr Richardson, Hepburn, and I, eagerly devoured the food, which they imprudently presented to us, in too great abundance, and in consequence we suffered dreadfully from indigestion, and had no rest the whole night. Adam being unable to feed himself, was more judiciously treated by them, and suffered less; his spirits revived hourly. The circumstance of our eating more food than was proper in our present condition, was another striking proof of the debility of our minds. We were perfectly aware of the danger, and Dr Richardson repeatedly cautioned us to be moderate; but he was himself unable to practise the caution he so judiciously recommended.

*[After wintering over at Fort Resolution, the party set off at the end of May 1822 and reached York Factory that July. Franklin's narrative ends: 'And thus terminated our long, fatiguing, and disastrous travels in North America, having journeyed by water and by land (including our navigation of the Polar Sea) five thousand five hundred and fifty miles.']*

1823

# Anna Brownell Jameson

## 1794–1860

## Travel Writing

Travel writing, a very old form, became increasingly popular and important after the Renaissance voyages of discovery. In the nineteenth century, readers increasingly looked to it for accounts of individuals' subjective experiences of distant milieus. British travellers went out from the centre of empire to experience Africa, Asia, the Americas, then came home to publish their accounts, not from the perspective of explorers who faced the unknown nor that of emigrants trying to establish new homes but as representatives of their culture who could serve as windows through which their compatriots could view the world abroad. In contrast to explorers' reports, which were initially prepared for the organizations that had sponsored their efforts, these narratives, aimed at a general readership, were not made up of scientific observation of non-narrative detail: in place of novel landscapes and geographies, they focused on the novelties of societies and cultures, often by contrasting distant ways of living to the customs that were familiar to the travellers and their readers. Unlike the tales sent home from emigrants such as Susanna Moodie, they did not chronicle the hardships of making a new home in a new place but were concerned with the sojourns of that new kind of visitor: the tourist. Although risk-taking and encounters with the sublime features of the landscape were sometimes found in these travel books, their narratives were more quietly adventuresome than were the tales of exploration or pioneering.

Sometimes, the excursions they described were made within Western Europe, where their *raison d'être* was exposing the traveller, and thus the reader, to the broadening experience of more 'sophisticated' cultures. In the nineteenth century, stories of visits to non-European environments grew increasingly popular: for their readers, the interest often lay in the tension between their confirmation of the traveller's and the reader's expectations and the discovery that some things are not as anticipated. Among these nineteenth-century travel narratives, the best-known book about Canada is Anna Jameson's *Winter Studies and Summer Rambles in Canada* (London, 1838). It was successful in its own day and has remained in print, if often in abridged form, ever since.

## Anna Brownell Jameson

Born in Dublin, Anna Brownell Murphy was a traveller from the time she was four. By the age of nine, she had moved with her parents—but without her older sisters—three times across England. Her family was finally reunited in London, where her father Denis Brownell Murphy became a court painter of miniatures. Anna Murphy was a precocious child—she read all of Shakespeare's plays between the ages of seven and ten—and she became a governess for the Marquis of Winchester when she was sixteen. While still in her teens, she met Robert Jameson, a lawyer and friend of Montagu, Coleridge, and Lamb. In 1821, after a long acquaintance, she consented to an engagement. However, though they shared interests in art and literature, both were strong-willed and seem to have been temperamentally unsuited to one another. Calling off their engagement, she travelled as governess with the Rowles family on their 1821 tour of Italy. Returning a year later, she took another position as governess, for the family of Mr Littleton (later Lord Hatherton), and lived with them in Staffordshire for three years. In 1825, she finally did consent to marry Robert Jameson; shortly after, she published, with Robert's encouragement, her first major work, *A Lady's Diary* (1826), subsequently retitled *The Diary of an Ennuyée* (a woman suffering from boredom). This well-received anonymous and sentimental account of travels in Italy received some notoriety when public knowledge of its little-disguised authorship revealed it to be highly fictionalized and less autobiographical than it seemed.

Following its success, she became part of a group of writers whose work was regularly published in magazines such as *Blackwoods*. In these recently established periodicals that catered to women eager to acquire knowledge and culture, Jameson's writing was valued because it dealt with the rights of women, emphasized the need for female education, and generally reflected attitudes aligned with the proto-feminism that developed in England in the years that followed the publication of Mary Wollstonecraft's *A Vindication of the Rights of Woman* (1792).

Although the Jamesons lived together in London for a few years, in 1829, Robert left for a post as a judge in Dominica while Anna went to the Continent with her father and his patron, Sir Gerard Noel. She did not rejoin her husband when, after a brief return to London, he became, in 1833, attorney-general of Upper Canada, but continued to travel, particularly in Germany where she met Robert Noel and his cousin Lady Byron, both of whom became close friends. Through Noel, Jameson was introduced to the Goethe family. Summoned back to England to attend to her father's illness, she returned in 1834 to live in Germany for another two years. During this period, she wrote five more books, four of which were about women: *Memoirs of the Lovers of the Poets* (1829), *Memoirs of the Celebrated Female Sovereigns* (1831), *Memoirs of the Beauties of the Court of Charles II*

(1831), and *Characteristics of Woman* (1832). The last of these, a series of psychological studies of the female characters in Shakespeare's dramas (subsequently retitled *Shakespeare's Heroines*), is the book for which she became best known. She also completed a second travel diary, *Visits and Sketches at Home and Abroad* (1834).

After a summer in England, Jameson agreed to join her husband in Canada in an attempt to resume their marriage. Arriving in the winter of 1836, she remained in Canada through the summer of 1837 and, after reaching an agreement with Robert for a formal separation and the settlement of an allowance, she left for New York for six months, before returning to England and then to Germany and Paris. She began to visit galleries and to write about the paintings and artists she saw. After her father's death in 1842, she stayed in England to arrange quarters for her mother and unmarried sisters, whom she had already been supporting for a number of years. During this period, she visited Scotland before returning to Germany and Italy. On her way to Italy, Jameson met Robert and Elizabeth Browning in Paris and aided them in their flight to Florence. (They remained close friends until her death.) When Robert Jameson died in 1854, Anna discovered that, counter to their agreement, he had willed his estate to others and left her with no source of income.

She began to give lectures that focused on women's issues of the day; they resulted in two books, *Sisters of Charity* (1855) and *The Communion of Labour* (1856). As her health failed, her friends put together an annuity to supplement her income. She died in 1860 after a brief illness.

## Winter Studies and Summer Rambles in Canada

While her stay in Canada was brief, it provided Jameson with the opportunity to write *Winter Studies and Summer Rambles in Canada*. Her unhappiness—the attempted reconciliation with her husband had been unsuccessful and she deeply regretted having left behind the culture and civilization of Europe—may have influenced her perceptions; her first entry in the book, for 20 December 1836, records her disillusionment on arriving at her new home:

*What Toronto may be in summer, I cannot tell; they say it is a pretty place. At present its appearance to me, a stranger, is most strangely mean and melancholy. A little ill-built town on low land, at the bottom of a frozen bay, with one very ugly church, without tower or steeple; some government offices, built of staring red brick, in the most tasteless, vulgar style imaginable; three feet of snow all around; and the grey, sullen, wintry lake, and the dark gloom of the pine forest bounding the prospects; such seems Toronto to me now. I did not expect much; but for this I was not prepared.*

To provide a written record of her Canadian experience, she first set about acquainting herself with Toronto society. In the 'Winter Studies' portion of her book, Jameson records her experiences, intermixed with reflections on literature and life, and quotations from the works of German literature she was then reading. 'I know no better way of coming at the truth,' she wrote, 'than by observing and recording faithfully the impressions made by objects and characters on my own mind—or, rather, the impress they receive from my own mind.' She took particular interest in the difficulties felt by women in the province, observing, 'I have not often in my life met with contented and cheerful-minded women, but I never met with so many repining and discontented women as in Canada'—though she also believed that 'really accomplished women, accustomed to what is called the best society, have more resources here, and manage better. . . .'

Deciding that she wanted to see more of Upper Canada, in June 1837, Jameson embarked—over her husband's objections and in an age when a woman travelling without friends or escort was extremely unusual, especially in such primitive conditions—on the journey that was to provide materials for the 'summer rambles' section of her account:

To undertake such a journey alone is rash perhaps—yet alone it must be achieved, I find, or not at all; I shall have neither companion nor manservant, nor femme de chambre, nor even a 'little foot-page', to give notice of my fate, should I be swamped in a bog, or eaten up by a bear, or scalped, or disposed of in some strange way; but shall I leave this fine country without seeing anything of its great characteristic features?

Her trip included visits to Niagara Falls (with which she expressed disappointment), Hamilton, London, and Port Talbot; she eventually made her way through Detroit and as far

north as Sault Ste Marie, which she called her 'Ultima Thule'. Her curiosity about North American Native peoples led her to call on Henry Schoolcraft—whose extensive collection of Aboriginal lore later furnished material for Longfellow's *Hiawatha*—and to attend a Native conclave at Manitoulin Island. In the more distant parts of her trip, Jameson travelled with only a few other passengers in small boats rowed by voyageurs, and she became the first European woman to pass through the rapids at the Sault. When she returned to Toronto in August, she recorded that 'the people here are in great enthusiasm about me and stare at me as if I had done some most wonderful thing; the most astonished of all is Mr Jameson.'

The publication of *Winter Studies and Summer Rambles* in 1838, the year Anna Jameson returned to England, proved timely: her compatriots were interested in observations of Canada made on the eve of the 1837 Rebellions. Readers were rewarded with shrewd insights about an unfamiliar land, parts of which its own inhabitants had rarely seen. As well, the morals she draws in passing, in which she makes little parables from her observations (as when she observes that the two ways of killing trees are like 'the two ways a woman's heart can be killed in this world of ours'), added to the work's charm for many readers. She was aware that her regrets about leaving behind an established career in England may have given a negative cast to her perceptions of Upper Canada, but the scope and acuity of her remarks, especially given the brevity of her visit, remain admirable. Particularly penetrating are her comments about the obstacles to forming a new society in Canada, which anticipate those of Susanna Moodie and later writers.

Jameson made drawings to accompany *Winter Studies and Summer Rambles in Canada*, but they were omitted by her publisher; eventually, they were published on their own as *Early Canadian Sketches* (1958).

# From *Winter Studies and Summer Rambles in Canada*

January 16.

Some philosopher has said or written, that our good and bad qualities, our virtues and our vices, depend more on the influence of climate, than the pride of civilised humanity would be willing to allow; and this is a truth or truism, which for my own part I cannot gainsay—yet which I do not much like to believe. Whatever may be the climate in which the human being is born or reared, can he not always by moral strength raise himself above its degrading, or benumbing, or exciting influence? and yet more, rather than less, easily, when, at a mature age and with habits formed, he is subjected accidentally to such influences? Is there most wisdom, in such a case, in passively assimilating ourselves, our habits, and our feelings, to external circumstances, or resisting and combating them, rather to defend the integrity of our own individual being, than with the hope of changing or controlling the physical or social influence around us?

How I might have settled this question with myself, long ago, when in possession of the health and energy and trusting spirit of my young years, I know—but now it is too late. I could almost wish myself a dormouse, or a she-bear, to sleep away the rest of this cold, cold winter, and wake only with the first green leaves, the first warm breath of the summer wind. I shiver through the day and through the night; and, like poor Harry Gill, 'my teeth they chatter, chatter still,'[1] and then at intervals I am burned up with a dry hot fever: this is what my maid, a good little Oxfordshire girl, calls the *hager* (the ague,) more properly the lake fever, or cold fever. From the particular situation of Toronto, the disorder is very prevalent here in the spring: being a stranger, and not yet *acclimatée*, it has attacked me thus unseasonably. Bark is the general and unfailing remedy.

The cold is at this time so intense, that the ink freezes while I write, and my fingers stiffen round the pen; a glass of water by my bed-side, within a few feet of the hearth, (heaped with logs of oak and maple kept burning all night long,) is a solid mass of ice in the morning. God help the poor emigrants who are yet unprepared against the rigour of the season!—yet this is nothing to the climate of the lower province, where, as we hear, the thermometer has been thirty degrees below zero. I lose all heart to write home, or to register a reflection or a feeling;—thought stagnates in my head as the ink in my pen—and this will never do!—I *must* rouse myself to occupation; and if I cannot find it without, I must create it from within. There are yet four months of winter and leisure to be disposed of. How?—I know not; but they *must* be employed, not wholly lost.

---

[1] Wordsworth's poem 'Goody Blake and Harry Gill: A True Story' (1798) recounts the legend of a man who beats a poor woman for gathering firewood from his hedge, and is thereafter cursed with feeling cold for the rest of his life. The poem opens: 'Oh! what's the matter? What's the matter? / What is't that ails young Harry Gill? / That evermore his teeth they chatter, / Chatter, chatter, chatter still.'

\* \* \*

Toronto, February 7.

Mr B. gave me a seat in his sleigh, and after a rapid and very pleasant journey, during which I gained a good deal of information, we reached Toronto yesterday morning.

The road was the same as before, with one deviation however—it was found expedient to cross Burlington Bay on the ice, about seven miles over, the lake beneath being twenty, and five-and-twenty fathoms in depth. It was ten o'clock at night, and the only light was that reflected from the snow. The beaten track, from which it is not safe to deviate, was very narrow, and a man, in the worst, if not the last stage of intoxication, noisy and brutally reckless, was driving before us in a sleigh. All this, with the novelty of the situation, the tremendous cracking of the ice at every instant, gave me a sense of apprehension just sufficient to be exciting, rather than very unpleasant, though I will confess to a feeling of relief when we were once more on the solid earth.

B. is said to be a hard, active, clever, practical man. I liked him, and thought him intelligent and good-natured: we had much talk. Leaving his servant to drive, he would jump down, stand poised upon one of runners, and, thus gliding smoothly along, we conversed.

It is a remarkable fact, with which you are probably acquainted, that when one growth of timber is cleared from the land, another of quite a different species springs up spontaneously in its place. Thus, the oak or the beech succeeds to the pine, and the pine to the oak or maple. This is not accounted for, at least I have found no one yet who can give me a reason for it. We passed by a forest lately consumed by fire, and I asked why, in clearing the woods, they did not leave groups of the finest trees, or even single trees, here and there, to embellish the country? But it seems that this is impossible—for the trees thus left standing, when deprived of the shelter and society to which they have been accustomed, uniformly perish—which, for mine own poor part, I thought very natural.

A Canadian settler *hates* a tree, regards it as his natural enemy, as something to be destroyed, eradicated, annihilated by all and any means. The idea of useful or ornamental is seldom associated here even with the most magnificent timber trees, such as among the Druids had been consecrated, and among the Greeks would have sheltered oracles and votive temples. The beautiful faith which assigned to every tree of the forest its guardian nymph, to every leafy grove its tutelary divinity, would find no votaries here. Alas! for the Dryads and Hamadryads of Canada![2]

There are two principal methods of killing trees in this country, besides the quick, unfailing destruction of the axe; the first by setting fire to them, which sometimes leaves the root uninjured to rot gradually and unseen, or be grubbed up at leisure, or, more generally, there remains a visible fragment of a charred and blackened stump, deformed and painful to look upon: the other method is slower, but even more effectual; a deep gash is cut through the bark into the stem, quite round the bole of the tree.

2  Wood nymphs.

This prevents the circulation of the vital juices, and by degrees the trees droops and dies. This is technically called *ringing* timber. Is not this like the two ways in which a woman's heart may be killed in this world of ours—by passion and by sorrow? But better far the swift fiery death than this 'ringing', as they call it!

\* \* \*

February 17.

'There is no *society* in Toronto,' is what I hear repeated all around me—even by those who compose the only society we have. 'But', you will say, 'what could be expected in a remote town, which forty years ago was an uninhabited swamp, and twenty years ago only began to exist?' I really do not know what I expected, but I will tell you what I did *not* expect. I did not expect to find here in this capital of a new country, with the boundless forest within half a mile of us on almost every side,—concentrated as it were the worst evils of our old and most artificial social system at home, with none of its *agrémens*, and none of its advantages. Toronto is like a fourth or fifth rate provincial town, with the pretensions of a capital city. We have here a petty colonial oligarchy, a self-constituted aristocracy, based upon nothing real, nor even upon anything imaginary; and we have all the mutual jealousy and fear, and petty gossip, and mutual meddling and mean rivalship, which are common in a small society of which the members are well known to each other, a society composed, like all societies, of many heterogeneous particles; but as these circulate within very confined limits, there is no getting out of the way of what one most dislikes: we must necessarily hear, see, and passively endure much that annoys and disgusts any one accustomed to the independence of a large and liberal society, or the ease of continental life. It is curious enough to see how quickly a new fashion, or a new folly, is imported from the old country, and with what difficulty and delay a new idea finds its way into the heads of the people, or a new book into their hands. Yet, in the midst of all this, I cannot but see that good spirits and corrective principles are at work; that progress is making: though the march of intellect be not here in double quick time, as in Europe, it does not absolutely stand stock-still.

There reigns here a hateful factious spirit in political matters, but for the present no public or patriotic feeling, no recognition of general or generous principles of policy: as yet I have met with none of these. Canada is a colony, not a *country*; it is not yet identified with the dearest affections and associations, remembrances, and hopes of its inhabitants: it is to them an adopted, not a real mother. Their love, their pride, are not for poor Canada, but for high and happy England; but a few more generations must change all this.

We have here Tories, Whigs, and Radicals, so called; but these words do not signify exactly what we mean by the same designations at home.

You must recollect that the first settlers in Upper Canada were those who were obliged to fly from the United States during the revolutionary war, in consequence of their attachment to the British government, and the soldiers and non-commissioned officers who had fought during the war. These were recompensed for their losses, sufferings, and services, by grants of land in Upper Canada. Thus the very first elements out of which our social system was framed, were repugnance and contempt for the new institutions of the United States, and a dislike to the people of that country,—a very natural result of foregone causes; and thus it has happened that the slightest tinge of democratic, or even liberal principles in politics, was for a long time a sufficient impeachment of the loyalty, a stain upon the personal character, of those who held them. The Tories have therefore been hitherto the influential party; in their hands we find the government patronage, the principal offices, the sales and grants of land, for a long series of years.

Another party, professing the same boundless loyalty to the mother country, and the same dislike for the principles and institutions of their Yankee neighbours, may be called the Whigs of Upper Canada; these look with jealousy and scorn on the power and prejudices of the Tory families, and insist on the necessity of many reforms in the colonial government. Many of these are young men of talent, and professional men, who find themselves shut out from what they regard as their fair proportion of social consideration and influence, such as, in a small society like this, their superior education and character ought to command for them.

Another set are the Radicals, whom I generally hear mentioned as 'those scoundrels', or 'those rascals', or with some epithet expressive of the utmost contempt and disgust. They are those who wish to see this country erected into a republic, like the United States. A few among them are men of talent and education, but at present they are neither influential nor formidable.

There is among all parties a general tone of complaint and discontent—a mutual distrust—a languor and supineness—the causes of which I cannot as yet understand. Even those who are enthusiastically British in heart and feeling, who sincerely believe that it is the true interest of the colony to remain under the control of the mother country, are as discontented as the rest: they bitterly denounce the ignorance of the colonial officials at home, with regard to the true interests of the country: they ascribe the want of capital for improvement on a large scale to no mistrust in the resources of the country, but to a want of confidence in the measures of the government, and the security of property.

In order to understand something of the feelings which prevail here, you must bear in mind the distinction between the two provinces of Upper and Lower Canada. The project of uniting them once more into one legislature, with a central metropolis, is most violently opposed by those whose personal interests and convenience would suffer materially by a change in the seat of government. I have heard some persons go so far as to declare, that if the union of the two provinces were to be established by law, it were sufficient to absolve a man from his allegiance. On the other hand, the measure has powerful advocates in both provinces. It seems, on looking over the map of this vast and magnificent country, and reading its whole history, that the political division into five provinces,[3] each with its independent governor

---

3  Viz. Upper Canada, Lower Canada, Nova Scotia, New Brunswick, and Prince Edward's Island. [Jameson's note]

and legislature, its separate correspondence with the Colonial-office, its local laws, and local taxation, must certainly add to the amount of colonial patronage, and perhaps render more secure the subjection of the whole to the British crown; but may it not also have perpetuated local distinctions and jealousies—kept alive divided interests, narrowed the resources, and prevented the improvement of the country on a large and general scale?

But I had better stop here, ere I get beyond my depth. I am not one of those who opine sagely, that women have nothing to do with politics. On the contrary; but I do seriously think that no one, be it man or woman, ought to talk, much less write, on what they do not understand. Not but that I have my own ideas on these matters, though we were never able to make out, either to my own satisfaction or to yours, whether I am Whig or Tory or Radical. In politics I acknowledge but two parties,—those who hope and those who fear. In morals, but two parties—those who lie and those who speak the truth: and all the world I divide into those who love, and those who hate. This comprehensive arrangement saves me a vast deal of trouble, and answers all my own purposes to admiration.

\* \* \*

July 5.

. . . Here, as everywhere else, I find the women of the better class lamenting over the want of all society, except of the lowest grade in manners and morals. For those who have recently emigrated, and are settled more in the interior, there is absolutely no social intercourse whatever; it is quite out of the question. They seem to me perishing of ennui, or from the want of sympathy which they cannot obtain, and, what is worse, which they cannot feel: for being in general unfitted for out-door occupations, unable to comprehend or enter into the interests around them, and all their earliest prejudices and ideas of the fitness of things continually outraged in a manner exceedingly unpleasant, they may be said to live in a perpetual state of inward passive discord and fretful endurance—

> 'All too timid and reserved
> For onset, for resistance too inert—
> Too weak for suffering, and for hope too tame.'[4]

A gentleman well known to me by name, who was not a resident of London, but passing through it on his way from a far western settlement up by Lake Huron, was one of my morning visitors. He had been settled in the bush for five years, had a beautiful farm, well cleared, well stocked. He was pleased with his prospects, his existence, his occupations: all he wanted was a wife, and on this subject he poured forth a most eloquent appeal.

---

4 'Despondency', from Wordsworth's *The Excursion* (1814).

'Where', said he, 'shall I find such a wife as I could, with a safe conscience, bring into these wilds, to share a settler's fate, a settler's home? You, who know your own sex so well, point me out such a one, or tell me at least where to seek her. I am perishing and deteriorating, head and heart, for want of a companion—a wife, in short. I am becoming as rude and coarse as my own labourers, and as hard as my own axe. If I wait five years longer, no woman will be able to endure such a fellow as I shall be by that time—no woman, I mean, whom I could marry—for in this lies my utter unreasonableness. Habituated to seek in woman those graces and refinements which I have always associated with her idea, I must have them here in the forest, or dispense with all female society whatever. With some one to sympathise with me—to talk to—to embellish the home I return to at night—such a life as I now lead, with all the cares and frivolities of a too artificial society cast behind us, security and plenty all around us, and nothing but hope before us, a life of "cheerful yesterdays and confident to-morrows"[5]—were it not delicious? I want for myself nothing more, nothing better; but—perhaps it is a weakness, an inconsistency!—I could not love a woman who was inferior to all my preconceived notions of feminine elegance and refinement—inferior to my own mother and sisters. You know I was in England two years ago;—well, I have a vision of a beautiful creature, with the figure of a sylph and the head of a sibyl, bending over her harp, and singing *A te, O cara*;[6] and when I am logging in the woods with my men, I catch myself meditating on that vision, and humming *A te, O cara*, which somehow or other runs strangely in my head. Now, what is to be done? What could I do with that fair vision here? Without coxcombry may I not say, that I need not entirely despair of winning the affections of an amiable, elegant woman, and might even persuade her to confront, for my sake, worse than all this? For what will not your sex do and dare for the sake of us men creatures, savages that we are? But even for that reason shall I take advantage of such sentiments? You know what this life is—this isolated life in the bush—and so do I; but by what words could I make it comprehensible to a fine lady? Certainly I might draw such a picture of it as should delight by its novelty and romance, and deceive even while it does not deviate from the truth. A cottage in the wild woods—solitude and love—the world forgetting, by the world forgot—the deer come skipping by—the red Indian brings game, and lays it at her feet—how pretty and how romantic! And for the first few months, perhaps the first year, all goes well; but how goes it the next, and the next? I have observed with regard to the women who come out, that they do well enough the first year, and some even the second; but the third is generally fatal: and the worst with you women—or the best shall I not say?—is, that you cannot, and do not, forget domestic ties left behind. We men go out upon our land, or to the chase, and the women, poor souls, sit, and sew, and *think*. You have seen Mrs A. and Mrs B., who came out here, as I well remember, full of health and bloom—what are they now? premature old women, sickly, careworn, without nerve or cheerfulness:— and as for C —, who brought his wife to his place by Lake Simcoe only three years

5 Also from *The Excursion*; a peasant seen by the poet is idealized as 'A Man . . . of cheerful yesterday / And confident to-morrows' (VII. 557–8).
6 The Italian song she sings begins, 'To you, O love'.

ago, I hear the poor fellow must sell all off, or see his wife perish before his eyes. Would you have me risk the alternative? Or perhaps you will say, marry one of the women of the country—one of the daughters *of the bush*. No, I cannot; I must have something different. I may not have been particularly fortunate, but the women I have seen are in general coarse and narrow-minded, with no education whatever, or with an education which apes all I most dislike, and omits all I could admire in the fashionable education of the old country. What could I do with such women? In the former I might find an upper servant, but no companion—in the other, neither companionship nor help!'

To this discontented and fastidious gentleman I ventured to recommend two or three very amiable girls I had known at Toronto and Niagara; and I told him, too, that among the beautiful and spirited girls of New England he might also find what would answer his purpose. But with regard to Englishwomen of that grade in station and education, and personal attraction, which would content him, I could not well speak; not because I knew of none who united grace of person and lively talents with capabilities of strong affection, ay, and sufficient energy of character to meet trials and endure privations; but in women, as now educated, there is a strength of local habits and attachments, a want of cheerful self-dependence, a cherished physical delicacy, a weakness of temperament,—deemed, and falsely deemed, in deference to the pride of man, essential to feminine grace and refinement,—altogether unfitting them for a life which were otherwise delightful:—the active out-of-door life in which she must share and sympathise, and the in-door occupations which in England are considered servile; for a woman who cannot perform for herself and others all household offices, has no business here. But when I hear some men declare that they cannot endure to see women eat, and others speak of brilliant health and strength in young girls as being rude and vulgar, with various notions of the same kind too grossly absurd and perverted even for ridicule, I cannot wonder at any nonsensical affectations I meet with in my own sex; nor do I otherwise than pity the mistakes and deficiencies of those who are sagely brought up with the one end and aim—to get married. As you always used to say, 'Let there be a demand for a better article, and a better article will be supplied.'

\*     \*     \*

1838

# Thomas Chandler Haliburton
## 1796–1865

## Early Humour

The comic writing that emerged in nineteenth-century North America drew on British traditions—especially the humorous sketches and biting satire of the eighteenth century—while at the same time responding to the colonial conditions and the wilderness experience that produced an interest in the tall tale, a fascination with the way formal language breaks down and reconstitutes itself in new societies, and concerns about the social and cultural changes produced by a new location. As can be seen in Thomas Chandler Haliburton's *Clockmaker* sketches, this meeting of the Old World with the New World could lead to a humour that looked both ways: its half-ironic longing for the values, customs, and sophistication of the empire joined to an admiration for freedoms that crossed class boundaries and challenged the status quo. With his irreverent tone and his use for comic effect of broad dialect, of folk and oral traditions, and of the eccentric character type known in the eighteenth and nineteenth centuries as 'an original', Haliburton became one of the key figures in the emergence of the new North American literary humour, influencing, among others, Mark Twain (who called Haliburton 'the father of American humor').

Addressing readers who were first of all the colonists themselves, rather than a distant audience 'back home', Haliburton employed this new humour in its satiric mode, using it for social commentary. In contrast to the gentler comedy favoured by some American contemporaries such as Washington Irving, who celebrated more than criticized his new post-colonial society and its values, Haliburton attacked the complacent acceptance of things as they were. At the same time, he didn't, in the fashion of many satirists, look back to a past era whose values had been better. In contrast to the more conservative satire of *The Mephibosheth Stepsure Letters* (originally published serially in 1821–2), created by his fellow Nova Scotian Dr Thomas McCulloch, Haliburton's sketches were aimed at improving his colonial society. While Haliburton's humour does play off the old against the new, he was willing to affirm what he saw as admirable in the new ways: indeed, as he continued to dramatize the rough, even uncultured, aspects of the emerging North American code embodied in his American salesman Sam Slick, he seems to have grown increasingly fond of his main character and found more worth valuing.

Satire has been an important form in Canada, even more than in the United States. From earlier Canadian writers such as Haliburton, McCulloch, and Stephen Leacock, through later writers such as W.O. Mitchell, Mordecai Richler, Robert Kroetsch, Jack Hodgins, Margaret Atwood, Douglas Coupland, Will Ferguson, and Thomas King, along with the caustic pop culture satirists and comedians for which Canada has become well known, Canadian humorists have developed a reputation for an iconoclastic ability to look sidelong at things and see them anew: perennial outsiders, they call attention to what mass culture has too often been willing to ignore.

## Thomas Chandler Haliburton

Born in Windsor, Nova Scotia, of Loyalist stock, Haliburton grew up in a colony that seemed to him a well-established society on the eve of its industrial age. He was eager to participate in Nova Scotia's future development and in righting its social inequities: his education at King's College in Windsor, the accepted preparation for a young Anglican Tory professional, was a means of readying himself for his place in society, and after establishing a successful law practice in Annapolis Royal, he became a member of the legislative assembly, where he argued for various social and governmental reforms that were intended to maintain the strong colonial relationship with England. Haliburton lacked political effectiveness, however: a man of blunt and undiplomatic manners, he alienated the Tories, by supporting reforms, and the reformers, by arguing for close ties to the British Empire. In 1829, he accepted a propitious call to the bench, taking the judgeship in the Court of Common Pleas that had recently been vacated after his father's death. In 1841, Haliburton became chief justice of the Supreme Court of Nova Scotia, a position he held until his retirement in 1856. As he grew older, Haliburton was attracted to Britain, and he moved there after his retirement. In England, he took up politics once more, becoming a Conservative MP at the end of his life, often arguing in the British Parliament against the reforms he had supported as a young man.

Haliburton's first two books—*A General Description of Nova Scotia* (1823) and *An Historical and Statistical Account of Nova Scotia* (1829)—are not works of humour, but they do show his deep knowledge of, and wide-ranging interest in, the colony. By becoming a circuit judge, Haliburton was able to learn still more of the particulars of daily life as he travelled widely through Nova Scotia—good preparation for his creation of Sam Slick, another circuit rider. Indeed, it was in his first years as a judge, when he was disenchanted with politics and convinced that the only changes of real importance would come through a transformation in the character of his compatriots (who struck him as apathetic) that he hit on the idea of writing satirical sketches that would hold up a mirror to Nova Scotians and goad them into action. To this end, he created two principal characters, using their dialogues to debate his chief ideas. One of these was Sam Slick from Slickville, an American clock salesman who, though a trickster who could not be trusted, exemplified the new unrestrained individual and the virtues of 'Industry, Enterprise, Economy', qualities associated with, in Slick's phrase, the 'Go ahead' of American society. Haliburton's counterbalancing character was the Squire, a representative of the old traditions of the British hierarchy—and of Haliburton's own Tory colonial ideals. Through their biting discussions about the somnambulant colonial society of Nova Scotia, their creator sought to awaken his readers to the charged political climate that followed the American and French Revolutions, to shake his fellow colonials from the stupor induced by their lack of enfranchisement and freedom, and to make them conscious of a middle way that blended the opposing values of revolution and empire by marrying energy and assertiveness with moral behaviour. These sketches unite Burkeian Tory principles such as stability, respect for law, and fair-mindedness, with an appreciation of the attributes Haliburton most admired in New Englanders, their outspoken self-confidence, adaptability, and work ethic.

The *Clockmaker* sketches began to appear in 1835 in *The Nova Scotian*, a newspaper edited by Joseph Howe, a friend and a reformer with whom Haliburton had once been politically allied. In 1836, Howe gathered thirty-three of the sketches and published *The Clockmaker; or, The Sayings and Doings of Samuel Slick, of Slickville*, the first of what eventually became eleven volumes chronicling Slick. Their success was so great that in 1858, Haliburton became the first colonial to be given an honorary degree for literary merit by Oxford University. Within fifty years of the Yankee clock peddler's first appearance, there were more than a hundred editions of these books, and Haliburton was being read not only in Canada, England, and the United States but, in translation, in France and Germany, making him the first Canadian author to gain an international readership.

As the years passed, Haliburton's humour became less satiric and the clockmaker less morally complex. By the time Haliburton published his last set of sketches, *The Old Judge; or, Life in a Colony* (1849), a book notable for its observations of society, Sam Slick had disappeared altogether, and the presentation of Nova Scotian life had become a sympathetic one.

# The Trotting Horse

I was always well mounted. I am fond of a horse, and always piqued[1] myself on having the fastest trotter in the Province. I have made no great progress in the world. I feel doubly, therefore, the pleasure of not being surpassed on the road. I never feel so well or so cheerful as on horseback, for there is something exhilarating in quick motion; and, old as I am, I feel a pleasure in making any person whom I meet on the way put his horse to the full gallop, to keep pace with my trotter. Poor Ethiope! You recollect him, how he was wont to lay back his ears on his arched neck, and push away from all competition. He is done, poor fellow! The spavin[2] spoiled his speed, and he now roams at large upon 'my farm at Truro'. Mohawk never failed me till this summer.

I pride myself (you may laugh at such childish weaknesses in a man of my age), but still I pride myself in taking the conceit out of coxcombs I meet on the road, and on the ease with which I can leave a fool behind, whose nonsense disturbs my solitary musings.

On my last journey to Fort Lawrence, as the beautiful view of Colchester had just opened upon me, and as I was contemplating its richness and exquisite scenery, a tall thin man, with hollow cheeks and bright twinkling black eyes, on a good bay horse, somewhat out of condition, overtook me; and drawing up, said, 'I say, stranger, I guess you started early this morning, didn't you?' 'I did sir,' I replied. 'You did not come from Halifax, I presume, sir, did you?' in a dialect too rich to be mistaken as genu*ine* Yankee. 'And which way may you be travelling?' asked my inquisitive companion. 'To Fort Lawrence.' 'Ah!' said he, 'so am I, it is *in my circuit*.'[3] The word *circuit* sounded so professional, I looked again at him to ascertain whether I had ever seen him before, or whether I had met with one of those nameless but innumerable limbs of the law who now flourish in every district of the Province. There was a keenness about his eye, and an acuteness of expression, much in favour of the law; but the dress, and general bearing of the man, made against the supposition. His was not the coat of a man who can afford to wear an old coat, nor was it one of 'Tempest and More's'[4] that distinguish country lawyers from country boobies. His clothes were well made, and of good materials, but looked as if their owner had shrunk a little since they were made for him; they hung somewhat loose on him. A large brooch, and some superfluous seals and gold keys, which ornamented his outward man, looked 'New England' like. A visit to the States had, perhaps, I thought, turned this Colchester beau into a Yankee fop. Of what consequence was it to me who he was—in either case I had nothing to do with him, and I desired neither his acquaintance nor his company—still I could not but ask myself who can this man be? 'I am not aware', said I, 'that there is a court sitting at this time at Cumberland?' 'Nor am I,' said my friend. What then could he have to do with the circuit? It occurred to me he must be a Methodist preacher. I looked again, but his appearance again puzzled me. His attire might do—the colour might be suitable—the broad brim not out of place;

---

1 Prided.
2 A bony tumour on a horse's leg, which causes inflammation and pain.
3 The regular journey through an area made by certain itinerant professionals such as preachers and judges.
4 A tailor shop in Halifax run by John Tempest and William More.

but there was a want of that staidness of look, that seriousness of countenance, that expression, in short, so characteristic of the clergy.

I could not account for my idle curiosity—a curiosity which, in him, I had the moment before viewed both with suspicion and disgust; but so it was—I felt a desire to know who he could be who was neither lawyer nor preacher, and yet talked of his *circuit* with the gravity of both. How ridiculous, I thought to myself, is this; I will leave him. Turning towards him, I said, I feared I should be late for breakfast, and must, therefore, bid him good morning. Mohawk felt the pressure of my knees, and away we went at a slapping pace. I congratulated myself on conquering my own curiosity, and on avoiding that of my travelling companion. This, I said to myself, this is the value of a good horse; I patted his neck—I felt proud of him. Presently I heard the steps of the unknown's horse—the clatter increased. Ah, my friend, thought I, it won't do; you should be well mounted if you desire my company; I pushed Mohawk faster, faster, faster—to his best. He outdid himself; he had never trotted so handsomely—so easily—so well.

'I guess that is a pretty considerable smart horse,' said the stranger as he came beside me, and apparently reined in, to prevent his horse passing me. 'There is not, I reckon, so spry a one on *my circuit.*'

*Circuit, or no circuit,* one thing was settled in my mind; he was a Yankee, and a very impertinent Yankee too. I felt humbled, my pride was hurt, and Mohawk was beaten. To continue this trotting contest was humiliating; I yielded, therefore, before the victory was palpable, and pulled up.

'Yes,' continued he, 'a horse of pretty considerable good action, and a pretty fair trotter, too, I guess.' Pride must have a fall—I confess mine was prostrate in the dust. These words cut me to the heart. What! is it come to this, poor Mohawk, that you, the admiration of all but the envious, the great Mohawk, the standard by which all other horses are measured—trots next to Mohawk, only yields to Mohawk, looks like Mohawk—that you are, after all, only a counterfeit, and pronounced by a straggling Yankee to be merely a 'pretty fair trotter'!

'If he was trained, I guess that he might be made to do a little more. Excuse me, but if you divide your weight between the knee and the stirrup, rather most on the knee, and rise forward on the saddle, so as to leave a little daylight between you and it, I hope I may never ride *this circuit again*, if you don't get a mile more an hour out of him.'

What! not enough, I mentally groaned, to have my horse beaten, but I must be told that I don't know how to ride him; and that, too, by a Yankee. Aye, there's the rub—a Yankee what? Perhaps a half-bred puppy, half yankee, half blue-nose.[5] As there is no escape, I'll try to make out my riding master. '*Your circuit*', said I, my looks expressing all the surprise they were capable of—'your circuit, pray what may that be?' 'Oh,' said he, 'the eastern circuit—I am on the eastern circuit, sir.' 'I have heard,' said I, feeling that I now had a lawyer to deal with, 'that there is a great deal of business on this circuit—pray, are there many cases of importance?' 'There is a pretty fair business

---

5 A Nova Scotian is 'known throughout America as Mr Blue Nose, a sobriquet acquired from a superior potato of that name' (Haliburton's Preface to *The Old Judge*).

to be done, at least there has been,' said he, 'but the cases are of no great value—we don't make much out of them. We get them up very easy, but they don't bring much profit.' What a beast, thought I, is this; and what a curse to a country, to have such an unfeeling pettifogging rascal practising in it—a horse jockey,[6] too, what a finished character! I'll try him on that branch of his business.

'That is a superior animal you are mounted on,' said I. 'I seldom meet one that can keep pace with mine.' 'Yes,' said he coolly, 'a considerable fair traveller, and most particular good bottom.'[7] I hesitated: this man who talks with such unblushing effrontery of getting up cases, and making profit out of them, cannot be offended at the question—yes, I will put it to him. 'Do you feel an inclination to part with him?' 'I never part with a horse, sir, that suits me,' said he. 'I am fond of a horse—I don't like to ride in the dust after every one I meet, and I allow no man to pass me but when I choose.' Is it possible, I thought, that he can know me? that he has heard of my foible, and is quizzing[8] me, or have I this feeling in common with him? 'But', continued I, 'you might supply yourself again.' 'Not on *this circuit*, I guess,' said he, 'nor yet in Campbell's circuit.' 'Campbell's circuit—pray, sir, what is that?' 'That', said he, 'is the western—and Lampton rides the shore circuit; and as for the people on the shore, they know so little of horses that Lampton tells me a man from Aylesford once sold a hornless ox there, whose tail he had cut and nicked, for a horse of the Goliath breed.' 'I should think', said I, 'that Mr Lampton must have no lack of cases among such enlightened clients.' 'Clients, sir!' said my friend, 'Mr Lampton is not a lawyer.' 'I beg pardon, I though you said he rode the *circuit*.' 'We call it a circuit,' said the stranger, who seemed by no means flattered by the mistake. 'We divide the Province, as in the Almanack, into circuits, in each of which we separately carry on our business of manufacturing and selling clocks. There are few, I guess,' said the Clockmaker, 'who go upon *tick*[9] as much as we do, who have so little use for lawyers. If attornies could wind a *man up again*, after he has been fairly *run down*, I guess they'd be a pretty harmless sort of folks.'

This explanation restored my good humour, and as I could not quit my companion, and he did not feel disposed to leave, I made up my mind to travel with him to Fort Lawrence, the limit of *his circuit*.

6  Horse trader.
7  Physical endurance; strength.
8  Mocking.
9  To be 'on tick' has two idiomatic meanings, both available here: 'punctually' and 'on credit'.

# The Clockmaker

I had heard of Yankee clock pedlars, tin pedlars, and bible pedlars, especially of him who sold Polyglot Bibles[1] (*all in English*) to the amount of sixteen thousand pounds. The house of every substantial farmer had three substantial ornaments, a wooden clock, a tin reflector, and a Polyglot Bible. How is it that an American can sell his

1  Bibles published in several Biblical languages as well as in modern translation; used to settle textual disputes; 'tin reflector': a reflector placed behind a candle to allow it to serve as a lamp.

wares, at whatever price he pleases, where a blue-nose would fail to make a sale at all? I will inquire of the Clockmaker the secret of his success.

'What a pity it is, Mr *Slick*,' (for such was his name), 'what a pity it is', said I, 'that you, who are so successful in teaching these people the value of *clocks*, could not also teach them the value of *time*.' 'I guess', said he, 'they have got that ring to grow on their horns yet,[2] which every four-year-old has in our country. We reckon hours and minutes to be dollars and cents. They do nothin in these parts but eat, drink, smoke, sleep, ride about, lounge at taverns, make speeches at temperance meetings, and talk about "*House of Assembly*". If a man don't hoe his corn, and he don't get a crop, he says it is all owin to the Bank; and if he runs into debt and is sued, why he says lawyers are a cuss to the country. They are a most idle set of folks, I tell *you*.'

'But how is it', said I, 'that you manage to sell such an immense number of clocks (which certainly cannot be called necessary articles) among a people with whom there seems to be so great a scarcity of money?'

Mr Slick paused, as if considering the propriety of answering the question, and looking me in the face, said, in a confidential tone, 'Why I don't care if I do tell you, for the market is glutted, and I shall quit this circuit. It is done by a knowledge of *soft sawder* and *human natur*. But here is Deacon Flint's,' said he. 'I have but one clock left, and I guess I will sell it to him.'

At the gate of a most comfortable-looking farmhouse stood Deacon Flint, a respectable old man, who had understood the value of time better than most of his neighbours, if one might judge from the appearance of everything about him. After the usual salutation, an invitation to 'alight' was accepted by Mr Slick, who said he wished to take leave of Mrs Flint before he left Colchester.

We had hardly entered the house before the Clockmaker pointed to the view from the window, and addressing himself to me, said, 'If I was to tell them in Connecticut there was such a farm as this away down east here in Nova Scotia, they wouldn't believe me—why there ain't such a location in all New England. The deacon has a hundred acres of dyke.'[3] 'Seventy,' said the Deacon, 'only seventy.' 'Well, seventy; but then there is your fine deep bottom. Why I could run a ramrod into it.' 'Interval, we call it,' said the Deacon, who, though evidently pleased at this eulogium,[4] seemed to wish the experiment of the ramrod to be tried in the right place. 'Well, interval if you please (though Professor Eleazer Cumstick, in his work on Ohio, calls them bottoms) is just as good as dyke. Then there is that water privilege,[5] worth 3,000 or 4,000 dollars, twice as good as what Governor Cass paid 15,000 dollars for.[6] I wonder, Deacon, you don't put up a carding mill[7] on it: the same works would carry a turning lathe, a shingle machine, a circular saw, grind bark, and—' 'Too old,' said the Deacon, 'too old for all those speculations.' 'Old,' repeated the Clockmaker, 'not you; why you are worth half

2  Cattle and oxen grow rings on their horns as they mature.
3  Land built up to hold water back; a 'bottom' or an 'interval' is low-lying land, usually along a river.
4  Formal expression of praise.
5  Right to use water, especially running water to turn machinery.
6  A governor of the territory of Michigan who paid $12,000 for 500 acres at the mouth of the Detroit River; though the sum was deemed exorbitant at the time, the property made the governor's personal fortune.
7  Mill for combing and cleansing raw wool.

a dozen of the young men we see now-a-days; you are young enough to have—' Here he said something in a lower tone of voice, which I did not distinctly hear; but whatever it was, the Deacon was pleased. He smiled, and said he did not think of such things now.

'But your beasts, dear me, your beasts must be put in and have a feed,' saying which he went out to order them to be taken to the stable.

As the old gentleman closed the door after him, Mr Slick drew near to me, and said in an undertone, 'Now that is what I call "*soft sawder*". An Englishman would pass that man as a sheep passes a hog in a pastur, without lookin at him. Or,' said he, looking rather archly, 'if he was mounted on a pretty smart horse, I guess he'd trot away, *if he could*. Now I find—' Here his lecture on '*soft sawder*' was cut short by the entrance of Mrs Flint. 'Jist come to say goodbye, Mrs Flint.' 'What, have you sold all your clocks?' 'Yes, and very low, too, for money is scarce, and I wished to close the consarn.[8] No, I am wrong in saying all, for I have jist one left. Neighbour Steel's wife asked to have the refusal of it, but I guess I won't sell it. I had but two of them, this one and the feller of it that I sold Governor Lincoln.[9] General Green, the Secretary of State for Maine, said he'd give me 50 dollars for this here one—it has composition wheels and patent axles, it is a beautiful article—a real first chop[10]—no mistake. Genuine superfine. But I guess I'll take it back; and beside, Squire Hawk might think kinder harder that I didn't give him the offer.' 'Dear me,' said Mrs Flint, 'I should like to see it. Where is it?' 'It is in a chist of mine over the way, at Tom Tape's store. I guess he can ship it on to Eastport.' 'That's a good man,' said Mrs Flint, 'jist let's look at it.'

Mr Slick, willing to oblige, yielded to these entreaties, and soon produced the clock—a gawdy, highly varnished, trumpery looking affair. He placed it on the chimney-piece, where its beauties were pointed out and duly appreciated by Mrs Flint, whose admiration was about ending in a proposal, when Mr Flint returned from giving his directions about the care of the horses. The Deacon praised the clock. He too thought it a handsome one; but the Deacon was a prudent man, he had a watch—he was sorry, but he had no occasion for a clock. 'I guess you're in the wrong furrow this time, Deacon, it an't for sale,' said Mr Slick. 'And if it was, I reckon neighbour Steel's wife would have it, for she gives me no peace about it.' Mrs Flint said that Mr Steel had enough to do, poor man, to pay his interest, without buying clocks for his wife. 'It's no consarn of mine,' said Mr Slick, 'so long as he pays me what he has to do. But I guess I don't want to sell it, and besides it comes too high; that clock can't be made at Rhode Island under 40 dollars. Why it an't possible,' said the Clockmaker, in apparent surprise, looking at his watch, 'why as I'm alive, it is 4 o'clock, and if I hav'nt been two blessed hours here—how on airth shall I reach River Philip tonight? I'll tell you what, Mrs Flint, I'll leave the clock in your care till I return on my way to the States—I'll set it a goin, and put it to the right time.'

As soon as this operation was performed, he delivered the key to the Deacon with a sort of serio-comic injunction to wind up the clock every Saturday night, which

8  Concern.
9  Fourth governor of Maine, 1827–9.
10  First-rate article.

Mrs Flint said she would take care should be done, and promised to remind her husband of it in case he should chance to forget it.

'That,' said the Clockmaker, as soon as we were mounted, 'that I call "*human natur*"! Now that clock is sold for 40 dollars—it cost me jist 6 dollars and 50 cents. Mrs Flint will never let Mrs Steel have the refusal—nor will the Deacon larn, until I call for the clock, that having once indulged in the use of a superfluity, how difficult it is to give it up. We can do without any article of luxury we have never had, but when once obtained, it isn't "*in human natur*" to surrender it voluntarily. Of fifteen thousand sold by myself and partners in this Province, twelve thousand were left in this manner, and only ten clocks were ever returned—when we called for them, they invariably bought them. We trust to "*soft sawder*" to get them into the house, and to "human natur" that they never come out of it.

1836

---

# Catharine Parr Traill
## 1802–1899

### Pioneer Memoirs

Pioneer memoirs are a non-fiction genre that enjoyed some popularity in the nineteenth and early twentieth centuries. A form that often lacks dramatic shape, the account of a pioneer was usually a story of hardship and struggle against nature. Its appeal was its realistic representation of an experience that often was shared by its readers, either first-hand or in family memory. Unlike the explorers' stories of extreme privation in what seemed to Europeans a virtually uninhabitable landscape, and in contrast to the traveller's tales of romantic and exotic trips, the pioneer memoir tends to be a narrative of the ordinary marked by long years of repetitious combat against the environment—an enemy that can also be a friend and a resource. It is the story of human spirit exposed to Job-like trials by the land and climate. The tendency in recent years to call these memoirs 'settlement narratives' emphasizes the way individual accounts come to be seen as representative of or a collective experience in the development of a nation. Their later fictional equivalent is the pioneer novel, a form made popular in Canada by several early-twentieth-century prairie authors, including Martha Ostenso (in *Wild Geese*, 1925), Robert Stead (see especially *Grain*, 1926), and Frederick Philip Grove in his several accounts of the life of Manitoba farmers (such as *Fruits of the Earth*, 1933).

### Catharine Parr Traill

Catharine Strickland was born in London into a large and literary family. Writing as Catharine Parr Traill, she became one of three siblings to provide accounts of pioneer experience in nineteenth-century Canada. Her brother, Samuel Strickland, was the author of *Twenty-seven Years in Canada West* (1853), while her younger sister, Susanna Moodie, became famous as the author of *Roughing It in the Bush* (1852). It was through Susanna and her new husband, Lieutenant John

Moodie, that Catharine first met Lieutenant Thomas Traill, a half-pay officer. The Traills were married in 1832, and both they and the Moodies emigrated to Upper Canada in that year, departing within a week of one another. The Traills settled in Douro Township (near Peterborough), at Rice Lake; their farm was next to that of Samuel Strickland, who had preceded them in 1825.

By the time she came to Canada, Catharine Traill had already written children's stories as well as a book on her future homeland—*The Young Emigrants; or, Pictures of Canada* (1826), based on the experiences of family friends and on information from travel books. Four years after her arrival, she published *The Backwoods of Canada* (1836), a work drawing on letters she had written home. It was undertaken, as she later said, 'with the view of preparing females of my class . . . for the changes that awaited them in the life of a Canadian emigrant's wife.' In 1852, she published a children's book about her adopted country, *Canadian Crusoes*, which remains interesting both for its idealized treatment of the union in Canada of English and French, Scots and Indians, and also because Crusoe, like Noah, has been an emblematic figure in Canadian writing: the individual who carries with him and recreates the civilization from which he has been separated. In 1854, Traill published *The Female Emigrant's Guide* (reprinted as *The Canadian Settler's Guide*), a work that continues the project begun in *The Backwoods of Canada* of conveying to emigrating gentlewomen the knowledge Traill won through hard experience. Already interested in nature, she displayed considerable talents as a naturalist once in Canada, collecting and cataloguing the plant life she found around her. Her chapter on flowers in *The Backwoods of Canada* and in such later studies as *Canadian Wild Flowers* (1869) and *Studies of Plant Life in Canada* (1885) are botanical landmarks. Traill, whose life spanned the nineteenth century, continued to write even into her nineties: *Pearls and Pebbles; or, Notes of an Old Naturalist* was published when she was ninety-two.

*The Backwoods of Canada* is often contrasted with Susanna Moodie's *Roughing It in the Bush*. Though Traill, like her younger sister, does tell of many hardships, her overall outlook is much more optimistic. Indeed, she so buoyed the despairing Susanna's spirits, that Moodie writes midway through *Roughing It*, 'My conversation with her [Catharine] had quite altered the aspect of the country, and predisposed me to view things in the most favourable light.' Traill saw the pleasanter traits of nature as expressing God's benevolence, and she believed that in adversity the individual's duty to self and to God lay in strong-willed determination: 'In cases of emergency, it is folly to fold one's hands and sit down to bewail in abject terror: it is better to be up and doing' (*The Female Emigrant's Guide*). Hers was clearly an attitude valuable to new pioneers; lacking it, they tended, as she observed, to 'blame the Colony for the failure of the individual.' In *The Diviners* (1974), Margaret Laurence has her central character enter into imaginary dialogues with Catharine Traill, even to the point of invoking her: 'Saint Catharine: Where are you now that we need you?'

# From *The Backwoods of Canada*

## LETTER IX

Lake House
April 18, 1833

But it is time that I should give you some account of our log-house, into which we moved a few days before Christmas. Many unlooked-for delays having hindered its completion before that time, I began to think it would never be habitable.

The first misfortune that happened was the loss of a fine yoke of oxen that were purchased to draw in the house-logs, that is, the logs for raising the walls of the house.

Not regarding the bush as pleasant as their former master's cleared pastures, or perhaps foreseeing some hard work to come, early one morning they took into their heads to ford the lake at the head of the rapids, and march off, leaving no trace of their route excepting their footing at the water's edge. After many days spent in vain search for them, the work was at a stand, and for one month they were gone, and we began to give up all expectation of hearing any news of them. At last we learned they were some twenty miles off, in a distant township, having made their way through bush and swamp, creek and lake, back to their former owner, with an instinct that supplied to them the want of roads and compass.

Oxen have been known to traverse a tract of wild country to a distance of thirty or forty miles going in a direct line for their former haunts by unknown paths, where memory could not avail them. In the dog we consider it is scent as well as memory that guides him to his far-off home;—but how is this conduct of the oxen to be accounted for? They returned home through the mazes of interminable forests, where man, with all his reason and knowledge, would have been bewildered and lost.

It was the latter end of October before even the walls of our house were up. To effect this we called 'a bee'.[1] Sixteen of our neighbours cheerfully obeyed our summons; and though the day was far from favourable, so faithfully did our hive perform their tasks, that by night the outer walls were raised.

The work went merrily on with the help of plenty of Canadian nectar (whiskey), the honey that our *bees* are solaced with. Some huge joints of salt pork, a peck of potatoes, with a rice-pudding, and a loaf as big as an enormous Cheshire cheese, formed the feast that was to regale them during the raising. This was spread out in the shanty,[2] in a *very rural style*. In short, we laughed, and called it a *pic-nic in the backwoods*; and rude as was the fare, I can assure you, great was the satisfaction expressed by all the guests of every degree, our 'bee' being considered as very well conducted. In spite of the difference of rank among those that assisted at the bee, the greatest possible harmony prevailed, and the party separated well pleased with the day's work and entertainment.

The following day I went to survey the newly-raised edifice, but was sorely puzzled, as it presented very little appearance of a house. It was merely an oblong square of logs raised one above the other, with open spaces between every row of logs. The spaces for the doors and windows were not then chopped out, and the rafters were not up. In short, it looked a very queer sort of a place, and I returned home a little disappointed, and wondering that my husband should be so well pleased with the progress that had been made. A day or two after this I again visited it. The *sleepers*[3] were laid to support the floors, and the places for the doors and windows cut out of the solid timbers, so that it had not quite so much the look of a bird-cage as before.

After the roof was shingled, we were again at a stand, as no boards could be procured nearer than Peterborough, a long day's journey through horrible roads. At that time no saw-mill was in progress; now there is a fine one building within a little distance of us. Our flooring-boards were all to be sawn by hand, and it was some time

1 Any gathering for communal work.
2 Used here in its French-Canadian sense: 'workshop'.
3 Supporting beams.

before any one could be found to perform this necessary work, and that at high wages—six-and-sixpence per day. Well, the boards were at length down, but of course of unseasoned timber: this was unavoidable; so as they could not be planed we were obliged to put up with their rough unsightly appearance, for no better were to be had. I began to recall to mind the observation of the old gentleman with whom we travelled from Cobourg to Rice Lake.[4] We console ourselves with the prospect that by next summer the boards will all be seasoned, and then the house is to be turned topsy-turvy, by having the floors all relaid, jointed, and smoothed.

The next misfortune that happened, was, that the mixture of clay and lime that was to plaster the inside and outside of the house between the chinks of the logs was one night frozen to stone. Just as the work was about half completed, the frost suddenly setting in, put a stop to our proceeding for some time, as the frozen plaster yielded neither to fire nor to hot water, the latter freezing before it had any effect on the mass, and rather making bad worse. Then the workman that was hewing the inside walls to make them smooth, wounded himself with the broad axe, and was unable to resume his work for some time.

I state these things merely to show the difficulties that attend us in the fulfilment of our plans, and this accounts in a great measure for the humble dwellings that settlers of the most respectable description are obliged to content themselves with at first coming to this country,—not, you may be assured, from inclination, but necessity: I could give you such narratives of this kind as would astonish you. After all, it serves to make us more satisfied than we should be on casting our eyes around to see few better off than we are, and many not half so comfortable, yet of equal, and, in some instances, superior pretensions as to station and fortune.

Every man in this country is his own glazier; this you will laugh at: but if he does not wish to see and feel the discomfort of broken panes, he must learn to put them in his windows with his own hands. Workmen are not easily to be had in the backwoods when you want them, and it would be preposterous to hire a man at high wages to make two days' journey to and from the nearest town to mend your windows. Boxes of glass of several different sizes are to be bought at a very cheap rate in the stores. My husband amused himself by glazing the windows of the house preparatory to their being fixed in.[5]

To understand the use of carpenter's tools, I assure you, is no despicable or useless kind of knowledge here. I would strongly recommend all young men coming to Canada to acquire a little acquaintance with this valuable art, as they will often be put to great inconvenience for the want of it.

---

4 ' "If you go into the backwoods your house must necessarily be a log-house," said an elderly gentleman, who had been a settler many years in the country, "for you will most probably be out of the way of a saw-mill, and you will find so much to do, and so many obstacles to encounter, for the first two or three years, that you will hardly have opportunity for carrying these improvements into effect.

' "There is an old saying," he added: . . . "'first creep and then go.' Matters are not carried on quite so easily here as at home. . . . At the end of ten or fifteen years you may begin to talk of these pretty improvements and elegancies and you will then be able to see a little what you are about. . . ." ' (Letter V)

5 That is, he placed the glass in the window frames before putting the frames in place.

I was once much amused with hearing the remarks made by a very fine lady, the reluctant sharer of her husband's emigration, on seeing the son of a naval officer of some rank in the service busily employed in making an axe-handle out of a piece of rock-elm.

'I wonder that you allow George to degrade himself so,' she said, addressing his father.

The captain looked up with surprise. 'Degrade himself? In what manner, madam? My boy neither swears, drinks whiskey, steals, nor tells lies.'

'But you allow him to perform tasks of the most menial kind. What is he now better than a hedge carpenter;[6] and I suppose you allow him to chop, too?'

'Most assuredly I do. That pile of logs in the cart there was all cut by him after he had left study yesterday,' was the reply.

'I would see my boys dead before they should use an axe like common labourers.'

'Idleness is the root of all evil,' said the captain. 'How much worse might my son be employed if he were running wild about the street with bad companions.'

'You will allow this is not a country for gentlemen or ladies to live in,' said the lady.

'It is the country for gentlemen that will not work and cannot live without, to starve in,' replied the captain bluntly; 'and for that reason I make my boys early accustom themselves to be usefully and actively employed.'

'My boys shall never work like common mechanics,'[7] said the lady, indignantly.

'Then, madam, they will be good for nothing as settlers; and it is a pity you dragged them across the Atlantic.'

'We were forced to come. We could not live as we had been used to do at home, or I never would have come to this horrid country.'

'Having come hither you would be wise to conform to circumstances. Canada is not the place for idle folks to retrench a lost fortune in. In some parts of the country you will find most articles of provision as dear as in London, clothing much dearer, and not so good, and a bad market to choose in.'

'I should like to know, then, who Canada is good for?' said she, angrily.

'It is a good country for the honest, industrious artisan. It is a fine country for the poor labourer, who, after a few years of hard toil, can sit down in his own log-house, and look abroad on his own land, and see his children well settled in life as independent freeholders.[8] It is a grand country for the rich speculator, who can afford to lay out a large sum in purchasing land in eligible situations; for if he have any judgment, he will make a hundred per cent as interest for his money after waiting a few years. But it is a hard country for the poor gentleman, whose habits have rendered him unfit for manual labour. He brings with him a mind unfitted to his situation; and even if necessity compels him to exertion, his labour is of little value. He has a hard struggle to live. The certain expenses of wages and living are great, and he is obliged to endure many privations if he would keep within compass, and be free of debt. If he have a large family, and brings them up wisely, so as to adapt themselves early to a settler's life, why he does well for them, and soon feels the benefit on his own land; but if he is idle himself, his wife extravagant and discontented, and the children taught to despise labour,

6 Fence repairer.
7 Manual labourers.
8 Those that own land without restrictions on its sale or use.

why, madam, they will soon be brought down to ruin. In short, the country is a good country for those to whom it is adapted; but if people will not conform to the doctrine of necessity and expediency, they have no business in it. It is plain Canada is not adapted to every class of people.'

'It was never adapted for me or my family,' said the lady, disdainfully.

'Very true,' was the laconic reply; and so ended the dialogue.

But while I have been recounting these remarks, I have wandered far from my original subject, and left my poor log-house quite in an unfinished state. At last I was told it was in a habitable condition, and I was soon engaged in all the bustle and fatigue attendant on removing our household goods. We received all the assistance we required from ———, who is ever ready and willing to help us. He laughed and called it a '*moving* bee'; I said it was a 'fixing bee'; and my husband said it was a 'settling bee'; I know we were unsettled enough till it was over. What a din of desolation is a small house, or any house under such circumstances. The idea of chaos[9] must have been taken from a removal or a setting to rights, for I suppose the ancients had their *flitting*,[10] as the Scotch call it, as well as the moderns.

Various were the valuable articles of crockery-ware that perished in their short but rough journey through the woods. Peace to their manes.[11] I had a good helper in my Irish maid, who soon roused up famous fires, and set the house in order.

We have not got quite comfortably settled, and I shall give you a description of our little dwelling. What is finished is only a part of the original plan; the rest must be added next spring, or fall, as circumstances may suit.

A nice small sitting-room with a store closet, a kitchen, pantry, and bed-chamber form the ground floor; there is a good upper floor that will make three sleeping-rooms.

'What a nut-shell!' I think I hear you exclaim. So it is at present; but we purpose adding a handsome frame front as soon as we can get boards from the mill, which will give us another parlour, long hall, and good spare bed-room. The windows and glass door of our present sitting-room command pleasant lake-views to the west and south. When the house is completed, we shall have a verandah in front; and at the south side, which forms an agreeable addition in the summer, being used as a sort of outer room, in which we can dine, and have the advantage of cool air, protected from the glare of the sunbeams. The Canadians call these verandahs 'stoups'. Few houses, either log or frame, are without them. The pillars look extremely pretty, wreathed with the luxuriant hop-vine, mixed with the scarlet creeper and 'morning glory', the American name for the most splendid of major convolvuluses. These stoups are really a considerable ornament, as they conceal in a great measure the rough logs, and break the barnlike form of the building.

Our parlour is warmed by a handsome Franklin stove with brass galley, and fender. Our furniture consists of a brass-railed sofa, which serves upon occasion for a bed, Canadian painted chairs, a stained pine table, green and white curtains, and a handsome Indian mat that covers the floor. One side of the room is filled up with our books.

9 That is, the ancient idea that chaos preceded and furnished the materials for the creation of the world.
10 Moving from place to place.
11 Spirits (Latin: the deified souls of departed ancestors).

Some large maps and a few good prints nearly conceal the rough wall, and form the decoration of our little dwelling. Our bed-chamber is furnished with equal simplicity. We do not, however, lack comfort in our humble home; and though it is not exactly such as we could wish, it is as good as, under existing circumstances, we could have.

\*   \*   \*

## LETTER X

Lake House
May the 9th, 1833

\*   \*   \*

Though the Canadian winter has its disadvantages, it also has its charms. After a day or two of heavy snow the sky brightens, and the air becomes exquisitely clear and free from vapour; the smoke ascends in tall spiral columns till it is lost: seen against the saffron-tinted sky of an evening, or early of a clear morning, when the hoar-frost sparkles on the trees, the effect is singularly beautiful.

I enjoy a walk in the woods of a bright winter-day, when not a cloud, or the faint shadow of a cloud, obscures the soft azure of the heavens above; when but for the silver covering of the earth I might look upwards to the cloudless sky and say, 'It is June, sweet June.' The evergreens, as the pines, cedars, hemlock, and balsam firs, are bending their pendent branches, loaded with snow, which the least motion scatters in a mimic shower around, but so light and dry is it that it is shaken off without the slightest inconvenience.

The tops of the stumps look quite pretty, with their turbans of snow; a blackened pine-stump, with its white cap and mantle, will often startle you into the belief that some one is approaching you thus fancifully attired. As to ghosts or spirits they appear totally banished from Canada. This is too matter-of-fact country for such supernaturals to visit. Here there are no historical associations, no legendary tales of those that came before us. Fancy would starve for lack of marvellous food to keep her alive in the backwoods. We have neither fay nor fairy, ghost nor bogle,[1] satyr nor wood-nymph; our very forests disdain to shelter dryad or hamadryad. No naiad haunts the rushy margin of our lakes, or hallows with her presence our forest-rills. No Druid claims our oaks; and instead of poring with mysterious awe among our curious limestone rocks, that are often singularly grouped together, we refer them to the geologist to exercise his skill in accounting for their appearance: instead of investing them with the solemn characters of ancient temples or heathen altars, we look upon them with the curious eye of natural philosophy alone.

Even the Irish and Highlanders of the humblest class seem to lay aside their ancient superstitions on becoming denizens of the woods of Canada. I heard a friend exclaim, when speaking of the want of interest this country possessed, 'It is the most

---

1   Goblin; 'dryad' and 'hamadryad': wood nymphs; 'naiad': water nymph; 'Druid': primitive Celtic priest.

unpoetical of all lands; there is no scope for imagination; here all is new—the very soil seems newly formed; there is no hoary ancient grandeur in these woods; no recollections of former deeds connected with the country. The only beings in which I take any interest are the Indians, and they want the warlike character and intelligence that I had pictured to myself they would possess.'

This was the lamentation of a poet. Now, the class of people to whom this country is so admirably adapted are formed of the unlettered and industrious labourers and artisans. They feel no regret that the land they labour on has not been celebrated by the pen of the historian or the lay of the poet. The earth yields her increase to them as freely as if it had been enriched by the blood of heroes. They would not spare the ancient oak from feelings of veneration, nor look upon it with regard for any thing but its use as timber. They have no time, even if they possessed the taste, to gaze abroad on the beauties of Nature, but their ignorance is bliss.

After all, these are imaginary evils, and can hardly be considered just causes for dislike to the country. They would excite little sympathy among every-day men and women, though doubtless they would have their weight with the more refined and intellectual members of society, who naturally would regret that taste, learning, and genius should be thrown out of its proper sphere.

For myself, though I can easily enter into the feelings of the poet and the enthusiastic lover of the wild and the wonderful of historic lore, I can yet make myself very happy and contented in this country. If its volume of history is yet a blank, that of Nature is open, and eloquently marked by the finger of God; and from its pages I can extract a thousand sources of amusement and interest whenever I take my walks in the forest or by the borders of the lakes.

1836

# Susanna Moodie
## 1803–1885

Susanna Moodie, like her older sister Catharine Parr Traill, began her literary career early, publishing her first novel by the time she was nineteen. She continued writing and published a collection of her poetry in 1831, the year she married John Dunbar Moodie, a retired army officer from the Orkneys (northern Scotland). The couple immigrated to Upper Canada in 1832, settling near Cobourg. After two difficult years, they relocated to Douro Township to be closer to Susanna's brother Samuel Strickland and her sister Catharine. Farming was still so difficult, however, that only when Dunbar Moodie was recalled to active service because of the Rebellions of 1837 did the family gain some measure of financial security. When, in 1839,

Mr Moodie was appointed sheriff of Victoria District (later Hastings County), it was with relief that the couple moved to Belleville, abandoning forever their attempts at managing a bush farm.

Once Susanna Moodie left rural life behind, she was able to return to her faltering literary career. Between 1829 and 1851, she contributed seventy-five poems and twenty pieces of prose to various magazines, including *The Canadian Literary Magazine*, *The North American Review*, and *The Literary Garland*. She integrated several of her published sketches into a larger narrative recounting her years of struggle as a farm wife, entitling it *Roughing It in the Bush; or, Forest Life in Canada*; it appeared in 1852. In Moodie's lifetime, this book was republished in several editions, the contents of which varied somewhat; in some later versions, whole chapters were deleted. (In 1988, the Centre for Editing Early Canadian Texts brought out a scholarly edition of *Roughing It in the Bush*.) A sequel, *Life in the Clearings versus the Bush*, appeared in 1853. There, Moodie explained that while *Roughing It* was intended 'to point out the error of gentlemen bringing delicate women and helpless children to toil in woods,' she nevertheless affirmed 'the REAL benefits to be derived from a judicious choice of settlement in this great and rising country.' Moodie wrote very rapidly in the years that followed, turning out several novels and helping to fill the pages of *The Literary Garland* and other magazines. Most of what she wrote is little read today except *Roughing It*, to which is sometimes added *Life in the Clearings* and the introduction to her novel *Mark Hurdlestone* for its account of literary activity in Canada in 1853. Her letters and those of her husband have been preserved and published: Susanna's correspondence to friends and literary acquaintants was gathered as *Letters of a Lifetime* (1985), and the letters that she and her husband exchanged during their periods of separation (their existence was not known until 1987) were collected as *Letters of Love and Duty* (1993). These two volumes add considerable depth to our knowledge of Moodie and her social milieu.

*Roughing It in the Bush*, originally published in London, was not immediately popular in Canada, where it was not published until 1871. In a preface to that first Canadian edition, the author expressed her hard-won affection for her adopted country. Perhaps because of those comments, or because the events were now sufficiently distant, the book gained its Canadian readership at last. It has maintained one since, even though Moodie's real purpose in writing was to warn unwary immigrants about the deceptive appearances they would find in Canada. In fact, Moodie has become an archetype of the early settler for modern Canadians—so much so that Margaret Atwood responded to her Canadian chronicles with a collection of poems, *The Journals of Susanna Moodie* (1970; a selection is included in this anthology), which in its own way has become as much of a classic as *Roughing It*.

Moodie's book is made up of a series of anecdotes that reveal its author as a practised storyteller with a remarkable ability to convey the variety of characters she met in the bush by using their colourful, idiomatic speech in lively dialogue. As a whole, *Roughing It* takes the form of a complaint: a speech in Chapter 19 by an acquaintance seems almost to capture its essence: 'Bah!—The only consolation one feels for such annoyances is to complain. Oh, the woods!—the cursed woods!—how I wish I were out of them.' In her afterword to *Journals*, Atwood sees Moodie as 'divided down the middle'—an emblem of the 'violent duality' of Canada itself. Indeed, what most engages the modern reader is that, although Moodie reveals herself as melancholy, inflexible, and proud to the point of condescension, she still continues to struggle against the perpetual defeat of her hopes, all the while giving vent to a confused mixture of feelings. Combining in her narrative the perspective of the time of the events described with the 'reconciled' viewpoint of the older woman recalling those events, she shows us her exhilaration in small victories, a degree of pleasure in enduring painful experiences, and even the tearful sadness she felt at leaving the scene of her hardships. It is in watching Moodie make her choice and achieve—if almost despite herself—her reconciliation with the land that the greatest attraction of her story lies.

# From *Roughing It in the Bush*

## INTRODUCTION TO THE THIRD EDITION

In most instances, emigration is a matter of necessity, not of choice; and this is more especially true of the emigration of persons of respectable connections, or of any station or position in the world. Few educated persons, accustomed to the refinements and luxuries of European society, ever willingly relinquish those advantages, and place themselves beyond the protective influence of the wise and revered institutions of their native land, without the pressure of some urgent cause. Emigration may, indeed, generally be regarded as an act of severe duty, performed at the expense of personal enjoyment, and accompanied by the sacrifice of those local attachments which stamp the scenes amid which our childhood grew, in imperishable characters, upon the heart. Nor is it until adversity has pressed sorely upon the proud and wounded spirit of the well-educated sons and daughters of old but impoverished families, that they gird up the loins of the mind, and arm themselves with fortitude to meet and dare the heart-breaking conflict.

The ordinary motive for the emigration of such persons may be summed up in a few brief words;—the emigrant's hope of bettering his condition, and of escaping from the vulgar sarcasms too often hurled at the less wealthy by the purse-proud, common-place people of the world. But there is a higher motive still, which has its origin in that love of independence which springs up spontaneously in the breasts of the high-souled children of a glorious land. They cannot labour in a menial capacity in the country where they were born and educated to command. They can trace no difference between themselves and the more fortunate individuals of a race whose blood warms their veins, and whose name they bear. The want of wealth alone places an impassable barrier between them and the more favoured offspring of the same parent stock; and they go forth to make for themselves a new name and to find another country, to forget the past and to live in the future, to exult in the prospect of their children being free and the land of their adoption great.

The choice of the country to which they devote their talents and energies depends less upon their pecuniary means than upon the fancy of the emigrant or the popularity of a name. From the year 1826 to 1829, Australia and the Swan River were all the rage. No other portions of the habitable globe were deemed worthy of notice. These were the *El Dorados*[1] and land of Goshen to which all respectable emigrants eagerly flocked. Disappointment, as a matter of course, followed their high-raised expectations. Many of the most sanguine of these adventurers returned to their native shores in a worse condition than when they left them. In 1830, the great tide of emigration flowed westward. Canada became the great land-mark for the rich in hope and poor in purse. Public newspapers and private letters teemed with the unheard-of advantages to be derived from a settlement in this highly-favoured region.

---

1 A fabled city of gold sought by early Spanish explorers of the New World. In the Book of Exodus, Goshen was the fertile land alloted the Israelites in Egypt, in which there was light during the plague of darkness; hence, a land of light and plenty.

Its salubrious climate, its fertile soil, commercial advantages, great water privileges, its proximity to the mother country, and last, not least, its almost total exemption from taxation—that bugbear which keeps honest John Bull in a state of constant ferment—were the theme of every tongue, and lauded beyond all praise. The general interest, once excited, was industriously kept alive by pamphlets, published by interested parties, which prominently set forth all the *good* to be derived from a settlement in the Backwoods of Canada; while they carefully concealed the toil and hardship to be endured in order to secure these advantages. They told of lands yielding forty bushels to the acre, but they said nothing of the years when these lands, with the most careful cultivation, would barely return fifteen; when rust and smut, engendered by the vicinity of damp over-hanging woods, would blast the fruits of the poor emigrant's labour, and almost deprive him of bread. They talked of log houses to be raised in a single day, by the generous exertions of friends and neighbours, but they never ventured upon a picture of the disgusting scenes of riot and low debauchery exhibited during the raising, or upon a description of the dwellings when raised—dens of dirt and misery, which would, in many instances, be shamed by an English pig-sty. The necessaries of life were described as inestimably cheap; but they forgot to add that in remote bush settlements, often twenty miles from a market town, and some of them even that distance from the nearest dwelling, the necessaries of life which would be deemed indispensable to the European, could not be procured at all, or, if obtained, could only be so by sending a man and team through a blazed forest road,—a process far too expensive for frequent repetition.

Oh, ye dealers in wild lands—ye speculators in the folly and credulity of your fellow-men—what a mass of misery, and of misrepresentation productive of that misery, have ye not to answer for! You had your acres to sell, and what to you were the worn-down frames and broken hearts of the infatuated purchasers? The public believed the plausible statements you made with such earnestness, and men of all grades rushed to hear your hired orators declaim upon the blessings to be obtained by the clearers of the wilderness.

Men who had been hopeless of supporting their families in comfort and independence at home, thought that they had only to come out to Canada to make their fortunes; almost even to realize the story told in the nursery, of the sheep and oxen that ran about the streets, ready roasted, and with knives and forks upon their backs. They were made to believe that if it did not actually rain gold, that precious metal could be obtained, as is now stated of California and Australia, by stooping to pick it up.

The infection became general. A Canada mania pervaded the middle ranks of British society; thousands and tens of thousands, for the space of three or four years, landed upon these shores. A large majority of the higher class were officers of the army and navy, with their families—a class perfectly unfitted by their previous habits and education for contending with the stern realities of emigrant life. The hand that has long held the sword, and been accustomed to receive implicit obedience from those under its control, is seldom adapted to wield the spade and guide the plough, or try its strength against the stubborn trees of the forest. Nor will such persons submit cheerfully to the saucy familiarity of servants, who, republicans in spirit, think themselves as good as their employers. Too many of these brave and honourable men were easy dupes to the designing land-speculators. Not having counted the cost, but only looked upon the bright side of the picture held up to their admiring gaze, they fell easily into the snares of their artful seducers.

To prove their zeal as colonists, they were induced to purchase large tracts of wild land in remote and unfavourable situations. This, while it impoverished and often proved the ruin of the unfortunate immigrant, possessed a double advantage to the seller. He obtained an exorbitant price for the land which he actually sold, while the residence of a respectable settler upon the spot greatly enhanced the value and price of all other lands in the neighbourhood.

It is not by such instruments as those I have just mentioned, that Providence works when it would reclaim the waste places of the earth, and make them subservient to the wants and happiness of its creatures. The Great Father of the souls and bodies of men knows the arm which wholesome labour from infancy has made strong, the nerves which have become iron by patient endurance, by exposure to weather, coarse fare, and rude shelter; and he chooses such, to send forth into the forest to hew out the rough paths for the advance of civilisation. These men become wealthy and prosperous, and form the bones and sinews of a great and rising country. Their labour is wealth, not exhaustion; its produce independence and content, not home-sickness and despair. What the Backwoods of Canada are to the industrious and ever-to-be-honoured sons of honest poverty, and what they are to the refined and accomplished gentleman, these simple sketches will endeavour to portray. They are drawn principally from my own experience, during a sojourn of nineteen years in the colony.

In order to diversify my subject, and make it as amusing as possible, I have between the sketches introduced a few small poems, all written during my residence in Canada, and descriptive of the country.

In this pleasing task I have been assisted by my husband, J.W. Dunbar Moodie, author of 'Ten Years in South Africa'.[2]

BELLEVILLE, UPPER CANADA

1854

2 Published in 1835, the story of Dunbar Moodie's years (1819–29) with his brother at his farm near Swellendam, South Africa.

## I. A VISIT TO GROSSE ISLE

\*   \*   \*

As the sun rose above the horizon, all these matter-of-fact circumstances were gradually forgotten and merged in the surpassing grandeur of the scene that rose majestically before me. The previous day had been dark and stormy; and a heavy fog had concealed the mountain chain, which forms the stupendous background to this sublime view, entirely from our sight. As the clouds rolled away from their grey, bald brows, and cast into denser shadow the vast forest belt that girdled them round, they loomed out like mighty giants—Titans of the earth, in all their rugged and awful beauty—a thrill of wonder and delight pervaded my mind. The spectacle floated dimly on my sight—my eyes were blinded with tears—blinded with the excess of beauty. I turned to the right and to the left, I looked up and down the glorious river; never had I beheld so many striking objects blended into one mighty whole! Nature had lavished all her noblest features in producing that enchanting scene.

The rocky isle in front, with its neat farm-houses at the eastern point, and its high bluff at the western extremity, crowned with the telegraph—the middle space occupied by tents and sheds for the cholera patients, and its wooded shores dotted over with motley groups—added greatly to the picturesque effect of the land scene. Then the broad glittering river, covered with boats darting to and fro, conveying passengers from twenty-five vessels, of various size and tonnage, which rode at anchor, with their flags flying from the mast-head, gave an air of life and interest to the whole. Turning to the south side of the St Lawrence, I was not less struck with its low fertile shores, white houses, and neat churches, whose slender spires and bright tin roofs shone like silver as they caught the first rays of the sun. As far as the eye could reach, a line of white buildings extended along the bank; their background formed by the purple hue of the dense, interminable forest. It was a scene unlike any I had ever beheld, and to which Britain contains no parallel. Mackenzie, an old Scotch dragoon, who was one of our passengers, when he rose in the morning and saw the parish of St Thomas for the first time, exclaimed: 'Weel, it beats a'! Can thae white clouts[1] be a' houses? They look like claes hung out to drie!' There was some truth in this odd comparison, and for some minutes I could scarcely convince myself that the white patches scattered so thickly over the opposite shore could be the dwellings of a busy, lively population.

'What sublime views of the north side of the river those *habitans* of St Thomas must enjoy,' thought I. Perhaps familiarity with the scene has rendered them indifferent to its astonishing beauty.

Eastward, the view down the St Lawrence towards the Gulf is the finest of all, scarcely surpassed by anything in the world. Your eye follows the long range of lofty mountains until their blue summits are blended and lost in the blue of the sky. Some of these, partially cleared round the base, are sprinkled over with neat cottages, and the green slopes that spread around them are covered with flocks and herds. The surface of the splendid river is diversified with islands of every size and shape, some in wood, others partially cleared, and adorned with orchards and white farm-houses. As the early sun streamed upon the most prominent of these, leaving the others in deep shade, the effect was strangely novel and imposing. In more remote regions, where the forest has never yet echoed to the woodman's axe, or received the impress of civilisation, the first approach to the shore inspires a melancholy awe which becomes painful in its intensity.

> Land of vast hills, and mighty streams,
> The lofty sun that o'er thee beams
> On fairer clime sheds not his ray,

---

1 Cloths; 'claes', clothes.

When basking in the noon of day
Thy waters dance in silver light,
And o'er them frowning, dark as night,
Thy shadowy forests, soaring high,
Stretch forth beyond the aching eye,
And blend in distance with the sky.

And silence—awful silence broods
Profoundly o'er these solitudes;
Not but the lapsing of the floods
Breaks the deep stillness of the woods;
A sense of desolation reigns
O'er these unpeopled forest plains
Where sounds of life ne'er wake a tone
Of cheerful praise round Nature's throne,
Man finds himself with God—alone.

My daydreams were dispelled by the return of the boat, which brought my husband and the captain from the island.

'No bread,' said the latter, shaking his head; 'you must be content to starve a little longer. Provision-ship not in till four o'clock.' My husband smiled at the look of blank disappointment with which I received these unwelcome tidings. 'Never mind, I have news which will comfort you. The officer who commands the station sent a note to me by an orderly, inviting us to spend the afternoon with him. He promises to show us everything worthy of notice on the island. Captain ——— claims acquaintance with me; but I have not the least recollection of him. Would you like to go?'

'Oh, by all means. I long to see the lovely island. It looks a perfect paradise at this distance.'

The rough sailor-captain screwed his mouth on one side, and give me one of his comical looks; but he said nothing until he assisted in placing me and the baby in the boat.

'Don't be too sanguine, Mrs Moodie; many things look well at a distance which are bad enough when near.'

I scarcely regarded the old sailor's warning, so eager was I to go on shore—to put my foot upon the soil of the new world for the first time. I was in no humour to listen to any depreciation of what seemed so beautiful.

It was four o'clock when we landed on the rocks, which the rays of an intensely scorching sun had rendered so hot that I could scarcely place my foot upon them. How the people without shoes bore it I cannot imagine. Never shall I forget the extraordinary spectacle that met our sight the moment we passed the low range of bushes which formed a screen in front of the river. A crowd of many hundred Irish emigrants had been landed during the present and former day and all this motley crew—men, women, and children, who were not confined by sickness to the sheds (which greatly resembled cattle-pens)— were employed in washing clothes or spreading them out on the rocks and bushes to dry.

The men and boys were *in* the water, while the women, with their scanty garments tucked above their knees, were tramping their bedding in tubs or in holes in the rocks, which the retiring tide had left half full of water. Those who did not possess washing tubs, pails, or iron pots, or could not obtain access to a hole in the rocks, were running to and fro, screaming and scolding in no measured terms. The confusion of Babel was among them. All talkers and no hearers—each shouting and yelling in his or her uncouth dialect, and all accompanying their vociferations with violent and extra-ordinary gestures, quite incomprehensible to the uninitiated. We were literally stunned by the strife of tongues. I shrank, with feelings almost akin to fear, from the hard-featured, sun-burnt harpies as they elbowed rudely past me.

I had heard and read much of savages, and have since seen, during my long residence in the bush, somewhat uncivilised life; but the Indian is one of Nature's gentlemen—he never says or does a rude or vulgar thing. The vicious, uneducated bar-barians, who form the surplus of overpopulous European countries, are far behind the wild man in delicacy of feeling or natural courtesy. The people who covered the island appeared perfectly destitute of shame, or even a sense of common decency. Many were almost naked, still more but partially clothed. We turned in disgust from the revolting scene, but were unable to leave the spot until the captain had satisfied a noisy group of his own people, who were demanding a supply of stores.

And here I must observe that our passengers, who were chiefly honest Scotch labourers and mechanics from the vicinity of Edinburgh, and who while on board ship had conducted themselves with the greatest propriety, and appeared the most quiet, orderly set of people in the world, no sooner set foot upon the island than they became infected by the same spirit of insubordination and misrule, and were just as insolent and noisy as the rest.

While our captain was vainly endeavouring to satisfy the unreasonable demands of his rebellious people, Moodie had discovered a woodland path that led to the back of the island. Sheltered by some hazel-bushes from the intense heat of the sun, we sat down by the cool, gushing river, out of sight, but, alas! not out of hearing of the noisy, riotous crowd. Could we have shut out the profane sounds which came to us on every breeze, how deeply should we have enjoyed an hour amid the tranquil beauties of that retired and lovely spot!

The rocky banks of the island were adorned with beautiful evergreens, which sprang up spontaneously in every nook and crevice. I remarked many of our favourite garden shrubs among these wildings of nature: the fillagree, with its narrow, dark glossy-green leaves; the privet, with its modest white blossoms and purple berries; the lignum-vitae, with its strong resinous odour; the burnet rose; and a great variety of ele-gant unknowns.

Here, the shores of the island and mainland, receding from each other, formed a small cove, overhung with lofty trees, clothed from the base to the summit with wild vines, that hung in graceful festoons from the topmost branches to the water's edge. The dark shadows of the mountains, thrown upon the water, as they towered to the height of some thousand feet above us, gave to the surface of the river an ebon hue. The sunbeams, dancing through the thick, quivering foliage, fell in stars of gold, or long lines of dazzling brightness, upon the deep black waters, producing the most novel and beautiful effects. It was a scene over which the spirit of peace might brood in silent adoration; but how spoiled by the discordant yells of the filthy beings who were sullying the purity of the air and water with contaminating sights and sounds!

We were now joined by the sergeant, who very kindly brought us his capful of ripe plums and hazelnuts, the growth of the island: a joyful present, but marred by a note from Captain ———, who had found that he had been mistaken in his supposed knowledge of us, and politely apologized for not being allowed by the health-officers to receive any emigrant beyond the bounds appointed for the performance of quarantine.

I was deeply disappointed, but my husband laughingly told me that I had seen enough of the island, and, turning to the good-natured soldier, remarked that 'it could be no easy task to keep such wild savages in order.'

'You may well say that, sir—but our night scenes far exceed those of the day. You would think they were incarnate devils, singing, drinking, dancing, shouting, and cutting antics that would surprise the leader of a circus. They have no shame—are under no restraint—nobody knows them here, and they think they can speak and act as they please; and they are such thieves that they rob one another of the little they possess. The healthy actually run the risk of taking the cholera by robbing the sick. If you have not hired one or two stout, honest fellows from among your fellow-passengers to guard your clothes while they are drying, you will never see half of them again. They are a sad set, sir, a sad set. We could, perhaps, manage the men; but the women, sir!—the women! Oh, sir!'

Anxious as we were to return to the ship, we were obliged to remain until sundown in our retired nook. We were hungry, tired, and out of spirits; the mosquitoes swarmed in myriads around us, tormenting the poor baby, who, not at all pleased with her visit to the new world, filled the air with cries, when the captain came to tell us that the boat was ready. It was a welcome sound. Forcing our way once more through the still squabbling crowd, we gained the landing place. Here we encountered a boat, just landing a fresh cargo of emigrants from the Emerald Isle. One fellow, of gigantic proportions, whose long, tattered great-coat just reached below the middle of his bare red legs and, like charity, hid the defects of his other garments, or perhaps concealed his want of them, leaped upon the rocks, and flourishing aloft his shilelagh, bounded and capered like a wild goat from his native mountains. 'Whurrah! my boys!' he cried. 'Shure we'll all be jintlemen!'

'Pull away, my lads!' said the captain. Then turning to me, 'Well, Mrs Moodie, I hope that you have had enough of Grosse Isle. But could you have witnessed the scenes that I did this morning—'

Here he was interrupted by the wife of the old Scotch dragoon, Mackenzie, running down to the boat and laying her hand familiarly upon his shoulder, 'Captain, dinna forget.'

'Forget what?'

She whispered something confidentially in his ear.

'Oh, ho! the brandy!' he responded aloud. 'I should have thought, Mrs Mackenzie, that you had had enough of *that same* on yon island?'

'Aye, sic a place for *decent* folk,' returned the drunken body, shaking her head. 'One needs a drap o'comfort, captain, to keep up one's heart avá.'[2]

The captain set up one of his boisterous laughs as he pushed the boat from the shore. 'Hello! Sam Frazer! steer in, we have forgotten the stores.'

'I hope not, captain,' said I; 'I have been starving since daybreak.'

'The bread, the butter, the beef, the onions, and potatoes are here, sir,' said honest Sam, particularizing each article.

'All right; pull for the ship. Mrs Moodie, we will have a glorious supper, and mind you don't dream of Grosse Isle.'

In a few minutes we were again on board. Thus ended my first day's experience of the land of all our hopes.

2 At all.

*       *       *

[*Leaving Montreal, the Moodies travelled by steamboat to Cobourg, Upper Canada (Ontario), near Peterborough. There they purchased a farm that had been lost by a bankrupt Loyalist identified as 'Old Joe R——' (called Uncle Joe in the next chapter). Though the purchase was concluded in the September following the Moodies' arrival, they were prevented from occupying their new home immediately by an agreement allowing Joe and his family to remain in the house (while his mother lived in a nearby shanty) until 'the commencement of sleighing'. Until then the Moodies were to live in an adjoining farm in 'a small dilapidated log tenement', which they rented from an especially untrustworthy Loyalist known as Old Satan.*]

## 8. UNCLE JOE AND HIS FAMILY

Ay, your rogue is a laughing rogue, and not a whit the less dangerous for the smile on his lip, which comes not from an honest heart, which reflects the light of the soul through the eye. All is hollow and dark within; and the contortion of the lip, like the prehistoric glow upon decayed timber, only serves to point out the rottenness within.

Uncle Joe! I see him now before me, with his jolly red face, twinkling black eyes, and rubicund nose. No thin, weasel-faced Yankee was he, looking as if he had lived upon 'cute[1] ideas and speculations all his life; yet Yankee he was by birth, ay, and in mind, too; for a more knowing fellow at a bargain never crossed the lakes to abuse British institutions and locate himself comfortably among the despised Britishers. But, then, he had such a good-natured, fat face, such a mischievous, mirth-loving smile, and such a merry, roguish expression in those small, jet-black, glittering eyes, that you

1 Acute, cunning.

suffered yourself to be taken in by him, without offering the least resistance to his impositions.

Uncle Joe's father had been a New England loyalist, and his doubtful attachment to the British government had been repaid by a grant of land in the township of H——. He was the first settler in that township, and chose his location in a remote spot, for the sake of a beautiful natural spring, which bubbled up in a small stone basin in the green bank at the back of the house.

'Father might have had the pick of the township,' quoth Uncle Joe; 'but the old coon preferred that sup of good water to the site of a town. Well, I guess it's seldom I trouble the spring; and whenever I step that way to water the horses, I think what a tarnation fool the old one was, to throw away such a chance of making his fortune for such cold lap.'[2]

'Your father was a temperance man?'[3]

'Temperance!—He had been fond enough of the whiskey bottle in his day. He drank up a good farm in the United States, and then he thought he could not do better than turn loyal, and get one here for nothing. He did not care a cent, not he, for the King of England. He thought himself as good, anyhow. But he found that he would have to work hard here to scratch along, and he was mightily plagued with the rheumatics, and some old woman told him that good spring water was the best cure for that; so he chose this poor, light, stony land on account of the spring, and took to hard work and drinking cold water in his old age.'

'How did the change agree with him?'

'I guess better than could have been expected. He planted that fine orchard, and cleared his hundred acres, and we got along slick enough as long as the old fellow lived.'

'And what happened after his death, that obliged you to part with your land?'

'Bad times—bad crops,' said Uncle Joe, lifting his shoulders. 'I had not my father's way of scraping money together. I made some deuced clever speculations, but they all failed. I married young, and got a large family; and the women critters ran up heavy bills at the stores, and the crops did not yield enough to pay them; and from bad we got to worse, and Mr C——put in an execution,[4] and seized upon the whole concern. He sold it to your man for double what it cost him; and you got all that my father toiled for during the last twenty years of his life for less than half the cash he laid out upon clearing it.'

'And had the whiskey nothing to do with this change?' said I, looking him in the face suspiciously.

'Not a bit! When a man gets into difficulties, it is the only thing to keep him from sinking outright. When your husband has had as many troubles as I have had, he will know how to value the whiskey bottle.'

This conversation was interrupted by a queer-looking urchin of five years old, dressed in a long-tailed coat and trowsers, popping his black shock head in at the door, and calling out,

2 Weak drink.
3 A man advocating abstinence from liquor, or one who has sworn to abstain.
4 The seizure of goods under law in default of payment.

'Uncle Joe!—You're wanted to hum.'[5]

'Is that your nephew?'

'No! I guess 'tis my woman's eldest son,' said Uncle Joe, rising, 'but they call me Uncle Joe. 'Tis a spry chap that—as cunning as a fox. I tell you what it is—he will make a smart man. Go home, Ammon, and tell your ma that I am coming.'

'I won't,' said the boy; 'you may go hum and tell her yourself. She has wanted wood cut this hour, and you'll catch it!'

Away ran the dutiful son, but not before he had applied his forefinger significantly to the side of his nose, and, with a knowing wink, pointed in the direction of home.

Uncle Joe obeyed the signal, drily remarking that he could not leave the barn door without the old hen clucking him back.

At this period we were still living in Old Satan's log house, and anxiously looking out for the first snow to put us in possession of the good substantial log dwelling occupied by Uncle Joe and his family, which consisted of a brown brood of seven girls, and the highly prized boy who rejoiced in the extraordinary name of Ammon.

Strange names are to be found in this free country. What think you, gentle reader, of *Solomon Sly*, *Reynard Fox*, and *Hiram Dolittle*; all veritable names, and belonging to substantial yeomen? After Ammon and Ichabod,[6] I should not be at all surprised to meet with Judas Iscariot, Pilate, and Herod. And then the female appellations! But the subject is a delicate one, and I will forbear to touch upon it. I have enjoyed many a hearty laugh over the strange affectations which people designate here *very handsome names*. I prefer the old homely Jewish names, such as that which it pleased my godfather and godmothers to bestow upon me, to one of those high-sounding christianities, the Minervas, Cinderellas, and Almerias of Canada. The love of singular names is here carried to a marvellous extent. It is only yesterday that, in passing through one busy village, I stopped in astonishment before a tombstone headed thus:—'Sacred to the memory of *Silence* Sharman, the beloved wife of Asa Sharman.' Was the woman deaf and dumb, or did her friends hope by bestowing upon her such an impossible name to still the voice of Nature, and check, by an admonitory appellative, the active spirit that lives in the tongue of woman? Truly, Asa Sharman, if thy wife was silent by name as well as by nature, thou wert a fortunate man!

But to return to Uncle Joe. He made many fair promises of leaving the residence we had bought, the moment he had sold his crops and could remove his family. We could see no interest which could be served by his deceiving us, and therefore we believed him, striving to make ourselves as comfortable as we could in the meantime in our present wretched abode. But matters are never so bad but that they may be worse. One day when we were at dinner, a waggon drove up to the door, and Mr ———— alighted, accompanied by a fine-looking, middle-aged man, who proved to be Captain

5  At home.

6  Ammon is the name of a Biblical land inhabited by a warlike people with whom the Israelites came into conflict. Ichabod can be found in 1 Samuel 4:21: 'She named the child Ichabod, meaning "The glory has departed from Israel, for the ark of God had been captured."' Moodie's point is that names from the Old Testament are being used without consideration of their negative connotations, as foolish in its way as would be using those of New Testament villains such as Judas, Pilate, and Herod.

S——, who had just arrived from Demerara[7] with his wife and family. Mr ——, who had purchased the farm of Old Satan, had brought Captain S—— over to inspect the land, as he wished to buy a farm, and settle in that neighbourhood. With some difficulty, I contrived to accommodate the visitors with seats, and provide them with a tolerable dinner. Fortunately, Moodie had brought in a brace of fine fat partridges that morning; these the servant transferred to a pot of boiling water, in which she immersed them for the space of a minute—a novel but very expeditious way of removing the feathers, which then come off at the least touch. In less than ten minutes they were stuffed, trussed, and in the bake-kettle; and before the gentlemen returned from walking over the farm, the dinner was on the table.

To our utter consternation, Captain S—— agreed to purchase, and asked if we could give him possession in a week!

'Good heavens!' cried I, glancing reproachfully at Mr ——, who was discussing[8] his partridge with stoical indifference. 'What will become of us? Where are we to go?'

'Oh, make yourself easy; I will force that old witch, Joe's mother, to clear out.'

'But 'tis impossible to stow ourselves into that pig-sty.'

'It will only be for a week or two, at farthest. This is October; Joe will be sure to be off by the first of sleighing.'

'But if she refuses to give up the place?'

'Oh, leave her to me. I'll talk her over,' said the knowing land speculator. 'Let it come to the worst,' he said, turning to my husband, 'she will go out for the sake of a few dollars. By-the-by, she refused to bar the dower[9] when I bought the place; we must cajole her out of that. It is a fine afternoon; suppose we walk over the hill, and try our luck with the old nigger?'

I felt so anxious about the result of the negotiation, that, throwing my cloak over my shoulders, and tying on my bonnet without assistance of a glass, I took my husband's arm, and we walked forth.

It was a bright, clear afternoon, the first week in October, and the fading woods, not yet denuded of their gorgeous foliage, glowed in a mellow, golden light. A soft, purple haze rested on the bold outline of the Haldemand hills, and in the rugged beauty of the wild landscape I soon forgot the purport of our visit to the old woman's log hut.

On reaching the ridge of the hill, the lovely valley in which our future home lay smiled peacefully upon us from amidst its fruitful orchards, still loaded with their rich, ripe fruit.

'What a pretty place it is!' thought I, for the first time feeling something like a local interest in the spot springing up in my heart. 'How I wish those odious people would give us possession of the home which for some time has been our own!'

The log hut that we were approaching, and in which the old woman, H——, resided, by herself—having quarrelled years ago with her son's wife—was of the smallest dimensions, only containing one room, which served the old dame for kitchen, and

---

7 British Guiana.
8 Consuming (humorous).
9 Void her right to legal tenancy. Joe had inherited the land from his father, but his mother had use of it during her lifetime.

bed-room, and all. The open door, and a few glazed panes, supplied it with light and air; while a huge hearth, on which crackled two enormous logs—which are technically termed a front and a back stick—took up nearly half the domicile; and the old woman's bed, which was covered with an unexceptionably clean patched quilt, nearly the other half, leaving just room for a small home-made deal[10] table, of the rudest workmanship, two basswood-bottomed chairs, stained red, one of which was a rocking-chair, appropriated solely to the old woman's use, and a spinning-wheel. Amidst this muddle of things—for, small as was the quantum of furniture, it was all crowded into such a tiny space that you had to squeeze your way through it in the best manner you could—we found the old woman, with a red cotton handkerchief tied over her grey locks, hood-fashion, shelling white bush-beans into a wooden bowl. Without rising from her seat, she pointed to the only remaining chair. 'I guess, miss, you can sit there; and if the others can't stand, they can make a seat of my bed.'

The gentlemen assured her that they were not tired, and could dispense with seats. Mr ——— then went up to the old woman, and proffering his hand, asked after her health in his blandest manner.

'I'm none the better for seeing you, or the like of you,' was the ungracious reply. 'You have cheated my poor boy out of his good farm; and I hope it may prove a bad bargain to you and yours.'

'Mrs H———,' returned the land speculator, nothing ruffled by her unceremonious greeting, 'I could not help your son giving way to drink, and getting into my debt. If people will be so imprudent, they cannot be so stupid as to imagine that others can suffer for their folly.'

'*Suffer!*' repeated the old woman, flashing her small, keen black eyes upon him with a glance of withering scorn. 'You suffer! I wonder what the widows and orphans you have cheated would say to that! My son was a poor, silly fool to be sucked in by the like of you. For a debt of eight hundred dollars—the goods never cost you four hundred—you take from us our good farm; and these, I s'pose,' pointing to my husband and me, 'are the folk you sold it to. Pray, miss,' turning quickly to me, 'what might your man give for the place?'

'Three hundred pounds in cash.'

'Poor sufferer!' again sneered the hag. 'Four hundred dollars is a very *small* profit in as many weeks. Well, I guess, you beat the Yankees hollow. And pray, what brought you here to-day, scenting about you like a carrion-crow? We have no more land for you to seize from us.'

Moodie now stepped forward, and briefly explained our situation, offering the old woman anything in reason to give up the cottage and reside with her son until he removed from the premises; which, he added, must be in a very short time.

The old dame regarded him with a sarcastic smile. 'I guess, Joe will take his own time. The house is not built which is to receive him; and he is not a man to turn his back upon a warm hearth to camp in the wilderness. You were *green* when you bought a farm of that man, without getting along with it the right of possession.'[11]

10 Pine wood.
11 Right of occupancy as distinguished from ownership.

'But, Mrs H——, your son promised to go out the first of sleighing.'

'Wheugh!' said the old woman. 'Would you have a man give away his hat and leave his own head bare? It's neither the first snow nor the last frost that will turn Joe out of his comfortable home. I tell you that he will stay here, if it is only to plague you.'

Threats and remonstrances were alike useless, the old woman remained inexorable; and we were just turning to leave the house, when the cunning old fox exclaimed, 'And now, what will you give me to leave my place?'

'Twelve dollars, if you give us possession next Monday,' said my husband.

'Twelve dollars! I guess you won't get me out for that.'

'The rent would not be worth more than a dollar a month,' said Mr ——, pointing with his cane to the dilapidated walls. 'Mr Moodie has offered you a year's rent for the place.'

'It may not be worth a cent,' returned the woman, 'for it will give everybody the rheumatism that stays a week in it—but it is worth that to me, and more nor[12] double that just now to him. But I will not be hard with him,' continued she, rocking herself to and fro. 'Say twenty dollars, and I will turn out on Monday.'

'I dare say you will,' said Mr ——, 'and who do you think would be fool enough to give you such an exorbitant sum for a ruined old shed like this?'

'Mind your own business, and make your own bargains,' returned the old woman, tartly. 'The devil himself could not deal with you, for I guess he would have the worst of it. What do you say sir?' and she fixed her keen eyes upon my husband, as if she would read his thought. 'Will you agree to my price?'

'It is a very high one, Mrs H——; but as I cannot help myself, and you take advantage of that, I suppose I must give it.'

''Tis a bargain,' cried the old crone, holding out her hard, bony hand. 'Come, cash down!'

'Not until you give me possession on Monday next; or you might serve me as your son has done.'

'Ha!' said the old woman, laughing and rubbing her hands together; 'you begin to see daylight, do you? In a few months, with the help of him', pointing to Mr ——, 'you will be able to go alone; but have a care of your teacher, for it's no good that you will learn from him. But will you *really* stand to your word, mister?' she added, in a coaxing tone, 'if I go out on Monday?'

'To be sure I will; I never break my word.'

'Well, I guess you are not so clever as our people, for they only keep it as long as it suits them. You have an honest look; I will trust you; but I will not trust him,' nodding to Mr ——, 'he can buy and sell his word as fast as a horse can trot. So on Monday I will turn out my traps. I have lived here six-and-thirty years; 'tis a pretty place, and it vexes me to leave it,' continued the poor creature, as a touch of natural feeling softened and agitated her world-hardened heart. 'There is not an acre in cultivation but I helped to clear it, nor a tree in yonder orchard but I held it while my poor man, who is dead and gone, planted it; and I have watched the trees bud from year to year, until their

12 Than.

boughs over-shadowed the hut, where all my children, but Joe, were born. Yes, I came here young, and in my prime; and must leave it in age and poverty. My children and husband are dead, and their bones rest beneath the turf in the burying-ground on the side of the hill. Of all that once gathered about my knees, Joe and his young ones alone remain. And it is hard, very hard, that I must leave their graves to be turned by the plough of a stranger.'

I felt for the desolate old creature—the tears rushed to my eyes; but there was no moisture in hers. No rain from the heart could filter through that iron soil.

'Be assured, Mrs H——,' said Moodie, 'that the dead will be held sacred; the place will never be disturbed by me.'

'Perhaps not; but it is not long that you will remain here. I have seen a good deal in my time; but I never saw a gentleman from the old country make a good Canadian farmer. The work is rough and hard, and they get out of humour with it, and leave it to their hired helps, and then all goes wrong. They are cheated on all sides, and in despair take to the whiskey bottle, and that fixes them. I tell you what it is, mister— I give you just three years to spend your money and ruin yourself; and then you will become a confirmed drunkard, like the rest.'

The first part of her prophecy was only too true. Thank God! the last has never been fulfilled, and never can be.

Perceiving that the old woman was not a little elated with her bargain, Mr —— urged upon her the propriety of barring the dower. At first, she was outrageous, and very abusive, and rejected all his proposals with contempt; vowing that she would meet him in a certain place below, before she would sign away her right to the property.

'Listen to reason, Mrs H——,' said the land speculator. 'If you will sign the papers before the proper authorities, the next time that your son drives you to C——, I will give you a silk gown.'

'Pshaw! Buy a shroud for yourself; you will need it before I want a silk gown,' was the ungracious reply.

'Consider, woman; a black silk of the best quality.'

'To mourn in for my sins, or for the loss of the farm?'

'Twelve yards,' continued Mr ——, without noticing her rejoinder, 'at a dollar a yard. Think what a nice church-going gown it will make.'

'To the devil with you! I never go to church.'

'I thought as much,' said Mr ——, winking to us. 'Well, my dear madam, what will satisfy you?'

'I'll do it for twenty dollars,' returned the old woman, rocking herself to and fro in her chair; her eyes twinkling, and her hands moving convulsively, as if she already grasped the money so dear to her soul.

'Agreed,' said the land speculator. 'When will you be in town?'

'On Tuesday, if I be alive. But, remember, I'll not sign till I have my hand on the money.'

'Never fear,' said Mr ——, as we quitted the house; then, turning to me, he added, with a peculiar smile, 'That's a devilish smart woman. She would have made a clever lawyer.'

Monday came, and with it all the bustle of moving, and, as is generally the case on such occasions, it turned out a very wet day. I left Old Satan's hut without regret, glad, at any rate, to be in a place of my own, however humble. Our new habitation, though small, had a decided advantage over the one we were leaving. It stood on a gentle slope; and a narrow but lovely stream, full of speckled trout, ran murmuring under the little window; the house, also, was surrounded by fine fruit trees.

I know not how it was, but the sound of that tinkling brook, for ever rolling by, filled my heart with a strange melancholy, which for many nights deprived me of rest. I loved it, too. The voice of waters, in the stillness of night, always had an extraordinary effect upon my mind. Their ceaseless motion and perpetual sound convey to me the idea of life—eternal life; and looking upon them, glancing and flashing on, now in sunshine, now in shade, now hoarsely chiding with the opposing rock, now leaping triumphantly over it,—creates within me a feeling of mysterious awe of which I never could wholly divest myself.

A portion of my own spirit seemed to pass into that little stream. In its deep wailings and fretful sighs, I fancied myself lamenting for the land I had left for ever; and its restless and impetuous rushings against the stones which choked its passage, were mournful types of my own mental struggles against the strange destiny which hemmed me in. Through the day the stream still moaned and travelled on,—but, engaged in my novel and distasteful occupations, I heard it not; but whenever my winged thoughts flew homeward, then the voice of the brook spoke deeply and sadly to my heart, and my tears flowed unchecked to its plaintive and harmonious music.

In a few hours I had my new abode more comfortably arranged than the old one, although its dimensions were much smaller. The location was beautiful, and I was greatly consoled by this circumstance. The aspect of Nature ever did, and I hope ever will, continue—

'To shoot marvellous strength into my heart'.[13]

As long as we remain true to the Divine Mother, so long will she remain faithful to her suffering children.

At that period my love for Canada was a feeling very nearly allied to that which the condemned criminal entertains for his cell—his only hope of escape being through the portals of the grave.

The fall rains had commenced. In a few days the cold wintry showers swept all the gorgeous crimson from the trees, and a bleak and desolate waste presented itself to the shuddering spectator. But, in spite of wind and rain, my little tenement was never free from the intrusion of Uncle Joe's wife and children. Their house stood about a stone's-throw from the hut we occupied, in the same meadow, and they seemed to look upon it still as their own, although we had literally paid for it twice over. Fine strapping girls

13 Moodie is recasting a passage from Coleridge's verse-drama 'The Death of Wallenstein: "If I but saw him, 'twould be well with me. / He, is the star of my nativity, / And often marvellously hath his aspect / Shot strength into my heart"' (V. i. 33–6).

they were, from five years old to fourteen, but rude and unnurtured as so many bears. They would come in without the least ceremony, and, young as they were, ask me a thousand impertinent questions; and when I civilly requested them to leave the room, they would range themselves upon the door-step, watching my motions, with their black eyes gleaming upon me through their tangled, uncombed locks. Their company was a great annoyance, for it obliged me to put a painful restraint upon the thoughtfulness in which it was so delightful to me to indulge. Their visits were not visits of love, but of mere idle curiosity, not unmingled with malicious hatred.

The simplicity, the fond, confiding faith of childhood is unknown in Canada. There are no children here. The boy is a miniature man—knowing, keen, and wide awake; as able to drive a bargain and take an advantage of his juvenile companion as the grown-up, world-hardened man. The girl, a gossipping flirt, full of vanity and affectation, with a premature love of finery, and an acute perception of the advantages to be derived from wealth, and from keeping up a certain appearance in the world.

The flowers, the green grass, the glorious sunshine, the birds of the air, and the young lambs gambolling down the verdant slopes, which fill the heart of the British child with a fond ecstacy, bathing the young spirit in Elysium, would float unnoticed before the vision of a Canadian child; while the sight of a dollar, or a new dress, or a gay bonnet, would swell its proud bosom with self-importance and delight. The glorious blush of modest diffidence, the tear of gentle sympathy, are so rare on the cheek, or in the eye of the young, that their appearance creates a feeling of surprise. Such perfect self-reliance in beings so new to the world is painful to a thinking mind. It betrays a great want of sensibility and mental culture, and a melancholy knowledge of the arts of life.

For a week I was alone, my good Scotch girl having left me to visit her father. Some small baby-articles were needed to be washed, and after making a great preparation, I determined to try my unskilled hand upon the operation. The fact is, I knew nothing about the task I had imposed upon myself, and in a few minutes rubbed the skin off my wrists without getting the clothes clean.

The door was open, as it generally was, even during the coldest winter days, in order to let in more light, and let out the smoke, which otherwise would have enveloped us like a cloud. I was so busy that I did not perceive that I was watched by the cold, heavy, dark eyes of Mrs Joe, who, with a sneering laugh, exclaimed,

'Well, thank God! I am glad to see you brought to work at last. I hope you may have to work as hard as I have. I don't see, not I, why you, who are no better than me, should sit still all day, like a lady!'

'Mrs H——,' said I, not a little annoyed at her presence, 'what concern is it of yours whether I work or sit still? I never interfere with you. If you took it into your head to lie in bed all day, I should never trouble myself about it.'

'Ah, I guess you don't look upon us as fellow-critters, you are so proud and grand. I s'pose you Britishers are not made of flesh and blood, like us. You don't choose to sit down at meat with your helps. Now, I calculate, we think them a great deal better nor you.'

'Of course,' said I, 'they are more suited to you than we are; they are uneducated, and so are you. This is no fault in either; but it might teach you to pay a little more respect to those who are possessed of superior advantages. But, Mrs H——, my helps, as you call them, are civil and obliging, and never make unprovoked and malicious speeches. If they could so far forget themselves, I should order them to leave the house.'

'Oh, I see what you are up to,' replied the insolent dame; 'you mean to say that if I were your help, you would turn me out of your house; but I'm a free-born American, and I won't go at your bidding. Don't think I come here out of regard to you. No, I hate you all; and I rejoice to see you at the wash-tub, and I wish that you may be brought down upon your knees to scrub the floors.'

This speech caused a smile, and yet I felt hurt and astonished that a woman whom I had never done anything to offend should be so gratuitously spiteful.

In the evening she sent two of her brood over to borrow my 'long iron', as she called an Italian iron.[14] I was just getting my baby to sleep, sitting upon a low stool by the fire. I pointed to the iron upon the shelf, and told the girl to take it. She did so, but stood beside me, holding it carelessly in her hand, and staring at the baby, who had just sunk to sleep upon my lap.

The next moment the heavy iron fell from her relaxed grasp, giving me a severe blow upon my knee and foot; and glanced so near the child's head that it drew from me a cry of terror.

'I guess that was nigh braining the child,' quoth Miss Amanda, with the greatest coolness, and without making the least apology. Master Ammon burst into a loud laugh. 'If it had, Mandy, I guess we'd have cotched it.' Provoked at their insolence, I told them to leave the house. The tears were in my eyes, for I felt certain that had they injured the child, it would not have caused them the least regret.

The next day, as we were standing at the door, my husband was greatly amused by seeing fat Uncle Joe chasing the rebellious Ammon over the meadow in front of the house. Joe was out of breath, panting and puffing like a small steam-engine, and his face flushed to deep red with excitement and passion.

'You ———— young scoundrel!' he cried, half choked with fury, 'if I catch up to you, I'll take the skin off you!'

'You ———— old scoundrel, you may have my skin if you can get at me,' retorted the precocious child, as he jumped up upon the top of the high fence, and doubled his fist in a menacing manner at his father.

'That boy is growing too bad,' said Uncle Joe, coming up to us out of breath, the perspiration streaming down his face. 'It is time to break him in, or he'll get the master of us all.'

'You should have begun that before,' said Moodie. 'He seems a hopeful pupil.'

'Oh, as to that, a little swearing is manly,' returned the father; 'I swear myself, I know, and as the old cock crows, so crows the young one. It is not his swearing that I care a pin for, but he will not do a thing I tell him to.'

---

14 An iron of a special shape for pressing clothes. In Chapter 5, 'Our First Settlement, & the Borrowing System', Moodie describes how this woman perpetually borrowed items: 'Day after day I was tormented by this importunate creature; she borrowed of me tea, sugar, candles, starch, blueing, irons, pots, bowls—in short, every article in common domestic use—while it was with utmost difficulty we could get them returned. . . . This method of living upon their neighbours is a most convenient one to unprincipled people.'

'Swearing is a dreadful vice,' said I, 'and, wicked as it is in the mouth of a grown-up person, it is perfectly shocking in a child; it painfully tells he has been brought up without the fear of God.'

'Pooh! pooh! that's all cant; there is no harm in a few oaths, and I cannot drive oxen and horses without swearing. I dare say that you can swear, too, when you are riled, but you are too cunning to let us hear you.'

I could not help laughing outright at this supposition, but replied very quietly, 'Those who practise such iniquities never take any pains to conceal them. The concealment would infer a feeling of shame; and when people are conscious of their guilt, they are in the road to improvement.' The man walked whistling away, and the wicked child returned unpunished to his home.

The next minute the old woman came in. 'I guess you can give me a piece of silk for a hood,' said she, 'the weather is growing considerable cold.'

'Surely it cannot well be colder than it is at present,' said I, giving her the rocking-chair by the fire.

'Wait a while; you know nothing of a Canadian winter. This is only November; after the Christmas thaw, you'll know something about cold. It is seven-and-thirty years ago since I and my man left the U-ni-ted States. It was called the year of the great winter. I tell you, woman, that the snow lay deep on the earth, that it blocked up all the roads, and we could drive a sleigh whither we pleased, right over the snake fences.[15] All the cleared land was one wide white level plain; it was a year of scarcity, and we were half starved; but the severe cold was far worse nor the want of provisions. A long and bitter journey we had of it; but I was young then, and pretty well used to trouble and fatigue; my man stuck to the British government. More fool he! I was an American born, and my heart was with the true cause. But his father was English, and, says he, "I'll live and die under their flag." So he dragged me from my comfortable fireside to seek a home in the far Canadian wilderness. Trouble! I guess you think you have your troubles; but what are they to mine?' She paused, took a pinch of snuff, offered me the box, sighed painfully, pushed the red handkerchief from her high, narrow, wrinkled brow, and continued:—'Joe was a baby then, and I had another helpless critter in my lap—an adopted child. My sister had died from it, and I was nursing it at the same breast with my boy. Well, we had to perform a journey of four hundred miles in an ox-cart, which carried, besides me and the children, all our household stuff. Our way lay chiefly through the forest, and we made but slow progress. Oh! what a bitter cold night it was when we reached the swampy woods where the city of Rochester now stands. The oxen were covered with icicles, and their breath sent up clouds of steam. "Nathan," says I to my man, "you must stop and kindle a fire; I am dead with cold, and I fear the babes will be frozen." We began looking about for a good spot to camp in, when I spied a light through the trees. It was a lone shanty, occupied by two French lumberers. The men were kind; they rubbed our frozen limbs with snow, and shared with us their supper and buffalo skins. On that very spot where we camped that night, where we heard nothing but the wind soughing amongst the trees, and the rushing of

15 Zigzag fences made of split rails.

the river, now stands the great city of Rochester. I went there two years ago, to the funeral of a brother. It seemed to me like a dream. Where we foddered our beasts by the shanty fire, now stands the largest hotel in the city; and my husband left this fine growing country to starve here.'

I was so much interested in the old woman's narrative—for she was really possessed of no ordinary capacity, and, though rude and uneducated, might have been a very superior person under different circumstances—that I rummaged among my stores, and soon found a piece of black silk, which I gave her for the hood she required.

The old woman examined it carefully over, smiled to herself, but, like all her people, was too proud to return a word of thanks. One gift to the family always involved another.

'Have you any cotton-batting, or black sewing-silk, to give me, to quilt it with?'

'No.'

'Humph!' returned the old dame, in a tone which seemed to contradict my assertion. She then settled herself in her chair, and, after shaking her foot a while, and fixing her piercing eyes upon me for some minutes, she commenced the following list of interrogatories:—

'Is your father alive?'

'No; he died many years ago, when I was a young girl.'

'Is your mother alive?'

'Yes.'

'What is her name?' I satisfied her on this point.

'Did she ever marry again?'

'She might have done so, but she loved her husband too well, and preferred living single.'

'Humph! We have no such notions here. What was your father?'

'A gentleman, who lived upon his own estate.'

'Did he die rich?'

'He lost the greater part of his property from being surety for another.'[16]

'That's a foolish business. My man burnt his fingers with that. And what brought you out to this poor country—you, who are no more fit for it than I am to be a fine lady?'

'The promise of a large grant of land, and the false statements we heard regarding it.'

'Do you like the country?'

'No; and I fear I never shall.'

'I thought not; for the drop is always on your cheek, the children tell me; and those young ones have keen eyes. Now, take my advice: return while your money lasts; the longer you remain in Canada the less you will like it; and when your money is all spent, you will be like a bird in a cage; you may beat your wings against the bars, but you can't get out.' There was a long pause. I hoped that my guest had sufficiently gratified her curiosity, when she again commenced:—

'How do you get your money? Do you draw it from the old country, or have you it with you in cash?'

16 Guaranteeing a loan by becoming responsible for the debt.

Provoked by her pertinacity, and seeing no end to her cross-questioning, I replied very impatiently, 'Mrs H——, is it the custom in your country to catechize strangers whenever you meet with them?'

'What do you mean?' said she, colouring, I believe, for the first time in her life.

'I mean', quoth I, 'an evil habit of asking impertinent questions.'

The old woman got up, and left the house without speaking another word.

[*During the winter of 1883 the Moodies finally moved into their new house. When spring came they brought in a man and his wife to help work the farm in return for a share of the produce. These people unfortunately proved to be untrustworthy. With them, Mrs Moodie writes, 'commenced that long series of losses and troubles to which their conduct formed the prelude'.*]

## 9. BRIAN, THE STILL-HUNTER

> O'er memory's glass I see his shadow flit,
> Though he was gathered to the silent dust
> Long years ago. A strange and wayward man,
> That shunn'd companionship, and lived apart;
> The leafy covert of the dark brown woods,
> The gleamy lakes, hid in their gloomy depths,
> Whose still, deep waters never knew the stroke
> Of cleaving oar, or echoed to the sound
> Of social life, contained for him the sum
> Of human happiness. With dog and gun
> Day after day he track'd the nimble deer
> Through all the tangled mazes of the forest.

It was early day. I was alone in the old shanty, preparing breakfast, and now and then stirring the cradle with my foot, when a tall, thin, middle-aged man walked into the house, followed by two large, strong dogs.

Placing the rifle he had carried on his shoulder in a corner of the room, he advanced to the hearth, and, without speaking, or seemingly looking at me, lighted his pipe, and commenced smoking. The dogs, after growling and snapping at the cat, who had not given the strangers a very courteous reception, sat down on the hearthstone on either side of their taciturn master, eyeing him from time to time, as if long habit had made them understand all his motions. There was a great contrast between the dogs. The one was a brindled bull dog of the largest size, the most formidable and powerful brute; the other a stag hound, tawny, deep-chested, and strong-limbed. I regarded the man and his hairy companions with silent curiosity.

He was between forty and fifty years of age; his head, nearly bald, was studded at the sides with strong, coarse, black curling hair. His features were high, his compexion brightly dark, and his eyes, in size, shape, and colour, greatly resembling the eyes of a hawk. The face itself was sorrowful and taciturn; and his thin, compressed lips looked as if they were not much accustomed to smile, or often to unclose to hold social communion with any one. He stood at the side of the huge hearth, silently smoking, his eyes bent on the fire, and now and then he patted the heads of his dogs, reproving their exuberant expressions of attachment with—'Down, Music, down, Chance!'

'A cold, clear morning,' said I, in order to attract his attention and draw him into conversation.

A nod, without raising his head, or withdrawing his eyes from the fire, was his only answer; and, turning from my unsociable guest, I took up the baby, who just then awoke, sat down on a low stool by the table, and began feeding her. During this operation, I once or twice caught the stranger's hawk-eye fixed upon me and the child, but word spoke he none; and presently, after whistling to his dogs, he resumed his gun, and strode out.

When Moodie and Monaghan[1] came in to breakfast, I told them what a strange visitor I had had; and Moodie laughed at my vain attempt to induce him to talk.

'He is a strange being,' I said; 'I must find out who and what he is.'

In the afternoon an old soldier, called Layton, who had served during the American war, and got a grant of land about a mile in the rear of our location, came in to trade for a cow. Now, this Layton was a perfect ruffian; a man whom no one liked, and whom all feared. He was a deep drinker, a great swearer, in short, a perfect reprobate; who never cultivated his land, but went jobbing about from farm to farm, trading horses and cattle, and cheating in a pettifogging way. Uncle Joe had employed him to sell Moodie a young heifer, and he had brought her over for him to look at. When he came in to be paid, I described the stranger of the morning; and as I knew that he was familiar with every one in the neighbourhood, I asked if he knew him.

'No one should know him better than myself,' he said, ''tis old Brian B——, the still-hunter,[2] and a near neighbour of your'n. A sour, morose, queer chap he is, and as mad as a March hare! He's from Lancashire, in England, and came to this country some twenty years ago, with his wife, who was a pretty young lass in those days, and slim enough then, though she's so awfully fleshy now. He had lots of money, too, and he bought four hundred acres of land, just at the corner of the concession line,[3] where it meets the main road. And excellent land it is; and a better farmer, while he stuck to his business, never went into the bush, for it was all bush here then. He was a dashing, handsome fellow, too, and did not hoard the money either; he loved his pipe and his pot too well; and at last he left off farming, and gave himself to them altogether. Many a jolly booze he and I have had, I can tell you. Brian was an awful passionate man, and, when the liquor was in, and the wit was out, as savage and as quarrelsome as a bear. At such times there was no one but Ned Layton dared go near him. We once had a pitched battle, in which I was conqueror, and ever arter he yielded a sort of sulky obedience to all I said to him. Arter being on the spree for a week or two, he would take fits of remorse, and

1  The Moodies' new hired man.
2  One who hunts game on foot or in a quiet or stealthy manner.
3  Rural road separating concessions (grants of land).

return home to his wife; would fall down at her knees, and ask her forgiveness, and cry like a child. At other times he would hide himself up in the woods, and steal home at night, and get what he wanted out of the pantry, without speaking a word to any one. He went on with these pranks for some years, till he took a fit of the blue devils.

'"Come away, Ned, to the ———— lake, with me," said he; "I am weary of my life, and I want a change."

'"Shall we take the fishing-tackle?" says I. "The black bass are in prime season, and F——— will lend us the old canoe. He's got some capital rum up from Kingston. We'll fish all day, and have a spree at night."

'"It's not to fish I'm going," says he.

'"To shoot, then? I've bought Rockwood's new rifle."

'"It's neither to fish nor to shoot, Ned; it's a new game I'm going to try; so come along."

'Well, to the ———— lake we went. The day was very hot, and our path lay through the woods, and over those scorching plains, for eight long miles. I thought I should have dropped by the way; but during our long walk my companion never opened his lips. He strode on before me, at a half-run, never once turning his head.

'"The man must be a devil!" says I, "and accustomed to a warmer place, or he must feel this. Hollo, Brian! Stop there! Do you mean to kill me?"

'"Take it easy," says he; "you'll see another day arter this—I've business on hand and cannot wait."

'Well, on we went, at the same awful rate, and it was midday when we got to the little tavern on the lake shore, kept by one F———, who had a boat for the convenience of strangers who came to visit the place. Here we got our dinner, and a glass of rum to wash it down. But Brian was moody, and to all my jokes he only returned a sort of grunt; and while I was talking with F———, he steps out, and a few minutes arter we saw him crossing the lake in the old canoe.

'"What's the matter with Brian?" says F———; "all does not seem right with him, Ned. You had better take the boat and look arter him."

'"Pooh!" says I; "he's often so, and grows so glum now-a-days that I will cut his acquaintance altogether if he does not improve."

'"He drinks awful hard," says F———; "maybe he's got a fit of the delirium-tremulous. There is no telling what he may be up to at this minute."

'My mind misgave me too, so I e'en takes the oars, and pushes out, right upon Brian's tracks; and by the Lord Harry! if I did not find him, upon my landing on the opposite shore, lying wallowing in his blood, with his throat cut. "Is that you, Brian?" says I, giving him a kick with my foot, to see if he was alive or dead. "What upon earth tempted you to play me and F——— such a dirty, mean trick, as to go and stick yourself like a pig, bringing such a discredit upon the house?—and you so far from home and those who should nurse you."

'I was so mad with him, that (saving your presence, ma'am) I swore awfully, and called him names that would be ondacent to repeat here; but he only answered with groans and a horrid gurgling in his throat. "It's a choking you are," said I; "but you shan't have your own way and die so easily either, if I can punish you by keeping you alive." So I just turned him upon his stomach, with his head down the steep bank; but he still kept choking and growing black in the face.'

Layton then detailed some particulars of his surgical practice which it is not necessary to repeat. He continued—

'I bound up his throat with my handkerchief, and took him neck and heels, and threw him into the bottom of the boat. Presently he came to himself a little, and sat up in the boat; and—would you believe it?—made several attempts to throw himself into the water. "This will not do," says I; "you've done mischief enough already by cutting your weasand![4] If you dare to try that again, I will kill you with the oar." I held it up to threaten him; he was scared, and lay down as quiet as a lamb. I put my foot upon his breast. "Lie still, now! or you'll catch it." He looked piteously at me; he could not speak, but his eyes seemed to say, "Have pity on me, Ned; don't kill me."

'Yes, ma'am, this man, who had just cut his throat, and twice arter that had tried to drown himself, was afraid that I should knock him on the head and kill him. Ha! ha! I never shall forget the work that F—— and I had with him arter I got him up to the house.

'The doctor came and sewed up his throat; and his wife—poor crittur!—came to nurse him. Bad as he was, she was mortal fond of him! He lay there, sick and unable to leave his bed, for three months, and did nothing but pray to God to forgive him, for he thought the devil would surely have him for cutting his own throat; and when he got about again, which is now twelve years ago, he left off drinking entirely, and wanders about the woods with his dogs, hunting. He seldom speaks to any one, and his wife's brother carries on the farm for the family. He is so shy of strangers that 'tis a wonder he came in here. The old wives are afraid of him; but you need not heed him—his troubles are to himself, he harms no one.'

Layton departed, and left me brooding over the sad tale which he had told in such an absurd and jesting manner. It was evident from the account he had given of Brian's attempt at suicide, that the hapless hunter was not wholly answerable for his conduct—that he was a harmless maniac.

The next morning, at the very same hour, Brian again made his appearance; but instead of the rifle across his shoulder, a large stone jar occupied the place, suspended by a stout leather thong. Without saying a word, but with a truly benevolent smile that flitted slowly over his stern features, and lighted them up like a sunbeam breaking from beneath a stormy cloud, he advanced to the table, and unslinging the jar, set it down before me, and in a low and gruff, but by no means an unfriendly, voice, said, 'Milk, for the child,' and vanished.

'How good it was of him! How kind!' I exclaimed, as I poured the precious gift of four quarts of pure new milk out into a deep pan. I had not asked him—had never said that the poor weanling wanted milk. It was the courtesy of a gentleman—of a man of benevolence and refinement.

For weeks did my strange, silent friend steal in, take up the empty jar, and supply its place with another replenished with milk. The baby knew his step, and would hold

4  Windpipe or throat.

out her hands to him and cry, 'Milk!' and Brian would stoop down and kiss her, and his two great dogs lick her face.

'Have you any children, Mr B——?'

'Yes, five; but none like this.'

'My little girl is greatly indebted to you for your kindness.'

'She's welcome, or she would not get it. You are strangers; but I like you all. You look kind, and I would like to know more about you.'

Moodie shook hands with the old hunter, and assured him that we should always be glad to see him. After this invitation, Brian became a frequent guest. He would sit and listen with delight to Moodie while he described to him elephant-hunting at the Cape;[5] grasping his rifle in a determined manner, and whistling an encouraging air to his dogs. I asked him one evening what made him so fond of hunting.

' 'Tis the excitement,' he said; 'it drowns thought, and I love to be alone. I am sorry for the creatures, too, for they are free and happy; yet I am led by an instinct I cannot restrain to kill them. Sometimes the sight of their dying agonies recalls painful feelings; and then I lay aside the gun, and do not hunt for days. But 'tis fine to be alone with God in the great woods—to watch the sunbeams stealing through the thick branches, the blue sky breaking in upon you in patches, and to know that all is bright and shiny above you, in spite of the gloom that surrounds you.'

After a long pause, he continued, with much solemn feeling in his look and tone—

'I lived a life of folly for years, for I was respectably born and educated, and had seen something of the world, perhaps more than was good, before I left home for the woods; and from the teaching I had received from kind relatives and parents I should have known how to have conducted myself better. But, madam, if we associate long with the depraved and ignorant, we learn to become even worse than they. I felt deeply my degradation—felt that I had become the slave to low vice, and in order to emancipate myself from the hateful tyranny of evil passions, I did a very rash and foolish thing. I need not mention the manner in which I transgressed God's holy laws; all the neighbours know it, and must have told you long ago. I could have borne reproof, but they turned my sorrow into indecent jests, and, unable to bear their coarse ridicule, I made companions of my dogs and gun, and went forth into the wilderness. Hunting became a habit. I could no longer live without it, and it supplies the stimulant which I lost when I renounced the cursed whiskey-bottle.

'I remember the first hunting excursion I took alone in the forest. How sad and gloomy I felt! I thought that there was no creature in the world so miserable as myself. I was tired and hungry, and I sat down upon a fallen tree to rest. All was still as death around me, and I was fast sinking to sleep, when my attention was aroused by a long, wild cry. My dog, for I had not Chance then, and he's no hunter, pricked up his ears, but instead of answering with a bark of defiance, he crouched down, trembling, at my feet. "What does this mean?" I cried, and I cocked my rifle and sprang upon the log. The sound came nearer upon the wind. It was like the deep baying of a pack of hounds in full cry. Presently a noble deer rushed past me, and fast upon his trail—

5 Cape of Good Hope, South Africa.

I see them now, like so many black devils—swept by a pack of ten or fifteen large, fierce wolves, with fiery eyes and bristling hair, and paws that seemed hardly to touch the ground in their eager haste. I thought not of danger, for, with their prey in view, I was safe; but I felt every nerve within me tremble for the fate of the poor deer. The wolves gained upon him at every bound. A close thicket intercepted his path, and, rendered desperate, he turned at bay. His nostrils were dilated, and his eyes seemed to send forth long streams of light. It was wonderful to witness the courage of the beast. How bravely he repelled the attacks of his deadly enemies, how gallantly he tossed them to the right and left, and spurned them from beneath his hoofs; yet all his struggles were useless, and he was quickly overcome and torn to pieces by his ravenous foes. At that moment he seemed more unfortunate even than myself, for I could not see in what manner he had deserved his fate. All his speed and energy, his courage and fortitude, had been exerted in vain. I had tried to destroy myself; but he, with every effort vigorously made for self-preservation, was doomed to meet the fate he dreaded! Is God just to his creatures?'

With this sentence on his lips, he started abruptly from his seat and left the house.

One day he found me painting some wild flowers, and was greatly interested in watching the progress I made in the group. Late in the afternoon of the following day he brought me a large bunch of splendid spring flowers.

'Draw these,' said he; 'I have been all the way to the ——— lake plains to find them for you.'

Little Katie, grasping them one by one, with infantile joy, kissed every lovely blossom.

'These are God's pictures,' said the hunter, 'and the child, who is all nature, understands them in a minute. Is it not strange that these beautiful things are hid away in the wilderness, where no eyes but the birds of the air, and the wild beasts of the wood, and the insects that live upon them, ever see them? Does God provide, for the pleasures of such creatures, these flowers? Is His benevolence gratified by the admiration of animals whom we have been taught to consider as having neither thought nor reflection? When I am alone in the forest, these thoughts puzzle me.'

Knowing that to argue with Brain was only to call into action the slumbering fires of his fatal malady, I turned the conversation by asking him why he called his favourite dog Chance?

'I found him', said he, 'forty miles back in the bush. He was a mere skeleton. At first I took him for a wolf, but the shape of his head undeceived me. I opened my wallet,[6] and called him to me. He came slowly, stopping and wagging his tail at every step, and looking me wistfully in the face. I offered him a bit of dried venison, and he soon became friendly, and followed me home, and has never left me since. I called him Chance, after the manner I happened with him; and I would not part with him for twenty dollars.'

Alas, for poor Chance! he had, unknown to his master, contracted a private liking for fresh mutton, and one night he killed no less than eight sheep that belonged to Mr D——, on the front road; the culprit, who had been long suspected, was caught

6 Knapsack.

in the very act, and this *mischance* cost him his life. Brian was sad and gloomy for many weeks after his favourite's death.

'I would have restored the sheep fourfold', he said, 'if he would but have spared the life of my dog.'

\* \* \*

## 22. THE FIRE

> Now, Fortune, do thy worst! For many years,
> Thou, with relentless and unsparing hand,
> Hast sternly pour'd on our devoted heads
> The poison'd phials of thy fiercest wrath.

The early part of the winter of 1837, a year never to be forgotten in the annals of Canadian history, was very severe. During the month of February, the thermometer often ranged from eighteen to twenty-seven degrees below zero. Speaking of the coldness of one particular day, a genuine brother Jonathan[1] remarked, with charming simplicity, that it was thirty degrees below zero that morning, and it would have been much colder if the thermometer had been longer.

The morning of the seventh was so intensely cold that everything liquid froze in the house. The wood that had been drawn for the fire was green, and it ignited too slowly to satisfy the shivering impatience of women and children; I vented mine inaudibly grumbling over the wretched fire, at which I in vain endeavoured to thaw frozen bread, and to dress crying children.

It so happened that an old friend, the maiden lady before alluded to,[2] had been staying with us for a few days. She had left us for a visit to my sister, and as some relatives of hers were about to return to Britain, by the way of New York, and had offered to convey letters to friends at home, I had been busy all the day before preparing a packet for England.

It was my intention to walk to my sister's with this packet, directly the important affair of breakfast had been discussed; but the extreme cold of the morning had occasioned such delay, that it was late before breakfast-things were cleared away.

After dressing, I found the air so keen that I could not venture out without some risk to my nose, and my husband kindly volunteered to go in my stead.

I had hired a young Irish girl the day before. Her friends were only just located in our vicinity, and she had never seen a stove until she came to our house. After Moodie left, I suffered the fire to die away in the Franklin stove in the parlour, and went into the kitchen to prepare bread for the oven.

---

1 Typical Yankee.
2 In the chapter that precedes this one, Moodie writes: 'I was surprised by a visit from an old maiden lady, a friend of mine from C———. She had walked up with a Mr. Crowe, from Peterborough, a young, brisk-looking farmer, in breeches and top-boots, just out from the old country, who, naturally enough thought he would like to roost among the woods.'

The girl, who was a good-natured creature, had heard me complain bitterly of the cold, and the impossibility of getting the green wood to burn, and she thought that she would see if she could not make a good fire for me and the children, against[3] my work was done. Without saying one word about her intention, she slipped out through a door that opened from the parlour into the garden, ran round to the woodyard, filled her lap with cedar chips, and, not knowing the nature of the stove, filled it entirely with the light wood.

Before I had the least idea of my danger, I was aroused from the completion of my task by the crackling and roaring of a large fire, and a suffocating smell of burning soot. I looked up at the kitchen cooking-stove. All was right there. I knew I had left no fire in the parlour stove; but not being able to account for the smoke and smell of burning, I opened the door, and, to my dismay, found the stove red-hot, from the front plate to the topmost pipe that let out the smoke through the roof.

My first impulse was to plunge a blanket, snatched from the servant's bed, which stood in the kitchen, into cold water. This I thrust into the stove, and upon it I threw water, until all was cool below. I then ran up to the loft, and, by exhausting all the water in the house, even to that contained in the boilers upon the fire, contrived to cool down the pipes which passed through the loft. I then sent the girl out of doors to look at the roof, which, as a very deep fall of snow had taken place the day before, I hoped would be completely covered, and safe from all danger of fire.

She quickly returned, stamping, and tearing her hair, and making a variety of uncouth outcries, from which I gathered that the roof was in flames.

This was terrible news, with my husband absent, no man in the house, and a mile and a quarter from any other habitation. I ran out to ascertain the extent of the misfortune, and found a large fire burning in the roof between the two stove-pipes. The heat of the fires had melted off all the snow, and a spark from the burning pipe had already ignited the shingles. A ladder, which for several months had stood against the house, had been moved two days before to the barn, which was at the top of the hill near the road; there was no reaching the fire through that source. I got out the dining-table, and tried to throw water upon the roof by standing on a chair placed upon it, but I only expended the little water that remained in the boiler, without reaching the fire. The girl still continued weeping and lamenting.

'You must go for help,' I said. 'Run as fast as you can to my sister's, and fetch your master.'

'And lave you, ma'arm, and the childher alone wid the burnin' house?'

'Yes, yes! Don't stay one moment.'

'I have no shoes, ma'arm, and the snow is so deep.'

'Put on your master's boots; make haste, or we shall be lost before help comes.'

The girl put on the boots and started, shrieking 'Fire!' the whole way. This was utterly useless, and only impeded her progress by exhausting her strength. After she had vanished from the head of the clearing into the wood, and I was left quite alone, with the house burning over my head, I paused one moment to reflect what had best be done.

3 Until.

The house was built of cedar logs; in all probability it would be consumed before any help could arrive. There was a brisk breeze blowing up from the frozen lake, and the thermometer stood at eighteen degrees below zero. We were placed between the two extremes of heat and cold, and there was as much danger to be apprehended from the one as the other. In the bewilderment of the moment, the direful extent of the calamity never struck me; we wanted but this to put the finishing stroke to our misfortunes, to be thrown naked, houseless, and penniless, upon the world. '*What shall I save first?*' was the thought just then uppermost in my mind. Bedding and clothing appeared the most essentially necessary, and, without another moment's pause, I set to work with a right good will to drag all that I could from my burning home.

While little Agnes, Dunbar, and baby Donald filled the air with their cries, Katie, as if fully conscious of the importance of exertion, assisted me in carrying out sheets and blankets, and dragging trunks and boxes some way up the hill, to be out of the way of the burning brands when the roof should fall in.

How many anxious looks I gave to the head of the clearing as the fire increased, and large pieces of burning pine began to fall through the boarded ceiling about the lower rooms where we were at work. The children I had kept under a large dresser in the kitchen, but it now appeared absolutely necessary to remove them to a place of safety. To expose the young, tender things to the direct cold, was almost as bad as leaving them to the mercy of the fire. At last I hit upon a plan to keep them from freezing. I emptied all the clothes out of a large, deep chest of drawers, and dragged the empty drawers up the hill; these I lined with blankets, and placed a child in each drawer, covering it well over with the bedding, giving to little Agnes the charge of the baby to hold between her knees, and keep well covered until help should arrive. Ah, how long it seemed coming!

The roof was now burning like a brush-heap, and, unconsciously, the child and I were working under a shelf upon which were deposited several pounds of gunpowder, which had been procured for blasting a well, as all our water had to be brought uphill from the lake. This gunpowder was in a stone jar, secured by a paper stopper; the shelf upon which it stood was on fire, but it was utterly forgotten by me at the time, and even afterwards, when my husband was working on the burning loft over it.

I found that I should not be able to take many more trips for goods. As I passed out of the parlour for the last time, Katie looked up at her father's flute, which was suspended upon two brackets, and said,

'Oh, dear mamma! do save papa's flute; he will be so sorry to lose it.'

God bless the dear child for the thought! the flute was saved; and, as I succeeded in dragging out a heavy chest of clothes, and looked up once more despairingly to the road, I saw a man running at full speed. It was my husband. Help was at hand, and my heart uttered a deep thanksgiving as another and another figure came upon the scene.

I had not felt the intense cold, although without cap, or bonnet, or shawl; with my hands bare and exposed to the bitter, biting air. The intense excitement, the anxiety to save all I could, had so totally diverted my thoughts from myself, that I had felt nothing of the danger to which I had been exposed; but now that help was near, my knees trembled under me, I felt giddy and faint, and dark shadows seemed dancing before my eyes.

The moment my husband and brother-in-law entered the house, the latter exclaimed, 'Moodie, the house is gone; save what you can of your winter stores and furniture.'

Moodie thought differently. Prompt and energetic in danger, and possessing admirable presence of mind and coolness when others yield to agitation and despair, he sprang upon the burning loft and called for water. Alas, there was none!

'Snow, snow; hand me pailfuls of snow!'

Oh! it was bitter work filling those pails with frozen snow; but Mr T—— and I worked at it as fast as we were able.

The violence of the fire was greatly checked by covering the boards of the loft with this snow. More help had now arrived. Young B—— and S—— had brought the ladder down with them from the barn, and were already cutting away the burning roof, and flinging the flaming brands into the deep snow.

'Mrs Moodie, have you any pickled meat?'

'We have just killed one of our cows and salted it for winter stores.'

'Well, then, fling the beef into the snow, and let us have the brine.'

This was an admirable plan. Wherever the brine wetted the shingles, the fire turned from it, and concentrated into one spot.

But I had not time to watch the brave workers on the roof. I was fast yielding to the effects of over excitement and fatigue, when my brother's team dashed down the clearing, bringing my excellent old friend, Miss B——, and the servant-girl.

My brother sprang out, carried me back into the house, and wrapped me up in one of the large blankets scattered about. In a few minutes I was seated with the dear children in the sleigh, and on the way to a place of warmth and safety.

Katie alone suffered from the intense cold. The dear little creature's feet were severely frozen, but were fortunately restored by her uncle discovering the fact before she approached the fire, and rubbing them well with snow.

In the meanwhile, the friends we had left so actively employed at the house, succeeded in getting the fire under before it had destroyed the walls. The only accident that occurred was to a poor dog that Moodie had called Snarleyowe. He was struck by a burning brand thrown from the house, and crept under the barn and died.

Beyond the damage done to the building, the loss of our potatoes and two sacks of flour, we had escaped in a manner almost miraculous. This fact shows how much can be done by persons working in union, without bustle and confusion, or running in each other's way. Here were six men, who, without the aid of water, succeeded in saving a building, which, at first sight, almost all of them had deemed past hope. In after-years, when entirely burnt out in a disastrous fire that consumed almost all we were worth in the world, some four hundred persons were present, with a fire-engine to second their endeavours, yet all was lost. Every person seemed in the way; and though the fire was discovered immediately after it took place, nothing was done beyond saving some of the furniture.

\* \* \*

[*After the fire, circumstances improved for the Moodies, so much so that Mrs Moodie writes of that time: 'We were always cheerful, and sometimes contented and happy.' The Rebellion of 1837 brought this period to a sudden close, and in 1839, the Moodies departed from the bush to begin their 'life in the clearings'. In the final chapter, Mrs Moodie bids a somewhat sentimental 'Adieu to the Woods,' but concludes her book with two paragraphs of stern warning.*]

## 25. ADIEU TO THE WOODS

\*    \*    \*

Reader! it is not my intention to trouble you with the sequel of our history. I have given you a faithful picture of a life in the backwoods of Canada, and I leave you to draw from it your own conclusions. To the poor, industrious working man it presents many advantages; to the poor gentleman, none! The former works hard, puts up with coarse, scanty fare, and submits, with good grace, to hardships that would kill a domesticated animal at home. Thus he becomes independent, inasmuch as the land that he has cleared finds him in the common necessaries of life; but it seldom, if ever, in remote situations, accomplishes more than this. The gentleman can neither work so hard, live so coarsely, nor endure so many privations as his poorer but more fortunate neighbour. Unaccustomed to manual labour, his services in the field are not of a nature to secure for him a profitable return. The task is new to him, he knows not how to perform it well; and, conscious of his deficiency, he expends his little means in hiring labour, which his bush-farm can never repay. Difficulties increase, debts grow upon him, he struggles in vain to extricate himself, and finally sees his family sink into hopeless ruin.

If these sketches should prove the means of deterring one family from sinking their property, and shipwrecking all their hopes, by going to reside in the backwoods of Canada, I shall consider myself amply repaid for revealing the secrets of the prison-house, and feel that I have not toiled and suffered in the wilderness in vain.

1852

# Charles Sangster
## 1822–1893

## Colonial Poetry

Even before Confederation in 1867, many thought that to read, write, and value poetry in the colonies was one way of supplying cultural values for the incipient nation. The first poets to live and write in Canada were United Empire Loyalists, who made their way across the border as a result of the American Revolution and who used their verses to defend the King and to protest what they viewed as America's folly. The best-remembered of these writers may be Jonathan Odell, who wrote of how the Americans had 'broken the most sacred ties', and of how

> When civil madness first from man to man
> In these devoted climes like wildfire ran,
> There were who gave the moderating hint,
> In conversation some, and some in print;
> Wisely they spake–and what was their
>     reward?—
> The tar, the rail, the prison, and the cord!

The Loyalists' descendents and the generation of immigrants who came after them paid more attention to the space they actually found themselves inhabiting, but they continued to take British writers as their models when they wrote—using inherited poetic forms for their new content and employing old conventions to describe new situations. As we have seen in *The Rising Village*, New Brunswick's Oliver Goldsmith closely imitated his great-uncle's long pastoral poem, *The Deserted Village*, to create his response. Versions of Goldsmith's argument, that an emerging Canadian agrarian society would compensate Britain for its loss of village society, are frequent: early poets emphasized the potential of the new land but only once it was conquered, ordered, and civilized. Although links to England became less important, the post-colonial drive to both describe and praise the distinctive features of the new

land and its emerging social structures (which, for a long time, remained those of the farm and the village) was strong in the formative periods of Canadian poetry.

As Canada approached nationhood, the desire for a 'native' poetry written for Canadian consumption, and not first of all for British readers, began to manifest itself. A year after immigrating from Ireland in 1857, Thomas D'Arcy McGee, later one of the Fathers of Confederation, expressed anxieties about the lack of such literary expression—and to address its absence, wrote his own book of poems, *Canadian Ballads and Occasional Verses* (1858), in which he gave early expression to the idea that the strengths and freedom of Canada was the result of its northern climate. In 1864, Edward Hartley Dewart put together the first significant anthology of Canadian poems. In his introductory essay, he argued that Canada's status as a colony left its writers neither part of the mainstream of British literature nor able to develop an independent voice in the way that authors in the United States had; indifference to Canadian subject matter resulted from a colonial mentality that respected only the products and associations of the mother country.

The most famous of the poets in that volume and the first Canadian poet to achieve recognition in Canada in his lifetime was Charles Sangster; Dewart said he occupied 'first place' among his peers. Called in his own time 'Canada's national bard' and the 'first important national poet', Sangster became, by virtue of two books published in his thirties, the unofficial poet laureate of his day. Because he elected to work in the tradition of the English Romantics, his poetry is important for the way it responded to his immediate milieu rather than staying within the bounds of the neo-classic mode of his predecessors. One of Sangster's attempts to depict a Canadian landscape resulted in his 1856 poem 'The St Lawrence and the Saguenay', a work indebted to Wordsworth's late sonnet sequence 'The River Duddon'. However, Sir Daniel Wilson, in his review of the poem (which became an important commentary), thought that Sangster's long poem was no more than an adapting of English expression—neither true to its Canadian environment nor successful in finding a native idiom:

*Were we to transport the scene to the firth of Clyde, or any other islanded home river, and change only a single term; that of the* Red Man *for the* old Pict *. . . there is nothing in the description that would betray its new-world parentage. At best it is no true Indian, but only the white man dressed in*

*his attire; strip him of his paint and feathers, and it is our old-world familiar acquaintance. . . . However much taste and refinement may be displayed in such echoes of the old thought and fancy of Europe, the path to success lies not in this direction for the poet of the new world. (The Canadian Journal of Industry, Science, and Art, January, 1858)*

Wilson's argument, one that has often been made since, may have had an effect, because Sangster's 1860 'Sonnets Written in the Orillia Woods' suffers much less from these defects: the sonnets in this work begin to evoke a recognizable Canadian experience and to move beyond an inherited poetics.

## Charles Sangster

Sangster was born at the Navy Yard in Kingston, Upper Canada, in 1822; his father died while he was still an infant. At the age of fifteen, he went to work full time at Fort Henry, where he was employed to make cartridges. After two years there, his job changed to one in which, as he later said, he was 'ranked as a messenger, received the pay of a labourer, and did the duty of a clerk.' Of the loss of schooling, which might have given him better preparation for a career as a poet, he wrote,

*like many leading Canadians, [I am] a self-made man . . . I have not the advantages of a classical education. All that I possess mentally has been acquired by careful reading of the best authors (chiefly Fiction), properly directed thought, and a tolerable share of industry. . . . Even as a boy my ear seems to have been tuned to the harmony of sounds. I would have read more in my younger days, but books were not to be had—the Bible, and the 'Citizen of the World' in two volumes, constituted my library for many years. That I have read the former attentively is apparent from my poems.*

Having begun to write poems for newspapers and magazines such as *The Literary Garland* and

*The Anglo-American Review*, Sangster quit Fort Henry in 1849 to become the editor of the *Courier* at Amherstburg. Unfortunately, the paper collapsed when its publisher died. In 1850, he took more menial employment with the Kingston *British Whig*, remaining there for the next fourteen years. Despite the arduousness of his tasks at the *Whig*, he managed to write *The St Lawrence and the Saguenay and Other Poems* (1856) and *Hesperus, and Other Poems, and Lyrics* (1860).

The presence of love poetry in these collections coincided with Sangster's two marriages—the first to Mary Kilborne, whose death eighteen months later greatly saddened the poet; the second to Henrietta Meagher. In 1864, Sangster became a reporter for the Kingston *Daily News*, and in 1868, he joined the newly formed federal post office in Ottawa as a clerk. In 1882, he was honoured with a charter membership in the Royal Society of Canada. A breakdown forced his retirement in 1886. He had hoped to ready two more volumes of his poetry for publication but was unable to do so (these were eventually edited by Frank Tierney and published in the 1970s).

# From *The St. Lawrence and the Saguenay*[1]

\* \* \*

The bark leaps love-fraught from the land; the sea
Lies calm before us. Many an isle is there,[2]                    20
Clad with soft verdure; many a stately tree
Uplifts its leafy branches through the air;
The amorous current bathes the islets fair,
As we skip, youth-like, o'er the limpid waves;
White cloudlets speck the golden atmosphere,
Through which the passionate sun looks down, and graves
His image on the pearls that boil from the deep caves,

And bathe the vessel's prow. Isle after isle
Is passed, as we glide tortuously through
The opening vistas, that uprise and smile                        30
Upon us from the ever-changing view.
Here nature, lavish of her wealth, did strew
Her flocks of panting islets on the breast
Of the admiring River, where they grew,
Like shapes of Beauty, formed to give a zest
To the charmed mind, like waking Visions of the Blest.

The silver-sinewed arms of the proud Lake
Love-wild, embrace each islet tenderly,
The zephyrs kiss the flowers when they wake
At morn, flushed with a rare simplicity;                         40
See how they bloom around yon birchen tree,
And smile along the bank, by the sandy shore,
In lovely groups—a fair community!
The embossed rocks glitter like golden ore,
And here, the o'erarching trees form a fantastic bower.

Red walls of granite rise on either hand,
Rugged and smooth; a proud young eagle soars
Above the stately evergreens, that stand
Like watchful sentinels on these God-built towers;
And near yon beds of many-colored flowers                        50
Browse two majestic deer, and at their side
A spotted fawn all innocently cowers;
In the rank brushwood it attempts to hide,
While the strong-antlered stag steps forth with lordly stride,

---

1 Stanzas 3 to 11.
2 The setting of this first section is the Thousand Islands region; 'bark': a sailing vessel.

And slakes his thirst, undaunted, at the stream.
Isles of o'erwhelming beauty! surely here
the wild enthusiast might live, and dream
His life away. No Nymphic trains appear,
To charm the pale Ideal Worshipper
Of Beauty; nor Neriads[3] from the deeps below;  60
Nor hideous Gnomes, to fill the breast with fear:
But crystal streams through endless landscapes flow,
And o'er the clustering Isles the softest breezes blow.

### LYRIC TO THE ISLES

Here the Spirit of Beauty keepeth
 Jubilee for evermore;
Here the Voice of Gladness leapeth,
 Echoing from shore to shore.
O'er the hidden watery valley,
 O'er each buried wood and glade,
Dances our delighted galley,  70
 Through the sunlight and the shade—
 Dances o'er the granite cells,
 Where the Soul of Beauty dwells:

Here the flowers are ever springing,
 While the summer breezes blow;
Here the Hours are ever clinging,
 Loitering before they go;
Playing round each beauteous islet,
 Loath to leave the sunny shore,
Where, upon her couch of violet,  80
 Beauty sits for evermore—
 Sits and smiles by day and night,
 Hand in hand with pure Delight.

Here the Spirit of Beauty dwelleth
 In each palpitating tree,
In each amber wave that welleth
 From its home, beneath the sea;
In the moss upon the granite,
 In each calm, secluded bay,
With the zephyr trains that fan it  90

3  Water nymphs.

With their sweet breaths all the day—
On the waters, on the shore,
Beauty dwelleth evermore!

Yes, here the Genius[4] of Beauty truly dwells.
I worship Truth and Beauty in my soul.
The pure prismatic globule that upwells
From the blue deep; the psalmy waves that roll
Before the hurricane; the outspread scroll
Of heaven, with its written tomes of stars;
The dew-drop on the leaf: These I extol,                    100
    And all alike—each one a Spirit-Mars,
Guarding my Victor-Soul above Earth's prison bars.

There was a stately Maiden once, who made
These Isles her home. Oft has her lightsome skiff
Toyed with the waters; and the velvet glade,
The shadowy woodland, and the granite cliff,
Joyed at her footsteps. Here the Brigand Chief,
Her Father, lived, an outlaw. Her soul's pride
Was ministering to his wants. In brief,
    The wildest midnight she would cross the tide,           110
Full of a daughter's love, to hasten to his side.

Queen of the Isles! she well deserved the name:
In look, in action, in repose a Queen!
Some Poet-Muse may yet hand down to fame
Her woman's courage, and her classic mien;
Some Painter's skill immortalize the scene,
And blend with it that Maiden's history;
Some Sculptor's hand from the rough marble glean
    An eloquent Thought, whose truthfulness shall be
The expounder of her worth and moral dignity.               120

On, through the lovely Archipelago,
Glides the swift bark. Soft summer matins ring
From every isle. The wild fowl come and go,
Regardless of our presence. On the wing,
And perched upon the boughs, the gay birds sing

4  Guardian spirit.

Their loves: This is their summer paradise;
From morn till night their joyous caroling
Delights the ear, and through the lucent skies
Ascends the choral hymn in softest symphonies.

        \*    \*    \*

1856


## From *Sonnets Written in the Orillia Woods*

### IV

The birds are singing merrily, and here
A squirrel claims the lordship of the woods,
And scolds me for intruding. At my feet
The tireless ants all silently proclaim
The dignity of labour. In my ear
The bee hums drowsily; from sweet to sweet
Careering, like a lover weak in aim.
I hear faint music in the solitudes;
A dreamlike melody that whispers peace
Imbues the calmy forest, and sweet rills            10
Of pensive feeling murmur through my brain,
Like ripplings of pure water down the hills
That slumber in the moonlight. Cease, oh, cease!
Some day my weary heart will coin these into pain.


### VII

Our life is like a forest, where the sun
Glints down upon us through the throbbing leaves;
The full light rarely finds us. One by one,
Deep rooted in our souls, there springeth up
Dark groves of human passion, rich in gloom,
At first no bigger than an acorn-cup.
Hope threads the tangled labyrinth, but grieves
Till all our sins have rotted in their tomb,
And made the rich loam of each yearning heart
To bring forth fruits and flowers to new life.       10
We feel the dew from heaven, and there start

From some deep fountain little rills whose strife
Is drowned in music. Thus in light and shade
We live, and move, and die, through all this earthly glade.


### XIII

I've almost grown a portion of this place;
I seem familiar with each mossy stone;
Even the nimble chipmunk passes on,
And looks, but never scolds me. Birds have flown
And almost touched my hand; and I can trace
The wild bees to their hives. I've never known
So sweet a pause from labour. But the tone
Of a past sorrow, like a mournful rill
Threading the heart of some melodious hill,
Or the complainings of the whippoorwill,                    10
Passes through every thought, and hope, and aim.
It has its uses; for it cools the flame
Of ardent love that burns my being up—
Love, life's celestial pearl, diffused through all its cup.

1860

# Isabella Valancy Crawford
## 1850–1887

Born in Dublin, Isabella Valancy Crawford emigrated with her family to North America in 1858; they settled in Canada West, in the town of Paisley (near the Bruce Peninsula). Her father was the first doctor there, but his practice was never profitable, likely because of his alcoholism. Treasurer of the township, he may have misappropriated funds, leading the Crawford family to retreat to the Kingston area in 1862. They relocated to Lakefield (where they lived for a time with Robert Strickland,

nephew of Susanna Moodie and Catharine Parr Traill), and then to Peterborough around 1870. This series of moves exacerbated the family's impoverishment.

Dr Crawford died in Peterborough in 1875. Nine of Isabella's eleven siblings had already died in childhood, possibly because of a congenital heart condition aggravated by malnutrition. Since her remaining sister died in 1876 as a young woman, either from consumption (tuberculosis) or of heart failure, it is hardly surprising that mortality is a recurring concern in Crawford's poetry. After her only surviving sibling, a brother, went north to seek his livelihood, Crawford was left to care for her mother.

Educated at home by her parents, who instructed her in Latin and French as well as in English, Crawford's rich imagination was shaped by the classics—Horace and Dante were said to be her favourite poets—as well as by contemporary English and French literature. Her poetry has affinities with that of Tennyson and the Pre-Raphaelites, but it also shows her knowledge of earlier writers such as Shakespeare and Milton. Crawford depended on her classical education and on British tradition to create a unique blend that drew on her Canadian background for landscape and milieu as well as for Native imagery and mythology.

Her work stands apart from the poetry of her time: Crawford so imbues nature with life that the settings become animistic; and her images (as in 'Said the Canoe') have a quality so sensual that critics have offered Freudian interpretations. She shows remarkable control over a wide range of forms, including long narrative poems such as *Malcolm's Katie* (perhaps her best-known work), song-like lyrics, poems in dialect, and dramatic monologues. Her poetic vision is one of forces in opposition, sometimes universalized to a cosmic struggle between darkness and light, hope and despair.

Having begun to publish poems in the Toronto *Mail*, Crawford moved with her mother to Toronto around 1876 to be close to publishers. Because she hoped to support herself as a commercial writer, much of what she published was in newspapers and periodicals. Her poems began to appear regularly in the Toronto *Evening Telegram* but earned her little. The only book of her work published in her lifetime—*Old Spookses' Pass, Malcolm's Katie, and Other Poems*—was issued at her own expense in 1884 and sold few copies, despite receiving good reviews in Canada and Britain.

From an early age, by supplementing her poetry with fiction written with a popular readership in mind, she was able to earn enough to live on, if only barely. Because of the ephemeral nature of the papers in which Crawford published, many of her works of fiction have been lost. None seems to have been of the quality of her poems. In 1873, she won a $500 prize from the weekly story paper *The Favorite* for the publication (in twelve instalments) of a novel, *Winona; or, The Foster Sisters*. Unfortunately, she received only $100 from the financially distressed publisher, and that after suing for payment. That novel was published in book form for the first time in 2007, in a critical edition edited by Len Early and Michael Peterman: they describe it as anticipating Crawford's later work 'in its representation of women, its ethical vision, its use of Native materials, its exuberant engagement with high as well as popular culture, and its peculiar deployment of irony and romance.' The growth of interest and scholarship in her work led not only to the recovery of *Winona* but of two additional novels: *Wrecked! Or, The Rosclerras of Mistree* (1872–3) and *Hate* (1875), both of which had originally appeared in the US magazine, *Frank Leslie's Chimney Corner*. Two collections of her surviving short pieces were gathered in the 1970s, *Selected Stories of Isabella Valancy Crawford* and *Fairy Tales of Isabella Valancy Crawford*.

Crawford died of heart failure at the age of thirty-six, having gained neither the financial success nor the readership she longed for; her work began to receive critical recognition following the publication of *The Collected Poems of Isabella Valancy Crawford*, edited by John Garvin, in 1905. Her reputation was further enhanced when the poets James Reaney (who joined Northrop Frye in emphasizing her 'mythopoeic' qualities) and Dorothy Livesay became interested in her poetry. In 1972, *The Collected Poems* were reprinted with a new introduction by Reaney. Livesay's work on Crawford's unpublished manuscripts led to the recovery (in an incomplete and fragmented state) of a major long poem. The version Livesay assembled from these fragments was published in *Canadian Literature* in 1973 (with her commentary) as 'The Hunters Twain'; a more satisfactory if still speculative reconstruction by Glen Clever was published as a chapbook in 1977 under the title, *Hugh and Ion*.

## Malcolm's Katie: A Love Story

The long narrative poem was already an important form of literary expression in the Canadian tradition before Crawford came to it. The precursors of *Malcolm's Katie* stretch from Thomas Cary's *Abram's Plains* (1789), Goldsmith's *Rising Village* (1825), and John Richardson's *Tecumseh* (1828), through William Kirby's *The U.E.: A Tale of Upper Canada* (1859), and Alexander McLachlan's *The Emigrant* (1861), among others. These are poems of nation-building—a theme also important in *Malcolm's Katie*, which describes how the labourers from the Old World find opportunity in the New World:

> . . . the lean weaver ground anew his axe,
> Nor backward look'd upon the vanish'd loom,
> But forward to the ploughing of his fields,
> And to the rose of Plenty in the cheeks.

As we have seen in early works such as *The History of Emily Montague*, and as Crawford's poem also makes clear, it is the availability of land that brings these settlers to Canada:

> *The pallid clerk look'd on his blister'd palms*
> *And sigh'd and smil'd, but girded up his loins*
> *And found new vigour as he felt new hope.*
> *The lab'rer with train'd muscles, grim and grave,*
> *Look'd at the ground and wonder'd in his soul,*
> *What joyous anguish stirr'd his darken'd heart,*
> *At the mere look of the familiar soil,*
> *And found his answer in the words—'Mine own!'*

Thus, poems such as these gave aesthetic form to settlement narratives like Traill's and Moodie's. In Crawford's poem, the axe of the hero (Max) becomes a potent metonym for the work to be done in claiming the land.

In shaping her story of European settlers bringing civilization to the New World, Crawford created a poem that does new things with familiar elements. Her narrative—with its pure and faithful heroine, and its noble and brave hero appearing in the nick of time to save her from the black-hearted and duplicitous villain—might at first seem too indebted to Victorian melodrama, but Crawford's heightened expression of these conventions moves the poem beyond melodramatic to operatic. The

lyrics she intersperses throughout, such as Max's song to his axe (IV.39–52) or the hymn to 'Sorrow' that opens Part VI, contribute to this quality—as do the set pieces such as the animistic dramatization of the coming of autumn, which opens Part II, or Alfred's speech on 'Nothingness' (V.152–167). As well, Crawford's interest in the transcendental and the mythic added new dimensions to her plot's familiar outlines; her characters prove more complicated psychologically than we expect; her wide-ranging reading allowed her to enrich the text with echoes and allusions; and her engagement with ideas being debated at the time of her writing is evident in the philosophical questions raised by the poem.

If one thinks of this poem as descending, by way of Tennyson, from medieval romance, we can see that, in Crawford's Canada, the woodsman has displaced the knight, both in courtship and on the field of battle (which, for Max, is first of all with his noble foe, the forest, and only secondarily with Alfred). The question of love that the romance elements raise is worth thinking about: in one of several doublings that run through the poem, Katie and Max's belief in love allows them to oppose Alfred's belief that life is nothing but a prologue to death; as well, Katie uses a logic of love to maintain her faith against Alfred's stern rationalism.

At the same time, there are aspects of *Malcolm's Katie* that move us from romance to epic, that oldest poem on nation-building: Max has all the characteristics of an epic hero, and his tasks are epic in scale. (Note, too, how the triangle of Max, Katie, and Alfred recalls that of Odysseus, Penelope, and her suitors.) Adding to these large patterns and extending the emerging-nation theme is the culminating allusion to the Adam and Eve story, making Canada the new Eden and Alfred, with his nihilistic materialism, the serpent in this garden. These biblical echoes show more evidence of Crawford's epic ambitions, since some lines in the poem recall Milton's *Paradise Lost*, reminding us that for the nineteenth century, *Paradise Lost* was the mediating text for understanding the Garden of Eden story: Crawford is clearly sympathetic to Milton's notion that the fallen state of Eden is necessary and that it brings with it the 'Paradise within thee, happier far.'

It is no wonder that readers such as Reaney responded to this poetry as mythopoeic, especially when we see that still larger patterns haunt *Malcolm's Katie*. It anticipates the investigations that came in the generation following Crawford—one that was preoccupied with the archetypes of fisher king, questing knight, and grail legend. Malcolm is the aging ruler of the land: as such, he must eventually yield to the new order, which is identified with the knightlike Max; and in the end, Malcolm himself is renewed by Max's actions. The sacrificial pattern of the scapegoat is also evident here: for his task to be accomplished, Max must be seen to die and be reborn. (And Katie later thinks, 'If he should perish, 'twill be as a God.') All of this is played out against a cycle of seasonal change, while Crawford employs imagery that includes Katie being compared to a 'pale chalice' filled with distilled dew.

The richness of this poem has invited a range of interpretations. Critics have noted the social commentary implied in its engagement with the question of progress and with the materialism espoused by Alfred. The complexity of Katie's role, who is as much the hero of the poem as Max is, has invited discussions of the poem's feminist dimensions and of its implied critique of a patriarchal order that has its most negative aspects embodied in Alfred, for whom Katie is merely the key to a transfer of wealth. Finally, for some readers, because of the way Victorian propriety constrained free expression of women's sexuality, the lushness of the poem's imagery has invited readings that plumb Crawford's own psyche.

# Malcolm's Katie: A Love Story[1]

## PART I

Max plac'd a ring on little Katie's hand,
A silver ring that he had beaten out
From that same sacred coin—first well-priz'd wage
For boyish labour, kept thro' many years.
'See, Kate,' he said, 'I had no skill to shape
Two hearts fast bound together, so I grav'd[2]
Just K. and M., for Katie and for Max.'
'But, look; you've run the lines in such a way,
That M. is part of K., and K. of M.,'
Said Katie, smiling. 'Did you mean it thus?                    10
I like it better than the double hearts.'
'Well, well,' he said, 'but womankind is wise!
Yet tell me, dear, will such a prophecy
Not hurt you sometimes, when I am away?
Will you not seek, keen ey'd, for some small break
In those deep lines, to part the K. and M.
For you? Nay, Kate, look down amid the globes
Of those large lilies that our light canoe

---

1 Literary echoes and debts have generally not been indicated in these annotations. D.M.R. Bentley's 1987 critical edition of *Malcolm's Katie* notes a number, especially those that show Crawford's engagement with Tennyson's poetry.
2 Engraved.

Divides, and see within the polish'd pool
That small, rose face of yours—so dear, so fair—                    20
A seed of love to cleave into a rock,
And bourgeon³ thence until the granite splits
Before its subtle strength. I being gone—
Poor soldier of the axe—to bloodless fields
(Inglorious battles, whether lost or won)⁴
That sixteen-summer'd heart of yours may say:
"I but was budding, and I did not know
My core was crimson and my perfume sweet;
I did not know how choice a thing I am;
I had not seen the sun, and blind I sway'd⁵                          30
To a strong wind, and thought because I sway'd,
'Twas to the wooer of the perfect rose—
That strong, wild wind has swept beyond my ken⁶—
The breeze I love sighs thro' my ruddy leaves.'"
'O, words!' said Katie, blushing, 'only words!
You build them up that I may push them down;
If hearts are flow'rs, I know that flow'rs can root—
Bud, blossom, die—all in the same lov'd soil;
They do so in my garden. I have made
Your heart my garden. If I am a bud                                  40
And only feel unfoldment feebly stir
Within my leaves, wait patiently; some June,
I'll blush a full-blown rose, and queen it,⁷ dear,
In your lov'd garden. Tho' I be a bud,
My roots strike deep, and torn from that dear soil
Would shriek like mandrakes⁸—those witch things I read
Of in your quaint old books. Are you content?'
'Yes—crescent-wise—but not to round, full moon.⁹
Look at yon hill that rounds so gently up
From the wide lake;¹⁰ a lover king it looks,                        50

3  Variant of burgeon: to bud, grow, or flourish.
4  The beginning of an extended pattern of images depicting farmers as soldiers in battle with the land.
5  Max suggests, in this extended metaphor, that, like a rosebud that has not yet opened, Katie has not yet seen the larger world.
6  Understanding; comprehension.
7  Rule over.
8  Mandrakes were plants that, probably because their forked roots recalled human forms, were said to cry out when pulled from the ground. Among 'old books' alluding to the mandrake, see Shakespeare's *Romeo and Juliet*, IV.iii.47–48.
9  Max is comparing his contentment in Katie's love with the new, or crescent, moon: that is, he is content in part because of his anticipation that their love will, over time, grow to fullness.
10  As the setting sun goes over the horizon, it looks like a hill on the other side of the lake. Max compares it to a 'lover king' leaving behind his Queen, the silver moon. His shoulders and the fringes of his garment are the colours and shades of the sunset. Malcolm's maple trees, seen on the same horizon, supply the plumes of his feathered crest (like that worn by a knight on his helmet).

In cloth of gold, gone from his bride and queen:
And yet delay'd, because her silver locks
Catch in his gilded fringes; his shoulders sweep
Into blue distance, and his gracious crest,
Not held too high, is plum'd with maple groves;—
One of your father's farms. A mighty man,
Self-hewn from rock, remaining rock through all.'
'He loves me, Max,' said Katie. 'Yes, I know—
A rock is cup to many a crystal spring.
Well, he is rich; those misty, peak-roof'd barns—                    60
Leviathans[11] rising from red seas of grain—
Are full of ingots, shaped like grains of wheat.
His flocks have golden fleeces, and his herds
Have monarchs worshipful, as was the calf
Aaron call'd from the furnace; and his ploughs,
Like Genii chained, snort o'er his mighty fields.
He has a voice in Council and in Church—'
'He work'd for all,' said Katie, somewhat pain'd.
'Aye, so, dear love, he did; I heard him tell
How the first field upon his farm was ploughed.                      70
He and his brother Reuben, stalwart lads,
Yok'd themselves, side by side, to the new plough;
Their weaker father, in the grey of life
(But rather the wan age of poverty
Than many winters), in large, gnarl'd hands
The plunging handles held: with mighty strains
They drew the ripping beak[12] through knotted sod,
Thro' tortuous lanes of blacken'd, smoking stumps;
And past great flaming brush heaps, sending out
Fierce summers, beating on their swollen brows.                      80
O, such a battle! had we heard of serfs
Driven to like hot conflict with the soil,
Armies had march'd and navies swiftly sail'd
To burst their gyves.[13] But here's the little point—
The polish'd di'mond pivot on which spins

---

11 Leviathan, mentioned in the Bible as a giant aquatic monster, is, by application, anything of enormous size;
   'golden fleece': the magic fleece for which the mythic hero Jason and his men, the Argonauts, quested; Aaron
   was Moses' brother who, when Moses was on the mountain receiving the Ten Commandments, lost faith and
   had the Jews in the wilderness melt their gold jewellery in a furnace so it could be 'call'd' (forged) into a golden
   calf, which they worshipped as an idol; 'Genii' were household gods from whom the Romans sought protection
   for their families.
12 The ploughshare.
13 That is, if we had learned of men in servitude who were forced into similar struggle in efforts to make the land
   yield, we would have called out the military to release them from their shackles.

The wheel of Difference[14]—they OWN'D the rugged soil,
And fought for love—dear love of wealth and pow'r,
And honest ease and fair esteem of men;
One's blood heats at it!' 'Yet you said such fields
Were all inglorious,' Katie, wondering, said.                    90
'Inglorious? Yes; they make no promises
Of Star or Garter,[15] or the thundering guns
That tell the earth her warriors are dead.
Inglorious![16] Aye, the battle done and won
Means not—a throne propp'd up with bleaching bones;
A country sav'd with smoking seas of blood;
A flag torn from the foe with wounds and death;
Or Commerce, with her housewife foot upon
Colossal bridge of slaughter'd savages,
The Cross laid on her brawny shoulder, and                       100
In one sly, mighty hand her reeking sword,
And in the other all the woven cheats
From her dishonest looms.[17] Nay, none of these.
It means—four walls, perhaps a lowly roof;
Kine[18] in a peaceful posture; modest fields;
A man and woman standing hand in hand
In hale old age, who, looking o'er the land,
Say: "Thank the Lord, it all is mine and thine!"
It means, to such thew'd[19] warriors of the Axe
As your own father;—well, it means, sweet Kate,                  110
Outspreading circles of increasing gold,
A name of weight; one little daughter heir,
Who must not wed the owner of an axe,
Who owns naught else but some dim, dusky woods

---

14  That is, the Wheel of Fortune, or fate—used here as determining class or status. Even though Malcolm and his brother work like slaves, they are not doomed to be labourers forever because they own the land they cultivate and thus will gain from its profits.

15  Orders of knighthood; the Order of the Garter is the highest order, the one to which the Royal Family itself belongs.

16  Max argues that although the action of Malcolm and his brother (and soon of Max himself) is heroic, it will not gain them the glory that warriors deserve.

17  Though they may win their battles against the land, the farmers do not gain the glory associated with the violence of patriotic warfare in defence of country—bloody conflicts that leave bones bleaching in the sun in support of the monarch. But neither have they engaged in the more recent wars of exploitation being fought on behalf of commerce instead of country. The sinister quality Crawford here gives to a personified Commerce recalls the social commentary in earlier poems—particularly 'War' (1879), written in response to British military interventions in Africa: there she writes that modern war will 'feast with Commerce, be her spouse!' Here, she suggests that a rapacious market-driven imperialism has had the effect of building a bridge from the dead bodies of pre-industrial peoples, and that Europeans have, as the cross and the sword carried by Commerce suggest, combined their belief in their superior religious enlightenment with their military might in order to produce and sell their tawdry goods ('woven cheats').

18  Cattle.

19  Sinewed; well-muscled; strong.

In a far land; two arms indifferent strong—'
'And Katie's heart,' said Katie, with a smile;
For yet she stood on that smooth, violet plain,
Where nothing shades the sun; nor quite believed
Those blue peaks closing in were aught but mist
Which the gay sun could scatter with a glance.[20]                    120
For Max, he late had touch'd their stones, but yet
He saw them seam'd with gold and precious ores,
Rich with hill flow'rs and musical with rills.
'Or that same bud that will be Katie's heart,
Against the time your deep, dim woods are clear'd,
And I have wrought[21] my father to relent.'
'How will you move him, sweet? Why, he will rage
And fume and anger, striding o'er his fields,
Until the last-bought king of herds lets down
His lordly front, and rumbling thunder from                          130
His polish'd chest, returns his chiding tones.[22]
How will you move him, Katie, tell me how?'
'I'll kiss him and keep still—that way is sure,'
Said Katie, smiling. 'I have often tried.'
'God speed the kiss,' said Max, and Katie sigh'd,
With pray'rful palms close seal'd, 'God speed the axe!'

        \*     \*     \*

*O, light canoe, where dost thou glide?*
*Below thee gleams no silver'd tide.*
*But concave Heaven's chiefest pride.*

        \*     \*     \*

*Above thee burns Eve's rosy bar;*                                   140
*Below thee throbs her darling star;[23]*
*Deep 'neath thy keel her round worlds are!*

        \*     \*     \*

20  That is, Katie is still innocently optimistic and thinks of the world as a smooth and sunny plain, with no
     mountains to obscure that sunlight. The lines that follow suggest that Max is less optimistic because he has
     'late' (recently) encountered life's mountains; nevertheless, just as mountains may contain gold, flowers, and
     'rills' (streams), he sees these obstacles as filled with possibilities.
21  Moved.
22  That is, Malcolm will, in his fury, so bellow like a beast that his most recently acquired bull will respond in
     kind.
23  This lyric, which forms the close to Part I, has caused difficulties for readers—chiefly because the capitalization
     of Eve has been misread for the biblical character (who is not alluded to by Crawford until the end of the poem),
     rather than as the evening personified. The canoe in which Katie and Max sit talking is said to have the sky both
     above it and (because of the sky's reflection in the water) below it. (In Crawford's unrevised manuscript, lines
     140–1 read, 'Above, below, Eve's rosy bar— / Above, below her darling star—'.) Thus, the 'silvered tide' is the
     reflection of the stars and of one in particular, Evening's 'darling star' Venus, traditionally known as the Evening
     Star. The 'rosy bar' is the afterglow of sunset on the horizon.

*Above, below, O sweet surprise.*
*To gladden happy lover's eyes;*
*No earth, no wave—all jewell'd skies!*

## PART II

The South Wind laid his moccasins aside,
Broke his gay calumet of flow'rs,[1] and cast
His useless wampum, beaded with cool dews,
Far from him, northward: his long, ruddy spear
Flung sunward, whence it came,[2] and his soft locks
Of warm, fine haze grew silver as the birch,
His wigwam of green leaves began to shake;
The crackling rice-beds scolded harsh like squaws;
The small ponds pouted up their silver lips;
The great lakes ey'd the mountains, whisper'd 'Ugh!                    10
Are ye so tall, O chiefs? Not taller than
Our plumes can reach,'[3] and rose a little way,
As panthers stretch to try their velvet limbs,
And then retreat to purr and bide their time.
At morn the sharp breath of the night arose
From the wide prairies, in deep-struggling seas,[4]
In rolling breakers, bursting to the sky;
In tumbling surfs, all yellow'd faintly thro'
With the low sun—in mad, conflicting crests,
Voic'd with low thunder from the hairy throats                        20
Of the mist-buried herds; and for a man
To stand amid the cloudy roll and moil,[5]
The phantom waters breaking overhead,
Shades of vex'd billows bursting on his breast,
Torn caves of mist wall'd with a sudden gold,[6]

1  A calumet is a clay pipe used in Native peace ceremonies and ordinarily filled with tobacco. The South Wind, associated with Summer, fills his with flowers; the later use of calumet, at the beginning of Part IV, suggests its smoke is the flowers' perfume.
2  Lines 1–147 of Part II form an extended passage on seasonal change. The South Wind, personified as a Native warrior, puts aside his accoutrements—moccasins, calumet, wampum (money in the form of shell beads), and spear—as he prepares to yield to colder weather. In the lines that immediately follow, the landscape is personi-fied as it gives way to the frost that silvers the birch and the ice that closes the surface of the ponds, making them look as if they were mouths with their lips protruded in a sullen expression.
3  That is, the lakes say to the mountains that their plumes of fog or mist can reach to mountain's heights.
4  Crawford here begins an extended metaphor comparing a storm to an ocean rolling through the heavens. Within the storm is a herd—perhaps the bison seen later—that takes on its characteristics: their bellowing echoes the sound of its thunder; their 'broad, shaggy fronts' recall its dark clouds, their 'fire-eyes' reflect its light-ning.
5  Turmoil; mire.
6  Sunlight briefly breaking through the clouds.

Reseal'd as swift as seen—broad, shaggy fronts,
Fire-ey'd and tossing on impatient horns
The wave impalpable—was but to think
A dream of phantoms held him as he stood.
The late, last thunders of the summer crash'd,                    30
Where shrieked great eagles, lords of naked cliffs.
The pulseless forest,[7] lock'd and interlock'd
So closely, bough with bough, and leaf with leaf,
So serf'd[8] by its own wealth, that while from high
The Moons of Summer kiss'd its green-gloss'd locks,
And round its knees the merry West Wind[9] danc'd,
And round its ring, compacted emerald,[10]
The South Wind crept on moccasins of flame,
And the red fingers of th' impatient Sun
Pluck'd at its outmost fringes—its dim veins              40
Beat with no life—its deep and dusky heart,
In a deep trance of shadow, felt no throb
To such soft wooing answer:[11] thro' its dream
Brown rivers of deep waters sunless stole;
Small creeks sprang from its mosses, and amaz'd,
Like children in a wigwam curtain'd close
Above the great, dead heart of some red chief,
Slipp'd on soft feet, swift stealing through the gloom,
Eager for light and for the frolic winds.
In this shrill Moon the scouts of Winter[12] ran            50
From the ice-belted north, and whistling shafts
Struck maple and struck sumach   and a blaze
Ran swift from leaf to leaf, from bough to bough;
Till round the forest flash'd a belt of flame
And inward lick'd its tongues of red and gold
To the deep, tranced inmost heart of all.
Rous'd the still heart—but all too late, too late,
Too late, the branches welded fast with leaves,
Toss'd, loosen'd, to the winds—too late the Sun
Pour'd his last vigor to the deep, dark cells              60
Of the dim wood. The keen, two-bladed Moon

---

7 As the lines that follow suggest, the forest at the end of Summer is so verdant that its greenery becomes an
   impervious and unmoving barrier to outside forces, including the moon, the winds, and even the sun.
8 Enslaved.
9 Associated with Autumn.
10 That is, densely green.
11 The heart of the forest, protected from the sun by its foliage, does not 'throb' in answering response to the
   'wooing' of the sun.
12 That is, the autumn winds—their 'tongues of red and gold' are their cold blasts, which bring the colour of fall
   to the leaves. In the compressed vision of seasonal change that follows, the moon, associated with cold weather,
   is able to penetrate the forest's heart after the leaves fall from the branches.

Of Falling Leaves roll'd up on crested mists;
And where the lush, rank[13] boughs had foiled the Sun
In his red prime, her pale, sharp fingers crept
After the wind and felt about the moss,
And seem'd to pluck from shrinking twig and stem
The burning leaves—while groan'd the shudd'ring wood.
Who journey'd where the prairies made a pause,
Saw burnish'd ramparts flaming in the sun,
With beacon fires, tall on their rustling walls.[14]                70
And when the vast, horn'd herds[15] at sunset drew
Their sullen masses into one black cloud,
Rolling thund'rous o'er the quick pulsating plain,
They seem'd to sweep between two fierce red suns
Which, hunter-wise, shot at their glaring balls
Keen shafts, with scarlet feathers and gold barbs.[16]
By round, small lakes with thinner forests fring'd,
More jocund[17] woods that sung about the feet
And crept along the shoulders of great cliffs,
The warrior stags, with does and tripping fawns,                80
Like shadows black upon the throbbing mist
Of evening's rose, flash'd thro' the singing woods—
Nor tim'rous,[18] sniff'd the spicy, cone-breath'd air;
For never had the patriarch of the herd
Seen, limn'd[19] against the farthest rim of light
Of the low-dipping sky, the plume or bow
Of the red hunter; nor, when stoop'd to drink,
Had from the rustling rice-beds heard the shaft
Of the still hunter hidden in its spears;
His bark canoe close-knotted in its bronze,                90
His form as stirless as the brooding air,
His dusky eyes, too, fix'd, unwinking, fires;
His bow-string tighten'd till it subtly sang
To the long throbs, and leaping pulse that roll'd
And beat within his knotted, naked breast.
There came a morn. The Moon of Falling Leaves,
With her twin silver blades, had only hung

13 Luxuriant in growth, often with a suggestion of excess.
14 That is, if someone were to journey to where the forests gave way to the prairies, he or she would see the forest's walls as red as if illuminated by beacons.
15 Bison on the prairie.
16 The autumn or harvest moon is often red, especially when rising as the sun is setting. The sun and the moon together in the sky, therefore, look like two suns (the moon on the east, the sun on the west), and their rays of light are like sharp arrows directed at the eyeballs of the bison, which are thereby illuminated ('glaring').
17 Merry.
18 Fearful.
19 Outlined; here, silhouetted.

Above the low-set cedars of the swamp
For one brief quarter, when the Sun arose
Lusty with light and full of summer heat, 100
And, pointing with his arrows at the blue,
Clos'd, wigwam curtains of the sleeping Moon,
Laugh'd with the noise of arching cataracts,[20]
And with the dove-like cooing of the woods,
And with the shrill cry of the diving loon,
And with the wash of saltless, rounded seas,[21]
And mock'd the white Moon of the Falling Leaves.
'Esa! esa! shame upon you, Pale Face![22]
Shame upon you, Moon of Evil Witches!
Have you kill'd the happy, laughing Summer? 110
Have you slain the mother of the flowers
With your icy spells of might and magic?
Have you laid her dead within my arms?
Wrapp'd her, mocking, in a rainbow blanket?
Drown'd her in the frost-mist of your anger?
She is gone a little way before me;
Gone an arrow's flight beyond my vision;
She will turn again and come to meet me,
With the ghosts of all the slain flowers.
In a blue mist round her shining tresses, 120
In a blue smoke in her naked forests—
She will linger, kissing all the branches;
She will linger, touching all the places,
Bare and naked, with her golden fingers,
Saying, "Sleep, and dream of me, my children;
Dream of me, the mystic Indian Summer;
I, who, slain by the cold Moon of Terror,
Can return across the Path of Spirits,[23]
Bearing still my heart of love and fire,
Looking with my eyes of warmth and splendour, 130
Whisp'ring lowly thro' your sleep of sunshine,
I, the laughing Summer, am not turn'd
Into dry dust, whirling on the prairies—

20  Waterfalls.
21  The Great Lakes (mentioned above, in II.10).
22  In the speech that begins here, the Sun challenges the Autumn Moon for thinking she has successfully killed
    Summer with her 'frost-mist', arguing that 'Indian Summer' (the expression for a period of warm weather com-
    ing after the first onset of cold weather and seasonal colour change) will prove her wrong. (The Sun then per-
    sonifies Indian Summer in a long speech: II.125–45. After the conclusion of the Sun's speech, at II.147,
    Crawford returns the reader to the story of Max.)
23  The path connecting this world with the Native afterlife, the Happy Hunting Ground where great Manitou—
    the Great Spirit that rules over all creation—resides (mentioned in II.137–8).

Into red clay, crush'd beneath the snowdrifts.
I am still the mother of sweet flowers
Growing but an arrow's flight beyond you—
In the Happy Hunting Ground—the quiver
Of great Manitou, where all the arrows
He has shot from his great bow of Pow'r,
With its clear, bright, singing cord of Wisdom,                  140
Are re-gather'd, plum'd again and brighten'd,
And shot out, re-barb'd[24] with Love and Wisdom;
Always shot, and evermore returning.
Sleep, my children, smiling in your heart-seeds
At the spirit words of Indian Summer!"
Thus, O Moon of Falling Leaves, I mock you!
Have you slain my gold-ey'd squaw, the Summer?'
The mighty morn strode laughing up the land,
And Max, the labourer and the lover, stood
Within the forest's edge, beside a tree;                         150
The mossy king of all the woody tribes,
Whose clatt'ring branches rattl'd, shuddering,
As the bright axe cleav'd moon-like thro' the air,
Waking strange thunders, rousing echoes link'd
From the full, lion-throated roar, to sighs
Stealing on dove-wings thro' the distant aisles.
Swift fell the axe, swift follow'd roar on roar,
Till the bare woodland bellow'd in its rage,
As the first-slain slow toppl'd to his fall.
'O King of Desolation, art thou dead?'                           160
Thought Max, and laughing, heart and lips, leap'd on
The vast, prone trunk. 'And have I slain a King?
Above his ashes will I build my house—
No slave beneath its pillars, but—a King!'
Max wrought alone, but for a half-breed lad,
With tough, lithe sinews and deep Indian eyes,
Lit with a Gallic sparkle.[25] Max, the lover, found
The labourer's arms grow mightier day by day—
More iron-welded as he slew the trees;
And with the constant yearning of his heart                      170
Towards little Kate, part of a world away,
His young soul grew and shew'd a virile front,
Full muscl'd and large statur'd, like his flesh,
Soon the great heaps of brush were builded high,

24 'Plum'd . . . rebarbed': the arrows (the souls of the departed) are given new feathers and points and sent back out into the world.
25 That is, Max's companion in his work is a strong and graceful boy of mixed Native and French descent.

And, like a victor, Max made pause to clear
His battle-field, high strewn with tangl'd dead.
Then roar'd the crackling mountains, and their fires
Met in high heaven, clasping flame with flame.[26]
The thin winds swept a cosmos of red sparks
Across the bleak, midnight sky: and the sun                    180
Walk'd pale behind the resinous, black smoke.
And Max car'd little for the blotted sun,
And nothing for the startl'd, outshone stars;
For Love, once set within a lover's breast,
Has its own Sun—its own peculiar sky,
All one great daffodil[27]—on which do lie
The sun, the moon, the stars—all seen at once,
And never setting; but all shining straight
Into the faces of the trinity—
The one belov'd, the lover, and sweet Love!                    190
It was not all his own, the axe-stirr'd waste.[28]
In these new days men spread about the earth
With wings at heel—and now the settler hears,
While yet his axe rings on the primal woods,
The shrieks of engines rushing o'er the wastes;
Nor parts his kind[29] to hew his fortune out.
And as one drop glides down the unknown rock
And the bright-threaded stream leaps after it
With welded billions, so the settler finds out
His solitary footsteps beaten out,                             200
With the quick rush of panting, human waves
Upheav'd by throbs of angry poverty,
And driven by keen blasts of hunger, from
Their native strands[30]—so stern, so dark, so dear!
O, then, to see the troubl'd, groaning waves,
Throb down to peace in kindly, valley beds,
Their turbid bosoms clearing in the calm
Of sun-ey'd Plenty—till the stars and moon,
The blessed sun himself, has leave to shine

26  Like an ancient warrior, Max stops his battle and creates funeral pyres for the fallen.
27  This conceit seems particularly indebted to Tennyson's *Maud*, where in the early morning, the 'planet of love'
    (i.e., Venus), pictured on 'a bed of daffodil [pale yellow] sky', is beginning to 'faint in the light of the sun.'
28  That is, Max is not the only woodsman chopping down trees in this 'waste' land, i.e., the uncultivated wilder-
    ness. In the lines that follow, Crawford speaks of how machine labour will soon follow these settlers, and how,
    in clearing the wilderness, men such as Max are the first 'drop' of a river to come. Ironically, the settlers
    Crawford describes in the lines that follow come partly to escape their slavery to machines. The 'smooth-coated
    men' that conclude this progression are entrepreneurs and developers, who, for better or worse, complete the
    transformation of wilderness into civilization.
29  Nor does he have to leave behind his peers.
30  Shores.

And laugh in their dark hearts! So shanties grew 210
Other than his amid the blacken'd stumps;
And children ran with little twigs and leaves
And flung them, shouting, on the forest pyres
Where burn'd the forest kings—and in the glow
Paus'd men and women when the day was done.
There the lean weaver ground anew his axe,
Nor backward look'd upon the vanish'd loom,
But forward to the ploughing of his fields,
And to the rose of Plenty in the cheeks
Of wife and children—nor heeded much the pangs 220
Of the rous'd muscles tuning to new work.
The pallid clerk look'd on his blister'd palms
And sigh'd and smil'd, but girded up his loins
And found new vigour as he felt new hope.
The lab'rer with train'd muscles, grim and grave,
Look'd at the ground and wonder'd in his soul,
What joyous anguish stirr'd his darken'd heart,
At the mere look of the familiar soil,
And found his answer in the words—'*Mine own!*'
Then came smooth-coated men, with eager eyes, 230
And talk'd of steamers on the cliff-bound lakes;
And iron tracks across the prairie lands;
And mills to crush the quartz of wealthy hills;
And mills to saw the great, wide-arm'd trees;
And mills to grind the singing stream of grain;
And with such busy clamour mingled still
The throbbing music of the bold, bright Axe—
The steel tongue of the Present, and the wail
Of falling forests—voices of the Past.
Max, social-soul'd, and with his practised thews, 240
Was happy, boy-like, thinking much of Kate,
And speaking of her to the women-folk,
Who, mostly, happy in new honeymoons
Of hope themselves, were ready still to hear
The thrice-told tale of Katie's sunny eyes
And Katie's yellow hair, and household ways;
And heard so often, 'There shall stand our home—
On yonder slope, with vines about the door!'
That the good wives were almost made to see
The snowy walls, deep porches, and the gleam 250
Of Katie's garments flitting through the rooms;
And the black slope all bristling with burn'd stumps
Was known amongst them all as 'Max's House.'

\* \* \*

*O, Love builds on the azure sea,*
*And Love builds on the golden sand;*
*And Love builds on the rose-wing'd cloud.*
*And sometimes Love builds on the land.*

*O, if Love build on sparkling sea—*
*And if Love build on golden strand—*
*And if Love build on rosy cloud—* 260
*To Love these are the solid land.*

*O, Love will build his lily walls,*
*And Love his pearly roof will rear—*
*On cloud or land, or mist or sea—*
*Love's solid land is everywhere!*

## PART III

The great farm house of Malcolm Graem stood
Square shoulder'd and peak roof'd upon a hill,
With many windows looking everywhere;
So that no distant meadow might lie hid,
Nor corn-field hide its gold—nor lowing herd
Browse in far pastures, out of Malcolm's ken.
He lov'd to sit, grim, grey, and somewhat stern,
And thro' the smoke-clouds from his short clay pipe
Look out upon his riches; while his thoughts
Swung back and forth between the bleak, stern past, 10
And the near future, for his life had come
To that close balance, when, a pendulum,
The memory swings between the 'Then' and 'Now';
His seldom speech ran thus two diff'rent ways:
'When I was but a laddie, thus I did';
Or, 'Katie, in the fall I'll see to build
Such fences or such sheds about the place;
And next year, please the Lord, another barn.'
Katie's gay garden foam'd about the walls,
'Leagur'd[1] the prim-cut modern sills, and rush'd 20
Up the stone walls—and broke on the peak'd roof.
And Katie's lawn was like a poet's sward,[2]

1  That is, beleaguered: overwhelmed; 'prim-cut': neatly cut; 'sills': the horizontal timbers that form the foundation
   of the house.
2  A sward is a plot of grass; thus, it was a lawn such as a poet might imagine for a poem.

Velvet and sheer and di'monded with dew;
For such as win their wealth most aptly take
Smooth, urban ways and blend them with their own;
And Katie's dainty raiment was as fine
As the smooth, silken petals of the rose;
And her light feet, her nimble mind and voice,
In city schools had learn'd the city's ways,
And grafts upon the healthy, lovely vine                           30
They shone, eternal blossoms 'mid the fruit.³
For Katie had her sceptre in her hand
And wielded it right queenly there and here,
In dairy, store-room, kitchen—ev'ry spot
Where women's ways were needed on the place.
And Malcolm took her through his mighty fields,
And taught her lore about the change of crops;
And how to see a handsome furrow plough'd;
And how to choose the cattle for the mart;
And how to know a fair day's work when done;                       40
And where to plant young orchards; for he said,
'God sent a lassie, but I need a son—
Bethankit⁴ for His mercies all the same.'
And Katie, when he said it, thought of Max—
Who had been gone two winters and two springs,
And sigh'd, and thought, 'Would he not be your son?'
But all in silence, for she had too much
Of the firm will of Malcolm in her soul
To think of shaking that deep-rooted rock;
But hop'd the crystal current of his love                          50
For his one child, increasing day by day,
Might fret with silver lip until it wore
Such channels thro' the rock that some slight stroke
Of circumstance might crumble down the stone.⁵
The wooer, too, had come, Max prophesied;
Reputed wealthy; with the azure eyes
And Saxon-gilded⁶ locks—the fair, clear face,
And stalwart form that most women love,
And with the jewels of some virtues set
On his broad brow. With fires within his soul                      60

3  That is, Katie takes the 'smooth' ways of contemporary urban society and joins these with the healthy vigour of
   her rural background. In the passage that follows, Katie similarly masters both the women's realms of Malcolm's
   farm and the male knowledge needed for farming.
4  God be thanked; often said at the end of grace before meals.
5  Returning to the idea of her father as a rock and of love as a crystal spring (I.59), Katie hopes that his love for
   her will be as a 'crystal current' of water that will slowly erode her father's resistance to Max.
6  Blond.

He had the wizard skill to fetter down
To that mere pink, poetic, nameless glow,
That need not fright a flake of snow away—
But, if unloos'd, could melt an adverse rock
Marrow'd with iron, frowning in his way.[7]
And Malcolm balanc'd[8] him by day and night;
And with his grey-ey'd shrewdness partly saw
He was not one for Kate; but let him come,
And in chance moments thought: 'Well, let it be—
They make a bonnie pair—he knows the ways          70
Of men and things: can hold the gear I give,[9]
And, if the lassie wills it, let it be.'
And then, upstarting from his midnight sleep,
With hair erect and sweat upon his brow
Such as no labor e'er had beaded there;
Would cry aloud, wide-staring thro' the dark—
'Nay, nay; she shall not wed him—rest in peace.'
Then fully waking, grimly laugh and say:
'Why did I speak and answer when none spake?'
But still lie staring, wakeful, through the shades;[10]          80
List'ning to the silence, and beating still
The ball of Alfred's merits to and fro—
Saying, between the silent arguments:
'But would the mother like it, could she know?
I would there was a way to ring a lad
Like a silver coin,[11] and so find out the true;
But Kate shall say him "Nay" or say him "Yea"
At her own will.' And Katie said him 'Nay,'
In all the maiden, speechless, gentle ways
A woman has. But Alfred only laugh'd          90
To his own soul, and said in his wall'd mind:
'O, Kate, were I a lover, I might feel
Despair flap o'er my hopes with raven wings;
Because thy love is giv'n to other love.
And did I love—unless I gain'd thy love,
I would disdain the golden hair, sweet lips,
Air-blown form and true violet eyes;

---

7 'With fires . . . in his way': That is, Alfred burned within, but had the cunning to chain ('fetter') his passions—
  though they are in fact strong enough to melt a challenging rock (an adversary such as Malcolm or Max), even
  one threaded through with veins of iron.
8 Weighed; assessed.
9 Can take over and maintain Malcolm's farm.
10 Shadows, but also ghosts. As will later be made clear, Malcolm is dreaming of and speaking to his dead wife.
11 Coins were tested for the purity of their metal content by the ringing sound they made when struck; those
  adulterated with base metals did not ring true.

Nor crave the beauteous lamp without the flame;
Which in itself would light a charnel house.[12]
Unlov'd and loving, I would find the cure          100
Of Love's despair in nursing Love's disdain—
Disdain of lesser treasure than the whole.
One cares not much to place against the wheel
A di'mond lacking flame[13]—nor loves to pluck
A rose with all its perfume cast abroad
To the bosom of the gale. Not I, in truth!
If all man's days are three-score years and ten,[14]
He needs must waste them not, but nimbly seize
The bright, consummate blossom that his will
Calls for most loudly. Gone, long gone the days          110
When Love within my soul for ever stretch'd
Fierce hands of flame, and here and there I found
A blossom fitted for him—all up-fill'd
With love as with clear dew—they had their hour
And burn'd to ashes with him, as he droop'd
In his own ruby fires. No Phoenix he,[15]
To rise again because of Katie's eyes,
On dewy wings, from ashes such as his!
But now, another Passion bids me forth,
To crown him with the fairest I can find,          120
And makes me lover—not of Katie's face,
But of her father's riches! O, high fool,
Who feels the faintest pulsing of a wish
And fails to feed it into lordly life!
So that, when stumbling back to Mother Earth,
His freezing lip may curl in cold disdain
Of those poor, blighted fools who starward stare
For that fruition, nipp'd and scanted here.
And, while the clay o'ermasters all his blood—
And he can feel the dust knit with his flesh—          130
He yet can say to them, "Be ye content;
I tasted perfect fruitage thro' my life,
Lighted all lamps of passion, till the oil
Fail'd from their wicks; and now, O now, I know
There is no Immortality could give
Such boon as this—to simply cease to be!

12 A dark place where dead bodies, or the bones of the dead, are kept.
13 That is, a diamond without natural lustre is not worth putting on the polishing wheel.
14 Seventy years: the traditional length of human life according to the Bible (Psalm 90). In the speech that follows, Alfred, believing that there is no afterlife, affirms his philosophy of living for the moment and not deny-
   ing himself any pleasure in this brief span.
15 The legendary bird of Greek myth that, after being consumed by fire, rises again from its ashes.

There lies your Heaven, O ye dreaming slaves,
If ye would only live to make it so;
Nor paint upon the blue skies lying shades[16]
Of—what *is not*. Wise, wise and strong the man          140
Who poisons that fond haunter of the mind,
Craving for a hereafter with deep draughts
Of wild delights—so fiery, fierce, and strong,
That when their dregs are deeply, deeply drain'd,
What once was blindly crav'd of purblind[17] Chance,
Life, life eternal—throbbing thro' all space,
Is strongly loath'd—and with his face in dust.
Man loves his only Heav'n—six feet of Earth!"
So, Katie, tho' your blue eyes say me "Nay",
My pangs of love for gold must needs be fed,          150
And shall be, Katie, if I know my mind.'
Events were winds close nestling in the sails
Of Alfred's bark,[18] all blowing him direct
To his wish'd harbour. On a certain day,
All set about with roses and with fire;
One of three days of heat which frequent slip,
Like triple rubies, in between the sweet,
Mild, emerald days of summer, Katie went,
Drawn by a yearning for the ice-pale blooms,[19]
Natant and shining—firing all the bay          160
With angel fires built up of snow and gold.
She found the bay close pack'd with groaning logs,
Prison'd between great arms of close-hing'd wood.
All cut from Malcolm's forests in the west,
And floated hither to his noisy mills;
And all stamp'd with the potent 'G.' and 'M.',
Which much he lov'd to see upon his goods,
The silent courtiers owning him their king.
Out clear beyond, the rustling ricebeds sang,
And the cool lilies starr'd the shadow'd wave.          170
'This is a day for lily-love,' said Kate,
While she made bare the lilies of her feet,
And sang a lily-song that Max had made,
That spoke of lilies—always meaning Kate.

16 Here, illusions.
17 Here, completely blind.
18 A sailing vessel.
19 Water lilies; 'Natant': floating.

'White Lady of the silver'd lakes,
Chaste Goddess of the sweet, still shrines,
   The jocund river fitful makes,
By sudden, deep gloom'd brakes,[20]
Close shelter'd by close weft and woof of vine,
Spilling a shadow gloomy-rich as wine,            180
Into the silver throne where thou dost sit,
Thy silken leaves all dusky round thee knit!

Mild soul of the unsalted wave!
   White bosom holding golden fire!
Deep as some ocean-hidden cave
   Are fix'd the roots of thy desire,
Thro' limpid currents stealing up,
And rounding to the pearly cup.
   Thou dost desire,
With all thy trembling heart of sinless fire,      190
   But to be fill'd
   With dew distill'd
From clear, fond skies that in their gloom
Hold, floating high, thy sister moon.
Pale chalice of a sweet perfume,
Whiter-breasted than a dove—
To thee the dew is—love!'

Kate bared her little feet, and pois'd herself
On the first log close grating on the shore;
And with bright eyes of laughter, and wild hair—     200
A flying wind of gold—from log to log
Sped, laughing as they wallow'd in her track,
Like brown-scal'd monsters rolling, as her foot
Spurn'd each in turn with its rose-white sole.
A little island, out in middle wave,
With its green shoulder held the great drive[21] brac'd
Between it and the mainland: here it was
The silver lilies drew her with white smiles;
And as she touch'd the last great log of all,
It reel'd, upstarting, like a column brac'd       210
A second on the wave—and when it plung'd
Rolling upon the froth and sudden foam,
Katie had vanish'd, and with angry grind

---

20 Ferns; 'weft and woof': i.e., as if woven on a loom.
21 Log-drive: a quantity of logs transported by floating them downstream.

The vast logs roll'd together—nor a lock
Of drifting, yellow hair—an upflung hand,
Told where the rich man's chiefest treasure sank
Under his wooden wealth. But Alfred, laid
With pipe and book upon the shady marge[22]
Of the cool isle, saw all, and seeing hurl'd
Himself, and hardly knew it, on the logs.                                220
By happy chance a shallow lapp'd the isle
On this green bank; and when his iron arms
Dash'd the bark'd monsters, as frail stems of rice,
A little space apart, the soft, slow tide
But reach'd his chest, and in a flash he saw
Kate's yellow hair, and by it drew her up,
And lifting her aloft, cried out, 'O, Kate!'
And once again said, 'Katie! is she dead?'
For like the lilies broken by the rough
And sudden riot of the armor'd logs,                                     230
Kate lay upon his hands; and now the logs
Clos'd in upon him, nipping his great chest,
Nor could he move to push them off again
For Katie in his arms. 'And now,' he said,
'If none should come, and any wind arise
To weld these woody monsters 'gainst the isle,
I shall be crack'd like any broken twig;
And as it is, I know not if I die,
For I am hurt—aye, sorely, sorely hurt!'
Then look'd on Katie's lily face, and said,                              240
'Dead, dead or living? Why, an even chance.
O lovely bubble on a troubl'd sea,
I would not thou shouldst lose thyself again
In the black ocean whence thy life emerg'd,
But skyward steal on gales as soft as love,
And hang in some bright rainbow overhead,
If only such bright rainbow spann'd the earth.'
Then shouted loudly, till the silent air
Rous'd like a frighten'd bird, and on its wings
Caught up his cry and bore it to the farm.                              250
There Malcolm, leaping from his noontide sleep,
Upstarted as at midnight, crying out,
'She shall not wed him—rest you, wife, in peace!'
They found him, Alfred, haggard-ey'd and faint,
But holding Katie ever towards the sun,

22 Bank.

Unhurt, and waking in the fervent heat.
And now it came that Alfred, being sick
Of his sharp hurts and tended by them both,
With what was like to love, being born of thanks,
Had choice of hours most politic to woo,                                  260
And used his deed as one might use the sun,
To ripen unmellow'd fruit; and from the core
Of Katie's gratitude hop'd yet to nurse
A flow'r all to his liking—Katie's love.
But Katie's mind was like the plain, broad shield
Of a table di'mond,²³ nor had a score of sides;
And in its shield, so precious and so plain,
Was cut, thro' all its clear depths—Max's name.
And so she said him 'Nay' at last, in words
Of such true-sounding silver that he knew                                 270
He might not win her at the present hour,
But smil'd and thought—'I go, and come again!
Then shall we see. Our three-score years and ten
Are mines of treasure, if we hew them deep,
Nor stop too long in choosing out our tools!'

23 The table, and in this passage the shield, is the large horizontal plane at the top of a cut diamond.

## PART IV

From his far wigwam sprang the strong North Wind
And rush'd with war-cry down the steep ravines,
And wrestl'd with the giants of the woods;
And with his ice-club beat the swelling crests
Of the deep watercourses into death;
And with his chill foot froze the whirling leaves
Of dun and gold and fire in icy banks;
And smote the tall reeds to the harden'd earth;
And sent his whistling arrows o'er the plains,
Scatt'ring the ling'ring herds—and sudden paus'd                          10
When he had frozen all the running streams,
And hunted with his war-cry all the things
That breath'd about the woods, or roam'd the bleak
Bare prairies swelling to the mournful sky.
'White squaw,'¹ he shouted, troubl'd in his soul,
'I slew the dead, wrestl'd with naked chiefs
Unplum'd before, scalped of their leafy plumes;²

1 A personification of Winter.
2 The trees, which have already been scalped of their leaves by Autumn, long before Winter conquered them.

I bound sick rivers in cold thongs of death,
And shot my arrows over swooning plains,
Bright with the paint of death—and lean and bare. 20
And all the braves of my loud tribe will mock
And point at me—when our great chief the Sun,
Relights his Council fire in the Moon
Of Budding Leaves: "Ugh, ugh! he is a brave!
He fights with squaws and takes the scalps of babes!"
And the least wind[3] will blow his calumet—
Fill'd with the breath of smallest flow'rs—across
The war-paint on my face, and pointing with
His small, bright pipe, that never moved a spear
Of bearded rice, cry, "Ugh! he slays the dead!" 30
O, my white squaw, come from thy wigwam grey,
Spread thy white blanket on the twice-slain dead,
And hide them, ere the waking of the Sun!'

> *High grew the snow beneath the low-hung sky,*
> *And all was silent in the Wilderness;*
> *In trance of stillness Nature heard her God*
> *Rebuilding her spent fires, and veil'd her face*
> *While the Great Worker brooded o'er His work.*

'Bite deep and wide, O Axe, the tree,[4]
What doth thy bold voice promise me?' 40

'I promise thee all joyous things,
That furnish forth the lives of kings!

For ev'ry silver ringing blow,
Cities and palaces shall grow!'

'Bite deep and wide, O Axe, the tree
Tell wider prophecies to me.'

'When rust hath gnaw'd me deep and red,
A nation strong shall lift his head!

His crown the very Heav'ns shall smite,
Æons shall build him in his might!' 50

---

3  The East Wind, associated with Spring.
4  The fourteen lines that begin here are Max's song to his axe: he asks it to foretell the future that he and it will help bring into being and imagines it replying.

'Bite deep and wide, O Axe, the tree;
Bright Seer, help on thy prophecy!'

Max smote the snow-weigh'd tree and lightly laugh'd.
'See, friend,'⁵ he cried to one that look'd and smil'd,
'My axe and I—we do immortal tasks—
We build up nations—this my axe and I!'
'O,' said the other with a cold, short smile,
'Nations are not immortal! Is there now
One nation thron'd upon the sphere of earth,
That walk'd with the first Gods, and saw                          60
The budding world unfold its slow-leav'd flow'r?
Nay; it is hardly theirs to leave behind
Ruins so eloquent that the hoary sage
Can lay his hand upon their stones, and say:
"These once were thrones!" The lean, lank lion peals
His midnight thunders over lone, red plains.
Long-ridg'd and crested on their dusty waves
With fires from moons red-hearted as the sun;
And deep re-thunders all the earth to him.
For, far beneath the flame-fleck'd, shifting sands,               70
Below the roots of palms, and under stones
Of younger ruins, thrones, tow'rs and cities
Honeycomb the earth. The high, solemn walls
Of hoary ruins—their foundings all unknown
(But to the round-ey'd worlds that walk
In the blank paths of Space and blanker Chance)—
At whose stones young mountains wonder, and the seas'
New-silv'ring, deep-set valleys pause and gaze,
Are rear'd upon old shrines, whose very Gods
Were dreams to the shrine-builders of a time                      80
They caught in far-off flashes—as the child
Half thinks he can remember how one came
And took him in her hand and shew'd him that,
He thinks, she call'd the sun. Proud ships rear high
On ancient billows that have torn the roots
Of cliffs, and bitten at the golden lips
Of firm, sleek beaches, till they conquer'd all,
And sow'd the reeling earth with salted waves.

5 Alfred, who has come to visit Max. Contrary to Max's belief that he and his axe are—by contributing to the
building up of civilization—accomplishing tasks that will endure, Alfred will argue that nothing lasts forever,
even though Time, which he personifies in lines IV.100–34, repeatedly deludes herself and others into believing
that there are beginnings and permanence. Alfred concludes that only Death endures; Max will counter with
his belief that Love is the one immortal thing.

Wrecks plunge, prow foremost, down still, solemn slopes,
And bring their dead crews to as dead a quay;                    90
Some city built before that ocean grew,
By silver drops from many a floating cloud,
By icebergs bellowing in their throes of death,
By lesser seas toss'd from their rocking cups,
And leaping each to each; by dew-drops flung
From painted sprays, whose weird leaves and flow'rs
Are moulded for new dwellers on the earth,
Printed in hearts of mountains and of mines.
Nations immortal? Where the well-trimm'd lamps
Of long-past ages, when Time seem'd to pause                     100
On smooth, dust-blotted graves that, like the tombs
Of monarchs, held dead bones and sparkling gems?
She saw no glimmer on the hideous ring
Of the black clouds; no stream of sharp, clear light
From those great torches, pass'd into the black
Of deep oblivion. She seem'd to watch, but she
Forgot her long-dead nations. When she stirr'd
Her vast limbs in the dawn that forc'd its fire
Up the black East, and saw the imperious red
Burst over virgin dews and budding flow'rs,                      110
She still forgot her molder'd thrones and kings,
Her sages and their torches, and their Gods,
And said, "This is my birth—my primal day!"
She dream'd new Gods, and rear'd them other shrines,
Planted young nations, smote a feeble flame
From sunless flint, re-lit the torch of mind;
Again she hung her cities on the hills,
Built her rich tow'rs, crown'd her kings again,
And with the sunlight on her awful[6] wings
Swept round the flow'ry cestus of the earth,                    120
And said, "I build for Immortality!"
Her vast hand rear'd her tow'rs, her shrines, her thrones;
The ceaseless sweep of her tremendous wings
Still beat them down and swept their dust abroad;
Her iron finger wrote on mountain sides
Her deeds and prowess—and her own soft plume
Wore down the hills! Again drew darkly on
A night of deep forgetfulness; once more
Time seem'd to pause upon forgotten graves—

---

6  Evoking awe; cestus: belt or girdle; particularly the embroidered girdle of the goddess Aphrodite, capable of
   arousing passion.

Once more a young dawn stole into her eyes—                      130
Again her broad wings stirr'd, and fresh, clear airs,
Blew the great clouds apart;—again Time said,
"This is my birth—my deeds and handiwork
Shall be immortal." Thus and so dream on
Fool'd nations, and thus dream their dullard sons.
Naught is immortal save immortal—Death!'
Max paus'd and smil'd: 'O, preach such gospel, friend,
To all but lovers who most truly love;
For them, their gold-wrought scripture glibly reads,
All else is mortal but immortal—Love!'                          140
'Fools! fools!' his friend said, 'most immortal fools!—
But pardon, pardon, for, perchance, you love?'
'Yes,' said Max, proudly smiling, 'thus do I
Possess the world and feel eternity!'
Dark laughter blacken'd in the other's eyes:
'Eternity! why, did such Iris-arch
Enring our worm-bored planet, never liv'd
One woman true enough such tryst to keep!'[7]
'I'd swear by Kate,' said Max: and then, 'I had
A mother, and my father swore by her.'                          150
'By Kate? Ah, that were lusty oath, indeed!
Some other man will look into her eyes,
And swear me roundly, "By true Catherine!"
As Troilus swore by Cressèd[8]—so they say.'
'You never knew my Kate,' said Max, and pois'd
His axe again on high. 'But let it pass—
You are too subtle[9] for me; argument
Have I none to oppose yours with—but this,
Get you a Kate, and let her sunny eyes
Dispel the doubting darkness in your soul.'                     160
'And have not I a Kate? Pause, friend, and see.
She gave me this faint shadow[10] of herself
The day I slipp'd the watch-star[11] of our loves—

---

7  Alfred challenges Max's statement about the immortality of love with the argument that love cannot be immortal because women are untrue: beginning with an echo of a famous passage in Henry Vaughn's poem 'The
   World', in which the poet says he has had a vision of eternity as a 'great Ring of pure and endless light,' Alfred
   says that even if any such 'Iris-arch' (rainbow) did encircle our planet riddled with mortality (suggested by the
   way worms bore through it), women would still not be faithful to their trysts (here, promises).
8  Cressèd: the central female figure in Chaucer's long poem *Troilus and Criseyde*, infamous for her betrayal of her
   faithful lover. This spelling suggests that Crawford's allusion is to *Troilus and Cressida*, Shakespeare's version of
   the story, in which the name often appears in this form.
9  Abstruse; cunning, especially in the sense of deceptive.
10 Alfred shows Max an image of Katie: the word 'shadow' suggests it is a silhouette (i.e., a miniature profile in
   solid black that outlines a loved one's face).
11 Guiding star; the North Star, the fixed point used by sailors in navigation.

A ring—upon her hand—she loves me, too;
Yet tho' her eyes be suns, no Gods are they
To give me worlds, or make me feel a tide
Of strong Eternity set towards my soul;
And tho' she loves me, yet am I content
To know she loves me by the hour—the year—
Perchance the second—as all women love.'                    170
The bright axe falter'd in the air, and ripp'd
Down the rough bark, and bit the drifted snow,
For Max's arm fell, wither'd in its strength,
'Long by his side. 'Your Kate,' he said; 'your Kate!'
'Yes, mine, while holds her mind that way, my Kate;
I sav'd her life, and had her love for thanks;
Her father is Malcolm Graem—Max, my friend,
You pale! What sickness seizes on your soul?'
Max laugh'd, and swung his bright axe high again:
'Stand back a pace—a too far-reaching blow           180
Might level your false head with yon prone trunk—
Stand back and listen while I say, "You lie!"
That is my Katie's face upon your breast,
But 'tis my Katie's love lives in my breast—
Stand back, I say! My axe is heavy, and
Might chance to cleave a liar's brittle skull.
Your Kate! your Kate! your Kate!—hark, how the woods
Mock at your lie with all their woody tongues.
O, silence, ye false echoes! Not his Kate
But mine—I'm certain I will have your life!'           190
All the blue heav'n was dead in Max's eyes;
Doubt-wounded lay Kate's image in his heart,
And could not rise to pluck the sharp spear out.
'Well, strike, mad fool,' said Alfred, somewhat pale;
'I have no weapon but these naked hands.'
'Aye, but,' said Max, 'you smote my naked heart!
O shall I slay him?—Satan, answer me—
I cannot call on God for answer here.
O Kate—!'
A voice from God came thro' the silent woods           200
And answer'd him—for suddenly a wind
Caught the great tree-tops, con'd with high-pil'd snow,
And smote them to and fro, while all the air
Was sudden fill'd with busy drifts, and high
White pillars whirl'd amid the naked trunks,
And harsh, loud groans, and smiting, sapless boughs
Made hellish clamour in the quiet place.

With a shrill shriek of tearing fibres, rock'd
The half-hewn tree above his fated head;
And, tott'ring, asked the sudden blast, 'Which way?'                    210
And, answ'ring its windy arms, crash'd and broke
Thro' other lacing boughs, with one loud roar
Of woody thunder; all its pointed boughs
Pierc'd the deep snow—its round and mighty corpse,
Bark-flay'd and shudd'ring, quiver'd into death.
And Max—as some frail, wither'd reed, the sharp
And piercing branches caught at him, as hands
In a death-throe, and beat him to the earth—
And the dead tree upon its slayer lay.
'Yet hear we much of Gods;—if such there be,                           220
They play at games of chance with thunderbolts,'
Said Alfred, 'else on me this doom had come.
This seals my faith in deep and dark unfaith![12]
Now, Katie, are you mine, for Max is dead—
Or will be soon, imprison'd by those boughs,
Wounded and torn, sooth'd by the deadly palms
Of the white, trait'rous frost; and buried then
Under the snows that fill those vast, grey clouds,
Low-sweeping on the fretted forest roof.
And Katie shall believe you false—not dead;                           230
False, false!—and I? O, she shall find me true—
True as a fabl'd devil to the soul
He longs for with the heat of all Hell's fires.
These myths serve well for simile, I see.[13]
And yet—down, Pity! Knock not at my breast,
Nor grope about for that dull stone my heart;
I'll stone thee with it, Pity! Get thee hence,
Pity, I'll strangle thee with naked hands;
For thou dost bear upon thy downy breast
Remorse, shap'd like a serpent, and her fangs                         240
Might dart at me and pierce my marrow thro'.[14]
Hence, beggar, hence—and keep with fools, I say!
He bleeds and groans! Well, Max, thy God or mine,

---

12 Feeling that if the Gods were just, the tree would have fallen on him in punishment for his lies and not on Max, Alfred sees the event as further confirmation of his belief that blind chance rules the universe.

13 That is, though Alfred does not believe in Hell, it provides him with a useful myth in constructing his comparison.

14 Personified as a threatening giant, Pity has remorse, seen as a serpent, at his breast: Alfred fears that it might travel from there and attach itself to him. The idea of remorse as a fanged viper that creeps into and dwells in one's breast or bosom is developed later in the poem as a way of showing Alfred's struggles with his emotions; this conceit can be found in earlier texts such as Mary Shelley's *Frankenstein* and Nathaniel Hawthorne's 'Egotism; or, The Bosom Serpent'.

Blind Chance, here play'd the butcher—'twas not I.
Down hands! Ye shall not lift his fall'n head.
What cords tug at ye? What? Ye'd pluck him up
And staunch his wounds? There rises in my breast
A strange, strong giant, throwing wide his arms
And bursting all the granite of my heart!
How like to quiv'ring flesh a stone may feel!                                    250
Why, it has pangs! I'll none of them. I know
Life is too short for anguish and for hearts—
So I wrestle with thee, giant! and my will
Turns the thumb, and thou shalt take the knife.[15]
Well done! I'll turn thee on the arena dust,
And look on thee. What? thou wert Pity's self,
Stol'n in my breast; and I have slaughter'd thee—
But hist[16]—where hast thou hidden thy fell snake,
Fire-fang'd Remorse? Not in my breast, I know,
For all again is chill and empty there,                                          260
And hard and cold—the granite knitted up.
So lie there, Max—poor fond and simple Max,
'Tis well thou diest; earth's children should not call
Such as thee father—let them ever be
Father'd by rogues and villains, fit to cope
With the foul dragon Chance, and the black knaves
Who swarm in loathsome masses in the dust.
True Max, lie there, and slumber into death.'

15  That is, like a Roman emperor watching a contest between gladiators, Alfred's Will gives a thumb's down sign,
     calling for the execution of the giant, Pity.
16  Hush; 'fell': cruel.


## PART V

Said the high hill, in the morning: 'Look on me—
Behold, sweet earth, sweet sister sky, behold
The red flames on my peaks, and how my pines
Are cressets[1] of pure gold; my quarried scars
Of black crevasse and shadow-till'd canon,
Are trac'd in silver mist. Now on my breast
Hang the soft purple fringes of the night;
Close to my shoulder droops the weary moon,
Dove-pale, into the crimson surf the sun
Drives up before his prow;[2] and blackly stands                                  10

1  Torches; 'canon': canyon.
2  That is, the sun, like a ship, throws up a surf (the red light of dawn) as its prow cuts through the waves.

On my slim, loftiest peak, an eagle with
His angry eyes set sunward, while his cry
Falls fiercely back from all my ruddy heights;
And his bald eaglets, in their bare, broad nest,
Shrill pipe their angry echoes: "Sun, arise,
And show me that pale dove, beside her nest,
Which I shall strike with piercing beak and tear
With iron talons for my hungry young." '
And that mild dove, secure for yet a space,
Half waken'd, turns her ring'd and glossy neck          20
To watch dawn's ruby pulsing on her breast,
And see the first bright golden motes slip down
The gnarl'd trunks about her leaf-deep nest,
Nor sees nor fears the eagle on the peak.

'Aye, lassie, sing—I'll smoke my pipe the while,[3]
And let it be a simple, bonnie song,
Such as an old, plain man can gather in
His dulling ear, and feel it slipping thro'
The cold, dark, stony places of his heart.'
'Yes, sing, sweet Kate,' said Alfred in her ear;          30
'I often heard you singing in my dreams
When I was far away the winter past.'
So Katie on the moonlit window lean'd,
And in the airy silver of her voice
Sang of the tender, blue 'Forget-me-not.'

> 'Could every blossom find a voice,
>     And sing a strain to me,
> I know where I would place my choice,
>     Which my delight should be.
>     I would not choose the lily tall,          40
>     The rose from musky grot;[4]
> But I would still my minstrel call
>     The blue "Forget-me-not!"
>
> And I on mossy bank would lie
>     Of brooklet, ripp'ling clear;
> And she of the sweet azure eye,
>     Close at my list'ning ear,

---

3  The poem here returns us to Malcolm.
4  Grotto; cave.

Should sing into my soul a strain
    Might never be forgot—
So rich with joy, so rich with pain,                50
    The blue "Forget-me-not!"

Ah, ev'ry blossom hath a tale
    With silent grace to tell,
From rose that reddens to the gale
    To modest heather bell;
But O, the flow'r in ev'ry heart
    That finds a sacred spot
To bloom, with azure leaves apart,
    Is the "Forget-me-not!"

Love plucks it from the mosses green            60
    When parting hours are nigh,
And places it Love's palms between,
    With many an ardent sigh;
And bluely up from grassy graves
    In some lov'd churchyard spot,
It glances tenderly and waves,
    The dear "Forget-me-not!" '

And with the faint, last cadence, stole a glance
At Malcolm's soften'd face—a bird-soft touch
Let flutter on the rugged, silver snarls         70
Of his thick locks, and laid her tender lips
A second on the iron of his hand.
'And did you ever meet,' he sudden ask'd
Of Alfred, sitting pallid in the shade,
'Out by yon unco[5] place, a lad—a lad
Nam'd Maxwell Gordon; tall, and straight, and strong;
About my size, I take it, when a lad?'
And Katie at the sound of Max's name,
First spoken for such a space by Malcolm's lips,
Trembl'd and started, and let down her brow,      80
Hiding its sudden rose on Malcolm's arm.
'Max Gordon? Yes. Was he a friend of yours?'
'No friend of mine, but of the lassie's here—
How comes he on? I wager he's a drone,
And never will put honey in the hive.'[6]

---

5 Unknown.
6 Drones are male bees; they do not contribute to honey gathering.

'No drone,' said Alfred, laughing; 'when I left,
He and his axe were quarr'ling with the woods
And making forests reel—love steels a lover's arm.'
O, blush that stole from Katie's swelling heart,
And with its hot rose brought the happy dew                                    90
Into her hidden eyes. 'Aye, aye! is that the way?'
Said Malcolm, smiling. 'Who may be his love?
In that he is a somewhat simple soul,
Why, I suppose he loves—' he paused, and Kate
Look'd up with two 'Forget-me-nots' for eyes,
With eager jewels in their centres set
Of happy, happy tears, and Alfred's heart
Became a closer marble than before.
'—Why I suppose he loves—his lawful wife.'
'His wife! his wife!' said Malcolm, in amaze,                                   100
And laid his heavy hand on Katie's head;
'Did you two play me false, my little lass?'[7]
Speak and I'll pardon! Katie, lassie, what?'
'He has a wife,' said Alfred, 'lithe and bronz'd,
An Indian woman, comelier than her kind;
And on her knee a child with yellow locks,
And lake-like eyes of mystic Indian brown.
And so you knew him? He is doing well.'
'False, false!' said Katie, lifting up her head.
'O, you know not the Max my father means!'                                     110
'He came from yonder farm-house on the slope.'
'Some other Max—we speak not of the same.'
'He has a red mark on his temple set.'
'It matters not—'tis not the Max we know.'
'He wears a turquoise ring slung round his neck.'
'And many wear them—they are common stones.'
'His mother's ring—her name was Helen Wynde.'
'And there be many Helens who have sons.'
'O Katie, credit me—it is the man.'
'O not the man! Why, you have never told                                       120
Us of the true soul that the true Max has;
The Max we know has such a soul, I know.'
'How know you that, my foolish little lass?'
Said Malcolm, a storm of anger bound
Within his heart, like Samson with green withs[8]—

7   That is, Malcolm thinks Katie and Max may have secretly married.
8   Ropes. In the story of Samson (Judges 13–16), this heroic figure was betrayed to the Philistines by his wife
    Delilah: tied to the pillars of their temple, he used his great strength to pull down the building, killing himself
    as well as his enemies.

'Belike it is the false young cur we know!'
'No, no,' said Katie, simply, and low-voic'd;
'If he were traitor I must needs be false,
For long ago love melted our two hearts,
And time has moulded those two hearts in one.            130
And he is true since I am faithful still.'
She rose and parted, trembling as she went,
Feeling the following steel of Alfred's eyes,
And with the icy hand of scorn'd mistrust
Searching about the pulses of her heart—
Feeling for Max's image in her breast.
'To-night she conquers Doubt; to-morrow's noon
His following soldiers sap the golden wall,[9]
And I shall enter and possess the fort,'
Said Alfred, in his mind. 'O Katie, child,                140
Wilt thou be Nemesis,[10] with yellow hair,
To rend my breast? For I do feel a pulse
Stir when I look into thy pure-barb'd eyes—
O, am I breeding that false thing, a heart,
Making my breast all tender for the fangs
Of sharp Remorse to plunge their hot fire in?
I am a certain dullard! Let me feel
But one faint goad, fine as a needle's point,
And it shall be the spur in my soul's side
To urge the madd'ning thing across the jags[11]          150
And cliffs of life, into the soft embrace
Of that cold mistress,[12] who is constant too,
And never flings her lovers from her arms—
Not Death, for she is still a fruitful wife,
Her spouse the Dead, and their cold marriage yields
A million children, born of mould'ring flesh—
So Death and Flesh live on—immortal they!
I mean the blank-ey'd queen whose wassail bowl

9 Doubt commands soldiers that will, like sappers (i.e., by digging), weaken or undermine their opposition's defences (Katie is seen as a walled fort), allowing Alfred to conquer her.
10 The Greek goddess of retributive justice and vengeance.
11 Sharp projections of rock.
12 In the lines that follow, Alfred delays identifying this figure of the 'cold mistress'; instead, he tells us, in the fashion of a riddle, who she is not and with what she is associated. She is not Death, who, as spouse to the Dead, produces new life from their corpses (that is, the insects that seem to be born from rotting flesh and the plants that are fertilized by decomposition). The lover he seeks brings a wassail bowl (a punch bowl used for toasts) from which she serves the Waters of Forgetfulness (taken from the River Lethe, which, according to Greek mythology, marks the border of Hades and from which the dead drink to forget the joys of living they once had). The entrance to the home of this mistress is by way of a porch covered with red poppies (the opium poppy, which can produce forgetfulness, sleep, and death) on which she stands awaiting the 'panting' (breathless) soul. This mistress is not a slave to man or god; indeed, Alfred says, even if a single god exists, she would mock him.

Is brimm'd from Lethe, and whose porch is red
With poppies, as it waits the panting soul—                         160
She, she alone is great! No scepter'd slave
Bowing to blind, creative giants, she;
No forces seize her in their strong, mad hands,
Nor say, "Do this—be that!" Were there a God,
His only mocker, she, great Nothingness![13]
And to her, close of kin, yet lover too,
Flies this large nothing that we call the soul.'

> *Doth true Love lonely grow?*[14]
>     *Ah, no! ah, no!*
> *Ah, were it only so—*                                           170
> *That it alone might show*
> *Its ruddy rose upon its sapful tree,*
>     *Then, then in dewy morn,*
>     *Joy might his brow adorn*
> *With Love's young rose as fair and glad as he.*

> *But with Love's rose doth blow,*[15]
>     *Ah, woe! ah, woe!*
> *Truth with its leaves of snow,*
> *And Pain and Pity grow*
> *With Love's sweet roses on its sapful tree!*                    180
>     *Love's rose buds not alone,*
>     *But still, but still doth own*
> *A thousand blossoms cypress-hued*[16] *to see!*

---

13 The cold mistress is Nothingness personified. Alfred's viewpoint and philosophical perspective throughout is
   drawn from the nihilism that emerged in the middle of the nineteenth century—the belief that existence has
   no meaning, no moral value, and no purpose. His is not the extreme form of nihilism—which believes that
   nothing exists—but the kind that denies any systematic order, leading him to embrace chance as the determiner
   of all action and to put material gain for himself above all else.
14 That is, Does true love grow in isolation?
15 Bloom.
16 Dark green. In Greek tradition and mythology, the cypress was associated with mourning: it was often planted
   to shade a grave and its wood used to make coffins.

## PART VI

*Who curseth Sorrow knows her not at all.*
*Dark matrix*[1] *she, from which the human soul*
*Has its last birth; whence, with its misty thews,*
*Close-knitted in her blackness, issues out.*
*Strong for immortal toil up such great heights.*
*As crown o'er crown rise through Eternity.*
*Without the loud, deep clamour of her wail,*
*The iron of her hands, the biting brine*
*Of her black tears, the Soul but lightly built*
*Of indeterminate spirit, like a mist*            10
*Would lapse to Chaos in soft, gilded dreams,*
*As mists fade in the gazing of the sun.*
*Sorrow, dark mother of the soul, arise!*
*Be crown'd with spheres where thy bless'd children dwell.*
*Who, but for thee, were not. No lesser seat*
*Be thine, thou Helper of the Universe,*
*Than planet on planet pil'd!—thou instrument*
*Close-clasp'd within the great Creative Hand!*

The Land had put his ruddy gauntlet[2] on,
Of harvest gold, to dash in Famine's face.            20
And like a vintage wain,[3] deep dy'd with juice,
The great moon falter'd up the ripe, blue sky,
Drawn by silver stars—like oxen white
And horn'd with rays of light. Down the rich land
Malcolm's small valleys, fill'd with grain, lip-high,
Lay round a lonely hill that fac'd the moon,
And caught the wine-kiss of its ruddy light.
A cusp'd, dark wood caught in its black embrace
The valleys and the hill, and from its wilds,
Spic'd with dark cedars, cried the Whip-poor-will.            30
A crane, belated, sail'd across the moon.
On the bright, small, close-link'd lakes green islets lay,
Dusk knots of tangl'd vines, or maple boughs,

1 Womb. This passage on the value of Sorrow (personified) suggests that, for an individual's soul or inner being, to experience sorrow is like being nourished inside Sorrow's womb; when the soul emerges from that period of suffering it is as if it is reborn, its muscles no longer insubstantial ('misty'). Now it can toil immortally, as each generation builds for the next to ensure humankind's eternal existence. Without Sorrow, the soul would be vulnerable to the power of Chaos (here, another name for nothingness). Sorrow is so important that she resides in the highest heaven, held in the Creator's hand.
2 Glove used for work or in battle.
3 Work wagon or cart. Lines 107–37 present a pastoral picture of evening, but the presence of elements such as the Whip-poor-will's cry (a sad-sounding call in the evening and night) and the image of the crane (a bad omen in the classical tradition), flying across the moon, forebode the violent scene that follows.

Or tuft'd cedars, boss'd upon the waves.[4]
The gay, enamell'd[5] children of the swamp
Roll'd a low bass to treble, tinkling notes
Of little streamlets leaping from the woods.
Close to old Malcolm's mills, two wooden jaws[6]
Bit up the water on a sloping floor;
And here, in season, rush'd the great logs down,                    40
To seek the river winding on its way.
In a green sheen, smooth as a Naiad's locks,
The water roll'd between the shudd'ring jaws—
Then on the river-level roar'd and reel'd—
In ivory-arm'd conflict with itself.
'Look down,' said Alfred, 'Katie, look and see
How that but pictures my mad heart to you.
It tears itself in fighting that mad love
You swear is hopeless—hopeless—is it so?'
'Ah, yes!' said Katie, 'ask me not again.'                    50
'But Katie, Max is false; no word has come,
Nor any sign from him for many months,
And—he is happy with his Indian wife.'
She lifted eyes fair as the fresh, grey dawn
With all its dews and promises of sun.
'O, Alfred!—saver of my little life—
Look in my eyes and read them honestly.'
He laugh'd till all the isles and forests laugh'd.
'O simple child! what may the forest flames
See in the woodland ponds but their own fires?[7]                    60
And have you, Katie, neither fears nor doubts?'
She, with the flow'r-soft pinkness of her palm
Cover'd her sudden tears, then quickly said:
'Fears—never doubts, for true love never doubts.'
Then Alfred paus'd a space, as one who holds
A white doe by the throat and searches for
The blade to slay her. 'This your answer still—
You doubt not—doubt not this far love of yours,

4  The small islands look as if they are embossed upon the water.
5  That is, bright and shiny. The 'children of the swamp' are the creatures that inhabit it—probably, as Bentley
   suggests, frogs, whose bass notes form a counterpart to the treble-noted tinkling of the swamp's 'streamlets'.
6  The jaws are part of Crawford's description of a chute or slide, a 'sloping floor' set up to move logs from that
   level of water to a lower one; the opening of the chute resembles jaws that allow the inclined slide to catch the
   logs and carry them down to the larger body of water, the river below. The vortex that the chute creates in the
   upper level pulls the logs down and into otherwise peaceful water that Crawford compares to the smooth green
   hair of a naiad (a water nymph in Greek mythology). As the water flows down the chute with the logs and combines with the river below, it becomes agitated, producing what looks like a battle between the two flows.
7  That is, Katie's eyes, like a woodland lake, reflect what is near them; Alfred, looking into them, can see only a
   reflection of himself.

Tho' sworn a false young recreant,[8] Kate, by me?'
'He is as true as I am,' Katie said;                                        70
'And did I seek for stronger simile,
I could not find such in the universe!'
'And were he dead? What, Katie, were he dead—
A handful of brown dust, a flame blown out—
What then would love be strongly true to—Naught?'
'Still true to Love my love would be,' she said,
And, faintly smiling, pointed to the stars.
'O fool!' said Alfred, stirr'd—as craters rock
To their own throes—and over his pale lips
Roll'd flaming stone, his molten heart. 'Then, fool—          80
Be true to what thou wilt—for he is dead.
And there have grown this gilded summer past
Grasses and buds from his unburied flesh.
I saw him dead. I heard his last, loud cry,
"O Kate!" ring thro' the woods; in truth I did.'
She half raised up a piteous, pleading hand,
Then fell along the mosses at his feet.
'Now will I show I love you, Kate,' he said,
'And give you gift of love; you shall not wake
To feel the arrow, feather-deep, within                            90
Your constant heart. For me, I never meant
To crawl an hour beyond what time I felt
The strange, fang'd monster that they call Remorse
Fold round my waken'd heart. The hour has come;
And as Love grew, the welded folds of steel
Slipp'd round in horrid zones.[9] In Love's flaming eyes
Stared its fell eyeballs, and with Hydra head[10]
It sank hot fangs in breast, and brow and thigh.
Come, Kate! O Anguish is a simple knave[11]
Whom hucksters could outwit with small trade lies,              100
When thus so easily his smarting thralls
May flee his knout! Come, come, my little Kate;
The black porch with its fringe of poppies waits—
A propylaeum[12] hospitably wide—

8  A coward or deserter.
9  Terrible, frightful steel-like bands that, here, encircle Alfred's heart.
10  The Hydra is the many-headed snake of Greek myth.
11  That is, Anguish, though it can hold its captives in painful bondage ('smarting thrall'), can be escaped because,
    like a boy or fool, it can be tricked by an obvious ruse, similar to the weak lies that petty traders, or peddlers,
    make about the goods they try to sell. A knout is a whip or scourge designed to inflict severe injury.
12  A porch or entrance to a temple or sacred enclosure; here, the gateway to death and oblivion.

No lictors with their fasces at its jaws,[13]
Its floor as kindly to my fire-vein'd feet
As to thy silver, lilied, sinless ones.
O you shall slumber soundly, tho' the white,
Wild waters pluck the crocus[14] of your hair,
And scaly spies stare with round, lightless eyes    110
At your small face laid on my stony breast.
Come, Kate! I must not have you wake, dear heart,
To hear you cry, perchance, on your dead Max.'
He turn'd her still face close upon his breast,
And with his lips upon her soft, ring'd hair,
Leap'd from the bank, low shelving[15] o'er the knot
Of frantic waters at the long slide's foot.
And as the sever'd waters crash'd and smote
Together once again—within the wave
Stunn'd chamber of his ear there peal'd a cry:    120
'O Kate! stay, madman; traitor, stay! O Kate!'

Max, gaunt as prairie wolves in famine time,
With long-drawn sickness, reel'd upon the bank—
Katie, new-rescu'd, waking in his arms.
On the white riot of the waters gleam'd,
The face of Alfred, calm, with close-seal'd eyes,
And blood red on his temple where it smote
The mossy timbers of the groaning slide.
'O God!' said Max, as Katie's opening eyes
Looked up to his, slow budding to a smile    130
Of wonder and of bliss, 'My Kate, my Kate!'
She saw within his eyes a larger soul
Than that light spirit that before she knew,
And read the meaning of his glance and words.
'Do as you will, my Max. I would not keep
You back with one light-falling finger-tip!'[16]
And cast herself from his large arms upon
The mosses at his feet, and hid her face

13 That is, in Nothingness's house, unlike in the courts of ancient Rome, no lictor (Roman official) stands at the entrance holding the fasces (his symbol of magisterial authority: a bundle of rods in which an axe is wrapped, an emblem of the power to sentence someone to death or flogging).

14 Saffron-colour, like the flower that is compared here to Katie's hair. In other words, the water will move her hair while fish ('scaly spies') look at her face.

15 Sloping.

16 Katie realizes that Max has grown (now has a larger soul) since he left her and that he must decide on his own whether to risk his life again by attempting to rescue Alfred or stay with Katie on the shore. In the lines that follow, she does not want to influence his decision, though she cannot bear to think of losing him. A voice within tells her that even if Max dies in his attempt, it will be a Christ-like sacrifice. When Max emerges from the water with Alfred, he achieves heroic 'triumph' in having acted to save his enemy.

That she might not behold what he would do;
Or lest the terror in her shining eyes 140
Might bind him to her, and prevent his soul
Work out its greatness; and her long, wet hair
Drew, mass'd, about her ears, to shut the sound
Of the vex'd waters from her anguish'd brain.
Max look'd upon her, turning as he look'd.
A moment came a voice in Katie's soul:
'Arise, be not dismay'd, arise and look;
If he should perish, 'twill be as a God,
For he would die to save his enemy.'
But answer'd her torn heart: 'I cannot look— 150
I cannot look and see him sob and die
In those pale, angry arms.[17] O, let me rest
Blind, blind and deaf until the swift-pac'd end.
My Max! O God—was that his Katie's name?'
Like a pale dove, hawk-hunted, Katie ran,
Her fear's beak in her shoulder;[18] and below,
Where the coil'd waters straighten'd to a stream,
Found Max all bruis'd and bleeding on the bank,
But smiling with man's triumph in his eyes,
When he has on fierce Danger's lion neck 160
Plac'd his right hand and pluck'd the prey away.
And at his feet lay Alfred, still and white,
A willow's shadow tremb'ling on his face.
'There lies the false, fair devil, O my Kate,
Who would have parted us, but could not, Kate!'
'But could not, Max,' said Katie. 'Is he dead?'
But, swift perusing Max's strange, dear face,
Close clasp'd against his breast—forgot him straight
And ev'ry other evil thing upon
The broad green earth. 170

17 The clutch of the river.
18 That is, Katie, while hiding her face, hears Max call her name; though fear penetrates her like a hawk with its
   beak in its prey's shoulder, she runs to him. In the lines that follow, this image is paralleled with the metaphor
   of Max's placing one hand on the neck of Danger, personified as a lion, and with the other pulling the lion's
   prey (Alfred) from the water.


## PART VII

Again rang out the music of the axe,
And on the slope, as in his happy dreams,
The home of Max with wealth of drooping vines
On the rude walls; and in the trellis'd porch

Sat Katie, smiling o'er the rich, fresh fields;
And by her side sat Malcolm, hale and strong;
Upon his knee a little, smiling child,
Nam'd—Alfred, as the seal of pardon set
Upon the heart of one who sinn'd and woke
To sorrow for his sins—and whom they lov'd                    10
With gracious joyousness—nor kept the dusk
Of his past deeds between their hearts and his.[1]
Malcolm had follow'd with his flocks and herds
When Max and Katie, hand in hand, went out
From his old home; and now, with slow, grave smile,
He said to Max, who twisted Katie's hair
About his naked arm, bare from his toil:
'It minds me of old times, this house of yours;
It stirs my heart to hearken to the axe,
And hear the windy crash of falling trees;                    20
Aye, these fresh forests make an old man young.'
'Oh, yes!' said Max, with laughter in his eyes;
'And I do truly think that Eden bloom'd
Deep in the heart of tall, green maple groves,
With sudden scents of pine from mountain sides,
And prairies with their breasts against the skies.[2]
And Eve was only little Katie's height.'
'Hoot, lad! you speak as ev'ry Adam speaks
About his bonnie Eve; but what says Kate?'
'O Adam had not Max's soul,' she said;                        30
'And these wild woods and plains are fairer far
Than Eden's self. O bounteous mothers they!
Beck'ning pale starvelings with their fresh, green hands,
And with their ashes mellowing the earth,
That she may yield her increase willingly.
I would not change these wild and rocking woods,
Dotted by little homes of unbark'd trees,
Where dwell the fleers from the waves of want—
For the smooth sward of selfish Eden bowers,
Nor—Max for Adam, if I knew my mind!'                         40

1884

---

1  They have forgiven Alfred, despite his dark actions.
2  Max here claims that the nature around Eden—the perfect garden made by the Creator for the first of the
   human race, Adam and Eve—must have been like that now surrounding Max and Katie's new home. Katie
   replies that their nature is better than the walled garden of 'selfish' Eden because it welcomes famished settlers
   ('starvelings') who flee from the Old World's inability to nourish them, and because it rewards their own hard
   work. Thus, Max, who has helped by his labours to create this new Eden, is better than Adam.

# Esther [1]

Unheard of others, voices called all night:—
The babble of young voices, the strong cries
Of men and women mourned amid the palms,
And gathered in mine ear, as winds that blow
About the earth and, gathering in some cave,
Give ghostly utterance of ghostly things—
'Esther, the Queen, arise and move the King
To sheathe the sword that lies upon the throats
Of thine own people!'

       When the sun sprang up          10
His tresses were as blood that stained the courts
And beat upon the walls, and sent its tide
To bathe my naked feet when I thrust back
The golden tissue of the door to catch
Some sweetness of the morn upon my brow;
And lo! my God, a sweetness filled my soul
That came not from the morning but from Thee!

The winds that stirred the foldings of my robe
Were children's fingers—ghostly, clinging clasps
That said, 'O Esther, plead before the King!'        20
Ah me! how often when a little maid,
Playing amid the fountains and the flowers
Of mine own people, have such dimpled hands
Caught at my flying robe in mimic fright,
And great round eyes buried themselves therein;
But then the voices laughed, 'O Esther, stay
That wicked brother, for he chases us,
And pelts with blushing roses.' Now I hear,
'O Esther, stay the King, he slaughters us!'

Alas! my courage is so weak a blade        30
It trembles at a breath. God, temper it to strength!
I perish if I go uncalled before the King.
Yea! let him smite me down a sacrifice
For Israel! Perchance that, dying thus, my blood
May creep about his heart and soften it

---

1  The Biblical Book of Esther explains how the Persian king chooses the Jewish maiden Esther to be his queen. When
   Esther's uncle, Mordecai, angers the king's vizier, the latter decides to take revenge by slaughtering all of Persia's
   Jews. Mordecai asks Esther to intercede with the king, even though for Esther to enter the throne room without
   being summoned is a breach of protocol that, if it meets with the king's disfavour, will result in her execution.

To those for whom I die. O God, when Thou
Didst veil Thy handmaid's soul in this fair flesh
'Twas for some strait sore as the present need!

What is it that glimmers ready by my couch?
The symbol of my state, the crown the King                40
Hath set upon my brows. On, crown, and deck
My triumph or my death! O robes of state,
Ye jewelled splendours, how ye mock this flesh
That quivers with monitions of that hour
When this night's moon shall peer above the palms
And find no life in Esther but that cold, cold life,
Blazing from diamond crown and golden robe,
Mocks of her life's brief sun and briefer state.

But still will Esther go. Jehovah calls!
And if I die—Hark! as I go by court                      50
And golden pillar, sweet, shrill voices cry,
Unheard of others, 'Esther, stay the King!'
O yea, my lambs of Israel! how your hands
Cling to my robes and pluck me to the King!
God, lift his sceptre up before my face!
But if I die—I die!

[c. 1874], 1905


# Canada to England

Gone are the days, old Warrior of the Seas,
When thine armed head, bent low to catch my voice,
Caught but the plaintive sighings of my woods,
And the wild roar of rock-dividing streams,
And the loud bellow of my cataracts,
Bridged with the seven splendours of the bow.
When Nature was a Samson yet unshorn,[1]
Filling the land with solitary might,
Or as the Angel of the Apocalypse,
One foot upon the primeval bowered land                  10
One foot upon the white mane of the sea,[2]

1  That is, Samson before losing his innate strength when his hair—which, as a sign of his dedication to God, he
   must not cut—is cut by the Philistine Delilah.
2  An image from the Book of Revelation 10:5–10.

My voice but faintly swelled the ebb and flow
Of the wild tides and storms that beat upon
Thy rocky girdle,—loud shrieking from the Ind³
Ambrosial-breathing furies; from the north
Thundering with Arctic bellows, groans of seas
Rising from tombs of ice disrupted by
The magic kisses of the wide-eyed sun.

The times have won a change. Nature no more
Lords it alone and binds the lonely land                        20
A serf to tongueless solitudes; but Nature's self
Is led, glad captive, in light fetters rich
As music-sounding silver can adorn;
And man has forged them, and our silent God
Behind His flaming worlds smiles on the deed.
'Man hath dominion'—words of primal might;⁴
'Man hath dominion'—thus the words of God.

If destiny is writ on night's dusk scroll,
Then youngest stars are dropping from the hand
Of the Creator, sowing on the sky                               30
My name in seeds of light. Ages will watch
Those seeds expand to suns, such as the tree
Bears on its boughs, which grows in Paradise.⁵

How sounds my voice, my warrior kinsman, now?
Sounds it not like to thine in lusty youth—
A word-possessing shout of busy men,
Veined with the clang of trumpets and the noise
Of those who make them ready for the strife,
And in the making ready bruise its head?
Sounds it not like to thine—the whispering vine,               40
The robe of summer rustling thro' the fields,
The lowing of the cattle in the meads,
The sound of Commerce, and the music-set,
Flame-brightened step of Art in stately halls,—
All the infinity of notes which chord
The diapason⁶ of a Nation's voice?

---

3  India (poetic). The 'furies' (Maenads)—ecstatic followers of Dionysus—are said to have followed him to India
   and back.
4  An allusion to the naming of 'the Dominion of Canada', which is based on Psalm 72:8: 'He shall have dominion also from sea to sea, and from the river unto the ends of the earth' (Psalm 72:8).
5  That is, the Tree of Knowledge, which in the Book of Genesis, is found in the Garden of Eden.
6  The entire musical range of an instrument or voice.

My infants' tongues lisp word for word with thine;
We worship, wed, and die, and God is named
That way ye name Him,—strong bond between
Two mighty lands when as one mingled cry,                    50
As of one voice, Jehovah turns to hear.
The bonds between us are no subtle links
Of subtle minds binding in close embrace,
Half-struggling for release, two alien lands,
But God's own seal of kindred, which to burst
Were but to dash His benediction from
Our brows. 'Who loveth not his kin,
Whose face and voice are his, how shall he love
God whom he hath not seen?'[7]

1874, 1905

7  A paraphrase of 1 John 4:20: 'If a man say, I love God, and hateth his brother, he is a liar: for he that loveth not
   his brother whom he hath seen, how can he love God whom he hath not seen?'

## Said the Canoe

My masters twain made me a bed
Of pine-boughs resinous, and cedar;
Of moss, a soft and gentle breeder
Of dreams of rest; and me they spread
With furry skins and, laughing, said:
'Now she shall lay her polished sides
As queens do rest, or dainty brides,
Our slender lady of the tides!'

My masters twain their camp-soul[1] lit;
Streamed incense from the hissing cones;                    10
Large crimson flashes grew and whirled;
Thin golden nerves of sly light curled
Round the dun camp; and rose faint zones,
Half way about each grim bole knit,
Like a shy child that would bedeck
With its soft clasp a Brave's red neck,
Yet sees the rough shield on his breast,
The awful plumes shake on his crest,
And, fearful, drops his timid face,
Nor dares complete the sweet embrace.                       20

1  i.e. the campfire.

Into the hollow hearts of brakes²—
Yet warm from sides of does and stags
Passed to the crisp, dark river-flags—
Sinuous, red as copper-snakes,
Sharp-headed serpents, made of light,
Glided and hid themselves in night.

My masters twain the slaughtered deer
Hung on forked boughs with thongs of leather:
Bound were his stiff, slim feet together,
His eyes like dead stars cold and drear.          30
The wandering firelight drew near
And laid its wide palm, red and anxious,
On the sharp splendour of his branches,
On the white foam grown hard and sere
    On flank and shoulder.
Death—hard as breast of granite boulder—
    Under his lashes
Peered thro' his eyes at his life's grey ashes.

My masters twain sang songs that wove—
As they burnished hunting-blade and rifle—          40
A golden thread with a cobweb trifle,
Loud of the chase and low of love:

'O Love! art thou a silver fish,
Shy of the line and shy of gaffing,
Which we do follow, fierce, yet laughing,
Casting at thee the light-winged wish?
And at the last shall we bring thee up
From the crystal darkness, under the cup
    Of lily folden
    On broad leaves golden?          50

'O Love! art thou a silver deer
With feet as swift as wing of swallow,
While we with rushing arrows follow?
And at the last shall we draw near
And o'er thy velvet neck cast thongs
Woven of roses, stars and songs—
    New chains all moulden
    Of rare gems olden?'

2 Thickets; 'flags': reeds or fronds.

They hung the slaughtered fish like swords
   On saplings slender; like scimitars,                   60
   Bright, and ruddied from new-dead wars,
Blazed in the light the scaly hordes.

They piled up boughs beneath the trees,
   Of cedar web and green fir tassel.
   Low did the pointed pine tops rustle,
The camp-fire blushed to the tender breeze.

The hounds laid dewlaps on the ground
   With needles of pine, sweet, soft and rusty,
   Dreamed of the dead stag stout and lusty;
A bat by the red flames wove its round.              70

The darkness built its wigwam walls
   Close round the camp, and at its curtain
   Pressed shapes, thin, woven and uncertain
As white locks of tall waterfalls.

1884, 1905

---

# Charles G.D. Roberts
## 1860–1945

Charles G.D. Roberts, his cousin Bliss Carman, Archibald Lampman, and Duncan Campbell Scott are the most significant members of the group referred to as the Poets of the Confederation—poets who came to prominence between the founding of Canada in 1867 and the First World War. Although Roberts eventually left Canada for an extended period, and although Carman spent his career in the United States, their concern with nationalism, their sense that they were bringing Canadian poetry to its maturity, and their interrelated lives make this group truly a school of poetry. The oldest and the first to publish, Roberts seemed to the others their founding father. A famous essay by Lampman suggests his importance:

*It was almost ten years ago, and I was very young, an undergraduate at college. One May evening somebody lent me* Orion and Other Poems, *then recently published. Like most of the young fellows about me I had been under the depressing conviction that we were situated hopelessly on the outskirts of civilization, where no art and no literature could be, and it was useless to expect that anything great could be done by any of our companions, still more useless to expect that we could do it ourselves. I sat up all night reading and re-reading* Orion *in a state of the wildest excitement and when I went to bed I could not sleep. It seemed to me a wonderful thing that such work could be done by a Canadian, by a young man, one of ourselves.* ('Two Canadian Poets: A Lecture', 1891)

Roberts's youth, the resource out of which much of his best poetry is constructed, combined many of the common elements of Confederation life: an English and Loyalist background, a rural boyhood in close contact with the wilderness, and a broad classical education received at home. When Roberts was fourteen, his father, an Anglican clergyman, accepted a post at Fredericton, moving the boy away from New Brunswick's Tantramar marshes region, which he had loved while growing up. At Fredericton Collegiate School, he expanded his classical education to include recent British poets; later, at the University of New Brunswick, he added philosophy and political economy to his studies. While completing his degree, he began writing poetry. By the time he was twenty-three, Roberts had married, been head of two schools, and published three books of verse. *Orion* (1880), the first of these, received international praise.

Although Matthew Arnold, among others, hailed *Orion* as distinctively Canadian, it was criticized at home for being too regional. Roberts took this criticism to heart and by 1886 was calling for a more national approach in the writing of Canadian poetry: 'We must forget to ask of a work whether it is Nova Scotian or British Columbian, of Ontario, or of New Brunswick, until we have inquired if it be broadly and truly Canadian.' This changed attitude was partly due to his having come in contact with the Canada First Movement, a loose union of individuals who were intent on developing national pride by celebrating Anglo-Canadian history, encouraging Canadian arts, and strengthening Canada politically.

In 1883, Roberts became literary editor of Goldwin Smith's important Canadian journal of ideas, *The Week* (Smith was active in the Canada First Movement). During his brief association with *The Week*, Roberts used it as a forum to encourage young writers, and he himself became more involved with the literary community. In 1885, he returned to teaching, accepting a post at King's College, Windsor, Nova Scotia, and during his ten years there, he wrote prolifically and was elected to the Royal Society of Canada in 1893. Roberts left teaching in 1895; shortly after, he also left his wife, his five children, and then Canada—becoming an expatriate for many years while working as an editor and writing numerous books, including collections of highly popular animal stories, historical romances, works of non-fiction, and new poetry. He lived in New York until 1907; he moved to Europe, finally settling in London from 1912. In 1925, he returned to Canada for a triumphant and extended lecture tour. He became active in the Canadian literary scene once more and settled permanently in Toronto. He was knighted in 1935 and died ten years later at the age of eighty-five.

Like many of his contemporaries, Roberts was marked by contradictions. A man of letters who valued poetry, at various times in his life he earned most of his income through commercial writing; a nationalist who wrote patriotic verse and a history of Canada, he lived in exile for an extended period. Though he preached the primacy of nation over region, his best poems—like the sonnet sequence in *Songs of the Common Day* (1893)—portray the New Brunswick landscape through the seasons. And though he owes a considerable debt to the Romantics, the pre-Raphaelite tradition, and Transcendentalism, a surprisingly modern vision pervades his best-known poem, 'Tantramar Revisited', in which man's belief in permanence is seen as an illusion in a world dominated by 'chance and change'. (In 'A Note on Modernism', which first appeared in *Open House*, 1931, a collection of his essays, Roberts sees the Confederation poets as having played a role in breaking ground for the modernist movement in Canada.)

This vision, of continual flux, informed his poetry throughout his career. It is also central in the animal tales to which Roberts turned once he began to support himself by his pen. Roberts created a new kind of animal story, one based on realistic observation of wildlife and told from the animals' point of view. Collected in *The Kindred of the Wild* (1902) and many other books, these stories express a Darwinian vision in which, as in 'Under the Ice-Roof', every creature lives in danger both from nature's caprices and from what another Roberts story calls 'all the foraging world'. In such a world, survival is a matter of luck as much as of fitness.

The massive savagery of the First World War, which Roberts responded to in 'Going Over (The Somme, 1917)', moved him to

expand his understanding of Darwinian existence, in which all prey on all, to include
humans. In 'As Down the Woodland Ways', a
poem written late in his life, Roberts finds in the
cyclic pattern of nature one solution to the
apparent random flux of the modern world:
emphasizing that pattern allows him to see that,
because the seasons bring constant renewal,
death is 'but a travail-pang of life, / Destruction
but a name.'

# Tantramar Revisited[1]

Summers and summers have come, and gone with the flight of the swallow;
Sunshine and thunder have been, storm, and winter, and frost;
Many and many a sorrow has all but died from remembrance,
Many a dream of joy fall'n in the shadow of pain.
Hands of chance and change have marred, or moulded, or broken,
Busy with spirit or flesh, all I most have adored;
Even the bosom of Earth is strewn with heavier shadows,—
Only in these green hills, aslant to the sea, no change!
Here where the road that has climbed from the inland valleys and woodlands,
Dips from the hill-tops down, straight to the base of the hills,—                     10
Here, from my vantage-ground, I can see the scattering houses,
Stained with time, set warm in orchards, meadows, and wheat,
Dotting the broad bright slopes outspread to southward and eastward,
Wind-swept all day long, blown by the south-east wind.

Skirting the sunbright uplands stretches a riband[2] of meadow,
Shorn of the labouring grass, bulwarked well from the sea,
Fenced on its seaward border with long clay dikes from the turbid
Surge and flow of the tides vexing the Westmoreland shores.
Yonder, toward the left, lie broad the Westmoreland marshes,—
Miles on miles they extend, level, and grassy, and dim,                               20
Clear from the long red sweep of flats to the sky in the distance,
Save for the outlying heights, green-rampired[3] Cumberland Point;
Miles on miles outrolled, and the river-channels divide them,—
Miles on miles of green, barred by the hurtling gusts.

Miles on miles beyond the tawny bay is Minudie.
There are the low blue hills; villages gleam at their feet.
Nearer a white sail shines across the water, and nearer
Still are the slim, grey masts of fishing boats dry on the flats.

---

1   The Tantramar is a tidal river that empties into the Cumberland Basin of the Bay of Fundy. The region includes
    the village of Westcock in Westmoreland County, NB, and the fertile farmlands, tidal flats, and marshes that
    slope down to the river. Cumberland Point, now called Dorchester, is a village west of Westcock; Minudie is a
    village that lies across the bay in Nova Scotia.
2   Ribbon.
3   Barricaded. 'Green-rampired' refers to the natural fortification of the sloping land.

Ah, how well I remember those wide red flats, above tide-mark
Pale with scurf[4] of the salt, seamed and baked in the sun!                              30
Well I remember the piles of blocks and ropes, and the net-reels
Wound with the beaded nets, dripping and dark from the sea!
Now at this season the nets are unwound; they hang from the rafters
Over the fresh-stowed hay in upland barns, and the wind
Blows all day through the chinks, with the streaks of sunlight, and sways them
Softly at will; or they lie heaped in the gloom of a loft.

Now at this season the reels are empty and idle; I see them
Over the lines of the dikes, over the gossiping grass.
Now at this season they swing in the long strong wind, thro' the lonesome
Golden afternoon, shunned by the foraging gulls.                                          40
Near about sunset the crane will journey homeward above them;
Round them, under the moon, all the calm night long,
Winnowing soft grey wings of marsh-owls wander and wander,
Now to the broad, lit marsh, now to the dusk of the dike.
Soon, thro' their dew-wet frames, in the live keen freshness of morning,
Out of the teeth of the dawn blows back the awakening wind.
Then, as the blue day mounts, and the low-shot shafts of the sunlight
Glance from the tide to the shore, gossamers jewelled with dew
Sparkle and wave, where late sea-spoiling fathoms of drift-net
Myriad-meshed, uploomed sombrely over the land.                                           50

Well I remember it all. The salt, raw scent of the margin;
While, with men at the windlass, groaned each reel, and the net,
Surging in ponderous lengths, uprose and coiled in its station;
Then each man to his home,—well I remember it all!

Yet, as I sit and watch, this present peace of the landscape,—
Stranded boats, these reels empty and idle, the hush,
One grey hawk slow-wheeling above yon cluster of haystacks,—
More than the old-time stir this stillness welcomes me home.
Ah, the old-time stir, how once it stung me with rapture,—
Old-time sweetness, the winds freighted with honey and salt!                             60
Yet will I stay my steps and not go down to the marshland,—
Muse and recall far off, rather remember than see,—
Lest on too close sight I miss the darling illusion,
Spy at their task even here the hands of chance and change.

1886

4  Scaly flakes.

# The Mowing

This is the voice of high midsummer's heat.
   The rasping vibrant clamour soars and shrills
   O'er all the meadowy range of shadeless hills,
As if a host of giant cicadae beat
The cymbals of their wings with tireless feet,
   Or brazen grasshoppers with triumphing note
   From the long swath proclaimed the fate that smote
The clover and timothy-tops[1] and meadowsweet.

The crying knives glide on; the green swath lies.
   And all noon long the sun, with chemic ray,           10
   Seals up each cordial essence in its cell,
That in the dusky stalls, some winter's day,
   The spirit of June, here prisoned by his spell,
May cheer the herds with pasture memories.

1893

1 The flower spikes of a common pasture grass; 'meadowsweet' is a plant with white fragrant flowers that grows in moist meadows.

# In an Old Barn

Tons upon tons the brown-green fragrant hay
   O'erbrims the mows[1] beyond the time-warped eaves,
   Up to the rafters where the spider weaves,
Though few flies wander his secluded way.
Through a high chink one lonely golden ray,
   Wherein the dust is dancing, slants unstirred.
   In the dry hush some rustlings light are heard,
Of winter-hidden mice at furtive play.

Far down, the cattle in their shadowed stalls,
   Nose-deep in clover fodder's meadowy scent,          10
   Forget the snows that whelm their pasture streams,
The frost that bites the world beyond their walls.
   Warm housed, they dream of summer, well content
   In day-long contemplation of their dreams.

1893

1 Haylofts.

# The Flight of the Geese

I hear the low wind wash the softening snow,
   The low tide loiter down the shore. The night,
   Full filled with April forecast, hath no light.
The salt wave on the sedge-flat[1] pulses slow.
Through the hid furrows lisp in murmurous flow
   The thaw's shy ministers; and hark! The height
   Of heaven grows weird[2] and loud with unseen flight
Of strong hosts prophesying as they go!

High through the drenched and hollow night their wings
   Beat northward hard on Winter's trail. The sound       10
Of their confused and solemn voices, borne
Athwart the dark to their long Arctic morn,
   Comes with a sanction and an awe profound,
A boding of unknown, foreshadowed things.

1893

1 A flat terrain covered with rushes or rough grasses.
2 Mysterious.


# The Skater

My glad feet shod with the glittering steel
I was the god of the wingèd heel.

The hills in the far white sky were lost;
The world lay still in the wide white frost;

And the woods hung hushed in their long white dream
By the ghostly, glimmering, ice-blue stream.

Here was a pathway, smooth like glass,
Where I and the wandering wind might pass

To the far-off palaces, drifted deep,
Where Winter's retinue rests in sleep.       10

I followed the lure, I fled like a bird,
Till the startled hollows awoke and heard

A spinning whisper, a sibilant twang,
As the stroke of the steel on the tense ice rang;

And the wandering wind was left behind
As faster, faster I followed my mind;

Till the blood sang high in my eager brain,
And the joy of my flight was almost pain.

Then I stayed the rush of my eager speed
And silently went as a drifting seed,—                    20

Slowly, furtively, till my eyes
Grew big with the awe of a dim surmise,

And the hair of my neck began to creep
At hearing the wilderness talk in sleep.

Shapes in the fir-gloom drifted near.
In the deep of my heart I heard my fear.

And I turned and fled, like a soul pursued,
From the white, inviolate solitude.

1901


# Going Over[1]
(The Somme, 1917)


A girl's voice in the night troubled my heart
Across the roar of the guns, the crash of the shells,
Low and soft as a sigh, clearly I heard it.

Where was the broken parapet, crumbling about me?
Where my shadowy comrades, crouching expectant?
A girl's voice in the dark troubled my heart.

---

1 This poem takes place during World War I among soldiers stationed on the Allied front at the Somme River, in the aftermath, or 'Second Phase', of the Battle of the Somme. The original battle, waged for five months in 1916, is remembered as the most disastrous and futile battle of the war, and as perhaps the bloodiest single battle in history. (The combined German and Allied losses in the 1916 battle are estimated at nearly 1.3 million, of which almost 25,000 were Canadians and Newfoundlanders.) The fighting at the Somme was characteristic of World War I trench warfare, in which men huddled for weeks and months at a time at the front of the action in fortified trenches strung with barbed wire, trenches that were often filled with water and mud. They left these positions to charge out periodically, often under heavy gunfire from machine-gun emplacements or barrages of heavier artillery, in an attempt to gain a few additional yards of territory. The men in such charges were said to be 'going over the top' as they left the relative safety of the trenches, in that they stepped up onto the top, or parapet, of the trench as they charged out into the open. Roberts was well informed about these events: in England when the war broke out, he lied about his age and enlisted as a private. He was subsequently made a major and attached to the Canadian War Records Office in London. In that capacity he visited the Western Front in December 1916 and saw the Allied and German lines entrenched at the Somme not long after winter had brought an end to the first round of fighting there. He was subsequently commissioned to write the story of Canadian involvement in the Battle of the Somme when he was asked to complete the third volume of Lord Beaverbrook's war history, *Canada in Flanders*.

A dream was the ooze of the trench, the wet clay slipping.
A dream the sudden out-flare of the wide-flung Verys.[2]
I saw but a garden of lilacs, a-flower in the dusk.

What was the sergeant saying?—I passed it along.—                    10
Did *I* pass it along? I was breathing the breath of the lilacs.
For a girl's voice in the night troubled my heart.

Over! How the mud sucks! Vomits red the barrage.
But I am far off in the hush of a garden of lilacs.
For a girl's voice in the night troubled my heart.
Tender and soft as a sigh, clearly I heard it.

1919

2  Verys Lights were red flares.

## As Down the Woodland Ways

As down the woodland ways I went
   With every wind asleep
I felt the surge of endless life
   About my footsteps creep.

I felt the urge of quickening mould
   That had been once a flower
Mount with the sap to bloom again
   At its appointed hour.

I saw gray stumps go crumbling down
   In sodden, grim decay,                                    10
To soar in pillared green again
   On some remoter day.

I saw crushed beetles, mangled grubs,
   All crawling, perished things,
Whirl up in air, an ecstasy
   Of many-coloured wings.

Through weed and world, through worm and star,
   The sequence ran the same:—
Death but the travail-pang of life,
   Destruction but a name.                                  20

1937

# Under the Ice-Roof

I

Filtering thinly down through the roof of snow and clean blue ice, the sharp winter sunshine made almost a summer's glow upon the brown bottom of the pond. Beneath the ice the water was almost as warm now as in summer, the pond being fed by springs from so deep a source that their temperature hardly varied with the seasons. Here and there a bit of water-weed stood up from the bottom, green as in June. But in the upper world, meanwhile, the wind that drove over the ice and snow was so intensely cold that the hardy northern trees snapped under it, and few of the hardy northern creatures of the wilderness, though fierce with hunger, had the fortitude to face it. They crouched shivering in their lairs, under fallen trunks or in the heart of dense fir thickets, and waited anxiously for the rigour of cold and the savagery of wind to abate. Only down in the pond, in the generous spaces of amber water beneath the ice-roof, life went on busily and securely. The wind might rage unbridled, the cold might lay its hand of death heavily on forest and hill; but the beavers in their unseen retreat knew nothing of it. All it could do was to add an inch or two of thickness to the icy shelter above them, making their peaceful security more secure.

The pond was a large one, several acres in extent, with a depth of fully five feet in the deeper central portions, which were spacious enough to give the beavers room for play and exercise. Around the shallow edges the ice, which was fully fifteen inches thick beneath its blanket of snow, lay solid on the bottom.

The beavers of this pond occupied a lodge on the edge of the deep water, not far above the dam. This lodge was a broad-based, low-domed house of mud, turf, and sticks cunningly interwoven, and rising about four feet above the surface of the ice-roof. The dome, though covered deep with snow, was conspicuous to every prowler of the woods, who would come at times to sniff greedily at the warm smell of beaver steaming up from the minute air-vents in the apex. But however greedy, however ravenous, the prowling vagrants might be, the little dome-builders and dam-builders within neither knew nor cared about their greed. The dome was fully two feet thick, built solidly, and frozen almost to the hardness of granite. There were no claws among all the ravening forest kindred strong enough to tear their way through such defences. In the heart of the lodge, in a dry grass-lined chamber just above high-water level, the beavers dwelt warm and safe.

But it was not from the scourge of the northern cold alone, and the ferocity of their enemies, that the beavers were protected by their ice-roof and their frozen dome. The winter's famine, too, they had well guarded themselves against. Before the coming of the frost, they had gnawed down great quantities of birch, poplar, and willow, cut them into convenient, manageable lengths, and dragged them to a spot a little above the centre of the dam, where the water was deepest. Here the store of logs, poles, and brush made a tangled mass from the bottom up to the ice. When it was feeding-time in the hidden chamber of the lodge, a beaver would swim to the brush pile, pull out a suitable stick, and drag it into the chamber. Here the family would feast at their ease, in the dry, pungent gloom, eating the bark and the delicate outer layer of young wood. When the stick was stripped clean, another beaver would drag it out and tow it down to the dam, there to await its final use as material for repairs. Every member of the colony was blest with a good appetite, and there was nearly always at least one beaver to be seen swimming through the amber gloom, either with a green stick from the brush pile, or a white stripped one to deposit on the base of the dam.

For these most diligent of all the four-foot kindreds this was holiday time. Under the ice-roof, they had no dam-building, no tree-cutting, no house-repairing. There was nothing to do but eat, sleep, and play. There was not much variety to their play, to be sure; but the monotony of it did not trouble them. Sometimes two would indulge in a sort of mad game of tag, swimming at marvellous speed close beneath the ice, their powerful hind legs propelling them, their tiny little fore paws held up demurely under their chins, and their broad, flat, hairless tails stretched straight out behind to act as rudders. As they swam this way and that, they loosed a trail of silvery bubbles behind them, from the air carried under their close fur. At last one of the players, unable to hold his breath any longer, would whisk sharply into the mouth of the black tunnel leading into the lodge, scurry up into the chamber, and lie there panting, to be joined a moment later by his equally breathless pursuer. One by one the other members of the colony would dip in, till the low chamber was full of furry, snuggling warmth and well-fed content. Little cared the beavers whether it was night or day in the wide, frozen, perilous world above the ice-roof, whether the sun shone from the bitter blue, or the wolf-haunted moonlight lay upon the snow, or the madness of the blizzard made the woods cower before its fury.

As long as the cold endured and the snow lay deep upon the wilderness, the beavers lived their happy, uneventful life beneath the ice-roof. But in this particular winter the untempered cold of December and January, which slew many of the wood folk and drove the others wild with hunger, broke suddenly in an unprecedented thaw. Not the oldest bear of the Bald Mountain caves could remember any such thaw. First there were days on days, and nights on nights, of bland, melting rain, softer than April's. The snow vanished swiftly from the laden branches of fir and spruce and hemlock, and the silent woods stood up black and terrible against the weeping sky. On the ground and on the ice of pond and stream the snow shrank, settled, and assumed a grayish complexion. Water, presently, gathered in great spreading, leaden-coloured pools on the ice; and on the naked knolls the bare moss and petty shrubs began to emerge. Every narrow watercourse soon carried two streams,—the temperate, fettered, summer-mindful stream below the ice, and the swollen, turbulent flood above. Then the rain stopped. The sun came out warm and urgent as in latter May. And snow and ice together dwindled under the unnatural caress.

The beavers, in their safe seclusion, had knowledge in two ways of this strange visitation upon the world. Not all the soft flood of the melting snow ran over the surface of their ice, but a portion got beneath it, by way of the upper brooks. This extra flow disturbed both the colour and the temperature of the clear amber water of the pond. It lifted heavily against the ice, pressed up the tunnels to the very edge of the dry chamber of the lodge, and thrust ponderously at the outlets of the dam. Understanding the peril, the wise little dam-builders sallied forth in a flurry, and with skilful tooth and claw lost no time in enlarging the outlets. They were much too intelligent to let the flood escape by a single outlet, lest the concentrated flow should become too heavy for them to control it. They knew the spirit of that ancient maxim of tyrants, '*divide et impera*'.

By dividing the overflow into many feeble streams they knew how to rule it. This done, they rested in no great anxiety, expecting the thaw to end with a stringent frost.

Then, however, came the second, and more significant, manifestation of peril. The snow on the ice-roof had vanished; and looking up through the ice they saw the flood eddying riotously over the naked expanse. It was a portent which the wiser elders understood. The whole colony fell to work strengthening the dam where the weight of the current bore down upon it, and increasing the outlet along the farther edges.

A thaw so persistent, however, and at the same time so violent, overpassed their cunning calculations. One night, when all had done their best and, weary, but reassured, had withdrawn into the warm chamber of the lodge, something happened that they had never looked for. In their snug retreat they were falling to sleep, the rush of the overflow and the high clamour of the side vents coming dimly to their ears, when suddenly they were startled by the water being forced up over the dry floor of the chamber. The pressure of water beneath the ice had suddenly increased. They were more than startled. They were badly frightened. If the water should rise much higher they would be drowned helplessly, for the ice lay close all over the pond. The younger ones scurried this way and that with plaintive squeaks, and several dashed forth into the pond in a panic, forgetting that there was no escape in that direction. A moment later a low crashing penetrated to the dark chamber; and the invading water retreated down the tunnel. The ice-roof, worn thin, honey-combed, and upheaved by the pressure from below, had gone to pieces.

It was the older and wiser beavers who had remained in the chamber, terrified, but not panic-stricken. When the water retreated to its normal level,—about two inches below the chamber floor,—they were satisfied. Then, however, a louder and heavier note in the rush of the overflow came to their ears, and their anxiety returned with fresh force. Thrusting their whiskered noses inquiringly down the tunnel, they observed that the water was sinking far below its proper level. Well they knew what that meant. The dam was broken. The water, which was their one protection from the terrors of the forest, was escaping.

This was the kind of an emergency which a beaver will always rise to. Shy as they are, under ordinary circumstances, when the dam is attacked their courage is unfailing. In a moment every beaver in the colony was out among the swirling ice, under the broad, white moonlight which they had not seen for so long.

It was at its very centre, where the channel was deepest and the thrust of the water most violent, that the dam had given way. The break was about ten feet wide, and not, as yet, of any great depth. It was the comparatively narrow and unsubstantial crust of the embankment which had yielded, disintegrated by the thaw and ripped by the broken edges of the ice.

The vehemence of the torrent was rapidly cutting down into the firmer body of the dam, when the beavers flung themselves valiantly into the breach. In the face of the common danger they forgot all caution, and gave no heed to any hungry eyes that might be glaring at them from the woods on either shore. Without any apparent leadership in the work, they all seemed to help each other in whatever way would be most effective. Some dragged up the longest and heaviest poles from the pile of stripped stuff, floated them carefully into the break, butt end up-stream and parallel with the flow, and held them there doggedly with their teeth and fore paws till others could come with more timbers to hold the first lot down. Meanwhile, from the soft bottom along the base of the dam, big lumps of mingled clay and grass-roots, together with small stones to add weight, were grabbed up and heaped solidly upon the layers of sticks for anchorage. This loose stuff, though deposited along the upper ends of the sticks where the flow was least violent, and swiftly packed down into the interstices, was mostly washed away in the process. It was seemingly an even struggle, for a time, and the beavers could do no more than hold the breach from deepening and widening. But they were quite undaunted; and they seemed to know no such thing as fatigue. Little by little they gained upon the torrent, making good the hold of a mass of turf here, a few stones there, and everywhere the long straight sticks upon which the water could get but slight grip. The flood grew shallower and less destructive. More sticks were brought, more stones, and clay, and grass-roots; and then a layer of heavy, clean poles, over which the water slid thinly and smoothly without danger to the structure beneath.

The dam was now strongest at this point, its crest being broader and formed of heavier timbers than elsewhere. But no sooner had the hard-won victory been secured, and the plucky little architects paused for breath, than there came an ominous crackling from far over to the extreme left of the dam, where a subsidiary channel had offered a new vantage to the baffled torrent. The crackling was mingled with a loud rushing noise. Another section of the crest of the dam had been swept away. A white curtain of foam sprang into the moonlight, against the darkness of the trees.

## II

While the brave little dam-builders had been battling with the flood, out there in the wide-washing moonlight, hungry eyes had been watching them from the heart of a dense spruce thicket, a little below the left end of the dam. The watching had been hopeless enough, as the owner of those fierce, narrow eyes knew it was no use trying to surprise a beaver in the open, when the whole pond was right there for him to dive into. But now when the new break brought the whole colony swimming madly to the left-hand shore, and close to the darkness of the woods, those watching eyes glowed with a savage expectancy, and began slowly, noiselessly, steadily, floating nearer through the undisturbed underbrush.

The tremendous thaw, loosing the springs and streams on the high flanks of Bald Mountain, had washed out the snow from the mouth of a shallow cave and rudely aroused a young bear from his winter sleep. As soon as he had shaken off his heaviness the bear found himself hungry. But his hunting thus far had not been successful. His training had not been in the winter woods. He hardly knew what to look for, and the soft slumping snow hampered him. One panic-stricken white rabbit, and a few ants from a rotten stump, were all that he had found to eat in three days. His white fangs in his red jaws had slavered with craving as he watched the plump beavers at their work, far out on the brightly moonlit dam. When, at last, they came hurrying toward him, and fell to work on the new break within thirty or forty yards of his hiding-place, he could hardly contain himself. He did contain himself, however; for he had hunted beaver before, and not with a success to make him overconfident. Right by the termination of the dam, where the beavers were working, the woods came down thick and dark to within eight or ten feet of the water. Toward this point he made his way patiently, and with such control of every muscle that, for all his apparent clumsiness, not a twig snapped, not a branch rustled, any more than if a shadow were gliding through them. He saw one old beaver sitting stiffly erect on the crest of the dam, a wary sentinel, sniffing the still air and scanning the perilous woods; but he planned to make his final rush so swift that the sentinel would have no time to give warning.

But the fierce little eyes of the bear, dark and glinting red, were not the only ones that watched the beavers at their valorous toil. In the juniper scrub, a short distance up the bank of the pond, crouched two big gray lynxes, glaring down upon the scene with wide, round, pale greenish eyes, unspeakably sinister. The lynxes were gaunt with famine. Fired with the savage hope that some chance might bring a beaver within reach of their mighty spring, they had crept down, on their great, furred, stealthy pads, to the patch of juniper scrub. Here they had halted, biding their time with that long, painful patience which is the price of feeding—the price of life—among the winter-scourged kindreds. Now, when the beavers had so considerately come over to the edge of the woods, and appeared to be engrossed in some incomprehensible pulling and splashing and mud-piling, the two lynxes felt that their opportunity had arrived. Their bellies close to the snow, their broad, soft-padded feet stepping lightly as the fall of feathers, their light gray fur all but invisible among the confused moon-shadows, their round, bright eyes unwinking, they seemed almost to drift down through the thickets toward their expected prey.

Neither the bear creeping up from below the dam, nor the two lynxes stealing down from above it, had eyes or thought for anything in the world but the desperately toiling beavers. Their hunger was gnawing at their lean stomachs, the fever of the hunt was in their veins, and the kill was all but within reach. A few moments more, and the rush would come, up from the fir thickets—the long, terrible spring and pounce, down from the juniper scrub.

The work of repairing the breach was making good progress. Already the roaring overflow was coming into subjection, its loud voice dwindling to a shallow clamour. Then, something happened. Perhaps the wary sentinel on the crest of the dam detected a darker shade stirring among the firs, or a lighter grayness moving inexplicably between the bushes up the bank. Perhaps his quick nostrils caught a scent that meant danger. Perhaps the warning came to him mysteriously, flashed upon that inner sense, sometimes alert and sometimes densely slumbering, which the forest furtiveness seems to develop in its creatures. However it came, it came. Dropping forward as if shot, the sentinel beaver brought his flat tail down upon the surface of the water with a smack that rang all up and around the borders of the pond, startling the quiet of the night. In a fraction of a second every beaver had vanished beneath the shining surface.

At the same moment, or an eye-wink later, a strange thing happened—one of those violent surprises with which the vast repression of the forest sometimes betrays itself. Maddened to see his prey escaping, the bear made his rush, launching himself, a black and uncouth mass, right down to the water's edge. Simultaneously the two lynxes shot into the air from higher up the bank, frantic with disappointed hunger.

With a screech of fury, and a harsh spitting and snarling, they landed a few feet distant from the bear, and crouched flat, their stub tails twitching, their eyes staring, their tufted ears laid back upon their skulls.

Like a flash the bear wheeled, confronting the two great cats with uplifted paw and mouth wide open. Half-sitting back upon his haunches, he was ready for attack or defence. His little eyes glowed red with rage. To him it was clearly the lynxes who had frightened off the beavers and spoiled his hunting; and interference of this kind is what the wild kindreds will not tolerate. To the lynxes, on the other hand, it was obvious that the bear had caused the whole trouble. He was the clumsy interloper who had come between them and their quarry. They were on the verge of that blindness of fury which might hurl them, at any instant, tooth and claw, upon their formidable foe. For the moment, however, they had not quite lost sight of prudence. The bear was master of the forest, and they knew that even together they two were hardly a match for him.

The bear, on the other hand, was not quite sure that he was willing to pay the price of vengeance. His blood surging in the swollen veins, he growled with heavy menace, and rocking forward upon his haunches he seemed on the point of rushing in. But he knew how those powerful knife-edged claws of the lynxes could rend. He knew that their light bodies were strong and swift and elusive, their teeth almost as punishing as his own. He felt himself the master; nevertheless he realized that it would cost dear to enforce that mastery. He hesitated. Had he made the slightest forward move, the lynxes would have thrown caution to the winds, and sprung upon him. On the other hand, had the lynxes even tightened up their sinews to spring, he would have hurled himself with a roar into the battle. But as it was, both sides held themselves in leash, tense, ready, terrible in restraint. And as the moments dragged by, out on the bright surface of the pond small heads appeared, with little bright eyes watching curiously.

For perhaps three or four long, intense minutes there was not a move made. Then the round eyes of the lynxes shifted ever so little, while the bear's eyes never faltered. The bear's was the steadier purpose, the more tenacious and resolute temper. Almost imperceptibly the lynxes shrank backward, gliding inch by inch. A swift side-glance showed them that the way of retreat was open. Then, as if both were propelled by the one vehement impulse, they bounded into the air, one whirling aside and the other almost doubling back upon his own trail. Quicker than it takes to tell it, they were fleeing like gray shadows, one over the bank and through the juniper bushes, the other up along the snowy shore of the pond, their discomfiture apparently driving them to part company. The bear, as if surprised, sat up on his haunches to stare after them. Then, with a hungry look at the beavers, now swimming openly far out in the moonlight, he turned and shambled off to find some more profitable hunting.

For a few minutes all was stillness, save for the rushing of the water over the dam. The solitude of the night had resumed its white and tranquil dominion as if nothing had ever occurred to jar its peace. Then once more the watchful sentinel appeared, sitting erect on the dam, and the diligent builders busied themselves to complete the mending of the breach.

1906

# Bliss Carman
## 1861–1929

William Bliss Carman grew up in Fredericton, New Brunswick, where, like his one-year-older cousin Charles G.D. Roberts, he attended Fredericton Collegiate and the University of New Brunswick. Gripped by indecisiveness after his graduation in 1881, he was unable for some years to establish his independence. He did not complete the degrees he began at Oxford and Edinburgh (nor later at Harvard), and he vacillated about his choice of profession, making stabs at teaching, law, and surveying. Except for brief ventures, he lived with his parents until their deaths in 1885 and 1886. He left Canada to take up the study of literature at Harvard from 1886 to 1888, never returning permanently.

At Harvard, he became close friends with the American poet Richard Hovey, who encouraged him in the writing of poetry and later became his collaborator in the Vagabondia series. In 1890, he took an editorial job on a religious weekly, *The Independent*, where he stayed for two years—his longest term of employment. After leaving that post he supported himself through various short-lived journalistic positions, as well as, once he achieved success as a poet, through lecturing and reading his poetry on tour. Lacking sufficient income to support himself, from 1892, he lived as a visitor with friends and relatives, often with Roberts, moving cyclically with the seasons. Finally, in 1908, he found a home with Dr Morris King and his wife Mary, in New Canaan, Connecticut: he remained with them for the rest of his life.

Despite his unpromising beginnings, Carman proved very successful once he took up poetry. Writing in the tradition of English Romanticism and of the American Transcendentalism of his distant kinsman Ralph Waldo Emerson, he became the best-known Canadian poet of his day. He was even sometimes hailed as Canada's unofficial poet laureate. However, most of his life's work was published in the United States, where he was regarded as an American writer. (Carman was dubbed the 'American High Priest of Symbolism' by a New York newspaper in the 1890s.) Although much of his verse appeared only in periodicals, he still produced over fifty books and chapbooks, the first and best of which remains *Low Tide on Grand Pré* (1893). The Vagabondia books that followed, begun in 1894 and running to four volumes by 1912, proved so successful that Carman followed with a similar series, the *Pipes of Pan* (five volumes, 1902–5). Collections of light verse, the volumes in these series celebrate a nostalgic carefree world in which the landscape is pastoral and life is simple.

Carman's interest in creating such Edenic settings eventually gave way to his investigations of quasi-religious philosophies, especially the ideas of Mary King, with whom he helped found the Unitrinian School of Personal Harmonizing. His book *The Making of Personality* (1908) is an articulation of her ideas, and he collaborated with her on several lyric masques meant to express her beliefs. In 1925, Carman delivered a series of lectures at the University of Toronto, subsequently published as *Talks on Poetry and Life*. He was made a Fellow of the Royal Society of Canada that year. Two volumes of his letters have been collected and published. After his death, he was cremated in New Canaan; at first reluctant, Mary King was persuaded to allow his ashes to be buried in Fredericton.

From the beginning of his adulthood, Carman suffered from bouts of depression, often interspersed with manic joy, and his most effective poetry reflects this emotional flux. Unlike Roberts and Lampman, he writes chiefly of feelings, not thoughts, provides impressions, not descriptions, and is sometimes given to vague hints of mysterious forces, as in 'The Eavesdropper'. His poetry at its best—'Low Tide on Grand Pré' is generally regarded as his finest poem—captures the ephemeral quality of a world that seems always remote yet somehow within reach. Though it was viewed as an important body of work in its day, the bulk of his verse has not worn well, leading the critic

Donald Stephens to begin his book-length study of Carman with the warning: 'As a poet he is a sentimentalist, an eternal child.'

## The Eavesdropper

In a still room at hush of dawn,
    My Love and I lay side by side
And heard the roaming forest wind
    Stir in the paling autumn-tide.

I watched her earth-brown eyes grow glad
    Because the round day was so fair;
While memories of reluctant night
    Lurked in the blue dusk of her hair.

Outside, a yellow maple tree,
    Shifting upon the silvery blue                 10
With tiny multitudinous sound,
    Rustled to let the sunlight through.

The livelong day the elvish leaves
    Danced with their shadows on the floor;
And the lost children of the wind
    Went straying homeward by our door.

And all the swarthy afternoon
    We watched the great deliberate sun
Walk through the crimsoned hazy world,
    Counting his hilltops one by one.             20

Then as the purple twilight came
    And touched the vines along our eaves,
Another Shadow stood without
    And gloomed the dancing of the leaves.

The silence fell on my Love's lips;
    Her great brown eyes were veiled and sad
With pondering some maze of dream,
    Though all the splendid year was glad.

Restless and vague as a gray wind
    Her heart had grown, she knew not why.        30
But hurrying to the open door,
    Against the verge of western sky

I saw retreating on the hills,
    Looming and sinister and black,
The stealthy figure swift and huge
    Of One who strode and looked not back.

1893

## Low Tide on Grand Pré [1]

The sun goes down, and over all
    These barren reaches by the tide
Such unelusive glories fall,
    I almost dream they yet will bide
    Until the coming of the tide.

And yet I know that not for us,
    By any ecstasy of dream,
He lingers to keep luminous
    A little while the grievous stream,
    Which frets, uncomforted of dream—          10

A grievous stream, that to and fro
    Athrough the fields of Acadie
Goes wandering, as if to know
    Why one beloved face should be
    So long from home and Acadie.

Was it a year or lives ago
    We took the grasses in our hands,
And caught the summer flying low
    Over the waving meadow lands,
    And held it there between our hands?        20

The while the river at our feet—
    A drowsy inland meadow stream—
At set of sun the after-heat
    Made running gold, and in the gleam
    We freed our birch upon the stream.

---

1  Marshlands on Minas Basin at the mouth of the Gaspéreau River in Nova Scotia; when dyked by the Acadians, they became rich farmlands. In 1755, the Acadians were expelled from the village of Grand Pré by the British. It was near Windsor, Nova Scotia, where Carman stayed several summers with Roberts.

There down along the elms at dusk
    We lifted dripping blade to drift,
Through twilight scented fine like musk,
    Where night and gloom awhile uplift,
    Nor sunder soul and soul adrift.                    30

And that we took into our hands
    Spirit of life or subtler thing—
Breathed on us there, and loosed the bands
    Of death, and taught us, whispering,
    The secret of some wonder-thing.

Then all your face grew light, and seemed
    To hold the shadow of the sun;
The evening faltered, and I deemed
    That time was ripe, and years had done
    Their wheeling underneath the sun.                   40

So all desire and all regret,
    And fear and memory, were naught;
One to remember or forget
    The keen delight our hands had caught;
    Morrow and yesterday were naught.

The night has fallen, and the tide . . .
    Now and again comes drifting home,
Across these aching barrens wide,
    A sigh like driven wind or foam:
    In grief the flood is bursting home.                 50

1893


# Lord of My Heart's Elation

Lord of my heart's elation,
Spirit of things unseen,
Be thou my aspiration
Consuming and serene!

Bear up, bear out, bear onward
This mortal soul alone,
To selfhood or oblivion,
Incredibly thine own,—

As the foamheads are loosened
And blown along the sea,                    10
Or sink and merge forever
In that which bids them be.

I, too, must climb in wonder,
Uplift at thy command,—
Be one with my frail fellows
Beneath the wind's strong hand,

A fleet and shadowy column
Of dust or mountain rain,
To walk the earth a moment                  20
And be dissolved again.

Be thou my exaltation
Or fortitude of mien,
Lord of the world's elation,
Thou breath of things unseen!

1903


## Morning in the Hills

How quiet is the morning in the hills!
The stealthy shadows of the summer clouds
Trail through the cañon,[1] and the mountain stream
Sounds his sonorous music far below
In the deep-wooded wind-enchanted cove.

Hemlock and aspen, chestnut, beech, and fir
Go tiering down from storm-worn crest and ledge,
While in the hollows of the dark ravine
See the red road emerge, then disappear
Towards the wide plain and fertile valley lands.    10

My forest cabin half-way up the glen
Is solitary, save for one wise thrush,
The sound of falling water, and the wind
Mysteriously conversing with the leaves.

1 Canyon.

Here I abide unvisited by doubt,
Dreaming of far-off turmoil and despair,
The race of men and love and fleeting time,
What life may be, or beauty, caught and held
For a brief moment at eternal poise.

What impulse now shall quicken and make live          20
This outward semblance and this inward self?
One breath of being fills the bubble world,
Coloured and frail, with fleeting change on change.

Surely some God contrived so fair a thing
In the vast leisure of uncounted days,
And touched it with the breath of living joy,
Wondrous and fair and wise! It must be so.

1912


## The World Voice

I heard the summer sea
Murmuring to the shore
Some endless story of a wrong
The whole world must deplore.

I heard the mountain wind
Conversing with the trees
Of an old sorrow of the hills
Mysterious as the sea's.

And all that haunted day
It seemed that I could hear          10
The echo of an ancient speech
Ring in my listening ear.

And then it came to me,
That all that I had heard
Was my own heart in the sea's voice
And the wind's lonely word.

1916

# Sara Jeannette Duncan
## 1861–1922

Before settling on the form of her name by which she is now remembered, the woman who became Canada's first modernist writer was born Sarah Janet Duncan in Brantford, Canada West. She used several versions of her name and some pseudonyms: after she married, the author's name on most of her books was Mrs Everard Cotes—though she continued to be identified parenthetically on the title pages as Sara Jeannette Duncan.

Almost as various as her pen names were the roles Duncan played and the voices she made use of in her writing. Trained to be a schoolteacher, she established herself in her twenties as a breezy, colloquial journalist, and her first books—light fiction made up of loosely linked sketches—are written in a casual, journalistic style. She soon abandoned the masculine pseudonym 'Garth' that she had found necessary in order to be taken seriously in the journalistic world of her day, and she adopted instead the role of a late-nineteenth-century 'American girl'—an emancipated, brash, slangy young woman, the ambiguous union of innocence and immodesty portrayed by Henry James in *Daisy Miller* (1878)—and she often played this persona off against British national stereotypes, as in *A Social Departure: How Orthodocia and I Went Round the World by Ourselves* (1890), *An American Girl in London* (1891), and *A Voyage of Consolation* (1898). A restless traveller, Duncan chronicled her visit to New Orleans in 1884, where she met the flamboyant American poet Joaquin Miller. (With Miller, along with other 'Bohemians', she travelled to Florida in a whimsical search for the Fountain of Youth.) She also described her brief sojourn in British Honduras, and her world tour with fellow Canadian journalist Lily Lewis, a trip that took them through Western Canada on the recently completed Canadian Pacific Railway—they daringly rode on the cowcatcher fastened to

the front of the train through the Rockies—as well as to Japan and India.

After failing to secure a staff position at the Toronto *Globe* in 1885 (she later complained about the conservatism of Canadian journalism with regard to its employment of women), Duncan accepted a job at the Washington *Post*. The following year, however, she was hired by the *Globe* after all and, placed in charge of the 'Woman's World' section, she became the first woman to hold a full-time position in Canadian journalism. Always interested in politics, she moved, in 1888, to the Montreal *Star* to become its parliamentary correspondent.

Between 1886 and 1888, Duncan also contributed columns and book reviews to Goldwin Smith's *The Week*; in them, she struck a more elevated and intellectual (and sometimes more rhetorical) tone than in her other journalism. Interested in literary fiction and the arts, she found *The Week* gave her an opportunity to discuss questions of Canadian culture and to stress the need for Canada to move beyond colonial self-definition:

*In our character as colonists we find the root of all our sins of omission in letters. . . . Our enforced political humility is the distinguishing characteristic of every phase of our national life. We are ignored, and we ignore ourselves. . . . So long as Canada remains in political obscurity, content to thrive only at the roots, so long will the leaves and blossoms of art and literature be scanty and stunted products of our national energy. . . . A national literature cannot be looked for as an outcome of anything less than a complete national existence.* (1886)

She was nevertheless convinced that 'national literature cannot be wholly evoked from within,' and she took a lively interest in the novelists then emerging in the United States, particularly Henry James and W.D. Howells (whom she met in Washington), and in the controversies that arose from Howells's advocacy of realism.

In 1890, Duncan married Everard Cotes, a museum official she had met during her earlier trip to Calcutta; in 1891, she moved to India. Though she later wearied of it, her new home seems at first to have both engaged and energized her, and she began to write serious fiction. In *The Simple Adventures of a Memsahib* (1893), she tells of a young English woman's difficult entry into the somewhat cloistered world of the Anglo-Indian community. *A Daughter of To-day* (1894) is an account of a non-conformist woman who leaves the United States for a career as an expatriate artist and writer in Europe but eventually commits suicide over her lack of success. *His Honour, and a Lady* (1896), an acutely observed portrait of Anglo-Indian politics, shows Duncan's continued interest in women who play untraditional roles.

In 1901, Duncan published *On the Other Side of the Latch*, an affecting memoir that describes her summer convalescence from tuberculosis, which had probably been brought on by conditions in India. Her only short fiction, the highly polished novellas and the short story collected in *The Pool in the Desert* (1903), which treat in a Jamesian manner the emotions suppressed beneath the formal surfaces of the highly mannered Anglo-Indian community,

were written around this time. Their subtle psychological nuances of situation outweigh external events, as these stories carefully filter the narrative through the consciousness of one highly subjective character.

Although initially attracted to its exoticism, Duncan came to feel that India was, as she wrote in a letter, 'too far out upon the periphery of the Empire.' She increasingly made use of her earnings as a writer to get away, making return visits to Canada and living for extended periods in London, England, where her health seemed better. In the first decade of the twentieth century, she published the two books that deal extensively with Canada: *The Imperialist* (1904; an extract from that novel has been chosen to represent Duncan here) and *Cousin Cinderella: A Canadian Girl in London* (1908).

Duncan's later career, which was increasingly spent in England, saw the publication of *Set in Authority* (1906), a second examination of political themes and of the relationship of colony and empire, this time using an Anglo-Indian context; followed by a Kensington memoir, *Two in a Flat* (1908); several more novels, most of which rework the international theme that preoccupied James; and popular plays. By the time she died in England in 1922, Duncan had written twenty books, in addition to numerous plays and a great quantity of journalism.

## The Imperialist

Now regarded as Duncan's masterpiece, *The Imperialist* was not initially well received. In England, its Canadian subject matter was not of interest; in Canada, male reviewers seemed to feel a woman could not be a shrewd enough observer to carry off a political novel. Nonetheless, her precise descriptive powers did receive praise—as in a review published in *Saturday Night*, which lauded the novel for its 'photographic . . . fidelity to local conditions' as well as for its 'subtle humour and literary finish'.

Despite the high quality of several of her books of fiction, Duncan's reputation today rests chiefly on *The Imperialist*, which, after it was brought back into print in 1961, found a place in the Canadian canon. In a 1905 letter to Lord Lansdowne, then governor general of Canada, Duncan wrote, 'It seemed to me that

among the assumptions and disputes over here [she was writing from England] as to what the "colonial view" really is, it might be worth while to present the situation as it appears to the average Canadian of the average small town, inarticulate except at election times.'

Her complexly ironic tale is set in the town of Elgin, Ontario, easily recognized as a fictional version of Brantford, and it focuses on the Murchisons, a Scottish-Canadian family. ('No one could say the Murchisons were demonstrative.') In it, *balance* is both a theme and a technique, and the way the second and third chapters, reprinted here, are counterpoised—so that the public world of Mr Murchison, dominated by commerce, religion, and politics, is set against the domestic world of Mrs Murchison, the demands of family, and the home—suggests the artful design of this novel. Its plot revolves around Lorne Murchison, a young man who romanticizes England and all its values, and the balancing figure of his perspicacious (and undomestic) older sister Advena. As their town becomes involved in an election in which the central debate is over the strengthening of Canada's ties to the British Empire, Lorne campaigns for office as an enthusiastic supporter of Canada's becoming more closely tied to the empire. This was not an anti-national concept at the time; he speaks for those who saw Canada as having an important role in the future of the British Empire. (Lorne tells his auditors in his climactic election speech, 'The centre of the Empire must shift—and where, if not to Canada?' And he later stresses the importance of resisting American dominance of the Canadian economy.) Against this ambition, however, the novel suggests that bringing together the values of the Old World and the New World may be the best course. It also reminds us of the distance that Elgin (and Canada) actually lies from the centres of power. As with Leacock's depiction of Mariposa in the later *Sunshine Sketches of a Little Town*, much of the humour in the novel stems from Duncan's sharp eye for the exact nuance of manners combined with an ability to skewer a small town's tendency to take itself too seriously.

# From *The Imperialist*

## CHAPTER II

'We've seen changes, Mr Murchison. Aye. We've seen changes.'

Dr Drummond and Mr Murchison stood together in the store door, over which the sign, 'John Murchison: Hardware', had explained thirty years of varying commercial fortune. They had pretty well begun life together in Elgin. John Murchison was one of those who had listened to Mr Drummond's trial sermon, and had given his vote to 'call' him to the charge. Since then there had been few Sundays when, morning and evening, Mr Murchison had not been in his place at the top of his pew, where his dignified and intelligent head appeared with the isolated significance of a strong individuality. People looked twice at John Murchison in a crowd; so did his own children at home. Hearing some discussion of the selection of a Premier, Alec, looking earnestly at him once said, 'Why don't they tell Father to be it?' The young minister looked twice at him that morning of the trial sermon, and asked afterward who he was. A Scotchman, Mr Drummond was told, not very long from the old country, who had bought the Playfair business on Main Street, and settled in the 'Plummer Place', which already had a quarter of a century's standing in the annals of the town. The Playfair business was a respectable business to buy; the Plummer Place, though it stood in an unfashionable outskirt, was a respectable place to settle in; and the minister, in casting his lot in Elgin, envisaged John Murchison as part of it, thought of him confidently as a 'dependence',[1] saw him among the future elders and office-bearers of the congregation, a man who would be punctual with his pew-rent, sage in his judgments, and whose views upon church attendance would be extended to his family.

So the two came, contemporaries, to add their labour and their lives to the building of this little outpost of Empire. It was the frankest transfer, without thought of return;

1 A person or thing on which one relies or may rely; the object of one's trust.

they were there to spend and be spent within the circumference of the spot they had chosen, with no ambition beyond. In the course of nature, even their bones and their memories would enter into the fabric. The new country filled their eyes; the new town was their opportunity, its destiny their fate. They were altogether occupied with its affairs, and the affairs of the growing Dominion, yet obscure in the heart of each of them ran the undercurrent of the old allegiance. They had gone the length of their tether, but the tether was always there. Thus, before a congregation that always stood in the early days, had the minister every Sunday morning for thirty years besought the Almighty, with ardour and humility, on behalf of the Royal Family. It came in the long prayer, about the middle. Not in the perfunctory words of a ritual, but in the language of his choice, which varied according to what he believed to be the spiritual needs of the reigning House, and was at one period, touching certain of its members, though respectful, extremely candid.[2] The General Assembly of the Church of Scotland, 'now in session', also—was it ever forgotten once? And even the Prime Minister, 'and those who sit in council with him', with just a hint of extra commendation if it happened to be Mr Gladstone.[3] The minister of Knox Church, Elgin, Ontario, Canada, kept his eye on them all. Remote as he was, and concerned with affairs of which they could know little, his sphere of duty could never revolve too far westward to embrace them, nor could his influence, under any circumstances, cease to be at their disposal. It was noted by some that after Mr Drummond had got his 'D.D.'[4] from an American University he also prayed occasionally for the President of the neighbouring Republic; but this was rebutted by others, who pointed out that it happened only on the occurrence of assassinations, and held it reasonable enough. The cavillers mostly belonged to the congregation of St Andrew's, 'Established'[5]—a glum, old-fashioned lot indeed, who now and then dropped in of a Sunday evening to hear Mr Drummond preach. (There wasn't much to be said for the preaching at St Andrew's.) The Established folk went on calling the minister of Knox Church 'Mr' Drummond long after he was 'Doctor' to his own congregation, on account of what they chose to consider the dubious source of the dignity; but the Knox Church people had their own theory to explain this hypercriticism, and would promptly turn the conversation to the merits of the sermon.

2 In Duncan's serialized version of *The Imperialist*, published in England in 1903 (in *The Queen: The Lady's Newspaper*), the phrase 'touching the Heir Apparent'—deleted in the book's subsequent publication—made it clear that this was a reference to the Prince of Wales, who had ascended to the throne in 1901, and whose social life had given much scandal. (The specific incident referred to may be a libel case about cheating at cards, in which he had to appear in 1891.) In the following chapter, there is an allusion to the young Prince's celebrated visit to Canada in 1860, when he was just eighteen. (It included a stopover in Brantford.)

3 Liberal prime minister of England during the periods 1868–74, 1880–5, 1886, and 1892–4.

4 Doctor of Divinity. (Since Dr Drummond receives the degree from an American university after his ministry has begun, it is presumably an honorary one.) The 'occurrence of assassinations' alludes to the assassinations of the US presidents James Garfield in 1881 and William McKinley in 1901.

5 Because the church of the 'cavillers' is named after St Andrew (the patron saint of Scotland), it is clear that the competition here is not between Dr Drummond's Presbyterian faith and the Anglican Church of Canada—which is what would ordinarily be meant in Canada when someone spoke of the 'Established' church, i.e. that recognized as the national church or religion. (The Anglican church is instead referred to, later in this chapter, as Episcopalian, its usual designation in the US, where no church is 'Established'). Duncan's joke here is that Elgin is so Scottish that 'Established' is understood in this context as referring to the Established Church of Scotland—as opposed to Dr Drummond's own Presbyterian congregation, which is associated with one of the strains of Presbyterianism that had dissociated itself from the Established Presbyterian faith.

Twenty-five years it was, in point, this Monday morning when the Doctor—not being Established we need not hesitate, besides by this time nobody did—stood with Mr Murchison in the store door and talked about having seen changes. He had preached his anniversary sermon the night before to a full church, when, laying his hand upon his people's heart, he had himself to repress tears. He was aware of another strand completed in their mutual bond: the sermon had been a moral, an emotional, and an oratorical success; and in the expansion of the following morning Dr Drummond had remembered that he had promised his housekeeper a new gas cooking-range, and that it was high time he should drop into Murchison's to inquire about it. Mrs Forsyth had mentioned at breakfast that they had ranges with exactly the improvement she wanted at Thompson's, but the minister was deaf to the hint. Thompson was a Congregationalist,[6] and, improvement or no improvement, it wasn't likely that Dr Drummond was going 'outside the congregation' for anything he required. It would have been on a par with a wandering tendency in his flock, upon which he systematically frowned. He was as great an autocrat in this as the rector of any country parish in England undermined by Dissent;[7] but his sense of obligation worked unfailingly both ways.

John Murchison had not said much about the sermon; it wasn't his way, and Dr Drummond knew it. 'You gave us a good sermon last night, Doctor;' not much more than that, 'and I noticed the Milburns there; we don't often get Episcopalians;' and again, 'The Wilcoxes'—Thomas Wilcox, wholesale grocer, was the chief prop of St Andrew's—'were sitting just in front of us. We overtook them going home, and Wilcox explained how much they liked the music. "Glad to see you," I said. "Glad to see you for any reason," ' Mr Murchison's eye twinkled. 'But they had a great deal to say about "the music." ' It was not an effusive form of felicitation; the minister would have liked it less if it had been, felt less justified, perhaps, in remembering about the range on that particular morning. As it was, he was able to take it with perfect dignity and good humour, and to enjoy the point against the Wilcoxes with that laugh of his that did everybody good to hear; so hearty it was, so rich in the grain of the voice, so full of the zest and flavour of the joke. The range had been selected, and their talk of changes had begun with it, Mr Murchison pointing out the new idea in the boiler, and Dr Drummond remembering his first kitchen stove that burned wood and stood on its four legs, with nothing behind but the stove pipe, and if you wanted a boiler you took off the front lids and put it on, and how remarkable even that had seemed to his eyes, fresh from the conservative kitchen notions of the old country. He had come, unhappily, a widower to the domestic improvements on the other side of the Atlantic. 'Often I used to think', he said to Mr Murchison, 'if my poor wife could have seen that stove how delighted she would have been! But I doubt this would have been too much for her altogether!'

6 Another Protestant denomination. (The Congregationalists, Presbyterians, and Methodists were later united, in 1925, to form the United Church of Canada.)

7 Duncan here continues her joke about the Scottishness of Elgin and its treating Presbyterianism as the Established religion. Dr Drummond views Protestant faiths other than Presbyterianism in the way Anglican rectors in England would view Dissenting faiths (those Protestant faiths, including Presbyterianism, that broke away from both Roman Catholicism and the Established faith of the Church of England).

'That stove!' answered Mr Murchison. 'Well I remember it. I sold it myself to your predecessor, Mr Wishart, for thirty dollars—the last purchase he ever made, poor man. It was great business for me—I had only two others in the store like it. One of them old Milburn bought—the father of this man, d'ye mind him?—the other stayed by me a matter of seven years. I carried a light stock in those days.'

It was no longer a light stock. The two men involuntarily glanced round them for the satisfaction of the contrast Murchison evoked, though neither of them, from motives of vague delicacy, felt inclined to dwell upon it. John Murchison had the shyness of an artist in his commercial success, and the minister possibly felt that his relation toward the prosperity of a member had in some degree the embarrassment of a tax-gatherer's. The stock was indeed heavy now. You had to go upstairs to see the ranges, where they stood in rows, and every one of them bore somewhere upon it, in raised black letters, John Murchison's name. Through the windows came the iterating ring on the iron from the foundry in Chestnut Street which fed the shop, with an overflow that found its way from one end of the country to the other. Finicking visitors to Elgin found this wearing, but to John Murchison it was the music that honours the conqueror of circumstances. The ground floor was given up to the small wares of the business, chiefly imported; two or three young men, steady and knowledgeable-looking, moved about in their shirt sleeves among shelves and packing cases. One of them was our friend Alec; our other friend Oliver[8] looked after the books at the foundry. Their father did everything deliberately; but presently, in his own good time, his commercial letter paper would be headed, with regard to these two, 'John Murchison and Sons'. It had long announced that the business was 'Wholesale and Retail'.

Dr Drummond and Mr Murchison, considering the changes in Elgin from the store door, did it at their leisure, the merchant with his thumbs thrust comfortably in the armholes of his waist-coat, the minister, with that familiar trick of his, balancing on one foot and suddenly throwing his slight weight forward on the other. 'A bundle of nerves' people called the Doctor: to stand still would have been a penance to him; even as he swayed backward and forward in talking his hand must be busy at the seals on his watch chain and his shrewd glance travelling over a dozen things you would never dream so clever a man would take notice of. It was a prospect of moderate commercial activity they looked out upon, a street of mellow shop-fronts, on both sides, of varying height and importance, wearing that air of marking a period, a definite stop in growth, that so often co-exists with quite a reasonable degree of activity and independence in colonial towns. One could almost say, standing there in the door at Murchison's, where the line of

---

8 Alec and Oliver are two of John Murchison's sons. In Chapter One the narrator explains: 'We must take this matter of names seriously; the Murchisons always did,' and explains that the full names given the boys are Alexander Mackenzie Murchison and Oliver Mowat Murchison because 'neither an Alexander Mackenzie nor an Oliver Mowat could very well grow up into anything but a sound Liberal in that part of the world without feeling himself an unendurable paradox.' (Mackenzie was the Liberal prime minister of Canada, 1873–8; Mowat, the Liberal premier of Ontario, 1872–96.) The narrator also informs us of the source of Lorne Murchison's name, which was given him 'at the period of a naïve fashion of christening the young sons of Canada in the name of her Governor-General' (i.e. Sir John Campbell, Marquis of Lorne, Governor-General of Canada 1878–83). In contrast, the two oldest children, the daughters Advenna and Abigail, are named for their grandmothers; and the youngest child, also a daughter, is named Stella because Mrs Murchison 'was thankful to have a girl at last whom she could name without regard to her own relations or anybody else's.'

legitimate enterprise had been over-passed and where its intention had been none too sanguine—on the one hand in the faded and pretentious red brick building with the false third story, occupied by Cleary, which must have been let at a loss to dry-goods or anything else; on the other hand in the solid 'Gregory block', opposite the market, where rents were as certain as the dividends of the Bank of British North America.

Main Street expressed the idea that, for the purpose of growing and doing business, it had always found the days long enough. Drays[9] passed through it to the Grand Trunk station, but they passed one at a time; a certain number of people went up and down about their affairs, but they were never in a hurry; a street car jogged by every ten minutes or so, but nobody ran after it. There was a decent procedure; and it was felt that Bofield—he was dry-goods, too—in putting in an elevator was just a little unnecessarily in advance of the times. Bofield had only two stories, like everybody else, and a very easy staircase, up which people often declared they preferred to walk rather than wait in the elevator for a young man to finish serving and work it. These, of course, were the sophisticated people of Elgin; country folk, on a market day, would wait a quarter of an hour for the young man, and think nothing of it; and I imagine Bofield found his account in[10] the elevator, though he did complain sometimes that such persons went up and down on frivolous pretexts or to amuse the baby. As a matter of fact, Elgin had begun as the centre of 'trading' for the farmers of Fox County, and had soon over-supplied that limit in demand; so that when other interests added themselves to the activity of the town there was still plenty of room for the business they brought. Main Street was really, therefore, not a fair index; nobody in Elgin would have admitted it. Its appearance and demeanour would never have suggested that it was now the chief artery of a thriving manufacturing town, with a collegiate institute, eleven churches, two newspapers, and an asylum for the deaf and dumb, to say nothing of a fire department unsurpassed for organization and achievement in the Province of Ontario. Only at twelve noon it might be partly realized, when the prolonged 'toots' of seven factory whistles at once let off, so to speak, the hour. Elgin liked the demonstration; it was held to be cheerful and unmistakable, an indication of 'go-ahead' proclivities which spoke for itself. It occurred while yet Dr Drummond and Mr Murchison stood together in the store door.

'I must be getting on,' said the minister, looking at his watch. 'And what news have you of Lorne?'

'Well, he seems to have got through all right.'

'What—you've heard already, then?'

'He telegraphed from Toronto on Saturday night.' Mr Murchison stroked his chin, the better to retain his satisfaction. 'Waste of money—the post would have brought it this morning—but it pleased his mother. Yes, he's through his Law Schools examination, and at the top, too, as far as I can make out.'

'Dear me, and you never mentioned it!' Dr Drummond spoke with the resigned impatience of a familiar grievance. It was certainly a trying characteristic of John Murchison that he never cared about communicating anything that might seem to ask for congratulation. 'Well, well! I'm very glad to hear it.'

---

9  Low carts without sides, used for hauling.
10  Brought in a profit because of.

'It slipped my mind,' said Mr Murchison. 'Yes, he's full-fledged "barrister and solicitor" now; he can plead your case or draw you up a deed with the best of them. Lorne's made a fair record, so far. We've no reason to be ashamed of him.'

'That you have not.' Personal sentiments between these two Scotchmen were rather indicated than indulged. 'He's going in with Fulke and Warner, I suppose—you've got that fixed up?'

'Pretty well. Old man Warner was in this morning to talk it over. He says they look to Lorne to bring them in touch with the new generation. It's a pity he lost that son of his.'

'Oh, a great pity. But since they had to go outside the firm they couldn't have done better; they couldn't have done better. I hope Lorne will bring them a bit of Knox Church business too; there's no reason why Bob Mackintosh should have it all. They'll be glad to see him back at the Hampden Debating Society. He's a great light there, is Lorne; and the Young Liberals, I hear, are wanting him for chairman this year.'

'There's some talk of it. But time enough—time enough for that! He'll do first-rate if he gets the law to practise, let alone the making of it.'

'Maybe so; he's young yet. Well, good-morning to you. I'll just step over the way to the *Express* office and get a proof out of them of that sermon of mine. I noticed their reporter fellow—what's his name?—Rawlins with his pencil out last night, and I've no faith in Rawlins.'

'Better cast an eye over it,' responded Mr Murchison, cordially, and stood for a moment or two longer in the door watching the crisp, significant little figure of the minister as he stepped briskly over the crossing to the newspaper office. There Dr Drummond sat down, before he explained his errand, and wrote a paragraph.

'We are pleased to learn', it ran, 'that Mr Lorne Murchison, eldest son of Mr John Murchison, of this town, has passed at the capital of the Province his final examination in Law, distinguishing himself by coming out at the top of the list. It will be remembered that Mr Murchison, upon entering the Law Schools, also carried off a valuable scholarship. We are glad to be able to announce that Mr Murchison, junior, will embark upon his profession in his native town, where he will enter the well-known firm of Fulke and Warner.'

The editor, Mr Horace Williams, had gone to dinner, and Rawlins was out, so Dr Drummond had to leave it with the press foreman. Mr Williams read it appreciatively on his return, and sent it down with the following addition—

'This is doing it as well as it can be done. Elgin congratulates Mr L. Murchison upon having produced these results, and herself upon having produced Mr L. Murchison.'

## CHAPTER III

From the day she stepped into it Mrs Murchison knew that the Plummer Place was going to be the bane of her existence. This may have been partly because Mr Murchison had bought it, since a circumstance welded like that into one's life is very apt to assume the character of a bane, unless one's temperament leads one to philosophy, which Mrs Murchison's didn't. But there were other reasons more difficult to traverse: it was plainly true that the place did require a tremendous amount of 'looking after', as such things were measured in Elgin, far more looking after than the Murchison's could afford to give it. They could never have afforded, in the beginning, to possess it, had it not been sold, under mortgage, at a dramatic sacrifice. The house was a dignified old affair, built of wood and painted white, with wide green verandahs compassing the four sides of it, as they often did in days when the builder had only to turn his hand to the forest. It stood on the very edge of the town; wheatfields in the summer billowed up to its fences, and cornstacks in the autumn camped around it like a besieging army. The plank sidewalk finished there; after that you took the road, or, if you were so inclined, the river, into which you could throw a stone from the orchard of the Plummer Place. The house stood roomily and shadily in ornamental grounds, with a lawn in front of it and a shrubbery at each side, an orchard behind, and a vegetable garden, the whole intersected by winding gravel walks, of which Mrs Murchison was wont to say that a man might do nothing but weed them and have his hands full. In the middle of the lawn was a fountain, an empty basin with a plaster Triton,[1] most difficult to keep looking respectable and pathetic in his frayed air of exile from some garden of Italy sloping to the sea. There was also a barn with stabling, a loft, and big carriage doors opening on a lane to the street. The originating Plummer, Mrs Murchison often said, must have been a person of large ideas, and she hoped he had the money to live up to them. The Murchisons at one time kept a cow in the barn, till a succession of 'girls' left on account of the milking, and the lane was useful as an approach to the back yard by the teams that brought the cordwood in the winter. It was trying enough for a person with the instinct of order to find herself surrounded by out-of-door circumstances which she simply could not control, but Mrs Murchison often declared that she could put up with the grounds if it had stopped there. It did not stop there. Though I was compelled to introduce Mrs Murchison in the kitchen, she had a drawing-room in which she might have received the Lieutenant Governor, with French windows and a cut-glass chandelier, and a library with an Italian marble mantelpiece. She had an ice-house and wine cellar, and a string of bells in the kitchen that connected with every room in the house; it was a negligible misfortune that not one of them was in order. She had far too much, as she declared, for any one pair of hands and a growing family, and if the ceiling was not dropping in the drawing-room, the cornice was cracked in the library, or the gas was leaking in the dining-room, or the verandah wanted re-flooring if any one coming to the house was not to put his foot through it; and as to the barn, if it was dropping to pieces it would just have to drop. The barn was definitely outside the radius of possible amelioration—it passed gradually, visibly, into decrepitude, and Mrs Murchison often wished she could afford to pull it down.

It may be realized that in spite of its air of being impossible to 'overtake'—I must, in this connection, continue to quote its mistress—there was an attractiveness about the dwelling of the Murchisons, the attractiveness of the large ideas upon which it had been built and designed, no doubt by one of those gentlefolk of reduced income who wander out to the colonies with a nebulous view to economy and occupation, to perish of the readjustment. The case of such persons, when they arrive, is at once felt to be pathetic; there is a tacit local understanding that they have made a mistake. They

1 A god of the sea, having the head and trunk of a man and the tail of a fish.

may be entitled to respect, but nothing can save them from the isolation of their difference and their misapprehension. It was like that with the house. The house was admired—without enthusiasm—but it was not copied. It was felt to be outside the general need, misjudged, adventitious; and it wore its superiority in the popular view like a folly. It was in Elgin, but not of it; it represented a different tradition; and Elgin made the same allowance for its bedroom bells and its old-fashioned dignities as was conceded to its original master's habit of a six o'clock dinner, with wine.

The architectural expression of the town was on a different scale, beginning with 'frame', rising through the semi-detached, culminating expensively in Mansard roofs, cupolas and modern conveniences, and blossoming, in extreme instances, into Moorish fretwork and silk portières for interior decoration.[2] The Murchison house gained by force of contrast: one felt, stepping into it, under influences of less expediency and more dignity, wider scope and more leisured intention; its shabby spaces had a redundancy the pleasanter and its yellow plaster cornices a charm the greater for the numerous close-set examples of contemporary taste in red brick which made, surrounded by geranium beds, so creditable an appearance in the West Ward. John Murchison in taking possession of the house had felt in it these satisfactions, had been definitely penetrated and soothed by them, the more perhaps because he brought to them a capacity for feeling the worthier things of life which circumstances had not previously developed. He seized the place with a sense of opportunity leaping sharp and conscious out of early years in the grey 'wynds'[3] of a northern Scottish town; and its personality sustained him, very privately but none the less effectively, through the worry and expense of it for years. He would take his pipe and walk silently for long together about the untidy shrubberies in the evening for the acute pleasure of seeing the big horse-chestnuts in flower; and he never opened the hall door without a feeling of gratification in its weight as it swung under his hand. In so far as he could, he supplemented the idiosyncrasies he found. The drawing-room walls, though mostly bare in their old-fashioned French paper—lavender and gilt, a grape vine pattern—held a few good engravings; the library was reduced to contain a single bookcase, but it was filled with English classics. John Murchison had been made a careful man, not by nature, by the discipline of circumstances; but he would buy books. He bought them between long periods of abstinence, during which he would scout[4] the expenditure of an unnecessary dollar, coming home with a parcel under his arm for which he vouchsafed no explanation, and which would disclose itself to be Lockhart, or Sterne, or Borrow, or Defoe. Mrs Murchison kept a discouraging eye upon such purchases; and

2  Here, 'frame' refers to simple wood buildings. Mansard roofs form an additional upper story by being pitched sharply vertical, then topped with a nearly horizontal peak; cupolas are small domed structures surmounting a roof; fretwork is an ornamental design of repeated, interlaced, and symmetrical figures, and Moorish fretwork an ornate form of this; portières are ornamental curtains hung across doorways.

3  Sidestreets (Scottish).

4  Deride. The four authors John Murchison does decide to spend money on are John Gibson Lockhart (1794–1854), the Scottish novelist and author of a celebrated multi-volume biography of Sir Walter Scott (1837–8); Laurence Stern (1713–68) the Irish-born writer now chiefly remembered for his novel *The Life and Opinions of Tristram Shandy, Gentleman,* (Murchison may have valued him for *A Sentimental Journey Through France and Italy* and his sermons and memoirs); the polyglot George Henry Borrow (1803–81), whose accounts of exotic travel (often on foot or on horseback) and records of Gypsy life were based on his first-hand experiences; and Daniel Defoe (*c.* 1659–1731), the author of *Robinson Crusoe,* who published on a wide variety of topics, including politics, religion, and moral philosophy. Murchison also purchases the compendious reference work on, and collection of extracts by, British writers that was compiled in 1840 by the Scottish scholar Robert Chambers.

when her husband brought home Chambers' *Dictionary of English Literature*, after shortly and definitely repulsing her demand that he should get himself a new winter overcoat, she declared that it was beyond all endurance. Mrs Murchison was surrounded, indeed, by more of 'that sort of thing' than she could find use or excuse for; since, though books made but a sporadic appearance, current literature, daily, weekly, and monthly, was perpetually under her feet. The Toronto paper came as a matter of course, as the London daily takes its morning flight into the provinces, the local organ as simply indispensable, the Westminster as the corollary of church membership and for Sunday reading. These were constant, but there were also mutables—*Once a Week, Good Words for the Young, Blackwood's* and the *Cornhill*,[5] they used to be; years of back numbers Mrs Murchison had packed away in the attic, where Advena on rainy days came into the inheritance of them, and made an early acquaintance of fiction in *Ready Money Mortiboy* and *Verner's Pride*, while Lorne, flat on his stomach beside her, had glorious hours on *The Back of the North Wind*. Their father considered such publications and their successors essential, like tobacco and tea. He was also an easy prey to the subscription agent, for works published in parts and paid for in instalments, a custom which Mrs Murchison regarded with abhorrence. So much so that when John put his name down for *Masterpieces of the World's Art* which was to cost twenty dollars by the time it was complete, he thought it advisable to let the numbers accumulate at the store.

Whatever the place represented to their parents, it was pure joy to the young Murchisons. It offered a margin and a mystery to life. They saw it far larger than it was; they invested it, arguing purely by its difference from other habitations, with a romantic past. 'I guess when the Prince of Wales came to Elgin, mother, he stayed here,' Lorne remarked, as a little boy. Secretly he and Advena took up boards in more than one unused room, and rapped on more than one thick wall to find a hollow chamber; the house revealed so much that was interesting, it was apparent to the meanest understanding that it must hide even more. It was never half lighted, and there was a passage in which fear dwelt—wild were the gallopades[6] from attic to cellar in the early nightfall, when every young Murchison tore after every other, possessed, like cats, by a demoniac ecstasy of the gloaming. And the garden, with the autumn moon coming over the apple trees and the neglected asparagus thick for ambush, and a casual untrimmed boy or two with the delicious recommendation of being utterly without credentials, to join in the rout and be trusted to make for the back fence without further hint at the voice of Mrs Murchison—these were joys of the very fibre, things to push ideas and envisage life with an attraction that made it worth while to grow up.

And they had all achieved it—all six. They had grown up sturdily, emerging into sobriety and decorum by much the same degrees as the old house, under John Murchison's improving fortunes, grew cared for and presentable. The new roof went on, slate replacing shingles, the year Abby put her hair up; the bathroom was contemporary with Oliver's leaving school; the electric light was actually turned on for the first time in honour of Lorne's return from Toronto, a barrister and solicitor; several rooms

---

5  Victorian weeklies, which serialized literary fiction but also contained works of popular fiction such as those mentioned later in this sentence, the romances *Ready Money Mortiboy* and *Verner's Pride* and the children's novel *The Back of the North Wind* by George Macdonald.
6  Lively dances; 'gloaming': twilight.

had been done up for Abby's wedding. Abby had married, early and satisfactorily, Dr Harry Johnson, who had placidly settled down to await the gradual succession of his father's practice; 'Dr Harry and Dr Henry' they were called. Dr Harry lived next door to Dr Henry, and had a good deal of the old man's popular manner. It was an unacknowledged partnership, which often provided two opinions for the same price; the town prophesied well of it. That left only five at home, but they always had Abby over in the West Ward, where Abby's housekeeping made an interest and Abby's baby a point of pilgrimage. These considerations almost consoled Mrs Murchison, declaring, as she did, that all of them might have gone but Abby, who alone knew how to be 'any comfort or any dependence' in the house; who could be left with a day's preserving; and I tell you that to be left by Mrs Murchison with a day's preserving, be it cherries or strawberries, damsons or pears, was a mark of confidence not easy to obtain. Advena never had it; Advena, indeed, might have married and removed no prop of the family economy. Mrs Murchison would have been 'sorry for the man'—she maintained a candour toward and about those belonging to her that permitted no illusions—but she would have stood cheerfully out of the way on her own account. When you have seen your daughter reach and pass the age of twenty-five without having learned properly to make her own bed, you know, without being told, that she will never be fit for the management of a house—don't you? Very well then. And for ever and for ever, no matter what there was to do, with a book in her hand—Mrs Murchison would put an emphasis on the 'book' which scarcely concealed a contempt for such absorption. And if, at the end of your patience, you told her for any sake to put it down and attend to matters, obeying in a kind of dream that generally drove you to take the thing out of her hands and do it yourself, rather than jump out of your skin watching her.

Sincerely Mrs Murchison would have been sorry for the man if he had arrived, but he had not arrived. Advena justified her existence by taking the university course for women at Toronto, and afterward teaching the English branches to the junior forms in the Collegiate Institute, which placed her arbitrarily outside the sphere of domestic criticism. Mrs Murchison was thankful to have her there—outside—where little more could reasonably be expected of her than that she should be down in time for breakfast. It is so irritating to be justified in expecting more than seems likely to come. Mrs Murchison's ideas circulated strictly in the orbit of equity and reason; she expected nothing from anybody that she did not expect from herself; indeed, she would spare others in far larger proportion. But the sense of obligation which led her to offer herself up to the last volt of her energy made her miserable when she considered that she was not fairly done by in return. Pressed down and running over were the services she offered to the general good, and it was on the ground of the merest justice that she required from her daughters 'some sort of interest' in domestic affairs. From her eldest she got no sort of interest, and it was like the removal of a grievance from the hearth when Advena took up employment which ranged her definitely beyond the necessity of being of any earthly use in the house. Advena's occupation to some extent absorbed her shortcomings, which was much better than having to attribute them to her being naturally 'through-other', or naturally clever, according to the bias of the moment. Mrs Murchison no longer excused or complained of her daughter; but she still pitied the man.

'The boys', of course, were too young to think of matrimony. They were still the boys, the Murchison boys; they would be the boys at forty if they remained under their father's roof. In the mother country, men in short jackets and round collars emerge from the preparatory schools; in the daughter lands boys in tail coats conduct serious affairs. Alec and Oliver, in the business, were frivolous enough as to the feminine interest. For all Dr Drummond's expressed and widely-known views upon the subject, it was a common thing for one or both of these young men to stray from the family pew on Sunday evenings to the services of other communions, thereafter to walk home in the dusk under the maples with some attractive young person, and be sedately invited to finish the evening on her father's verandah. Neither of them was guiltless of silk ties knitted or handkerchiefs initialled by certain fingers; without repeating scandal, one might say by various fingers. For while the ultimate import of these matters was not denied in Elgin, there was a general feeling against giving too much meaning to them, probably originating in a reluctance among heads of families to add to their responsibilities. These early spring indications were belittled and laughed at; so much so that the young people themselves hardly took them seriously, but regarded them as a form of amusement almost conventional. Nothing would have surprised or embarrassed them more than to learn that their predilections had an imperative corollary, that anything should, of necessity, 'come of it'. Something, of course, occasionally did come of it; and, usually after years of 'attention', a young man of Elgin found himself mated to a young woman, but never under circumstances that could be called precipitate or rash. The cautious blood and far sight of the early settlers, who had much to reckon with, were still preponderant social characteristics of the town they cleared the site for. Meanwhile, however, flowers were gathered, and all sorts of evanescent idylls came and went in the relations of young men and maidens. Alec and Oliver Murchison were already in the full tide of them.

From this point of view they did not know what to make of Lorne. It was not as if their brother were in any way ill calculated to attract that interest which gave to youthful existence in Elgin almost the only flavour that it had. Looks are looks, and Lorne had plenty of them; taller by an inch than Alec, broader by two than Oliver, with a fine square head and blue eyes in it, and features which conveyed purpose and humour, lighted by a certain simplicity of soul that pleased even when it was not understood. 'Open', people said he was, and 'frank'—so he was, frank and open, with horizons and intentions; you could see them in his face. Perhaps it was more conscious of them than he was. Ambition, definitely shining goals, adorn the perspectives of young men in new countries less often than is commonly supposed. Lorne meant to be a good lawyer, squarely proposed to himself that the country should hold no better; and as to more selective usefulness, he hoped to do a little stumping for the right side when Frank Jennings ran for the Ontario House in the fall. It wouldn't be his first electioneering: from the day he became chairman of the Young Liberals the party had an eye on him, and when occasion arose, winter or summer, by bobsleigh or buggy, weatherbeaten local bosses would convey him to country schoolhouses for miles about to keep a district sound on railway policy, or education, or tariff reform. He came home smiling with the triumphs of these occasions, and offered them, with the slow, good-humoured, capable drawl that inspired such confidence in him, to his family at breakfast, who said 'Great!' or 'Good for you, Lorne!' John Murchison oftenest said nothing, but would glance significantly at his wife, frowning and pursing his lips when she, who had most spirit of them all, would exclaim, 'You'll be Premier yet, Lorne!' It was no part of the Murchison policy to draw against future balances: they might believe everything, they would express nothing; and I doubt whether Lorne himself had any map of the country he meant to travel over in that vague future, already defining in local approbation, and law business coming freely in with a special eye on the junior partner. But the tract was there, sub-conscious, plain in the wider glance, the alerter manner; plain even in the grasp and stride which marked him in a crowd; plain, too, in the preoccupation with other issues, were it only turning over a leader in the morning's *Dominion*, that carried him along indifferent to the allurements I have described. The family had a bond of union in their respect for Lorne, and this absence of nugatory inclinations in him was among its elements. Even Stella, who, being just fourteen, was the natural mouthpiece of family sentiment, would declare that Lorne had something better to do than go hanging about after girls, and for her part she thought all the more of him for it.

1904

# E. Pauline Johnson
## 1861–1913

Emily Pauline Johnson was born in Chiefswood, a mansion built on the Six Nations Reserve in the Grand River valley near Brantford, Ontario. Chiefswood was constructed by her Mohawk father (Chief George Henry Martin Johnson) for his English bride, Emily Susanna Howells. Johnson's early learning was derived from stories told by her grandfather, John Smoke Johnson, and from her governesses. Although her formal education was limited—she spent two years at a school on the reserve and graduated from Central Collegiate in Brantford (1875–7)— her mother introduced her to the work of Longfellow, Byron, Shakespeare, and Emerson. Johnson also read the important poets and prose writers of her own day. At school, she pursued her interest in the performing arts, and learned the rhetorical skills that would be the cornerstone of her career.

After her return to Chiefswood, Johnson began to write poetry. In 1886, she adopted the Mohawk name Tekahionwake or 'Double Life'; and she published her first poem that year, after reading it at the unveiling of the Joseph Brant statue in Brantford's Victoria Park. In 1892, her reading of 'A Cry from an Indian Wife' at the Young Liberals' Club in Toronto was so well received that it launched her career as a poet-performer. She toured as the 'Mohawk Princess', emphasizing her ability to move between the two cultures by wearing a buckskin costume when reading Indian poems and then, during the interval, changing into an evening dress for the remainder of her performance. She performed with the comedian and musician Owen Smiley (until 1897) and with Walter McRaye (after 1901). In 1909, she retired to Vancouver.

Johnson's reputation as a poet was established when two of her poems were included in the anthology *Songs of the Great Dominion* (London, 1889). By the time her first collection of poetry, *The White Wampum*, was published in Britain in 1895, she was a popular performer both there and in North America. This collection and her next, *Canadian Born* (1903), increased the interest in her performances. Her last collection, *Flint and Feather* (1912), published just before her death, is drawn principally from the two previous volumes. In 2002, all of her poems (together with some prose selections) were published as *Tekahionwake*, edited by Carole Gerson and Veronica Strong-Boag.

A tension in Johnson's work, a product of her mixed traditions, is evident in such poems as 'A Cry from an Indian Wife'. Although she makes use of her Mohawk heritage for both content and perspective, the poem (which conveys an Indian wife's thoughts on the Northwest Rebellion of 1869–70 led by Louis Riel) also draws heavily on Johnson's knowledge of the tradition and conventions of English verse. The speaker's hesitations, for instance, are more reminiscent of a Shakespearean soliloquy than of the oral tradition of Johnson's Mohawk ancestors. This combination was the key to Johnson's appeal to her white audiences: this 'Mohawk Princess' communicated the unfamiliar in a way wholly familiar to them. In 'Silhouette', for example—part of a Smiley–Johnson performance routine called 'There and Back'—Johnson uses the familiar ballad form to paint a picture of a noble and endangered way of life and to make it readily accessible to her audience. No wonder she was so well received in England in 1894 and again in 1906, or that her first book was brought out by the distinguished British publisher Bodley Head.

After 1904, Johnson began to concentrate on writing prose, and scompleted three collections of short fiction: *Legends of Vancouver* (1911), *The Shagganappi*, and *The Moccasin Maker*, the latter two being published posthumously in 1913. Perhaps the most interesting manifestation of Johnson's complex relationships with the First Nations communities may be seen in *Legends of Vancouver*. Prior to writing *Legends*, she had spent her career generalizing about Aboriginal groups; mixing the myths and customs of a number of peoples; and expressing this mélange in a language alien to its subject matter. For the stories in *Legends*, she uses a form closer to that of oral narrative and more suited to its Native content. The tales in this volume are told by an elder to a westernized listener, the pattern of Johnson's own experience. She first heard most of these narratives, which she describes as legends previously 'unknown to . . . Pale-faces', from Squamish Chief Joe Capilano. The oral quality of Capilano's narration is retained in such stories as 'The Lost Island', a tale explaining earlier Squamish power and providing for the possibility of its return.

# The Song My Paddle Sings

West wind, blow from your prairie nest,
Blow from the mountains, blow from the west
The sail is idle, the sailor too;
O! wind of the west, we wait for you.
Blow, blow!
I have wooed you so,
But never a favour you bestow.
You rock your cradle the hills between,
But scorn to notice my white lateen.[1]

I stow the sail, unship the mast:
I wooed you long but my wooing's past;
My paddle will lull you into rest.
O! drowsy wind of the drowsy west,
Sleep, sleep,
By your mountain steep,

10

1 A small triangular sail.

Or down where the prairie grasses sweep!
Now fold in slumber your laggard wings,
For soft is the song my paddle sings.

August is laughing across the sky,
Laughing while paddle, canoe and I,          20
Drift, drift,
Where the hills uplift
On either side of the current swift.

The river rolls in its rocky bed;
My paddle is plying its way ahead;
Dip, dip,
While the waters flip
In foam as over their breast we slip.

And oh, the river runs swifter now;
The eddies circle about my bow.              30
Swirl, swirl!
How the ripples curl
In many a dangerous pool awhirl!

And forward far the rapids roar,
Fretting their margin for evermore.
Dash, dash,
With a mighty crash,
They seethe, and boil, and bound, and splash.

Be strong, O paddle! be brave, canoe!
The reckless waves you must plunge into.      40
Reel, reel.
On your trembling keel,
But never a fear my craft will feel.

We've raced the rapid, we're far ahead!
The river slips through its silent bed.
Sway, sway,
As the bubbles spray
And fall in tinkling tunes away.

And up on the hills against the sky,
A fir tree rocking its lullaby,               50
Swings, swings,
Its emerald wings,
Swelling the song that my paddle sings.

[1891–2], 1895

# His Majesty the West Wind

Once in a fit of mental aberration
I wrote some stanzas to the western wind,
A very stupid, maudlin invocation
That into ears of audiences I've dinned.

A song about a sail, canoe and paddle
Recited by a sailor flannel dressed,
And when they heard it, people would skedaddle,
Particularly those who had been west.

For they alas had knowledge I was missing
To write of something I had never known,                    10
That I had never experienced the driving
Of western winds across a prairie blown.

I never thought when grinding out those stanzas
I'd have to swallow specks of prairie dust,
That I'd deny my old extravaganzas
And wish His Majesty distinctly—cussed!

1894, 1990[1]

1 Johnson wrote this ironic commentary on her immensely popular performance piece 'The Song My Paddle
Sings' in August 1894 when a late summer tour with Smiley took her, for the first time, to the Canadian prairies;
she published it in the Toronto *Globe* that December. Many of Johnson's fans were offended by this poem's
descent from the high rhetoric to which they were accustomed to 'slang'; this controversy prompted a debate
over Johnson's merits as a poet in the letters column of *The Week*. Johnson never republished this poem, and it
was not reprinted anywhere until it appeared in *The Beaver* (Dec. 1986/Jan. 1987); its appearance in the 1990
*Anthology of Canadian Literature in English* marked its first book publication.

# A Cry from an Indian Wife

My Forest Brave, my Red-skin love, farewell;
We may not meet to-morrow; who can tell
What mighty ills befall our little band,
Or what you'll suffer from the white man's hand?
Here is your knife! I thought 'twas sheathed for aye.
No roaming bison calls for it to-day;
No hide of prairie cattle will it maim;
The plains are bare, it seeks a nobler game:
'Twill drink the life-blood of a soldier host.
Go; rise and strike, no matter what the cost.                 10

Yet stay. Revolt not at the Union Jack,
Nor raise Thy hand against this stripling pack
Of white-faced warriors, marching West to quell
Our fallen tribe that rises to rebel.
They all are young and beautiful and good;
Curse to the war that drinks their harmless blood.
Curse to the fate that brought them from the East
To be our chiefs—to make our nation least
That breathes the air of this vast continent.
Still their new rule and council is well meant.                    20
They but forget we Indians owned the land
From ocean unto ocean; that they stand
Upon a soil that centuries agone
Was our sole kingdom and our right alone.
They never think how they would feel to-day,
If some great nation came from far away,
Wresting their country from their hapless braves,
Giving what they gave us—but wars and graves.
Then go and strike for liberty and life,
And bring back honour to your Indian wife.                         30
Your wife? Ah, what of that, who cares for me?
Who pities my poor love and agony?
What white-robed priest prays for your safety here,
As prayer is said for every volunteer
That swells the ranks that Canada sends out?
Who prays for vict'ry for the Indian scout?
Who prays for our poor nation lying low?
None—therefore take your tomahawk and go.
My heart may break and burn into its core,
But I am strong to bid you go to war.                              40
Yet stay, my heart is not the only one
That grieves the loss of husband and of son;
Think of the mothers o'er the inland seas;
Think of the pale-faced maiden on her knees;
One pleads her God to guard some sweet-faced child
That marches on toward the North-West wild.
The other prays to shield her love from harm,
To strengthen his young, proud uplifted arm.
Ah, how her white face quivers thus to think,
*Your* tomahawk his life's best blood will drink.                  50
She never thinks of my wild aching breast,
Nor prays for your dark face and eagle crest
Endangered by a thousand rifle balls,
My heart the target if my warrior falls.

O! coward self I hesitate no more;
Go forth, and win the glories of the war.
Go forth, nor bend to greed of white men's hands,
By right, by birth we Indians own these lands,
Though starved, crushed, plundered, lies our nation low . . . .
Perhaps the white man's God has willed it so.          60

1895

# The Flight of the Crows

The autumn afternoon is dying o'er
   The quiet western valley where I lie
Beneath the maples on the river shore,
   Where tinted leaves, blue waters and fair sky
   Environ all; and far above some birds are flying by

To seek their evening haven in the breast
   And calm embrace of silence, while they sing
Te Deums to the night, invoking rest
   For busy chirping voice and tired wing—
   And in the hush of sleeping trees their sleeping cradles swing.          10

In forest arms the night will soonest creep,
   Where sombre pines a lullaby intone,
Where Nature's children curl themselves to sleep,
   And all is still at last, save where alone
   A band of black, belated crows arrive from lands unknown.

Strange sojourn has been theirs since waking day,
   Strange sights and cities in their wanderings blend
With fields of yellow maize, and leagues away
   With rivers where their sweeping waters wend
   Past velvet banks to rocky shores, in cañons bold to end.          20

O'er what vast lakes that stretch superbly dead,
   Till lashed to life by storm-clouds, have they flown?
In what wild lands, in laggard flight have led
   Their aërial career unseen, unknown,
   'Till now with twilight come their cries in lonely monotone?

The flapping of their pinions in the air
    Dies in the hush of distance, while they light
Within the fir tops, weirdly black and bare,
    That stand with giant strength and peerless height,
    To shelter fairy, bird and beast throughout the closing night.      30

Strange black and princely pirates of the skies,
    Would that your wind-tossed travels I could know!
Would that my soul could see, and, seeing, rise
    To unrestricted life where ebb and flow
    Of Nature's pulse would constitute a wider life below!

Could I but live just here in Freedom's arms,
    A kingly life without a sovereign's care!
Vain dreams! Day hides with closing wings her charms,
    And all is cradled in repose, save where
    Yon band of black, belated crows still frets the evening air.      40

1895

## Silhouette

The sky-line melts from russet into blue,
Unbroken the horizon, saving where
A wreath of smoke curls up the far, thin air,
And points the distant lodges of the Sioux.

Etched where the lands and cloudlands touch and die
A solitary Indian tepee stands,
The only habitation of these lands,
That roll their magnitude from sky to sky.

The tent poles lift and loom in thin relief,
The upward floating smoke ascends between,      10
And near the open doorway, gaunt and lean,
And shadow-like, there stands an Indian Chief.

With eyes that lost their lustre long ago,
With visage fixed and stern as fate's decree,
He looks towards the empty west, to see
The never-coming herd of buffalo.

Only the bones that bleach upon the plains,
Only the fleshless skeletons that lie
In ghastly nakedness and silence, cry
Out mutely that naught else to him remains.                    20

1903


## 'Through Time and Bitter Distance'[1]

Unknown to you, I walk the cheerless shore.
    The cutting blast, the hurl of biting brine
May freeze, and still, and bind the waves at war,
    Ere you will ever know, O! Heart of mine,
That I have sought, reflected in the blue
    Of these sea depths, some shadow of your eyes;
Have hoped the laughing waves would sing of you,
    But this is all my starving sight descries—


              I
Far out at sea a sail
        Bends to the freshening breeze,
Yields to the rising gale                                      10
        That sweeps the seas;


              II
Yields, as a bird wind-tossed,
        To saltish waves that fling
Their spray, whose rime and frost
        Like crystals cling


              III
To canvas, mast and spar,
        Till, gleaming like a gem,
She sinks beyond the far
        Horizon's hem.                                         20


1  'For this title the author is indebted to Mr Charles G.D. Roberts. It occurs in his sonnet, "Rain" [Johnson's note].
   The longer passage from which this line comes reads: 'Ah God, if love had power / To voice its utmost yearning,
   even tho' / Thro' time and bitter distance, not in vain, / Surely Her heart would hear me at this hour.'

IV

Lost to my longing sight,
    And nothing left to me
Save an oncoming night,—
    An empty sea.

1903

# The Lost Island

'Yes,' said my old tillicum,[1] 'we Indians have lost many things. We have lost our lands, our forests, our game, our fish; we have lost our ancient religion, our ancient dress; some of the younger people have even lost their fathers' language and the legends and traditions of their ancestors. We cannot call those old things back to us; they will never come again. We may travel many days up the mountain trail, and look in the silent places for them. They are not there. We may paddle many moons on the sea, but our canoes will never enter the channel that leads to the yesterdays of the Indian people. These things are lost, just like "The Island of the North Arm". They may be somewhere near by, but no one can find them.'

'But there are many islands up the North Arm,' I asserted.

'Not the island we Indian people have sought for many tens of summers,' he replied sorrowfully.

'Was it ever there?' I questioned.

'Yes, it was there,' he said. 'My grandsires and my great-grandsires saw it; but that was long ago. My father never saw it, though he spent many days in many years searching, always searching for it. I am an old man myself, and I have never seen it, though from my youth, I, too, have searched. Sometimes in the stillness of the nights I have paddled up in my canoe.' Then, lowering his voice: 'Twice I have seen its shadow: high rocky shores, reaching as high as the tree tops on the mainland, then tall pines and firs on its summit like a king's crown. As I paddled up the Arm one summer night, long ago, the shadow of these rocks and firs fell across my canoe, across my face, and across the waters beyond. I turned rapidly to look. There was no island there, nothing but a wide stretch of waters on both sides of me, and the moon almost directly overhead. Don't say it was the shore that shadowed me,' he hastened, catching my thought. 'The moon was above me; my canoe scarce made a shadow on the still waters. No, it was not the shore.'

'Why do you search for it?' I lamented, thinking of the old dreams in my own life whose realization I have never attained.

'There is something on that island that I want. I shall look for it until I die, for it is there,' he affirmed.

There was a long silence between us after that. I had learned to love silences when with my old tillicum, for they always led to a legend. After a time he began voluntarily:

1  Friend (from Chinook Jargon, a trade language of the Pacific Northwest).

'It was more than one hundred years ago. This great city of Vancouver was but the dream of the Sagalie Tyee [God] at that time. The dream had not yet come to the white man; only one great Indian medicine man knew that some day a great camp for Pale-faces would lie between False Creek and the Inlet. This dream haunted him; it came to him night and day—when he was amid his people laughing and feasting, or when he was alone in the forest chanting his strange songs, beating his hollow drum, or shaking his wooden witch-rattle to gain more power to cure the sick and the dying of his tribe. For years this dream followed him. He grew to be an old, old man, yet always he could hear voices, strong and loud, as when they first spoke to him in his youth, and they would say: "Between the two narrow strips of salt water the white men will camp, many hundreds of them, many thousands of them. The Indians will learn their ways, will live as they do, will become as they are. There will be no more great war-dances, no more fights with other powerful tribes; it will be as if the Indians had lost all bravery, all courage, all confidence." He hated the voices, he hated the dream; but all his power, all his big medicine, could not drive them away. He was the strongest man on all the North Pacific Coast. He was mighty and very tall, and his muscles were as those of Leloo, the timber wolf, when he is strongest to kill his prey. He could go for many days without food; he could fight the largest mountain lion; he could overthrow the fiercest grizzly bear; he could paddle against the wildest winds and ride the highest waves. He could meet his enemies and kill whole tribes single-handed. His strength, his courage, his power, his bravery, were those of a giant. He knew no fear; nothing in the sea, or in the forest, nothing in the earth or the sky, could conquer him. He was fearless, fearless. Only this haunting dream of the coming white man's camp he could not drive away; it was the only thing in life he had tried to kill and failed. It drove him from the feasting, drove him from the pleasant lodges, the fires, the dancing, the story-telling of his people in their camp by the water's edge, where the salmon thronged and the deer came down to drink of the mountain streams. He left the Indian village, chanting his wild songs as he went. Up through the mighty forests he climbed, through the trailless deep mosses and matted vines, up to the summit of what the white men call Grouse Mountain. For many days he camped there. He ate no food, he drank no water, but sat and sang his medicine songs through the dark hours and through the day. Before him—far beneath his feet—lay the narrow strip of land between the two salt waters. Then the Sagalie Tyee gave him the power to see far into the future. He looked across a hundred years, just as he looked across what you call the Inlet, and he saw mighty lodges built close together, hundreds and thousands of them—lodges of stone and wood, and long straight trails to divide them. He saw these trails thronging with Palefaces; he heard the sound of the white man's paddle dip on the waters, for it is not silent like the Indian's; he saw the white man's trading posts, saw the fishing nets, heard his speech. Then the vision faded as gradually as it came. The narrow strip of land was his own forest once more.

"'I am old," he called, in his sorrow and his trouble for his people. "I am old, O Sagalie Tyee! Soon I shall die and go to the Happy Hunting Grounds of my fathers. Let not my strength die with me. Keep living for all time my courage, my bravery, my fearlessness. Keep them for my people that they may be strong enough to endure the white man's rule. Keep my strength living for them; hide it so that the Paleface may never find or see it."

'Then he came down from the summit of Grouse Mountain. Still chanting his medicine songs, he entered his canoe and paddled through the colours of the setting sun far up the North Arm. When night fell he came to an island with misty shores of great grey rock; on its summit tall pines and firs encircled like a king's crown. As he neared it he felt all his strength, his courage, his fearlessness, leaving him; he could see these things drift from him on to the island. They were as the clouds that rest on the mountains, grey-white and half transparent. Weak as a woman, he paddled back to the Indian village; he told them to go and search for "The Island", where they would find all his courage, his fearlessness and his strength, living, living for ever. He slept then, but—in the morning he did not wake. Since then our young men and our old have searched for "The Island." It is there somewhere, up some lost channel, but we cannot find it. When we do, we will get back all the courage and bravery we had before the white man came, for the great medicine man said those things never die—they live for one's children and grandchildren.'

His voice ceased. My whole heart went out to him in his longing for the lost island. I thought of all the splendid courage I knew him to possess, so made answer: 'But you say that the shadow of this island has fallen upon you; is it not so, tillicum?'

'Yes,' he said half mournfully. 'But only the shadow.'

1911, 1920, 1961

# Archibald Lampman
## 1861–1899

Archibald Lampman—like Charles G.D. Roberts—was born into a Loyalist Anglican family. Although he grew up on the edge of the wilderness, his education and career carried him into the increasingly urban world of the emerging Canadian nation. Born in Morpeth, a village in Canada West on Lake Erie, Lampman spent his childhood in the Rice Lake district, first at Gore's Landing—where he met the Strickland sisters, Susanna Moodie and Catharine Parr Traill—and then, after a brief time in Cobourg, where his clergyman father had taken a new parish, as a boarder at Trinity College School in Port Hope. He next went to Trinity College, Toronto, on a scholarship, but his pursuit of the less academic side of undergraduate life cost him a first-class degree and an academic career.

After realizing that he disliked teaching high school, he settled into a permanent position in the civil service, working as a clerk in the Post Office Department. In 1887, Lampman married Maud Playter, against his family's wishes; the union was apparently unhappy for both partners. However, he found kinship with a group of people, members of the Ottawa Literary and Scientific Society, who shared his national and intellectual interests; among them were two other poets and civil servants, Wilfred Campbell and Duncan Campbell Scott.

Scott and Lampman became close friends, for they shared a love of the wilderness, joining in many canoeing expeditions while they discussed their real work, the writing of poetry. As a naturalist poet, Lampman learned to employ vivid yet simple images and diction, to build poems out of the sounds, the motion, and even the colours of the wilderness. His importance lies in his attempts to capture a uniquely Canadian landscape, for he believed that 'climate and scenic conditions have much to do with the molding of national character.' He considered Canada to be 'still in the house-building, land-breaking stage,' feeling that the growth and materialism of the new Confederation were necessary in order for future generations to have the leisure to create a balanced culture.

Lampman's writing was well received in his time, appearing in various journals in Canada and the United States. In spite of this popularity, he had to publish his first volume of poetry, *Among the Millet* (Ottawa, 1888), at his own expense. Though he was unable to interest anyone in a book of sonnets, Lampman found an American publisher who accepted a volume of nature poems, *Lyrics of the Earth* (Boston, 1895). Around this time his infant son died (1894), his marriage deteriorated, and he learned that his heart had been weakened by the rheumatic fever he had contracted in childhood. Early in 1899, while working on the proofs of his third volume, *Alcyone*, he caught pneumonia and died a few days later. (Shortly after his death in 1899, D.C. Scott ordered a printing of twelve copies of *Alcyone*.) As Lampman's literary executor, Scott then published a memorial collection of his friend's poems in 1900. In 1943, Scott and E.K. Brown discovered 'At the Long Sault' in manuscript and published it in a new edition of Lampman's poems. Among other unpublished poems Lampman left behind when he died were a group of love poems inspired by his close friendship with Katherine Waddell, a fellow

civil servant. Suppressed by Scott—except for six sonnets that appeared in *At the Long Sault and Other New Poems* (1943)—they were finally published in *Lampman's Kate* (1975), edited by Margaret Coulby Whitridge.

Charles G.D. Roberts presents an informative contrast with Lampman. Where Roberts found change at the heart of things, Lampman saw change as existing only in the superficialities of appearance, and he sought instead the vision (he often called it a dream) of the true and unchanging reality that lies beneath the surface. His poetry, which records moments of intense experience with nature that offer glimpses of eternal truth, may therefore be said to look backwards to the English Romantics, in a way that Roberts's poetry does not—but its expression is so effective, that Lampman is now generally thought of as the best of the Confederation poets. His description of how Emerson responded to the 'cosmic sympathy' of the universe might well be applied to himself: 'He is drawn to nature because in the energy of his own soul he is aware of a kinship to the forces of nature, and feels with an elemental joy as if it were a part of himself the eternal movement of life' ('At the Mermaid Inn', 22 April 1893). Although nature played a large role in Lampman's writing, his poetry also looks at the urban landscape, though, like the Romantics, he generally saw the city as a threat to nature. The disturbing images in 'The Railway Station', with its fiery engine and dazed crowds, take on an apocalyptic cast in the later dreamlike poem 'The City of the End of Things', in which the individual is endangered by a nightmarish city that, increasingly mechanical and industrialized, seems like a version of Milton's hellish Pandemonium.

# Heat

From plains that reel to southward, dim,
    The road runs by me white and bare;
Up the steep hill it seems to swim
    Beyond, and melt into the glare.

1 Daisies; a midge is a small gnat-like insect.

Upward half-way, or it may be
    Nearer the summit, slowly steals
A hay-cart, moving dustily
    With idly clacking wheels.

By his cart's side the wagoner
    Is slouching slowly at his ease,              10
Half-hidden in the windless blur
    Of white dust puffing to his knees.
This wagon on the height above,
    From sky to sky on either hand,
Is the sole thing that seems to move
    In all the heat-held land.

Beyond me in the fields the sun
    Soaks in the grass and hath his will;
I count the marguerites[1] one by one;
    Even the buttercups are still.           20
On the brook yonder not a breath
    Disturbs the spider or the midge.
The water-bugs draw close beneath
    The cool gloom of the bridge.

Where the far elm-tree shadows flood
    Dark patches in the burning grass,
The cows, each with her peaceful cud,
    Lie waiting for the heat to pass.
From somewhere on the slope near by
    Into the pale depth of the noon          30
A wandering thrush slides leisurely
    His thin revolving tune.

In intervals of dreams I hear
    The cricket from the droughty ground;
The grasshoppers spin into mine ear
    A small innumerable sound.
I lift mine eyes sometimes to gaze:
    The burning sky-line blinds my sight:
The woods far off are blue with haze:
    The hills are drenched in light.          40

And yet to me not this or that
    Is always sharp or always sweet;
In the sloped shadow of my hat

I lean at rest, and drain the heat;
Nay more, I think some blessèd power
  Hath brought me wandering idly here:
In the full furnace of this hour
  My thoughts grow keen and clear.

1888

## The Frogs

### I

Breathers of wisdom won without a quest,
  Quaint uncouth dreamers, voices high and strange,
  Flutists of lands where beauty hath no change,
And wintry grief is a forgotten guest,
Sweet murmurers of everlasting rest,
  For whom glad days have ever yet to run,
  And moments are as aeons, and the sun
But ever sunken half-way toward the west.

Often to me who heard you in your day,
  With close rapt ears, it could not choose but seem      10
That earth, our mother, searching in what way
  Men's hearts might know her spirit's inmost dream;
  Ever at rest beneath life's change and stir,
Made you her soul, and bade you pipe for her.

### II

In those mute days when spring was in her glee,
  And hope was strong, we knew not why or how,
  And earth, the mother, dreamed with brooding brow,
Musing on life, and what the hours might be,
When love should ripen to maternity
  Then like high flutes in silvery interchange      20
  Ye piped with voices still and sweet and strange,
And ever as ye piped, on every tree

---

1 A common spring wildflower (*Claytonia virginica*) having small white or pinkish flowers; 'windflower': an
anemone, a flower of the buttercup family; 'adder-tongue': a spring flower with mottled leaves, also known as the
dogtooth violet or trout lily.

The great buds swelled; among the pensive woods
    The spirits of first flowers awoke and flung
From buried faces the close fitting hoods,
    And listened to your piping till they fell,
    The frail spring-beauty[1] with her perfumed bell,
The wind-flower, and the spotted adder-tongue.

### III

All the day long, wherever pools might be
    Among the golden meadows, where the air          30
    Stood in a dream, as it were moorèd there
Forever in a noon-tide reverie,
Or where the birds made riot of their glee
    In the still woods, and the hot sun shone down,
    Crossed with warm lucent shadows on the brown
Leaf-paven pools, that bubbled dreamily,

Or far away in whispering river meads[2]
    And watery marshes where the brooding noon,
    Full with the wonder of its own sweet boon,
Nestled and slept among the noiseless reeds,         40
    Ye sat and murmured, motionless as they,
    With eyes that dreamed beyond the night and day.

### IV

And when day passed and over heaven's height,
    Thin with the many stars and cool with dew,
    The fingers of the deep hours slowly drew
The wonder of the every-healing night,
No grief or loneliness or rapt delight
    Or weight of silence ever brought to you
    Slumber or rest; only your voices grew
More high and solemn; slowly with hushèd flight         50

Ye saw the echoing hours go by, long-drawn,
    Nor ever stirred, watching with fathomless eyes,
    And with your countless clear antiphonies
Filling the earth and heaven, even till dawn,
    Last-risen, found you with its first pale gleam,
    Still with soft throats unaltered in your dream.

2 Meadows.

V

And slowly as we heard you, day by day,
    The stillness of enchanted reveries
    Bound brain and spirit and half-closed eyes,
In some divine sweet wonder-dream astray;                    60
To us no sorrow or upreared dismay
    Nor any discord came, but evermore
    The voices of mankind, the outer roar,
Grew strange and murmurous, faint and far away.

Morning and noon and midnight exquisitely,
    Rapt with your voices, this alone we knew,
Cities might change and fall, and men might die,
    Secure were we, content to dream with you
    That change and pain are shadows faint and fleet,
And dreams are real, and life is only sweet.                 70

1888


# The Railway Station

The darkness brings no quiet here, the light
    No waking: ever on my blinded brain
    The flare of lights, the rush, and cry, and strain,
The engines' scream, the hiss and thunder smite:
I see the hurrying crowds, the clasp, the flight,
    Faces that touch, eyes that are dim with pain:
    I see the hoarse wheels turn, and the great train
Move labouring out into the bourneless night.
So many souls within its dim recesses,
    So many bright, so many mournful eyes:                   10
Mine eyes that watch grow fixed with dreams and guesses;
    What threads of life, what hidden histories,
What sweet or passionate dreams and dark distresses,
    What unknown thoughts, what various agonies!

1888

# In November[1] ——

With loitering step and quiet eye,
Beneath the low November sky,
I wandered in the woods, and found
A clearing, where the broken ground
Was scattered with black stumps and briers,
And the old wreck of forest fires.
It was a bleak and sandy spot,
And, all about, the vacant plot
Was peopled and inhabited
By scores of mulleins[2] long since dead.          10
A silent and forsaken brood
In that mute opening of the wood,
So shrivelled and so thin they were,
So grey, so haggard, and austere,
Not plants at all they seemed to me,
But rather some spare company
Of hermit folk, who long ago,
Wandering in bodies to and fro,
Had chanced upon this lonely way,
And rested thus, till death one day          20
Surprised them at their compline[3] prayer,
And left them standing lifeless there.

There was no sound about the wood
Save the wind's secret stir. I stood
Among the mullein-stalks as still
As if myself had grown to be
One of their sombre company,
A body without wish or will.
And as I stood, quite suddenly,
Down from a furrow in the sky          30
The sun shone out a little space
Across that silent sober place,
Over the sand heaps and brown sod,
The mulleins and dead goldenrod,
And passed beyond the thickets gray,
And lit the fallen leaves that lay,
Level and deep within the wood,
A rustling yellow multitude.

1  This has the same title as an earlier poem, a sonnet later retitled 'Late November'.
2  Flower of the figwort family with velvety leaves.
3  Last church service of the day.

And all around me the thin light,
So sere, so melancholy bright,
Fell like the half-reflected gleam
Or shadow of some former dream;
A moment's golden reverie
Poured out on every plant and tree
A semblance of weird joy, or less,
A sort of spectral happiness;
And I, too, standing idly there,
With muffled hands in the chill air,
Felt the warm glow about my feet,
And shuddering betwixt cold and heat,                    50
Drew my thoughts closer, like a cloak,
While something in my blood awoke,
A nameless and unnatural cheer,
A pleasure secret and austere.

1895


# A Summer Dream[1]

Once in a dream, between two troubled slips
Of sleep, I saw you in your brightest guise.
Methought you stood, but tears were in your eyes,
Softer than rain or any dew that drips.
On my cold hand you laid your finger tips
And I, touched by a sudden sweet surprise,
Caught you in both mine arms with sobs and sighs
And kissed your brow, beloved, and your lips.

And you—ah yes! even you, upon my breast
Leaned for a moment, with cheeks wet and wan,                    10
Then smiled and vanished; but for many hours
I wandered in a speechless dream, caressed
By winds from such a magic summer dream
As never wantoned over earthly flowers.

[1896], 1975

---

1  One of the poems addressed to Katherine Waddell that remained in manuscript until 1975.

# The City of the End of Things

Beside the pounding cataracts
Of midnight streams unknown to us
'Tis builded in the leafless tracts
And valleys huge of Tartarus.[1]
Lurid and lofty and vast it seems;
It hath no rounded name that rings,
But I have heard it called in dreams
The City of the End of Things.

Its roofs and iron towers have grown
None knoweth how high within the night,          10
But in its murky streets far down
A flaming terrible and bright
Shakes all the stalking shadows there,
Across the walls, across the floors,
And shifts upon the upper air
From out a thousand furnace doors;
And all the while an awful sound
Keeps roaring on continually,
And crashes in the ceaseless round
Of a gigantic harmony.                            20
Through its grim depths re-echoing
And all its weary height of walls,
With measured roar and iron ring,
The inhuman music lifts and falls.
Where no thing rests and no man is,
And only fire and night hold sway;
The beat, the thunder and the hiss
Cease not, and change not, night nor day.

And moving at unheard commands,
The abysses and vast fires between,               30
Flit figures that with clanking hands
Obey a hideous routine;
They are not flesh, they are not bone,
They see not with the human eye,
And from their iron lips is blown
A dreadful and monotonous cry;
And whoso of our mortal race
Should find that city unaware,

1  Infernal abyss below Hades, where Zeus threw the rebel Titans.

Lean Death would smite him face to face,
And blanch him with its venomed air:                          40
Or caught by the terrific spell,
Each thread of memory snapt and cut,
His soul would shrivel and its shell
Go rattling like an empty nut.

It was not always so, but once,
In days that no man thinks upon,
Fair voices echoed from its stones,
The light above it leaped and shone:
Once there were multitudes of men,
That built that city in their pride,                          50
Until its might was made, and then
They withered age by age and died.
But now of that prodigious race,
Three only in an iron tower,
Set like carved idols face to face,
Remain the masters of its power;
And at the city gate a fourth,
Gigantic and with dreadful eyes,
Sits looking toward the lightless north,
Beyond the reach of memories;                                 60
Fast rooted to the lurid floor,
A bulk that never moves a jot,
In his pale body dwells no more,
Or mind or soul,—an idiot!
But sometime in the end those three
Shall perish and their hands be still,
And with the master's touch shall flee
Their incommunicable skill.
A stillness absolute as death
Along the slacking wheels shall lie,                          70
And, flagging at a single breath,
The fires shall moulder out and die.
The roar shall vanish at its height,
And over that tremendous town
The silence of eternal night
Shall gather close and settle down.
All its grim grandeur, tower and hall,
Shall be abandoned utterly,
And into rust and dust shall fall
From century to century;                                      80
Nor ever living thing shall grow,

Nor trunk of tree, nor blade of grass;
No drop shall fall, no wind shall blow,
Nor sound of any foot shall pass:
Alone of its accursèd state,
One thing the hand of Time shall spare,
For the grim Idiot at the gate
Is deathless and eternal there.

1899

## Voices of Earth ———

We have not heard the music of the spheres,[1]
The song of star to star, but there are sounds
More deep than human joy and human tears,
That Nature uses in her common rounds;
The fall of streams, the cry of winds that strain
The oak, the roaring of the sea's surge, might
Of thunder breaking afar off, or rain
That falls by minutes in the summer night.
These are the voices of earth's secret soul,
Uttering the mystery from which she came.                    10
To him who hears them grief beyond control,
Or joy inscrutable without a name,
Wakes in his heart thoughts bedded there, impearled,
Before the birth and making of the world.

1899

1  Cosmic harmonies, supposed to be produced by the movement of heavenly bodies.

## Winter Evening ———

To-night the very horses springing by
Toss gold from whitened nostrils. In a dream
The streets that narrow to the westward gleam
Like rows of golden palaces; and high
From all the crowded chimneys tower and die
A thousand aureoles. Down in the west
The brimming plains beneath the sunset rest,
One burning sea of gold. Soon, soon shall fly

The glorious vision, and the hours shall feel
A mightier master; soon from height to height,    10
With silence and the sharp unpitying stars,
Stern creeping frosts, and winds that touch like steel,
Out of the depth beyond the eastern bars,
Glittering and still shall come the awful night.

1899


# To a Millionaire

The world in gloom and splendor passes by,
And thou in the midst of it with brows that gleam,
A creature of that old distorted dream
That makes the sound of life an evil cry.
Good men perform just deeds, and brave men die,
And win not honor such as gold can give,
While the vain multitudes plod on, and live,
And serve the curse that pins them down: But I
Think only of the unnumbered broken hearts,
The hunger and the mortal strife for bread,    10
Old age and youth alike mistaught, misfed,
By want and rags and homelessness made vile,
The griefs and hates, and all the meaner parts
That balance thy one grim misgotten pile.

1900


# At the Long Sault: May, 1660[1]

Under the day-long sun there is life and mirth
    In the working earth,
And the wonderful moon shines bright
    Through the soft spring night,
The innocent flowers in the limitless woods are springing
    Far and away
    With the sound and the perfume of May,

1 On 1 May 1660 Adam Dollard des Ormeaux (sometimes called Daulac), with 16 companions and 44 Hurons and Algonquins, laid an ambush for some Iroquois at an abandoned fort on the Ottawa River. The Iroquois were joined by a reinforcement of 500, but it took them ten days to vanquish the Frenchmen and their allies. Until fairly recently this event was considered to have saved the colony of Montreal from Iroquois attack, and the Frenchmen were considered martyrs for the faith.

And ever up from the south the happy birds are winging,
    The waters glitter and leap and play
      While the gray hawk soars.                            10

But far in an open glade of the forest set
    Where the rapid plunges and roars,
Is a ruined fort with a name that men forget,—
    A shelterless pen
      With its broken palisade,
      Behind it, musket in hand,
      Beyond message or aid
      In this savage heart of the wild,
      Mere youngsters, grown in a moment to men,
      Grim and alert and arrayed,                 20
      The comrades of Daulac stand.
      Ever before them, night and day,
      The rush and skulk and cry
      Of foes, not men but devils, panting for prey;
Behind them the sleepless dream
Of the little frail-walled town, far away by the plunging stream.
    Of maiden and matron and child,
With ruin and murder impending, and none but they
To beat back the gathering horror
Deal death while they may,                        30
    And then die.

Day and night they have watched while the little plain
Grew dark with the rush of the foe, but their host
Broke ever and melted away, with no boast
But to number their slain;
And now as the days renew
Hunger and thirst and care
Were they never so stout, so true,
Press at their hearts; but none
Falters or shrinks or utters a coward word,          40
Though each setting sun
Brings from the pitiless wild new hands to the Iroquois horde,
And only to them despair.

Silent, white-faced, again and again
Charged and hemmed round by furious hands,
Each for a moment faces them all and stands
In his little desperate ring; like a tired bull moose
Whom scores of sleepless wolves, a ravening pack,

Have chased all night, all day
Through the snow-laden woods, like famine let loose;                    50
And he turns at last in his track
Against a wall of rock and stands at bay;
Round him with terrible sinews and teeth of steel
They charge and recharge; but with many a furious plunge and wheel,
Hither and thither over the trampled snow,
He tosses them bleeding and torn;
Till, driven, and ever to and fro
Harried, wounded, and weary grown,
His mighty strength gives way
And all together they fasten upon him and drag him down.               60

So Daulac turned him anew
With a ringing cry to his men
In the little raging forest glen,
And his terrible sword in the twilight whistled and slew.
And all his comrades stood
With their backs to the pales,² and fought
Till their strength was done;
The thews that were only mortal flagged and broke
Each struck his last wild stroke,
And they fell one by one,                                              70
And the world that had seemed so good
Passed like a dream and was naught.

And then the great night came
With the triumph-songs of the foe and the flame
Of the camp-fires.
Out of the dark the soft wind woke,
The song of the rapid rose alway
And came to the spot where the comrades lay,
Beyond help or care,
With none but the red men round them                                  80
To gnash their teeth and stare.

All night by the foot of the mountain
    The little town lieth at rest,
The sentries are peacefully pacing;
    And neither from East nor from West

---

2  Row of spiked wooden poles, here the walls of the fort.

Is there rumor of death or of danger;
  None dreameth tonight in his bed
That ruin was near and the heroes
    That met it and stemmed it are dead.

But afar in the ring of the forest,
  Where the air is so tender with May
And the waters are wild in the moonlight
    They lie in their silence of clay.

      90

The numberless stars out of heaven
  Look down with a pitiful glance;
And the lilies asleep in the forest
    Are closed like the lilies of France.[3]

[1899], 1943

3 That is, the fleur-de-lis, the emblematic flower of France—often appearing as a heraldic emblem on the shields of French warriors.

# Duncan Campbell Scott
## 1862–1947

The writing of Duncan Campbell Scott, like that of other Confederation poets, developed out of a profound response to the Canadian landscape and its people, influenced by mid-nineteenth-century British and American thought. Born in Ottawa and raised in villages in Ontario and Quebec, where his father served as a Methodist minister, Scott became interested as a boy in the life and customs of Aboriginal peoples, frontier lumbermen, and French-Canadian *habitants*—all of whom became important subjects in his writing.

Unlike Charles G.D. Roberts and Archibald Lampman, Scott was unable to attend university for financial reasons. In 1879, after an interview with the prime minister, Sir John A. Macdonald, he accepted a clerkship at $1.50 a day in the Department of Indian Affairs, where he remained for over fifty years, eventually assuming that department's highest permanent office. He began to write in the mid-1880s, after meeting Lampman, another civil servant. As Roberts had earlier inspired Lampman, so Lampman supplied Scott with the confidence he needed. Within the next few years, Scott's stories and poems began to appear in periodicals. He published his first book of poetry, *The Magic House and Other Poems*, in 1893, and in 1896, his first volume of short stories, *In the Village of Viger*. In 1892, Scott and Lampman joined another civil servant, Wilfred Campbell, in writing 'At the Mermaid Inn' for the Toronto *Globe*, a column in which they commented on the Canadian cultural milieu and developed their own literary theories. Scott also continued his interest in wilderness life, taking long recreational canoe trips with Lampman, as well as making an increasing number of professional expeditions to visit Native bands.

In his second book of verse, *Labour and the Angel* (1898), Scott began to move away from the shadowy, lush poetry of his earlier volume and introduce poems on First Nations subjects, for which he became well known. In this book, and the books that follow, Scott's depiction of large conflicts between contrasting forces—producing a dialectic that recurs throughout his work—emerges. For him, the natural struggle often resolves itself in moments of beauty and serenity that are, like those in 'The Height of Land', 'deeper than peace.' As well as continuing to write poetry and prose throughout his lifetime, Scott edited several volumes of Lampman's verse after his friend died in 1899. Among Scott's other books are *New World Lyrics* (1905); *Lundy's Land and Other Poems* (1916); *Beauty and Life* (1921); *The Poems of Duncan Campbell Scott* (1926); *The Green Cloister and Other Poems* (1935); and the short story collection, *The Witching of Elspie* (1923).

While Scott continued to work within the more conservative traditions of Confederation poetry, he helped open the doors of what had become a staid literary establishment to the post-war writers, many of whom were proponents of modernism. In a 1922 speech he gave as president of the Royal Society, he condemned the static condition of Canadian writing and recommended new voices:

*It is the mission of new theories in the arts, and particularly of new theories that come to us illustrated by practice, to re-examine the grounds of our preferences, and to retest our accepted dogmas. . . . We require more rage of our poets. We should like them to put to the proof that saying of William Blake: 'The tigers of wrath are wiser than the horses of instruction.'*

Scott's request for poetic rage may derive from his own strong sense of man in confrontation with a violent universe. His answer to that violence was, when the struggle was a losing one, an affirmation of death as a part of life. In 'At the Cedars', the lumberman Isaàc Dufour, swept along by forces beyond his control, keeps his balance and sings; when neither his skill nor his nonchalance can continue to protect him, he makes a gesture of graceful acceptance: 'And when he was there / In the air, / Kissed his hand / To the land.' Scott saw this calm way of meeting death as heroism whether it took place in war, as in 'The Battle of Lundy's Lane', or in extraordinary conditions of peace, as in 'The Forsaken'.

Although the heroic Chipewyan woman in 'The Forsaken' follows a similar pattern to that found in non-Native poems—she stays alive when she must by bravely fishing with her own flesh, but years later accepts her inevitable death unflinchingly, as she meets the 'silence deeper than silence'—the way we read this and other of Scott's poems about Natives has changed. It is not just that many readers now have some difficulty accepting depictions of Natives that come to us through the eyes and voice of a non-Aboriginal but also that we view Scott himself differently from the way readers once did. In contrast to readers who simply saw him as writing sympathetically about Native peoples (in poems such as 'The Onondaga Madonna') based on his extensive contact with them, we find it hard today to ignore the fact that the same people about whom he seems objective or idealizing in his poems are those who in real life were adversely affected by Scott's role in Indian Affairs.

The isolation of the individual apparent in several of his poems is often a feature of Scott's fiction as well, as may be seen in the story printed here. In 'Labrie's Wife', which borrows the form of many exploration narratives—a Hudson's Bay Company journal—the first-person narrator's inability to respond to people not only cuts him off from society but also leads him into foolish self-deception.

# At the Cedars

You had two girls—Baptiste—
One is Virginie—
Hold hard—Baptiste!
Listen to me.

The whole drive was jammed
In that bend at the Cedars,
The rapids were dammed
With the logs tight rammed
And crammed; you might know
The Devil had clinched them below.                    10

We worked three days—not a budge,
'She's as tight as a wedge, on the ledge,'
Says our foreman;
'Mon Dieu! boys, look here,
We must get this thing clear.'
He cursed at the men
And we went for it then;
With our cant-dogs[1] arow,
We just gave he-yo-ho;
When she gave a big shove                             20
From above.

The gang yelled and tore
For the shore,
The logs gave a grind
Like a wolf's jaws behind,
And as quick as a flash,
With a shove and a crash,
They were down in a mash,
But I and ten more,
All but Isaàc Dufour,                                 30
Were ashore.

He leaped on a log in the front of the rush,
And shot out from the bind
While the jam roared behind;
As he floated along
He balanced his pole

---

1 Hooked tools that bite into logs.

And tossed us a song.
But just as we cheered,
Up darted a log from the bottom,
Leaped thirty feet square and fair,                    40
And came down on his own.

He went up like a block
With the shock,
And when he was there
In the air,
Kissed his hand
To the land;
When he dropped
My heart stopped,
For the first logs had caught him                    50
And crushed him;
When he rose in his place
There was blood on his face.

There were some girls, Baptiste,
Picking berries on the hillside,
Where the river curls, Baptiste,
You know—on the still side
One was down by the water,
She saw Isaàc
Fall back.                                            60

She did not scream, Baptiste,
She launched her canoe;
It did seem, Baptiste,
That she wanted to die too,
For before you could think
The birch cracked like a shell
In that rush of hell,
And I saw them both sink—

Baptiste!—
He had two girls,                                     70
One is Virginie,
What God calls the other
Is not known to me.

1893

# The Onondaga[1] Madonna

She stands full-throated and with careless pose,
This woman of a weird and waning race,
The tragic savage lurking in her face,
Where all her pagan passion burns and glows;
Her blood is mingled with her ancient foes,
And thrills with war and wildness in her veins;
Her rebel lips are dabbled with the stains
Of feuds and forays and her father's woes.

And closer is the shawl about her breast,
The latest promise of her nation's doom,                    10
Paler than she her baby clings and lies,
The primal warrior gleaming from his eyes;
He sulks, and burdened with his infant gloom,
He draws his heavy brows and will not rest.

1898

1  An Iroquois tribe.

# Watkwenies[1]

Vengeance was once her nation's lore and law:
When the tired sentry stooped above the rill,
Her long knife flashed, and hissed, and drank its fill;
Dimly below her dripping wrist she saw,
One wild hand, pale as death and weak as straw,
Clutch at the ripple in the pool; while shrill
Sprang through the dreaming hamlet on the hill,
The war-cry of the triumphant Iroquois.

Now clothed with many an ancient flap and fold,
And wrinkled like an apple kept till May,                    10
She weighs the interest-money[2] in her palm,
And, when the Agent calls her valiant name,
Hears, like the war-whoops of her perished day,
The lads playing snow-snake in the stinging cold.

1898

1  'The woman who Conquers' (Scott's note).
2  That is, government money paid to the Natives, here disbursed by the Indian Affairs bureaucrat known to them as
   the 'Agent'. 'Snow-snake' is a traditional Native game in which a carved stick is thrown along a trough in the snow.

# Night Hymns on Lake Nipigon

Here in the midnight, where the dark mainland and island
Shadows mingle in shadow deeper, profounder,
Sing we the hymns of the churches, while the dead water
　　　　Whispers before us.

Thunder is travelling slow on the path of the lightning;
One after one the stars and the beaming planets
Look serene in the lake from the edge of the storm-cloud,
　　　　Then have they vanished.

While our canoe, that floats dumb in the bursting thunder,
Gathers her voice in the quiet and thrills and whispers,
Presses her prow in the star-gleam, and all her ripple
　　　　Lapses in blackness.

Sing we the sacred ancient hymns of the churches,
Chanted first in old-world nooks of the desert,
While in the wild, pellucid Nipigon reaches
　　　　Hunted the savage.

Now have the ages met in the Northern midnight,
And on the lonely, loon-haunted Nipigon reaches
Rises the hymn of triumph and courage and comfort,
　　　　Adeste Fideles.

Tones that were fashioned when the faith brooded in darkness,
Joined with sonorous vowels in the noble Latin,
Now are married with the long-drawn Ojibway,
　　　　Uncouth and mournful.

Soft with the silver drip of the regular paddles
Falling in rhythm, timed with the liquid, plangent
Sounds from the blades where the whirlpools break and are carried
　　　　Down into darkness;

Each long cadence, flying like a dove from her shelter
Deep in the shadow, wheels for a throbbing moment,
Poises in utterance, returning in circles of silver
　　　　To nest in the silence.

10

20

30

All wild nature stirs with the infinite, tender
Plaint of a bygone age whose soul is eternal,
Bound in the lonely phrases that thrill and falter
      Back into quiet.

Back they falter as the deep storm overtakes them,
Whelms them in splendid hollows of booming thunder,
Wraps them in rain, that, sweeping, breaks and onrushes
      Ringing like cymbals.          40

1905

# The Forsaken

     I

Once in the winter
Out on a lake
In the heart of the north-land,
Far from the Fort
And far from the hunters,
A Chippewa woman
With her sick baby,
Crouched in the last hours
Of a great storm.
Frozen and hungry,
She fished through the ice
With a line of the twisted
Bark of the cedar,
And a rabbit-bone hook
Polished and barbed;
Fished with the bare hook
All through the day,
Fished and caught nothing;
While the young chieftain
Tugged at her breasts,          20
Or slept in the lacings
Of the warm *tikanagan*.[1]

10

1   Moss-filled cradle board.

All the lake-surface
Streamed with the hissing
Of millions of iceflakes,
Hurled by the wind;
Behind her the round
Of a lonely island
Roared like a fire
With the voice of the storm                                    30
In the deeps of the cedars.
Valiant, unshaken,
She took of her own flesh,
Baited the fish-hook,
Drew in a grey-trout,
Drew in his fellows,
Heaped them beside her,
Dead in the snow.
Valiant, unshaken,
She faced the long distance,                                   40
Wolf-haunted and lonely,
Sure of her goal
And the life of her dear one;
Tramped for two days,
On the third in the morning,
Saw the strong bulk
Of the Fort by the river,
Saw the wood-smoke
Hang soft in the spruces,
Heard the keen yelp                                            50
Of the ravenous huskies
Fighting for whitefish:
Then she had rest.


                  II


Years and years after,
When she was old and withered,
When her son was an old man
And his children filled with vigour,
They came in their northern tour on the verge of winter,
To an island in a lonely lake.

There one night they camped, and on the morrow
Gathered their kettles and birch-bark[1]
Their rabbit-skin robes and their mink-traps,
Launched their canoes and slunk away through the islands,                    10
Left her alone forever,
Without a word of farewell,
Because she was old and useless,
Like a paddle broken and warped,
Or a pole that was splintered.
Then, without a sigh,
Valiant, unshaken,
She smoothed her dark locks under her kerchief,
Composed her shawl in state,
Then folded her hands ridged with sinews and corded with veins,              20
Folded them across her breasts spent with the nourishing of children,
Gazed at the sky past the tops of the cedars,
Saw two spangled nights arise out of the twilight,
Saw two days go by filled with the tranquil sunshine,
Saw, without pain, or dread, or even a moment of longing:
Then on the third great night there came thronging and thronging
Millions of snowflakes out of a windless cloud;
They covered her close with a beautiful crystal shroud,
Covered her deep and silent.
But in the frost of the dawn,                                                30
Up from the life below,
Rose a column of breath
Through a tiny cleft in the snow,
Fragile, delicately drawn,
Wavering with its own weakness,
In the wilderness a sign of the spirit,
Persisting still in the sight of the sun
Till day was done,
Then all light was gathered up by the hand of God and hid in His breast,
Then there was born a silence deeper than silence,                           40
Then she had rest.

1905

---

1  Waterproof birch-bark bowls or buckets.

# The Battle of Lundy's Lane[1]

Rufus Gale speaks—1852

Yes,—in the Lincoln Militia,—in the war of eighteen-twelve;
Many's the day I've had since then to dig and delve—
But those are the years I remember as the brightest years of all,
When we left the plow in the furrow to follow the bugle's call.
Why, even our son Abner wanted to fight with the men!
'Don't you go, d'ye hear, sir!'—I was angry with him then.
'Stay with your mother!' I said, and he looked so old and grim—
He was just sixteen that April—I couldn't believe it was him;
But I didn't think—I was off—and we met the foe again,
Five thousand strong and ready, at the hill by Lundy's Lane.                    10
There as the night came on we fought them from six to nine,
Whenever they broke our line we broke their line,
They took our guns and we won them again, and around the levels
Where the hill sloped up—with the Eighty-ninth,—we fought like devils
Around the flag—and on they came and we drove them back,
Until with its very fierceness the fight grew slack.

It was then about nine and dark as a miser's pocket,
When up came Hercules Scott's[2] brigade swift as a rocket,
And charged,—and the flashes sprang in the dark like a lion's eyes;
The night was full of fire—groans, and cheers, and cries;                      20
Then through the sound and the fury another sound broke in—
The roar of a great old duck-gun shattered the rest of the din;
It took two minutes to charge it and another to set it free.
Every time I heard it an angel spoke to me;
Yes, the minute I heard it I felt the strangest tide
Flow in my veins like lightning, as if, there, by my side,
Was the very spirit of Valour. But 'twas dark—you couldn't see—
And the one who was firing the duck-gun fell against me
And slid down to the clover, and lay there still;
Something went through me—piercing—with a strange, swift thrill;               30
The noise fell away into silence, and I heard as clear as thunder

1  In June 1812, the US declared war on Britain and attacked the only British possession on the continent—Canada.
   Lundy's Lane, near Niagara Falls, was the site of one of the bitterest encounters of the War of 1812 (24–5 July
   1814), fought between US troops and British regulars, including the Royal Scots and the 8th, 41st, and 89th reg-
   iments on foot, aided by Canadian militia. Both sides suffered heavy losses, and the battle was inconclusive,
   although the Americans were forced to withdraw to Fort Erie. The War itself ended in a stalemate, with all conquered territories restored to their pre-war owners under conditions set out in the Treaty of Ghent (signed 24 Dec.
   1814); nevertheless, for Canadians it helped develop a sense of identity and community, as Scott's poem illustrates.
2  A hero in the Lundy's Lane battle, Lieutenant Colonel Hercules Scott (1775–1814), brought his 103rd regiment
   up in urgent fashion to reinforce the Canadian troops holding off the invading Americans. (Scott died at the
   subsequent Siege of Fort Erie.)

The long, slow roar of Niagara: O the wonder
Of that deep sound. But again the battle broke
And the foe, driven before us desperately—stroke upon stroke,
Left the field to his master, and sullenly down the road
Sounded the boom of his guns, trailing the heavy load
Of his wounded men and his shattered flags, sullen and slow,
Setting fire in his rage to Bridgewater mills, and the glow
Flared in the distant forest. We rested as we could,
And for a while I slept in the dark of a maple wood: 40
But when the clouds in the east were red all over,
I came back there to the place we made the stand in the clover;
For my heart was heavy then with a strange, deep pain,
As I thought of the glorious fight, and again and again
I remembered the valiant spirit and the piercing thrill;
But I knew it all when I reached the top of the hill,—
For there, there with the blood on his dear, brave head,
There on the hill in the clover lay our Abner—dead!—
No—thank you—no, I don't need it; I'm solid as granite rock,
But every time that I tell it I feel the old, cold shock, 50
I'm eighty-one my next birthday—do you breed such fellows now?
There he lay with the dawn cooling his broad fair brow,
That was no dawn for him; and there was the old duck-gun
That many and many's the time,—just for the fun,
We together, alone, would take to the hickory rise,
And bring home more wild pigeons than ever you saw with your eyes.
Up with Hercules Scott's brigade, just as it came on night—
He was the angel beside me in the thickest of the fight—
Wrote a note to his mother—He said, 'I've got to go;
Mother, what would home be under the heel of the foe!' 60
Oh! she never slept a wink, she would rise and walk the floor;
She'd say this over and over, 'I knew it all before!'
I'd try to speak of the glory to give her a little joy.
'What is the glory to me when I want my boy, my boy!'
She'd say, and she'd wring her hands; her hair grew white as snow—
And I'd argue with her up and down, to and fro,
Of how she had mothered a hero, and his was a glorious fate,
Better than years of grubbing to gather an estate.
Sometimes I'd put it this way: 'If God was to say to me now
"Take him back as he once was helping you with the plow," 70
I'd say, "No, God, thank You kindly; 'twas You that he obeyed;
You told him to fight and he fought, and he wasn't afraid;
You wanted to prove him in battle, You sent him to Lundy's Lane,
'Tis well!"' But she only would answer over and over again,
'Give me back my Abner—give me back my son!'

It was so all through the winter until the spring had begun,
And the crocus was up in the dooryard, and the drift by the fence was thinned,
And the sap drip-dropped from the branches wounded by the wind,
And the whole earth smelled like a flower,—then she came to me one night—
'Rufus!' she said, with a sob in her throat,—'Rufus, you're right.'                    80
I hadn't cried till then, not a tear—but then I was torn in two—
There, it's all right—my eyes don't see as they used to do!

But O the joy of that battle—it was worth the whole of life,
You felt immortal in action with the rapture of the strife,
There in the dark by the river, with the flashes of fire before,
Running and crashing along, there in the dark, and the roar
Of the guns, and the shrilling cheers, and the knowledge that filled your heart
That there was a victory making and you must do your part,
But—there's his grave in the orchard where the headstone glimmers white:
We could see it, we thought, from our window even on the darkest night;          90
It is set there for a sign that what one lad could do
Would be done by a hundred hundred lads whose hearts were stout and true.
And when in the time of trial you hear the recreant[3] say,
Shooting his coward lips at us, 'You shall have had your day:
For all your state and glory shall pass like a cloudy wrack,
And here some other flag shall fly where flew the Union Jack,'—
Why tell him a hundred thousand men would spring from these sleepy farms,
To tie that flag in its ancient place with the sinews of their arms;
And if they doubt you and put you to scorn, why you can make it plain,
With the tale of the gallant Lincoln men and the fight at Lundy's Lane.          100

1916

3  Coward; 'wrack': drifting clouds.

# The Height of Land[1] ——

Here is the height of land:
The watershed on either hand
Goes down to Hudson Bay
Or Lake Superior;
The stars are up, and far away
The wind sounds in the wood, wearier
Than the long Ojibway cadence[2]

1  Here, the Arctic watershed; north of that point all rivers flow into the Arctic Ocean.
2  The multi-syllabic language of the Native guides mentioned in the lines that follow, Potan the wise (introduced in a previous poem in the volume) and Chees-que-ne-e.

In which Potàn the Wise
Declares the ills of life
And Chees-que-ne-ne makes a mournful sound                    10
Of acquiescence. The fires burn low
With just sufficient glow
To light the flakes of ash that play
At being moths, and flutter away
To fall in the dark and die as ashes:
Here there is peace in the lofty air,
And Something comes by flashes
Deeper than peace;—
The spruces have retired a little space
And left a field of sky in violet shadow                      20
With stars like marigolds in a water-meadow.

Now the Indian guides are dead asleep;
There is no sound unless the soul can hear
The gathering of the waters in their sources.

We have come up through the spreading lakes
From level to level,—
Pitching our tents sometimes over a revel
Of roses that nodded all night,
Dreaming within our dreams,
To wake at dawn and find that they were captured              30
With no dew on their leaves;
Sometimes mid sheaves
Of bracken and dwarf-cornel,[3] and again
On a wide blueberry plain
Brushed with the shimmer of a bluebird's wing;
A rocky islet followed
With one lone poplar and a single nest
Of white-throat-sparrows that took no rest
But sang in dreams or woke to sing,—
To the last portage and the height of land—:                  40
Upon one hand
The lonely north enlaced with lakes and streams,
And the enormous targe[4] of Hudson Bay,
Glimmering all night
In the cold arctic light;

3  Large ferns and bunchberry (a kind of dogwood).
4  Shield.

On the other hand
The crowded southern land
With all the welter of the lives of men.
But here is peace, and again
That Something comes by flashes                                          50
Deeper than peace,—a spell
Golden and inappelable[5]
That gives the inarticulate part
Of our strange being one moment of release
That seems more native than the touch of time,
And we must answer in chime;
Though yet no man may tell
The secret of that spell
Golden and inappellable.

Now are there sounds walking in the wood,                                60
And all the spruces shiver and tremble,
And the stars move a little in their courses.
The ancient disturber of solitude
Breathes a pervasive sigh,
And the soul seems to hear
The gathering of the waters at their sources;
Then quiet ensues and pure starlight and dark;
The region-spirit murmurs in meditation,
The heart replies in exaltation
And echoes faintly like an inland shell                                  70
Ghost tremors of the spell;
Thought reawakens and is linked again
With all the welter of the lives of men.

Here on the uplands where the air is clear
We think of life as of a stormy scene,—
Of tempest, of revolt and desperate shock;
And here, where we can think, on the bright uplands
Where the air is clear, we deeply brood on life
Until the tempest parts, and it appears
As simple as to the shepherd seems his flock:                           80
A Something to be guided by ideals—
That in themselves are simple and serene—
Of noble deed to foster noble thought,
And noble thought to image noble deed,
Till deed and thought shall interpenetrate,

5  Here, ineffable; that which cannot be named.

Making life lovelier, till we come to doubt
Whether the perfect beauty that escapes
Is beauty of deed or thought or some high thing
Mingled of both, a greater boon than either:
Thus we have seen in the retreating tempest                    90
The victor-sunlight merge with the ruined rain,
And from the rain and sunlight spring the rainbow.

The ancient disturber of solitude
Stirs his ancestral potion in the gloom,
And the dark wood
Is stifled with the pungent fume
Of charred earth burnt to the bone
That takes the place of air.
Then sudden I remember when and where,—
The last weird lakelet foul with weedy growths              100
And slimy viscid things the spirit loathes,
Skin of vile water over viler mud
Where the paddle stirred unutterable stenches,
And the canoes seemed heavy with fear,
Not to be urged toward the fatal shore
Where a bush fire, smouldering, with sudden roar
Leaped on a cedar and smothered it with light
And terror. It had left the portage-height
A tangle of slanted spruces burned to the roots,
Covered still with patches of bright fire                        110
Smoking with incense of the fragrant resin
That even then began to thin and lessen
Into the gloom and glimmer of ruin.

'Tis overpast.[6] How strange the stars have grown;
The presage of extinction glows on their crests
And they are beautied with impermanence;
They shall be after the race of men
And mourn for them who snared their fiery pinions,
Entangled in the meshes of bright words.

A lemming stirs the fern and in the mosses                     120
Eft-minded things feel the air change, and dawn
Tolls out from the dark belfries of the spruces.
How often in the autumn of the world
Shall the crystal shrine of dawning be rebuilt

6 Over, ended.

With deeper meaning! Shall the poet then,
Wrapped in his mantle on the height of land,
Brood on the welter of the lives of men
And dream of his ideal hope and promise
In the blush sunrise? Shall he base his flight
Upon a more compelling law than Love                    130
As Life's atonement; shall the vision
Of noble deed and noble thought immingled
Seem as uncouth to him as the pictograph
Scratched on the cave side by the cave-dweller
To us of the Christ-time? Shall he stand
With deeper joy, with more complex emotion,
In closer commune with divinity,
With the deep fathomed, with the firmament charted,
With life as simple as a sheep-boy's song,
What lies beyond a romaunt[7] that was read          140
Once on a morn of storm and laid aside
Memorious with strange immortal memories?
Or shall he see the sunrise as I see it,
In shoals of misty fire the deluge-light
Dashes upon and whelms with purer radiance,
And feel the lulled earth, older in pulse and motion,
Turn the rich lands and the inundant[8] oceans
To the flushed colour, and hear as now I hear
The thrill of life beat up the planet's margin
And break in the clear susurrus[9] of deep joy         150
That echoes and reëchoes in my being?
O Life is intuition the measure of knowledge
And do I stand with heart entranced and burning
At the zenith of our wisdom when I feel
The long light flow, the long wind pause, the deep
Influx of spirit, of which no man may tell
The Secret, golden and inappellable?

1916

---

7 Romantic tale or poem.
8 Flooding.
9 Whisper.

# To a Canadian Aviator Who Died for His Country in France

Tossed like a falcon from the hunter's wrist,
A sweeping plunge, a sudden shattering noise,
And thou hast dared, with a long spiral twist,
The elastic stairway to the rising sun.
Peril below thee and above, peril
Within thy car;[1] but peril cannot daunt
Thy peerless heart: gathering wing and poise,
Thy plane transfigured, and thy motor-chant
Subduèd to a whisper—then silence,—
And thou art but a disembodied venture                    10
In the void.

But Death, who has learned to fly,
Still matchless when his work is to be done,
Met thee between the armies and the sun;
Thy speck of shadow faltered in the sky;
Then thy dead engine and thy broken wings
Drooped through the arc and passed in fire,
A wreath of smoke—a breathless exhalation.
But ere that came a vision sealed thine eyes,
Lulling thy senses with oblivion;                         20
And from its sliding station in the skies
Thy dauntless soul upward in circles soared
To the sublime and purest radiance whence it sprang.

In all their eyries,[2] eagles shall mourn thy fate,
And leaving on the lonely crags and scaurs
Their unprotected young, shall congregate
High in the tenuous heaven and anger the sun
With screams, and with a wild audacity
Dare all the battle danger of thy flight;
Till weary with combat one shall desert the light,       30
Fall like a bolt of thunder and check his fall
On the high ledge, smoky with mist and cloud,
Where his neglected eaglets shriek aloud,
And drawing the film across his sovereign sight
Shall dream of thy swift soul immortal
Mounting in circles, faithful beyond death.

1917[3]

1 Cockpit.
2 Nests built on a high cliff or mountain; scaurs: cliffs.
3 Published in a chapbook, *'To the Canadian Mothers' and Three Other Poems*, in support of the Prisoners of War Fund.

# Labrie's Wife

*Being an excerpt from the manuscript journal of Archibald Muir, Clerk of The Honourable The Hudson's Bay Company at Nipigon House in the year of our Lord, 1815.*

*May Twenty-second, 1815*

Today something happened which is bound to be of consequence in this outlandish place, and that I will set down here and make of record. Alec, who is getting more gumption now, although as unsteady in all his performances as he was ever, returned from his trip to the Flat Rock, and arrived safe with his two canoes and Ogemah-ga-bow, little Needic and his two sons. It appears that they had, by reason of the rough weather, to lay by at Dry Beaver Islands and had like to have starved if the wind had not gone down, for these fools of Indians will never learn not to devour half their rations in the first day out from the Post. They came in looking like wasps, their belts girt so tightly about their middles.

I could tell the moment I clapped eyes upon Alec that he had some bee in his bonnet, for he can no more control his countenance than an otter can help fishing. His face was all of a jump, and he spoke as if he had no spittle under his tongue. I have a plan to let the youngster speak when he is ready, and by this means I have the enjoyment of witnessing him cast about to get me to question him and assist him out with his story. When we were having a bit of dinner he fairly simmered, but he did not boil until I lit my pipe. Then he could stand my coolness no longer.

'We're to have opposition!' he blurted out. I did not want to show any astonishment, but I nearly dropped my pipe, such a matter never having been thought of in Nipigon before. 'You see,' he went on, 'I determined when I was at that part of the lake to go over to Keg Island and see if the cache was all right, and on St Paul's Island, when we went ashore to roast some fish, we found two canoes loaded, and a Frenchman and three Indians.

'He asked me if I was with the English, and I lied to him straight enough, and said No! I was trading alone. Then he wanted to know where our Post was, and I said it was beyond the large island to the west. He said his name was Labrie, and that he was for the North West Company, and was sent in opposition to the English on the lake. So I decided to camp where I was, and not to go to Keg Island, but to come on here. I told him to keep due west, and not to land until he struck the big island, which was Cariboo Island, and not for any reason to camp on a little flat island half way there, which was full of snakes.'

The youngster was mighty proud of himself at outwitting the Frenchman, but to take down his pride a bit, I provoked him by saying, 'Well, poor Donald used to call you a clavering[1] idiot, but if he had lived to this day he'd have had to invent a new kind of word for you. If your Labrie is anything of a trader he watched you away in the morning, and he will treat us in good Hudson's Bay Company rum when we first meet, having visited your little flat island full of snakes.' Off went Alec trying to bite

1 Babbling.

his beard, aping Donald's manner, poor lad; but he had yet a beard no longer than a pinfeather.

*May Twenty-third, 1815*

I was up before sun this day, as I had a restless night, thinking what I should do now we were to have opposition on the lake, a thing new to me who have scant experience. I determined to be smooth with them and observe them closely, and spoil them if I might with a fair face, and in all events to fight them with what weapons they may choose. I had wakened from a light doze with a sudden thought that I should posses myself of the point of land below the Post where I have always said the buildings should have been placed, which commands and oversees our present position. If it were seized by these pirates of Frenchmen, what then would become of our trade? They would eat it like a bear eats honey-comb. Alec could not see that, and provoked me with much grumbling that it was a useless work and a weary waste of muscle. It is curious how block-headed he is about all matters connected with trade; he has some acuteness belike but of what sort God alone knows. In the end I was mightily satisfied to see a stout staff with the ensign flying, and a small boat-landing, with one of the boats moored. We had the work done before midday, and for the rest of the time I had pleasure in looking down at the point which had an inhabited and secure look, under the Hudson's Bay Company's flag. If the Frenchmen have any idea of the shore about here there will be some *sacréing*[2] when they find the point taken up, for northwards there is no place for a foothold, and only in a cove, half a mile to the south, can they find level land enough for building upon. So when our Indians come down, and they should be here in a matter of four weeks, they are bound to reach the Post first, and I can keep my eye upon the rascals, who would, if they could, trade with the newcomers and forget old kindnesses and obligations.

*May Twenty-fourth, 1815*

Ogemah-ga-bow came up to say that one of Needic's boys had died last night, having over-eaten himself after his fast on the Dry Beaver Islands. Rain today.

*May Twenty-sixth, 1815*

Sundown yesterday on my bench before the door, whereby Needic had made a smudge[3] to keep off the flies, which are now very bad, when I saw a canoe that was none of ours land at the point, and a man step out onto the new boat-landing. He looked all about him as if he was making an inventory of the place, and then he came slowly up the hill. He was a stout-shouldered, low-set fellow, with a black beard and small, bad eyes. Said I to myself as I saw him approach, 'There is something mainly dishonest in your make-up, my man, and whatever one may have to do to keep trade from you it won't be very savoury in the doing if your methods are to be used.'

'My name's Labrie,' he said, running a hand through his hair.

---

2  That is, cursing, swearing. *'Sacré'* (literally 'holy') is a common French expletive.
3  A fire with a dense smoke, used to repel insects.

I got upon my legs and said politely, 'I heard of your being in the Lake from my man. Will you be seated?'

He said, 'No' and looked over his shoulders at the Point.

'You have the Point under your flag,' he remarked.

'Aye,' I said, as dry as I could.

'The work has marks of newness.'

'You are right, it was only finished yesterday.'

The blood came into his face in an ugly way.

'Well, there can be no great objection to my trading a little.'

'Not there,' said I bluntly. 'Under my company's flag what we take we claim and keep.'

He breathed rather heavily, but held his tongue, and was going to walk away.

'Hold on,' said I, 'strangers are not treated so here, you must have a dram.'

I called Alec, who brought the rum and the glasses. We drank health courteously, then were ready to cut one another's throats.

'Did you ever taste better than that?' said I.

'I have as good,' said he, 'though it is the best, I can match it.'

'Match it!' said I in a tone of surprise, winking at Alec, who flew as red as a bubble jock.[4] We parted then but just as he was getting away he said over his shoulder, 'Your man there has a damned queer idea of direction.'

*May Twenty-seventh, 1815*

Sent Needic and his live boy and Ogemah-ga-bow's brother to Poplar Lodge, to have news of the hunters. The Osnaburgh packs from the north should now be two weeks out, unless the ice is later this year than last. Tomorrow I will put Alec and Ogemah-ga-bow to work clearing out the storehouse and setting things to rights. I am much exercised in mind over my responsibilities. It was bad enough last year, but now I have the whole management, and this opposition to contend with upon the back of it. I begin to be worn with it, what with loss of sleep at night, and thinking about nought else in the day. No sign of Labrie or any of his party.

*May Thirtieth, 1815*

This morning Labrie came up to borrow an adze, which I lent to him without any question. He seemed to want to be civil enough. When I asked him, however, if Madame Labrie had arrived, he seemed quite put about and mumbled something in his beard, which sounded nearly like 'What affair is that of yours?' I paid no attention to him, not wishing to quarrel yet awhile, and without any further parley off he went with the adze, which I am fortunate if I ever see again.

Heat intense today, bring on a great storm of thunder and much rain. Had a great debate with Alec, when we were indoors, as to when the Osnaburgh packs will be in. I calculated in three weeks, as the water is like to be high, they will take the route through Mud Lakes to Negodina, as I wrote Godfrey. The old route to Wabinosh

4  A male turkey (Scottish); usually 'bubbly jock'.

would take them much longer and, what with broken water and two desperate, long carries, there is a great risk of loss by that way. Alec thinks they will be down sooner. There is no doubt they have had a fine winter and if the pack can be safely landed it will be a great matter, and no doubt I shall hear good of it from the partners.

*May Thirty-first, 1815*

This morning when I was cleaning my pistols I heard a clear sound of laughter. Now laughter is an uncommon thing in this country, visiting us very infrequently. To be sure the Indians laugh, but that to me always has an unmeaning sound, and sometimes a bestial. Moreover, this laugher was different in kind, and one must have listened to it however absorbed he might have been. It was high-pitched and very clear and had something merry and withal innocent about it. It was contagious also and the mere sound of it made my very muscles twitch. There was no one visible, but after I had gazed awhile I saw Alec come up the steps from the warehouse. Not to appear interested before the lad I went back to my work. After a little he came in. I noticed his face was flushed and his manner excited. I paid no attention to him until he had knocked a dish off the table. It broke in three pieces. I was angry with him, good crockery not being by any means very plentiful in this country.

'Good God, man!' I cried. 'If you're in such a state that you cannot avoid breaking the dishes, will you lie upon your bed for a while.' He glared at me terribly, but had not a word to say. Then I kept quiet for as much as a quarter of an hour, and I could see it was fretting him; he fidgeted about greatly. Then he got up and went to the door.

'It seems to me you take mighty small interest in things.'

I said never a word.

'Are you deaf this morning?'

I made no sound. He made no move for a minute, then he said, just as he was going out of the door, in an exasperated way, 'That was Labrie's wife.'

I could have laughed to myself, but when I had thought upon it for a time I began to perceive something bitter in his tone, and I reflected that of late I had treated him much as poor Donald used unthinkingly to treat me, and that he must be occupying my old position of complaint, and my heart was softened a bit, and I resolved to be more kind to him in the future, who is in much a good boy and canny in a sort about many things.

*June First, 1815*

I saw Labrie's wife for the first time this morning. An uncommon looking wench, with black hair and eyes and a mouthful of white teeth. I discussed her thoroughly with Alec, who sticks up for it that she is a handsome one. So she is, after her manner, though that I do not acknowledge to Alec. She looked me all over as if I were for sale, and when I coolly turned my back on her, that she might have a good look at that, she went off in a mighty huff.

Alec reports that there are two other women in Labrie's party, rather old and haggish. I have not clapped eyes upon them, not having visited the Cove. Although she went off in a huff, the young wench is a merry one, and it amuses her to hear Alec so aboundingly polite to her with his 'Madame Labrie'. 'Madame Labrie' this and 'Madame Labrie' that, whereupon she giggles or breaks out into wild laughter.

*June Third, 1815*

Needic back from Poplar Lodge, where everything is all right. Had an amusing conversation with the lad Alec anent[5] Labrie's wife. The hussy comes about the house constantly, even when we are not here.

'Now what is she after?' said I.

'You have no understanding of women,' he replied. 'Of course she will come back when you treat her in that way.'

'Now in what way?' said I. 'Never do I look at her or pass the time of day with her.

'That is it,' he retorts. 'You are fairly insulting her, and she comes back.'

'Do you try and be sweet to her and mayhap she would stay away.'

'It is different with me,' he says, biting his whiskers and shrugging up his shoulders, just as the wench does herself. He has taken on a sort of mincing, balancing, half-Frenchified accent, and shrugs his shoulders.

'Are you afraid she would fall into love weez you, Alec?' I remarked, trying hard to imitate the accent.

'It is not me she will be in love with.'

'No, who then? Needic?'

'Needic!' he cried, going off with a great French shrug.

*June Fourth, 1815*

No word from Godfrey about the packs. I am getting a trifle anxious. Alec says there are more guns than yardsticks in Labrie's quarters, and makes out they are on for a fight. Labrie's wife came up at noon and made us an omelette with gull's eggs and fresh onion-tops. She is a clever wench and sat looking at me as I devoured it. I talked a bit to her. After she left, Alec sat frowning.

'You were very free with her.'

'I merely spoke to her, but then she made a good omelette.'

'You said too much to her. You nearly told her we expected the packs at Negodina by the Mud Lake route this year instead of Wabinosh.'

'Well, and if I did?'

'It is all she wanted to know.'

'Well, you seem to be always ready to stand up for the spy, if she be one,' said I, turning the French accent upon him. This made him wroth, as it always does.

'You never seem to understand that a woman's not like a man. The best of them you have to watch, and more particularly when one of them is in love with you.'

'That does not apply here,' I said, 'unless you have her assurances yourself.'

'I would not make love to a married woman,' he said hotly.

'That's why you guard yourself so carefully, is it? You are mighty pious. It is a pity you are not like me. Now for me Mr Labrie's wife has no attraction whatever, commandments or no commandments.'

5 About, concerning (chiefly Scottish).

This set him off again.

'Be careful you, Archibald Muir, that is what I have to say to you.'

We could hear the lady herself laughing down at the landing, and it sounded so innocent that I could not refrain from smiling at the boy.

*June Fifth, 1815*

We had a scene last night with Labrie's wife, for which Alec has to be thanked, and in which I think he had a small revenge for my baiting of him. I will set down the occurrence here although it be against myself, and our national instrument. She had been hardly before the house, and it was in the dusk of the evening, when she asked me to play upon the pipes.

'Will you play upon the bag-pipes, Mr Muir?' she said in a very civil voice. 'I have never heard the bag-pipes.'

Now I am always at pains to oblige a lady, if it be possible, so I went in and got the pipes, hearing Alec urge me also, so I had two willing to be pleased.

Well, scarcely had I begun to get the skin filled with wind when Labrie's wife began to laugh. Now I am willing to admit that the foreword to a performance on the pipes may be dispiriting, but I charge that what follows after when the instrument is well controlled, and when the melody pours forth in full cry, would serve to obliterate a greatly more dispiriting prelude. But in this case I did not get beyond that stage, for Labrie's wife laughed with so little judgement that I was put about. I saw something in Alec's face which led me to think that the whole matter was preconceived by him, and with that I laid down my pipes on the bench beside me. Not another note would I play. I am not much versed in women's ways, and what Labrie's wife did puzzled me. But of that I shall give Alec's explanation. At first she kept on laughing, and then she stopped suddenly and came forward looking sober enough, but with the wrinkles of the laugher not yet gone out of her face. There she stood about four feet from me with a bit of her dress in her hand, as I have seen school girls stand abashed having been found at fault.

'You are angry because I laughed?' she said.

I did not answer.

Then she came close to me and made as if to put her hands upon my shoulders, and when I looked straight upon her eyes she dropped her hands, made a sound in her throat, and turned and went away.

Then young Alec began to strut about like a bantam cock.

'I have to thank you for that performance,' I said.

'Why would you prevent a woman from laughing?' says he, in a rage. 'Don't you know enough of women to let them laugh and let them talk?'

'I can lay no claim to such knowledge as yourself.' said I, in a mighty sneering voice. 'In truth I know naught about them.'

'You have proved that this night,' retorted Alec.

'Expound that, you young oracle,' said I.

'Expound? You have sent her away with a sore heart, and she was minded to be playful with you, and that cuts sore on a heart such as hers. Don't you see it, man?' he cried, sort of dashing his hands down.

'I see nothing of the sort. She was angry simply because I wouldn't speak back to her.'

'You might have spoken to her or not spoken, and she would never have minded if you hadn't looked at her in the way you did.'

I saw it was no use my trying to fathom the young donkey, so I would speak no more to him.

*June Sixth, 1815*

Labrie's wife was up last night but I would not go out to see her, being tired of the body and her endless chatter. Alec and she talked for an hour; the boy would be contented to go on vapouring forever, I believe. I pretended to be busy with my papers, and in the end she went away. She came to the window just before she went, and I heard her fingers on the sash, but I did not look up, and I heard her low gurgling laugh as she ran away from Alec, who would go down to the landing with her.

He is as polite to her and as formal as if he were living by a code of court etiquette. I twitted him with that.

'Well,' he says, mighty stiff, and pulling a solemn face, 'she is a woman, and she is another man's wife.'

'That last is her great virtue,' said I, with a tone of sarcasm, at which he looked scornful and exceeding pious.

*June Seventh, 1815*

Good news yesterday. Toma came in with a message from Godfrey. The Osnaburgh packs are safe at Cache point on the Mud Lake route. The water is high and they have not had a mishap. In three days they should reach Negodina at the end of the lake. It is, as I have always said, a route more clean and handy than the Wabinosh route, and it will be adopted now from this out.

Woke up with a mighty sore head this morning and had words with Alec. It is inconceivable how domineering that lad has become.

'You were drinking with Madame Labrie last night,' he said.

'And my lord is jealous,' I replied, sneering at him.

'Ye have made a fool of yourself. What did you tell her?'

'Nothing that I rightly remember. Since when were you ordained my catechist?'

'Now I have told you many times', he said in a parsoning way, 'that you did not understand the nature of women, and that you would let slip something that Labrie wanted to know. Now you have done so, I believe, between a glass too much of whisky and a pretty woman.'

'Do you call yon a pretty woman?' I said, mocking his accent.

'I pity you!' he said, with great contempt.

He went away swinging his shoulders, much more the master than the man.

To set down the truth, although it be against myself, Labrie's wife came up in the evening of yesterday. I was more decent with the bitch, having had good news, and I treated her to some whisky, and drank with her. Alec was off watching Toma, as he thought Labrie might try to get hold of him. I do not just remember when she went away. God forgive me, I do not rightly remember anything about it.

Hardly had Alec dismissed himself when he came back very greatly excited, but in anger this time.

'They have gone,' said he.

'Who?' said I, not thinking for a moment.

'Who! My God! Who? Why Labrie.'

'Well what of that?' I said. 'It is a good riddance of a vile lot of thieves out of God's country.'

'That is all you see to it?' he said.

'Well, what more?' I replied.

'I seem to see that last night you told Madame Labrie the packs were coming by the Mud Lake route to Negodina, and that they have gone to stop them. I have my doubt they will not barter with them. I seem to see that they will capture the furs and that by no very gentle means.'

'You have said it before,' I cried out, wroth with him and with myself. 'So yon slut is what I have always supposed her to be.'

A dark look came into his face. 'Choose your words!' he cried, taking a step towards me.

'I'll neither pick nor choose my words,' I said. 'What do you call her then that would take our hospitality and then do us wrong?'

'Madaline would do no such thing,' he cried, strutting about in a way that looked comical to me. I laughed at him.

'Madaline! Madaline! We shall see what Madaline will have done when we lose our furs. Why, man, you said out of your own mouth that she had done it.'

'You lie,' he cried, but it was here not impudence, so I paid no attention to him.

After some parley and conversation, I sent him with three canoes and all the able men, except Needic, to Negodina to see what had fallen out. He is to send me back a letter, as soon as he can, with the word. I am here now quite alone, and in mind very much put about. I have been striving to recall what passed between Labrie's wife and myself, but without any clear recollection. Ah, those women! I well remember my father used to say, 'At the bottom of every trouble, there you will find a woman,' and my mother used to retort, 'And likewise at the bottom of every happiness.' Whereupon he would kiss her.

*June Tenth, 1815*

Last night—waiting for word from Alec. This morning I went down to Labrie's camp with Needic. They had left two tents and some rubbish, and a little green box marked 'M.L.'. Turning the lot over I found two empty kegs marked 'H.B. Co.', once full of rum, which they had stolen from the cache on Keg Island. So we heaped all together and set fire to it. It burned merrily, and they are at least by that much poorer.

*June Eleventh, 1815*

I am in great spirits today. Last night I was awakened by Needic, who had his boy with him. Everything had reached Negodina safely, and there was no sign anywhere of Labrie's party. They will push on at once.

*June Twelfth, 1815*

This morning Labrie came back. Needic came up and told me, so about noon I took my pistols and went down with him to the cove. They had one tent up and the women were making the fire. The men went off and none of them would speak to us. I stood smiling in a taunting way, and just as I was about to leave, Labrie's wife came over to me. I perceived she had her arm wound in a cloth.

'Well, Madame Labrie, how did you hurt your arm?'

'Why do you call me Madame Labrie?'

'One must call you something. My boy, Alec, calls you Madaline.'

Her face grew a darker red.

'You have been away for a while?'

'Yes,' she said, 'we were at Wabinosh, and I see you burned my box when I was gone.'

'Were you ever in love?' she asked suddenly.

'Never,' said I, 'praise be to God.'

'When you are I pray heaven you may be tortured in it.'

'I am thankful of your good wishes.'

'The other night you told me your packs were coming by Negodina. You understand? It was Labrie who shot me through the arm. He wanted to kill me for taking them to Wabinosh, but the others would not let him.'

'The low rascal,' I said, 'to shoot a woman.'

'And *you* have nothing to say about *me*?' She looked at me curiously, and put an odd emphasis on the *you* and the *me*.

'It is fortunate you made a mistake.'

'A mistake!' she said. 'Your boy Alec is twice the man you are.'

The hussy said that with a fluff of pride.

'Goodbye,' said I from my canoe.

'Is that all, Archibald Muir, is that all?'

'Goodbye,' said I, 'and I hope your husband won't shoot at you again.'

I looked back when we had gone a bit, and she still stood there. She did not make any sign towards me, though I waved to her in courtesy. Then she covered up her face in her hands.

No word of Godfrey and Alec. I sent Needic to Labrie's wife with two gold guineas for the box I had burned, probably the only gold she ever clapped her eyes on, as it is unknown in this trade almost.

*June Thirteenth, 1815*

The packs came in yesterday evening. Godfrey and the men all well. I mixed a keg of spirits for them and they made a hideous night of it. Too busy to write much now, but can do nothing more tonight. Looking back in the store ledgers I can see no such winter's catch. Great good luck. Labrie's party still hanging around. Alec went down as soon as he got back, and stayed longer than he ought, so I berated him soundly. Tonight at supper he said:

'Labrie shot her through the arm because she had taken them to Wabinosh and had misled them.'

I paid no attention to him. By and by he said:

'You will be glad to know that she says you told her nothing about the packs.'

'Did she?' said I, puzzled, as she had told me the contrary.

'I don't believe her,' he added.

'You're complimentary to the ladies,' I remarked.

'Here is something she asked me to give you.'

It was the money I had sent her for that box of hers I burnt.

*June Fourteenth, 1815*

Busy all day between the storehouse and the fur press. Half the Indians are drunk yet. Alec says Labrie and his party have gone. May the devil's luck go with them. I thought Alec looked a trifle white in the face, and as if he was impatient to make me talk, but I had no time to be spending with him.

A wonderfully warm day, and the flies very bad, enough to madden one. Have pressed all the packs and now everything is in order for a move. What a grand night for the partners it will be when they see our canoes full of the finest come to land at Fort William. It should be of profit to me, and I expect to come back here or go somewhere a factor,[6] if I comprehend the rules properly. About an hour ago I had just finished writing the last words when Alec's shadow came over the window. He seemed to stand there over long, and I was just on the point of crying out to him when he moved off. In a moment he came in to me. I did not look up from my writing when he flung a scrap of paper down before me.

'There!' he said, in an odd voice. 'I found it under the sash. It fell face down, so I saw printing on the back, I thought it was but a scrap torn off a fur bill.

'Read it,' said he.

I turned it over and observed that there were some words in writing on the other side. I made them out to be: 'Why do you call me Labrie's wife? She is my aunt. Do you think I would marry an ugly fellow like Labrie? They brought me up here to help their plans. We shall see. If you want to know my name it's Madaline Lesage. I learned to write from the Sister St Theresa at Wikwemikong. Is it not pretty? M.L.'

Then I recalled how she had come to the window, one night not very long ago, when, I opine, she had left the paper there.

'Well!' I said coolly, 'and what is it now that you have to say about Madaline Lesage?'

His face had a tortured look upon it. He tried to speak. 'She was—she was the bravest, the dearest'—he stopped there and hung down his head. 'Oh, my God, you cannot understand. You can never understand!'

He moved away and stood by the door. I thought upon what he had said. No, I did not understand. Then I tried once more to go on with my page. But I was detained by the sound which is as uncommon as that of laughter in these outlandish parts. The sound of sobbing. Just for a moment it brought back to me the sound of my sister's voice as she sobbed for her lover when they brought him back dead and

---

6  An agent or trader; a rank higher than that of clerk.

dripping out of the sea. I had a vision of it as if it were snapped upon my eye in a flash of lightning, she leaning her forehead upon her wrists against the wall. I looked up at Alec and there he was leaning at the door-post, his shoulders all moving with his sobs. I understood in a flash. I pray God to forgive me for the sin of blindness, and for always being so dead to others in my own affairs. I went towards him knowing that I could not give him any comfort. So he went out from the house and walked alone through the gloaming.[7] I perceived that a change had come over him. I had always considered him a bit of a boy to be ordered about, but there was a man walking away from me, resolute in his steps, big in his bulk, and weighed down as if he was carrying a load, bearing it as if he was proud of it, with energy and trust in himself.

1923

7 Twilight.

# Jessie Georgina Sime
## 1868–1958

Canons can evolve. That is, because literary tastes, contexts for judgment, and canonical criteria change over time, some writers come to seem less significant while others find a new readership. Among Canadian writers who benefited from reassessment in the 1990s is Georgina Sime, whose work presents readers with a realist's perspective on women in the early twentieth century, a period of significant cultural change.

From an early age, Sime was exposed to socialism and to reform politics, and was generally made aware of literary and social issues. Born in Edinburgh, Scotland, she was the only child of Jessie Wilson and James Sime—writers and educators who moved in literary circles. Growing up in London, England, and in Chiswick (then a suburb of London); Sime became acquainted, through her parents, with such notable authors and thinkers as Thomas Hardy, George Bernard Shaw, and William Morris. As a result of her employment as secretary to Dr Freeland Barbour (an eminent gyne-

cologist associated with the University of Edinburgh), she met and worked for William James, one of the pioneers of North American psychology. Sime also assisted her father by working for him as a reader for Macmillan Press, which had been founded by her mother's friend, Daniel Macmillan; as well, she worked as a journalist in London and as an editor in London and Edinburgh.

Sime attended Queen's College in London, an institution founded in the mid-nineteenth century to promote the education of women. At seventeen, she travelled alone to Berlin for a year to study singing. After she returned, Sime became still more deeply involved in the intellectual ferment of the time, especially the debate over the 'New Woman'. Following her father's death in 1895 she returned to Edinburgh but, after London and Berlin, found the city puritanical and unreceptive. Around this time, she became involved both professionally and personally with a young married Canadian physician two years her senior. He completed his degree at the University of Edinburgh in 1898 and remained for two further years of post-graduate study before returning to Montreal, where he rejoined his wife in her life of social privilege. Sime stayed in Scotland until her mother's death in 1907; she then moved to Montreal to renew her relationship with this doctor and to work as his secretary. It has been suggested that Sime's frequent portrayals of an 'irregular union' (the title of one of the stories in *Sister Woman*) were reflections on her own situation, which was quite unconventional at that time.

Even before she arrived, Canada was a place known to Sime. Her maternal uncle, Daniel Wilson—a professor and the chancellor of the University of Toronto—had told her about the country that now became her home and that was to provide the subject matter of her fiction for the next three decades. After arriving in Canada, Sime took up professional life as a businesswoman, which included serving as vice president of the Quebec branch of the Canadian Women's Press Club, and became a well-known writer and an effective lecturer on women, women's writing, and the literary depiction of women. She also served as the president and founding member of the Montreal chapter of the international literary organization PEN and as the president of the Montreal branch of the new Canadian Author's Association.

Although Sime wrote on a variety of topics in her journalism, sketches, and early short stories, her interest in the social, economic, and emotional impact on women of the changes taking place in modern life and culture was of particular importance. In the years immediately following the First World War, British librarian Frank Carr Nicholson, a friend and long-time correspondent acted on her behalf as literary agent and editor: he found her a supportive publisher in England, Grant Richards, who brought out her first two books with serious literary aspirations: *Sister Woman* (1919; reprinted in 1992) and *Our Little Life: A Novel of Today* (1921; reprinted in 1994).

Breaking with the idealistic portrayals of the pre-war era, these books offer unfamiliar pictures of women. Sime's characters vary in class and economic security but, like Bertha Martin, the protagonist of 'Munitions!', they all face the emerging challenges encountered by women at the beginning of the twentieth century. In her books, Sime emphasizes, from a female perspective, the way lives of working-class women have been altered by the move into the city from small towns and farms; the particular problems immigrants confront; and the way issues around national identity affect newcomers. The way the women in *Our Little Life* and *Sister Woman* often lose their companions and must live alone, even raise their children on their own, shows them facing the new complexities of the age without support.

In a framing prologue and epilogue to *Sister Woman*, Sime makes clear her desire to use her fiction to change the world. In the first of these two self-reflexive sketches, a man wants to discuss 'The Woman's Question' with the dramatized author, who responds by saying, 'The woman's [question] and the man's. It's the same thing. There's no difference.' When he challenges her to 'state your grievance,' she seats herself at her typewriter, making it evident that the book that follows is her response. In the concluding sketch, that book has now been written. The same man now distresses the author by asking her if that is 'all you have to say'; the sketch's conclusion is her response, a commitment to go on writing:

*'Why, I'm not even started yet,' I said. . . . 'I've got reams and reams and reams to say . . . Let me tell you what we women want is simple—but the world isn't simple. Don't you see,' I said, 'you've got to start the world again if—We can't fight the world the way it is. You—you've got to . . .'*

*. . . I ran my fingers over the typewriter keys—and felt them lovingly.*

A pioneer in Canadian realist and urban Modernist fiction, Sime's prose met with a range of critical reception: some readers were shocked by her subject matter and her focus on what seemed to them women's trivialities; others praised her for her spare style and her close and frank attention to the details of everyday life. She continued to publish throughout her long lifetime, although her emphasis shifted, with the times, from her earlier urban realism to a focus on the interior life of the mind. As well as additional works of fiction, her later books include a critical study, *Thomas Hardy of the Wessex Novels: An Essay and a Biographical Note* (1928), and an autobiographical sketch, *In a Canadian Shack* (1937). With Nicholson she co-authored *A Tale of Two Worlds* (1953), a consideration of German life after the Second World War.

# Munitions!

Bertha Martin sat in the street car in the early morning going to her work. Her work was munitions. She had been at it exactly five weeks.

She sat squeezed up into a corner, just holding on to her seat and no more, and all round her were women and girls also working at munitions—loud, noisy, for ever talking—extraordinarily happy. They sat there filling the car with their two compact rows, pressed together, almost in one another's laps, joking, chewing tobacco—flinging the chewed stuff about.

It wasn't in the least that they were what is technically known as 'bad women'. Oh no—no! If you thought that, you would mistake them utterly. They were decent women, good, self-respecting girls, for the most part 'straight girls'—with a black sheep here and there, to be sure, but where aren't there black sheep here and there? And the reason they made a row and shrieked with laughter and cracked an unseemly jest or two was simply that they were turned loose. They had spent their lives caged, most of them, in shop or house, and now they were drunk with the open air and the greater freedom and the sudden liberty to do as they liked and damn whoever stopped them.

Bertha Martin looked round at her companions. She saw the all sorts that make the world. Here and there was a pretty, young, flushed face, talking—talking—trying to express something it felt inside and couldn't get out. And here and there Bertha Martin saw an older face, a face with a knowledge of the world in it and that something that comes into a woman's eyes if certain things happen to her, and never goes out of them again. And then Bertha Martin saw quite elderly women, or so they seemed to her—women of forty or so, decent bodies, working for someone besides themselves—they had it written on their faces; and she saw old women—old as working women go—fifty and more, sitting there with their long working lives behind them and their short ones in front. And now and then some woman would draw her snuff-box from her shirt-waist and it would pass up and down the line and they would all take great pinches of the brown, pungent powder and stuff it up their noses—and laugh and laugh. . . . Bertha Martin looked round the car and she couldn't believe it was she who was sitting in it.

It was the very early spring. The white March sunshine came streaming into the car, and when Bertha, squeezed sideways in her corner, looked through the window, she saw the melting snow everywhere—piles and piles of it uncleared because the men whose job it was to clear it were at the war. She saw walls of snow by the sides of the streets—they went stretching out into infinity. And the car went swinging and lurching between them, out through the city and into the country where the factory was.

There were puddles and little lakes of water everywhere; winter was melting away before the birth of another spring.

Bertha looked. She looked up into the clear—into the crystal clearness of the morning sky. It was the time of the spring skies of Canada—wonderful, delicate, diaphanous skies that come every spring to the Northern Land—skies the colour of bluebells and primroses—transparent, translucent, marvellously beautiful. Bertha looked up into the haze of colour—and she smiled. And then she wondered why she smiled.

It was the very early springtime.

Just five weeks before and Bertha had been a well-trained servant in a well-kept, intensely self-respecting house—a house where no footfall was heard on the soft, long-piled rugs; where the lights were shaded and the curtains were all drawn at night; where the mistress lay late in bed and 'ordered' things; where life was put to bed every night with hot bottles to its feet; where no one ever spoke of anything that mattered; where meals were paramount. There had Bertha Martin lived five long, comfortable years.

She had gone about her business capably. She had worn her uniform like any soldier—a white frock in the mornings and a cap upon her head, and her hair had been orderly, her apron accurately tied. She had been clean. There were no spring skies in sight—or else she had not looked to see them. She had got up—not too unreasonably early—had had her early morning cup of tea with the other servants, had set the dining-room breakfast, waited on it—quiet—respectful—as self-respecting as the house. And in the afternoons there she had been in her neat black gown with her cap and apron immaculate—her hair still orderly and unobtrusive—everything about her, inside and out, still self-respecting and respectful. She had 'waited on table', cleaned silver, served tea, carried things everlastingly in and out, set them on tables, taken them off again, washed them, put them away, taken them out again, reset tables with them—it was a circular game with never any end to it. And she had done it well. 'Martin is an excellent servant,' she had heard the lady of the house say once. 'I can trust her thoroughly.'

One afternoon in the week she went out. At a certain hour she left the house; at another certain hour she came back again. If she was half-an-hour late she was liable to be questioned: 'Why?' And when she had given her explanation then she would hear the inevitable 'Don't let it occur again.' And Sunday—every other Sunday—there was the half day, also at certain hours. Of course—how otherwise could a well-run house *be* well run? And down in the kitchen the maids would dispute as to whether you got out half-an-hour sooner last time and so must go half-an-hour later this—they would quarrel and squabble over the silliest little things. Their horizon was so infinitesimally small, and they were so much too comfortable—they ate so much too much and they did so far too little—what could they do but squabble? They were never all on speaking-terms at one time together. Either the old cook was taking the housemaid's part or she and the housemaid were at daggers drawn; and they all said the same things over and over and over again—to desperation.

Bertha Martin looked up at the exquisite sky—and she smiled. The sun came streaming in, and the girls and women talked and jabbered and snuffed and chewed their tobacco and spat it out. And sometimes when the car conductor put his head in at the door they greeted him with a storm of chaff—a hail of witticisms—a tornado of personalities. And the little French-Canadian, overpowered by numbers, would never even try to break a lance with them. He would smile and shrug and put his hand up to his ears and run the door back between himself and them. And the women would laugh and clap their hands and stamp with their feet and call things to him—shout. . . .

Bertha turned to the girl next her—nearly atop of her—and looked her over. She was a fragile-looking, indoors creature—saleslady was written all over her—with soft rings of fair curled hair on her temples, and a weak, smiling mouth, and little useless feet in her cheap, high-heeled pumps. She was looking intently at a great strap of a girl opposite, with a great mouth on her, out of which was reeling a broad story.

'My, ain't she the girl!' said Bertha's little neighbour; and with the woman's inevitable gesture, she put her two hands up to her hair behind, and felt, and took a hairpin out here and there and put it in again.

She turned to Bertha.

'Say, ain't she the girl alright? Did you hear?'

Bertha nodded.

The little indoors thing turned and glanced at Bertha—took her in from head to foot with one feminine look.

'You gittin' on?' she said.

'Fine!' said Bertha.

The eyes of the women met. They smiled at one another. Fellow-workers—out in the world together. That's what their eyes said: Free! And then the little creature turned away from Bertha—bent forward eagerly. Another of the stories was coming streaming out.

'Ssh! . . . ssh!' cried some of the older women. But their voices were drowned in the sea of laughter as the climax took possession of the car. The women rocked and swayed—they clutched each other—they shrieked.

'Where's the harm?' the big strap cried.

Five weeks ago and Bertha had never heard a joke like that. Five weeks ago she would hardly have taken in the utter meaning of that climax. Now! Something in her ticked—something went beating. She smiled—not at the indecency, not at the humour. What Bertha smiled at was the sense of liberty it gave her. She could hear stories if she liked. She could *act* stories if she liked. She was earning money—good money—she was capable and strong. Yes, she was strong, not fragile like the little thing beside her, but a big, strong girl—twenty-four—a woman grown—alive.

It seemed a long, dim time ago when all of them sat round that kitchen table to their stated meals at stated hours. Good, ample, comfortable meals. Plenty of time to eat them. No trouble getting them—that was the cook's affair—just far too much to eat and too much time to eat it in. Nothing to think about. Inertia. A comfortable place. What an age ago it seemed! And yet she had expected to spend her life like that—till she married someone! She never would have thought of 'giving in her notice' if it hadn't been for Nellie Ford. How well Bertha remembered it—that Sunday she met Nellie—a Nellie flushed, with shining eyes.

'I'm leaving,' Nellie had said to her. 'I'm leaving—for the factory!'

And Bertha had stopped, bereft of words.

'*The factory* . . . !' she had said. That day the factory had sounded like the bottomless pit. 'The factory . . . !'

'Come on,' Nellie had said, 'come on—it's fine out there. You make good money. Give in your notice—it's the life.'

And Bertha had listened helplessly, feeling the ground slipping.

'But, Nellie——' she kept saying.

'It's the life,' Nellie had kept reiterating; 'it's the life, I tell you. Come on, Bert, *sure* it's the life. Come on—it's great out there. We'll room together if you'll come.'

Then Nellie had told her hurriedly, brokenly, as they walked along that Sunday afternoon, all that she knew about the factory. What Agnes Dewie, that was maid to Lady Something once—what *she* said. 'It was great!' That's what she said. 'Liberty,' said Agnes Dewie, 'a room you paid for, good money, disrespect to everything, nothing above you—freedom. . . .'

Nellie had panted this out to Bertha. 'Come on, come *on*, Bert,' she had said; 'it's time we lived.'

And slowly the infection had seized on Bertha. The fever touched her blood—ran through it. Her mental temperature flew up. She was a big girl, a slow-grower, young for her years, with a girl's feelings in her woman's body. But Nellie Ford had touched the spring of life in her. After that Sunday when Bertha looked round the quiet, self-respecting house—she hated it. She hated the softness of it—the quietness—hated the very comfort. What did all these things matter? Nellie Ford had said: 'It's time we *lived*. . . .'

Bertha gazed upward through the window of the car—twisted and turned so that she could look right into the morning blue. The car was clear of city life. It sped along a country road. Fields were on either side, and only now and then a solitary house. Great trees stretched out bare branches.

Then in that far-off life came the giving in of the notice. Bertha remembered the old cook's sour face—that old sour face past every hope of life and living. Could one grow to look like that? Can such things be? 'You'll live to rue the day, my lady!' said the cook. And Bertha remembered how the lady at the head of things had said: 'Do you realise that you'll *regret* leaving a good place like this?' And then, more acidly: 'I wouldn't have believed it of you, Martin.' And as she turned to go: 'If you choose to reconsider——'

Regret! Reconsider! Never again would she hear bells and have to answer them. Never again would someone say to her: 'Take tea into the library, Martin.' Never again need she say: 'Yes, ma'am.' Think of it! Bertha smiled. The sun came streaming in on her—she smiled.

Liberty! Liberty to work the whole day long—ten hours at five and twenty cents an hour—in noise and grime and wet. Damp floors to walk on. Noise—distracting noise all round one. No room to turn or breathe. No time to stop. And then at lunch-time no ample comfortable meal—some little hurried hunch of something you brought with you. Hard work. Long hours. Discomfort. Strain. That was about the sum of it, of all that she had gained . . . but then, the sense of freedom! The joy of being done with cap and apron. The feeling that you could draw your breath—speak as you liked—wear overalls like men—curse if you wanted to.

Oh, the relief of it! The going home at night, dead-tired, to where you had your room. Your own! The poor, ill-cooked suppers—what a taste to them! The deep, dreamless sleep. And Sunday—if you ever got a Sunday off—when you could lie abed, no one to hunt you up, no one to call you names and quarrel with you. Just Nellie there.

What did it matter if you had no time to stop or think or be? What did anything matter if life went pulsing through you amidst dirt and noise and grime? The old life—that treading round with brush and dust-pan—that making yourself noiseless with a duster: 'Martin, see you dust well *beneath* the bed.' 'Yes, ma'am.' And now the factory! A new life with other women working round you—bare-armed—grimy—roughened—unrestrained. What a change! What a sense of broadening out! What . . . !

Bertha Martin smiled. She smiled so that a woman opposite smiled back at her; and then she realised that she was smiling. She felt life streaming to her very finger-tips. She felt the spring pass through her being—insistent and creative. She felt her blood speak to her—say things it never said when she was walking softly in the well-ordered house she helped to keep for five long, comfortable years. 'Selfish to leave me.' That was what the lady of the house had said to her. 'Selfish—you're all selfish. You think of nothing but yourselves.'

Well—why not? What if that were true? Let it go anyway. That half-dead life was there behind . . . and Bertha Martin looked out at the present. The car went scudding in the country road. There was the Factory—the Factory, with its coarse, strong, beckoning life—its noise—its dirt—its men.

Its men! And suddenly into Bertha Martin's cheek a wave of colour surged. Yesterday—was it yesterday?—that man had caught her strong, round arm as she was passing him—and held it.

Her breath came short. She felt a throbbing. She stopped smiling—and her eyes grew large.

It was the very early spring.

Then suddenly the flock of women rose—felt in the bosoms of their shirt-waists for their cigarettes and matches—surged to the door—talking—laughing—pushing one another—the older ones expostulating.

And, massed together in the slushy road, they stood, lighting up, passing their matches round—happy—noisy—fluttered—not knowing what to do with all the life that kept on surging up and breaking in them—waves of it—wave on wave. Willingly would they have fought their way to the Munitions Factory. If they had known the *Carmagnole* they would have danced it in the melting snow. . . .

It was the spring.

1919

# Nellie McClung

## 1873–1951

A prolific writer who was highly popular in her day, Nellie McClung has never been completely accepted into the Canadian literary canon and is now mostly remembered for her accomplishments as a social activist rather than for her achievements as a writer. She was involved in the most important and contested issues of her times: among the many reforms she fought for were women's suffrage, improved labour laws, temperance, birth control, medical care for children, safety in the workplace, women's property rights, and the ordination of women. McClung was largely responsible for women in Manitoba gaining both the vote and the right to run for political office. (Her province became the first to give suffrage to both married and single women.) She was a member—with Henrietta Muir Edwards, Louise McKinney, Emily Murphy, and Irene Parlby—of what came to be known as the Famous Five, a group that, by winning the Persons Case, gave Canadian women full recognition under federal law and, thus, federal enfranchisement. McClung's involvement in the Temperance movement has sometimes been seen as misguided, but it should be understood as part of her larger efforts at social amelioration. In McClung's day, when male heads of the household drank away their incomes—as many did—they left their families without food or housing or means of support (and children were plentiful in a time when birth control was both illegal and unreliable). Although Prohibition proved an unworkable solution, making the efforts of women Prohibitionists seem misdirected, they did lead to changes in social attitudes and to the creation of responsible laws regulating alcohol sales and consumption.

McClung's social activism was complemented by her writing, which often took the form of social satire. But, because the political and even homiletic dimensions of her fiction were as important to her as its aesthetic merit, it sometimes doesn't seem 'literary' by contemporary standards. She thought an important function of stories was to dramatize the common social problems her readers encountered and to show how those problems could be overcome. Her best work stands up well because she combined these didactic aims with a sharp comic wit and an observant eye that caught the follies of her time, placing her on a par with other Canadian satirists. Though McClung's sympathies were mostly aligned with Liberal Party policies, she was equally caustic about 'partyism' on both sides. This is evident in her short story 'The Live Wire', with its ironic treatment of what would later be called 'spin'. There, in the Reform newspaper,

*you might read of a distressing accident which befell one Simon Henry (also a Reformer), while that great and good man was abroad upon an errand of mercy, trying to induce a drunken man to go quietly to his home and family. Mr Henry was eulogised for his kind act, and regret was expressed that Mr Henry should have met with such rough usage while endeavouring to hold out a helping hand to one unfortunate enough to be held in the demon chains of intemperance.*

While the account in the Conservative paper read,

*We regret to hear that Simon Henry, secretary of the Young Liberal Club, got mixed up in a drunken brawl last evening and as a result will be confined to his house for a few days. We trust his injuries are not serious, as his services are indispensable to his party in the coming campaigns.*

'The Elusive Vote', the story collected here, shows how McClung's style employs a Western humour, more like that of mid-twentieth-century writer W.O. Mitchell than that of Stephen Leacock, in that she humanizes, and sympathizes with, her characters—even John Thomas Green, much as he may also be a perfect example of why women should have the vote.

Nellie Letitia Mooney was born in Ontario, but Nellie McClung was shaped by her upbringing in Western Canada—in Manitoba—where her family moved in 1880. Raised by strongly contrasting parents, she seems to have inherited a good-natured way of seeing the world from her easygoing Irish father, who was known for his wry sense of fun; her Scottish-Presbyterian mother, who had a strong work ethic and a belief in enduring in the face of adversity, provided her daughter with a powerful female role model. Although Nellie did not learn to read until she was ten, which was when she was first able to attend school, by the time she was sixteen, she was herself a schoolteacher working near Manitou, Manitoba. There, she met Anne McClung, a WCTU (Women's Christian Temperance Union) member, who became her landlady and, in 1896, her mother-in-law. After she married Robert Wesley 'Wes' McClung, who owned and ran the town's pharmacy, she stopped teaching and began a family: they eventually had five children. She became deeply involved in her church and in other organizations related to the Social Gospel movement, which focused on legal reforms benefiting workers, aid for the poor, and voting rights for women.

Wes had a breakdown in 1905, which caused them to sell the pharmacy. McClung had already begun to write short pieces for magazines and newspapers, and Anne, believing her talent could be a source of income, encouraged her to enter a short-story contest and took over Nellie's domestic duties to provide the younger woman time to write. The story McClung wrote proved the real start of her career, becoming the basis for McClung's best-selling first novel, *Sowing Seeds in Danny* (1908). (The novel's ironic title refers to the satiric portrait, in the first chapter, of a wealthy and childless woman who wants to improve the lot of the poor in her neighbourhood by seeding the young with ideals when what they really need is food and clothes.)

The income from *Sowing Seeds in Danny* was a godsend. Wes recovered his health and started a new career, working for a large insurance company: that job took the family to Winnipeg in 1911, to Edmonton in 1914, and to Calgary in 1923. McClung continued the tale of Pearlie Watson, the young girl at the centre of *Sowing Seeds in Danny*, in two more novels: *The Second Chance* (1910) and *Purple Springs* (1921). Her other novels include *When Christmas*

*Crossed 'The Peace'* (1923), and *Painted Fires* (1925). Her short fiction and her many sketches were collected in *The Black Creek Stopping House and Other Stories* (1912), *All We like Sheep* (1926), *Flowers for the Living* (1931), and *Be Good to Yourself* (1930); a new selection of her short fiction, *Stories Subversive: Through the Field with Gloves Off,* appeared in 1996. Her non-fiction includes *In Times like These* (1915), *The Next of Kin* (1917), *Three Times and Out* (1918), *Leaves from Lantern Lane* (1936), and *More Leaves from Lantern Lane* (1937). Among her last works are her memoirs, *Clearing in the West* (1935) and *The Stream Runs Fast* (1945).

McClung's success as a writer led to a career as a public speaker, a role in which she excelled by winning over listeners with a delivery that was both nuanced and somewhat informal. Her ability to inject humour into her serious topics not only eased tensions but helped McClung make her political points, even with those who disagreed with her. One particularly recalcitrant opponent who felt the sting of her wit was Sir Rodmond Roblin, the Conservative premier of Manitoba from 1900 to 1915. After he couldn't be persuaded directly by argument, McClung used his own words to turn the public against him when women from the Manitoba chapter of the Canadian Women's Press Club and the new Political Equality League staged four performances of her play, *The Women's Parliament*, to packed houses. It parodied Roblin as the head of a women-only legislature in a world in which men had no vote, and the words and arguments he uses, largely drawn from Roblin's own statements about why women should not vote, startled audiences when they now heard them applied to men. The play became a point of reference for discussions of equity in Manitoba for years.

After McClung and her family moved to Edmonton, she entered politics in order to challenge the provincial Conservatives' refusal to entertain the idea of women's suffrage. She was elected as a Liberal to the Legislative Assembly of Alberta in 1921, and served until 1926. In 1932, she and her husband retired and moved to Victoria. A heart condition brought an end to her speaking tours and eventually to her writing.

# The Elusive Vote: An Unvarnished Tale of September 21st, 1911

John Thomas Green did not look like a man on whom great issues might turn. His was a gentle soul encased in ill-fitting armour. Heavy blue eyes, teary and sad, gave a wintry droop to his countenance; his nose showed evidence of much wiping, and the need of more. When he spoke, which was infrequent, he stammered; when he walked he toed in.

He was a great and glorious argument in favor of woman suffrage; he was the last word, the *piece de resistance*; he was a living, walking, yellow banner, which shouted 'Votes for Women', for in spite of his many limitations there was one day when he towered high above the mightiest woman in the land; one day that the plain John Thomas was clothed with majesty and power; one day when he emerged from obscurity and placed an impress on the annals of our country. Once every four years John Thomas Green came forth (at the earnest solicitation of friends) and stood before kings.

The Reciprocity fight was on,[1] and nowhere did it rage more hotly than in Morton, where Tom Brown, the well-beloved and much-hated Conservative member, fought for his seat with all the intensity of his Irish blood. Politics were an incident to Tom—the real thing was the fight! and so fearlessly did he go after his assailants—and they were many—that every day greater enthusiasm prevailed among his followers, who felt it a privilege to fight for a man who fought so well for himself.

The night before the election the Committee[2] sat in the Committee Rooms and went carefully over the lists. They were hopeful but not hilarious[3]—there had been disappointments, desertions, lapses!

Billy Weaver, loyal to the cause, but of pessimistic nature, testified that Sam Cowery had been 'talkin' pretty shrewd about reciprocity', by which Billy did not mean 'shrewd' at all, but rather crooked and adverse. However, there was no mistaking Billy's meaning of the word when one heard him say it with his inimitable 'down-the-Ottaway' accent.[4] It is only the feeble written word which requires explanation.

George Burns was reported to have said he did not care whether he voted or not; if it were a wet day he might, but if it were weather for stacking he'd stack, you bet![5] This was a gross insult to the President of the Conservative Association, whose farm he had rented and lived on for the last five years, during which time there had been two elections, at both of which he had voted 'right'. The President had not thought it necessary

---

1 'Reciprocity' was the name given to the free trade battle of the time, specifically the plan to abolish protective tariffs on natural resources imported and exported between the United States and Canada. A particularly hot issue in the Prairies because grain farmers wanted increased access to the US market, free trade between the United States and Canada had been debated among the political parties since Canada's founding. In McClung's era it was the Conservatives who opposed free trade, while the Grits (the Liberals) supported it and gained control of Parliament in 1896 with a reciprocity plank in their platform. The trade agreement the Liberals had recently negotiated with the United States became a major issue in the 1911 federal election, which was ultimately won by the Conservatives, whose slogan was, 'No truck or trade with the Yankees'.

2 That is, the Conservative Party committee for the local riding.

3 Merry.

4 That is, parodying the dialect or accent of speakers who live in the Ottawa Valley.

5 That is, if it was good weather he wouldn't stop his farm work, such as stacking hay, in order to vote.

to interview him at all this time, feeling sure that he was within the pale.[6] But now it seemed that some trifler had told him that he would get more for his barley and not have to pay so much for his tobacco if Reciprocity carried, and it was reported that he had been heard to say, with picturesque eloquence, that you could hardly expect a man to cut his throat both ways by voting against it!

These and other kindred reports filled the Committee with apprehension.

The most unmoved member of the company was the redoubtable Tom himself, who, stretched upon the slippery black leather lounge, hoarse as a frog from much addressing of obdurate electors, was endeavoring to sing 'Just Before the Battle, Mother',[7] hitting the tune only in the most inconspicuous places!

The Secretary, with the list in his hand, went over the names:

'Jim Stewart—Jim's solid; he doesn't want Reciprocity, because he sent to the States once for a washing-machine for his wife, and smuggled it through from St Vincent, and when he got it here his wife wouldn't use it!

'Abe Collins—Abe's not right and never will be—he saw Sir Wilfrid once—[8]

'John Thomas Green—say, how about Jack? Surely we can corral Jack. He's working for you, Milt, isn't he?' addressing one of the scrutineers.

'Leave him to me,' said Milt, with an air of mystery; 'there's no one has more influence with Jack than me. No, he isn't with me just now, he's over with my brother Angus; but when he comes in to vote I'll be there, and all I'll have to do is to lift my eyes like this' (he showed them the way it would be done) 'and he'll vote—right.'

'How do you know he will come, though?' asked the Secretary, who had learned by much experience that many and devious are the bypaths which lead away from the polls!

'Yer brother Angus will be sure to bring him in, won't he, Milt?' asked John Gray, the trusting one, who believed all men to be brothers.

There was a tense silence.

Milt took his pipe from his mouth. 'My brother Angus,' he began, dramatically, girding himself for the effort—for Milt was an orator of Twelfth of July[9] fame—'Angus Kennedy, my brother, bred and reared, and reared and bred, in the principles of Conservatism, as my poor old father often says, has gone over—has deserted our banners, has steeped himself in the false teachings of the Grits. Angus, my brother,' he concluded, impressively, 'is—not right!'

'What's wrong with him?' asked Jim Grover, who was of an analytical turn of mind.

'Too late to discuss that now!' broke in the Secretary; 'we cannot trace Angus's downfall, but we can send out and get in John Thomas. We need his vote—it's just as good as anybody's.'

Jimmy Rice volunteered to go out and get him. Jimmy did not believe in leaving anything to chance. He had been running an auto all week and would just as soon

---

6  An idiom meaning 'safely inside the enclosure'—i.e., part of the trusted in-group (from an old use of the word *pale*, a fence that marked off a limit beyond which individuals were not supposed to venture).

7  A US Civil War song about preparing to go into battle. In the later nineteenth century, it became popular among members of the Conservative Party in the United Kingdom. Around the same time, it was often sung in Canada at Victoria Day celebrations.

8  Wilfrid Laurier, who was the leader of the Liberal Party and the prime minister of Canada from 1896 to 1911.

9  Orangeman's Day, an annual celebration (originating in Ireland) of Protestantism.

work at night as any other time. Big Jack Moore, another enthusiastic Conservative, agreed to go with him.

When they made the ten-mile run to the home of the apostate Angus, they met him coming down the path with a lantern in his hand on the way to feed his horses.

They, being plain, blunt men, unaccustomed to the amenities of election time, and not knowing how to skilfully approach a subject of this kind, simply announced that they had come for John Thomas.

'He's not here,' said Angus, looking around the circle of light that the lantern threw.

'Are you sure?' asked James Rice, after a painful pause.

'Yes,' said Angus, with exaggerated ease, affecting not to notice the significance of the question. 'Jack went to Nelson to-day, and he ain't back yet. He went about three o'clock,' went on Angus, endeavoring to patch up a shaky story with a little interesting detail. 'He took over a bunch of pigs for me that I am shippin' into Winnipeg, and he was goin' to bring back some lumber.'

'I was in Nelson to-day, Angus,' said John Moore, sternly; 'just came from there, and I did not see John Thomas.'

Angus, though fallen and misguided, was not entirely unregenerate; a lie sat awkwardly on his honest lips, and now that his feeble effort at deception had miscarried, he felt himself adrift on a boundless sea. He wildly felt around for a reply, and was greatly relieved by the arrival of his father on the scene, who, seeing the lights of the auto in the yard, had come out hurriedly to see what was the matter. Grandpa Kennedy, although nearing his ninetieth birthday, was still a man of affairs, and what was still more important on this occasion, a lifelong Conservative. Grandpa knew it was the night before the election; he also had seen what he had seen. Grandpa might be getting on, but he could see as far through a cellar door as the next one. Angus, glad of a chance to escape, went on to the stable, leaving the visiting gentlemen to be entertained by Grandpa.

Grandpa was a diplomat; he wanted to have no hard feelings with anyone.

'Good-night, boys,' he cried, in his shrill voice; he recognized the occupants of the auto and his quick brain took in the situation. 'Don't it beat all how the frost keeps off? This reminds me of the fall, 'leven years ago—we had no frost till the end of the month. I ripened three bushels of Golden Queen tomatoes!' All this was delivered in a very high voice for Angus's benefit—to show him, if he were listening, how perfectly innocent the conversation was.

Then as Angus's lantern disappeared behind the stable, the old man's voice was lowered, and he gave forth this cryptic utterance:

*'John Thomas is in the cellar.'*

Then he gaily resumed his chatter, although Angus was safe in the stable; but Grandpa knew what he knew, and Angus's woman might be listening at the back door. 'Much election talk in town, boys?' he asked, breezily.

They answered him at random. Then his voice fell again. 'Angie's dead against Brown—won't let you have John Thomas—put him down cellar soon as he saw yer lights; Angie's woman is sittin on the door knittin'—she's wors'n him—don't let on I give it away—I don't want no words with her!—Yes, it's grand weather for threshin';

won't you come on away in? I guess yer horse will stand.' The old man roared with laughter at his own joke.[10]

John Moore and James Rice went back to headquarters for further advice. Angus's woman sitting on the cellar door knitting was a contingency that required to be met with guile.

Consternation sat on the face of the Committee when they told their story. They had not counted on this. The wildest plans were discussed. Tom Stubbins began a lengthy story of an elopement that happened down at the 'Carp', where the bride made a rope of the sheets and came down from an upstairs window. Tom was not allowed to finish his narrative, though, for it was felt that the cases were not similar.

No one seemed to be particularly anxious to go back and interrupt Mrs Angus's knitting.

Then there came into the assembly one of the latest additions to the Conservative ranks, William Batters, a converted and reformed Liberal. He had been an active member of the Liberal party for many years, but at the last election he had been entirely convinced of their unworthiness by the close-fisted and niggardly way in which they dispensed the election money.

He heard the situation discussed in all its aspects. Milton Kennedy, with inflamed oratory, bitterly bewailed his brother's defection—'not only wrong himself, but leadin' others, and them innocent lambs!'—but he did not offer to go out and see his brother. The lady who sat knitting on the cellar door seemed to be the difficulty with all of them.

The reformed Liberal had a plan.

'I will go for him,' said he. 'Angus will trust me—he doesn't know I have turned. I'll go for John Thomas, and Angus will give him to me without a word, thinkin' I'm a friend,' he concluded, brazenly.

'Look at that now!' exclaimed the member elect. 'Say, boys, you'd know he had been a Grit—no honest, open-faced Conservative would ever think of a trick like that!'

'There is nothing like experience to make a man able to see every side,' said the reformed one, with becoming modesty.

An hour later Angus was roused from his bed by a loud knock on the door. Angus had gone to bed with his clothes on, knowing that these were troublesome times.

'What's the row?' he asked, when he had cautiously opened the door.

'Row!' exclaimed the friend who was no longer a friend, 'You're the man that's makin' the row. The Conservatives have 'phoned in to the Attorney-General's Department to-night to see what's to be done with you for standin' between a man and his heaven-born birthright, keeping' and confining' of a man in a cellar, owned by and closed by you!'

This had something the air of a summons, and Angus was duly impressed.

'I don't want to see you get into trouble. Angus,' Mr Batters went on; 'and the only way to keep out of it is to give him to me, and then when they come out here with a search-warrant they won't find nothin'.'

10 That is, because his 'horse' is actually a car, Rice does not need to worry about it wandering off if he leaves it unattended.

Angus thanked him warmly, and, going upstairs, roused the innocent John from his virtuous slumbers. He had some trouble persuading John, who was a profound sleeper, that he must arise and go hence; but many things were strange to him, and he rose and dressed without very much protest.

Angus was distinctly relieved when he got John Thomas off his hands—he felt he had had a merciful deliverance.

On the way to town, roused by the night air, John Thomas became communicative.

'Them lads in the automobile, they wanted me pretty bad, you bet,' he chuckled, with the conscious pride of the much-sought-after; 'but gosh, Angus fixed them. He just slammed down the cellar door on me, and says he, "Not a word out of you, Jack; you've as good a right to vote the way you want to as anybody, and you'll get it, too, you bet."'

The reformed Liberal knitted his brows. What was this simple child of nature driving at?

John Thomas rambled on: 'Tom Brown can't fool people with brains, you bet you—Angus's woman explained it all to me. She says to me, "Don't let nobody run you, Jack—and vote for Hastings. You're all right, Jack—and remember Hastings is the man. Never mind why—don't bother your head—you don't have to—but vote for Hastings." Says she, "Don't let on to Milt, or any of his folks, or Grandpa, but vote the way you want to, and that's for Hastings!"'

When they arrived in town the reformed Liberal took John Thomas at once to the Conservative Hotel, and put him in a room, and told him to go to bed, which John cheerfully did. Then he went for the Secretary, who was also in bed. 'I've got John Thomas,' he announced, 'but he says he's a Grit and is going to vote for Hastings. I can't put a dint in him—he thinks I'm a Grit, too. He's only got one idea, but it's a solid one, and that is "Vote for Hastings".'

The Secretary yawned sleepily. 'I'll not go near him. It's me for sleep. You can go and see if any of the other fellows want a job. They're all down at a ball at the station. Get one of those wakeful spirits to reason with John.'

The conspirator made his way stealthily to the station, from whence there issued the sound of music and dancing. Not wishing to alarm the Grits, many of whom were joining in the festivities, and who would have been quick to suspect that something was on foot, if they saw him prowling around, he crept up to the window and waited until one of the faithful came near. Gently tapping on the glass, he got the attention of the editor, the very man he wanted, and, in pantomime, gave him to understand that his presence was requested. The editor, pleading a terrific headache, said goodnight, or rather good-morning, to his hostess, and withdrew. From his fellow-worker who waited in the shadow of the trees outside, he learned that John Thomas had been secured in the body but not in spirit.

The newspaper man readily agreed to labor with the erring brother and hoped to be able to deliver his soul alive.

Once again was John Thomas roused from his slumbers, and not by a familiar voice this time, but by an unknown vision in evening dress.

The editor was a convincing man in his way, whether upon the subject of reciprocity or apostolic succession,[11] but John was plainly bored from the beginning, and though he offered no resistance, his repeated 'I know that!' 'That's what I said!' were more disconcerting than the most vigorous opposition. At daylight the editor left John, and he really had the headache that he had feigned a few hours before.

Then John Thomas tried to get a few winks of unmolested repose, but it was election day, and the house was early astir. Loud voices sounded through the hall. Innumerable people, it seemed, mistook his room for their own. Jack rose at last, thoroughly indignant and disposed to quarrel. He had a blame good notion to vote for Brown after all, after the way he had been treated.

When he had hastily dressed himself, discussing his grievances in a loud voice, he endeavored to leave the room, but found the door securely locked. Then his anger knew no bounds. He lustily kicked on the lower panel of the door and fairly shrieked his indignation and rage.

The chambermaid, passing, remonstrated with him by beating on the other side of the door. She was a pert young woman with a squeaky voice, and she thought she knew what was wrong with the occupant of 17. She had heard kicks on doors before.

'Quiet down, you, mister, or you'll get yourself put in the cooler—that's the best place for noisy drunks.'

This, of course, annoyed the innocent man beyond measure, but she was gone far down the hall before he could think of the retort suitable.

When she finished her upstairs work and came downstairs to peel the potatoes, she mentioned casually to the bartender that whoever he had in number 17 was 'smashin' things up pretty lively!'

The bartender went up and liberated the indignant voter, who by this time had his mind made up to vote against both Brown and Hastings, and furthermore to renounce politics in all its aspects for evermore.

However, a good breakfast and the sincere apologies of the hotel people did much to restore his good humor. But a certain haziness grew in his mind as to who was who, and at times the disquieting thought skidded through his murky brain that he might be in the enemy's camp for all he knew. Angus and Mrs Angus had said, 'Do what you think is right and vote for Hastings,' and that was plain and simple and easily understood. But now things seemed to be all mixed up.

The committee were ill at ease about him. The way he wagged his head and declared he knew what was what, you bet, was very disquieting, and the horrible fear haunted them that they were perchance cherishing a serpent in their bosom.[12]

The Secretary had a proposal: 'Take him out to Milt Kennedy's. Milt said he could work him. Take him out there! Milt said all he had to do was to raise his eyes and John Thomas would vote right.'

---

11  In those Christian churches that have bishops, 'apostolic succession' is the idea that these bishops can trace an unbroken succession of their authority from Jesus's original twelve apostles.

12  That is, were being deceived into treating someone like a child to be loved and nurtured, when they should be viewing him as a poisonous snake to be avoided.

The erstwhile Liberal again went on the road with John Thomas, to deliver him over to the authority of Milt Kennedy. If Milt could get results by simply elevating his eyebrows, Milt was the man who was needed.

Arriving at Milt's, he left the voter sitting in the buggy, while he went in search of the one who could control John's erring judgment.

While sitting there alone, another wandering thought zig-zagged through John's brain. They were making a fool of him, some way! Well, he'd let them see, b'gosh!

He jumped out of the buggy, and hastily climbed into the hay-mow. It was a safe and quiet spot, and was possessed of several convenient eye-holes through which he could watch with interest the search which immediately began.

He saw the two men coming up to the barn, and as they passed almost below him, he heard Milt say, 'Oh, sure, John Thomas will vote right—I can run him all right!—he'll do as I say. Hello, John! Where is he?'

They went into the house—they searched the barn—they called, coaxed, entreated. They ran down to the road to see if he had started back to town; he was as much gone as if he had never been!

'Are you dead sure you brought him?' Milt asked at last in desperation, as he turned over a pile of sacks in the granary.

'Gosh! ain't they lookin' some!' chuckled the elusive voter, as he watched with delight their unsuccessful endeavors to locate him. 'But there's lots of places yet that they hain't thought of; they hain't half looked for me yet. I may be in the well for all they know.' Then he began to sing to himself, 'I know something I won't tell!'

It was not every day that John Thomas Green found himself the centre of attraction, and he enjoyed the sensation.

Having lost so much sleep the night before, a great drowsiness fell on John Thomas, and curling himself up in the hay, he sank into a sweet, sound sleep.

While he lay there, safe from alarms, the neighborhood was shaken with a profound sensation. John Thomas was lost. Lost, and his vote lost with him!

Milton Kennedy, who had to act as scrutineer at the poll in town, was forced to leave home with the mystery unsolved. Before going, he 'phoned to Billy Adams, one of the faithful, and in guarded speech, knowing that he was surrounded by a cloud of witnesses,[13] broke the news! Billy Adams immediately left his stacking, and set off to find his lost compatriot.

Mrs Alex Porter lived on the next farm to Billy Adams, and being a lady of some leisure, she usually managed to get in on most of the 'phone conversations. Billy Adams' calls were very seldom overlooked by her,[14] for she was on the other side of politics, and it was always well to know what was going on. Although she did not know all that was said by the two men, she heard enough to assure her that crooked work was going on. Mrs Alex Porter declared she was not surprised. She threw her apron over her head and went to the field and told Alex. Alex was not surprised. In fact, it seems Alex had expected it!

---

13 Milton is using a phrase drawn from the Bible to suggest that he is being watched by hostile eyes (see Hebrews 12:1).

14 That is, she eavesdropped on his phone calls. At this time, most homes had shared (or party) lines, which meant that individuals could listen in on the calls of all others sharing that line.

They 'phoned in cipher to Angus, Mrs Angus being a sister of Mrs Alex Porter. Mrs Angus told them to speak out plain, and say what they wanted to, even if all the Conservatives on the line were listening. Then Mrs Porter said that John Thomas was lost over at Milt Kennedy's. They had probably drugged him or something.

Then Angus's wife said he was safe enough. Billy Batters had come and got him the night before. At the mention of Billy Batters there was a sound of suppressed mirth all along the line. Mrs Angus's sister fairly shrieked. 'Billy Batters! Don't you know he has turned Conservative!—he's working tooth and nail for Brown.' Mrs Angus called Angus excitedly. Everybody talked at once; somebody laughed; one or two swore. Mrs Porter told Milt Kennedy's wife she'd caught her eavesdropping this time sure. She'd know her cackle any place, and Milt's wife told Mrs Porter to shut up—she need-n't talk about eavesdroppers,—good land! and Mrs Porter told Mrs Milt she should try something for that voice of hers, and recommended machine oil, and Central[15] rang in and told them they'd all have their 'phones taken out if they didn't stop quarreling; and John Thomas, in the hay-mow, slept on, as peacefully as an innocent babe!

In the Committee rooms, Jack's disappearance was excitedly discussed. The Conservatives were not sure that Bill Batters was not giving them the double cross— once a Grit, always a Grit! Angus was threatening to have him arrested for abduc-tion—he had beguiled John Thomas from the home of his friends, and then carelessly lost him.

William Batters realized that he had lost favor in both places, and anxiously longed for a sight of John Thomas's red face, vote or no vote.

At four o'clock John Thomas awoke much refreshed, but very hungry. He went into the house in search of something to eat. Milton and his wife had gone into town many hours before, but he found what he wanted, and was going back to the hay-mow to finish his sleep, just as Billy Adams was going home after having cast his vote.

Billy Adams seized him eagerly, and rapidly drove back to town. Jack's vote would yet be saved to the party!

It was with pardonable pride that Billy Adams reined in his foaming team, and rushed John Thomas into the polling booth, where he was greeted with loud cheers. Nobody dare ask him where he had been—time was too precious. Milton Kennedy, scrutineer, lifted his eyebrows as per agreement. Jack replied with a petulant shrug of his good shoulder and passed in to the inner chamber.

The Conservatives were sure they had him. The Liberals were sure, too. Mrs Angus was sure Jack would vote right after the way she had reasoned with him and showed him!

When the ballots were counted, there were several spoiled ones, of course. But there was one that was rather unique. After the name of Thomas Brown, there was written in lead pencil, 'None of yer business!' which might have indicated a preference for the other name of John Hastings, only for the fact that opposite his name was the curt remark, 'None of yer business, either!'

Some thought the ballot was John Thomas Green's.

---

15  The telephone operator, who, by operating a central switchboard, put through all calls (and could listen in on them).

# Stephen Leacock
## 1869–1944

Stephen Leacock once explained his having left England at the age of six in this way: 'My parents migrated to Canada in 1876, and I decided to go with them.' We recognize in this line the ironic and often self-mocking quality that characterizes much of Leacock's best writing—the sense of deflation that comes when individuals try to assert more control over their fate than they can ever really have. Perhaps it was Leacock's early years that led him to regard the world as an unreliable place: after coming to Canada, he grew up on a farm (near Ontario's Lake Simcoe) that, as a result of his father's mismanagement, teetered continually on the edge of financial collapse. Although Leacock's mother provided the family with stability, she may also have sharpened his sense of the absurd as she engaged in her constant struggle to instill into eleven children the manners of a distant British aristocracy. The Leacock family's insecure life never reached the point of complete disaster only because occasional financial assistance from England kept the family afloat, even allowing Stephen to attend Upper Canada College in Toronto as a boarder.

As an adult, Leacock lived two lives: he was an academic first and only later a humorist. He began his teaching career at Upper Canada College (UCC) while completing a BA at the University of Toronto. He later left UCC to pursue graduate work at the University of Chicago, where he studied economics under Thorstein Veblen. His PhD completed, Leacock joined the Department of Economics and Political Science at McGill University in 1903. He gained distinction as an engaging classroom lecturer, and his first book, *Elements of Political Science* (1906), which earned him a reputation for clarity of thought and vigour of expression, soon became a standard text. In 1907, at the request of the governor general, Leacock undertook a year-long tour of the British Empire to speak on Imperial unity; upon his return, he was placed in charge of his department at McGill.

Leacock began his second career in 1910 when—against the advice of a friend who thought he would harm his scholarly reputation—he collected the occasional pieces of humour he had written for magazines and published them at his own expense as *Literary Lapses*. An immediate success, the collection was reprinted in England and the United States, as well as in Canada. Leacock quickly followed it with *Nonsense Novels* (1911), a book that gave the world his famous description of the young man who 'flung himself upon his horse and rode madly off in all directions.' His third book of humour, *Sunshine Sketches of a Little Town*, was published in 1912, after appearing as a series in the *Montreal Star*.

*Sunshine Sketches* was based on Leacock's experiences in Orillia, near which, in 1908, he had bought a farm for his annual summer holidays. His friend B.K. Sandwell later observed of the book that 'it was the only really large-scale commission ever received [by Leacock] for a fictional job to be done for a purely Canadian audience. . . . He had a wealth of material not too suitable for his American buyers.' Leacock's decision to write this book for a Canadian readership was probably the reason the book achieved neither the international popularity nor the commercial success of his others, although it is now generally regarded as his best and most unified work. It remains in print, and in 1996 and 2002, critical editions appeared. In 1914, Leacock made use, in a similar fashion, of events and scenes drawn from Montreal life for *Arcadian Adventures with the Idle Rich*, a companion volume to *Sunshine Sketches*—but he transposed the setting of that work to a US city.

For the rest of his career, Leacock worked at an intense pace, averaging a book of humour a year, as well as writing biographies, social commentary, and popular histories. The quality of his humorous writing suffered as a result of this industry, which was fuelled by a strong desire for money and prestige. In 1921, he was instrumental in organizing the Canadian Authors' Association as a means of working out a satisfactory agreement on Canadian copyright. After his enforced retirement from McGill at the age of sixty-five, Leacock, already a popular public speaker, embarked on a lecture tour of Western Canada that led to *My Discovery of the West* (1937), for which he won a Governor General's Award.

Despite its satire and comedy, *Sunshine Sketches* is Leacock's version of the 'regional idyll' that was the dominant literary form in Canada between 1900 and 1920. Although many Orillia citizens were angered by Leacock's failure to disguise the identities of the people on whom he modelled his characters, there is an evident fondness in the book for its fictional town of Mariposa—an affection most evident in the nostalgic sketch that closes the work, 'L'Envoi: The Train to Mariposa'. There, Leacock writes of how we all dream of returning to that 'little Town in the Sunshine that once we knew':

*Look from the window as you go. The city is far behind now and right and left of you there are trim farms with elms and maples near them and with tall windmills beside the old barns that you can still see in the gathering dusk. There is a dull red light from the windows of the farmstead. It must be comfortable there after the roar and clatter of the city, and only think of the still quiet of it. . . .*

*What? It feels nervous and strange to be coming here again after all these years? It must indeed. No, don't bother to look at the reflection of your face in the window-pane shadowed by the night outside. Nobody could tell you now after all these years. Your face has changed in these long years of money-getting in the city. Perhaps if you had come back now and again, just at odd times, it wouldn't have been so.*

# The Marine Excursion of the Knights of Pythias

Half-past six on a July morning? The *Mariposa Belle* is at the wharf, decked in flags, with steam up ready to start.

Excursion day!

Half-past six on a July morning, and Lake Wissanotti lying in the sun as calm as glass. The opal colours of the morning light are shot from the surface of the water.

Out on the lake the last thin threads of the mist are clearing away like flecks of cotton wool.

The long call of the loon echoes over the lake. The air is cool and fresh. There is in it all the new life of the land of the silent pine and the moving waters. Lake Wissanotti in the morning sunlight! Don't talk to me of the Italian lakes, on the Tyrol or the Swiss Alps. Take them away. Move them somewhere else. I don't want them.

Excursion Day, at half-past six of a summer morning! With the boat all decked in flags and all the people in Mariposa on the wharf, and the band in peaked caps with big cornets tied to their bodies ready to play at any minute! I say! Don't tell me about the Carnival of Venice and the Delhi Durbar.[1] Don't! I wouldn't look at them. I'd shut my eyes! For light and colour give me every time an excursion out of Mariposa down the lake to the Indian's Island out of sight in the morning mist. Talk of your Papal

---

1  During the period of the British Empire in India, a durbar was a state reception given for a British sovereign. The Coronation Durbar at Delhi for King Edward VII, which lasted from 31 December 1902 to 7 January 1903, was a highly elaborate spectacle that attracted international attention.

Zouaves[2] and your Buckingham Palace Guard! I want to see the Mariposa band in uniform and the Mariposa Knights of Pythias with their aprons and their insignia and their picnic baskets and their five-cent cigars!

Half-past six in the morning, and all the crowd on the wharf and the boat due to leave in half an hour. Notice it!—in half an hour. Already she's whistled twice (at six, and at six fifteen), and at any minute now, Christie Johnson will step into the pilot house and pull the string for the warning whistle that the boat will leave in half an hour. So keep ready. Don't think of running back to Smith's Hotel for the sandwiches. Don't be fool enough to try to go up to the Greek Store, next to Netley's, and buy fruit. You'll be left behind for sure if you do. Never mind the sandwiches and the fruit! Anyway, here comes Mr Smith himself with a huge basket of provender that would feed a factory. There must be sandwiches in that. I think I can hear them clinking. And behind Mr Smith is the German waiter from the caff[3] with another basket—indubitably lager beer; and behind him, the bartender of the hotel, carrying nothing, as far as one can see. But of course if you know Mariposa you will understand that why he looks so nonchalant and empty-handed is because he has two bottles of rye whisky under his linen duster.[4] You know, I think, the peculiar walk of a man with two bottles of whisky in the inside pockets of a linen coat. In Mariposa, you see, to bring beer to an excursion is quite in keeping with public opinion. But, whisky—well, one has to be a little careful.

Do I say that Mr Smith is here? Why, everybody's here. There's Hussell, the editor of the *Newspacket*, wearing a blue ribbon on his coat, for the Mariposa Knights of Pythias are, by their constitution, dedicated to temperance; and there's Henry Mullins, the manager of the Exchange Bank, also a Knight of Pythias, with a small flask of Pogram's Special in his hip pocket as a sort of amendment to the constitution. And there's Dean Drone, the Chaplain of the Order, with a fishing-rod (you never saw such green bass as lie among the rocks at Indian's Island), and with a trolling line in case of maskinonge,[5] and a landing-net in case of pickerel, and with his eldest daughter, Lilian Drone, in case of young men. There never was such a fisherman as the Rev. Rupert Drone.

Perhaps I ought to explain that when I speak of the excursion as being of the Knights of Pythias, the thing must not be understood in any narrow sense. In Mariposa practically everybody belongs to the Knights of Pythias just as they do to everything else. That's the great thing about the town and that's what makes it so different from the city. Everybody is in everything.

2  A troop of soldiers (eventually including more than 500 Canadian volunteers—who became the first substantial body of troops from Canada to take part in an overseas campaign), formed in 1860 to protect the Vatican. Their colourful uniforms of baggy trousers, braided jacket, and tasselled fez were patterned after the North African-inspired uniforms of the French Zouaves, who had a romantic reputation as dashing daredevils.
3  In 'The Hostelry of Mr Smith', the first of Leacock's *Sunshine Sketches*, Josh Smith, the proprietor of the local hotel, has—in order to persuade the town to support the renewal of his liquor license—opened the Ladies' and Gent's Café. (Once his licence is renewed, he fires his French chef and gets rid of all of its distinctive flourishes.) Mr Smith explains that he has patterned it after 'a real French Caff' with a 'Rat's Cooler' (his misunderstanding of rathskeller): these mistakes made by Mariposans in pronunciation (as in 'Gothey' for Goethe later in this story) are a source of humour for Leacock throughout *Sunshine Sketches*.
4  A loose full-length coat.
5  Pike.

You should see them on the seventeenth of March, for example, when everybody wears a green ribbon and they're all laughing and glad—you know what the Celtic nature is—and talking about Home Rule.[6]

On St Andrew's Day every man in town wears a thistle and shakes hands with everybody else, and you see the fine old Scotch honesty beaming out of their eyes.

And on St George's Day!—well, there's no heartiness like the good old English spirit, after all; why shouldn't a man feel glad that he's an Englishman?

Then on the Fourth of July there are stars and stripes flying over half the stores in town, and suddenly all the men are seen to smoke cigars, and to know all about Roosevelt and Bryan and the Philippine Islands.[7] Then you learn for the first time that Jeff Thorpe's people came from Massachusetts and that his uncle fought at Bunker Hill[8] (anyway Jefferson will swear it was in Dakota all right enough); and you find that George Duff has a married sister in Rochester and that her husband is all right; in fact, George was down there as recently as eight years ago. Oh, it's the most American town imaginable is Mariposa—on the fourth of July.

But wait, just wait, if you feel anxious about the solidity of the British connexion, till the twelfth of the month,[9] when everybody is wearing an orange streamer in his coat and the Orangemen (every man in town) walk in the big procession. Allegiance! Well, perhaps you remember the address they gave to the Prince of Wales[10] on the platform of the Mariposa station as he went through on his tour to the west. I think that pretty well settled that question.

So you will easily understand that of course everybody belongs to the Knights of Pythias and the Masons and Oddfellows, just as they all belong to the Snow Shoe Club and the Girls' Friendly Society.

And meanwhile the whistle of the steamer has blown again for a quarter to seven—loud and long this time, for anyone not here now is late for certain, unless he should happen to come down in the last fifteen minutes.

What a crowd upon the wharf and how they pile onto the steamer! It's a wonder that the boat can hold them all. But that's just the marvellous thing about the *Mariposa Belle*.

I don't know—I have never known—where the steamers like the *Mariposa Belle* come from. Whether they are built by Harland and Wolff of Belfast, or whether, on

---

6 Home Rule for Ireland (that is, Irish independence from British rule) was a popular cause among Irish Catholics and those sympathetic to them, and was therefore promoted when St Patrick's Day was celebrated.

7 During the Spanish-American War (1898) Theodore Roosevelt led the First US Volunteer Calvary (the 'Rough Riders') in a famous charge up San Juan Hill in Cuba. (Roosevelt subsequently became the vice president and then president of the US in 1901, following the assassination of William McKinley.) One outcome of the US victory in that war was the annexation of Philippines from Spain. Although this development stirred anti-imperialist debate in the US, pro-imperialists carried the tide of opinion. One of the strongest of the pro-imperialist speeches was made by William Jennings Bryan, who, in his 'White Man's Burden' oration on the fourth of July in 1906, argued that the US was performing the same noble service in governing the Philippines that England was performing by ruling over the people of India.

8 A famous battle (in Boston) of the American Revolutionary War.

9 July twelfth is the date of the annual Orange parade. This affirmation of Irish Protestantism is, of course, entirely contrary to the affirmation of Irish Catholicism shown by Mariposa's residents on St Patrick's Day.

10 The narrator here is apparently referring to the 1860 visit of Albert Edward, Prince of Wales, to Upper and Lower Canada, rather than to the visit of George Prince of Wales to Quebec in 1908—though the former is not likely to actually be in the living memory of those addressed.

the other hand, they are not built by Harland and Wolff of Belfast, is more than one would like to say offhand.

The *Mariposa Belle* always seems to me to have some of those strange properties that distinguish Mariposa itself. I mean, her size seems to vary so. If you see her there in the winter, frozen in the ice beside the wharf with a snowdrift against the windows of the pilot house, she looks a pathetic little thing the size of a butternut. But in the summer time, especially after you've *been* in Mariposa for a month or two, and have paddled alongside of her in a canoe, she gets larger and taller, and with a great sweep of black sides, till you see no difference between the *Mariposa Belle* and the *Lusitania*.[11] Each one is a big steamer and that's all you can say.

Nor do her measurements help you much. She draws about eighteen inches forward[12], and more than that—at least half an inch more, astern, and when she's loaded down with an excursion crowd she draws a good two inches more. And above the water—why, look at all the decks on her! There's the deck you walk onto, from the wharf, all shut in, with windows along it, and the after cabin with the long table, and above that the deck with all the chairs piled upon it, and the deck in front where the band stand round in a circle, and the pilot house is higher than that, and above the pilot house is the board with the gold name and the flag pole and the steel ropes and the flags; and fixed in somewhere on the different levels is the lunch counter where they sell the sandwiches, and the engine room, and down below the deck level, beneath the water line, is the place where the crew sleep. What with steps and stairs and passages and piles of cordwood for the engine—oh, no, I guess Harland and Wolff didn't build her. They couldn't have.

Yet even with a huge boat like the *Mariposa Belle*, it would be impossible for her to carry all of the crowd that you see in the boat and on the wharf. In reality, the crowd is made up of two classes—all of the people in Mariposa who are going on the excursion and all those who are not. Some come for the one reason and some for the other.

The two tellers of the Exchange Bank are both there standing side by side. But one of them—the one with the cameo pin and the long face like a horse—is going, and the other—with the other cameo pin and the face like another horse—is not. In the same way, Hussell of the *Newspacket* is going, but his brother, beside him, isn't. Lilian Drone is going, but her sister can't; and so on all through the crowd.

And to think that things should look like that on the morning of a steamboat accident.

How strange life is!

To think of all these people so eager and anxious to catch the steamer, and some of them running to catch it, and so fearful that they might miss it—the morning of a steamboat accident. And the captain blowing his whistle, and warning them so severely that he would leave them behind—leave them out of the accident! And everybody crowding so eagerly to be in the accident.

Perhaps life is like that all through.

11  When it was launched in June 1906, RMS *Lusitania* took the title of largest liner afloat.
12  That is, about eighteen inches of the boat is submerged.

Strangest of all to think, in a case like this, of the people who were left behind, or in some way or other prevented from going, and always afterwards told of how they had escaped being on board of the *Mariposa Belle* that day!

Some of the instances were certainly extraordinary.

Nivens, the lawyer, escaped from being there merely by the fact that he was away in the city.

Towers, the tailor, only escaped owing to the fact that, not intending to go on the excursion he had stayed in bed till eight o'clock and so had not gone. He narrated afterwards that waking up that morning at half-past five, he had thought of the excursion and for some unaccountable reason had felt glad that he was not going.

The case of Yodel, the auctioneer, was even more inscrutable. He had been to the Oddfellows' excursion on the train the week before and to the Conservative picnic the week before that, and had decided not to go on this trip. In fact, he had not the least intention of going. He narrated afterwards how the night before someone had stopped him on the corner of Nippewa and Tecumseh Streets (he indicated the very spot) and asked: 'Are you going to take in the excursion tomorrow?' and he had said, just as simply as he was talking when narrating it: 'No.' And ten minutes after that, at the corner of Dalhousie and Brock Street (he offered to lead a party of verification to the precise place) somebody else had stopped him and asked: 'Well, are you going on the steamer trip tomorrow?' Again he had answered: 'No,' apparently almost in the same tone as before.

He said afterwards that when he heard the rumour of the accident it seemed like the finger of Providence, and he fell on his knees in thankfulness.

There was the similar case of Morison (I mean the one in Glover's hardware store that married one of the Thompsons). He said afterwards that he had read so much in the papers about accidents lately—mining accidents, and aeroplanes and gasoline— that he had grown nervous. The night before his wife had asked him at supper: 'Are you going on the excursion?' He had answered: 'No, I don't think I feel like it,' and had added: 'Perhaps your mother might like to go.' And the next evening just at dusk, when the news ran through the town, he said the first thought that flashed through his head was: 'Mrs Thompson's on that boat.'

He told this right as I say it—without the least doubt or confusion. He never for a moment imagined she was on the *Lusitania* or the *Olympic* or any other boat. He knew she was on this one. He said you could have knocked him down where he stood. But no one had. Not even when he got halfway down—on his knees, and it would have been easier still to knock him down or kick him. People do miss a lot of chances.

Still, as I say, neither Yodel nor Morison nor anyone thought about there being an accident until just after sundown when they—

Well, have you ever heard the long booming whistle of a steamboat two miles out on the lake in the dusk, and while you listen and count and wonder, seen the crimson rockets going up against the sky and then heard the fire bell ringing right there beside you in the town, and seen the people running to the town wharf?

That's what the people of Mariposa saw and felt that summer evening as they watched the Mackinaw lifeboat go plunging out into the lake with seven sweeps to a side and the foam clear to the gunwale with the lifting stroke of fourteen men!

But, dear me, I am afraid that this is no way to tell a story. I suppose the true art would have been to have said nothing about the accident till it happened. But when you write about Mariposa, or hear of it, if you know the place, it's all so vivid and real, that a thing like the contrast between the excursion crowd in the morning and the scene at night leaps into your mind and you must think of it.

But never mind about the accident—let us turn back again to the morning.

The boat was due to leave at seven. There was no doubt about the hour—not only seven, but seven sharp. The notice in the *Newspacket* said: 'The boat will leave sharp at seven'; and the advertising posters on the telegraph poles on Missinaba Street that began, 'Ho, for Indian's Island!' ended up with the words: 'Boat leaves at seven sharp.' There was a big notice on the wharf that said: 'Boat leaves sharp on time.'

So at seven, right on the hour, the whistle blew loud and long, and then at seven-fifteen three short peremptory blasts, and at seven-thirty one quick angry call—just one—and very soon after that they cast off the last of the ropes and the *Mariposa Belle* sailed off in her cloud of flags, and the band of the Knights of Pythias, timing it to a nicety, broke into the 'Maple Leaf for Ever!'

I suppose that all excursions when they start are much the same. Anyway, on the *Mariposa Belle* everybody went running up and down all over the boat with deck chairs and camp stools and baskets, and found places, splendid places to sit, and then got scared that there might be better ones and chased off again. People hunted for places out of the sun and when they got them swore that they weren't going to freeze to please anybody; and the people in sun said that they hadn't paid fifty cents to get roasted. Others said that they hadn't paid fifty cents to get covered with cinders, and there were still others who hadn't paid fifty cents to get shaken to death with the propeller.

Still, it was all right presently. The people seemed to get sorted out into the places on the boat where they belonged. The women, the older ones, all gravitated into the cabin on the lower deck and by getting round the table with needlework, and with all the windows shut, they soon had it, as they said themselves, just like being at home.

All the young boys and the toughs and the men in the band got down on the lower deck forward, where the boat was dirtiest and where the anchor was and the coils of rope.

And upstairs on the after deck there were Lilian Drone and Miss Lawson, the high-school teacher, with a book of German poetry—Gothey I think it was—and the bank teller and the young men.

In the centre, standing beside the rail, were Dean Drone and Dr Gallagher, looking through binocular glasses at the shore.

Up in front on the little deck forward of the pilot house was a group of the older men, Mullins and Duff and Mr Smith in a deck chair, and beside him Mr Golgotha Gingham, the undertaker of Mariposa, on a stool. It was part of Mr Gingham's principles to take in an outing of this sort, a business matter, more or less—for you never know what may happen at these water parties. At any rate, he was there in a neat suit of black, not, of course, his heavier or professional suit, but a soft clinging effect as of burnt paper that combined gaiety and decorum to a nicety.

'Yes,' said Mr Gingham, waving his black glove in a general way towards the shore, 'I know the lake well, very well. I've been pretty much all over it in my time.'

'Canoeing?' asked somebody.

'No,' said Mr Gingham, 'not in a canoe.' There seemed a peculiar and quiet meaning in his tone.

'Sailing, I suppose,' said somebody else.

'No,' said Mr Gingham. 'I don't understand it.'

'I never knowed that you went onto the water at all, Gol,' said Mr Smith, breaking in.

'Ah, not now,' explained Mr Gingham; 'it was years ago, the first summer I came to Mariposa. I was on the water practically all day. Nothing like it to give a man an appetite and keep him shape.'

'Was you camping?' asked Mr Smith.

'We camped at night,' assented the undertaker, 'but we put in practically the whole day on the water. You see, we were after a party that had come up here from the city on his vacation and gone out in a sailing canoe. We were dragging. We were up every morning at sunrise, lit a fire on the beach and cooked breakfast, and then we'd light our pipes and be off with the net for a whole day. It's great life,' concluded Mr Gingham wistfully.

'Did you get him?' asked two or three together.

There was a pause before Mr Gingham answered.

'We did,' he said '—down in the reeds past Horseshoe Point. But it was no use. He turned blue on me right away.'

After which Mr Gingham fell into such a deep reverie that the boat had steamed another half-mile down the lake before anybody broke the silence again. Talk of this sort—and after all what more suitable for a day on the water?—beguiled the way.

Down the lake, mile by mile over the calm water, steamed the *Mariposa Belle*. They passed Poplar Point where the high sand-banks are with all the swallows' nests in them, and Dean Drone and Dr Gallagher looked at them alternately through the binocular glasses, and it was wonderful how plainly one could see the swallows and the banks and the shrubs—just as plainly as with the naked eye.

And a little farther down they passed the Shingle Beach, and Dr Gallagher, who knew Canadian history, said to Dean Drone that it was strange to think that Champlain had landed there with his French explorers three hundred years ago;[13] and Dean Drone, who didn't know Canadian history, said it was stranger still to think that the hand of the Almighty had piled up the hills and rocks long before that; and Dr Gallagher said it was wonderful how the French had found their way through such a

---

13  The French explorer Samuel de Champlain (1567–1635); he travelled to Lake Simcoe in 1615, visiting a Huron village in the area close to the site of present-day Orillia.

pathless wilderness; and Dean Drone said that it was wonderful also to think that the Almighty had placed even the smallest shrub in its appointed place. Dr Gallagher said it filled him with admiration. Dean Drone said it filled him with awe. Dr Gallagher said he'd been full of it ever since he was a boy and Dean Drone said so had he.

Then a little further, as the *Mariposa Belle* steamed on down the lake, they passed the Old Indian Portage where the great grey rocks are; and Dr Gallagher drew Dean Drone's attention to the place where the narrow canoe track wound up from the shore to the woods, and Dean Drone said he could see it perfectly well without the glasses.

Dr Gallagher said that it was just here that a party of five hundred French had made their way with all their baggage and accoutrements across the rocks of the divide and down to the Great Bay. And Dean Drone said that it reminded him of Xenophon leading his ten thousand Greeks over the hill passes of Armenia down to the sea.[14] Dr Gallagher said that he had often wished he could have seen and spoken to Champlain, and Dean Drone said how much he regretted to have never known Xenophon.

And then after that they fell to talking of relics and traces of the past, and Dr Gallagher said that if Dean Drone would come round to his house some night he would show him some Indian arrow heads that he had dug up in his garden. And Dean Drone said that if Dr Gallagher would come round to the rectory any afternoon he would show him a map of Xerxes' invasion of Greece.[15] Only he must come some time between the Infant Class and the Mothers' Auxiliary.

So presently they both knew that they were blocked out of one another's houses for some time to come, and Dr Gallagher walked forward and told Mr Smith, who had never studied Greek, about Champlain crossing the rock divide.

Mr Smith turned his head and looked at the divide for half a second and then said he had crossed a worse one up north back of the Wahnipitae and that the flies were Hades—and then went on playing freezeout poker with the two juniors in Duff's bank.

So Dr Gallagher realized that that's always the way when you try to tell people things, and that as far as gratitude and appreciation goes one might as well never read books or travel anywhere or do anything.

In fact, it was at this very moment that he made up his mind to give the arrows to the Mariposa Mechanics' Institute—they afterwards became, as you know, the Gallagher Collection. But, for the time being, the doctor was sick of them and wandered off around the boat and watched Henry Mullins showing George Duff how to make a John Collins[16] without lemons, and finally went and sat down among the Mariposa band and wished that he hadn't come.

So the boat steamed on and the sun rose higher and higher, and the freshness of the morning changed into the full glare of noon, and pretty soon the *Mariposa Belle* had floated out onto the lake again and they went on to where the lake began to narrow in at its foot, just where the Indian's Island is—all grass and trees and with a log

---

14  In 401 BCE, Xenophon, one of the leaders of Greek mercenaries, guided some 10,000 men across the middle of the Persian empire, away from a battle that had ended in a draw, with heavy military losses for the Persians.

15  'Xerxes': ruler of the Persian Empire in 486 BCE, invaded Greek territories with a massive army and navy. A turning point was the battle of Thermopylae in which a large part of his army was destroyed. His navy also in pieces, Xerxes withdrew. A 'map of Xerxes invasion' would be a map of losses.

16  A John Collins is a mixed drink made with sweet gin, lemon juice, and sugar.

wharf running into the water. Below it the Lower Ossawippi runs out of the lake, and quite near are the rapids, and you can see down among the trees the red brick of the power house and hear the roar of the leaping water.

.The Indian's Island itself is all covered with trees and tangled vines, and the water about it is so still that it's all reflected double and looks the same either way up. Then when the steamer's whistle blows as it comes into the wharf, you hear it echo among the trees of the island, and reverberate back from the shores of the lake.

The scene is all so quiet and still and unbroken, that Miss Cleghorn[17]—the sallow girl in the telephone exchange, that I spoke of—said she'd like to be buried there. But all the people were so busy getting their baskets and gathering up their things that no one had time to attend to it.

I mustn't even try to describe the landing and the boat crunching against the wooden wharf and all the people running to the same side of the deck and Christie Johnson calling out to the crowd to keep to the starboard and nobody being able to find it. Everyone who has been on a Mariposa excursion knows all about that.

Nor can I describe the day itself and the picnic under the trees. There were speeches afterwards, and Judge Pepperleigh gave such offence by bringing in Conservative politics that a man called Patriotus Canadiensis wrote and asked for some of the invaluable space of the *Mariposa Times-Herald* and exposed it.

I should say that there were races too, on the grass on the open side of the island, graded mostly according to ages—races for boys under thirteen and girls over nineteen and all that sort of thing. Sports are generally conducted on that plan in Mariposa. It is realized that a woman of sixty has an unfair advantage over a mere child.

Dean Drone managed the races and decided the ages and gave out the prizes; the Wesleyan minister helped, and he and the young student, who was relieving in the Presbyterian Church, held the string at the winning point.

They had to get mostly clergymen for the races because all the men had wandered off, somehow, to where they were drinking lager beer out of two kegs stuck on pine logs among the trees.

But if you've ever been on a Mariposa excursion you know all about these details anyway.

So the day wore on and presently the sun came through the trees on a slant and the steamer whistle blew with a great puff of white steam and all the people came straggling down to the wharf and pretty soon the *Mariposa Belle* had floated out onto the lake again and headed for the town, twenty miles away.

I suppose you have often noticed the contrast there is between an excursion on its way out in the morning and what it looks like on the way home.

17 Miss Cleghorn is mentioned in the preceding sketch, 'The Speculations of Jefferson Thorpe', where she serves as a foil for Myra Thorpe, with whom she works in the Telephone Exchange: 'Myra had golden hair and a Greek face. . . . As you saw her swinging up the street to the Telephone Exchange . . . there was style written all over her—the kind of thing that Mariposa recognized and did homage to. . . . [Y]ou could understand why it was that the commercial travellers would stand round the Exchange calling up all sorts of impossible villages, and waiting about so pleasant and genial!—it made one realize how naturally good-tempered men are. And then when Myra would go off duty and Miss Cleghorn, who was sallow, would come on, the commercial men would be off again like autumn leaves.' To be 'sallow' is to have a sickly yellow complexion.

In the morning everybody is so restless and animated and moves to and from all over the boat and asks questions. But coming home, as the afternoon gets later and later and the sun sinks beyond the hills, all the people seem to get so still and quiet and drowsy.

So it was with the people on the *Mariposa Belle*. They sat there on the benches and the deck chairs in little clusters, and listened to the regular beat of the propeller and almost dozed off asleep as they sat. Then when the sun set and the dusk drew on, it grew almost dark on the deck and so still that you could hardly tell there was anyone aboard.

And if you had looked at the steamer from the shore or from one of the islands, you'd have seen the row of lights from the cabin windows shining on the water and the red glare of the burning hemlock from the funnel, and you'd have heard the soft thud of the propeller miles away over the lake.

Now and then, too, you could have heard them singing on the steamer—the voices of the girls and the men blended into unison by the distance, rising and falling in long-drawn melody: '*O—Can-a-da—O—Can-a-da*'.

You may talk as you will about the intoning choirs of your European cathedrals, but the sound of '*O—Can-a-da*', borne across the waters of a silent lake at evening is good enough for those of us who know Mariposa.

I think that it was just as they were singing like this: '*O—Can-a-da*', that word went round that the boat was sinking.

If you have ever been in any sudden emergency on the water, you will understand the strange psychology of it—the way in which what is happening seems to become known all in a moment without a word being said. The news is transmitted from one to the other by some mysterious process.

At any rate, on the *Mariposa Belle* first one and then the other heard that the steamer was sinking. As far as I could ever learn the first of it was that George Duff, the bank manager, came very quietly to Dr Gallagher and asked him if he thought that the boat was sinking. The doctor said no, that he had thought so earlier in the day but that he didn't now think that she was.

After that Duff, according to his own account, had said to Macartney, the lawyer, that the boat was sinking, and Macartney said that he doubted it very much.

Then somebody came to Judge Pepperleigh and woke him up and said that there was six inches of water in the steamer and that she was sinking. And Pepperleigh said it was perfect scandal and passed the news on to his wife and she said that they had no business to allow it and that if the steamer sank that was the last excursion she'd go on.

So the news went all round the boat and everywhere the people gathered in groups and talked about it in the angry and excited way that people have when a steamer is sinking on one of the lakes like Lake Wissanotti.

Dean Drone, of course, and some others were quieter about it, and said that one must make allowances and that naturally there were two sides to everything. But most of them wouldn't listen to reason at all. I think, perhaps, that some of them were frightened. You see the last time but one that the steamer had sunk, there had been a man drowned and it made them nervous.

What? Hadn't I explained about the depth of Lake Wissanotti? I had taken it for granted that you knew; and in any case parts of it are deep enough, though I don't suppose in this stretch of it from the big reed beds up to within a mile of the town wharf, you could find six feet of water in it if you tried. Oh, pshaw! I was not talking about a steamer sinking in the ocean and carrying down its screaming crowds of people into the hideous depths of green water. Oh, dear me, no! That kind of thing never happens on Lake Wissanotti.

But what does happen is that the *Mariposa Belle* sinks every now and then, and sticks there on the bottom till they get things straightened up.

On the lakes round Mariposa, if a person arrives late anywhere and explains that the steamer sank, everybody understands the situation.

You see when Harland and Wolff built the *Mariposa Belle*, they left some cracks in between the timbers that you fill up with cotton waste every Sunday. If this is not attended to, the boat sinks. In fact, it is part of the law of the province that all the steamers like the *Mariposa Belle* must be properly corked[18]—I think that is the word—every season. There are inspectors who visit all the hotels in the province to see that it is done.

So you can imagine now that I've explained it a little straighter, the indignation of the people when they knew that the boat had come uncorked and that they might be stuck out there on a shoal or a mud-bank half the night.

I don't say either that there wasn't any danger; anyway, it doesn't feel very safe when you realize that the boat is settling down with every hundred yards that she goes, and you look over the side and see only the black water in the gathering night.

Safe! I'm not sure now that I come to think of it that it isn't worse than sinking in the Atlantic. After all, in the Atlantic there is wireless telegraphy, and a lot of trained sailors and stewards. But out on Lake Wissanotti—far out, so that you can only just see the lights of the town away off to the south—when the propeller comes to a stop—and you hear the hiss of steam as they start to rake out the engine fires to prevent explosion—and when you turn from the red glare that comes from the furnace doors as they open them, to the black dark that is gathering over the lake—and there's a night wind beginning to run among the rushes—and you see the men going forward to the roof of the pilot house to send up the rockets to rouse the town—safe? Safe yourself, if you like; as for me, let me once get back to Mariposa again, under the night shadow of the maple trees, and this shall be the last, last time I'll go on Lake Wissanotti.

Safe! Oh, yes! Isn't it strange how safe other people's adventures seem after they happen? But you'd have been scared, too, if you'd been there just before the steamer sank, and seen them bringing up all the women on to the top deck.

I don't see how some of the people took it so calmly; how Mr Smith, for instance, could have gone on smoking and telling how he'd had a steamer 'sink on him' on Lake Nipissing and a still bigger one, a side-wheeler, sink on him in Lake Abbitibbi.

Then, quite suddenly, with a quiver, down she went. You could feel the boat sink, sink—down, down—would it never get to the bottom? The water came flush up to

---

18 A malapropism for 'caulked'; also slang for very drunk.

the lower deck, and then—thank heaven—the sinking stopped and there was the *Mariposa Belle* safe and tight on a reed bank.

Really, it made one positively laugh! It seemed so queer and, anyway, if a man has a sort of natural courage, danger makes him laugh. Danger? pshaw! fiddlesticks! everybody scouted the idea. Why, it is just the little things like this that give zest to a day on the water.

Within half a minute they were all running round looking for sandwiches and cracking jokes and talking of making coffee over the remains of the engine fires.

I don't need to tell at length how it all happened after that.

I suppose the people on the *Mariposa Belle* would have had to settle down there all night or till help came from the town, but some of the men who had gone forward and were peering out into the dark said that it couldn't be more than a mile across the water to Miller's Point. You could almost see it over there to the left—some of them, I think, said 'off on the port bow', because you know when you get mixed up in these marine disasters, you soon catch the atmosphere of the thing.

So pretty soon they had the davits swung out over the side and were lowering the old lifeboat from the top deck into the water.

There were men leaning out over the rail of the *Mariposa Belle* with lanterns that threw the light as they let her down, and the glare fell on the water and the reeds. But when they got the boat lowered, it looked such a frail, clumsy thing as one saw it from the rail above, that the cry was raised: 'Women and children first!' For what was the sense, if it should turn out that the boat wouldn't even hold women and children, of trying to jam a lot of heavy men into it?

So they put in mostly women and children and the boat pushed out into the darkness so freighted down it would hardly float.

In the bow of it was the Presbyterian student who was relieving the minister, and he called out that they were in the hands of Providence. But he was crouched and ready to spring out of them at the first moment.

So the boat went and was lost in the darkness except for the lantern in the bow that you could see bobbing on the water. Then presently it came back and they sent another load, till pretty soon the decks began to thin out and everybody got impatient to be gone.

It was about the time that the third boat-load put off that Mr Smith took a bet with Mullins for twenty-five dollars, that he'd be home in Mariposa before the people in the boats had walked round the shore.

No one knew just what he meant, but pretty soon they saw Mr Smith disappear down below the lowest part of the steamer with a mallet in one hand and a big bundle of marline in the other.

They might have wondered more about it, but it was just at this time that they heard the shouts from the rescue boat—the big Mackinaw lifeboat—that had put out from the town with fourteen men at the sweeps when they saw the first rockets go up.

I suppose there is always something inspiring about a rescue at sea, or on the water.

After all, the bravery of the lifeboat man is the true bravery—expended to save life, not to destroy it.

Certainly they told for months after of how the rescue boat came out to the *Mariposa Belle*.

I suppose that when they put her in the water the lifeboat touched it for the first time since the old Macdonald Government placed her on Lake Wissanotti.

Anyway, the water poured in at every seam. But not for a moment—even with two miles of water between them and the steamer—did the rowers pause for that.

By the time they were halfway there the water was almost up to the thwarts, but they drove her on. Panting and exhausted (for mind you, if you haven't been in a fool boat like that for years, rowing takes it out of you), the rowers stuck to their task. They threw the ballast over and chucked into the water the heavy cork jackets and lifebelts that encumbered their movements. There was no thought of turning back. They were nearer to the steamer than the shore.

'Hang to it, boys,' called the crowd from the steamer's deck, and hang they did.

They were almost exhausted when they got them; men leaning from the steamer threw them ropes and one by one every man was hauled aboard just as the lifeboat sank under their feet.

Saved! by heaven, saved by one of the smartest pieces of rescue work ever seen on the lake.

There's no use describing it; you need to see rescue work of this kind by lifeboats to understand it.

Nor were the lifeboat crew the only ones that distinguished themselves.

Boat after boat and canoe after canoe had put out from Mariposa to the help of the steamer. They got them all.

Pupkin, the other bank teller with a face like a horse, who hadn't gone on the excursion—as soon as he knew that the boat was signalling for help and that Miss Lawson was sending up rockets—rushed for a row boat, grabbed an oar (two would have hampered him)—and paddled madly out into the lake. He struck right out into the dark with the crazy skiff almost sinking beneath his feet. But they got him. They rescued him. They watched him, almost dead with exhaustion, make his way to the steamer, where he was hauled up with ropes. Saved! Saved!

They might have gone on that way half the night, picking up the rescuers, only, at the very moment when the tenth load of people left for the shore—just as suddenly and saucily as you please, up came the *Mariposa Belle* from the mud bottom and floated.

*Floated?*

Why, of course she did. If you take a hundred and fifty people off a steamer that has sunk, and if you get a man as shrewd as Mr Smith to plug the timber seams with mallet and marline, and if you turn ten bandsmen of the Mariposa band onto your hand pump on the bow of the lower decks—float? why, what else can she do?

Then, if you stuff in hemlock into the embers of the fire that you were raking out, till it hums and crackles under the boiler, it won't be long before you hear the propeller thud—thudding at the stern again, and before the long roar of the steam whistle echoes over to the town.

And so the *Mariposa Belle*, with all steam up again and with the long train of sparks careering from the funnel, is heading for the town.

But no Christie Johnson at the wheel in the pilot house this time.

'Smith! Get Smith!' is the cry.

Can he take her in? Well, now! Ask a man who has had steamers sink on him in half the lakes from Temiscaming to the Bay, if he can take her in? Ask a man who has run a York boat down the rapids of the Moose when the ice is moving, if he can grip the steering wheel of the *Mariposa Belle*? So there she steams safe and sound to the town wharf!

Look at the lights and the crowds! If only the federal census taker could count us now! Hear them calling and shouting back and forward from the deck to the shore! Listen! There is the rattle of the shore ropes as they get them ready, and there's the Mariposa band—actually forming in a circle on the upper deck just as she docks, and the leader with his baton—one—two—ready now—

'O CAN-A-DA!'

1912

---

# L.M. Montgomery
## 1874–1942

Lucy Maud Montgomery, now known world-wide as the author of *Anne of Green Gables* (1908), was a fifth-generation Prince Edward Islander. Her childhood resembled that of several of her heroines, most particularly Emily (whose life is chronicled in a series of books beginning with *Emily of New Moon*, 1923). Her mother died when Montgomery was two, and her father left her behind with her maternal grandparents when he moved to Saskatchewan shortly after (he remarried and began a new family). Her grandparents were harsh and critical of the child, causing her to turn inward at a young age and to begin to write stories. Educated at Prince of Wales College, Charlottetown, and at Dalhousie University, Montgomery taught school in PEI and worked briefly for the Halifax *Daily Echo* (1901–2) before returning home to care for her grandmother.

Montgomery began publishing poems and stories while still a teenager, but she had difficulty getting her first novel, *Anne of Green Gables*, into print. However, once she did find a publisher (L.C. Page, a US company), her story of a spirited and imaginative orphan's passage from childhood into adolescence was an immediate success: within five months, it went through six printings, selling 19,000 copies and eliciting praise from Mark Twain, among others. It has now been translated into at least fifteen languages, and its heroine, Anne Shirley, is a cult hero in Japan. Its seven sequels include *Anne of Avonlea* (1909), *Anne of the Island* (1915), and *Anne of Ingleside* (1939).

After the death of her grandmother in 1911, Montgomery married the Rev. Ewan Macdonald and moved to Leaskdale, Ontario. She continued to pursue her writing career while taking care of a young family and performing the duties of a minister's wife.

The Emily series, which followed *Emily of New Moon* with *Emily Climbs* (1925) and *Emily's Quest* (1927), brought Montgomery continued popularity and recognition, as did later books for young readers such as *Pat of Silver Bush* (1933) and *Jane of Lantern Hill* (1937). *The Story Girl* (1911), from which the story reprinted in this anthology comes, is one of Montgomery's several collections of short stories. (One of these—*Further Chronicles of Avonlea*, 1920—became the occasion of a nine-year legal battle with her first publisher, which Montgomery ultimately won.) She wrote two novels for adults: *The Blue Castle* (1926) and *A Tangled Web* (1931), which were less successful, and also produced a volume of poetry, *The Watchman and Other Poems* (1916). Among her many posthumously published works are *The Road to Yesterday* (1974), *The Doctor's Sweetheart and Other Stories* (1979), *The Alpine Path: The Story of My Career* (1974; a collection of autobiographical magazine articles), and five volumes of selections from her journals. These published journals have been much admired and have deepened our understanding of Montgomery by showing the shadows (including her growing restiveness because her 'publishers keep me at this sort of stuff because it sells. . . . they claim that the public, having become used to this from my pen, would not tolerate a change' [26 December 1918] and, especially in her later years, her husband's declining mental health) that sometimes hung over the woman whose pastoral landscapes hold few hints of darkness.

Like later writers, such as the novelist Hugh MacLennan, Montgomery is important in part because she wrote about a particular place within the Canadian landscape, giving Canadians vivid depictions of places and individuals in their world at a time when such representations were not yet common. While the nostalgic quality of her rural idylls may make them seem backward looking, Montgomery created within the body of her work a picture of modern girlhood that is itself as important as any one of her books. Anne, Emily, Pat, Jane, and the Story Girl captured the imagination of twentieth-century readers (not just those who were adolescent and female) in much the same way Mark Twain's earlier depictions of Tom Sawyer and Huckleberry Finn—also the subject of several sequels—provided an image of boyhood in a changing United States. Just as endangered American definitions of masculinity and nationhood are played out in Huck's innocence of social restraint and his restless boundary crossing in the face of the impending loss of the frontier—and the imaginative freedom it symbolized—so in Montgomery's young women, readers found individuals similarly testing the restraints of conformity and discovering new outlets at a time of changing social structures. Because the emerging society will force Montgomery's girls to grow up with the knowledge that they will no longer be insulated from the world, they must find a way to exist within social constraints without compromising their values and intelligence; and they must learn to become self-sufficient. If for Huck and the American male he spoke to, the world is free yet somehow diminishing, for Montgomery's newly modern girls, the world is restraining yet expanding, and the women who read her fiction knew their horizons were broadening.

## The Story Girl

*The Story Girl* is a good example of the way Montgomery's work functions in a sphere that goes beyond fiction for young readers. It captures a timeless world in PEI and also shows us the development of a new kind of woman, the Story Girl, who shakes hands 'with an air of frank comradeship, which was very different from the shy, feminine advances' of other girls. The framing device of this collection of stories—the trip of two brothers, Beverley and Felix, to their father's old PEI home (with 'the glamour of old family traditions and tales . . . lending its magic to all sights and sounds around us') and their adventures with a group of children, including the coquettish Felicity and her opposite number, the master storyteller known to the neighbourhood as the Story Girl (she is another of Montgomery's orphaned girls)—creates a container for remembered tales that show the character of the early days of Prince Edward Island. Of the Story Girl herself, the young boy who narrates the frame tells us,

*Never had we heard a voice like hers. Never, in all my life since, have I heard such a voice. I cannot describe it. I might say it was clear; I might say it was sweet; I might say it was vibrant and far-reaching and bell-like; all this would be true, but would give you no real idea of the peculiar quality which made the Story Girl's voice what it was.*

*If voices had colour, hers would have been like a rainbow. It made words live. Whatever she said became a breathing entity, not a mere verbal statement or utterance.*

In 'How Betty Sherman Won a Husband', the Story Girl tells an old curmudgeon (and the other children, who have reluctantly come along) a story about one of his ancestors. In *The Alpine Path*, Montgomery explains that the tale is based on the experiences of her own great-grandmother, Betsy Penman. The horse and cutter that Donald Fraser takes in the Story Girl's narrative were much less romantic in real life: a 'half-broken steer, hitched to a rude, old wood-sled.' And Montgomery adds, 'If Betsy were alive today, I have no doubt, she would be an ardent suffragette. The most advanced feminist could hardly spurn old conventions more effectually than she did when she proposed to David.'

# How Betty Sherman Won a Husband

The rest of us did not share the Story Girl's enthusiasm regarding our call on Mr Campbell. We secretly dreaded it. If, as was said, he detested children, who knew what sort of a reception we might meet?

Mr Campbell was a rich, retired farmer, who took life easily. He had visited New York and Boston, Toronto and Montreal; he had even been as far as the Pacific coast. Therefore he was regarded in Carlisle as a much travelled man; and he was known to be 'well read' and intelligent. But it was also known that Mr Campbell was not always in a good humour. If he liked you there was nothing he would not do for you; if he disliked you—well, you were not left in ignorance of it. In short, we had the impression that Mr Campbell resembled the famous little girl with the curl in the middle of her forehead. 'When he was good, he was very, very good, and when he was bad he was horrid.' What if this were one of his horrid days?

'He can't *do* anything to us, you know,' said the Story Girl. 'He may be rude, but that won't hurt any one but himself.'

'Hard words break no bones,' observed Felix philosophically.

'But they hurt your feelings. *I* am afraid of Mr Campbell,' said Cecily candidly.

'Perhaps we'd better give up and go home,' suggested Dan.

'You can go home if you like,' said the Story Girl scornfully. 'But *I* am going to see Mr Campbell. I know I can manage him. But if I have to go alone, and he gives me anything, I'll keep it all for my own collection, mind you.'[1]

That settled it. We were not going to let the Story Girl get ahead of us in the matter of collecting.

---

1 In an earlier story in the volume, we are told that the children's 'teacher thought it would be an excellent thing to have a library in connection with the school; and he suggested that each of the pupils should try to see how much money he or she could raise for the project during the month of June. We might earn it by honest toil, or gather it in by contributions levied on our friends,' and that: 'The result was a determined rivalry as to which pupil should collect the largest sum.'

Mr Campbell's housekeeper ushered us into his parlour and left us. Presently Mr Campbell himself was standing in the doorway, looking us over. We took heart of grace.[2] It seemed to be one of his good days, for there was a quizzical smile on his broad, clean-shaven, strongly-featured face. Mr Campbell was a tall man, with a massive head, well thatched with thick, black hair, gray-streaked. He had big, black eyes, with many wrinkles around them, and a thin, firm, long-lipped mouth. We thought him handsome, for an old man.

His gaze wandered over us with uncomplimentary indifference until it fell on the Story Girl, leaning back in an armchair. She looked like a slender red lily in the unstudied grace of her attitude. A spark flashed into Mr Campbell's black eyes.

'Is this a Sunday School deputation?' he inquired rather ironically.

'No. We have come to ask a favour of you,' said the Story Girl.

The magic of her voice worked its will on Mr Campbell, as on all others. He came in, sat down, hooked his thumb into his vest pocket, and smiled at her.

'What is it?' he asked.

'We are collecting for our school library, and we have called to ask you for a contribution,' she replied.

'Why should *I* contribute to your school library?' demanded Mr Campbell.

This was a poser for us. Why should he, indeed? But the Story Girl was quite equal to it. Leaning forward, and throwing an indescribable witchery into tone and eyes and smile, she said,

'Because a lady asks you.'

Mr Campbell chuckled.

'The best of all reasons,' he said. 'But see here, my dear young lady, I'm an old miser and curmudgeon, as you may have heard. I *hate* to part with my money, even for a good reason. And I *never* part with any of it, unless I am to receive some benefit from the expenditure. Now, what earthly good could I get from your three by six school library? None whatever. But I shall make you a fair offer. I have heard from my housekeeper's urchin of a son that you are a 'master hand' to tell stories. Tell me one, here and now. I shall pay you in proportion to the entertainment you afford me. Come now, and do your prettiest.'

There was a fine mockery in his tone that put the Story Girl on her mettle instantly. She sprang to her feet, an amazing change coming over her. Her eyes flashed and burned; crimson spots glowed in her cheeks.

'I shall tell you the story of the Sherman girls, and how Betty Sherman won a husband,' she said.

We gasped. Was the Story Girl crazy? Or had she forgotten that Betty Sherman was Mr Campbell's own great-grandmother, and that her method of winning a husband was not exactly in accordance with maidenly traditions.

But Mr Campbell chuckled again.

'An excellent test,' he said. 'If you can amuse *me* with that story you must be a wonder. I've heard it so often that it has no more interest for me than the alphabet.'

2  Took courage.

'One cold winter day, eighty years ago,' began the Story Girl without further parley, 'Donald Fraser was sitting by the window of his new house, playing his fiddle for company, and looking out over the white, frozen bay before his door. It was bitter, bitter cold, and a storm was brewing. But, storm, or no storm, Donald meant to go over the bay that evening to see Nancy Sherman. He was thinking of her as he played "Annie Laurie", for Nancy was more beautiful than the lady of the song. "Her face, it is the fairest that e'er the sun shone on," hummed Donald—and oh, he thought so, too! He did not know whether Nancy cared for him or not. He had many rivals. But he knew that if she would not come to be the mistress of his new house no one else ever should. So he sat there that afternoon and dreamed of her, as he played sweet old songs and rollicking jigs on his fiddle.

'While he was playing a sleigh drove up to the door, and Neil Campbell came in. Donald was not overly glad to see him, for he suspected where he was going. Neil Campbell, who was Highland Scotch and lived down at Berwick, was courting Nancy Sherman, too; and, what was far worse, Nancy's father favoured him, because he was a richer man than Donald Fraser. But Donald was not going to show all he thought— Scotch people never do—and he pretended to be very glad to see Neil, and made him heartily welcome.

'Neil sat down by the roaring fire, looking quite well satisfied with himself. It was ten miles from Berwick to the bay shore, and a call at a half way house[3] was just the thing. Then Donald brought out the whisky. They always did that eighty years ago, you know. If you were a woman, you could give your visitors a dish of tea; but if you were a man and did not offer them a "taste" of whisky, you were thought either very mean or very ignorant.

' "You look cold," said Donald, in his great, hearty voice. "Sit nearer the fire, man, and put a bit of warmth in your veins. It's bitter cold the day. And now tell me the Berwick news. Has Jean McLean made up with her man yet? And is it true that Sandy McQuarrie is to marry Kate Ferguson? 'Twill be a match now! Sure, with her red hair, Sandy will not be like to lose his bride past finding."

'Neil had plenty of news to tell. And the more whisky he drank the more he told. He didn't notice Donald was not taking much. Neil talked on and on, and of course he soon began to tell things it would have been much wiser not to tell. Finally he told Donald that he was going over the bay to ask Nancy Sherman that very night to marry him. And if she would have him, then Donald and all the folks should see a wedding that *was* a wedding.

'Oh, wasn't Donald taken aback! This was more than he had expected. Neil hadn't been courting Nancy very long, and Donald never dreamed he would propose to her *quite* so soon.

'At first Donald didn't know what to do. He felt sure deep down in his heart, that Nancy liked *him*. She was very shy and modest, but you know a girl can let a man see she likes him without going out of her way. But Donald knew that if Neil proposed first he would have the best chance. Neil was rich and the Shermans were poor, and old Elias Sherman would have the most to say in the matter. If he told Nancy she must

---

3 A house situated midway between the beginning and the end of a journey; a convenient stopping point.

take Neil Campbell she would never dream of disobeying him. Old Elias Sherman was a man who had to be obeyed. But if Nancy had only promised some one else first her father would not make her break her word.

'Wasn't it a hard plight for poor Donald? But he was a Scotchman, you know, and it's pretty hard to stick a Scotchman long. Presently a twinkle came into his eyes, for he remembered that all was fair in love and war. So he said to Neil, oh, so persuasively,

' "Have some more, man, have some more. 'Twill keep the heart in you in the teeth of that wind. Help yourself. There's plenty more where that came from."

'Neil didn't want *much* persuasion. He took some more, and said slyly,

' "Is it going over the bay the night that yourself will be doing?"

'Donald shook his head.

' "I had thought of it," he owned, "but it looks a wee like a storm, and my sleigh is at the blacksmith's to be shod. If I went it must be on Black Dan's back, and he likes a canter over the ice in a snow-storm as little as I. His own fireside is the best place for a man to-night, Campbell. Have another taste, man, have another taste."

'Neil went on "tasting", and that sly Donald sat there with a sober face, but laughing eyes, and coaxed him on. At last Neil's head fell forward on his breast, and he was sound asleep. Donald got up, put on his overcoat and cap, and went to the door.

' "May your sleep be long and sweet, man," he said, laughing softly, "and as for the waking, 'twill be betwixt you and me."

'With that he untied Neil's horse, climbed into Neil's sleigh, and tucked Neil's buffalo robe about him.

' "Now, Bess, old girl, do your bonniest," he said. "There's more than you know hangs on your speed. If the Campbell wakes too soon Black Dan could show you a pair of clean heels for all your good start. On, my girl."

'Brown Bess went over the ice like a deer, and Donald kept thinking of what he should say to Nancy—and more still of what she would say to him. *Suppose* he was mistaken. *Suppose* she said "no"!

' "Neil will have the laugh on me then. Sure he's sleeping well. And the snow is coming soon. There'll be a bonny swirl on the bay ere long. I hope no harm will come to the lad if he starts to cross. When he wakes up he'll be in such a fine Highland temper that he'll never stop to think of danger. Well, Bess, old girl, here we are. Now, Donald Fraser, pluck up heart and play the man. Never flinch because a slip of a lass looks scornful at you out of the bonniest dark-blue eyes on earth."

'But in spite of his bold words Donald's heart was thumping as he drove into the Sherman yard. Nancy was there, milking a cow by the stable door, but she stood up when she saw Donald coming. Oh, she was very beautiful! Her hair was like a skein of golden silk, and her eyes were as blue as the gulf water when the sun breaks out after a storm. Donald felt more nervous than ever. But he knew he must make the most of his chance. He might not see Nancy alone again before Neil came. He caught her hand and stammered out,

' "Nan, lass, I love you. You may think 'tis a hasty wooing, but that's a story I can tell you later maybe. I know well I'm not worthy of you, but if true love could make a man worthy there'd be none before me. Will you have me, Nan?"

'Nancy didn't *say* she would have him. She just *looked* it, and Donald kissed her right there in the snow.

'The next morning the storm was over. Donald knew Neil must be soon on his track. He did not want to make the Sherman house the scene of a quarrel, so he resolved to get away before the Campbell came. He persuaded Nancy to go with him to visit some friends in another settlement. As he brought Neil's sleigh up to the door he saw a black speck far out on the bay and laughed.

' "Black Dan goes well, but he'll not be quick enough," he said.

'Half an hour later Neil Campbell rushed into the Sherman kitchen and oh, how angry he was! There was nobody there but Betty Sherman, and Betty was not afraid of him. She was never afraid of anybody. She was very handsome, with hair as brown as October nuts and black eyes and crimson cheeks; and she had always been in love with Neil Campbell herself.

' "Good morning, Mr Campbell," she said, with a toss of her head. "It's early abroad you are. And on Black Dan, no less! Was I mistaken in thinking that Donald Fraser said once that his favourite horse should never be backed by any man but him? But doubtless a fair exchange is no robbery, and Brown Bess is a good mare in her way."

' "Where is Donald Fraser?" said Neil, shaking his fist. "It's him I'm seeking, and it's him I will be finding. Where is he, Betty Sherman?"

' "Donald Fraser is far enough away by this time," mocked Betty. "He is a prudent fellow, and has some quickness of wit under that sandy thatch of his. He came here last night at sunset, with a horse and sleigh not his own, or lately gotten, and he asked Nan in the stable yard to marry him. Did a man ask *me* to marry him at the cow's side, with a milking pail in my hand, it's a cold answer he'd get for his pains. But Nan thought differently, and they sat late together last night, and 'twas a bonny story Nan wakened me to hear when she came to bed—the story of a braw[4] lover who let his secret out when the whisky was above the wit, and then fell asleep while his rival was away to woo and win his lass. Did you ever hear a like story, Mr Campbell?"

' "Oh, yes," said Neil fiercely. "It is laughing at me over the country side and telling that story that Donald Fraser will be doing, is it? But when I meet him it is not laughing he will be doing. Oh, no. There will be another story to tell!"

' "Now, don't meddle with the man," cried Betty. "What a state to be in because one good-looking lass likes sandy hair and gray eyes better than Highland black and blue! You have not the spirit of a wren, Neil Campbell. Were I you, I would show Donald Fraser that I could woo and win a lass as speedily as any Lowlander of them all; that I would! There's many a girl would gladly say 'yes' for your asking. And here stands one! Why not marry *me*, Neil Campbell? Folks say I'm as bonny as Nan—and I could love you as well as Nan loves her Donald—ay, and ten times better!"

'What do you suppose the Campbell did? Why, just the thing he ought to have done. He took Betty at her word on the spot; and there was a double wedding soon after. And it is said that Neil and Betty were the happiest couple in the world—happier even than Donald and Nancy. So all was well because it ended well!'

4  Brave, splendid, worthy (Scottish).

The Story Girl curtsied until her silken skirts swept the floor. Then she flung herself in her chair and looked at Mr Campbell, flushed, triumphant, daring.

The story was old to us. It had once been published in a Charlottetown paper, and we had read in Aunt Olivia's scrapbook, where the Story Girl had learned it. But we had listened entranced. I have written down the bare words of the story, as she told it; but I can never reproduce the charm and colour and spirit she infused into it. It *lived* for us. Donald and Neil, Nancy and Betty, were there in that room with us. We saw the flashes of expression on their faces, we heard their voices, angry or tender, mocking or merry, in Lowland and Highland accent. We realized all the mingled coquetry and feeling and defiance and archness in Betty Sherman's daring speech. We had even forgotten all about Mr Campbell.

That gentlemen, in silence, took out his wallet, extracted a note therefrom, and handed it gravely to the Story Girl.

'There are five dollars for you,' he said, 'and your story was well worth it. You *are* a wonder. Some day you will make the world realize it. I've been about a bit, and heard some good things, but I've never enjoyed anything more than that threadbare old story I heard in my cradle. And now, will you do me a favour?'

'Of course,' said the delighted Story Girl.

'Recite the multiplication table for me,' said Mr Campbell.

We stared. Well might Mr Campbell be called eccentric. What on earth did he want the multiplication table recited for? Even the Story Girl was surprised. But she began promptly, with twice one and went through it to twelve times twelve. She repeated it simply, but her voice changed from one tone to another as each in succession grew tired. We had never dreamed that there was so much in the multiplication table. As she announced it, the fact that three times three was nine was exquisitely ridiculous, five times six almost brought tears to our eyes, eight times seven was the most tragic and frightful thing ever heard of, and twelve times twelve rang like a trumpet call to victory.

Mr Campbell nodded his satisfaction.

'I thought you could do it,' he said. 'The other day I found this statement in a book. "Her voice would have made the multiplication table charming!" I thought of it when I heard yours. I didn't believe it before, but I do now.'

Then he let us go.

'You see,' said the Story Girl as we went home, 'you need never be afraid of people.'

'But we are not all Story Girls,' said Cecily.

That night we heard Felicity talking to Cecily in their room.

'Mr Campbell never noticed one of us except the Story Girl,' she said, 'but if *I* had put on *my* best dress as she did maybe she wouldn't have taken all the attention.'

'Could you ever do what Betty Sherman did, do you suppose?' asked Cecily absently.

'No; but I believe the Story Girl could,' answered Felicity rather snappishly.

1911

# Frederick Philip Grove

## 1879–1948

Frederick Philip Grove was a writer not only devoted to the idea of literary realism—that is, to the depiction of fictional characters, events, and milieus in such an unidealized way as to convince the reader that the narrative was based in real life and was objective and accurate—but to applying such 'realism' to the presentation of his own life story. His two apparently auto-biographical books, *A Search for America* (1927) and *In Search of Myself* (1946; it received the Governor General's Award for non-fiction) were regarded as generally accurate accounts when they were published. They are now, how-ever, recognized as more fiction than fact.

According to *In Search of Myself*, Grove was born in 1871 in Russia of mixed Swedish, Scottish, and English descent, and was edu-cated in Paris, Munich, and Rome. The son of a wealthy Swedish landowner, he came to North America in 1891, and, after working for some months as a waiter in Toronto, began an odyssey that carried him across the North American continent in a twenty-year search for an identity and a true home. In *A Search for America*, he describes how, drawn by the American myth of equal opportunity, his search became a quest for an idealized 'America' as defined by Lincoln and Thoreau, which para-doxically leads him in the end to choose Canada, finding it the place in North America where the positive values of an agrarian order still endured, as opposed to the 'graft . . . cruelty . . . failure' that, by the beginning of the twen-tieth century, seemed to him to have corrupted a once-noble American way of living.

Grove's 'realist' presentation of himself as a simple man who, through difficult experience, comes to find a simple and healthful rural life, one where hard work and moral integrity are their own reward, was in sharp contrast to the more romantic existence that we now know he himself led as a young man. In 1973, Douglas O. Spettigue's biography, *F.P.G.: The European Years*, revealed the background of the man who

had transformed himself into Frederick Philip Grove. Spettigue had discovered that his name before he came to North America was Felix Paul Greve, and that he had been born—eight years later than 'Grove'—in Radomno, a German town on the Russian border. Greve was raised in Hamburg, educated in the famous Gymnasium Johanneum, and attended univer-sities in Bonn and Munich—where he studied classical philology and archaeology and was part of several literary circles that blossomed in early-twentieth-century Germany. Though his literary interests brought him at least a marginal living translating English and French texts into German, he was an unprincipled young man who deceitfully borrowed large sums from friends (one incident led to his serving a year in prison for fraud) and who double-sold at least one of his translations. He also formed a trian-gular relationship with Else and August Endell, and the three lived together in Switzerland, France, and Berlin.

While living in Europe, Greve began his career as a writer with *Wanderungen* (1902), a book of poems, and (in the same year) *Helena und Damon*, a verse drama, and followed these with two novels, *Fanny Essler* (1905) and *Maurermeister Ihles Haus* (1906). In 1909, with his irregular financial practices catching up with him again, he faked a suicide, adopted a new name, and fled to the United States, where Else followed him a year later. He seems to have lived with her for a while on a farm in Kentucky, before leaving her in 1911. In 1912, he emerged in Manitoba, as 'Grove'. Else, for her part, made her way to New York, married again, and became a well-known participant in the avant-garde Dada movement, which embraced delib-erate nonsense in the name of art.

Grove chose a life very different from Else's. In Manitoba, he became a teacher; and married a fellow teacher, Catherine Wiens, in 1914. He attended the University of Manitoba part-time, graduating in 1922 with a BA in

French and German. As early as 1914, he had become part of the German-Canadian community, publishing an essay in the German-language newspaper *Der Nordwesten*. However, although he never entirely lost his European identity or his connections to its culture (he and André Gide had a long correspondence), to the Canadian reading public, he was thought of as a pioneer writer rather than as an immigrant author. His early non-fiction accounts of life in Manitoba—*Over Prairie Trails* (1922) and *The Turn of the Year* (1923)—his occasional short stories, and his four prairie novels—*Settlers of the Marsh* (1925), *Our Daily Bread* (1928), *Yoke of Life* (1930), and *Fruits of the Earth* (1933)—show us why his commitment to a realistic, unsentimental treatment of prairie life and his deliberate use of language that doesn't strive for literary elegance made Grove one of the founders of prairie realism, a mode of writing that had a powerful influence on twentieth-century Canadian fiction.

As with early realists in Europe and America, the frankness of his fiction got him into trouble with the moral arbiters of his time: in particular, *Settlers of the Marsh* was condemned as pornographic. The part of the novel considered most offensive—a striking passage about a prairie wife who deliberately induces abortions by engaging in punishing work—now seems to readers simply one of the many instances in which Grove was responding compassionately and sensitively to the suffering and deprivation that was endured by women on lonely northern farms.

In his depiction of pioneer men, Grove was more ambivalent. He showed that in the monumental task of clearing the land there lay the possibility of acts of noble stoicism and even grandeur, and that the common materials of daily rural life could, therefore, be given epic sweep, even take on mythic dimensions. But he also depicted the ways in which the sense of a heroic contest with the environment could lead men to great folly.

Grove and his wife had one daughter, Phyllis May, who died of appendicitis in 1927, shortly before she was twelve. Two years later, he quit teaching and moved to Ontario to become a full-time writer. The couple settled

first in Ottawa, where Grove founded the short-lived Ariston Press and where their son Leonard was born, and then on a farm north of Lake Simcoe. Although he never gained the financial security he sought, he continued to write and publish until he died.

All of Grove's prairie writing deals in some ways with change—whether the changing aspects of the natural cycle or the tremendous social and technological transformations that were affecting the fabric of life around him. In *Two Generations* (1939) and *The Master of the Mill* (1944), the two novels set in Ontario after he moved there, the difficult demands of pioneer life are no longer his subject; instead, the way technological change and new economic structures disrupt the family and produce social conflicts becomes more important. In particular, *The Master of the Mill* offers a trenchant critique of monopoly capitalism.

Grove's last novel, *Consider Her Ways*, is a social satire in the form of an allegory about ants: published in 1947, the year before his death, it marked a departure from his realistic mode. His short stories remained uncollected until they were gathered by Desmond Pacey as *Tales from the Margin* (1971). He was also a frequent public speaker and his speeches were published as *It Needs to be Said* (1929). In them, Grove emphasizes his commitment to realism in opposition to romance, and explains his tragic view of life: 'It remains my impression—as, American authors excepted, it is the universal verdict of mankind—that all of us who conceive a great aim must necessarily fail and fall short of achieving it.' The last of the pieces collected there, 'Nationhood', was a speech Grove gave to more than twenty Canadian Clubs while travelling across the country. In it, he argued that Canada was achieving real nationhood at last; that it had to resist the influence of the United States; and that there was a distinctive Canadian character, which could best be seen among 'plain, rough people of the prairies.'

The sketch that follows is one of seven that make up *Over Prairie Trails*. Each tells of one of Grove's weekend trips between the school where he taught to the house where his wife and daughter waited. In the Author's Preface, Grove wrote,

*I procured a buggy and horse and went 'home' on Fridays, after school was over, to return to my town on Sunday evening—covering thus, while the season was clement and allowed straight cross-country driving, coming and going, a distance of sixty-eight miles. Beginning with the second week of January this distance was raised to ninety miles because . . . the straight cross-country roads became impassable through snow.*

*These drives, the fastest of which was made in somewhat over four hours and the longest of which took me nearly eleven . . . soon became what made my life worth living. . . . I made thirty-six of these trips: seventy-two drives in all. I think I could still rehearse every smallest incident of every single one of them. With all their weird-ness, with all their sometimes dangerous adventure—most of them were made at night, and with hardly ever any regard being paid to the weather*

*or to the state of the roads—they stand out in the vast array of memorable trifles that constitute the story of my life as among the most memorable ones. Seven drives seem, as it were, lifted above the mass of others as worthy to be described in some detail.*

'Snow' is an account of the most difficult of these trips, a heroic contest against a hostile climate; it is an excellent example of Grove's realist writing, objective in its detailing of the northern Manitoba milieu, while using its close observations to suggest larger ideas.

In 1932, Grove returned to the material of 'Snow' in a short story by the same name. (It has become Grove's most often reprinted story.) It pairs strikingly with the earlier sketch, showing now not the heroic exuberance of overcoming nature but the potentially tragic consequences of challenging the harsh prairie winter storms.

## Snow

The blizzard started on Wednesday morning. It was that rather common, truly western combination of a heavy snowstorm with a blinding northern gale—such as piles the snow in hills and mountains and makes walking next to impossible.

I cannot exactly say that I viewed it with unmingled joy. There were special reasons for that. It was the second week in January; when I had left 'home' the Sunday before, I had been feeling rather bad; so my wife would worry a good deal, especially if I did not come at all. I knew there was such a thing as its becoming quite impossible to make the drive. I had been lost in a blizzard once or twice before in my lifetime. And yet, so long as there was the least chance that horse-power and human will-power combined might pull me through at all, I was determined to make or anyway to try it.

At noon I heard the first dismal warning. For some reason or other I had to go down into the basement of the school. The janitor, a highly efficient but exceedingly bad-humoured cockney, who was dissatisfied with all things Canadian because 'in the old country we do things differently'—whose sharp tongue was feared by many, and who once remarked to a lady teacher in the most casual way, 'If you *was* a lidy, I'd wipe my boot on you!'—this selfsame janitor, standing by the furnace, turned slowly around, showed his pale and hollow-eyed face, and smiled a withering and commiserating smile. 'Ye won't go north this week,' he remarked—not without sympathy, for somehow he had taken a liking to me, which even prompted him off and on to favour me with caustic expressions of what he thought of the school board and the leading citizens of the town. I, of course, never encouraged him in his communicativeness which seemed to be just what he would expect, and no rebuff ever goaded him into the slightest show of resentment. 'We'll see,' I said briefly. 'Well, Sir,' he repeated apodeictically,[1] 'ye won't.' I smiled and went out.

But in my classroom I looked from the window across the street. Not even in broad daylight could you see the opposite houses or trees. And I knew that, once a storm like that sets in, it is apt to continue for days at a stretch. It was one of those orgies in which Titan Wind indulges ever so often on our western prairies. I certainly needed something to encourage me, and so, before leaving the building, I went upstairs to the third story and looked through a window which faced north. But, though I was now above the drifting layer, I could not see very far here either; the snowflakes were small and like little round granules, hitting the panes of the windows with little sounds of 'ping-ping'; and they came, driven by a relentless gale, in such numbers that they blotted out whatever was more than two or three hundred yards away.

The inhabitant of the middle latitudes of this continent has no data to picture to himself what a snowstorm in the north may be. To him snow is something benign that comes soft-footedly over night, and on the most silent wings like an owl, something that suggests the sleep of Nature rather than its battles. The further south you go, the more, of course, snow loses of its aggressive character.

At the dinner table in the hotel I heard a few more disheartening words. But after four I defiantly got my tarpaulin out and carried it to the stable. If I had to run the risk of getting lost, at least I was going to prepare for it. I had once stayed out, snowbound, for a day and a half, nearly without food and altogether without shelter; and I was not going to get thus caught again. I also carefully overhauled my cutter.[2] Not a bolt but I tested it with a wrench; and before the stores were closed, I bought myself enough canned goods to feed me for a week should through any untoward accident the need arise. I always carried a little alcohol stove, and with my tarpaulin I could convert my cutter within three minutes into a windproof tent. Cramped quarters, to be sure, but better than being given over to the wind at thirty below!

More than any remark on the part of friends or acquaintances one fact depressed me when I went home. There was not a team in town which had come in from the country. The streets were deserted: the stores were empty. The north wind and the snow had the town to themselves.

On Thursday the weather was unchanged. On the way to the school I had to scale a snowdrift thrown up to a height of nearly six feet, and, though it was beginning to harden, from its own weight and the pressure of the wind, I still broke in at every step and found the task tiring in the extreme. I did my work, of course, as if nothing oppressed me, but in my heart I was beginning to face the possibility that, even if I tried, I might fail to reach my goal. The day passed by. At noon the school-children, the teachers, and a few people hurrying to the post-office for the mail lent a fleeting appearance of life to the street. It nearly cheered me; but soon after four the whole town again took on that deserted look which reminded me of an abandoned mining camp. The lights in the store windows had something artificial about them, as if they were merely painted on the canvas-wings of a stage-setting. Not a team came in all day.

1  As if based on incontrovertible evidence.
2  A light horse-drawn sleigh.

On Friday morning the same. Burroughs[3] would have said that the weather had gone into a rut. Still the wind whistled and howled through the bleak, dark, hollow dawn; the snow kept coming down and piling up, as if it could not be any otherwise. And as if to give notice of its intentions, the drift had completely closed up my front door. I fought my way to the school and thought things over. My wife and I had agreed, if ever the weather should be so bad that there was danger in going at night, I was to wait till Saturday morning and go by daylight. Neither one of us ever mentioned the possibility of giving the attempt up altogether. My wife probably understood that I would not bind myself by any such promise. Now even on this Friday I should have liked to go by night, if for no other reason, then for the experience's sake; but I reflected that I might get lost and not reach home at all. The horses knew the road—so long as there was any road; but there was none now. I felt it would not be fair to wife and child. So, reluctantly and with much hesitation, but definitely at last, I made up my mind that I was going to wait till morning. My cutter was ready—I had seen to that on Wednesday. As soon as the storm had set in, I had instinctively started to work in order to frustrate its designs.

At noon I met in front of the post-office a charming lady who with her husband and a young Anglican curate constituted about the only circle of real friends I had in town. 'Why!' I exclaimed, 'what takes you out into this storm, Mrs _____?' 'The desire', she gasped against the wind and yet in her inimitable way, as if she were asking a favour, 'to have you come to our house for tea, my friend. You surely are not going this week?' 'I am going to go to-morrow morning at seven,' I said. 'But I shall be delighted to have tea with you and Mr _____.' I read her at a glance. She knew that in not going out at night I should suffer—she wished to help me over the evening, so I should not feel too much thwarted, too helpless, and too lonesome. She smiled. 'You really want to go? But I must not keep you. At six, if you please.' And we went our ways without a salute, for none was possible at this gale-swept corner.

After four o'clock I took word to the stable to have my horses fed and harnessed by seven in the morning. The hostler[4] had a tale to tell. 'You going out north?' he enquired although he knew perfectly well I was. 'Of course,' I replied. 'Well,' he went on, 'a man came in from ten miles out; he was half dead; come, look at his horses! He says, in places the snow is over the telephone posts.' 'I'll try it anyway,' I said. 'Just have the team ready. I know what I can ask my horses to do. If it cannot be done, I shall turn back, that is all.'

When I stepped outside again, the wind seemed bent upon shaking the strongest faith. I went home to my house across the bridge and dressed. As soon as I was ready, I allowed myself to be swept past stable, past hotel and post-office till I reached the side street which led to the house where I was to be the guest.

How sheltered, homelike, and protected everything looked inside. The hostess, as usual, was radiantly amiable. The host settled back after supper to talk old country. The Channel Islands, the French Coast, Kent and London—those were from common knowledge our most frequently recurring topics. Both host and hostess, that was easy to

---

3 John Burroughs (1837–1921), a popular and prolific American nature writer to whom Grove alludes several times in *Over Prairie Trails*.
4 Stableman.

see, were bent upon beguiling the hours of their rather dark-humoured guest. But the howling gale outside was stronger than their good intentions. It was not very long before the conversation got around—reverted, so it seemed—to stories of storms, or being lost, of nearly freezing. The boys were sitting with wide eager eyes, afraid they might be sent to bed before the feast of yarns was over. I told one or two of my most thrilling escapes, the host contributed a few more, and even the hostess had had an experience, driving on top of a railroad track for several miles, I believe, with a train, snowbound, behind her. I leaned over. 'Mrs _____,' I said, 'do not try to dissuade me. I am sorry to say it, but it is useless. I am bound to go.' 'Well,' she said, 'I wish you would not.' 'Thanks,' I replied and looked at my watch. It was two o'clock. 'There is only one thing wrong with coming to have tea in this home,' I continued and smiled; 'it is so hard to say good-bye.'

I carefully lighted my lantern and got into my wraps. The wind was howling dismally outside. For a moment we stood in the hall, shaking hands and paying the usual compliments; then one of the boys opened the door for me; and in stepping out I had one of the greatest surprises. Not far from the western edge of the world there stood the setting half-moon in a cloudless sky; myriads of stars were dusted over the vast, dark blue expanse, twinkling and blazing at their liveliest. And though the wind still whistled and shrieked and rattled, no snow came down, and not much seemed to drift. I pointed to the sky, smiled, nodded, and closed the door. As far as the drifting of the snow went, I was mistaken, as I found out when I turned to the north, into the less sheltered street, past the post-office, hotel, and stable. In front of a store I stopped to read a thermometer which I had found halfways reliable the year before. It read minus thirty-two degrees. . . .[5]

It was still dark, of course, when I left the house on Saturday morning to be on my way. Also, it was cold, bitterly cold, but there was very little wind. In crossing the bridge which was swept nearly clean of snow I noticed a small, but somehow ominous-looking drift at the southern end. It had such a disturbed, lashed-up appearance. The snow was still loose, yet packed just hard enough to have a certain degree of toughness. You could no longer swing your foot through it: had you run into it at any great speed, you would have fallen; but as yet it was not hard enough to carry you. I knew that kind of a drift; it is treacherous. On a later drive one just like it, only built on a vastly larger scale, was to lead to the first of a series of little accidents which finally shattered my nerve. That was the only time that my temerity failed me. I shall tell you about that drive later on.[6]

At the stable I went about my preparations in a leisurely way. I knew that a supreme test was ahead of myself and the horses, and I meant to have daylight for tackling it. Once more I went over the most important bolts; once more I felt and pulled at every strap in the harness. I had a Clark footwarmer[7] and made sure that it functioned properly. I pulled the flaps of my military fur cap down over neck, ears, and cheeks. I tucked a pillow under the sweater over my chest and made sure that my leggings

5 The ellipsis mark is frequently used by Grove to punctuate these sketches. There are no editorial deletions.
6 In the seventh and concluding sketch, 'Skies and Scares', Grove tells this story of how 'the cumulative effect of three mishaps, one following the other,' combined with 'the aspect of the skies' and 'broke my nerve that night'.
7 A kind of metal box containing coal.

clasped my furlined moccasins well. Then, to prevent my coat from opening even under the stress of motion, just before I got into the cutter, I tied a rope around my waist.

The hostler brought the horses into the shed. They pawed the floor and snorted with impatience. While I rolled my robes about my legs and drew the canvas curtain over the front part of the box, I weighed Dan with my eyes. I had no fear for Peter, but Dan would have to show to-day that he deserved the way I had fed and nursed him. Like a chain, the strength of which is measured by the strength of its weakest link, my team was measured by Dan's pulling power and endurance. But he looked good to me as he danced across the pole and threw his head, biting back at Peter who was teasing him.

The hostler was morose and in a biting mood. Every motion of his seemed to say, 'What is the use of all this? No teamster would go out on a long drive in this weather, till the snow has settled down; and here a schoolmaster wants to try it.'

At last he pushed the slide doors aside, and we swung out. I held the horses tight and drove them into that little drift at the bridge to slow them down right from the start.

The dawn was white, but with a strictly localised angry glow where the sun was still hidden below the horizon. In a very few minutes he would be up, and I counted on making that first mile just before he appeared.

This mile is a wide, well levelled road, but ever so often, at intervals of maybe fifty to sixty yards, steep and long promontories of snow had been flung across—some of them five to six feet high. They started at the edge of the field to the left where a rank growth of shrubby weeds gave shelter for the snow to pile in. Their base, alongside the fence, was broad, and they tapered across the road, with a perfectly flat top, and with concave sides of a most delicate, smooth, and finished looking curve, till at last they ran out into a sharp point, mostly beyond the road on the field to the right.

The wind plays strange pranks with snow; snow is the most plastic medium it has to mould into images and symbols of its moods. Here one of these promontories would slope down, and the very next one would slope upward as it advanced across the open space. In every case there had been two walls, as it were, of furious blow, and between the two a lane of comparative calm, caused by the shelter of a clump of brush or weeds, in which the snow had taken refuge from the wind's rough and savage play. Between these capes of snow there was an occasional bare patch of clean swept ground. Altogether there was an impression of barren, wild, bitter-cold windiness about the aspect that did not fail to awe my mind; it looked inhospitable, merciless, and cruelly playful.

As yet the horses seemed to take only delight in dashing through the drifts, so that the powdery crystals flew aloft and dusted me all over. I peered across the field to the left, and a curious sight struck me. There was apparently no steady wind at all, but here and there, and every now and then a little swirl of snow would rise and fall again. Every one of them looked for all the world like a rabbit reconnoitring in deep grass. It jumps up on its hindlegs, while running, peers out, and settles down again. It was as if the snow meant to have a look at me, the interloper at such an early morning hour. The snow was so utterly dry that it obeyed the lightest breath; and whatever there was of motion in the air, could not amount to more than a cat's-paw's sudden reach.

At the exact moment when the snow where it stood up highest became suffused with a rose-red tint from the rising sun, I arrived at the turn to the correction line.[8] Had I been a novice at the work I was engaged in, the sight that met my eye might well have daunted me. Such drifts as I saw here should be broken by drivers who have short hauls to make before the long distance traveller attempts them. From the fence on the north side of the road a smoothly curved expanse covered the whole of the road allowance and gently sloped down into the field at my left. Its north edge stood like a cliff, the exact height of the fence, four feet I should say. In the centre it rose to probably six feet and then fell very gradually, whaleback fashion, to the south. Not one of the fence posts to the left was visible. The slow emergence of the tops of these fence posts became during the following week, when I drove out here daily, a measure for me of the settling down of the drift. I believe I can say from my observations that if no new snow falls or drifts in, and if no very considerable evaporation takes place, a newly piled snowdrift, undisturbed except by wind-pressure, will finally settle down to about from one-third to one-half of its original height, according to the pressure of the wind that was behind the snow when it first was thrown down. After it has, in this contracting process, reached two-thirds of its first height, it can usually be relied upon to carry horse and man.

The surface of this drift, which covered a ditch besides the grade and its grassy flanks, showed that curious appearance that we also find in the glaciated surfaces of granite rock and which, in them, geologists call exfoliation. In the case of rock it is the consequence of extreme changes in temperature. The surface sheet in expanding under sudden heat detaches itself in large, leaflike layers. In front of my wife's cottage up north there lay an exfoliated rock in which I watched the process for a number of years. In snow, of course, the origin of this appearance is entirely different; snow is laid down in layers by the waves in the wind. 'Adfoliation' would be a more nearly correct appellation of the process. But from the analogy of the appearance I shall retain the more common word and call it exfoliation. Layers upon layers of paperlike sheets are superimposed upon each other, their edges often 'cropping out' on sloping surfaces; and since these edges, according to the curvatures of the surfaces, run in wavy lines, the total aspect is very often that of 'moire' silk.

I knew the road as well as I had ever known a road. In summer there was a grassy expanse some thirty feet wide to the north; then followed the grade, flanked to the south by a ditch; and the tangle of weeds and small brush beyond reached right up to the other fence. I had to stay on or rather above the grade; so I stood up and selected the exact spot where to tackle it. Later, I knew, this drift would be harmless enough; there was sufficient local traffic here to establish a well-packed trail. At present, however, it still seemed a formidable task for a team that was to pull me over thirty-three miles or more. Besides it was a first test for my horses; I did not know yet how they would behave in snow.

But we went at it. For a moment things happened too fast for me to watch details. The horses plunged wildly and reared on their hind feet in a panic, straining against

---

8 A correction made along the longitudinal line of a survey to compensate for the curvature of the earth. On the Prairies, roads are generally laid out along survey lines; north-south roads, therefore, turn east-west for a short distance along the correction line.

each other, pulling apart, going down underneath the pole, trying to turn and retrace their steps. And meanwhile the cutter went sharply up at first, as if on the crest of a wave, then toppled over into a hole made by Dan, and altogether behaved like a boat tossed on a stormy sea. Then order returned into the chaos. I had the lines short, wrapped doubled and treble around my wrists; my feet stood braced in the corner of the box, knees touching the dashboard; my robes slipped down. I spoke to the horses in a soft, quiet, purring voice; and at last I pulled in. Peter hated to stand. I held him. Then I looked back. This first wild plunge had taken us a matter of two hundred yards into the drift. Peter pulled and champed at the bit; the horses were sinking nearly out of sight. But I knew that many and many a time in the future I should have to go through just this and that from the beginning I must train the horses to tackle it right. So, in spite of my aching wrists I kept them standing till I thought that they were fully breathed. Then I relaxed my pull the slightest bit and clicked my tongue. 'Good,' I thought, 'they are pulling together!' And I managed to hold them in line. They reared and plunged again like drowning things in their last agony, but they no longer clashed against nor pulled away from each other. I measured the distance with my eye. Another two hundred yards or thereabout, and I pulled them in again. Thus we stopped altogether four times. The horses were steaming when we got through this drift which was exactly half a mile long; my cutter was packed level full with slabs and clods of snow; and I was pretty well exhausted myself.

'If there is very much of this', I thought for the moment, 'I may not be able to make it.' But then I knew that a north-south road will drift in badly only under exceptional circumstances. It is the east-west grades that are most apt to give trouble. Not that I minded my part of it, but I did not mean to kill my horses. I had sized them up in their behaviour towards snow. Peter, as I had expected, was excitable. It was hard to recognize in him just now, as he walked quietly along, the uproar of playing muscle and rearing limbs that he had been when we first struck the snow. That was well and good for a short, supreme effort; but not even for Peter would it do in the long, endless drifts which I had to expect. Dan was quieter, but he did not have Peter's staying power; in fact, he was not really a horse for the road. Strange, in spite of his usual keenness on the level road, he seemed to show more snow sense in the drift. This was to be amply confirmed in the future. Whenever an accident happened, it was Peter's fault. As you will see if you read on, Dan once lay quiet when Peter stood right on top of him.

On this road north I found the same 'promontories' that had been such a feature of the first one, flung across from the northwest to the southeast. Since the clumps of shrubs to the left were larger here, and more numerous, too, the drifts occasionally also were larger and higher; but not one of them was such that the horses could not clear it with one or two leaps. The sun was climbing, the air was winter-clear and still. None of the farms which I passed showed the slightest sign of life. I had wrapped up again and sat in comparative comfort and at ease, enjoying the clear sparkle and glitter of the virgin snow. It was not till considerably later that the real significance of the landscape dawned upon my consciousness. Still there was even now in my thoughts a speculative undertone. Subconsciously I wondered what might be ahead of me.

We made Bell's corner[9] in good time. The mile to the west proved easy. There were drifts, it is true, and the going was heavy, but at no place did the snow for any length of time reach higher than the horses' hocks. We turned to the north again, and here, for a while, the road was very good indeed; the underbrush to the left, on those expanses of wild land, had fettered, as it were, the feet of the wind. The snow was held everywhere, and very little of it had drifted. Only one spot I remember where a clump of Russian willow close to the trail had offered shelter enough to allow the wind in the narrow road-gap to a depth of maybe eight or nine feet; but here it was easy to go around to the west. Without any further incident we reached the point where the useless, supernumerary fence post had caught my eye on my first trip out. I had made nearly eight miles now.

But right here I was to get my first inkling of sights that might shatter my nerve. You may remember that a grove of tall poplars ran to the east, skirted along its southern edge by a road and a long line of telephone posts. Now here, in this shelter of the poplars, the snow from the more or less level and unsheltered spaces to the northwest had piled in indeed. It sloped up to the east; and never shall I forget what I beheld.

The first of the posts stood a foot in snow; at the second one the drift reached six or seven feet up; the next one looked only half as long as the first one, and you might have imagined, standing as it did on a sloping hillside, that it had intentionally been made so much shorter than the others; but at the bottom of the visible part the wind, in sweeping around the pole, had scooped out a funnel-shaped crater which seemed to open into the very earth like a sinkhole. The next pole stood like a giant buried up to this chest and looked singularly helpless and footbound; and the last one I saw showed just its crossbar with three glassy, green insulators above the mountain of snow. The whole surface of this gigantic drift showed again that 'exfoliated' appearance which I have described. Strange to say, this very exfoliation gave it something of a quite peculiarly desolate aspect. It looked so harsh, so millennial-old, so antediluvian and pre-adamic! I still remember with particular distinctness the slight dizziness that overcame me, the sinking feeling in my heart, the awe, and the foreboding that I had challenged a force in Nature which might defy all tireless effort and the most fearless heart.

So the hostler had not been fibbing after all!

But not for a moment did I think of turning back. I am fatalistic in temperament. What is to be, is to be, that is not my outlook.[10] If at last we should get bound up in a drift, well and good, I should then see what the next move would have to be. While the wind blows, snow drifts; while my horses could walk and I was not disabled, my road led north, not south. Like the snow I obeyed the laws of my nature. So far the road was good, and we swung along.

Somewhere around here a field presented a curious view. Its crop had not been harvested; it still stood in stooks.[11] But from my side I saw nothing of the sheaves—it

9 The corner of a farm that served Grove as a landmark, signalling the completion of the first leg of his journey, a distance of about six miles from town. Later in this sketch he mentions other landmarks by which he judges his progress, such as the 'hovel', 'half way farms', and the 'White Range Line House'.

10 The sense of this passage seems to call for this sentence to conclude with the words, '. . . that is my outlook', but Grove's original manuscript does not support an emendation.

11 Sheaves.

seemed to be flax, for here and there a flag of loose heads showed at the top. The snow had been blown up from all directions, so it looked, by the counter-currents that set up in the lee of every obstacle. These mounds presented one and all the appearance of cones or pyramids of butter patted into shape by upward strokes made with a spoon. There were the sharp ridges, irregular and erratic, and there were the hollows running up their flanks—exactly as such a cone of butter will show them. And the whole field was dotted with them, as if there were so many fresh graves.

I made the twelve-mile bridge—passing through the cottonwood gate—reached the 'hovel', and dropped into the wilderness again. Here the bigger trees stood strangely bare. Winter reveals the bark and the 'habit'[12] of trees. All ornaments and unessentials have been dropped. The naked skeletons show. I remember how I was more than ever struck by that dappled appearance of the bark of the balm:[13] an olive-green, yellowish hue, ridged and spotted with the black of ancient, overgrown leaf-scars; there was actually something gay about it; these poplars are certainly beautiful winter trees. The aspens were different. Although their stems stood white on white in the snow, that greenish tinge in their white gave them a curious look. From the picture that I carry about in my memory of this morning I cannot help the impression that they looked as if their white were not natural at all; they looked whitewashed! I have often since confirmed this impression when there was snow on the ground.

In the copses of saplings the zigzagging of the boles from twig to twig showed very distinctly, more so, I believe, than to me it had ever done before. How slender and straight they look in their summer garb—now they were stripped, and bone and sinew appeared.

We came to the 'half way farms', and the marsh lay ahead. I watered the horses, and I do not know what made me rest them for a little while, but I did. On the yard of the farm where I had turned in there was not a soul to be seen. Barns and stables were closed—and I noticed that the back door of the dwelling was buried tight by the snow. No doubt everybody preferred the neighbourhood of the fire to the cold outside. While stopping, I faced for the first time the sun. He was high in the sky by now—it was half-past ten—and it suddenly came home to me that there was something relentless, inexorable, cruel, yes, something of a sneer in the pitiless way in which he looked down on the infertile waste around. Unaccountably two Greek words formed on my lips: Homer's Pontos atrygetos—the barren sea.[14] Half an hour later I was to realize the significance of it.

I turned back to the road and north again. For another half mile the fields continued on either side; but somehow they seemed to take on a sinister look. There was more snow on them than I had found on the level land further south; the snow lay more smoothly, again under those 'exfoliated' surface sheets which here, too, gave it an inhuman, primeval look; in the higher sun the vast expanse looked, I suppose, more blindingly white; and nowhere did buildings or thickets seem to emerge. Yet, so long as the grade continued, the going was fair enough.

---

12  In botany, the characteristic growth and appearance of a plant.
13  Balsam poplar.
14  A common Homeric formula in *The Odyssey*.

Then I came to the corner which marked half the distance, and there I stopped. Right in front, where the trail had been and where a ditch had divided off the marsh, a fortress of snow lay now: a seemingly impregnable bulwark, six or seven feet high, with rounded top, fitting descriptions which I had read of the underground bomb-proofs around Belgian strongholds—those forts which were hammered to pieces by the Germans in their first, heartbreaking forward surge in 1914. There was not a wrinkle in this inverted bowl. There it lay, smooth and slick—curled up in security, as it were, some twenty, thirty feet across; and behind it others, and more of them to the right and to the left. This had been a stretch, covered with brush and bush, willow and poplar thickets; but my eye saw nothing except a mammiferous[15] waste, cruelly white, glittering in the heatless, chuckling sun, and scoffing at me, the intruder. I stood up again and peered out. To the east it seemed as if these buttes of snow were a trifle lower; but maybe the ground underneath also sloped down. I wished I had travelled here more often by daytime, so I might know. As it was, there was nothing to it; I had to tackle the task. And we plunged in.

I had learned something from my first experience in the drift one mile north of town, and I kept my horses well under control. Still, it was a wild enough dash. Peter had lost his footing two or three times and worked himself into a mild panic. But Dan—I could not help admiring the way in which, buried over his back in snow, he would slowly and deliberately rear on his hindfeet and take his bound. For fully five minutes I never saw anything of the horses except their heads. I inferred their motions from the dusting snowcloud that rose above their bodies and settled on myself. And then somehow we emerged. We reached a stretch of ground where the snow was just high enough to cover the hocks of the horses. It was a hollow scooped out by some freak of the wind. I pulled in, and the horses stood panting. Peter no longer showed any desire to fret and to jump. Both horses apparently felt the wisdom of sparing their strength. They were all white with the frost of their sweat and the spray of the snow. . . .

While I gave them their time, I looked around, and here a lesson came home to me. In the hollow where we stood, the snow did not lie smoothly. A huge obstacle to the northwest, probably a buried clump of brush, had made the wind turn back upon itself, first downward, then, at the bottom of the pit, in a direction opposite to that of the main current above, and finally slantways upward again to the summit of the obstacle, where it rejoined the parent blow. The floor of the hollow was cleanly scooped out and chiselled in low ridges; and these ridges came from the southeast, running their points to the northwest. I learned to look out for this sign, and I verily believe that, had I not learned that lesson right now, I should never have reached the creek which was still four or five miles distant.

The huge mound in the lee of which I was stopping was a matter of two hundred yards away; nearer to it the snow was considerably deeper; and since it presented an appearance very characteristic of Prairie bush-drifts, I shall describe it in some detail. Apparently the winds had first bent over all the stems of the clump; for whenever I saw one of them from the north, it showed a smooth, clean upward sweep. On the south

15 Breast-like.

side the snow first fell in a sheer cliff; then there was a hollow which was partly filled by a talus-shaped[16] drift thrown in by the counter currents from the southern pit in which we were stopping; the sides of this talus again showed the marks that reminded of those left by the spoon when butter is roughly stroked into the shape of a pyramid. The interesting parts of the structure consisted in the beetling brow of the cliff and the roof of the cavity underneath. The brow had a honey-combed appearance; the snow had been laid down in layers of varying density (I shall discuss this more fully in the next chapter when we are going to look in on the snow while it is actually at work[17]); and the counter currents that here swept upward in a slanting direction had bitten out the softer layers, leaving a fine network of little ridges which reminded strangely of the delicate fretwork-tracery in wind-sculptured rock—as I had seen it in the Black Hills in South Dakota. This piece of work of the wind is exceedingly short-lived in snow, and it must not be confounded with the honeycombed appearance of those faces of snow cliffs which are 'rotting' by reason of their exposure to the heat of the noonday sun. These latter are coarse, often dirty, and nearly always have something bristling about them which is entirely absent in the sculptures of the wind. The under side of the roof in the cavity looked very much as a very stiff or viscid treacle would look when spread over a meshy surface, as, for instance, over a closely woven netting of wire. The stems and the branches of the bush took the place of the wire, and in their meshes the snow had been pressed through by its own weight, but held together by its curious ductility or tensile strength of which I was to find further evidence soon enough. It thus formed innumerable, blunted little stalactites, but without the corresponding stalagmites which you find in limestone caves or on the north side of buildings when the snow from the roof thaws and forms icicles and slender cones of ice growing up to meet them from the ground where the trickling drops fall and freeze again.

By the help of these various tokens I had picked my next resting place before we started up again. It was on this second dash that I understood why those Homeric words had come to my lips a while ago. This was indeed like nothing so much as like being out on rough waters and in a troubled sea, with nothing to brace the storm with but a wind-tossed nutshell of a one-man sailing craft. I knew that experience for having outridden many a gale in the mouth of the mighty St Lawrence River. When the snow reached its extreme depth, it gave you the feeling which a drowning man may have when fighting his desperate fight with the salty waves. But more impressive than that was the frequent outer resemblance. The waves of the ocean rise up and reach out and batter against rocks and battlements of the shore, retreating again and ever returning to the assault, covering the obstacles thrown in the way of their progress with thin sheets of licking tongues at least. And if such a high crest wave had suddenly been frozen into solidity, its outline would have mimicked to perfection many a one of the snow shapes that I saw around.

Once the horses had really learned to pull exactly together—and they learned it thoroughly here—our progress was not too bad. Of course, it was not like going on a

---

16 Like a sloping wall in a fortification, wider at its base than at its top.

17 In the fifth sketch, 'Wind and Waves', Grove describes his return trip to school, taken the next day during a blowing snowstorm—the experience of which he details with the scientific detachment of a naturalist.

grade, be it ever so badly drifted in. Here the ground underneath, too, was uneven and overgrown with a veritable entanglement of brush in which often the horses' feet would get caught. As for the road, there was none left, nothing that even by the boldest stretch of imagination could have been considered even as the slightest indication of one. And worst of all, I knew positively that there would be no trail at any time during the winter. I was well aware of the fact that, after it once snowed up, nobody ever crossed this waste between the 'half-way farms' and the 'White Range Line House'. This morning it took me two and a half solid hours to make four miles.

But the ordeal had its reward. Here where the fact that there was snow on the ground, and plenty of it, did no longer need to be sunk into my brain—as soon as it has lost its value as a piece of news and a lesson, I began to enjoy it just as the hunter in India will enjoy the battle of wits when he is pitted against a yellow-black tiger. I began to catch on to the ways of this snow; I began, as it were, to study the mentality of my enemy. Though I never kill, I am after all something of a sportsman. And still another thing gave me back that mental equilibrium which you need in order to see things and to reason calmly about them. Every dash of two hundred yards or so brought me that much nearer to my goal. Up to the 'half-way farms' I had, as it were, been working uphill: there was more ahead than behind. This was now reversed: there was more behind than ahead, and as yet I did not worry about the return trip.

Now I have already said that snow is the only really plastic element in which the wind can carve the vagaries of its mood and leave a record of at least some permanency. The surface of the sea is a wonderful book to be read with a lightning-quick eye; I do not know anything better to do as a cure for ragged nerves—provided you are a good sailor. But the forms are too fleeting, they change too quickly—so quickly, indeed, that I have never succeeded in so fixing their record upon my memory as to be able to develop one form from the other in descriptive notes. It is that very fact, I believe, upon which hinges the curative value of the sight: you are so completely absorbed by the moment, and all other things fall away. Many and many a day have I lain on my deck chair on board a liner and watched the play of the waves; but the pleasure, which was very great indeed, was momentary; and sometimes, when in an unsympathetic mood, I have since impatiently wondered in what that fascination may have consisted. It was different here. Snow is very nearly as yielding as water and, once it fully responds in its surface to the carving of forces of the wind, it stays—as if frozen into the glittering marble image of its motion. I know few things that are as truly fascinating as the sculptures of the wind in snow; for here you have time and opportunity a-plenty to probe not only into the what, but also into the why. Maybe that one day I shall write down a fuller account of my observations. In this report I shall have to restrict myself to a few indications, for this is not the record of the whims of the wind, but merely the narrative of my drives.

In places, for instance, the rounded, 'bomb-proof' aspect of the expanses would be changed into the distinct contour of gigantic waves with a very fine, very sharp crest-line. The upsweep from the northwest would be ever so slightly convex, and the downward sweep into the trough was always very distinctly concave. This was not the ripple which we find in beach sand. That ripple was there, too, and in places it covered the wide backs of these huge waves all over; but never was it found on the concave side. Occasionally, but rarely, one of these great waves would resemble a large breaker with a curly crest. Here the onward sweep from the northwest had built the snow out, beyond the supporting base, into a thick overhanging ledge which here and there had sagged; but by virtue of that tensile strength and cohesion in snow which I have mentioned already, it still held together and now looked convoluted and ruffled in the most deceiving way. I believe I actually listened for the muffled roar which the breaker makes when its subaqueous part begins to sweep the upward sloping beach. To make this illusion complete, or to break it by the very absurdity and exaggeration of a comparison drawn out too far— I do not know which—there would, every now and then, from the crest of one of these waves, jut out something which closely resembled the wide back of a large fish diving down into the concave side towards the trough. This looked very much like porpoises or dolphins jumping in a heaving sea; only that in my memory picture the real dolphins always jump in the opposite direction, against the run of the waves, bridging the trough.

In other places a fine, exceedingly delicate crest-line would spring up from the high point of some buried obstacle and sweep along in the most graceful curve as far as the eye would carry. I particularly remember one of them, and I could discover no earthy reason for the curvature in it.

Again there would be a triangular—or should I say 'tetrahedral'?—up-sweep from the direction of the wind, ending in a sharp, perfectly plane down-sweep on the south side; and the point of this three-sided but oblique pyramid would hang over like the flap of a tam. There was something of the consistency of very thick cloth about this overhanging flap.

Or an up-slope from the north would end in a long, nearly perpendicular cliffline facing south. And the talus formation which I have mentioned would be perfectly smooth; but it did not reach quite to the top of the cliff, maybe to within a foot of it. The up sloping layer from the north would hang out again, with an even brow; but between this smooth cornice and the upper edge of the talus the snow looked as if it had been squeezed out by tremendous pressure from above, like an exceedingly viscid liquid—cooling glue, for instance, which is being squeezed out from between the core and the veneer in a veneering press.

Once I passed close to and south of, two thickets which were completely buried by the snow. Between them a ditch had been scooped out in a very curious fashion. It resembled exactly a winding river bed with its water drained off; it was two or three feet deep, and wherever it turned, its banks were undermined on the 'throw'[18] side by the 'wash' of the furious blow. The analogy between the work of the wind and the work of flowing water constantly obtrudes, especially where this work is one of 'erosion'.

But as flowing water will swing up and down in the most surprising forms where the bed of the river is rough with rocks and throws it into choppy waves which do not seem to move, so the snow was thrown up into the most curious forms where the frozen swamp ground underneath had bubbled, as it were, into phantastic shapes. I remember several places where a perfect circle was formed by a sharp crestline that bounded an hemispherical, crater-like hollow. When steam bubbles up through thick porridge,

18  In geology, a displacement of a bed or strata.

in its leisurely and impeded way, and the bubble bursts with a clucking sound, then for a moment a crater is formed just like these circular holes; only here in the snow they were on a much larger scale, of course, some of them six to ten feet in diameter.

And again the snow was thrown up into a bulwark, twenty and more feet high, with that always repeating cliff-face to the south, resembling a miniature Gibraltar, with many smaller ones of most curiously similar form on its back: bulwarks upon bulwarks, all lowering to the south. In these the aggressive nature of storm-flung snow was most apparent. They were formidable structures; formidable and intimidating, more through the suggestiveness of their shape than through mere size.

I came to places where the wind had had its moments of frolicsome humour, where it had made grim fun of its own massive and cumbersome and yet so pliable and elastic majesty. It has turned around and around, running with breathless speed, with its tongue lolling out, as it were, and probably yapping and snapping in mocking mimicry of a pup trying to catch its tail; and it had scooped out a spiral trough with overhanging rim. I felt sorry that I had not been there to watch it, because after all, what I saw, was only the dead record of something that had been very much alive and vociferatingly noisy. And in another place it had reared and raised its head like a boa constrictor, ready to strike at its prey; up to the flashing, forked tongue it was there. But one spot I remember, where it looked exactly as if quite consciously it had attempted the outright ludicrous: it had thrown up the snow into the semblance of some formidable animal—more like a gorilla than anything else it looked, a gorilla that stands on its four hands and raises every hair on its back and snarls in order to frighten that which it is afraid of itself—a leopard maybe.

And then I reached the 'White Range Line House'. Curiously enough, there it stood, sheltered by its majestic bluff to the north, as peaceful looking as if there were no such thing as that record, which I had crossed, of the uproar and fury of one of the forces of Nature engaged in an orgy. And it looked so empty, too, and so deserted, with never a wisp of smoke curling from its flue-pipe, that for a moment I was tempted to turn in and see whether maybe the lonely dweller was ill. But then I felt as if I could not be burdened with any stranger's worries that day.

The effective shelter of the poplar forest along the creek made itself felt. The last mile to the northeast was peaceful driving. I felt quite cheered, though I walked the horses over the whole of the mile since both began to show signs of wear. The last four miles had been a test to try any living creature's mettle. To me it had been one of the culminating points in that glorious winter, but the horses had lacked the mental stimulus, and even I felt rather exhausted.

On the bridge I stopped, threw the blankets over the horses, and fed. Somehow this seemed to be the best place to do it. There was no snow to speak of, and I did not know yet what might follow. The horses were drooping, and I gave them an additional ten minutes' rest. Then I slowly made ready. I did not really expect serious trouble.

We turned at a walk, and the chasm of the bush road opened up. Instantly I pulled the horses in. What I saw, baffled me for a moment so completely that I just sat there and gasped. There was no road. The trees to both sides were not so overly high, but the snow had piled in level with their tops; the drift looked like a gigantic barricade. It was that fleeting sight of the telephone posts over again, though on a slightly smaller scale; but this time it was in front. Slowly I started to whistle and then looked around. I remembered now. There was newly cut-out road running north past the school which lay embedded in the bush. It had offered a lane to the wind; and the wind, going there, in cramped space, at a doubly furious stride, had picked up and carried along all the loose snow from the grassy glades in its path. The road ended abruptly just north of the drift, where the east-west grade sprang up. When the wind had reached this end of the lane, where the bush ran at right angles to its direction, it had found itself in something like a blind alley, and, sweeping upward, to clear the obstacle, it had dropped every bit of its load into the shelter of the brush, gradually, in the course of three long days, building up a ridge that buried underbrush and trees. I might have known it, of course. I knew enough about snow; all the conditions for an exceptionally large drift were provided for here. But it had not occurred to me, especially after I had found the northern fringe of the marsh so well sheltered. Here I felt for a moment as if all the snow of the universe had piled in. As I said, I was so completely baffled that I could have turned the horses then and there.

But after a minute or two my eyes began to cast about. I turned to the south, right into the dense underbrush and towards the creek which here swept south in a long, flat curve. Peter was always intolerant of anything that moved underfoot. He started to bolt when the dry and hard-frozen stems snapped and broke with reports resembling pistol shots. But since Dan kept quiet, I held Peter well in hand. I went along the drift for maybe three to four hundred yards, reconnoitring. Then the trees began to stand too dense for me to proceed without endangering my cutter. Just beyond I saw the big trough of the creek bed, and though I could not make out how conditions were at its bottom, the drift continued on its southern bank, and in any case it was impossible to cross the hollow. So I turned; I had made up my mind to try the drift.

About a hundred and fifty yards from the point where I had turned off the road there was something like a fold in the flank of the drift. At its foot I stopped. For a moment I tried to explain that fold to myself. This is what I arrived at. North of the drift, just about where the new cut-out joined the east-west grade, there was a small clearing caused by a bush fire which a few years ago had penetrated thus far into this otherwise virgin corner of the forest. Unfortunately it stood so full of charred stumps that it was impossible to get through there. But the main currents of the wind would have free play in this opening, and I knew that, when the blizzard began, it had been blowing from a more northerly quarter than later on, when it veered to the northwest. And though the snow came careering along the lane of the cut-out, that is, from due north, its 'throw' and therefore, the direction of the drift would be determined by the direction of the wind that took charge of it on this clearing. Probably, then, a first, provisional drift whose long axis lay nearly in a north-south line, had been piled up by the first, northerly gale. Later a second larger drift had been superimposed upon it at an angle, with its main axis running from the northwest to the southeast. The fold marked the point where the first, smaller drift still emerged from the second larger one. This reasoning was confirmed by a study of the clearing itself which I came to make two or three weeks after.

Before I called on the horses to give me their very last ounce of strength, I got out of my cutter once more and made sure that my lines were still sound. I trusted my ability to guide the horses even in this crucial test, but I dreaded nothing so much as that the lines might break; and I wanted to guard against any accident. I should mention that, of course, the top of my cutter was down, that the traces of the harness were new, and that the cutter itself during its previous trials had shown an exceptional stability. Once more I thus rested my horses for five minutes; and they seemed to realize what was coming. Their heads were up, their ears were cocked. When I got back into my cutter, I carefully brushed the snow from moccasins and trousers, laid the robe around my feet, adjusted my knees against the dashboard, and tied two big loops into the lines to hold them by.

Then I clicked my tongue. The horses bounded upward in unison. For a moment it looked as if they intended to work through, instead of over, the drift. A wild shower of angular snow-slabs swept in upon me. The cutter reared up and plunged and reared again—and then the view cleared. The snow proved harder than I had anticipated— which bespoke the fury of the blow that had piled it. It did not carry the horses, but neither—once we had reached a height of five or six feet—did they sink beyond their bellies and out of sight. I had no eye for anything except them. What lay to right or left, seemed not to concern me. I watched them work. They went in bounds, working beautifully together. Rhythmically they reared, and rhythmically they plunged. I had dropped back to the seat, holding them with a firm hand, feet braced against the dash-board; and whenever they got ready to rear, I called to them in a low and quiet voice, 'Peter—Dan—now!' And their muscles played with the effort of desperation. It probably did not take more than five minutes, maybe considerably less, before we had reached the top, but to me it seemed like hours of nearly fruitless endeavour. I did not realize at first that we were high. I shall never forget the weird kind of astonishment when the fact came home to me that what snapped and crackled in the snow under the horses' hoofs, were the tops of trees. Nor shall the feeling of estrangement, as it were—as if I were not myself, but looking on from the outside at the adventure of somebody who yet was I—the feeling of other-worldliness, if you will pardon the word, ever fade from my memory—a feeling of having been carried beyond my depth where I could not swim—which came over me when with two quick glances to right and left I took in the fact that there were no longer any trees to either side, that I was above that forest world which had so often engulfed me.

Then I drew my lines in. The horses fought against it, did not want to stand. But I had to find my way, and while they were going, I could not take my eyes from them. It took a supreme effort on my part to make them obey. At last they stood, but I had to hold them with all my strength, and with not a second's respite. Now that I was on top of the drift, the problem of how to get down loomed larger than that of getting up had seemed before. I knew I did not have half a minute in which to decide upon my course; for it became increasingly difficult to hold the horses back, and they were fast sinking away.

During this short breathing spell I took in the situation. We had come up in a northeast direction, slanting along the slope. Once on top, I had instinctively turned to the north. Here the drift was about twenty feet wide, perfectly level and with an exfoliated surface layer. To the east the drift fell steeply, with a clean, smooth cliff-line marking off the beginning of the descent; this line seemed particularly disconcerting, for it betrayed the concave curvature of the down-sweep. A few yards to the north I saw below, at the foot of the cliff, the old logging-trail, and I noticed that the snow on it lay as it had fallen, smooth and sheer, without a ripple of a drift. It looked like mockery. And yet that was where I had to get down.

The next few minutes are rather a maze in my memory. But two pictures were photographed with great distinctness. The one is of the moment when we went over the edge. For a second Peter reared up, pawing the air with his forefeet; Dan tried to back away from the empty fall. I had at this excruciating point no purchase whatever on the lines. Then apparently Peter sat or fell down, I do not know which, on his haunches and began to slide. The cutter lurched to the left as if it were going to spill all it held. Dan was knocked off his hind feet by the drawbar—and we plunged. . . . We came to with a terrific jolt that sent me in a heap against the dash board. One jump, and I stood on the ground. The cutter—and this is the second picture which is etched clearly on the plate of my memory—stood on its pole, leaning at an angle of forty-five degrees against the drift. The horses were as stunned. 'Dan, Peter!' I shouted, and they struggled to their feet. They were badly winded, but otherwise everything seemed all right. I looked wistfully back and up at the gully which we had torn into the flank of the drift.

I should gladly have breathed the horses again, but they were hot, the air was at zero or colder, the rays of the sun had begun to slant. I walked for a while alongside the team. They were drooping sadly. Then I got in again, driving them slowly till we came to the crossing of the ditch. I had no eye for the grade ahead. On the bush road the going was good—now and then a small drift, but nothing alarming anywhere. The anti-climax had set in. Again the speckled trunks of the balm poplars struck my eye, now interspersed with the scarlet stems of the red osier dogwood. But they failed to cheer me—they were mere facts, unable to stir moods. . . .

I began to think. A few weeks ago I had met that American settler with the French sounding name who lived alongside the angling dam further north. We had talked snow, and he had said, 'Oh, up here it never is bad except along this grade',—we were stopping on the last east-west grade, the one I was coming to—'there you cannot get through. You'd kill your horses. Level with the treetops.' Well, I had had just that a little while ago—I could not afford any more of it. So I made up my mind to try a new trail, across a section which was fenced. It meant getting out of my robes twice more, to open the gates, but I preferred that to another tree-high drift. To spare my horses was now my only consideration. I should not have liked to take the new trail by night, for fear of missing the gates; but that objection did not hold just now. Horses and I were pretty well spent. So, instead of forking off the main trail to the north we went straight ahead.

In due time I came to the bridge which I had to cross in order to get up on the dam. Here I saw—in an absent-minded, half unconscious, and uninterested way—one more structure built by architect wind. The deep master ditch from the north emptied here, to the left of the bridge, into the grade ditch which ran east and west. And at the corner the snow had very nearly bridged it—so nearly that you could easily have stepped across the remaining gap. But below it was hollow—nothing supported the bridge—it was a mere arch, with a vault underneath that looked temptingly sheltered and rosy to wearied eyes.

The dam was bare, and I had to pull off to the east, on to the swampy plain. I gave my horses the lines, and slowly, slowly they took me home! Even had I not always lost interest here, to-day I should have leaned back and rested. Although the horses had done all the actual work, the strain of it had been largely on me. It was the after-effect that set in now.

I thought of my wife, and how she would have felt had she been able to follow the scenes in some magical mirror through every single vicissitude of my drive. And once more I saw with the eye of recent memory the horses in that long, endless plunge through the corner of the marsh. Once more I felt my muscles a-quiver with the strain of that last wild struggle over that last, inhuman drift. And slowly I made up my mind that the next time, the very next day, on my return trip, I was going to add another eleven miles to my already long drive and to take a different road. I knew the trail over which I had been coming so far was closed for the rest of the winter—there was no traffic there—no trail would be kept open. That other road of which I was thinking and which lay further west was the main cordwood trail to the towns in the south. It was out of my way, to be sure, but I felt convinced that I could spare my horses and even save time by making the detour.

Being on the east side of the dam, I could not see school or cottage till I turned up on the correction line. But when at last I saw it, I felt somewhat as I had felt coming home from my first big trip overseas. It seemed a lifetime since I had started out. I seemed to be a different man.

Here, in the timber land, the snow had not drifted to any extent. There were signs of the gale, but its record was written in fallen tree trunks, broken branches, a litter of twigs—not in drifts of snow. My wife would not surmise what I had gone through.

She came out with a smile on her face when I pulled in on the yard. It was characteristic of her that she did not ask why I came so late; she accepted the fact as something for which there were no doubt compelling reasons. 'I was giving our girl a bath,' she said; 'she cannot come.' And then she looked wistfully at my face and at the horses. Silently I slipped the harness off their backs. I used to let them have their freedom for a while on reaching home. And never yet but Peter at least had had a kick and a caper and a roll before they sought their mangers. To-day they stood for a moment knock-kneed, without moving, then shook themselves in a weak, half-hearted way and went with drooping heads and weary limbs straight to the stable.

'You had a hard trip?' asked my wife; and I replied with as much cheer as I could muster, 'I have seen sights to-day that I did not expect to see before my dying day.' And taking her arm, I looked at the westering sun and turned towards the house.

1922

# Snow

Towards morning the blizzard had died down, though it was still far from daylight. Stars without number blazed in the dark-blue sky which presented that brilliant and uncompromising appearance always characterizing, on the northern plains of America, those nights in the dead of winter when the thermometer dips to its lowest levels.

In the west, Orion was sinking to the horizon. It was between five and six o'clock.

In the bush-fringe of the Big Marsh, sheltered by thick but bare bluffs of aspens, stood a large house, built of logs, white-washed, solid—such as a settler who is still single would put up only when he thinks of getting married. It, too, looked ice-cold, frozen in the night. Not a breath stirred where it stood; a thin thread of whitish smoke, reaching up to the level of the tree-tops, seemed to be suspended into the chimney rather than to issue from it.

Through the deep snow of the yard, newly packed, a man was fighting his way to the door. Arrived there, he knocked and knocked, first tapping with his knuckles, then hammering with his fists.

Two, three minutes passed. Then a sound awoke in the house, as of somebody stirring, getting out of bed.

The figure on the door-slab—a medium-sized, slim man in sheepskin and high rubber boots into which his trousers were tucked, with the ear-flaps of his cap pulled down—stood and waited, bent over, hands thrust into the pockets of the short coat, as if he wished to shrink into the smallest possible space so as to offer the smallest possible surface to the attack of the cold. In order to get rid of the dry, powdery snow which filled every crease in his foot-gear and trousers, he stamped his feet. His chin was drawn deep into the turned-up collar on whose points his breath had settled in the form of a thick layer of hoar frost.

At last a bolt was withdrawn inside.

The face of a man peered out, just discernible in the starlight.

Then the door was opened; in ominous silence the figure from the outside entered, still stamping its feet.

Not a word was spoken till the door had been closed. Then a voice sounded through the cold and dreary darkness of the room.

'Redcliff hasn't come home. He went to town about noon and expected to get back by midnight. We're afraid he's lost.'

The other man, quite invisible in the dark, had listened, his teeth chattering with the cold. 'Are you sure he started out from town?'

'Well,' the newcomer answered hesitatingly, 'one of the horses came to the yard.'

'One of his horses?'

'Yes. One of those he drove. The woman worked her way to my place to get help.'

The owner of the house did not speak again. He went, in the dark, to the door in the rear and opened it. There, he groped about for matches, and, finding them, lighted a lamp. In the room stood a big stove, a coal-stove of the self-feeder type; but the fuel used was wood. He opened the drafts and shook the grate clear of ashes; there were two big blocks of spruce in the fire-box, smouldering away for the night. In less than a minute they blazed up.

The newcomer entered, blinking in the light of the lamp, and looked on. Before many minutes the heat from the stove began to tell.

'I'll call Bill,' the owner of the house said. He was himself of medium height or only slightly above it, but of enormous breadth of shoulder: a figure built for lifting loads. By his side the other man looked small, weakly, dwarfed.

He left the room and, returning through the cold bare hall in front, went upstairs.

A few minutes later a tall, slender, well-built youth bolted into the room where the newcomer was waiting. Bill, Carroll's hired man, was in his underwear and carried his clothes, thrown in a heap over his arm. Without loss of time, but jumping, stamping, swinging his arms, he began at once to dress.

He greeted the visitor. 'Hello, Mike! What's that Abe tells me? Redcliff got lost?'

'Seems that way,' Mike said listlessly.

'By gringo,' Bill went on. 'I shouldn't wonder. In that storm! I'd have waited in town. Wouldn't catch me going out over the marsh in that kind of weather!'

'Didn't start till late in the afternoon,' Mike Sobotski said in his shivering way.

'No. And didn't last long, either,' Bill agreed while he shouldered into his overalls. 'But while she lasted . . .'

At this moment Abe Carroll, the owner of the farm, reentered, with sheep-skin, fur cap, and long, woollen scarf on his arms. His deeply lined, striking, square face bore a settled frown while he held the inside of his sheep-skin to the stove to warm it up. Then, without saying a word, he got deliberately into it.

Mike Sobotski still stood bent over, shivering, though he had opened his coat and, on his side of the stove, was catching all the heat it afforded.

Abe, with the least motion needed to complete dressing, made for the door. In passing Bill, he flung out an elbow which touched the young man's arm. 'Come on,' he said; and to the other, pointing to the stove, 'Close the drafts.'

A few minutes later a noise as of rearing and snorting horses in front of the house . . .

Mike, buttoning up his coat and pulling his mitts over his hands, went out.

They mounted three unsaddled horses. Abe leading, they dashed through the new drifts in the yard and out through the gate to the road. Here, where the shelter of the bluffs screening the house was no longer effective, a light but freshening breeze from the north-west made itself felt as if fine little knives were cutting into the flesh of their faces.

Abe dug his heels into the flank of his rearing mount. The horse was unwilling to obey his guidance, for Abe wanted to leave the road and to cut across wild land to the south-west.

The darkness was still inky-black, though here and there, where the slope of the drifts slanted in the right direction, starlight was dimly reflected from the snow. The drifts were six, eight, in places ten feet high; and the snow was once more crawling up their flanks, it was so light and fine. It would fill the tracks in half an hour. As the horses plunged through, the crystals dusted up in clouds, flying aloft over horses and riders.

In less than half an hour they came to a group of two little buildings, of logs, that seemed to squat on their haunches in the snow. Having entered the yard through a gate, they passed one of the buildings and made for the other, a little stable; their horses snorting, they stopped in its lee.

Mike dismounted, throwing the halter-shank of his horse to Bill. He went to the house, which stood a hundred feet or so away. The shack was even smaller than the stable, twelve by fifteen feet perhaps. From its flue-pipe a thick, white plume of smoke blew to the south-east.

Mike returned with a lantern; the other two sprang to the ground; and they opened the door to examine the horse which the woman had allowed to enter.

The horse was there, still excited, snorting at the leaping light and shadows from the lantern, its eyes wild, its nostrils dilated. It was covered with white frost and fully harnessed, though its traces were tied up to the back-band.

'He let him go,' said Mike, taking in these signs. 'Must have stopped and unhitched him.'

'Must have been stuck in a drift,' Bill said, assenting.

'And tried to walk it,' Abe added.

For a minute or so they stood silent, each following his own gloomy thoughts. Weird, luminous little clouds issued fitfully from the nostrils of the horse inside.

'I'll get the cutter,' Abe said at last.

'I'll get it,' Bill volunteered. 'I'll take the drivers along. We'll leave the filly here in the stable.'

'All right.'

Bill remounted, leading Abe's horse. He disappeared into the night.

Abe and Mike, having tied the filly and the other horse in their stalls, went out, closed the door and turned to the house.

There, by the light of a little coal-oil lamp, they saw the woman sitting at the stove, pale, shivering, her teeth a-chatter, trying to warm her hands, which were cold with fever, and looking with lack-lustre eyes at the men as they entered.

The children were sleeping; the oldest, a girl, on the floor, wrapped in a blanket and curled up like a dog; four others in one narrow bed, with hay for a mattress, two at the head, two at the foot; the baby on, rather than in, a sort of cradle made of a wide board slung by thin ropes to the pole-roof of the shack.

The other bed was empty and unmade. The air was stifling from a night of exhalations.

'We're going to hunt for him,' Mike said quietly. 'We've sent for a cutter. He must have tried to walk.'

The woman did not answer. She sat and shivered.

'We'll take some blankets,' Mike went on. 'And some whisky if you've got any in the house.'

He and Abe were standing by the stove, opposite the woman, and warming their hands, their mitts held under their arm-pits.

The woman pointed with a look to a home-made little cupboard nailed to the wall and apathetically turned back to the stove. Mike went, opened the door of the cupboard, took a bottle from it, and slipped it into the pocket of his sheep-skin. Then he raised the blankets from the empty bed, rolled them roughly into a bundle, dropped it, and returned to the stove where, with stiff fingers, he fell to rolling a cigarette.

Thus they stood for an hour or so.

Abe's eye was fastened on the woman. He would have liked to say a word of comfort, of hope. What was there to be said?

She was the daughter of a German settler in the bush, some six or seven miles northeast of Abe's place. Her father, an oldish, unctuous, bearded man had, some ten years ago, got tired of the hard life in the bush where work meant clearing, picking stones, and digging stumps. He had sold his homestead and bought a prairie-farm, half a section, on crop payments, giving notes for the equipment which he needed to handle the place. He had not been able to make it 'a go'. His bush farm had fallen back on his hands; he had lost his all and returned to the place. He had been counting on the help of his two boys—big, strapping young fellows who were to clear much land and to raise crops which would lift the debt. But the boys had refused to go back to the bush; they could get easy work in town. Ready money would help. But the ready money had melted away in their hands. Redcliff, the old people's son-in-law, had been their last hope. They were on the point of losing even their bush farm. Here they might perhaps still have found a refuge for their old age—though Redcliff's homestead lay on the sand-flats bordering on the marsh where the soil was thin, dreadfully thin; it drifted when the scrub-brush was cleared off. Still, with Redcliff living, this place had been a hope. What were they to do if he was gone? And this woman, hardly more than a girl, in spite of her six children!

The two tiny, square windows of the shack began to turn grey.

At last Abe, thinking he heard a sound, went to the door and stepped out. Bill was there; the horses were shaking the snow out of their pelts; one of them was pawing the ground.

Once more Abe opened the door and gave Mike a look for a signal. Mike gathered the bundle of blankets into his arms, pulled on his mitts, and came out.

Abe reached for the lines; but Bill objected.

'No. Let me drive. I found something.'

And as soon as the two older men had climbed in, squeezing into the scant space on the seat, he clicked his tongue.

'Get up there!' he shouted, hitting the horses' backs with his lines. And with a leap they darted away.

Bill turned, heading back to the Carroll farm. The horses plunged, reared, snorted, and then, throwing their heads, shot along in a gallop, scattering snow-slabs right and left and throwing wing-waves of the fresh, powdery snow, especially on the lee side. Repeatedly they tried to turn into the wind which they were cutting at right angles. But Bill plied the whip and guided them expertly.

Nothing was visible anywhere; nothing but the snow in the first grey of dawn. Then, like enormous ghosts, or like evanescent apparitions, the trees of the bluff were adumbrated behind the lingering veils of the night.

Bill turned to the south, along the straight trail which bordered Abe Carroll's farm. He kept looking out sharply to right and left. But after a while he drew his galloping horses in.

'Whoa!' he shouted, tearing at the lines in see-saw fashion. And when the rearing horses came to a stop, excited and breathless, he added, 'I've missed it.' He turned.

'What is it?' Abe asked.

'The other horse,' Bill answered. 'It must have had the scent of our yard. It's dead . . . frozen stiff.'

A few minutes later he pointed to a huge white mound on top of a drift to the left. 'That's it,' he said, turned the horses into the wind, and stopped.

To the right, the bluffs of the farm slowly outlined themselves in the morning greyness.

The two older men alighted and, with their hands, shovelled the snow away. There lay the horse, stiff and cold, frozen into a rocklike mass.

'Must have been here a long while,' Abe said.

Mike nodded. 'Five, six hours.' Then he added, 'Couldn't have had the smell of the yard. Unless the wind has turned.'

'It has,' Abe answered and pointed to a fold in the flank of the snow-drift which indicated that the present drift had been superimposed on a lower one whose longitudinal axis ran to the north-east.

For a moment longer they stood and pondered.

Then Abe went back to the cutter and reached for the lines.

'I'll drive,' he said.

Mike climbed in.

Abe took his bearings, looking for landmarks. They were only two or three hundred feet from his fence. That enabled him to estimate the exact direction of the breeze. He clicked his tongue. 'Get up!'

And the horses, catching the infection of a dull excitement, shot away. They went straight into the desert of drifts to the west, plunging ahead without any trail, without any landmark in front to guide them.

They went for half an hour, an hour, and longer.

None of the three men said a word. Abe knew the sandflats better than any other; Abe reasoned better than they. If anyone could find the missing man, it was Abe.

Abe's thoughts ran thus. The horse had gone against the wind. It would never have done so without good reason; that reason could have been no other than a scent to follow. If that was so, however, it would have gone in as straight a line as it could. The sand-flats stretched away to the south-west for sixteen miles with not a settlement, not a farm but Redcliff's. If Abe managed to strike that line of the scent it must take him to the point whence the horses had started.

Clear and glaring, with an almost indifferent air, the sun rose to their left.

And suddenly they saw the wagon-box of the sleigh sticking out of the snow ahead of them.

Abe stopped, handed Bill the lines, and got out. Mike followed. Nobody said a word.

The two men dug the tongue of the vehicle out of the snow and tried it. This was part of the old, burnt-over bush land south of the sand-flats. The sleigh was tightly wedged in between several charred stumps which stuck up through the snow. That was the reason why the man had unhitched the horses and turned them loose. What else, indeed, could he have done?

The box was filled with a drift which, toward the tail-gate, was piled high, for there three bags of flour were standing on end and leaning against a barrel half-filled with small parcels the interstices between which were packed with mealy snow.

Abe waded all around the sleigh, reconnoitring; and as he did so, wading at the height of the upper edge of the wagon-box, the snow suddenly gave way beneath him; he broke in; the drift was hollow.

A suspicion took hold of him; with a few quick reaches of his arm he demolished the roof of the drift all about.

And there, in the hollow, lay the man's body as if he were sleeping, a quiet expression, as of painless rest, on his face. His eyes were closed; a couple of bags were wrapped about his shoulders. Apparently he had not even tried to walk! Already chilled to the bone, he had given into that desire for rest, for shelter at any price, which overcomes him who is doomed to freeze.

Without a word the two men carried him to the cutter and laid him down on the snow.

Bill, meanwhile, had unhitched the horses and was hooking them to the tongue of the sleigh. The two others looked on in silence. Four times the horses sprang, excited because Bill tried to make them pull with a sudden twist. The sleigh did not stir.

'Need an axe,' Mike said at last, 'to cut the stumps. We'll get the sleigh later.'

Mike hitched up again and turned the cutter. The broken snowdrifts through which they had come gave the direction.

Then they laid the stiff, dead body across the floor of their vehicle, leaving the side doors open, for it protruded both ways. They themselves climbed up on the seat and crouched down, so as not to put their feet on the corpse.

Thus they returned to Abe Carroll's farm where, still in silence, they deposited the body in the granary.

That done, they stood for a moment as if in doubt. Then Bill unhitched the horses and took them to the stable to feed.

'I'll tell the woman,' said Mike. 'Will you go tell her father?'

Abe nodded. 'Wait for breakfast,' he added.

It was ten o'clock; and none of them had eaten since the previous night.

On the way to Altmann's place in the bush, drifts were no obstacles to driving. Drifts lay on the marsh, on the open sand-flats.

Every minute of the time Abe, as he drove along, thought of that woman in the shack: the woman, alone, with six children, and with the knowledge that her man was dead.

Altmann's place in the bush looked the picture of peace and comfort: a large log-house of two rooms. Window-frames and door were painted green. A place to stay with, not to leave. . . .

When Abe knocked, the woman, whom he had seen but once in his life, at the sale where they had lost their possessions, opened the door—an enormously fat woman, overflowing her clothes. The man, tall, broad, with a long, rolling beard, now grey, stood behind her, peering over her shoulder. A visit is an event in the bush!

'Come in,' he said cheerfully when he saw Abe. 'What a storm that was!'

Abe entered the kitchen which was also dining and living room. He sat down on the chair which was pushed forward for him and looked at the two old people, who remained standing.

Suddenly, from the expression of his face, they anticipated something of his message. No use dissembling.

'Redcliff is dead,' he said. 'He was frozen to death last night on his way from town.'

The two old people also sat down; it looked as if their knees had given way beneath them. They stared at him, dumbly, a sudden expression of panic fright in their eyes.

'I thought you might want to go to your daughter,' Abe added sympathetically.

The man's big frame seemed to shrink as he sat there. All the unctuousness and the conceit of the handsome man dwindled out of his bearing. The woman's eyes had already filled with tears.

Thus they remained for two, three minutes.

Then the woman folded her fat, pudgy hands; her head sank low on her breast; and she sobbed, 'God's will be done!'

# E.J. Pratt
## 1882–1964

The publication in 1923 of Pratt's *Newfoundland Verse* marked a turning point in Canadian literary history, introducing Imagism into Canada in poems such as 'The Shark'. Imagism was a precursor of modernism that prepared Canadian writing for the poetics of that later movement. Pratt himself, however, was never a member of any school but a poet who went his own way: although his subsequent work remained strongly imagistic, it was also often narrative and dramatic, focusing on individuals, their sense of place, and the elements with which they were often in conflict (see, for example, 'Silences'). Unlike most of his contemporaries, Pratt worked extensively in longer poetic forms. Indeed, the magnitude of Pratt's long poems has sometimes overshadowed his shorter lyrics, though they remain important in their own right. The density and complex dramatic construction of 'Come Away, Death', for example, make it one of the most memorable poems in Canadian literature.

E.J. Pratt—'Ned' as he was called by his many friends, who remembered his personal warmth and conviviality with affection—was born in 1882 in Western Bay, Newfoundland. Growing up on the Newfoundland coast gave him an intense feeling for the sea, especially as a place where the individual is tested by nature. As a young man, Pratt prepared himself to follow his father into the Methodist ministry and, after his education at St John's Methodist College, he served as both a student-minister and a teacher in several small Newfoundland communities. In 1907, he came to Toronto to continue his education, enrolling in Victoria College, University of Toronto, where he studied theology, philosophy, and psychology. Despite taking his Bachelor of Divinity and being ordained in 1913, he remained at the university, becoming a demonstrator for the Department of Psychology and completing a PhD thesis on the eschatology of St Paul. In 1919, Pelham Edgar, the chair of the Department of English and a staunch supporter of Canadian poetry, provided Pratt with an alternative to a religious career by making him an associate professor of English at Victoria, largely on the strength of his promise as a poet. Pratt remained there until he retired in 1953.

Pratt's decision not to enter the ministry, apparently the result of a crisis of faith not uncommon in the late Victorian era, was specifically rooted in his childhood encounters with the tragedies of Newfoundland seafaring life. As he later wrote, he was puzzled by 'the ironic enigma of Nature in relation to the Christian view of the world.' Struggling with traditional perceptions of God and human existence, he turned toward Darwinian ideas that came in his poetry to express what Sandra Djwa has called his 'evolutionary vision'. The philosophical position in this poetry is not, however, entirely clear: it variously commends humanism, stoic heroism, and aspects of Christianity. Perhaps the closest Pratt came to synthesizing his beliefs was in a radio broadcast about the self-sacrificing heroism shown in the sea-rescue that was the subject of *The Roosevelt and the Antinoe* (1930): 'Science in league with good will; individual courage and humanity behind the machine. It's that sort of thing that's the hope of the world.'

*Newfoundland Verse* was followed by *The Witches' Brew* (1925), a comic saga about the intoxication of the ocean's creatures that demonstrates the exuberant humour often found in Pratt's writing. The next year, Pratt published *Titans*, a volume made up of two long poems, 'The Cachalot', about a hunt for a great whale, and 'The Great Feud', a fable of prehistoric war among the animals. Especially striking among Pratt's long poems is his 1935 *The Titanic*, with its journalistic style, dramatic dialogue, and fragmented form. It is an example of the way Pratt used historical details in most of his poetry (he was a painstaking researcher) and of what Dorothy Livesay has called a new kind of poetry, one that is 'neither epic nor narrative, but documentary.' This documentary quality in Pratt's poetry, also visible in the Second World War poems *Dunkirk* (1941) and *Behind the Log* (1947), derives not only from subject matter but also from its specialized language, filled with technical names, precise bits of knowledge, and arcane facts. Pratt also continued to publish collections of his shorter poems, including *The Fable of the Goats* (1937) and *Still Life* (1943).

Pratt turned to Canadian history to create his two national epics—extended considerations of crucial episodes in the nation's development: *Brébeuf and His Brethren* (1940), the story of seventeenth-century Jesuit missionaries to the Hurons, and *Towards the Last Spike* (1952), about the building of the CPR (both won Governor General's Awards). To Northrop Frye, who edited Pratt's *Collected Poems* (1958), Pratt took on the role of epic bard in Canada—a 'poet of an oral and pre-literate society,' transforming the history and, in *Towards the Last Spike*, the scientific knowledge of a culture into a heroic and mythic whole (*The Bush Garden*). In 1983 and 1985, Pratt's collected prose was published in two volumes: *E.J. Pratt on His Life and Poetry and Pursuits Amateur and Academic*. A two-volume edition of his *Complete Poems* was followed by a new edition of his *Selected Poems* in 2000.

## Towards the Last Spike

Pratt's choice of subject was a considered one: the building of the Canadian Pacific Railroad was viewed both in its own day and in Pratt's as a crucial act of bringing the new Dominion of Canada into existence by giving the country the sea-to-sea span its national motto promised. The belief that the unification of the provinces into a single nation had become necessary following the end of the US Civil War—if British North America was not to be taken over by the States—along with the developing demographics of Canada, with the bulk of its population stretched along the border, created an enduring sense that Canadian union depended on drawing the country together with an east–west transportation system that did not necessitate crossing into the United States at any point. Thus, the successful completion of the CPR—symbolized by the driving of the last spike—meant much more than the conquest of the wilderness by commercial interests: it came to be understood as a heroic struggle for national and cultural independence and autonomy.

In 'The Truant', Pratt showed himself impressed by the immense technological and scientific achievements of his age. In *Towards the Last Spike* he carried that sense of the new age still further: the hero of his epic is the whole community of engineers, builders, and politicians who, by joining together, achieve what seemed almost impossible. Perhaps because the rhetoric of the Second World War was still lingering when Pratt composed the poem, their struggle to succeed is frequently cast in martial terms, but this lexicon also suggests that the building of the railroad is what, in Canada, took the place of a revolutionary war—a long battle fought against both a landscape that resists with all the energy of a prehistoric monster and the competition of the American entrepreneurial railroads, which had more funds at their disposal and much easier terrain to cross. That Canada's railroad depended on a mix of government and private participation, that Pratt's epic hero is a community of individuals rather than a single man, that the main quality of epic heroism in

*Towards the Last Spike* is endurance and faith in the future, and that the final victory is celebrated modestly made this poem one that spoke out of, and to, Canada at mid-twentieth century.

The poem reprinted here is abridged. Pratt saw the struggle to build the CPR as one that had to be fought politically as well as physically; in *Towards the Last Spike*, he sets two combats in balanced counterpoint, the one led by William Van Horne against the resistant landscape made possible by the other, led by Sir John A. Macdonald, who must engage in heroic debates and endure grave conflicts in the Canadian Parliament to maintain support for the venture. Although the political passages retain considerable interest, for contemporary readers the sections detailing the opening of the railway—through the north, across the prairies, and in the difficult passage across the Rockies—hold a greater attraction. Pratt supplied subheads and brief synopses at key moments in the poem, and these have been retained, giving readers a sense of what has been elided.

## The Shark

He seemed to know the harbour,
So leisurely he swam;
His fin,
Like a piece of sheet-iron,
Three-cornered,
And with knife-edge,
Stirred not a bubble
As it moved
With its base-line on the water.

His body was tubular                                        10
And tapered
And smoke-blue,
And as he passed the wharf
He turned,
And snapped at a flat-fish
That was dead and floating.
And I saw the flash of a white throat,

And a double row of white teeth,
And eyes of metallic grey,
Hard and narrow and slit.                                     20

Then out of the harbour,
With that three-cornered fin
Shearing without a bubble the water
Lithely,
Leisurely,
He swam—
That strange fish,
Tubular, tapered, smoke-blue,
Part vulture, part wolf,
Part neither—for his blood was cold.                         30

1923

# Newfoundland

Here the tides flow,
And here they ebb;
Not with that dull, unsinewed tread of waters
Held under bonds to move
Around unpeopled shores—
Moon-driven through a timeless circuit
Of invasion and retreat;
But with a lusty stroke of life
Pounding at stubborn gates,
That they might run                                          10
Within the sluices of men's hearts,
Leap under throb of pulse and nerve,
And teach the sea's strong voice
To learn the harmonies of new floods,
The peal of cataract,
And the soft wash of currents
Against resilient banks,
Or the broken rhythms from old chords
Along dark passages
That once were pathways of authentic fires.                  20

*Red is the sea-kelp on the beach,*
*Red as the heart's blood,*
*Nor is there power in tide or sun*
*To bleach its stain.*
*It lies there piled thick*
*Above the gulch-line.*
*It is rooted in the joints of rocks,*
*It is tangled around a spar,*
*It covers a broken rudder,*
*It is red as the heart's blood,*                                    30
*And salt as tears.*

Here the winds blow,
And here they die,
Not with that wild, exotic rage
That vainly sweeps untrodden shores,
But with familiar breath
Holding a partnership with life,
Resonant with the hopes of spring,
Pungent with the airs of harvest.
They call with the silver fifes of the sea,            40
They breathe with the lungs of men,
They are one with the tides of the sea,
They are one with the tides of the heart,
They blow with the rising octaves of dawn,
They die with the largo[1] of dusk,
Their hands are full to the overflow,
In their right is the bread of life,
In their left are the waters of death.

*Scattered on boom*
*And rudder and weed*                                    50
*Are tangles of shells;*
*Some with backs of crusted bronze,*
*And faces of porcelain blue,*
*Some crushed by the beach stones*
*To chips of jade;*
*And some are spiral-cleft*
*Spreading their tracery on the sand*
*In the rich veining of an agate's heart;*
*And others remain unscarred,*
*To babble of the passing of the winds.*              60

---

1  A musical passage in a slow, dignified style.

Here the crags
Meet with winds and tides—
Not with that blind interchange
Of blow for blow
That spills the thunder of insentient seas;
But with the mind that reads assault
In crouch and leap and the quick stealth,
Stiffening the muscles of the waves.
Here they flank the harbours,
Keeping watch                                                    70
On thresholds, altars and the fires of home,
Or, like mastiffs,
Over-zealous,
Guard too well.

*Tide and wind and crag,*
*Sea-weed and sea-shell*
*And broken rudder—*
*And the story is told*
*Of human veins and pulses,*
*Of eternal pathways of fire,*                                    80
*Of dreams that survive the night,*
*Of doors held ajar in storms.*

1923


# Silences

There is no silence upon the earth or under the earth like the
        silence under the sea;
No cries announcing birth,
No sounds declaring death.
There is silence when the milt is laid on the spawn in the
        weeds and fungus of the rock-clefts;
And silence in the growth and struggle for life.
The bonitoes pounce upon the mackerel,
And are themselves caught by the barracudas,
The sharks kill the barracudas                                   10
And the great molluscs rend the sharks,
And all noiselessly—
Though swift be the action and final the conflict,
The drama is silent.

There is no fury upon the earth like the fury under the sea.
For growl and cough and snarl are the tokens of spendthrifts
 who know not the ultimate economy of rage.
Moreover, the pace of the blood is too fast.
But under the waves the blood is sluggard and has the same
 temperature as that of the sea.        20

There is something pre-reptilian about a silent kill.

Two men may end their hostilities just with their battle-cries.
'The devil take you,' says one.
'I'll see you in hell first,' says the other.
And these introductory salutes followed by a hail of gutturals
 and sibilants are often the beginning of friendship, for who
 would not prefer to be lustily damned than to be half-
 heartedly blessed?
No one need fear oaths that are properly enunciated, for they
 belong to the inheritance of just men made perfect, and, for  30
 all we know, of such may be the Kingdom of Heaven.
But let silent hate be put away for it feeds upon the heart of
 the hater.
Today I watched two pairs of eyes. One pair was black and
 the other grey. And while the owners thereof, for the space
 of five seconds, walked past each other, the grey snapped at
 the black and the black riddled the grey.
One looked to say—'The cat,'
And the other—'The cur.'
But no words were spoken;          40
Not so much as a hiss or a murmur came through the perfect
 enamel of the teeth; not so much as a gesture of enmity.
If the right upper lip curled over the canine, it went unnoticed.
The lashes veiled the eyes not for an instant in the passing.
And as between the two in respect to candour of intention or
 eternity of wish, there was no choice, for the stare was
 mutual and absolute.
A word would have dulled the exquisite edge of the feeling.
An oath would have flawed the crystallization of the hate.
For only such culture could grow in a climate of silence—  50
Away back before emergence of fur or feather, back to the
 unvocal sea and down deep where the darkness spills its
 wash on the threshold of light, where the lids never close
 upon the eyes, where the inhabitants slay in silence and are
 as silently slain.

1937

# The Prize Cat

Pure blood domestic, guaranteed,
Soft-mannered, musical in purr,
The ribbon had declared the breed,
Gentility was in the fur.

Such feline culture in the gads[1]
No anger ever arched her back—
What distance since those velvet pads
Departed from the leopard's track!

And when I mused how Time had thinned
The jungle strains within the cells,         10
How human hands had disciplined
Those prowling optic parallels;

I saw the generations pass
Along the reflex of a spring,
A bird had rustled in the grass,
The tab had caught it on the wing:

Behind the leap so furtive-wild
Was such ignition in the gleam,
I thought an Abyssinian child
Had cried out in the whitethroat's[2] scream.     20

1937

---

1 Claws.
2 Sparrow's. Pratt said that this poem 'refers to Mussolini's attack on Ethiopia just before the Second World War. I had been pondering over the illusion that, with the growth of civilization and culture, human savager was disappearing.'

# Come Away, Death[1]

Willy-nilly, he comes or goes, with the clown's logic,
Comic in epitaph, tragic in epithalamium.[2]
And unseduced by any mused rhyme.
However blow the winds over the pollen,
Whatever the course of the garden variables,
He remains the constant,
Ever flowering from the poppy seeds.

There was a time he came in formal dress,
Announced by Silence tapping at the panels
In deep apology.                                          10
A touch of chivalry in his approach,
He offered sacramental wine,
And with acanthus[3] leaf
And petals of the hyacinth
He took the fever from the temples
And closed the eyelids,
Then led the way to his cool longitudes
In the dignity of the candles.

His mediaeval grace is gone—
Gone with the flame of the capitals[4]                    20
And the leisured turn of the thumb
Leafing the manuscripts,
Gone with the marbles
And the Venetian mosaics,
With the bend of the knee
Before the rose-strewn feet of the Virgin.

---

1  In the opening scene of Shakespeare's *Twelfth Night*, a clown sings an 'old and plain' song that begins 'Come away, come away, death'. Sandra Djwa has pointed out an echo of another of Shakespeare's clowns in the poem's first line—the gravedigger in the opening of Act V of *Hamlet*, who (in an example of his 'clown's logic') says: 'if the man go to this water, and drown himself, it is, will he, nill he, he goes—mark you that; but if the water come to him and drown him, he drowns not himself: argal, he that is not guilty of his own death shortens not his own life.'

2  A formal poem on the occasion of a wedding.

3  A herb once in wide use for its supposed mollifying properties. Hyacinth petals were associated with the ancient festival honouring the mythic youth Hyacinthus, who was turned into a hyacinth after his death at the hands of Apollo; the festival began with funeral offerings and lamentations but ended with songs of joy for his achievement of immortality.

4  That is, the illustrated letters that begin passages in illuminated medieval manuscripts—but with a possible pun on capital cities consistent with the movement in the passage from the death of individuals to the multiple deaths resulting from modern warfare. (This poem was inspired by the Aug.-Sept. 1940 Battle of Britain—the first German bombing raids against England.)

The *paternosters* of his priests,
Committing clay to clay,
Have rattled in their throats
Under the gride[5] of his traction tread.                                          30

One night we heard his footfall—one September night—
In the outskirts of a village near the sea.
There was a moment when the storm
Delayed its fist, when the surf fell
Like velvet on the rocks—a moment only;
The strangest lull we ever knew!
A sudden truce among the oaks
Released their fratricidal arms;
The poplars straightened to attention
As the winds stopped to listen                                                      40
To the sound of a motor drone—
And then the drone was still.[6]
We heard the tick-tock on the shelf,
And the leak of valves in our hearts.
A calm condensed and lidded
As at the core of a cyclone ended breathing.
This was the monologue of Silence
Grave and unequivocal.

What followed was a bolt
Outside the range and target of the thunder,                                        50
And human speech curved back upon itself
Through Druid runways[7] and the Piltdown scarps,
Beyond the stammers of the Java caves,
To find its origins in hieroglyphs
On mouths and eyes and cheeks
Etched by a foreign stylus never used
On the outmoded page of the Apocalypse.[8]

1941, 1943

5  Grating sound; perhaps also with its alternate meaning of a spasm of pain. The whole line refers to the introduction of tanks in modern warfare.
6  The reference here is to the German bombs that fell during the Battle of Britain in 1940. (Pratt's poem was first published in April 1941.) After the planes passed over, there was a moment of silence before the explosion of the bombs.
7  The paths that form a part of primitive religious monuments such as those at Avebury and Stonehenge, which
   were formerly believed to be the work of the Druids (early Celtic priests). 'Piltdown', 'Java': when Pratt wrote
   the poem, Piltdown man and Java man were believed to be among the most primitive ancestors of modern man
   (the fossil evidence for Piltdown man was subsequently discovered to be fraudulent).
8  Another name for Revelation, the last book of the Bible, which predicts the events leading up to the end of the
   world, including Armageddon—the final battle between good and evil.

# The Truant[1]

'What have you there?' the great Panjandrum[2] said
To the Master of the Revels[3] who had led
A bucking truant with a stiff backbone
Close to the foot of the Almighty's throne.

'Right Reverend, most adored,
And forcibly acknowledged Lord
By the keen logic of your two-edged sword!
This creature has presumed to classify
Himself—a biped, rational, six feet high
And two feet wide; weighs fourteen stone;                    10
Is guilty of a multitude of sins.
He has abjured his choric origins,
And like an undomesticated slattern,
Walks with tangential step unknown
Within the weave of the atomic pattern.
He has developed concepts, grins
Obscenely at your Royal bulletins,
Possesses what he calls a will
Which challenges your power to kill.'

'What is his pedigree?'                                      20

'The base is guaranteed, your Majesty—
Calcium, carbon, phosphorus, vapour
And other fundamentals spun
From the umbilicus[4] of the sun,
And yet he says he will not caper
Around your throne, nor toe the rules
For the ballet of the fiery molecules.'

'His concepts and denials—scrap them, burn them—
To the chemists with them promptly.'

---

1  For the intellectual debate that provides the context for this poem, see Djwa, *E.J. Pratt: The Evolutionary Vision* (1974), pp. 114–20. Pratt wrote to Desmond Pacey: 'My own profession of faith was expressed in "The Truant", a comparatively late poem. . . . It is an indictment of absolute power without recognition of moral ends.'
2  A pompous and pretentious official; here, God, not as traditionally conceived but as a deity embodying mechanistic theories of the universe as a set of explicable scientific principles.
3  Formerly, a person appointed to organize merrymaking; here a satanic figure. The dramatic situation of the poem recalls the opening of the Book of Job.
4  Core (literally, navel).

'Sire,             30
The stuff is not amenable to fire.
Nothing but their own kind can overturn them.
The chemists have sent back the same old story—
"With our extreme gelatinous apology,
We beg to inform your Imperial Majesty,
Unto whom be dominion and power and glory,
There still remains that strange precipitate
Which has the quality to resist
Our oldest and most trusted catalyst.
It is a substance we cannot cremate      40
By temperatures known to our Laboratory." '

And the great Panjandrum's face grew dark—
'I'll put those chemists to their annual purge,
And I myself shall be the thaumaturge[5]
To find the nature of this fellow's spark.
Come, bring him nearer by yon halter rope:
I'll analyse him with the cosmoscope.'

Pulled forward with his neck awry,
The little fellow six feet short,
Aware he was about to die,      50
Committed grave contempt of court
By answering with a flinchless stare
The Awful Presence seated there.

The ALL HIGH swore until his face was black.
He called him a coprophagite.[6]
A genus *homo*, egomaniac,
Third cousin to the family of worms,
A sporozoan[7] from the ooze of night,
Spawn of a spavined troglodyte:
He swore by all the catalogue of terms      60
Known since the slang of carboniferous[8] Time.
He said that he could trace him back
To pollywogs and earwigs in the slime.
And in his shrillest tenor he began
Reciting his indictment of the man,
Until he closed upon this capital crime—

5  Miracle worker.
6  Feces eater.
7  A parasitic protozoan, a primitive form of life; 'spavined': lame; 'troglodyte': prehistoric cave dweller.
8  The Carboniferous period, in the latter part of the Paleozoic era, began about 345 million years ago.

'You are accused of singing out of key,
(A foul unmitigated dissonance)
Of shuffling in the measures of the dance,
Then walking out with that defiant, free                                70
Toss of your head, banging the doors,
Leaving a stench upon the jacinth[9] floors.
You have fallen like a curse
On the mechanics of my Universe.

'Herewith I measure out your penalty—
Hearken while you hear, look while you see:
I send you now upon your homeward route
Where you shall find
Humiliation for your pride of mind.
I shall make deaf the ear, and dim the eye,                             80
Put palsy in your touch, make mute
Your speech, intoxicate your cells and dry
Your blood and marrow, shoot
Arthritic needles through your cartilage,
And having parched you with old age,
I'll pass you wormwise through the mire;
And when your rebel will
Is mouldered, all desire
Shrivelled, all your concepts broken,
Backward in dust I'll blow you till                                     90
You join my spiral festival of fire.[10]
Go, Master of the Revels—I have spoken.'

And the little genus *homo*, six feet high,
Standing erect, countered with this reply—
'You dumb insouciant invertebrate,
You rule a lower than a feudal state—
A realm of flunkey decimals that run,
Return; return and run; again return,
Each group around its little sun,
And every sun a satellite.                                             100
There they go by day and night,
Nothing to do but run and burn,
Taking turn and turn about,

9  A reddish-orange gem.
10  According to *Dante's Inferno* (the first part of *The Divine Comedy*), hell is a downward spiralling pit. The three
   sections of this long poem trace Dante's spiralling descent into hell, where he finds Satan at its deepest point,
   and then (in the *Purgatorio* and *Paradiso*) his spiralling ascent up to the pinnacle of Heaven, where god resides,
   providing, as suggested later in 'The Truant', a blueprint of 'spiral stairs / From nadir depth to zenith height'.

Light-year in and light-year out,
Dancing, dancing in quadrillions,[11]
Never leaving their pavilions.

'Your astronomical conceit
Of bulk and power is anserine.[12]
Your ignorance so thick,
You did not know your own arithmetic.                    110
We flung the graphs about your flying feet;
We measured your diameter—
Merely a line
Of zeros prefaced by an integer.
Before we came
You had no name.
You did not know direction or your pace;
We taught you all you ever knew
Of motion, time and space.
We healed you of your vertigo                             120
And put you in our kindergarten show,
Perambulated you through prisms, drew
Your mileage through the Milky Way,
Lassoed your comets when they ran astray,
Yoked Leo, Taurus, and your team of Bears
To pull our kiddy cars of inverse squares.[13]

'Boast not about your harmony,
Your perfect curves, your rings
Of *pure and endless light*[14]—'Twas we
Who pinned upon your seraphim their wings,                130
And when your brassy heavens rang
With joy that morning while the planets sang
Their choruses of archangelic lore,
'Twas we who ordered the notes upon their score
Out of our winds and strings.
Yes! all your shapely forms
Are ours—parabolas of silver light,
Those blueprints of your spiral stairs
From nadir depth to zenith height,

11  $10^{15}$; with a pun on 'quadrille', a square dance for four couples.
12  Goose-like, foolish.
13  Leo, Taurus, and the Great and Lesser Bears (that is, Ursa Major and Ursa Minor, also known as the Big and
    Little Dippers) are constellations. The inverse square law is the principle in physics for calculating such things
    as the force of gravity over distance. (Like the intensity of light, the force of gravity decreases as the inverse
    square of the distance travelled.)
14  An allusion to the opening lines of 'The World' by the seventeenth-century mystical poet Henry Vaughan: 'I saw
    Eternity the other night / Like a great Ring of pure and endless light.'

Coronas, rainbows after storms,                                        140
Auroras on your eastern tapestries
And constellations over western seas.

'And when, one day, grown conscious of your age,
While pondering an eolith,[15]
We turned a human page
And blotted out a cosmic myth
With all its baby symbols to explain
The sunlight in Apollo's eyes,[16]
Our rising pulses and the birth of pain,
Fear, and that fern-and-fungus breath                                  150
Stalking our nostrils to our cave of death—
That day we learned how to anatomize
Your body, calibrate your size
And set a mirror up before your face
To show you what you really were—a rain
Of dull Lucretian atoms[17] crowding space,
A series of concentric waves which any fool
Might make by dropping stones within a pool,
Or an exploding bomb forever in flight[18]
Bursting like hell through Chaos and Old Night.                        160

'You oldest of the hierarchs
Composed of electronic sparks,
We grant you speed,
We grant you power, and fire
That ends in ash, but we concede
To you no pain nor joy nor love nor hate,
No final tableau of desire,
No causes won or lost, no free
Adventure at the outposts—only
The degradation of your energy[19]                                     170
When at some late
Slow number of your dance your sergeant-major Fate

---

15  Stone-Age artifact.
16  Apollo, especially under his epithet Phoebus ('The Bright One'), was identified as the god of the sun in Greek myth.
17  Lucretius (96?–55 BC) was a Roman poet and philosopher and one of the early atomists; he believed the universe was made of primordial 'seeds' of infinitesimal size dropping through a void.
18  The concept of the universe as beginning with an explosion from a single point and continuing to expand as matter moves away from this point was first formulated in the 1920s and became a well-established scientific theory during the 1930s. 'Chaos and Old Night': In Milton's *Paradise Lost* the fallen angels give 'A shout that tore Hell's Concave, and beyond / Frighted the Reign of *Chaos* and Old Night' (I. 542–3). 'Old Night' or 'eldest night', the outer limit of the universe in Milton's cosmology, was the eternal uncreated aspect of God out of which God derived Chaos, undifferentiated inchoate matter; God then produced Creation from Chaos.
19  A reference to the concept of entropy, the idea—implicit in the second law of thermodynamics—that the universe is running down because of a continuing loss of available energy.

Will catch you blind and groping and will send
You reeling on that long and lonely
Lockstep of your wave-lengths towards your end.

'We who have met
With stubborn calm the dawn's hot fusillades;
Who have seen the forehead sweat
Under the tug of pulleys on the joints,
Under the liquidating tally[20]                                    180
Of the cat-and-truncheon[21] bastinades;
Who have taught our souls to rally
To mountain horns and the sea's rockets
When the needle ran demented through the points;
We who have learned to clench
Our fists and raise our lightless sockets
To morning skies after the midnight raids,
Yet cocked our ears to bugles on the barricades,
And in cathedral rubble found a way to quench
A dying thirst within a Galilean[22] valley—                      190
No! by the Rood, we will not join in your ballet.'

1943

20 Record or score, but with a possible pun on the original meaning of 'tally', a notched stick, because 'bastinade' is a beating with a stick.
21 Whip (cat-o'-nine-tails) and club.
22 Of Galilee, the area, in northern Palestine, associated with Jesus's ministry; 'Rood': the cross.

## Towards the Last Spike

It was the same world then as now—the same,
Except for little differences of speed
And power, and means to treat myopia
To show an axe-blade infinitely sharp
Splitting things infinitely small, or else
Provide the telescopic sight to roam
Through curved dominions never found in fables.
The same, but for new particles[1] of speech—
Those algebraic substitutes for nouns
That sky cartographers would hang like signboards             10
Along the trespass of our thoughts to stop
The stutters of our tongues with their equations.

1 Here, referring to the new discoveries about sub-atomic particles, but punning on the fact that 'particle' is a term from grammar for minor parts of speech or common prefixes and suffixes.

As now, so then, blood kept its ancient colour,
And smoothly, roughly, paced its banks; in calm
Preserving them, in riot rupturing them.
Wounds needed bandages and stomachs food:
The hands outstretched had joined the lips in prayer—
'Give us our daily bread, give us our pay.'
The past flushed in the present and tomorrow
Would dawn upon today; only the rate                          20
To sensitize or numb a nerve would change;
Only the quickening of a measuring skill
To gauge the onset of a birth or death
With the precision of micrometers.
Men spoke of acres then and miles and masses,
Velocity and steam, cables that moored
Not ships but continents, world granaries,
The east-west cousinship, a nation's rise,
Hail of identity, a world expanding,
If not the universe: the feel of it                          30
Was in the air—'Union required the Line.'[2]
The theme was current at the banquet tables,
And arguments profane and sacred rent
God-fearing families into partisans.
Pulpit, platform and floor were sounding-boards;
Cushions beneath the pounding fists assumed
The hues of western sunsets; nostrils sniffed
The prairie tang; the tongue rolled over texts:
Even St Paul was being invoked to wring
The neck of Thomas in this war of faith                      40
With unbelief.[3] Was ever an adventure
Without its cost? Analogies were found
On every page of history or science.
A nation, like the world, could not stand still.
What was the use of records but to break them?
The tougher armour followed the new shell;
The newer shell the armour; lighthouse rockets
Sprinkled their stars over the wake of wrecks.
Were not the engineers at work to close
The lag between the pressures and the valves?                 50

2 When British Columbia was admitted into Confederation in 1871 it was with the promise that a railway would be built within ten years to connect that province with eastern Canada. Sir John A. Macdonald and his Conservative Party argued in Parliament that Canada's hold on the West and Northwest depended on the fulfillment of that promise, and that an all-Canadian route was essential to future national unity.
3 St Paul preached a doctrine of faith. The unbelievers are like the apostle Thomas who, before acknowledging the resurrected Christ, required physical proof (hence 'doubting Thomas'). Pratt is playfully alluding to the fact that men who built the CPR gained their railroad experience revitalizing the St Paul and Pacific Railway (see p. 359, note 8).

The same world then as now thirsting for power
To crack those records open, extra pounds
upon the inches, extra miles per hour.
The mildewed static schedules which before
Had like asbestos been immune to wood
Now curled and blackened in the furnace coal.
This power lay in the custody of men
From down-and-outers needing roofs, whose hands
Were moulded by their fists, whose skins could feel
At home incorporate with dolomite.[4]                                    60
To men who with the marshal instincts in them,
Deriving their authority from wallets,
Directed their battalions from the trestles.


## THE GATHERING

(*'Oats—a grain which in England is generally given to horses, but in Scotland supports the people.'*
*—Dr Samuel Johnson. 'True, but where will you find such horses, where such men?'—Lord Elibank's*
*reply as recorded by Sir Walter Scott.)*


Oatmeal was in their blood and in their names.
Thrift was the title of their catechism.
It governed all things but their mess of porridge
Which, when it struck the hydrochloric acid
With treacle and skim-milk, became a mash.
Entering the duodenum, it broke up
Into amino acids: then the liver                                         70
Took on its natural job as carpenter:
Foreheads grew into cliffs, jaws into juts.
The meal, so changed, engaged the follicles:
Eyebrows came out as gorse, the beards as thistles,
And the chest-hair the fell[5] of Grampian rams.
It stretched and vulcanized the human span:
Nonagenarians worked and thrived upon it.
Out of such chemistry run through by genes,
The food released its fearsome racial products:—
The power to strike a bargain like a foe,                                80
To win an argument upon a burr,


4  An important mineral in building, found in much limestone and some marble.
5  Fleece; the Grampians are the principal mountains of Scotland.

Invest the language with a Bannockburn,[6]
Culloden or the warnings of Lochiel,
Weave loyalties and rivalries in tartans,
Present for the amazement of the world
Kilts and the civilized barbaric Fling,
And pipes which, when they acted on the mash,
Fermented lullabies to *Scots wha hae*.[7]


Their names were like a battle-muster—Angus[8]
(He of the Shops) and Fleming (of the Transit),                 90
Hector (of the *Kicking Horse*), Dawson,
'Cromarty' Ross, and Beatty (Ulster Scot),
Bruce, Allan, Galt and Douglas, and the 'twa'—
Stephen (Craigellachie) and Smith (Strathcona)—
Who would one day climb from their Gaelic hide-outs,
Take off their plaids and wrap them round the mountains.
And then the everlasting tread of the Macs,
Vanguard, centre and rear, their roving eyes
On summits, rivers, contracts, beaver, ledgers;

6  Famous battles between Scotland and England. The English were beaten back by the Scots at the Battle of
   Bannockburn in 1314. In 1746 the forces of Prince Charles Edward Stuart (Bonnie Prince Charlie) were defeated
   at Culloden, a celebrated battle that marked the breakup of the Highland Clans. Donald Cameron of Lochiel
   was a famous Highland chieftain allied with Stuart; in 'Lochiel's Warning' (1802), the poet Thomas Campbell
   tells of a wizard appearing to Lochiel and forecasting the coming defeat. 'Fling': a vigorous but graceful dance,
   often performed to the point of exhaustion.
7  A reference to 'Robert Bruce's March to Bannockburn' by Robert Burns (1759–96), a famous war-glorifying
   patriotic song about the Scottish hero William Wallace, beginning, 'Scots wha hae wi' Wallace bled, / Scots,
   wham Bruce has aften led, / Welcome to your gory bed / Or to Victorie!'
8  Richard B. Angus (1831–1922) became general manager in 1879 of the St Paul and Pacific Railway following its
   purchase in 1877 by Donald Smith, George Stephen, Jim Hill, John S. Kennedy, Duncan McIntyre, and
   Norman Kittson; in 1880 Angus became part of the syndicate—with Smith, Stephen, McIntyre, and Henry
   Beatty—that was formed for the construction of the Canadian Pacific Railway. He later established shops in
   Montreal for the building of railway equipment. Sandford Fleming (1827–1915) was appointed engineer-in-chief
   for the CPR in 1871 and made the original surveys through the mountain ranges that presented the greatest obstacle between east and west. (A transit is a surveyor's instrument.) James Hector (1834–1907), geologist, discovered the Kicking Horse Pass through the Rocky Mountains, the pass eventually chosen over the more northerly
   Yellowhead Pass favoured by Fleming. Simon James Dawson (1820–1902), a civil engineer, first opened communications with the Red River country by means of the 'Dawson Route', and therefore was an important forerunner of the railway builders. James Ross (1848–1913), born in Cromarty, Scotland, took charge of the CPR west
   of Winnipeg in 1883. Randolph Bruce (1863–1942) was an engineer on surveys investigating alternate passes
   through the Rockies in 1891. Sir Hugh Allan (1810–82), one of the original projectors of the CPR, was given the
   initial contract for its construction in 1872; subsequent revelations of financial improprieties resulted in the fall
   of the Macdonald government and the loss of the contract. Alexander Galt (1817–93), one of the chief architects
   of the British North America Act, was an early railroad builder in Canada, associated with the Grand Trunk
   Railway. Sir James Douglas (1803–77) was the first governor of British Columbia (1858–64). George Stephen
   (1829–1921) was president of the syndicate formed to build the CPR and one of its two most important members along with Donald Smith (1820–1914), later Baron Strathcona. It was Smith who drove the last spike in
   1885, symbolizing the completion of the laying of tracks. In 1884 Stephen, who had gone to England to raise
   funds to keep the railway solvent in a period of financial crisis, sent a famous cable to Smith with the message
   'Stand Fast. Craigellachie'—the defiant war cry of the Clan Grant, which refers to a sentinel rock in the Scottish
   countryside familiar to both men. All of the men named in these lines came from Scotland except for Galt, who
   was born in England but was the son of the Scottish novelist John Galt.

Their ears cocked to the skirl of Sir John A.,  100
The general of the patronymic march.[9]

*(Sir John revolving round the Terms of Union with British*
*Columbia. Time, late at night.)*

Insomnia had ripped the bed-sheets from him
Night after night. How long was this to last?
Confederation had not played this kind
Of trickery on him. That was rough indeed,
So gravelled,[10] that a man might call for rest
And take it for a life accomplishment.
It was his laurel though some of the leaves
Had dried. But this would be a longer tug
Of war which needed for his team thick wrists  110
And calloused fingers, heavy heels to dig
Into the earth and hold—men with bull's beef
Upon their ribs. Had he himself the wind,
The anchor-waist to peg at the rope's end?
'Twas bad enough to have these questions hit
The waking mind: 'twas much worse when he dozed;
For goblins had a way of pinching him,
Slapping a nightmare on to dwindling snoozes.
They put him and his team into a tug
More real than life. He heard a judge call out—  120
'Teams settle on the rope and take the strain!'
And with the coaches' *heave*, the running welts
Reddened his palms, and then the gruelling *backlock*
Inscribed its indentations on his shoulders.
This kind of burn he knew he had to stand;
It was the game's routine; the other fire
Was what he feared the most for it could bake him—
That white dividing rag tied to the rope
Above the centre pole had with each heave
Wavered with chances equal. With the backlock,  130
Despite the legs of Tupper[11] and Cartier,
The western anchor dragged; the other side
Remorselessly was gaining, holding, gaining.
No sleep could stand this strain and, with the nightmare
Delivered of its colt, Macdonald woke.

9 That is, many of those involved in the railroad had the patronymic prefix 'Mac' on their names, chief among
   them Sir John A. Macdonald. 'Skirl': the shrill sound of a bagpipe.
10 Mired; run aground.
11 Charles Tupper (1812–1915) and George Etienne Cartier (1811–73) were Macdonald's staunchest allies in
   Parliament during the 1871 debate with Alexander Mackenzie's Liberals over the proposed transcontinental railway. Tupper later served as Macdonald's minister of railways and canals (1879–84).

Tired with the midnight toss, lock-jawed with yawns,
He left the bed and, shuffling to the window,
He opened it. The air would cool him off
And soothe his shoulder burns. He felt his ribs:
Strange, nothing broken—how those crazy drowses      140
Had made the fictions tangle with the facts!
He must unscramble them with steady hands.
Those Ranges pirouetting in his dreams
Had their own knack of standing still in light,
Revealing peaks whose known triangulation
Had to be read in prose severity.
Seizing a telescope, he swept the skies,
The north-south drift, a self-illumined chart.
Under Polaris was the Arctic Sea
And the sub-Arctic gates well stocked with names:      150
Hudson, Davis, Baffin, Frobisher;[12]
And in his own day Franklin, Ross and Parry
Of the Canadian Archipelago;
Kellett, McClure, McClintock, of *The Search*.
Those straits and bays had long been kicked by keels,
And flags had fluttered on the Capes that fired
His youth, making familiar the unknown.
What though the odds were nine to one against,
And the Dead March was undertoning trumpets,
There was enough of strychnine[13] in the names      160
To make him flip a penny for the risk,
Though he had palmed the coin reflectively
Before he threw and watched it come down *heads*.
That stellar path looked too much like a road map
Upon his wall—the roads all led to market—
The north-south route. He lit a candle, held
It to a second map full of blank spaces
And arrows pointing west. Disturbed, he turned
The lens up to the zenith, followed the course
Tracked by a cloud of stars that would not keep      170
Their posts—Capella,[14] Perseus, were reeling;

12 That is, these early explorers gave their names to Hudson Bay, Davis Strait, Baffin Bay, and Frobisher Bay. John
    Ross accompanied by Edward Parry in 1818, and Parry in 1819, made voyages that added vastly to knowledge
    about the region, as did John Franklin's expeditions into the Arctic archipelago between 1819 and 1825. After
    Franklin departed on a third voyage in 1845, from which he never returned, a reward was offered for informa-
    tion about his fate, and a famous search was mounted that lasted from 1847 until 1859; Henry Kellett, Robert
    McClure, and Leopold McClintock were among those who took part. For details see the headnote to Franklin,
    pp. 65–6.
13 Although highly toxic, strychnine was formerly used for its properties as a stimulant.
14 Brightest star in the constellation Auriga, which is one of the prominent constellations of the northern celes-
    tial hemisphere, with Perseus, Cassiopeia (a queen seated on a throne), Aries (the ram), and Cygnus (the swan).

Low in the north-west, Cassiopeia
Was qualmish, leaning on her starboard arm-rest,
And Aries was chasing, butting Cygnus,
Just diving. Doubts and hopes struck at each other.
Why did those constellations look so much
Like blizzards? And what lay beyond the blizzards?

'Twas chilly at the window. He returned
To bed and savoured soporific terms:
*Superior*, the *Red River, Selkirk, Prairie*,                    180
*Port Moody* and *Pacific*. Chewing them,
He spat out *Rocky* grit before he swallowed.
*Selkirk*![15] This had the sweetest taste. Ten years
Before, the Highland crofters had subscribed
Their names in a memorial[16] for the Rails.
Sir John reviewed the story of the struggle,
That four months' journey from their native land—
The Atlantic through the Straits to Hudson Bay,
Then the Hayes River to Lake Winnipeg
Up to the Forks of the Assiniboine.                              190
He could make use of that—just what he needed,
A Western version of the Arctic daring,
Romance and realism, double dose.
How long ago? Why, this is '71.
Those fellows came the time Napoleon
Was on the steppes.[17] For sixty years they fought
The seasons, 'hoppers, drought, hail, wind and snow;
Survived the massacre at Seven Oaks,
The 'Pemmican War' and the Red River floods.
They wanted now the Road—those pioneers                          200
Who lived by spades instead of beaver traps.
Most excellent word that, pioneers! Sir John
Snuggled himself into his sheets, rolling
The word around his tongue, a theme for song,
Or for a peroration to a speech.

15  The town founded by the Red River settlers. The lines that follow recapitulate the progress of these distressed
    Highlanders who came to Canada under the leadership of Lord Selkirk (1771–1820) as they journeyed to the Red
    River to found a settlement there, on land granted to Selkirk by the Hudson's Bay Company; crucial events in the
    history of the Settlement are mentioned in lines 186–99. The massacre at Seven Oaks took place in 1816 when the
    governor of the colony and twenty of his men were killed by Métis; this hostility had been prompted by the North
    West Company, which found that the location of the Red River Settlement cut off its vital supply of pemmican
    (preserved buffalo meat); the union in 1821 of the rival Hudson's Bay Company with the North West Company
    ended that conflict, but flooding in 1826 (and again in 1852) brought new hardship to the Selkirk settlers.
    'Crofters': tenant farmers; 'memorial': petition.
16  Petition.
17  Napoleon invaded Russia in 1812 (the year the Red River Settlement was founded), although he never actually
    reached the steppes, the treeless grassland southeast of Moscow.

## THE HANGOVER AT DAWN

He knew the points that had their own appeal.
These did not bother him: the patriot touch,
The Flag, the magnetism of explorers,
The national unity. These could burn up
The phlegm in most of the provincial throats.                    210
But there was one tale central to his plan
(The focus of his headache at this moment),
Which would demand the limit of his art—
The ballad of his courtship in the West:
Better reveal it soon without reserve.


## THE LADY OF BRITISH COLUMBIA

Port Moody and Pacific! He had pledged
His word the Line should run from sea to sea.
'From sea to sea', a hallowed phrase.[18] Music
Was in that text if the right key were struck,
And he must strike it first, for, as he fingered                  220
The clauses of the pledge, rough notes were rasping—
'No Road, No Union', and the converse true.
East-west against the north-south run of trade,
For California like a sailor-lover
Was wooing over-time. He knew the ports.
His speech was as persuasive as his arms,
As sinuous as Spanish arias—
Tamales, Cazadero, Mendocino,
Curling their baritones around the Lady.
Then Santa Rosa, Santa Monica,[19]                               230
Held absolution in their syllables.
But when he saw her stock of British temper
Starch at ironic sainthood in the whispers—
'Rio de nuestra señora de Buena guia',[20]
He had the tact to gutturalize the liquids,[21]

18 'Hallowed' because its original source is Psalm 72:8: 'He shall have dominion also from sea to sea'; the phrase (in Latin, *'a mari usque ad mari'*) was adopted as Canada's national motto in 1866, when the word 'dominion' was chosen to designate Canada.

19 The Bay of Tamoles (or Tamales) and the other places named here are in California, chiefly northern California. The temptation of linking a north-south rail line to California with its seaports was very real, and Pratt seems to be specifically alluding to the California coastal rail line that ran north from Sausalito to Cazadero, beginning in 1875, and eventually on to Mendocino.

20 'River of Our Lady of Safe Conduct' [Pratt's note].

21 Pratt is playing here with the sense of 'liquids' in the linguistic sense, i.e. the sounds of the *r* and the *l* in the Spanish place names, which the personified California is gutturalizing to make them sound more familiar to English Canadian ears, and the fact that these names are associated with coastal ports and therefore with literal liquids.

Steeping the tunes to drinking songs, then take
Her on a holiday where she could watch
A roving sea-born Californian pound
A downy chest and swear by San Diego.

Sir John, wise to the tricks, was studying hard,                    240
A fresh proposal for a marriage contract.[22]
He knew a game was in the ceremony.
That southern fellow had a healthy bronze
Complexion, had a vast estate, was slick
Of manner. In his ardour he could tether
Sea-roses to the blossoms of his orchards,
And for his confidence he had the prime
Advantage of his rival—*he was there*.


## THE LONG-DISTANCE PROPOSAL

A game it was, and the Pacific lass
Had poker wisdom on her face. Her name                    250
Was rich in values—*British*; this alone
Could raise Macdonald's temperature: so could
*Columbia*[23] with a different kind of fever,
And in between the two, *Victoria*.
So the *Pacific* with its wash of letters
Could push the Fahrenheit another notch.
She watched for bluff on those Disraeli features,[24]
Impassive but for arrowy chipmunk eyes,
Engaged in fathoming a contract time.
With such a dowry she could well afford                    260
To take the risk of tightening the terms—
'Begin the Road in two years, end in ten'[25]—
Sir John, a moment letting down his guard,
Frowned at the Rocky skyline, but agreed.


22  Pratt's image of British Columbia as a prospective bride has its source in popular journalism of the period; for example, on 2 January 1871 the *British Colonist* wrote: 'Clad in bridal attire, she is about to unite her destinies with a country which is prepared to do much for her.'
23  A name used to personify the United States.
24  Benjamin Disraeli (1804–88) was prime minister of England in 1868 (and again in 1874–80). Both Macdonald and Disraeli were thought of as being physically unattractive, with prominent noses.
25  The first clause of the agreement negotiated with British Columbia in 1870 read: 'The Government of the Dominion undertake to secure the commencement simultaneously, within two years from the date of the union, of the construction of a railway, from the Pacific towards the Rocky Mountains, and from such point as may be selected, east of the Rocky Mountains towards the Pacific, to connect the seaboard of British Columbia with the railway system of Canada, and further, to secure the completion of such railway within ten years from the date of such union.'

*(The Terms ratified by Parliament, British Columbia enters Confederation July, 1871, Sandford Fleming being appointed engineer-in-chief of the proposed Railway, Walter Moberly[26] to cooperate with him in the location of routes. 'Of course, I don't know how many millions you have, but it is going to cost you money to get through those canyons.'—Moberly to Macdonald.)*

## THE PACIFIC SCANDAL[27]

*(Huntingdon's charges of political corruption based on correspondence and telegrams rifled from the offices of the solicitor of Sir Hugh Allan, Head of the Canada Pacific Company; Sir John's defence; and the appearance of the Honourable Edward Blake[28] who rises to reply to Sir John at 2 a.m.)*

\* \* \*

*(The Charter granted to The Canadian Pacific Railway, February 17, 1881, with George Stephen as first President . . . One William Cornelius Van Horne[29] arrives in Winnipeg, December 31, 1881, and there late at night, forty below zero, gives vent to a soliloquy.)*

Stephen had laid his raw hands on Van Horne,
Pulled him across the border, sent him up
To get the feel of northern temperatures.
He knew through Hill[30] the story of his life
And found him made to order. Nothing less
Than geologic space his field of work,                    680
He had in Illinois explored the creeks
And valleys, brooded on the rocks and quarries.
Using slate fragments, he became a draughtsman,
Bringing to life a landscape or a cloud,
Turning a tree into a beard, a cliff
Into a jaw, a creek into a mouth

26  (1852–1915); Moberly had had extensive experience in railway construction prior to taking charge of the difficult Rocky Mountain and British Columbia surveys in 1871.

27  Name given the general charges of bribery, corruption, and underhand dealing that were brought by Liberal MP L.S. Huntingdon in 1872 against Macdonald and Hugh Allan. The charges, based on correspondence and papers stolen from Allan's office, suggested that Allan had paid Macdonald and Cartier for railway contracts. Subsequent investigation showed that at the very least the prime minister had acted unwisely in accepting substantial campaign contributions from Allan. On 3 November 1873 Macdonald defended himself in Parliament in a famous speech that lasted five hours.

28  Although Alexander Mackenzie was the formally chosen leader of the Liberals, Blake (1833–1912)—famous for his intellectual capacity and for his long and meticulously argued orations—was regarded as the party's real leader. He responded to Macdonald's speech for about half an hour immediately after it was over, and then for a further four hours the next day. The Macdonald government fell on 5 November 1873.

29  (1843–1915); Van Horne, an American, became general manager of the CPR in 1881.

30  James Hill (1838–1916); the Canadian-born American investor who was responsible for the formation of the Canadian group (which included George Stephen) that purchased the St Paul and Pacific Railway in 1877, recommended Van Horne to Stephen as 'a man of great mental and physical power to carry this line through'.

With banks for lips. He loved to work on shadows.
Just now the man was forcing the boy's stature,
The while the youth tickled the man within.
Companioned by the shade of Agassiz,[31]                        690
He would come home, his pockets stuffed with fossils—
Crinoids and fish-teeth—and his tongue jabbering
Of the earth's crust before the birth of life,
Prophetic of the days when he would dig
Into Laurentian rock. The morse-key tick
And tape were things mesmeric—space and time
Had found a junction. Electricity
And rock, one novel to the coiling hand,
The other frozen in the lap of age,
Were playthings for the boy, work for the man.                 700
As man he was the State's first operator;[32]
As boy he played a trick upon his boss
Who, cramped with current, fired him on the instant;
As man at school, escaping Latin grammar,
He tore the fly-leaf from the text to draw
The contour of a hill; as boy he sketched
The principal, gave him flapdoodle ears,
Bristled his hair, turned eyebrows into quills,
His whiskers into flying buttresses,
His eye-tusks into rusted railroad spikes,                     710
And made a truss between his nose and chin.
Expelled again, he went back to the keys,
To bush and rock and found companionship
With quarry-men, stokers and station-masters,
Switchmen and locomotive engineers.

Now he was transferred to Winnipeg.
Of all the places in an unknown land
Chosen by Stephen for Van Horne, this was
The pivot on which he could turn his mind.
Here he could clap the future on the shoulder                  720
And order Fate about as his lieutenant,
For he would take no nonsense from a thing
Called Destiny—the stars had to be with him.
He spent the first night in soliloquy,

31  Jean-Louis Agassiz (1807–73) was a Swiss-American naturalist who greatly added to the knowledge of North
    American zoology and geology; 'Crinoids': small plantlike sea animals ('crinoid' means 'lily-shaped').
32  Van Horne became a telegraph operator on the Illinois Central Railway when he was fourteen, thereby begin-
    ning a lifelong association with railroads; however, he lost that first job because he set up a ground plate that
    would give a mild shock to anyone who stepped on it.

Like Sir John A. but with a difference.
Sir John wanted to sleep but couldn't do it:
Van Horne could sleep but never wanted to.
It was a waste of time, his bed a place
Only to think or dream with eyes awake.
Opening a jack-knife, he went to the window,      730
Scraped off the frost. Great treks ran through his mind,
East-west. Two centuries and a half gone by,
One trek had started from the Zuyder Zee
To the new Amsterdam.[33] 'Twas smooth by now,
Too smooth. His line of grandsires and their cousins
Had built a city from Manhattan dirt.
Another trek to Illinois; it too
Was smooth, but this new one it was his job
To lead, then build a highway which men claimed
Could not be built. Statesmen and engineers      740
Had blown their faces blue with their denials:
The men who thought so were asylum cases
Whose monomanias harmless up to now
Had not swept into cells. His bearded chin
Pressed to the pane, his eyes roved through the west.
He saw the illusion at its worst—the frost,
The steel precision of the studded heavens,
Relentless mirror of a covered earth.
His breath froze on the scrape: he cut again
And glanced at the direction west-by-south.      750
That westward trek was the American,
Union-Pacific—easy so he thought,
Their forty million stacked against his four.
Lonely and desolate this. He stocked his mind
With items of his task: the simplest first,
Though hard enough, the Prairies, then the Shore
North of the Lake—a quantity half-guessed.
Mackenzie like a balky horse had shied
And stopped at this. Van Horne knew well the reason,
But it was vital for the all-land route.      760
He peered through at the South. Down there Jim Hill
Was whipping up his horses on a road[34]
Already paved. The stations offered rest
With food and warmth, and their well-rounded names
Were tossed like apples to the public taste.

33 The former name for New York City; i.e., from an area in the Netherlands to a city in North America named
     after one in the Netherlands.
34 The St Paul and Pacific Railway.

He made a mental note of his three items.
He underlined the Prairies, double-lined
The Shore and triple-lined *Beyond the Prairies*,
Began counting the Ranges—first the Rockies;
The Kicking Horse ran through them, this he knew;                    770
The Selkirks? Not so sure. Some years before
Had Moberly and Perry[35] tagged a route
Across the lariat loop of the Columbia.
Now Rogers was traversing it on foot,
Reading an aneroid and compass, chewing
Sea-biscuit and tobacco. Would the steel
Follow this trail? Van Horne looked farther west.
There was the Gold Range, there the Coastal Mountains.
He stopped, putting a period to the note,
As rivers troubled nocturnes in his ears.                           780
His plans must not seep into introspection—
Call it a night, for morning was at hand,
And every hour of daylight was for work.

* * *

## NUMBER ONE

Oak Lake to Calgary. Van Horne took off
His coat. The North must wait, for that would mean
His shirt as well. First and immediate
This prairie pledge—five hundred miles,[36] and it
Was winter. Failure of this trial promise
Would mean—no, it must not be there for meaning.
An order from him carried no repeal:
It was as final as an execution.                                    820
A cable started rolling mills in Europe:
A tap of Morse sent hundreds to the bush,
Where axes swung on spruce and the saws sang,
Changing the timber into pyramids
Of poles and sleepers. Clicks, despatches, words,
Like lanterns in a night conductor's hands,

35  Albert Perry accompanied Moberly (see p. 365, note 26) on his 1866 search for a pass through the Selkirk Mountains. Though the quest was unsuccessful then, and also when Moberly returned in 1871–2, Major A.B. Rogers later found in Moberly's journal a description of a valley that was partially investigated by Perry in 1866. Acting on that lead, Rogers eventually found the pass (named after him) that would take the CPR from the Kicking Horse Pass in the Rockies through the Selkirks. The Columbia River system forms a large, elliptical loop in the Selkirks, with Rogers Pass lying in the middle. An aneroid barometer measures elevation. 'Seabiscuit': a kind of dried bread once used to provision long ocean voyages.
36  When Van Horne became manager of the CPR he promised the directors that he would lay 500 miles of track in the 1882 season.

Signalled the wheels: a nod put Shaughnessy[37]
In Montreal: supplies moved on the minute.
Thousands of men and mules and horses slipped
Into their togs and harness night and day.                830
The grass that fed the buffalo was turned over,
The black alluvial mould laid bare, the bed
Levelled and scraped. As individuals
The men lost their identity; as groups,
As gangs, they massed, divided, subdivided,
Like numerals only—sub-contractors, gangs
Of engineers, and shovel gangs for bridges,
Culverts, gangs of mechanics stringing wires,
Loading, unloading and reloading gangs,
Gangs for the fish-plates[38] and the spiking gangs,        840
Putting a silver polish on the nails.
But neither men nor horses ganged like mules:
Wiser than both they learned to unionize.
Some instinct in their racial nether regions
Had taught them how to sniff the five-hour stretch
Down to the fine arithmetic of seconds.
They tired out their rivals and they knew it.
They'd stand for overwork, not overtime.
Faster than workmen could fling down their shovels,
They could unhinge their joints, unhitch their tendons;    850
Jumping the foreman's call, they brayed 'Unhook'
With a defiant, corporate instancy.
The promise which looked first without redemption
Was being redeemed. From three to seven miles
A day the parallels were being laid,
Though Eastern throats were hoarse with the old question—
Where are the settlements? And whence the gift
Of tongues which could pronounce place-names that purred
Like cats in relaxation after kittens?
Was it a part of the same pledge to turn                  860
A shack into a bank for notes renewed;
To call a site a city when men saw
Only a water-tank? This was an act
Of faith indeed—substance of things unseen—
Which would convert preachers to miracles,
Lure teachers into lean-to's for their classes.
And yet it happened that while labourers

37 Thomas Shaughnessy (1853–1933), known for his organizing ability, joined the CPR in 1882 as its purchasing
   agent; and became its president in 1899.
38 Connecting metal plates, bolted alongside two rails where they meet to make them stable.

Were swearing at their blisters in the evening
And straightening out their spinal kinks at dawn,
The tracks joined up Oak Lake to Calgary. 870

## NUMBER TWO

On the North Shore a reptile[39] lay asleep—
A hybrid that the myths might have conceived,
But not delivered, as progenitor
Of crawling, gliding things upon the earth.
She lay snug in the folds of a huge boa
Whose tail had covered Labrador and swished
Atlantic tides, whose body coiled itself
Around the Hudson Bay, then curled up north
Through Manitoba and Saskatchewan
To Great Slave Lake. In continental reach 880
The neck went past the Great Bear Lake until
Its head was hidden in the Arctic Seas.
This folded reptile was asleep or dead:
So motionless, she seemed stone dead—just seemed:
She was too old for death, too old for life,[40]
For as if jealous of all living forms
She had lain there before bivalves began
To catacomb their shells on western mountains.
Somewhere within this life-death zone she sprawled,
Torpid upon a rock-and-mineral mattress. 890
Ice-ages had passed by and over her,
But these, for all their motion, had but sheared
Her spotty carboniferous hair or made
Her ridges stand out like the spikes of molochs.[41]
Her back grown stronger every million years,
She had shed water by the longer rivers
To Hudson Bay and by the shorter streams
To the great basins to the south, had filled
Them up, would keep them filled until the end
Of Time. 900

39 Pratt uses two images of reptiles as personifications of the Laurentian Shield. The first, a sleeping reptile, is a
female lizard that corresponds to the area of the shield along the North Shore of Lake Superior; it lies 'snug'
against a larger reptile, a huge boa constrictor that represents the full extent of the Laurentian Shield itself.
40 Because the Shield is composed of rock from the Precambrian period, dating mostly from before the advent of
recorded life on earth.
41 Spiny-backed lizard of Australia, said to be the most grotesque of living reptiles; also the name of one of Satan's
company in John Milton's *Paradise Lost*.

Was this the thing Van Horne set out
To conquer? When Superior lay there
With its inviting levels? Blake, Mackenzie,
Offered this water like a postulate.
'Why those twelve thousand men sent to the North?
Nonsense and waste with utter bankruptcy.'
And the Laurentian monster at the first
Was undisturbed, presenting but her bulk
To the invasion. All she had to do
Was lie there neither yielding nor resisting.            910
Top-heavy with accumulated power
And overgrown survival without function,
She changed her spots as though brute rudiments
Of feeling foreign to her native hour
Surprised her with a sense of violation
From an existence other than her own—
Or why take notice of this unknown breed,
This horde of bipeds that could toil like ants,
Could wake her up and keep her irritated?
They tickled her with shovels, dug pickaxes,              920
Into her scales and got under her skin,
And potted holes in her with drills and filled
Them up with what looked like find grains of sand,
Black sand. It wasn't noise that bothered her,
For thunder she was used to from her cradle—
The head-push and nose-blowing of the ice,
The height and pressure of its body: these
Like winds native to clime and habitat
Had served only to lull her drowsing coils.
It was not size or numbers that concerned her.           930
It was their foreign build, their gait of movement.
They did not crawl—nor were they born with wings.
They stood upright and walked, shouted and sang;
They needed air—that much was true—their mouths
Were open but the tongue was alien.
The sounds were not the voice of winds and waters,
Nor that of any beasts upon the earth.
She took them first with lethargy, suffered
The rubbing of her back—those little jabs
Of steel were like the burrowing of ticks                940
In an elk's hide needing an antler point,
Or else left in a numb monotony.
These she could stand but when the breed
Advanced west on her higher vertebrae,

Kicking most insolently at her ribs,
Pouring black powder in her cavities,
And making not the clouds but her insides
The home of fire and thunder, then she gave
Them trial of her strength: the trestles tottered;
Abutments, bridges broke; her rivers flooded:                               950
She summoned snow and ice, and then fell back
On the last weapon in her armoury—
The first and last—her passive corporal bulk,
To stay or wreck the schedule of Van Horne.


## NUMBER THREE

The big one was the mountains—seas indeed!
With crests whiter than foam: they poured like seas,
Fluting the green banks of the pines and spruces.
An eagle-flight above they hid themselves
In clouds. They carried space upon their ledges.
Could these be overridden frontally,                                        960
Or like typhoons outsmarted on the flanks?
And what were on the flanks? The troughs and canyons,
Passes more dangerous to the navigator
Than to Magellan when he tried to read
The barbarous language of his Strait by calling
For echoes from the rocky hieroglyphs
Playing their pranks of hide-and-seek in fog:
As stubborn too as the old North-West Passage,
More difficult, for ice-packs could break up;
And as for bergs, what polar architect                                      970
Could stretch his compass points to draught such peaks
As kept on rising there beyond the foothills?
And should the bastions of the Rockies yield
To this new human and unnatural foe,
Would not the Selkirks stand? This was a range
That looked like some strange dread outside a door
Which gave its name but would not show its features,
Leaving them to the mind to guess at. This
Meant tunnels—would there be no end to boring?
There must be some day. Fleming and his men                                 980
Had nosed their paths like hounds; but paths and trails,
Measured in every inch by chain and transit,
Looked easy and seductive on a chart.
The rivers out there did not flow: they tumbled.

The cataracts were fed by glaciers;
Eddies were thought as whirlpools in the Gorges,
And gradients had paws that tore up tracks.

Terror and beauty like twin signal flags
Flew on the peaks for men to keep their distance.
The two combined as in a storm at sea—                           990
'Stay on the shore and take your fill of breathing,
But come not to the decks and climb the rigging.'
The Ranges could put cramps in hands and feet
Merely by the suggestion of the venture.
They needed miles to render up their beauty,
As if the gods in high aesthetic moments,
Resenting the profanity of touch,
Chiselled this sculpture for the eye alone.

*(Van Horne in momentary meditation at the Foothills.)*

His name was now a legend. The North Shore,
Though not yet conquered, yet had proved that he                 1000
Could straighten crooked roads by pulling at them,
Shear down a hill and drain a bog or fill
A valley overnight. Fast as a bobcat,
He'd climb and run across the shakiest trestle
Or, with a locomotive short of coal,
He could supply the head of steam himself.
He breakfasted on bridges, lunched on ties,
Drinking from gallon pails, he dined on moose.
He could tire out the lumberjacks; beat hell
From workers but no more than from himself.                      1010
Only the devil or Paul Bunyan shared
With him the secret of perpetual motion,
And when he moved among his men they looked
For shoulder sprouts upon the Flying Dutchman.[42]

But would his legend crack upon the mountains?
There must be no retreat: his bugles knew
Only one call—the summons to advance
Against two fortresses: the mind, the rock.
To prove the first defence was vulnerable,
To tap the treasury at home and then                             1020

42 The ghostly captain of a legendary ship doomed to sail the seas forever.

Untie the purse-strings of the Londoners,
As hard to loosen as salt-water knots—
That job was Stephen's, Smith's, Tupper's, Macdonald's.
He knew its weight: had heard, as well as they,
Blake pumping at his pulmonary bellows,
And if the speeches made the House shock-proof
Before they ended, they could still peal forth
From print more durable than spoken tones.
Blake had returned to the attack and given
Sir John the ague with another phrase        1030
As round and as melodious as the first:
'The Country's wealth, its millions after millions
Squandered—LOST IN THE GORGES OF THE FRASER':[43]
A beautiful but ruinous piece of music
That could only be drowned with drums and fifes.
Tupper, fighting with fists and nails and toes,
Had taken the word *scandal* which had cut
His master's ballots, and had turned the edge
With his word *slander*, but Blake's *sea*, how turn
That edge? Now this last devastating phrase!      1040
But let Sir John and Stephen answer this
Their way. Van Horne must answer it in his.


## INTERNECINE STRIFE

The men were fighting foes which had themselves
Waged elemental civil wars and still
Were hammering one another at this moment.
The peaks and ranges flung from ocean beds
Had wakened up one geologic morning
To find their scalps raked off, their lips punched in,
The colour of their skins charged with new dyes.
Some of them did not wake or but half-woke;      1050
Prone or recumbent with the eerie shapes
Of creatures that would follow them. Weather
Had acted on their spines and frozen them
To stegosaurs[44] or, taking longer cycles,
Divining human features, had blown back
Their hair and, pressing on their cheeks and temples,
Bestowed on them the gravity of mummies.

---

43 On 15–16 April 1880 Blake delivered his long speech opposing construction west of the Rockies, concluding in part: 'All that we can raise by taxes or loans, all that we can beg or borrow, is to be sunk in the gorges of the Fraser. . . . do not by your present action based on airy dreams and vain imaginings risk the ruin of your country.'
44 Dinosaurs with a double row of upright bony plates along their backs.

But there was life and power which belied
The tombs. Guerrilla evergreens were climbing
In military order: at the base                                    1060
The *ponderosa* pine; the fir backed up
The spruce; and it the Stoney Indian lodge-poles;[45]
And these the white-barks; then, deciduous,
The outpost suicidal Lyell larches[46]
Aiming at summits, digging scraggy roots
Around the boulders in the thinning soil,
Till they were stopped dead at the timber limit—
Rock *versus* forest with the rock prevailing.
Or with the summer warmth it was the ice,
In treaty with the rock to hold a line                           1070
As stubborn as a Balkan boundary,
That left its caves to score the Douglases,[47]
And smother them with half a mile of dirt,
And making snow-sheds, covering the camps,
Futile as parasols in polar storms.
One enemy alone had battled rock
And triumphed: searching levels like lost broods,
Keen on their ocean scent, the rivers cut
The quartzite, licked the slate and softened it,
Till mud solidified was mud again,                               1080
And then, digesting it like earthworms, squirmed
Along the furrows with one steering urge—
To navigate the mountains in due time
Back to their home in worm-casts on the tides.

Into this scrimmage came the fighting men,
And all but rivers were their enemies.
Whether alive or dead the bush resisted:
Alive, it must be slain with axe and saw,
If dead, it was in tangle at their feet.
The ice could hit men as it hit the spruces.                    1090
Even the rivers had betraying tricks,
Watched like professed allies across a border.
They smiled from fertile plains and easy runs
Of valley gradients: their eyes got narrow,
Full of suspicion at the gorges where
They leaped and put the rickets in the trestles.

45  The lodge-pole pine, characterized by slim, straight trunks; 'white-barks': the white-bark pine.
46  Or subalpine larch, which thrives at the timberline. The larch is the only tree with needlelike leaves that sheds
    them; hence it is deciduous.
47  Douglas firs, but with an echo of ancient Scottish battles, in which the Douglases were often prominent.

Though natively in conflict with the rock,
Both leagued against invasion. At Hell's Gate[48]
A mountain laboured and brought forth a bull
Which, stranded in mid-stream, was fighting back                 1100
The river, and the fight turned on the men,
Demanding from this route their bread and steel.
And there below the Gate was the Black Canyon
With twenty-miles-an-hour burst of speed.

*(Onderdonk[49] builds the 'skuzzy' to force the passage.)*

'Twas more than navigation: only eagles
Might follow up this run; the spawning salmon
Gulled by the mill-race had returned to rot
Their upturned bellies in the canyon'eddies.
Two engines at the stern, a forrard[50] winch,
Steam-powered, failed to stem the cataract.                      1110
The last resource was shoulders, arms and hands.
Fifteen men at the capstan,[51] creaking hawsers,
Two hundred Chinese tugging at shore ropes
To keep her bow-on from the broadside drift,
The *Skuzzy* under steam and muscle took
The shoals and rapids, and warped through the Gate,
Until she reached the navigable water—
The adventure was not sailing: it was climbing.

As hard a challenge were the precipices
Worn water-smooth and sheer a thousand feet.                     1120
Surveyors from the edges looked for footholds,
But, finding none, they tried marine manoeuvres.
Out of a hundred men they drafted sailors
Whose toes as supple as their fingers knew
The wash of reeling decks, whose knees were hardened
Through tying gaskets[52] at the royal yards:
They lowered them with knotted ropes and drew them
Along the face until the lines were strung
Between the juts. Barefooted, dynamite

48  The most treacherous section of the Fraser canyon because of its swift and turbulent rapids.
49  Andrew Onderdonk (1848–1905) supervised the building of the BC section of the CPR; 'skuzzy': a small, sturdy steamboat that Onderdonk had built when he became unhappy with the cost of hauling freight ('bread and steel') over the wagon road.
50  Forward.
51  Vertical revolving barrel onto which the cables ('hawsers') were wound; it was turned by men walking around it, pushing on horizontal levers. This was used to supplement the steam-driven forward winch.
52  A small rope that secures a furled sail to its supporting yard-arm.

Strapped to their waists, the sappers[53] followed, treading      1130
The spider films and chipping holes for blasts,
Until the cliffs delivered up their features
Under the civil discipline of roads.

## RING, RING THE BELLS

*Ring, ring the bells, but not the engine bells:*
*Today only the ritual of the steeple*
*Chanted to the dull tempo of the toll.*
*Sorrow is stalking through the camps, speaking*
*A common mother-tongue. 'Twill leave tomorrow*
*To turn that language on a Blackfoot tepee,*
*Then take its leisurely Pacific time*      1140
*To tap its fingers on a coolie's door.*
*Ring, ring the bells but not the engine bells:*
*Today only that universal toll,*
*For granite, mixing dust with human lime,*
*Had so compounded bodies into boulders*
*As to untype the blood, and, then, the Fraser,*
*Catching the fragments from the dynamite,*
*Had bleached all birthmarks from her swirling dead.*

Tomorrow and the engine bells again!

\*    \*    \*

## DYNAMITE ON THE NORTH SHORE

The lizard was in sanguinary mood.
She had been waked again: she felt her sleep      1240
Had lasted a few seconds of her time.
The insects had come back—the ants, if ants
They were—dragging *those* trees, *those* logs athwart
Her levels, driving in *those* spikes; and how
The long grey snakes unknown within her region
Wormed from the east, unstriped, sunning themselves
Uncoiled upon the logs and then moved on,
Growing each day, ever keeping abreast!
She watched them, waiting for a bloody moment,
Until the borers halted at a spot,      1250
The most invulnerable of her whole column,

---

53 Men who dig tunnels or trenches for blasting to undermine the mountain walls; 'films': filaments, fine threads,
     i.e., the men climbing down the rock walls on ropes are like spiders walking along their webs.

Drove in that iron, wrenched it in the holes,
Hitting, digging, twisting. Why that spot?
Not this the former itch. That sharp proboscis
Was out for more than self-sufficing blood
About the cuticle:[54] 'twas out for business
In the deep layers and the arteries.
And this consistent punching at her belly
With fire and thunder slapped her like an insult,
As with the blasts the caches of her broods                    1260
Broke—nickel, copper, silver and fool's gold,
Burst from their immemorial dormitories
To sprawl indecent in the light of day.
Another warning—this time different.

Westward above her webs she had a trap—
A thing called muskeg, easy on the eyes
Stung with the dust of gravel. Cotton grass,
Its white spires blending with the orchids,
Peeked through green table-cloths of sphagnum moss.
Carnivorous bladder-wort studded the acres,                    1270
Passing the water-fleas through their digestion.
Sweet-gale and sundew[55] edged the dwarf black spruce;
And herds of cariboo had left their hoof-marks,
Betraying visual solidity,
But like the thousands of the pitcher plants,
Their downward-pointing hairs alluring insects,
Deceptive—and the men were moving west!
Now was her time. She took three engines, sank them
With seven tracks down through the hidden lake
To the rock bed, then over them she spread                     1280
A counterpane of leather-leaf[56] and slime.
A warning, that was all for now. 'Twas sleep
She wanted, sleep, for drowsing was her pastime
And waiting through eternities of seasons.
As for intruders bred for skeletons—
Some day perhaps when ice began to move,
Or some convulsion ran fires through her tombs,
She might stir in her sleep and far below
The reach of steel and blast of dynamite,

54 Here, the epidermis, i.e., the surface.
55 A shrub and a flower that, like the other plants mentioned in this passage, attests to the bog-like quality of the
   apparently solid muskeg. The sundew, like the bladder-wort and the pitcher plant, is carnivorous, trapping and
   consuming insects in its sticky leaves.
56 A low evergreen shrub, so called because of the texture of its leaves.

She'd claim their bones as her possessive right                  1290
And wrap them cold in her pre-Cambrian folds.

*   *   *

## BACK TO THE MOUNTAINS

As grim an enemy as rock was time.
The little men from five-to-six feet high,
From three-to-four score years in lease of breath,
Were flung in double-front[57] against them both
In years a billion strong; so long was it                        1330
Since brachiopods[58] in mollusc habitats
Were clamping shells on weed in ocean mud.
Now only yesterday had Fleming's men,
Searching for toeholds on the sides of cliffs,
Five thousand feet above sea-level, set
A tripod's leg upon a trilobite.[59]
And age meant pressure, density. Sullen
With aeons, mountains would not stand aside;
Just block the path—morose but without anger,
No feeling in the menace of their frowns,                        1340
Immobile for they had no need of motion;
Their veins possessed no blood—they carried quartzite.
Frontal assault! To go through them direct
Seemed just as inconceivable as ride
Over their peaks. But go through them the men
Were ordered and their weapons were their hands
And backs, pickaxes, shovels, hammers, drills
And dynamite—against the rock and time;
For here the labour must be counted up
In months subject to clauses of a contract                       1350
Distinguished from the mortgage-run an age
Conceded to the trickle of the rain
In building river-homes. The men bored in,
The mesozoic rock arguing the inches.

This was a kind of surgery unknown
To mountains or the mothers of the myths.
These had a chloroform in leisured time,
Squeezing a swollen handful of light-seconds,

---

57 That is, they were like soldiers engaged in battles on two fronts.
58 A bivalve mollusc that Charles Darwin singled out as an example of a life-form that had not changed much
    from a remote geological epoch.
59 Fossil marine arthropods from the Paleozoic era (600 million to 230 million years ago).

When water like a wriggling casuist[60]
Had probed and found the areas for incision.                    1360
Now time was rushing labour—inches grew
To feet, to yards: the drills—the single jacks,
The double jacks—drove in and down; the holes
Gave way to excavations, these to tunnels,
Till men sodden with mud and roof-drip steamed
From sunlight through the tar-black to the sunlight.

*   *   *

*(The last gap in the mountains—between the Selkirks and
Savona's Ferry—is closed.)*

The Road itself was like a stream that men
Had coaxed and teased or bullied out of Nature.
As if watching for weak spots in her codes,                     1520
It sought for levels like the watercourses.
It sinuously took the bends, rejoiced
In plains and easy grades, found gaps, poured through them,
But hating steep descents avoided them.
Unlike the rivers which in full rebellion
Against the canyons' hydrophobic slaver[61]
Went to the limit of their argument:
Unlike again, the stream of steel had found
A way to climb, became a mountaineer.
From the Alberta plains it reached the Summit,                  1530
And where it could not climb, it cut and curved,
Till from the Rockies to the Coastal Range
It had accomplished what the Rivers had,
Making a hundred clean Caesarian cuts,
And bringing to delivery in their time
Their smoky, lusty-screaming locomotives.

## THE SPIKE

Silver or gold? Van Horne had rumbled '*Iron*'.
No flags or bands announced this ceremony,
No Morse in circulation through the world,
And though the vital words like Eagle Pass,                     1540

---

60  Here, one who specializes in quibbling, convoluted arguments.
61  That is, the canyons' walls seem to drool as would the jaws of a rabid dog.

Craigellachie,[62] were trembling in their belfries,
No hands were at the ropes. The air was taut
With silences as rigid as the spruces
Forming the background in November mist.
More casual than camera-wise, the men
Could have been properties upon a stage,[63]
Except for road maps furrowing their faces.

Rogers, his both feet planted on a tie,
Stood motionless as ballast. In the rear,
Covering the scene with spirit-level eyes,                               1550
Predestination on his chin, was Fleming.[64]
The only one groomed for the ritual
From smooth silk hat and well-cut square-rig beard
Down through his Caledonian[65] longitude,
He was outstaturing others by a foot,
And upright as the mainmast of a brig.
Beside him, barely reaching to his waist,
A water-boy had wormed his way in front
To touch this last rail with his foot, his face
Upturned to see the cheek-bone crags of Rogers.                          1560
The other side of Fleming, hands in pockets,
Eyes leaden-lidded under square-crowned hat,
And puncheon-bellied[66] under overcoat,
Unsmiling at the focused lens—Van Horne.
Whatever ecstasy played round that rail
Did not leap to his face. Five years had passed,
Less than five years—so well within the pledge.

The job was done. Was this the slouch of rest?
Not to the men he drove through walls of granite.
The embers from the past were in his soul,                               1570
Banked for the moment at the rail and smoking,
Just waiting for the future to be blown.

---

62 The driving of the last spike signifying the completion of the CPR (which was deliberately done without the
 elaborate ritual that marked the completion of the Union Pacific in the States) took place in the Eagle Pass; the
 place was called Craigellachie because of the name's significance for Smith and Stephen (see p. 359, conclusion
 of note 8).
63 The lines that follow are based on a famous photograph of the driving of the last spike.
64 That is, Fleming's square-cut beard made him look like the typical Scots-Calvinist that he was. (Calvinists
 believe in the doctrine of predestination, i.e. that one was born already destined for Heaven or Hell.)
65 Scottish (poetic).
66 Pot-bellied (a puncheon is a large cask of liquor).

At last the spike and Donald with the hammer!
His hair like frozen moss from Labrador
Poked out under his hat, ran down his face
To merge with streaks of rust in a white cloud.
What made him fumble the first stroke?[67] Not age:
The snow belied his middle sixties. Was
It lapse of caution or his sense of thrift,
That elemental stuff which through his life            1580
Never pockmarked his daring but had made
The man the canniest trader of his time,
Who never missed a rat-count,[68] never failed
To gauge the size and texture of a pelt?
Now here he was caught by the camera,
Back bent, head bowed, and staring at a sledge,
Outwitted by an idiotic nail.
Though from the crowd no laughter, yet the spike
With its slewed[69] neck was grinning up at Smith.
Wrenched out, it was replaced. This time the hammer     1590
Gave a first tap as with apology,
Another one, another, till the spike
Was safely stationed in the tie and then
The Scot, invoking his ancestral clan,
Using the hammer like a battle-axe,
His eyes bloodshot with memories of Flodden,[70]
Descended on it, rammed it to its home.

The stroke released a trigger for a burst
Of sound that stretched the gamut of the air.
The shouts of engineers and dynamiters,            1600
Of locomotive-workers and explorers,
Flanking the rails, were but a tuning-up
For a massed continental chorus. Led
By Moberly (of the Eagles and *this* Pass)
And Rogers (of *his own*), followed by Wilson,[71]

67 Smith bent the first spike and had to drive a second.
68 That is, who never miscounted muskrat pelts.
69 Twisted.
70 A Scottish battle against the English in 1513, of which John Hill Burton writes, in his *History of Scotland*: 'From other battles Scotland has suffered more unhappy political results, but this was the most disastrous of all in immediate loss. As a calamity rather than a disgrace, it has ever been spoken of with a mournful pride for the unavailing devotedness which it called out.'
71 All the men named in this passage were present at the driving of the last spike: Tom Wilson had served as Rogers' guide in the Kicking Horse surveys; John Egan was general superintendent of the CPR western division under Van Horne; Henry J. Cambie was a government engineer who supervised a difficult section of the road in the Fraser Canyon; Marcus Smith took over the BC surveys in 1873; George Harris was a Boston financier and company director; John H. McTavish was the CPR land commissioner.

And Ross (charged with the Rocky Mountain Section),
By Egan (general of the Western Lines),
Cambie and Marcus Smith, Harris of Boston,
The roar was deepened by the bass of Fleming,
And heightened by the laryngeal fifes                    1610
Of Dug McKenzie and John H. McTavish.
It ended when Van Horne spat out some phlegm
To ratify the tumult with 'Well Done'[72]
Tied in a knot of monosyllables.

Merely the tuning up! For on the morrow
The last blow on the spike would stir the mould
Under the drumming of the prairie wheels,
And make the whistles from the steam out-crow
The Fraser. Like a gavel it would close
Debate, making Macdonald's 'sea to sea'                  1620
Pour through two oceanic megaphones—
Three thousand miles of *Hail* from port to port;
And somewhere in the middle of the line
Of steel, even the lizard heard the stroke.
The breed had triumphed after all. To drown
The traffic chorus, she must blend the sound
With those inaugural, narcotic notes
Of storm and thunder which would send her back
Deeper than ever in Laurentian sleep.

1952

---

72 Van Horne's famous speech at the driving of the last spike was brief and to the point: 'All I can say is that the
   work has been done well in every way.'

# Marjorie Pickthall

## 1883–1922

Born in Middlesex, England, Marjorie Lowry Christie Pickthall immigrated with her parents to Toronto in 1889. She attended Saint Mildred's Girls' School and the Bishop Strachan School for Girls, selling her first story, 'Two Ears', to the *Toronto Globe* in 1898. After her mother's death in 1910 (an event that upset her greatly), she became an assistant librarian at Victoria College. In 1912, she returned to England to live with relatives, in an attempt to improve her failing health. There, she contributed to the war effort as much as her health permitted, working as an ambulance driver, farm labourer, and assistant librarian in a meteorological office. She returned briefly to Toronto in 1919 before moving to Victoria and then to Vancouver, where she died of complications following heart surgery.

Although Pickthall had turned more toward prose at the time of her death (she was working on a novel, *The Beaten Man*), she was known primarily in Canada as a poet. Only two collections of poetry, however, were published during her lifetime: *The Drift of Pinions* (1913) and *The Lamp of Poor Souls* (1916; rpr. 1972). The others were published posthumously: *The Woodcarver's Wife and Other Poems* (a one-act verse drama; 1922), *Little Songs* (1925), and *The Naiad and Five Other Poems* (1931). *The Complete Poems of Marjorie Pickthall* (1925), collected by her father, Arthur C. Pickthall, saw a series of editions including that of 1936, to which several newly discovered poems were added.

A prolific writer, Pickthall worked in a variety of forms and published her work in well-known magazines, both in North America and in England. Twenty-four of her many short stories were collected in *Angels' Shoes* (1922). As well, she wrote three juvenile novels—*Dick's Desertion: A Boy's Adventures in Canadian Forests* (1905), *The Straight Road* (1906), and *Billy's Hero; or, The Valley of Gold* (1908)—and two adult novels, *Little Hearts* (1915) and *The Bridge: A Story of the Great Lakes* (1921). *The Bridge* was

serialized both in *Everybody's* (New York) and *Sphere* (London); the juvenile novels were published serially in *East and West*, a paper sponsored by the Presbyterian Church.

In her day, Pickthall received both popular and critical acclaim, earning great praise from such influential critics as Archibald MacMechan, Sir Andrew Macphail, and Lorne Pierce (who wrote her biography in 1925). The Montreal Branch of the Canadian Authors' Association noted at the time of her death that 'her place is secure, not only as the first poet of Canada, but one of the first poets of the English language' (23 April). Condemned, however, in the 1940s by E.K. Brown, and then in the 1950s by Desmond Pacey, her poetry fell out of fashion at a time when literary tastes favoured irony over reverie, and a realistic vision over a stylized romantic one.

Ironically, Pickthall's early success may have contributed to her decline in popularity. She received public recognition even before the publication of her first collection of poetry by winning the Christmas poetry competition sponsored by the *The Mail and Empire* in 1900, and because of her many smaller publications in prominent magazines across North America. The poems of her first volume were collected at the suggestion of Andrew Macphail, which guaranteed its success; the first edition of a thousand copies sold out in ten days. Because of the early praise she received, she was never pushed to develop beyond the lyric conventions she inherited from the English Romantics and Pre-Raphaelites, though some of poems do reflect the Symbolist and Decadent writing important in Europe at the end of the nineteenth century. It is unfortunate that her career was cut short by her untimely death, because there is evidence in her poetry to suggest that she was beginning to question her use of these conventions. As Diana Relke points out, Pickthall, as a female poet, had difficulty locating herself in a lyric tradition that deals with the relationship between man and nature (*Canadian Literature*, 1987). Pickthall's own comments about gender are striking. In a letter to Lorne Pierce (27 Dec 1919) she wrote:

*To me the trying part is being a woman at all. I've come to the ultimate conclusion that I'm a misfit of the worst kind, in spite of a superficial feminity— emotion with a foreknowledge of impermanence, a daring mind with only the tongue as an outlet, a greed for experience plus a slavery to convention— what the deuce are you to make of that—as a woman? As a man, you could go ahead and stir things up fine.*

Her discomfort is evident in 'The Sleep-Seekers', for example, where the poetic voice, striving to identify itself in terms of 'there/here' and 'you/we', finally affirms a dream world lying beyond life and nature.

Much of Pickthall's poetry deals with this mystical and imaginative space, characterized by the colour silver and accessible only through a kind of artistic reverie. In 'Made in His Image', she expresses some of her concerns about a God who may be all-powerful, even all-knowing, but ultimately unfeeling. This troubled tone in her work led a contemporary essayist, John Daniel Logan, to describe her as not 'a natural, happy poet of Nature' but as a 'wistful, sorrowing poet of the Spirit' torn between a naturally 'pagan' spirit and a learned Christian 'asceticism' that did not wholly satisfy her (*Marjorie Pickthall: Her Poetic Genius and Art*, 1922).

The speaker's discomfort with her subject is echoed in the halting repetitions and alliterations of 'Made in His Image'. Unlike the flowing internal rhymes of 'The Sleep-Seekers', which inspired Archibald MacMehan to mourn the loss of 'the truest, sweetest singing voice ever heard in Canada,' the play with rhythm and repetition in such poems as 'Made in His Image' and 'The Bird in the Room' demonstrates the range and variety of Pickthall's skill.

'The Third Generation,' a good example of a Gothic form popular throughout the twentieth century—the ironic ghost story—suggests the guilt European settlers felt about their effect on the First Nations. It also serves as a prose continuation of Pickthall's concerns with the spirit, with sorrow, and with death.

## The Sleep-Seekers

Lift thou the latch whereon the wild rose clings,
Touch the green door to which the briar has grown.
If you seek sleep, she dwells not with these things,—
The prisoned wood, the voiceless reed, the stone.
But where the day yields to one star alone,
Softly Sleep cometh on her brown owl-wings,
Sliding above the marshes silently
To the dim beach between the black pines and the sea.

There; or in one leaf-shaken loveliness
Of birchen light and shadow, deep she dwells,          10
Where the song-sparrow and the thrush are heard,
And once a wandering flute-voiced mocking-bird,
Where, when the year was young,
Grew sweet faint bloodroot, and the adder-tongue
Lifting aloft her spire of golden bells.[1]

---

1  Bloodroot, adder-tongue (or adder's tongue, a kind of lily), and golden bells (a kind of daffodil) are all flowers that bloom in early spring.

Here shall we lift our lodge against the rain,
Walling it deep
With tamarac branches and the balsam fir,
Sweet even as sleep,
And aspen boughs continually astir                    20
To make a silver-gleaming,—
Here shall we lift our lodge and find again
A little space for dreaming.

1925


## The Bird in the Room

Last autumn when they aired the house
A bird got in, and died in this room.
Here it fluttered
Close to the shuttered
Window, and beat in the airless gloom,
No space for its wing, no drop for its mouth,—
A swallow, flying south.


And the velvet-creeping unsleeping mouse
Trampled that swiftness where it fell
On the dusty border                                   10
Pattern'd in order
With a citron flower and a golden shell,—
But it might not fly and it might not drink,
On the carpet's sunless brink.


A thought of you beat into my mind,
Empty and shuttered, dark, and spread
With dusty sheeting
To hide the beating
Tread of the hours. But the thought was dead
When I opened the door of that room, to find          20
If the Spring
Had left me anything—

1936

# Made in His Image

Between the archangels and the old eclipse
Of glory on perfect glory, does He feel
A vision, thin as frost at midnight, steal
And lay a nameless shadow on His lips?
Does He, Who gave the power, endure the pain?—
Look down the hollow'd universe, and see
His works, His worlds, choiring Him endlessly,—
His worlds, His works, all made, and made in vain?
Then does He bid all heaven beneath His hand,
In blossom of worship, flame on flame of praise,                    10
And taste their thunders, and grow sick, and gaze
At some gray silence that He had not planned,
And shiver among His stars, and nurse each spark
That wards Him from the uncreated dark?

1936

# The Third Generation[1]

> No shanty fires shall cheer them,
> No comrades march beside,
> But the northern lights shall beckon
> And the wandering winds shall guide.
> They shall cross the silent waters
> By a trail that is wild and far,
> To the place of the lonely lodges
> Under a lonely star.
>                    —*La Longue Traverse.*

'Bob, is this Lake Lemaire?'

Bob Lemaire, leaning against a wind-twisted tamarack on the ridge above the portage, looked long and very long at the desolate country spread out beneath them. Then he looked at a map, drawn on parchment in faded ink, which he had just unfolded from a waterproof case. 'I can't identify it,' he confessed at last, 'but I think—'

'If you say another word', groaned Barrett, 'about the reliability of your grandfather, I—I'll heave rocks at you.' Lemaire smiled slowly, and the smile transfigured his lean, serious face; he folded the map and replaced it in the little case. 'Well,' he answered, comfortingly, 'we can't mistake P'tite Babiche, anyway, when we come to it.'

---

1  An allusion to a passage in the Bible about 'visiting the iniquity of the fathers upon the children, and upon the children's children, unto the third and to the fourth generation' (Exodus 34:7).

'If the thing exists . . . Oh, I know your grandfather said he found it, and stuck it on his map. But no one else has ever found it since.'

'No one else', said Lemaire, quietly, 'has been so far west from the Gran' Babiche.'

He looked again at the land, one of the most desolate in the world, across which they must go. Lake, rapid, river; rock, scrub, pine, and caribou moss—here the world held only these things, repeated to infinity. But as Lemaire's grave eyes rested on them, those eyes showed nothing but stillness and a strange content. And Barrett, who had been watching his friend and not the new chain of lakes ahead, cried suddenly, 'Bob, I believe you like it!'

'Yes, I like it—if like is the word.'

'O gosh! And you never saw it till five years ago?'

'No.'

'And your father never saw it at all?'

'No. He married young, you know, and had no money. He worked in an office all his life. My mother said he used to talk in his sleep of—all this—which he had never seen. And when I saw it, it just seemed to—come natural.' He smiled again. 'We've three—four—more portages', he went on, 'before we camp.'

'And it's along of having Forbes Lemaire for a grandfather,' groaned Barrett, as he limped after Lemaire's light stride, down the rocky slope to the little beach where they had left their canoe.

They launched the canoe, thigh deep in the rush of the ice-clear water, and put out into yet another of that endless chain of unknown and uncharted lakes whose course they were following. Only one map in the world showed these lakes, those low iron hills, that swamp—the map made by Bob Lemaire's grandfather fifty years before; as far as was known, only one white man before themselves had ever tried the journey from the Gran' Babiche due west to the P'tite Babiche, that mythical river; and that had been Forbes Lemaire. As Barrett said, it was a tour personally conducted by the ghost of a grandfather.

Another wet portage—tripping and sliding under a low cliff among fallen shale and willow bushes—another lake, as wide, as lonely, as the former one. So for three hours. And then the afternoon shut down in drive on drive of damp gray mist; and they edged the canoe inshore, and beached it at last upon a dun ridge of sand, the shadows of dwarfed bullpines promising firing.

Too tired to speak, they made their camp, deftly, as long practice had taught them. Tinned beef, flapjacks and coffee had power, however, to change the very aspect of the weather. And Barrett, smoking the pipe of repletion, under a wisp of tent, had time to admire the Japanese effect of the writhed pines in the fog, to hear a sort of wild music in the voices of rain and water, and to meditate on the chances of an ouananiche for the morning's meal.

The shadows of the fog were changing to the shadows of night, and the silent Lemaire rose and flung wood on the fire. It sent out a warm glow; and as if it had been a signal, a living shadow crept from the shadow of the rocks, and very timidly approached the light.

Both men rose with an exclamation; for they had not seen a human being for nearly a month. Barrett said, 'An Indian,' and sank back on his blanket, leaving Lemaire to ask questions. Lemaire went round the fire, and stooped over the queer huddled shadow on the ground.

'Well?' Barrett called after him at last.

'A Montagnais,' Lemaire answered after a pause, some trouble in his voice. 'About the oldest old Indian I've ever seen; they aren't long-lived. . . . He seems a bit wrong in the head. He doesn't seem to know his name or where he comes from. But—he says he's going to a big encampment many days' journey west. He says he's been following us. He says he's a friend of mine.'

'Is he?'

'I never saw him before. . . . That's all I can get out of him. He's probably been cast off by his tribe. Why? Oh, too old to be useful.'

'Cruel brutes.'

'Not so cruel as some white men,' said Lemaire, half to himself. He had come back to the firelight, and was rummaging among their stores, none too plentiful. He returned to the old Indian, carrying food; and presently Barrett heard snapping sounds, as of a hungry dog feeding. Lemaire came again to his nook under the tent; and Barrett smoked out his pipe in silence. Then, as he knocked the ashes, fizzling, into a little pool of rain, he said gently, 'Bob, what makes you so uncommonly good to the Indians?'

Quiet Lemaire did not attempt to evade the direct question. But a rather shy flush rose to his dark, lean cheeks as he said diffidently, 'I suppose—because I feel my family—any one of my name—owes 'em something.'

'The grandfather·again, eh?'

'Yes. . . . Men had no souls in those days, Barrett. I think the tremendous loneliness—the newness—the lack of responsibility—something killed their souls. . . . Wait.'

Leaning forward, he flung more wood on the fire. And the red light flickered on his strong and gentle face. He glanced at his friend, and went on abruptly. 'I've my grandfather's maps and journals, you know—what my father called the shameful records of his fame. He was absolutely explicit in 'em. I never saw them in father's lifetime, but he left them to me, saying I could read them or not, as I liked. I was very proud of them. I read them. And upon my word—though from them I got the hints that may lead us to the rediscovery of the Lost Babiche—I'm almost sorry I did. It leaves a bad taste in the mind, if you know what I mean, to think that one's father's father was such a heroic scoundrel.'

'A bad record, Bobby?'

'Bad even for those days. Listen to me. While he was on this very expedition we're on now, he was taken sick. He was very sick, and going to be worse. He knew what it was. He was near the big summer camp of a tribe of Indians that had been very kind to him, coast Indians, come inland for the caribou hunting; he went to them. He was sick, and they took him in, and nursed him. And all the time he knew what it was he had. It was the smallpox.

'You know what La Picotte is in the wilds. They've a song about it still, down along the Lamennais. . . . For of all that tribe, only one family, they say, escaped. All the others died; they died as if the Angel of Destruction had come among them with his sword—they died like flies, they died in heaps. And over the bones of the dead the tepees stood for years, ragged, blowing in the winds. And then the skins rotted, and the bare poles stood, gleaming white, over the rotting bones that covered an acre of ground, they say. No one ever went to that place any more. It was cursed . . . because of my grandfather.'

'Monsieur Forbes made his get-away?'

'Yes, or I shouldn't be telling you about it.' Lemaire summoned a smile, but his eyes were sombre. 'And so I guess—that's one reason why. One among many.'

'You're a likeable old freak,' murmured Barrett affectionately, 'but—*you* ain't responsible you know!'

'As I look at it, we're all responsible.'

'Well—anyway, I wouldn't give that old scarecrow too much of our grubstake, old man. We've none too much, if the Babiche doesn't turn up according to schedule.'

'Probably we won't see any more of him. He'll be gone by the morning.'

He was gone with the morning. But as day followed weary day, and there was still no sign of the lakes narrowing to the long-sought river, Barrett was increasingly conscious that the old man was close upon their trail. Sometimes, in the brief radiance of the September dawns, he would see, far and far behind on the wrinkled silver water, a warped canoe paddling feebly. They always hauled away, by miles, from that decrepit canoe. But always, some time in the dark hours, it crept up again. Sometimes, he would see, in the sunset, a wavering thread of smoke arising from the site of their last-camp-but-one. It irritated him at last; the thought of that ragged, cranky canoe, paddled by the ragged, dirty, old imbecile, forever following them—creeping, creeping, under the great gaunt stars, creeping, creeping, under the flying dawns, the stormy moons; when he found Lemaire leaving little scraps of precious tobacco, a pinch of flour in a screw of paper, or a fresh-caught fish beside the trodden ashes of their cooking-place, he exploded.

'I can't help it,' Lemaire apologized, 'I *know* I'm all kinds of a fool, Barrett. But the poor old wretch is nearly blind—from long-ago smallpox, I should think. He can't catch things for himself much.'

Barrett, aware that wisdom was on his side, yet felt sorry for his explosion. He said nothing more. Soon he forgot the matter, having much else to think about.

For the Lost Babiche, the once-discovered river, did not 'turn up according to schedule.'

The chain of lakes they had been following turned due south. They left them, and, after a terrible portage, launched the canoe in a stream that ran west. Here their progress was very slow, for there were rapids, and consequent portages, every mile or so. This stream, instead of feeding another lake, died out in impassable quaking mosses. They saw a range of low hills some four or five miles ahead; so again they left the canoe and struck out for them on foot, half-wading, half-walking. It was exhausting work. At last they climbed the barren spurs and saw beyond, under a flaring sunset, a world of interlacing waterways, unvisited and unknown, that seemed then as if they smoked under the vast clouds and spirals of wildfowl settling homeward to the reeds. The two men watched that wonderful sight in silence.

At last, 'They're gathering to go south,' said Lemaire briefly. And Barrett answered, 'D'you know what date it is? It's the day on which we said we'd turn back if we hadn't found the Lost Babiche. It's the fifteenth of September.'

'Well . . . are we going back?'

'Not till we've found our river,' cried Barrett, with half a laugh and half a curse. They gripped hands, smiling rather grimly. They made a miserable, fireless camp, and went back the next day, carrying canoe and supplies, in four toilsome trips, across the hills; repacking and relaunching the second day on a new lake, where in all probability no white man—but one—had ever before dipped paddle.

They had been in the wilderness so long that they had fallen into the habit of carrying on conversations as if the lapse of two or three days had been as many minutes. Barrett knew to what Lemaire referred when he said abruptly, 'After all, it isn't as if you were ignorant of the risks.'

'I guess I know just as much about them as you,' said Barrett, cheerily. 'We're taking chances on the grub, aren't we? If we find the Lost Babiche before the game moves, we'll be alright, though our own supplies won't take us there. Once there, Bob, we're pretty sure to find friendly Indians when we link up with the Silver Fork—which we do seventy miles down the P'tite Babiche if your grandpa's map's correct. Well there are a good many 'if's' in the programme, but don't you worry. We'll get through or out, somehow. There's always fish. I've a feeling that this country *can't* go back on a Lemaire!'

They went on to a pleasant camp that night on a sandy islet overgrown with dwarf willow, and a wild-duck supper. The current of these new lakes went west with such increasing strength that Lemaire thought they were feeling the 'pull' of some big river into which the system drained; and if so, it could be no river but the lost Babiche. They slept, all a-tingle with the fever of discovery and re-made maps in their dreams.

Behind them many miles, a wandering smoke arose from the ashes of their last camp. The old Indian, about whom they had almost forgotten, had gained on them while they packed their supplies over the hills. Now he was close upon them again.

The life of that old savage seemed thin and wavering as the smoke of the fire he made. All night he sat in the ashes, motionless as a stone. Only once, just before the fierce dawn, he rose to his feet with an inarticulate cry, stirred to some instinctive excitement. For in a moment the vast, chill dusk was filled with a musical thrill, a tremendous clamour and rush of life, as thousand by thousand after their kinds, teal and widgeon, mallard and sheldrake, lifted from the reeds and fled before the coming cold. As the old man dimly watched, two delicate things fell and touched his face; one was a feather, the second was a flake of snow.

In those few delicate flakes, Lemaire and Barrett seemed to feel for the first time the ever-present hostility of nature; with such a brief, exquisite touch were they first made aware of the powers against which they strove. The new waterways seemed to stretch interminably. Each time they cleared one of the deep-cut channels which linked lake with lake regularly as a thread links beads, they looked ahead with the same question. Each time they saw the same expanse of gray water, low islets, barren shores; the country passed them changing and unchanging as a dream. They seemed to be moving in a dream, conscious of nothing but the pressure of the current on their paddles.

Then came the mist.

It shut them into a circle ten feet wide, a pearl-white prison. Outside the circle were shadows, wandering voices, trees as men walking. For two days they felt their way westward through this fog; two nights they shivered over a damp-wood fire, hearing nothing but water beading and dripping everywhere with a sound of grief. It strangely broke Lemaire's steel nerve. On the second night he said, restlessly, 'We must turn back to-morrow.'

'Bob!'

He flung out a tanned hand passionately. 'I know. . . . But can't you feel it? Things have turned against us. These things.' He pointed at the veiled sky, the milky water. 'I daren't go on. If we don't find the river to-morrow, we'll go back. And then . . . the land will have done for me what it never did for my grandfather.'

'What, Bob, old fellow?'

'Beaten me,' said Lemaire, and rolled into his blankets without another word.

He woke next morning with the touch of clear sunlight on his eyelids. He leaped to his feet silently, without waking Barrett, and as he did so, ice broke and tinkled like glass where the edge of the blankets had lain in a little pool of moisture. The last of the fog was draining in golden smoke from the low, dark hills. He strode to the edge of the water, and stopped, shaking suddenly as if he were cold. Then he went to Barrett, and stooped over him.

'Hullo, Bob, is it morning?' Then, as he saw Lemaire's face, 'My God, what is it?'

Twice Lemaire tried to speak. Then he pointed eastward to three high rocky islands which lay across the water, exactly spaced, like the ruined spans of a great bridge which once had stretched from shore to shore.

'Barrett,' he said huskily, 'We entered the Lost Babiche yesterday in the fog, and never knew. Those islands are ten miles down the river on Forbes Lemaire's map.'

They faced each other in silence, too much moved to speak. Their hands met in a long grip. Then Barrett said suddenly, 'Anything else.'

'Yes. It's freezing hard.'

'But . . . we've won, Bob, we've won!'

'Not yet,' said the man whose fathers had been bred in the wilderness, and wed to it. 'Not yet. It's still against us.'

But there was no talk now of turning back.

The Lost Babiche—lost no more—was a noble river; a gray and ice-clear stream winding in generous curves between high cliffs of slate-coloured rock. These cliffs were much cut into ravines and gullies, where grew timber of fine size for that country. But as their tense excitement lessened a little, they were struck by the absence of all life; even in the deep rock-shadows they saw no fish. Of human life there was not a sign; though in Forbes Lemaire's days the country had supported many Indians. And now—'Not a soul but ourselves,' said Barrett, in an awed voice; 'not a living soul . . .'

Yes. One soul yet living. Far behind them, in the staggering old canoe, the old Indian paddled valiantly on their trail. But he had forgotten them now, as they had long forgotten him. He stopped no more for the offal of their camps. A stronger instinct even than that of hunger was drawing him on the way they also went; down the Lost Babiche. Had they looked, they would not have seen him. And soon, between him and them, the clouds which had been gathering all day dropped a curtain of fine snow.

The first sting of the tiny balled flakes on his knuckles was to Lemaire like the thunder of guns, the opening of a battle.

He had no need to speak to Barrett. They bent over the paddles and the canoe surged forward. It was a race; a race between the early winter and themselves. If the cold weather set in so soon, if they found no Indians on the little-known Silver Fork—there were a dozen 'ifs' in their minds as, mile after mile, they fled down the P'tite Babiche. Even as they fled from the winter, so that other white man long ago had fled from the sickness; seen those stark bluffs unrolling; viewed perhaps those very trees.

They made a record distance that day. 'We're winning, Bob, we're winning,' said Barrett over the fire that night. Lemaire had not the heart to contradict him; but Lemaire's instincts, inherited from generations, told him that the wilderness was still mysteriously their enemy. He sat smoking, silent, hearing nothing but the faint, innumerable hiss of the snowflakes falling into the flames.

The snow was thickening in the morning, and by noon a bitter wind arose, blowing in their faces and against the stream. Soon the canoe was smack-smack-smacking on the waves, and the snow was driving almost level. The continual pressure of wind and snow drugged their senses. They never heard the voice of the rapids until, rounding an abrupt bend, the ravelled water seemed to leap at them from under the very bow of the canoe.

There was only one thing to be done, and—'Let her go!' yelled Lemaire, crouching tense as a spring above the steering paddle.

Now for the trained eye, the strong hand—the eye to see the momentary chance, the hand to obey without a falter.

Now for the sleeping instincts of a brain inherited from far generations of wanderers and voyageurs. Flash on flash of leaping water, the drive of spray and snow, the canoe staggering and checking like a thing hurt, but always recovering.

Barrett, in the bows, paddled blindly. His life lay in Bob Lemaire's hands, and he was content to leave it there during those roaring moments. But those hands failed—by an inch.

They were in smooth water. Barrett would have paused to take a breath, but Lemaire's voice barked at him from the stern. He obeyed. The canoe drove forward again—forward in great leaps, towards the point of a small island ahead, dimly seen through the snow—something was wrong, though, thought Barrett, grunting; he could get no 'beef' on the thing—it dragged; you'd have thought Bob was paddling against him. Then, suddenly, he understood. He called up the last of his strength, drove the paddle in, once, twice—again—heard a shout, flung himself overside into water waist-deep, and just as the canoe was sinking under them, he and Lemaire caught it and ran it ashore. Then, dripping, they looked each other in the face, and each seemed to see the face of disaster.

'It was a rock,' said Lemaire at last, very quietly, 'a few inches below the surface. It has almost cut the canoe in two.'

'What's to be done?'

'Find shelter, I suppose.'

They were very quiet about it. There was no shelter on their islet but a few rocks and a dead spruce in the middle. Here they set up their tent as a wind-break. It was bitterly cold; the island was sheathed in white ice, for the spray from the rough water froze now as it fell; everything in the canoe was wet; they were wet to their waists. They tried to induce the dead tree to burn, but the wood was so rotted with wet it only smouldered and went out. They had a little cooking lamp and a few squares of compressed fuel for it; they lighted this, and Lemaire made tea with numbed hands. It renewed the life in them, but could not dry them. They huddled against the little lamp in silence, waiting—waiting.

After some time Lemaire heard a curious sound from Barrett; his teeth were chattering. Lemaire saw that his face had taken a waxy white hue. He spoke to him, and Barrett looked up, but his eyes were dim and glazed. 'It'll be all right,' he said, thickly, 'we'll get through, somehow. I've a feeling that this country can't go back on a Lemaire.'

They were the first symptoms of collapse. Lemaire groaned. He got to his feet, and staggered across the slippery rocks. He shook his fist in the implacable face of the desolation. He shouted, foolish rage and defiance, caught back at his sanity; shouted again. . . . This time he thought he heard a faint cry in the snow. It whipped him back to self-control. He splashed out into the curdling shallows, shouting desperately.

Out of the gray drive of snow loomed the ghost of a canoe; paddled, as it seemed, by a ghost. It was the old Indian, whom Lemaire had long forgotten; the weather had not hindered him, the rapids had not wrecked him. At Lemaire's cry he raised his head, and the canoe put inshore, waveringly. Lemaire splashed to meet it, met the incurious gaze of the half-blind old eyes under the scarred lids, and read into the wrinkled, foul old face, a sort of animal kindness.

Five minutes later he was desperately trying to rouse Barrett. Barrett looked at him at last, and Lemaire saw that the brief delirium was past. 'What is it, Bob?' he asked, weakly. And Lemaire broke into a torrent of words.

'The old Indian—the old Indian you said was a hoodoo—don't you remember? He's here. He has caught us up, God knows how. He says his canoe'll hold three. He says that a very little way on there's a big camp, and that he'll take us there—in a very little while. He says his tribe is always kind to strangers, to white men. . . . I can't make out all he says, he's queer in his head. But he's dead sure of the encampment. He says it's always there . . .'

Still talking eagerly, Lemaire snatched together a few things, got an arm round Barrett, lifted him up to his feet, got him reeling to the canoe, laid him in the bottom, and helped the old Indian push off. There was no second paddle. There was no need of it. The current took them at once.

The cold was increasing, as the wind died and the snow thinned. Lemaire ceased to be conscious of the passing of time, but within himself the stubborn life burned; he was strongly curious to know the end, to discover what it was the wilderness had in store for him after five years, to read the riddle of that relationship with himself which had called him from the cities to this.

He was aware, at last, of a vast, golden light. The clouds were parting behind the snow, and the sunset was gleaming through. It turned the snow into a mist of rose and molten gold. The old Indian feebly turned the canoe. It crept toward the shore.

'The lodges of my people,' muttered the old Indian. He stood erect, and pointed with his bleached paddle. 'They are very many—a very strong tribe.'

Lemaire also looked, and saw.

Silently, the canoe took the half-frozen sand. Silently, very slowly, Lemaire stepped out. The old Indian waited for him. It seemed that the whole world was waiting for him.

He, like a man in a dream, moved slowly into the midst of a level stretch of sand, and stood there. All about him, covering the whole level, were the ridgepoles of wigwams, but the coverings had long fallen away and rotted, and the sunset glowed through the gaunt poles. Lemaire stretched out his hand, and touched the nearest; they fell into dust and rot. . . . Under his feet he crushed the bones of the dead—the dead, who had died fifty years before, and had waited for him here ever since, under the blown sand and the ground willows. . . . 'They've a song about it, down along the Lamennais. For of all that tribe, only one family, they say, escaped. All the others died . . . they died like flies, they died in heaps. And over the bones of the dead the tepees stood for years. . . . No one ever went to that place any more. It was cursed . . . because of my grandfather.'

He went back to the canoe. Whining like an old animal, the old Indian was busied above Barrett. 'The lodges of my people,' he muttered, 'a very strong tribe, and kind to the white men.'

Very gently, Lemaire put aside the blind old hands that touched Barrett's unconscious face. 'Don't wake him,' he said.

1922

# Ethel Wilson
## 1888–1980

Ethel Wilson, born Ethel Davis Bryant, began her life in Port Elizabeth, South Africa, where her English parents were missionaries. Her mother, who was tubercular, died in childbirth eighteen months later. Ethel remained with her father, a Methodist minister, who had returned to England, until his death from pneumonia in 1897. Then, after a year with various relatives in England—an experience that left her painfully shy and with a lifelong sense of displacement— she went to live with her maternal grandmother in Vancouver. She attended school there until she was sent to a boarding school in Britain for her secondary-school years. After graduating, she continued to live with her grandmother and her two aunts while training as a teacher (1906–7) and then while teaching elementary school. She left teaching in 1920, when she became engaged to Dr Wallace Wilson, an internist and medical ethicist she married the following year. Except for two extended trips abroad and frequent holidays in northern British Columbia, they spent the rest of their lives in Vancouver.

Wilson's first short story was published in England in 1937. However, her wartime work—including the editing of a Red Cross magazine—interrupted her writing career for almost ten years. In 1947, Wilson, nearing sixty, published *Hetty Dorval*, her first novel. Over the next fourteen years, she produced three more novels: *The Innocent Traveller* (1949), which began as a series of family sketches; *Swamp Angel* (1954); and *Love and Salt Water* (1956). Her shorter fiction includes two novellas, published together in *The Equations of Love* (1952), and *Mrs Golightly and Other Stories* (1961), which draws together her published short stories. A number of previously unpublished stories appeared in a posthumous volume, *Ethel Wilson: Stories, Essays and Letters* (1987), edited by David Stouck.

Drawing on the early British Modernists as her models, Wilson wrote with an elegant, balanced style that, in its seemingly artless surfaces, belies the complex structures of her narratives. The most-often-read of her novels, *Swamp Angel*—the story of a woman freeing herself from a failed marriage and stifling social expectations—depicts the peace and beauty of northern nature in counterpoint to the troubled actions of its characters and the disquiet the narrative produces in the reader. As is true of much of Wilson's fiction, *Swamp Angel* also deals with women's relationships across generations showing the differences in generational expectations and opportunities. (While not a feminist herself, Wilson is someone whose work later feminists found of value.)

Her stories—which seem tales of slightly absurd characters, often living in the isolation of their dreamlike worlds—achieve their effect through the imposition of a comic, even biting, vision upon a meticulously realistic presentation. This yoking of literary modes allows her to examine two important topics in twentieth-century Canadian literature: the universe as a tricky, unreliable place and society as an increasingly dehumanized milieu, in which individuals are in danger of losing their place in the community. 'The Window' deals with both these themes. Hugo McPherson suggests that Wilson's 'title image, the window framing by day the empty scene and mirroring by night the sterile life of the protagonist, is central not only to her but to much Canadian fiction.'

# The Window

The great big window must have been at least twenty-five feet wide and ten feet high. It was constructed in sections divided by segments of something that did not interfere with the view; in fact the eye by-passed these divisions and looked only at the entrancing scenes beyond. The window, together with a glass door at the western end, composed a bland shallow curve and formed the entire transparent north-west (but chiefly north) wall of Mr Willy's living-room.

Upon his arrival from England Mr Willy had surveyed the various prospects of living in the quickly growing city of Vancouver with the selective and discarding characteristics which had enabled him to make a fortune and retire all of a sudden from business and his country in his advanced middle age. He settled immediately upon the very house. It was a small old house overlooking the sea between Spanish Banks and English Bay. He knocked out the north wall and made the window. There was nothing particular to commend the house except that it faced immediately on the sea-shore and the view. Mr Willy had left his wife and her three sisters to play bridge together until death should overtake them in England. He now paced from end to end of his living-room, that is to say from east to west, with his hands in his pockets, admiring the northern view. Sometimes he stood with his hands behind him looking through the great glass window, seeing the wrinkled or placid sea and the ships almost at his feet and beyond the sea the mountains, and seeing sometimes his emancipation. His emancipation drove him into a dream, and sea sky mountains swam before him, vanished, and he saw with immense release his wife in still another more repulsive hat. He did not know, nor would have cared, that much discussion went on in her world, chiefly in the afternoons, and that he was there alleged to have deserted her. So he had, after providing well for her physical needs which were all the needs of which she was capable. Mrs Willy went on saying '. . . and he would come home my dear and never speak a word I can't tell you my dear how *frightful* it was night after night I might say for *years* I simply can't tell you . . .' No, she could not tell but she did, by day and night. Here he was at peace, seeing out of the window the crimped and wrinkled sea and the ships which passed and passed each other, the seabirds and the dream-inducing sky.

At the extreme left curve of the window an island appeared to slope into the sea. Behind this island and to the north, the mountains rose very high. In the summer time the mountains were soft, deceptive in their innocency, full of crags and crevasses and arêtes and danger. In the winter they lay magnificent, white and much higher, it seemed, than in the summer time. They tossed, static, in almost visible motion against the sky, inhabited only by eagles and—so a man had told Mr Willy, but he didn't believe the man—by mountain sheep and some cougars, bears, wild cats and, certainly, on the lower slopes, deer, and now a ski camp far out of sight. Mr Willy looked at the mountains and regretted his past youth and his present wealth. How could he endure to be old and rich and able only to look at these mountains which in his youth he had not known and did not climb. Nothing, now, no remnant of his youth would come and enable him to climb these mountains. This he found hard to believe, as old people do. He was shocked at the newly realized decline of his physical powers which had proved good enough on the whole for his years of success, and by the fact that now he had, at last, time and could not swim (heart), climb mountains (heart and legs), row a boat in a rough enticing sea (call that old age). These things have happened to other people, thought Mr Willy, but not to us, now, who have been so young, and yet it will happen to those who now are young.

Immediately across the water were less spectacular mountains, pleasant slopes which in winter time were covered with invisible skiers. Up the dark mountain at night sprang the lights of the ski-lift, and ceased. The shores of these mountains were strung with lights, littered with lights, spangled with lights, necklaces, bracelets, constellations, far more beautiful as seen through this window across the dark water than if Mr Willy had driven his car across the Lions' Gate Bridge and westwards among those constellations which would have disclosed only a shopping centre, people walking the streets, street lights, innumerable cars and car lights like anywhere else and, up the slopes, peoples' houses. Then, looking back to the south across the dark water towards his own home and the great lighted window which he would not have been able to distinguish so far away, Mr Willy would have seen lights again, a carpet of glitter thrown over the slopes of the city.

Fly from one shore to the other, fly and fly back again, fly to a continent or to an island, but you are no better off than if you stayed all day at your own window (and such a window), thought Mr Willy pacing back and forth, then into the kitchen to put the kettle on for a cup of tea which he will drink beside the window, back for a glass of whisky, returning in time to see a cormorant flying level with the water, not an inch too high not an inch too low, flying out of sight. See the small ducks lying on the water, one behind the other, like beads on a string. In the mornings Mr Willy drove into town to see his investment broker and perhaps to the bank or round the park. He lunched, but not at a club. He then drove home. On certain days a woman called Mrs Ogden came in to 'do' for him. This was his daily life, very simple, and a routine was formed whose pattern could at last be discerned by an interested observer outside the window.

One night Mr Willy beheld a vast glow arise behind the mountains. The Arctic world was obviously on fire—but no, the glow was not fire glow, flame glow. The great invasion of colour that spread up and up the sky was not red, was not rose, but of a synthetic cyclamen colour. This cyclamen glow remained steady from mountain to zenith and caused Mr Willy, who had never seen the Northern Lights, to believe that these were not Northern Lights but that something had occurred for which one must be prepared. After about an hour, flanges of green as of putrefaction, and a melodious yellow arose and spread. An hour later the Northern Lights faded, leaving Mr Willy small and alone.

Sometimes as, sitting beside the window, he drank his tea, Mr Willy thought that nevertheless it is given to few people to be as happy (or contented, he would say), as he was, at his age, too. In his life of decisions, men, pressures, more men, antagonisms, fusions, fissions and Mrs Willy, in his life of hard success, that is, he had sometimes looked forward but so vaguely and rarely to a time when he would not only put this life down; he would leave it. Now he had left it and here he was by his window. As time went on, though, he had to make an effort to summon this happiness, for it seemed to elude him. Sometimes a thought or a shape (was it?), gray, like wood ash that falls in pieces when it is touched, seemed to be behind his chair, and this shape teased him and communicated to him that he had left humanity behind, that a man needs humanity and that if he ceases to be in touch with man and is not in touch with God, he does not matter. 'You do not matter any more', said the spectre like wood ash before it fell to pieces, 'because you are no longer in touch with any one and so you do not exist. You are in a vacuum and so you are nothing.' Then Mr Willy, at first uneasy, became satisfied again for a time after being made uneasy by the spectre. A storm would get up and the wind, howling well, would lash the windows sometimes carry-ing the salt spray from a very high tide which it flung against the great panes of glass. That was a satisfaction to Mr Willy and within him something stirred and rose and met the storm and effaced the spectre and other phantoms which were really vague regrets. But the worst that happened against the window was that from time to time a little bird, sometimes but not often a seabird, flung itself like a stone against the strong glass of the window and fell, killed by the passion of its flight. This grieved Mr Willy, and he could not sit unmoved when the bird flew at the clear glass and was met by death. When this happened, he arose from his chair, opened the glass door at the far end of the window, descended three or four steps and sought in the grasses for the body of the bird. But the bird was dead, or it was dying, its small bones were smashed, its head was broken, its beak split, it was killed by the rapture of its flight. Only once Mr Willy found the bird a little stunned and picked it up. He cupped the bird's body in his hands and carried it into the house.

Looking up through the grasses at the edge of the rough terrace that descended to the beach, a man watched him return into the house, carrying the bird. Still looking obliquely through the grasses the man watched Mr Willy enter the room and vanish from view. Then Mr Willy came again to the door, pushed it open, and released the bird which flew away, who knows where. He closed the door, locked it, and sat down on the chair facing east beside the window and began to read his newspaper. Looking over his paper he saw, to the east, the city of Vancouver deployed over rising ground with low roofs and high buildings and at the apex the tall Electric Building which at night shone like a broad shaft of golden light.

This time, as evening drew on, the man outside went away because he had other business.

Mr Willy's investment broker was named Gerald Wardho. After a time he said to Mr Willy in a friendly but respectful way, 'Will you have lunch with me at the Club tomorrow?' and Mr Willy said he would. Some time later Gerald Wardho said, 'Would you like me put you up at the Club?'

Mr Willy considered a little the life which he had left and did not want to re-enter and also the fact that he had only last year resigned his membership in three clubs, so he said, 'That's very good of you, Wardho, but I think no. I'm enjoying things as they are. It's a novelty, living in a vacuum . . . I like it, for a time anyway.'

'Yes, but,' said Gerald Wardho, 'you'd be some time on the waiting list. It wouldn't hurt—'

'No,' said Mr Willy, 'no.'

Mr Willy had, Wardho thought, a distinguished appearance or perhaps it was an affable accustomed air, and so he had. When Mrs Wardho said to her husband, 'Gerry, there's not an extra man in this town and I need a man for Saturday,' Gerald Wardho said, 'I know a man. There's Willy.'

Mrs Wardho said doubtfully, 'Willy? Willy who? Who's Willy?'

Her husband said, 'He's fine, he's okay, I'll ask Willy.'

'How old is he?'

'About a hundred . . . but he's okay.'

'Oh-h-h,' said Mrs Wardho, 'isn't there anyone anywhere unattached young any more? Does he play bridge?'

'I'll invite him, I'll find out,' said her husband, and Mr Willy said he'd like to come to dinner.

'Do you care for a game of bridge, Mr Willy?' asked Gerald Wardho.

'I'm afraid not,' said Mr Willy kindly but firmly. He played a good game of bridge but had no intention of entering servitude again just yet, losing his freedom, and being enrolled as what is called a fourth. Perhaps later; not yet. 'If you're having bridge I'll come another time. Very kind of you, Wardho.'

'No no no,' said Gerald Wardho, 'there'll only be maybe a table of bridge for anyone who wants to play. My wife would be disappointed.'

'Well thank you very much. Black tie?'

'Yes. Black tie,' said Gerald Wardho.

And so, whether he would or no, Mr Willy found himself invited to the kind of
evening parties to which he had been accustomed and which he had left behind, given
by people younger and more animated than himself, and he realized that he was on his
way to becoming old odd man out. There was a good deal of wood ash at these
parties—that is, behind him the spectre arose, falling to pieces when he looked at it,
and said 'So this is what you came to find out on this coast, so far from home, is it, or
is there something else. What else is there?' The spectre was not always present at these
parties but sometimes awaited him at home and said these things.

One night Mr Willy came home from an evening spent at Gerald Wardho's
brother-in-law's house, a very fine house indeed. He had left lights burning and begun
to turn out the lights before he went upstairs. He went into the living-room and
before turning out the last light gave a glance at the window which had in the course
of the evening behaved in its accustomed manner. During the day the view through
the window was clear or cloudy, according to the weather or the light or absence of
light in the sky; but there it was—the view—never quite the same though, and that
is owing to the character of oceans or of any water, great or small, and of light. Both
water and light have so great an effect on land observed on any scene, rural, urban or
wilderness, that one begins to think that life, that a scene, is an illusion produced by
influences such as water and light. At all events, by day the window held this fine view
as in a frame, and the view was enhanced by ships at sea of all kinds, but never was
the sea crowded, and by birds, clouds, and even aeroplanes in the sky—no people to
spoil this fine view. But as evening approached, and moonless night, all the view (illusion again) vanished slowly. The window, which was not illusion, only the purveyor
of illusion, did not vanish, but became a mirror which reflected against the blackness
every detail of the shallow living-room. Through this clear reflection of the whole
room, distant lights from across the water intruded, and so chains of light were
thrown across the reflected mantel-piece, or a picture, or a human face, enhancing it.
When Mr Willy had left his house to dine at Gerald Wardho's brother-in-law's house
the view through the window was placidly clear, but when he returned at 11:30 the
window was dark and the room was reflected from floor to ceiling against the blackness. Mr Willy saw himself entering the room like a stranger, looking at first debonair
with such a gleaming shirt front and then—as he approached himself—a little shabby,
his hair perhaps. He advanced to the window and stood looking at himself with the
room in all its detail behind him.

Mr Willy was too often alone, and spent far too much time in that space which
lies between the last page of the paper or the turning-off of the radio in surfeit, and
sleep. Now as he stood at the end of the evening and the beginning of the night, looking at himself and the room behind him, he admitted that the arid feeling which he
had so often experienced lately was probably what is called loneliness. And yet he did

not want another woman in his life. It was a long time since he had seen a woman whom he wanted to take home or even to see again. Too much smiling. Men were all right, you talked to them about the market, the emergence of the Liberal Party, the impossibility of arriving anywhere with those people while that fellow was in office, nuclear war (instant hell opened deep in everyone's mind and closed again), South Africa where Mr Willy was born, the Argentine where Mr Wardho's brother-in-law had spent many years—and then everyone went home.

Mr Willy, as the months passed by, was dismayed to find that he had entered an area of depression unknown before, like a tundra, and he was a little frightened of this tundra. Returning from the dinner party he did not at once turn out the single last light and go upstairs. He sat down on a chair beside the window and at last bowed his head upon his hands. As he sat there, bowed, his thoughts went very stiffly (for they had not had much exercise in that direction throughout his life), to some area that was not tundra but that area where there might be some meaning in creation which Mr Willy supposed must be the place where some people seemed to find a God, and perhaps a personal God at that. Such theories, or ideas, or passions had never been of interest to him, and if he had thought of such theories, or ideas, or passions he would have dismissed them as invalid and having no bearing on life as it is lived, especially when one is too busy. He had formed the general opinion that people who hold such beliefs were either slaves to an inherited convention, hypocrites, or nit-wits. He regarded such people without interest, or at least he thought them negligible as he returned to the exacting life in hand. On the whole, though, he did not like them. It is not easy to say why Mr Willy thought these people were hypocrites or nit-wits because some of them, not all, had a strong religious faith, and why he was not a hypocrite or nit-wit because he had not a strong religious faith; but there it was.

As he sat on and on looking down at the carpet with his head in his hands he did not think of these people, but he underwent a strong shock of recognition. He found himself looking this way and that way out of his aridity for some explanation or belief beyond the non-explanation and non-belief that had always been sufficient and had always been his, but in doing this he came up against a high and solid almost visible wall of concrete or granite, set up between him and a religious belief. This wall had, he thought, been built by him through the period of his long life, or perhaps he was congenitally unable to have a belief; in that case it was no fault of his and there was no religious belief possible to him. As he sat there he came to have the conviction that the absence of a belief which extended beyond the visible world had something to do with his malaise; yet the malaise might possibly be cirrhosis of the liver or a sort of delayed male menopause. He recognized calmly that death was as inevitable as tomorrow morning or even tonight and he had a rational absence of fear of death. Nevertheless his death (he knew) had begun, and had begun—what with his awareness of age and this malaise of his—to assume a certainty that it had not had before. His death did not trouble him as much as the increasing tastelessness of living in this tundra of mind into which a belief did not enter.

The man outside the window had crept up through the grasses and was now watching Mr Willy from a point rather behind him. He was a morose man and strong. He had served two terms for robbery with violence. When he worked, he worked up the coast. Then he came to town and if he did not get into trouble it was through no fault of his own. Last summer he had lain there and, rolling over, had looked up through the grasses and into—only just into—the room where this guy was who seemed to live alone. He seemed to be a rich guy because he wore good clothes and hadn't he got this great big window and—later, he discovered—a high-price car. He had lain in the grasses and because his thoughts always turned that way, he tried to figger out how he could get in there. Money was the only thing that was any good to him and maybe the old guy didn't keep money or even carry it but he likely did. The man thought quite a bit about Mr Willy and then went up the coast and when he came down again he remembered the great big window and one or two nights he went around and about the place and figgered how he'd work it. The doors was all locked, even that glass door. That was easy enough to break but he guessed he'd go in without warning when the old guy was there so's he'd have a better chance of getting something off of him as well. Anyways he wouldn't break in, not that night, but if nothing else offered he'd do it some time soon.

Suddenly Mr Willy got up, turned the light out, and went upstairs to bed. That was Wednesday.

On Sunday he had his first small party. It seemed inevitable if only for politeness. Later he would have a dinner party if he still felt sociable and inclined. He invited the Wardhos and their in-laws and some other couples. A Mrs Lessways asked if she might bring her aunt and he said yes. Mrs Wardho said might she bring her niece who was arriving on Saturday to meet her fiancé who was due next week from Hong Kong, and the Wardhos were going to give the two young people a quiet wedding, and Mr Willy said 'Please do.' Another couple asked if they could bring another couple.

Mr Willy, surveying his table, thought that Mrs Ogden had done well. 'Oh I'm so glad you think so,' said Mrs Ogden, pleased. People began to arrive. 'Oh!' they exclaimed without fail, as they arrived, 'what a beautiful view!' Mrs Lessways' aunt who had blue hair fell delightedly into the room, turning this way and that way, acknowledging smiles and tripping to the window. 'Oh,' she cried turning to Mr Willy in a fascinating manner, 'isn't that just lovely! Edna says you're quite a recluse! I'm sure I don't blame you! Don't you think that's the loveliest view Edna . . . oh how d'you do how d'you do, isn't that the loveliest view? . . .' Having paid her tribute to the view she turned away from the window and did not see it again. The Aunt twirled a little bag covered with iridescent beads on her wrist. 'Oh!' and 'Oh!' she exclaimed, turning, 'Mr dear how *lovely* to see you! I didn't even know you were back! Did you have a good time?' She reminded Mr Willy uneasily of his wife. Mr and Mrs Wardho arrived accompanied by their niece Sylvia.

A golden girl, thought Mr Willy taking her hand, but her young face surrounded by sunny curls was stern. She stood, looking from one to another, not speaking, for people spoke busily to each other and the young girl stood apart, smiling only when need be and wishing that she had not had to come to the party. She drifted to the window and seemed (and was) forgotten. She looked at the view as at something seen for the first and last time. She inscribed those notable hills on her mind because had she not arrived only yesterday? And in two days Ian would be here and she would not see them again.

A freighter very low laden emerged from behind a forest and moved slowly into the scene. So low it was that it lay like an elegant black line upon the water with great bulkheads below. Like an iceberg, thought Sylvia, and her mind moved along with the freighter bound for foreign parts. Someone spoke to her and she turned. 'Oh thank you!' she said for her cup of tea.

Mr Willy opened the glass door and took with him some of the men who had expressed a desire to see how far his property ran. 'You see, just a few feet, no distance,' he said.

After a while day receded and night came imperceptibly on. There was not any violence of reflected sunset tonight and mist settled down on the view with only distant dim lights aligning the north shore. Sylvia, stopping to respond to ones and twos, went to the back of the shallow room and sat down behind the out-jut of the fireplace where a wood fire was burning. Her mind was on two levels. One was all Ian and the week coming, and one—no thicker than a crust on the surface—was this party and all these people talking, the Aunt talking so busily that one might think there was a race on, or news to tell. Sylvia, sitting in the shadow of the corner and thinking about her approaching lover, lost herself in this reverie, and her lips, which had been so stern, opened slightly in a tender smile. Mr Willy who was serving drinks from the dining-room where Mrs Ogden had left things ready, came upon her and, struck by her beauty, saw a different sunny girl. She looked up at him. She took her drink from him with a soft and tender smile that was grateful and happy and was only partly for him. He left her, with a feeling of beauty seen.

Sylvia held her glass and looked towards the window. She saw, to her surprise, so quickly had black night come, that the end of the room which had been a view was now a large black mirror which reflected the glowing fire, the few lights, and the people unaware of the view, its departure, and its replacement by their own reflections behaving to each other like people at a party. Sylvia watched Mr Willy who moved amongst them, taking a glass and bringing a glass. He was removed from the necessities, now, of conversation, and looked very sad. Why does he look sad, she wondered and was young enough to think, he shouldn't look sad, he is well off. She took time off to like Mr Willy and to feel sorry that he seemed melancholy.

People began to look at their watches and say good-bye. The Aunt redoubled her vivacity. The women all thanked Mr Willy for his tea party and for the beautiful beautiful view. They gave glances at the window but there was no view.

When all his guests had gone, Mr Willy, who was an orderly man, began to collect glasses and take them into the kitchen. In an armchair lay the bag covered with iridescent beads belonging to the Aunt. Mr Willy picked it up and put it on a table, seeing the blue hair of the Aunt. He would sit down and smoke for awhile. But he found that when, lately, he sat down in the evening beside the window and fixed his eyes upon the golden shaft of the Electric Building, in spite of his intention of reading or smoking, his thoughts turned towards this subject of belief which now teased him, eluded, yet compelled him. He was brought up, every time, against the great stone wall, how high, how wide he knew, but not how thick. If he could, in some way, break through the wall which bounded the area of his aridity and his comprehension, he knew without question that there was a light (not darkness) beyond, and that this light could in some way come through to him and alleviate the sterility and lead him, lead him. If there was some way, even some conventional way—although he did not care for convention—he would take it in order to break the wall down and reach the light so that it would enter his life; but he did not know the way. So fixed did Mr Willy become in contemplation that he looked as though he were graven in stone.

Throughout the darkened latter part of the tea party, the man outside had lain or crouched near the window. From the sands, earlier, he had seen Mr Willy open the glass door and go outside, followed by two or three men. They looked down talking, and soon went inside again together. The door was closed. From anything the watcher knew, it was not likely that the old guy would turn and lock the door when he took the other guys in. He'd just close it, see.

As night came on the man watched the increased animation of the guests preparing for departure. Like departing birds they moved here and there in the room before taking flight. The man was impatient but patient because when five were left, then three, then no one but the old guy who lived in the house, he knew his time was near. (How gay and how meaningless the scene had been, of these well-dressed persons talking and talking, like some kind of a show where nothing happened—or so it might seem, on the stage of the lighted room from the pit of the dark shore.)

The watcher saw the old guy pick up glasses and take them away. Then he came back into the room and looked around. He took something out of a chair and put it on a table. He stood still for a bit, and then he found some kind of a paper and sat down in the chair facing eastward. But the paper dropped in his hand and then it dropped to the floor as the old guy bent his head and then he put his elbows on his knees and rested his head in his hands as if he was thinking, or had some kind of headache.

The watcher, with a sort of joy and a feeling of confidence that the moment had come, moved strongly and quietly to the glass door. He turned the handle expertly, slid inside, and slowly closed the door so that no draught should warn his victim. He moved cat-like to the back of Mr Willy's chair and quickly raised his arm. At the self-same moment that he raised his arm with a short blunt weapon in his hand, he was aware of the swift movement of another person in the room. The man stopped still, his arm remained high, every fear was aroused. He turned instantly and saw a scene clearly enacted beside him in the dark mirror of the window. At the moment and shock of turning, he drew a sharp intake of breath and it was this that Mr Willy heard and that caused him to look up and around and see in the dark mirror the intruder, the danger, and the victim who was himself. At that still moment, the telephone rang shrilly, twice as loud in that still moment, on a small table near him.

It was not the movement of that figure in the dark mirror, it was not the bell ringing close at hand and insistently. It was an irrational and stupid fear lest his action, reproduced visibly beside him in the mirror, was being faithfully registered in some impossible way that filled the intruder with fright. The telephone ringing shrilly, Mr Willy now facing him, the play enacted beside him, and this irrational momentary fear caused him to turn and bound towards the door, to escape into the dark, banging the glass door with a clash behind him. When he got well away from the place he was angry—everything was always against him, he never had no luck, and if he hadn't a lost his head it was a cinch he coulda done it easy.

'Damn you!' shouted Mr Willy in a rage, with his hand on the telephone, 'you might have broken it! Yes?' he said into the telephone, moderating the anger that possessed him and continuing within himself a conversation that said It was eighteen inches away, I was within a minute of it and I didn't know, it's no use telephoning the police but I'd better do that, it was just above me and I'd have died not knowing. 'Yes? Yes?' he said impatiently, trembling a little.

'Oh,' said a surprised voice, 'It is Mr Willy, isn't it? Just for a minute it didn't sound like you Mr Willy that was the *loveliest* party and what a lovely view and I'm sorry to be such a nuisance I kept on ringing and ringing because I though you couldn't have gone out so soon' (tinkle tinkle) 'and you couldn't have gone to bed so soon but I do believe I must have left my little bead bag it's not the *value* but . . .' Mr Willy found himself shaking more violently now, not only with death averted and the rage of the slammed door but with the powerful thoughts that had usurped him and were interrupted by the dangerous moment which was now receding, and the tinkling voice on the telephone.

'I have it here. I'll bring it tomorrow,' he said shortly. He hung up the telephone and at the other end the Aunt turned and exclaimed, 'Well if he isn't the rudest man I never was treated like that in my whole life d'you know what he . . .'

Mr Willy was in a state of abstraction.

He went to the glass door and examined it. It was intact. He turned the key and drew the shutter down. Then he went back to the telephone in this state of abstraction. Death or near-death was still very close, though receding. It seemed to him at that moment that a crack had been coming in the great wall that shut him off from the light but perhaps he was wrong. He dialled the police, perfunctorily not urgently. He knew that before him lay the hardest work of his life—in his life out of the country. He must in some way and very soon break the great wall that shut him off from whatever light there might be. Not for fear of death oh God not for fear of death but for fear of something else.

1961

# F.R. Scott
## 1899–1985

Francis Reginald Scott was a second-generation Canadian poet, the son of Frederick George Scott (1861–1944), one of the Confederation poets. Born in Quebec City, where his father was rector of St Matthew's Church, Frank Scott received a traditional Anglican upbringing. Attending his father's alma mater, Bishop's College, he won a Rhodes Scholarship to Oxford University in 1920 and read history at Magdalen College. As Scott once said, 'I spent three blissful years at Oxford soaking up everything I could learn about the past and paying very little attention to the present.' On his return to Canada in 1923, he taught for a brief period at Lower Canada College before enrolling in law at McGill University. He was called to the bar in 1927 and was made a professor in McGill's Faculty of Law in 1928. Scott served as its dean from 1961 to 1964 and retired in 1968.

His father's writing and literary concerns nurtured Scott's interest in poetry, both as a reader and a writer, but before 1925, this interest progressed little beyond reading the Georgian poets and writing sonnets. At McGill, he was befriended by A.J.M. Smith, who introduced him to the new American poets, including Pound and Eliot. Together, Scott and Smith founded the *McGill Fortnightly Review* (1925–27), for which they wrote so prolifically that it became necessary for them to invent pseudonyms.

The Modernist poets changed Scott's conception of poetry, and the social decay of the Depression altered his ideas about politics and economics. He rejected not only the romantic poetry of his father's generation ('Amid the crash of systems, was Romantic poetry to survive?' he wrote in *The Canadian Forum* in 1931) but also its capitalism. He became a social reformer and a socialist, an authority on constitutional law, and a defender of civil liberties and social justice. He assisted in the formation of the Co-operative Commonwealth Federa-

tion (CCF, the forerunner to the NDP), of which he was national chair from 1942 to 1950. In the 1950s, he fought three celebrated court cases in Quebec: against Premier Maurice Duplessis' padlock law, against the censorship of D.H. Lawrence's *Lady Chatterley's Lover*, and Roncarelli v. Duplessis, a famous civil-liberties case. In the 1960s, he was a member of the Royal Commission on Bilingualism and Bi-culturalism. A sampler of his political writings, *A New Endeavour: Selected Political Essays, Letters, and Addresses* (1986), has been compiled by Michiel Horn.

Scott's literary career reflected his activist nature. As early as 1928, he joined other writers in helping to found the *Canadian Mercury*, a literary magazine that gave voice to three members of the Montreal Group, Leo Kennedy, A.M. Klein, and Scott himself. With Smith, Scott edited an anthology of this 'new' poetry, *New Provinces* (1936), which served as a public announcement that Canadian poetry was indeed changing. Over the years, Scott continued to be interested in helping to provide a public outlet for new voices, often by his support of literary magazines. He helped to found *Preview* in 1942, which, like the *Canadian Mercury* and the *McGill Fortnightly Review* before it, gave a new generation of writers a public forum. Then in 1956, he became one of the founding editors of the *Tamarack Review*, which for more than a quarter of a century was the leading literary journal in Canada. His commitment to a fully bicultural Canada was reflected in his continuing interest in French-Canadian culture and in his activities as a translator. His *St-Denys Garneau and Anne Hébert* (1962) helped make two important francophone writers more visible in English Canada; in 1977, his *Poems of French Canada* won a Canada Council Translation Prize.

Scott's poems were collected in *Overture* (1945), *Events and Signals* (1954), *The Eye of the*

*Needle: Satires, Sorties, Sundries* (1957), *Signature* (1964), and *The Dance Is One* (1973). His *Selected Poems* appeared in 1966, and his *Collected Poems*, which won a Governor General's Award, was published in 1981. With Smith, Scott compiled a popular anthology, *The Blasted Pine: An Anthology of Satire, Invective and Disrespectful Verse; Chiefly by Canadian Writers* (1957).

Scott's poetry has sometimes been divided into 'public' and 'private' poems. But even the public satire of a poem like 'The Canadian Authors Meet' is not without a personal voice. Whether he is treating a political subject such as Mackenzie King's role as prime minister or responding to the developments of technology (in 'Trans Canada') or recording his plunge into the elemental world of nature in 'Lakeshore', his is a comprehensive poetry that can unite the mythic nature of the land with the reality of personal experience, and that can scrutinize the trivialities of a self-indulgent society while also seeing with the eye of a visionary.

# The Canadian Authors¹ Meet

Expansive puppets percolate self-unction
Beneath a portrait of the Prince of Wales.
Miss Crotchet's muse has somehow failed to function,
Yet she's a poetess. Beaming, she sails

From group to chattering group, with such a dear
Victorian saintliness, as is her fashion,
Greeting the other unknowns with a cheer—
Virgins of sixty who still write of passion.

The air is heavy with Canadian topics,
And Carman, Lampman, Roberts, Campbell, Scott,                    10
Are measured for their faith and philanthropics,
Their zeal for God and King, their earnest thought.

The cakes are sweet, but sweeter is the feeling
That one is mixing with the *literati*;
It warms the old, and melts the most congealing.
Really, it is a most delightful party.

Shall we go round the mulberry bush, or shall
We gather at the river, or shall we
Appoint a Poet Laureate this fall,²
Or shall we have another cup of tea?                              20

---

1 The Canadian Authors' Association, founded in 1921, appeared to Scott a self-congratulatory and self-indulgent group that was mostly a refuge for poetasters and that celebrated safely established poets while ignoring modern innovators. He wrote this poem after attending a meeting of the CAA in the spring of 1925.
2 At the meeting Scott attended the appointment of a Canadian poet laureate was discussed.

O Canada, O Canada, Oh can
A day go by without new authors springing
To paint the native maple, and to plan
More ways to set the selfsame welkin[3] ringing?

1927,[4] 1945

3  Sky (poetic archaism).
4  When first published in the *McGill Fortnightly Review* (27 April 1927), this poem concluded with an additional
   stanza:
   *Far in a corner sits (though none would know it)*
   *The very picture of disconsolation,*
   *A rather lewd and most ungodly poet*
   *Writing these verses, for his soul's salvation.*

# Trans Canada

Pulled from our ruts by the made-to-order gale
We sprang upward into a wider prairie
And dropped Regina below like a pile of bones.[1]

Sky tumbled upon us in waterfalls,
But we were smarter than a Skeena salmon
And shot our silver body over the lip of air
To rest in a pool of space
On the top storey of our adventure.

A solar peace
And a six-way choice.[2]                                                    10

Clouds, now, are the solid substance,
A floor of wool roughed by the wind
Standing in waves that halt in their fall.
A still of troughs.

The plane, our planet,
Travels on roads that are not seen or laid
But sound in instruments on pilots' ears,
While underneath
The sure wings
Are the everlasting arms of science.                                        20

1  Early settlers' name for Regina.
2  In that 'up and down' have been added to the usual four points of the compass.

Man, the lofty worm, tunnels his latest clay,
And bores his new career.

This frontier, too, is ours.
This everywhere whose life can only be led
At the pace of a rocket
Is common to man and man,
And every country below is an I land.    pun

The sun sets on its top shelf,
And stars seem farther from our nearer grasp.

I have sat by night beside a cold lake      30
And touched things smoother than moonlight on still water,
But the moon on this cloud sea is not human,
And here is no shore, no intimacy,
Only the start of space, the road to suns.

1945


# Lakeshore

The lake is sharp along the shore
Trimming the bevelled edge of land
To level curves; the fretted sands
Go slanting down through liquid air
Till stones below shift here and there
Floating upon their broken sky
All netted by the prism wave
And rippled where the currents are.

I stare through windows at this cave
Where fish, like planes, slow-motioned, fly.      10
Poised in a still of gravity
The narrow minnow, flicking fin,
Hangs in a paler, ochre sun,
His doorways open everywhere.

And I am a tall frond that waves
Its head below its rooted feet
Seeking the light that draws it down

To forest floors beyond its reach
Vivid with gloom and eerie dreams.

The water's deepest colonnades                    20
Contract the blood, and to this home
That stirs the dark amphibian
With me the naked swimmers come
Drawn to their prehistoric womb.

They too are liquid as they fall
Like tumbled water loosed above
Until they lie, diagonal,
Within the cool and sheltered grove
Stroked by the fingertips of love.

Silent, our sport is drowned in fact             30
Too virginal for speech or sound
And each is personal and laned
Along his private aqueduct.

Too soon the tether of the lungs
Is taut and straining, and we rise
Upon our undeveloped wings
Toward the prison of our ground
A secret anguish in our thighs
And mermaids in our memories.

This is our talent, to have grown                40
Upright in posture, false-erect,
A landed gentry, circumspect,
Tied to a horizontal soil
The floor and ceiling of the soul;
Striving, with cold and fishy care
To make an ocean of the air.

Sometimes, upon a crowded street,
I feel the sudden rain come down
And in the old, magnetic sound
I hear the opening of a gate                      50
That loosens all the seven seas.
Watching the whole creation drown
I muse, alone, on Ararat.[1]

1954

1 The mountain on which Noah is said to have landed after the flood (Genesis 8:4).

# Poetry

Nothing can take its place. If I write 'ostrich'
Those who have never seen the bird see it
With its head in the sand and its plumes fluffed with the wind
Like Mackenzie King talking on Freedom of Trade.[1]

And if I write 'holocaust', and 'nightingales',
I startle the insurance agents and the virgins
Who belong, by this alchemy, in the same category,
Since both are very worried about their premiums.

A rose and a rose are two roses; a rose is a rose is a rose.[2]
Sometimes I have walked down a street marked No Outlet          10
Only to find that what was blocking my path
Was a railroad track roaring away to the west.

So I know it will survive. Not even the decline of reading
And the substitution of advertising for genuine pornography
Can crush the uprush of the mushrooming verb
Or drown the overtone of the noun on its own.

1954

---

1  In the late 1930s King supported closer economic ties with the US as a way of distancing Canada from Britain.
   In the period after the end of World War II, King abandoned free trade talks with the US, increasingly fearful
   of American domination of the Canadian economy. For details on King as a political leader and Scott's opinion
   of him, see the following poem and its notes.
2  This alludes to a line from Gertrude Stein's poem 'Sacred Emily' (1913)—'Rose is a rose is a rose is a rose'—that
   came to exemplify her particular brand of difficult modern writing.

# W.L.M.K.[1]

How shall we speak of Canada,
Mackenzie King dead?
The Mother's boy in the lonely room
With his dog, his medium and his ruins?[2]

He blunted us.

We had no shape
Because he never took sides,
And no sides
Because he never allowed them to take shape.

He skilfully avoided what was wrong                                    10
Without saying what was right,
And never let his on the one hand
Know what his on the other hand was doing.

The height of his ambition
Was to pile a Parliamentary Committee on a Royal Commission,
To have 'conscription if necessary
But not necessarily conscription',
To let Parliament decide—
Later.

Postpone, postpone, abstain.                                          20

Only one thread was certain:
After World War I
Business as usual,
After World War II
Orderly decontrol.
Always he led us back to where we were before.

1  William Lyon Mackenzie King (1874–1950) became the leader of the Liberal Party in 1919 and served as prime
   minister of Canada for twenty-two years (non-consecutively) between 1921 and 1948. His administration was
   characterized by caution and compromise; his critics found him weak and evasive. In the 1942 debate about
   whether or not the Liberals would abandon their previous anti-conscription stand (English Canadians believed
   they should; French Canadians strongly opposed conscription), King famously declared, 'Not necessarily conscription, but conscription if necessary.' He kept detailed diaries, which revealed, after his death, that he doted
   on his pet dog and that he had occasionally invited mediums to his home to hold seances, believing that he could
   communicate with departed spirits—especially that of his mother, to whom he had always been deeply devoted.
2  King lived on a lavish family estate, Kingsmere, to which he added false 'ruins' to make it look more like an
   English estate of significant antiquity.

He seemed to be in the centre
Because we had no centre,
No vision
To pierce the smoke-screen of his politics. · 30

Truly he will be remembered
Wherever men honour ingenuity,
Ambiguity, inactivity, and political longevity.

Let us raise up a temple
To the cult of mediocrity,
Do nothing by halves
Which can be done by quarters.

1957

# All the Spikes But the Last[1]

Where are the coolies in your poem, Ned?
Where are the thousands from China who swung
    their picks with bare hands at forty below?

Between the first and the million other spikes
    they drove, and the dressed-up act of
    Donald Smith,[2] who has sung their story?

Did they fare so well in the land they helped to
    unite? Did they get one of the 25,000,000 CPR acres?

Is all Canada has to say to them written in the Chinese
    Immigration Act?[3] 10

1957

---

1 A response to E.J. ('Ned') Pratt's Towards the Last Spike. For the completion of the CPR in British Columbia, some 6,000 labourers, referred to as coolies, were brought over from China because of their willingness to accept low wages and endure brutal conditions. Pratt's poem alludes to them only in passing (at lines 1113 and 1114).
2 Donald Smith (1820–1913) was recognized for his role in the building of the CPR by being chosen to drive the last spike in 1884, a ritual he performed in frock-coat and high hat.
3 The Chinese Immigration Act, more commonly known as the Chinese Exclusion Act, was passed in 1923. A late outgrowth of continued reaction against this imported labour, it virtually prohibited further entry into Canada by Chinese. The act was repealed in 1947.

# Harry Robinson

## 1900–1990

One of the important tellers of Native tales and experiences in twentieth-century Canada was Harry Robinson, who, late in his long life, said he could tell stories 'twenty-one hours or more . . . because this is my job. I'm a storyteller.' His stories have been important for younger First Nations writers such as Thomas King, who describes thus his first encounter:

*I couldn't believe the power and the skill with which Robinson could work up a story—in English: they weren't translated, they were simply transcribed—and how well he understood the power of the oral voice in a written piece. . . . It was inspirational . . . I remember sitting in my office, just sort of sweating, reading this stuff: it was so good.*

Born in Oyama, near Kelowna, British Columbia, in the Okanagan Valley, Robinson grew up in the Similkameen Valley near Keremeos. An Okanagan, he was a member of the Lower Similkameen Band of the Interior Salish people. Because he received only five months of formal schooling, Robinson didn't learn to read and write until he was twenty-two. He spent most of his early life in a primarily oral culture, learning many of his stories from his grandmother and other elders in the community. Until 1971, he worked as a rancher. Following the death of his wife, he retired to a small bungalow on a friend's ranch.

As a storyteller in an age of electronic media, Robinson considered himself among the last of a dying breed: he therefore retold the stories he had heard as a boy, not only for their own value, but also as a way of keeping alive both the tales themselves and the tradition of storytelling. At first, he told his stories in his native Okanagan; however, he found, as he grew older, that even Okanagan listeners could not always understand the language, so he began to tell his stories in English.

Robinson's tales have been compiled into three volumes by the ethnologist Wendy Wickwire, who first met Robinson in 1977. Becoming a friend, she recorded and transcribed more than a hundred of his stories during twelve years of interviews. The first of these collections, *Write It on Your Heart: The Epic World of an Okanagan Storyteller* (1989), was published shortly before his death. *Nature Power: In the Spirit of an Okanagan Storyteller*, appeared three years later, followed by *Living by Stories: A Journey of Landscape and Memory* in 2005. In the introduction to the 1989 collection, she describes how she would visit the 'quiet setting beside the Similkameen River in British Columbia's southern interior, [where] in a neat and simple house without television, radio or newspapers, Harry lives with an unbroken contact to a deep past.'

Robinson divided his stories into two kinds: *chap-TEEK-whl* and *shmee-MA-ee* (these are Wickwire's phonetic spellings). *Chap-TEEK-whl* stories, of which 'Coyote Challenges God' is an example, explain the nature of the world and its creation, often featuring animal-creators and animal-people who existed in a timeless period before the Okanagan people became fully human. *Shmee-MA-ee* stories, such as 'Indian Doctor', deal with human beings and take place within time.

Publication of oral stories, especially those that also involve translation, can distort the style if not the content of oral narratives. The nuances of speech are lost when transcribers reshape tales to the conventions of the print culture—for example, regularizing syntax, or compressing the repetition that is present in, and important to, all spoken communication. Wickwire, sensing that the oral stories she was hearing were 'really performed events', worked with Robinson to avoid these losses as much as possible. Robinson told her his stories in English, not in Okanagan, and he taught Wickwire about the oral structure of his narratives. Wickwire's transcriptions retain much of their oral nature through the use of line breaks that show the rhythm of Robinson's speech, including his pauses and repetitions: the result feels more like speech than writing.

In reading such transcriptions, we should nevertheless remember that, in contrast to the fixed nature of written texts, oral narratives are protean. Though many of Robinson's stories have their origins at least as far back as the 1840s (the period of his grandmother's girlhood), they have not remained unaffected by Robinson's own experiences or by the conditions of their telling. One reason oral stories continually change shape is that their tellers tailor each rendition to suit their audience. Robinson told his stories to Wickwire, who was a friend but also a woman of European descent, with the knowledge that they would later be read by an audience comprised mostly of non-Okanagans—factors that would have influenced what he told and his way of telling it.

## Coyote Challenges God

*Coyote travels along and meets an old man. He claims he's the older of the two. The old man invites Coyote into a contest of his power.*

Coyote was walking.
And then he see somebody walking ahead of him.
Looks like this man is walking from here.
And he walks.
And pretty soon they get together.
And they met.
And he looked at him.
He was an old man, a very old man,
    that one he met.
White hair.                 10
Look old.

And he talk to him.
And I do not know for sure what they were saying.
But anyway, they talking to one another.
But Coyote says to him,
   'I'm the oldest.
   You young.
   I'm the oldest.'
Coyote, he claims himself, he's older than him.
And this man told him,           20
   'No, you young.
   I'm the older.'
   'Oh no,' Coyote says,
   'I'm older.
   I been walking all over the place.'

And he tell him all what he have done,
   and explain him how much power he was,
      and so on.
But he didn't know he was the one who gave him that power.

So the old man told him,                             30
   'All right, if you got the full power, I like to see.'

All right.
They walked a little ways and they see a little mountain.
Not small.
It's kinda big mountain.
He stopped there.
And then this old man told him,
   'If you got the power the way you say,
      a lot of power,
         I want to see you move this mountain         40
           and put 'em in another place,
              if you got the power.'
Coyote says,
   'Why sure, I got the power.'
He says,
   'All right.
   I like to see you move that mountain.'

So Coyote, he use his power
   and he moved that mountain just by his thought.
And the mountain,                              50
   it seems to move and sit in another place.

All right.
The old man told 'em,
   'All right, you've got the power.'
Then they go a little ways and they see a lake.
Pretty good sized lake.
And the old man told 'em,
   'Now you move this lake from that place
      and set it in another place.
   Same as you do that mountain,               60
      if you got power.'
Coyote said,
   'Sure, I'll move 'em.'
   'All right, let's see you move it.'

So he use his power and he move that lake
    and set it in a different place.
And he told the old man,
    'Now you see, I move it.
    I told you I got the power.'

All right.                         70
The old man told 'em,
    'All right, we go back
        and I like to see you move that mountain
            back into place.'
Coyote said,
    'All right, I can do it.'
So they went back.
And he going to move that mountain.
The old man takes the power away from him.
He didn't know.                   80
He try to move the mountain back to the place.
He couldn't make it.
Can't do it.
Old man told him,
    'All right, we go back to that lake
        and you can move that back in place.'
So they went back and he said,
    'All right, you move that back in place.'
Try to move but they couldn't move it.
And the old man told 'em,         90
    'You always say you got a lot of power.
    But you can't move 'em back.'
    'Well,' he says, 'I don't know.'
    'Yeah, you don't know but I do.
    I am the one that give you that power in the first place.
    So you used that power
        and you've got the power and you moved that.
     But now I take that power away from you
        for a little while.
    And then you couldn't move it.        100
    All right.
    Now I give you the power back.
    Then move it.'

Well, still he didn't know,
    but he get the power back.
Then he moved the lake into place.

And he moved the mountain into place.
Then told him,
    'Now, that's the last thing you can do.
    Now I take the power away from you        110
        and I'm going to take you
        and I'm going to put you in a certain place
        and you're going to stay there till
            the end of the world.
    Because the reason why I'm going to do that with you,
        you've done a lot of good things
            and you've done a lot of bad things.
    And it seems to be the bad you have done,
        it's more than the good.
    So that's why I'm going to put you in one place.        120
    And you going to stay there until the end of the world.
    Just before the world is going to be the end,
        I can let you go.
    Then you can go in the place all over again
        just like you do before.'

And the old man left him on a boat on the water
    and told him,
        'You're going to be there at all time.'

The boat, it goes around itself by wind.
And Coyote stay in there all the time.        130
For a long time Coyote was there on the water
    sitting on that boat.
And he eat right there.
And he got a fire,
    and the fire never go out.
Just like it was when he first set the fire.
It was like that all the time.
And been there a long time.
Just like he put him in jail.

1989

# Indian Doctor

*A woman announces at a winter dance that she has power to doctor people. When a man is seriously stabbed a short while later, they go and get this woman to work on him. It is her first doctoring, but her power is strong.*

There's one woman down in Okanogan Washington,
    just the other side of Omak.
She put up a *shnay-WUM* herself, you know.
Susan Joseph, her name was.
And they put up a *shnay-WUM*.
And some other people, they goes in there
    and they have the *shnay-WUM* for one winter.
Second winter, they went and make a *shnay-WUM*,
    but in the third winter they had a *shnay-WUM*,
        she put up the *shnay-WUM* herself,       10
            alone.
And when they finish, they give away blankets,
    and clothes and buckskin, you know, and stuff like that.

When she finish, she says to the people,
    'I'm going to tell you what I'm going to be from now on.'
She says,
    'If anybody got hurt, and he got blood inside of him,
        supposing if somebody got stabbed with knife,
        or somebody got shot with gun,
        or somebody fall off from a horse,       20
        or from something, and get hurt,
            as long as they got injured, let me know.
    See what I'll do.'
All right.

The people remember that.
In winter she say that.
That summer, in the month of June,
    and one fella, he got stabbed.
Someone stabbed him in the belly here with a knife, you know,
    cut him open.       30
Then, the other people they says,
    'That Susan, she says she is going to be good for the people
        that get hurt. Go get her.'

So they went and get her.
She was at home and she see somebody in the morning,
    about eight o'clock in the morning,
        somebody come, come down the hill pretty fast,
            leading a horse.

They come and tell Susan,
    'I coming to get you.                                                40
        My brother got hurt.
        He was stabbed with a knife.
        Maybe he's going to die.
        Badly stabbed. Big opening here.'
    'All right, I go.'

So she got a special dress.
She can put that on to do the work.
She made that dress and keep 'em,
    never wear 'em.
Only when she go to work, she put them on.                              50
Just like the priests, you know,
    the priests, put them on for the mass.
Something like that.
And then she went.
They got to go up the hill.
Kinda sandy ground and the horses, they gallop.
But they couldn't gallop fast enough up the hill,
    and kinda sandy.
They going slow.
Then, the horses kind of played out till they get up to the top.       60
It's not steep, you know, but it's uphill.
When they get to the top, and she says to this man,
    whoever come and get her, she says to him,
        'When we get to the top of the hill, we turn off the road,
            and we get off and set down there for a while.
                I want to smoke.'

So, this man, he think,
    Well, why did she have to stop there to smoke?
    My brother, he going to die.
    She should get there right away.                                   70
He think, but he didn't say it, but he think in his heart.

So they turn off the road, stop, and they get off their horses.
And this man hold the horses,
   and she got a pipe,
      a handmade pipe, you know.
They make 'em out of stone.
And she fill up with tobacco.
She have to cut the plug.
Hard tobacco.
It's been in a plug.                              80
And she cut that with a knife,
   and cut 'em and cut 'em and cut 'em.
Then she put 'em in the pipe.
Then the kinnikinnik, she smash that and put them mixed,
   then light and then she smoked in the pipe.
And it takes a while to do that before she smoke.
And this man, he think,
   What the heck do we have to smoke here for?
He never said, but he think that.

When she finish smoking, then she put that away           90
   and she says to him,
      'Don't you think that.
         When I smoke, I'm looking at that man
            and now I know I'm going to get there
               and I know I'm going to get him to be all right.
        That's why I smoke.
        If I don't smoke I don't know
           if I'm going to get him to be all right or not.
        But when I smoke, I know.
        Now, we go.'                          100
She know what he thinks, but she didn't say.
She's Indian doctor.
She knows that by her power.

So, they got on, and went and get to the place.
There was a camp, bunch of people,
   lot of camp.
Quite a few camp along the creek there.
They were camping there.
They were supposed to be go to church there,
   they call that Corpus Christi.                   110
And they go to church about a couple days,
   the priest, you know.

That's why all the people gather there.
Some people were drinking, you know.
They always do.
Some people go to the church and some people drink.
They always do that.

So, there's a lot of people there.
The Indian doctor, she come,
    and she see that man that get hurt,            120
        they pile up the blanket and pillows
            and they lay him there just kind of half sitting,
                lay there.
Just like you lay on that chair and sit back, like that.
And quite a little ways,
    when they get off the saddlehorse, you know in the cabin,
        get off the saddle horse and stepped on the ground.
You know, if you get off the saddlehorse
    and you step on the ground first
        before you pull your other foot off the stirrup,        130
            step on the ground.
Just as soon as she hit the ground with her foot,
    and up comes her song,
        come out.
And she started to sing loud, right away.
Then, she turn,
    and she walk towards the injured man kinda slow.
Walk slow,
    and when she get from about here to that wall there
        and she stop.            140
Sing there for a while and she put her hand like that.
Put it like that,
    and sing her song.
And some of the people, they all watching.
Turn around and look at the one lady and says,
    'Get me water. Get me water right from the creek.'
And the creek is quite a little ways down.
And this lady, she pick up a bucket
    and run down to the creek
        and get fresh water.        150
And she come and she says,
    'Put 'em in the basin.'
And they take the basin, and they put this water in the basin
    and they set it right alongside of 'em.

And they said that injured man,
   he was laying like from here to the corner over there,
      just about that far, laying,
And she said,
   'You pick up the water.'
   'I can't see.'
   'Pick up the water.'                    160
She says,
   'I throw the water to 'em.
   When I throw the water to 'em it's just like little balls.'
And it hit him right in the forehead.

Then again she sing awhile
   and get another one.
Then she throw that one.
Who can hold the water and throw 'em?
Nobody.                            170

Then, after that, and she walked over there,
   and she get to that man.
This man was lay against the pillow,
   the blanket, high, you know,
      laying there.
And she kind of sit alongside of him.
And she put her hands like that.
See, there's hole here, like that.
Put her hands like that,
   and then she put it, she don't put 'em like that,      180
     about four inches away from her mouth,
       and about four inch away from the body.
Then she 'ssssss',
   she suck the blood,
     and they could never see the blood come through here
       because her hand was about four inch away from her mouth,
        and four inch away from the body.
You could never see the blood come through there
   in the open.
Then she turn around and spit in the water.        190
Just blood.
Black blood.
Then sing her song, sing her song for a while.
Same way—'ssssssss',
Spit, and the blood was just straight blood.

On the third time, the blood was just kind of a yellow.
She said,
   'No more.'
She suck that blood out of him
   because if that blood builds up inside
     then it comes to the heart and die.              200
Says, 'All right, that's all.
   I go down and get some medicine
     and fix the medicine for you,
       and then you okay.'

She went down to the creek herself.
Get some of them willow.
She get the bark off the willow,
   and she kind of smash that and mix 'em with the water
     and wet it, you know.                    210
And she put them on the cut, you know, on the open.
Put them on and wrap 'em up with the handkerchief or something
Said,
   'You keep that, and you lay there for a while.
     When the sun goes about halfways from noon to sunset,
       you get up and you walk around.
     In the morning, just as soon as the sun comes
       out from the mountain,
         and you get up and walk around.
     And after that you'll be all right.'          220

That man, he get better.
That's the first one, she did that work.
But another time, I watching 'em.
I was there.
She suck the blood the same way.
Just like that.
And I was stand right alongside of her.
And I could never see the blood come.
But she spit blood.
It's pretty hard to believe that.              230

1989

# A.J.M. Smith

## 1902–1980

Poet, anthologist, critic, teacher, and one of the founders of the modernist literary movement in Canada, Arthur James Marshall Smith had a profound effect on modern Canadian poetry, beginning in his student days and carrying on through a long career. Born in Montreal, he entered McGill University in 1921, completing an undergraduate degree in science before taking an MA in literature. While at McGill, he began two literary publications: the *Literary Supplement of the McGill Daily* (1924–5), which lasted less than a year, and then, with F.R. Scott, the *McGill Fortnightly Review* (1925–7). The *McGill Fortnightly Review* published the poetry of the nascent 'Montreal group' (F.R. Scott, Leo Kennedy, and Smith himself, among others), along with Smith's early critical statements about the need for a modernist poetry in Canada.

In 1927, Smith married and left Montreal for Edinburgh, where he began a PhD in English on seventeenth-century poetry. While he was in Scotland, his brief but influential critical article, 'Wanted—Canadian Criticism', appeared in the *Canadian Forum* (April 1928). In it, he called for a modern criticism that would guide Canadian writers into twentieth-century aesthetics and away from the moral patriotism and subservience to commerce that he saw seducing contemporary writers. He thought that Canadian critics had so far been misguided because they applied moral rather than artistic criteria and supported writers who used clichéd themes and trite Canadian images. He argued that Canada's adolescence was now over and that the 'adult' writing to come would be realistic; would be able to utilize irony, cynicism, and liberalism without stigma; and would be conscious not so much of its position in space as of its location in time. This article was his formal declaration of a split between those in Canada who supported modernist sensibilities and those who adhered to nationalistic goals in order to promote Canadian literature. Around this time, he also contributed poems to the *Canadian*

*Mercury* (1928–9), which, in its brief lifetime, continued the policies that had guided the *McGill Fortnightly Review.*

In 1929, he returned briefly to Montreal. Unable to find a university teaching position in Canada during the Depression, Smith took several temporary ones in the United States. He completed his doctorate in 1931 and in 1938 was appointed to the faculty of Michigan State University in East Lansing. That became his permanent home, though he retuned to Canada to spend his summers at a family cottage in Quebec. When Smith retired in 1972, he stayed on at Michigan State as writer-in-residence.

Despite being based in the United States, Smith maintained a deep interest in, and editorial involvement with, Canadian literature. In the 1930s, Smith and Scott compiled *New Provinces* (1936); containing work by four members of the now-dispersed 'Montreal group' (Kennedy, A.M. Klein, Scott, and Smith), along with work by E.J. Pratt and Robert Finch of Toronto, it was presented as an anthology of 'new' Canadian poets intended to define Canadian modernist poetry. Its publication was clouded, however, by the rejection of Smith's deliberately provocative preface by Hugh Eayrs, the publisher of Macmillan, and by Finch and Pratt. They objected to the way Smith criticized 'romantic' poetry of feeling as inferior to impersonal poetry of intellect, knowing that this preference would be understood as an attack on earlier Canadian poets and would convey an implicit suggestion that worthwhile Canadian poetry began with the *New Provinces* writers. Scott replaced it with a less-controversial preface. Smith's objectionable one was finally published in 1965, in the journal *Canadian Literature,* as 'A Rejected Preface'.

Although Raymond Knister, Dorothy Livesay, and W.W.E. Ross were writing imagist and modernist poetry before the Montreal group, it was Smith who—responding to his reading of Yeats, to the Imagist movement defined by Pound, and to Eliot's *The Waste Land*—attempted, in a series of critical pronouncements, to establish the poetic principles of Canadian modernism. Writing in 1926, he described the job of the early modernists, such as Yeats, as having been 'to overthrow an effete and decadent diction and to bring the subject matter of poetry out of the library and the afternoon-tea salon into the open air, dealing in the language of present-day speech with subjects of living interest'; Smith believed that the undertaking of his own generation of modernists was 'a turning back to the Seventeenth Century, a renewed interest in the poems of John Donne, an attempt to recapture and exploit in a new way the poetics of the Metaphysical poets'. By incorporating into that endeavour 'various psychological theories of the subconscious', this type of modernism would be able to 'forge . . . what is almost a new form of expression—a form which has found so far its culmination in the prose of James Joyce and the poetry of T.S. Eliot'. These were writers, he observed, who 'turned aside from the world, concerned themselves with abstruse questions of technique', and emphasized 'the importance of form'.

In the 1940s, Smith applied his formalist principles to national literature by making a controversial distinction, in his 1943 preface to *The Book of Canadian Poetry*, between 'cosmopolitan' and 'native' verse. For Smith, the 'cosmopolitan' poet responded to what Canadian life 'had in common with life everywhere', while the 'native' poet 'concentrated on what was individual and unique in Canadian life'. Historically, Smith saw the native poet as having sought to 'come to terms with an environment that is only now ceasing to be colonial', while the cosmopolitan writer 'from the very beginning has made a heroic effort to transcend colonialism by entering into the universal, civilizing culture of ideas'. For Smith, colonialism, which he equated with parochialism, was a threat to Canadian writing, while cosmopolitanism admitted Canadian writers to the world of international modernism.

This preface to the 1943 anthology began a dispute between Smith and another group of contemporary writers whose work often appeared in the literary magazine *First Statement*, edited by John Sutherland. In his preface to *Other Canadians: An Anthology of the New Poetry in Canada, 1940–1946* (1947), Sutherland defended the 'hardfisted' proletarian writers who valued not the civilized poetry of 'cosmopolitanism' but a more local verse that was 'racy and vigorous', 'healthy and masculine'—exemplified by poets like Irving Layton, Louis Dudek, and Raymond Souster. These, he argued, were poets who wrote a kind of native poetry that was different from that which Smith disliked, one not focused on the physical world but on the people within it, a poetry 'of the common man'. The debate between Smith and Sutherland came to be viewed as a debate between two schools of Canadian modernist poetry, the writers associated with *First Statement* and those with *Preview*, a Montreal literary magazine that was publishing the work of Scott, Klein, and P.K. Page, and it reflected a growing division between those who valued an elegant and simple verse and those who rejected the refined diction and form associated with Eliot's brand of modernism. (Often ignored was the fact that both groups had turned away from the nature-based poetry of earlier Canadian writing and embraced a simpler, more natural diction.)

The debate was not merely about aesthetics. In the 1940s, modernism was being increasingly criticized as an anti-national approach to writing at a time when national literature and identity were once again becoming important goals. In the same year as Smith's advocacy of cosmopolitan poetry, E.K. Brown argued, in his influential book *On Canadian Poetry*, that Canadian literature had always been colonial because it had first looked to Britain for its models and then to the United States rather than developing an independent literature that confidently drew on its own traditions and reflected back its own experiences and places.

Smith's influence on Canadian writing went beyond his role as spokesperson for modernism. As an anthologist, he helped shape the Canadian literary canon. The collections of poetry and prose he compiled include *The Oxford Book of Canadian Verse* (1960); *Modern Canadian Verse* (1967); *The Blasted Pine: An Anthology of Satire, Invective and Disrespectful Verse, Chiefly by Canadian Writers* (with F.R. Scott, 1957); and two anthologies of critical essays, *Masks of Fiction* (1961) and *Masks of*

**The Lonely Land** | **427**

*Poetry* (1962). His own criticism was collected in *Towards a View of Canadian Poetry: Selected Critical Essays, 1928–1971* (1973) and *On Poetry and Poets* (1977).

Although Smith published his own poetry over the years—mostly in periodicals such as the *Canadian Forum*—he long refrained from collecting them in a book. His first volume of poems, *News of the Phoenix*, which won a Governor General's Award, did not appear until 1943. There followed *A Sort of Ecstasy* (1954), *Collected Poems* (1963), *Poems: New and Collected* (1967), and *The Classic Shade: Selected Poems* (1978). In 2007, Brian Trehearne published an edition of *The Complete Poems of A.J.M. Smith*.

All of Smith's poetry is characterized by an assured command of form that controls his intricate allusions; by a style that can combine, within a single poem, a convoluted syntax

derived from seventeenth-century poetry ('How all men wrongly death to dignify / Conspire. I tell') and the wry humour and colloquial speech rhythms of the jazz world ('a worth / Beyond all highfalutin' woes or shows'). A severe critic of his own efforts, and a constant reviser, Smith believed that a poem should be

*a highly organized, complex, and unified re-creation of experience in which the maximum use of meaning and suggestion in the sounds of words has been achieved with the minimum essential outlay of words. A poem is not the description of an experience, it is itself an experience, and it awakens in the mind of the alert and receptive reader a new experience analogous to the one in the mind of the poet ultimately responsible for the creation of the poem.* ('The Refining Fire: The Meaning and Use of Poetry', 1954)

# The Lonely Land[1]

Cedar and jagged fir
uplift sharp barbs
against the gray
and cloud-piled sky;
and in the bay
blown spume and windrift
and thin, bitter spray
snap
at the whirling sky;
and the pine trees                          10
lean one way.

A wild duck calls
to her mate,
and the ragged
and passionate tones
stagger and fall,
and recover,
and stagger and fall,
on these stones—

1 Originally subtitled 'Group of Seven' (in the *McGill Fortnightly Review*, 1926), this poem was revised for two other periodical publications, in 1927 and again in 1929.

are lost
in the lapping of water
on smooth, flat stones.

This is a beauty
of dissonance,
this resonance
of stony strand,
this smoky cry
curled over a black pine
like a broken
and wind-battered branch
when the wind
bends the tops of the pines
and curdles the sky
from the north.

This is the beauty
of strength
broken by strength
and still strong.

1926; 1943

# Far West

Among the cigarettes and the peppermint creams
Came the flowers of fingers, luxurious and bland,
Incredibly blossoming in the little breast.
And in the Far West
The tremendous cowboys in goatskin pants
Shot up the town of her ignorant wish.

In the gun flash she saw the long light shake
Across the lake,[1] repeating that poem
At Finsbury Park.

1 An allusion to Tennyson's 'The Princess', iv, Introductory Song:

> The splendour falls on castle walls
> And snowy summits old in story:
> The long light shakes across the lakes,
> And the wild cataract leaps in glory.
> Blow, bugle, blow, set the wild echoes flying,
> Blow, bugle; answer, echoes, dying, dying, dying.

'Finsbury Park' is an area in northwest London, apparently the location of the movie theatre in the poem.

But the echo was drowned in the roll of the trams—  10
Anyway, who would have heard? Not a soul.
Not one noble and toxic like Buffalo Bill.

In the holy name *bang! bang!* the flowers came
With the marvellous touch of fingers
Gentler than the fuzzy goats
Moving up and down up and down as if in ecstasy
As the cowboys rode their skintight stallions
Over the barbarous hills of California.

1943

## Sea Cliff

Wave on wave
and green on rock
and white between
the splash and black
the crash and hiss
of the feathery fall,
the snap and shock
of the water wall
and the wall of rock:

after—                                    10
after the ebb-flow,
wet rock,
high—
high over the slapping green,
water sliding away
and the rock abiding,
new rock riding
out of the spray.

1943

# Business as Usual: 1946[1]

Across the craggy indigo
Come rumours of the flashing spears,
And in the clank of rancid noon
There is a tone, and such a tone.

How tender! How insidious!
The air grows gentle with protecting bosks,[2]
And furry leaves take branch and root.
Here we are safe, we say, and slyly smile.

In this delightful forest, fluted so,
We burghers of the sunny central plain                    10
Fable a still refuge from the spears
That clank—but gently clank—but clank again!

1954

1    'Business as Usual' was first published in *The Fiddlehead* in 1946. When including it in *A Sort of Ecstasy* (1954),
     Smith added the date to the title and paired it with the poem that follows ('Fear as Normal: 1954') to show
     that, though he had been pessimistic about North America's returning to a 'business as usual' post-war
     economy instead of trying to deal with the after-effects of the war on Europe, he had failed to anticipate the
     Cold War that followed.
2    Thickets.

# Fear as Normal: 1954[1]

But gently clank? The clank has grown
A flashing crack—the crack of doom.
It mushrooms high above our salty plain,
And plants the sea with rabid fish.[2]

How skilful! How efficient!
The active cloud is our clenched fist.
Hysteria, dropping like the gentle dew,[3]
Over the bent world broods with ah! bright wings.

1    Anxieties associated with the Cold War reached new heights in North America following the Soviet Union's test
     of a hydrogen bomb in 1953, spurring construction of backyard fallout shelters (often lead-lined) and intensify-
     ing preparations for a possible nuclear attack.
2    The test by the United States of a hydrogen bomb in March, 1954, produced much greater nuclear fallout than
     anticipated, causing widespread radiation poisoning; one effect was the death of a Japanese fisherman and the
     contamination of the catch on board his boat.
3    This allusion to Portia's famous speech in *The Merchant of Venice*, arguing for mercy as superior to justice ('The
     quality of mercy is not strain'd, / It droppeth as the *gentle dew* from heaven'), is followed in the next line by an
     allusion to Gerard Manley Hopkins's poem 'God's Grandeur', which begins by promising that the 'world is
     charged with the grandeur of God. / It will flame out' and concludes that 'nature is never spent' because 'the Holy
     Ghost over the bent / World broods with warm breast and with ah! bright wings.'

We guess it dazzles our black foe;
But that it penetrates and chars                     10
Our own Christ-laden lead-encasèd hearts
Our terrified fierce dreamings know.

1954

# On Reading an Anthology of Popular Poetry

What shall we say now
To these whose shrill voice,
Giving the game away, now
Less by chance than by choice,

Cries from the stitched heart
In soft melodious screams
The sweet sweet songs that start
Out of alluvial dreams?

The old eternal frog
In the throat that comes                              10
With the words *mother, sweetheart, dog*
Excites, and then numbs.

Is there no katharsis
But 'song' for this dull
Pain, that every Saul of Tarsus
Must pant himself into a Paul?[1]

1943

---

1  In the Book of Acts, Saul of Tarsus has a sudden moment of enlightenment bringing on a conversion experience
   that turns him from a persecutor of Christianity to its leading advocate.

# The Wisdom of Old Jelly Roll[1]

How all men wrongly death to dignify
Conspire, I tell. Parson, poetaster, pimp,
Each acts or acquiesces. They prettify,
Dress up, deodorize, embellish, primp,
And make a show of Nothing. Ah, but met-
aphysics laughs; she touches, tastes, and smells
—Hence knows—the diamond holes that make a net.
Silence resettled testifies to bells.
'Nothing' depends on 'Thing', which is or was:
So death makes life or makes life's worth, a worth          10
Beyond all highfalutin' woes or shows
To publish and confess, 'Cry at the birth,
Rejoice at the death,' old Jelly Roll said,
Being on whiskey, ragtime, chicken, and the scriptures fed.

1962

1 Ferdinand Joseph La Menthe ('Jelly Roll') Morton (1885–1941), American jazz pianist and composer.

# Morley Callaghan
## 1903–1990

Morley Callaghan's short stories are structured around a character who faces a crisis that will determine the course of his life. The crossroads in Callaghan's stories do not merely serve a melodramatic purpose—they have a didactic function. A committed Catholic, Callaghan saw himself as a writer who, in giving 'a shape and form to human experience', had to 'become a moralist'.

Born and educated in Toronto, Callaghan took a General BA in 1925 from St Michael's College, University of Toronto, and completed law school in 1928. While a student, he spent his summers working as a cub reporter for the Toronto *Daily Star*. It was there, in 1923, that he met Ernest Hemingway. Having already begun

to compose fiction, Callaghan showed the American writer his stories. Hemingway, who left for France shortly after, passed them on to some of the editors of Paris literary magazines and presses. As a result, Callaghan's first published story, 'A Girl with Ambition', made its appearance in Paris in 1926, in the important modernist literary magazine *This Quarter*. (His work was later published in other distinguished European literary magazines of the time, *transition* and Ezra Pound's *Exile*.) Callaghan was also successful when he submitted his fiction to American magazines, publishing, from 1928 on, in such journals as *Atlantic Monthly*, *Scribner's Magazine*, *Harper's Bazaar*, and *The New Yorker*. F. Scott Fitzgerald, after reading some of

Callaghan's stories, recommended him to his editor at Scribner's, Maxwell Perkins, who oversaw the publication of Callaghan's first novel, *Strange Fugitive* (1928), and his first collection of stories, *A Native Argosy* (1929).

During this period, Callaghan lived and worked as a journalist in Toronto and Montreal. In 1929, he and his wife travelled to Paris, where he met writers in the expatriate community. (Many years later, in 1963, he published a memoir of his visit, *That Summer in Paris*, the best-known episode of which describes his victory in a boxing match with Hemingway; Fitzgerald was the time-keeper.) Returning to North America later in the year, the Callaghans settled in Toronto.

In the 1930s, Callaghan wrote prolifically. In addition to placing sixty-five stories in high-paying American magazines, he published seven volumes of fiction in eight years: *It's Never Over* (1930), *No Man's Meat* (1931), *A Broken Journey* (1932), *Such Is My Beloved* (1934), *They Shall Inherit the Earth* (1935), *Now That April's Here and Other Stories* (1936), and *More Joy in Heaven* (1937). In 1938, however, Callaghan entered a decade he described as a 'period of spiritual dryness' during which he produced little new fiction. During that time, he worked as a journalist, a scriptwriter, and even as a moderator and panellist on CBC radio.

In 1948, he returned to fiction; among his later works are *The Loved and the Lost* (1951), *Morley Callaghan's Stories* (1959), and *A Passion in Rome* (1961). His last two novels, *A Fine and Private Place* (1975), and *A Wild Old Man on the Road* (1988), contain loosely autobiographical portraits. In 1985, Callaghan's son, the poet, short-story writer, and editor Barry Callaghan, brought together a number of his father's previously uncollected stories as *The Lost and Found Stories of Morley Callaghan*. He subsequently oversaw the publication of *The New Yorker Stories* (2001) and *The Complete Stories* in four volumes (2003), with introductions by Alistair MacLeod, André Alexis, Anne Michaels, and Margaret Atwood.

Though Callaghan received early international recognition, praise in Canada was not always forthcoming; it was not until 1951 that he received a Governor General's Award; this was followed by the Lorne Pierce Medal in 1960 and, in 1970, the Molson Prize and the Royal Bank Award. Callaghan had been criticized at home by both academics and newspaper reviewers for universalizing his characters and settings, a strategy that helped him gain an international market—at the denial of his own Canadian identity. In particular, E.K. Brown ridiculed him, first in a lecture on CBC radio, reprinted in 1938, and then in *On Canadian Poetry* (1943), as being representative of the Canadian colonial mentality. However, one could argue that Callaghan's tendency to blur or make transparent particular features was not limited to the lack of Canadian locales in his fiction: as the American critic Edmund Wilson, a long-time admirer, pointed out, Callaghan was more abstract than writers like Fitzgerald and Hemingway—removing even his own presence from his writing: 'Callaghan is so much interested in moral character as exhibited in other people's behavior that, unlike his two exhibitionistic friends, he never shows himself at all.' In choosing to obscure both himself and his environment, Callaghan took the option A.J.M. Smith had seen as the choice of modernist 'cosmopolitan' writers. That turned out, however, to run counter to the choice made by most twentieth-century Canadian writers, who often employed recognizable places, people, and events as a way of establishing Canadian identity.

Callaghan strove instead to portray the universal problem of humankind's imperfect condition. Early in his career he employed a Marxist-framed social realism as a way of framing his responses to humanity's difficulties; however, after the mid-1930s, he found his solution in Christian humanism. Following his meetings in 1933 with the French philosopher Jacques Maritain, Callaghan developed the view that, in an increasingly oppressive society, the individual needs to control not so much his physical destiny as his personal salvation. This position resulted in a preoccupation with a particular kind of 'criminality' that sets itself in opposition to rigid moral codes and social laws: his hero is often a criminal saint, a social martyr of individual conscience.

Nowhere is the extremity of the individual's situation more evident than in Callaghan's short stories, where this conflict is internalized inside a single character, one who must often choose between personal relationships and his desire to be part of an impersonal society. The merits of Callaghan's novels have sometimes been debated, but the quality of his best stories has always been clear. They are crystallizations of humanity's sense of loss, of its longing for Edens that are no longer attainable. In the short stories especially, Callaghan's laconic style suggests objectivity, an unemotional mirroring of life. At the same time, beneath this surface detachment, a homiletic voice sounds a warning against a dehumanized world and a law that has largely forgotten the personal dimensions of morality.

# Watching and Waiting

Whenever Thomas Hilliard, the lawyer, watched his young wife dancing with men of her own age, he was very sad, for she seemed to glow with a laughter and elation that didn't touch her life with him at all. He was jealous, he knew; but his jealousy at that time made him feel humble. It gave him the fumbling tenderness of a young boy. But as time passed and he saw that his humility only added to her feeling of security, he grew sullen and furtive and began to spy on her.

At times he realized that he was making her life wretched, and in his great shame he struggled hard against the distrust of her that was breaking the peace of his soul. In his longing to be alone with her, so that he would be free to offer her whatever goodness there was in him, he insisted that they move out to the country and renovate the old farmhouse on the lake where he had been born. There they lived like two scared prisoners in the house that was screened from the lane by three old oak trees. He went into the city only three days a week and his business was soon ruined by such neglect.

One evening Thomas Hilliard was putting his bag in the car, getting ready to return to the city. He was in a hurry, for the sky was darkening; the wind had broken the surface of the lake into choppy little waves with whitecaps, and soon it would rain. A gust of wind slammed an open window. Above the noise of the water on the beach, he heard his wife's voice calling, rising eagerly as it went farther away from the house.

She was calling, 'Just a minute, Joe,' and she was running down to the gate by the lane, with the wind blowing her short fair hair back from her head as she ran.

At the gate a young man was getting out of a car, waving his hand to her like an old friend, and calling: 'Did you want to speak to me, Mrs Hilliard?'

'I wanted to ask you to do something for me,' she said.

The young man, laughing, lifted a large green bass from a pail in the back of his car, and he said: 'I caught it not more than half an hour ago. Will you take it, Mrs Hilliard?'

'Isn't it a beauty!' she said, holding it out at arm's length on the stick he had thrust through the jaws. 'You shouldn't be giving such a beauty away.' And she laughed, a free careless laugh that was carried up to the house on the wind.

For a while there was nothing Thomas Hilliard could hear but the murmur of his wife's voice mixed with the murmur of the young man's voice; but the way the laughter had poured out of her, and the look of pleasure on the young man's face, made him tense with resentment. He began to feel sure he had been actually thinking of that one man for months without ever naming him, that he had even been wondering about him while he was packing his bag and thinking of the drive into the city. Why was the young man so friendly that first time he had stopped them, on the main street of the town, when they were doing their weekend shopping, to explain that his name was Joe Whaley and he was their neighbour? That was something he had been wondering about for a long time. And every afternoon when Joe Whaley was off shore in his motorboat, he used to stand up and wave to them, the length of his lean young body outlined against the sky. It was as though all these things had been laid aside in Thomas Hilliard's head, to be given a sudden meaning now in the eager laughter of his wife, in her voice calling, and the pleasure on the young man's face.

He became so excited that he started to run down to the gate; and as he ran, his face was full of yearning and despair. They watched him coming, looking at each other doubtfully. When his wife saw how old and broken he looked, she suddenly dropped the fish in the dust of the road.

'Hey, there! Wait a minute,' he was calling to the young man, who had turned away awkwardly.

'Did you want to speak to me, Mr Hilliard?' Joe Whaley said.

'Is there something you want?' Hilliard asked.

'I just stopped a moment to give you people the fish.'

'I'd like to know, that's all,' Hilliard said, and he smiled foolishly.

The young man, who was astonished, mumbled some kind of an apology and got into his car. He drove up the lane with the engine racing, and the strong wind from the lake whirling the dust in a cloud across the fields.

Speaking quietly, as if nothing had happened to surprise her, Mrs Hilliard began, 'Did you think there was something the matter, Tom?' But then her voice broke, and she cried out: 'Why did you come running down here like that?'

'I heard the way you laughed,' he said.

'What was the matter with the way I laughed?'

'Don't you see how it would strike me? I haven't heard you laugh like that for such a long time.'

'I was only asking him if he'd be passing by the station tonight. I was going to ask him if he'd bring my mother here, if she was on the right train.'

'I don't believe that. You're making up a story,' he shouted.

It was the first time he had openly accused her of deceit; and when she tried to smile at him, her eyes were full of terror. It was as though she knew she was helpless at last, and she said slowly: 'I don't know why you keep staring at me. You're frightening me. I can't bear the way you watch me. It's been going on for such a long time. I've got to speak to someone—can't you see? It's dreadfully lonely here.'

She was staring out over the choppy wind-swept water: she turned and looked up with a child's wonder at the great oak trees that shut the house off from the road. 'I can't stand it any longer,' she said, her voice soft and broken. 'I've been a good wife. I had such an admiration for you when we started. There was nothing I wouldn't have trusted you with. And now—I don't know what's happened to us.' This was the first time she had ever tried to tell him of her hidden desolation; but all he could see was that her smile as she pleaded with him was pathetically false.

'You're lying. You're scared of what might happen,' he shouted.

'I've known how you've been watching me, and I've kept asking myself what the both of us have been waiting for,' she said. As the wind, driving through the leaves of the trees, rattled a window on the side of the house, and the last of the light faded from the lake, she cried out: 'What are we waiting for, day after day?'

'I'm not waiting any more,' he shouted. 'I'm going. You don't need to worry about me watching you any more. I'll not come back this time.' He felt crazy as he started to run over to the car.

Running after him, she cried out: 'I've kept hoping something would happen to make it different, something that would save us. I've prayed for it at night, just wanting you to be like you were three years ago.'

But he had started the car, and it came at her so suddenly that she had to jump out of the way. When the car lurched up the lane, he heard her cry out, but the words were blown away on the wind. He looked back, and saw her standing stiff by the gate, with both hands up to her head.

He drove up to the highway, swinging the car around so wildly at the turn by the grocery-store that the proprietor shouted at him. He began to like the way the car dipped at high speed down the deep valleys, and rose and fell with him always rigid and unthinking. When he reached the top of the highest hill in the country, the first of the rain whipped across his face, slashing and cutting at him in the way they slap the face of a fighter who has been beaten and is coming out of a stupor. His arms were trembling so he stopped the car; and there he sat for a long time, looking out over the hills in the night rain, at the low country whose roll and rise could be followed by the line of lights curving around the lake through the desolation of the wooded valleys and the rain-swept fields of this country of his boyhood, a gleaming line of light leading back to the farm and his wife.

There was a flash of lightning, and the fields and pasture-land gleamed for a moment in the dark. Then he seemed to hear her voice crying out above the wind: 'I've been waiting for so long!' And he muttered: 'How lost and frightened she'll be alone there on a night like this.' He knew then that he could go no farther. With his heart full of yearning for the tenderness he knew she had offered to him, he kept repeating: 'I can't leave her. I can't ever leave her. I'll go back and ask her to forgive me.'

So he sighed and was ashamed; and he drove back slowly along the way he had come, making up in his head fine little speeches that would make his wife laugh and forgive him.

But when he had turned off the highway and was going down the lane that led to the house, he suddenly thought it could do no harm if he stopped the car before it was heard, and went up to the house quietly to make sure no one else was there.

Such a notion made him feel terribly ashamed. As the car rocked in the ruts and puddles of the dirt road, and the headlights gleamed on the wet leaves from over-hanging branches, he was filled with a profound sadness, as if he knew instinctively that no matter how he struggled, he would not be able to stop himself from sneaking up to the house like a spy. Stopping the car, he sat staring at the shuttered windows through which the light hardly filtered, mumbling: 'I've got a heart like a snake's nest. I've come back to ask her to forgive me.' Yet as he watched the strips of light on the shutters, he found himself thinking it could do no harm to make sure she was alone, that this would be the last time he would ever spy on her.

As he got out of the car, he stood a while in the road, getting soaking wet, assuring himself he had no will to be evil. And then as he started to drag his feet through the puddles, he knew he was helpless against his hunger to justify his lack of faith in her.

Swinging open the gate and crossing the grass underneath the oak tree, he stopped softly on the veranda and turned the door-knob slowly. When he found that the door was locked, his heart began to beat unevenly, and he went to pound the door with his fist. Then he grew very cunning. Jumping down to the grass, he went cautiously around to the side of the house, pressed his head against the shutters and listened. The rain streamed down his face and ran into his open mouth.

He heard the sound of his wife's voice, and though he could not make out the words, he knew she was talking earnestly to someone. Her voice seemed to be breaking; she seemed to be sobbing, pleading that she be comforted. His heart began to beat so loud he was sure they would be able to hear it. He grabbed at the shutter and tried to pry it open with his hand, but his fingers grew numb, and the back of his hand began to bleed. Stepping back from the house, he looked around wildly for some heavy stick or piece of iron. He remembered where there was an old horseshoe imbedded in the mud by the gate, and running there, he got down on his knees and scraped with his fingers, and he grinned in delight when he tugged the old horseshoe out of the mud.

But when he had inserted the iron prongs of the shoe between the shutters, and had started to use his weight, he realized that his wife was no longer talking. She was coming over to the window. He heard her gasp and utter a little cry. He heard her running from the room.

Full of despair, as though he were being cheated of the discovery he had been patiently seeking for years, he stepped back from the house, trembling with eagerness. The light in the room where he had loosened the shutter was suddenly turned out. He turned and ran back up the lane to the car, and got his flashlight.

This time he went round to the other side of the house, listening for the smallest sounds which might tell him where they were hiding, but it was hard to hear anything above the noise of the wind in the trees and the roll of the waves on the shore. At the kitchen window at the back of the house he pulled at the shutter. He heard them running out of the room.

The longing to look upon the face of the one who was with his wife became so great that he could hardly think of his wife at all. 'They probably went upstairs to the bedroom. That's where they'll be. I think I heard them going up the stairs.' He went over to the garage and brought out the ladder they had used to paint the house, and put it up against the bedroom window and started to climb on the slippery rungs with the flashlight clutched in his hand, eager for the joy that would be his if he could see without being seen.

The voices he heard as he lay against the ladder were broken with fright; he began to feel all the terror that grew in them as they ran from room to room and whispered and listened and hid in the darkness and longed to cry out.

But they must have heard some noise he made at the window, for before he was ready to use the flashlight, they ran from the room; they hurried downstairs in a way that showed they no longer cared what noise they made, they fled as though they intended to keep on going out of the front door and up the lane.

If he had taken the time to climb down the ladder, they might have succeeded; but instead of doing that, he wrapped his arms and legs around the wet rails and slid to the ground; he got over to the oak tree, and was hidden, his flashlight pointed at the door, before they came out.

As they came running from the house, he kept hidden and flashed the light on them, catching his wife in the strong beam of light, and making her stop dead and scream. She was carrying the rifle he used for hunting in the fall.

With a crazy joy he stepped out and swung the light on the other one; it was his wife's mother, stooped in horror. They were both held in the glare of the light, blinking and cringing in terror, while he tried to remember that the mother was to come to the house. And then his wife shrieked and pointed the gun into the darkness at the end of the beam of light, and fired; and he called out helplessly: 'Marion—'

But it was hurting him on his breast. The light dropped from his hand as he sank to the ground and began to cough.

Then his wife snatched up the light and let it shine on his face: 'Oh, Tom, Tom! Look what I've done,' she moaned.

The mother was still on her knees, stiff with fright.

His hand held against his breast was wet with warm blood; and as his head sank back on the grass he called out jerkily to the mother: 'Go on—hurry! Get someone—for Marion. I'm dying. I want to tell them how it happened.'

The mother, shrieking, hobbled over to the lane, and her cries for help were carried away on the wind.

With his weeping wife huddled over him, he lay dying in the rain. But when he groped with his hand and touched her head, his soul was suddenly overwhelmed by an agony of remorse for his lack of faith in her: in these few moments he longed to be able to show her all the comforting tenderness she had missed in the last three years. 'Forgive me,' he whispered. 'It was my fault—if only you could forgive me.' He wanted to soothe the fright out of her before the others came running up from the lane.

1936, 1959

# Earle Birney

## 1904–1995

Born in Alberta, Alfred Earle Birney was raised there and in rural British Columbia on small frontier farms and in Banff. As a boy and young man, Birney worked to help support his family and to earn enough money to attend university. The jobs he held—'chain-and-rod man with a Waterton survey party, pick-and-shovel and sledge-hammer man on a road crew, mountain guide, fossil hunter, axeman and oiler in a mosquito-control project,' as well as suburban newspaper editor—influenced his poetry. In 1926, he graduated with a first-class honours BA in English literature from the University of British Columbia. He took a PhD (1936) in Old and Middle English at the University of Toronto, writing a dissertation on Chaucer's irony, while he held temporary positions at UBC and the University of California and studied at the University of London. In the year he completed his degree, he accepted a teaching post at the University of Toronto, and remained there until he left, in 1942, to serve in the Second World War. While posted in the Netherlands, he contracted dysentery and diphtheria and was invalided out of the army in 1945. On his return to Canada, Birney worked briefly for the CBC in Montreal before accepting a professorship in medieval literature at UBC. After his retirement in 1965, he was writer-in-residence at the Universities of Toronto (1965–7), Waterloo (1967–8), and Western Ontario (1981–2), as well as Regents Professor at the University of California. In 1987, he suffered a catastrophic heart attack from which he never recovered.

Birney received wide recognition: he won Governor General's Awards for poetry in 1942 and 1945; the Leacock Medal for Humour, for his novel *Turvey*, in 1949; the Lorne Pierce Medal for Literature from the Royal Society of Canada; and the Canada Council Medal 'for outstanding achievement' in 1968.

An extensive traveller, he gave readings of his work throughout the world under Canada Council grants and fellowships. Geographical location even became the organizing principle of his *Collected Poems* (1975). Believing that geography linked humanity to its history, Birney took pains in his poetry to mark, document, and define the significance of being in a particular place at a specific time.

No mere observer, Birney forged new pathways in Canadian writing. Although he deprecated his role as innovator, he was the first poet in Canada to emphasize a metrics based on normal speech rhythms rather than artificial cadences; his 'doodles' (Birney's description of his visual poems) coincided with the beginnings of concrete poetry; and his need to write down 'the particular sound of my own voice' resulted in the first sound poems in Canada. Birney also helped to provide Canadian writers with new outlets for publication, both as literary editor of the *Canadian Forum* (1936–40) and as editor of the *Canadian Poetry Magazine* (1946–8). He further contributed to Canadian writing by organizing one of the first creative writing courses in Canada (at the University of Toronto in 1941) and the first department of creative writing (at the University of British Columbia in 1963). Out of this teaching experience came *The Creative Writer* (1966) and a book in which he discusses the composition of his own poems, *The Cow Jumped Over the Moon* (1972).

Around the time Birney began to edit and to teach creative writing, he also made a serious commitment to his own poetry. His first book, *David and Other Poems*, was published in 1942, and his second, *Now Is Time*, in 1945. He published some fifteen volumes of verse, as well as the novels *Turvey* and *Down the Long Table* (1955). He also wrote widely on poetry and poetics; some of his essays are collected in *Spreading Time: Remarks on Canadian Writing and Writers, 1904–1949* (1980).

Birney's poetry reflects a range of interests, from political beliefs (in the 1930s and early 40s, he was an active Trotskyite) to Anglo-Saxon poetics; but despite the seriousness of many of his poems, they are rarely without a sense of playfulness. Always a public poet, Birney reacted both to A.J.M. Smith's notion of 'cosmopolitanism' and to the more radical theories of the leftist poets of the 1940s by setting out his ideas for a Canadian poetics:

*A revolutionary approach to the world today is somehow associated with a revolt against syntax and the beauties of lucidity. In all this what is lost sight of is that the true cosmopolite in poetry, the great world figure, always had his roots deep in the peculiar soil of his own country, and made himself international because he spoke from his own nation even when he spoke for and to the world. . . . The most cosmopolitan service a Canadian poet can do is to make himself . . . a clear and memorable and passionate interpreter of Canadians themselves, in the language of Canada. . . .*
('Has Poetry a Future in Canada?', 1946)

# Vancouver Lights

About me the night    moonless    wimples the mountains
wraps ocean    land    air    and mounting
sucks at the stars    The city    throbbing below
webs the sable peninsula    The golden
strands overleap the seajet[1]    by bridge and buoy
vault the shears of the inlet    climb the woods
toward me    falter    and halt    Across to the firefly
haze of a ship on the gulf's erased horizon
roll the lambent spokes of a lighthouse

Through the feckless years we have come to the time    10
when to look on this quilt of lamps is a troubling delight
Welling from Europe's bog    through Africa flowing
and Asia    drowning the lonely lumes[2] on the oceans
tiding up over Halifax    now to this winking
outpost comes flooding the primal ink[3]

On this mountain's brutish forehead with terror of space
I stir    of the changeless night and the stark ranges
of nothing    pulsing down from beyond and between
the fragile planets    We are a spark beleaguered
by darkness    this twinkle we make in a corner of emptiness    20
how shall we utter our fear that the black Experimentress[4]
will never in the range of her microscope find it?    Our Phoebus

1 Black sea.
2 Lights.
3 In this stanza Birney describes the progress of the Axis powers in the Second World War, which had caused 'the blackouts spreading from Europe through North Africa, over to Halifax, and [was] now threatening the lights of Vancouver' (Birney, *The Cow Jumped Over the Moon*, hereafter abbreviated as *CJOM*).
4 Night, and the larger concept of the cosmic void, are personified as a black woman, a Nubian, whose experiment is the universe. Our sun, Phoebus, is only a small star or bubble to her; the nebulae or galaxies are but a necklace she has casually chosen to wear. This myth of a female progenitor of the universe recalls the Orphic legend of creation.

himself is a bubble that dries on Her slide     while the Nubian
wears for an evening's whim a necklace of nebulae

Yet we must speak     we the unique glowworms
Out of the waters and rocks of our little world
we conjured these flames     hooped these sparks
by our will     From blankness and cold we fashioned stars
to our size     and signalled Aldebaran[5]
This must we say     whoever may be to hear us     30
if murk devour     and none weave again in gossamer:

           These rays were ours
we made and unmade them     Not the shudder of continents
doused us     the moon's passion     nor crash of comets
In the fathomless heat of our dwarfdom     our dream's combustion
we contrived the power     the blast that snuffed us
No one bound Prometheus     Himself he chained
and consumed his own bright liver[6]     O stranger
Plutonian     descendant     or beast in the stretching night—
there was light                            40

1945, rev. 1966[7]

5 One of the twenty brightest stars in the sky, Aldebaran is used for navigation.
6 When Prometheus stole divine fire for mankind, Zeus punished him by having him chained to a rock where a vulture perpetually devoured his liver. 'Plutonian': (i) pertaining to the god of the dead; (ii) of the planet Pluto.
7 Birney revised many of his poems for *Selected Poems* (1966), mostly by replacing traditional punctuation with spaces.

# Anglosaxon Street[1]

Dawndrizzle ended     dampness steams from
blotching brick and     blank plasterwaste
Faded housepatterns     hoary and finicky
unfold stuttering     stick like a phonograph

Here is a ghetto     gotten for goyim[2]
O with care denuded     of nigger and kike

1 This poem utilizes conventions of Old English, or Anglo-Saxon, poetry, including a caesura that breaks each line in two; single and double alliteration connecting the two halves; accented speech rhythms; kennings (metaphoric compounds substituted for ordinary words—e.g. 'learninghall' for school and 'whistleblow' for the end of the workday); and litotes (ironic understatement by negation—'not humbly' for proudly).
2 Yiddish for those who are not Jews. The poem plays off on the second meaning of Anglo-Saxon—i.e., those who identify themselves as of white British descent—as a way of attacking the exclusivity and racism of the period, exacerbated by the nationalism of the war.

No coonsmell rankles     reeks only cellarrot
attar³ of carexhaust     catcorpse and cookinggrease
Imperial hearts     heave in this haven
Cracks across windows     are welded with slogans     10
There'll Always Be An England     enhances geraniums
and V's for Victory     vanquish the housefly

Ho! with climbing sun     march the bleached beldames
festooned with shopping bags     farded⁴ flatarched
bigthewed Saxonwives     stepping over buttrivers
waddling back wienerladen     to suckle smallfry

Hoy! with sunslope     shrieking over hydrants
flood from learninghall     the lean fingerlings
Nordic nobblecheeked⁵     not all clean of nose
leaping Commandowise     into leprous lanes     20

What! after whistleblow!     spewed from wheelboat
after daylight doughtiness     dire handplay
in sewertrench or sandpit     come Saxonthegns⁶
Junebrown Jutekings     jawslack for meat

Sit after supper     on smeared doorsteps
not humbly swearing     hatedeeds on Huns⁷
profiteers politicians     pacifists Jews

Then by twobit magic     to muse in movie
unlock picturehoard⁸     or lope to alehall
soaking bleakly     in beer skittleless     30

Home again to hotbox     and humid husbandhood
in slumbertrough adding     sleepily to Anglekin

---

3 Fragrant essence, usually rose-like.
4 Rouged.
5 Pimpled. Compare Chaucer's description of the Summoner, who could not find an ointment to cure him of the 'knobbes sittynge on his cheeks' ('General Prologue' to *The Canterbury Tales*, I. 633).
6 Freemen who provided military services for the Saxon lords; 'Jute kings' refers to the Jutes, the German tribe which, invading England in the fifth century, spearheaded the Anglo-Saxon conquest.
7 The people who invaded Europe in the fourth century; also a modern term of contempt for Germans.
8 A play on the opening of an Anglo-Saxon poem, from the sixth or seventh century, that describes a bard beginning to tell a tale: 'Widswith [the far-wanderer] spoke, unlocked his wordhoard.' To be 'in beer skittless' would be to fall short of a life of 'beer and skittles' (that is, one of indulgence and plenty).

Alongside in lanenooks     carling and leman
caterwaul and clip[9]    careless of Saxonry
with moonglow and haste    and a higher heartbeat

Slumbers now slumtrack    unstinks cooling
waiting brief for milkmaid    mornstar and worldrise

*Toronto 1942*

1945, rev. 1966

9 Churl, surly individual; 'leman': lover, 'clip': embrace.

# The Ebb Begins from Dream

The stars like stranded starfish pale and die
and tinted sands of dawning dry
The ebb begins from dream    leaving a border
of milk and morning paper on the porches

From crusted reefs of homes    from unkempt shores
the workers slip reluctant    half-asleep
lapse back into the city's deep
The waves of factory hands and heads    of salesman
eyes and waiting waitress faces
slide soughing out from night's brief crannies      10
suck back along the strand of streets
rattling pebbled smalltalk

O then the curves and curls
of girl stenographers
the loops and purls[1]
of children foaming in the ooze
that by the ceaseless moon of living moves
through heaving flats of habit down the day

And late    from tortuous coves    remoter bays
there sets[2] the sinuous undertow      20
of brokers    and the rolling politicians flow
to welter in the one pelagic motion

1 Murmuring ripples.
2 Flows; 'pelagic': deep sea.

Housewives      beached like crabs in staling pools
crisscross     are swashed in search of food
down to the midtown breakers' booming

At last with turning earth     relentless moon
slow but flooding comes the swell once more
with gurge[3] and laughter's plash and murmur
back to the fraying rocks     far-freighted now
with briny flotsam of each morning vow         30
a wrack of deeds that dulls with neaping[4]
dead thoughts that float again to sea
salt evening weeds that lie
and rot between the cracks of life
and hopes that waterlogged will never link
with land     but will be borne until they sink

Now tide is full and sighing creeps
into the clean sought coigns[5] of sleep
And yet in sleep begins to stir
to mutter in the dark its yearning         40
and to the round possessive mother turning
dreams of vaster wellings
makes the last cliff totter
cradles all the globe in swaying water

The ebb begins from dream. . . .

*Toronto 1945 / Eaglecliff 1947*

1948, rev. 1966

---

3 Whirlpool.
4 The coming of neap tide (here synonymous with ebbing).
5 Corners.

# Pacific Door[1]

Through or over the deathless feud
of the cobra sea and the mongoose wind
you must fare to reach us
Through hiss and throttle come
by a limbo of motion humbled
under cliffs of cloud
and over the shark's blue home
Across the undulations of this slate
long pain and sweating courage chalked
such names as glimmer yet                                    10
Drake's crewmen scribbled here their paradise
and dying Bering[2] lost in fog
turned north to mark us off from Asia still
Here cool Cook traced in sudden blood his final bay
and scurvied traders trailed the wakes of yesterday
until the otter rocks were bare
and all the tribal feathers plucked
Here Spaniards and Vancouver's boatmen scrawled
the problem that is ours and yours
that there is no clear Strait of Anian                        20
to lead us easy back to Europe
that men are isled in ocean or in ice
and only joined by long endeavour to be joined
Come then on the waves of desire that well forever
and think no more than you must

---

1   In early maps and explorers' accounts, the Strait of Anian was the name given to the body of water that, by connecting Frobisher's Strait with the Pacific, was supposed to provide the much-sought-for Northwest Passage. The explorers mentioned in this poem were all engaged in dangerous, often deadly, explorations to prove or disprove the existence of this 'Pacific door'. Birney's *The Strait of Anian: Selected Poems* (1948), which contains 'Pacific Door', begins with an epigraph concerning Sir Francis Drake (1540–90): '. . . *Sir Francis himselfe (as I haue heard) was of very good will to have sailed still more Northward hoping to find passage through the narrow sea Anian . . . and so from thence to haue taken his course Northeast, and so to retourne . . . into England, but his Mariners finding the coast of Noua Albion to be very cold, had no good will to sayle any further Northward . . .*' Thos. Blundeville, *Of Sir Francis Drake His First Voyage into the Indies,* 1594.
2   Vitas Jonassen Bering (1680–1741), Danish-born explorer for Russia, discovered Bering Strait and Alaska; he lost his life on this voyage when his ship was wrecked. James Cook (1728–79), master in the British Navy, in 1778 explored the northwest Pacific coast as far as Bering Strait and was killed the next year by native inhabitants of a Hawaiian beach. Spanish explorer Juan Perez sailed with his men in 1774 to take possession of Russian trading posts in the North Pacific; they were the first Europeans to sight the coast of British Columbia. Captain George Vancouver (1757–98) commanded a British expedition to the west coast to take over the Nootka Sound territory from Spanish officers, as provided for in the Nootka Convention.

of the simple unhuman truth of this emptiness
that down deep below the lowest pulsing of primal cell
tar-dark and still
lie the bleak and forever capacious tombs of the sea

*Dollarton 1947*

1948

# Bushed

He invented a rainbow but lightning struck it
shattered it into the lake-lap of a mountain
so big his mind slowed when he looked at it

Yet he built a shack on the shore
learned to roast porcupine belly and
wore the quills on his hatband

At first he was out with the dawn
whether it yellowed bright as wood-columbine
or was only a fuzzed moth in a flannel of storm
But he found the mountain was clearly alive                    10
sent messages whizzing down every hot morning
boomed proclamations at noon and spread out
a white guard of goat
before falling asleep on its feet at sundown

When he tried his eyes on the lake       ospreys
would fall like valkyries
choosing the cut-throat[1]
He took then to waiting
till the night smoke rose from the boil of the sunset

But the moon carved unknown totems                    20
out of the lakeshore
owls in the beardusky woods derided him
moosehorned cedars circled his swamps and tossed
their antlers up to the stars

---

1 Cut-throat: (i) BC trout that osprey prey upon; (ii) the slain upon the field of battle who are gathered up by the Valkyries, the spirit-guides to the afterlife (Valkyries take the form of both women and birds of prey).

then he knew      though the mountain slept      the winds
were shaping its peak to an arrowhead
poised

And now he could only
bar himself in and wait
for the great flint to come singing into his heart      30

*Wreck Beach 1951*

1952


# Can. Lit.

(or *them able leave her ever*[1])

since we'd always sky about
when we had eagles they flew out
leaving no shadow bigger than wren's
to trouble even our broodiest hens

too busy bridging loneliness
to be alone
we hacked in railway ties
what Emily[2] etched in bone

we French&English never lost
our civil war      10
endure it still
a bloody civil bore

the wounded sirened off
no Whitman[3] wanted
it's only by our lack of ghosts
we're haunted

*Spanish Banks, Vancouver 1947/1966*

1962, rev. 1966

1  Word play on 'The Maple Leaf Forever'.
2  Emily Dickinson.
3  Walt Whitman (1819–92), American poet. His poem 'The Wound Dresser' describes his experience in the
   American Civil War of 'Bearing the bandages, water and sponge, / Straight and swift to my wounded I go, /
   Where they lie on the ground after the battle brought in'.

# El Greco: *Espolio*[1]

The carpenter is intent on the pressure of his hand

on the awl      and the trick of pinpointing his strength
through the awl to the wood      which is tough
He has no effort to spare for despoilings
or to worry if he'll be cut in on the dice
His skill is vital to the scene      and the safety of the state
Anyone can perform the indignities      It's his hard arms
and craft that hold the eyes of the convict's women
There is the problem of getting the holes exact
(in the middle of this elbowing crowd)                                        10
and deep enough to hold the spikes
after they've sunk through those bared feet
and inadequate wrists he knows are waiting behind him

He doesn't sense perhaps that one of the hands
is held in a curious gesture over him—
giving      or asking      forgiveness?—
but he'd scarcely take time to be puzzled by poses
Criminals come in all sorts
as anyone knows who makes crosses
are as mad or sane as those who decide on their killings      20
Our one at least has been quiet so far
though they say he talked himself into this trouble
a carpenter's son who got notions of preaching

Well here's a carpenter's son who'll have carpenter sons
God willing      and build what's wanted
temples or tables      mangers or crosses
and shape them decently
working alone in that firm and profound abstraction
which blots out the bawling of rag-snatchers
To construct with hands      knee-weight      braced thigh      30
keeps the back turned from death

But it's too late now for the other carpenter's boy
to return to this peace before the nails are hammered

*Point Grey 1960*

1962, rev. 1966

1 'Espolio [is] an imagining of the scene when Christ waited on the Hill of Calvary before his execution. Meantime he endured the Espolio or "spoliation" (latin *expolio*, that is "despoiling"), a tearing away of his clothes by greedy spectators who would then gamble for the strips. In [El Greco's] painting, there is a prominent figure in the right foreground, in workmen's clothes, whom I take to be the carpenter; he is busy putting holes in the cross' *(CJOM)*.

# Newfoundland

*(for E.J. Pratt)*

ne*w*foun*d*land
new***found***land
***new***found***land***
new*foun*dland
new*fo*und*l*and
new*fo*und*l*and
newfoundl*and*
ne*w*foundl*and*
ne*w*fo*u*ndl*and*
new***found***land
newfound*lan*d
newfoundl*and*
***newfoun***dland
new***foundl******and***
ne*wfo*undl*an*d
n*e*w*fo*und*l*and
newfoundla*nd*

*St. John's, Newfoundland*

1971

# Sinclair Ross
## 1908–1996

The youngest of three children, James Sinclair Ross was born on his parents' homestead near Prince Albert, Saskatchewan. While Ross was a small child, his father suffered a severe injury when he was thrown from a horse. The permanent personality change that followed resulted in a breakup of the family, and from the age of seven, Ross lived alone with his mother. They moved from place to place, with her working as a housekeeper on farms in the area, until the need for a stable income led Ross to leave school after grade eleven. At the age of sixteen, he took a job with the Union Bank of Canada (later part of the Royal Bank) and, except for four years' service in the Royal Canadian Ordinance Corps during the Second World War, spent his life working in banks, first in three small Saskatchewan towns (between 1924 and 1933), then in Winnipeg (1933–42), and finally in Montreal (1946–68). He lived with his mother until his wartime service, and supported her until her death in 1957. After retiring in 1968, he lived for three years in Greece and then for a decade in Spain before returning to Canada in

1981. He spent his last years in Vancouver, suffering from Parkinson's disease.

Ross's experience in banking would have provided him ample opportunity to learn about the aspirations and disappointments of those around him. As a witness to the difficulties of farm life in the Prairies, and especially to the economic failures caused by the Depression and the disastrous weather of the 1930s, he created stories (published between 1934 and 1952, chiefly in *Queen's Quarterly*) and a first novel, *As for Me and My House* (1941), that captured the sense of oppression and desolation felt by a whole generation. Written in a style that does not call attention to itself, this fiction is both more crafted and more colloquial than that of the Prairie realists, like Grove, who preceded him. In the introduction to Ross's *The Lamp at Noon and Other Stories* (1968), Margaret Laurence observed, 'Ross's style is always beautifully matched to his material—spare, lean, honest, no gimmicks, and yet in its very simplicity setting up continuing echoes in the mind.'

The struggle and alienation depicted in this fiction is not limited to agrarian life: in *As for Me and My House*, the narrator, Mrs Bentley, describes the gulf that separates her from her husband, a minister in the small town of Horizon, and from the town's other residents. This novel, like Ross's short stories, carries an intense emotional impact. It did not, however, find a readership when it was originally published (it appeared only in the United States) in the early years of the Second World War. It was rediscovered in 1957 when it was (with works by Grove, Leacock, and Callaghan) one of the first four books selected by Malcolm Ross for reprint in his New Canadian Library series. Following this republication, the novel came to be recognized as a classic of Canadian literature and a touchstone of Western fiction.

As with other classics, the way *As for Me and My House* has been understood changed over time. Originally seen primarily as a fictional journal that revealed the hidden depths in the lives of a quiet couple or as a narrative that recorded hardship and celebrated endurance, it later came to be read as a story told by an unreliable narrator who reveals more than she knows. It has also been viewed as a window into Ross's own complex psyche.

Laurence is one of many writers who said that Ross gave impetus to her own writing. The poet Lorna Crozier has described *As for Me and My House* as her most important influence, adding, 'It was the first book I read that was set in the landscape where I grew up. It made me realize that someone from my area could actually be a writer and, in some ways, it gave me the courage to try.' In 1996, Crozier paid tribute to the novel by creating *A Saving Grace: The Collected Poems of Mrs. Bentley*, a series of poems that she imagines Ross's protagonist having written.

Ross did not publish a second novel until *The Well* (1958), the story of a troubled city boy who finds redemption by returning to rural Saskatchewan. His third novel, *Whir of Gold* (1970), brings a character that first appeared in one of his early stories to Montreal and shows the difficulties he encounters in an urban world. In his last novel, *Sawbones Memorial* (1974), Ross returned to the milieu of a small Western town and to the period of his own prairie experiences—but now with 'a little humour in the face of the inscrutable'. In its interweaving of dialogue with monologues and its complex use of multiple points of view, *Sawbones Memorial* is Ross's most experimental novel. In 1982, the short fiction that remained uncollected was published as *The Race and Other Stories*.

None of Ross's later fiction ever quite matched the achievement of his early writing, with its powerful delineations of individuals working out private destinies within a profoundly shaping landscape. In these moving accounts, such as 'The Runaway', each individual clings to a faint but abiding hope; Laurence described it as 'desperate persistence':

*The real wonder is that so many of these men and women continue somehow—stumbling, perhaps, but still going on. Hope never quite vanishes. In counterpoint to desolation runs the theme of renewal. Tomorrow it may rain. The next spring will ultimately come.*

In *As for Me and My Body: A Memoir of Sinclair Ross* (1997), the Canadian fiction writer Keath Fraser tells of visiting Ross in the latter's last years, many of which were spent in a nursing home, and of how, near the end of his life, Ross revealed to Fraser that he was gay; however, David Stouck, in his 2005 scholarly biography, has argued that Ross's sexual identity was more ambiguous. In any case, Ross's need to conceal his sexual longings in an era of intense homophobia may explain why he became one of the most solitary figures in Canadian writing and why he wrote so often about thwarted dreams and desires.

# The Runaway

You would have thought that old Luke Taylor was a regular and welcome visitor, the friendly, unconcerned way he rode over that afternoon, leading two of his best Black Diamond mares.

'Four-year-olds,' he said with a neighbourly smile. 'None better in my stable. But I'm running short of stall room—six more foals last spring—so I thought if you were interested we might work out a trade in steers.'

My father was interested. We were putting a load of early alfalfa in the loft, and he went on pitching a minute, aloof, indifferent, but between forkfuls he glanced down stealthily at the Diamonds, and at each glance I could see his suspicion and resistance ebb.

For more than twenty years old Luke had owned a stableful of Diamonds. They were his special pride, his passion. He bred them like a man dedicated to an ideal, culling and matching tirelessly. A horse was a credit to the Black Diamond Farm, a justification of the name, or it disappeared. There were broad-rumped, shaggy-footed work horses, slim-legged runners, serviceable in-betweens like the team he had with him now, suitable for saddle or wagon—at a pinch, even for a few days on the plough—but all, whatever their breed, possessed a flawless beauty, a radiance of pride and spirit, that quickened the pulse and brought a spark of wonder to the dullest eye. When they passed you turned from what you were doing and stood motionless, transfixed. When you met them on the road you instinctively gave them the right of way. And it didn't wear off. The hundredth time was no different from the first.

'None better in my stable,' old Luke repeated, and for once it was easy to believe him. Black coats shining in the sun like polished metal; long, rippling manes; imperious heads—the mares were superb, and they knew it. First, in a fine display of temperament, rearing rebelliously, they pretended astonishment and indignation: a barn with peeling paint and a sway-backed roof—it wasn't their due, they wouldn't submit to it! A moment later, all coy conciliation, they minced forward daintily for a nibble of our alfalfa.

I knew that since it was old Luke making the offer there must be a trick in it, that the bland voice and shifty smile must conceal some sly design, but far from trying to warn my father I held my breath, and hoped he would be weak and take them.

He was weak. A frown of annoyance at being interrupted in his work, a few critical preliminaries, looking at their teeth, feeling their knees, then a dubious, 'I've seen worse, but right now I've no real need of them. What would you be wanting in the way of trade?'

Old Luke was reasonable. He began with seven steers, and after a brief argument settled for four. 'Since we're old neighbours', he agreed, 'and I'm running short of stall room.'

I saddled my pony Gopher and helped him home with the steers. He was talkative and friendly on the way, and when the pasture gate was safely closed he invited me into the house for a glass of lemonade. I made my excuses, of course—a barrel of lemonade, and he would still have been the man who foreclosed on a quarter-section of our land in a dry year, who up and down the countryside was as notorious for his shady deals as he was famous for his Diamonds; but cantering home I found myself relenting a little, deciding that maybe he had some good points after all.

I had wavered, it was true, before. Riding past the Taylor place it had always been a point of honour with me to keep my eyes fixed straight ahead, disdainfully, yet somehow the details of the barnyard and the aspect of the buildings had become as familiar to me as our own. My scorn had never been quite innocent of envy. The handsome greystone house might be the abode of guile, but I knew from one of the boys at school, whose parents sometimes visited the Taylors, that it contained a bathroom with hot and cold running water, just like the ones in town, and a mechanical piano that you played with pedals instead of your fingers. The big red hip-roofed barn might have been built with what my mother called 'his ill-gotten gains', but in its stalls there were never fewer than twenty-four Black Diamonds. So I had my lapses. Sometimes I wished for a miracle harvest which would enable us to buy old Taylor out. Sometimes I went so far as to speculate on reconciliation and partnership.

Today, though, I wasn't just coveting the bathroom and piano. I was taking a critical look at ourselves, wondering whether our attitude towards Luke wasn't uncharitably severe, whether some of the stories told about him mightn't have been exaggerated. This time, in any case, he had been more than fair. Ten steers instead of four, and the trade would still have been in our favour.

My father had been similarly impressed. 'Luke must be getting close to seventy,' he met my mother's anger at the supper-table, 'and for all you know he's starting to repent. If he wants to turn honest and God-fearing at last it's for us to help him, not to keep raking up his past.'

'Old Luke turn God-fearing!' my mother cried bitterly. 'That's something I'll believe when I see him trying to mend a little of the harm he's done. And you of all people to be taken in again! For a team of fancy horses!'

'But you can trust him where the Diamonds are concerned. They're his whole life. You'll find nothing in his stable but the best.'

'That's what I mean—those there's something wrong with he trades off for good fat steers.'

'Come out and look at them,' my father persisted. 'See for yourself.'

'I don't need to see. I know. If Luke got rid of them he had his reasons. They're spavined,[1] or roarers, or old.'

'Four-year-olds, and I checked them—teeth, feet—'

---

1  Suffering from a disorder of the hock, often leading to lameness; 'roarers': horses that makes a loud noise in breathing as a symptom of disease of the larynx.

'But there are things you can't check. All the years we've known him has he once done what was right or decent? Do you know a man for twenty miles who'd trust him? Didn't he get your own land away from you for half what it was worth?' And she went on, shrill and exasperated, to pour out instance upon instance of his dishonesty and greed, everything from foreclosures on mortgages and bribes at tax and auction sales to the poker games in which, every fall for years, he had been fleecing his harvest-hands right after paying them.

Now, though, it all fell a little flat. I sat bored and restless, wondering when she would be done, and with a mild, appeasing gesture my father said, 'A lot of it's talk. For once let's give him the benefit of the doubt. We owe it to him till we're sure. It's only Christian charity.'

For a moment my mother struggled to control her anger. Then, her voice withering, she said, 'He's a sneak thief, one of the meanest, but with such fools for neighbours, just waiting to be taken in, I don't know that I can blame him.'

'We'll see,' my father answered. 'I'm going to town with them tomorrow, to see what they can do. Why don't you come along?'

My mother sat up straight and scornful. 'I'd walk first barefoot, and be less ashamed.'

The next day, however, she changed her mind. She even primped and curled a little, and found a brighter ribbon for her hat. My father, too, made his preparations. He washed the democrat,[2] greased the axles, carefully cleaned and polished his two best sets of harness, and finally, after dinner, changed into his Sunday suit and a clean white shirt. His hands shook as he dressed. He called me in twice to crawl under the bed for a cuff button, and my mother had to help him with his tie.

At the last minute it was decided that I should stay home and hoe potatoes. For a while I sulked indignantly, but watching their departure I understood why they didn't want me with them. My father, driving up to the door with a reckless flourish of the whip, was so jaunty and important, and above the pebbly whirl of wheels as the Diamonds plunged away there was such a girlish peal of laughter from my mother! They were young again. My father had a team of Diamonds, and my mother had something that his envious passion for them had taken from her twenty years ago. Walking over to the potato patch I realized that they couldn't possibly have taken me with them. Today's events, properly understood, were all before my time.

It was shortly after one o'clock when they set out. The round trip to town, travelling light, was about five hours with an ordinary team, and I expected, therefore, that with the Diamonds they would easily be back in good time for supper. But I had bedded down the stable, taken my own supper cold from the pantry and begun to fear there must have been a runaway or accident, when at last they arrived.

It was a return as dejected and shamefaced as the departure had been dashing and high-spirited. No whirl of wheels, no peal of laughter, no snorts or capers from the Diamonds. For a minute or two, peering through the dusk, I thought that my father must have made another trade. Then I ran out to meet them, and my shout of welcome sagged to silence and bewilderment. It was a strange team of nondescript bays hitched to the democrat. The Diamonds were jogging along ignominiously behind.

2 Light wagon seating two or more people, usually drawn by two horses.

'Did you think we were never coming?' my mother greeted me, the false brightness of her voice worse than the defeat of my father's rounded shoulders. 'Run along
and help your father with the horses. I'll have a good supper ready in no time.'

My father's face, drawn and grey in the late twilight, restrained my curiosity as we
unhitched. It wasn't till we had finished at the stable and were on our way to the house
that he explained. 'They're balky—you know what that means. Not worth their keep.
Trust old Luke—I might have known he'd put it over me.'

It was a bitter word. I swallowed hard and asked hopefully, 'Both of them?'

'Both of them. Right in Main Street, wouldn't take a step. Just as we were ready
to start for home. Two hours—the whole town watching. I even took the whip to
them, but with balky horses nothing helps. The longer they stand the worse they get.
I had to unhitch at last, and hire a team from the livery stable.'

Nothing more was said, by either him or my mother, but not much imagination
was needed to reconstruct the scene. His pride as he spanked[3] up Main Street, the same
pride I had witnessed earlier that day, the same youth and showmanship; and then the
sudden collapse of it all, the unbearable moment of humiliation when the Diamonds,
instead of springing away with flying manes and foaming mouths, striking sparks of
envy and wonder from the heart of every beholder, simply stood there, chewed their
bits and trembled.

For my mother, too, it had been a memorably cruel experience. Doubly cruel, for
in addition to her embarrassment—and perched up on the democrat seat with the
crowd around her, a town-shy woman, sensitive to her rough hands and plain clothes,
she must have suffered acutely—in addition to that there was the burden of concealing it from my father, suppressing criticism and anger, pretending not to have noticed
that he had made a fool of himself. For of the two she was in many ways the stronger,
the more responsible, and she must have known instantly, even as they sat there in the
democrat, that the Diamonds were a crisis in his life, and that to bring him safely
through there was urgent need of all her skill and sympathy.

Even so, he came through badly. For it wasn't just four good steers against two
balky Diamonds. It wasn't just a matter of someone getting the better of him. It was
that after all these years old Taylor should still be practising fraud and trickery, still getting away with it, still prospering.

According to his lights my father was a good man, and his bewilderment was in
proportion to his integrity. For years he had been weakened and confused by a conflict, on the one hand resentment at what Luke had done and got away with, on the
other sincere convictions imposing patience and restraint; but through it all he had
been sustained by the belief that scores were being kept, and that he would live to see
a Day of Reckoning. Now, though, he wasn't sure. You could see in his glance and
frown that he was beginning to wonder which he really was: the upright, God-fearing
man that he had always believed himself to be, or a simple, credulous dupe. There was
the encounter with the Taylors at church, for instance, just a Sunday or two after his
trip to town with the Diamonds. It wasn't an accidental or inevitable encounter. After

3 Moved briskly.

the service they deliberately came over and spoke to us. There were a few polite remarks; then old Luke, screwing up his little eyes and leering, enquired about the Diamonds. He understood we had been having trouble with them, and hoped that they were doing better now. 'They're touchy and high-strung, you know,' he said blandly. 'You can't treat them just like ordinary horses.'

My father turned without a word and walked over to the democrat. 'He's an old man,' he said quietly as we drove off. 'It's for the Lord to judge, not me.' But his expression belied the charity of his words. His mouth was hard with the suspicion that the Lord saw nothing in his behaviour to condemn.

We drove a while in silence. Then I suggested, 'He traded them off on you—why don't you try it now on someone else?'

'Two wrongs never make a right,' my mother reproved me quickly. 'Besides, they're good mares, and we'll get good colts out of them. They may even turn out all right themselves, if your father separates them, and gives them a spell of good hard work. Touchy and high-strung is right. What they need is to be brought down a peg or two.'

How could she? My father glanced at her sidewise without answering, and I saw the reproach in his eyes. Had she no feelings, then, at all? Did she not know that it was only as a team, flashing along in unison, striking sparks, taking corners on two wheels, that they were Diamonds? That separated, their identities lost among old Bill and Ned and Bessie, they would be clods, nonentities? And watching the lines around his mouth grow firm I knew that he would never consent to such a degradation. They would always be a team of Diamonds. Their foam-flecked, sun-sparked loveliness might disappoint his vanity, might elude his efforts to exploit it, but it would live on, in stall and pasture, finally in memory, resplendent and inviolate.

His vanity, though, died hard. 'Balky horses', he remarked casually a few days later, 'are just scared horses. Nerves—a fright, maybe, when they were colts. Treat them right and they should get over it. Keep cool, I mean, and help them through their bad spells.'

Of course he was wrong. He should have known what every horseman knows, that a balky horse is never cured. If you're unscrupulous, you'll trade it off or sell it. If you're honest, you'll shoot it. Promptly, humanely, before it exasperates you to moments of rage and viciousness from which your self-respect will never quite recover. For weeks and months on end it will be a model horse, intelligent, co-operative, and then one fine day, when you're least expecting trouble, it will be a balky one again. You'll waste time and patience on it. You'll try persuasion first, then shouts and curses. You'll go back to persuasion, then degrade yourself to blows. And at last, weary and ashamed, you'll let the traces down and lead it to its stall.

But to renounce the Diamonds, now that he actually owned them, wasn't easy. He was a simple, devout man, but not by any means an other-worldly one, and all these years, struggling along in the shadow of Luke's prosperity, he had suffered, discipline himself as he would, the pangs of envy and frustration. Three hundred acres against two thousand, weather-beaten old buildings against the big stone house and hip-roofed barn, plodding work-horses against the handsome, show-off Diamonds—comparisons and a sense of failure had been inevitable.

From the beginning it was the Diamonds that had hurt him most. If Luke had indulged himself in anything else, tractors or pedigreed bulls, it would have been comparatively easy. But a horseman more passionate and discerning than my father never lived. In ordinary circumstances, being genuine, he would probably have found satisfaction in ordinary horses, like the ones he owned—humble, worthy creatures, their only fault a lack of grace and fire—but there was a splendour about the Diamonds, a poise, a dramatic loftiness, that left in its wake a blight of shabbiness and discontent. Arching their necks like emperor horses, flinging their heads up, pealing trumpet neighs—how could my father *help* wanting them? How could he turn to his own dull, patient brutes and feel anything but shame?

Yet he had never tried to acquire Black Diamonds or their equals for himself. At least one team would have been possible. He was a poor farmer, but he managed other things. In part, no doubt, it was because of his faith, his childlike sincerity. He prayed for deliverance from the vanities of the world because he wanted deliverance, and while unable to control his desire for the Diamonds, he could at least resist the temptation to possess them. But if it was in part because he struggled against the vanities of the world, it was also in part because he yielded to the vanity within himself. For one team would have been to reveal his desire, his ambition. One team would have been to set himself up for public comparison, two Black Diamonds against twenty-four.

But all that was forgotten now, lost in the excitement of actual possession. 'Nothing but nerves,' he kept saying, 'scared when they were little. I'd be balky too, if old Luke had ever had the handling of me.'

Give him his due, he worked intelligently. He took them out, for instance, when he wasn't pressed for time. He kept to quiet side-roads, where he wasn't likely to be watched or flustered. Usually he had me go along on Gopher, because it was their nature to resent another horse in front of them, and if I rode ahead they invariably responded with a competitive burst of speed. In the main things went well. So well that as the summer wore on he gradually became a little careless, and absently, as it were, began to leave the unfrequented side-roads for the highway. At that, the highway was safe enough so long as they kept going. They never stopped of their own accord. There was no danger except when it came time to start them.

Mindful of this, my father always left the front gate open. His route was always a non-stop square, cross-road to cross-road, with right angle turns that could be taken at a trot. He never went so far that it was necessary to rest the Diamonds. When he met a neighbour, he resisted the temptation to discuss crops and weather, and sailed past grandly with a nod or wave.

There was one hazard, however, that he overlooked. A gust of wind took his hat one day, and impulsively, before he could think of the possible consequences, or notice old Taylor approaching from the opposite direction on horseback, he reined in the Diamonds to a standstill.

And after weeks without a single lapse, that had to be the moment for them to balk again. Was it the arrival of Taylor, I have often wondered, something about his smell or voice, that revived colthood memories? Or was it my father's anger that flared at the sight of him, and ran out through his fingers and along the reins like an electric current, communicating to them his own tensions, his conflicting impulses of hatred and forbearance? No matter—they balked, and as if to enjoy my father's mortification, old Luke too reined in and sat watching. 'Quite a man with horses,' he laughed across at me. 'One of the finest teams for miles and just look at the state he's got them in. Better see what you can do, son, before he ruins them completely.' And then, squinting over his shoulder as he rode off, he added. 'I'll tell you how to get a balky horse going. It's easy—just build a little fire under him.'

'I wouldn't put it past him at that,' my father muttered, as he climbed down and started to unhitch. 'Being what he is, the idea of fire comes natural.'

But for the time being that was all. Harvest was on us, and for the next two months the Diamonds pawed their stall. It wasn't till November, after threshing was finished and the grain hauled, that my father was free to hitch them up again. And by that time, eager as colts after their long idleness, they were in no mood for balking. Instead, they seemed ashamed of their past, and to want nothing more than to live it down, to establish themselves as dependable members of our little farmyard community. 'All they needed was the right care,' my father said complacently one day. 'They're not mean or stubborn horses by nature. It's as I've always said—something must have happened when they were colts.'

And for a week or two he was young again. Young, light-hearted, confident. Confident in the Diamonds, confident in the rightness of the world. Old Luke had traded off balky horses on him, but now, in the service of an upright man, they were already willing, loyal ones. It showed you. Plant potatoes eyes down, and up they come the right way. They were such fine, mettled horses, such a credit to creation. Watching and working with them it was impossible to doubt that at the heart of things there was wisdom, goodness and a plan. They were an affirmation, a mighty Yea. They made the world right, and old Taylor unimportant.

With it all, though, my father was a practical man, and soon he decided that the Diamonds must be put to work. There had been enough driving round the country in the democrat. It was time they got used to pulling loads and spending an entire day in harness.

Care and patience were still necessary, and as a cautious beginning he hitched them up one afternoon and went for straw. (We used straw in considerable quantities for bedding down the stable, and not having loft room for it, brought it in, a rackful at a time, from the field, every week or ten days.) It was a short haul, and a light load. The day, moreover, was cold and windy, and it was to be expected that after standing while we built the load they would be impatient for their stall. As usual I rode Gopher, and set off for home a minute or two ahead of them.

But it was one of their bad days. I looked back after a short distance, and they hadn't moved. My father was up on the load, clicking them forward vainly.

We both tried to be nonchalant. My father climbed down and lit his pipe, threw on another forkful of straw as if he hadn't noticed anything. I led Gopher close to the Diamonds so that they could sniff at one another, then mounted him and started home a second time.

But to no avail. My father picked up the reins again; they only mouthed their bits and trembled. He tried to lead them forward; they only braced themselves, cowering against each other as if in fear of a blow.

'Let's unhitch,' I said uneasily. 'It's nearly dark, and we're only wasting time.' But ignoring me, he turned his back and lit his pipe again.

I knew there was trouble brewing. I knew from the way he was standing that the contagion had spread, that his real nature, too, was paralyzed and darkened.

'Let's unhitch,' I repeated. 'They're only getting worse. First thing they'll be as bad as when you started.'

'They're that already,' he replied, hunching his shoulders and scowling at the Diamonds. 'Unhitching's getting us nowhere. It's only giving in. I think I'll take old Luke's advice, and see what a fire will do.'

I began to protest, but he assured me that it would be a small fire. 'Not enough to burn them—just so they'll feel the heat coming up around their legs. I've heard of it before. They'll take a jump ahead, and then keep going.'

It sounded sensible enough. There was something about his voice and shoulders that forbade further protest, anyway. Without looking round again he tossed a small forkful of straw under the Diamonds, then bent cautiously to light it.

I closed my eyes a moment. When I opened them he had straightened and stepped back, and there on the ground between the Diamonds' feet, like something living that he had slipped out of his coat, was a small yellow flame, flickering up nervously against the dusk.

For a second or two, feeling its way slowly round the straw, it remained no larger than a man's outspread hand. Then, with a spurt of sparks and smoke, it shot up right to the Diamonds' bellies.

They gave a frightened snort, lunged ahead a few feet, stopped short again. The fire now, burning briskly, was directly beneath the load of straw, and even as I shouted to warn my father a tongue of flame licked up the front of the rack, and the next instant, sudden as a fan being flicked open, burst into a crackling blaze.

The Diamonds shook their heads and pawed a moment, then in terror of the flames and my father's shouts, set off across the field at a thundering, break-neck gallop. I followed on Gopher, flogging him with the ends of the reins, but straining his utmost he couldn't overtake or pass them. A trail of smoke and sparks was blowing back, and as we galloped along he kept shaking his head and coughing. Through my half-closed eyes I could see the wagon lurching dangerously over the frozen ruts of the rough wagon-trail we were following, and it flashed across my mind that if the rack upset we would ride right into it. But still I kept on lashing Gopher, pounding him with my heels. The gate was open, and there were oatstacks beside the stable. If I didn't get ahead and turn them, they would set the buildings on fire.

They turned, though, of their own accord. About a quarter of a mile from where we started the road forked, one branch turning into the barnyard, the other circling out to the highway. Riding close behind, my head lowered against the smoke and sparks, I didn't realize, till the wagon took the little ditch onto the highway at a sickening lurch, that the Diamonds were going home. Not to their new home, where they belonged now, but to old Luke Taylor's place.

I lashed and pommelled Gopher even harder, but still we couldn't gain. The highway stretched out straight and smooth, and the Diamonds were going home. Terror in their hearts, hitched to a load of fire. Through the clatter of wheels their hoof-beats sounded sharp and rhythmic like an urgent drum. Telephone poles leaped up startled and pale as we tore along, and an instant later flicked out again into the dark. Once I caught a glimpse of a horse and buggy down in the ditch, the horse rearing and white-eyed, the man leaning back on the reins with all his strength. Once it was a frantic cow, struggling to escape through the barbed-wire fence that ran alongside the road. Gopher, meanwhile, was gaining, and presently the hot smoke in our faces was a cold blast of wind. Then I could see the Diamonds, the flying manes, the sheen of the flames on their glossy hides. Then we were riding neck and neck with them.

It was a good ride. The sparks flew and the hooves thundered, and all the way I knew that for months to come the telling of it would be listened to. A good ride, but a fatal finish. The Taylor gate was open, and still galloping hard the Diamonds made a sharp swerve off the road and through it. There was a faint, splintering sound as the hind hub caught one of the posts; the next instant, only twenty or thirty feet in front of the big hip-roofed barn, wagon and rack turned over.

It was a well-built, solid load of straw, scarcely half burned away, and what was left spilled out across the yard in loose, tumbling masses that blazed up fiercely as if drenched with gasoline. I was sick with fright by this time, scarcely able to control Gopher, but even as I turned him through the gate, jerking and sawing at his bit, yelling at the top of my voice for old Taylor, I realized the danger. The loft door, where they had been putting in feed, was standing wide open. Sparks and bits of burning straw were already shooting up towards it in a steady stream.

I knew the door had to be closed, that there wasn't a second to lose, but as I jumped down from Gopher Mrs Taylor ran out of the house and began shouting at me to get back on my horse and go for Luke. He and his man had been away all after-noon to town. By this time, though, they should be nearly home again, and while I went to meet them she would telephone the neighbours.

There wasn't time to go for Luke, and I had sense enough to turn my back on her, but the Diamonds now, still hitched to the overturned wagon, were kicking and snort-ing wildly about the barnyard, and for two or three minutes, until the whiffle-tree[4] snapped and they plunged off free into the darkness, I could only stand petrified and watch them. Gopher too was excited. Getting him quietened and tied meant another delay. Then I had to make my way into the barn, completely strange to me, and grope along through the darkness in search of a stairway leading to the loft.

The flames were ahead of me. Already they were licking across the littered, clear space round the door, and up the hay that was stacked and mounded to within a few

4 Crossbar pivoted in the middle to which the harness traces of a horse are attached and which is, in turn, attached to a wagon.

feet of the roof. I watched helplessly for a minute, then sprang down the stairs again. Mrs Taylor had come as far as the door, and was still shouting at me to go for Luke. I knew that the barn was lost, but responding to the urgency in her voice, I ran across the yard and untied Gopher. I had mounted, and was two or three hundred yards down the road to meet Luke, before I came abruptly to my senses and realized that there were horses in the barn.

By the time I had Gopher tied again the loft door was a bright rectangle of flame, and when I reached the barn the air was already dense with smoke. Shrill neighs greeted me, but for a moment I could see nothing. Then there was a sudden blaze at the far end of the feed-ally, and an instant later the out-thrust nose and flattened ears of one of the Diamonds were silhouetted against the glow.

I ran forward and squeezed in past its heels, then untied the halter-shank, but when I tried to lead it out it trembled and crushed its body tight against the side of the stall. I climbed into the manger, struck it hard across the nose; it only stamped and tossed its head. Then I tried the next stall, then the next and the next. Each time I met the same fear-crazed resistance. One of the Diamonds lashed out with its heels. Another caught me such a blow with a swing of its head that I leaned half-stunned for a minute against the manger. Another, its eyes rolling white and glassy, slashed with its teeth as I turned, and ripped my smock from shoulder to shoulder.

Meanwhile the smoke was thickening, biting at my throat and eyes like acid, and suddenly panic-stricken, racked by a violent fit of coughing, I stumbled out dizzily to safety.

The cold wind revived me. The sight of the leaping flames cleared my eyes of smoke and sting.

I stood rooted a minute, staring. The roof by this time had burned through in several places, and huge spouts of flame and smoke were shooting up high against the darkness, spark-streaked and swift, as if blown out by a giant forge. Then I was roused by the sound of galloping hooves and the rattle of wheels, and a minute or two later the neighbours began to arrive. They came in buggies and wagons and on horseback. All at once the yard was alive with them, shouting advice and warnings to one another, running about aimlessly. A few entered the barn, only to stagger out again retching and coughing. My father was among them, and in his relief at finding me unhurt he clutched the collar of my smock and shook me till fire and men and horses were all spinning. Then old Luke arrived, and agile as a boy he leapt down from his wagon and started across the yard towards the barn. Three or four of the neighbours closed in to intercept him, but swerving sharply, then doubling back, he sprang away from them and through the door.

The same moment that he disappeared the floor of the loft collapsed. It was as if when running through the door he had sprung a trap, the way the great, billowy masses of burning hay plunged down behind him. There were tons and tons of it. The air caught it as it fell, and it blazed up throbbing like a furnace. We put our hands to our faces before the heat, and fell back across the yard.

A cry came from Mrs Taylor that was sucked up quickly into the soft, roaring silence of the flames. One of the neighbours helped her into the house. The rest of us stood watching. It was terrible and long because we didn't know whether it had already happened, whether it was happening now, or whether it was still to happen. At last my father slipped away, and presently returned leading our own team of Diamonds. They stood quiet and spent, their heads nearly to the ground, while we righted the wagon and tied up the broken whiffle-tree. Afraid they might balk again, I mounted Gopher as usual and rode through the gate ahead of them, but at the first click of the reins they trotted off obediently. Obediently and dully, like a team of reliable old ploughhorses. Riding along beside them, listening to the soft creak and jingle of the harness, I had the feeling that we, too, had lost our Diamonds.

It was nearly nine o'clock when we reached home, but my mother was still waiting supper. 'It's as I've always said,' she kept repeating, filling our plates and taking them away untouched. '*Though the mills of God grind slowly, yet they grind exceeding small.*[5] His own balky Diamonds, and look what they carried home to him.' She hadn't been there to see it—that was why she could say such things. 'You sow the wind and you reap the whirlwind.[6] Better for him today if he had debts and half-a-section like the rest of us.'

But my father sat staring before him as though he hadn't heard her. There was a troubled, old look in his eyes, and I knew that for him it was not so simple as that to rule off a man's account and show it balanced. Leave Luke out of it now—say that so far as he was concerned the scores were settled—but what about the Diamonds? What kind of reckoning was it that exacted life and innocence for an old man's petty greed? Why, if it was retribution, had it struck so clumsily?

'All of them,' he said at last, 'all of them but the team he was driving and my own two no-good balky ones. Prettiest horses a man ever set eyes on. It wasn't coming to them.'

'But you'll raise colts,' my mother said quickly, pouring him a fresh cup of coffee, 'and there'll be nothing wrong with them. Five or six years—why, you'll have a stableful.'

He sipped his coffee in silence a moment and then repeated softly, 'Prettiest horses a man ever set eyes on. No matter what you say, it wasn't coming to them.' But my mother's words had caught. Even as he spoke his face was brightening, and it was plain that he too, now, was thinking of the colts.

1935, 1968

---

5 The lines are those of the seventeenth-century German epigrammatist Friedrich von Logau (1604–55). The full translation is: 'Though the mills of God grind slowly, yet they grind exceeding small; / Though with patience He stands waiting, with exactness grinds He all.'
6 A paraphrase of Hosea 8:7: 'For they have sown the wind, and they shall reap the whirlwind.'

# A.M. Klein

## 1909–1972

Abraham Moses Klein was born in Ratno, Ukraine, one of twin sons (his brother died in his first year). In 1910, his family, seeking freedom from persecution, moved to Montreal, settling in the Jewish ghetto.

Klein received an orthodox upbringing, supplementing his lessons in Montreal's English Protestant schools with instruction in Hebrew and in the Torah (the first five books of the Bible attributed to Moses) and the Talmud (commentaries on the Torah). A natural scholar from his early days, Klein steeped himself in the Talmudic tradition of textual study and learned commentary, and also became fluent in five languages (English, Yiddish, Hebrew, French, and Latin). He graduated from McGill University in 1930, then took a law degree at the University of Montreal. He was called to the bar in 1933; in 1939, he established his own firm.

Klein began his studies at McGill in 1926, the last year of publication of the *McGill Fortnightly Review*. Although his only submission to the journal was not accepted, he was deeply affected by the poetic fervour he found among the *Fortnightly* group, which included Leon Edel, Leo Kennedy, F.R. Scott, and A.J.M. Smith. When the *Canadian Mercury* (1928–9) was created to take the *Fortnightly's* place, Klein was one of the first contributors. Within twelve months, he had published thirty poems in periodicals ranging from the *Canadian Mercury* and the *Canadian Forum* through the *Menorah Journal* to the prestigious *Poetry* (Chicago). Seven years later, when *New Provinces* (1936) belatedly affirmed the existence of modern poetry in Canada, Klein was one of the six poets represented in that volume.

In the decade that followed, Klein, while continuing to practise law and write poetry, became increasingly active in the Jewish community, especially in the Zionist movement. From 1936 to 1937, he edited the *Canadian Zionist*, and in 1939, he became the editor of the

*Canadian Jewish Chronicle*, a position he held for the next fifteen years. In 1948, combining his Zionism with political activism, Klein unsuccessfully campaigned as a CCF candidate for public office.

Klein's poetry passed through two major stages. The first comprises the poems published between 1929 and 1944—most of which were collected in *Hath Not a Jew . . .* (1940) and *Poems* (1944). These draw heavily on his Jewish background and are written in a style that combines biblical rhetoric on the one hand and varied English-language influences, such as the Renaissance poets and T.S. Eliot, on the other. In 1944, Klein also published the *Hitleriad*, a satire on Nazism, written in a form and style derived from Alexander Pope. The growing anti-Semitism of the era must have been extremely painful for a man who has been described as 'easily bruised', and his poetry often reflects his struggle to understand a world that permits evil and injustice. However, even when the poems depict a grim existence, their irony and humour save them from being despairing. What Irving Layton wrote of the sequence of Psalms that opens *Poems* might be said about much of Klein's work up to this time:

*They wonderfully express the Jew's attitude towards his God, an attitude which is a rich and puzzling alloy of self-abasement and pride, of humility and defiance; it is one of accepting the heavenly scourge while establishing at the same time his human dignity by questioning its necessity or its timing.*

The second stage of Klein's poetry coincided with the emergence in the 1940s of the new and vigorous poetry in Montreal that was associated with the journals *Preview* and *First Statement*. These literary magazines received submissions from a number of younger poets with whom Klein was in contact—including P.K. Page, Patrick Anderson, Layton, and Louis

Dudek—and the influence of these poets, combined with an appointment from 1945 to 1948 as a lecturer in English at McGill University, encouraged Klein to experiment with a more broadly based poetry and a somewhat simpler style. A collection of this new poetry, *The Rocking Chair and Other Poems* (1948), won a Governor General's Award.

For the poems in *The Rocking Chair*, Klein turned mostly to the milieu of French Quebec for inspiration. He explained in a letter to the American poet Karl Shapiro: 'Two books I wrote, both stemming out of my ancestral traditions; both praised ancient virtues; when I looked around for those virtues in the here and now, I found them in Quebec. . . . here was a minority, like my own, which led a compact life; continued, unlike my own, an ancient tradition, preserved inherited values, felt that it "belonged".'

After *The Rocking Chair*, Klein devoted most of his creative energies to a study of Joyce's *Ulysses*, a book that had long preoccupied him, and to writing a novel that showed Joyce's influence, *The Second Scroll*. The first three chapters of his Joyce study, appearing in journals between 1949 and 1951, are detailed and insightful critiques of the textual complexities of Joyce's elaborate, mythic fiction. They, along with Klein's other critical pieces, are reprinted in *Literary Essays and Reviews* (1987).

Klein's novel, published in 1951, is, like *Ulysses*, a radical departure from the conventions of storytelling. The tale of a young Jew in search of his heroic and mysterious uncle, *The Second Scroll* combines traditional narrative with poetry, essay, and even drama, and casts the whole into a complicated structure based on the Torah and its Talmudic commentaries.

Around 1954, Klein suffered a nervous breakdown from which he never fully recovered.

He retired from active life and gave up his writing, leaving his work on Joyce unfinished. In 1957, he was awarded the Lorne Pierce Medal by the Royal Society of Canada. After his death in 1972, Miriam Waddington edited *The Collected Poems of A.M. Klein* (1974), a volume that brought together his four books of poetry as well as previously uncollected poems from periodicals and *The Second Scroll*.

Since Klein's day, a substantial contribution to the writing of poetry and fiction in Canada has been made by Jewish writers as diverse as Irving Layton, Leonard Cohen, Eli Mandel, Mordecai Richler, Miriam Waddington, Adele Wiseman, Matt Cohen, Joe Rosenblatt, Norman Levine, Marian Engel, Anne Michaels, and Michael Redhill. Klein, the first of this distinguished company, paved the way. Indeed, as the critic Ludwig Lewisohn suggested in his foreword to Klein's first book, *Hath Not a Jew . . .*, Klein is 'the first contributor of authentic Jewish poetry to the English language.' Lewisohn adds that by not trying to disguise his Jewishness as earlier Jewish writers in English had done, Klein also became 'the first Jew to contribute authentic poetry to the literatures of English speech'.

A uniform edition of *The Collected Works of A.M. Klein*, published by the University of Toronto Press, includes *Beyond Sambation: Selected Essays and Editorials, 1928–1955* (1982), *The Short Stories of A.M. Klein* (1983), *Literary Essays and Reviews* (1987), *The Complete Poems* (1990), *Notebooks: Selections from the A.M. Klein Papers* (1994), *Selected Poems* (1997), and a scholarly edition of *The Second Scroll* (2000). Within the pages of those volumes, the reader can discover how well Klein fulfilled the task he set himself in one of his earliest lyrics: 'I will disguise the drab in mystery, / . . . I will contrive to fill days with strange words.'

# Reb Levi Yitschok[1] Talks to God

Reb Levi Yitschok, crony of the Lord,
Familiar of heaven, broods these days.
His heart erupts in sighs. He will have a word
At last, with Him of the mysterious ways.

He will go to the synagogue of Berditchev,[2]
And there sieve out his plaints in a dolorous sieve.

*Rebono shel Olam*[3]—he begins—
Who helps you count our little sins?
Whosoever it be, saving your grace,
I would declare before his face,
He knows no ethics,
No, nor arithmetics.

For if from punishments we judge the sins,
Thy midget Hebrews, even when they snore,
Are most malefic djinns,[4]
And wicked to the core of their heart's core;
Not so didst thou consider them,
Thy favourite sons of yore.

How long wilt thou ordain it, Lord, how long
Will Satan fill his mickle-mouth[5] with mirth,                    20

---

1 Reb (or Rabbi) Levi Yitschok, also spelled Yitzchak, (1740–1809) was one of the early followers of the Baal Shem Tov, the founder of Chassidic Judaism in the eighteenth century. Chassidism was a populist movement that to some extent replaced the Messianic preoccupations of earlier Judaism, shifting away from an emphasis on some future deliverer to an ecstatic affirmation of the here and now achieved through a knowledge of an immanent God expressed in his visible creation. Among the Chassidic rabbis, Levi Yitschok was especially noted for his intimate and direct address to God (as opposed to the traditional Judaic manner of reverential and indirect address), and for the fact that he would even call God to account and demand of him an explanation for the suffering of the Jews. G.K. Fischer (in *In Search of Jerusalem*, 1975) suggests that Klein may have been partly inspired by the traditional Yiddish folksong 'Levi Yitschok's Kaddish', which begins:

> *Good morning, Lord of the Universe!*
> *I, Levi Yitschok, son of Sarah, of Berditchev,*
> *Have come to you in a law-suit*
> *On behalf of your people Israel.*
> *What have you against your people Israel?*
> *And why do you oppress*
> *Your people Israel?*

For more information about the influences of Chassidism on the poetry of Klein, see also the essays by Phyllis Gotlieb and Fischer in *The A.M. Klein Symposium* (1975).

2 Town in Ukraine of which Levi Yitschok was rabbi.
3 'Master of the universe' (Hebrew).
4 Or 'jinn': here, evil spirits.
5 Large mouth (archaic).

Beholding him free, the knave who earned the thong,[6]
And Israel made the buttocks of the earth?

*The moon grinned from the window-pane; a cat*
*Standing upon a gable, humped and spat;*
*Somewhere a loud mouse nibbled at a board,*
*A spider wove a niche in the House of the Lord.*

Reb Levi Yitschok talking to himself,
Addressed his infant arguments to God:
Why hast thou scattered him like biblic dust,
To make a union with unhallowed sod,                                    30
Building him temples underneath a mound,
Compatriot of the worm in rain-soaked ground?

The lion of Judah![7] no such parable
Is on my lips; no lion, nor lion's whelp,
But a poor bag o'bones goat[8] which seeks thy help,
A scrawny goat, its rebel horns both broken,
Its beard uncouthly plucked, its tongue so dumbly lolling
Even its melancholy ma-a- remains unspoken.

*The candles flicker,*
*And peeping through the windows, the winds snicker.*          40
*The mice digest some holy rune,*
*And gossip of the cheeses of the moon. . . .*

Where is the trumpeted Messiah? Where
The wine long-soured into vinegar?
Have cobwebs stifled his mighty shofar?[9] Have
Chilblains weakened his ass's one good hoof?[10]

So all night long Reb Levi Yitschok talked,
Preparing words on which the Lord might brood.
How long did even angels guard a feud?

---

6 Whip, lash.
7 Judah is the ancestor of the Israelite tribe of Judah; in Genesis 49:9 Jacob, Judah's father, prophesies power for
   him, saying: 'Judah is a lion's whelp.'
8 Recalling the sacrificial goat (e.g. of Leviticus 16:8); in general, that which suffers for the sins of others.
9 A horn made of ram's horn, the shofar is sounded on ceremonial occasions; traditionally, when the Messiah
   finally comes he will be 'trumpeted' by a great shofar, the sounding of which will also denote the final defeat
   of Satan.
10 Traditionally the Messiah will first manifest himself riding on an ass. That his ass is lame seems to be Reb Levi's
   own ironic jest.

When would malign Satanas[11] be unfrocked?                    50
Why were the tortured by their echoes mocked?
Who put Death in his ever-ravenous mood?
Good men groaned: Hunger; bad men belched of food;
Wherefore? And why? Reb Levi Yitschok talked . . .
Vociferous was he in his monologue.
He raged, he wept. He suddenly went mild
Begging the Lord to lead him through the fog;
Reb Levi Yitschok, an ever-querulous child,
Sitting on God's knees in the synagogue,
Unanswered even when the sunrise smiled.                        60


1940

11 Satan.


# Heirloom

My father bequeathed me no wide estates;
No keys and ledgers were my heritage;
Only some holy books with *yahrzeit*[1] dates
Writ mournfully upon a blank front page—

Books of the Baal Shem Tov,[2] and of his wonders;
Pamphlets upon the devil and his crew;
Prayers against road demons, witches, thunders;
And sundry other tomes for a good Jew.

Beautiful: though no pictures on them,[3] save
The scorpion crawling on a printed track;                       10
The Virgin floating on a scriptural wave,
Square letters twinkling in the Zodiac.

The snuff left on this page, now brown and old,
The tallow stains of midnight liturgy—
These are my coat of arms, and these unfold
My noble lineage, my proud ancestry!

1  'Literally anniversary. It is customary to inscribe the date of the passing of an ancestor on the flyleaf of some
   sacred book. Special prayers are said on that anniversary date' [Klein's note; the notes by Klein to this poem,
   and to 'Autobiographical', are from a 1945 letter to A.J.M. Smith, reprinted in *The A.M. Klein Symposium*].
2  'Literally, the Master of the Good Name—a saintly rabbi of the eighteenth century, founder of the movement
   known as Chassidism; he placed good works above scholarship. He was a simple good man, a St Francis of
   Assisi, without birds or flowers' [Klein].
3  'Hebrew prayer books are never illustrated. The only drawings that appear in the liturgy are the signs of the
   Zodiac illustrating the prayers for rain and fertility' [Klein].

And my tears, too, have stained this heirloomed ground,
When reading in these treatises some weird
Miracle, I turned a leaf and found
A white hair fallen from my father's beard.                    20

1940

# The Rocking Chair

It seconds the crickets of the province. Heard
in the clean lamplit farmhouses of Quebec,—
wooden,—it is no less a national bird;
and rivals, in its cage, the mere stuttering clock.
To its time, the evenings are rolled away;
and in its peace the pensive mother knits
contentment to be worn by her family,
grown-up, but still cradled by the chair in which she sits.

It is also the old man's pet, pair to his pipe,
the two aids of his arithmetic and plans,                      10
plans rocking and puffing into market-shape;
and it is the toddler's game and dangerous dance.
Moved to the verandah, on summer Sundays, it is,
among the hanging plants, the girls, the boy-friends,
sabbatical and clumsy, like the white haloes
dangling above the blue serge suits of the young men.

It has a personality of its own;
is a character (like that old drunk Lacoste,
exhaling amber,[1] and toppling on his pins);
it is alive; individual; and no less                           20
an identity than those about it. And
it is tradition. Centuries have been flicked
from its arcs, alternately flicked and pinned.
It rolls with the gait of St Malo.[2] It is act

and symbol, symbol of this static folk
which moves in segments, and returns to base,—
a sunken pendulum; *invoke, revoke*;
loosed yon, leashed hither, motion on no space.

1  The fumes of amber-coloured beverages such as beer or whiskey.
2  With the walk of sailors. (St Malo is a town on the coast of France.)

O, like some Anjou ballad, all refrain,[3]
which turns about its longing, and seems to move          30
to make a pleasure out of repeated pain,
its music moves, as if always back to a first love.

1948

3 Anjou is a former province of western France. What Klein seems to have in mind is the repetitive quality of
  those French-Canadian songs that had their roots in medieval France. About these, Edith Fowke quotes an early
  traveller in Canada: '[the song] seems endless. After each short line comes the refrain, and the story twines itself
  along like a slender creeping plant' (*The Penguin Book of Canadian Folk Songs*, 1973).

# Political Meeting

*for Camillien Houde*[1]

On the school platform, draping the folding seats,
they wait the chairman's praise and glass of water.
Upon the wall the agonized Y[2] initials their faith.

Here all are laic;[3] the skirted brothers have gone.
Still, their equivocal absence is felt, like a breeze
that gives curtains the sounds of surplices.

The hall is yellow with light, and jocular;
suddenly some one lets loose upon the air
the ritual bird which the crowd in snares of singing

catches and plucks, throat, wings, and little limbs.          10
Fall the feathers of sound, like *alouette's*.[4]
The chairman, now, is charming, full of asides and wit,

building his orators, and chipping off
the heckling gargoyles popping in the hall.
(Outside, in the dark, the street is body-tall,

flowered with faces intent on the scarecrow thing
that shouts to thousands the echoing
of their own wishes.) The Orator has risen!

1 (1889–1958), mayor of Montreal almost continuously from 1928 to 1954; also MLA for Quebec in the 1920s, later
  elected MP in 1949. During the Second World War, Houde was interned because of his stand against conscription: he advised French Canadians to resist serving in what he viewed as an English cause.
2 The figure of Christ on the crucifix.
3 Of the laity; in contrast to the discreetly departed priests, the 'skirted brothers' (a reference to the surplices, or
  tunics, that are worn in a priest's performance of his liturgical duties).
4 Banquets and social gatherings in Quebec traditionally opened or closed with the singing of the folk song
  '*Alouette*'. Klein's lines here play with the fact that in the refrain ('*je t'y plumerai*'), the singers promise to pluck
  the skylark's head, beak, nose, eyes, wings, feet, etc.

Worshipped and loved, their favourite visitor,
a country uncle with sunflower seeds in his pockets,                    20
full of wonderful moods, tricks, imitative talk,

he is their idol: like themselves, not handsome,
not snobbish, not of the *Grande Allée! Un homme!*[5]
Intimate, informal, he makes bear's compliments

to the ladies; is gallant; and grins;
goes for the balloon, his opposition, with pins;
jokes also on himself, speaks of himself

in the third person, slings slang, and winks with folklore;
and knows now that he has them, kith and kin.
Calmly, therefore, he begins to speak of war,                          30

praises the virtue of being *Canadien*,
of being at peace, of faith, of family,
and suddenly his other voice: *Where are your sons?*[6]

He is tearful, choking tears; but not he
would blame the clever English; in their place
he'd do the same; maybe.

Where *are* your sons?
                The whole street wears one face,
shadowed and grim; and in the darkness rises
the body-odour of race.                                                40

1948

5  That is, a man of the people, not from an aristocratic neighbourhood.
6  A rallying cry among Québécois in their opposition to conscription.

# Portrait of the Poet as Landscape

    I

Not an editorial-writer, bereaved with bartlett,[1]
mourns him, the shelved Lycidas.[2]
No actress squeezes a glycerine tear for him.
The radio broadcast lets his passing pass.
And with the police, no record. Nobody, it appears,
either under his real name or his alias,
missed him enough to report.

1  That is, looking up useful stock phrases in *Bartlett's Familiar Quotations*.
2  *Lycidas* (1637) is Milton's pastoral elegy mourning the death by drowning of the young poet Edward King.

It is possible that he is dead, and not discovered.
It is possible that he can be found some place
in a narrow closet, like the corpse in a detective story,          10
standing, his eyes staring, and ready to fall on his face.
It is also possible that he is alive
and amnesiac, or mad, or in retired disgrace,
or beyond recognition lost in love.

We are sure only that from our real society
he has disappeared; he simply does not count,
except in the pullulation[3] of vital statistics—
somebody's vote, perhaps, an anonymous taunt
of the Gallup poll, a dot in a government table—
but not felt, and certainly far from eminent—          20
in a shouting mob, somebody's sigh.

O, he who unrolled our culture from his scroll—
the prince's quote, the rostrum-rounding roar—
who under one name made articulate
heaven, and under another the seven-circled air,[4]
is, if he is at all, a number, an x,
a Mr Smith in a hotel register,—
incognito, lost, lacunal.[5]

II

The truth is he's not dead, but only ignored—
like the mirroring lenses forgotten on a brow          30
that shine with the guilt of their unnoticed world.
The truth is he lives among neighbours, who, though they will allow
him a passable fellow, think him eccentric, not solid,
a type that one can forgive, and for that matter, forgo.

Himself he has his moods, just like a poet.
Sometimes, depressed to nadir, he will think all lost,
will see himself as throwback, relict,[6] freak,
his mother's miscarriage, his great-grandfather's ghost,
and he will curse his quintuplet senses, and their tutors
in whom he put, as he should not have put, his trust.          40

3  Rapid breeding; teeming.
4  According to early pre-Copernican versions of the universe, the earth was surrounded by seven concentric
   spheres (the sun, the moon, and the five known planets).
5  That is, of a lacuna or empty space.
6  An organism from a previous age surviving in a changed environment.

Then he will remember his travels over that body—
the torso verb, the beautiful face of the noun,
and all those shaped and warm auxiliaries!
A first love it was, the recognition of his own.
Dear limbs adverbial, complexion of adjective,
dimple and dip of conjugation!

And then remember how this made a change in him
affecting for always the glow and growth of his being;
how suddenly was aware of the air, like shaken tinfoil,[7]
of the patents of nature, the shock of belated seeing,                    50
the lonelinesses peering from the eyes of crowds;
the integers of thought; the cube-roots of feeling.

Thus, zoomed to zenith, sometimes he hopes again,
and sees himself as a character, with a rehearsed role:
the Count of Monte Cristo,[8] come for his revenges;
the unsuspected heir, with papers; the risen soul;
or the chloroformed prince awaking from his flowers;
or—deflated again—the convict on parole.


             III

He is alone; yet not completely alone.
Pins on a map of a colour similar to his,                                 60
each city has one, sometimes more than one;
here, caretakers of art, in colleges;
in offices, there, with arm-bands, and green-shaded;
and there, pounding their catalogued beats in libraries,—

everywhere menial, a shadow's shadow.
And always for their egos—their outmoded art.
Thus, having lost the bevel[9] in the ear,
they know neither up nor down, mistake the part
for the whole, curl themselves in a comma,
talk technics, make a colon their eyes. They distort—                     70

---

7 An echo of the opening lines of Gerard Manley Hopkins' 'God's Grandeur': 'The world is charged with the
  grandeur of God. / It will flame out, like shining from shook foil.'
8 In the novel *The Count of Monte Cristo* (1844–5), by Alexandre Dumas, an innocent man, imprisoned on
  trumped-up charges, escapes to the Island of Monte Cristo, where he finds fabulous riches. He returns to Paris
  a powerful man and, under various guises, takes revenge on those responsible for his ill treatment.
9 A tool for ascertaining angles; that is, the poet has lost his sense of direction.

such is the pain of their frustration—truth
to something convolute and cerebral.
How they do fear the slap of the flat of the platitude!
Now Pavlov's victims, their mouths water at bell,
the platter empty.
            See they set twenty-one jewels
into their watches; the time they do not tell!

Some, patagonian[10] in their own esteem,
and longing for the multiplying word,
join party and wear pins, now have a message,           80
an ear, and the convention-hall's regard.
Upon the knees of ventriloquists, they own,
of their dandled[11] brightness, only the paint and board.

And some go mystical, and some go mad.
One stares at a mirror all day long, as if
to recognize himself; another courts
angels,—for here he does not fear rebuff;
and a third, alone, and sick with sex, and rapt,
doodles him symbols convex and concave.

O schizoid solitudes! O purities           90
curdling upon themselves! Who live for themselves,
or for each other, but for nobody else;
desire affection, private and public loves;
are friendly, and then quarrel and surmise
the secret perversions of each other's lives.

      IV

He suspects that something has happened, a law
been passed, a nightmare ordered. Set apart,
he finds himself, with special haircut and dress,
as on a reservation. Introvert.
He does not understand this; sad conjecture           100
muscles and palls thrombotic on his heart.

---

10 Gigantic. Klein is referring to old travellers' tales about a mythical race of giant Natives in South America.
11 Moved lightly up and down on the knee.

He thinks an imposter, having studied his personal biography,
his gestures, his moods, now has come forward to pose
in the shivering vacuums his absence leaves.
Wigged with his laurel, that other, and faked with his face,
he pats the heads of his children, pecks his wife,
and is at home, and slippered, in his house.

So he guesses at the impertinent silhouette
that talks to his phone-piece and slits open his mail.
Is it the local tycoon who for a hobby                                    110
plays poet, he so epical in steel?
The orator, making a pause? Or is that man
he who blows his flash of brass in the jittering hall?

Or is he cuckolded by the troubadour
rich and successful out of celluloid?
Or by the don who unrhymes atoms? Or
the chemist death built up? Pride, lost impostor'd pride,
it is another, another, whoever he is,
who rides where he should ride.

V

*Fame*, the adrenalin: to be talked about;                                120
to be a verb; to be introduced as *The*:
to smile with endorsement from slick paper; make
caprices anecdotal; to nod to the world; to see
one's name like a song upon the marquees played;
to be forgotten with embarrassment; to be—
to be.

It has its attractions, but is not the thing;
nor is it the ape mimesis[12] who speaks from the tree
ancestral; nor the merkin joy[13] . . .
Rather it is stark infelicity                                             130
which stirs him from his sleep, undressed, asleep
to walk upon roofs and window-sills and defy
the gape of gravity.

---

12 Imitation; perhaps in reference to Aristotle's mimetic concept of poetry as an imitation of an action.
13 A deceptive joy; 'merkin': a wig for the female pubic area.

## VI

Therefore he seeds illusions. Look, he is
the nth Adam taking a green inventory
in world but scarcely uttered, naming, praising,
the flowering fiats in the meadow, the
syllabled fur, stars aspirate, the pollen
whose sweet collision sounds eternally.
For to praise                                                                          140

the world—he, solitary man—is breath
to him. Until it has been praised, that part
has not been. Item by exciting item—
air to his lungs, and pressured blood to his heart.—
they are pulsated, and breathed, until they map,
not the world's, but his own body's chart!

And now in imagination he has climbed
another planet, the better to look
with single camera view upon this earth—
its total scope, and each afflated[14] tick,                                          150
its talk, its trick, its tracklessness—and this,
this, he would like to write down in a book!

To find a new function for the *déclassé* craft
archaic like the fletcher's;[15] to make a new thing;
to say the word that will become sixth sense;
perhaps by necessity and indirection bring
new forms to life, anonymously, new creeds—
O, somehow pay back the daily larcenies of the lung!

These are not mean ambitions. It is already something
merely to entertain them. Meanwhile, he                                               160
makes of his status as zero a rich garland,
a halo of his anonymity,
and lives alone, and in his secret shines
like phosphorus. At the bottom of the sea.

1948

---

14  Breathed upon, inspired.
15  Arrow maker's.

# Autobiographical[1]

Out of the ghetto streets where a Jewboy
Dreamed pavement into pleasant Bible-land,
Out of the Yiddish slums where childhood met
The friendly beard, the loutish Sabbath-goy,[2]
Or followed, proud, the Torah-escorting band,[3]
Out of the jargoning city I regret,
Rise memories, like sparrows rising from
The gutter-scattered oats,
Like sadness sweet of synagogal hum,
Like Hebrew violins                                                  10
Sobbing delight upon their Eastern notes.

Again they ring their little bells, those doors[4]
Deemed by the tender-year'd, magnificent:
Old Ashkenazi's[5] cellar, sharp with spice;
The widows' double-parloured candy-stores
And nuggets sweet bought for one sweaty cent;
The warm fresh-smelling bakery, its pies,
Its cakes, its navel'd bellies of black bread;
The lintels candy-poled
Of barber-shop, bright-bottled, green, blue, red;                    20
And fruit-stall piled, exotic,
And the big synagogue door, with letters of gold.

Again my kindergarten home is full—
Saturday night—with kin and compatriot:
My brothers playing Russian card-games; my
Mirroring sisters looking beautiful,
Humming the evening's imminent fox-trot;
My uncle Mayer, of blessed memory,
Still murmuring Maariv,[6] counting holy words;
And the two strangers, come                                           30

---

1  This poem first appeared in the *Canadian Forum* in 1943; it later became one of the 'glosses' in *The Second Scroll*.
2  'A Gentile employed by Jews to kindle their fires on the Sabbath, such labour being prohibited on that day to the children of Israel. Goy = Gentile' [Klein].
3  'The Torah is the scroll of the Law, written on parchment. When such a scroll is donated to a synagogue by a rich knave who seeks with his piety to atone for the wretchedness of his soul, the said scroll is customarily carried from the home of the donor through the streets leading to the synagogue, the whole to the accompaniment of music, to wit, a couple of violins and a flute' [Klein].
4  'The impression of my childhood days is that the only people who kept groceries were widows, who always had little bells over their doors, so that they might hear the entering customer, even from the remoteness of the back kitchen, the emporium usually being located in the front double-parlor' [Klein].
5  Jews of central European descent, as opposed to Sephardic Jews (from Spain and Portugal); also a surname.
6  Evening prayer (Hebrew).

Fiery from Volhynia's[7] murderous hordes—
The cards and humming stop.
And I too swear revenge for that pogrom.

Occasions dear: the four-legged aleph[8] named
And angel pennies dropping on my book;[9]
The rabbi patting a coming scholar-head;
My mother, blessing candles, Sabbath-flamed,
Queenly in her Warsovian perruque;[10]
My father pickabacking me to bed
To tell tall tales about the Baal Shem Tov[11]—                    40
Letting me curl his beard.
Oh memory of unsurpassing love,
Love leading a brave child
Through childhood's ogred corridors, unfear'd!

The week in the country at my brother's—(May
He own fat cattle in the fields of heaven!)
Its picking of strawberries from grassy ditch,
Its odour of dogrose and of yellowing hay—
Dusty, adventurous, sunny days, all seven!—
Still follow me, still warm me, still are rich                     50
With the cow-tinkling peace of pastureland.
The meadow'd memory
Is sodded with its clover, and is spanned
By that same pillow'd sky
A boy on his back one day watched enviously.

And paved again the street: the shouting boys,
Oblivious of mothers on the stoops,
Playing the robust robbers and police,
The corncob battle—all high-spirited noise
Competitive among the lot-drawn groups.                           60
Another day, of shaken apple trees
In the rich suburbs, and a furious dog,
And guilty boys in flight;

---

7 Province in northwestern Ukraine; the site of pogroms against the Jews.
8 'The first letter of the Hebrew alphabet, cf. Alpha. Called "running" because written with four legs . . .' [Klein].
9 'If I knew my lesson well, my father would, unseen, drop a penny on my book, and then proclaim it the reward of angels for good study' [Klein].
10 'Jewesses (married and pious) wear perruques. The custom has died out in America; but not for my mother' [Klein]. A perruque (also spelled 'peruke') is a wig. 'Warsovian': in the style of Warsaw.
11 See p. 464, note 1.

Hazelnut games,[12] and games in the synagogue—
The burrs, the Haman rattle,[13]
The Torah dance on Simchas-Torah night.[14]

Immortal days of the picture calendar
Dear to me always with the virgin joy
Of the first flowering of senses five,
Discovering birds, or textures, or a star,                    70
Or tastes sweet, sour, acid, those that cloy;
And perfumes. Never was I more alive.
All days thereafter are a dying off,
A wandering away
From home and the familiar. The years doff
Their innocence.
No other day is ever like that day.

I am no old man fatuously intent
On memoirs, but in memory I seek
The strength and vividness of nonage days,                    80
Not tranquil recollection of event.[15]
It is a fabled city that I seek;
It stands in Space's vapours and Time's haze;
Thence comes my sadness in remembered joy
Constrictive of the throat;
Thence do I hear, as heard by a Jewboy,
The Hebrew violins,
Delighting in the sobbed Oriental note.

1951

12 *Nisslach*, or 'Nuts', a game played during Passover. In one version, players tossed handfuls of hazelnuts at a small hole dug in the ground, guessing in advance whether the number to drop in would be odd or even.
13 'The Ninth of Ab (a month in the Jewish calendar) commemorates the destruction of the Temple. It is a day of mourning and fasting. It is customary on that day for youngsters to gather burrs and thistles, bring them to the synagogue, and throw them—not always with impunity—into the beards of the mourning elders—so as to give a touch or realism to their historic weeping. For the kids, this is a lot of fun' [Klein]. 'Haman rattle': 'Haman is the villain of the Book of Esther. On Purim, which is the festival commemorating its events, the Book of Esther is read in the synagogue. Every time the name of Haman is uttered by the reader of the scroll, the youngsters, armed with rattles, make a furious noise, so as to drown out those unspeakable syllables' [Klein].
14 Festival celebrating God's giving his law to Moses; it is marked by the carrying of the parchment scrolls containing the Law seven (or more) times around the synagogue in a dancing procession.
15 Arguing that his own 'nonage' (youth) remains vivid, Klein here rejects Wordsworth's famous formula about poetry being an expression of 'emotion recollected in tranquility'.

# Sheila Watson
## 1909–1998

Although her literary output was small, Sheila Watson's influence on Canadian writing was substantial. Born Sheila Martin Doherty in New Westminster, British Columbia, she grew up on the grounds of the mental hospital there (her father, a physician, was its superintendent), next door to the provincial penitentiary. Initially educated at home, she entered convent school at age seven. Her father died when she was ten, leaving the Dohertys dependent on the support of friends and family; after her mother suffered an emotional collapse, Watson assumed much of the care for her three siblings. In 1927, she enrolled at the University of British Columbia in a program of English study that was exceptional for its time in that its curriculum included contemporary writers such as Joyce, Pound, and Eliot.

Watson continued her studies after completing her BA, taking a teaching certificate and, in 1933, an MA in English. Finding employment scarce during the Depression, she accepted a position at a school in Dog Creek, an isolated community in the Cariboo region of central British Columbia. Living alone in a log cabin and learning how to shoot in order to put food on her table, she taught there for two years until the school closed, and then found work in other districts of the provincial school system. During these years, she wrote a novel about the Cariboo that began her testing of the limits of regional realism. It remained unpublished until 1992, when she finally allowed it to appear as *Deep Hollow Creek*. She had already published a short story about this period in her life. 'Rough Answer', which appeared in *The Canadian Forum* in 1938, is, like *Deep Hollow Creek*, a short realist narrative about a schoolteacher unsuited to the tiny community in which she finds herself.

In 1941, she married the poet Wilfred Watson, and, in 1945, moved with him to Toronto so he could pursue graduate studies at the University of Toronto. Watson taught English and drama at a private girls' school and also enrolled in graduate courses at the University of Toronto. Finding that the east gave her fresh perspective on the west, she began a new novel, also based on her Cariboo experiences—she worked for more than a decade on what would eventually become *The Double Hook*—and she wrote another brief short story, 'And the Four Animals', which resembles *The Double Hook* in that it is a cryptic fable written in a prose of oblique surfaces and allusive depths.

Although 'And the Four Animals' begins with what seems a poetic description of reality (a 'reality'—like that of *The Double Hook*—inhabited by Coyote, the Native trickster figure), it shifts to fantastic, even hallucinatory or visionary, events that allegorically comment about human intervention in the natural world. A significant departure from Watson's earlier fiction, it was not published until 1980.

In 1949, Watson became an instructor at UBC. In the decade that followed she began publishing short stories in the *Queen's Quarterly* and *Tamarack Review*, in which the principal characters are named after, and share some qualities with, the mythic characters in Sophocles' plays about Oedipus. She used these characters to investigate her own family dynamics by reconsidering her personal experiences as archetypal. Watson moved with her husband to Calgary in 1952 and then to Edmonton, where she continued to work on *The Double Hook*, revising it in 1955–6 while spending a year in Paris. On their return to Canada, the two writers found themselves increasingly incompatible emotionally and separated for the next five years, while Watson returned to graduate study at the University of Toronto. There, she wrote one more of her Oedipus stories (they were eventually collected, as *Four Stories*, in 1979). Marshall McLuhan became her mentor and her adviser on a dissertation dealing with the fiction and art of the British modernist Wyndham Lewis.

Having previously failed to interest a publisher in *The Double Hook*, she finally found one adventurous enough to take it on: Jack McClelland, whose publishing house, McClelland & Stewart, was aggressively expanding its support of Canadian writing. Structured around evocative images, stark tableaux, and archetypal echoes drawn from a variety of cultural resources, and told with a dramatic economy, *The Double Hook* became, when published in 1959, the first Canadian novel in which form and style takes precedence over character and event. Watson had found her way out of the impasse that she and other Canadian writers faced at the middle of the twentieth century: the need to escape the constraints of realism and regionalism that were then dominating Canadian fiction, and also the need to avoid Morley Callaghan's literary approach, which was to obscure his Canadian identity. Occupying a middle ground between the realism of 'A Rough Answer' and the complete departure from the real in 'And the Four Animals', *The Double Hook* focuses on a definite region but gives to its setting a symbolic and dreamlike quality, transforming it into a landscape of the imagination.

When *The Double Hook* appeared, Ethel Wilson hailed as an example of 'the very best writing in our country', adding that it exemplified the 'incandescence which takes place in a prepared mind where forces meet'. George Bowering later called it the 'most important book to be published since World War II,' and declared that 'innovative fiction writers and poets across the country constantly refer to [it] in their writing and conversation. I call the interesting stuff written since 1959 the "Sheila Watson canon".' Robert Kroetsch and bpNichol

have spoken about how the book opened up possibilities for their own writing; and Mordecai Richler, Michael Ondaatje, and Margaret Atwood are among the many Canadian writers touched by its influence.

In 1961, Watson rejoined her husband in the English Department at the University of Alberta while continuing to work on her dissertation (completed in 1965). Except for a return to Toronto in 1968–9, when she and Wilfred helped McLuhan (who had suffered a stroke) teach his courses, Watson taught at the University of Alberta until her retirement in 1975. During those years, she was actively involved in Edmonton's literary community and in Canadian writing more generally, encouraging and fostering the talent of many younger writers, translating the stories of the French-Canadian writer Madeleine Ferron, and helping to found and co-edit *White Pelican: A Quarterly Review of the Arts* (1971–5).

A 1975 special issue of *Open Letter*, published on the occasion of Watson's retirement, brought together all four Oedipus stories, her commentary on *The Double Hook*, and her literary essays on Wyndham Lewis, Gertrude Stein, Jonathan Swift, and Michael Ondaatje. It also contains a reproduction of the first page of the manuscript of *The Double Hook*, which shows how Watson's revisions worked to make the novel more elliptical. Near the end of her life, Watson consigned her papers, correspondence, and journals to her literary executor, Fred Flahiff. All six of her short stories were collected in 2004 as *A Father's Kingdom*. Falhiff's *Always Someone to Kill the Doves: A Life of Sheila Watson* (2005) contains selections from her journals and tells the story of this woman who, throughout her life, remained intensely private.

# And the Four Animals[1]

The foothills slept. Over their yellow limbs the blue sky crouched. Only a fugitive green suggested life which claimed kinship with both and acknowledged kinship with neither.

Around the curve of the hill, or out of the hill itself, came three black dogs. The watching eye could not record with precision anything but the fact of their presence. Against the faded contour of the earth the things were. The watcher could not have said whether they had come or whether the eye had focused them into being. In the place of the hills before and after have no more meaning than the land gives. Now there were the dogs where before were only the hills and the transparent stir of the dragonfly.

Had the dogs worn the colour of the hills, had they swung tail round leg, ears oblique and muzzles quivering to scent carrion, or mischief, or the astringency of grouse mingled with the acrid smell of low-clinging sage, the eye might have recognized a congruence between them and the land. Here Coyote, the primitive one, the god-baiter and troublemaker, the thirster after power, the vainglorious, might have walked since the dawn of creation—for Coyote had walked early on the first day.

The dogs, however, were elegant and lithe. They paced with rhythmic dignity. In the downshafts of light their coats shone ebony. The eye observed the fineness of bone, the accuracy of adjustment. As the dogs advanced they gained altitude, circling, until they stood as if freed from the land against the flat blue of the sky.

The eye closed and the dogs sank back into their proper darkness. The eye opened and the dogs stood black against the blue of the iris for the sky was in the eye yet severed from it.

In the light of the eye the dogs could be observed clearly—three Labrador retrievers, gentle, courteous, and playful with the sedate bearing of dogs well schooled to know their worth, to know their place, and to bend willingly to their master's will. One stretched out, face flattened. Its eyes, darker than the grass on which it lay, looked over the rolling hills to the distant saw-tooth pattern of volcanic stone. Behind it the other two sat, tongues dripping red over the saw-tooth pattern of volcanic lip.

The dogs were against the eye and in the eye. They were in the land but not of it. They were of Coyote's house, but became aristocrats in time which had now yielded them up to the timeless hills. They, too, were gods, but civil gods made tractable by use and useless by custom. Here in the hills they would starve or lose themselves in wandering. They were aliens in this spot or exiles returned as if they had never been. The eye closed. It opened and closed again. Each time the eye opened the dogs circled the hill to the top and trained their gaze on the distant rock. Each time they reached the height of land with more difficulty. At last all three lay pressing thin bellies and jaws against the unyielding earth.

---

1 The phrase 'and the four animals' comes from the Book of Revelation in the Jerusalem Bible. (In other translations, such as the King James Version, 'the four animals' is rendered as 'the four beasts'.) The 'four animals'—later described as a lion, a bull, a creature with a human face, and an eagle—first appear in Revelation 5:13–14: 'Then I heard all the living things in creation—everything that lives in the air, and on the ground, and under the ground, and in the sea, crying "To the One who is sitting on the throne and to the Lamb, be all praise, honour, glory and power, for ever and ever." And the four animals said, "Amen".' Traditionally, this passage has been interpreted as showing the ceaseless worship due to God from all his creation.

Now when the eye opened there were four dogs and a man and the eye belonged to the man and stared from the hill of his head along the slope of his arm on which the four dogs lay. And the fourth which he had whistled up from his own depths was glossy and fat as the others had been. But this, too, he knew in the end would climb lackluster as the rest.

So he opened the volcanic ridge of his jaws and bit the tail from each dog and stood with the four tails in his hand and the dogs fawned graciously before him begging decorously for food. And he fed the tail of the first dog to the fourth and the tail of the fourth to the first. In the same way he disposed of the tails of the second and the third. And the dogs sat with their eyes on his mouth.

Then he bit the off-hind leg from each and offered it to the other; then the near-hind leg, and the dogs grew plump and shone in the downlight of his glance. Then the jaw opened and closed on the two forelegs and on the left haunch and the right and each dog bowed and slavered and ate what was offered.

Soon four fanged jaws lay on the hill and before them the man stood rolling the amber eyes in his hands and these he tossed impartially to the waiting jaws. Then he fed the bone of the first jaw to the fourth and that of the second to the third. And taking the two jaws that lay before him he fed tooth to tooth until one tooth remained and this he hid in his own belly.

# Dorothy Livesay
## 1909–1996

Winnipeg was a focal point for Dorothy Livesay. There her parents, both newspaper reporters, met; there she was born; and there she often returned. Livesay grew up in a household in which her mother, Florence Randal Livesay, wrote her own poetry and translated Ukrainian poems and novels, while her iconoclast father, John F.B. Livesay, pursued his interest in politics and economics. In *A Winnipeg Childhood* (1973), a series of stories based on her early childhood, Livesay describes this home life, against a backdrop of the First World War and the Winnipeg General Strike of 1919.

When Livesay's father organized the Canadian Press and became its first manager, the family moved to Toronto. There, John Livesay encouraged his daughter to read great books, especially those written by women, and to attend lectures and listen to speakers—including advocates of women's and worker's rights. At the same time, Florence Livesay's acquaintance with both new and established Canadian writers brought her daughter into contact not only with the Victorian sensibilities that still dominated Canada's literature but also with the new movements that were developing.

In this politicized and literary atmosphere, Livesay herself began to write. When she was just thirteen, her first published poem appeared in the Vancouver *Province*; and in her second year at Trinity College, University of Toronto, Livesay, still in her teens, not only won the Jardine Memorial Prize for her poem 'City Wife' but also had her first book, *Green Pitcher* (1928), published. After a year of graduate work at the Sorbonne in Paris, she returned to Canada in 1932 and published her second book, *Signposts*. In these early books, Livesay established herself as a member of the Imagist movement in Canada. Like Raymond Knister and W.W.E. Ross, she sought simplicity of form and the direct impact of the image to express unromanticized observations about everyday life.

Livesay divided her writing into four categories: *agit-prop*, *documentary*, *lyric*, and *confessional*. The latter two divisions include the writing of both her very early career before the Depression and her 'second season'—work done after her middle age. *Agit-prop* is a term that arose in the Communist Party during the 1930s to describe writing, usually drama, in which political techniques of agitation (oral persuasion) and propaganda (written proselytizing) are united in simple pieces for working-class audiences. In the 1930s, Livesay wrote a number of agit-prop plays as part of her activities in communist and proletarian artist groups. At the same time, she earned a living as a social worker in Montreal and in Englewood, New Jersey. In the reminiscences, essays, letters, and poems gathered in *Right Hand, Left Hand* (1977) she provided an account of this period.

Out of her experiences in the Depression, Livesay fashioned 'Day and Night', a poem that expresses the concerns of the agit-prop plays while working primarily as a 'documentary'. In applying this term to poetry, Livesay was describing what she considered a particularly Canadian genre,

*in which historical or other 'found' material is incorporated into a writer's own thoughts, in order to create a dialectic between the objective facts and the subjective feeling of the poet. The effect is often ironic; it is always intensely personal.*

Livesay viewed most of her longer poems— those collected in *The Documentaries* (1968)—as working in this tradition, which descends from Crawford, Lampman, and D.C. Scott, and includes later poets such as Pratt and Birney.

In 1936, Livesay moved west, settling in Vancouver. Remaining politically active (especially as a member of the CCF), she and her future husband, Duncan Macnair, organized a writers' group that originally served as a conduit for stories and articles for the Toronto-based *New Frontier* (1936–7). She herself became a contributor to this periodical, which stood politically between the radically communist *Masses* (1932–4), which she had earlier helped to found, and the more moderate *Canadian Forum*. During this period, Livesay also began to teach creative writing. As a result of her suggestion that a poetry magazine be started on the West Coast to complement Pratt's *Canadian Poetry Magazine* in the East, Alan Crawley founded *Contemporary Verse* (1941–53). (In 1975, Livesay established the Winnipeg-based journal *CV/II*, its title a tribute to Crawley's magazine, which had been generally known as *CV*).

The poetry Livesay wrote in the 1940s and early 1950s often lacked the assured voice that her earlier political militancy had given her. Nevertheless, it was during this period that she received two Governor General's Awards—one for *Day and Night* (1944), a collection of poems actually written in the mid-1930s, and one for *Poems for People* (1947).

In 1958, Livesay returned to school to prepare herself for a teaching career. While at the University of London, she learned of her husband's death. In 1960, with her children grown, she took a job in what is now Zambia, teaching for UNESCO. The three years she spent there revitalized her poetry. After her return, she published *The Unquiet Bed* (1967), which drew new attention to her work—partly because of the frank sensuality of some of the poems. That was followed by several books of new poetry, including *Plainsongs* (1969), *The Woman I Am* (1977), *Phases of Love* (1983), and *Feeling the Worlds* (1984). As well, her new and earlier poems were gathered in *Collected Poems: The Two Seasons* (1972) and *The Self-Completing Tree: Selected Poems* (1986).

*Archive for Our Times: The Previously Uncollected and Unpublished Poems of Dorothy Livesay* (1998), edited by Dean J. Irvine, was published posthumously. Livesay created a body of poetry that is frequently epigrammatic yet also personal—even confessional—and always socially engaged. In poems like 'Day and Night', which assimilates the rhythms of the factory worksong and those of popular music, she celebrated the flux of life by adapting form to suit her content. Livesay's prose works include *The Husband: A Novella* (1990)—a story of a woman's search for personal and artistic ful-fillment and the strains it puts on her marriage—and *Journey With My Selves: A Memoir, 1909–1963* (1991). Her autobiographical story collection *A Winnipeg Childhood* was reprinted in an expanded version as *Beginnings* in 1988.

# Green Rain

I remember long veils of green rain
Feathered like the shawl of my grandmother—
Green from the half-green of the spring trees
Waving in the valley.

I remember the road
Like the one which leads to my grandmother's house,
A warm house, with green carpets,
Geraniums, a trilling canary
And shining horse-hair chairs;
And the silence, full of the rain's falling
Was like my grandmother's parlour
Alive with herself and her voice, rising and falling—
Rain and wind intermingled.

I remember on that day
I was thinking only of my love
And of my love's house.
But now I remember the day
As I remember my grandmother.
I remember the rain as the feathery fringe of her shawl.

1932

# The Difference

Your way of loving is too slow for me.
For you, I think, must know a tree by heart
Four seasons through, and note each single leaf
With microscopic glance before it falls—
And after watching soberly the turn
Of autumn into winter and the slow
Awakening again, the rise of sap—
Then only will you cry: 'I love this tree!'

As if the beauty of the thing could be
Made lovelier or marred by any mood                    10
Of wind, or by the sun's caprice; as if
All beauty had not sprung up with the seed—
With such slow ways you find no time to love
A falling flame, a flower's brevity.

1932


## Day and Night[1]


       I

Dawn, red and angry, whistles loud and sends
A geysered shaft of steam searching the air.
Scream after scream announces that the churn
Of life must move, the giant arm command.
Men in a stream, a moving human belt
Move into sockets, every one a bolt.
The fun begins, a humming, whirring drum—
Men do a dance in time to the machines.


    2

One step forward
Two steps back
Shove the lever,                                       10
Push it back

While Arnot[2] whirls
A roundabout
And Geoghan shuffles
Bolts about.


1 In her 1968 'Commentary on "Day and Night"' Livesay wrote: 'This documentary is dominated by themes of struggle: class against class, race against race. The sound of Negro spirituals mingled in my mind with Cole Porter's "Night and Day" and Lenin's words (I quote from memory): "To go two steps forward we may have to take one step back." That phrase captured my imagination for it seemed to me that the capitalist system was putting that concept in reverse.'
2 'Arnot' and 'Geoghan' are names Livesay gives to two workers.

One step forward
Hear it crack
Smashing rhythm—
Two steps back                                                    20

Your heart-beat pounds
Against your throat
The roaring voices
Drown your shout

Across the way
A writhing whack
Sets you spinning
Two steps back—

One step forward
Two steps back.                                                  30


3

Day and night are rising and falling
Night and day shift gears and slip rattling
Down the runway, shot into storerooms
Where only arms and a note-book remember
The record of evil, the sum of commitments.
We move as through sleep's revolving memories
Piling up hatred, stealing the remnants,
Doors forever folding before us—
And where is the recompense, on what agenda
Will you set love down? Who knows of peace?              40

Day and night
Night and day                      .
Light rips into ribbons
What we say.

I called to love
Deep in dream:
Be with me in the daylight
As in gloom.

Be with me in the pounding
In the knives against my back                                    50
Set your voice resounding
Above the steel's whip crack.

High and sweet
Sweet and high
Hold, hold up the sunlight
In the sky!

Day and night
Night and day
Tear up all the silence
Find the words I could not say . . .                             60


            4

We were stoking coal in the furnaces; red hot
They gleamed, burning our skins away, his and mine.
We were working together, night and day, and knew
Each other's stroke; and without words, exchanged
An understanding about kids at home,
The landlord's jaw, wage-cuts and overtime.
We were like buddies, see? Until they said
That nigger is too smart the way he smiles
And sauces back the foreman; he might say
Too much one day, to others changing shifts.                     70
Therefore they cut him down, who flowered at night
And raised me up, day hanging over night—
So furnaces could still consume our withered skin.

Shadrach, Meshach and Abednego[3]
Turn in the furnace, whirling slow.
        Lord, I'm burnin' in the fire
        Lord, I'm steppin' on the coals
        Lord, I'm blacker than my brother
        Blow your breath down here.


3  In Daniel 3, Shadrach, Meshack, and Abednego, sent by Daniel to help rule Babylon, were condemned by its
   king, Nebuchadnezzar, to the 'fiery furnace' for failing to worship his golden idol. These men were saved by God
   and emerged from the fire unharmed.

Boss, I'm smothered in the darkness                                 80
Boss, I'm shrivellin' in the flames
Boss, I'm blacker than my brother
Blow your breath down here.
Shadrach, Meshach and Abednego
Burn in the furnace, whirling slow.


5

Up in the roller room, men swing steel
Swing it, zoom; and cut it, crash.
Up in the dark the welder's torch
Makes sparks fly like lightning reel.

Now I remember storm on a field                                    90
The trees bow tense before the blow
Even the jittering sparrows' talk
Ripples into the still tree shield.

We are in storm that has no cease
No lull before, no after time
When green with rain the grasses grow
And air is sweet with fresh increase.

We bear the burden home to bed
The furnace glows within our hearts:
Our bodies hammered through the night                              100
Are welded into bitter bread.

Bitter, yes:
But listen, friend:
We are mightier
In the end.

We have ears
Alert to seize
A weakness
In the foreman's ease

We have eyes
To look across                                                     110
The bosses' profit
At our loss.

Are you waiting?
Wait with us
After evening
There's a hush—

Use it not
For love's slow count:
Add up hate                                               120
And let it mount

Until the lifeline
Of your hand
Is calloused with
A fiery brand!

Add up hunger,
Labour's ache
These are figures
That will make

The page grow crazy                                      130
Wheels go still,
Silence sprawling
On the till—

Add your hunger,
Brawn and bones,
Take your earnings:
Bread, not stones!


            6


Into thy maw I commend my body[4]
But the soul shines without
A child's hands as a leaf are tender                      140
And draw the poison out.

Green of new leaf shall deck my spirit
Laughter's roots will spread:
Though I am overalled and silent
Boss, I'm far from dead!

4  Compare Luke 23:46: 'Father, into thy hand I commit my spirit'—Jesus' final words on the cross.

One step forward
Two steps back
Will soon be over:
Hear it crack!

The wheels may whirr                                    150
A roundabout
And neighbour's shuffle
Drown your shout

The wheel must limp
Till it hangs still
And crumpled men
Pour down the hill.

Day and night
Night and day
Till life is turned                                    160
The other way!

1944


# Bartok[1] and the Geranium

She lifts her green umbrellas
Towards the pane
Seeking her fill of sunlight
Or of rain;
Whatever falls
She has no commentary
Accepts, extends,
Blows out her furbelows,[2]
Her bustling boughs;

And all the while he whirls                            10
Explodes in space,
Never content with this small room:
Not even can he be
Confined to sky

---

1 Béla Bartók (1881–1945), Hungarian composer who profoundly influenced modern music by his departure from the traditional diatonic scale; his compositions are noted for their emotional intensity.
2 Flounces; used figuratively here to suggest that the petals are like the ornamental pleats on the hem of a gown or petticoat.

But must speed high and higher still
From galaxy to galaxy,
Wrench from the stars their momentary notes
Steal music from the moon.

She's daylight
He is dark                                                    20
She's heaven-held breath
He storms and crackles
Spits with hell's own spark.

Yet in this room, this moment now
These together breathe and be:
She, essence of serenity,
He in a mad intensity
Soars beyond sight
Then hurls, lost Lucifer,
From heaven's height.                                        30

And when he's done, he's out:
She leans a lip against the glass
And preens herself in light.

1955


# The Secret Doctrine of Women

### I

The solution is always at hand:
lurking unsuspected just around
the corner; on the wave-torn shore
or vivid on a path in springing woods;
in the gnarled patience of that oak—look there!
or deep in a crowd at traffic halt
once face alight
one woman's hair


### 2

In a dream I heard the familiar words:
*Knock, and it shall be opened unto you;*                     10
*Seek, and ye shall find.*

All day I hugged that message
close to my heart—
all month I remembered it—
all year I groped
aching for that truth, as yet unlocked
searching far and wide
and all the while you bided there
close by
offering yourself, your love.                           20
As at a stroke of lightning I awoke
and found you at my side
and saw revealed
the secret doctrine we must share—
share and divide


3


A private eye, only the sun
sees us
stretched on the shore
your torso gleaming against rock
I on sand alongside                                        30
soaking up the whiteness of your skin
marble flow of flesh
whose veins
explore with rock
the pathway to the sea.


4


I am amazed at me
so joined
my blood racing and pounding
beside yours
my mind hooded within your head                    40
the pressure of our fingers locked
as ankle is to foot
knee to thigh
heart to lung—

5

The solution
opens up like morning
seizes us     every day
with a new song:
you are the watcher in my brain
who tells me how to dream                                    50


6

Beside you without needing any dream
here on the boundary of land, sea, sky
I am a more living, pulsing, breathing one
than on that first blind naked thrust—
my journey into the world's light.


7

The secret doctrine of women
despair and creation

1983


# The Artefacts: West Coast

In the middle of the night
I hear this old house breathing
a steady sigh
when oak trees and rock shadows
assemble silence
under a high
white moon


I hear the old house turn
in its sleep
shifting the weight of long dead footsteps          10
from one wall to another

echoing the children's voices
shrilly calling
from one room to the next
repeating those whispers in the master bedroom
a cry, a long sigh of breath
from one body to another
when the holy ghost takes over

In the middle of the night
I wake                                                          20
and hear time speaking

First it was forest; rock;
hidden ups and downs
a hill where oaks and pines
struggled
and if a stranger climbed
the topmost pine
he'd see the ocean flattening the mountains
the forest, serried—
below, only the sculpted bays                                   30
native encampments
ceremonial lodges, totem poles
and winter dances
the Raven overall
giver-of-light, supervising
and the white whale imminent
evil lurking
to be appeased with ritual
long hair dancing
feathered masks                                                 40

      *But history begins*
the woman said
      *when you are thirty*
      *that tomtom, time*
      *begins to beat*
      *to beat for you*

And in this city on the brink
of forest—sea—
history delights that Queen Victoria
made marriage with the totem wilderness                         50
the cedar silences
the raven's wing

Now ravens build here still
seagulls spiral
the happy children in these attics
breathe and cry
unwittingly
the names of history
tumble from their lips:
Nootka[1]    Nanaimo                                                          60
Masset      Ucluelet
The map leaps up
       *here did I live*
         *was born and reared*
       *here died*


So also said Chief Maquinna[2]    Jewitt    Emily Carr

The map leaps up
from namelessness
to history
each place made ceremonial                                                    70
when named
and its name
peopled!
events shouted!

     *here the waters divided*
     *here the whale bellowed*

In the middle of the night
the house heaves, unmoored
launched on a vast sea.

1986

---

1 Historic fur-trading centre and former summer village of the Mowach'ath group of the Nuu-chah-nulth (or Nootka) First Nation; 'Nanaimo': city on the east coast of Vancouver Island, originally inhabited by the Central Coast Salish; 'Masset': village on Graham Island, the largest of the Queen Charlotte Islands, the traditional home of the Haida; 'Ucluelet': village on the west coast of Vancouver Island, originally home to the Nuu-chah-nulth.

2 Ranking leader of the Mowach'ath during the early years of European contact, when Nootka Sound became an important fur-trading centre. John Jewitt (1783–1821), armourer aboard the American fur-trading ship Boston, whose life was spared by Maquinna when the boat was destroyed by the Mowach'ath in Nootka Sound, 22 March 1803. Emily Carr (1871–1945), Canadian painter who grew up in Victoria, BC; the nature and Native art of the Pacific Northwest were profound influences on her.

# Anne Wilkinson

## 1910–1961

Born Anne Gibbons in Toronto, Anne Wilkinson grew up there and in London, Ontario. Educated privately at home and then in schools in the United States and England, she eventually returned to Toronto, where she married and raised three children. In her forties, Wilkinson published two volumes of poetry—*Counterpoint to Sleep* (1951) and *The Hangman Ties the Holly* (1955)—and two prose works, *Lions in the Way* (1956; a history of the Osler family, of which she was a member), and *Swann and Daphne* (1960; a fantasy for children). In 1956, she also became one of the founding editors of the *Tamarack Review*. A few years after her death at age fifty, her published poetry, some unpublished poems selected from her notebooks, and a brief memoir, 'Four Corners of My World', were gathered in *The Collected Poems of Anne Wilkinson and a Prose Memoir* (1968), with an introduction by its editor, A.J.M. Smith.

In her poetry, Wilkinson uses classical and literary allusions and combines the rhythms and diction of folk songs, hymns, and nursery rhymes with wordplay reminiscent both of children's language and of James Joyce. All these devices serve to illuminate the connection between the sensual experience of the physical world and its transformation in the mind of the perceiver. As her poem 'Letter to My Children' suggests, tangible experience is her source of wisdom:

> Mind the senses and the soul
> Will take care of itself
> Being five times blessed.

This union between spirit and body brings to her poetry a sense of universal metamorphosis and flux. We are not only what we experience—'The stone in my hand / IS my hand'—but in experiencing it, we 'Touch everything available / To consciousness' ('Poem in Three Parts').

As A.J.M. Smith pointed out, the world-view of much of Wilkinson's poetry is grounded in classical Greek theories of a natural order in which the organic and the inorganic unite in the four elements: air, earth, fire, and water. As part of this totality, several of her poems are about the place of death as an aspect of universal flux. When she writes, in 'Nature Be Damned', of how 'we're kin in appetite / Tree, bird in the tree and I' because the 'feaster is reborn / The feast, and feasted on,' she recalls the sentiment in Charles G.D. Roberts's poem, 'As Down the Woodland Ways' (which ends with 'Death but a travail-pang of life, / Destruction but a name')—as well as that of Irving Layton's 'Birth of Tragedy'.

In Wilkinson's memoir, written while she was dying from lung cancer, her love of humorous anecdote, as she recalls her childhood, reveals her vitality and spirit in the face of her own death:

*London* [Ontario] *is more prone to eccentric happenings than the reticent Toronto. The case of a well-known golfer, for instance. Not a pro, just an enthusiast. After his death the mourners gathered at his house for funeral, found him dead indeed, though he hardly appeared so, seated as he was in the chair, his feet on a stool, a familiar figure in his plus fours, a putter clasped between his hands. Not a Toronto funeral, certainly.* ('Four Corners of My World')

Although interest in Wilkinson's work faded for a time, there has been a revival of attention. Michael Ondaatje made Wilkinson a recognizable character in his 1987 novel, *In the Skin of a Lion* (she is the woman in whose house the thief Caravaggio takes refuge), and he makes references to her writing in both that book and its sequel, *The English Patient* (1992). In 1990, her collected poems were republished as *The Poetry of Anne Wilkinson and a Prose Memoir* with a new biographical introduction by Joan Coldwell; and in 1992, Coldwell brought together the journals Wilkinson kept from 1948 to 1955, some personal poems, and the autobiography Wilkinson was working on at the time of her death as *The Tightrope Walker: Autobiographical Writings of Anne Wilkinson*. Dean Irvine afforded readers the ability to judge the extent of Wilkinson's achievement by editing *Heresies: The Complete* *Poems of Anne Wilkinson, 1924–61* (2003), a scholarly edition of the poetry that brings together all the published poems, along with poems that had previously only existed in manuscript form.

# The Great Winds

I'll tell you why the great winds trouble us:
Once upon a briny while ago
The sea was home and land lay sunning, cliff
And cove and dune a-doze
In unproved element of air;
A gale ago the ocean granaries
Ran low in the sea one harvest season,
Foes swam surly through a hedge of friends
And Sea Lords fought for each sea-stalk of pasture.
One among them, Marco Polo                                        10
Swimming low in shallow water, slid to shore;
He conjured solid land, he raised a flag,
A lung, our pledge to plunge from a still water
No more moving of a mother's womb.
Each birth repeats the first howled breath in time,
Reversing all the levels of the world
Till seas come up on land,
Submerged in you and me; in bog and swamp
Released, they sing amphibian noel.

The great winds trouble when a summer storm                       20
Breaks, blowing waves from hiding, drowning
Land-baked puff and pride in childish seas
Till we're unbeached, awash,
A native-stranger in contrary gardens;
Green and liquid shutters dim the sun
Where coral builds pink cities on the sand;
Little horses chase their tails
Among a maze of cockle shells and silver-sides
And sea-cows, udderless,
Hung, tethered to the herd by tongue-tied bells.                  30
Here flotsam is the sloughed-off memory,
Delirium or octopus or clue
To beat the walls of water in escape,
Though tentacles are ours, were always there
Growing in the harvest of our hair;

Here sharks, all lazy but their teeth
Come swimming sweet and slow, the easier
To you know what, my dear;
And tiny barnacles that love too much
Stick, clinging till their millions anchor us;                40
Here mouths are raw, are filled with sorrow, washed
With salt by shocked sea-silence when we scream.

The great winds trouble till a winter storm
Breaks, frosting brine to flesh and wrecking
With a breath our web to earth;
And long before the wind's cried out
We're bound in six cold feet of Arctic ice;
No leaway anywhere to move as in
A glass-walled room, and nothing here molests
But the weight of the dying albatross                        50
Whose two white wings lie cooling on our breast.

1951


## Winter Sketch, Rockcliffe, Ottawa

Down domestic roads the snow plough, snorting
Stacks a crop of winter, spills it high
To hedgerows alped with lilies; in the valley
White is wag, is daisy till
The sun aloft and hot with husbandry
Beheads the flowers.

Behind the plough the cold air flies a spume
As soft and adamant as swans
Where snow's vocation is to etherize
The wood and choke the town's                                10
Hard arteries with drifts of chloroform.
And all the long excessive day the ploughman
Steers his dreaming over the hill
To the faraway hour that carries his frostbite home.

Such storm of white
Bound by the black extravagance of night
Makes winding sheet[1] our myth-told-many-a-bed-time tale
Till April babble swells the shroud to breast

1 Shroud.

So milky full the whole north swills, licking
A world of sugar from encrusted nipples                     20
Springful and swollen with love.

And tusked with icicles, the houses here
Bog stuporous in slow white sand, guard
Their docile lawns with walls that boast
Immaculate conception in a cloud
Made big by polar ghost.[2]
In suburb of the forest, men walk shy,
Dismembered by two worlds;
Only the uncurled ears of children hear
The coyotes mating in a neighbour's acre,                   30
Theirs the only hands whose thumbs work free
To sculpt a tower leaning tipsy with unPisan laughter;
And being young, flexible pink tongues
Rename a carrot, nose;
Nose on hump of snow they crystal christen
Christ, the stillborn man;
Then herd their feet to kick the undefiled
When eyes still whey with vision see
That chastity, though white, is wormed with sleep.

O watch the child lie down and lusty swing                  40
His arms to angel in his image, sing
'I dare the snow my wings to keep.'

1951

2  A metaphor comparing a cloud's being 'impregnated' by the north wind to the impregnation of Mary, the virgin
   mother of Christ, by the Holy Spirit. The idea that the term 'Immaculate Conception' refers to Mary's pregnancy
   is popular error.

# Easter Sketches, Montreal

### I

South of North
Men grow soft with summer,
Lack the winter muscle
Set to tauten at the miracle;
Boom and shrapnel,
March of Easter, loud
Where guns of ice salute
The cracking god.

Vision dims where flowers
Blur the lens                                    10
But here, intemperate
The ropes of air
Whip the optic nerve
Till eyes are clean with crying
For the melting hour
When flocks of snow stampede
And rocks are split by spring
And intimations of fertility
In water ring.

South of North                                   20
Men grow deaf with summer,
Sound is muffled by the pile of lawns,
But where the air is seeded fresh
And skies can stretch their cloudy loins
To the back of the long north wind
The ear is royal pitched
And hears the dying snows
Sing like swans.[1]


            II

Where campanile of rock steeples the town
Water bells the buoy of all our birthdays;       30
Rivers swell in tumbling towers of praise,
Ice in aqua risen hails
The bearing down in labour of the sun.
And after sun, guards of northern lights
Stand their swords; green fires kindled
By the green shoots in our wood
Cut the natal cord,

Freeing the animal sensual man with astral
Spears of grass.
Cerebral ore conceives when pollen               40
Falls from heaven in a buzz of stars

And time and the rolling world
Fold the birthday children in their arms.

---

1 i.e., make their swan-songs or last appearances; the term *swan song* refers to the legendary notion that the swan
  sings only once—just before its death.

III

North of South
Winter is Jehovah, we
The Jobs who scold the frosty Lord
Till wings of weather
Clap the air
And crows unfrock the melting God.

On our nativity
The mellowed sun is grown,
A man to kill our father,
A sun with breath so warm
It seeds the body of our summer.

1955


## In June and Gentle Oven

In June and gentle oven
Summer kingdoms simmer
As they come
And flower and leaf and love
Release
Their sweetest juice.
No wind at all
On the wide green world
Where fields go stroll-
Ing by                                                10
And in and out
An adder of a stream
Parts the daisies
On a small Ontario farm.

And where, in curve of meadow,
Lovers, touching, lie,
A church of grass stands up
And walls them, holy, in.

Fabulous the insects
Stud the air                                          20
Or walk on running water,

Klee-drawn[1] saints
And bright as angels are.

Honeysuckle here
Is more than bees can bear
And time turns pale
And stops to catch its breath
And lovers slip their flesh

And light as pollen
Play on treble water
Till bodies reappear
And a shower of sun
To dry their languor.

Then two in one the lovers lie
And peel the skin of summer
With their teeth
And suck its marrow from a kiss
So charged with grace
The tongue, all knowing
Holds the sap of June
Aloof from seasons, flowing.

1955

30

40

1 Paul Klee (1879–1940), Swiss painter, who saw his work as an attempt to imitate 'the play of those forces which create and are still creating the world'.

# Nature Be Damned

## I

Pray where would lamb and lion be
If they lay down in amity?
Could lamb then nibble living grass?
Lamb and lion both must starve;
For none may live if all do love.

## II

I go a new dry way, permit no weather
Here, on undertaker's false green sod

Where I sit down beneath my false tin tree.
There's too much danger in a cloud,
In wood or field, or close to moving water.                    10
With my black blood—who can tell?
The dart of one mosquito might be fatal;

Or in the flitting dusk a bat
Might carry away my destiny,
Hang it upside down from a rafter
In a barn unknown to me.

I hide my skin within the barren city
Where artificial moons pull no man's tide,
And so escape my green love till the day
Vine breaks through brick and strangles me.                    20


### III

I was witch and I could be
Bird or leaf
Or branch and bark of tree.

In rain and two by two my powers left me;
Instead of curling down as root and worm
My feet walked on the surface of the earth,
And I remember a day of evil sun
When forty green leaves withered on my arm.

And so I damn the font where I was blessed,[1]
Am unbeliever; was deluded lover; never                        30
Bird or leaf or branch and bark of tree.
Each, separate as curds from whey,
Has signature to prove identity.

And yet we're kin in appetite;
Tree, bird in the tree and I.
We feed on dung, a fly, a lamb
And burst with seed
Of tree, of bird, of man,
Till tree is bare
And bird and I are bone                                        40
And feaster is reborn
The feast, and feasted on.

---

1  i.e. baptized.

IV

I took my watch beside the rose;
I saw the worm move in;
And by the tail I yanked him out
And stamped him dead, for who would choose
To leave alive a sin?

The pale rose died of grief. My heel
Had killed darling foe,
Worm that cuddles in the heart                                    50
 To ravish it. If worm not tell
How should rose its fairness know?


V

Once a year in the smoking bush
A little west of where I sit
I burn my winter caul[2] to a green ash.
This is an annual festival,
Nothing to stun or startle;
A coming together—water and sun
In summer's first communion.

Today again I burned my winter caul                              60
Though senses nodded, dulled by ritual.

One hundred singing orioles
And five old angels wakened me;
Morning sky rained butterflies
And simple fish, bass and perch,
Leapt from the lake in salutation.
St Francis, drunk among the daisies,
Opened his ecstatic eye.

Then roused from this reality I saw
Nothing, anywhere, but snow.                                     70

1957, 1968

---

2  Portion of the membrane that surrounds a fetus and sometimes covers its head at birth; also, formerly, a woman's
   indoor cap or headdress worn to protect the head from drafts.

# Irving Layton

## 1912–2006

Born Israel Pincu Lazarovitch, Irving Layton became one of Canada's best-known authors, not only because of his sizeable body of writing, but also because of his ability to keep himself in the public eye and his reputation for controversy. He was often at the centre of bitter feuds and he discussed his sexual adventures and offered opinions in language sufficiently frank and bawdy for the time to offend readers and to lose his first connection with a commercial press in Canada.

Layton acknowledged that he deliberately assumed 'the role of public exhibitionist'. Indeed, he, more than any other poet in Canada, he played the part of the artist as it was defined in the early days of the modernist movement: the gadfly and rebel, outraging the middle class and challenging the assumptions of an anaesthetized society. He seems, at that same time, to have been a battler by instinct. 'I would not have had it any other way,' he wrote in the preface to *Engagements: The Prose of Irving Layton* (1972), adding that his many conflicts had brought him 'some of the most delicious moments of my life'.

Layton was more complex, however, than his public persona might suggest. Despite his oft-expressed scorn for academics, he took a master's degree and devoted almost as much of his career to teaching as to writing. As a young man, he worked patiently with new immigrants to help them master English and taught in a parochial school in Montreal; subsequently, he was an instructor at Sir George Williams (now Concordia) University and at York University and spent a year as writer-in-residence at the University of Toronto. And for all his disparaging remarks about rival poets, he was extremely solicitous toward beginning writers and his own creative-writing students, and often took time to encourage an understanding and appreciation of the fellow poets he publicly criticized. Indeed, though he some-

times seemed to hold a generalized contempt for humankind, Layton was always generous with his time and energy, answering correspondence from readers he had never met, chatting patiently after his public readings, and working with students in his classes.

Born in Romania to Jewish parents, Layton and his family moved to the Montreal's St Urbain Street ghetto when he was an infant. His developmental years there made him 'suspicious of both literature and reality':

*Let me explain. My father was an ineffectual visionary; he saw God's footprint in a cloud and lived only for his books and meditations. A small bedroom in a slum tenement which in the torrid days steamed and blistered and sweated, he converted into a tabernacle for the Lord of Israel; and here, like the patriarch Abraham, he received his messengers. Since there was nothing angelic about me or his other children, he no more noticed us than if we had been flies on a wall. Had my mother been as otherworldly as he was, we should have starved. Luckily for us, she was not; she was tougher than nails, shrewd and indomitable. Moreover, she had a gift for cadenced vituperation; to which, doubtless, I owe my impeccable ear for rhythm. With parents so poorly matched and dissimilar, small wonder my entelechy [realization of potential] was given a terrible squint from the outset. I am not at ease in the world (what poet ever is?); but neither am I fully at ease in the world of the imagination. I require some third realm, as yet undiscovered, in which to live. My dis-ease has spurred me on to bridge the two with the stilts of poetry, or to create inside me an ironic balance of tensions. (*Foreword, A Red Carpet for the Sun,* 1959*)*

Like A.M. Klein before him and Mordecai Richler after him, Layton attended Baron Byng High School, while working at a variety of jobs to earn the monthly school fee of $1.50.

Although he fell in love with poetry there, he was—because of an argument with one of his teachers—expelled in his last year. He plunged into what may have been the most important phase of his education, an extended period of reading and self-instruction, supplemented by tutoring and mentorship by Klein (which allowed him to pass his junior matriculation exams), and debates in the evenings at Horn's Cafeteria (a gathering place during the Depression for many of Montreal's radicals and disaffected intellectuals). Eventually, he returned to school, completing a B.Sc. in agricultural science at Macdonald College in 1939. (Of this, Layton remarked, 'You can see the agricultural images in my poems. I worked on farms for three or four summers, something significant for an urban Jew.') After a period of wartime military service, he resumed his education, entering graduate studies in political science at McGill University in 1945. The subtitle of his master's thesis on British labourite Harold Laski—'The Paradoxes of a Liberal Marxist'— testifies to Layton's 'ironic balance of tensions'.

The post-war era was a period of intense activity for Layton, a time of 'exciting personalities, living poetry twenty-four hours a day, thinking, talking, analyzing, arguing, reading and above all writing.' At McGill, he met the poet Louis Dudek (both men published poems in the *McGill Daily*) and heard about John Sutherland's newly established mimeographed magazine *First Statement* (1942–5). Layton sent Sutherland some poems and later, with Dudek, joined him in editing the often-controversial little magazine. Together, the three of them set out to establish a new poetry movement in Canada, one that would challenge the 'cosmopolitan' writers who had grouped themselves around Patrick Anderson's rival magazine *Preview* (1942–5) with less abstract and more earthy poetry. In 'Montreal Poets of the Forties' (*Canadian Literature*, No. 14), Wynn Francis describes how the rivalry, though sometimes acrimonious, stimulated the more-established poets of *Preview*, while making the younger ones at *First Statement* work harder. 'Not that we wanted to be like them,' she quotes Layton as saying, 'but we wanted to be as good as they were in our way.'

In 1945, the *First Statement* group launched a series of printed chapbooks with a collection of Layton's poems, *Here and Now*, following this with Layton's second book, *Now is the Place*, in 1948. When the group around Sutherland broke up, Layton and Dudek joined Raymond Souster to found Contact Press, a co-operative venture in which the editors and several younger writers funded the publication of their own books. In addition to *Cerberus* (1952), an anthology of the work of the three editors, Contact Press published a number of Layton's most important books of poetry, including *The Black Huntsman* (1951), *Love the Conqueror Worm* (1952), *The Long Pea-Shooter* (1954), *The Cold Green Element* (1955), and *The Bull-Calf and Other Poems* (1956). These books were not much noticed in Canada, but Layton caught the attention of US poets and editors. Robert Creeley praised Layton's poetry in the first issue of the *Black Mountain Review* and published Layton's *In the Midst of My Fever* (1954) under his Divers Press; the American small-press editor Jonathan Williams brought out Layton's first substantial volume of selected poems, *The Improved Binoculars* (1956), and a collection of new poems, *A Laughter in the Mind* (1958). Even though the Ryerson Press reneged on its agreement to distribute *The Improved Binoculars* in Canada, this book gained Layton his first sustained Canadian readership, partly as a result of a preface by William Carlos Williams, in which, after avowing his admiration for the younger poet, Williams concluded, 'In short, I believe this poet to be capable, to be capable of anything. . . . There will, if I am not mistaken, be a battle: Layton against the rest of the world.'

Soon after this, Layton was approached by McClelland & Stewart, who agreed to publish a compilation of the poems Layton valued most from his previous books. Entitled *A Red Carpet for the Sun*, this collection won the Governor General's Award for poetry in 1959. With a commercial publisher now supporting him and an established Canadian audience, Layton began to publish even more frequently during the next three decades, sometimes producing one or two volumes a year. He published more than forty books of poetry in all, including the 589-page

*Collected Poems of Irving Layton* (1971); two collections of prose; a memoir of his formative years, *Waiting for the Messiah* (1985); and several volumes of correspondence, including *Wild Gooseberries: The Selected Letters of Irving Layton* (1989), and *Irving Layton and Robert Creeley: The Complete Correspondence, 1953–1978* (1990).

From his first poem to his last, two aspects of Layton's personality dominated: his exuberance and his drive to enlighten his readers. Deeply influenced by Nietzsche, Layton declared that the 'poet has a public function as a prophet'. With an existential sense that life was to be understood in physical as well as intellectual terms and that death gave life its meaning, his poems frequently drew their vitality through their depiction of animals, often suffering and dying. These poems express his concern over human failings and reflect on human mortality.

While humans are threatening predators, they, in turn, live in a predatory world. 'The Cold Green Element' gives one of the fullest accounts of Layton's vision: the universe is seen variously here: as an indifferent sea in which we swim or drown; or, in the image of the robin devouring the worm, as actively hostile, a consumer of life. But the poem suggests that "worm-like" humanity need not go meekly to annihilation. Instead, like a poet, we should strive to become one with 'the worm / who sang for an hour in the throat of a robin.'

## The Birth of Tragedy[1]

And me happiest when I compose poems.
      Love, power, the huzza of battle
      are something, are much;
yet a poem includes them like a pool
      water and reflection.
In me, nature's divided things—
      tree, mould on tree—
      have their fruition;
I am their core. Let them swap,
bandy, like a flame swerve           10
I am their mouth; as a mouth I serve.

And I observe how the sensual moths
      big with odour and sunshine
      dart into the perilous shrubbery;
or drop their visiting shadows
      upon the garden I one year made

1 A reference to *The Birth of Tragedy Out of the Spirit of Music* (1872), a work by the German philosopher Friedrich Nietzsche (1844–1900). In that book—ostensibly an attempt to explain the origins of Greek tragedy—Nietzsche discusses classical Greek culture as a union of two religious systems: the first based on the worship of the immortal gods of Olympus (such as Apollo), the second celebrating a dying god in rituals for Dionysus, the god of fertility and wine. From this observation Nietzsche generalizes two responses to the universe: 'Apollonian', which seeks the ideal world and believes in order and restraint, and 'Dionysiac', which confronts the chaos that actually underlies the appearance of order. Identifying Apollonian with 'dream' and Dionysiac with 'vision', he sees the power of Greek tragic playwrights deriving from their ability to unite Apollonian form and Dionysiac content.

of flowering stone to be a footstool
  for the perfect gods,
   who, friends to the ascending orders,
sustain all passionate meditations       20
and call down pardons
for the insurgent blood.

A quiet madman, never far from tears,
  I lie like a slain thing
   under the green air the trees
inhabit, or rest upon a chair
   towards which the inflammable air
tumbles on many robins' wings;
   noting how seasonably
    leaf and blossom uncurl     30
and living things arrange their death,
while someone from afar off
blows birthday candles for the world.

1954

# The Cold Green Element

At the end of the garden walk
the wind and its satellite wait for me;
their meaning I will not know
  until I go there,
but the black-hatted undertaker

who, passing, saw my heart beating in the grass,
is also going there. Hi, I tell him,
a great squall in the Pacific blew a dead poet
  out of the water,
who now hangs from the city's gates.     10

Crowds depart daily to see it, and return
with grimaces and incomprehension;
if its limbs twitched in the air
  they would sit at its feet
peeling their oranges.

And turning over I embrace like a lover
the trunk of a tree, one of those
for whom the lightning was too much
    and grew a brilliant
hunchback with a crown of leaves.           20

The ailments escaped from the labels
of medicine bottles are all fled to the wind;
I've seen myself lately in the eyes
    of old women,
spent streams mourning my manhood,

in whose old pupils the sun became
a bloodsmear on broad catalpa[1] leaves
and hanging from ancient twigs,
    my murdered selves
sparked the air like the muted collisions          30

of fruit. A black dog howls down my blood,
a black dog with yellow eyes;
he too by someone's inadvertence
    saw the bloodsmear
on the broad catalpa leaves.

But the Furies clear a path for me to the worm
who sang for an hour in the throat of a robin,
and misled by the cries of young boys
    I am again
a breathless swimmer in that cold green element.      40

1955

1  Tree with large heart-shaped leaves.

# The Fertile Muck

There are brightest apples on those trees
    but until I, fabulist, have spoken
they do not know their significance
or what other legends are hung like garlands
    on their black boughs twisting
like a rumour. The wind's noise is empty.

Nor are the winged insects better off
   though they wear my crafty eyes
wherever they alight. Stay here, my love;
you will see how delicately they deposit          10
   me on the leaves of elms
or fold me in the orient dust of summer.

And if in August joiners and bricklayers
   are thick as flies around us
building expensive bungalows for those
who do not need them, unless they release
   me roaring from their moth-proofed cupboards
their buyers will have no joy, no ease.

I could extend their rooms for them without cost
   and give them crazy sundials                    20
to tell the time with, but I have noticed
how my irregular footprint horrifies them
   evenings and Sunday afternoons:
they spray for hours to erase its shadow.

How to dominate reality? Love is one way;
   imagination another. Sit here
beside me, sweet; take my hard hand in yours.
We'll mark the butterflies disappearing over the hedge
   with tiny wristwatches on their wings:
our fingers touching the earth, like two Buddhas.    30

1956

# Whatever Else Poetry Is Freedom

Whatever else poetry is freedom.
Forget the rhetoric, the trick of lying
All poets pick up sooner or later. From the river,
Rising like the thin voice of grey castratos[1]—the mist;
Poplars and pines grow straight but oaks are gnarled;
Old codgers must speak of death, boys break windows;
Women lie honestly by their men at last.

1 Historically, males castrated before puberty in order to retain their soprano or alto singing voices into adulthood.

And I who gave my Kate a blackened eye[2]
Did to its vivid changing colours
Make up an incredible musical scale;                              10
And now I balance on wooden stilts and dance
And thereby sing to the loftiest casements.
See how with polish I bow from the waist.
Space for these stilts! More space or I fail!

And a crown I say for my buffoon's head.
Yet no more fool am I than King Canute,[3]
Lord of our tribe, who scanned and scorned;
Who half-deceived, believed; and, poet, missed
The first white waves come nuzzling at his feet;
Then damned the courtiers and the foolish trial              20
With a most bewildering and unkingly jest.

It was the mist. It lies inside one like a destiny.
A real Jonah it lies rotting like a lung.
And I know myself undone who am a clown
And wear a wreath of mist for a crown;
Mist with the scent of dead apples,
Mist swirling from black oily waters at evening,
Mist from the fraternal graves of cemeteries.

It shall drive me to beg my food and at last
Hurl me broken I know and prostrate on the road;            30
Like a huge toad I saw, entire but dead,
That Time mordantly had blacked; O pressed
To the moist earth it pled for entry.
I shall be I say that stiff toad for sick with mist
And crazed I smell the odour of mortality.

And Time flames like a paraffin stove
And what it burns are the minutes I live.
At certain middays I have watched the cars
Bring me from afar their windshield suns;
What lay to my hand were blue fenders,                        40
The suns extinguished, the drivers wearing sunglasses.
And it made me think I had touched a hearse.

---

2  Apparently a reference to Shakespeare's *The Taming of the Shrew*, though Kate, the Shrew, is not actually struck
   in the play. (She strikes Petruchio, who threatens to hit her back.)
3  Eleventh-century king of England who is said to have placed his throne on the shore and commanded the tide
   not to rise. In some versions, when the tide rolled over him anyway, he explained that he had done this to rebuke
   his courtiers, who thought or acted as if he had God-like powers.

So whatever else poetry is freedom. Let
Far off the impatient cadences reveal
A padding for my breathless stilts. Swivel,
O hero, in the fleshy groves, skin and glycerine,
And sing of lust, the sun's accompanying shadow
Like a vampire's wing, the stillness in dead feet—
Your stave[4] brings resurrection, O aggrievèd king.


1958

4  Rod, lance; but also with the punning meaning of 'stanza'.


# Keine Lazarovitch
# 1870–1959

When I saw my mother's head on the cold pillow,
Her white waterfalling hair in the cheeks' hollows,
I thought, quietly circling my grief, of how
She had loved God but cursed extravagantly his creatures.

For her final mouth was not water but a curse,
A small black hole, a black rent in the universe,
Which damned the green earth, stars and trees in its stillness
And the inescapable lousiness of growing old.

And I record she was comfortless, vituperative,
Ignorant, glad, and much else besides; I believe          10
She endlessly praised her black eyebrows, their thick weave,
Till plagiarizing Death leaned down and took them for his mould.

And spoiled a dignity I shall not again find,
And the fury of her stubborn limited mind;
Now none will shake her amber beads and call God blind,
Or wear them upon a breast so radiantly.

O fierce she was, mean and unaccommodating;
But I think now of the toss of her gold earrings,
Their proud carnal assertion, and her youngest sings
While all the rivers of her red veins move into the sea.          20


1961

# Butterfly on Rock

The large yellow wings, black-fringed,
were motionless

They say the soul of a dead person
will settle like that on the still face

But I thought: the rock has borne this;
this butterfly is the rock's grace,
its most obstinate and secret desire
to be a thing alive made manifest

Forgot were the two shattered porcupines
I had seen die in the bleak forest.                                    10
Pain is unreal; death, an illusion:
There is no death in all the land,
I heard my voice cry;
And brought my hand down on the butterfly
And felt the rock move beneath my hand.

1963

# A Tall Man Executes a Jig

                    I

So the man spread his blanket on the field
And watched the shafts of light between the tufts
And felt the sun push the grass towards him;
The noise he heard was that of whizzing flies,
The whistlings of some small imprudent birds,
And the ambiguous rumbles of cars
That made him look up at the sky, aware
Of the gnats that tilted against the wind
And in the sunlight turned to jigging motes.
Fruitflies he'd call them except there was no fruit                    10
About, spoiling to hatch these glitterings,

These nervous dots for which the mind supplied
The closing sentences from Thucydides,[1]
Or from Euclid having a savage nightmare.

## II

Jig, jig, jig, jig. Like miniscule black links
Of a chain played with by some playful
Unapparent hand or the palpitant
Summer haze bored with the hour's stillness.
He felt the sting and tingle afterwards
Of those leaving their orthodox unrest,                    20
Leaving their undulant excitation
To drop upon his sleeveless arm. The grass,
Even the wildflowers became black hairs
And himself a maddened speck among them.
Still the assaults of the small flies made him
Glad at last, until he saw purest joy
In their frantic jiggings under a hair,
So changed from those in the unrestraining air.

## III

He stood up and felt himself enormous.
Felt as might Donatello[2] over stone,                     30
Or Plato, or as a man who has held
A loved and lovely woman in his arms
And feels his forehead touch the emptied sky
Where all antinomies[3] flood into light.
Yet jig jig jig, the haloing black jots
Meshed with the wheeling fire of the sun:
Motion without meaning, disquietude
Without sense or purpose, ephemerids[4]
That mottled the resting summer air till
Gusts swept them from his sight like wisps of smoke.       40
Yet they returned, bringing a bee who, seeing
But a tall man, left him for a marigold.

---

1  The conclusion to *The Peloponnesian War* by the Greek historian Thucydides (*c.* 470–*c.* 400 BCE) is missing.
   The poet here connects the gnats with the ellipses used in texts to indicate incompleteness, while in the line that
   follows they become like the points that are the smallest defining element in Euclid's geometry.
2  Name taken by Donato di Niccolò (*c.* 1386–1466), considered to be the father of Renaissance sculpture because
   he was the first to portray the human figure in realistic and dynamic terms.
3  Paradoxes, especially contradictions in law.
4  Small insects that live only a day in their adult form.

### IV

He doffed his aureole of gnats and moved
Out of the field as the sun sank down,
A dying god upon the blood-red hills.
Ambition, pride, the ecstasy of sex,
And all circumstance of delight and grief,
That blood upon the mountain's side, that flood
Washed into a clear incredible pool
Below the ruddied peaks that pierced the sun.          50
He stood still and waited. If ever
The hour of revelation was come
It was now, here on the transfigured steep.
The sky darkened. Some birds chirped. Nothing else.
He thought the dying god had gone to sleep:
An Indian fakir on his mat of nails.


### V

And on the summit of the asphalt road
Which stretched towards the fiery town, the man
Saw one hill raised like a hairy arm, dark
With pines and cedars against the stricken sun          60
—The arm of Moses or of Joshua.[5]
He dropped his head and let fall the halo
Of mountains, purpling and silent as time,
To see temptation coiled before his feet:
A violated grass snake that lugged
Its intestine like a small red valise.
A cold-eyed skinflint it now was, and not
The manifest of that joyful wisdom,
The mirth and arrogant green flame of life;
Or earth's vivid tongue that flicked in praise of earth.          70


### VI

And the man wept because pity was useless.
'Your jig's up; the flies come like kites,' he said
And watched the grass-snake crawl towards the hedge,

5 A reference to Exodus 10:22: 'And Moses stretched forth his hand toward heaven; and there was a thick darkness in all the land of Egypt'; and to Joshua 10:12, in which Joshua commands the sun to stand still (glossed by
   later commentators as also being a command for darkness).

Convulsing and dragging into the dark
The satchel filled with curses for the earth,
For the odours of warm sedge, and the sun,
A blood-red organ in the dying sky.
Backwards it fell into a grassy ditch
Exposing its underside, white as milk,
And mocked by wisps of hay between its jaws;    80
And then it stiffened to its final length.
But though it opened its thin mouth to scream
A last silent scream that shook the black sky,
Adamant and fierce, the tall man did not curse.


VII

Beside the rigid snake the man stretched out
In fellowship of death; he lay silent
And stiff in the heavy grass with eyes shut,
Inhaling the moist odours of the night
Through which his mind tunnelled with flicking tongue
Backwards to caves, mounds, and sunken ledges    90
And desolate cliffs where come only kites,
And where of perished badgers and raccoons
The claws alone remain, gripping the earth.
Meanwhile the green snake crept upon the sky,
Huge, his mailed coat glittering with stars that made
The night bright, and blowing thin wreaths of cloud
Athwart the moon; and as the weary man
Stood up, coiled above his head, transforming all.

1963

# P.K. Page

## 1916–2010

Patricia Kathleen Page called herself a traveller without a map. Certainly, journeys played an important role in her life and work. Born in England, she was raised in Alberta and Manitoba. In *Hand Luggage: A Memoir in Verse* (2006), she writes,

> Calgary. The twenties. Cold and the sweet
> melt of Chinooks. . . .
> This was the wilderness: western Canada.
> Tomahawk country—teepees, coyotes,
> cayuses, lariats. The land that Ontario
> looked down its nose at. Nevertheless
> we thought it civilized.

In 1935, she moved with her family to Saint John, New Brunswick, and from there, in the 1940s, to Montreal, where she worked as a clerk and then a scriptwriter for the National Film Board. She met NFB head W. Arthur Irwin, whom she later married. When Irwin began to work for the Department of External Affairs, his career took the two of them abroad in the early 1950s to Australia, where Irwin served as Canadian high commissioner, then Brazil and Mexico, where Irwin served as ambassador. It was not until 1964 that they returned to Canada and settled in Victoria, British Columbia.

In *Hand Luggage*, Page describes how she was enamoured with visual art, music, and literature from an early age. Poetry, especially, appealed to her:

> The pattern of vowels in a poem,
> the clicking of consonants, cadence, and stress—
> were magic and music. What matter the
> meaning?
> the sound was the meaning—a mantra, a route
> to the noumenon[1]

Page published her first poem when she was eighteen; soon, her poems were appearing in the major Canadian literary magazines of the 1940s, including Alan Crawley's *Contemporary Verse* (1941–52) and *Canadian Poetry Magazine* (edited for a time by Earle Birney), as well as in the prestigious American journal, *Poetry*. Shortly after moving to Montreal, Page began working on and contributing to Patrick Anderson's *Preview* (1942–5). The influence of Anderson and the social movements in 1940s Montreal is evident in the way her early work expresses concerns about the dehumanizing effect of social institutions.

In 1944, Page's work appeared in *Unit of Five*, a collection of a small group of poets—including Louis Dudek, Raymond Souster, James Wreford, and its editor, Ronald Hambleton—which, like the 1930s anthology *New Provinces*, showed the artistic and philosophical positions of a new generation of Canada's emerging poets. These poets were also included in John Sutherland's *Other Canadians*, a large anthology that was published in 1947 to counter the 1943 edition of A.J.M. Smith's *Book of Canadian Poetry*—which itself contained four poems by Page. In 1946, Page produced her first book of poetry, *As Ten, As Twenty*. Her second book, *The Metal and the Flower*, appeared in 1954, and won a Governor General's Award.

Though Page continued with her poetry during her three years in Australia, she found herself unable to write in Latin America. Drawing and painting became her chief creative outlets. After she returned to Canada, Page worked both as a writer and (under the name P.K. Irwin) as a visual artist. A few years after *Cry Ararat: Poems New and Selected* was published (1967), Page showed her strengths as a prose writer in *The Sun and the Moon and Other Fictions* (1973), which contains a novella, *The Sun and the Moon*, that she had previously published (in 1944) under the pseudonym 'Judith Cape'. Her *Poems Selected and New* (1974) was

---

1 An object not available to the senses but intuited by the intellect.

followed by *Evening Dance of the Grey Flies* (1981), which contains, in addition to new poems, the short story, 'Unless the Eye Catch Fire . . .'. *The Glass Air* (1985), a collection of selected and new poems also includes two essays and nine drawings. In 1987, Page released *Brazilian Journal,* based on letters, journal entries, and reproductions of watercolours created during her 1957–9 stay in Brazil. *Hologram* (1994), from which 'The Gold Sun' and 'Poor Bird' are drawn, is a selection of fourteen poems based on the Spanish glosa, a poetic form of the early Renaissance, which begins with a *cabeza,* a four-line stanza taken from another poet, followed by four ten-line stanzas, each with a line from the cabeza. In 1997, *The Hidden Room* brought her poetry together in two volumes, while *Planet Earth: Poems Selected and New* (2002) provided a judicious selection and showed Page continuing to revise previously published work. In 2001, Page collected the stories she had been publishing since 1941 as *A Kind of Fiction.* She also wrote several books for children: *The Travelling Musicians of Bremen* (1992), an adaptation of the Grimm fairy tale; *A Flask of Sea Water* (1989), followed by two sequels, *The Old Woman and the Hen* and *The Sky Tree* (both 2009); *The Goat that Flew* (1993); and *A Brazilian Alphabet for the Younger Reader* (2005).

Page's poetry owes what she called her 'nourishment' to several lyric traditions: that of the English poets of the 1930s, particularly Spender, Wilfred Owen, and Auden; continental writers such as Rainer Maria Rilke and Federico Garcia Lorca; and Middle Eastern poets, especially those who were part of the mystical Sufi tradition. Central also to Page's use of imagery and to her philosophy are the writings of Jung and Yeats who, along with the Sufi writers, have provided the basis for her markedly Platonic poetics. She believes that poetry is an inspired creativity that calls not only for craft but also for 'a state of purity . . . a burning with some clear enough light' from which the poet receives poetic vision.

This sense that 'the theme chooses you' and that 'you have to be worthy of being chosen' is central to Page's poetry. Underlying her work is the image of the poet as dreamer, one who has a lifeline to the 'collective unconscious', to a 'memory of Eden or heaven'—which, as she observed, gives the artist a 'seed' that grants access to another dimension in which she must search for the dismembered parts of her poem in order to assemble them in the real world.

Despite her preoccupation with the unseen world, Page's poems are neither vague nor abstract; they employ highly sensual images that integrate mystical and worldly dimensions so effectively that the mystery becomes part of sensory experience. She achieves this integration by means of visual cues—references to eyes and seeing, to space and shape, and to colour. But Page's readers discover that, though sensory experience remains necessary as the pathway to revelation, visual images can be distorting lenses that obscure the truth. One way of understanding this paradox is suggested in 'Where the Wasteland Ends', the 1973 poem by Theodore Roszak (the opening line of which furnished Page the title of her short story reprinted here):

> Unless the eye catch fire
>     The God will not be seen
> Unless the ear catch fire
>     The God will not be heard
> Unless the tongue catch fire
>     The God will not be names
> Unless the heart catch fire
>     The God will not be loved
> Unless the mind catch fire
>     The God will not be known

At the time of her death, after more than seventy years of a highly distinguished career, Page was still writing. A new collection of fiction, *Up on the Roof,* and a collection of her wide-ranging essays, *The Filled Pen,* appeared in 2007, followed by a new book of glosas, entitled *Coal and Roses,* in 2009. Her poetic memoir *Hand Luggage* closes with a stanza that sums up her way of seeing the world:

> Though sickness and death take their
>     trouble toll
> and they did and they do—one's astonish-
>     ing heart
> almost sings through its grief like a bird—
>     water bird—
> in the wind and the waves of some vast
>     salty sea.

*Explain it? I can't. But it's true I'm in love*
*With some point beyond sight, with some*
*singular star*
*for which words won't suffice, which reduce*
*it, in fact.*

Words may not manage to express the ineffable
toward which Page's inner eye was always
turned, but she did her best to respond, because
'what interests me most / is beyond me: the
hologram, fractals and "god".'

## Stories of Snow

Those in the vegetable rain retain
an area behind their sprouting eyes
held soft and rounded with the dream of snow
precious and reminiscent as those globes—
souvenir of some nether nether land—
which hold their snowstorms circular, complete,
high in a tall and teakwood cabinet.

In countries where the leaves are large as hands
where flowers protrude their fleshy chins
and call their colours,
an imaginary snowstorm sometimes falls
among the lilies.
And in the early morning one will waken
to think the glowing linen of his pillow
a northern drift, will find himself mistaken
and lie back weeping.
And there the story shifts from head to head,
of how, in Holland, from their feather beds
hunters arise and part the flakes and go
forth to the frozen lakes in search of swans—
the snow light falling white along their guns,
their breath in plumes.
While tethered in the wind like sleeping gulls
ice boats await the raising of their wings
to skim the electric ice at such a speed
they leap jet strips of naked water,
and how these flying, sailing hunters feel
air in their mouths as terrible as ether.
And on the story runs that even drinks
in that white landscape dare to be no colour;
how flasked and water clear, the liquor slips
silver against the hunters' moving hips.
And of the swan in death these dreamers tell
of its last flight and how it falls, a plummet,
pierced by the freezing bullet

10

20

30

and how three feathers, loosened by the shot,
descend like snow upon it.
While hunters plunge their fingers in its down
deep as a drift, and dive their hands
up to the neck of the wrist                                    40
in that warm metamorphosis of snow
as gentle as the sort that woodsmen know
who, lost in the white circle, fall at last
and dream their way to death.

And stories of this kind are often told
in countries where great flowers bar the roads
with reds and blues which seal the route to snow—
as if, in telling, raconteurs unlock
the colour with its complement and go
through to the area behind the eyes                           50
where silent, unrefractive whiteness lies.

1946

## Photos of a Salt Mine

How innocent their lives look,
how like a child's
dream of caves and winter, both combined:
the steep descent to whiteness
and the stope[1]
with its striated walls
their folds all leaning as if pointing to
the greater whiteness still,
that great white bank
with its decisive front,                                       10
that seam upon a slope,
salt's lovely ice.

And wonderful underfoot the snow of salt
the fine
particles a broom could sweep,
one thinks
muckers might make angels in its drifts,
as children do in snow,
lovers in sheets,

1 An excavation in the form of steps made as ore is mined from vertical or steeply inclined veins.

lie down and leave imprinted where they lay       20
a feathered creature holier than they.

And in the outworked stopes
with lamps and ropes
up miniature Matterhorns
the miners climb
probe with their lights
the ancient folds of rock—
syncline[2], anticline—
and scoop from darkness an Aladdin's cave:      30
rubies and opals glitter from its walls.

But hoses douse the brilliance of these jewels,
melt fire to brine.
Salt's bitter water trickles thin and forms
slow fathoms down
a lake within a cave
lacquered with jet—
white's opposite.
There grey on black the boating miners float
to mend the stays and struts of that old stope
and deeply underground       40
their words resound,
are multiplied by echo, swell and grow
and make a climate of a miner's voice.

So all the photographs like children's wishes
are filled with caves or winter,
innocence
has acted as a filter,
selected only beauty from the mine.
Except in the last picture shot
from an acute high angle. In a pit       50
figures the size of pins are strangely lit
and might be dancing but you know they're not.
Like Dante's vision of the nether hell[3]
men struggle with the bright cold fires of salt
locked in the black inferno of the rock:
the filter here, not innocence but guilt.

1954

---

2  Low, troughlike fold in stratified rock, the opposite of 'anticline': fold with strata sloping downwards on both
   sides away from a common crest.
3  In *Inferno*, which forms the first part of Dante's fourteenth-century poem *The Divine Comedy*, hell is divided
   into three parts. The lowest part contains both fire and ice.

# Cry Ararat!¹

### I

In the dream the mountain near
but without sound.
A dream through binoculars
seen sharp and clear:
the leaves moving, turning
in a far wind
no ear can hear.

First soft in the distance,
blue in blue air
then sharpening, quickening                    10
taking on green.
Swiftly the fingers
seek accurate focus
(the bird
has vanished so often
before the sharp lens
could deliver it)
then as if from the sea
the mountain appears
emerging new-washed                            20
growing maples and firs.
The faraway, here.

Do not reach to touch it
nor labour to hear.
Return to your hand
the sense of the hand;
return to your ear
the sense of the ear.
Remember the statue,
that space in the air                          30
which with nothing to hold
what the minute is giving
*is* through each point
where its marble touches air.

1 Mountain range on which Noah's ark landed. As the flood waters began to recede, Noah—believing that God would once again provide a fertile earth—sent out a dove which, on its second excursion, returned bearing an olive branch.

Then will each leaf and flower
each bird and animal
become as perfect as
the thing its name evoked
when busy as a child
the world stopped at the Word                                40
and Flowers more real than flowers
grew vivid and immense;
and Birds more beautiful
and Leaves more intricate
flew, blew and quilted all
the quick landscape.

So flies and blows the dream
embracing like a sea
all that in it swims
when dreaming, you desire                                    50
and ask for nothing more
than stillness to receive
the I-am animal,
the We-are leaf and flower,
the distant mountain near.


              II


So flies and blows the dream that haunts us when we wake
to the unreality of bright day:
the far thing almost sensed by the still skin
and then the focus lost, the mountain gone.
This is the loss that haunts our daylight hours             60
leaving us parched at nightfall
blowing like last year's leaves
sibilant on blossoming trees
and thirsty for the dream of the mountain
more real than any event:
more real than strangers passing on the street
in a city's architecture white as bone
or the immediate companion.

But sometimes there is one
raw with the dream of flying:                               70
'I, a bird,
landed that very instant

and complete—
as if I had drawn a circle in my flight
and filled its shape—
find air a perfect fit.
But this my grief,
that with the next tentative lift
of my indescribable wings
the ceiling looms                                                    80
heavy as a tomb.

'Must my most exquisite and private dream
remain unleavened?
Must this flipped and spinning coin that sun
could gild and make miraculous become
so swiftly pitiful?
The vision of the flight it imitates
burns brightly in my head as if a star
rushed down to touch me where I stub against
what must forever be my underground.'                               90


### III

These are the dreams that haunt us,
these the fears.
Will the grey weather wake us,
toss us twice in the terrible night to tell us
the flight is cancelled
and the mountain lost?

O, then cry Ararat!

The dove believed
in her sweet wings and in the rising peak
with such a washed and easy innocence                               100
that she found rest on land for the sole of her foot
and, silver, circled back,
a green twig in her beak.

The leaves that make the tree by day,
the green twig the dove saw fit
to lift across a world of water
break in a wave about our feet.
The bird in the thicket with his whistle

the crystal lizard in the grass
the star and shell
tassel and bell
of wild flowers blowing where we pass,
this flora-fauna flotsam, pick and touch,
requires the focus of the total I.

A single leaf can block a mountainside;
all Ararat be conjured by a leaf.

1967

## Evening Dance of the Grey Flies

Grey flies, fragile, slender-winged and slender-legged
scribble a pencilled script across the sunlit lawn.

As grass and leaves grow black
the grey flies gleam—
their cursive flight a gold calligraphy.

It is the light that gilds their frail
bodies, makes them fat and bright as bees—
reflected or refracted light—

as once my fist
burnished by some beam I could not see
glowed like gold mail and conjured Charlemagne

as once your face
grey with illness and with age—
a silverpoint against the pillow's white—

shone suddenly like the sun
before you died.

1981

# Arras[1]

Consider a new habit—classical,
and trees espaliered[2] on the wall like candelabra.
How still upon that lawn our sandalled feet.

But a peacock rattling his rattan tail and screaming
has found a point of entry. Through whose eye
did it insinuate in furled disguise
to shake its jewels and silk upon that grass?

The peaches hang like lanterns. No one joins
those figures on the arras.
        Who am I             10
or who am I become that walking here
I am observer, other, Gemini,
starred for a green garden of cinema?

I ask, what did they deal me in this pack?
The cards, all suits, are royal when I look.
My fingers slipping on a monarch's face
twitch and grow slack.
I want a hand to clutch, a heart to crack.

No one is moving now, the stillness is
infinite. If I should make a break . . .            20
take to my springy heels . . . ? But nothing moves.
The spinning world is stuck upon its poles,
the stillness points a bone[3] at me. I fear
the future on this arras.
        I confess:

It was my eye.
Voluptuous it came.
Its head the ferrule[4] and its lovely tail
folded so sweetly; it was strangely slim
to fit the retina. And then it shook            30
and was a peacock—living patina,
eye-bright, maculate!
Does no one care?

1 Wall hanging, particularly a tapestry.
2 That is, with trees' branches trained to grow flat against a wall, supported on a lattice or framework of stakes.
3 'Aboriginal projective magic. A prepared human or kangaroo bone is pointed by a sorcerer at an intended victim (who may be miles away) to bring about his death' (from Page's glossary of Australian terms in *Cry Ararat!*).
4 Metal cap used to reinforce or secure the end of a pole or handle—here belonging to an umbrella.

I thought their hands might hold me if I spoke.
I dreamed the bite of fingers in my flesh,
their poke smashed by an image, but they stand
as if within a treacle,[5] motionless,
folding slow eyes on nothing. While they stare
another line has trolled the encircling air,
another bird assumes its furled disguise.                    40

1967

5  Molasses or sweet syrup; here referring to the fact that it entraps the insects it attracts.

# The Gold Sun

> *Trace the gold sun about the whitened sky*
> *Without evasion by a single metaphor.*
> *Look at it in its essential barrenness*
> *And say this, this is the centre that I seek.*

—Wallace Stevens, 'Credences of Summer'

Sky whitened by a snow on which no swan
is visible, and no least feather falling
could possibly or impossibly be seen,
sky whitened like the blank page of a book,
no letters forming into words unless
written in paleness—a pallidity
faint as the little rising moons on nails—
and so, forgettable and so, forgot.
Blue eyes dark as lapis lazuli[1]
*trace the gold sun about the whitened sky.*                10

You'll see the thing itself no matter what.
Though it may blind you, what else will suffice?
To smoke a glass or use a periscope
will give you other than the very thing,
or more, or elements too various.
So let the fabulous photographer
catch Phaeton[2] in his lens and think he is

1  An intensely blue rock, often with light streaks, used in jewellery and, before 1828, in the preparation of the
   pigment ultramarine. Hex 0038A8 is one of its shades of dark blue.
2  In Greek mythology, Phaeton is the son of Helios, the sun god who brought each day into existence when he
   rode his solar chariot across the sky. Phaeton lost control when he rashly attempted to drive his father's chariot
   and Zeus killed him with a thunderbolt to save the world from destruction.

the thing itself, not knowing all the else
he is become. But you will see it clear
*without evasion by a single metaphor.*                    20

How strip the sun of all comparisons?
That spinning coin—moving, yet at rest
in its outflinging course across the great
parabola of space—is Phoebus,[3]
sovereign: heroic principle,
the heat and light of us. And gold—no less
a metaphor than sun—is not the least
less multiple and married. Therefore how
rid the gold sun of all its otherness?
*Look at it in its essential barrenness.*                  30

Make a prime number of it, pure, and know
it indivisible and hold it so
in the white sky behind your lapis eyes.
Push aside everything that isn't sun
the way a sculptor works his stone,
the way a mystic masters the mystique
of making more by focusing on one
until at length, all images are gone
except the sun, the thing itself, deific,
*and say this, this is the centre that I seek.*            40

1994

---

3  An epithet of the Greek god Apollo, used when he is identified with the sun.

# Poor Bird

> *. . . looking for something, something, something.*
> *Poor bird, he is obsessed!*
> *The millions of grains are black, white, tan, and gray,*
> *mixed with quartz grains, rose and amethyst.*
>
>                     —Elizabeth Bishop, 'Sandpiper'

From birth, from the first astonishing moment
when he pecked his way out of the shell, pure fluff,
he was looking for something—warmth, food, love
or light, or darkness—we are all the same stuff,
all have the same needs: to be one of the flock

or to stand apart, a singular fledgling.
So the search began—the endless search
that leads him onward—a vocation
year in, year out, morning to evening
*looking for something, something, something.* 10

Nothing will stop him. Although distracted
By nest-building, eggs, high winds, high tides
and too short a lifespan for him to plan
an intelligent search—still, on he goes
with his delicate legs and spillikin[1] feet
and the wish to know what he's almost guessed.
Can't leave it alone, that stretch of sand.
Thinks himself Seurat[2] (pointilliste)
Or a molecular physicist.
*Poor bird, he is obsessed!* 20

And just because he has not yet found
what he doesn't know he is searching for
is not a sign he's off the track.
His track is the sedge, the sand, the suck
of the undertow, the line of shells.
Nor would he have it another way.
And yet—the nag—is there something else?
Something more, perhaps, or something less.
And though he examine them, day after day
*the millions of grains are black, white, tan and gray.* 30

But occasionally, when he least expects it,
in the glass of a wave a painted fish
like a work of art across his sight
reminds him of something he doesn't know
that he has been seeking his whole long life—
something that may not even exist!
Poor bird, indeed! Poor dazed creature!
Yet when his eye is sharp and sideways seeing
oh, *then* the quotidian unexceptional sand is
*mixed with quartz grains, rose and amethyst.* 40

1994

1 That is, thin, straw-like. Spillikins, also called jackstraws or pick-up sticks, is a game played with a heap of small, thin rods of wood, bone, or plastic (called 'spillikins'), that players try to remove one at a time without disturbing the others.
2 Georges Pierre Seurat (1859–91), French painter chiefly associated with pointillism, a painting technique that uses dots of various pure colours, rather than unbroken fields of blended colours, to suggest shapes.

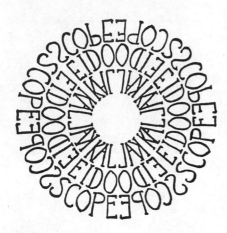

*I. A Little Fantasy*

> *I send you a very well-constructed Kaleidoscope, a recently invented Toy.*

> —John Murray to Byron, 1818[1]

So—Murray to Byron in Italy
when B. was falling in love again. In love.
Teresa this time. Guiccioli.
What a gift
to view her through that tube!
Her palms, sand dollars—
pale, symmetrical—
changed with his breathing
into petalled stars.
Four hearts her mouth, then eight,                    10
a single flower
become a bunch
to kiss and kiss and kiss
and kiss a fourth time.
What a field of mouths!
Her navel—curling, complex—
shells and pearls
quadrupling for him
and her soft hair—ah,
the flat, sweet plait of it                           20
beneath the glass—

---

1 John Murray was Alfred Lord Byron's publisher and correspondent. He published the early cantos of *Don Juan*, Byron's epic satire about a legendary Spanish nobleman famous for his dissolute lifestyle and his many seductions of women; Byron's last major work, it was left unfinished at its death, in spite of Murray's letters asking Byron to send him more sections of the poem. In 1818 Byron was living in Italy; in 1821 the Contessa Teresa Guiccioli (*c.* 1800–73) left her husband to become Byron's last lover.

a private hair brooch[2]
such as ladies wear
pinned to their *peau de soie.*

Byron is breathing heavily
the tube—a lover's perfect toy—
weighting his palm.
'Quite a celestial kaleidoscope.'
But Murray demands more cantos.
(Damn the man!)                                    30
Oh, multiple Terese,
'*Don Juan*' calls.


*II. A Little Reality*

My eye falls headlong
down this slender tube,
its eyebeam glued
to shift and flux and flow.
(Mirrors. A trick with mirrors.)
I cannot
budge from this cylinder.
An octagonal rose                                  40
holds me as though I were its stem.
We move
interdependent
paired in serious play
that is not play.
Part of the art
of dance.

Gwendolyn,
your garden of square roots[3]
grows in this circle:                              50

---

2 A brooch that carries 'hair art', usually hair plaited in an abstract pattern or hair braided around an armature in a shape such as a flower. These brooches, along with hair bracelets and rings, were often a form of mourning jewellery, preserving the hair of a departed loved one—and sometimes combining hair from more than one person. '*Peau de soie*' is smooth, finely ribbed, but dull-finished silk fabric.

3 'The Garden of Square Roots: An Autobiography' is a 1968 poem by Gwendolyn MacEwen. It reads in part:

>           this city i live in i built with bones
>           . . . . . . . . . .
>           for i was the i interior
>           . . . . . . . . . .
>           and all my gardens grew backwards
>           and all the roots were finally square
>           and Ah! the flowers grew there like algebra

from my pots and pans—
a silver chaparral of leaves and flowers—
the tap's drip dew
upon them—diamonds, stars;
the yellow plastic
of my liquid soap—
a quatrefoil of buttercups—
unfolds
in four-leaf clovers on a field of gold.

Nothing is what it seems.                                   60
Through this glass eye
each single thing is other—
all-ways joined
to every other thing.
Familiar here is foreign
fresh and fair
as never-seen-before.
And this kaleidoscope uniting all,
this tube, this conduit optical,
this lens                                                   70
is magic. Through it—see
(who dares?)
the perfect, all-inclusive metaphor.

1997

# Unless the Eye Catch Fire

*Unless the eye catch fire*
*The God will not be seen . . .*

—Theodore Roszak, *Where the Wasteland Ends*

**Wednesday, September 17.** The day began normally enough. The quail cockaded[1] as antique foot soldiers, arrived while I was having my breakfast. The males black-faced, white-necklaced, cinnamon-crowned, with short, sharp, dark plumes. Square bibs, Payne's grey;[2] belly and sides with a pattern of small stitches. Reassuring, the flock of them. They tell me the macadamization[3] of the world is not complete.

---

1 That is, with its distinctive plume of feathers standing up from its crown. A cockade is a rosette or knot of ribbons worn in a hat as a badge of office.
2 A very dark blue-grey (hex 808080).
3 That is, the process of paving the world. Macadam is broken stone used for building roads, usually combined with tar or asphalt.

A sudden alarm, and as if they had one brain among them, they were gone in a rush—a sideways ascending Niagara—shutting out the light, obscuring the sky and exposing a rectangle of lawn, unexpectedly emerald. How bright the berries on the cotoneaster. Random leaves on the cherry twirled like gold spinners. The garden was high-keyed, vivid, locked in aspic.

Without warning, and as if I were looking down the tube of a kaleidoscope, the merest shake occurred—moiréed[4] the garden—rectified itself. Or, more precisely, as if a range-finder through which I had been sighting found of itself a more accurate focus. Sharpened, in fact, to an excoriating exactness.

And then the colours changed. Shifted to a higher octave—a *bright spectrum*. Each colour with its own *light*, its own *shape*. The leaves of the trees, the berries, the grasses—as if shedding successive films—disclosed layer after layer of hidden perfections. And upon these rapidly changing surfaces the 'range-finder'—to really play hob with metaphor!—sharpened its small invisible blades.

I don't know how to describe the intensity and speed of focus of this gratuitous zoom lens through which I stared, or the swift and dizzying adjustments within me. I became a 'sleeping top', perfectly centred, perfectly sighted. The colours vibrated beyond the visible range of the spectrum. Yet I saw them. With some matching eye. Whole galaxies of them, blazing and glowing, flowing in rivulets, gushing in fountains—volatile, mercurial, and making lacklustre and off-key the colours of the rainbow.

I had no time or inclination to wonder, intellectualize. My mind seemed astonishingly clear and quite still. Like a crystal. A burning glass.

And then the range-finder sharpened once again. To alter space.

The lawn, the bushes, the trees—still super-brilliant—were no longer *there*. *There*, in fact, had ceased to exist. They were now, of all places in the world, *here*. Right in the centre of my being. Occupying an immense inner space. Part of me. Mine. Except the whole idea of ownership was beside the point. As true to say I was theirs as they mine. I and they were here; they and I, there. (*There, here* . . . odd . . . but for an irrelevant, inconsequential 't' which comes and goes, the words are the same.)

As suddenly as the world had altered, it returned to normal. I looked at my watch. A ridiculous mechanical habit. As I had no idea when the experience began it was impossible to know how long it had lasted. What had seemed eternity couldn't have been more than a minute or so. My coffee was still steaming in its mug.

The garden, through the window, was as it had always been. Yet not as it had always been. Less. Like listening to mono after hearing stereo. But with a far greater loss of dimension. A grievous loss.

I rubbed my eyes. Wondered, not without alarm, if this was the onset of some disease of the retina—glaucoma or some cellular change in the eye itself—superlatively packaged, fatally sweet as the marzipan cherry I ate as a child and *knew* was poison.

If it *is* a disease, the symptoms will recur. It will happen again.

---

4 That is, gave the garden a luminous, rippled appearance like that of moiré silk, which has a pattern of lustrous, irregular wavy lines that seem to shimmer.

***Tuesday, September 23.*** It has happened again.

Tonight, taking Dexter for his late walk, I looked up at the crocheted tangle of boughs against the sky. Dark silhouettes against the lesser dark, but beating now with an extraordinary black brilliance. The golden glints in obsidian or the lurking embers in black opals are the nearest I can come to describing them. But it's a false description, emphasizing as it does the wrong end of the scale. This was a *dark spectrum.* As if the starry heavens were translated into densities of black—black Mars, black Saturn, black Jupiter; or a master jeweller had crossed his jewels with jet and set them to burn and wink in the branches and twigs of oaks whose leaves shone luminous—a leafy Milky Way—fired by black chlorophyll.

Dexter stopped as dead as I. Transfixed. His thick honey-coloured coat and amber eyes, glowing with their own intense brightness, suggested yet another spectrum. A *spectrum of light.* He was a constellated dog, shining, supra-real, against the foothills and mountain ranges of midnight.

I am reminded now, as I write, of a collection of lepidoptera in Brazil—one entire wall covered with butterflies, creatures of daylight—enormous or tiny—blue, orange, black. Strong-coloured. And on the opposite wall their antiselves—pale night flyers spanning such a range of silver and white and lightest snuff-colour that once one entered their spectral scale there was no end to the subleties and delicate nuances. But I didn't think like this then. All thought, all comparisons were prevented by the startling infinities of darkness and light.

Then, as before, the additional shake occurred and the two spectrums moved swiftly from without to within. As if two equal and complementary circles centred inside me—or I in them. How explain that I not only *saw* but actually *was* the two spectrums? (I underline a simple, but in this case exactly appropriate, anagram.)

Then the range-finder lost its focus and the world, once again, was back to normal. Dexter, a pale, blurred blob, bounded about within the field of my peripheral vision, going on with his doggy interests just as if a moment before he had not been frozen in his tracks, a dog entranced.

I am no longer concerned about my eyesight. Wonder only if we are both mad, Dexter and I? Angelically mad, sharing hallucinations of epiphany. *Folie à deux?*

***Friday, October 3.*** It's hard to account for my secrecy, for I *have* been secretive. As if the cat had my tongue. It's not that I don't long to talk about the colours but I can't risk the wrong response—(as Gaby once said of a companion after a faultless performance of *Giselle*: 'If she had criticized the least detail of it, I'd have hit her!').

Once or twice I've gone so far as to say, 'I had the most extraordinary experience the other day . . .' hoping to find some look or phrase, some answering, 'So did I.' None has been forthcoming.

I can't forget the beauty. Can't get it out of my head. Startling, unearthly, indescribable. Infuriatingly indescribable. A glimpse of—somewhere else. Somewhere alive, miraculous, newly made yet timeless. And more important still—significant, luminous, with a meaning of which I was part. Except that I—the I who is writing this—did not exist: was flooded out, dissolved in that immensity where subject and object are one.

I have to make a deliberate effort now not to live my life in terms of it; not to sit, immobilized, awaiting the shake that heralds a new world. Awaiting the transfiguration.

Luckily the necessities of life keep me busy. But upstream of my actions, behind a kind of plate glass, some part of me waits, listens, maintains a total attention.

**Tuesday, October 7.** Things are moving very fast.

Some nights ago my eye was caught by a news item. 'Trucker Blames Colours', went the headline. Reading on: 'R.T. Ballantyne, driver for Island Trucks, failed to stop on a red light at the intersection of Fernhill and Spender. Questioned by traffic police, Ballantyne replied: "I didn't see it, that's all. There was this shake, then all these colours suddenly in the trees. Real bright ones I'd never seen before. I guess they must have blinded me." A breathalyzer test proved negative.' Full stop.

I had an overpowering desire to talk to R.T. Ballantyne. Even looked him up in the telephone book. Not listed. I debated reaching him through Island Trucks in the morning.

Hoping for some mention of the story, I switched on the local radio station, caught the announcer mid-sentence:

'. . . to come to the studio and talk to us. So far no one has been able to describe just what the "new" colours are, but perhaps Ruby Howard can. Ruby, you say you actually *saw* "new" colours?'

What might have been a flat, rather ordinary female voice was sharpened by wonder. 'I was out in the garden, putting it to bed, you might say, getting it ready for winter. The hydrangeas are dried out—you know the way they go. Soft beiges and greys. And I was thinking maybe I should cut them back, when there was this—shake, like—and there they were shining. Pink. And blue. But not like they are in life. Different. Brighter. With little lights, like . . .'

The announcer's voice cut in, 'You say "not like they are in life". D'you think this wasn't life? I mean, do you think maybe you were dreaming?'

'Oh, no,' answered my good Mrs Howard, positive, clear, totally unrattled. 'Oh, no, I wasn't *dreaming*. Not *dreaming*— . . . Why—*this* is more like dreaming.' She was quiet a moment and then, in a matter-of-fact voice, 'I can't expect you to believe it,' she said. 'Why should you? I wouldn't believe it myself if I hadn't seen it.' Her voice expressed a kind of compassion as if she was really sorry for the announcer.

I picked up the telephone book for a second time, looked up the number of the station. I had decided to tell Mrs Howard what I had seen. I dialled, got a busy signal, depressed the bar and waited, cradle in hand. I dialled again. And again.

**Later.** J. just phoned. Curious how she and I play the same game over and over.

J: Were you watching Channel 8?

ME: No, I . . .

J: An interview. With a lunatic. One who sees colours and flashing lights.

ME: Tell me about it.

J: He was a logger—a high-rigger—not that that has anything to do with it. He's retired now and lives in an apartment and has a window-box with geraniums. This morning the flowers were like neon, he said, flashing and shining . . . *Honestly!*

ME: Perhaps he saw something you can't . . .
J: (*Amused*) I might have known you'd take his side. Seriously, what *could* he have seen?
ME: Flashing and shining—as he said.
J: But they couldn't. Not geraniums. And you know it as well as I do. *Honestly*, Babe . . . (She is the only person left who calls me the name my mother called me.) Why are you always so perverse?

I felt faithless. I put down the receiver, as if I had not borne witness to my God.

**October 22.** Floods of letters to the papers. Endless interviews on radio and TV. Pros, cons, inevitable spoofs.

One develops an eye for authenticity. It's as easy to spot as sunlight. However they may vary in detail, true accounts of the colours have an unmistakable common factor—a common factor as difficult to convey as sweetness to those who know only salt. True accounts are inarticulate, diffuse, unlikely—impossible.

It's recently crossed my mind that there may be some relationship between having seen the colours and their actual manifestation—something as improbable as *the more one sees them the more they are able to be seen*. Perhaps they are always there in some normally invisible part of the electro-magnetic spectrum and only become visible to certain people at certain times. A combination of circumstances or some subtle refinement in the organ of sight. And then—from quantity to quality perhaps, like water to ice—a whole community changes, is able to see, catches fire.

For example, it was seven days between the first time I saw the colours and the second. During that time there were no reports to the media. But once the reports began, the time between lessened appreciably *for me*. Not proof, of course, but worth noting. And I can't help wondering why some people see the colours and others don't. Do some of us have extra vision? Are some so conditioned that they're virtually blind to what's there before their very noses? Is it a question of more, or less?

Reports come in from farther and farther afield; from all walks of life. I think now there is no portion of the inhabited globe without 'shake freaks' and no acceptable reason for the sightings. Often, only one member of a family will testify to the heightened vision. In my own small circle, I am the only witness—or so I think. I feel curiously hypocritical as I listen to my friends denouncing the 'shakers'. Drugs, they say. Irrational—possibly dangerous. Although no sinister incidents have occurred yet—just some mild shake-baiting here and there—one is uneasily reminded of Salem.

Scientists pronounce us hallucinated or mistaken, pointing out that so far there is no hard evidence, no objective proof. That means, I suppose, no photographs, no spectroscopic measurement—if such is possible. Interestingly, seismographs show very minor earthquake tremors—showers of them, like shooting stars in August.[5] Pundits claim 'shake fever'—as it has come to be called—is a variant on flying saucer fever and that it will subside in its own time. Beneficent physiologists suggest we are suffering (why is it *always* suffering, never enjoying?) a distorted form of *ocular spectrum* or after-image. (An after-image of what?) Psychologists disagree among themselves. All in all, it is not surprising that some of us prefer to keep our experiences to ourselves.

5  That is, during the Perseids meteor shower, visible every August.

***January 9.*** Something new has occurred. Something impossible. Disturbing. So disturbing, in fact, that according to rumour it is already being taken with the utmost seriousness at the highest levels. TV, press and radio—with good reason—talk of little else.

What seemingly began as a mild winter has assumed sinister overtones. Farmers in southern Alberta are claiming the earth is unnaturally hot to the touch. Golfers at Harrison[6] complain that the soles of their feet burn. Here on the coast, we notice it less. Benign winters are our speciality.

Already we don't lack for explanations as to why the earth could not be hotter than usual, nor why it is naturally 'un-naturally' hot. Vague notes of reassurance creep into the speeches of public men. They may be unable to explain the issue, but they can no longer ignore it.

To confuse matters further, reports on temperatures seem curiously inconsistent. What information we get comes mainly from self-appointed 'earth touchers'. And now that the least thing can fire an argument, their conflicting readings lead often enough to inflammatory debate.

For myself, I can detect no change at all in my own garden.

***Thursday . . .?*** There is no longer any doubt. The temperature of the earth's surface *is* increasing.

It is unnerving, horrible, to go out and feel the ground like some great beast, warm, beneath one's feet. As if another presence—vast, invisible—attends one. Dexter, too, is perplexed. He barks at the earth with the same indignation and, I suppose, fear, with which he barks at the first rumblings of earthquake.

Air temperatures, curiously, don't increase proportionately—or so we're told. It doesn't make sense, but at the moment nothing makes sense. Countless explanations have been offered. Elaborate explanations. None adequate. The fact that the air temperature remains temperate despite the higher ground heat must, I think, be helping to keep panic down. Even so, these are times of great tension.

Hard to understand these two unexplained—unrelated?—phenomena: the first capable of dividing families; the second menacing us all. We are like animals trapped in a burning building.

***Later.*** J. just phoned. Terrified. Why don't I move in with her, she urges. After all she has the space and we have known each other forty years. (Hard to believe when I don't feel even forty!) She can't bear it—the loneliness.

Poor J. Always so protected, insulated by her money. And her charm. What one didn't provide, the other did . . . diversions, services, attention.

What do I think is responsible for the heat, she asks. But it turns out she means who. Her personal theory is that the 'shake-freaks' are causing it—involuntarily, perhaps, but the two are surely linked.

'How could they possibly cause it?' I enquire. 'By what reach of the imagination . . . ?'

'Search *me*!' she protests. 'How on earth should *I* know?' And the sound of the dated slang makes me really laugh.

6  Harrison Hot Springs, a resort village, with a golf course, on Harrison Lake, northeast of Chilliwack, BC.

But suddenly she is close to tears. 'How can you *laugh*?' she calls. 'This is night-mare. Nightmare!'

Dear J. I wish I could help but the only comfort I could offer would terrify her still more.

*September.* Summer calmed us down. If the earth was hot, well, summers *are* hot. And we were simply having an abnormally hot one.

Now that it is fall—the season of cool nights, light frosts—and the earth like a feverish child remains worryingly hot, won't cool down, apprehension mounts.

At last we are given official readings. For months the authorities have assured us with irrefutable logic that the temperature of the earth could not be increasing. Now, without any apparent period of indecision of confusion, they are warning us with equal conviction and accurate statistical documentation that it has, in fact, increased. Something anyone with a pocket-handkerchief of lawn has known for some time.

Weather stations, science faculties, astronomical observatories all over the world are measuring and reporting. Intricate computerized tables are quoted. Special depart-ments of Government have been set up. We speak now of a new Triassic Age[7]—the Neo-Triassic—and of the accelerated melting of the ice caps. But we are elaborately assured that this could not, repeat not, occur in our lifetime.

Interpreters and analysts flourish. The media are filled with theories and explana-tions. The increased temperature has been attributed to impersonal agencies such as bacteria from outer space; a thinning of the earth's atmosphere; a build-up of carbon-dioxide in the air; some axial irregularity; a change in the earth's core (geologists are reported to have begun test borings). No theory is too far-fetched to have its support-ers. And because man likes a scapegoat, blame has been laid upon NASA, atomic physi-cists, politicians, the occupants of flying saucers, and finally upon mankind at large—improvident, greedy mankind—whose polluted, strike-ridden world is endan-gered now by the fabled flames of hell.

Yet, astonishingly, life goes on. The Pollack baby was born last week. I received the news as if it were a death. Nothing has brought the irony of our situation home to me so poignantly. And when I saw the perfect little creature in its mother's arms, the look of adoration on her face, I found myself saying the things one always says to a new mother—exactly as if the world had not changed. Exactly as if our radio was not informing us that Nostradamus,[8] the Bible, and Jeane Dixon have all foreseen our plight. A new paperback, *Let Edgar Cayce Tell You Why*, sold out in a matter of days. Attendance at churches has doubled. Cults proliferate. Yet even in this atmosphere, we, the 'shake freaks', are considered lunatic fringe. Odd men out. In certain quarters

7  The Triassic Age, from about 65 million to 2 million years ago, seems, in North America, to have been a period of unusually warm, perhaps even tropical, temperatures. Volcanoes spewed out lava flows, and forests and lush vegetation grew in many places where it does not today.

8  Michel de Nostredame (1503–66), French physician and astrologer who produced two collections of cryptic and apocalyptic predictions in rhymed quatrains (1555; 1558); Jeane Dixon (1918–97), popular American psychic and astrologer who became associated with predicting the death of US president John F. Kennedy; Edgar Cayce (1877–1945), the so-called 'sleeping prophet', who either fell asleep or entered a trance state during which he dis-cussed cures or exhibited knowledge of which he claimed to have no awareness when awake. In one of these ses-sions he 'revealed' the fate of the legendary continent Atlantis.

I believe we are seriously held responsible for the escalating heat, so J. is not alone. There have now been one or two nasty incidents. It is not surprising that even the most vocal among us have grown less willing to talk. I am glad to have kept silent. As a woman living alone, the less I draw attention to myself the better.

But, at the same time, we have suddenly all become neighbours. Total strangers greet each other on the street. And the almost invisible couple behind the high hedge appears every time I pass with Dexter—wanting to talk. Desperately wanting to talk.

For our lives are greatly altered by this overhanging sense of doom. It is already hard to buy certain commodities. Dairy products are in very short supply. On the other hand, the market is flooded with citrus fruits. We are threatened with severe shortages for the future. The authorities are resisting rationing but it will have to come, if only to prevent artificial shortages resulting from hoarding.

Luckily the colours are an almost daily event. I see them now, as it were, with my entire being. It is as if all my cells respond to their brilliance and become light too. At such times I feel I might shine in the dark.

**No idea of the date.** It is evening and I am tired but I am so far behind in my notes I want to get something down. Events have moved too fast for me.

Gardens, parks—every tillable inch of soil—have been appropriated for food crops. As an able, if aging body, with an acre of land and some knowledge of gardening, I have been made responsible for soybeans—small trifoliate plants rich with the promise of protein. Neat rows of them cover what were once my vegetable garden, flower beds, lawn.

Young men from the Department of Agriculture came last month, bulldozed, cultivated, planted. Efficient, noisy desecrators of my twenty years of landscaping. Dexter barked at them from the moment they appeared and I admit I would have shared his indignation had the water shortage not already created its own desolation.

As a Government gardener I'm a member of a new privileged class. I have watering and driving permits and coupons for gasoline and boots—an indication of what is to come. So far there has been no clothes rationing.

Daily instructions—when to water and how much, details of mulching, spraying—reach me from the Government radio station to which I tune first thing in the morning. It also provides temperature readings, weather forecasts and the latest news releases on emergency measures, curfews, rationing, insulation. From the way things are going I think it will soon be our only station. I doubt that newspapers will be able to print much longer. In any event, I have already given them up. At first it was interesting to see how quickly drugs, pollution, education, women's lib., all became bygone issues; and, initially, I was fascinated to see how we rationalized. Then I became bored. Then disheartened. Now I am too busy.

**Evening.** A call came from J. Will I come for Christmas?

*Christmas!* Extraordinary thought. Like a word from another language learned in my youth, now forgotten.

'I've still got some Heidseck. We can get tight.'

The word takes me back to my teens. 'Like old times . . .'

'Yes.' She is eager. I hate to let her down. 'J., I can't. How could I get to you?'

'In your *car*, silly. *You* still have gas. You're the only one of us who has.' Do I detect a slight hint of accusation, as if I had acquired it illegally?

'But J., it's only for emergencies.'

'My God, Babe, d'you think *this* isn't an emergency?'

'J. dear . . .'

'*Please*, Babe,' she pleads. 'I'm so afraid. Of the looters. The eeriness. You must be afraid too. *Please!*'

I should have said, yes, that of course I was afraid. It's only natural to be afraid. Or, unable to say that, I should have made the soothing noises a mother makes to her child. Instead, 'There's no reason to be afraid, J.,' I said. It must have sounded insufferably pompous.

'No reason!' She was exasperated with me. 'I'd have thought there was every reason.'

She will phone again. In the night perhaps when she can't sleep. Poor J. She feels so alone. She *is* so alone. And so idle. I don't suppose it's occurred to her yet that telephones will soon go. That a whole way of life is vanishing completely.

It's different for me. I have the soybeans which keep me busy all the daylight hours. And Dexter. And above all I have the colours and with them the knowledge that there are others, other people, whose sensibilities I share. We are as invisibly, inviolably related to one another as the components of a molecule. I say 'we'. Perhaps I should speak only for myself, yet I feel as sure of these others as if they had spoken. Like the quail, we share one brain—no, I think it is one heart—between us. How do I know this? How *do* I know? I know by knowing. We are less alarmed by the increasing heat than those who have not seen the colours. I can't explain why. But seeing the colours seems to change one—just as certain diagnostic procedures cure the complaint they are attempting to diagnose.

In all honesty I admit to having had moments when this sense of community was not enough, when I have had a great longing for my own kind—for so have I come to think of these others—in the way one has a great longing for someone one loves. Their presence in the world is not enough. One must see them. Touch them. Speak with them.

But lately that longing has lessened. All longing, in fact. And fear. Even my once great dread that I might cease to see the colours has vanished. It is as if through seeing them I have learned to see them. Have learned to be ready to see—passive; not striving to see—active. It keeps me very wide awake. Transparent even. Still.

The colours come daily now. Dizzying. Transforming. Life-giving. My sometimes back-breaking toil in the garden is lightened, made full of wonder, by the incredible colours shooting in the manner of children's sparklers from the plants themselves and from my own work-worn hands. I hadn't realized that I too am part of this vibrating luminescence.

*Later.* I have no idea how long it is since I abandoned these notes. Without seasons to measure its passing, without normal activities—preparations for festivals, occasional outings—time feels longer, shorter or—more curious still—simultaneous, undifferentiated. Future and past fused in the present. Linearity broken.

I had intended to write regularly, but the soybeans keep me busy pretty well all day and by evening I'm usually ready for bed. I'm sorry however to have missed recording the day-by-day changes. They were more or less minor at first. But once the heat began its deadly escalation, the world as we have known it—'our world'—had you been able to put it alongside 'this world'—would have seemed almost entirely different.

No one, I think, could have foreseen the speed with which everything has broken down. For instance, the elaborate plans made to maintain transportation became useless in a matter of months. Private traffic was first curtailed, then forbidden. If a man from another planet had looked in on us, he would have been astonished to see us trapped who were apparently free.

The big changes only really began after the first panic evacuations from the cities. Insulated by concrete, sewer pipes and underground parkades, high density areas responded slowly to the increasing temperatures. But once the heat penetrated their insulations, Gehennas[9] were created overnight and whole populations fled in hysterical exodus, jamming highways in their futile attempts to escape.

Prior to this the Government had not publicly acknowledged a crisis situation. They had taken certain precautions, brought in temporary measures to ease shortages and dealt with new developments on an *ad hoc* basis. Endeavoured to play it cool. Or so it seemed. Now they levelled with us. It was obvious that they must have been planning for months, only awaiting the right psychological moment to take everything over. That moment had clearly come. What we had previously thought of as a free world ended. We could no longer eat, drink, move without permits or coupons. This was full-scale emergency.

Yet nothing proceeds logically. Plans are made only to be remade to accommodate new and totally unexpected developments. The heat, unpatterned as disseminated sclerosis,[10] attacks first here, then there. Areas of high temperature suddenly and inexplicably cool off—or vice versa. Agronomists are doing everything possible to keep crops coming—taking advantage of hot-house conditions to force two crops where one had grown before—frantically playing a kind of agriculture roulette, gambling on the length of time a specific region might continue to grow temperate-zone produce.

Mails have long since stopped. And newspapers. And telephones. As a member of a new privileged class, I have been equipped with a two-way radio and a permit to drive on Government business. Schools have of course closed. An attempt was made for a time to provide lessons on TV. Thankfully the looting and rioting seem over. Those desperate gangs of angry citizens who for some time made life additionally difficult, have now disappeared. We seem at last to understand that we are all in this together.

Life is very simple without electricity. I get up with the light and go to bed as darkness falls. My food supply is still substantial and because of the soybean crop I am all

9  Places of fiery suffering, hells. This New Testament word comes from Hebrew *ge' hinnom*, literally 'valley of Hinnom', a place near Jerusalem where worshippers of foreign gods supposedly sacrificed children by burning; later this place was used continuously to burn refuse, hence the imagery of a burning pit where the damned were forever consumed.

10  That is, like the intermittent pattern occurring in some cases of multiple sclerosis, in which the illness flares up in one area of the body and then goes into remission before showing up in a new location.

right for water. Dexter has adapted well to his new life. He is outdoors less than he used to be and has switched to a mainly vegetable diet without too much difficulty.

***Evening.*** This morning a new order over the radio. All of us with special driving privileges were asked to report to our zone garage to have our tires treated with heat-resistant plastic.

I had not been into town for months. I felt rather as one does on returning home from hospital—that the world is unexpectedly large, with voluminous airy spaces. This was exaggerated perhaps by the fact that our whole zone had been given over to soybeans. Everywhere the same rows of green plants—small pods already formed—march across gardens and boulevards. I was glad to see the climate prove so favourable. But there was little else to make me rejoice as I drove through ominously deserted streets, paint blistering and peeling on fences and houses, while overhead a haze of dust, now always with us, created a green sun.

The prolonged heat has made bleak the little park opposite the garage. A rocky little park, once all mosses and rhododendrons, it is bare now, and brown. I was seeing the day as everyone saw it. Untransmuted.

As I stepped out of my car to speak to the attendant I cursed that I had not brought my insulators. The burning tarmac made me shift rapidly from foot to foot. Anyone from another planet would have wondered at this extraordinary quirk of earthlings. But my feet were forgotten as my eyes alighted a second time on the park across the way. I had never before seen so dazzling and variegated a display of colours. How could there be such prismed brilliance in the range of greys and browns? It was as if the perceiving organ—wherever it is—sensitized by earlier experience, was now correctly tuned for this further perception.

The process was as before: the merest shake and the whole park was 'rainbow, rainbow, rainbow'. A further shake brought the park from *there* to *here*. Interior. But this time the interior space had increased. Doubled. By a kind of instant knowledge that rid me of all doubt, I knew that the garage attendant was seeing it too. *We saw the colours.*

Then, with that slight shift of focus, as if a gelatinous film had moved briefly across my sight, everything slipped back.

I really looked at the attendant for the first time. He was a skinny young man standing up naked inside a pair of loose striped overalls cut off at the knee, *Sidney* embroidered in red over his left breast pocket. He was blond, small-boned, with nothing about him to stick in the memory except his clear eyes which at that moment bore an expression of total comprehension.

'You . . .' we began together and laughed.

'Have you seen them before?' I asked. But it was rather as one would say 'how do you do'—not so much a question as a salutation.

We looked at each other for a long time, as if committing each other to memory.

'Do you know anyone else?' I said.

'One or two. Three, actually. Do you?

I shook my head. 'You are the first. Is it . . . is it . . . always like that?'

'You mean . . . ?' he gestured towards his heart.

I nodded.

'Yes,' he said. 'Yes, it is.'

There didn't seem anything more to talk about. Your right hand hasn't much to say to your left, or one eye to the other. There was comfort in the experience, if comfort is the word, which it isn't. More as if an old faculty had been extended. Or a new one activated.

Sidney put my car on the hoist and sprayed its tires.

***Some time later.*** I have not seen Sidney again. Two weeks ago when I went back he was not there and as of yesterday, cars have become obsolete. Not that we will use that word publicly. The official word is *suspended*.

Strange to be idle after months of hard labour. A lull only before the boys from the Department of Agriculture come back to prepare the land again. I am pleased that the soybeans are harvested, that I was able to nurse them along to maturity despite the scorching sun, the intermittent plagues and the problems with water. Often the pressure was too low to turn the sprinklers and I would stand, hour after hour, hose in hand, trying to get the most use from the tiny trickle spilling from the nozzle.

Sometimes my heart turns over as I look through the kitchen window and see the plants shrivelled and grotesque, the baked earth scored by a web of fine cracks like the glaze on a plate subjected to too high an oven. Then it comes to me in a flash that of course, the beans are gone, the harvest is over.

The world is uncannily quiet. I don't think anyone had any idea of how much noise even distant traffic made until we were without it. It is rare indeed for vehicles other than Government mini-cars to be seen on the streets. And there are fewer and fewer pedestrians. Those who do venture out move on their thick insulators with the slow gait of rocking-horses. Surreal and alien, they heighten rather than lessen one's sense of isolation. For one *is* isolated. We have grown used to the sight of helicopters like large dragon-flies hovering overhead—addressing us through their PA systems, dropping supplies—welcome but impersonal.

Dexter is my only physical contact. He is delighted to have me inside again. The heat is too great for him in the garden and as, officially, he no longer exists, we only go out under cover of dark.

The order to destroy pets, when it came, indicated more clearly than anything that had gone before, that the Government had abandoned hope. In an animal-loving culture, only direct necessity could validate such an order. It fell upon us like a heavy pall.

When the Government truck stopped by for Dexter, I reported him dead. Now that the welfare of so many depends upon our co-operation with authority, law-breaking is a serious offence. But I am not uneasy about breaking this law. As long as he remains healthy and happy, Dexter and I will share our dwindling provisions.

No need to be an ecologist or dependent on non-existent media to know all life is dying and the very atmosphere of our planet is changing radically. Already no birds sing in the hideous hot dawns as the sun, rising through a haze of dust, sheds its curious bronze-green light on a brown world. The trees that once gave us shade stand leafless now in an infernal winter. Yet as if in the masts and riggings of ships, St Elmo's fire[11] flickers and shines in their high branches, and bioplasmic pyrotechnics light the dying soybeans. I am reminded of how the ghostly form of a limb remains attached to the body from which it has been amputated. And I can't help thinking of all the people who don't see the colours, the practical earth-touchers with only their blunt senses to inform them. I wonder about J. and if, since we last talked, she has perhaps been able to see the colours too. But I think not. After so many years of friendship, surely I would be able to sense her, had she broken through.

***Evening. . . ?*** The heat has increased greatly in the last few weeks—in a quantum leap. This has resulted immediately in two things: a steady rising of the sea level through-out the world—with panic reactions and mild flooding in coastal areas; and, at last, a noticeably higher air temperature. It is causing great physical discomfort.

It was against this probability that the authorities provided us with insulator spray. Like giant cans of pressurized shaving cream. I have shut all rooms but the kitchen and by concentrating my insulating zeal on this one small area, we have managed to keep fairly cool. The word is relative, of course. The radio has stopped giving temperature readings and I have no thermometer. I have filled all cracks and crannies with the foaming plastic, even applied a layer to the exterior wall. There are no baths, of course, and no cold drinks. On the other hand I've abandoned clothes and given Dexter a shave and a haircut. Myself as well. We are a fine pair. Hairless and naked.

When the world state of emergency was declared we didn't need to be told that science had given up. The official line had been that the process would reverse itself as inexplicably as it had begun. The official policy—to hold out as long as possible. With this in mind, task forces worked day and night on survival strategy. On the municipal level, which is all I really knew about, everything that could be centralized was. Telephone exchanges, hydro plants, radio stations became centres around which vital activities took place. Research teams investigated the effects of heat on water mains, sewer pipes, electrical wiring; work crews were employed to prevent, protect, or even destroy incipient causes of fires, flood, and asphyxiation.

For some time now the city has been zoned. In each zone a large building has been selected, stocked with food, medical supplies, and insulating materials. We have been provided with zone maps and an instruction sheet telling us to stay where we are until ordered to move to what is euphemistically called our 'home'. When ordered, we are to load our cars with whatever we still have of provisions and medicines and drive off *at once*. Helicopters have already dropped kits with enough gasoline for the trip and a small packet, somewhat surprisingly labelled 'emergency rations', which contains one cyanide capsule—grim reminder that all may not go as the planners plan. We have been asked to mark out maps, in advance, with the shortest route from our house to our 'home', so that in a crisis we will know what we are doing. These instructions are repeated *ad nauseam* over the radio, along with hearty assurances that everything is under control and that there is no cause for alarm. The Government station is now all

---

11 A phenomenon in which a luminous electrical discharge appears as a ball of fire on a ship during a storm.

that remains of our multimedia. When it is not broadcasting instructions, its mainly pre-recorded tapes sound inanely complacent and repetitive. Evacuation Day, as we have been told again and again, will be announced by whistle blast. Anyone who runs out of food before that or who is in need of medical aid is to use the special gas ration and go 'home' at once.

As a long-time preserver of fruits and vegetables, I hope to hold out until E. Day. When that time comes it will be a sign that broadcasts are no longer possible, that contact can no longer be maintained between the various areas of the community, that the process will not reverse itself in time and that, in fact, our world is well on the way to becoming—oh, wonder of the modern kitchen—a self-cleaning oven.

***Spring, Summer, Winter, Fall. What season is it after all?*** I sense the hours by some inner clock. I have applied so many layers of insulating spray that almost no heat comes through from outside. But we have to have air and the small window I have left exposed acts like a furnace. Yet through it I see the dazzling colours; sense my fellow-men.

***Noon.*** The sun is hidden directly overhead. The world is topaz. I see it through the minute eye of my window. I, the perceiving organ that peers through the house's only aperture. We are one, the house and I—parts of some vibrating sensitive organism in which Dexter plays his differentiated but integral role. The light enters us, dissolves us. We are the golden motes in the jewel.

***Midnight.*** The sun is directly below. Beneath the burning soles of my arching feet it shines, a globe on fire. Its rays penetrate the earth. Upward beaming, they support and sustain us. We are held aloft, a perfectly balanced ball in the jet of a golden fountain. Light, dancing, infinitely upheld.

***Who knows how much later.*** I have just 'buried' Dexter.

This morning I realized this hot little cell was no longer a possible place for a dog.

I had saved one can of dog food against this day. As I opened it Dexter's eyes swivelled in the direction of so unexpected and delicious a smell. He struggled to his feet, joyous, animated. The old Dexter. I was almost persuaded to delay, to wait and see if the heat subsided. What if tomorrow we awakened to rain? But something in me, stronger than this wavering self, carried on with its purpose.

He sat up, begging, expectant.

I slipped the meat out of the can.

'You're going to have a really good dinner,' I said, but as my voice was unsteady, I stopped.

I scooped a generous portion of the meat into his dish and placed it on the floor. He was excited, and as always when excited about food, he was curiously ceremonial, unhurried—approaching his dish and backing away from it, only to approach it again at a slightly different angle. As if the exact position was of the greatest importance. It was one of his most amusing and endearing characteristics. I let him eat his meal in his own leisurely and appreciative manner and then, as I have done so many times before,

I fed him his final *bonne bouche* by hand. The cyanide pill, provided by a beneficent Government for me, went down in a gulp.

I hadn't expected it to be so sudden. Life and death so close. His small frame convulsed violently, then collapsed. Simultaneously, as if synchronized, the familiar 'shake' occurred in my vision. Dexter glowed brightly, whitely, like phosphorus. In that dazzling, light-filled moment he was no longer a small dead dog lying there. I could have thought him a lion, my sense of scale had so altered. His beautiful body blinded me with its fires.

With the second 'shake' his consciousness must have entered mine for I felt a surge in my heart as if his loyalty and love had flooded it. And like a kind of ground bass, I was aware of scents and sounds I had not known before. Then a great peace filled me— an immense space, light and sweet—and I realized that this was death. Dexter's death.

But how describe what is beyond description?

As the fires emanating from his slight frame died down, glowed weakly, residually, I put on my insulators and carried his body into the now fever-hot garden. I laid him on what had been at one time an azalea bed. I was unable to dig a grave in the baked earth or to cover him with leaves. But there are no predators now to pick the flesh from his bones. Only the heat which will, in time, desiccate it.

I returned to the house, opening the door as little as possible to prevent the barbs and briars of burning air from entering with me. I sealed the door from inside with foam sealer.

The smell of the canned dog food permeated the kitchen. It rang in my nostrils. Olfactory chimes, lingering, delicious. I was intensely aware of Dexter. Dexter immanent. I contained him as simply as a dish contains water. But the simile is not exact. For I missed his physical presence. One relies on the physical more than I had known. My hands sought palpable contact. The flesh forgets slowly.

Idly, abstractedly, I turned on the radio. I seldom do now as the batteries are low and they are my last. Also, there is little incentive. Broadcasts are intermittent and I've heard the old tapes over and over.

But the Government station was on the air. I tuned with extreme care and placed my ear close to the speaker. A voice, faint, broken by static, sounded like that of the Prime Minister.

'. . . all human beings can do, your Government has done for you.' (Surely not a political speech *now*?) 'But we have failed. Failed to hold back the heat. Failed to protect ourselves against it; to protect you against it. It is with profound grief that I send this farewell message to you all.' I realized that this, too, had been pre-recorded, reserved for the final broadcast. 'Even now, let us not give up hope . . .'

And then, blasting through the speech, monstrously loud in the stone-silent world, the screech of the whistle summoning us 'home'. I could no longer hear the PM's words.

I began automatically, obediently, to collect my few remaining foodstuffs, reaching for a can of raspberries, the last of the crop to have grown in my garden when dawns were dewy and cool and noon sun fell upon us like golden pollen. My hand stopped in mid-air.

*I would not go 'home'.*

The whistle shrilled for a very long time. A curious great steam-driven cry—man's last. Weird that our final utterance should be this anguished inhuman wail.

***The end.*** Now that it is virtually too late, I regret not having kept a daily record. Now that the part of me that writes has become nearly absorbed, I feel obliged to do the best I can.

I am down to the last of my food and water. Have lived on little for some days—weeks, perhaps. How can one measure passing time? Eternal time grows like a tree, its roots in my heart. If I lie on my back I see winds moving in its high branches and a chorus of birds is singing in its leaves. The song is sweeter than any music I have ever heard.

My kitchen is as strange as I am myself. Its walls bulge with many layers of spray. It is without geometry. Like the inside of an eccentric Styrofoam coconut. Yet, with some inner eye, I see its intricate mathematical structure. It is as ordered and no more random than an atom.

My face is unrecognizable in the mirror. Wisps of short damp hair. Enormous eyes. I swim in their irises. Could I drown in the pits of their pupils?

Through my tiny window when I raise the blind, a dead world shines. Sometimes dust storms fill the air with myriad particles burning bright and white as the lion body of Dexter. Sometimes great clouds swirl, like those from which saints receive revelations.

The colours are almost constant now. There are times when, light-headed, I dance a dizzying dance, feel part of that whirling incandescent matter—what I might once have called inorganic matter!

On still days the blameless air, bright as a glistening wing, hangs over us, hangs its extraordinary beneficence over us.

We are together now, united, indissoluble. Bonded.

Because there is no expectation, there is no frustration.

Because there is nothing we can have, there is nothing we can want.

We are hungry of course. Have cramps and weakness. But they are as if in *another body*. Our body is inviolate. Inviolable.

We share one heart.

We are one with the starry heavens and our bodies are stars.

Inner and outer are the same. A continuum. The water in the locks is level. We move to a higher water. A high sea.

A ship could pass through.

1981

# Margaret Avison
## 1918–2007

Born in Galt, Ontario, Margaret Avison was the daughter of a Methodist minister whose pastorship took him and his family (while Avison was still quite young), to Regina and then to Calgary. In 1931, they moved to Toronto, where Avison finished her secondary education and took a BA in English literature at the University of Toronto. There, she began to publish her poetry in campus magazines. After graduating in 1940, she remained in Toronto except for eight months that she spent in Chicago on a 1956 Guggenheim Fellowship to work on her poetry. (The manuscript that eventually became *Winter Sun* took shape in this period.) She held a number of jobs over the years—first working in the University of Toronto library, then as an editor, a social worker, an instructor at University of Toronto's Scarborough campus, and a secretary. She also volunteered extensively, and served as a caregiver in her own family. During this time, she returned for a while to academic studies, taking an MA in 1963 and continuing toward, but not completing, a PhD.

Although she had published poems in journals since the 1930s and was already known as an outstanding poet whose work had appeared in several anthologies, Avison was diffident about publishing a book-length collection. Finally, in 1960, encouraged by friends, she brought out *Winter Sun*, which won a Governor General's Award. Her early poems recall T.S. Eliot and Wallace Stevens in the way they present brilliant surfaces that—because they draw on a wide knowledge of history and poetic tradition, of contemporary events and universal myths— challenge their readers. A.J.M. Smith described her diction in this period as 'erudite, complex, archaic, simple, modern—an amalgam of the scientific and philosophical with the familiar and the new, a high style and low, pillaged and put to work.' Dense and witty, these are poems that can freshly reconsider traditional Christianity by contrasting it with the views of modern science ('Neverness'); can juxtapose the painter's rules of vanishing-point perspective with our everyday view of the world as we move through it ('Perspective'); and can turn the sonnet into a weapon against sonnets ('Butterfly Bones').

In 1962, the American literary magazine *Origin* featured her poetry, printing thirteen poems and a letter to its editor, Cid Corman, in which Avison wrote of the necessity for 'self-effacement' that permits a poet to 'listen long and thoughtfully to the experience of living'. This statement anticipates the most important event in Avison's life. Having witnessed the terrible deprivation of the Depression, she felt her childhood faith had become little more than an abstraction; then, in 1963, she underwent a powerful spiritual experience that led her back to a deeply personal Christianity. (Her account of this conversion can be found in *A Kind of Perseverance*, the published version of the Pascal Lectures on Christianity and the University that she gave at the University of Waterloo in 1992.) By 1968, she left her graduate studies to commit herself to a life of contemplation and service, and began working for the Presbyterian Church Mission; she later worked for the Mustard Seed Mission, until her retirement in 1986. While engaged in this urban missionary service, she continued to write, publishing book reviews and translating poetry, as well as working steadily on her own poems.

The poems that followed her 1963 conversion experience show a change—though religious concerns were already present in her early poetry, as may be seen in 'The Butterfly'—in that there is a more evident striving to close the distance between the human and the divine. The difficulties presented by the earlier poetry, written in a high modernist mode, began to give way, in *The Dumfounding* (1966), to poems written in a more accessible style. Avison's third collection, *Sunblue*, which appeared in 1978, shows still more clearly the influence of her Christianity on both style and content. That book was followed in 1989 by *No Time*, which earned her a second Governor General's Award.

Avison's Christian poetry often reflects her social concerns, particularly in its frequent use of the theme of suffering, which is notably explored in 'The Jo Poems'—a sequence that opens *No Time* and, later, in 'Job: Word and Action', her 1997 meditation on the biblical book that takes up the question of why the innocent and virtuous suffer.

Having long refused to publish a selection of her poems or to reprint those early poems that had been anthologized but not collected in one of her books, she finally permitted a volume of *Selected Poems* to be brought together in 1991. In her last years she published more often, beginning with *Not Yet, but Still* (1997), she also began publishing somewhat more often in her later years. *Concrete and Wild Carrot*, which appeared in 2002, won her the Griffin Poetry Prize. The three-volume edition of her collected poems, *Always Now*, published in 2003–5, includes a number of new poems. In 2006, at the age of eighty-eight, she published the last book of poems to appear in her lifetime, *Momentary Dark*. In 2009, both *Listening: The Last Poems of Margaret Avison* and a memoir, *I Am Here and Not Not-There*, were published posthumously.

# The Butterfly

An uproar,
a spruce-green sky, bound in iron,
the murky sea running a sulphur scum:
I saw a butterfly suddenly;
it clung between the ribs of the storm, wavering
and flung against the battering bone-wind.
I remember it, glued to the grit of that rain-strewn beach
that glowered around it, swallowed its startled design
in the larger iridescence of unstrung dark.

That wild, sour air, the miles of crouching forest, those wings,       10
when all-enveloping air is a
thin glass globe, swirling with storm,
tempt one to the abyss.

The butterfly's meaning, even though smashed.
Imprisoned in endless cycle? No. The meaning!
Can't we stab that one angle[1]
into the curve of space[2] that sweeps beyond
our farthest knowing, out into light's
place of invisibility?

1943; rev. 1989

1 Probably in the sense of perspective. In revising this poem, Avison added a note saying that 'the "angle" seems indicated' in Romans 8:21 ('the creature itself shall also be delivered from the bondage of corruption into the glorious liberty of the children of God') and Ephesians 1:10 (which says God has promised that in 'the fulness of times he might gather together in one all things in Christ')— that is, in two New Testament passages about the possibility of escape from the mortal sphere into an infinite realm of immortality.
2 Wide-ranging discussions of the new science of Einstein's theories were in the air when Avison wrote this poem, including the notion that the universe was not infinite but curved back upon itself.

# Neverness

OR, THE ONE SHIP BEACHED
ON ONE FAR DISTANT SHORE

Old Adam, with his fist-full of plump earth,
His sunbright gaze on his eternal hill[1]
Is not historical:
His tale is never done
For us who know a world no longer bathed
In harsh splendor of economy.
We millions hold old Adam in our thoughts
A pivot for the future-past, a core
Of the one dream that never goads to action
But stains our entrails with nostalgia                    10
And wrings the sweat of death in ancient eyes.

The one-celled plant is not historical.
Leeuwenhoek[2] peered through his magic window
And in a puddle glimpsed the tiny grain
Of firmament that was before the Adam.

I'd like to pull that squinting Dutchman's sleeve
And ask what were his thoughts, lying at night,
And smelling the sad spring, and thinking out
Across the fullness of night air, smelling
The dark canal, and dusty oat-bag, cheese,                20
And wet straw-splintered wood, and rust-seamed leather
And pearly grass and silent deeps of sky
Honey-combed with its million years' of light
And prune-sweet earth
Honey-combed with the silent worms of dark.
Old Leeuwenhoek must have had ribby thoughts
To hoop the hollow pounding of his heart
Those nights of spring in 1600-odd.
It would be done if he could tell it us.

---

1 Eden. 'Old Adam' here refers to the idea of pre-fallen Adam as described in Genesis, the first book of the Bible
—alone in Eden, before the creation of Eve. He is a pivot, or hinge, 'for the future-past' because the archetype
of Adam allows those of us who hold him in mind to look back to an idealized past and form an idea of an
idealized future.
2 Anton van Leeuwenhoek (1632–1723), Dutch naturalist and an important pioneer in microscopy, is considered
the father of microbiology: he was the first to refine the microscope to the point that one-celled organisms were
made visible and the first to observe bacteria, spermatozoa, and blood cells.

The tissue of our metaphysic cells                                          30
No magic window yet has dared reveal.
Our bleared world welters on
Far past the one-cell instant. Points are spread
And privacy is unadmitted prison.

Why, now I know the lust of omnipresence!
You thousands merging lost,
  I call to you
Down the stone corridors that wall me in.

I am inside these days, snug in a job
In one of many varnished offices                                            40
Bleak with the wash of daylight
And us, the human pencils wearing blunt.
Soon I'll be out with you,
Another in the lonely unshut world
Where sun blinks hard on yellow brick and glazed,
On ads in sticky posterpaint
  And fuzzy
   At midday intersections.
The milk is washed down corded throats at noon
Along a thousand counters, and the hands                                    50
That count the nickel from a greasy palm
Have never felt an udder.
  The windy dark
That thrums high among towers and nightspun branches
Whirs through our temples with a dry confusion.
We sprawl abandoned into disbelief
And feel the pivot-picture of old Adam
On the first hill that ever was, alone,
And see the hard earth seeded with sharp snow
And dream that history is done.                                             60

    *

And if that be the dream that whortles[3] out
Into unending night
Then must the pivot Adam be denied
And the whole cycle ravelled and flung loose.
Is this the epoch[4] when the age-old Serpent

---

3 Here, 'hurtles'.
4 For a believer in Christianity, the end of history is described in the Book of Revelation, the last book of the
 bible. A new Eden, restoring that lost by Adam and Eve is promised but only after the final battle of good and
 evil (of the forces of God versus the Serpent — i.e. Satan), the battle of Armageddon.

Must writhe and loosen, slacking out
To a new pool of time's eternal sun?
O Adam, will your single outline blur
At this long last when slow mist wells
Fuming from all the valleys of the earth? 70
Or will our unfixed vision rather blind
Through agony to the last gelid stare
And none be left to witness the blank mist?

1943, 2003


# Perspective

A sport,[1] an adventitious sprout
These eyeballs, that have somehow slipped
The mesh of generations since Mantegna?[2]

Yet I declare, your seeing is diseased
That cripples space. The fear has eaten back
Through sockets to the caverns of the brain
    And made of it a sifty habitation.

We stand beholding the one plain
And in your face I see the chastening
Of its small tapering design 10
That brings up *punkt*.[3]
    (The Infinite, you say,
    Is an unthinkable—and pointless too—
        Extension of that *punkt*.)

But do you miss the impact of that fierce
Raw boulder five miles off? You are not pierced
By that great spear of grass on the horizon?
    You are not smitten with the shock
        Of that great thundering sky?

Your law of optics is a quarrel 20
Of chickenfeet on paper. Does a train
Run pigeon-toed?

1  A mutation, used later in the poem in the more familiar sense of the word; 'adventitious': unneeded; out of place.
2  Andrea Mantegna (1431–1506), Italian painter and engraver famous for his use of perspective of great depth.
3  German for point or dot.

I took a train from here to Ottawa
On tracks that did not meet. We swelled and roared
Mile upon mightier mile, and when we clanged
Into the vasty Station we were indeed
Brave company for giants.

   Keep your eyes though,
You, and not I, will travel safer back
       To Union station.                                        30

Your fear has me infected, and my eyes
That were my sport so long, will soon be apt
Like yours to press out dwindling vistas from
The massive flux massive Mantegna knew
And all its sturdy everlasting foregrounds.

1948,[4] 2003

4 This poem and the two preceding poems received their first book publication in *The Book of Canadian Poetry*,
edited by A.J.M. Smith: 'Neverness' and 'The Butterfly' in the first edition (1943), and 'Perspective' in the
second edition (1948).

## Snow

Nobody stuffs the world in at your eyes.
The optic heart must venture: a jail-break
And re-creation. Sedges[1] and wild rice
Chase rivery pewter. The astonished cinders quake
With rhizomes. All ways through the electric air
Trundle candy-bright disks; they are desolate
Toys if the soul's gates seal, and cannot bear,
Must shudder under, creation's unseen freight.
But soft, there is snow's legend: colour of mourning
Along the yellow Yangtze[2] where the wheel                    10
Spins an indifferent stasis that's death's warning.
Asters of tumbled quietness reveal
Their petals. Suffering this starry blur
The rest may ring your change,[3] sad listener.

1960

1 Grassy plants that grow in marshy areas; they propagate by rhizomes, root-like stems that run under the soil and
from which new plants grow.
2 River in China, the longest in Asia.
3 Change ringing is the ringing of church bells in all the permutations of a given pattern; thus, to ring changes is
to play with permutations.

# Butterfly Bones;
# or Sonnet Against Sonnets

The cyanide jar seals life, as sonnets move
towards final stiffness. Cased in a white glare
these specimens stare for peering boys, to prove
strange certainties. Plane dogsled and safari
assure continuing range. The sweep-net skill,
the patience, learning, leave all living stranger.
Insect—or poem—waits for the fix, the frill
precision can effect, brilliant with danger.
What law and wonder the museum spectres
bespeak is cryptic for the shivery wings,                          10
the world cut-diamond-eyed, those eyes' reflectors,
or herbal grass, sunned motes, fierce listening.
Might sheened and rigid trophies strike men blind
like Adam's lexicon locked in the mind?

1960

# Tennis

Service is joy, to see or swing. Allow
All tumult to subside. Then tensest winds
Buffet, brace, viol and sweeping bow.
Courts are for love and volley. No one minds
The cruel ellipse of service and return,
Dancing white galliards[1] at tape or net
Till point, on the wire's tip, or the long burn-
ing arc to nethercourt marks game and set.
Purpose apart, perched like an umpire, dozes,
Dreams golden balls whirring through indigo.           10
Clay blurs the whitewash but day still encloses
The albinos, bonded in their flick and flow.
Playing in musicked gravity, the pair
Score liquid Euclids in foolscaps of air.[2]

1960

1  Spirited dances in triple time, popular in Elizabethan England.
2  Geometric figures; Euclid was a Greek mathematician of the third century who systematized the essentially
   undefined concepts of point, line, and plane; foolscap is a kind of writing paper, longer than the standard page.

# The Swimmer's Moment

For everyone
The swimmer's moment at the whirlpool comes,
But many at that moment will not say
'This is the whirlpool, then.'
By their refusal they are saved
From the black pit, and also from contesting
The deadly rapids, and emerging in
The mysterious, and more ample, further waters.
And so their bland-blank faces turn and turn
Pale and forever on the rim of suction                    10
They will not recognize.
Of those who dare the knowledge
Many are whirled into the ominous centre
That, gaping vertical, seals up
For them an eternal boon of privacy,
So that we turn away from their defeat
With a despair, not for their deaths, but for
Ourselves, who cannot penetrate their secret
Nor even guess at the anonymous breadth
Where one or two have won:                                20
(The silver reaches of the estuary).

1962


# We the Poor Who Are Always with Us[1]

The cumbering hungry
and the uncaring ill
become too many
try as we will.

Try on and on, still?
In fury, fly
out, smash shards? (And quail
at tomorrow's new supply,
and fail anew to find and smash the why?)

---

1 See Matthew 26:6–11: 'Now when Jesus was in Bethany . . . there came unto him a woman having an alabaster box of very precious ointment, and poured it on his head, as he sat at meat. But when his disciples saw it, they had indignation, saying, "To what purpose is this waste? For this ointment might have been sold for much, and given to the poor." When Jesus understood it, he said unto them, "Why trouble ye the woman? for she hath wrought a good work upon me. For ye have the poor always with you; but me ye have not always."'

It is not hopeless.                                     10
One can crawling move
too there, still free to love
past use, where none survive.

And there is reason in
the hope that then can shine
when other hope is none.

1978


# Job: Word and Action

*Confrontation and Resolution, In* Job[1]

## PROEM[2]

Devastation is the seed-bed
for a new era.
Fifteen months of flood waters
recede at last.
Lazarus dies with the saver of lives
summoned, not responding
in time.
John the Baptist grimaces from
Salome's salver.
Jerusalem's stones and golden                           10
ritual vessels
become flesh and blood, and
know it, in
rubble and in
time.

---

1  The sixth or fifth century Book of Job—found in the Hebrew Scriptures (the Christian Old Testament) and set
   in the (now unknown) land of Uz—deals with the question of why the righteous suffer. Satan, God's adversary,
   seeks to test Job, arguing that he is a figure of exemplary righteousness and piety only because his life is going
   well, and God accepts this challenge. Satan takes away all Job's livestock, servants, and children; when that does
   not deter his faith, he covers Job's body with sores. Though he laments, Job still does not yield to the temptation
   to curse God for his afflictions. Friends come to comfort Job, but their comfort is hollow and they increase his
   misery by suggesting that if God is just then Job must deserve his fate. In the conclusion, God breaks his silence
   and 'answered Job out of the whirlwind', telling him that God's ways are beyond human comprehension.
2  This proem (prologue) uses two biblical narratives as examples of devastation, recasting the first. The story of
   Jesus bringing Lazarus back from the dead by can be found in John 11. The story of the death of John the Baptist
   in Matthew 14:1–12: John, a prophet who has announced Jesus's ministry, is killed by Herod when his step-
   daughter Salome—having been promised whatever she wants as a reward for her dancing—asks for the head of
   John the Baptist on a 'salver' (platter). The concluding six lines are a reference to the destruction of the Jewish
   temple in 70 C.E. and suggest a traditional Christian interpretation of the event—that its 'stones and golden
   ritual vessels' have been superseded by Christianity 'flesh and blood' saviour.

## A BOOK REVIEW

Idle to do this.
Nothing will do
but to r e a d the book.
For one thing, it is
immeasurably better,                                      20
and clearer, and probably more accessible.

Why write about it then?
Because I want to,
to cope with it
in human company.

Words written down
centuries and many centuries
ago in a
faraway land, were properly
special and enigmatic                                     30
in some ways
to be studied and pondered. I
thought. And found
the reading put me in
the midst, not as the self I knew
and certainly not by being manipulated into an other's
identity, but—
on purpose.
I found myself belonging
without surprise, in a new setting.                       40

Anyone who reads this book
risks losing forever any belonging that
he thought defined himself.

Stop here and read the book, if you
want that, not just
a book review.

## THE SUBJECT

Job was a good man.
His biographer gives a
picture of parental and
political reliability.                                     50

When Job refers to his own life
and doings, he elaborates;
the account squares with his three friends'
opinions too.
He was a good man.

(It's not a usual situation
for someone to
define in action what he knows is
perfect polity.)

## THE CONTEXT

If Job did what he said—           60
and I believe him when he
said it, only because
by then his back was
up against the wall—
if in the dismissive eye
of all the disbelievers, also
facing himself, even then,
he said it,
anyone would believe:

> he had not once       70
> failed a hungry man or a
> defenceless child or an
> abandoned woman or
> the stranger at his door.

If he did give what it took
always (and yet
he also said
his table, and all his sons', also his servants'
tables were unfailingly
bountiful—and I believe him),      80
then was he something like a spring-fed brook
irrigating the places that would be
too dry for growing, otherwise;
and did that leave him, like
the other wealthy ones
around—and with the help of
sons and servants—
thriving by giving, able
increasingly to raise more crops?

That would have been a                                           90
government by the richest, then—
who were to be rewarded
for having done the right thing
always.

The book of Job is no 'Utopia' though.


## EVENTS

No seeds of the disasters
that struck were in
the having done it well
surely.
     In one night                                            100
everything was wiped out.
Pain and revulsion and
indignities
only, remained.


## THE REVIEWER SPECULATES

Was there a jaundiced eye watching and
hoping perfection somehow would be marred?
Perhaps the followers of his
example, kindly citizens, might
have been inclined, later, to speculate
about some flaw in him                                           110
that brought him down.

But they were friends.
They waited
for days for some
evidence, first.


## THE ISSUE

A conviction was at stake for
Job—and for his friends.
Job felt it keenly and
for them it mattered too:
to affirm the fairness of                                        120

the ethical order. Perhaps they also
felt an obligation to
blame someone—yes, blame Job.
He and his situation
would not fit, otherwise.

Their rock-solid convictions
steadied them in the rough
sea of their friend's
grief, magnificent courage, and
refusal to despair.                                    130

His struggle to take it, and
to take it in, they did
recognize—but not the
appalling loneliness.

He listened—for
one word to break
in upon the core of his
desolation. Their
speaking only defined
a special doom he stoutly                              140
denied himself
i.e. that he was quite
alone in a
though baffling and beautiful
yet meaninglessly devastating
homeless wilderness.

## THE REVIEWER INTERPOLATES

Your reviewer had expected
something quite different in the
working out of the story.
Visitors spent days counselling                        150
contrition as a therapy,
or equanimity (from
someone in *extremis*!). Distance
lends its own perspective.

Surely God would come and
console His child.
After all, it was Job
who, in the first shock,
nonetheless kept his grip
firm on one reality:                                         160
the One with all
power was in the end the
only trustworthy one.

He was not consoled.

Was Job being honoured then
for enduring?

Was it that either comfort or
compensation would have seemed . . .
patronising?

In any case it only                                          170
made sense—read it yourself and
see what you think—
this way, for me, right now:


## WRATH IS FELT FROM ITS SOURCE

What was pushing the Other
past patience?
      Of course there is no parallel
      anywhere.
      But a person can
      remember standing at a bedside
      ineffectually and                                180
      seeing somebody in dire distress,
      who is isolated by it
      and fights off isolation, and
      gropes for vital contact.
      The person keeping vigil
      trembles within, knowing
      no means but touch, and voice.
      These don't get through.
      Words evaporate then.

## SOLILOQUY

There is no way                                                    190
to open my counsel.
I have been close by
knowing ahead that I would have to choose
powerlessness. No
intervening. And would be
unable to explain—
and all because I
trusted your integrity, Job.

But searing is this
wordlessness.                                                      200

> He was the One to whom
> Job shouted, whispered, always addressing
> the ultimate question.
> Job was tormented to know
> how it could all make sense.

I knew,
but oh, out of Job's range.

                    *    *    *

And so the Lord endured—
His Presence like white sound—
while His child struggled to find foothold           210
in faith, anticipating
deliverance, when the One
who secures all that holds would heed
and show the way and
finally force his battered
misunderstandings to be gone.

## UNDERSTANDING?

No words but His own
word can be
reliable, or safely used
in speculation.                                                    220

When he confused their language
at Babel, and the achievements
crumbled, wasn't that
merciful?[3]

> Somebody said
> (I'm quoting) 'There is a
> danger that everything, through being misnamed
> will be misunderstood', something like that.

I.e. we go on building on our self-
generated constructs, with a self-                                    230
referent valuing. But in a not
self-generated universe.
Is our communal language—
dollars and megabytes and so on—
just a few stages past our
Meccano sets?

Hard-won are the words
we need to truly
converse with someone close
and yet mysterious to us.                                             240


## IMPASSE

Why can't Job glimpse
the truth of feeling on both sides?
And the sufferer
presses, presses.

> It would be unworthy to
> speak some approximating
> word, not a real answer,
> thus negating your respect
> for the true question. Would you break
> the other's integrity?                                              250

---

3 According to Genesis, Chapter 10, 'the whole earth was of one language, and of one speech' before those living
in the ancient city of Babel attempted to build a tower that would reach the heavens. To prevent this, God
decided he would 'confound their language, that they may not understand one another's speech.'

No. You plunge him in
terror, and awe:
through indigo ocean currents, among
shelves where coral builds on
coral. To Job's stunned
absorption, teeming creation flashed and,
intricate and monstrous,
its creatures sublimely
untroubled, burned with their being.
Job awoke then to a                                                         260
newly vivid sense of his littleness.

Someone had after all been
listening to him all through
the times he ranted, through his
desperate appeals. Someone had let
the barriers build up
between you, in pure pain.

It came then.
Job was scathed—although
but briefly—by the wrath.                                                   270

Whatever Job felt when the voice
stormed at him, any reader of this book
is outraged!

> 'Will the one who contends with the Almighty
> correct Him?
> Let him who accuses God
> answer Him!'[4]
> and
> 'Would you discredit My justice
> Would you condemn Me to justify yourself?'                                280

## RESTIVE INTERLUDE

Did you too, reader,
have to put down the book
to let your seething settle?

---

4  Job 40:2; the passage that follows is Job 40:8. (Avison is quoting from the New English Bible.)

E.g. did you too
ask, Was Job wrong
to cry out,
      'If I have sinned
      how do I injure Thee,
      Thou Watcher of the
      hearts of men?'[5]                        290

      or, 'I call for help but
      Thou dost not answer. I stand up
      to plead, but Thou
      sittest aloof'?

And then Job listened

even through that storm, intent,
he listened.

## THE BRIEF WORDS OF ANGER, OVER

      That part breaks off, Magenta
      clouds boil away and blanch.
      The thunderer abruptly, but               300
      wholly encompasses His man:
      plunges him through
      night's plotted skies; then floundering
      light-flooded skies during a March gale;
      vast unvisited snowfields, and
      Galapagos's coast.

      Then, after those
      avalanching wonders,
      every creature's every detail was revealed,
      a centre of this Other's               310
      acute awareness. Equally.
      Prairie crocus or coyote or
      seas braiding around Leviathan.[6]

---

5  Job 7:20; the passage that follows is Job 30:20.
6  A monstrous sea creature, mentioned twice in the Book of Job—the second time in God's concluding speech
   to Job, emphasizing human limitations: 'Can you pull in the leviathan with a fishhook?'

By then Job knew
what it is to be broken and
to be overwhelmed in his littleness by
power, and the glory.

FINIS

It ends up not to be
a biography.
Another Presence turns out to be                               320
dominant—yet without Job's
dwindling.
The other is
beyond any biographer.
When He speaks for Himself
word and action are all but identical.

When were they not
identical?

1997


# Poetry Is

Poetry is always in
unfamiliar territory.

At a ballgame when
the hit most matters
and the crowd is half-standing
already hoarse, then poetry's
eye is astray to a
quiet area to find out
who picks up the bat the runner
flung out of his runway.                    10

Little stuff like that
poetry tucks away in
the little basket of other
scraps. There's the

cradling undergrowth in
the scrub beside a
wild raspberry bush where
a bear lay feet up feeding
but still three rubied berries
glow in the green.                                    20
He had had enough.

Then there's the way
a child's watering can
forgotten in the garden
no faucet, but the far
sky has filled. When sun
shines again it has
become a dragonfly's pretend
skating rink.

Scraps. Who carries the basket?                       30
What will the scraps be used for?
Poetry does not care
what things are for but *is*
willing to listen to
any, if not everyone's,
questions.

It can happen that poetry
basket and all *is*
the unfamiliar territory
that poetry is in.                                    40

2006

# Al Purdy

## 1918–2000

Alfred Wellington Purdy (before settling on 'Al Purdy' he signed his poems 'Alfred W. Purdy' and 'A.W. Purdy') is strongly associated with Prince Edward Country, Ontario, and its environs near the eastern end of Lake Ontario. Descended from what he characterized as 'degenerate Loyalist stock', Purdy was born in Wooler—a small town he claimed was 'mythological because the same village could not now be found'—and attended school in Trenton, until dropping out at the age of sixteen. In the opening lines of 'The Country North of Belleville', Purdy describes his home territory as 'bush land scrub land,' a landscape that can give a man 'some sense of what beauty / is', yet is also 'the country of our defeat'. Though calling it a region 'where the young / leave quickly', he spent most of his life in this landscape of contradictions, making it the subject of his most powerful poetry. As Michael Ondaatje wrote in his foreword to Purdy's final book,

*Cashel and Ameliasburg and Elzevir and Weslemkoon are names we can now put on a literary map alongside the Mississippi and the Strand. For a person of my generation, Al Purdy's poems mapped and named the landscape of Ontario.*

His attachment to place as a source of identity and self-worth can be seen as a desire to articulate the 'true language' that 'speaks from inside / the land itself' ('A Handful of Earth'). In 'Say the Names', the very place-names of Canada become a lyric and moving tribute to the landscape they denominate.

Purdy held a number of casual jobs in the Trenton–Belleville area before deciding, in 1936, to travel west, first hitchhiking, then riding the rails. After working his way across Canada to Vancouver, he returned to Ontario in time for the beginning of the Second World War, enlisting in the Royal Canadian Air Force.

He remained in the RCAF until 1945. In 1941, he married Eurithe Parkhurst, who became his wife of forty-nine years. (She makes many appearances in his poems as his straight man.) After the war, the Purdys lived in Ontario for a few years, and then moved to the West Coast until the late 1950s, when they settled permanently in Ameliasburg, Prince Edward County, on Roblin Lake. Though they frequently travelled away from that home base—Purdy's journeys to the Cariboo country of British Columbia, to Baffin Island, to Hiroshima, to the site of ancient Troy, and throughout Latin America served to reinvigorate his poetry and to provide occasions for further reflections on the relationship of the individual to place—the house Purdy built on Roblin Lake remained the centre of his psychic universe.

Having begun to write poetry in his teens, Purdy paid to have his amateurish first book, *The Enchanted Echo*, published in 1944 (only a few copies still exist to record the fact that his poems once contained lines like, 'Now oft, anon, as in a dream, / Oe'r sculptured heights ascending'). In the 1950s, Purdy produced three more collections of largely derivative work, patterned on traditional models, including that of Rudyard Kipling and Confederation poets Charles G.D. Roberts and Bliss Carman. He credits two influences with bringing about the maturation of his poetic style. One of these was the Vancouver bookseller Steve McIntyre, who, around this time, told him that he couldn't pretend to be a serious writer without having first steeped himself in the great works of the literary tradition. As a result, Purdy became an omnivorous reader and one of the great autodidacts, eventually turning himself into a remarkably erudite man. The other, and balancing, influence was the friendship he formed with the Maritime poet Milton Acorn, whose use of a vigorous and highly vernacular voice and humble subject matter earned him the title of 'the People's Poet'. Acorn's example showed Purdy that knowing the poetic tradition and techniques didn't mean having to write imitations of poems long out of date.

The result was that Purdy made a remarkable breakthrough with the publication of *Poems for All the Annettes* (1962). As Dennis Lee has observed, 'the mature Purdy simply vaults free of three decades of dead-end and marking time, in a riot of exuberant, full-throated energy'. Purdy continued to develop this newly found power in *The Cariboo Horses* (1965), which earned him his first Governor General's Award. *Poems for All the Annettes* was reissued in 1968 in an expanded edition that collected and revised all the earlier poetry Purdy wished to preserve.

Though he became a prolific poet—by the mid-1980s, he estimated that he had written over a thousand poems and published more than seven hundred of them—Purdy was also a stern judge of his own work, publishing only two hundred and fifty poems in his first *Collected Poems* (1986; Governor General's Award). Near the end of his life, Purdy co-edited, with Sam Solecki, *Beyond Remembering*, a somewhat expanded and updated version of the collected poems published posthumously in 2000.

Purdy's success in the 1960s and 1970s introduced into Canada a loose, colloquial style that strongly influenced the generation of poets who came after him, including Bronwen Wallace and Lorna Crozier. In his distinctive voice—relaxed in tone, conversational, unaffected, sometimes gruff, often joking—he wrote not only of the landscape and history of his home place, but also of the jobs he took in his early years, the people he met in his own region of Canada, and his travels. His subject was often his own clumsy encounters with the world, and the 'I' who dominates these poems is a half-autobiographical and half-fictional character Purdy created to embody this awkward humanity.

Because Purdy never stopped maturing as a writer, some of his best work can be found in the five books published in the last years of his nearly sixty-year career: *The Stone Bird* (1981), *Piling Blood* (1984), *A Woman on the Shore* (1990), *Naked with Summer in Your Mouth* (1994), and *To Paris Never Again* (1997). In these later poems, he began to risk a more serious tone, abandoning much of his jokingly ironic manner for more intense and reflective lines.

Since time is as important as place in Purdy's poetry, the connections made in his poems are often temporal—they move from present to past and back again, discovering lost continuities. In poems such as 'Elegy for a Grandfather' and 'Roblin Mills (2)', he seeks to understand the vanished era glimpsed in his childhood. In 1974, Purdy assembled a number of his poems on the Loyalist heritage and history of rural Ontario into a book-length investigation of the past, *In Search of Owen Roblin*. It concludes,

> First my grandfather, then Owen Roblin
> me hanging on their coattails
> gaining strength from them
> Then I went still further back
> trying to enter the minds and bodies
> of the first settlers and pioneers here
> . . . . . . . . . . . . . . . . .
>
> In search of Owen Roblin
> I discovered a whole era
> that was really a backward extension of myself.

In some poems, the time span is much longer than the history of a family or community, because Purdy—like Pratt and many other modern Canadian writers—found the sources of the present in the vestiges of a remote past that still lives and gives meaning in such poems as 'On the Flood Plain' and 'Lament for the Dorsets'. In the latter, Purdy shows the continuing life of a work of art, while at the same time revealing how that work contains its own history, stretching back to the earliest human moments. The most striking feature of these investigations of time and place may be the sense they convey of a mind in motion, a mind synthesizing its environment and looking for connections and meaning—and even (as in 'Trees at the Arctic Circle') a mind still engaged in composing the poem that we are now reading.

In addition to this voluminous body of poetry, Purdy wrote a large number of prose pieces—book reviews, critical essays, anecdotes, and vignettes. A representative selection of these is gathered in *Starting from Ameliasburg* (1995). Near the end of his career, he also wrote a novel, *A Splinter in the Heart* (1990)—an account of how a boy's life is shaken by the 1918 explosion of the British Chemical plant in Trenton, Ontario—and published a memoir, *Reaching for the Beaufort Sea* (1993). Several volumes of his correspondence have also been published, including *Margaret Laurence—Al Purdy: A Friendship in Letters* (1993) and *Yours: The Collected Letters of Al Purdy* (1998).

# The Country North of Belleville

Bush land scrub land—
      Cashel Township and Wollaston
Elzevir Mclure and Dungannon
green lands of Weslemkoon Lake
where a man might have some
      opinion of what beauty
is and none deny him
      for miles—

Yet this is the country of defeat
where Sisyphus[1] rolls a big stone           10
year after year up the ancient hills
picnicking glaciers have left strewn
with centuries' rubble
      backbreaking days
      in the sun and rain
when realization seeps slow in the mind
without grandeur or self-deception in
      noble struggle
of being a fool—

A country of quiescence and still distance       20
a lean land
      not like the fat south
with inches of black soil on
      earth's round belly—
And where the farms are
      it's as if a man stuck
both thumbs in the stony earth and pulled

---

1 As a punishment for his misdeeds, Sisyphus was condemned to Hades, where his task was to roll a large boulder to the top of a hill, at which point it rolled back down. In *Le Mythe de Sisyphe* (1942) Albert Camus depicts him as a symbol of the absurd nature of daily life.

        it apart
        to make room
enough between the trees             30
for a wife
        and maybe some cows and
        room for some
of the more easily kept illusions—
And where the farms have gone back
to forest
        are only soft outlines
        shadowy differences—

Old fences drift vaguely among the trees
        a pile of moss-covered stones     40
gathered for some ghost purpose
has lost meaning under the meaningless sky
        —they are like cities under water
and the undulating green waves of time
        are laid on them—

This is the country of our defeat
        and yet
during the fall plowing a man
might stop and stand in a brown valley of the furrows
        and shade his eyes to watch for the same    50
        red patch mixed with gold
        that appears on the same
        spot in the hills
        year after year
        and grow old
plowing and plowing a ten-acre field until
the convolutions run parallel with his own brain—

And this is a country where the young
        leave quickly
unwilling to know what their fathers know    60
or think the words their mothers do not say—

Herschel Monteagle and Faraday
lakeland rockland and hill country
a little adjacent to where the world is
a little north of where the cities are and
sometime

we may go back there
           to the country of our defeat
Wollaston Elzevir and Dungannon
and Weslemkoon lake land                                    70
where the high townships of Cashel
           McClure and Marmora once were—
But it's been a long time since
and we must enquire the way
           of strangers—


1965, rev. 1972



# Trees at the Arctic Circle
*(Salix cordifolia—Ground Willow)*

They are 18 inches long
or even less
crawling under rocks
grovelling among the lichens
bending and curling to escape
making themselves small
finding new ways to hide
Coward trees
I am angry to see them
like this                                                   10
not proud of what they are
bowing to weather instead
careful of themselves
worried about the sky
afraid of exposing their limbs
like a Victorian married couple

I call to mind great Douglas firs
I see tall maples waving green
and oaks like gods in autumn gold
the whole horizon jungle dark                               20
and I crouched under that continual night
But these
even the dwarf shrubs of Ontario
mock them
Coward trees

And yet—and yet—
their seed pods glow
like delicate grey earrings
their leaves are veined and intricate
like tiny parkas                                         30
They have about three months
to make sure the species does not die
and that's how they spend their time
unbothered by any human opinion
just digging in here and now
sending their roots down down down
And you know it occurs to me
         about 2 feet under
those roots must touch permafrost
ice that remains ice forever                             40
and they use it for their nourishment
they use death to remain alive

I see that I've been carried away
in my scorn of the dwarf trees
most foolish in my judgments
To take away the dignity
         of any living thing
even tho it cannot understand
         the scornful words
is to make life itself trivial                          50
and yourself the Pontifex Maximus[1]
         of nullity
I have been stupid in a poem
I will not alter the poem
but let the stupidity remain permanent
as the trees are
in a poem
the dwarf trees of Baffin Island

PANGNIRTUNG

1967

---

1 The chief priest in ancient Rome; in later use, the Pope.

# Wilderness Gothic

Across Roblin Lake, two shores away,
they are sheathing the church spire
with new metal. Someone hangs in the sky
over there from a piece of rope,
hammering and fitting God's belly-scratcher,
working his way up along the spire
until there's nothing left to nail on—

Perhaps the workman's faith reaches beyond:
touches intangibles, wrestles with Jacob,[1]
replacing rotten timber with pine thews,                    10
pounds hard in the blue cave of the sky,
contends heroically with difficult problems of
gravity, sky navigation and mythopoeia,
his volunteer time and labour donated to God,
minus sick benefits of course on a non-union job—

Fields around are yellowing into harvest,
nestling and fingerling are sky and water borne,
death is yodelling quiet in green woodlots,
and bodies of three young birds have disappeared
in the sub-surface of the new county highway—          20

That picture is incomplete, part left out
that might alter the whole Dürer[2] landscape:
gothic ancestors peer from medieval sky,
dour faces trapped in photograph albums escaping
to clop down iron roads with matched greys:
work-sodden wives groping inside their flesh
for what keeps moving and changing and flashing
beyond and past the long frozen Victorian day.
A sign of fire and brimstone? A two-headed calf
born in the barn last night? A sharp female agony?      30
An age and a faith moving into transition,
the dinner cold and new-baked bread a failure,
deep woods shiver and water drops hang pendant,

---

1  Jacob wrestled with God, or with an angel, until he was given a blessing; see Genesis 32:24–9. In this line 'with' should probably be understood in the sense of 'alongside'.

2  Albrecht Dürer (1471–1528), painter and engraver, the greatest artist of the northern Renaissance; caught up in a period of intense change, and influential in bringing Italian Renaissance styles into Germany, Dürer also maintained some of the dominant Gothic style of earlier German art.

double yolked eggs and the house creaks a little—
Something is about to happen. Leaves are still.
Two shores away, a man hammering in the sky.
Perhaps he will fall.

1968

## Lament for the Dorsets
*(Eskimos extinct in the 14th century* AD*)* [1]

Animal bones and some mossy tent rings
scrapers and spearheads     carved ivory swans
all that remains of the Dorset giants
who drove the Vikings back to their long ships
talked to spirits of earth and water
—a picture of terrifying old men
so large they broke the backs of bears
so small they lurk behind bone rafters
in the brain of modern hunters
among good thoughts and warm things                    10
and come out at night
to spit on the stars

The big men with clever fingers
who had no dogs and hauled their sleds
over the frozen northern oceans
awkward giants
               killers of seal
they couldn't compete with little men
who came from the west with dogs
Or else in a warm climatic cycle                       20
the seals went back to cold waters
and the puzzled Dorsets scratched their heads
with hairy thumbs around 1350 AD
—couldn't figure it out
went around saying to each other
plaintively
          'What's wrong? What happened?
          Where are the seals gone!'
And died

1  The date of the mysterious disappearance of the Dorset, who were probably absorbed or expelled by the Thule Inuit,
   is now placed at around AD 1000, during a gradual warming period that began around then. To preserve good
   relations with the spirits of the animals they hunted, Dorset craftsmen carved finely detailed miniature replicas.

Twentieth-century people                                       30
apartment dwellers
executives of neon death
warmakers with things that explode
—they have never imagined us in their future
how could we imagine them in the past
squatting among the moving glaciers
six hundred years ago
with glowing lamps?
As remote or nearly
as the trilobites[2] and swamps                                40
when coal became
or the last great reptile hissed
at a mammal the size of a mouse
that squeaked and fled

Did they ever realize at all
what was happening to them?
Some old hunter with one lame leg
a bear had chewed
sitting in a caribou-skin tent
—the last Dorset?                                              50
Let's say his name was Kudluk
and watch him sitting there
carving 2-inch ivory swans
for a dead grand-daughter
taking them out of his mind
the places in his mind
where pictures are
He selects a sharp stone tool
to gouge a parallel pattern of lines
on both sides of the swan                                      60
holding it with his left hand
bearing down and transmitting
his body's weight
from brain to arm and right hand
and one of his thoughts
turns to ivory
The carving is laid aside
in beginning darkness
at the end of hunger

---

2  Fossil marine arthropods from the Paleozoic era (600 million to 230 million years ago).

and after a while wind                                    70
blows down the tent and snow
begins to cover him

After 600 years
the ivory thought
is still warm

1968


# At the Quinte Hotel

I am drinking
I am drinking beer with yellow flowers
in underground sunlight
and you can see that I am a sensitive man
And I notice that the bartender is a sensitive man too
so I tell him about his beer
I tell him the beer he draws
is half fart and half horse piss
and all wonderful yellow flowers
But the bartender is not quite                            10
so sensitive as I supposed he was
the way he looks at me now
and does not appreciate my exquisite analogy
Over in one corner two guys
are quietly making love
in the brief prelude to infinity
Opposite them a peculiar fight
enables the drinkers to lay aside
their comic books and watch with interest
as I watch with interest                                  20
A wiry little man slugs another guy
then tracks him bleeding into the toilet
and slugs him to the floor again
with ugly red flowers on the tile
three minutes later he roosters over
to the table where his drunk friend sits
with another friend and slugs both
of em ass-over-electric-kettle
so I have to walk around
on my way for a piss                                      30

Now I am a sensitive man
so I say to him mildly as hell
'You shouldn'ta knocked over that good beer
with them beautiful flowers in it'
So he says to me 'Come on'
So I Come On
like a rabbit with weak kidneys I guess
like a yellow streak charging
on flower power I suppose
& knock the shit outa him & sit on him                    40
(he is just a little guy)
and say reprovingly
'Violence will get you nowhere this time chum
Now you take me
I am a sensitive man
and would you believe I write poems?'
But I could see the doubt in his upside down face
in fact in all the faces
'What kinda poems?'
'Flower poems'                                            50
'So tell us a poem'
I got off the little guy but reluctantly
for he was comfortable
and told them this poem
They crowded around me with tears
in their eyes and wrung my hands feelingly
for my pockets for
it was a heart-warming moment for Literature
and moved by the demonstrable effect
of great Art and the brotherhood of people I remarked     60
'—the poem oughta be worth some beer'
It was a mistake of terminology
for silence came
and it was brought home to me in the tavern
that poems will not really buy beer or flowers
or a goddam thing
and I was sad
for I am a sensitive man

1968

# Roblin's Mills (2)[1]

The wheels stopped
and the murmur of voices
behind the flume's tremble
stopped
          and the wind-high ships
that sailed from Rednersville[2]
to the sunrise ports of Europe
are delayed somewhere
in a toddling breeze
The black millpond                                        10
turns an unreflecting eye
to look inward
like an idiot child
locked in the basement
when strangers come
whizzing past on the highway
above the dark green valley
a hundred yards below
The mill space is empty
even stones are gone                                      20
where hands were shaken
and walls enclosed laughter
saved up and brought here
from the hot fields
where all stories
are rolled into one
And white dust floating
above the watery mumble
and bright human sounds
to shimmer among the pollen                               30
where bees dance now
Of all these things
no outline remains
no shadow on the soft air
no bent place in the heat glimmer
where the heavy walls pressed
And some of those who vanished

---

1  Originally published as 'Roblin's Mills: Circa 1842'. Purdy later retitled this poem 'Roblin's Mills (2)' to distinguish it from an earlier poem entitled 'Roblin's Mills'. Purdy used 'Roblin's Mills (2)' as the conclusion of his long poem *In Search of Owen Roblin* (1974).
2  Town on the Bay of Quinte, not far from Roblin Mills.

lost children of the time
kept after school
left alone in a graveyard                    40
who may not change
or ever grow six inches
in one hot summer
or turn where the great herons
graze the sky's low silver
—stand between the hours
in a rotting village
near the weed-grown eye
that looks into itself
deep in the black crystal                     50
that holds and contains
the substance of shadows
manner and custom
          of the inarticulate
departures and morning rumours
gestures and almost touchings
announcements and arrivals
gossip of someone's marriage
when a girl or tired farm woman
whose body suddenly blushes                    60
beneath a faded house dress
with white expressionless face
turns to her awkward husband
to remind him of something else
The black millpond
                    holds them
movings and reachings and fragments
the gear and tackle of living
under the water eye
all things laid aside                          70
          discarded
                    forgotten
but they had their being once
and left a place to stand on

1968, rev. 1972

# Elegy for a Grandfather [1986]

Well, he died I guess. They said he did.
His wide whalebone hips will make a prehistoric barrow
men of the future may find or maybe not:
where this man's relatives ducked their heads
in real and pretended sorrow
for the dearly beloved gone thank Christ to God,
after a bad century, a tough big-bellied Pharaoh,
with a deck of cards in his pocket and a Presbyterian grin—

Maybe he did die, but the boy didn't understand it;
the man knows now and the scandal never grows old            10
of a happy lumberjack who lived on rotten whiskey,
and died of sin and Quaker oats age 90 or so.
But all he was was too much for any man to be,
a life so full he couldn't include one more thing,
nor tell the same story twice if he'd wanted to,
and didn't and didn't—

Just the same he's dead. A sticky religious voice
folded his century sideways to get it out of sight,
and lowered him into the ground like someone still alive
who had to be handled very carefully,                        20
even after death he made people nervous:
and earth takes him as it takes more beautiful things:
populations of whole countries,
museums and works of art,
and women with such a glow
it makes their background vanish
                        they vanish too,
and Lesbos' singer[1] in her sunny islands
stopped when the sun went down—

No, my grandfather was decidedly unbeautiful,               30
260 pounds of scarred slag,
barnraiser and backwoods farmer:
become an old man in a one-room apartment
over a drygoods store,
become anonymous as a dead animal
whose chemicals may not be reconstituted.

---

1 Lesbos, an island in the northeastern Aegean Sea, was the home of the ancient Greek poet Sappho. Though only
  fragments remain, her passionate writing has been called the greatest lyric poetry of ancient Greece.

There is little doubt that I am the sole
repository of his remains: which consist of
these flashing pictures in my mind,
which I can't bequeath to anyone,                                    40
which stop here: juice and flavour
of the old ones, whose blood runs thin
in us: mustard, cayenne, ammonia,
brimstone (trace only above his grave)
                    —a dying soup-stained giant
I will never let go of—not yet.
He scared hell out of me sometimes,
but sometimes I caught myself, fascinated,
overhearing him curse God in my own arteries:
even after death I would never dare                                 50
admit to loving him, which he'd despise,
and his ghost haunt the poem forever
(which is an exaggeration of course,
but he liked those)—

1956; rev. 1986



## For Steve McIntyre
(1912–1984)

He said I was ignorant
and didn't mince words about it
my deficiency was GREAT BOOKS
—so I read Proust Woolf Cervantes
Dostoyevsky Joyce the works
and they were just as boring
as I'd always suspected
—but one night just before sleep
words were suddenly shining in the dark
like false teeth in a glass of water                                10
like the laughter of Australopithecus
mocking other beasts surrounding his tree
like *Thalassa* for Xenophon and the Greeks
like Joshua's trumpet at Jericho
like sunlight under the bedsheets
with her arms around my neck
And I climbed down from the tree
instructed Darwin's non-evoluted

critters to get lost
delighted in the Black Sea with Xenophon                    20
and the Greek Ten Thousand
and stole the wavetips' green diamonds
for my ballpoint—
All because of Steve McIntyre
a dead man who hears nothing
not *Thalassa* nor Joshua's trumpet
not Australopithecus inventing laughter
nor the tenderness I softly withdraw
from my breast in the form of
words that say *Goodbye*                                    30
beyond his hearing—

1986


# On the Flood Plain

Midnight:  ·
it's freezing on the lake
and wind whips ice eastward
but most of the water remains open
—and stars visit earth
tumbled about like floating candles
on the black tumulus[1]
then wind extinguishes the silver fire
but more flash down
and even those reflections reflect                          10
on the sides of waves
even the stars' reflections reflect stars

Ice:
far older than earth
primordial as the Big Bang
—cold unmeasured by Celsius and Fahrenheit
quarrelling about it on a Jurassic shingle[2]

---

1  An ancient burial mound or barrow.
2  That is, a stretch of gravelled beach from the Jurassic period (the second period of the Mesozoic Era, 65 million
   to 230 million years ago). 'Pangaea' is the name given, in theories of continental drift, to a vast 'supercontinent',
   comprising all the continental crust of the earth, postulated to have existed in late Palaeozoic and Mesozoic
   times before it broke into two smaller, but still immense, landmasses: Laurasia and Gondwanaland.

—before Pangaea and Gondwanaland
arrive here in the 20th century
born like a baby                                          20
under the flashlight beam
Bend down and examine the monster
and freeze for your pains
—tiny oblong crystals
seem to come from nowhere
little transparent piano keys
that go tinkle tinkle tinkle
while the wind screams
—and you feel like some shivering hey
presto god grumbling at his fucked-up weather            30
hurry indoors hurry indoors to heaven

People have told us we built too near the lake
'The flood plain is dangerous' they said
and no doubt they know more about it than we do
—but here wind pressed down on new-formed ice
trembles it like some just-invented musical instrument
and that shrieking obbligato to winter
sounds like the tension in a stretched worm
when the robin has it hauled halfway out of the lawn
I stand outside                                          40
between house and outhouse
feeling my body stiffen in fossilized rigor mortis
and listening
thinking
this is the reason we built on the flood plain
damn right
the seriousness of things beyond your understanding

Whatever I have not discovered and enjoyed
is still waiting for me
and there will be time                                   50
but now are these floating stars on the freezing lake
and music fills the darkness
holds me there listening
—it's a matter of separating these instants from others
that have no significance
so that they keep reflecting each other
a way to live and contain eternity
in which the moment is altered and expanded

my consciousness hung like a great silver metronome
suspended between stars                                          60
on the dark lake
and time pours itself into my cupped hands shimmering

1990


## Grosse Isle

> *Look, stranger, at this island now*
> *The leaping light for your delight discovers*

—W.H. Auden

Look stranger
a diseased whale in the St Lawrence
this other island than Auden's
dull grey when the weather is dull grey
and an east wind brings rain
this Appalachian outcrop
a stone ship foundered in the river estuary
now in the care and keeping of Parks Canada
—a silence here like no mainland silence
at Cholera Bay where the dead bodies                            10
awaited high tide and the rough kindness
of waves sweeping them into the dark—

Look stranger
at this other island
weedgrown graves in the three cemeteries
be careful your clothes don't get hooked
by wild raspberry canes and avoid the poison ivy
—here children went mad with cholera fever
and raging with thirst they ran into the river
their parents following a little way                           20
before they died themselves
—and don't stumble over the rusted tricycle
somehow overlooked at the last big cleanup
or perhaps left where it is for the tourists?

Look stranger
where the sea wind sweeps westward
down the estuary

this way the other strangers came
potato-famine Irish and Scotch crofters
refugees from the Highland clearances                                    30
and sailing ships waited here
to remove their corpses
and four million immigrants passed through
—now there's talk of a Health Spa and Casino
we could situate our billboard
right under the granite cross by the river:
          UNLIMITED INVESTMENT OPPORTUNITIES

Look stranger
see your own face reflected in the river
stumble up from the stinking hold                                          40
blinded by sunlight and into the leaky dinghy
only half-hearing the sailors taunting you
          'Shanty Irish! Shanty Irish!'
gulp the freshening wind and pinch yourself
trying to understand if the world is a real place
stumble again and fall when you reach the shore
and bless this poisoned earth
but stranger no longer
for this is home

1994


## Say the Names

—say the names say the names
and listen to yourself
an echo in the mountains
Tulameen     Tulameen
say them like your soul
was listening and overhearing
and you dreamed you dreamed
you were a river
and you were a river
Tulameen     Tulameen                                                      10
—not the flat borrowed imitations
of foreign names
not Brighton Windsor Trenton
but names that ride the wind

Spillimacheen and Nahanni
Kleena Kleene and Horsefly
Illecillewaet and Whachamacallit
Lillooet and Kluane
Head-Smashed-In Buffalo Jump
and the whole sky falling                                       20
when the buffalo went down
Similkameen and Nahanni
names that make you an exile
if you ever wander elsewhere
'the North as a deed and forever'[1]
where we lost our way one evening
and the spines of Devil's Club
stuck to our lost behinds
— say them say them remember
Kleena Kleene    Nahanni                                        30
Similkameen and Buffalo Jump
say the names
soft fermenting syllables
in the brain's closet
the memory of white shadows
spangling the river bottom
where moonlight remembers sunlight
say the names
as if they were your soul
lost among the mountains                                        40
a soul you mislaid
and found again rejoicing
and slipped it quickly away
into your breast pocket
till the heart stops beating
Tulameen    Tulameen

say the names

1999, rev. 2000[2]

---

1  From A.J.M. Smith's 'To Hold in a Poem', which asks for 'words / As crisp and white / As our snow' to contain
   what is 'Lonely, unbuyable, dear, / The North, as a deed, and forever'.
2  Purdy revised this poem in his last weeks, for a limited edition broadside.

# Raymond Souster

## b. 1921

Raymond Holmes Souster was born and educated in Toronto. After high school, he began a career in banking, which—with the exception of four years' wartime service in the RCAF—he continued until his retirement in 1985. Over the last sixty-five years, Souster has, through his poetry, chronicled his own life as a middle-class, white-collar worker, as well as the lives of the people he sees on his way to work, over the lunch counter, and in his Toronto neighbourhood.

Souster began writing poetry as a boy: his first poem, which he has described as 'a typical Lampman sonnet', was published in the *Toronto Star* in the early 1930s. During the Second World War, his poems appeared in John Sutherland's *First Statement* (1942–5); in *Direction* (1943–6), a little magazine he edited with Bill Goldberg from their RCAF station in Sydney, Nova Scotia; and in the anthology *Unit of Five* (1944). After the war, he published his first two books, *When We Are Young* (1946) and *Go to Sleep World* (1947). Then, frustrated over what he felt was a growing bias for safe, conventional poetry in Canadian literary magazines and presses, he started the journal *Contact* (1952–4). In its first issue, Louis Dudek set the tone with an article urging young Canadians to contribute to the shaping of modernist poetry in Canada. The journal published the poetry of such Canadians—including Irving Layton and Phyllis Webb, in addition to Dudek—and of American poets as the Black Mountain writers Charles Olson and Robert Creeley, as well as poems in translation by contemporary Europeans. With Dudek and Layton, Souster also began Contact Press (1952–67), a loosely organized publishing operation that not only printed the work of its editors—its first book, *Cerberus* (1952), was an anthology of their own poetry—but also that of writers such as D.G. Jones, F.R. Scott, W.W.E. Ross, and Eli Mandel, along with the first full-length books

of Gwendolyn MacEwen and Margaret Atwood. In 1957, Souster began a new journal, *Combustion* (1957–60), to replace Cid Corman's *Origin*, a US literary magazine that had temporarily ceased publication. Like *Contact* and *Origin*, *Combustion* was an international magazine, publishing Canadians alongside the innovative poets of Europe and Britain, and showcasing emerging American poets from the west coast, the Beat movement, and the Black Mountain School. Souster's support of new poetry in Canada also manifested itself in his anthology *New Wave Canada* (1966), which announced a new generation in Canadian poetry by bringing together poets of the *Tish* movement (including Daphne Marlatt and Fred Wah) with the work of young Ontario poets such as Victor Coleman, Roy MacSkimming, David McFadden, bpNichol, and Michael Ondaatje.

After Contact Press ceased publication, Souster co-edited several school anthologies and helped to found the League of Canadian Poets—serving as its first president from 1967 to 1972. Since the mid-1960s, collections of his own poetry have appeared under the imprint of various presses, including *The Colour of the Times* (1964, Governor General's Award), *As Is* (1967), *Selected Poems* (1972), *Extra Innings* (1977), *Hanging In* (1979), *Jubilee of Death* (1984), *Running Out the Clock* (1991), and *Close to Home* (1996). Oberon Press has published a uniform edition (through his 2000 book *Of Time and Toronto*) of his collected poems in ten volumes—comprising more than 2,500 pages of poetry.

Souster feels that poetry belongs not in the study but—as one of the poems below declares—'outdoors', on the streets. He depends upon intuitive, empathetic observations of external circumstances and outward behaviour to animate his work. As he once said in an interview with Jon Pearce,

*When I write a poem, I'm first of all concerned with my own reaction to the subject matter, how it affects me, and I'm also concerned with communicating the emotion that subject matter arouses in me.* (Twelve Voices, 1980)

Rather than relying upon rhetoric or conceptualized 'ideas', Souster usually employs images (sometimes combined with brief narrative). His technique owes much to that of the Imagist poets William Carlos Williams and W.W.E. Ross (who was one of the first modernist poets in Canada).

Although Souster has always shown interest in experimental writing, his own poetry has never departed much from its Imagist origins. Except for some experiments with the long poem ('Death Chants for Mr. Johnson's America', 'Pictures of a Long Lost World'), and the novel (he published, under the pseudonyms Raymond Holmes and John Holmes, two novels dealing with the Second World War), he has written mainly short, unadorned poems—often devoted to a single observation—that are colloquial in tone and diction. While each is carefully crafted in itself, when viewed cumulatively as part of an enormous body of work, the individual poems take an additional dimension, having the character of journal entries in an ongoing chronicle of a writer's life.

Many of Souster's poems make social statements. They show the dehumanization and degradation that technological society inflicts upon its members, and the need to seek out the simple pleasures of nature and of the pre-industrial past. Souster's impulse, more reportorial than revolutionary, acknowledges the imperfections of the world but offers no plan for social change. In contrast to Layton and Dudek, proclaiming, polemicizing, or theorizing, has never been consistent with his famous personal reticence. Although very active in writing and publishing, he has remained almost invisible as a physical presence in the world—refusing even to attend a gala evening that was held in his honour.

Baseball has been a frequent source of images for Souster. In 'Waiting for the Poem to Come through' (from *Extra Innings*) the poet-as-batter, waiting for the pitch, may tell the reader more about Souster's poetics and philosophy of life than any discursive statement can:

> *Then you're ready,*
> *the umpire behind you*
> *growls 'play ball'*
> *you give that last little wiggle,*
> *look straight ahead at the kid*
> *standing tall on the rubber,*
> *murmur under your breath*
> *'throw it over and duck',*
>
> *wait for the poem to come whipping*
> *curving*
> *sinking in.*

## The Penny Flute

On the side street as we came along it in the darkness,
an old man, hat in front of him on the pavement,
was playing a penny flute.
                    The sound was small and sweet,
almost a whisper beside the heavy beat
of the cloth factory's machinery, across the street,
(as if somehow he wasn't playing
for an audience at all, but only for himself).

We wondered who he was, and how long he'd been standing
piping that thin string of music.                                               10
                                 But we were late for where
   we were going,
and young and impatient: we really didn't have time for old
   men and thin, lonely tunes,
especially tunes played on a penny flute. . . .

1941; rev. 1980


## At Split Rock Falls

At Split Rock Falls I first saw my death
in a sudden slip the space of a breath;
my windmill body met the crazy shock
of uncounted centuries of stubborn rock.

At Split Rock Falls I saw green so green
it was almost as though grass had never been;
in the dappled depth of that pure pool
my eyes looked at me, recognized a fool.

From Split Rock Falls as I came away
the hint of a rainbow topped the spray,                                         10
while the trees tossed down: O let nothing matter
if not beautiful, swift as that singing water!

1958


## Like the Last Patch of Snow

That's the way
we've got to hang on—

like the last patch of snow
clinging to the hillside
crouching at the wood edge
with April done

dirty-white
but defiant

lonely
fighting death.                                              10

1964


## Get the Poem Outdoors

Get the poem outdoors under any pretext,
reach through the open window if you have to,
    kidnap it right off the poet's desk,
then walk the poem in the garden, hold it up
    among the soft yellow garlands of the
    willow,
command of it no further blackness, no silent
    cursing at midnight, no puny whimpering
    in the endless small hours, no more
    shivering in the cold-storage room of the          10
    winter heart,
tell it to sing again, loud and then louder so it
    brings the whole neighbourhood out, but
    who cares,
ask of it a more human face, a new tenderness,
    even the sentimental allowed between the
    hours of nine to five,
then let it go, stranger in a fresh green world, to
    wander down the flower beds, let it go to
    welcome each bird that lights on the still          20
    barren mulberry tree.

1969


## Queen Anne's Lace

It's a kind of flower
that if you didn't know it
you'd pass by the rest of your life.

But once it's pointed out
you'll look for it always,
even in places
where you know it can't possibly be.

You will never tire
of bending over to examine,
to marvel at this,                                        10
the shyest filigree of wonder
born among grasses.

You will imagine poems
as brief, as spare,
so natural with themselves
as to take breath away.

1972


## Trying One on for Size

'What made me, John Stirling Cameron,
decide to cut through Mount Pleasant Cemetery
that balmy summer evening? For one thing
I was late getting out from the bank
with a walk ahead of me to Well's Hill,
a good step or two; and besides,
the soft green of the grass, the full-leafed trees,
seemed to beckon through the still-open gates.

'So I found myself wandering
off the road inside, strolling among the gravestones,               10
trying for a short-cut to Yonge Street.
And so busy trying to read
the more interesting inscriptions,
that I wasn't watching where I was going
to say the least. Suddenly my feet
seemed to leave the good feel of earth,
my body dropping like a stone
tossed down an unused well.
                            Luckily
it was only a half-dug grave                                          20

that had set its trap for me;
I landed on soft sand only five feet down,
which meant I was able (only just)
to pull myself out again.

'So I brushed myself off,
walked on as if nothing had happened,
still, couldn't help laughing to myself
thinking of the possibilities:
                        one of which was
that the hole being deeper I'd have had to stay there          30
the whole night through, then sweat it out
till someone came or heard me in the morning—
which wasn't that much worse, I decided,
than crouching in a fox-hole overnight
the way I'd been doing in Europe
just the year before . . .
                while a much worse misfortune
(a long shot but still conceivable),
could have been breaking my neck, then having my body found
by the grave-diggers next day when they came to finish their job    40
(the corpse having shown up much too early
for its own decent burial . . .).

'Anyway, that's enough of my raving, my rambling. . . .
As for you who may have your own grave-plots ready,
I simply say I'm a mile ahead of you,
because last night I took my trial run, so to speak,
lay back on the earth well down in the earth,
was, one could say, rudely measured out for the grave. . . .'

1979

# Mavis Gallant

## b. 1922

Mavis Gallant, born Mavis de Trafford Young in Montreal, entered, at age four, a strict French-Catholic boarding school where, as a Protestant child of English-speaking parents, she was an anomaly. That experience may have initiated the sense of being an outsider that became part of her life and a theme in her stories. Certainly, her father's death when she was ten and her peripatetic education thereafter—she attended seventeen schools in Canada and the United States—prepared her for an independent and, by choice, solitary life. After high school, she worked briefly for the National Film Board and then as a reporter for the *Montreal Standard*. She began to write fiction during these years but was at first disinclined to submit her work for publication. Two of her stories—'Good Morning and Goodbye' and 'Three Brick Walls'—were published in 1944 in the Montreal magazine *Preview* after a friend forwarded them to its editor, Patrick Anderson.

In 1950, after a brief marriage, Gallant committed herself to becoming a full-time writer. She quit reporting and left Canada for Europe, settling eventually in Paris. Before leaving, she submitted a story to *The New Yorker*, which returned it—saying that it was too Canadian for their American readers—but asked to see more of her work. In 1951, *The New Yorker* published her second submission; subsequently, most of her stories—even the 'Canadian' ones—appeared first in that magazine. Her highly polished style, her pervasive but understated irony, and her urbane tone were influential in defining what came to be thought of as the '*New Yorker* story' and soon established her as one of the leading writers of short fiction in English; as Robert Fulford suggested, 'One begins comparing her best moments to those of major figures in literary history. Names like Henry James, Chekhov, and George Eliot dance across the mind.'

Substantial collections of Gallant's new fiction appeared in each of the next five decades: *The Other Paris* (1956); *My Heart Is Broken* (1964); *The Pegnitz Junction* (1973), which linked stories to investigate the sources of German fascism; *Overhead in a Balloon: Stories of Paris* (1985); and *Across the Bridge* (1993). Although her early work was neglected in Canada, the 1974 selection Robert Weaver made for the New Canadian Library, *The End of the World and Other Stories*, helped to bring recognition at home. Many of her stories are set in Paris, but a substantial number are about Canadians both at home and abroad, and these (including the story reprinted here) were gathered in a volume called *Home Truths* (1981), which won a Governor General's Award.

In 1988, Gallant brought together her previously uncollected stories from the 1950s and 60s in *In Transit*. In 1994, Mordecai Richler edited a selection of her fiction—*The Moslem Wife and Other Stories* (1994)—for which he also provided an afterword. In 1996, Gallant drew together all the short fiction she wished to preserve at that time in *The Selected Stories*, a nine-hundred-page volume of over fifty stories that demonstrates her extraordinary accomplishment. In 2002, Michael Ondaatje put together a new selection as *Paris Stories*. In 2003, the American writer Russell Banks edited and wrote an introduction for a selection—*Varieties of Exile*—that emphasized the theme of exile in her work, and the following year, Banks edited *Montreal Stories*, a companion to Ondaatje's selection.

Although Gallant clearly prefers short fiction to longer forms (she has described writing a story as 'like being on tip-toe the whole time . . . It's very tense'), she has published two novels, *Green Water, Green Sky* (1959) and *A Fairly Good Time* (1970). Her play, *What Is To Be Done* (published in 1984), was produced by Toronto's Tarragon Theatre in 1982.

Gallant occasionally writes non-fiction as well, reporting and reviewing from her position as an observer of France. Her views on French life can be found in such pieces as 'The Events in May: A Paris Notebook', her first-hand account of the 1968 Paris student riots, and her long introduction to *The Affair of Gabrielle Russier* (1971), a book about a complex French legal scandal involving a teacher and her student. These, as well as many of her essays and reviews, are collected in *Paris Notebooks* (1986).

Bilingual from childhood, Gallant has immersed herself in French culture and life. But she writes only in English, believing that 'one needs a strong, complete language, fully understood to anchor one's understanding.' She has always been concerned with the individual's experience of an unfamiliar culture, and, while her stories capture the sense of alienation so commonly found in modern society, she shows especially deep sympathy for the isolated individual. Like the remittance man Frank Cairns in 'Varieties of Exile', her characters struggle to hang onto threads of their former cultures while seeking to understand environments that are physically and psychologically alien. They stand apart, their psychic distance intensified by the loss of traditional codes, and, as in the fiction of Henry James, what remains is truncated communication in the twilight of an obsolescent world.

Gallant portrays characters obliquely, often focusing on social custom and unconscious behaviour. In dialogues filled with nuance, little is said directly—but what *is* said takes on great importance. Her characters, detached and unable to express judgments, join those many reticent figures who share the malady Northrop Frye thought was a theme in Canadian writing: 'strangled articulateness'. Both burdened by history and isolated by it, they find their society moving away from the familiar patterns that bind and reassure.

Gallant's recurrent examination of dislocation and exile can be seen in the short story reprinted here, 'Varieties of Exile', which is from the Linnet Muir cycle, the most autobiographical of Gallant's fiction. In it, an expatriate Brit finds himself in Canada during the Second World War, neither able to fit into Montreal's social, cultural, and political milieu, nor belonging to its crowd of refugees and displaced persons. Linnet, the narrator and protagonist, is also struggling to find and understand her own place in this changing city—partly because she is uncomfortable with its gendered society (an experience like Gallant's own: she had difficulty being accepted as a female reporter.)

Despite Gallant's own long exile, she has returned to Canada from time to time (in 1983–4 she was writer-in-residence at the University of Toronto) and she retains a cultural identity with her homeland, which in turn has bestowed many honours upon her. She was made a Companion of the Order of Canada in 1993 and has been awarded honorary degrees by several Canadian universities. In 2006, Gallant was deeply moved to learn that she had received the Prix Athanase-David Award, the only English-language writer ever given this Quebec honour.

# Varieties of Exile

In the third summer of the war I began to meet refugees. There were large numbers of them in Montreal—to me a source of infinite wonder. I could not get enough of them. They came straight out of the twilit Socialist-literary landscape of my reading and my desires. I saw them as prophets of a promised social order that was to consist of justice, equality, art, personal relations, courage, generosity. Each of them—Belgian, French, Catholic German, Socialist German, Jewish German, Czech—was a book I tried to read from start to finish. My dictionaries were films, poems, novels, Lenin, Freud. That the refugees tended to hate one another seemed no more than a deplorable accident. Nationalist pigheadedness, that chronic, wasting, and apparently incurable disease, was known to me only on Canadian terms and I did not always recognize its symptoms. Anything I could not decipher I turned into fiction, which was my way of untangling knots. At the office where I worked I now spent my lunch hour writing stories about people in exile. I tried to see Montreal as an Austrian might see it and to feel whatever he felt. I was entirely at home with foreigners, which is not surprising— the home was all in my head. They were the only people I had met until now who believed, as I did, that our victory would prove to be a tidal wave nothing could stop. What I did not know was how many of them hoped and expected their neighbours to be washed away too.

I was nineteen and for the third time in a year engaged to be married. What I craved at this point was not love, or romance, or a life added to mine, but conversation, which was harder to find. I knew by now that a man in love does not necessarily have anything interesting to say: If he has, he keeps it for other men. Men in Canada did not talk much to women and hardly at all to young ones. The impetus of love—of infatuation, rather—brought on a kind of conversation I saw no reason to pursue. A remand such as 'I can't live without you' made the speaker sound not only half-witted to me but almost truly, literally, insane. There is a girl in a Stefan Zweig[1] novel who says to her lover, 'Is that all?' I had pondered this carefully many years before, for I supposed it had something unexpected to do with sex. Now I gave it another meaning, which was that where women were concerned men were satisfied with next to nothing. If every woman was a situation, she was somehow always the same situation, and what was expected from the woman—the situation—was so limited it was insulting. I had a large opinion of what I could do and provide, yet it came down to 'Is that all? Is that all you expect?' Being promised to one person after another was turning into a perpetual state of hesitation and refusal: I was not used to hesitating over anything and so I supposed I must be wrong. The men in my office had warned me of the dangers of turning into a married woman; if this caution affected me it was only because it coincided with a misgiving of my own. My private name for married women was Red Queens. They looked to me like the Red Queen in *Through the Looking-Glass*,[2] chasing after other people and minding their business for them. To get out of the heat that summer I had taken a room outside Montreal in an area called simply 'the Lakeshore'. In those days the Lakeshore was a string of verdant towns with next to no traffic. Dandelions grew in the pavement cracks. The streets were thickly shaded. A fragrance I have never forgotten of mown grass and leaf smoke drifted from yard to yard. As I walked to my commuters' train early in the morning I saw kids still in their pajamas digging holes in the lawns and Red Queen wives wearing housecoats. They stuck their heads out of screen doors and yelled instructions—to husbands, to children, to dogs, to postmen, to a neighbour's child.

1 Zweig (1881–1942) was a cosmopolitan Austrian Jewish poet, essayist, and novelist whose books were immensely popular throughout Europe in the 1930s, when the Nazi party took control he went into exile in 1934, eventually committing suicide.

2 In *Through the Looking-Glass, and What Alice Found There* (Lewis Carroll's 1872 sequel to *Alice in Wonderland*), Alice finds herself in a world where the pieces of the chess set have come alive. The Red Queen, the most prominent among them, is given to declarations such as 'open your mouth a little wider when you speak, and always say "your Majesty"' and she famously explains to Alice that 'here it takes all the running you can do, to keep in the same place'.

How could I be sure I wouldn't sound that way—so shrill, so discontented? As for a family, the promise of children all stamped with the same face, cast in the same genetic mould, seemed a cruel waste of possibilities. I would never have voiced this to anyone, for it would have been thought unnatural, even monstrous. When I was very young, under seven, my plan for the future had been to live in every country of the world and have a child in each. I had confided it: with adult adroitness my listener led me on. How many children? Oh, one to a country. And what would you do with them? Travel in trains. How would they go to school? I hate schools. How will they learn to read and write, then? They'll know already. What would you live on? It will all be free. That's not very sensible, is it? Why not? As a result of this idyll, of my divulgence of it, I was kept under watch for a time and my pocket money taken away lest I save it up and sail to a tropical island (where because of the Swiss Family Robinson I proposed to begin) long before the onset of puberty. I think no one realized I had not even a nebulous idea of how children sprang to life. I merely knew two persons were required for a ritual I believed had to continue for nine months, and which I imagined in the nature of a long card game with mysterious rules. When I was finally 'told'—accurately, as it turned out—I was offended at being asked to believe something so unreasonable, which could not be true because I had never come across it in books. This trust in the printed word seems all the more remarkable when I remember that I thought children's books were written by other children. Probably at nineteen I was still dim about relevant dates, plain facts, brass tacks, consistent reasoning. Perhaps I was still hoping for magic card games to short-circuit every sort of common sense—common sense is only an admission we don't know much. I know that I wanted to marry this third man but that I didn't want to be anybody's Red Queen.

The commuters on the Montreal train never spoke much to each other. The mystifying and meaningless 'Hot enough for you?' was about the extent of it. If I noticed one man more than the anonymous others it was only because he looked so hopelessly English, so unable or unwilling to concede to anything, even the climate. Once, walking a few steps behind him, I saw him turn into the drive of a stone house, one of the few old French-Canadian houses in that particular town. The choice of houses seemed to me peculiarly English too—though not, of course, what French Canadians call 'English', for that includes plain Canadians, Irish, Swedes, anything you like not natively French. I looked again at the house and at the straight back going along the drive. His wife was on her knees holding a pair of edging shears. He stopped to greet her. She glanced up and said something in a carrying British voice so wild and miserable, so resentful, so intensely disagreeable that it could not have been the tag end of a morning quarrel; no, it was the thunderclap of some new engagement. After a second he went on up the walk, and in another I was out of earshot. I was persuaded that he had seen me; I don't know why. I also thought it must have been humiliating for him to have had a witness.

Which of us spoke first? It could not have been him and it most certainly could not have been me. There must have been a collision, for there we are, speaking, on a station platform. It is early morning, already hot. I see once again, without surprise, that he is not dressed for the climate.

He said he had often wondered what I was reading. I said I was reading 'all the Russians'. He said I really ought to read Arthur Waley.[3] I had never heard of Arthur Waley. Similar signalling takes place between galaxies rushing apart in the outer heavens. He said he would bring me a book by Arthur Waley the next day.

'Please don't. I'm careless with books. Look at the shape this one's in.' It was the truth. 'All the Russians' were being published in a uniform edition with flag-red covers, on greyish paper, with microscopic print. The words were jammed together; you could not have put a pin between the lines. It was one of those cheap editions I think we were supposed to be sending the troops in order to cheer them up. Left in the grass beside a tennis court *The Possessed*[4] now curved like a shell. A white streak ran down the middle of the shell. The rest of the cover had turned pink. That was nothing, he said. All I needed to do was dampen the cover with a sponge and put a weight on the book. *The Wallet of Kai Lung*[5] had been to Ceylon with him and had survived. Whatever bait 'Ceylon' may have been caught nothing. Army? Civil Service? I did not take it up. Anyway I thought I could guess.

'You'd better not bring a book for nothing. I don't always take this train.'

He had probably noticed me every morning. The mixture of reserve and obstinacy that next crossed his face I see still. He smiled, oh, not too much: I'd have turned my back on a grin. He said, 'I forgot to . . . Frank Cairns.'

'Muir, Linnet Muir.' Reluctantly.

The thing is, I knew all about him. He was, one, married and, two, too old. But there was also three: Frank Cairns was stamped, labelled, ticketed by his tie (club? regiment? school?); by his voice, manner, haircut, suit; by the impression he gave of being stranded in a jungle, waiting for a rescue party—from England, of course. He belonged to a species of British immigrant known as remittance men. Their obsolescence began on 3 September 1939 and by 8 May 1945 they were extinct. I knew about them from having had one in the family. Frank Cairns worked in a brokerage house—he told me later—but he probably did not need a job, at least not for a living. It must have been a way of ordering time, a flight from idleness, perhaps a means of getting out of the house.

The institution of the remittance man was British, its genesis a chemical structure of family pride, class insanity, and imperial holdings that seemed impervious to fission but in the end turned out to be more fragile than anyone thought. Like all superfluous and marginal persons, remittance men were characters in a plot. The plot began with a fixed scene, an immutable first chapter, which described a powerful father's taking umbrage at his son's misconduct and ordering him out of the country. The pound was then one to five dollars, and there were vast British territories everywhere you looked. Hordes of young men who had somehow offended their parents were shipped

3 (1889–1966); poet, translator, and scholar, Waley introduced Chinese and Japanese literature and culture to a broad twentieth-century public through his English translations of East Asian classics.
4 Fyodor Dostoevsky's novel (1871–2), which contains negative portraits of radical political movements in Russia, including Nihilism, Anarchism, and Socialism.
5 Like *Kai Lung's Golden Hours*, mentioned subsequently, a pseudo-Oriental tale (published in 1900) by Ernest Bramah. Bramah's Kai Lung stories are written in an ornate, whimsical manner and have no authentic Chinese background.

out, golden deportees, to Canada, South Africa, New Zealand, Singapore. They were reluctant pioneers, totally lacking any sense of adventure or desire to see that particular world. An income—the remittance—was provided on a standing banker's order, with one string attached: 'Keep out of England'. For the second chapter the plot allowed a choice of six crimes as reasons for banishment: Conflict over the choice of a profession—the son wants to be a tap-dancer. Gambling and debts—he has been barred from Monte Carlo. Dud cheques—'I won't press a charge, sir, but see that the young rascal is kept out of harm's way.' Marriage with a girl from the wrong walk of life—'Young man, you have made your bed!' Fathering an illegitimate child: '. . . and broken your mother's heart'. Homosexuality, if discovered: too grave for even a lecture—it was a criminal offence.

This is the plot of the romance: this is what everyone repeated and what the remittance man believed of himself. Obviously, it is a load of codswallop. A man legally of age could marry the tattooed woman in a circus, be arrested for cheque-bouncing or for soliciting boys in Green Park, be obliged to recognize his by-blow and even to wed its mother, become a ponce or a professional wrestler, and still remain where he was born. All he needed to do was eschew the remittance and tell his papa to go to hell. Even at nineteen the plot was a story I wouldn't buy. The truth came down to something just as dramatic but boring to tell: a classic struggle for dominance with two protagonists—strong father, pliant son. It was also a male battle. No son was ever sent into exile by his mother, and no one has ever heard of a remittance *woman*. Yet daughters got into scrapes nearly as often as their brothers. Having no idea what money was, they ran up debts easily. Sometimes, out of ignorance of another sort, they dared to dispose of their own virginity, thus wrecking their value on the marriage market and becoming family charges for life. Accoucheurs[6] had to be bribed to perform abortions; or else the daughters were dispatched to Austria and Switzerland to have babies they would never hear of again. A daughter's disgrace was long, expensive, and hard to conceal, yet no one dreamed of sending her thousands of miles away and forever: on the contrary, she became her father's unpaid servant, social secretary, dog walker, companion, sick nurse. Holding on to a daughter, dismissing a son were relatively easy: it depended on having tamely delinquent children, or a thunderous personality no child would dare to challenge, and on the weapon of money—bait or weapon, as you like.

Banished young, as a rule, the remittance man (the RM, in my private vocabulary) drifted for the rest of his life, never quite sounding or looking like anyone around him, seldom raising a family or pursuing an occupation (so much for the 'choice of profession' legend)—remote, dreamy, bored. Those who never married often became low-key drunks. The remittance was usually ample without being handsome, but enough to keep one from doing a hand's turn; in any case few remittance men were fit to do much of anything, being well schooled but half educated, in that specifically English way, as well as markedly unaggressive and totally uncompetitive, which would have meant early death in the New World for anyone without an income. They were like children waiting for the school vacation so that they could go home, except that at home

6  Midwives (French).

nobody wanted them: the nursery had been turned into a billiards room and Nanny dismissed. They were parted from mothers they rarely mentioned, whom in some way they blended with a Rupert Brooke[7] memory of England, of the mother country, of the Old Country as everyone at home grew old. Often as not the payoff, the keep-away blackmail funds, came out of the mother's marriage settlement—out of the capital her own father had agreed to settle upon her unborn children during the wear and tear of Edwardian engagement negotiations. The son disgraced would never see more than a fixed income from this; he was cut off from a share of inheritance by his contract of exile. There were cases where the remittance ended abruptly with the mother's death, but that was considered a bad arrangement. Usually the allowance continued for the exile's lifetime and stopped when he died. No provision was made for his dependants, if he had them, and because of his own subject attitude to money he was unlikely to have made any himself. The income reverted to his sisters and brothers, to an estate, to a cat-and-dog hospital—whatever his father had decreed on some black angry day long before.

Whatever these sons had done their punishment was surely a cruel and singular one, invented for naughty children by a cosmic headmaster taking over for God: they were obliged to live over and over until they died the first separation from home, and the incomparable trauma of rejection. Yes, they were like children, perpetually on their way to a harsh school; they were eight years of age and sent 'home' from India to child-hoods of secret grieving among strangers. And this wound, this amputation, they would mercilessly inflict on their own children when the time came—on sons always, on daughters sometimes—persuaded that early heartbreak was right because it was British, hampered only by the financial limit set for banishment: it costs money to get rid of your young.

And how they admired their fathers, those helpless sons! They spoke of them with so much admiration, with such a depth of awe: only in memory can such voices still exist, the calm English voice on a summer night—a Canadian night so alien to the speaker—insisting, with sudden firmness, with a pause between words. 'My . . . father . . . once . . . said . . . to . . . me . . .' and here would follow something utterly trivial, some advice about choosing a motorcar or training a dog. To the Canadian grandchildren the unknown grandfather was seven foot tall with a beard like George V, while the grandmother came through weepy and prissy and not very interesting. It was the father's Father, never met, never heard, who made Heaven and Earth and Eve and Adam. The father in Canada seemed no more than an apostle transmitting a paternal message from the Father in England—the Father of us all. It was, however, rare for a remittance man to marry, rarer still to have any children; how could he become a father when he had never stopped being a son?

If the scattered freemasonry of offspring the remittance man left behind, all adult to elderly now, had anything in common it must have been their degree of incompetence. They were raised to behave well in situations that might never occur, trained to become genteel poor on continents where even the concept of genteel poverty has

---

7 (1887–1915); English poet famous for his wartime poetry and his idealized patriotism, Brooke came to be remem-bered as an emblem of the flower of young British manhood lost in World War I.

never existed. They were brought up with plenty of books and music and private lessons, a nurse sometimes, in a household where certain small luxuries were deemed essential—a way of life that, in North America at least, was supposed to be built on a sunken concrete base of money; otherwise you were British con men, a breed of gypsy, and a bad example.

Now, your remittance man was apt to find this assumption quite funny. The one place he would never take seriously was the place he was in. The identification of prominent local families with the name of a product, a commodity, would be his running joke: 'The Allseeds are sugar, the Bilges are coal, the Cumquats are cough medicine, the Doldrums are coffins, the Earwigs are saucepans, the Fustians are timber, the Grindstones are beer.' But his young, once they came up against it, were bound to observe that their concrete base was the dandelion fluff of a banker's order, their commodity nothing but 'life in England before 1914', which was not negotiable. Also, the constant, nagging 'What does your father really do?' could amount to persecution.

'Mr Bainwood wants to know what you do.'

'Damned inquisitive of him.'

Silence. Signs of annoyance. Laughter sometimes. Or something silly: 'What do *you* do when you aren't asking questions?'

No remittance man's child that I know of ever attended a university, though care was taken over the choice of schools. There they would be, at eighteen and nineteen, the boys wearing raincoats in the coldest weather, the girls with their hair ribbons and hand-knits and their innocently irritating English voices, well read, musical, versed in history, probably because they had been taught that the past is better than now, and somewhere else better than here. They must have been the only English-Canadian children to speak French casually, as a matter of course. Untidy, unpunctual, imperially tactless, they drifted into work that had to be 'interesting', 'creative', never demeaning, and where—unless they'd had the advantage of a rough time and enough nous[8] to draw a line against the past—they seldom lasted. There was one in every public-relations firm, one to a radio station, two to a publisher—forgetting appointments, losing contracts, jamming typewriters, sabotaging telephones, apologizing in accents it would have taken elocution lessons to change, so strong had been paternal pressure against the hard Canadian 'r', not to mention other vocables:

'A-t-e is *et* darling, not *ate*.'

'I can't say *et*. Only farmers say it.'

'Perhaps here, but you won't always be here.'

Of course the children were guilt-drenched, wondering which of the six traditional crimes they ought to pin on their father, what his secret was, what his past included, why he had been made an outcast. The answer was quite often 'Nothing, no reason,' but it meant too much to be unravelled and knit up. The saddest were those unwise enough to look into the families who had caused so much inherited woe. For the family was often as not smaller potatoes than the children had thought,

8  Common sense (chiefly British informal).

and their father's romantic crime had been just the inability to sit for an examination, to stay at university, to handle an allowance, to gain a toehold in any profession, or even to decide what he wanted to do—an ineptitude so maddening to live with that the Father preferred to shell out forever rather than watch his heir fall apart before his eyes. The male line, then, was a ghost story. A mother's vitality would be needed to create ectoplasm, to make the ghost offspring visible. Unfortunately the exiles were apt to marry absentminded women whose skirts are covered with dog hairs—the drooping, bewildered British-Canadian mouse, who counts on tea leaves to tell her 'what will happen when Edward goes'. None of us is ever saved entirely, but even an erratic and alarming maternal vitality could turn out to be better than none.

Frank Cairns was childless, which I thought wise of him. He had been to Ceylon, gone back to England with a stiff case of homesickness disguised as malaria, married, and been shipped smartly out again, this time to Montreal. He was a neat, I think rather a small, man, with a straight part in his hair and a quick, brisk walk. He noticed I was engaged. I did not reply. I told him I had been in New York, had come back about a year ago, and missed 'different things'. He seemed to approve. 'You can't make a move here,' he said more than once. I was not sure what he meant. If he had been only the person I have described I'd have started taking an earlier train to be rid of him. But Frank Cairns was something new, unique of his kind, and almost as good as a refugee, for he was a Socialist. At least he said he was. He said he had never voted anywhere but that if he ever in the future happened to be in England when there was an election he would certainly vote Labour. His Socialism did not fit anything else about him, and seemed to depend for its life on the memory of talks he'd once had with a friend whom he described as brilliant, philosophical, farseeing, and just. I thought, Like Christ, but did not know Frank Cairns well enough to say so. The nonbeliever I had become was sometimes dogged by the child whose nightly request had been 'Gentle Jesus, meek and mild, look upon a little child,' and I sometimes got into ferocious arguments with her, as well as with other people. I was too curious about Frank Cairns to wish to quarrel over religion—at any rate not at the beginning. He talked about his friend without seeming able to share him. He never mentioned his name. I had to fill in the blank part of this conversation without help; I made the friend a high-ranking civil servant in Ceylon, older than anyone—which might have meant forty-two—an intellectual revolutionary who could work the future out on paper, like arithmetic.

Wherever his opinions came from, Frank Cairns was the first person ever to talk to me about the English poor. They seemed to be a race, different in kind from other English. He showed me old copies of *Picture Post* he must have saved up from the Depression. In our hot summer train, where everyone was starched and ironed and washed and fed, we considered slum doorways and the faces of women at the breaking point. They looked like Lenin's 'remnants of nations' except that there were too many of them for a remnant. I thought of my mother and her long preoccupation with the fate of the Scottsboro Boys.[9] My mother had read and mooned and fretted about the Scottsboro case, while I tried to turn her attention to something urgent, such as that my school uniform was now torn in three places. It is quite possible that my mother had seldom seen a black except on railway trains. (If I say 'black' it is only because it is expected. It was a rude and offensive term in my childhood and I would not have been allowed to use it. 'Black' was the sort of thing South Africans said.) Had Frank Cairns actually seen those *Picture Post* faces, I wondered. His home, his England, was every other remittance man's—the one I called 'Christopher-Robin-land' and had sworn to keep away from. He hated Churchill, I remember, but I was used to hearing that. No man who remembered the Dardanelles[10] really trusted him. Younger men (I am speaking of the handful I knew who had any opinions at all) were not usually irritated by his rhetoric until they got into uniform.

Once in a book I lent him he found a scrap of paper on which I had written the title of a story I was writing, 'The Socialist RM', and some scrawls in, luckily, a private shorthand of mine. A perilous moment: 'remittance man' was a term of abuse all over the Commonwealth and Empire.

'What is it?' he asked. 'Resident Magistrate?'

'It might be Royal Marine. Royal Mail. I honestly don't remember. I can't read my own writing sometimes.' The last sentence was true.

His Socialism was unlike a Czech's or a German's; though he believed that one should fight hard for social change, there was a hopelessness about it, an almost moral belief that improving their material circumstances would get the downtrodden nowhere. At the same time, he thought the poor *were* happy, that they had some strange secret of happiness—the way people often think all Italians are happy because they have large families. I wondered if he really believed that a man with no prospects and no teeth in his head was spiritually better off than Frank Cairns and why, in that case, Frank Cairns did not let him alone with his underfed children and his native good nature. This was a British left-wing paradox I was often to encounter later on. What it seemed to amount to was leaving people more or less as they were, though he did speak about basic principles and the spread of education. It sounded dull. I was Russian-minded; I read Russian books, listened to Russian music. After Russia came Germany and Central Europe—that was where the real mystery and political

9 The nine black youths who were indicted in 1931 at Scottsboro, Alabama, on charges of raping two white women. Despite the paucity of evidence against the young men, all nine were found guilty by an all-white jury. The decision sparked outrage outside the southern US, particularly among Northern liberal and radical groups, who championed and sometimes exploited the cause of the Scottsboro Boys. (The US Supreme Court twice reversed guilty decisions on procedural grounds, but retrials of the youths resulted in reconvictions. In response to persistent pressure from citizens' groups, charges against five of the youths were dropped in 1937, while two of the youths were paroled in 1944 and another in 1951. The remaining Scottsboro boy, Haywood Patterson, escaped prison in 1948 and was later convicted of manslaughter in a separate incident.)

10 As the first lord of the admiralty, William Churchill championed the 1915 campaign for the Dardanelles, a narrow strip of water that divided European from Asiatic Turkey. The campaign, thought to be critical to the Allies in World War I, ended with a difficult Allied retreat and became emblematic of strategic bungling and lost opportunities. Churchill lost his admiralty post and his political power as a result.

excitement lay. His Webbs[11] and his Fabians were plodding and grey. I saw the men with thick moustaches, wearing heavy boots, sharing lumpy meals with moral women. In the books he brought me I continued to find his absent friend. He produced Housman and Hardy (I could not read either), Siegfried Sassoon and Edmund Blunden, H.G. Wells and Bernard Shaw. The friend was probably a Scot—Frank Cairns admired them. The Scots of Canada, to me, stood for all that was narrow, grasping, at a standstill. How I distrusted those granite bankers who thought it was sinful to smoke! I was wrong, he told me. The true Scots were full of poetry and political passion. I said, 'Are you sure?' and turned his friend into a native of Aberdeen and a graduate from Edinburgh. I also began a new notebook: 'Scottish Labour Party. Keir Hardie.[12] Others'. This was better than the Webbs but still not as good as Rosa Luxemburg.

It was Frank Cairns who said to me 'Life has no point,' without emphasis, in response to some ignorant assumption of mine. This was his true voice. I recall the sidelong glance, the lizard's eye that some men develop as they grow old or when they have too much to hide. I was no good with ages. I cannot place him even today. Early thirties, probably. What else did he tell me? That 'Scotch' was the proper term and 'Scots' an example of a genteelism overtaking the original. That unless the English surmounted their class obsessions with speech and accent Britain would not survive in the world after the war. His remedy (or his friend's) was having everyone go to the same schools. He surprised me even more by saying, 'I would never live in England, not as it is now.'

'Where, then?'

'Nowhere. I don't know.'

'What about Russia? They all go to the same schools.'

'Good Lord,' said Frank Cairns.

He was inhabited by a familiar who spoke through him, provided him with jolting outbursts but not a whole thought. Perhaps that silent coming and going was the way people stayed in each other's lives when they were apart. What Frank Cairns was to me was a curio cabinet. I took everything out of the cabinet, piece by piece, examined the objects, set them down. Such situations, riddled with ambiguity, I would blunder about with for a long time until I learned to be careful.

---

11  Beatrice (1858–1943) and Sidney (1859–1947) Webb, English socialists and economists who helped establish the London School of Economics (1895) and were prominent members of the Fabian Society, an organization of British socialists favouring the gradual rather than revolutionary achievement of socialism. (Shaw was also a member.) Much of the point of the list of authors that follows is that while the literary works that we have seen Linnet reading are by Continental European and non-European writers and all have a strong philosophical character, Cairns prefers writers like A.E. Housman, Thomas Hardy, Edmund Blunden (a lesser-known English poet, whose poetry speaks of his love for the English countryside), and others, all of whom are strongly identified with the United Kingdom and who created works that are descriptions of English life.

12  (1856–1915); Scottish labour activist, lay minister, temperance leader, supporter of women's suffrage, and eventually Labour politician. Rosa Luxemburg (1871–1919), a Polish-born German revolutionary leader, co-founder of the revolutionary group known as the Spartacus League (1916) and the German Communist party (1918), gained considerable international attention through her fiery manner, stirring platform rhetoric, and rabble-rousing approach—not least because she was a charismatic woman espousing a radical left political agenda.

The husband of the woman from whom I rented my summer room played golf every weekend. On one of those August nights when no one can sleep and the sky is nearly bright enough to read by, I took to the back yard and found him trying to cool off with a glass of beer. He remembered he had offered to give me golf lessons. I did not wish to learn, but did not say so. His wife spoke up from a deck chair: 'You've never offered to teach me, I notice.' She then compounded the error by telling me everyone was talking about me and the married man on the train. The next day I took the Käthe Kollwitz[13] prints down from the walls of my room and moved back to Montreal without an explanation. Frank Cairns and I met once more that summer to return some books. That was all. When he called me at my office late in November, I said, 'Who?'

He came into the coffee shop at Windsor Station, where I was waiting. He was in uniform. I had not noticed he was good-looking before. It was not something I noticed in men. He was a first lieutenant. I disapproved: 'Couldn't they make you a private?'

'Too old,' he said. 'As it is I am too old for my rank.' I thought he just meant he might be promoted faster because of that.

'You don't look old.' I at once regretted this personal remark, the first he had heard from me. Indeed, he had shed most of his adult life. He must have seemed as young as this when he started out to Ceylon. The uniform was his visa to England; no one could shut him away now. His face was radiant, open: he was halfway there. This glimpse of a purpose astonished me; why should a uniform make the change he'd been unable to make alone? He was not the first soldier I saw transfigured but he was the first to affect me.

He kept smiling and staring at me. I hoped he was not going to make a personal remark in exchange for mine. He said, 'That tam makes you look, I don't know. Canadian. I've always thought of you as English. I still think England is where you might be happy.'

'I'm happy here. You said you'd never live there.'

'It would be a good place for you,' he said. 'Well, well, we shall see.'

He would see nothing. My evolution was like freaky weather then: a few months, a few weeks even, were the equivalent of long second thoughts later on. I was in a completely other climate. I no longer missed New York and 'different things'. I had become patriotic. Canadian patriotism is always anti-American in part, and feeds upon anecdotes. American tourists were beginning to arrive in Montreal looking for anything expensive or hard to find in the United States; when they could not buy rationed food such as meat and butter, or unrationed things such as nylon stockings (because they did not exist), they complained of ingratitude. This was because Canada was thought to be a recipient of American charity and on the other end of Lend-Lease.[14] Canadians were, and are, enormously touchy. Great umbrage had been taken over a story that was

---

13 (1867–1945); German graphic artist and sculptor, as well as a socialist, Kollwitz's stark and powerful images reflect her compassion for the poor.

14 Lend-lease was an arrangement for the transfer of war supplies, including food, machinery, and services, to nations whose defence was considered vital to the defence of the United States in World War II. In effect, Lend-Lease allowed the executive branch of the American government to enter the war indirectly, circumventing the desire of its citizenry and the Congress for continued US neutrality. Many Americans resented the cost of Lend-Lease and believed Allied and Commonwealth countries were benefiting at the expense of the US taxpayer.

going around in the States about Americans who had been soaked for black-market butter in Montreal; when they got back across the border they opened the package and found the butter stamped 'Gift of the American People'. This fable persisted throughout the war and turned up in print. An American friend saw it in, I think, Westbrook Pegler's column and wrote asking me if it was true. I composed a letter I meant to send to the *New York Times*, demolishing the butter story. I kept rewriting and reshaping it, trying to achieve a balance between crippling irony and a calm review of events. I never posted it, finally, because my grandmother appeared to me in a dream and said that only fools wrote to newspapers.

Our coffee was tepid, the saucers slopped. He complained, and the waitress asked if we knew there was a war on. 'Christ, what a bloody awful country this is,' he said.

I wanted to say, Then why are you with a Canadian regiment? I provided my own answer: They pay more than the Brits. We were actually quarrelling in my head, and on such a mean level. I began to tear up a paper napkin and to cry.

'I have missed you,' he remarked, but quite happily; you could tell the need for missing was over. I had scarcely thought of him at all. I kept taking more and more napkins out of the container on the table and blotting my face and tearing the paper up. He must be the only man I ever cried about in a public place. I hardly knew him. He was not embarrassed, as a Canadian would have been, but looked all the happier. The glances we got from other tables were full of understanding. Everything gave the wrong impression—his uniform, my engagement ring, my tears. I told him I was going to be married.

'Nonsense,' he said.

'I'm serious.'

'You seem awfully young.'

'I'll soon be twenty.' A slip. I had told him I was older. It amazed me to remember how young I had been only the summer before. 'But I won't actually be a married woman,' I said, 'because I hate everything about them. Another thing I won't be and that's the sensitive housewife—the one who listens to Brahms while she does the ironing and reads all the new books still in their jackets.'

'No, don't be a sensitive housewife,' he said.

He gave me *The Wallet of Kai Lung* and *Kai Lung's Golden Hours*, which had been in Ceylon with him and had survived.

Did we write to each other? That's what I can't remember. I was careless then; I kept moving on. Also I really did, that time, get married. My husband was posted three days afterward to an American base in the Aleutian Islands—I have forgotten why. Eight months later he returned for a brief embarkation leave and then went overseas. I had dreaded coming in to my office after my wedding for fear the men I worked with would tease me. But the mixture of war and separation recalled old stories of their own experiences, in the First World War. Also I had been transformed into someone with a French surname, which gave them pause.

'Does he—uh—speak any French?'

'Not a word. He's from the West.' Ah. 'But he ought to. His father is French.' Oh.

I had disappeared for no more than four days, but I was Mrs Something now, not young Linnet. They spoke about me as 'she', and not 'Linnet' or 'the kid'. I wondered what they saw when they looked at me. In every head bent over a desk or a drawing board there was an opinion about women; expressed, it sounded either prurient or coarse, but I still cannot believe that is all there was to it. I know I shocked them profoundly once by saying that a wartime ditty popular with the troops, 'Rock me to sleep, Sergeant-Major, tuck me in my little bed', was innocently homosexual. That I could have such a turn of thought, that I could use such an expression, that I even knew it existed seemed scandalous to them. 'You read too damned much,' I was told. Oddly enough, they had never minded my hearing any of the several versions of the song, some of which were unspeakable; all they objected to was my unfeminine remark. When I married they gave me a suitcase, and when I left for good they bought me a Victory Bond. I had scrupulously noted every detail of the office, and the building it was in, yet only a few months later I would walk by it without remembering I had ever been inside, and it occurs to me only now that I never saw any of them again.

I was still a minor, but emancipated by marriage. I did not need to ask parental consent for anything or worry about being brought down on the wing. I realized how anxious I had been once the need for that particular anxiety was over. A friend in New York married to a psychiatrist had sent me a letter saying I had her permission to marry. She did not describe herself as a relative or state anything untrue—she just addressed herself to whom it may concern, said that as far as *she* was concerned I could get married, and signed. She did not tell her husband, in case he tried to put things right out of principle, and I mentioned to no one that the letter was legal taradiddle and carried about as much weight as a library card. I mention this to show what essential paperwork sometimes amounts to. My husband, aged twenty-four, had become my legal guardian under Quebec's preposterous Napoleonic law, but he never knew that. When he went overseas he asked me not to join any political party, which I hadn't thought of doing, and not to enlist in the Army or the Air Force. The second he vanished I tried to join the Wrens,[15] which had not been on the list only because it slipped his mind. Joining one of the services had never been among my plans and projects— it was he who accidentally put the idea in my head. I now decided I would turn up overseas, having made it there on my own, but I got no further than the enlistment requirements, which included '. . . of the white race only.' This barrier turned out to be true of nearly all the navies of the Commonwealth countries. I supposed everyone must have wanted it that way, for I never heard it questioned. I was only beginning to hear the first rumblings of hypocrisy on our side—the right side; the wrong side seemed to be guilty of every sin humanly possible except simulation of virtue. I put the blame for the racial barrier on Churchill, who certainly *knew*, and had known since the First World War; I believed that Roosevelt, Stalin, Chiang Kai-shek, and de Gaulle did not know, and that should it ever come to their attention they would be as shocked as I was.

15 The Women's Royal Canadian Naval Service, whose members served at Royal Canadian Navy establishments in North American and in the UK, participating in a wide range of support trades, including clerical and signals work.

Instead of enlisting I passed the St John Ambulance first-aid certificate, which made me a useful person in case of total war. The Killed-Wounded-Missing columns of the afternoon paper were now my daily reading. It became a habit so steadfast that I would automatically look for victims even after the war ended. The summer of the Scottish Labour Party, Keir Hardie, and Others fell behind, as well as a younger, discarded Linnet. I lighted ferocious autos-da-fé.[16] Nothing could live except present time. In the ever-new present I read one day that Major Francis Cairns had died of wounds in Italy. Who remembers now the shock of the known name? It was like a flat white light. One felt apart from everyone, isolated. The field of vision drew in. Then, before one could lose consciousness, vision expanded, light and shadow moved, voices pierced through. One's heart, which had stopped, beat hard enough to make a room shudder. All this would occupy about a second. The next second was inhabited by disbelief. I saw him in uniform, so happy, halfway there, and myself making a spectacle of us tearing a paper napkin. I was happy for him that he would never need to return to the commuting train and the loneliness and be forced to relive his own past. I wanted to write a casual letter saying so. One's impulse was always to write to the dead. Nobody knew I knew him, and in Canada it was not done to speak of the missing. I forgot him. He went under. I was doing a new sort of work and sharing a house with another girl whose husband was also overseas. Montreal had become a completely other city. I was no longer attracted to refugees. They were going through a process called 'integrating'. Some changed their names. Others applied for citizenship. A refugee eating cornflakes was of no further interest. The house I now lived in contained a fireplace, in which I burned all my stories about Czech and German anti-Fascists. In the picnic hamper I used for storing journals and notebooks I found a manila envelope marked 'Lakeshore'. It contained several versions of 'The Socialist RM' and a few other things that sounded as if they were translated from the Russian by Constance Garnett.[17] I also found a brief novel I had no memory of having written, about a Scot from Aberdeen, a left-wing civil servant in Ceylon—a man from somewhere, living elsewhere, confident that another world was entirely possible, since he had got it all down. It had a shape, density, voice, but I destroyed it too. I never felt guilt about forgetting the dead or the living, but I minded about that one manuscript for a time. All this business of putting my life through a sieve and then discarding it was another variety of exile; I knew that even then, but it seemed quite right and perfectly natural.

1981

---

16 The term applied to the burning of heretics by the Spanish Inquisition. (Its literal meaning is 'acts of faith', that is, acts of pious sacrifice.)

17 (1861–1946); the English translator famous for having made the literary works of the great Russian writers such as Dostoyevsky, Tolstoy, and Chekhov available to an English-speaking audience. (It is her translation of *The Possessed* that Linnet would have been reading.)

# Margaret Laurence

## 1926–1987

Born and raised Jean Margaret Wemys in the small Manitoba town of Neepawa, Margaret Laurence drew on her milieu to create the complexly realized town of Manawaka, the setting of a series of five interrelated works of fiction beginning with *The Stone Angel* (1964) and concluding with *The Diviners* (1974). Laurence's early years in Neepawa—including her struggle to reconcile the experience of several deaths in the family (among these, her mother's when she was four and her father's when she was nine) with the vision of a powerful and just God handed down from her Scots-Presbyterian grandparents—colour her Manawaka fiction, especially the autobiographical Vanessa MacLeod stories collected in *A Bird in the House* (1970). Like Vanessa, the adolescent Laurence felt herself trapped in her grandfather's home. In 1943, a Manitoba scholarship allowed her to attend United College in Winnipeg (now the University of Winnipeg) and begin an independent life, freed from Neepawa and a restrictive family. Interested in writing from an early age, as an undergraduate, Laurence took an honours English degree at United College and began to work on and publish stories and poems in the college newspaper. After graduating in 1947, she took a job as a reporter for the *Winnipeg Citizen*. That same year, she married Jack Laurence.

In 1949, Laurence and her husband moved to England, where he took a civil engineering job building dams for the British Overseas Development Service. In 1950, his work took them to the British Protectorate of Somaliland (now Somalia) and, two years later, to the Gold Coast (now Ghana). Responding deeply to Africa's culture, Laurence, while raising their two children, began her career as a writer, first with *A Tree for Poverty* (1954), a translation and recasting of Somali poetry and tales, and then with a series of stories about the people she saw caught in a transitional moment between the old tribal world and the modern one. These stories, set in the Gold Coast, began to appear in

periodicals in 1954 and were collected as *The Tomorrow-Tamer* in 1963. Three other books grew out of Laurence's African years: *This Side Jordan* (1960), a novel that deals with Ghana's struggle for independence; *The Prophet's Camel Bell* (1963), an account of her residence in Somaliland based on the journal she kept while there; and *Long Drums and Cannons* (1968), a critical study of the English-language writers emerging in Nigeria. Her experience of the various African struggles for freedom and nationhood sharpened her sense of Canada as also a new country coming to terms with its own colonial influences.

Laurence seems to have valued the perspective gained through expatriation. Five years after she and her husband returned to Canada, settling in Vancouver in 1957, they separated and she returned to England: it was there she wrote the first three Manawaka novels—*The Stone Angel*, *A Jest of God* (1966), and *The Fire-Dwellers* (1969). These books had enormous impact in Canada: demonstrating the power and universality of regionalism, they established her as the foremost novelist of the decade.

In 1969, Laurence began returning to Canada, spending summers at a cottage on the Otonabee River, near Peterborough, Ontario; she also returned to serve as writer-in-residence at the University of Toronto, Trent University, and the University of Western Ontario. In 1971, she was named a Companion of the Order of Canada. She moved back to Canada permanently in 1974, settling in Lakefield, Ontario. In the same year, she published *The Diviners*: her most ambitious work of fiction, it draws together characters and themes from the four other Manawaka books and, by use of reciprocal parallels with *The Stone Angel*, provides a formal close to the sequence. Like *A Jest of God*, *The Diviners* won a Governor General's Award.

After *The Diviners*, Laurence published only children's stories and short non-fiction pieces. *Heart of a Stranger* (1976) draws together a selection of essays and magazine articles from the previous twelve years. Throughout the 1980s, she was active in causes that mattered to her, such as nuclear disarmament, energy conservation, and environmental protection. From 1981 through 1983, she also served as chancellor of Trent University. After her death in 1987, her daughter Jocelyn completed the memoir that Laurence had begun in 1985, *Dance on the Earth* (1989). In addition, four selections of her letters have appeared: *A Very Large Soul: Selected Letters from Margaret Laurence to Canadian Writers* (1995), edited by J.A. Wainwright, and the volumes collecting her exchanges with the poet Al Purdy, the French-Canadian novelist Gabrielle Roy, and the novelist Adele Wiseman, her oldest friend. Laurence was an excellent correspondent and her letters offer insights into her development as a writer and the importance of her role in the Canadian literary community.

From her early African writing through her later novels and even in her children's book, *Jason's Quest* (1970), Laurence chronicled a search for freedom, autonomy, and joy. Powerful forces work against the individual in this search, as ninety-year-old Hagar Shipley at last realizes in the moving conclusion to *The Stone Angel*:

*This knowing comes upon me so forcefully, so shatteringly, and with such bitterness as I have never felt before. I must always, always, have wanted that—simply to rejoice. How is it I never could? . . . Every good joy I might have held, in my man or any child of mine or even the plain light of morning, of walking the earth, all were forced to a standstill by some brake of proper appearances—oh, proper to whom? When did I ever speak the heart's truth?*

*Pride was my wilderness, and the demon that led me there was fear. I was alone, never anything else, and never free, for I carried my chains within me, and they spread out from me and shackled all I touched.*

Though Hagar and the women of her era seem unable to fully escape their bonds, the protagonists who follow come closer to Laurence's ideal of freedom. In *The Diviners* Laurence suggests that Hagar's struggle (her name is the same as that of Abraham's bondswoman in the Bible) has helped to free the protagonist of *The Diviners*, Morag (whose name is the Scottish equivalent of Sarah, Abraham's wife).

The way Hagar's experiences cross generations to touch Morag is an example of inheritance being an important theme for Laurence. Inheritance—not only genetic makeup but also the profoundly shaping influences of one's culture, society, and environment—is sometimes a restraint against which her characters struggle but it is always their chief source of strength, the thing that allows them to survive in a world characterized by bewildering uncertainty.

Laurence left her own legacy: her fiction gave the life and landscape of Canada a new place in the nation's imagination while showing the complexity of the country's cultural heritage. For some readers, she spoke as a regionalist, telling them about Prairie life and history; for others, she chronicled the progress of women in Canadian society; for many, she was the voice of a child of immigrants struggling with a tradition partly frozen in time and partly created out of the meeting of old with the new; for everyone, she recorded the new social freedoms that came about in the 1960s and 70s.

# To Set Our House in Order

When the baby was almost ready to be born, something went wrong and my mother had to go into hospital two weeks before the expected time. I was wakened by her crying in the night, and then I heard my father's footsteps as he went downstairs to phone. I stood in the doorway of my room, shivering and listening, wanting to go to my mother but afraid to go lest there be some sight there more terrifying than I could bear.

'Hello—Paul?' my father said, and I knew he was talking to Dr Cates. 'It's Beth. The waters have broken, and the fetal position doesn't seem quite—well, I'm only thinking of what happened the last time, and another like that would be—I wish she were a little huskier, damn it—she's so—no, don't worry, I'm quite all right. Yes, I think that would be the best thing. Okay, make it as soon as you can, will you?'

He came back upstairs, looking bony and dishevelled in his pyjamas, and running his fingers through his sand-coloured hair. At the top of the stairs, he came face to face with Grandmother MacLeod, who was standing there in her quilted black satin dressing gown, her slight figure held straight and poised, as though she were unaware that her hair was bound grotesquely like white-feathered wings in the snare of her coarse night-time hairnet.

'What is it, Ewen?'

'It's all right, Mother. Beth's having—a little trouble. I'm going to take her into the hospital. You go back to bed.'

'I told you,' Grandmother MacLeod said in her clear voice, never loud, but distinct and ringing like the tap of a sterling teaspoon on a crystal goblet, 'I did tell you, Ewen, did I not, that you should have got a girl in to help her with the housework? She would have rested more.'

'I couldn't afford to get anyone in,' my father said. 'If you thought she should've rested more, why didn't you ever—oh God, I'm out of my mind tonight—just go back to bed, Mother, please. I must get back to Beth.'

When my father went down to the front door to let Dr Cates in, my need overcame my fear and I slipped into my parents' room. My mother's black hair, so neatly pinned up during the day, was startlingly spread across the white pillowcase. I stared at her, not speaking, and then she smiled and I rushed from the doorway and buried my head upon her.

'It's all right, honey,' she said. 'Listen, Vanessa, the baby's just going to come a little early, that's all. You'll be all right. Grandmother MacLeod will be here.'

'How can she get the meals?' I wailed, fixing on the first thing that came to mind. 'She never cooks. She doesn't know how.'

'Yes, she does,' my mother said. 'She can cook as well as anyone when she has to. She's just never had to very much, that's all. Don't worry—she'll keep everything in order, and then some.'

My father and Dr Cates came in, and I had to go, without ever saying anything I had wanted to say. I went back to my own room and lay with the shadows all around me. I listened to the night murmurings that always went on in that house, sounds which never had a source, rafters and beams contracting in the dry air, perhaps, or mice in the walls, or a sparrow that had flown into the attic through the broken skylight there. After a while, although I would not have believed it possible, I slept.

The next morning I questioned my father. I believed him to be not only the best doctor in Manawaka, but also the best doctor in the whole of Manitoba, if not in the entire world, and the fact that he was not the one who was looking after my mother seemed to have something sinister about it.

'But it's always done that way, Vanessa,' he explained. 'Doctors never attend members of their own family. It's because they care so much about them, you see, and—'

'And what?' I insisted, alarmed at the way he had broken off. But my father did not reply. He stood there, and then he put on that difficult smile with which adults seek to conceal pain from children. I felt terrified, and ran to him, and he held me tightly.

'She's going to be fine,' he said. 'Honestly she is. Nessa, don't cry—'

Grandmother MacLeod appeared beside us, steel-spined despite her apparent fragility. She was wearing a purple silk dress and her ivory pendant. She looked as though she were all ready to go out for afternoon tea.

'Ewen, you're only encouraging the child to give way,' she said. 'Vanessa, big girls of ten don't make such a fuss about things. Come and get your breakfast. Now, Ewen, you're not to worry. I'll see to everything.'

Summer holidays were not quite over, but I did not feel like going out to play with any of the kids. I was very superstitious, and I had the feeling that if I left the house, even for a few hours, some disaster would overtake my mother. I did not, of course, mention this feeling to Grandmother MacLeod, for she did not believe in the existence of fear, or if she did, she never let on. I spent the morning morbidly, in seeking hidden places in the house. There were many of these—odd-shaped nooks under the stairs, small and loosely nailed-up doors at the back of clothes closets, leading to dusty tunnels and forgotten recesses in the heart of the house where the only things actually to be seen were drab oil paintings stacked upon the rafters, and trunks full of outmoded clothing and old photograph albums. But the unseen presences in these secret places I knew to be those of every person, young or old, who had ever belonged to the house and had died, including Uncle Roderick who got killed on the Somme,[1] and the baby who would have been my sister if only she had managed to come to life. Grandfather MacLeod, who had died a year after I was born, was present in the house in more tangible form. At the top of the main stairs hung the mammoth picture of a darkly uniformed man riding upon a horse whose prancing stance and dilated nostrils suggested that the battle was not yet over, that it might indeed continue until Judgment Day. The stern man was actually the Duke of Wellington, but at the time I believed him to be my grandfather MacLeod, still keeping an eye on things.

We had moved in with Grandmother MacLeod when the Depression got bad and she could no longer afford a housekeeper, but the MacLeod house never seemed like home to me. Its dark red brick was grown over at the front with Virginia creeper that turned crimson in the fall, until you could hardly tell brick from leaves. It boasted a small tower in which Grandmother MacLeod kept a weedy collection of anaemic ferns. The verandah was embellished with a profusion of wrought-iron scrolls, and the circular rose-window upstairs contained glass of many colours which permitted an outlooking eye to see the world as a place of absolute sapphire or emerald, or if one wished to look with a jaundiced eye, a hateful yellow. In Grandmother MacLeod's opinion, their features gave the house style.

---

1 One of the most costly campaigns of the First World War. The British offensive at the Somme, which began in July 1915, was joined by the 4th Canadian Division in September; despite severe losses on both sides, the results were indecisive.

Inside a multitude of doors led to rooms where my presence, if not actually forbidden, was not encouraged. One was Grandmother MacLeod's bedroom, with its stale and old-smelling air, the dim reek of medicines and lavender sachets. Here resided her monogrammed dresser silver, brush and mirror, nail-buffer and button hook and scissors, none of which must even be fingered by me now, for she meant to leave them to me in her will and intended to hand them over in the same flawless and unused condition in which they had always been kept. Here, too, were the silver-framed photographs of Uncle Roderick—as a child, as a boy, as a man in his Army uniform. The massive walnut spool bed had obviously been designed for queens or giants, and my tiny grandmother used to lie within it all day when she had a migraine, contriving somehow to look like a giant queen.

The living room was another alien territory where I had to tread warily, for many valuable objects sat just-so on tables and mantelpiece, and dirt must not be tracked in upon the blue Chinese carpet with its birds in eternal motionless flight and its water-lily buds caught forever just before the point of opening. My mother was always nervous when I was in this room.

'Vanessa, honey,' she would say, half apologetically, 'why don't you go and play in the den, or upstairs?'

'Can't you leave her, Beth?' my father would say. 'She's not doing any harm.'

'I'm only thinking of the rug,' my mother would say, glancing at Grandmother MacLeod, 'and yesterday she nearly knocked the Dresden shepherdess off the mantel. I mean, she can't help it, Ewen, she has to run around—'

'Goddamn it, I know she can't help it,' my father would growl, glaring at the smirking face of the Dresden shepherdess.

'I see no need to blaspheme, Ewen,' Grandmother MacLeod would say quietly, and then my father would say he was sorry, and I would leave.

The day my mother went to the hospital, Grandmother MacLeod called me at lunch-time, and when I appeared, smudged with dust from the attic, she looked at me distastefully as though I had been a cockroach that had just crawled impertinently out of the woodwork.

'For mercy's sake, Vanessa, what have you been doing with yourself? Run and get washed this minute. Here, not that way—you use the back stairs, young lady. Get along now. Oh—your father phoned.'

I swung around. 'What did he say? How is she? Is the baby born?'

'Curiosity killed a cat,' Grandmother MacLeod said, frowning. 'I cannot understand Beth and Ewen telling you all these things, at your age. What sort of vulgar person you'll grow up to be, I dare not think. No, it's not born yet. Your mother's just the same. No change.'

I looked at my grandmother, not wanting to appeal to her, but unable to stop myself. 'Will she—will she be all right?'

Grandmother MacLeod straightened her already-straight back. 'If I said definitely yes, Vanessa, that would be a lie, and the MacLeods do not tell lies, as I have tried to impress upon you before. What happens is God's will. The Lord giveth, and the Lord taketh away.'

Appalled, I turned away so she would not see my face and my eyes. Surprisingly, I heard her sigh and felt her papery white and perfectly manicured hand upon my shoulder.

'When your Uncle Roderick got killed,' she said, 'I thought I would die. But I didn't die, Vanessa.'

At lunch, she chatted animatedly, and I realised she was trying to cheer me in the only way she knew.

'When I married your Grandfather MacLeod,' she related, 'he said to me, "Eleanor, don't think because we're going to the prairies that I expect you to live roughly. You're used to a proper house, and you shall have one." He was as good as his word. Before we'd been in Manawaka three years, he'd had this place built. He earned a good deal of money in his time, your grandfather. He soon had more patients than either of the other doctors. We ordered our dinner service and all our silver from Birks' in Toronto. We had resident help in those days, of course, and never had less than twelve guests for dinner parties. When I had a tea, it would always be twenty or thirty. Never any less than half a dozen different kinds of cake were ever served in this house. Well, no one seems to bother much these days. Too lazy, I suppose.'

'Too broke,' I suggested. 'That's what Dad says.'

'I can't bear slang,' Grandmother MacLeod said. 'If you mean hard up, why don't you say so? It's mainly a question of management, anyway. My accounts were always in good order, and so was my house. No unexpected expenses that couldn't be met, no fruit cellar running out of preserves before the winter was over. Do you know what my father used to say to me when I was a girl?'

'No,' I said. 'What?'

'God loves Order,' Grandmother MacLeod replied with emphasis. 'You remember that, Vanessa. God loves Order—he wants each one of us to set our house in order. I've never forgotten those words of my father's. I was a MacInnes before I got married. The MacInnes is a very ancient clan, the lairds of Morven and constables of the Castle of Kinlochaline. Did you finish that book I gave you?'

'Yes,' I said. Then, feeling some additional comment to be called for, 'It was a swell book, Grandmother.'

This was somewhat short of the truth. I had been hoping for her cairngorm[2] brooch on my tenth birthday, and had received instead the plaid-bound volume entitled *The Clans and Tartans of Scotland*.[3] Most of it was too boring to read, but I had looked up the motto of my own family and those of some of my friends' families. *Be then a wall of brass. Learn to suffer. Consider the end. Go carefully.* I had not found any of these slogans reassuring. What with Mavis Duncan learning to suffer, and Laura Kennedy considering the end, and Patsy Drummond going carefully, and me spending my time in being a wall of brass, it did not seem to me that any of us were going to lead very interesting lives. I did not say this to Grandmother MacLeod.

2 Also called 'Scotch topaz'; a semi-precious stone frequently worn as part of the Highland Scots costume.

3 Vanessa would have discovered in Robert Bain's *The Clans and Tartans of Scotland* (1938, and many subsequent editions; the mottoes were added later) that the MacInneses were 'a Celtic clan of ancient origin', their earliest-known territory that of Morven. Bain says that they 'remained in possession of Morven, and as late as 1645 it appears that a MacInnes was in command of the Castle of Kinlochaline when it was besieged and burnt. . . .'

'The MacInnes motto is *Pleasure Arises from Work*,' I said.

'Yes,' she agreed proudly. 'And an excellent motto it is, too. One to bear in mind.'

She rose from the table, rearranging on her bosom the looped ivory beads that held the pendant on which a fullblown ivory rose was stiffly carved.

'I hope Ewen will be pleased,' she said.

'What at?'

'Didn't I tell you?' Grandmother MacLeod said. 'I hired a girl this morning, for the housework. She's to start tomorrow.'

When my father got home that evening, Grandmother MacLeod told him her good news. He ran one hand distractedly across his forehead.

'I'm sorry, Mother, but you'll just have to unhire her. I can't possibly pay anyone.'

'It seems distinctly odd', Grandmother MacLeod snapped, 'that you can afford to eat chicken four times a week.'

'Those chickens', my father said in an exasperated voice, 'are how people are paying their bills. The same with the eggs and the milk. That scrawny turkey that arrived yesterday was for Logan MacCardney's appendix, if you must know. We probably eat better than any family in Manawaka, except Niall Cameron's. People can't entirely dispense with doctors or undertakers. That doesn't mean to say I've got any cash. Look, Mother, I don't know what's happening with Beth. Paul thinks he may have to do a Caesarean. Can't we leave all this? Just leave the house alone. Don't touch it. What does it matter?'

'I have never lived in a messy house, Ewen,' Grandmother MacLeod said, 'and I don't intend to begin now.'

'Oh Lord,' my father said. 'Well, I'll phone Edna, I guess, and see if she can give us a hand, although God knows she's got enough, with the Connor house and her parents to look after.'

'I don't fancy having Edna Connor in to help,' Grandmother MacLeod objected.

'Why not?' my father shouted. 'She's Beth's sister, isn't she?'

'She speaks in such a slangy way,' Grandmother MacLeod said. 'I have never believed she was a good influence on Vanessa. And there is no need for you to raise your voice to me, Ewen, if you please.'

I could barely control my rage. I thought my father would surely rise to Aunt Edna's defence. But he did not.

'It'll be all right,' he soothed her. 'She'd only be here for part of the day, Mother. You could stay in your room.'

Aunt Edna strode in the next morning. The sight of her bobbed black hair and her grin made me feel better at once. She hauled out the carpet sweeper and the weighted polisher and got to work. I dusted while she polished and swept, and we got through the living room and the front hall in next to no time.

'Where's her royal highness, kiddo?' she enquired.

'In her room,' I said. 'She's reading the catalogue from Robinson & Cleaver.'

'Good Glory, not again?' Aunt Edna cried. 'The last time she ordered three linen tea-cloths and two dozen serviettes. It came to fourteen dollars. Your mother was absolutely frantic. I guess I shouldn't be saying this.'

'I knew anyway,' I assured her. 'She was at the lace handkerchiefs section when I took up her coffee.'

'Let's hope she stays there. Heaven forbid she should get onto the banqueting cloths. Well, at least she believes the Irish are good for two things—manual labour and linen-making. She's never forgotten Father used to be a blacksmith, before he got the hardware store. Can you beat it? I wish it didn't bother Beth.'

'Does it?' I asked, and immediately realised this was the wrong move, for Aunt Edna was suddenly scrutinizing me.

'We're making you grow up before your time,' she said. 'Don't pay any attention to me, Nessa. I must've got up on the wrong side of the bed this morning.'

But I was unwilling to leave the subject.

'All the same,' I said thoughtfully, 'Grandmother MacLeod's family were the lairds of Morven and the constables of the Castle of Kinlochaline. I bet you didn't know that.'

Aunt Edna snorted. 'Castle, my foot. She was born in Ontario, just like your Grandfather Connor, and her father was a horse doctor. Come on, kiddo, we'd better shut up and get down to business here.'

We worked in silence for a while.

'Aunt Edna—' I said at last, 'what about Mother? Why won't they let me go and see her?'

'Kids aren't allowed to visit maternity patients. It's tough for you, I know that. Look, Nessa, don't worry. If it doesn't start tonight, they're going to do the operation. She's getting the best of care.'

I stood there, holding the feather duster like a dead bird in my hands. I was not aware that I was going to speak until the words came out.

'I'm scared,' I said.

Aunt Edna put her arms around me, and her face looked all at once stricken and empty of defences.

'Oh, honey, I'm scared, too,' she said.

It was this way that Grandmother MacLeod found us when she came stepping lightly down into the front hall with the order in her hand for two dozen lace-bordered handkerchiefs of pure Irish linen.


I could not sleep that night, and when I went downstairs, I found my father in the den. I sat down on the hassock beside his chair, and he told me about the operation my mother was to have the next morning. He kept on saying it was not serious nowadays.

'But you're worried,' I put in, as though seeking to explain why I was.

'I should at least have been able to keep from burdening you with it,' he said in a distant voice, as though to himself. 'If only the baby hadn't got itself twisted around—'

'Will it be born dead, like the little girl?'

'I don't know,' my father said. 'I hope not.'

'She'd be disappointed, wouldn't she, if it was?' I said bleakly, wondering why I was not enough for her.

'Yes, she would,' my father replied. 'She won't be able to have any more, after this. It's partly on your account that she wants this one, Nessa. She doesn't want you to grow up without a brother or sister.'

'As far as I'm concerned, she didn't need to bother,' I retorted angrily.

My father laughed. 'Well, let's talk about something else, and then maybe you'll be able to sleep. How did you and Grandmother make out today?'

'Oh, fine, I guess. What was Grandfather MacLeod like, Dad?'

'What did she tell you about him?'

'She said he made a lot of money in his time.'

'Well, he wasn't any millionaire,' my father said, 'but I suppose he did quite well. That's not what I associate with him, though.'

He reached across to the bookshelf, took out a small leather-bound volume and opened it. On the pages were mysterious marks, like doodling, only much neater and more patterned.

'What is it?' I asked.

'Greek,' my father explained. 'This is a play called *Antigone*. See, here's the title in English. There's a whole stack of them on the shelves there. *Oedipus Rex. Electra. Medea.* They belonged to your Grandfather MacLeod. He used to read them often.'

'Why?' I enquired, unable to understand why anyone would pore over those undecipherable signs.

'He was interested in them,' my father said. 'He must have been a lonely man, although it never struck me that way at the time. Sometimes a thing only hits you a long time afterwards.'

'Why would he be lonely?' I wanted to know.

'He was the only person in Manawaka who could read these plays in the original Greek,' my father said. 'I don't suppose many people, if anyone, had even read them in English translations. Maybe he would have liked to be a classical scholar—I don't know. But his father was a doctor, so that's what he was. Maybe he would have liked to talk to somebody about these plays. They must have meant a lot to him.'

It seemed to me that my father was talking oddly. There was a sadness in his voice that I had never heard before, and I longed to say something that would make him feel better, but I could not, because I did not know what was the matter.

'Can you read this kind of writing?' I asked hesitantly.

My father shook his head. 'Nope. I was never very intellectual, I guess. Rod was always brighter than I, in school, but even he wasn't interested in learning Greek. Perhaps he would've been later, if he'd lived. As a kid, all I ever wanted to do was go into the merchant marine.'

'Why didn't you, then?'

'Oh well,' my father said offhandedly, 'a kid who'd never seen the sea wouldn't have made much of a sailor. I might have turned out to be the seasick type.'

I had lost interest now that he was speaking once more like himself.

'Grandmother MacLeod was pretty cross today about the girl,' I remarked.

'I know,' my father nodded. 'Well, we must be as nice as we can to her, Nessa, and after a while she'll be all right.'

Suddenly I did not care what I said.

'Why can't she be nice to us for a change?' I burst out. 'We're always the ones who have to be nice to her.'

My father put his hand down and slowly tilted my head until I was forced to look at him.

'Vanessa,' he said, 'she's had troubles in her life which you really don't know much about. That's why she gets migraine sometimes and has to go to bed. It's not easy for her these days, either—the house is still the same, so she thinks other things should be, too. It hurts her when she finds they aren't.'

'I don't see—' I began.

'Listen,' my father said, 'you know we were talking about what people are interested in, like Grandfather MacLeod being interested in Greek plays? Well, your grandmother was interested in being a lady, Nessa, and for a long time it seemed to her that she was one.'

I thought of the Castle of Kinlochaline, and of horse doctors in Ontario.

'I didn't know—' I stammered.

'That's usually the trouble with most of us,' my father said. 'You go on up to bed now. I'll phone tomorrow from the hospital as soon as the operation's over.'

I did sleep at last, and in my dreams I could hear the caught sparrow fluttering in the attic, and the sound of my mother crying, and the voices of the dead children.

My father did not phone until afternoon. Grandmother MacLeod said I was being silly, for you could hear the phone ringing all over the house, but nevertheless I refused to move out of the den. I had never before examined my father's books, but now, at a loss for something to do, I took them out one by one and read snatches here and there. After I had been doing this for several hours, it dawned on me that most of the books were of the same kind. I looked again at the titles.

*Seven League Boots. Arabia Deserta. The Seven Pillars of Wisdom. Travels in Tibet. Count Lucknor, the Sea Devil.*[4] And a hundred more. On a shelf by themselves were copies of the *National Geographic* magazine, which I looked at often enough, but never before with the puzzling compulsion which I felt now, as though I were on the verge of some discovery, something which I had to find out and yet did not want to know. I riffled through the picture-filled pages. Hibiscus and wild orchids grew in a soft-petalled confusion. The Himalayas stood lofty as gods, with the morning sun on their peaks of snow. Leopards snarled from the vined depths of a thousand jungles. Schooners buffeted their white sails like the wings of giant angels against the great sea winds.

'What on earth are you doing?' Grandmother MacLeod enquired waspishly, from the doorway. 'You've got everything scattered all over the place. Pick it all up this minute, Vanessa, do you hear?'

So I picked up the books and magazines, and put them all neatly away, as I had been told to do.

4  Five classic works of travel literature, published between the two world wars, by Richard Halliburton, C.M. Doughty, T.E. Lawrence, H. Harrier, and Lowell Thomas respectively.

When the telephone finally rang, I was afraid to answer it. At last I picked it up. My father sounded faraway, and the relief in his voice made it unsteady.

'It's okay, honey. Everything's fine. The boy was born alive and kicking after all. Your mother's pretty weak, but she's going to be all right.'

I could hardly believe it. I did not want to talk to anyone. I wanted to be by myself, to assimilate the presence of my brother, towards whom, without ever having seen him yet, I felt such tenderness and such resentment.

That evening, Grandmother MacLeod approached my father, who, still dazed with the unexpected gift of neither life now being threatened, at first did not take her seriously when she asked what they planned to call the child.

'Oh, I don't know. Hank, maybe, or Joe. Fauntleroy, perhaps.'

She ignored his levity.

'Ewen,' she said, 'I wish you would call him Roderick.'

My father's face changed. 'I'd rather not.'

'I think you should,' Grandmother MacLeod insisted, very quietly, but in a voice as pointed and precise as her silver nail-scissors.

'Don't you think Beth ought to decide?' my father asked.

'Beth will agree if you do.'

My father did not bother to deny something that even I knew to be true. He did not say anything. Then Grandmother MacLeod's voice, astonishingly, faltered a little.

'It would mean a great deal to me,' she said.

I remembered what she had told me—*When your Uncle Roderick got killed, I thought I would die. But I didn't die.* All at once, her feeling for that unknown dead man became a reality for me. And yet I held it against her, as well, for I could see that it had enabled her to win now.

'All right,' my father said tiredly. 'We'll call him Roderick.'

Then, alarmingly, he threw back his head and laughed.

'Roderick Dhu!' he cried. 'That's what you'll call him, isn't it? Black Roderick. Like before. Don't you remember? As though he were a character out of Sir Walter Scott, instead of an ordinary kid who—'

He broke off, and looked at her with a kind of desolation in his face.

'God, I'm sorry, Mother,' he said. 'I had no right to say that.'

Grandmother MacLeod did not flinch, or tremble, or indicate that she felt anything at all.

'I accept your apology, Ewen,' she said.

My mother had to stay in bed for several weeks after she arrived home. The baby's cot was kept in my parents' room, and I could go in and look at the small creature who lay there with his tightly closed fists and his feathery black hair. Aunt Edna came in to help each morning, and when she had finished the housework, she would have coffee with my mother. They kept the door closed, but this did not prevent me from eavesdropping, for there was an air register in the floor of the spare room, which was linked somehow with the register in my parents' room. If you put your ear to the iron grille, it was almost like a radio.

'Did you mind very much, Beth?' Aunt Edna was saying.

'Oh, it's not the name I mind,' my mother replied. 'It's just the fact that Ewen felt he had to. You know that Rod had only had the sight of one eye, didn't you?'

'Sure, I knew. So what?'

'There was only a year and a half between Ewen and Rod,' my mother said, 'so they often went around together when they were youngsters. It was Ewen's air-rifle that did it.'

'Oh Lord,' Aunt Edna said heavily. 'I suppose she always blamed him?'

'No, I don't think it was so much that, really. It was how he felt himself. I think he even used to wonder sometimes if—but people shouldn't let themselves think like that, or they'd go crazy. Accidents do happen, after all. When the war came, Ewen joined up first. Rod should never have been in the Army at all, but he couldn't wait to get in. He must have lied about his eyesight. It wasn't so very noticeable unless you looked at him closely, and I don't suppose the medicals were very thorough in those days. He got in as a gunner, and Ewen applied to have him in the same company. He thought he might be able to watch out for him, I guess, Rod being—at a disadvantage. They were both only kids. Ewen was nineteen and Rod was eighteen when they went to France. And then the Somme. I don't know, Edna, I think Ewen felt that if Rod had had proper sight, or if he hadn't been in the same outfit and had been sent somewhere else—you know how people always think these things afterwards, not that it's ever a bit of use. Ewen wasn't there when Rod got hit. They'd lost each other somehow, and Ewen was looking for him, not bothering about anything else, you know, just frantically looking. Then he stumbled across him quite by chance. Rod was still alive, but—'

'Stop it, Beth,' Aunt Edna said. 'You're only upsetting yourself.'

'Ewen never spoke of it to me', my mother went on, 'until once his mother showed me the letter he'd written to her at the time. It was a peculiar letter, almost formal, saying how gallantly Rod had died, and all that. I guess I shouldn't have, but I told him she'd shown it to me. He was very angry that she had. And then, as though for some reason he were terribly ashamed, he said—*I had to write something to her, but men don't really die like that, Beth. It wasn't that way at all.* It was only after the war that he decided to come back and study medicine and go into practice with his father.'

'Had Rod meant to?' Aunt Edna asked.

'I don't know,' my mother said slowly. 'I never felt I should ask Ewen that.'

Aunt Edna was gathering up the coffee things, for I could hear the clash of cups and saucers being stacked on the tray.

'You know what I heard her say to Vanessa once, Beth? *The MacLeods never tell lies.* Those were her exact words. Even then, I didn't know whether to laugh or cry.'

'Please, Edna—' my mother sounded worn out now. 'Don't.'

'Oh Glory,' Aunt Edna said remorsefully, 'I've got all the delicacy of a two-ton truck. I didn't mean Ewen, for heaven's sake. That wasn't what I meant at all. Here, let me plump up your pillows for you.'

Then the baby began to cry, so I could not hear anything more of interest. I took my bike and went out beyond Manawaka, riding aimlessly along the gravel highway. It was late summer, and the wheat had changed colour, but instead of being high and bronzed in the fields, it was stunted and desiccated, for there had been no rain again this year. But in the bluff where I stopped and crawled under the barbed wire fence and lay stretched out on the grass, the plentiful poplar leaves were turning to a luminous yellow and shone like church windows in the sun. I put my head down very close to the earth and looked at what was going on there. Grasshoppers with enormous eyes ticked and twitched around me, as though the dry air were perfect for their purposes. A ladybird laboured mightily to climb a blade of grass, fell off, and started all over again, seeming to be unaware that she possessed wings and could have flown up.

I thought of the accidents that might easily happen to a person—or, of course, might not happen, might happen to somebody else. I thought of the dead baby, my sister, who might as easily have been I. Would she, then, have been lying here in my place, the sharp grass making its small toothmarks on her brown arms, the sun warming her to the heart? I thought of the leatherbound volumes of Greek, and the six different kinds of iced cakes that used to be offered always in the MacLeod house, and the pictures of leopards and green seas. I thought of my brother, who had been born alive after all, and now had been given his life's name.

I could not really comprehend these things, but I sensed their strangeness, their disarray. I felt that whatever God might love in this world, it was certainly not order.

1970

---

# James Reaney
## 1926–2008

---

Growing up as an only child on a farm near Stratford, Ontario, James Reaney responded deeply to his local surroundings while learning early to depend on his powerful imagination. He attended a one-room school and then Stratford Collegiate before he began his studies, in 1944, at the University of Toronto's Victoria College. While still an undergraduate, he published stories and poetry in such journals as *Contemporary Verse*, *Northern Review*, and *Canadian Forum*. After he received his BA in English in 1948, he completed an MA in 1949. He also published his first book of poems that year, *The Red Heart*, which won him his first Governor General's Award.

In the fall of 1949, Reaney joined the English department at the University of Manitoba, remaining there until 1960—the only period he lived outside Ontario. While on leave from UoM in 1956–8, he returned to the University of Toronto to complete his doctoral degree under the direction of Northrop Frye. His thesis, which investigated Edmund Spenser's influence on Yeats, inspired Reaney to create a witty imitation of *The Shepheardes Calender*, entitled *A Suit of Nettles* (1958): in it, he transformed Spenser's pastoral dialogues between shepherds tending their flocks into conversations among geese on an Ontario farm. The poem won Reaney his second Governor General's Award.

In the 1960s, Reaney became interested in creating poetic works for performance and established himself as a leading Canadian playwright. He also composed the libretto for *Night-Blooming Cereus* (1960)—an opera by John

Beckwith—and a sequence of poems about Stratford, Ontario for CBC radio, which was published in 1962 as *Twelve Letters to a Small Town*. His first collection of drama, *The Killdeer and Other Plays*, appeared later that same year, and Reaney was awarded his third Governor General's Award for the two books. His finest theatrical achievement and the work for which he may be best known is *The Donnellys*, a trilogy first staged in the early 1970s and published in 1975–7: set in the nineteenth century, it is the story of a contumacious Irish family who lived near London, Ontario, and were murdered as the result of conflicts carried over from Ireland. (In 2004, Reaney, who had done exhaustive research in preparing the drama, edited a collection of background sources about the event: *The Donnelly Documents: An Ontario Vendetta*.) Like Reaney's other plays, *The Donnellys* departed from the then-prevailing conventions of realistic theatre in its poetic style and frequent disruptions of linear narrative.

Reaney continued to explore opera by writing librettos that drew on local history. *The Shivaree* (1978) shows the mythic dimensions of the rural custom of mock serenades for newly-wed couples. *Serinette* tells the story of the Children of Peace, a pacifist and religious group that emigrated from the United States after they separated from the Quakers in 1812; in 1990, it was produced in the octagonal Sharon Temple built by that group. Four years later, Reaney dealt, in *Taptoo*, with events in Upper Canada in the years preceding *Serinette*.

Reaney also worked in prose. In addition to writing two novels for adolescents—*The Boy with an R in His Hand: A Tale of the Type-Riot at William Lyon Mackenzie's Printing Office* in 1886 (1965, revised 1980) and *Take the Big Picture* (1986)—he collected, in 1966, his influential short stories, mostly written in the 1940s and 1950s, as *The Box Social and Other Stories*. Several of the stories in this collection, particularly 'The Box Social' (which scandalized readers when it was first published) and 'The Bully', are early examples of what Timothy Findley identified as 'Southern Ontario Gothic', a narrative tradition, which includes, in addition to Reaney, Margaret Atwood (who has said 'The Bully' was a key reading experience for her), Findley, Alice Munro, and Barbara Gowdy—in which (as in the earlier American Southern Gothic) a strong sense of place is combined with macabre events.

Reaney's poetry and drama are intensely grounded in his experience of growing up in Perth County, Ontario. When he taught courses in Ontario culture and literature, he would have his students begin with a close consideration of the small actualities of daily existence and a careful scrutiny of maps of their area. At the same time, Reaney regarded myth and the archetypes drawn from the imagination as giving universal significance to the immediacy of existence, and as part of the construction and function of everyday culture. His contact with Frye when he was an undergraduate and again when he worked on his doctoral thesis led him to the theories contained in *Anatomy of Criticism* (published in 1957, shortly after Reaney began his study under Frye) and to Carl Jung and other theorists on the mythic dimensions of the mind.

In her essay on *Alphabet*, the important literary magazine that Reaney founded and edited from 1960 to 1971, Atwood discusses Reaney's goal as 'documentary on one side and myth on the other', and suggests that this tension between myth and documentary is not only central to Reaney's vision, but is peculiarly Canadian ('Eleven Years of *Alphabet*', *Canadian Literature*, No. 49, 1971). A special issue of the *University of Toronto Quarterly* on 'The Visionary Tradition in Canadian Writing' (2001) located Reaney as a central figure in that tradition, along with Frye, Margaret Avison, P.K. Page, Al Purdy, Atwood, Don McKay, Michael Ondaatje, and others.

The extent of Reaney's interest in the creative dimension and the power of the human mind is conveyed by the full title of his literary magazine: *Alphabet: A Semi-Annual Devoted to the Iconography of the Imagination*. Begun the year Reaney moved from Manitoba to take up a position at the University of Western Ontario, *Alphabet* coincided with Frye's critical theories and the work of poets such as Jay Macpherson to direct the attention of emerging Canadian writers to myth as a resource and suggested—by the often arbitrary juxtaposition of its diverse contents to the mythic figure announced for each issue—that the presence of myth in a work is derived as much from the mind's quest for meaning as from anything inherent in individual stories and poems. At the same time, the title of Reaney's journal sets against the universalizing tendency of myth the particulars out of which language grows, the very letters themselves. (Before beginning to publish his magazine, Reaney trained as a typesetter and for a time typeset each issue himself.) One of the many emerging writers of the decade who appeared in *Alphabet* was bpNichol, whose concrete poetry literally attempted to create art out of the alphabet by treating letters as things in themselves—an act which would influence Reaney in his later work.

While teaching, editing, and working on his plays, Reaney never stopped writing poetry. *The Dance of Death at London, Ontario* (1963) is a satiric sequence of poems about his new hometown. The 1972 volume entitled *Poems*, edited and with an introduction by Germaine Warkentin, is a large selection of Reaney's poetry. That same year, Reaney wrote an introduction to a new reprint of *The Collected Poems of Isabella Valancy Crawford*, Crawford's early mythologizing of nature and its opposing forces having long

interested him. In 1984, *Imprecations: The Art of Swearing* playfully explored the 'lost skill' of cursing. His *Performance Poems* (1990) is a collection of works arranged in a calendrical cycle from January to December.

In 'The Alphabet' and 'Starling with a Split-Tongue' language itself seems a source of magic, while the figure of the child, which recurs throughout Reaney's work, holds secret truths that we as adults yearn for. It is to this child in all of us that Reaney, in his constant playfulness, was ultimately speaking. Because Reaney was less interested in objective reality than in the imaginative structures into which the mind orders that reality—that is, not in what happens but in what we make of what happens—what he most valued in his rural community was the power of words to transform reality into stories, song, folktales, nursery rhymes, and individual flights of fancy. In all his works, the mind is striving to make the world comprehensible—but since both mind and world oscillate between innocence and experience, and between dreaming and waking (in ways that make it hard to say which is which) comprehension remains intriguingly elusive.

# The School Globe

Sometimes when I hold
Our faded old globe
That we used at school
To see where oceans were
And the five continents,
The lines of latitude and longitude,
The North Pole, the Equator and the South Pole—
Sometimes when I hold this
Wrecked blue cardboard pumpkin
I think: here in my hands                                    10
Rest the fair fields and lands
Of my childhood
Where still lie or still wander
Old games, tops and pets;
A house where I was little
And afraid to swear
Because God might hear and

Send a bear
To eat me up;
Rooms where I was as old                                          20
As I was high;
Where I loved the pink clenches,
The white, red and pink fists
Of roses; where I watched the rain
That Heaven's clouds threw down
In puddles and rutfuls
And irregular mirrors
Of soft brown glass upon the ground.
This school globe is a parcel of my past,
A basket of pluperfect[1] things.                                 30
And here I stand with it
Sometime in the summertime
All alone in an empty schoolroom
Where about me hang
Old maps, an abacus, pictures,
Blackboards, empty desks.
If I raise my hand
No tall teacher will demand
What I want.
But if someone in authority                                       40
Were here, I'd say
Give me this old world back
Whose husk I clasp
And I'll give you in exchange
The great sad real one
That's filled
Not with a child's remembered and pleasant skies
But with blood, pus, horror, death, stepmothers, and lies.

1949

1   More than perfect; in grammar the tense that denotes completed action (expressed in English by the auxiliary *had*).

## The Lost Child

Long have I looked for my lost child.
I hear him shake his rattle
Slyly in the winter wind
In the ditch that's filled with snow.

He pinched and shrieked and ran away
At the edge of the November forest.
The hungry old burdock stood
By the dead dry ferns.

Hear him thud that ball!
The acorns fall by the fence.                                    10
See him loll in the St. Lucy sun,[1]
The abandoned sheaf in the wire.

Oh Life in Death! my bonny nursling
Merry drummer in the nut brown coffin,
With vast wings outspread I float
Looking and looking over the empty sea

And there! in the—on the rolling death
Rattling a dried out gourd
Floated the mysterious cradle
Filled with a source.                                            20

I push the shore and kingdom to you,
Oh winter walk with seedpod ditch:
I touch them to the floating child
And lo! Cities and gardens, shepherds and smiths.

1962[2]

---

1 St Lucy's Day, 13 December, was traditionally thought of as the shortest day of the year and the beginning of
  the winter solstice.
2 As the final poem in *One-Man Masque*, a one-man drama about the stages of life.

## The Alphabet

Where are the fields of dew?
I cannot keep them.
They quip and pun
The rising sun
Who plucks them out of view:
*But lay down fire-veined jasper!*

For out of my cloudy head
Come Ay Ee I Oh and U,
Five thunders shouted;
*Drive in sardonyx!*                                             10

And Ull Mm Nn Rr and hisSsings
Proclaim huge wings;
*Pour in sea blue sapphires!*


Through my bristling hair
Blows Wuh and Yuh
Puh, Buh, Phuh and Vuh,
The humorous air:
*Lift up skies of chalcedony!*


Huh, Cuh, Guh and Chuh
Grunt like pigs in my acorn mind:
*Arrange these emeralds in a meadow!*                    20


Come down Tuh, Duh and Thuh!
Consonantly rain
On the windowpane
Of the shrunken house of the heart;
*Lift up blood red sardius!*


*Lift up golden chrysolite!*
Juh, Quuh, Zuh and X
Scribble heavens with light
Steeples take fright.                    30


In my mouth like bread
Stands the shape of this glory;
Consonants and vowels
Repeat the story:
*And sea-green beryl is carried up!*


The candle tongue in my dark mouth
Is anguished with its sloth
And stung with self-scoff
As my eyes behold this treasure.
*Let them bring up topaz now!*                    40


*Dazzling chrysoprase!*
Dewdrops tempt dark wick to sparkle.
Growl Spark! you whelp and cur,
Leap out of tongue kennel
And candle sepulchre.

*I faint in the hyacinthine quarries!*
My words pursue
Through the forest of time
The fading antlers of this dew.

A B C D E F G H I J K L M                                          50
Take captive the sun
Slay the dew quarry
Adam's Eve is morning rib
Bride and bridegroom marry
Still coffin is rocking crib
Tower and well are one
The stone is the wind, the wind is the stone
New Jerusalem[1]
N O P Q R S T U V W X Y Z!

1960, 1972

1 The final paradise after Armageddon according to Revelation; see Revelation 21–2, which is the source of the imagery of the poem.

## Starling with a Split Tongue[1]

Some boys caught me
    In the yard
And with a jackknife they
Split my tongue into speech
So in a phrenological[2] cage
Here in the garage I stay
    And say
The cracklewords passersby taught.
I say I know not what
Though I pray I do not pray                                      10
Though I curse I do not curse
Though I talk I do not talk

'I thought that made it kinda nice'
I heard her say as she began slipping on the ice

1 Folk belief holds that splitting the tongues of crows, ravens, and starlings makes it possible to teach them how to speak.
2 That is, 'skull-like'; phrenology (literally the study of the mental faculties) is the pseudo-scientific theory that the shape of the skull gives evidence of personality and mental ability.

| | |
|---|---|
| The the I am | An a am I |
| I and am are the & a | Who is are? Who saw war? |
| I rock a little pronoun | It does instead of me |
| I rose as I | Nooned as you |
| Lay down as he or she | Begat we, you & they |
| My eggs are covered with commas | 20 |

'Yuh remember when she fell down in a fit?'
Reveries Jake from the bottom of the pit.

| | |
|---|---|
| Before beforeday | after St After's Massacre |
| While the while is on | Since since is since |
| Let's wait till till | Or until if you like |
| I come from from | to Whither Bay |
| Down Whence Road | but not To-day |

| | |
|---|---|
| As still as infinitives were the | Stones |
| Filled with adjectives were the | Trees |
| And with adverbs the | Pond          30 |

This all is a recorded announcement
            This all is a recorded announcement
'I thought that made it kinda nice'
'Yuh remember . . . . . . . . . . . . . in a fit?'
                        Darkness deep
Now fills the garage and its town
                With wordless sleep.

Who split their tongues? I ask.
Of Giant Jackknife in the sky.
Who split their tongues into lie mask              40
And lie face; split their hand
Into this way, that way, up and down,
Divided their love into restless hemispheres,
Split into two—one seeing left, one right
Their once one Aldebaran[3] all-seeing eye?
In the larger garage of the endless starlight
            Do they not croak as I?

1964, 1972

---

3  One of the brightest stars in the sky, Aldebaran is an orange giant that forms the bull's eye in the constellation
    Taurus.

# Phyllis Webb

## b. 1927

Phyllis Webb was born in Victoria, British Columbia, and grew up there and in Vancouver. In 1949, she received a BA in English and philosophy from the University of British Columbia. At twenty-two, she ran as a CCF candidate for the BC legislature; during the campaign, she met F.R. Scott, then chair of the CCF In 1950, Webb moved to Montreal, at Scott's suggestion, to join the poetic ferment there. She supported herself with secretarial jobs and copy-editing, took graduate courses at McGill, and made extended trips to England, Ireland, and, from 1957–9, Paris. (She wrote pieces about her experiences there for the *Victoria Daily Times*.) After teaching at UBC for four years from 1960 to 1963, Webb spent a year in San Francisco, where she met Robert Duncan, Allen Ginsberg, Charles Olson, Denise Levertov, and others. Returning to Canada, she settled in Toronto to accept a job with CBC radio, for which she had been freelancing since 1955. With William A. Young, she created the groundbreaking radio program *Ideas*: its explorations of contemporary intellectual and artistic developments and thought have been broadcast since 1965. (From 1967 to 1969, she was the show's executive producer.) Webb also interviewed a number of Canadian writers for CBC television, including Scott, A.J.M. Smith, Livesay, Atwood, and bpNichol. In the 1960s, she was instrumental in convincing the CBC to employ more female announcers. At the end of decade, she left full-time radio work; since 1969, she has made her home on the West Coast—chiefly on Salt Spring Island—while sometimes teaching creative writing at the University of Victoria. She has also taught at the Banff Centre and was writer-in-residence at the University of Alberta.

Webb's first book publication was in *Trio* (1954), a showcase for her work and that of Gael Turnbull and Eli Mandel, two other new writers then in Montreal; it was followed by *Even Your Right Eye* (1956). After her return to British Columbia, Webb published *The Sea Is Also a Garden* (1962). The book that followed, *Naked Poems* (1965), which has been described as the first poetry in Canada to deal with lesbian love, marked a shift from the formal style of her earlier work to a stark minimalist approach, reflected in its short lines of intense poetry.

By the time *Selected Poems, 1954–1965* was published in 1971, Webb had entered a period of poetic silence following *Naked Poems* that lasted until the publication of *Wilson's Bowl* (1980). The poems in this and subsequent volumes, though not so austere as the lyrics of *Naked Poems*, demonstrate her characteristic economy of form. Since 1980, Webb has produced four more volumes of poetry: *Sunday Water: Thirteen Anti Ghazals* (1982); *Selected Poems: The Vision Tree* (1982), a Governor General's Award–winner that includes some new work; *Water and Light: Ghazals and Anti Ghazals* (1984); and *Hanging Fire* (1990). Webb's essays on poetry and the creative process are gathered in two volumes: *Talking* (1982), which also contains scripts of some of her radio talks; and *Nothing But Brush Strokes: Selected Prose* (1995), which includes some of her photo-collages, reflecting her growing focus on visual art. In 2004, she edited *The Griffin Poetry Prize Anthology*.

Webb's early poetry often deals with despair and death but is rarely morbid and always leavened with wit: in 'To Friends Who Have Also Considered Suicide' she wrote, 'It has concerned our best philosophers / and inspired some of the most popular / of our politicians and financiers.' Her viewpoint during this early period was shaped by a conscious existentialism. Investigating what she sees as a sterile, even meaningless, world, she presents readers with strategies for survival. In the face of breakup and breakdown—topics important to late-twentieth-century culture and to her personally—Webb suggests that the individual should seek protective isolation and quietude. In her own life, she has found these in the beaches, water, and gardens of BC's Gulf Islands.

Webb's later poetry is more externally directed and sometimes angry, rejecting the patriarchal values and forms that she has inherited and has come to view as inimical to women's natural aesthetics. Her work has displayed a broad range of affinities—from the intricacies of metaphysical poetry techniques (as in 'Marvell's Garden') to the stylistic simplicity of the Black Mountain and San Francisco poetry movements (found in *Naked Poems*), as well as responding to the philosophy of Buddhism and to the aesthetic forms of Western Asia. The most important aspect of

her poetry, however—particularly from *Naked Poems* onward—has been her feminism and her need to create a poetics supportive of women's interests. Her wide familiarity with poetic traditions and her desire to find within them the tools she needs, have made her last poetry collection, *Hanging Fire* (1990), rewardingly rich in structure. She tries to obey what she calls

*the physics of the poem. Energy/Mass. Waxy splendour, the massive quiet of the fallen tulip petals. So much depends upon: the wit of the syntax, the rhythm and speed of the fall, the drop, the assumption of a specific light, curved. (Talking, 1982)*

# Marvell's Garden[1]

Marvell's garden, that place of solitude,[2]
is not where I'd choose to live
yet is the fixed sundial[3]
that turns me round
unwillingly
in a hot glade
as closer, closer I come to contradiction
to the shade green within the green shade.[4]

The garden where Marvell scorned love's solicitude[5]—
that dream—and played instead an arcane solitaire,      10
shuffling his thoughts like shadowy chance
across the shrubs of ecstasy,
and cast the myths away to flowering hours
as yes, his mind, that sea, caught at green
thoughts shadowing a green infinity.

1 This poem is built around responses and allusions to 'The Garden' by the British poet Andrew Marvell (1621–78).
2 Marvell chooses to be solitary in the garden, declaring: 'Society is all but rude / To this delicious solitude'.
3 The sundial in Marvell's poem is equated with the garden itself; in the seventeenth century the sundial was often a symbol of a stable point against which to measure the illusions of experience.
4 In this stanza and the next, Webb refers to lines in Marvell's poem:

> The mind, that ocean where each kind
> Does straight its own resemblance find;
> Yet it creates, transcending these,
> Far other worlds, and other seas;
> Annihilating all that's made
> To a green thought in a green shade.

5 Marvell rejects physical love, approving of the mythical stories in which young women escape seduction when they are transformed into a tree or a reed.

And yet Marvell's garden was not Plato's
garden[6]—and yet—he *did* care more for the form
of things than for the thing itself—
ideas and visions,
resemblances and echoes,                                          20
things seeming and being
not quite what they were.

That was his garden, a kind of attitude
struck out of an earth too carefully attended,
wanting to be left alone.
And I don't blame him for that.
God knows, too many fences fence us out
and his garden closed in on Paradise.[7]

On Paradise! When I think of his hymning
Puritans in the Bermudas,[8] the bright oranges           30
lighting up that night! When I recall
his rustling tinsel hopes
beneath the cold decree of steel.[9]
Oh, I have wept for some new convulsion
to tear together this world and his.

But then I saw his luminous plumèd Wings[10]
prepared for flight,
and then I heard him singing glory
in a green tree,
and then I caught the vest he'd laid aside                  40
all blest with fire.

6  Marvell, while affirming the Platonic concept of ideal forms, departed from most of his contemporary Neo-
   Platonists in his belief that man's mind—equated in 'The Garden' with the ocean, which was though, in the
   Renaissance, to contain a parallel to every land-based thing—was superior to nature, and thus to an ideal reality,
   because it not only had a pre-existent knowledge of all the 'forms' of reality but also could imaginatively create
   new 'forms' that have never before existed.
7  Marvell equates his garden to Eden before the creation of Eve and Adam's fall.
8  In the poem 'Bermudas', Marvell depicts religious dissenters rowing ashore to the Bermudas (celebrated by
   Europeans as a kind of earthly paradise), singing a hymn of praise to God that includes the lines: 'He hangs in
   shades the orange bright, / Like golden lamps in a green night'.
9  Marvell himself was twice exiled to the Bermudas as a result of ecclesiastical persecution. Throughout his life
   he sought a middle ground in the political strife of England, which was being torn apart by civil war.
10  In 'The Garden', the poet undergoes a rapturous identification with his setting:

   *Casting the body's vest aside,*
   *My soul into the boughs does glide:*
   *There like a bird it sits, and sings,*
   *Then whets and combs its silver wings.*

And I have gone walking slowly in
his garden of necessity
leaving brothers, lovers, Christ
outside my walls
where they have wept without
and I within.

1956

## From *Naked Poems*

## Suite I

MOVING
to establish distance
between our houses.

It seems
I welcome you in.

Your mouth blesses me
all over.

There is room.

AND
here                                                    10
and here and
here
and over      and
over      your mouth

TONIGHT
quietness.      In me
and the room.

I am enclosed
by a thought

and some walls.                                        20

THE BRUISE

Again you have left
your mark.

Or we
have.

Skins shuddered
secretly.

FLIES

tonight
in this room

two flies
on the ceiling
are making
love
quietly.    Or

so it seems
down here

YOUR BLOUSE

I people
this room                                    40
with things, a
chair,    a lamp,    a
fly,    two books by
Marianne Moore.

I have thrown my
blouse on the floor.

Was it only
last night?

YOU
took                                                                    50

with so much
gentleness

my dark


## Suite II

*While you were away*

*I held you like this*
*in my mind.*

*It is a good mind*
*that can embody*
*perfection     with exactitude.*

*The sun comes through*
*plum curtains.*

*I said*
*the sun is gold*                                                      10

*in your eyes.*

*It isn't the sun*
*you said.*

*On the floor your blouse.*
*The plum light*
*falls more golden*

*going down.*

*Tonight*
*quietness*
*in the room.*                    20

*We knew*

*Then you must go.*
*I sat cross-legged*
*on the bed.*
*There is no room*
*for self-pity*
*I said*

*I lied*

*In the gold darkening*
*light*                    30

*you dressed.*

*I hid my face*
*in my hair.*

*The room that held you*

*is still here.*

*You brought me clarity.*

*Gift after gift*
*I wear.*

*Poems      naked*
*in the sunlight*                    40

*on the floor.*

*1965*

# Spots of Blood

I am wearing absent-minded red
slippers and a red vest—
spots of blood
to match the broken English
of Count Dracula being interviewed
on the radio in the morning sun.
I touch the holes in my throat
where the poppies bud—spots of blood
spots of womantime. '14,000 rats,'[1]
Dracula is saying, and the interviewer                         10
echoes, '14,000 rats! So beautiful,'
he sighs, 'The Carpathian Mountains—
the photography, so seductive!' The Count
also loves the film; he has already seen it
several times. He tells in his dreamy voice
how he didn't need direction, didn't want
makeup, how he could have done it with his own
teeth. He glided in and out of this role
believing in reincarnation, in metamorphosis.
Yet 14,000 rats and the beleaguered                            20
citizens of the Dutch town where those scenes
were shot (without him) are of no interest.
'And Hollywood?' the interviewer asks, himself
an actor, 'Hollywood next?' Who knows?
Who knows?

The blood pounds at my temples.
The women of the world parade before me
in red slippers and red vests, back and
forth, back and forth, fists clenched.
My heart emerges from my breast for                            30
14,000 rats and the citizens of Delft,
for the women of the world in their menses.
Yet I too imitate a crime of passion:
Look at these hands. Look at the hectic

---

1  In *Nosferatu* (Germany, 1922), a film based on Bram Stoker's novel *Dracula* (1887), the vampire sets a plague of
   rats upon a city. The heroine, sacrificing her own life in an effort to save humankind, entices the vampire to her
   bed, where he remains until destroyed by the first rays of the morning sun.

red painting my cheekbones as I metamorphose
in and out of the Buddha's eye,[2] the *animus
mundi*.

In the morning sun Count Dracula leans
against my throat with his own teeth.
Breathing poppies. Thinking.                                    40

1980

2  Buddha is said to be the Eye of the World, the All-Seeing Eye in which all existence rests. '*Animus mundi*': the
   world soul or mind, usually in the feminine form, *anima mundi*; here Webb refers to (i) the Buddhist notion
   of an Absolute Mind out of which the world emanates, and (ii) the Jungian principle of one's idealized sexual
   opposite. (Since the speaker is female, her ideal is male, *animus*.)

# I Daniel[1]

*for Timothy Findley*

I.

But I Daniel was grieved
and the vision of my head troubled me,[2]

and I do not want to keep
the matter in my heart

for the heart of the matter
is something different.

Neither do I want happiness
without vision.

I am apocryphal and received.[3]
I live now and in time past                                    10

1  This poem utilizes the form of the ghazal (pronounced 'guzzle'): a series of couplets dealing with one subject, each
   of which can stand by itself, and usually concerned with love (either sensual or mystical) in images that are simple
   and local. A poetic structure first used in Persia (now Iran) that spread from Western Asia to India and nearby
   countries, the ghazal has some other conventions that Webb has not followed here, which may be why she
   subtitled her book 'Ghazals and Anti Ghazals'. Webb has described her ghazals and anti ghazals as emphasizing
   'the particular, the local, the dialectical and private'.
2  Webb's poem is a response to the Book of Daniel, one of the last books in the Hebrew Scriptures (the Old
   Testament). The second part of the book (Chapters 7–12) is spoken by Daniel in the first person, with the formula
   'I Daniel' appearing at 7:15: 'I Daniel was grieved in my spirit in the midst of my body, and the visions of my head
   troubled me.' This half of Daniel is made up of a series of prophecies concerning the rise and fall of empires in
   Daniel's time—prophecies that were eventually reinterpreted as being about the end of the world and later combined with those found in the Book of Revelation to form the apocalyptic belief system of evangelical Christianity.
3  The Book of Daniel is part of the 'received' or authorized canon of scripture; however, additions to the Book of
   Daniel (which are found in the Greek, but not in the Hebrew, text of Daniel) are collected in the Apocrypha,
   those books of scripture that were considered for inclusion in the Bible but not made part of the official canon.

among all kinds of musick—sackbut,
cornet, flute, psaltery, harp, and dulcimer.[4]

You come bearing jobs and treachery and money,

but I Daniel, servant to powers
that pass all understanding,

grieve into time, times, and the dividing of time.[5]


    2.

I also serve the kings,
but my own name fascinates me[6]

with its slippery syllables.
I live in a mysterious book;                        20

my imitators incline me to derision
for they too are fascinated by my name,

by the flagrant musick of the old lore,
sackbut and psaltery, by the grief

in all my actions.


    3.

The coin is dropped into my palm.
I become the messenger, see—

here, now, in my own hand
the printout of the King's text

4  A reference to Chapter 3 of Daniel, which tells the famous story of how Daniel and three of his companions are cast into a fiery furnace because they refuse to worship a golden idol set up by Nebuchadnezzar, King of Babylon, who commands his people, 'That at what time ye hear the sound of the cornet, flute, harp, sackbut, psaltery, dulcimer, and all kinds of musick, ye fall down worship the golden image' (3:5). (The sackbut is the ancestor of the modern trombone; the psaltery is a harp-like instrument.)

5  In one of Daniel's prophecies, he foresees the coming of four beasts, a lion with eagle's wings, a bear with tusks, a winged leopard, and a terrifying creature with iron teeth, bronze claws, and ten horns; this last beast will, according to Daniel 7:25, take power 'for a time and times and the dividing of time'. ('Time' is a conventional expression for a year, and 'times' is understood as two years; thus, here, three and a half years—though in later apocalyptic interpretation, these are understood as 'prophetic years' of much longer duration).

6  The name 'Daniel' means 'judged by God'; after being captured and made a servant to Nebuchadnezzar, Daniel goes to the king who—having become enraged by his wise men's failure to interpret a dream that has troubled him (he makes his demands especially difficult by requiring that they also tell him the content of his dream)—has decided to kill all the wise men in his kingdom. Given a revelation by God, Daniel both recounts and inter-prets the dream. In consequence he is made the king's counsellor. He later serves Belshazzar, Nebuchadnezzar's successor, and Darius and Cyrus, Belshazzar's successors.

which he has forgotten                                                              30
and I remember.

Listen, I dream the dream,
I deliver its coded message

and pocket the coin.
Keep your jobs and dollars.

I go into the dark on the King's business
and spend my time thanking him

for the privilege of my servitude.


4.

The musick of the dulcimer was a silver bird
flying about my ears                                                                40

when I closed my eyes and sealed them.
Nebuchadnezzar

tapped me on the shoulder
after I'd done the job;

but all I could hear was bird
song in the apparatus,

all I could hear were three notes
from the string of the dulcimer

and one on the cornet.


5.

I ate no pleasant bread. The fast                                                   50
unbroken for weeks,

then I Daniel looked and saw—
but what do you care for the grief

of what I Daniel understood by
books the number of the years of desolation?

Confusion of faces, yours among them,
the poetry tangled, no vision of my own to speak of.

The hand moved along the wall.
I was able to read, that's all.[7]


      6.

I, even I Daniel, whose countenance           60
changed, said nothing about a broken heart.

Always it was the dangerous ones
who needed me

in the garden, under the stars—
always I found what they needed

flat on my face in a deep sleep:
'Messenger, here is your message.'

And I Daniel fainted
and was sick certain days.[8]


      7.

In those days I Daniel           70
was mourning three full weeks.

Haunted by numbers: what 'passed seven
times,'[9] and what 'shall be for a time,

and times, and a half'? Four horns or one
or one becoming four in the breakdown

---

7 A reference to the story in Daniel 5 of a mysterious hand that appears during a feast held by Belshazzar and writes upon the wall. When the wise men at Belshazzar's court cannot read the words, Daniel is sent for and interprets them: 'God hath numbered thy kingdom, and finished it. Thou are weighed in the balances, and art found wanting.' Webb's dedication of this poem to Timothy Findley may be because Findley's 1981 novel *Famous Last Words* makes extensive use of the story in Daniel 5. That novel is dedicated to Phyllis Webb.

8 Daniel 8:27. Daniel faints at the end of this chapter, following a dream that has shown him a future in which the kingdoms of Media and Persia, having displaced Babylon, will be conquered by Alexander the Great, whose kingdom will in turn be divided into four. In the dream, these events are expressed allegorically: a ram with two horns is defeated by a goat with one horn, which subsequently becomes four horns. The archangel Gabriel appears to Daniel to explain that the ram represents Media and Persia, and the goat, Alexander's Grecia. This dream, far more wide-ranging than any of his previous visions and showing him the instability of great kingdoms and the fact that they all will eventually fall, leaves Daniel exhausted.

9 In Daniel 9, Daniel interprets a dream of Nebuchadnezzar as foretelling a period of madness for the king: 'and thy dwelling shall be with the beasts of the field, and they shall make thee to eat grass as oxen, and they shall wet thee with the dew of heaven, and seven times shall pass over thee, until thou know that the most High ruleth in the kingdom of men and giveth it to whomsoever he will.' The passage that follows is from the last chapter of Daniel; in it a figure appears saying: 'Go thy way, Daniel: for the words are closed up and sealed till the time of the end.'

of the bicameral mind[10]—wherein I Daniel
alone saw the vision—


       8.

It was only politics, wars and rumours
in the vision or dream:

four beasts of terror with their                        80
numbers game. I play and trick my way

out of this scene into the arms of Gabriel
who does not hear the tune performed

on sackbut, psaltery, harp and dulcimer.

1984

10 As Stephen Scobie points out: 'The reference here is to Julian Jaynes' book *The Origins of Consciousness in the Breakdown of the Bicameral Mind* (1976), in which Jaynes argues that prophetic "visions", of the type Daniel records, can be accounted for as the sudden intrusions into left-brain consciousness of right-brain impulses, which are then perceived as coming "from the outside"' (*Signature Event Cantext* 132).


# The Making of a Japanese Print

> *The first plate in the volume is the key block*
> *giving the outline. It is easy to see how each*
> *successive color is added by a separate block to*
> *achieve the final result.*
>
>       —from *The Making of a Japanese Print*


**IMPRINT NO. I**
Eye contact, and it's forever.
The first circle.

And then the breast
the left or right.
So choice.
Or grab what is given.

Rosebud and at the
periphery / eyelash
dark sandals pass by.

Add a chair in the corner                          10
with a white chemise.
This is the only way to go
—outward.

Door behind the mother
closing as father in blue
blows out.

White filled in, hatch-
crossings for negative space.
Decadent life.

Flesh tint laid on                                  20
with extreme caution.
All moves are dangerous:
open the door and wind pours in
with dust. Lift the head
of mother an inch
her attention goes
out the unseen window.

If baby sleeps
hand falling away from
the opening bud, rose                               30
becomes dream, memory
a praise of distance.

*Technique is all
a test of the artist's
sincerity.* Oh
we are *sincere*, we go
for the blade, cut close
to the bone. The splotch
of red in the lower right-hand
corner, a sign of the happy                         40
maker.

**IMPRINT NO. 2**
Knife. Chisel. Mallet.
Block of cherry wood.
Printing pad. Paper. Ink.

What does he think?

He floats a green
into the space
of its assignation.
A world divides
the view from an empty                                    50
chair shifts

a chair with a life of its own
an orange cushion.
Poppies arise from extinction
on the plane of the sun.

Harunobu,[1] your hand trembles.
You will die young and lucky.
Sit down in the chair you
yourself have provided.
The curved form is a fan                                  60
alarmingly pink.
Flutter the air.

Intaglio[2] for what you see best
the 'empty imprint'?
What you see best
is the ivory kimono
coming towards you.
It will stay in the same place
always, Harunobu, brocading[3]
the threat of advance.                                    70

A mere press of your hands
and your death flies
into a silken shadow.

Then washy blue three-quarters up.

---

1 Suzuki Harunobu (1724–70), Japanese artist, who was the first to use a wide range of colours effectively in
  printing. He is celebrated for his graceful female figures, idealized portraits of actors, courtesans, and young
  girls. In 1765 he created multicoloured calendar prints from wood blocks.
2 A design that is cut, etched, or engraved in a hard surface, such as metal or stone. When a print is made from
  an intaglio surface (here, wood), the colours are transferred to the negative space—that is, to the space *around*
  the objects being represented, rather than to the objects themselves.
3 The technique of weaving a raised pattern into silk. Here, Webb is suggesting a parallel with the layers created
  in the print as its different colours are added in.

## IMPRINT NO. 3

A fake. There was no chair
no washy blue in the 'Heron Maid'.
I made it up for my own artistic
purposes. I was thinking of
Van Gogh, of myself sitting down
for the last time and getting                                    80
up again to make this confession.

Tree, shrubs, a turquoise stream
a Japanese woman dressed for cold
her parasol a shield against the
snow which we can't see falling.
One ear pokes out, too high up
from under her brown hood
yet all is harmonious.

In the floating world[4]
she stands quite still                                          90
like the snowy heron
who is really always moving.
She is also winter and tells me
more about herself than Harunobu
wanted me to know.

## IMPRINT NO. 4

The Heron Maid steps
on her wooden blocks
off the path
into summer.
She removes her winter                                         100
cloak, her sandals
dips her feet
in the turquoise stream.
What does she think
as she sits on the verge
this side of anonymous water?
She uncoils her hair

---

4  A phrase designating an area of Edo (now Tokyo) from the seventeenth to mid-nineteenth centuries that was
   noted for its theatres, brothels, and tea-houses. 'Pictures of the floating world' were a popular subject for wood-
   block prints during the time.

slips off her rings
imagines a different future.
She thinks of Harunobu                                    110
working away at his
butcher blocks
his famous seasons.

She'll have to change
habits and colors
wash off her fear.
Perhaps she'll look
for another job
cut her hair short
change her expression.                                    120
And, it's possible, die
some day in foreign arms
under the new dispensation.

Each block is laid on
with extreme caution
then set aside
out of harm's way.

A woman emerges at last
on the finest paper, cursing
his quest for the line                                    130
and this damned delicate fan
carved in her hand
to keep her forever cool
factitious,[5] apparently pleasing.

1990

_____

5  Artificial.

# Robert Kroetsch

## b. 1927

Growing up on a farm in the small northern Alberta community of Heisler during the intense drought and Great Depression of the 1930s, Robert Kroetsch decided early in his life that he wanted to be a storyteller. His western environment—including the sense of humour that pervaded the wild and bawdy tall tales he heard as a young man in prairie beer halls—shaped his novels, his poetry, and even his critical essays. However, in writing about life in the Canadian west and north, Kroetsch heightened the experiences he depicted through the use of mythic parallels and allusions (often expressed through comedy and parody) that draw on the Bible, ancient tales from Mesopotamia such as the *Epic of Gilgamesh* and the myth of Marduk, Greek myths and narratives by Homer, the Norse epic cycle, North American Native Trickster stories, and a wide variety of literary texts including Conrad's *Heart of Darkness*, Joyce's *Ulysses*, and Twain's *Huckleberry Finn*.

After earning a BA at the University of Alberta in 1948, Kroetsch journeyed to the Canadian north as a young man, in a Hemingwayesque search for experience. In one of his essays in *A Likely Story: The Writing Life* (1995), he borrows from the Russian theorist Mikhail Bakhtin the idea of the carnival as an escape from normal social restrictions to explain his journey:

*I went up North, not to discover gold in The Yukon or to find Sir John Franklin's bones, not even to get rich or to escape from home, but rather because I wanted to write a novel. . . . Insofar as the North carnivalizes given Canadian assumptions—turning upside-down assumptions about time, about direction, about urban ambition, about America—it seemed an escape from the authority of tradition and hierarchy, an escape that would allow me to become a storyteller.*

He spent time as a labourer on the Fort Smith Portage, worked on Mackenzie riverboats for two seasons, and held jobs for several years in Labrador. He then travelled to Montreal to study at McGill under Hugh MacLennan. During his summers, he attended the Bread Loaf School of English at Middlebury College, Vermont, where he completed an MA In 1956, he entered the Writers' Workshop program at the University of Iowa, earning his PhD in 1961 with an early draft of what would eventually become *The Studhorse Man* (1969). Kroetsch remained in the United States for the next fourteen years, teaching at the State University of New York at Binghamton, before returning to Canada in 1975. He taught for short periods at the universities of Lethbridge and Calgary, then became a professor of English at the University of Manitoba, where he taught until his retirement to Victoria in 1999. Since then he has lived in Victoria, Winnipeg, and northern Alberta, While still at Binghamton, Kroetsch published *But We Are Exiles* (1965), the novel he had gone north to write, about the crew of a riverboat on the Mackenzie. He turned, in his next five novels, to his own province for material.

Kroetsch's Alberta novels begin with a trilogy: *The Words of My Roaring* (1966); *The Studhorse Man*, for which he won a Governor General's Award; and *Gone Indian* (1973). These are followed by *Badlands* (1975) and *What the Crow Said* (1978). At this point in his career, Kroetsch felt he was undertaking the chief task of the western Canadian novelist: to write his so-far-unimagined environment into existence. In an early conversation with Margaret Laurence, he stressed the importance of this act: 'In a sense we haven't got an identity until somebody tells our story. The fiction makes us real' (*Creation*, 1970). His 'Out West' trilogy (he calls it a triptych—like a set of three interrelated paintings) is an extended investigation of rural Alberta in the twentieth century: in it, a comic portrait of the politics of the Depression thirties is followed by a wild tale of horse-breeding—full of implication about technological change and changing sexual mores after the Second

World War—and then by a broad mythic take on the back-to-the-land pastoralism that sent US citizens looking for utopias in Canada during the unrest of the late 1960s and early 1970s. *Badlands* continues his investigation of the Prairies, with its early-twentieth-century tale of river-rafting through the Alberta Badlands in a mock-epic quest for dinosaur bones: it both looks back to the West's prehistoric past and opens into a future that has more room for women. *What the Crow Said* became Kroetsch's farewell to—he has referred to it as his deconstruction of—his Western material: its fantastic Rabelaisian narrative revolves around a printer and a talking crow in the fabulous town of Big Indian, ambiguously located on the border of Alberta and Saskatchewan. (In addition to these Western novels, *Alberta*, Kroetsch's 1968 travel book, provides a more personal and, at the same time, more concrete and objective response to his native province.)

In the early 1970s, at a time when the term 'postmodern' was just beginning to be used in the literary community, Kroetsch, with William Spanos, co-founded the Binghamton-based critical journal *Boundary 2: A Journal of Post-Modern Literature*, which became a shaping force in North American letters. He also began to articulate his theories of Canadian postmodernism in essays that were eventually collected in *The Lovely Treachery of Words: Essays Selected and New* (1989) and in *Labyrinths of Voice*, a book of conversations with Shirley Neuman and Robert Wilson (1981). In these two books, Kroetsch discusses postmodern literary techniques: parody as a way of responding to inherited forms and traditions; resistance to closure and to overriding unity as a method of rejecting modernist claims of a text having organic completeness; narratives that cast doubt on the veracity of their texts; and the foregrounding of writing and reading as a way of undermining the authority of both writer and reader. Why Kroetsch thought these postmodern tactics were especially important to Canadian writers is explained in his essay 'Unhiding the Hidden' (first published in 1974), which served as a manifesto. Here, he has changed his mind about the need for Canadian writers to name their landscape into existence. Instead, he argues, they need to free themselves from the burden of the

colonial cultural inheritances from Britain and the United States by 'un-naming' their surroundings—and even themselves. His poem 'F.P. Grove: The Finding', reprinted below, playfully suggests that Frederick Philip Grove is exemplary: his creation of a new world identity, after 'exfoliating' himself to blankness, is an act of this un-naming.

During the second half of the 1970s, Kroetsch devoted much of his creative energy to poetry. He published his short poems from the previous decade as *The Stone Hammer Poems* (1975). Then, fascinated by the problems of form and structure in the modern long poem, he began—with 'Stone Hammer Poem' and *The Ledger* in 1975 and *Seed Catalogue* in 1977—what he thought of as a loosely unified ongoing long poem, itself made out of long poems. In 1981, he brought together the nine long poems he had by then composed in *Field Notes*. In 1989, he added additional poems and published the whole as *Completed Field Notes: The Long Poems of Robert Kroetsch*.

Because of Kroetsch's feeling that for Canadian writers—and for prairie writers in particular—'uncreating' was needed if they were to come to terms with the essential elements of their 'home place', he wrote poems that showed the strangeness in familiar objects drawn from his own background: these initially took the form of meditations on a stone hammer his father had found while plowing, on a ledger left behind by his grandfather, and on the seed catalogue that was mailed each winter to farm families. 'Seed Catalogue' views that object as an embodiment of the promise of a new spring and it finds a kind of poetry in its glowing descriptions of what its seeds will bring—but its quotations from the catalogue's promotional copy also draw our attention to its inflated language and its picture of an ideal future that can never be realized. In Canada, perhaps all one can ever really assert about spring is that 'winter was ending'.

As early as *The Studhorse Man*, Kroetsch's interest in metafiction and self-reflexivity led him to play with the role of the narrator and his (or, as in *Badlands*, her) relationship to the reader. However, when Kroetsch returned to fiction in the 1980s—having written in *The Crow Journals* (1980) that 'I deconstruct even after I've come to the end of deconstruction'—his explorations of poststructuralist theory brought further testing of fiction's limits. *Alibi* (1983) and its sequel, *The Puppeteer* (1992), are novels that, while expanding Kroetsch's games with myth and narrative form, keep the reader off balance by refusing to provide stable, presiding narratives. These are the first two parts of a projected trilogy, but Kroetsch never wrote the third volume, possibly because his use of deconstructive methods had undermined the possibility of further storytelling. Instead, in 1998, Kroetsch published *The Man from the Creeks*—the 'untold' story behind Robert Service's popular poem of the Yukon gold rush, 'The Shooting of Dan McGrew'—a novel that was more in the spirit of his early fiction.

Though he had stated that *The Completed Field Notes* marked his farewell to poetry, Kroetsch published *The Hornbooks of Rita K* in 2001—a mixture of prose and poetry in which a fictional archivist gives an account of a vanished Prairie poet (whose initials happen to be the same as Kroetsch's) and offers an extensive selection of her poems—and *The Snowbird Poems* in 2004. That volume, which deals with aging and death, features a sequence in which a Canadian snowbird is on a Florida beachfront, having fled the Canadian winter. It concludes gnomically:

*We fly south to forget winter and instead
we remember the long color of snow.*

*We seek to recover the sun and instead
we imagine the uses of shade ...*

*Here by the salt sea, we dare to hope by remembering
salt eats the snow from the hidden road.*

At 83, Kroetsch is still at work, and his most recent book, *Too Bad: Sketches toward a Self-Portrait* (2010), features its own kind of remembering.

# F.P. Grove: The Finding[1]

I

Dreaming the well-born      hobo of yourself
against the bourgeois father[2]      dreaming Europe
if only to find      a place to be from

the hobo tragedian      pitching bundles
riding a freight      to the impossible city
the fallen archangel      of Brandon or Winnipeg

in all your harvesting      real
or imagined      did you really find
four aged stallions[3]      neigh

---

1 This poem is constructed around references to three of Grove's books, *Over Prairie Trails* (1922), *A Search for America* (1927), and *In Search of Myself* (1946). See pp. 315–41.

2 In *In Search of Myself*, Grove describes his father as a wealthy Swedish landowner. In *A Search for America*, he recounts twenty years of wandering across North America as a tramp and a hobo. Both books were long thought of as autobiographical accounts but eventually discovered to be highly dramatized fictions.

3 In Chapter Five of *In Search of Myself*, Grove writes, 'I was hired as a teamster, and I owed the job to one single fact, namely, that of not being afraid of handling any kind of horse, not even the team I was offered which consisted of four aged stallions.'

in your cold undertaking        on those trails north              10
in all the (dreamed) nights        in stooks
in haystacks        dreaming the purified dreamer

who lured you        to a new man (back
to the fatal earth)        inventing (beyond
America) a new world        did you find

did you dream        the French priest who hauled you
out of your *fleurs du mal*[4]        and headlong
into a hundred drafts        real

or imagined        of the sought form
(there are no models)        and always                          20
(there are only models)        alone


2

alone in the cutter        in the blizzard[5]
two horses        hauling you into the snow
that buries the road        burying the forest

the layered mind        exfoliating[6]
back to the barren sea        (Greek to us,
Grove)        back to the blank sun

and musing snow to yourself        new
to the old rite of burial        the snow
lifting the taught man        into the coyote self              30

the silence of sight        'as if I were not myself
who yet am I'        riding the drifted snow
to your own plummeting        alone and alone

the *wirklichkeit*[7]        of the word itself
the name under the name        the sought
and calamitous edge        of the white earth

4  According to Chapter Six of *In Search of Myself*, Grove was persuaded to begin his teaching career as the result of
   a chance encounter with a French priest who saw him reading Baudelaire's *Fleurs du mal* in a North Dakota train
   station.
5  From here to the conclusion, the poem is based on the sketch 'Snow' from *Over Prairie Trails* (reprinted on
   pp. 317–34), which describes a particularly harrowing winter journey.
6  Grove says that the snow drifts he was crossing 'showed that curious appearance that we also find in the glaciated
   surfaces of granite rock and which, in them, geologists call exfoliation' (p. 322). Later, Grove writes that as he
   looked at 'the infertile waste' around him, 'Unaccountably two Greek words formed on my lips: Homer's Pontos
   atrygetos—the barren sea' (p. 325).
7  Reality; actual fact (German).

the horses        pawing the empty fall
the hot breath on the zero day      the man
seeing the new man so vainly     alone

we say with your waiting wife      (but she      40
was the world      before you invented it
old liar)     'You had a hard trip?'

1975

# Seed Catalogue

I.

No. 176—Copenhagen Market Cabbage: 'This *new introduction, strictly speaking,* is
in every respect a *thoroughbred,* a *cabbage* of *highest pedigree,* and is *creating considerable
flurry* among *professional gardeners* all *over the world.'*

We took the storm windows/off
the south side of the house
and put them on the hotbed.[1]
Then it was spring. Or, no:
then winter was ending.

> 'I wish to say we had lovely success
> this summer with the seed purchased          10
> of you. We had the finest Sweet
> Corn in the country, and Cabbage
> were dandy.'
> —W.W. Lyon, South Junction, Man.

> My mother said:
> Did you wash your ears?
> You could grow cabbages
> in those ears.

---

1  Framed planting bed of enriched soil, covered by glass. (Here, the glass used is that of the house's storm windows,
i.e. the extra panes put up each fall to keep the house warm through the winter and taken down again in the
spring.) Because the glass of the hotbed holds in the sun's heat and protects the plant from frost, seeds can be
planted early in the spring to germinate and begin their growth sooner than the climate would otherwise permit.

Winter was ending.
This is what happened: 20
we were harrowing the garden.[2]
You've got to understand this:
I was sitting on the horse.
The horse was standing still.
I fell off.

> The hired man laughed: how
> in hell did you manage to
> fall off a horse that was
> *standing still?*

> Bring me the radish seeds, 30
> my mother whispered.

Into the dark of January
the seed catalogue bloomed

a winter proposition, if
spring should come, then,[3]

with illustrations:

No. 25—*McKenzie's Improved Golden Wax Bean:* 'THE MOST PRIZED OF ALL BEANS.
*Virtue* is its own reward. We have had *many expressions* from *keen discriminating
gardeners extolling our seed* and *this variety.* '

> Beans, beans,
> the musical fruit; 40
> the more you eat,
> the more you virtue.

My mother was marking the first row
with a piece of binder twine, stretched
between two pegs.

The hired man laughed: just
about planted the little bugger.
Cover him up and see what grows.

---

2  That is, breaking up the soil with a harrow, a plow-like instrument that has rows of sharp teeth or discs to prepare
   the soil for planting.
3  A rephrasing of W.B. Shelley's line in 'Ode to the West Wind': 'If Winter comes, can Spring be far behind?'

My father didn't laugh. He was puzzled                                    50
by any garden that was smaller than a
quarter-section[4] of wheat and summerfallow.

the home place: N.E. 17-42-16-W4th Meridian.

the home place:  one and a half miles west of Heisler, Alberta,
                 on the correction line road[5]
                 and three miles south.

No trees
around the house.
Only the wind.
Only the January snow.                                                    60
Only the summer sun.
The home place:
a terrible symmetry[6].

*How do you grow a gardener?*

                    Telephone Peas
                    Garden Gem Carrots
                    Early Snowcap Cauliflower
                    Perfection Globe Onions
                    Hubbard Squash
                    Early Ohio Potatoes                                   70

This is what happened—at my mother's wake. This
is a fact—the World Series was in progress. The
Cincinnati Reds were playing the Detroit Tigers.
It was raining. The road to the graveyard was barely
passable. The horse was standing still. Bring me
the radish seeds, my mother whispered.

                    2.

My father was mad at the badger: the badger was digging holes in the potato
patch, threatening man and beast with broken limbs (I quote). My father took the
double- barrelled shotgun out into the potato patch and waited.

---

4  A land unit measuring 800 m. on each side—65 hectares; 'summerfallow' is land tilled but not planted for a year
   so it can regain the moisture needed to grow productive crops.
5  See note 10 to Grove's sketch, 'Snow.'
6  'A terrible symmetry' (the phrase recurs at line 460) recalls William Blake's 'fearful symmetry' a phrase that
   appears twice in his poem 'The Tyger' and is thematically appropriate to that poem's role in Blake's exploration
   of the balance between innocence and experience.

Every time the badger stood up, it looked like a little man, come out of the ground.    80
Why, my father asked himself—Why would so fine a fellow live under the ground?
Just for the cool of roots? The solace of dark tunnels? The blood of gophers?

My father couldn't shoot the badger. He uncocked the shotgun, came back to the
house in time for breakfast. The badger dug another hole. My father got mad
again. They carried on like that all summer.

> Love is an amplification
> by doing/over and over.
> by doing/over and over.
>
> Love is a standing up
> to the loaded gun.                    90
>
> Love is a burrowing.

One morning my father actually shot at the badger. He killed a magpie that was
pecking away at a horse turd about fifty feet beyond and to the right of the spot
where the badger had been standing.

A week later my father told the story again. In that version he intended to hit the
magpie. Magpies, he explained, are a nuisance. They eat robins' eggs. They're harder
to kill than snakes, jumping around the way they do, nothing but feathers.

Just call me sure-shot,
my father added.


      3.


No. 1248—*Hubbard Squash*: 'As *mankind* seems to have a *particular fondness*    100
for squash, *Nature* appears to have *especially* provided this *matchless* variety of
*superlative flavour.*'

> Love is a leaping up
> and down.
>
> Love
> is a break in the warm flesh.

'As a cooker, it heads the list for warted squash. The
vines are of strong running growth; the fruits are large,
olive shaped, of a rich deep green colour, the rind is
smooth . . .                    110

*But how do you grow a lover?*

This is the God's own truth:
playing dirty is a mortal sin
the priest told us, you'll go to hell
and burn forever (with illustrations)—

It was our second day of cathechism
—Germaine and I went home that
afternoon     if it's that bad, we
laid to each other     we realized
We better quit     we realized                                    120

let's do it just one last time
and quit.

This is the God's own truth:
catechism, they called it,
the boys had to sit in the pews
on the right, the girls on the left.
Souls were like underwear that you
wore inside. If boys and girls sat
together—

*Adam and Eve got caught*                                        130
*playing dirty.*

This is the truth.
We climbed up into a granary[7]
full of wheat     to the gunny sacks
the binder twine was shipped in—

we spread the paper from the sacks
smooth sheets     on the soft wheat
Germaine and I     were we were like/one

we had discovered, don't ask me
how, where—but when the priest said                              140
*playing dirty* we knew—well—

he had named it     he had named
our world     out of existence
(the horse     was standing still)

—This is my first confession. Bless me father I played
    dirty so long, just the other day, up in the granary
    there by the car shed—up there on the Brantford Binder

7  Storeroom for grain.

Twine gunny sacks and the sheets of paper—Germaine
with her dress up and her bloomers down—

—Son. For penance, keep your peter in your pants                    150
for the next thirteen years.

*But how—*

      Adam and Eve and Pinch-Me
      went down to the river to swim—
      Adam and Eve got drownded.

*But how do you grow a lover?*

      We decided we could do it
      just one last time.


      4.


It arrived in winter, the seed catalogue, on a January
day. It came into town on the afternoon train.                     160

Mary Hauck, when she came west from Bruce County, Ontario,
arrived in town on a January day. She brought
along her hope chest.[8]

She was cooking in the Heisler Hotel. The Heisler Hotel
burned down on the night of June 21, 1919. Everything
in between: lost. Everything: an absence

of satin sheets
of embroidered pillowcases
of tea-towels and English china
of silver serving spoons.                                          170

*How do you grow a prairie town?*

                        The gopher was the model.
                        Stand up straight:
                        telephone poles
                        grain elevators
                        church steeples.
                        Vanish, suddenly: the
                        gopher was the model.

---

8  In an earlier era, young women kept hope chests in which they collected such things as the linens, china, silver,
    and clothing they would need to start their household when they married.

*How do you grow a past/*
to live in                                                                              180

the absence of silkworms
the absence of clay and wattles (whatever the hell
                    they are)
the absence of Lord Nelson
the absence of kings and queens

the absence of a bottle opener, and me with a vicious
                    attack of the 26-ounce flu

the absence of both Sartre and Heidegger

the absence of pyramids

the absence of lions                                                                190

the absence of lutes, violas and xylophones

the absence of a condom dispenser in the Lethbridge Hotel and
                    me about to screw an old Blood whore. I was
                    in love.

the absence of the Parthenon, not to mention the Cathédrale de
                    Chartres

the absence of psychiatrists

the absence of sailing ships

the absence of books, journals, daily newspapers and everything
                    else but the *Free Press Prairie Farmer* and *The*                200
                    *Western Producer*

the absence of gallows (with apologies to Louis Riel)

the absence of goldsmiths

the absence of the girl who said that if the Edmonton Eskimos
                    won the Grey Cup she'd let me kiss her
                    nipples in the foyer of the Palliser Hotel. I
                    don't know where she got to.

the absence of Heraclitus

the absence of the Seine, the Rhine, the Danube, the Tiber and
                    the Thames. Shit, the Battle River ran dry                        210

one fall. The Strauss boy could piss across it.
He could piss higher on a barn wall than any
of us. He could piss right clean over the
principal's new car.

the absence of ballet and opera

the absence of Aeneas

*How do you grow a prairie town?*

Rebuild the hotel when it bums down. Bigger. Fill it
full of a lot of A-I Hard Northern[9] Bullshitters.

—You ever hear the one about the woman who buried                                    220
  her husband with his ass sticking out of the ground
  so that every time she happened to walk by she could
  give it a swift kick?

—Yeh, I heard it.


              5.


I planted some melons, just to see what would
happen. Gophers ate everything.

                              I applied to the Government.
                              I wanted to become a postman,
                              to deliver real words
                              to real people.                                        230

                              There was no one to receive
                              my application

I don't give a damn if I do die do die do die do die do die
do die do die do die do die do die do die do die do
die do die do die do die do die do die do die do die
do

9 'Hard northern' is a variety of wheat grown on the Canadian prairies.

6.

No. 339—McKenzie's *Pedigreed Early Snowcap Cauliflower.* 'Of the many *varieties* of *vegetables* in *existence, Cauliflower* is *unquestionably* one of the *greatest inheritances* of the *present generation, particularly Western Canadians.* There is *no place* in the *world* where *better cauliflowers* can be *grown* than right    240 here in the *West.* The *finest specimens* we have *ever seen,* larger and of *better quality,* are *annually grown* here on our *prairies.* Being *particularly a high altitude plant* it *thrives* to a *point* of *perfection* here, *seldom seen* in *warmer climes.'*

*But how do you grow a poet?*

Start: with an invocation
invoke—

His muse is
his muse/if
memory is

and you have                                             250
no memory then
no meditation

no song (shit
we're up against it)

                             how about that girl
                             you felt up in the
                             school bam or that
                             girl you necked with
                             out by Hastings' slough
                             and ran out of gas with    260
                             and nearly froze to
                             death with/or that
                             girl in the skating
                             rink shack who had on
                             so much underwear you
                             didn't have enough
                             prick to get past her/
                             CCM skates

Once upon a time in the village of Heisler—

—Hey, wait a minute.                                           270
That's a story.

*How do you grow a poet?*

> For appetite: cod-liver
> oil.
> For bronchitis: mustard
> plasters.
> For pallor and failure to fill
> the woodbox: sulphur
> & molasses.
> For self-abuse: ten Our                                    280
> Fathers & ten Hail Marys.
> For regular bowels: Sunny Boy
> Cereal.

*How do you grow a poet?*

'It's a pleasure to advise that I
won the First Prize at the Calgary
Horticultural Show . . . This is my
first attempt. I used your seeds.'

> Son, this is a crowbar.
> This is a willow fencepost.                                290
> This is a sledge.
> This is a roll of barbed wire.
> This is a bag of staples.
> This is a claw hammer.

We give form to this land by running
a series of posts and three strands
of barbed wire around a quarter-section.

> First off I want to take that
> crowbar and drive 1,156 holes
> in that gumbo.[10]                                          300
> And the next time you want to
> write a poem
> we'll start the haying.

*How do you grow a poet?*

> This is a prairie road.
> This road is the shortest distance
> between nowhere and nowhere.
> This road is a poem.

---

10 Sticky, muddy, wet soil with a consistency comparable to the thick stew of the same name.

Just two miles up the road
you'll find a porcupine                                    310
dead in the ditch. It was
trying to cross the road.

As for the poet himself
we can find no record
of his having traversed
the land/in either direction

no trace of his coming
or going/only a scarred
page, a spoor of wording
a reduction to mere black                                   320

and white/a pile of rabbit
turds that tells us
all spring long
where the track was

poet . . . say uncle.

*How?*

Rudy Wiebe: 'You must lay great black steel lines of
fiction, break up that space with huge design and, like
the fiction of the Russian steppes, build a giant
artifact. No song can do that . . .'[11]                    330

February 14, 1976. Rudy, you
took us there: to the Oldman River
Lorna & Byrna, Ralph & Steve and me
you showed us where
the Bloods surprised the Crees[12]

in the next coulee/surprise.
them to death. And after

---

11  In his essay, 'Passage by Land' (1971), Rudy Wiebe argued that epic fiction, rather than poetry, is best suited to
respond to the Canadian prairie: 'To touch this land with words requires an architectural structure; to break
into the space of the reader's mind with the space of this western landscape and the people in it you must build
a structure of fiction like an engineer builds a skyscraper over and into space. A poem, a lyric, will not do. You
must lay great black steel lines of fiction, break up that space with huge design and, like the fiction of the
Russian steppes, build giant artifacts. No song can do that; it must be giant fiction.' The whole of Seed
Catalogue, a long poem about the prairies based on fragments of found prose, becomes Kroetsch's counter-
statement to Wiebe—as is his description, in Part 7, of Al Purdy's recital of his poem 'The Cariboo Horses',
which is so powerful it is as if Purdy had actually 'galloped a Cariboo horse/ . . . through the dining area'.
12  In 1870, a band of Cree attacked a camp of Blood on the Oldman River in what is now Lethbridge. Wiebe
included this event—it proved to be the last important battle among North American Native peoples—in his
novel *The Temptation of Big Bear*.

you showed us Rilke's word
*Lebensgliedes.*[13]

Rudy: Nature thou art.                                                                                          340


                            7.


*Brome Grass (Bromus lnermis)*: 'No amount of cold will kill it. It *withstands*
the summer suns. Water may stand on it for several weeks without apparent
injury. The roots push through the soil, throwing up new plants continually.
It *starts quicker* than other grasses in the spring. *Remains green* longer in the
fall. *Flourishes under absolute neglect.* '

The end of winter:
seeding/time.

*How do you grow*
*a poet?*

(a)
I was drinking with Al Purdy. We went round and round                               350
in the restaurant on top of the Chateau Lacombe. We
were the turning centre in the still world, the winter
of Edmonton was hardly enough to cool our out-sights.

The waitress asked us to leave. She was rather insistent;
we were bad for business, shouting poems at the paying
customers. Twice, Purdy galloped a Cariboo horse
right straight through the dining area.

Now that's what I call
a piss-up.

                                                    'No song can do that.'            360

(b)
No. 2362—*Imperialis Morning*
*Glory*: 'This is the wonderful Jap-
anise Morning Glory, celebrated the
world over for its *wondrous beauty*
of both flowers and foliage.'

---

13 The word comes in the first poem of a sequence by Rilke called Seven Poems (sometimes known as 'seven
   phallic poems' because of their central imagery). The first lines of the poem are *'Auf einmal fasst die*
   *Rosenpflückerin / die volle Knospe seines Lebensgliedes,'* which has been translated as 'The girl who gathers roses
   suddenly / grasps the full bud of his life-giving limb.' (*Lebensgliedes* in this poem has also been translated as
   'vital member'.)

Sunday, January 12, 1975. This evening after
rereading *The Double Hook*: looking at Japanese prints.
Not at actors. Not at courtesans. Rather: Hiroshige's
series, *Fifty-Three Stations on the Tokaido.*

From the *Tokaido* series: 'Shono-Haku-u.' The                    370
bare-assed travellers, caught in a sudden shower.
Men and trees, bending. How it is in a rain shower/
that you didn't see coming. And couldn't have avoided/
even if you had.

>            The double hook:
>            the home place.
>
>            The stations of the way:
>            the other garden
>
>            *Flourishes.*
>            *Under absolute neglect.*                           380

(c)
Jim Bacque said (I was waiting for a plane,
after a reading; Terminal 2, Toronto)—he said,
You've got to deliver the pain to some woman,
don't you?

—Hey, Lady.
You at the end of the bar.
I wanna tell you something.

—Yuh?

—Pete Knight—of Crossfield,
Alberta. Bronc-Busting Champion                                 390
of the World. You ever hear of
Pete Knight, the King of All
Cowboys, Bronc-Busting Champion
of the World?

—Huh-uh.

—You know what I mean? King
of *All* Cowboys . . . Got
killed—by a horse.
He fell off.

—You some kind of nut                                           400
or something?

8.

> We silence words
> by writing them down.

THIS IS THE LAST WILL AND TESTAMENT
OF ME, HENRY L. KROETSCH:

(a) [yes, his first bequest]

*To my son Frederick my carpenter tools.*

It was his first bequest. First,
a man must build.

Those horse-barns around Heisler—                                    410
those perfectly designed barns
With the rounded roofs—only Freddie
knew how to build them. He mapped
Ihe parklands with perfect horse-barns.

> I remember my Uncle Freddie.
> (The farmers no longer
> use horses.)
>
> Back in the 30s, I remember
> he didn't have enough money
> to buy a pound of coffee.          420
>
> Every morning at breakfast
> he drank a cup of hot water
> with cream and sugar in it.
>
> Why, I asked him one morning—
> I wasn't all that old—why
> do you do that? I asked him.
>
> Jesus Christ, he said. He was
> a gentle man, really. Don't you
> understand *anything?*

9.

*The danger of merely living.*                                              430

A shell/exploding
In the black sky: a
strange planting

a bomb/exploding
in the earth: a
strange

man/falling
on the city.
Killed him dead.

It was a strange                                                            440
planting.

the absence of my cousin who was shot down while bombing
the city that was his maternal great-grandmother's
birthplace. He was the navigator. He guided himself
to that fatal occasion:

> —a city he had
> forgotten

> —a woman he had
> forgotten

He intended merely to release a cargo of bombs on a                         450
target and depart. The exploding shell was:

a) an intrusion on a design that was not his, or

b) an occurrence which he had in fact, unintentionally,
   himself designed, or

c) it is essential that we understand this matter
   because:

He was the first descendant of that family to return
to the Old Country. He took with him: a cargo of bombs.

> Anna Weller: *Geboren* Köln, 1849.
> Kenneth MacDonald: Died Cologne, 1943.                                    460

A terrible symmetry.

A strange muse: forgetfulness. Feeding her far children
to ancestral guns, blasting them out of the sky, smack/
into the earth. Oh, she was the mothering sort. Blood/
on her green thumb.

10.

After the bomb/blossoms        *Poet, teach us*
After the city/falls           *to love our dying.*
After the rider/falls
(the horse                      *West is a winter place.*
standing still)                 *The palimpsest of prairie*        470

                                *under the quick erasure*
                                *of snow, invites a flight.*

*How/do you grow a garden?*

                    No. 3060—Spencer Sweet Pea:
                    Pkt $.10; oz $.25;
                    quarter lb $.75; half lb $1.25.

Your sweet peas
climbing the staked
chicken wire,
climbing the stretched                                             480
binder twine by
the front porch

taught me the smell
of morning, the grace
of your tired
hands, the strength
of a noon sun, the
colour of prairie grass
taught me the smell
of my sweating armpits.                                            490

(b)
*How do you a garden grow?*
*How do you grow a garden?*

'Dear Sir,
*The longest brome grass I remember seeing was one night in Brooks. We were on
our way up to the Calgary Stampede, and reached Brooks about 11 P.M., perhaps
earlier because there was still a movie on the drive-in screen. We unloaded Cindy,
and I remember tying her up to the truck box and the brome grass was up to her
hips. We laid down in the back of the truck—on some grass I pulled by hand—and
slept for about three hours, then drove into Calgary.*

*Amie'*       500

(c)
No trees
around the house.
only the wind.
Only the January snow.
Only the summer sun.

*Adam and Eve got drownded—
Who was left?*

1977

---

# Timothy Findley

## 1930–2002

As his family's fortune ebbed and waned, Toronto-born Timothy Irving Frederick Findley ('Tiff' to his friends) grew up in and out of that city's wealthy Rosedale community. When, at seventeen, he wanted to take ballet lessons, he had to drop out of high school and work in the foundry at the Massey-Harris factory to pay for them. After a back injury ended his dreams of being a dancer, he pursued a career in acting, appearing in a television production of Stephen Leacock's *Sunshine Sketches of a Little Town*. While playing small parts in the first season of Ontario's Stratford Shakespeare Festival, he met the renowned British actor Alec Guinness, who was so impressed that he sponsored Findley's drama education in London, England. That led to a

small role in a production of US playwright Thornton Wilder's *The Matchmaker*, which starred Ruth Gordon.

Gordon encouraged Findley to pursue his related interest in writing and provided him with some financial support; Wilder talked to him about how his ability as an actor to understand character should inform his creation of character as a writer. In 1956, around the time *The Matchmaker* ended its tour in Hollywood, Findley's first story, 'About Effie', appeared in the initial issue of the *Tamarack Review*. Findley remained in California in hopes of pursuing an acting career in film while developing scripts for the young medium of television. In 1958, he decided to return to work in Toronto theatre, where, after a brief marriage to actress Janet

Reid, he met his life partner William Whitehead, a producer, actor, and writer. Together, the two men retired from acting to focus on writing. In 1964, they purchased a farm near Cannington, Ontario, which they named Stone Orchard in homage to Chekhov's play, *The Cherry Orchard*, and from which they worked and lived until the late 1990s. In Findley's last years, the couple lived in France and in Toronto.

Though his first two novels, *The Last of the Crazy People* (1967) and *The Butterfly Plague* (1969), were rejected by Canadian publishers and published in the United States to limited success, the 1970s brought Findley wide recognition. He served as chief writer for *The Whiteoaks of Jalna* TV series (1971-4) and, with Whitehead, wrote *The National Dream* (1974), an award-winning television script about the building of the Canadian Pacific Railway. He became playwright-in-residence at the National Arts Centre in Ottawa (1974–5) and, in 1977–8, chair of the Writers' Union of Canada, an organization of which he was also a co-founder. He later served as president of the Canadian branch of PEN International. Most importantly, he received broad acclaim for his third novel, *The Wars* (1977), which won a Governor General's Award; he later wrote the script for the 1983 National Film Board adaptation.

*The Wars* marked the beginning of an extended period of creativity that included the novels *Famous Last Words* (1981), *Not Wanted on the Voyage* (1984), *The Telling of Lies* (1986), *Headhunter* (1993), *The Piano Man's Daughter* (1995), *Pilgrim* (1999), and *Spadework* (2001); the novella *You Went Away* (1996); and three short-story collections—*Dinner Along the Amazon* (1984), *Stones* (1988), and *Dust to Dust* (1997)—along with two works of non-fiction, *Inside Memory: Pages from a Writer's Workbook* (1990) and *From Stone Orchard: A Collection of Memories* (1998). He also wrote five plays, including *Elizabeth Rex* (2000) for which he won his second Governor General's Award. In 1986, Findley was made an Officer of the Order of Canada.

Although an individual deeply affected by the horrors of the contemporary world and famous for his love of animals and his support of humanitarian causes, Findley gave us stories marked by appalling violence—fires, killings, wars. In part, these narratives serve him as a way of showing the internal struggles waged by decent, but isolated, characters (such as Everett Menlo in the story 'Dreams') who find it difficult to retain their grip on reality in a world filled with pain. Findley frequently suggests that the source of both individual and social breakdowns is mistaken idealism—whether it manifests itself at the personal level as the drive for individual perfection or at the social level in the longing for a completely regulated state. He challenges the notion of the perfect family in *The Last of the Crazy People* and of a perfect America in *The Butterfly Plague*; in *The Wars*, he suggests misplaced ideas of chivalric honour produced the global conflict of the First World War; and in *Famous Last Words*—which is narrated by Hugh Selwyn Mauberley, the eponymous hero of Ezra Pound's 1920 poem—he shows readers the dangers that arise when (as in the ascension of Mussolini in Italy) 'a shared ideal became a single man'.

Although the factual and historical basis of *The Wars* and *Famous Last Words* is important, Findley's narratives move away from the conventions of mimetic realism by calling attention to their constructed nature. This kind of postmodern self-reflexivity is also apparent in *Headhunter*, in which a character from an earlier literary work—Kurtz, Joseph Conrad's emblem of evil and imperialism in *Heart of Darkness*—escapes into the daily world of contemporary Toronto. In *Not Wanted on the Voyage*, Findley goes even further in creating a provocative retelling of the biblical Noah story, a revisionary fable—its diverse cast of characters includes even the fallen Lucifer—that protests the violence of a Creator who would destroy his own creation. Such stories blur formal and conceptual borderlines: divisions between life and art, or—as in 'Dreams'—between dream-life and waking reality, break down, giving events a symbolic cast. These departures from realism have assisted Findley in his investigations of his tragic epoch, an age that, because of the traumatic effects of the First World War, exists in what the narrator of *Famous Last Words* calls 'the aftershock of a great catastrophe'.

# Dreams

Doctor Menlo was having a problem: he could not sleep and his wife—the other Doctor Menlo—was secretly staying awake in order to keep an eye on him. The trouble was that, in spite of her concern and in spite of all her efforts, Doctor Menlo—whose name was Mimi—was always nodding off because of her exhaustion.

She had tried drinking coffee, but this had no effect. She detested coffee and her system had a built-in rejection mechanism. She also prescribed herself a week's worth of Dexedrine to see if that would do the trick. *Five mg at bedtime*—all to no avail. And even though she put the plastic bottle of small orange hearts beneath her pillow and kept augmenting her intake, she would wake half an hour later with a dreadful start to discover the night was moving on to morning.

Everett Menlo had not yet declared the source of his problem. His restless condition had begun about ten days ago and had barely raised his interest. Soon, however, the time spent lying awake had increased from one to several hours and then, on Monday last, to all-night sessions. Now he lay in a state of rigid apprehension—eyes wide open, arms above his head, his hands in fists—like a man in pain unable to shut it out. His neck, his back and his shoulders constantly harried him with cramps and spasms. Everett Menlo had become a full-blown insomniac.

Clearly, Mimi Menlo concluded, her husband was refusing to sleep because he believed something dreadful was going to happen the moment he closed his eyes. She had encountered this sort of fear in one or two of her patients. Everett, on the other hand, would not discuss the subject. If the problem had been hers, he would have said *such things cannot occur if you have gained control of yourself.*

Mimi began to watch for the dawn. She would calculate its approach by listening for the increase of traffic down below the bedroom window. The Menlos' home was across the road from The Manulife Centre—corner of Bloor and Bay streets. Mimi's first sight of daylight always revealed the high white shape of its terraced storeys. Their own apartment building was of a modest height and colour—twenty floors of smoky glass and polished brick. The shadow of the Manulife would crawl across the bedroom floor and climb the wall behind her, grey with fatigue and cold.

The Menlo beds were an arm's length apart, and lying like a rug between them was the shape of a large, black dog of unknown breed. All night long, in the dark of his well, the dog would dream and he would tell the content of his dreams the way that victims in a trance will tell of being pursued by posses of their nameless fears. He whimpered, he cried and sometimes he howled. His legs and his paws would jerk and flail and his claws would scrabble desperately against the parquet floor. Mimi—who loved this dog—would lay her hand against his side and let her fingers dabble in his coat in vain attempts to soothe him. Sometimes, she had to call his name in order to rouse him from his dreams because his heart would be racing. Other times, she smiled and thought: *at least there's one of us getting some sleep.* The dog's name was Thurber[1] and he dreamed in beige and white.

1 The dog has been named after James Thurber (1894–1961), American humorist, short story writer, and cartoonist. Known for his work in *The New Yorker*, his most famous story is 'The Secret Life of Walter Mitty', in which a timid and mild-mannered man escapes repeatedly into adventuresome fantasies. Many of Thurber's stories and drawings feature dogs.

Everett and Mimi Menlo were both psychiatrists. His field was schizophrenia; hers was autistic children. Mimi's venue was the Parkin Institute at the University of Toronto; Everett's was the Queen Street Mental Health Centre. Early in their marriage they decided never to work as a team and not—unless it was a matter of financial life and death—to accept employment in the same institution. Both had always worked with the kind of physical intensity that kills, and yet they gave the impression this was the only tolerable way in which to function. It meant there was always a sense of peril in what they did, but the peril—according to Everett—made their lives worth living. This, at least, had been his theory twenty years ago when they were young.

Now, for whatever unnamed reason, peril had become his enemy and Everett Menlo had begun to look and behave and lose his sleep like a haunted man. But he refused to comment when Mimi asked him what was wrong. Instead, he gave the worst of all possible answers a psychiatrist can hear who seeks an explanation of a patient's silence: he said there was *absolutely nothing wrong*.

'You're sure you're not coming down with something?'

'Yes.'

'And you wouldn't like a massage?'

'I've already told you: no.'

'Can I get you anything?'

'No.'

'And you don't want to talk?'

'That's right.'

'Okay, Everett . . .'

'Okay, what?'

'Okay, nothing. I only hope you get some sleep tonight.'

Everett stood up. 'Have you been spying on me, Mimi?'

'What do you mean by *spying*?'

'Watching me all night long.'

'Well, Everett, I don't see how I can fail to be aware you aren't asleep when we share this bedroom. I mean—I can hear you grinding your teeth. I can see you lying there wide awake.'

'When?'

'All the time. You're staring at the ceiling.'

'I've never stared at the ceiling in my whole life. I sleep on my stomach.'

'You sleep on your stomach *if* you sleep. But you have not been sleeping. Period. No argument.'

Everett Menlo went to his dresser and got out a pair of clean pyjamas. Turning his back on Mimi, he put them on.

Somewhat amused at the coyness of this gesture, Mimi asked what he was hiding.

'Nothing!' he shouted at her.

Mimi's mouth fell open. Everett never yelled. His anger wasn't like that; it manifested itself in other ways, in silence and withdrawal, never shouts.

Everett was staring at her defiantly. He had slammed the bottom drawer of his dresser. Now he was fumbling with the wrapper of a pack of cigarettes.

Mimi's stomach tied a knot.

Everett hadn't touched a cigarette for weeks.

'Please don't smoke those,' she said. 'You'll only be sorry if you do.'

'And you', he said, 'will be sorry if I don't.'

'But dear . . .' said Mimi.

'Leave me for Christ's sake alone!' Everett yelled.

Mimi gave up and sighed and then she said: 'all right. Thurber and I will go and sleep in the living-room. Goodnight.'

Everett sat on the edge of his bed. His hands were shaking.

'Please,' he said—apparently addressing the floor. 'Don't leave me here alone. I couldn't bear that.'

This was perhaps the most chilling thing he could have said to her. Mimi was alarmed; her husband was genuinely terrified of something and he would not say what it was. If she had not been who she was—if she had not known what she knew—if her years of training had not prepared her to watch for signs like this, she might have been better off. As it was, she had to face the possibility the strongest, most sensible man on earth was having a nervous breakdown of major proportions. Lots of people have breakdowns, of course; but not, she had thought, the gods of reason.

'All right,' she said—her voice maintaining the kind of calm she knew a child afraid of the dark would appreciate. 'In a minute I'll get us something to drink. But first, I'll go and change. . . .'

Mimi went into the sanctum of the bathroom, where her nightgown waited for her—a portable hiding-place hanging on the back of the door. 'You stay there,' she said to Thurber, who had padded after her. 'Mama will be out in just a moment.'

Even in the dark, she could gauge Everett's tension. His shadow—all she could see of him—twitched from time to time and the twitching took on a kind of lurching rhythm, something like the broken clock in their living-room.

Mimi lay on her side and tried to close her eyes. But her eyes were tied to a will of their own and would not obey her. Now she, too, was caught in the same irreversible tide of sleeplessness that bore her husband backward through the night. Four or five times she watched him lighting cigarettes—blowing out the matches, courting disaster in the bedclothes—conjuring the worst of deaths for the three of them: a flaming pyre on the twentieth floor.

All of this behaviour was utterly unlike him: foreign to his code of principles and ethics; alien to everything he said and believed. *Openness, directness, sharing of ideas, encouraging imaginative response to every problem. Never hide troubles. Never allow despair*. . . These were his directives in everything he did. Now, he had thrown them over.

One thing was certain. She was not the cause of his sleeplessness. She didn't have affairs and neither did he. He might be ill—but whenever he'd been ill before, there had been no trauma; never a trauma like this one, at any rate. Perhaps it was something about a patient—one of his tougher cases; a wall in the patient's condition they could not break through; some circumstance of someone's lack of progress—a sudden veering towards a catatonic state, for instance—something that Everett had not foreseen that had stymied him and was slowly . . . what? Destroying his sense of professional control? His self-esteem? His scientific certainty? If only he would speak.

Mimi thought about her own worst case: a child whose obstinate refusal to communicate was currently breaking her heart and, thus, her ability to help. If ever she had needed Everett to talk to, it was now. All her fellow doctors were locked in a battle over this child; they wanted to take him away from her. Mimi refused to give him up; he might as well have been her own flesh and blood. Everything had been done—from gentle holding sessions to violent bouts of manufactured anger—in her attempt to make the child react. She was staying with him every day from the moment he was roused to the moment he was induced to sleep with drugs.

His name was Brian Bassett and he was eight years old. He sat on the floor in the furthest corner he could achieve in one of the observation-isolation rooms where all the autistic children were placed when nothing else in their treatment—nothing of love or expertise—had managed to break their silence. Mostly, this was a signal they were coming to the end of life.

There in his four-square, glass-box room, surrounded by all that can tempt a child if a child can be tempted—toys and food and story-book companions—Brian Bassett was in the process, now, of fading away. His eyes were never closed and his arms were restrained. He was attached to three machines that nurtured him with all that science can offer. But of course, the spirit and the will to live cannot be fed by force to those who do not want to feed.

Now in the light of Brian Bassett's utter lack of willing contact with the world around him—his utter refusal to communicate—Mimi watched her husband through the night. Everett stared at the ceiling, lit by the Manulife building's distant lamps, borne on his back further and further out to sea. She had lost him, she was certain.

When, at last, he saw that Mimi had drifted into her own and welcome sleep, Everett rose from his bed and went out into the hall, past the simulated jungle of the solarium, until he reached the dining-room. There, all the way till dawn, he amused himself with two decks of cards and endless games of Dead Man's Solitaire.

Thurber rose and shuffled after him. The dining-room was one of Thurber's favourite places in all his confined but privileged world, for it was here—as in the kitchen—that from time to time a hand descended filled with the miracle of food. But whatever it was that his master was doing up there above him on the table-top, it wasn't anything to do with feeding or with being fed. The playing cards had an old and dusty dryness to their scent and they held no appeal for the dog. So he once again lay down and he took up his dreams, which at least gave his paws some exercise. This way, he failed to hear the advent of a new dimension to his master's problem. This occurred precisely at 5:45 a.m. when the telephone rang and Everett Menlo, having rushed to answer it, waited breathless for a minute while he listened and then said: 'yes' in a curious, strangulated fashion. Thurber—had he been awake—would have recognized in his master's voice the signal for disaster.

For weeks now, Everett had been working with a patient who was severely and uniquely schizophrenic. This patient's name was Kenneth Albright, and while he was deeply suspicious, he was also oddly caring. Kenneth Albright loved the detritus of life, such as bits of woolly dust and wads of discarded paper. He loved all dried-up leaves that had drifted from their parent trees and he loved the dead bees that had curled up to die along the window-sills of his ward. He also loved the spiderwebs seen high up in the corners of the rooms where he sat on plastic chairs and ate with plastic spoons.

Kenneth Albright talked a lot about his dreams. But his dreams had become, of late, a major stumbling block in the process of his recovery. Back in the days when Kenneth had first become Doctor Menlo's patient, the dreams had been overburdened with detail: 'over-cast', as he would say, 'with characters' and over-produced, again in Kenneth's phrase, 'as if I were dreaming the dreams of Cecil B. de Mille.'

Then he had said: 'but a person can't really dream someone else's dreams. Or can they, Doctor Menlo?'

'No' had been Everett's answer—definite and certain.

Everett Menlo had been delighted, at first, with Kenneth Albright's dreams. They had been immensely entertaining—complex and filled with intriguing detail. Kenneth himself was at a loss to explain the meaning of these dreams, but as Everett had said, it wasn't Kenneth's job to explain. That was Everett's job. His job and his pleasure. For quite a long while, during these early sessions, Everett had written out the dreams, taken them home and recounted them to Mimi.

Kenneth Albright was a paranoid schizophrenic. Four times now, he had attempted suicide. He was a fiercely angry man at times—and at other times as gentle and as pleasant as a docile child. He had suffered so greatly, in the very worst moments of his disease, that he could no longer work. His job—it was almost an incidental detail in his life and had no importance for him, so it seemed—was returning reference books, in the Metro Library, to their places in the stacks. Sometimes—mostly late of an afternoon—he might begin a psychotic episode of such profound dimensions that he would attempt his suicide right behind the counter and even once, in the full view of everyone, while riding in the glass-walled elevator. It was after this last occasion that he was brought, in restraints, to be a resident patient at the Queen Street Mental Health Centre. He had slashed his wrists with a razor—but not before he had also slashed and destroyed an antique copy of *Don Quixote*, the pages of which he pasted to the walls with blood.

For a week thereafter, Kenneth Albright—just like Brian Bassett—had refused to speak or to move. Everett had him kept in an isolation cell, force-fed and drugged. Slowly, by dint of patience, encouragement and caring even Kenneth could recognize as genuine, Everett Menlo had broken through the barrier. Kenneth was removed from isolation, pampered with food and cigarettes, and he began relating his dreams.

At first there seemed to be only the dreams and nothing else in Kenneth's memory. Broken pencils, discarded toys and the telephone directory all had roles to play in these dreams but there were never any people. All the weather was bleak and all the landscapes were empty. Houses, motor cars and office buildings never made an appearance. Sounds and smells had some importance, the wind would blow, the scent of unseen fires was often described. Stairwells were plentiful, leading nowhere, all of them rising from a subterranean world that Kenneth either did not dare to visit or would not describe.

The dreams had little variation, one from another. The themes had mostly to do with loss and with being lost. The broken pencils were all given names and the discarded toys were given to one another as companions. The telephone books were the sources of recitations—hours and hours of repeated names and numbers, some of which—Everett had noted with surprise—were absolutely accurate.

All of this held fast until an incident occurred one morning that changed the face of Kenneth Albright's schizophrenia forever, an incident that stemmed—so it seemed—from something he had dreamed the night before.

Bearing in mind his previous attempts at suicide, it will be obvious that Kenneth Albright was never far from sight at the Queen Street Mental Health Centre. He was, in fact, under constant observation; constant, that is, as human beings and modern technology can manage. In the ward to which he was ultimately consigned, for instance, the toilet cabinet had no doors and the shower-rooms had no locks. Therefore, a person could not ever be alone with water, glass or shaving utensils. (All the razors were cordless automatics.) Scissors and knives were banned, as were pieces of string and rubber bands. A person could not even kill his feet and hands by binding up his wrists or ankles. Nothing poisonous was anywhere available. All the windows were barred. All the double doors between this ward and the corridors beyond were doors with triple locks and a guard was always near at hand.

Still, if people want to die, they will find a way. Mimi Menlo would discover this to her everlasting sorrow with Brian Bassett. Everett Menlo would discover this to his everlasting horror with Kenneth Albright.

On the morning of April 19th, a Tuesday, Everett Menlo, in the best of health, had welcomed a brand-new patient into his office. This was Anne Marie Wilson, a young and brilliant pianist whose promising career had been halted mid-flight by a schizophrenic incident involving her ambition. She was, it seemed, no longer able to play and all her dreams were shattered. The cause was simple, to all appearances: Ann Marie had a sense of how, precisely, the music should be and she had not been able to master it accordingly. 'Everything I attempt is terrible,' she had said—in spite of all her critical accolades and all her professional success. Other doctors had tried and failed to break the barriers in Anne Marie, whose hands had taken on a life of their own, refusing altogether to work for her. Now it was Menlo's turn and hope was high.

Everett had been looking forward to his session with this prodigy. He loved all music and had thought to find some means within its discipline to reach her. She seemed so fragile, sitting there in the sunlight, and he had just begun to take his first notes when the door flew open and Louise, his secretary, said: 'I'm sorry, Doctor Menlo. There's a problem. Can you come with me at once?'

Everett excused himself.

Anne Marie was left in the sunlight to bide her time. Her fingers were moving around in her lap and she put them in her mouth to make them quiet.

Even as he'd heard his secretary speak, Everett had known the problem would be Kenneth Albright. Something in Kenneth's eyes had warned him there was trouble on the way: a certain wariness that indicated all was not as placid as it should have been, given his regimen of drugs. He had stayed long hours in one position, moving his fingers over his thighs as if to dry them on his trousers; watching his fellow patients come and go with abnormal interest—never, however, rising from his chair. An incident was on the horizon and Everett had been waiting for it, hoping it would not come.

Louise had said that Doctor Menlo was to go at once to Kenneth Albright's ward. Everett had run the whole way. Only after the attendant had let him in past the double doors, did he slow his pace to a hurried walk and wipe his brow. He didn't want Kenneth to know how alarmed he had been.

Coming to the appointed place, he paused before he entered, closing his eyes, preparing himself for whatever he might have to see. *Other people have killed themselves: I've seen it often enough*, he was thinking, *I simply won't let it affect me.* Then he went in.

The room was small and white—a dining-room—and Kenneth was sitting down in a corner, his back pressed out against the walls on either side of him. His head was bowed and his legs drawn up and he was obviously trying to hide without much success. An intern was standing above him and a nurse was kneeling down beside him. Several pieces of bandaging with blood on them were scattered near Kenneth's feet and there was a white enamel basin filled with pinkish water on the floor beside the nurse.

'Morowetz,' Everett said to the intern. 'Tell me what has happened here.' He said this just the way he posed such questions when he took the interns through the wards at examination time, quizzing them on symptoms and prognoses.

But Morowetz the intern had no answer. He was puzzled. What had happened had no sane explanation.

Everett turned to Charterhouse, the nurse.

'On the morning of April 19th, at roughly ten-fifteen, I found Kenneth Albright covered with blood,' Ms Charterhouse was to write in her report. 'His hands, his arms, his face and his neck were stained. I would say the blood was fresh and the patient's clothing—mostly his shirt—was wet with it. Some—a very small amount of it—had dried on his forehead. The rest was uniformly the kind of blood you expect to find free-flowing from a wound. I called for assistance and meanwhile attempted to ascertain where Mister Albright might have been injured. I performed this examination without success. I could find no source of bleeding anywhere on Mr Albright's body.

Morowetz concurred.

The blood was someone else's.

'Was there a weapon of any kind?' Doctor Menlo had wanted to know.

'No, sir. Nothing,' said Charterhouse.

'And was he alone when you found him?'

'Yes, sir. Just like this in the corner.'

'And the others?'

'All the patients in the ward were examined,' Morowetz told him.

'And?'

'Not one of them was bleeding.'

Everett said: 'I see.'

He looked down at Kenneth.

'This is Doctor Menlo, Kenneth. Have you anything to tell me?'

Kenneth did not reply.

Everett said: 'When you've got him back in his room and tranquillized, will you call me, please?'

Morowetz nodded.

The call never came. Kenneth had fallen asleep. Either the drugs he was given had knocked him out cold, or he had opted for silence. Either way, he was incommunicado.

No one was discovered bleeding. Nothing was found to indicate an accident, a violent attack, an epileptic seizure. A weapon was not located. Kenneth Albright had not a single scratch on his flesh from stem, as Everett put it, to gudgeon. The blood, it seemed, had fallen like the rain from heaven: unexplained and inexplicable.

Later, as the day was ending, Everett Menlo left the Queen Street Mental Health Centre. He made his way home on the Queen streetcar and the Bay bus. When he reached the apartment, Thurber was waiting for him. Mimi was at a goddamned meeting.

That was the night Everett Menlo suffered the first of his failures to sleep. It was occasioned by the fact that, when he wakened sometime after three, he had just been dreaming. This, of course, was not unusual—but the dream itself was perturbing. There was someone lying there, in the bright white landscape of a hospital dining-room. Whether it was a man or a woman could not be told, it was just a human body, lying down in a pool of blood.

Kenneth Albright was kneeling beside this body, pulling it open the way a child will pull a Christmas present open—yanking at its strings and ribbons, wanting only to see the contents. Everett saw this scene from several angles, never speaking, never being spoken to. In all the time he watched—the usual dream eternity—the silence was broken only by the sound of water dripping from an unseen tap. Then, Kenneth Albright rose and was covered with blood, the way he had been that morning. He stared at Doctor Menlo, looked right through him and departed. Nothing remained in the dining-room but plastic tables and plastic chairs and the bright red thing on the floor that once had been a person. Everett Menlo did not know and could not guess who this person might have been. He only knew that Kenneth Albright had left this person's body in Everett Menlo's dream.

Three nights running, the corpse remained in its place and every time that Everett entered the dining-room in the nightmare he was certain he would find out who it was. On the fourth night, fully expecting to discover he himself was the victim, he beheld the face and saw it was a stranger.

*But there are no strangers in dreams;* he knew that now after twenty years of practice. *There are no strangers; there are only people in disguise.*

Mimi made one final attempt in Brian Bassett's behalf to turn away the fate to which his other doctors—both medical and psychiatric—had consigned him. Not that, as a group, they had failed to expend the full weight of all they knew and all they could do to save him. One of his medical doctors—a woman whose name was Juliet Bateman—had moved a cot into his isolation room and stayed with him twenty-four hours a day for over a week. But her health had been undermined by this and when she succumbed to the Shanghai flu she removed herself for fear of infecting Brian Bassett.

The parents had come and gone on a daily basis for months in a killing routine of visits. But parents, their presence and their loving, are not the answer when a child has fallen into an autistic state. They might as well have been strangers. And so they had been advised to stay away.

Brian Bassett was eight years old—*unlucky eight,* as one of his therapists had said—and in every other way, in terms of physical development and mental capability, he had always been a perfectly normal child. Now, in the final moments of his life, he weighed a scant thirty pounds, when he should have weighed twice that much.

Brian had not been heard to speak a single word in over a year of constant observation. Earlier—long ago as seven months—a few expressions would visit his face from time to time. Never a smile—but often a kind of sneer, a passing of judgment, terrifying in its intensity. Other times, a pinched expression would appear—a signal of the shyness peculiar to autistic children, who think of light as being unfriendly.

Mimi's militant efforts in behalf of Brian had been exemplary. Her fellow doctors thought of her as *Bassett's crazy guardian angel.* They begged her to remove herself in order to preserve her health. Being wise, being practical, they saw that all her efforts would not save him. But Mimi's version of being a guardian angel was more like being a surrogate warrior: a hired gun or a samurai. Her cool determination to thwart the enemies of silence, stillness and starvation gave her strengths that even she had been unaware were hers to command.

Brian Bassett, seated in his corner on the floor, maintained a solemn composure that lent his features a kind of unearthly beauty. His back was straight, his hands were poised, his hair was so fine he looked the very picture of a spirit waiting to enter a newborn creature. Sometimes Mimi wondered if this creature Brian Bassett waited to inhabit could be human. She thought of all the animals she had ever seen in all her travels and she fell upon the image of a newborn fawn as being the most tranquil and the most in need of stillness in order to survive. If only all the natural energy and curiosity of a newborn beast could have entered into Brian Bassett, surely, they would have transformed the boy in the corner into a vibrant, joyous human being. But it was not to be.

On the 29th of April—one week and three days after Everett had entered into his crisis of insomnia—Mimi sat on the floor in Brian Bassett's isolation room, gently massaging his arms and legs as she held him in her lap.

His weight, by now, was shocking—and his skin had become translucent. His eyes had not been closed for days—for weeks—and their expression might have been carved in stone.

'Speak to me. Speak,' she whispered to him as she cradled his head beneath her chin. 'Please at least speak before you die.'

Nothing happened. Only silence.

Juliet Bateman—wrapped in a blanket—was watching through the observation glass as Mimi lifted up Brian Bassett and placed him in his cot. The cot had metal sides—and the sides were raised. Juliet Bateman could see Brian Bassett's eyes and his hands as Mimi stepped away.

Mimi looked at Juliet and shook her head. Juliet closed her eyes and pulled her blanket tighter like a skin that might protect her from the next five minutes.

Mimi went around the cot to the other side and dragged the IV stand in closer to the head. She fumbled for a moment with the long plastic lifelines—anti-dehydrants, nutrients—and she adjusted the needles and brought them down inside the nest of the cot where Brian Bassett lay and she lifted up his arm in order to insert the tubes and bind them into place with tape.

This was when it happened—just as Mimi Menlo was preparing to insert the second tube.

Brian Bassett looked at her and spoke.

'No,' he said. 'Don't.'

*Don't* meant death.

Mimi paused—considered—and set the tube aside. Then she withdrew the tube already in place and she hung them both on the IV stand.

*All right*, she said to Brian Bassett in her mind, *you win*.

She looked down then with her arm along the side of the cot—and one hand trailing down so Brian Bassett could touch if he wanted to. She smiled at him and said to him: 'not to worry. Not to worry. None of us is ever going to trouble you again.' He watched her carefully. 'Goodbye, Brian,' she said. 'I love you.'

Juliet Bateman saw Mimi Menlo say all this and was fairly sure she had read the words on Mimi's lips just as they had been spoken.

Mimi started out of the room. She was determined now there was no turning back and that Brian Bassett was free to go his way. But just as she was turning the handle and pressing her weight against the door—she heard Brian Bassett speak again.

'Goodbye,' he said.

And died.

Mimi went back and Juliet Bateman, too, and they stayed with him another hour before they turned out his lights. 'Someone else can cover his face,' said Mimi. 'I'm not going to do it.' Juliet agreed and they came back out to tell the nurse on duty that their ward had died and their work with him was over.

On the 30th of April—a Saturday—Mimi stayed home and made her notes and she wondered if and when she would weep for Brian Bassett. Her hand, as she wrote, was steady and her throat was not constricted and her eyes had no sensation beyond the burning itch of fatigue. She wondered what she looked like in the mirror, but resisted that discovery. Some things could wait. Outside it rained. Thurber dreamed in the corner. Bay Street rumbled in the basement.

Everett, in the meantime, had reached his own crisis and because of his desperate straits a part of Mimi Menlo's mind was on her husband. Now he had not slept for almost ten days. *We really ought to consign ourselves to hospital beds*, she thought. Somehow, the idea held no persuasion. It occurred to her that laughter might do a better job, if only they could find it. The brain, when over-extended, gives us the most surprisingly simple propositions, she concluded. *Stop*, it says to us. *Lie down and sleep.*

Five minutes later, Mimi found herself still sitting at the desk with her fountain pen capped and her fingers raised to her lips in an attitude of gentle prayer. It required some effort to re-adjust her gaze and re-establish her focus on the surface of the window glass beyond which her mind had wandered. Sitting up, she had been asleep.

Thurber muttered something and stretched his legs and yawned, still asleep. Mimi glanced in his direction. *We've both been dreaming*, she thought, *but his dream continues.*

Somewhere behind her, the broken clock was attempting to strike the hour of three. Its voice was dull and rusty, needing oil.

Looking down, she saw the words *BRIAN BASSETT* written on the page before her and it occurred to her that, without his person, the words were nothing more than extrapolations from the alphabet—something fanciful we call a 'name' in the hope that, one day, it will take on meaning.

She thought of Brian Bassett with his building blocks—pushing the letters around on the floor and coming up with more acceptable arrangements: *TINA STERABBS . . . IAN BRETT BASS . . . BEST STAB the RAIN*: a sentence. He had known all along, of course, that *BRIAN BASSETT* wasn't what he wanted because it wasn't what he was. He had come here against his will, was held here against his better judgment, fought against his captors and finally escaped.

But where was here to Ian Brett Bass? Where was here to Tina Sterabbs? Like Brian Bassett, they had all been here in someone else's dreams, and had to wait for someone else to wake before they could make their getaway.

Slowly, Mimi uncapped her fountain pen and drew a firm, black line through Brian Bassett's name. *We dreamed him*, she wrote, that's all. *And then we let him go.*

Seeing Everett standing in the doorway, knowing he had just returned from another Kenneth Albright crisis, she had no sense of apprehension. All this was only as it should be. Given the way that everything was going, it stood to reason Kenneth Albright's crisis had to come in this moment. If he managed, at last, to kill himself then at least her husband might begin to sleep again.

Far in the back of her mind a carping, critical voice remarked that any such thoughts were *deeply unfeeling and verging on the barbaric*. But Mimi dismissed this voice and another part of her brain stepped forward in her defence. *I will weep for Kenneth Albright*, she thought, *when I can weep for Brian Bassett. Now, all that matters is that Everett and I survive.*

Then she strode forward and put out her hand for Everett's briefcase, set the briefcase down and helped him out of his topcoat. She was playing wife. It seemed to be the thing to do.

For the next twenty minutes Everett had nothing to say, and after he had poured himself a drink and after Mimi had done the same, they sat in their chairs and waited for Everett to catch his breath.

The first thing he said when he finally spoke was: 'finish your notes?'

'Just about,' Mimi told him. 'I've written everything I can for now.' She did not elaborate. 'You're home early,' she said, hoping to goad him into saying something new about Kenneth Albright.

'Yes,' he said. 'I am.' But that was all.

Then he stood up—threw back the last of his drink and poured another. He lighted a cigarette and Mimi didn't even wince. He had been smoking now three days. The atmosphere between them had been, since then, enlivened with a magnetic kind of tension. But it was a moribund tension, slowly beginning to dissipate.

Mimi watched her husband's silent torment now with a kind of clinical detachment. This was the result, she liked to tell herself, of her training and her discipline. The lover in her could regard Everett warmly and with concern, but the psychiatrist in her could also watch him as someone suffering a nervous breakdown, someone who could not be helped until the symptoms had multiplied and declared themselves more openly.

Everett went into the darkest corner of the room and sat down hard in one of Mimi's straight-backed chairs: the ones inherited from her mother. He sat, prim, like a patient in a doctor's office, totally unrelaxed and nervy; expressionless. Either he had come to receive a deadly diagnosis, or he would get a clean bill of health.

Mimi glided over to the sofa in the window, plush and red and deeply comfortable; a place to recuperate. The view—if she chose to turn only slightly sideways—was one of the gentle rain that was falling onto Bay Street. Sopping wet pigeons huddled on the window-sill; people across the street in the Manulife building were turning on their lights.

A renegade robin, nesting in their eaves, began to sing.

Everett Menlo began to talk.

'Please don't interrupt,' he said at first.

'You know I won't,' said Mimi. It was a rule that neither one should interrupt the telling of a case until they had been invited to do so.

Mimi put her fingers into her glass so the ice-cubes wouldn't click. She waited.

Everett spoke—but he spoke as if in someone else's voice, perhaps the voice of Kenneth Albright. This was not entirely unusual. Often, both Mimi and Everett Menlo spoke in the voices of their patients. What was unusual, this time, was that, speaking in Kenneth's voice, Everett began to sweat profusely—so profusely that Mimi was able to watch his shirt front darkening with perspiration.

'As you know,' he said, 'I have not been sleeping.'

This was the understatement of the year. Mimi was silent.

'I have not been sleeping because—to put it in a nutshell—I have been afraid to dream.'

Mimi was somewhat startled by this. Not by the fact that Everett was afraid to dream, but only because she had just been thinking of dreams herself.

'I have been afraid to dream, because in all my dreams there have been bodies. Corpses. Murder victims.'

Mimi—not really listening—idly wondered if she had been one of them.

'In all my dreams, there have been corpses,' Everett repeated. 'But I am not the murderer. Kenneth Albright is the murderer, and, up to this moment, he has left behind him fifteen bodies: none of them people I recognize.'

Mimi nodded. The ice-cubes in her drink were beginning to freeze her fingers. Any minute now, she prayed, they would surely melt.

'I gave up dreaming almost a week ago,' said Everett, 'thinking that if I did, the killing pattern might be altered; broken.' Then he said tersely, 'it was not. The killings have continued. . . .'

'How do you know the killings have continued, Everett, if you've given up your dreaming? Wouldn't this mean he had no place to hide the bodies?'

In spite of the fact she had disobeyed their rule about not speaking, Everett answered her.

'I know they are being continued because I have seen the blood.'

'Ah, yes. I see.'

'No, Mimi. No. You do not see. The blood is not a figment of my imagination. The blood, in fact, is the only thing not dreamed.' He explained the stains on Kenneth Albright's hands and arms and clothes and he said: 'It happens every day. We have searched his person for signs of cuts and gashes—even for internal and rectal bleeding. Nothing. We have searched his quarters and all the other quarters in his ward. His ward is locked. His ward is isolated in the extreme. None of his fellow patients was ever found bleeding—never had cause to bleed. There were no injuries—no self-inflicted wounds. We thought of animals. Perhaps a mouse—a rat. But nothing. Nothing. Nothing . . . We also went so far as to strip-search all the members of the staff who entered that ward and I, too, offered myself for this experiment. Still nothing. Nothing. No one had bled.'

Everett was now beginning to perspire so heavily he removed his jacket and threw it on the floor. Thurber woke and stared at it, startled. At first, it appeared to be the beast that had just pursued him through the woods and down the road. But, then, it sighed and settled and was just a coat; a rumpled jacket lying down on the rug.

Everett said: 'we had taken samples of the blood on the patient's hands—on Kenneth Albright's hands and on his clothing and we had these samples analyzed. No. It was not his own blood. No, it was not the blood of an animal. No, it was not the blood of a fellow patient. No, it was not the blood of any members of the staff. . . .'

Everett's voice had risen.

'Whose blood was it?' he almost cried. 'Whose the hell was it?'

Mimi waited.

Everett Menlo lighted another cigarette. He took a great gulp of his drink.

'Well . . .' He was calmer now; calmer of necessity. He had to marshal the evidence. He had to put it all in order—bring it into line with reason. 'Did this mean that—somehow—the patient had managed to leave the premises—do some bloody deed and return without our knowledge of it? That is, after all, the only possible explanation. Isn't it?'

Mimi waited.

'Isn't it?' he repeated.

'Yes,' she said. 'It's the only possible explanation.'

'Except there is no way out of that place. There is absolutely no way out.'

Now, there was a pause.

'But one,' he added—his voice, again, a whisper.

Mimi was silent. Fearful—watching his twisted face.

'Tell me,' Everett Menlo said—the perfect innocent, almost the perfect child in quest of forbidden knowledge. 'Answer me this—be honest: is there blood in dreams?'

Mimi could not respond. She felt herself go pale. Her husband—after all, the sanest man alive—had just suggested something so completely mad he might as well have handed over his reason in a paper bag and said to her, *burn this*.

'The only place that Kenneth Albright goes, I tell you, is into dreams,' Everett said. 'That is the only place beyond the ward into which the patient can or does escape.'

Another—briefer—pause.

'It is real blood, Mimi. Real. And he gets it all from dreams. My dreams.'

They waited for this to settle.

Everett said: 'I'm tired. I'm tired. I cannot bear this any more. I'm tired. . . .'

Mimi thought, *good. No matter what else happens, he will sleep tonight.*

He did. And so, at last, did she.

Mimi's dreams were rarely of the kind that engender fear. She dreamt more gentle scenes with open spaces that did not intimidate. She would dream quite often of water and of animals. Always, she was nothing more than an observer; roles were not assigned her; often, this was sad. Somehow, she seemed at times locked out, unable to participate. These were the dreams she endured when Brian Bassett died: field trips to see him in some desert setting; underwater excursions to watch him floating amongst the seaweed. He never spoke, and indeed, he never appeared to be aware of her presence.

That night, when Everett fell into his bed exhausted and she did likewise, Mimi's dream of Brian Bassett was the last she would ever have of him and somehow, in the dream, she knew this. What she saw was what, in magical terms, would be called a disappearing act. Brian Bassett vanished. Gone.

Sometime after midnight on May Day morning, Mimi Menlo awoke from her dream of Brian to the sound of Thurber thumping the floor in a dream of his own.

Everett was not in his bed and Mimi cursed. She put on her wrapper and her slippers and went beyond the bedroom into the hall.

No lights were shining but the street lamps far below and the windows gave no sign of stars.

Mimi made her way past the jungle, searching for Everett in the living-room. He was not there. She would dream of this one day; it was a certainty.

'Everett?'

He did not reply.

Mimi turned and went back through the bedroom.

'Everett?'

She heard him. He was in the bathroom and she went in through the door.

'Oh,' she said, when she saw him. 'Oh, my God.'

Everett Menlo was standing in the bathtub, removing his pyjamas. They were soaking wet, but not with perspiration. They were soaking wet with blood.

For a moment, holding his jacket, letting its arms hang down across his belly and his groin, Everett stared at Mimi, blank-eyed from his nightmare.

Mimi raised her hands to her mouth. She felt as one must feel, if helpless, watching someone burn alive.

Everett threw the jacket down and started to remove his trousers. His pyjamas, made of cotton, had been green. His eyes were blinded now with blood and his hands reached out to find the shower taps.

'Please don't look at me,' he said. 'I . . . Please go away.'

Mimi said: 'no.' She sat on the toilet seat. 'I'm waiting here,' she told him, 'until we both wake up.'

1988

---

# Alice Munro
b. 1931

---

Born Alice Laidlaw, Alice Munro grew up in Wingham, Ontario, before moving, at the age of nineteen, to nearby London to attend the University of Western Ontario (UWO). After two years there, she married Jim Munro and settled with him in British Columbia. She lived in Vancouver and then Victoria for more than twenty years, writing, helping her husband manage his bookstore, and raising three daughters. In 1972, she returned to southwestern Ontario where she now lives in Clinton, not far from Wingham, with her second husband.

Munro began writing early—her first published work appeared in UWO's undergraduate literary magazine in 1950—and by 1960,

when 'The Peace of Utrecht' was read over CBC radio and published in the *Tamarack Review*, her writing began to gain recognition. However, she did not publish her first collection of stories, *Dance of the Happy Shades*, until 1968. The accomplished level of this debut book was recognized when it received the Governor General's Award for fiction, the first of three Munro would win. She subsequently published nine more collections of short fiction—*Something I've Been Meaning to Tell You* (1974); *The Moons of Jupiter* (1982); *The Progress of Love* (1986; Governor General's Award); *Friend of My Youth* (1990), *Open Secrets* (1994), *The Love of a Good Woman* (1998; Giller Prize),

*Hateship, Friendship, Courtship, Loveship, Marriage* (2001), *Runaway* (2004; Giller Prize), and *Too Much Happiness* (2009). She has also published two linked story sequences sometimes described as novels, *Lives of Girls and Women* (1971) and *Who Do You Think You Are?* (1978; Governor General's Award). Her 2006 work, *The View from Castle Rock*, is a cycle of short narratives that are overtly biographical, dealing with her family history and tracing out the importance of a Scottish heritage that has both shaped her and surrounded her with a set of attitudes against which she has struggled. In 2001, Munro's daughter Sheila published a memoir, *Lives of Mothers and Daughters: Growing Up with Alice Munro*, that also gives readers a sense of the interrelated textures of Munro's life and art.

*Selected Stories*, published in 1996, contains twenty-eight stories chosen by Munro. In 2003, Jane Urquhart edited and wrote an afterword to a new work of selections, *No Love Lost* (2003). *Alice Munro's Best: A Selection of Stories*, introduced by Margaret Atwood, appeared in 2008. Most of her new stories—like those of Mavis Gallant's—are first published in *The New Yorker*. Several of her stories have been made into feature films for television and theatre. Most recently, 'The Bear Came over the Mountain', as adapted and directed by Sarah Polley as *Away from Her* (2006; starring Gordon Pinsent and Julie Christie), won international praise and awards. (In 2007, Polley wrote a foreword for a new edition of *Hateship, Friendship, Courtship, Loveship, Marriage*, now retitled *Away from Her*.)

Munro's narrative structures are frequently developed through oppositions—which may take the form of contrasting characters (such as the sisters Marietta and Beryl in 'The Progress of Love') or of dialectics between 'female' and 'male' worlds or of a tension between rural and urban cultures. One opposition especially evident in her work is her playing off of *then* against *now*, which gives her stories a complex movement back and forth across time (often reflected in a play of tenses), reproducing the mind's ability to recover and reassess the layers of the past and their relationships to the present.

Describing Munro's achievements, the American short-story writer Mona Simpson wrote:

*Her genius, like Chekhov's, is quiet and particularly hard to describe, because it has the simplicity of the best naturalism, in that it seems not translated from life but, rather, like life itself. . . . Like the highest practitioners of any craft, Alice Munro seems, in her four most recent collections, to have left old forms behind, or to have broken them open, so that she is now writing not short stories or novellas but something altogether new . . . symphonic, large, architecturally gorgeous.* (The Atlantic Monthly, December, 2001)

Critics often use building metaphors to describe the intricate structure of these later stories. Munro herself, in suggesting that her way of writing stories can be explained by how she reads those written by other people, speaks of fiction as if it were something to explore, even to inhabit:

*I can start reading anywhere; from beginning to end, from end to beginning, from any point in between in either direction. So obviously I don't take up a story and follow it as if it were a road, taking me somewhere, with views and neat diversions along the way. I go into it, and move back and forth and settle here and there, and stay in it for a while. It's more like a house.* (Making It New: Contemporary Canadian Stories, edited by John Metcalf, 1982)

Munro furnishes her fictional houses meticulously. Because she usually sets her stories in a recognizable small-town Ontario, working with material she knows intimately and evoking fully realized milieus, she is sometimes thought of as a regionalist. Yet the ordinariness of the world she creates can be deceptive; disaster lurks or is longed for; secrets are glimpsed but remain untold, truth is uncertain. Many of the stories read as if they are on the verge of becoming full-length mystery novels, but they resist neat solutions, leaving their readers instead with what 'The Progress of Love' calls 'the old puzzles you can't resist or solve'.

The stories found in *The Progress of Love* marked a new stage in Munro's writing. Earlier, she had created beautifully written narratives about the complexities of the individual life; her later stories emphasize the power of perception and memory in shaping those lives. Although memory and the way one tells the story of the past were already important themes in Munro's fiction, increasingly, her stories have become kaleidoscopic, suggesting a shifting array of understandings that can unfold from an event. The broken chronology of Munro's stories reminds us that there is no one story, only an assembly of fragments of memory—a point that's underlined by the way events look different to various characters ('Beryl's version . . . was slanted, seen from a new angle,' the narrator of 'The Progress of Love' tells us). The 'deceptive realism' of her earlier fiction, where unexpected uncertainties and irresolution lay *beneath* apparently stable surfaces, has developed into stories in which surfaces themselves have become less certain, both for the reader and for the characters—a way of telling that allows readers to share the disorientation of the characters.

Narrated by a woman called Fame, 'The Progress of Love' tells a story of loss, particularly of the loss of equilibrium. While this loss begins with the death of her mother, physical death may not prove as serious as the death of love. Fame and the women from whom she is descended have experienced—and caused—a 'progress' of love, one that Fame hopes not to pass on to her sons. The other stories in the collection by that title, and indeed much of the body of Munro's work, might be thought of as similarly tracing out this ever-changing progress of love over the course of several generations.

# The Progress of Love

I got a call at work, and it was my father. This was not long after I was divorced and started in the real-estate office. Both of my boys were in school. It was a hot enough day in September.

My father was so polite, even in the family. He took time to ask me how I was. Country manners. Even if somebody phones up to tell you your house is burning down, they ask first how you are.

'I'm fine,' I said. 'How are you?'

'Not so good, I guess,' said my father, in his old way—apologetic but self-respecting. 'I think your mother's gone.'

I knew that *gone* meant *dead*. I knew that. But for a second or so I saw my mother in her black straw hat setting off down the lane. The word *gone* seemed full of nothing but a deep relief and even an excitement—the excitement you feel when a door closes and your house sinks back to normal and you let yourself loose into all the free space around you. That was in my father's voice too—behind the apology, a queer sound like a gulped breath. But my mother hadn't been a burden—she hadn't been sick a day— and far from feeling relieved at her death, my father took it hard. He never got used to living alone, he said. He went into the Netterfield Country Home quite willingly.

He told me how he found my mother on the couch in the kitchen when he came in at noon. She had picked a few tomatoes, and was setting them on the windowsill to ripen; then she must have felt weak, and lain down. Now, telling this, his voice went wobbly—meandering, as you would expect—in his amazement. I saw in my mind the couch, the old quilt that protected it, right under the phone.

'So I thought I better call you,' my father said, and he waited for me to say what he should do now.

My mother prayed on her knees at midday, at night, and first thing in the morning. Every day opened up to her to have God's will done in it. Every night she totted up what she'd done and said and thought, to see how it squared with Him. That kind of life is dreary, people think, but they're missing the point. For one thing, such a life can never be boring. And nothing can happen to you that you can't make use of. Even if you're wracked by troubles, and sick and poor and ugly, you've got your soul to carry through life like a treasure on a platter. Going upstairs to pray after the noon meal, my mother would be full of energy and expectation, seriously smiling.

She was saved at a camp meeting[1] when she was fourteen. That was the same summer that her own mother—my grandmother—died. For a few years, my mother went to meetings with a lot of other people who'd been saved, some who'd been saved over and over again, enthusiastic old sinners. She could tell stories about what went on at those meetings, the singing and hollering and wildness. She told about one old man getting up and shouting, 'Come down, O Lord, come down among us now! Come down through the roof and I'll pay for the shingles!'

She was back to being just an Anglican, a serious one, by the time she got married. She was about twenty-five then, and my father was thirty-eight. A tall good-looking couple, good dancers, good cardplayers, sociable. But serious people—that's how I would try to describe them. Serious the way hardly anybody is anymore. My father was not religious in the way my mother was. He was an Anglican, an Orangeman, a Conservative, because that's what he had been brought up to be. He was the son who got left on the farm with his parents and took care of them till they died. He met my mother, he waited for her, they married; he thought himself lucky then to have a family to work for. (I have two brothers, and I had a baby sister who died.) I have a feeling that my father never slept with any woman before my mother, and never with her until he married her. And he had to wait, because my mother couldn't get married until she had paid back to her own father every cent he had spent on her since her mother died. She had kept track of everything—board, books, clothes—so that she could pay it back. When she married, she had no nest egg, as teachers usually did, no hope chest, sheets, or dishes. My father used to say, with a sombre, joking face, that he had hoped to get a woman with money in the bank. 'But you take money in the bank, you have to take the face that goes with it,' he said, 'and sometimes that's no bargain.'

The house we lived in had big, high rooms, with dark-green blinds on the windows. When the blinds were pulled down against the sun, I used to like to move my head and catch the light flashing through the holes and cracks. Another thing I liked looking at was chimney stains, old or fresh, which I could turn into animals, people's faces, even distant cities. I told my own two boys about that, and their father, Dan Casey, said, 'See, your mom's folks were so poor, they couldn't afford TV, so they got these stains on the ceiling—your mom had to watch the stains on the ceiling!' He always liked to kid me about thinking poor was anything great.

---

1 An evangelical religious rally (in Ontario, usually Methodist), held outdoors or in a tent, and characterized by enthusiastic worship and altar calls; for many individuals, such camp meetings were accompanied by the tremendous emotional release that followed a conversion experience.

When my father was very old, I figured out that he didn't mind people doing new sorts of things—for instance, my getting divorced—as much as he minded them having new sorts of reasons for doing them.

Thank God he never had to know about the commune.

'The Lord never intended,' he used to say. Sitting around with the other old men in the Home, in the long, dim porch behind the spirea bushes, he talked about how the Lord never intended for people to tear around the country on motorbikes and snowmobiles. And how the Lord never intended for nurses' uniforms to be pants. The nurses didn't mind at all. They called him 'Handsome', and told me he was a real old sweetheart, a real old religious gentleman. They marvelled at his thick black hair, which he kept until he died. They washed and combed it beautifully, wet-waved it with their fingers.

Sometimes, with all their care, he was a little unhappy. He wanted to go home. He worried about the cows, the fences, about who was getting up to light the fire. A few flashes of meanness—very few. Once, he gave me a sneaky, unfriendly look when I went in; he said, 'I'm surprised you haven't worn all the skin off your knees by now.'

I laughed. I said, 'What doing? Scrubbing floors?'

'Praying?' he said, in a voice like spitting.

He didn't know who he was talking to.

I don't remember my mother's hair being anything but white. My mother went white in her twenties, and never saved any of her young hair, which had been brown. I used to try to get her to tell me what colour brown.

'Dark.'

'Like Brent, or like Dolly?' Those were two workhorses we had, a team.

'I don't know. It wasn't horsehair.'

'Was it like chocolate?'

'Something like.'

'Weren't you sad when it went white?'

'No. I was glad.'

'Why?'

'I was glad that I wouldn't have hair anymore that was the same colour as my father's.'

Hatred is always a sin, my mother told me. Remember that. One drop of hatred in your soul will spread and discolour everything like a drop of black ink in white milk. I was struck by that and meant to try it, but knew I shouldn't waste the milk.

All these things I remember. All the things I know, or have been told, about people I never even saw. I was named Euphemia, after my mother's mother. A terrible name, such as nobody has nowadays. At home they called me Phemie, but when I started to work, I called myself Fame. My husband, Dan Casey, called me Fame. Then in the bar of the Shamrock Hotel, years later, after my divorce, when I was going out, a man said to me, 'Fame, I've been meaning to ask you, just what is it you are famous for?'

'I don't know,' I told him. 'I don't know, unless it's for wasting my time talking to jerks like you.'

After that I thought of changing it altogether, to something like Joan, but unless I moved away from here, how could I do that?

In the summer of 1947, when I was twelve, I helped my mother paper the downstairs bedroom, the spare room. My mother's sister, Beryl, was coming to visit us. These two sisters hadn't seen each other for years. Very soon after their mother died, their father married again. He went to live in Minneapolis, then in Seattle, with his new wife and his young daughter, Beryl. My mother wouldn't go with them. She stayed on in the town of Ramsay, where they had been living. She was boarded with a childless couple who had been neighbours. She and Beryl had met only once or twice since they were grown up. Beryl lived in California.

The paper had a design of cornflowers on a white ground. My mother had got it at a reduced price, because it was the end of a lot. This meant we had trouble matching the pattern, and behind the door we had to do some tricky fitting with scraps and strips. This was before the days of pre-pasted wallpaper. We had a trestle table set up in the front room, and we mixed the paste and swept it onto the back of the paper with wide brushes, watching for lumps. We worked with the windows up, screens fitted under them, the front door open, the screen door closed. The country we could see through the mesh of screens and the wavery old window glass was all hot and flowering—milkweed and wild carrot in the pastures, mustard rampaging in the clover, some fields creamy with the buckwheat people grew then. My mother sang. She sang a song she said her own mother used to sing when she and Beryl were little girls.

> 'I once had a sweetheart, but now I have none.
> He's gone and he's left me to weep and to moan.
> He's gone and he's left me, but contented I'll be,
> For I'll get another one, better than he!'

I was excited because Beryl was coming, a visitor, all the way from California. Also because I had gone to town in late June to write the Entrance Examinations,[2] and was hoping to hear soon that I had passed with honours. Everybody who had finished Grade 8 in the country schools had to go into town to write those examinations. I loved that—the rustling sheets of foolscap, the important silence, the big stone high-school building, all the old initials carved in the desks, darkened with varnish. The first burst of summer outside, the green and yellow light, the townlike chestnut trees, and honeysuckle. And all it was was this same town, where I have lived now more than half my life. I wondered at it. And at myself, drawing maps with ease and solving problems, knowing quantities of answers. I thought I was so clever. But I wasn't clever enough to understand the simplest thing. I didn't even understand that examinations made no difference in my case. I wouldn't be going to high school. How could I? That was before there were school buses; you had to board in town. My parents didn't have the money. They operated on very little cash, as many farmers did then. The payments from the cheese factory were about all that came in regularly. And they didn't think of

2 Examinations used throughout Ontario for entrance into secondary school, they divided students up into vocational and academic streams.

my life going in that direction, the high-school direction. They thought that I would stay at home and help my mother, maybe hire out to help women in the neighbourhood who were sick or having a baby. Until such time as I got married. That was what they were waiting to tell me when I got the results of the examinations.

You would think my mother might have a different idea, since she had been a schoolteacher herself. But she said God didn't care. God isn't interested in what kind of job or what kind of education anybody has, she told me. He doesn't care two hoots about that, and it's what He cares about that matters.

This was the first time I understood how God could become a real opponent, not just some kind of nuisance or large decoration.

My mother's name as a child was Marietta. That continued to be her name, of course, but until Beryl came I never heard her called by it. My father always said Mother. I had a childish notion—I knew it was childish—that Mother suited my mother better than it did other mothers. Mother, not Mama. When I was away from her, I could not think what my mother's face was like, and this frightened me. Sitting in school, just over a hill from home, I would try to picture my mother's face. Sometimes I thought that if I couldn't do it, that might mean my mother was dead. But I had a sense of her all the time, and would be reminded of her by the most unlikely things—an upright piano, or a tall white loaf of bread. That's ridiculous, but true.

Marietta, in my mind, was separate, not swallowed up in my mother's grown-up body. Marietta was still running around loose up in her town of Ramsay, on the Ottawa River. In that town, the streets were full of horses and puddles, and darkened by men who came in from the bush on weekends. Loggers. There were eleven hotels on the main street, where the loggers stayed, and drank.

The house Marietta lived in was halfway up a steep street climbing from the river. It was a double house, with two bay windows in front, and a wooden trellis that separated the two front porches. In the other half of the house lived the Sutcliffes, the people Marietta was to board with after her mother died and her father left town. Mr Sutcliffe was an Englishman, a telegraph operator. His wife was German. She always made coffee instead of tea. She made strudel. The dough for the strudel hung down over the edges of the table like a fine cloth. It sometimes looked to Marietta like a skin.

Mrs Sutcliffe was the one who talked Marietta's mother out of hanging herself.

Marietta was home from school that day, because it was Saturday. She woke up late and heard the silence in the house. She was always scared of that—a silent house—and as soon as she opened the door after school she would call, 'Mama! Mama!' Often her mother wouldn't answer. But she would be there. Marietta would hear with relief the rattle of the stove grate or the steady slap of the iron.

That morning, she didn't hear anything. She came downstairs, and got herself a slice of bread and butter and molasses, folded over. She opened the cellar door and called. She went into the front room and peered out the window, through the bridal fern. She saw her little sister, Beryl, and some other neighbourhood children rolling down the bit of grassy terrace to the sidewalk, picking themselves up and scrambling to the top and rolling down again.

'Mama?' called Marietta. She walked through the house to the back yard. It was late spring, the day was cloudy and mild. In the sprouting vegetable gardens, the earth was damp, and the leaves on the trees seemed suddenly full-sized, letting down drops of water left over from the rain of the night before.

'Mama?' calls Marietta under the trees, under the clothesline.

At the end of the yard is a small barn, where they keep firewood, and some tools and old furniture. A chair, a straight-backed wooden chair, can be seen through the open doorway. On the chair, Marietta sees her mother's feet, her mother's black laced shoes. Then the long, printed cotton summer work dress, the apron, the rolled-up sleeves. Her mother's shiny-looking white arms, and neck, and face.

Her mother stood on the chair and didn't answer. She didn't look at Marietta, but smiled and tapped her foot, as if to say, 'Here I am, then. What are you going to do about it?' Something looked wrong about her, beyond the fact that she was standing on a chair and smiling in this queer, tight way. Standing on an old chair with back rungs missing, which she had pulled out to the middle of the barn floor, where it teetered on the bumpy earth. There was a shadow on her neck.

The shadow was a rope, a noose on the end of a rope that hung down from a beam overhead.

'Mama?' says Marietta, in a fainter voice. 'Mama. Come down, please.' Her voice is faint because she fears that any yell or cry might jolt her mother into movement, cause her to step off the chair and throw her weight on the rope. But even if Marietta wanted to yell she couldn't. Nothing but this pitiful thread of a voice is left to her— just as in a dream when a beast or a machine is bearing down on you.

'Go and get your father.'

That was what her mother told her to do, and Marietta obeyed. With terror in her legs, she ran. In her nightgown, in the middle of a Saturday morning, she ran. She ran past Beryl and the other children, still tumbling down the slope. She ran along the sidewalk, which was at that time a boardwalk, then on the unpaved street, full of last night's puddles. The street crossed the railway tracks. At the foot of the hill, it inter- sected the main street of the town. Between the main street and the river were some warehouses and the buildings of small manufacturers. That was where Marietta's father had his carriage works. Wagons, buggies, sleds were made there. In fact, Marietta's father had invented a new sort of sled to carry logs in the bush. It had been patented. He was just getting started in Ramsay. (Later on, in the States, he made money. A man fond of hotel bars, barbershops, harness races, women, but not afraid of work—give him credit.)

Marietta did not find him at work that day. The office was empty. She ran out into the yard where the men were working. She stumbled in the fresh sawdust. The men laughed and shook their heads at her. No. Not here. Not a-here right now. No. Why don't you try upstreet? Wait. Wait a minute. Hadn't you better get some clothes on first?

They didn't mean any harm. They didn't have the sense to see that something must be wrong. But Marietta never could stand men laughing. There were always places she hated to go past, let alone into, and that was the reason. Men laughing. Because of that, she hated barbershops, hated their smell. (When she started going to dances later on with my father, she asked him not to put any dressing on his hair, because the smell reminded her.) A bunch of men standing out on the street, outside a hotel, seemed to Marietta like a clot of poison. You tried not to hear what they were saying, but you could be sure it was vile. If they didn't say anything, they laughed and vileness spread out from them—poison—just the same. It was only after Marietta was saved that she could walk right past them. Armed by God, she walked through their midst and nothing stuck to her, nothing scorched her; she was safe as Daniel.[3]

Now she turned and ran, straight back the way she had come. Up the hill, running to get home. She thought she had made a mistake leaving her mother. Why did her mother tell her to go? Why did she want her father? Quite possibly so that she could greet him with the sight of her own warm body swinging on the end of a rope. Marietta should have stayed—she should have stayed and talked her mother out of it. She should have run to Mrs Sutcliffe, or any neighbour, not wasted time this way. She hadn't thought who could help, who could even believe what she was talking about. She had the idea that all families except her own lived in peace, that threats and miseries didn't exist in other people's houses, and couldn't be explained there.

A train was coming into town. Marietta had to wait. Passengers looked out at her from its windows. She broke out wailing in the faces of those strangers. When the train passed, she continued up the hill—a spectacle, with her hair uncombed, her feet bare and muddy, in her nightgown, with a wild, wet face. By the time she ran into her own yard, in sight of the barn, she was howling. 'Mama!' she was howling, 'Mama!'

Nobody was there. The chair was standing just where it had been before. The rope was dangling over the back of it. Marietta was sure that her mother had gone ahead and done it. Her mother was already dead—she had been cut down and taken away.

But warm, fat hands settled down on her shoulders, and Mrs Sutcliffe said, 'Marietta. Stop the noise. Marietta. Child. Stop the crying. Come inside. She is well, Marietta. Come inside and you will see.'

Mrs Sutcliffe's foreign voice said, 'Mari-et-cha', giving the name a rich, important sound. She was as kind as could be. When Marietta lived with the Sutcliffes later, she was treated as the daughter of the household, and it was a household just as peaceful and comfortable as she had imagined other households to be. But she never felt like a daughter there.

In Mrs Sutcliffe's kitchen, Beryl sat on the floor eating a raisin cookie and playing with the black-and-white cat, whose name was Dickie. Marietta's mother sat at the table, with a cup of coffee in front of her.

'She was silly,' Mrs Sutcliffe said. Did she mean Marietta's mother or Marietta herself? She didn't have many English words to describe things.

Marietta's mother laughed, and Marietta blacked out. She fainted, after running all that way uphill, howling, in the warm, damp morning. Next thing she knew, she

---

3 Daniel was a Hebrew prophet who spent his life as a captive in the court of Babylon but who refrained from partaking of the Babylonian king's bounty so that he 'would not defile himself'. The Book of Daniel recounts two stories of God's protecting those who are faithful to him: first, when Daniel's compatriots Shadrach, Meshach, and Abednego escape unscathed from a fiery furnace to which they are consigned for refusing to worship gods they do not believe in; and then when Daniel himself is delivered from the lions' den into which he had been thrown for his faithful observance of his religious customs.

was taking black, sweet coffee from a spoon held by Mrs Sutcliffe. Beryl picked Dickie up by the front legs and offered him as a cheering present. Marietta's mother was still sitting at the table.

Her heart was broken. That was what I always heard my mother say. That was the end of it. Those words lifted up the story and sealed it shut. I never asked, Who broke it? I never asked. What was the men's poison talk? What was the meaning of the word *vile*?

Marietta's mother laughed after not hanging herself. She sat at Mrs Sutcliffe's kitchen table long ago and laughed. Her heart was broken.

I always had a feeling, with my mother's talk and stories, of something swelling out behind. Like a cloud you couldn't see through, or get to the end of. There was a cloud, a poison, that had touched my mother's life. And when I grieved my mother, I became part of it. Then I would beat my head against my mother's stomach and breasts, against her tall, firm front, demanding to be forgiven. My mother would tell me to ask God. But it wasn't God, it was my mother I had to get straight with. It seemed as if she knew something about me that was worse, far worse, than ordinary lies and tricks and meanness; it was a really sickening shame. I beat against my mother's front to make her forget that.

My brothers weren't bothered by any of this. I don't think so. They seemed to me like cheerful savages, running around free, not having to learn much. And when I just had the two boys myself, no daughters, I felt as if something could stop now—the stories, and griefs, the old puzzles you can't resist or solve.

Aunt Beryl said not to call her Aunt. 'I'm not used to being anybody's aunt, honey. I'm not even anybody's momma. I'm just me. Call me Beryl.'

Beryl had started out as a stenographer, and now she had her own typing and bookkeeping business, which employed many girls. She had arrived with a man friend, whose name was Mr Florence. Her letter had said she would be getting a ride with a friend, but she hadn't said whether the friend would be staying or going on. She hadn't even said if it was a man or woman.

Mr Florence was staying. He was a tall, thin man with a long, tanned face, very light-coloured eyes, and a way of twitching the corner of his mouth that might have been a smile.

He was the one who got to sleep in the room that my mother and I had papered, because he was the stranger, and a man. Beryl had to sleep with me. At first we thought that Mr Florence was quite rude, because he wasn't used to our way of talking and we weren't used to his. The first morning, my father said to Mr Florence, 'Well, I hope you got some kind of a sleep on that old bed in there?' (The spare-room bed was heavenly, with a feather tick.[4]) This was Mr Florence's cue to say that he had never slept better.

4 Mattress.

Mr Florence twitched. He said, 'I slept on worse.'

His favourite place to be was in his car. His car was a royal-blue Chrysler, from the first batch turned out after the war. Inside it, the upholstery and floor covering and roof and door padding were all pearl grey. Mr Florence kept the names of those colours in mind and corrected you if you said just 'blue' or 'grey'.

'Mouse skin is what it looks like to me,' said Beryl rambunctiously. 'I tell him it's just mouse skin!'

The car was parked at the side of the house, under the locust trees. Mr Florence sat inside with the windows rolled up, smoking, in the rich new-car smell.

'I'm afraid we're not doing much to entertain your friend,' my mother said.

'I wouldn't worry about him,' said Beryl. She always spoke about Mr Florence as if there was a joke about him that only she appreciated. I wondered long afterward if he had a bottle in the glove compartment and took a nip from time to time to keep his spirits up. He kept his hat on.

Beryl herself was being entertained enough for two. Instead of staying in the house and talking to my mother, as a lady visitor usually did, she demanded to be shown everything there was to see on a farm. She said that I was to take her around and explain things, and see that she didn't fall into any manure piles.

I didn't know what to show. I took Beryl to the icehouse, where chunks of ice the size of dresser drawers, or bigger, lay buried in sawdust. Every few days, my father would chop off a piece of ice and carry it to the kitchen, where it melted in a tin-lined box and cooled the milk and butter.

Beryl said she had never had any idea ice came in pieces that big. She seemed intent on finding things strange, or horrible, or funny.

'Where in the world do you get ice that big?'

I couldn't tell if that was a joke.

'Off of the lake,' I said.

'Off of the lake! Do you have lakes up here that have ice on them all summer?'

I told her how my father cut the ice on the lake every winter and hauled it home, and buried it in sawdust, and that kept it from melting.

Beryl said, 'That's amazing!'

'Well, it melts a little,' I said. I was deeply disappointed in Beryl.

'That's really amazing.'

Beryl went along when I went to get the cows. A scarecrow in white slacks (this is what my father called her afterward), with a white sun hat tied under her chin by a flaunting red ribbon. Her fingernails and toenails—she wore sandals—were painted to match the ribbon. She wore the small, dark sunglasses people wore at that time. (Not the people I knew—they didn't own sunglasses.) She had a big red mouth, a loud laugh, hair of an unnatural colour and a high gloss, like cherry wood. She was so noisy and shiny, so glamorously got up, that it was hard to tell whether she was good-looking, or happy, or anything.

We didn't have any conversation along the cowpath, because Beryl kept her distance from the cows and was busy watching where she stepped. Once I had them all tied in their stalls, she came closer. She lit a cigarette. Nobody smoked in the barn. My father and other farmers chewed tobacco there instead. I didn't see how I could ask Beryl to chew tobacco.

'Can you get the milk out of them or does your father have to?' Beryl said. 'Is it hard to do?'

I pulled some milk down through the cow's teat. One of the barn cats came over and waited. I shot a thin stream into its mouth. The cat and I were both showing off.

'Doesn't that hurt?' said Beryl. 'Think if it was you.'

I had never thought of a cow's teat as corresponding to any part of myself, and was shaken by this indecency. In fact, I could never grasp a warm, warty teat in such a firm and casual way again.

Beryl slept in a peach-coloured rayon nightgown trimmed with écru lace. She had a robe to match. She was just as careful about the word *écru* as Mr Florence was about his royal blue and pearl grey.

I managed to get undressed and put on my nightgown without any part of me being exposed at any time. An awkward business. I left my underpants on, and hoped that Beryl had done the same. The idea of sharing my bed with a grownup was a torment to me. But I did get to see the contents of what Beryl called her beauty kit. Hand-painted glass jars contained puffs of cotton wool, talcum powder, milky lotion, ice-blue astringent. Little pots of red and mauve rouge—rather greasy-looking. Blue and black pencils. Emery boards, a pumice stone, nail polish with an overpowering smell of bananas, face powder in a celluloid box shaped like a shell, with the name of a dessert— Apricot Delight.

I had heated some water on the coal-oil stove we used in summertime. Beryl scrubbed her face clean, and there was such a change that I almost expected to see makeup lying in strips in the washbowl, like the old wallpaper we had soaked and peeled. Beryl's skin was pale now, covered with fine cracks, rather like the shiny mud at the bottom of puddles drying up in early summer.

'Look what happened to my skin,' she said. 'Dieting. I weighed a hundred and sixty-nine pounds once, I took it off too fast and my face fell in on me. Now I've got this cream, though. It's made from a secret formula and you can't even buy it commercially. Smell it. See, it doesn't smell all perfumy. It smells serious.'

She was patting the cream on her face with puffs of cotton wool, patting away until there was nothing to be seen on the surface.

'It smells like lard,' I said.

'Christ almighty, I hope I haven't been paying that kind of money to rub lard on my face. Don't tell your mother I swear.'

She poured clean water into the drinking glass and wet her comb, then combed her hair wet and twisted each strand around her finger, clamping the twisted strand to her head with two crossed pins. I would be doing the same myself, a couple of years later.

'Always do your hair wet, else it's no good doing it up at all,' Beryl said. 'And always roll it under even if you want it to flip up. See?'

When I was doing my hair up—as I did for years—I sometimes thought of this, and thought that of all the pieces of advice people had given me, this was the one I had followed most carefully.

We put the lamp out and got into bed, and Beryl said, 'I never knew it could get so dark. I've never known a dark that was as dark as this.' She was whispering. I was slow to understand that she was comparing country nights to city nights, and I wondered if the darkness in Netterfield County could really be greater than that in California.

'Honey?' whispered Beryl. 'Are there any animals outside?'

'Cows,' I said.

'Yes, but wild animals? Are there bears?'

'Yes,' I said. My father had once found bear tracks and droppings in the bush, and the apples had all been torn off a wild apple tree. That was years ago, when he was a young man.

Beryl moaned and giggled. 'Think if Mr Florence had to go out in the night and he ran into a bear!'

Next day was Sunday. Beryl and Mr Florence drove my brothers and me to Sunday school in the Chrysler. That was at ten o'clock in the morning. They came back at eleven to bring my parents to church.

'Hop in,' Beryl said to me. 'You too,' she said to the boys. 'We're going for a drive.'

Beryl was dressed up in a satiny ivory dress with red dots, and a red-lined frill over the hips, and red high heeled shoes. Mr Florence wore a pale-blue summer suit.

'Aren't you going to church?' I said. That was what people dressed up for, in my experience.

Beryl laughed. 'Honey, this isn't Mr Florence's kind of religion.'

I was used to going straight from Sunday school into church, and sitting for another hour and a half. In summer, the open windows let in the cedary smell of the graveyard and the occasional, almost sacrilegious sound of a car swooshing by on the road. Today we spent this time driving through country I had never seen before. I had never seen it, though it was less than twenty miles from home. Our truck went to the cheese factory, to church, and to town on Saturday nights. The nearest thing to a drive was when it went to the dump. I had seen the near end of Bell's Lake, because that was where my father cut the ice in winter. You couldn't get close to it in summer; the shoreline was all choked up with bulrushes. I had thought that the other end of the lake would look pretty much the same, but when we drove there today, I saw cottages, docks and boats, dark water reflecting the trees. All this and I hadn't known about it. This too was Bell's Lake. I was glad to have seen it at last, but in some way not altogether glad of the surprise.

Finally, a white frame building appeared, with verandas and potted flowers, and some twinkling poplar trees in front. The Wildwood Inn. Today the same building is covered with stucco and done up with Tudor beams and called the Hideaway. The poplar trees have been cut down for a parking lot.

On the way back to the church to pick up my parents, Mr Florence turned in to the farm next to ours, which belonged to the McAllisters. The McAllisters were Catholics. Our two families were neighbourly but not close.

'Come on, boys, out you get,' said Beryl to my brothers. 'Not you,' she said to me. 'You stay put.' She herded the little boys up to the porch, where some McAllisters were watching. They were in their raggedy home clothes, because their church, or Mass, or whatever it was, got out early. Mrs McAllister came out and stood listening, rather dumbfounded, to Beryl's laughing talk.

Beryl came back to the car by herself. 'There,' she said. 'They're going to play with the neighbour children.'

Play with McAllisters? Besides being Catholics, all but the baby were girls.

'They've still got their good clothes on,' I said.

'So what? Can't they have a good time with their good clothes on? I do!'

My parents were taken by surprise as well. Beryl got out and told my father he was to ride in the front seat, for the legroom. She got into the back, with my mother and me. Mr Florence turned again onto the Bell's Lake road, and Beryl announced that we were all going to the Wildwood Inn for dinner.

'You're all dressed up, why not take advantage?' she said. 'We dropped the boys off with your neighbours. I thought they might be too young to appreciate it. The neighbours were happy to have them.' She said with a further emphasis that it was to be their treat. Hers and Mr Florence's.

'Well, now,' said my father. He probably didn't have five dollars in his pocket. 'Well, now. I wonder do they let the farmers in?'

He made various jokes along this line. In the hotel dining room, which was all in white—white tablecloths, white painted chairs—with sweating glass water pitchers and high, whirring fans, he picked up a table napkin the size of a diaper and spoke to me in a loud whisper, 'Can you tell me what to do with this thing? Can I put it on my head to keep the draft off?'

Of course he had eaten in hotel dining rooms before. He knew about table napkins and pie forks. And my mother knew—she wasn't even a country woman, to begin with. Nevertheless this was a huge event. Not exactly a pleasure—as Beryl must have meant it to be—but a huge, unsettling event. Eating a meal in public, only a few miles from home, eating in a big room full of people you didn't know, the food served by a stranger, a snippy-looking girl who was probably a college student working at a summer job.

'I'd like the rooster,' my father said. 'How long has he been in the pot?' It was only good manners, as he knew it, to joke with people who waited on him.

'Beg your pardon?' the girl said.

'Roast chicken,' said Beryl. 'Is that okay for everybody?'

Mr Florence was looking gloomy. Perhaps he didn't care for jokes when it was his money that was being spent. Perhaps he had counted on something better than ice water to fill up the glasses.

The waitress put down a dish of celery and olives, and my mother said, 'Just a minute while I give thanks.' She bowed her head and said quietly but audibly, 'Lord, bless this food to our use, and us to Thy service, for Christ's sake. Amen.' Refreshed, she sat up straight and passed the dish to me, saying, 'Mind the olives. There's stones in them.'

Beryl was smiling around at the room.

The waitress came back with a basket of rolls.

'Parker House!' Beryl learned over and breathed in their smell. 'Eat them while they're hot enough to melt the butter!'

Mr Florence twitched, and peered into the butter dish. 'Is that what this is—butter? I thought it was Shirley Temple's curls.'

His face was hardly less gloomy than before, but it was a joke, and his making it seemed to convey to us something of the very thing that had just been publicly asked for—a blessing.

'When he says something funny', said Beryl—who often referred to Mr Florence as 'he' even when he was right there—'you notice how he always keeps a straight face? That reminds me of Mama. I mean of our mama, Marietta's and mine. Daddy, when he made a joke you could see it coming a mile away—he couldn't keep it off his face—but Mama was another story. She could look so sour. But she could joke on her deathbed. In fact, she did that very thing. Marietta, remember when she was in bed in the front room the spring before she died?'

'I remember she was in bed in that room,' my mother said. 'Yes.'

'Well, Daddy came in and she was lying there in her clean nightgown, with the covers off, because the German lady from next door had just been helping her take a wash, and she was still there tidying up the bed. So Daddy wanted to be cheerful, and he said, "Spring must be coming. I saw a crow today." This must have been in March. And Mama said quick as a shot, "Well, you better cover me up then, before it looks in that window and gets any ideas!" The German lady—Daddy said she just about dropped the basin. Because it was true, Mama was skin and bones; she was dying. But she could joke.'

Mr Florence said, 'Might as well when there's no use to cry.'

'But she could carry a joke too far, Mama could. One time, one time, she wanted to give Daddy a scare. He was supposed to be interested in some girl that kept coming around to the works. Well, he was a big good-looking man. So Mama said, "Well, I'll just do away with myself, and you can get on with her and see how you like it when I come back and haunt you." He told her not to be so stupid, and he went off downtown. And Mama went out to the barn and climbed on a chair and put a rope around her neck. Didn't she, Marietta? Marietta went looking for her and she found her like that!'

My mother bent her head and put her hands in her lap, almost as if she was getting ready to say another grace.

'Daddy told me all about it, but I can remember anyway. I remember Marietta tearing off down the hill in her nightie, and I guess the German lady saw her go, and she came out and was looking for Mama, and somehow we all ended up in the barn—me too, and some kids I was playing with—and there was Mama up on a chair preparing to give Daddy the fright of his life. She'd sent Marietta after him. And the German lady starts wailing, "Oh, missus, come down missus, think of your little *kindren*"— "*kindren*" is the German for "*children*"—"think of your *kindren*," and so on. Until it was me standing there—I was just a little squirt, but I was the one noticed that rope. My eyes followed that rope up and up and I saw it was just hanging over the beam, just flung there—it wasn't tied at all! Marietta hadn't noticed that, the German lady hadn't noticed it. But I just spoke up and said, "Mama, how are you going to manage to hang yourself without that rope tied around the beam?"'

Mr Florence said, 'That'd be a tough one.'

'I spoiled her game. The German lady made coffee and we went over there and had a few treats, and, Marietta, you couldn't find Daddy after all, could you? You could hear Marietta howling, coming up the hill, a block away.'

'Natural for her to be upset,' my father said.

'Sure it was. Mama went too far.'

'She meant it,' my mother said. 'She meant it more than you give her credit for.'

'She meant to get a rise out of Daddy. That was their whole life together. He always said she was a hard woman to live with, but she had a lot of character. I believe he missed that, with Gladys.'

'I wouldn't know,' my mother said, in that particularly steady voice with which she always spoke of her father. 'What he did say or didn't say.'

'People are dead now,' said my father. 'It isn't up to us to judge.'

'I know,' said Beryl. 'I know Marietta's always had a different view.'

My mother looked at Mr Florence and smiled quite easily and radiantly. 'I'm sure you don't know what to make of all these family matters.'

The one time that I visited Beryl, when Beryl was an old woman, all knobby and twisted up with arthritis, Beryl said, 'Marietta got all Daddy's looks. And she never did a thing with herself. Remember her wearing that old navy-blue crêpe dress when we went to the hotel that time? Of course, I know it was probably all she had, but did it have to be all she had? You know, I was scared of her somehow. I couldn't stay in a room alone with her. But she had outstanding looks.' Trying to remember an occasion when I had noticed my mother's looks, I thought of the time in the hotel, my mother's pale-olive skin against the heavy white, coiled hair, her open, handsome face smiling at Mr Florence—as if he was the one to be forgiven.

I didn't have a problem right away with Beryl's story. For one thing, I was hungry and greedy, and a lot of my attention went to the roast chicken and gravy and mashed potatoes laid on the plate with an ice-cream scoop and the bright diced vegetables out of a can, which I thought much superior to those fresh from the garden. For dessert, I had a butterscotch sundae, an agonizing choice over chocolate. The others had plain vanilla ice cream.

Why shouldn't Beryl's version of the same event be different from my mother's? Beryl was strange in every way—everything about her was slanted, seen from a new angle. It was my mother's version that held, for a time. It absorbed Beryl's story, closed over it. But Beryl's story didn't vanish; it stayed sealed off for years, but it wasn't gone. It was like the knowledge of that hotel and dining room. I knew about it now, though I didn't think of it as a place to go back to. And indeed, without Beryl's or Mr Florence's money, I couldn't. But I knew it was there.

The next time I was in the Wildwood Inn, in fact, was after I was married. The Lions Club had a banquet and dance there. The man I had married, Dan Casey, was a Lion. You could get a drink there by that time. Dan Casey wouldn't have gone anywhere you couldn't. Then the place was remodelled into the Hideaway, and now they have strippers every night but Sunday. On Thursday nights, they have a male stripper. I go there with people from the real estate office to celebrate birthdays or other big events.

The farm was sold for five thousand dollars in 1965. A man from Toronto bought it, for a hobby farm or just an investment. After a couple of years, he rented it to a commune. They stayed there, different people drifting on and off, for a dozen years or so. They raised goats and sold the milk to the health-food store that had opened up in town. They painted a rainbow across the side of the barn that faced the road. They hung tie-dyed sheets over the windows, and let the long grass and flowering weeds reclaim the yard. My parents had finally got electricity in, but these people didn't use it. They preferred oil lamps and the woodstove, and taking their dirty clothes to town. People said they wouldn't know how to handle lamps or wood fires, and they would burn the place down. But they didn't. In fact, they didn't manage badly. They kept the house and barn in some sort of repair and they worked a big garden. They even dusted their potatoes against blight—though I heard that there was some sort of row about this and some of the stricter members left. The place actually looked a lot better than many of the farms round about that were still in the hands of the original families. The McAllister son had started a wrecking business on their place. My own brothers were long gone.

I knew I was not being reasonable, but I had the feeling that I'd rather see the farm suffer outright neglect—I'd sooner see it in the hands of hoodlums and scroungers—than see that rainbow on the barn, and some letters that looked Egyptian painted on the wall of the house. They seemed a mockery. I even disliked the sight of those people when they came to town—the men with their hair in ponytails, and with holes in their overalls that I believed were cut on purpose, and the women with long hair and no makeup and their meek, superior expressions. What do you know about life, I felt like asking them. What makes you think you can come here and mock my father and mother and their life and their poverty? But when I thought of the rainbow and those letters, I knew they weren't trying to mock or imitate my parent's life. They had displaced that life, hardly knowing it existed. They had set up in its place these beliefs and customs of their own, which I hoped would fail them.

That happened, more or less. The commune disintegrated. The goats disappeared. Some of the women moved to town, cut their hair, put on makeup, and got jobs as waitresses or cashiers to support their children. The Toronto man put the place up for sale, and after about a year it was sold for more than ten times what he had paid for it. A young couple from Ottawa bought it. They have painted the outside a pale grey with oyster trim, and have put in skylights and a handsome front door with carriage lamps on either side. Inside, they've changed it around so much that I've been told I'd never recognize it.

I did get in once, before this happened, during the year that the house was empty and for sale. The company I work for was handling it, and I had a key, though the house was being shown by another agent. I let myself in on a Sunday afternoon. I had a man with me, not a client but a friend—Bob Marks, whom I was seeing a lot at the time.

'This is that hippie place,' Bob Marks said when I stopped the car. 'I've been by here before.'

He was a lawyer, a Catholic, separated from his wife. He thought he wanted to settle down and start up a practice here in town. But there already was one Catholic lawyer. Business was slow. A couple of times a week, Bob Marks would be fairly drunk before supper.

'It's more than that,' I said. 'It's where I was born. Where I grew up.' We walked through the weeds, and I unlocked the door.

He said that he had thought, from the way I talked, that it would be farther out.

'It seemed farther then.'

All the rooms were bare, and the floors swept clean. The woodwork was freshly painted—I was surprised to see no smudges on the glass. Some new panes, some old wavy ones. Some of the walls had been stripped of their paper and painted. A wall in the kitchen was painted a deep blue, with an enormous dove on it. On a wall in the front room, giant sunflowers appeared, and a butterfly of almost the same size.

Bob Marks whistled. 'Somebody was an artist.'

'If that's what you want to call it,' I said, and turned back to the kitchen. The same woodstove was there. 'My mother once burned up three thousand dollars,' I said. 'She burned three thousand dollars in that stove.'

He whistled again, differently, 'What do you mean? She threw in a cheque?'

'No, no. It was in bills. She did it deliberately. She went into town to the bank and she had them give it all to her, in a shoebox. She brought it home and put it in the stove. She put it in just a few bills at a time, so it wouldn't make too big a blaze. My father stood and watched her.'

'What are you talking about?' said Bob Marks. 'I thought you were so poor.'

'We were. We were very poor.'

'So how come she had three thousand dollars? That would be like thirty thousand today. Easily. More than thirty thousand today.'

'It was her legacy,' I said. 'It was what she got from her father. Her father died in Seattle and left her three thousand dollars, and she burned it up because she hated him. She didn't want his money. She hated him.'

'That's a lot of hate,' Bob Marks said.

'That isn't the point. Her hating him, or whether he was bad enough for her to have a right to hate him. Not likely he was. That isn't the point.'

'Money,' he said. 'Money's always the point.'

'No. My father letting her do it is the point. To me it is. My father stood and watched and he never protested. If anybody had tried to stop her, he would have protected her. I consider that love.'

'Some people would consider it lunacy.'

I remember that that had been Beryl's opinion, exactly.

I went into the front room and stared at the butterfly, with its pink-and-orange wings. Then I went into the front bedroom and found two human figures painted on the wall. A man and a woman holding hands and facing straight ahead. They were naked, and larger than life size.

'It reminds me of that John Lennon and Yoko Ono picture,' I said to Bob Marks, who had come in behind me. 'That record cover, wasn't it?' I didn't want him to think that anything he had said in the kitchen had upset me.

Bob Marks said, 'Different colour hair.'

That was true. Both figures had yellow hair painted in a solid mass, the way they do it in comic strips. Horsetails of yellow hair curling over their shoulders and little pigtails of yellow hair decorating their not so private parts. Their skin was a flat beige pink and their eyes a staring blue, the same blue that was on the kitchen wall.

I noticed that they hadn't quite finished peeling the wallpaper away before making this painting. In the corner, there was some paper left that matched the paper on the other walls—a modernistic design of intersecting pink and grey and mauve bubbles. The man from Toronto must have put that on. The paper underneath hadn't been stripped off when this new paper went on. I could see an edge of it, the cornflowers on a white ground.

'I guess this was where they carried on their sexual shenanigans,' Bob Marks said, in a tone familiar to me. That thickened, sad, uneasy, but determined tone. The not particularly friendly lust of middle-aged respectable men.

I didn't say anything. I worked away some of the bubble paper to see more of the cornflowers. Suddenly I hit a loose spot, and ripped away a big swatch of it. But the cornflower paper came too, and a little shower of dried plaster.

'Why is it?' I said. 'Just tell me, why is it that no man can mention a place like this without getting around to the subject of sex in about two seconds flat? Just say the words *hippie* or *commune* and all you guys can think about is screwing! As if there wasn't anything at all behind it but orgies and fancy combinations and non-stop screwing! I get so sick of that—it's all so stupid it just makes me sick!'

In the car, on the way home from the hotel, we sat as before—the men in the front seat, the women in the back. I was in the middle, Beryl and my mother on either side of me. Their heated bodies pressed against me, through cloth; their smells crowded out the smells of the cedar bush we passed through, and the pockets of bog, where Beryl exclaimed at the water lilies. Beryl smelled of all those things in pots and bottles. My mother smelled of flour and hard soap and the warm crêpe of her good dress and the kerosene she had used to take the spots off.

'A lovely meal,' my mother said. 'Thank you, Beryl. Thank you, Mr Florence.'

'I don't know who is going to be fit to do the milking,' my father said. 'Now that we've all ate in such style.'

'Speaking of money,' said Beryl—though nobody actually had been—'do you mind my asking what you did with yours? I put mine in real estate. Real estate in California—you can't lose. I was thinking you could get an electric stove, so you wouldn't have to bother with a fire in summer or fool with that coal-oil thing, either one.'

All the other people in the car laughed, even Mr Florence.

'That's a good idea, Beryl,' said my father. 'We could use it to set things on till we get the electricity.'

'Oh, Lord,' said Beryl. 'How stupid can I get?'

'And we don't actually have the money, either,' my mother said cheerfully, as if she was continuing the joke.

But Beryl spoke sharply. 'You wrote me you got it. You got the same as me.'

My father half turned in his seat. 'What money are you talking about?' he said. 'What's this money?'

'From Daddy's will,' Beryl said. 'That you got last year. Look, maybe I shouldn't have asked. If you had to pay something off, that's still a good use, isn't it? It doesn't matter. We're all family here. Practically.'

'We didn't have to use it to pay anything off,' my mother said. 'I burned it.'

Then she told how she went into town in the truck, one day almost a year ago, and got them to give her the money in a box she had brought along for the purpose. She took it home, and put it in the stove and burned it.

My father turned around and faced the road ahead.

I could feel Beryl twisting beside me while my mother talked. She was twisting, and moaning a little, as if she had a pain she couldn't suppress. At the end of the story, she let out a sound of astonishment and suffering, an angry groan.

'So you burned up money!' she said. 'You burned up money in the stove.'

My mother was still cheerful. 'You sound as if I'd burned up one of my children.'

'You burned their chances. You burned up everything the money could have got for them.'

'The last thing my children need is money. None of us need his money.'

'That's criminal,' Beryl said harshly. She pitched her voice into the front seat: 'Why did you let her?'

'He wasn't there,' my mother said. 'Nobody was there.'

My father said, 'It was her money, Beryl.'

'Never mind,' Beryl said. 'That's criminal.'

'Criminal is for when you call in the police,' Mr Florence said. Like other things he had said that day, this created a little island of surprise and a peculiar gratitude.

Gratitude not felt by all.

'Don't you pretend this isn't the craziest thing you ever heard of,' Beryl shouted into the front seat. 'Don't you pretend you don't think so! Because it is, and you do. You think just the same as me!'

My father did not stand in the kitchen watching my mother feed the money into the flames. It wouldn't appear so. He did not know about it—it seems fairly clear, if I remember everything, that he did not know about it until that Sunday afternoon in Mr Florence's Chrysler, when my mother told them all together. Why, then, can I see the scene so clearly, just as I described it to Bob Marks (and to others—he was not the first)? I see my father standing by the table in the middle of the room—the table with the drawer in it for knives and forks, and the scrubbed oilcloth on top—and there is the box of money on the table. My mother is carefully dropping the bills into the fire.

She holds the stove lid by the blackened lifter in one hand. And my father, standing by, seems not just to be permitting her to do this but to be protecting her. A solemn scene, but not crazy. People doing something that seems to them natural and necessary. At least, one of them is doing what seems natural and necessary, and the other believes that the important thing is for that person to be free, to go ahead. They understand that other people might not think so. They do not care.

How hard it is for me to believe that I made that up. It seems so much the truth it is the truth; it's what I believe about them. I haven't stopped believing it. But I have stopped telling that story. I never told it to anyone again after telling it to Bob Marks. I don't think so. I didn't stop just because it wasn't, strictly speaking, true. I stopped because I saw that I had to give up expecting people to see it the way I did. I had to give up expecting them to approve of any part of what was done. How could I even say that I approved of it myself? If I had been the sort of person who approved of that, who could do it, I wouldn't have done all I have done—run away from home to work in a restaurant in town when I was fifteen, gone to night school to learn typing and bookkeeping, got into the real-estate office, and finally become a licensed agent. I wouldn't be divorced. My father wouldn't have died in the county home. My hair would be white, as it has been naturally for years, instead of a colour called Copper Sunrise. And not one of these things would I change, not really, if I could.

Bob Marks was a decent man—good-hearted, sometimes with imagination. After I had lashed out at him like that, he said, 'You don't need to be so tough on us.' In a moment, he said, 'Was this your room when you were a little girl?' He thought that was why the mention of the sexual shenanigans had upset me.

And I thought it would be just as well to let him think that. I said yes, yes, it was my room when I was a little girl. It was just as well to make up right away. Moments of kindness and reconciliation are worth having, even if the parting has to come sooner or later. I wonder if those moments aren't more valued, and deliberately gone after, in the setups some people like myself have now, than they were in those old marriages, where love and grudges could be growing underground, so confused and stubborn, it must have seemed they had forever.

1996

# Mordecai Richler

## 1931–2001

Born in Montreal at the beginning of the Depression, Mordecai Richler drew on the experience of growing up in the working-class neighbourhood around St Urbain Street and attending Baron Byng, the predominantly Jewish high school nearby, in several of his novels and in the semi-autobiographical sketches collected in *The Street* (1969). Having grown up during the conflicts incited by the fascist regimes of Europe—the Spanish Civil War and the Second World War—he expressed regret that his generation had been too young to take part in those heroic struggles. The anti-Semitism that had brought such horrifying consequences in Europe became a recurring concern in his fiction and non-fiction.

As a student at Sir George Williams College (now part of Concordia University), Richler became involved in student journalism (and also wrote occasional pieces for *The Montreal Herald*), met the individuals involved in the *Northern Review* literary magazine, and made friends among the older students, including the veterans who were returning to their studies after the war. When most of them graduated the following year, Richler dropped out. Introduced to Mavis Gallant by mutual friends, he found they agreed that, for aspiring writers, leaving Canada for Europe was the best thing to do: he travelled to Paris soon after and spent the next two years there and in Spain. He read André Malraux, Ernest Hemingway, Henry Miller, Louis Ferdinand Céline, Jean-Paul Sartre, and Albert Camus, and joined a group of aspiring expatriate writers who gathered in the cafés to try out their wit and irony on one another. (Richler later said Paris 'was, in the truest sense, my university. Saint-Germain-des-Prés was my campus, Montparnasse my frat house'.) He published some short stories in a Paris literary magazine and worked on a novel that remains unpublished. In Spain, he found material that became the basis for his first published novel, and that also made its way into his later fiction—but he got into trouble with the police there and had to return to France. His novel *The Acrobats*, set in the post–Spanish Civil War era, was published in England in 1954; it was subsequently given a US paperback reprint and translated into German, Norse, and Danish. Despite this reception, it is an apprenticeship work; Richler later disavowed it and would not allow it back into print in his lifetime (it was republished a year after his death, with an afterword by Richler's old friend, the film director Ted Kotcheff).

Richler returned to Canada in 1952, working briefly for the CBC, before moving to England in 1954. The following year, he published *Son of a Smaller Hero*, an account of a young Jew's struggle to free himself from the restrictions of family, religion, and mid-twentieth-century North American society. It is his version of James Joyce's *A Portrait of the Artist as a Young Man* and similarly ends with its protagonist's decision to go abroad. His treatment of Montreal Jews, along with his mocking descriptions of the London expatriate writers and filmmakers who had taken refuge from the persecutions of 'reds' during the era of McCarthyism in *A Choice of Enemies* (1957), revealed Richler's willingness to create biting portraits of communities of which he himself was a member.

Although Richler lived away from Montreal until 1972, he continued to write about his old neighbourhood. In 1959, he published the novel that established his reputation, *The Apprenticeship of Duddy Kravitz*, a morally ambiguous story about a bumptious young hustler from St Urbain Street who will go to any lengths to achieve his goals. In this novel, as in *St. Urbain's Horseman* (1971; Governor General's Award), as well as in *Joshua Then and Now* (1980) and *Barney's Version* (1997), Richler demonstrates his impressive ability to create fully developed characters and place them in authentic and densely textured milieus.

The two novels Richler published in the 1960s—*The Incomparable Atuk* (1963) and *Cocksure* (1968; Governor General's Award)—are works of a very different sort. They show his other great strength: his skill in creating sharply aimed satires that discomfit the complacent. Mordant and surreal fables, they marked him as the most vitriolic satirist of his generation. In particular, the savage and bawdy humour of *Cocksure* (one of Richler's own favourites) made it an object of controversy when it received a Governor General's Award.

*St. Urbain's Horseman* is the story of Canadian expatriate film director Jake Hersh (he first appears in *The Apprenticeship of Duddy Kravitz*; Duddy Kravitz reappears in this novel). Jake, all but overwhelmed by the 'competing mythologies' of the modern world and haunted by the catastrophe of the Holocaust, fantasizes a new mythic figure, a justice-bringer he calls 'the horseman'—part Jewish golem and part Batman—but he must eventually come to terms with the shortcomings of the myth he has created. Richler's next novel, *Joshua Then and Now* complements this story: Joshua Shapiro resembles Jake in his vulnerable humanity and in being another of Richler's misunderstood men. Where Jake wishes he could set right the wrongs of the Nazi era, Joshua looks back on the Spanish Civil War. Like Jake, Joshua must learn that the past can never be redeemed and that to be obsessed with it leads to dangerous neglect of the present. Its conclusion also echoes *St. Urbain's Horseman*: each novel ends with husband and wife clinging to one another, at last realizing that their affection and bond is a source of stability in a volatile world.

Although Richler had long enjoyed mocking the pretensions and parochial attitudes of the cultural nationalism that bloomed in the 1960s and 70s, *Solomon Gursky Was Here* (1989; Commonwealth Writers' Prize) is a celebration of Canada. In this version of a foundational Canadian epic—a sprawling narrative that takes over (and parodies) the form and conventions of the family saga—he traces four generations in a story that spans over 138 years of Canadian history, to chronicle the fabulous and sometimes mysterious Gursky clan, whose history makes Jews the fourth of the founding peoples of Canada. The novel plays with various historical events (the Franklin expedition gets an extended treatment) and individuals, including the early fur trader Ezekiel Solomons. The Gursky family is based on the Bronfman clan, who built their giant liquor company out of Prohibition-era bootlegging; the poet L.B. Berger is a version of A.M. Klein, a figure who had long troubled Richler because of Klein's having accepted employment as the Bronfmans' 'poet laureate'.

*Barney's Version*, Richler's valedictory novel and winner of the Giller Prize, is the story of a television producer, sixty-eight-year-old Barney Panofsky, a curiously loveable curmudgeon who, like Jake and Joshua before him, is suspected of wrongdoing of which he is innocent. In response to these suspicions, and particularly in answer to an old rival's account of him as a poseur, lecher, drunk, and worse, he writes out his own version of his life (Duddy Kravitz takes his final bow here). As well as providing another occasion for Richler to direct his barbs at mass media and other favourite targets, *Barney's Version* allowed him, near the end of his life, to reflect on the way one struggles against a failing memory to render one's final account.

Richler helped finance his career as a novelist and filled the time between novels by working as a freelance journalist and acerbic newspaper columnist. His journalism has been collected in *Hunting Tigers under Glass* (1968; Governor General's Award); *Shovelling Trouble* (1972); *The Great Comic Book Heroes and Other Essays* (1978); *Home Sweet Home: My Canadian Album* (1981); and *Broadsides: Reviews and Opinions* (1990). The many short pieces he had written over the years about sporting events were gathered in 2002 as *Dispatches from the Sporting Life*. Richler authored three popular children's books, *Jacob Two-Two Meets the Hooded Fang* (1975), *Jacob Two-Two and the Dinosaur* (1987), and *Jacob Two-Two's First Spy Case* (1995). He also wrote two travel books: the text of *Images of Spain* (1977) and *This Year in Jerusalem* (1994), an account of his year in Israel, during which he traced down Canadians he had known as a young person and who had emigrated to the newly founded country in the early 1950s. He edited two anthologies: *Canadian Writing Today* (1970) and *The Best of Modern Humour* (1983).

In the 1990s, Richler—increasingly troubled by what he saw as the extremes of language laws that were a part of the Quebec separatist movement—went on the attack in an article in *The New Yorker*. Assuming the role of the most prominent public defender of Quebec's anglophones and, revelling in the controversy he provoked, he expanded his journalistic polemics into a book-length diatribe, *Oh Canada! Oh Quebec! Requiem for a Divided Country* (1992), which deeply disturbed Québécois nationalists by pointing to French Quebec's history of anti-Semitism. The debate he generated led to the easing of the Quebec sign laws.

At the time of his death in 2001, Richler was working on another non-fiction work, this one about a private passion—the game of snooker. *On Snooker* was published posthumously in 2002.

Richler also supplemented his income by working as a scriptwriter for radio, television, and films (as well as scripting *Life at the Top*,

1965, he collaborated on several films, including *Room at the Top*, 1959; *The Young and the Willing*, 1962; and *Fun with Dick and Jane*, 1977). He also adapted his own works, including *The Apprenticeship of Duddy Kravitz* (1974; theatrical) and *Joshua Then and Now* (1985; television), both directed by Kotcheff. His experiences working in the film and television industries are frequently visible in his fiction—as in the biting depiction of European film community career politics and pretentious egoism in 'Playing Ball on Hampstead Heath', reprinted below. Originally published separately in 1966, this story reappeared in slightly revised form as a comic set piece midway through *St. Urbain's Horseman* and then as the final selection in *Dispatches from the Sporting Life*.

Richler's intense relationship, both jaundiced and joyous, with Canada and Canadians was recognized in 2001 when he was made a Companion of the Order of Canada, the highest civilian national honour.

# Playing Ball on Hampstead Heath

Sunday morning softball on Hampstead Heath in summer was unquestionably the fun thing to do. It was a ritual.

Manny Gordon tooled in all the way from Richmond, stowing a fielder's mitt and a thermos of martinis in the boot, clapping a sporty tweed cap over his bald head and strapping himself and his starlet of the night before into his Aston-Martin at nine a.m. C. Bernard Farber started out from Ham Common, picking up Al Levine, Bob Cohen, Jimmy Grief and Myer Gross outside Mary Quant's on the King's Road. Moey Hanover had once startled the staff at the Connaught by tripping down the stairs on a Sunday morning, wearing a peak cap and T-shirt and blue jeans, carrying his personal Babe Ruth bat in one hand and a softball in the other. Another Sunday Ziggy Alter had flown in from Rome, just for the sake of a restorative nine innings.

Frankie Demaine drove in from Marlow-on-Thames in his Maserati. Lou Caplan, Morty Calman, and Cy Levi usually brought their wives and children. Monty Talman, ever mindful of his latest twenty-one-year-old girlfriend, always cycled to the Heath from St. John's Wood. Wearing a maroon track suit, he usually lapped the field eight or nine times before anyone else turned up.

Jake generally strolled to the Heath, his tattered fielder's mitt and three enervating bagels filled with smoked salmon concealed under the *Observer* in his shopping bag. Some Sundays, like this one, possibly his last for a while, Nancy brought the kids along to watch.

The starting line-up on Sunday, June 28, 1963 was:

| AL LEVINE'S TEAM | LOU CAPLAN'S BUNCH |
|---|---|
| Manny Gordon, ss. | Bob Cohen, 3b. |
| C. Bernard Farber, 2b. | Myer Gross, ss. |
| Jimmy Grief, 3b. | Frankie Demaine, lf. |
| Al Levine, cf. | Morty Calman, rf. |
| Monty Talman, 1b. | Cy Levi, 2b. |
| Ziggy Alter, lf. | Moey Hanover, c. |
| Jack Monroe, rf. | Johnny Roper, cf. |
| Sean Fielding, c. | Jason Storm, 1b. |
| Alfie Roberts, p. | Lou Caplan, p. |

Jake, like five or six others who had arrived late and hung over (or who were unusually inept players), was a sub. A utility fielder, Jake sat on the bench with Lou Caplan's Bunch. It was a fine, all but cloudless morning, but looking around Jake felt there were too many wives, children, and kibitzers about. Even more ominous, the Filmmakers' First Wives Club or, as Ziggy Alter put it, the Alimony Gallery, was forming, seemingly relaxed but actually fulminating, on the grass behind home plate.

First Al Levine's Team and then Lou Caplan's Bunch, both sides made up mostly of men in their forties, trotted out, sunken bellies quaking, discs suddenly tender, hemorrhoids smarting, to take a turn at fielding and batting practice.

Nate Sugarman, once a classy shortstop, but since his coronary the regular umpire, bit into a digitalis pill, strode onto the field, and called, 'Play ball!'

'Let's go, boychick.'

'We need a hit,' Monty Talman, the producer, hollered.

'*You* certainly do,' Bob Cohen, who only yesterday had winced through a rough cut of Talman's latest fiasco, shouted back snidely from the opposite bench.

Manny, hunched over the plate cat-like, trying to look menacing, was knotted with more than his usual fill of anxiety. If he struck out, his own team would not be too upset because it was early in the game, but Lou Caplan, pitching for the first time since his Mexican divorce, would be grateful, and flattering Lou was a good idea because he was rumoured to be ready to go with a three-picture deal for Twentieth; and Manny had not been asked to direct a big-budget film since *Chase*. *Ball one, inside.* If, Manny thought, I hit a single I will be obliged to pass the time of day with that stomach-turning queen Jason Storm, 1b., who was in London to make a TV pilot film for Ziggy Alter. *Strike one, called.* He had never hit a homer, so that was out, but if come a miracle he connected for a triple, what then? He would be stuck on third sack with Bob Cohen, strictly second featuresville, a born loser, and Manny didn't want to be seen with Bob, even for an inning, especially with so many producers and agents about. K-NACK! *Goddammit, it's a hit! A double, for Chrissake!*

As the players on Al Levine's bench rose to a man, shouting encouragement—

'Go, man. Go.'

'Shake the lead out, Manny. Run!'

—Manny, conscious only of Lou Caplan glaring at him ('It's not my fault, Lou.'), scampered past first base and took myopic, round-shouldered aim on second, wondering should he say something shitty to Cy Levi, 2b., who he suspected was responsible for getting his name on the blacklist[1] years ago.

Next man up to the plate, C. Bernie Farber, who had signed to write Lou Caplan's first picture for Twentieth, struck out gracefully, which brought up Jimmy Grief. Jimmy swung on the first pitch, lifting it high and foul, and Moey Hanover, c., called for it, feeling guilty because next Saturday Jimmy was flying to Rome and Moey had already arranged to have lunch with Jimmy's wife on Sunday. Moey made the catch, which brought up Al Levine, who homered, bringing in Manny Gordon ahead of him. Monty Talman grounded out to Gross, ss., retiring the side.

Al Levine's Team, first inning: two hits, no errors, two runs.

Leading off for Lou Caplan's Bunch, Bob Cohen smashed a burner to centre for a single and Myer Gross fanned, bringing up Frankie Demaine and sending all the outfielders back, back, back. Frankie whacked the third pitch long and high, an easy fly had Al Levine been playing him deep left instead of inside right, where he was able to flirt hopefully with Manny Gordon's starlet, who was sprawled on the grass there in the shortest of possible Pucci prints. Al Levine was the only man on either team who always played wearing shorts—shorts revealing an elastic bandage which began at his left kneecap and ran almost as low as the ankle.

'Oh, you poor darling,' the starlet said, making a face at Levine's knee.

Levine, sucking in his stomach, replied, 'Spain,' as if he were the tossing the girl a rare coin.

'Don't tell me,' she squealed. 'The beach at Torremolinos. Ugh!'

'No, no,' Levine protested. 'The civil war, for Chrissake. Shrapnel. Defence of Madrid.'[2]

Demaine's fly fell for a homer, driving in a panting Bob Cohen.

Lou Caplan's Bunch, first inning: one hit, one error, two runs.

Neither side scored in the next two innings, which were noteworthy only because Moey Hanover's game began to slip badly. In the second Moey muffed an easy pop fly and actually let C. Bernie Farber, still weak on his legs after a cleansing, all but foodless, week at Forest Mere Hydro, steal a base on him. The problem was clearly Sean Fielding,

---

1  A reference to the individuals in the motion picture industry who, as a result of the American government's anti-Communist 'witch hunts' of the 1950s led by US senator Joseph McCarthy, were blacklisted and unable to find further employment in Hollywood. Careers were ruined without evidence. Many who found themselves on the blacklist became expatriates and continued their work in film in Europe.

2  A reference to the Spanish Civil War (1936–9), fought between Nationalist forces and Republicans. In the military uprising against the leftist Republican Popular Front government, the Nationalists, led by General Francisco Franco, repeatedly tried to capture the Spanish capital, Madrid; their success in early 1939 marked the end for the Republic. Franco established a Fascist dictatorship that lasted until his death in 1975. In its aftermath the Spanish Civil War came to be seen as a testing ground for Fascism before Hitler's aggression led the world into World War II: those from outside Spain who volunteered to fight on the Republican side—which included Ernest Hemingway and André Malraux (the war was a great chapter in the careers of each)—gained special heroic status. Torremolinos is a popular Mediterranean resort town on the Costa del Sol in southern Spain.

the young RADA[3] graduate whom Columbia had put under contract because, in profile, he looked like Peter O'Toole. The game had only just started when Moey Hanover's wife, Lilian, had ambled over to Al Levine's bench and stretched herself out on the grass, an offering, beside Fielding, and the two of them had been giggling together and nudging each other ever since, which was making Moey nervy. Moey, however, had not spent his young manhood at a yeshiva[4] to no avail. Not only had he plundered the Old Testament for most of his winning *Rawhide* and *Bonanza* plots, but now that his Lilian was obviously in heat again, his hard-bought Jewish education, which his father had always assured him was priceless, served him splendidly once more. Moey remembered his *David ha'Melech:*[5] *And it came to pass in the morning, that David wrote a letter to Joab, and sent it by the hand of Uriah. And he wrote in the letter, saying, Set Uriah in the forefront of the hottest battle, and retire ye from him, that he may be smitten, and die.*

Amen.

Lou Caplan yielded two successive hits in the third and Moey Hanover took off his catcher's mask, called for time, and strode to the mound, rubbing the ball in his hands.

'I'm all right,' Lou said. 'Don't worry. I'm going to settle down now.'

'It's not that. Listen, when do you start shooting in Rome?'

'Three weeks tomorrow. You heard something bad?'

'No.'

'You're a friend now, remember. No secrets.'

'No. It's just that I've had second thoughts about Sean Fielding. I think he's very exciting. He's got lots of appeal. He'd be a natural to play Domingo.'

As the two men began to whisper together, players on Al Levine's bench hollered, 'Let's go, gang.'

'Come on. Break it up, Moey.'

Moey returned to the plate, satisfied that Fielding was as good as in Rome already. May he do his own stunts, he thought.

'Play ball,' Nate Sugarman called.

Alfie Roberts, the director, ordinarily expected soft pitches from Lou, as he did the same for him, but today he wasn't so sure, because on Wednesday his agent had sent him one of Lou's properties to read and—Lou's first pitch made Alfie hit the dirt. That settles it, he thought, my agent already told him it doesn't grab me. Alfie struck out as quickly as he could. Better be put down for a rally-stopper than suffer a head fracture.

Which brought up Manny Gordon again, with one out and runners on first and third. Manny dribbled into a double play, retiring the side.

Multi-coloured kites bounced in the skies over the Heath. Lovers strolled on the tow paths and locked together on the grass. Old people sat on benches, sucking in the sun. Nannies passed, wheeling toddlers with titles. The odd baffled Englishman stopped to watch the Americans at play.

3  The Royal Academy of Dramatic Art, a government-subsidized acting school (est. 1904) in London, England.
4  An Orthodox Jewish school or seminary.
5  King David (Hebrew). The Biblical passage that follows is from Samuel 2:11, which tells the story of how David, King of Israel, adulterously impregnates Bathsheba while her husband is away fighting, then arranges with Joab, the leader of his forces, to have her husband die in battle.

'Are they air force chaps?'

'Filmmakers, actually. It's their version of rounders.'

'Whatever is that enormous thing that woman is slicing?'

'Salami.'

'*On the Heath?*'

'Afraid so. One Sunday they actually set up a bloody folding table, right over there, with cold cuts and herrings and mounds of black bread and a whole bloody side of smoked salmon. *Scotch. Ten and six a quarter, don't you know?*'

'On the Heath?'

'Champagne *in paper cups*. Mumm's. One of them had won some sort of award.'

Going into the bottom of the fifth, Al Levine's Team led 6–3, and Tom Hunt came in to play second base for Lou Caplan's Bunch. Hunt, a Negro actor, was in town shooting *Othello X* for Bob Cohen.

Moey Hanover lifted a lazy fly into left field, which Ziggy Alter trapped rolling over and over on the grass until—just before getting up—he was well placed to look up Natalie Calman's skirt. Something he saw there so unnerved him that he dropped the ball, turning pale and allowing Hanover to pull up safely at second.

Johnny Roper walked. Which brought up Jason Storm, to the delight of a pride of British fairies who stood with their dogs on the first base line, squealing and jumping. Jason poked a bouncer through the infield and floated to second, obliging the fairies and their dogs to move up a base.

With two out and the score tied 7–7 in the bottom half of the sixth, Alfie Roberts was unwillingly retired and a new pitcher came in for Al Levine's Team. It was Gordie Kaufman, a writer blacklisted for years, who now divided his time between Madrid and Rome, asking a hundred thousand dollars a spectacular. Gordie came in to pitch with the go-ahead run on third and Tom Hunt stepping up to the plate for the first time. Big black Tom Hunt, who had once played semi-pro ball in Florida, was a militant. If he homered, Hunt felt he would be put down for another buck nigger, good at games, but if he struck out, which would call for rather more acting skill than was required of him on the set of *Othello X*, what then? He would enable a bunch of fat, foxy, sexually worried Jews to feel big, goysy.[6] Screw them, Hunt thought.

Gordie Kaufman had his problems too. His stunning villa on Mallorca was run by Spanish servants, his two boys were boarding at a reputable British public school, and Gordie himself was president, sole stockholder, and the only employee of a company that was a plaque in Liechtenstein. And yet—and yet—Gordie still subscribed to the *Nation*;[7] he filled his Roman slaves with anti-apartheid dialogue and sagacious Talmudic sayings; and whenever the left-wing *pushke* was passed around he came through with a nice cheque. I must bear down on Hunt, Gordie thought, because if he

6 Goy-like; that is, not like a Jew.

7 An American weekly journal of opinion, then considered the leading voice of the North American political left. The Talmud is the collection of ancient Rabbinic writings constituting the basis of religious authority in Orthodox Judaism; a *pushke* is a charity or collection box (Yiddish); 'ofay': a mildly derogatory term used by blacks for whites.

touches me for even a scratch single I'll come off a patronizing ofay. If he homers, God forbid, I'm a shitty liberal. And so with the count 3 and 2, and a walk, the typical social-democrat's compromise, seemingly the easiest way out for both men, Gordie gritted his teeth, his proud Trotskyite past getting the best of him, and threw a fast ball right at Hunt, bouncing it off his head. Hunt threw away his bat and started for the mound, fist clenched, but not so fast that players from both sides couldn't rush in to separate the two men, both of whom felt vindicated, proud, because they had triumphed over impersonal racial prejudice to hit each other as individuals on a fun Sunday on Hampstead Heath.

Come the crucial seventh, the Filmmakers' First Wives Club grew restive, no longer content to belittle their former husbands from afar, and moved in on the baselines and benches, undermining confidence with their heckling. When Myer Gross, for instance, came to bat with two men on base and his teammates shouted, 'Go, man. Go,' one familiar grating voice floated out over the others. 'Hit, Myer. Make your son proud of you, *just this once.*'

What a reproach the first wives were. How steadfast! How unchanging! Still Waiting for Lefty after all these years.[8] Today maybe hair had greyed and chins doubled, necks had gone pruney, breasts drooped and stomachs dropped, but let no man say these crones had aged in spirit. Where once they had petitioned for the Scotsboro Boys, broken with their families over mixed marriages, sent their boy friends off to defend Madrid, split with old comrades over the Stalin-Hitler Pact, fought for Henry Wallace, demonstrated for the Rosenbergs, and never, never yielded to McCarthy . . . today they clapped hands at China Friendship Clubs, petitioned for others to keep hands off Cuba and Vietnam, and made their sons chopped liver sandwiches and sent them off to march to Aldermaston.

The wives, alimonied but abandoned, had known the early struggling years with their husbands, the self-doubts, the humiliations, the rejections, the cold-water flats, and the blacklist, but they had always remained loyal. They hadn't altered, their husbands had.

Each marriage had shattered in the eye of its own self-made hurricane, but essentially the men felt, as Ziggy Alter had once put it so succinctly at the poker table, 'Right, wrong, don't be silly, it's really a question of who wants to grow old with Anna Pauker when there are so many juicy little things we can now afford.'

8 An allusion to Clifford Odets's 1935 play *Waiting for Lefty.* This agitprop classic ends with the revelation that Lefty will never come—as the result of an injustice that is meant to stir the audience to social activism. The Scotsboro Boys were nine black youths found guilty by an all-white jury in Scotsboro, Alabama, in 1931 on charges of raping two white women—a decision that sparked outrage outside the US South, particularly among Northern liberal and radical groups. 'Henry Wallace' (1836–1916): American agricultural pioneer and statesman, vice president of the US during Franklin D. Roosevelt's third term (1941–5); he epitomized the 'common man' philosophy of 'New Deal' Democrats. In 1948 he broke with the party and ran for president as leader of the new left-wing Progressive party, which he helped form. 'The Rosenbergs': Julius (1918–53) and Ethel Rosenberg (1915–53) were found guilty of passing military secrets to Soviet intelligence agents and were executed, though at the time many felt they were victims of America's anti-Communist Cold War hysteria. 'Aldermaston': a village near Reading in southern England, site of the Atomic Weapons Research Establishment.

So there they were, out on the grass chasing fly balls on a Sunday morning, short men, overpaid and unprincipled, all well within the coronary and lung cancer belt, allowing themselves to look ridiculous in the hope of pleasing their new young wives and girlfriends. There was Ziggy Alter, who had once written a play 'with content' for the Group Theater. Here was Al Levine, who had used to throw marbles under horses' legs at demonstrations and now raced two horses of his own at Epsom. On the pitcher's mound stood Gordie Kaufman, who had once carried a banner that read *No Pasarán*[9] through the streets of Manhattan and now employed a man especially to keep Spaniards off the beach at his villa on Mallorca. And sweating under a catcher's mask there was Moey Hanover, who had studied at a yeshiva, stood up to the committee, and was now on a sabbatical from Desilu.

Usually the husbands were able to avoid their used-up wives. They didn't see them in the gaming rooms at the White Elephant or in the Mirabelle or Les Ambassadeurs. But come Brecht to Shaftesbury Avenue and without looking up from the second row centre they could feel them squatting in their cotton bloomers in the second balcony, burning holes in their necks.

And count on them to turn up on a Sunday morning in summer on Hampstead Heath just to ruin a game of fun baseball. Even homering, as Al Levine did, was no answer to the drones.

'It's nice for him, I suppose', a voice behind Levine on the bench observed, 'that on the playing field, with an audience, if you know what I mean, he actually appears virile.'

The game dragged on. In the eighth inning Jack Monroe had to retire to his Mercedes-Benz for his insulin injection and Jake Hersh, until now an embarrassed sub, finally trotted onto the field. Hersh, thirty-three, one-time relief pitcher for Room 41, Fletcher's Field High (2–7), moved into right field, mindful of his disc condition and hoping he would not be called on to make a tricksy catch. He assumed a loose-limbed stance on the grass, waving at his wife, grinning at his children, when without warning a sizzling line drive came right at him. Jake, startled, did the only sensible thing: he ducked. Outraged shouts and moans from the bench reminded Jake where he was, in a softball game, and he started after the ball.

'Fishfingers.'

'*Putz!*'

Runners on first and third started for home as Jake, breathless, finally caught up with the ball. It had rolled to a stop under a bench where a nanny sat watching over an elegant perambulator.

'Excuse me,' Jake said.

'Americans,' the nurse said.

'I'm a Canadian,' Jake protested automatically, fishing the ball out from under the bench.

9 'They shall not pass'. In the Spanish Civil War, a slogan of the Republicans in their opposition to the Nationalists; subsequently used generally for resistance. The 'committee' referred to in the next sentence was the House Unamerican Activities Committee, which called filmmakers and others before the US Congress to be grilled as suspected Communist sympathizers.

Three runs scored. Jake caught a glimpse of Nancy, unable to contain her laughter. The children looked ashamed of him.

In the ninth inning with the score tied again, 11–11, Sol Peters, another sub, stepped cautiously to the plate for Lou Caplan's Bunch. The go-ahead run was on second and there was only one out. Gordie Kaufman, trying to prevent a bunt, threw right at him and Sol, forgetting he was wearing his contact lenses, held the bat in front of him to protect his glasses. The ball hit the bat and rebounded for a perfectly laid down bunt.

'Run, you shmock.'

'Go, man.'

Sol, terrified, ran, carrying the bat with him.

Monty Talman phoned home.

'Who won?' his wife asked.

'We did. 13–12. But that's not the point. We had lots of fun.'

'How many you bringing back for lunch?'

'Eight.'

*'Eight?'*

'I couldn't get out of inviting Johnny Roper. He knows Jack Monroe is coming.'

'I see.'

'A little warning. Don't, for Chrissake, ask Cy how Marsha is. They're separating. And I'm afraid Manny Gordon is coming with a girl. I want you to be nice to her.'

*'Anything else?'*

'If Gershon phones from Rome while the guys are there please remember I'm taking the call upstairs. And please don't start collecting glasses and emptying ashtrays at four o'clock. It's embarrassing. Bloody Jake Hersh is coming and it's just the sort of incident he'd pick on and joke about for months.'

'I never coll—'

'All right, all right. Oh, shit, something else. Tom Hunt is coming.'

'The actor?'

'Yeah. Now listen, he's very touchy, so will you please put away Sheila's doll.'

'Sheila's doll?'

'If she comes in carrying that bloody golliwog[10] I'll die. Hide it. Burn it. Hunt gets script approval these days, you know.'

'All right, dear.'

'See you soon.'

1971

---

10 Dolls based on caricatures of the American minstrel show's portrayal of black males, they became the most popular doll in Europe in the first half of the twentieth century.

# Alden Nowlan
## 1933–1983

The sympathy for victims of emotional and economic poverty expressed in the writing of Alden Nowlan derives from his own experience. Nowlan grew up near Nova Scotia's Annapolis Valley, in Stanley, a small, 'thin-soil' settlement he described as little touched by the Depression that marked his childhood—because it was already so impoverished. Although he quit school in grade 5, he continued his education by reading whatever he could find while working in nearby lumber mills and on farms. At nineteen, he took a position on the *Hartland Observer* in New Brunswick. In his ten years as a journalist and editor at the *Observer*, and later at the *Saint John Telegraph-Journal*, he developed a simple, direct style, reflected in the poetry and short fiction he began writing in the mid-1950s. In 1957, he met the Maritime poet, editor, and educator Fred Cogswell, whose encouragement led to the publication of Nowlan's first collection of poems, *The Rose and the Puritan* (1958).

Nowlan documented his milieu while recording the inhibitions that made it so difficult to document ('I am a product of a culture that fears any display of emotion and attempts to repress any true communication,' he wrote), publishing ten more volumes of poetry, including *Bread, Wine and Salt* (1967; Governor General's Award); *The Mysterious Naked Man* (1969); *Playing the Jesus Game: Selected Poems* (1970); *Smoked Glass* (1977); and *I Might Not Tell Everybody This* (1982). He also wrote short stories, collected in *Miracle at Indian River* (1968), that depict the brutal socio-economic trap in which Maritimers are caught, and published a novel, *Various Persons Named Kevin O'Brien* (1973)—a lightly fictionalized account of his difficult boyhood. Some of his journalistic pieces are gathered in *Double Exposure* (1978).

Several more volumes of Nowlan's work were published posthumously. Among these were *Early Poems* (1983); a *Selected Poems* edited

and introduced by Patrick Lane and Lorna Crozier (1996); and a later selected poems, *Between Tears and Laughter*, published in 2004. Prose works that appeared after Nowlan's death included *Will Ye Let the Mummers In?* (1984), a book of previously uncollected short stories; *The Wanton Troopers* (1988), a novel that provides further details of the semi-autobiographical character Kevin O'Brien; and two selections of Nowlan's *Telegraph-Journal* columns, *White Madness* (1996) and *Road Dancers* (1999). Allison Mitcham edited *The Best of Alden Nowlan* (1993).

From 1969 on, Nowlan served as the writer-in-residence at the University of New Brunswick while also working as a writer and freelance journalist. In the 1970s, he collaborated with Walter Learning in writing three plays; two of these focus on popular figures—Dr Victor Frankenstein (in *Frankenstein: The Man Who Became God*, 1974), and Sherlock Holmes (in *The Incredible Murder of Cardinal Tosca*, 1978).

Nowlan once observed that when he moved to small-town New Brunswick, he had also moved from the eighteenth century into the twentieth because he had left behind a boyhood home that had 'no furnace, no plumbing, no electricity, no refrigerator, no telephone', where 'we used kerosene lamps and on the coldest winter nights water froze in the bucket in the kitchen.' The rural Maritime way of life of which he was a chronicler—he called himself a 'witness'—seems primitive even in comparison with that depicted in the nineteenth-century poetry of Charles G.D. Roberts and Bliss Carman. Where his predecessors sometimes chose the picturesque, Nowlan focused on the commonplace. An observer of his region as well as a participant in it—a dual role he found uncomfortable—he created poetry that was powerful, uncompromising, and sometimes harsh, but never sentimental.

# Temptation

The boy is
badgering the man
to lower him down the
face of the cliff
to a narrow shelf
about eight feet
below:
'Your hands are strong,
and I'm not afraid.
The ledge is wide enough,          10
I won't hurt myself
even if you let go.'

'Don't be a fool.
You'd break every bone
in your body.
Where in God's name
do you get such ideas?
It's time we went home.'

But there is no
conviction in the          20
man's voice and
the boy persists;
nagging his wrists,
dragging him nearer.
Their summer shirts
balloon in the wind.

While devils whisper
what god-like sport
it would be
to cling to the          30
edge of the world
and gamble
one's only son
against the wind
and rocks
and sea.

1967

## Country Full of Christmas

Country full of Christmas,
the stripped, suspicious elms
groping for the dun sky—
what can I give my love?

The remembrance—mouse hawks
scudding on the dykes, above
the wild roses; horses and cattle
separate in the same field.
It is not for my love.

Do you know that foxes                                    10
believe in nothing
but themselves—everything
is a fox disguised: men, dogs and rabbits.

1969


## Canadian January Night

Ice storm: the hill
a pyramid of black crystal
down which the cars
slide like phosphorescent beetles
while I, walking backwards in obedience
to the wind, am possessed
of the fearful knowledge
my compatriots share
but almost never utter:
this is a country                                        10
where a man can die
                    simply from being
caught outside.

1971

# The Broadcaster's Poem

I used to broadcast at night
alone in a radio station
but I was never good at it,
partly because my voice wasn't right
but mostly because my peculiar
metaphysical stupidity
made it impossible
for me to keep believing
there was somebody listening
when it seemed I was talking                    10
only to myself in a room no bigger
than an ordinary bathroom.
I could believe it for a while
and then I'd get somewhat
the same feeling as when you
start to suspect you're the victim
of a practical joke.
                    So one part of me
was afraid another part
might blurt out something                       20
about myself so terrible
that even I had never until
that moment suspected it.
                    This was like the fear
of bridges and other
high places: Will I take off my glasses
and throw them
into the water, although I'm
half-blind without them?
Will I sneak up behind                          30
myself and push?
                    Another thing:
as a reporter
I covered an accident in which a train
ran into a car, killing
three young men, one of whom
was beheaded. The bodies looked
boneless, as such bodies do.
More like mounds of rags.
And inside the wreckage                         40
where nobody could get at it

the car radio
was still playing.
            I thought about places
the disc jockey's voice goes
and the things that happen there
and of how impossible it would be for him
to continue if he really knew.

1974

## On the Barrens

'Once when we were hunting cattle
    on the barrens,'
  so began many of the stories they told,
  gathered in the kitchen, a fire still
    the focus of life then,
  the teapot on the stove as long as
    anyone was awake,
  mittens and socks left to thaw on
    the open oven door,
  chunks of pine and birch piled
    halfway to the ceiling,                               10
  and always a faint smell of smoke
    like spice in the air,
  the lamps making their peace with
    the darkness,
  the world not entirely answerable
    to man.

  They took turns talking, the listeners
    puffed their pipes,
  he whose turn it was to speak used his
    as an instrument,                                     20
  took his leather pouch from a pocket
    of his overalls,
  gracefully, rubbed tobacco between
    his rough palms
  as he set the mood, tamped it into
    the bowl
  at a moment carefully chosen, scratched
    a match when it was necessary

to prolong the suspense. If his pipe
   went out it was no accident,
if he spat in the stove it was done
   for a purpose.
When he finished he might lean back
   in his chair so that it stood
on two legs; there'd be a short silence.

The barrens were flat clay fields,
   twenty miles from the sea
and separated from it by dense woods
   and farmlands.
They smelled of salt and the wind
   blew there
constantly as it does on the shore
   of the North Atlantic.

There had been a time, the older men
   said, when someone had owned
the barrens but something had happened
long ago and now anyone who wanted to
   could pasture there.
The cattle ran wild all summer,
sinewy little beasts, ginger-coloured
   with off-white patches,
grazed there on the windswept barrens
   and never saw a human
until fall when the men came to round
   them up,
sinewy men in rubber boots and tweed caps
   with their dogs beside them.

Some of the cattle would by now have
   forgotten
there'd been a time before they'd
   lived on the barrens.
They'd be truly wild, dangerous, the
   men would loose the dogs on them,
mongrel collies, barn dogs with the
   dispositions of convicts
who are set over their fellows,
   the dogs would go for the nose,
sink their teeth in the tender flesh,
   toss the cow on its side,

30

40

50

60

70

bleating, hooves flying, but shortly
   tractable.
There were a few escaped,
   it was said, and in a little while
they were like no other cattle—
   the dogs feared them,
they roared at night and the men
   lying by their camp-fires
heard them and moaned in their sleep,
   the next day tracking them            80
found where they'd pawed the moss,
   where their horns had scraped
bark from the trees—all the stories
   agreed
in this: now there was nothing to do
   but kill them.

1977

# Leonard Cohen
## b. 1934

Leonard Cohen was born and raised in a tradi-tional Jewish family in Montreal's Westmount. When he was nine his father died, leaving him a small trust fund, which gave him some financial independence as a young man. Interested in folk music as a teenager, Cohen formed a country-folk group while attending McGill University (BA, 1955). His first collection of poetry, *Let Us Compare Mythologies*, written while he was still an undergraduate, was published in 1956. It shows him responding to the American beat movement—with its rejection of the strictures of post–World War II society for the ideal of per-sonal freedom, its romantic fascination with self-destruction, and its embrace of a bohemian way of life associated with drugs, sexual permis-siveness, and social experimentation—as well as

to fellow Montreal Jewish poets A.M. Klein and Irving Layton. As the title suggests, *Let Us Compare Mythologies* begins Cohen's project of reconciling his Jewish beliefs with those of other cultures—including Montreal's French Catholics. Much of Cohen's career has been shaped by this desire to transcend the dogmas of religion by synthesizing systems of belief, even when that has meant drawing on divergent, and sometimes hostile, traditions.

In 1961, his poems in *The Spice-Box of Earth* announced a second preoccupation: eroti-cism. The themes and symbol systems of the erotic and the divine combine in Cohen's later work—as in the poems in *Parasites of Heaven* (1966)—where sexual desire can become a path to saintliness.

In 1963, Cohen published the first of his two novels, *The Favourite Game*. Influenced by North American Jewish writers such as Saul Bellow, Philip Roth, and Mordecai Richler, and also (like Richler's *Son of a Smaller Hero*) by James Joyce's *Portrait of the Artist as a Young Man*, Cohen dramatizes the need for the artist and intellectual to break with binding traditions and to escape his confining milieus. By the time *The Favourite Game* appeared, Cohen had begun an extended period of expatriation, basing himself chiefly on the Greek island of Hydra.

In *Flowers for Hitler* (1964), Cohen blends death and violence with eroticism, while employing rhetoric that allies the poems in that book with the protest poetry beginning to appear elsewhere in the 1960s. His second novel, *Beautiful Losers* (1966), shows how far Cohen was willing to go in testing boundaries and experimenting with form. Called pornographic when it was published and criticized for being self-indulgent, *Beautiful Losers* is a dazzling, disturbing tour de force that has been seen as announcing postmodernism in Canada: in it, Eros meets Thanatos as myths and images collide in self-annihilating Dionysiac madness. Its narrator's research into the story of Kateri Tekakwitha (a seventeenth-century Mohawk woman considered for canonization by the Roman Catholic Church) allows Cohen to contemplate the meaning of sainthood in the contemporary world.

*What is a saint? A saint is someone who has achieved a remote human possibility . . . a kind of balance in the chaos of existence. . . . He rides the drifts like an escaped ski. His course is a caress of the hill. His track is a drawing of the snow in a moment of its particular arrangement with wind and rock. Something in him so loves the world that he gives himself to the laws of gravity and chance. Far from flying with the angels, he traces with the fidelity of a seismograph needle the state of the solid bloody landscape. His house is dangerous and finite, but he is at home with the world.*

Cohen later reprinted several selections from *Beautiful Losers* in *Stranger Music: Selected Poems and Songs* (1993), treating them there as prose poems.

Despite the positive critical reception his writing had been receiving, Cohen found that he could not support himself as a poet and novelist. Fascinated by the popular music culture emerging in the era of Bob Dylan and the Beatles, he began to set his poems to music and to write lyrics for songs. Returning to North America in 1967 to be near its music centres, he met folk singer Judy Collins in New York City. She became the first person to record his compositions, one of which, 'Suzanne'—his portrait of a secular saint, published in 1966 in slightly different form as 'Suzanne Takes You Down' became one of the most recorded songs of the period. Encouraged by the music producer John Hammond, Cohen made an appearance at the Newport Folk Festival in 1967. Early in 1968, he released his first album as a performer, *Songs of Leonard Cohen*. As a result of his success as a poet, novelist, songwriter, and singer, Cohen had become, by the end of the 1960s, an artist-hero of his own creation. A brooding, mysterious figure given to grand gestures such as refusing a Governor General's Award for his 1968 *Selected Poems*, he took as his first priority the investigation of his own experiences and the exhibition of his own pain.

In 1969, after releasing *Songs from a Room*, Cohen began to tour North America and Europe. He has released some sixteen albums, including *Various Positions* (1985), *I'm Your Man* (1988), *The Future* (1992), *Ten New Songs* (2001; with Sharon Robinson), and, from his latest tour, *Live in London* (2009). Though songwriting and performing have become his chief activities, Cohen has also continued to write for the page. In 1972, he published *The Energy of Slaves*, a grim collection of poems based on the themes of suicide and artistic burnout. In 1978, he mixed poetry, prose-poems, and prose excerpts from his unpublished memoir, 'My Life in Art' (still unpublished and now known as 'The Final Revision of My Life in Art') in *Death of a Lady's Man*, accompanying these with running commentaries and extensive quotations from his notebooks. The conflict seen there, between redemption and desire, becomes more explicit in the poetic meditations of *Book of Mercy* (1984); it remains apparent in the songs that have followed.

The psalm-like poems of *Book of Mercy* are testimonies to Cohen's spiritual quest. After its publication, he withdrew from the public eye for extended periods of meditation at the Mount Baldy Zen Center near Los Angeles. In the early 1990s, after releasing the album *The Future*, he entered the monastery full-time, becoming ordained as the Zen monk Jikan, meditating, practising monastic discipline, and assisting his teacher, Sasaki Roshi. Though Cohen left the monastery in 1999 to return to writing and performing, he remains both a Buddhist and a follower of Judaism. Feeling that he attained peace in his retreat, he has given renewed prominence in his recent work to his religious vision and to political and social issues.

Cohen's later songs, such as 'The Future' and 'Closing Time', seem bleak, yet their expression is jocular and they find hope in the possibilities of human love, which has remained a dominant theme throughout his career. While love was originally defined as a physical experience, Eros is fused with other impulses as early as 'Suzanne'; in Cohen's later work, love in all its meanings brings to the individual a path that transcends the suffering Cohen also records.

In 2006, Cohen published *Book of Longing*, a new collection of poems and songs (it was later set to music by Philip Glass) that also includes his visual art. In it, he brings together the themes of his life's work under the rubric of 'longing'—the space between the seeking of love and repose. In this late work and in recent interviews, his once-pervasive anxiety is now largely gone. He sounds comfortable, even while dwelling in a fear-filled world that largely lacks faith in the divine, or in secular authority, or in the self. His newer songs and poems still suggest that suffering is inevitable, but acceptance of the world as it is has become both possible and necessary. Martyrdom has been replaced by mindfulness and the attractions of nihilism are countered by the joy that can be found in small things including what Cohen calls 'duties': the everyday routines of life. In the song 'Anthem' (from *The Future*), he echoes an idea found in the Kabbalah when he tells his listeners that 'there is a crack in everything / That's how the light gets in'.

# You Have the Lovers

You have the lovers,
they are nameless, their histories only for each other,
and you have the room, the bed and the windows.
Pretend it is a ritual.
Unfurl the bed, bury the lovers, blacken the windows,
let them live in that house for a generation or two.
No one dares disturb them.
Visitors in the corridor tiptoe past the long closed door,
they listen for sounds, for a moan, for a song:
nothing is heard, not even breathing.                                  10
You know they are not dead,
you can feel the presence of their intense love.
Your children grow up, they leave you,
they have become soldiers and riders.
Your mate dies after a life of service.
Who knows you? Who remembers you?

But in your house a ritual is in progress:
it is not finished: it needs more people.
One day the door is opened to the lover's chambers.
The room has become a dense garden,
full of colours, smells, sounds you have never known.
The bed is smooth as a wafer of sunlight,
in the midst of the garden it stands alone.
In the bed the lovers, slowly and deliberately and silently,
perform the act of love.
Their eyes are closed,
as tightly as if heavy coins of flesh lay on them.
Their lips are bruised with new and old bruises.
Her hair and his beard are hopelessly tangled.
When he puts his mouth against her shoulder
she is uncertain whether her shoulder
has given or received the kiss.
All her flesh is like a mouth.
He carries his fingers along her waist
and feels his own waist caressed.
She holds him closer and his own arms tighten around her.
She kisses the hand beside her mouth.
It is his hand or her hand, it hardly matters,
there are so many more kisses.
You stand beside the bed, weeping with happiness,
you carefully peel away the sheets
from the slow-moving bodies.
Your eyes are filled with tears, you barely make out the lovers.
As you undress you sing out, and your voice is magnificent
because now you believe it is the first human voice
heard in that room.
The garments you let fall grow into vines.
You climb into bed and recover the flesh.
You close your eyes and allow them to be sewn shut.
You create an embrace and fall into it.
There is only one moment of pain or doubt
as you wonder how many multitudes are lying beside your body,
but a mouth kisses and a hand soothes the moment away.

20

30

40

50

1961

# Suzanne

Suzanne takes you down
to her place near the river
you can hear the boats go by
you can spend the night beside her
And you know that she's half crazy
but that's why you want to be there
and she feeds you tea and oranges
that come all the way from China
And just when you mean to tell her
that you have no love to give her      10
she gets you on her wavelength
and she lets the river answer
that you've always been her lover
> And you want to travel with her
> you want to travel blind
> and you know that she can trust you
> for you've touched her perfect body
> with your mind

And Jesus was a sailor
when he walked upon the water[1]      20
and he spent a long time watching
from his lonely wooden tower
and when he knew for certain
only drowning men could see him
he said All men will be sailors then
until the sea shall free them
but he himself was broken
long before the sky would open
forsaken, almost human
he sank beneath your wisdom like a stone      30
> And you want to travel with him
> you want to travel blind
> and you think maybe you'll trust him
> for he's touched your perfect body
> with his mind

Now Suzanne takes your hand
and she leads you to the river
she is wearing rags and feathers
from Salvation Army counters

---

1 The account of Jesus' walking on the wave-tossed sea to his disciples on a ship can be found in Matthew 14:
22–33. Peter tried to emulate him but lost faith and began to sink.

And the sun pours down like honey 40
on our lady of the harbour
And she shows you where to look
among the garbage and the flowers
There are heroes in the seaweed
there are children in the morning
they are leaning out for love
they will lean that way forever
while Suzanne holds the mirror
　　*And you want to travel with her*
　　*you want to travel blind* 50
　　*and you know that you can trust her*
　　*for she's touched your perfect body*
　　*with her mind*

1966

# From *Book of Mercy*

## In the Eyes of Men

In the eyes of men he falls, and in his own eyes too. He falls from his high place, he trips on his achievement. He falls to you, he falls to know you. It is sad, they say. See his disgrace, say the ones at his heel. But he falls radiantly toward the light to which he falls. They cannot see who lifts him as he falls, or how his falling changes, and he himself bewildered till his heart cries out to bless the one who holds him in his falling. And in his fall he hears his heart cry out, his heart explains why he is falling, why he had to fall, and he gives over to the fall. Blessed are you, clasp of the falling. He falls into the sky, he falls into the light, none can hurt him as he falls. Blessed are you, shield of the falling. Wrapped in his fall, concealed within his fall, he finds the place, he is gathered in. While his hair streams back and his clothes tear in the wind, he is held up, comforted, he enters into the place of his fall. Blessed are you, embrace of the falling, foundation of the light, master of the human accident.

## It Is All Around Me

It is all around me, the darkness. You are my only shield. Your name is my only light. What love I have, your law is the source, this dead love that remembers only its name, yet the name is enough to open itself like a mouth, to call down the dew, and drink. O dead name that through your mercy speaks to the living name, mercy harkening to the will that is bent toward it, the will whose strength is its pledge to you—O name of love, draw down the blessings of completion on the man you have cut in half to know you.

## Holy Is Your Name

Holy is your name, holy is your work, holy are the days that return to you. Holy are the years that you uncover. Holy are the hands that are raised to you, and the weeping that is wept to you. Holy is the fire between your will and ours, in which we are refined. Holy is that which is unredeemed, covered with your patience. Holy are the souls lost in your unnaming. Holy, and shining with a great light, is every living thing, established in this world and covered with time, until your name is praised forever.

1984

## Everybody Knows[1]

*from I'm Your Man*

Everybody knows that the dice are loaded
Everybody rolls with their fingers crossed
Everybody knows that the war is over
Everybody knows the good guys lost
Everybody knows the fight was fixed
The poor stay poor, the rich get rich
That's how it goes
Everybody knows

Everybody knows that the boat is leaking
Everybody knows that the captain lied                                    10
Everybody got this broken feeling
Like their father or their dog just died

Everybody talking to their pockets
Everybody wants a box of chocolates
And a long stem rose
Everybody knows

Everybody knows that you love me baby
Everybody knows that you really do
Everybody knows that you've been faithful
Ah give or take a night or two                                           20
Everybody knows you've been discreet
But there were so many people you just had to meet
Without your clothes
And everybody knows

1 Written with Sharon Robinson.

Everybody knows, everybody knows
That's how it goes
Everybody knows

Everybody knows, everybody knows
That's how it goes
Everybody knows                                                    30

And everybody knows that it's now or never
Everybody knows that it's me or you
And everybody knows that you live forever
Ah when you've done a line or two
Everybody knows the deal is rotten
Old Black Joe's still pickin' cotton
For your ribbons and bows[2]
And everybody knows

And everybody knows that the Plague is coming
Everybody knows that it's moving fast                               40
Everybody knows that the naked man and woman
Are just a shining artifact of the past
Everybody knows the scene is dead
But there's gonna be a meter on your bed
That will disclose
What everybody knows

And everybody knows that you're in trouble
Everybody knows what you've been through
From the bloody cross on top of Calvary
To the beach of Malibu                                             50
Everybody knows it's coming apart
Take one last look at this Sacred Heart
Before it blows
And everybody knows

Everybody knows, everybody knows
That's how it goes
Everybody knows

---

2  Old Black Joe, the title character of a song by Stephen Foster (1826–64), served for a time as a sentimentalized
   personification of the 'happy slave' on pre-Civil War plantations. Written in 1860 (when slavery was still an
   institution in the American South), the song begins with the verse, 'Gone are the days when my heart was young
   and gay, / Gone are my friends from the cotton fields away, / Gone from the earth to a better land I know, / I
   hear their gentle voices calling "Old Black Joe" '.

Oh everybody knows, everybody knows
That's how it goes
Everybody knows                                                    60

Everybody knows

(L. Cohen - S. Robinson) Stranger Music, Inc. (recorded 1988)

## Closing Time

So we're drinking and we're dancing
and the band is really happening
and the Johnny Walker wisdom running high
And my very sweet companion
she's the Angel of Compassion
and she's rubbing half the world against her thigh
Every drinker, every dancer
lifts a happy face to thank her
and the fiddler fiddles something so sublime
All the women tear their blouses off                               10
and the men they dance on the polka-dots
and it's partner found and it's partner lost
and it's hell to pay when the fiddler stops
*It's closing time*

We're lonely, we're romantic
and the cider's laced with acid
and the Holy Spirit's crying, 'Where's the beef?'
And the moon is swimming naked
and the summer night is fragrant
with a mighty expectation of relief                                20
So we struggle and we stagger
down the snakes and up the ladder
to the tower where the blessed hours chime
And I swear it happened just like this:
a sigh, a cry, a hungry kiss
the Gates of Love they budged an inch
I can't say much has happened since
*but closing time*

I loved you for your beauty
but that doesn't make a fool of me—                                30
you were in it for your beauty too

I loved you for your body
there's a voice that sounds like G-d to me
declaring that your body's really you
I loved you when our love was blessed
and I love you now there's nothing left
but sorrow and a sense of overtime

And I miss you since the place got wrecked
by the winds of change and the weeds of sex
looks like freedom but it feels like death                    40
it's something in between, I guess
*it's closing time*

We're drinking and we're dancing
but there's nothing really happening
the place is dead as Heaven on a Saturday night
and my very close companion
gets me fumbling, gets me laughing
she's a hundred but she's wearing something tight
And I lift my glass to the Awful Truth
which you can't reveal to the Ears of Youth                   50
except to say it isn't worth a dime
And the whole damn place goes crazy twice
and it's once for the Devil and it's once for Christ
but the Boss don't like these dizzy heights—
we're busted in the blinding lights
*of closing time*

1993 (recorded 1992)


# Thousand Kisses Deep

*for Sandy 1945–1998*

I.

You came to me this morning
And you handled me like meat
You'd have to be a man to know
How good that feels how sweet
My mirror twin my next of kin
I'd know you in my sleep
And who but you would take me in
A thousand kisses deep

I loved you when you opened
Like a lily to the heat
I'm just another snowman
Standing in the rain and sleet
Who loved you with his frozen love
His second-hand physique
With all he is and all he was
A thousand kisses deep

I know you had to lie to me
I know you had to cheat
To pose all hot and high behind
The veils of sheer deceit
Our perfect porn aristocrat
So elegant and cheap
I'm old but I'm still into that
A thousand kisses deep

And I'm still working with the wine
Still dancing cheek to cheek
The band is playing Auld Lang Syne
The heart will not retreat
I ran with Diz[1] and Dante
I never had their sweep
But once or twice they let me play
A thousand kisses deep

The autumn slipped across your skin
Got something in my eye
A light that doesn't need to live
And doesn't need to die
A riddle in the book of love
Obscure and obsolete
Till witnessed here in time and blood
A thousand kisses deep

I'm good at love I'm good at hate
It's in between I freeze
Been working out but it's too late
It's been too late for years
But you look fine you really do
The pride of Boogie Street
Somebody must have died for you
A thousand kisses deep

10

20

30

40

1  The virtuoso jazz trumpeter John 'Dizzy' Gillespie (1917–93).

*I loved you when you opened*
*Like a lily to the heat*
*I'm just another snowman*                    50
*Standing in the rain and sleet*
But you don't need to hear me now
And every word I speak
It counts against me anyhow
A thousand kisses deep.


2.

The ponies run the girls are young
The odds are there to beat
You win a while and then it's done
Your little winning streak                    60
And summoned now to deal
With your invincible defeat
You live your life as if it's real
A thousand kisses deep.

I'm turning tricks I'm getting fixed
I'm back on Boogie Street
You lose your grip and then you slip
Into the Masterpiece
And maybe I had miles to drive
*And promises to keep*[2]                      70
You ditch it all to stay alive
A thousand kisses deep

Confined to sex we pressed against
The limits of the sea
I saw there were no oceans left
For scavengers like me
I made it to the forward deck
I blessed our remnant fleet
And then consented to be wrecked
A thousand kisses deep                         80

2 A recasting of the lines that conclude Robert Frost's 'Stopping by Woods on a Snowy Evening': 'But I have promises to keep, / And miles to go before I sleep.'

I'm turning tricks, I'm getting fixed
I'm back on Boogie Street
I guess they won't exchange the gifts
That you were meant to keep
And sometimes when the night is slow
The wretched and the meek
We gather up our hearts and go
A thousand kisses deep

*And fragrant is the thought of you*
*The file on you complete*                               90
*Except what we forgot to do*
*A thousand kisses deep*

2006

## 'the truth of the line'

2006

# Looking Through My Dreams

I was looking through my dreams
when I saw myself
looking through my dreams
looking through my dreams
and so on and so forth
until I was consumed
in the mysterious activity
of expansion and contraction
breathing in and out at the same time
and disappearing naturally                    10
up my own asshole
I did this for 30 years
but I kept coming back
to let you know how bad it felt
Now I'm here at the end of the song
the end of the prayer
The ashes have fallen away at last
exactly as they're supposed to do
The chains have slowly
followed the anchors                           20
to the bottom of the sea
It's merely a song
merely a prayer
Thank you, Teachers
Thank you, Everyone

2006

# Rudy Wiebe
## b. 1934

Born in Speedwell, a Mennonite farm community in northern Saskatchewan, to parents who came from the Soviet Union in 1930, Rudy Wiebe grew up in a polyglot environment in which the Low German dialect was the language of everyday life, English the language of school, and High (or standard) German the language of their religion. After receiving his primary and secondary education in Saskatchewan and then in Alberta, where his family moved in 1947, Wiebe began writing while a student at the University of Alberta. After he graduated in 1956, he continued his studies at the University of Tübingen in Germany, and then returned to the University of Alberta for his master's degree in creative writing. In revised form, his MA thesis became *Peace Shall Destroy Many* (1962), the first novel to portray a Mennonite community: it depicts the crisis a young man faces, during the Second World War, when he realizes that the pacifism central to his religion may not be benign in all times and places.

After earning a teaching certificate at the University of Manitoba and a Bachelor of Theology from the Mennonite Brethren Bible College, Wiebe worked for a year and a half for the *Mennonite Brethren Herald*, a weekly church publication. He resigned after *Peace Shall Destroy Many* was published because its descriptions of Mennonite life proved controversial. He took a job teaching English at Goshen College, a Mennonite undergraduate school in Indiana. While there, he published his second novel, *First and Vital Candle* (1966), about a man, disaffected from modern society, who seeks spiritual meaning in the far north. Wiebe left Goshen in 1967 to accept a position in the English department of the University of Alberta, where he spent the rest of his teaching career; he retired in 1992.

Wiebe's next three books—epic stories of minority peoples who struggle to maintain the integrity of their communities—marked his emergence as a major novelist. *The Blue Mountains of China* (1970) is a complex, panoramic history of the Mennonites. (The Mennonites left Germany and the Netherlands in the eighteen and nineteenth centuries for Russia; in the late nineteenth and early twentieth centuries, they migrated to the Americas.) Research for this book took Wiebe to Paraguay in late 1966, where he was struck by the political oppression prevalent in Latin America and the need for revolutionary resistance. His next two books take up the topic of oppression and rebellion in a Canadian context. *The Temptations of Big Bear* (1973; Governor General's Award) tells how the Native people of the Prairies were drawn into the conflict between the government of Canada and Louis Riel. (In 2008, Wiebe returned to this material in his brief biography of Big Bear for Penguin's Extraordinary Canadians series.) *The Scorched-Wood People* (1977) is the related narrative of Riel's attempt to establish recognition for the Métis. (A later book, on the history of the Northwest Rebellion—*War in the West: Voices of the 1885 Rebellion*, edited by Wiebe and Bob Beal for the centenary of that event—is a collection of documents from that conflict.)

A fascination with the north, a desire to reimagine historical events, and a concern for individuals who have lost their place in society come together in his next novel, *The Mad Trapper* (1980). In it, Albert Johnson, an isolated and enigmatic individual whose turn to violence led the RCMP on a monumental pursuit through the northern wilds. Wiebe's engagement with the past is itself examined in his novel *My Lovely Enemy* (1983), a love story set against an account of a historian's efforts to make sense of history and of his relationship with it.

*A Discovery of Strangers* (1994; Governor General's Award), a narrative of the first Franklin expedition, draws on Wiebe's collection of essays on exploration and contemporary life in the North—*Playing Dead: A Contemplation Concerning the Arctic* (1989)—by interweaving an account of the expedition with passages from the journals kept by John Richardson and Robert Hood. Wiebe's novel, *Sweeter Than All the World* (2001), continues his investigations of history by telling the story of a man who, when his marriage and family life begin to collapse, looks back on his Mennonite ancestry, tracing his family history from the Netherlands in the sixteenth century through Russia and South America to the Alberta homestead where he was born in 1935.

Wiebe's short fiction was first collected in *Where Is the Voice Coming From?* (1974); he later provided stories for *Alberta, A Celebration* (1979). Stories selected from both books make up *The Angel of the Tar Sands and Other Stories* (1982). In *River of Stone: Fiction and Memories* (1995), Wiebe combines short fiction with personal narratives and memoirs. In *Of This Earth: A Mennonite Boyhood in the Boreal Forest* (2007), he records more of his memories of what daily life was like when he was a young boy in a pioneering community. Wiebe has also written a play, *Far As the Eye Can See* (1977), and edited several anthologies. He is the author of two books for children, *Chinook Christmas* (1992) and *Hidden Buffalo* (2003). In 2000, he was made an Officer of the Order of Canada.

The most important feature of Wiebe's writing is the moral vision that derives from his religious background. Central to Mennonite belief is the rejection of worldly loyalties and values, particularly those associated with the state, in favour of commitment to a Christian community. However, Wiebe is concerned that balance for the Mennonites—which would mean not becoming entrapped in a dead past, yet not sacrificing too much to remain relevant to the present—is difficult to achieve, and that some Mennonites in North America have become too assimilated into modern, urban culture, while others have become too rigid in trying to hold off change. Lost to both groups is their original vitality and revolutionary activism. He addresses these topics and discusses his role as an artist in essays and interviews in *A Voice in the Land: Essays by and about Rudy Wiebe* (1981; edited by W.J. Keith).

While finding a connection between present and past has been important for other Canadian writers, the extent of Wiebe's commitment to history is striking. Although he accepts the postmodern belief that history can never be completely recovered, he seeks its vitalizing force by adding imagined details of daily experience and individual perceptions to the artifacts that have survived. His awareness of the complex relationships between documents and the actual events they respond to—and the fiction that can be derived from them—is central to 'Where Is the Voice Coming From?', the story reprinted below. In it, the narrator considers the problematic fragments left behind from the last battle between whites and Natives in North America—one that pitted Kah-kee-say-mane-too-wayo ('Voice of the Great Spirit' or 'Almighty Voice', 1874–97) and two members of his family against the North-West Mounted Police. Wiebe shows us that the account of this event is unstable and can never be fully known, but he also suggests that one receptive individual, contemplating the vestiges of that battle, can intuit the life that lies behind it. Like the readers of Wiebe's fiction, the story's narrator begins to 'hear' the voices of the long dead, voices that enrich one's understanding. Wiebe, thus, confirms the paradox at the heart of his art: turning the past into fiction may be falsifying, yet it also allows that past to speak.

# Where Is the Voice Coming From?

The problem is to make the story.

One difficulty of this making may have been excellently stated by Teilhard de Chardin:[1] 'We are continually inclined to isolate ourselves from the things and events which surround us . . . as though we were spectators, not elements, in what goes on.' Arnold Toynbee does venture, 'For all that we know, Reality is the undifferentiated unity of the mystical experience', but that need not here be considered. This story ended long ago; it is one of the finite acts, of orders, of elemental feelings and reactions, of obvious legal restrictions and requirements.

Presumably all the parts of the story are themselves available. A difficulty is that they are, as always, available only in bits and pieces. Though the acts themselves seem quite clear, some written reports of the acts contradict each other. As if these acts were, at one time, too well known; as if the original nodule of each particular fact had from somewhere received non-factual accretions; or even more, as if, since the basic facts were so clear perhaps there were a larger number of facts than any one reporter, or several, or even any reporter had ever attempted to record. About facts that are still simply told by this mouth to that ear, of course, even less can be expected.

An affair seventy-five years old should acquire some of the shiny transparency of an old man's skin. It should.

Sometimes it would seem that it would be enough—perhaps more than enough— to hear the names only. The grandfather One Arrow; the mother Spotted Calf; the father Sounding Sky; the wife (wives rather, but only one of them seems to have a name, though their fathers are Napaise, Kapahoo, Old Dust, The Rump)—the one wife named, of all things, Pale Face; the cousin Going-Up-To-Sky; the brother-in-law (again, of all things) Dublin. The names of the police sound very much alike; they all begin with Constable or Corporal or Sergeant, but here and there an Inspector, then a Superintendent and eventually all the resonance of an Assistant Commissioner echoes down. More. Herself: Victoria, by the Grace of God etc., etc., QUEEN, defender of the Faith, etc., etc.; and witness 'Our Right Trusty and Right Well-beloved Cousin and Councillor the Right Honorable Sir John Campbell Hamilton-Gordon, Earl of Aberdeen; Viscount Formartine, Baron Haddo, Methlic, Tarves and Kellie, in the Peerage of Scotland; Viscount Gordon of Aberdeen, County of Aberdeen, in the Peerage of the United Kingdom; Baronet of Nova Scotia, Knight Grand Cross of Our Most Distinguished Order of Saint Michael and Saint George, etc., Governor General of Canada'. And of course himself: in the award proclamation named 'Jean-Baptiste' but otherwise known only as Almighty Voice.

But hearing cannot be enough; not even hearing all the thunder of A Proclamation: 'Now Hear Ye that a reward of FIVE HUNDRED DOLLARS will be paid to any person or persons who will give such information as will lead . . . (etc., etc.) this

---

1 Pierre Teilhard de Chardin (1881–1955), French Jesuit philosopher whose unorthodox views included the concept of the 'noosphere', a kind of evolving collective consciousness formed by humanity's mental activity. Arnold Toynbee (1889–1975), the English historian best known for his twelve-volume *Study of History* (1934–61), believed that history exhibited unitary order, which was evidence of a cosmic design.

Twentieth day of April, in the year of Our Lord one thousand eight hundred and ninety-six, and the Fifty-ninth year of Our Reign . . .' etc. and etc.

Such hearing cannot be enough. The first item to be seen is the piece of white bone. It is almost triangular, slightly convex—concave actually as it is positioned at this moment with its corners slightly raised—graduating from perhaps a strong eighth to a weak quarter of an inch in thickness, its scattered pore structure varying between larger and smaller on its perhaps polished, certainly shiny surface. Precision is difficult since the glass showcase is at least thirteen inches deep and therefore an eye cannot be brought as close as the minute inspection of such a small, though certainly quite adequate, sample of skull would normally require. Also, because of the position it cannot be determined whether the several hairs, well over a foot long, are still in some manner attached or not.

The seven-pounder cannon can be seen standing almost shyly between the showcase and the interior wall. Officially it is known as a gun, not a cannon, and clearly its bore is not large enough to admit a large man's fist. Even if it can be believed that this gun was used in the 1885 Rebellion and that on the evening of Saturday, May 29, 1897 (while the nine-pounder, now unidentified, was in the process of arriving with the police on the special train from Regina), seven shells (all that were available in Prince Albert at that time) from it were sent shrieking into the poplar bluffs as night fell, clearly such shelling could not and would not disembowel the whole earth. Its carriage is now nicely lacquered, the perhaps oak spokes of its petite wheels (little higher than a knee) have been recently scraped, puttied and varnished; the brilliant burnish of its brass breeching testifies with what meticulous care charmen and women have used nationally-advertised cleaners and restorers.

Though it can also be seen, even a careless glance reveals that the same concern has not been expended on the one (of two) .44 calibre 1866 model Winchesters apparently found at the last in the pit with Almighty Voice. It also is preserved in a glass case; the number 1536735 is still, though barely, distinguishable on the brass cartridge section just below the brass saddle ring. However, perhaps because the case was imperfectly sealed at one time (though sealed enough not to warrant disturbance now), or because of simple neglect, the rifle is obviously spotted here and there with blotches of rust and the brass itself reveals discolorations almost like mildew. The rifle bore, the three long strands of hair themselves, actually bristle with clots of dust. It may be that this museum cannot afford to be as concerned as the other; conversely, the disfiguration may be something inherent in the items themselves.

The small building which was the police guardroom at Duck Lake, Saskatchewan Territory, in 1895 may also be seen. It had subsequently been moved from its original place and used to house small animals, chickens perhaps, or pigs—such as a woman might be expected to have under her responsibility. It is, of course, now perfectly empty, and clean so that the public may enter with no more discomfort than a bend under the doorway and a heavy encounter with disinfectant. The door-jamb has obviously been replaced; the bar network at one window is, however, said to be original; smooth still, very smooth. The logs inside have been smeared again and again with whitewash, perhaps paint, to an insistent point of identity-defying characterlessness.

Within the small rectangular box of these logs not a sound can be heard from the streets of the, probably dead, town.

> *Hey Injun you'll get hung for stealing that steer*
> *Hey Injun for killing that government cow you'll get three*
> *weeks on the woodpile Hey Injun*

The place named Kinistino seems to have disappeared from the map but the Minnechinass Hills have not. Whether they have ever been on a map is doubtful but they will, of course, not disappear from the landscape as long as the grass grows and the rivers run. Contrary to general report and belief, the Canadian prairies are rarely, if ever, flat and the Minnechinass (spelled five different ways and translated sometimes as 'The Outside Hill', sometimes as 'Beautiful Bare Hills') are dissimilar from any other of the numberless hills that everywhere block out the prairie horizon. They are bare; poplars lie tattered along their tops, almost black against the straw-pale grass and sharp green against the grey soil of the plowing laid in half-mile rectangular blocks upon their western slopes. Poles holding various wires stick out of the fields, back down the bend of the valley; what was once a farmhouse is weathering into the cultivated earth. The poplar bluff where Almighty Voice made his stand has, of course, disappeared.

The policemen he shot and killed (not the ones he wounded, of course) are easily located. Six miles east, thirty-nine miles north in Prince Albert, the English Cemetery. Sergeant Colin Campbell Colebrook, North West Mounted Police Registration Number 605, lies presumably under a gravestone there. His name is seventeenth in a very long 'list of non-commissioned officers and men who have died in the service since the inception of the force'. The date is October 29, 1895, and the cause of death is anonymous: 'Shot by escaping Indian prisoner near Prince Albert.' At the foot of this grave are two others: Constable John R. Kerr, No. 3040, and Corporal C.H.S. Hockin, No. 3106. Their cause of death on May 28, 1897 is even more anonymous, but the place is relatively precise: 'Shot by Indians at Min-etch-inass Hills, Prince Albert District.'

The gravestone, if he has one, of the fourth man Almighty Voice killed is more difficult to locate. Mr Ernest Grundy, postmaster at Duck Lake in 1897, apparently shut his window the afternoon of Friday, May 28, armed himself, rode east twenty miles, participated in the second charge into the bluff at about 6:30 p.m., and on the third sweep of that charge was shot dead at the edge of the pit. It would seem that he thereby contributed substantially not only to the Indians' bullet supply, but his clothing warmed them as well.

The burial place of Dublin and Going-Up-To-Sky is unknown, as is the grave of Almighty Voice. It is said that a Métis named Henry Smith lifted the latter's body from the pit in the bluff and gave it to Spotted Calf. The place of burial is not, of course, of ultimate significance. A gravestone is always less evidence than a triangular piece of skull, provided it is large enough.

Whatever further evidence there is to be gathered may rest on pictures. There are, presumably, almost numberless pictures of the policemen in the case, but the only one with direct bearing is one of Sergeant Colebrook, who apparently insisted on advancing to complete an arrest after being warned three times that if he took another step he would be shot. The picture must have been taken before he joined the force; it reveals him a large-eared young man, hair brush-cut and ascot tie, his eyelids slightly drooping, almost hooded under thick brows. Unfortunately a picture of Constable R.C. Dickson, into whose charge Almighty Voice was apparently committed in that guardroom and who after Colebrook's death was convicted of negligence, sentenced to two months hard labour and discharged, does not seem to be available.

There are no pictures to be found of either Dublin (killed early by rifle fire) or Going-Up-To-Sky (killed in the pit), the two teenage boys who gave their ultimate fealty to Almighty Voice. There is, however, one said to be of Almighty Voice, Junior. He may have been born to Pale Face during the year, two hundred and twenty-one days that his father was a fugitive. In the picture he is kneeling before what could be a tent, he wears striped denim overalls and displays twin babies whose sex cannot be determined by the double-laced dark bonnets they wear. In the supposed picture of Spotted Calf and Sounding Sky, Sounding Sky stands slightly before his wife; he wears a white shirt and a striped blanket folded over his left shoulder in such a manner that the arm in which he cradles a long rifle cannot be seen. His head is thrown back; the rim of his hat appears as a black half-moon above eyes that are pressed shut as if in profound concentration; above a mouth clenched thin in a downward curve. Spotted Calf wears a long dress, a sweater which could also be a man's dress coat, and a large fringed and embroidered shawl which would appear distinctly Doukhobor[2] in origin if the scroll patterns on it were more irregular. Her head is small and turned slightly towards her husband so as to reveal her right ear. There is what can only be called a quizzical expression on her crumpled face; it may be she does not understand what is happening and that she would have asked a question, perhaps of her husband, perhaps of the photographers, perhaps even of anyone, anywhere in the world if such questioning were possible for a Cree woman.

There is one final picture. That is one of Almighty Voice himself. At least it is purported to be of Almighty Voice himself. In the Royal Canadian Mounted Police Museum on the Barracks Grounds just off Dewdney Avenue in Regina, Saskatchewan, it lies in the same showcase, as a matter of fact immediately beside that triangular piece of skull. Both are unequivocally labelled, and it must be assumed that a police force with a world-wide reputation would not label *such* evidence incorrectly. But here emerges an ultimate problem in making the story.

There are two official descriptions of Almighty Voice. The first reads: 'Height about five feet, ten inches, slight build, rather good looking, a sharp hooked nose with a remarkably flat point. Has a bullet scar on the left side of his face about 1½ inches long running from near corner of mouth towards ear. The scar cannot be noticed when his face is painted but otherwise is plain. Skin fair for an Indian.' The second description is on the Award Proclamation: 'About twenty-two years old, five feet ten inches in height, weight about eleven stone, slightly erect, neat small feet and hands; complexion inclined to be fair, wavy dark hair to shoulders, large dark eyes, broad forehead,

---

2 A Russian Christian sect, many members of which migrated to western Canada in 1899 after persecution for refusing military service.

sharp features and parrot nose with flat tip, scar on left cheek running from mouth towards ear, feminine appearance.'

So run the descriptions that were, presumably, to identify a well-known fugitive in so precise a manner that an informant could collect five hundred dollars—a considerable sum when a police constable earned between one and two dollars a day. The nexus of the problems appears when these supposed official descriptions are compared to the supposed official picture. The man in the picture is standing on a small rug. The fingers of his left hand touch a curved Victorian settee, behind him a photographer's backdrop of scrolled patterns merges to vaguely paradisiacal trees and perhaps a sky. The moccasins he wears make it impossible to deduce whether his feet are 'neat small'. He may be five feet, ten inches tall, may weigh eleven stone, he certainly is 'rather good looking' and, though it is a frontal view, it may be that the point of his long and flaring nose could be 'remarkably flat'. The photograph is slightly over-illuminated and so the unpainted complexion could be 'inclined to be fair'; however, nothing can be seen of a scar, the hair is not wavy and shoulder-length but hangs almost to the waist in two thick straight braids worked through with beads, fur, ribbons and cords. The right hand that holds the corner of the blanket-like coat in position is large and, even in the high illumination, heavily veined. The neck is concealed under coiled beads and the forehead seems more low than 'broad'.

Perhaps, somehow, these picture details could be reconciled with the official description if the face as a whole were not so devastating.

On a cloth-backed sheet two feet by two-and-one-half feet in size, under the Great Seal of the Lion and the Unicorn, dignified by the names of the Deputy of the Minister of Justice, the Secretary of State, the Queen herself and all the heaped detail of her 'Right Trusty and Right Well Beloved Cousin', this description concludes: 'feminine appearance'. But the pictures: any face of history, any believed face that the world acknowledges as *man*—Socrates, Jesus, Attila, Genghis Khan, Mahatma Gandhi, Joseph Stalin—no believed face is more *man* than this face. The mouth, the nose, the clenched brows, the eyes—the eyes are large, yes, and dark, but even in this watered-down reproduction of unending reproductions of that original, a steady look into those eyes cannot be endured. It is a face like an axe.

It is not evident that the de Chardin statement quoted at the beginning has relevance only as it proves itself inadequate to explain what has happened. At the same time, the inadequacy of Aristotle's much more famous statement becomes evident: 'The true difference [between the historian and the poet] is that one relates what *has* happened, the other what *may* happen.' These statements cannot explain the storyteller's activity, since, despite the most rigid application of impersonal investigation, the elements of the story have now run me aground. If ever I could, I can no longer pretend to objective, omnipotent disinterestedness. I am no longer *spectator* of what *has* happened or what *may* happen: I am become *element* in what is happening at this very moment.

For it is, of course, I myself who cannot endure the shadows on that paper which are those eyes. It is I who stand beside this broken veranda post where two corner shingles have been torn away, where barbed wire tangles the dead weeds on the edge of this field. The bluff that sheltered Almighty Voice and his two friends has not disappeared from the slope of the Minnechinass, no more than the sound of Constable Dickson's voice in that guardhouse is silent. The sound of his speaking is there even if it has never been recorded in an official report:

> hey injun you'll get
> hung
> for stealing that steer
> hey injun for killing that government
> cow you'll get three
> weeks on the woodpile hey injun

The unknown contradictory words about an unprovable act that move a boy to defiance, an implacable Cree warrior long after the three-hundred-and-fifty-year war is ended, a war already lost the day the Cree watch Cartier hoist his gun ashore at Hochelaga[3] and they begin the long retreat west; these words of incomprehension, of threatened incomprehensible law are there to be heard just as the unmoving tableau of the three-day siege is there to be seen on the slopes of the Minnechinass. Sounding Sky is somewhere not there, under arrest, but Spotted Calf stands on a shoulder of the Hills a little to the left, her arms upraised to the setting sun. Her mouth is open. A horse rears, riderless, above the scrub willow at the edge of the bluff, smoke puffs, screams tangle in rifle barrage, there are wounds, somewhere. The bluff is so green this spring, it will not burn and the ragged line of seven police and two civilians is staggering through, faces twisted in rage, terror, and rifles sputter. Nothing moves. There is no sound of frogs in the night; twenty-seven policemen and five civilians stand in cordon at thirty-yard intervals and a body also lies in the shelter of a gully. Only a voice rises from the bluff:

> We have fought well
> You have died like braves
> I have worked hard and am hungry
> Give me food

but nothing moves. The bluff lies, a bright green island on the grassy slope surrounded by men hunched forward rigid over their long rifles, men clumped out of rifle-range, thirty-five men dressed as for fall hunting on a sharp spring day, a small gun positioned on a ridge above. A crow is falling out of the sky into the bluff, its feathers sprayed as by an explosion. The first gun and the second gun are in position, the beginning and end of the bristling surround of thirty-five Prince Albert Volunteers, thirteen civilians, and fifty-six policemen in position relative to the bluff and relative to the unnumbered whites astride their horses, standing up in their carts, staring and pointing across the valley, in position relative to the bluff and the unnumbered Cree squatting silent along the higher ridges of the Hills, motionless mounds, faceless against the Sunday morning sunlight edging between and over them down along the tree tips, down into the

3  Former Native village, located at the present-day site of Montreal, where Jacques Cartier arrived in the fall of 1535.

shadows of the bluff. Nothing moves. Beside the second gun the red-coated officer has flung a handful of grass into the motionless air, almost to the rim of the red sun.

And there is a voice. It is an incredible voice that rises from among the young poplars ripped of their spring bark, from among the dead somewhere lying there, out of the arm-deep pit shorter than a man; a voice rises over the exploding smoke and thunder of guns that reel back in their positions, worked over, serviced by the grimed motionless men in bright coats and glinting buttons, a voice so high and clear, so unbelievably high and strong in its unending wordless cry.

The voice of 'Gitchie-Manitou Wayo'—interpreted as 'voice of the Great Spirit'—that is, The Almighty Voice. His death chant no less incredible in its beauty than in its incomprehensible happiness.

I say 'wordless cry' because that is the way it sounds to me. I could be more accurate if I had a reliable interpreter who would make a reliable interpretation. For I do not, of course, understand the Cree myself.

1982, rev. 1995

# George Bowering
## b. 1935

In addition to the substantial body of work that George Bowering has published under his own name, his playful sense of humour has led him to add so many poems and reviews under a variety of pseudonyms that his bibliographers may never straighten out all questions of authorship. He has similarly confused his biographers by naming at least three different towns in the Okanagan Valley of British Columbia as his birthplace: Penticton, Osoyoos, and Oliver ('A very slow birth in a fast-moving car' is how he once explained this). He was actually born in the first of these. Bowering grew up in Oliver, leaving to become an aerial photographer for the RCAF (1954–7). After his service, he enrolled at the University of British Columbia, where he earned a BA in history (1960) and an MA in English (1963).

At UBC, Bowering studied creative writing under Earle Birney, as well as with the prominent American poet Robert Creeley (who, as a visiting professor, was Bowering's MA thesis adviser), and became part of a group of aspiring poets that included Frank Davey, Fred Wah, Daphne Buckle (Marlatt), and Lionel Kearns. From UBC professor Warren Tallman, they learned about contemporary American literary movements, especially the aesthetic theories and poetic practices current on the US West Coast; then under the sway of the poetics of William Carlos Williams and the Black Mountain movement (an influential school of poetry begun at Black Mountain College in North Carolina by Charles Olson, Robert Duncan, and Creeley) and of avant-garde writers such as Jack Spicer and beat poet Allen Ginsberg. These young BC poets were inspired by a 1961 visit to Vancouver by Duncan—who discussed not only Black Mountain theories but also the importance of 'little magazines' for new poetry movements—

and launched their own literary periodical, *Tish*, a monthly poetry 'newsletter' that patterned itself in part after such magazines as *Origin* in the United States and Louis Dudek's *Delta* in Canada.

The writers associated with this newsletter came to be known as the '*Tish* group'. They were greatly influenced by the Black Mountain movement's spare style (an inheritance from the Imagist tradition and from Williams), as well as its use of a loose poetic line based on the rhythms and pauses of colloquial speech, its emphasis on local and regional aspects of experience, and its belief in the communal nature of writing. Especially attracted to the long poem (in the tradition of Williams's *Patterson*) and in the serial poem (as developed by Spicer), they rejected the lyric mode associated with what they decried as the 'humanism' and 'romanticism' of poetry from eastern Canada and the northeastern United States. Following Olson, they called for a poetry of essentials that would be accurate and objective, created by writers who, as Bowering later said, 'turned their attention upon the factual things that make up the world' (*Tish*, No. 20, 1963).

Although *Tish* lasted for eight years (forty-five issues), its founders left after issue No. 19 to pursue other interests. Bowering accepted a teaching position at the University of Calgary; he then went to the University of Western Ontario for further graduate studies before becoming writer-in-residence, and subsequently professor, at Sir George Williams University (now part of Concordia). Remaining committed to little-magazine publishing in Canada, he founded and edited *Imago* (1964–74) and then became a contributing editor for Frank Davey's influential literary and critical journal *Open Letter* (begun in 1965). In 1971, he returned to British Columbia, where he taught English and creative writing at Simon Fraser University until his retirement in 2001. His extensive contributions to Canadian letters were recognized when he was named Canada's first Parliamentary Poet Laureate for 2002–4.

The most prolific member of the *Tish* group, Bowering has published more than thirty books of poetry, mostly with small presses. His first book, *Sticks & Stones* (with a preface by Creeley), appeared in 1963. He received a Governor General's Award in 1969 for the two books of poetry he published that year: *Rocky Mountain Foot* and *The Gangs of Kosmos*. Among his later books are *Touch: Selected Poems, 1960–70* (1971); *Selected Poems: Particular Accidents* (1980); *Seventy-One Poems for People* (1985); and *Blonds on Bikes* (1997). *George Bowering: Selected Poems, 1961–1992* (1993) brings together a substantial sample of his work, as does *Changing on the Fly: The Best Lyric Poems of George Bowering* (2004). Like other poets of the *Tish* group, Bowering tends to avoid rhetorical devices and metaphor, preferring a language and style closer to common speech. This poetry is saved from prosiness by the subtle musical quality in its diction and rhythms, and from slackness by its sharply etched observations. (Several of Bowering's long works—such as *Autobiology* [1972] and *A Short Sad Book* [1977]—straddle the boundary between prose and poetry.)

In the 1970s and 80s, Bowering's most important poetry took the form of loosely unified long poems; several are reprinted in *The Catch* (1976) and in *West Window* (1982). The best known of these is the book-length poem, *Kerrisdale Elegies* (1985), in which his career-long love of responding to other poets and poems takes the form of a playful yet meditative rewriting of Rainer Maria Rilke's *Duino Elegies* (1923). Such acts link Bowering with postmodernism's repudiation of Romanticism's and modernism's obsessions with originality. Relocating Rilke in a contemporary Vancouver neighbourhood, the dramatized speaker in *Kerrisdale Elegies* functions as someone who, having himself experienced loss, can serve as mediator for all readers in their grief—while reminding us of the inevitability of mortality and the passing away of that which we have known and loved. (The elegiac tradition has been important in Canadian poetry, where it has found expression both at a personal level and in laments for lost heritages and national ideals.)

Bowering has often drawn from his life in his books. His long poem *His Life* (2000) documents his personal experiences from 1958 to 1988. He observed in *Errata* (1988), that while he 'never wanted to write an autobiography', he has often drawn from 'what looks like my life story'. He suggests such literary works 'should be called biotext', explaining that 'autobiography replaces the writer', while 'biotext is an extension of him'.

In 2006, Bowering published a new collection of shorter poems, *Vermeer's Light: Poems, 1996–2006*. At the end of that book, he includes an essay that looks back to 'Grandfather', one of his earliest and most-often reprinted poems, and playfully considers how he might rewrite it now using some of the experimental techniques that have since come into vogue (the kind Christian Bök has used, for example).

Bowering is also the author of a number of important works of fiction. His short-story collections include *Flycatcher & Other Stories* (1974); *Protective Footwear: Stories and Fables* (1978); *A Place to Die* (1983); *The Rain Barrel and Other Stories* (1994); and *The Box* (2009). He is the author of a novella, *Concentric Circles* (1977); and of five novels: *A Mirror on the Floor* (1967); *Burning Water* (1980), which won Bowering his second Governor General's Award; *Harry's Fragments*, a parody thriller (1990); and two mock-westerns, *Caprice* (1987) and *Shoot!* (1994). He co-authored *Piccolo Mondo* (1998), a fictionalized memoir written collaboratively with Angela Bowering (his wife until her death in 1999) and two of their friends. (He and Angela Bowering also co-authored a sequence called 'Pictures', from which the prose poem 'Prodigal', reprinted below, is drawn.) In 2006,

Bowering published a road-trip memoir, *Baseball Love* (2006): a testimony to his lasting fascination with baseball, which is visible in many other poems, including the chapbook *Poem and Other Baseballs* (1976) and Elegy Five of *Kerrisdale Elegies*.

· Having written critical pieces throughout his career, Bowering turned to criticism with particular intensity in the 1980s, publishing four collections: *A Way with Words* (1982); *The Mask in Place: Essays on Fiction in North America* (1983); *Craft Slices* (1985); and *Imaginary Hand* (1988). (In *Errata*, he combined critical and personal meditations.) He has written three books of history—*Bowering's B.C.: A Swashbuckling History* (1996); *Egotists and Autocrats: The Prime Ministers of Canada* (1999); and *Stone Country: An Unauthorized History of Canada* (2003)—that draw upon his humour and talents as a storyteller to offer fresh, but never objective, accounts of his subjects.

Like other members of the *Tish* group, Bowering strives in all this writing to communicate a sense of *process* rather than to deliver finished product. Rejecting the modernist doctrine of the artist as a detached maker of impersonal, objective, and permanent artifacts, he frequently conveys this quality by dramatizing the writer in the text as an author embodied in the act of writing and by locating the work within the subjectivities that surround the act of creation.

# Grandfather

Grandfather
      Jabez Harry Bowering
strode across the Canadian prairie
hacking down trees
          & building churches
delivering personal baptist sermons in them
leading Holy holy holy lord god almighty songs in them
red haired man squared off in the pulpit
reading Saul on the road to Damascus at them[1]

---

1 That is, he takes as the text for his sermon the story of Saul's conversion. According to the Book of Acts, Saul was journeying to Damascus in his energetic persecution of early Christians when he was struck blind by God; he was healed three days later and, renamed Paul, given the commission to proclaim Christianity to the Gentiles.

Left home
     big walled Bristol town
at age eight
       to make a living
buried his stubby fingers in root snarled earth
for a suit of clothes & seven hundred gruelly meals a year
taking an anabaptist[2] cane across the back every day
for four years till he was whipt out of England

Twelve years old
       & across the ocean alone
to apocalyptic Canada                20
       Ontario of bone bending labour
six years on the road to Damascus till his eyes were blinded
with the blast of Christ & he wandered west
to Brandon among wheat kings & heathen Saturday nights
young red haired Bristol boy shovelling coal
in the basement of Brandon College five in the morning

Then built his first wooden church & married
a sick girl who bore two live children & died
leaving several pitiful letters & the Manitoba night

He moved west with another wife & built children & churches   30
Saskatchewan Alberta British Columbia Holy holy holy
lord god almighty
       struck his laboured bones with pain
& left him a postmaster prodding grandchildren with crutches
another dead wife & a glass bowl of photographs
& holy books unopened save the bible by the bed

Till he died the day before his eighty-fifth birthday
in a Catholic hospital of sheets white as his hair

1963

---

2 Anabaptist (literally, 'rebaptizer') was a term applied to those Protestant sects opposed to the Roman Catholic
practice of infant baptism—teaching that only those old enough to decide for themselves should be baptized.

# From *Kerrisdale Elegies*

## ELEGY TWO

Dead poets' voices I have heard in my head
are not terrifying.
>They tell me like lovers
we are worth speaking to,
>>I am a branch
a singing bird will stand on for a moment.[1]

Like a singing branch I call out in return. How
do otherwise?
>Rather that than couple
with a swan on 41st Avenue.                                    10
>>When Hilda[2]
appeared in my dream, she did not visit, she
walked by, into the other room,
>>and I didn't fall
in fear, but in love.

Inside.

Out there was the fortunate fall,[3] mountains
glistening with creation,
>a glacier between them,
flowing bright out of the working god's fingers,                20
first orchards rising from the melt, light
shaped on crest and cut,
>the roll of storms
shaking new trees, flattening the grass,
>>quick lakes
a scatter of mirrors, clouds in them, all
favour, all breathing side to side, all
being outside,
>all blossom.

---

1  In keeping with a poem about hearing 'dead poets' voices', Elegy Two is filled with echoes and resonances of poems and songs. Here Bowering is playing with a line from W.B. Yeats's 'Byzantium', in which the golden bird, which serves Yeats as a metaphor for the way a poem outlives the poet, is described as 'Planted on the star-lit golden bough', beyond 'all complexities of mire or blood'. A few lines later Bowering recalls Yeats's 'Leda and the Swan', which describes how Zeus took on the form of a swan to rape Leda.

2  Hilda Doolittle (1886–1961), the American poet who signed her work H.D., was a contemporary of Ezra Pound's and one of the central figures of the Imagist movement.

3  The Christian doctrine of the Fortunate Fall (the idea that Adam and Eve's fall from grace into sin was fortunate because it permitted God to provide humanity with the sacrifice of his son) is central to Milton's Renaissance epic *Paradise Lost.*

As for us, we dissolve into hungers,                    30
                              our breath
disappears every minute,
                         our skin flakes off
and lies unseen on the pavement.
                              She says
I've got you under my skin, yes, she says
you walk with me wherever I go,
                              you are
the weather.
             I reply with a call for help,                    40
I'm disappearing,

             there's a change in the weather.

Half the beautiful ones I have known are gone,
what's the hurry?
                  On this street the school girls
grow up and disappear into kitchens,
                              a breeze
shakes the blossoms from my cherry tree,
there's cat hair all over the rug.
                              What happened                    50
to that smile that was on your face
a minute ago?
               God, there goes another breath,
and I go with it,
                  I was further from my grave
two stanzas back, I'm human.
                              Will the universe
notice my unattached molecules drifting thru?

Will the dead poets notice our lines appearing among them,
or are their ears filled with their own music?                    60

Will their faces look as blank as these I pass
on 41st Avenue?
               I'm not talking about
making that great anthology,
                              I am recalling that god
who said excuse me, I wasnt listening, sorry.

In love we have a secret language we dont remember.
We catch a word or two,
                              as the wind passes,
we turn an ear to the cool,                                    70
                              it's gone. The trees
shake their leaves to say look,
                              we're alive
The house you've sat in for years remains
against all odds,
                    a part of the earth.

We are wisps,
            we flit invisible
around all that wood.
                        They dont even hear us,          80
they may be waiting for us to say something important.

Late night on 37th Avenue I see lovers
on each other in a lamplit Chevrolet.

Do their hands know for certain that's skin
they glide over?
                  I have rubbed my neck in exhaustion,
and almost believe I've touched something.

Is that a reason to look forward to next year?
Still, being dead
is no bed of roses.                                            90

But the moony flesh in the sedan
turns like the firmament,
                              he is entangled
in legs and gearshift,
                              she likely says yes
and grows to meet his growth,
                              dumb imitation
of the burgeoning garden in the nearby yard.

I grow more frail as they fill the car,
already disappearing,                                         100
                        should I ask them
whether I exist?

Si me soubmectz, leur serviteur
En tout ce que puis faire et dire,
A les honnorer de bon cuer[4]

I know they put their hands there and there
because their early fancy now arrives,
                              an island
risen from a placid sea.
                    An actual breast, a leg                    110
that does not disappear below conflicting pictures.

But the ones who have touched me have
disintegrated into seraphs and books.

These half-undressed in the front seat
have nearly slipped from time,
                              elastic hours
making Pleiades of the street.

Yet if they see the morning,
                    safe from their first
rough sea,                                                    120
        if they smooth each other's hair,
talk about their weekend shopping—are they
what they were?
                    Are they as far from time?

Do they kiss, and try to kiss again, and say
inside, yes I remember this?
                         Does a mask
feel the touch of a mask;
                         does the face
beneath the mask feel the mask?                              130

Did you see ancient Fred and whitened Ginger[5]
in the morning paper,
                    June 25, 1982? Now
each time we see them glide by each other's
garments in black & white youth, we stand
amazed.

4  These lines come from stanza CIX of *Le Grand Testament* (1461), a collection of bequests to friends and enemies
   interspersed with ballads and rondeaux (including 'Ballade des Dames du Temps Jadis') written by French poet
   François Villon (1431–c.63).
5  Fred Astaire (1899–1987) and Ginger Rogers (1911–95), American actors and dancers, who starred together in a
   number of film musicals and were noted for their grace and sophistication.

How light that touch, how quick,                                    110
how foreign to the dull surge of our own passion,
we thought.
                   They generated enormous energy, yet              140
met like eyelashes.
                   They were exactly like us.
God, if he choose,

                   can press us into
sausage patties,
                   he can flatten a car,
furl up a street,
                   tuck us into our own shoes.

We step out of cars, finally,
                   movies come to an end,                           150
we need a place at last that will fit us,
we need a cabin, a creek, a few trees,
maybe a typewriter and a sink.
                   We are evaporating
as our heroes did.
                   We cannot pursue our fragments
as they separate into earth and stars.

1984

## The Great Local Poem

The great local poem begins
when someone pulls

out the last spike.[1]

We declare the hole that is left
the centre of everything.

1997

---

1 See pp. 342–3. For Pratt, the last spike driven at Craigellachie, British Columbia, symbolizes the joining of the Canadian nation from coast to coast.

# From 'Pictures', with Angela Bowering

## PRODIGAL

'Who are you?' she says, and the calf knows, one eye rolled white at the camera, is wary, is not seduced by the child's curiosity, though it leans against the rope into the innocence, fattening for the slaughter. The child reminds me of my little sister. I was the prodigal daughter, but I was fiercely protective of my sister. She who later took care of everyone else herself needed protection. Because I was older, though only by 22 months, I appointed myself her guardian. My sister loved cows. She used to love to ride out to the farther field to bring them home, through the stumps and trees, along a trail filled with surface-dried cow pies, soft in the centre when you stepped on them. She didn't seem to mind. Sometimes we threw them at the boys who worked at the farm. Sometimes they threw them at us. Often I would find her sitting in the sun, arm around the neck of a sleepy cow, her hair the same sheen and colour of the hide of the animal she embraced.

Later, when she was 14, she got her first job shovelling shit out of the barns, washing the gutters down, shovelling hay and feed into the mangers. She was dreadful to sleep with—never took off her clothes—jeans and shirts stinking of the cowshit smell for a week until my mother forced her to wash herself and her things, once a week on Saturdays. She spent all the time she wasnt at school in the barn, or around the cows. Finally, I made her sleep on the couch. What did she dream? She probably dreamed about cows. But this was much later. I am thinking of an earlier time, a time before adolescence made monsters of us all.

A creek ran across the farm just below the barnyard where the cows were brought to be milked, fed, and watered, and my sister would follow the cows to its edge when they went to drink. We werent allowed to go into the creek, but one hot summer day we broke the rule and went wading. We soon discovered that the creek was filled with what we later learned were leeches which had plastered their dark jelly bodies to our ankles. We did not know then about burning them off, and they were very difficult to dislodge, so we were occupied for some time pulling them off before we realized that my little sister had not joined the general squealing exodus from the water. She was, in fact, lying flat on her belly in the creek, paddling happily. When she finally stood up, thin-legged and blue with cold, she froze in midstream, covered with leeches black and swollen with her blood. I rushed in and pulled her onto the bank. The neighbours' children ran off at once, screaming. Filled with hatred and contempt for their cowardice, I began yanking them off her as fast as I could. It took a long time. 'Dont worry,' I said, 'I'll get them all.' 'Dont worry,' I said, as I yanked down her bathing suit to get the ones that had crawled inside it, 'I'll get them all.' She did not move until I had got every one, and then I put my arms around her and carried her home, legs dragging. She was taller than I. On that day, a terrible moral judgment was born in me. I've

---

1 Jesus's parable of the prodigal son can be found in Luke 15. The younger of two sons, having asked for his inheritance while his father is still alive, he has left home and spent all his wealth in riotous living. Reduced to poverty, he supports himself by feeding, living among, and sharing the food of a farmer's swine. When he returns home and repents of his misdeeds, his father welcomes him and slaughters a 'fatted' calf for a feast in his honour. His older brother, who has remained faithfully at home, feels he is being treated unjustly.

never been able to shake it, however hard I've tried. It has made trouble for me all my life. Judgment born of love is hardest to shake.

She was always taking care of things and I was always taking care of her. Things were always sticking to her, and because I stuck to her, they stuck to me too. She took care of the cats and they gave her ringworm. She took care of the chickens and they gave her fleas. She learned to blow bubbles with bubble gum that stuck to her face and got impetigo. But the thing that stuck hardest to me was that moral judgment. She brought stray kittens home and birds that had fallen out of nests and we dug worms all day long to feed them; pollywogs from the pond put into galvanized washtubs soon turned into shrivelled little corkscrews in the hot sun and she mourned their passing. They never turned into frogs. Sometimes she irritated her creatures with her care: the broody hen who grew impatient to be left alone, the rooster I had to save her from when it objected to her ministrations—rooster pecking my ass in outrage as I carried my little sister, legs dragging, across the vacant lot. It was her innocence I had to save her from. She would go up and down the street, calling at all the neighbours' houses looking for me. 'Have you seen the little Angelaw?' she'd say. 'Have you seen the little girl with the silk hair?' Why did I think I knew so much?

I lost her once in her little sunbonnet. My mother and father and I looked all over the neighbourhood for her. The fear was that she would wander into the nearby woods and into the bear trap set for the cougar who visited from time to time and screamed at the back fences, looking for chickens, I now suspect. After calling and searching had failed to find her, my parents and I walked down the back alley toward the woods where the trap had been set. We held our breaths as blue-bonneted innocence, four years old, came smiling, unscathed, out of the wood, happy to see us again. Terrifying miracle it seemed to me. Saved from mutilation; saved me from it. Didn't even know.

1997

---

# Joy Kogawa
## b. 1935

The 1941 attack on the American fleet at Pearl Harbor had terrible consequences for the many Japanese Canadians living on the West Coast. Because the Canadian government declared all those of Japanese descent, even native-born Canadian citizens, 'resident aliens', Joy Nozomi Kogawa (née Nakayama) and her family were forcibly relocated from her birth city of Vancouver to what she has described as a 'shack' in an internment camp at Slocan, British Columbia, and then to 'a smaller shack' in a camp at Coaldale, Alberta. Some 21,000 individuals similarly lost their homes and possessions and were compelled to remain inland, not only for the duration of the Second World War but also for four years afterwards.

The daughter of an Anglican clergyman, Kogawa grew up and was schooled in these camps. After studying for a year at the University of Alberta, she taught elementary school at Coaldale for a year. She left at the end of that year and studied music at the University of Toronto Conservatory, and theology at the Anglican Women's Training College from 1955–6. After that, she moved to Vancouver, where she married and had two children. Following a separation from her husband, she published her first book of poetry, *The Splintered Moon* (1967); after her divorce in 1968, she made her first visit to Japan. In 1974, she began working as a writer in the Prime Minister's Office and published her second book of poems, *A Choice of Dreams*. Two years later, she left government employment to become a full-time freelance writer to support herself. She served as writer-in-residence at the University of Ottawa from 1977–8. Kogawa has published three further volumes of poetry—*Jericho Road* (1977), *Woman in the Woods* (1985), and a volume of selected poems, *A Garden of Anchors* (2003), which includes some revised and new poetry.

Before taking up poetry, Kogawa wrote short fiction. The seed of her first novel lies in the story called 'Obasan', published in the *Canadian Forum* in 1978 and reprinted in *Stories by Canadian Women* (1984). Later, while researching in Ottawa's National Archives, Kogawa found records of other Japanese-Canadian experiences during the Second World War that gave broader context to the events of her own life. She was moved by these to expand her earlier story into *Obasan*, a novel published in 1981 to immediate acclaim. Writing *Obasan* led Kogawa into a life of political activism. Working from 1983 to 1985 with the National Association of Japanese Canadians, she became one of the leaders of the Redress Movement, which sought legal reparations for the injustices experienced during the war. In 1988, the federal government officially apologized and provided modest financial compensation to Japanese Canadians. (Kogawa's involvement in this successful cause is described in poet Roy Miki's *Redress: Inside the Japanese Canadian Call for Justice*, 2005.)

Kogawa's writing is rooted in specific events and images that evoke large philosophical issues—whether in her poetry, which has epigrammatic qualities, or in her fiction, which moves toward allegory. The facts, objects, and personal memories that form 'Road Building by Pick Axe', for example, combine to form something greater than their parts in the poem's conclusion. In 'Obasan', Naomi, a young woman returns to visit her elderly obasan (the Japanese word for 'aunt'), a quiet woman who is living alone following her husband's death. During her visit, the objects and memories she finds in her aunt's decaying house restore meaning to the elided experience of the war years: they point to a hidden love that made it possible for the family's honour and values to survive, and give Naomi an understanding of the silence of her obasan and of an entire generation. This story complements the lines in one of Kogawa's poems, 'What Do I Remember of the Evacuation':

> *I remember how careful my parents were*
> *Not to bruise us with bitterness.*

Just as the short story 'Obasan' provided a departure point for Kogawa's novel about the Japanese internment, so the novel *Obasan* gave rise to its sequel, *Itsuka* (1992); she substantially revised this novel and republished it in 2005 as *Emily Kato* (which is the name of Naomi's other aunt). It traces Naomi's adult life as she moves from the Prairies to Toronto to become involved in the fight for redress. The material in *Obasan* also became the basis for a children's book by Kogawa, *Naomi's Road* (1986), which in turn was used for the libretto of a children's opera produced by the Vancouver Opera Company; *Naomi's Road* was translated into Japanese as *Naomi no Michi* (1988), which became a school text in Japan. In 2008, Kogawa produced a second children's book about Naomi's family, *Naomi's Tree* (illustrated by Ruth Ohi, who also furnished the images for the earlier Naomi story). In all these versions of her family's history, Kogawa avoids imposing conclusions on the reader. Her techniques might be compared to those of Naomi's grandfather (referred to in the story reprinted below)—a Japanese craftsman who used a carpenter's plane requiring a *pulling* motion rather than a pushing one—'a fundamental difference in workmanship' .

Throughout her life and career, Kogawa has honoured her Japanese inheritance, but she also situates herself as a Christian: her ethics, based on compassion and love, emerge from both traditions. Kogawa's third novel *The Rain Ascends* (1995) examines a problem in Christian ethics as she looks at a different kind of familial silence, about a hidden secret that festers unless it is spoken of and examined. In it, a middle-aged woman struggles with her feelings for her father, a well-respected minister, as she tries to decide whether or not to reveal that he has been a child molester. Should she give him a chance for redemption—and the boys he abused, the relief of justice—or remain silent to save her family from public shame and him from prosecution?

In *A Song of Lilith* (2000), a long poem with illustrations by Lilian Broca, Kogawa broadens her concerns. A graphic novel, it recasts the legend of the woman who, according to Talmudic tradition, was Adam's first wife. When Lilith refused to subordinate herself to Adam, she was banished. In Kogawa's version of the story, Lilith, long demonized, becomes an allegorical figure—an emblem of women's loss of human equity.

# Obasan

She is sitting at the kitchen table when I come in. She is so deaf now that my knocking does not rouse her and when she sees me she is startled.

'O,' she says, and the sound is short and dry as if there is no energy left to put any inflection into her voice. She begins to rise but falters and her hands, outstretched in greeting, fall to the table. She says my name as a question.

I put my shoulder bag down, remove the mud-caked books and stand before her. 'Obasan,' I say loudly and take her hands. My aunt is not one for hugs and kisses. She peers into my face. 'O,' she says again.

I nod in reply. We stand for a long time in silence. I open my mouth to ask, 'Did he suffer very much?' but the question feels pornographic.

'Everyone dies some day,' she says eventually. She tilts her head to the side as if it's all too heavy inside.

I hang my jacket on a coat peg and sit beside her.

The house is familiar but has shrunk over the years and is even more cluttered than I remember. The wooden table is covered with a plastic table cloth over a blue and white cloth. Along one edge are African violets in profuse bloom, salt and pepper shakers, a soya sauce bottle, an old radio, a non-automatic toaster, a small bottle full of toothpicks. She goes to the stove and turns on the gas flame under the kettle.

'Everyone dies some day,' she says again and looks in my direction, her eyes unclear and sticky with a gum-like mucus. She pours the tea. Tiny twigs and bits of popcorn circle in the cup.

When I last saw her nine years ago, she told me her tear ducts were clogged. I have never seen her cry. Her mouth is filled with a gummy saliva as well. She drinks warm water often because her tongue sticks to the roof of her false plate.

'Thank you,' I say, taking the cup in both hands.

Uncle was disoriented for weeks, my cousin's letter told me. Towards the end he got dizzier and dizzier and couldn't move without clutching things. By the time they got him to the hospital, his eyes were rolling.

'I think he was beginning to see everything upside down again,' she wrote, 'the way we see when we are born.' Perhaps for Uncle, everything had started reversing and he was growing top to bottom, his mind rooted in an upstairs attic of humus and memory, groping backwards through cracks and walls to a moist cellar. Down to water. Down to the underground sea.

Back to the fishing boat, the ocean, the skiff moored off Vancouver Island where he was born. Like Moses, he was an infant of the waves, rocked to sleep by the lap lap and *'Nen, nen, korori'*, his mother's voice singing the ancient Japanese lullaby. His father, Japanese craftsman, was also a son of the sea which had tossed and coddled his boatbuilding ancestors for centuries. And though he had crossed the ocean from one island as a stranger coming to an island of strangers, it was the sea who was his constant landlord. His fellow tenants, the Songhee Indians of Esquimalt, and the fishermen, came from up and down the BC coast to his workshop in Victoria, to watch, to barter and to buy.

In the framed family photograph hanging above the sideboard, Grandfather sits on a chair with his short legs not quite square on the floor. A long black cape hangs from his shoulders. His left hand clutches a pair of gloves and the top of a cane. On a pedestal beside him is a top hat, open end up. Uncle stands slightly to his right, and behind, with his hand like Napoleon's in his vest. Sitting to their left is Grandmother in a lace and velvet suit with my mother in her arms. They all look in different directions, carved and rigid with their expressionless Japanese faces and their bodies pasted over with Rule Britannia. There is not a ripple out of place.

And then there is the picture, not framed, not on display, showing Uncle as a young man smiling and proud in front of an exquisitely detailed craft. Not a fishing boat, not an ordinary yacht—a creation of many years and many winter evenings—a work of art. Uncle stands, happy enough for the attention of the camera, eager to pass on the message that all is well. That forever and ever all is well.

But many things happen. There is the voice of the RCMP officer saying 'I'll keep that one,' and laughing as he cuts through the water. 'Don't worry, I'll make good use of her.' The other boats are towed away and left to rot. Hundreds of Grandfather's boats belonging to hundreds of fishermen.

The memories are drowned in a whirlpool of protective silence. 'For the sake of the children,' it is whispered over and over. *'Kodomo no tame.'*

And several years later, sitting in a shack on the edge of a sugar beet field in southern Alberta, Obasan is watching her two young daughters with their school books doing homework in the light of a coal oil lamp. Her words are the same, *'Kodomo no tame.'* For their sakes, they will survive the dust and the wind, the gumbo, the summer oven sun. For their sakes, they will work in the fields, hoeing, thinning acres of sugar beets, irrigating, topping, harvesting.

'We must go back,' Uncle would say on winter evenings, the ice thick on the windows. But later, he became more silent.

*'Nen nen.'* Rest, my dead uncle. The sea is severed from your veins. You have been cut loose.

They were feeding him intravenously for two days, the tubes sticking into him like grafting on a tree. But Death won against the medical artistry.

'Obasan, will you be all right?' I ask.

She clears her throat and wipes dry skin off her lips but does not speak. She rolls a bit of dried up jam off the table cloth. She isn't going to answer.

The language of grief is silence. She knows it well, its idioms, its nuances. She's had some of the best tutors available. Grief inside her body is fat and powerful. An almighty tapeworm.

Over the years, Grief has roamed like a highwayman down the channels of her body with its dynamite and its weapons blowing up every moment of relief that tried to make its way down the road. It grew rich off the unburied corpses inside her body.

Grief acted in mysterious ways, its melancholy wonders to perform. When it had claimed her kingdom fully, it admitted no enemies and no vengeance. Enemies belonged in a corridor of experience with sense and meaning, with justice and reason. Her Grief knew nothing of these and whipped her body to resignation until the kingdom was secure. But inside the fortress, Obasan's silence was that of a child bewildered.

'What will you do now?' I ask.

What choices does she have? Her daughters, unable to rescue her or bear the silent rebuke of her suffering have long since fled to the ends of the earth. Each has lived a life in perpetual flight from the density of her inner retreat—from the rays of her inverted sun sucking in their lives with the voracious appetite of a dwarf star.[1] Approaching her, they become balls of liquid metal—mercurial—unpredictable in their moods and sudden departures. Especially for the younger daughter, departure is as necessary as breath. What metallic spider is it in her night that hammers a constant transformation, lacing open doors and windows with iron bars.

'What will you do?' I repeat.

She folds her hands together. I pour her some more tea and she bows her thanks. I take her hands in mine, feeling the silky wax texture.

'Will you come and stay with us?' Are there any other words to say? Her hands move under mine and I release them. Her face is motionless. 'We could leave in a few days and come back next month.'

'The plants . . .'

'Neighbours can water them.'

'There is trouble with the house,' she says. 'This is an old house. If I leave . . .'

'Obasan,' I say nodding, 'it is your house.'

She is an old woman. Every homemade piece of furniture, each pot holder and child's paper doily, is a link in her lifeline. She has preserved in shelves and in cupboards, under layers of clothing in closets—a daughter's rubber ball, colouring books, old hats,

1  A white dwarf, a star in an advanced state of stellar evolution, is created when the star finally exhausts all of its possible sources of fuel for thermonuclear fusion, at which point it collapses under its own gravity into a dense, compressed mass.

children's dresses. The items are endless. Every short stub pencil, every cornflake box stuffed with paper bags and old letters is of her ordering. They rest in the corners of the house like parts of her body, hair cells, skin tissue, food particles, tiny specks of memory. This house is now her blood and bones.

She is all old women in every hamlet in the world. You see her on a street corner in a village in southern France, in her black dress and her black stockings. She is squatting on stone steps in a Mexican mountain village. Everywhere she stands as the true and rightful owner of the earth, the bearer of love's keys to unknown doorways, to a network of astonishing tunnels, the possessor of life's infinite personal details.

'I am old,' she says.

These are the words my grandmother spoke that last night in the house in Victoria. Grandmother was too old then to understand political expediency, race riots, the yellow peril. I was too young.

She stands up slowly. 'Something in the attic for you,' she says.

We climb the narrow stairs one step at a time carrying a flashlight with us. Its dull beam reveals mounds of cardboard boxes, newspapers, magazines, a trunk. A dead sparrow lies in the nearest corner by the eaves.

She attempts to lift the lid of the trunk. Black fly corpses fall to the floor. Between the wooden planks, more flies fill the cracks. Old spider webs hang like blood clots, thick and black from the rough angled ceiling.

Our past is as clotted as old webs hung in dark attics, still sticky and hovering, waiting for us to adhere and submit or depart. Or like a spider with its skinny hairy legs, the past skitters out of the dark, spinning and netting the air, ready to snap us up and ensnare our thoughts in old and complex perceptions. And when its feasting is complete, it leaves its victims locked up forever, dangling like hollowed out insect skins, a fearful calligraphy, dry reminders that once there was life flitting about in the weather.

But occasionally a memory that refuses to be hollowed out, to be categorized, to be identified, to be explained away, comes thudding into the web like a giant moth. And in the daylight, what's left hanging there, ragged and shredded is a demolished fly trap, and beside it a bewildered eight-legged spinning animal.

My dead refuse to bury themselves. Each story from the past is changed and distorted, altered as much by the present as the present is shaped by the past. But potent and pervasive as a prairie dust storm, memory and dream seep and mingle through cracks, settling on furniture, into upholstery. The attic and the living room encroach onto each other, deep into their invisible places.

I sneeze and dust specks pummel across the flashlight beam. Will we all be dust in the end—a jumble of faces and lives compressed and powdered into a few lines of statistics—fading photographs in family albums, the faces no longer familiar, the clothing quaint, the anecdotes lost?

I use the flashlight to break off a web and lift the lid of the trunk. A strong whiff of mothballs assaults us. The odour of preservation. Inside, there are bits of lace and fur, a 1920s nightgown, a shoe box, red and white striped socks. She sifts through the contents, one by one.

'That's strange,' she says several times.

'What are you looking for?' I ask.

'Not here. It isn't here.'

She turns to face me in the darkness. 'That's strange,' she says and leaves her questions enclosed in silence.

I pry open the folds of a cardboard box. The thick dust slides off like chocolate icing sugar—antique pollen. Grandfather's boat building tools are wrapped in heavy cloth. These are all he brought when he came to this country wearing a western suit, western shoes, a round black hat. Here is the plane with a wooden handle which he worked by pulling it towards him. A fundamental difference in workmanship—to pull rather than push. Chisels, hammer, a mallet, a thin pointed saw, the handle extending from the blade like that of a kitchen knife.

'What will you do with these?' I ask.

'The junk in the attic', my cousin's letter said, 'should be burned. When I come there this summer, I'll have a big bonfire. It's a fire trap. I've taken the only things that are worth keeping.'

Beneath the box of tools is a pile of *Life* magazines dated the 1950s. A subscription maintained while the two daughters were home. Beside the pile is another box containing shoe boxes, a metal box with a disintegrating elastic band, several chocolate boxes. Inside the metal box are pictures, duplicates of some I have seen in our family albums. Obasan's wedding photo—her mid-calf dress hanging straight down from her shoulders, her smile glued on. In the next picture, Uncle is a child wearing a sailor suit.

The shoe box is full of documents.

Royal Canadian Mounted Police, Vancouver, BC, March 4, 1942. A folded mimeographed paper authorizes Uncle as the holder of a numbered Registration Card to leave a Registered Area by truck for Vernon where he is required to report to the local Registrar of Enemy Aliens, not later than the following day. It is signed by the RCMP superintendant.

Uncle's face, young and unsmiling looks up at me from the bottom right hand corner of a wallet size ID card. 'The bearer whose photograph and specimen of signature appear hereon, has been duly registered in compliance with the provisions of Order-in-Council PC 117.' A purple stamp underneath states 'Canadian Born'. His thumb print appears on the back with marks of identification specified—scar on back of right hand.

There is a letter from the Department of the Secretary of State. Office of the Custodian. Japanese Evacuation Section. 506 Royal Bank Bldg. Hastings and Granville. Vancouver, BC.

Dear Sir.

Dear Uncle. With whom were you corresponding and for what did you hope? That the enmity would cease? That you could return to your boats? I have grown tired, Uncle, of seeking the face of the enemy hiding in the thick forests of the past. You were not the enemy. The police who came to your door were not the enemy. The men who rioted against you were not the enemy. The Vancouver alderman who said 'Keep BC

White' was not the enemy. The men who drafted the Order-in-Council were not the enemy. He does not wear a uniform or sit at a long meeting table. The man who read your timid letter, read your polite request, skimmed over your impossible plea, was not your enemy. He had an urgent report to complete. His wife was ill. The phone rang all the time. The senior staff was meeting in two hours. The secretary was spending too much time over coffee breaks. There were a billion problems to attend to. Injustice was the only constant in a world of flux. There were moments when expedience demanded decisions which would later be judged unjust. Uncle, he did not always know what he was doing. You too did not have an all compassionate imagination. He was just doing his job. I am just doing my work, Uncle. We are all just doing our jobs.

My dear dead Uncle. Am I come to unearth our bitterness that our buried love too may revive?

'Obasan, what shall we do with these?'

She has been waiting at the top of the stairs, holding the railing with both hands. I close the shoe box and replace the four interlocking flaps of the cardboard box. With one hand I shine the flashlight and with the other, guide her as I precede her slowly down the stairs. Near the bottom she stumbles and I hold her small body upright.

'Thank you, thank you,' she says. This is the first time my arms have held her. We walk slowly through the living room and back to the kitchen. Her lips are trembling as she sits on the wooden stool.

Outside, the sky of the prairie spring is painfully blue. The trees are shooting out their leaves in the fierce wind, the new branches elastic as whips. The sharp-edged clarity is insistent as trumpets.

But inside, the rooms are muted. Our inner trees, our veins, are involuted, cocooned, webbed. The blood cells in the trunks of our bodies, like tiny specks of light, move in a sluggish river. It is more a potential than an actual river—an electric liquid—the current flowing in and between us, between our generations. Not circular, as in a whirlpool, or climactic and tidal as in fountains or spray—but brooding. Bubbling. You expect to hear barely audible pip-pip electronic tones, a pre-concert tuning up behind the curtains in the darkness. Towards the ends of our branches and fingertips, tiny human-shaped flames or leaves break off and leap towards the shadows. My arms are suffused with a suppressed urge to hold.

At the edges of our flesh is a hint of a spiritual osmosis, an eagerness within matter, waiting to brighten our dormant neurons, to entrust our stagnant cells with movement and dance.

Obasan drinks her tea and makes a shallow scratching sound in her throat. She shuffles to the door and squats beside the boot tray. With a putty knife, she begins to scrape off the thick clay like mud that sticks to my boots.

1978, 1984

# Where There's a Wall

Where there's a wall
there's a way through a
gate or door. There's even
a ladder perhaps and a
sentinel who sometimes sleeps.
There are secret passwords you
can overhear. There are methods
of torture for extracting clues
to maps of underground passages.
There are zeppelins, helicopters,                    10
rockets, bombs, battering rams,
armies with trumpets whose
all at once blast shatters
the foundations.

Where there's a wall there are
words to whisper by loose bricks,
wailing prayers to utter, birds
to carry messages taped to their feet.
There are letters to be written—
poems even.                                          20

Faint as in a dream
is the voice that calls
from the belly
of the wall.

1985

# Road Building by Pick Axe

*The Highway*

Driving down the
highway from Revelstoke—
the road built by
forced labour—all the
Nisei[1] having no

---

1 Pronounced 'knee-say', a name for second-generation Japanese-Canadians; 'Issei' means the first-generation (i.e., those who immigrated, rather than being born in Canada). 'Sensei' (later in the poem) is an honorific title.

choice etcetera etcetera
and mentioning this in
passing to this Englishman
who says when he
came to Canada from
England he wanted to
go to Vancouver too but
the quota for professors
was full so he was
forced to go to Toronto.

*Found Poem*

Uazusu Shoji
who was twice wounded
while fighting with the Princess Pats
in World War I
had purchased nineteen acres of land
under the Soldiers Settlement Act
and established a chicken farm.

His nineteen acres
a two-storied house
four chicken houses
and electric incubator
and 2,500 fowl
were sold for $1,492.59.

After certain deductions
for taxes and sundries were made
Mr Shoji received a cheque
for $39.32.

*The Day After*

The day after Sato-sensei
received the Order of Canada
he told some of us Nisei
the honour he received
was our honour, our glory
our achievement.

And one Nisei remembered
the time Sensei went to Japan
met the emperor
and was given a rice cake                                    10
how Sensei brought it back to Vancouver
took the cake to a baker and
had it crushed into powder
so that each pupil might
receive a tiny bit.

And someone suggested
he take the Order of Canada medal
and grind it to bits
to share with us.


## Memento

Trapped in
a clear plastic
hockey-puck
paperweight
is a blank ink sketch
of a jaunty outhouse.

Slocan Reunion—
August 31, 1974
Toronto.


## May 3, 1981

I'm watching the flapping
green ferry flag on the
way to Victoria—
the white dogwood flower
centred by a yellow dot.

A small yellow dot
in a BC ferry boat—

In the Vancouver Daily Province
a headline today reads
'Western Canada Hatred                                       10
Due to Racism.'

Ah my British
British Columbia, my
first brief home.


*For Issei in Nursing Homes*

Beneath the waiting
in the garden in
late autumn—how
the fruit falls without
a thud, the white
hoary hair falls and
falls and strangers
tread the grey walk ways
of the concrete garden.

How without vegetation how                    10
without touch the old ones
lie in their slow days.

With pick axe then
or dynamite

that in their last breaths, a
green leaf, yes, and
grandchild bringing gifts.

1985


# Minerals from Stone

For many years
androgynous with truth
I molded fact and fantasy
and where they met
made the crossroads home.

Here the house built
by lunatic limbs
fashioning what is not
into what might be—

a palace cave            10
for savage saints with
hunting knife still moist.

Bring me no longer
your spoils.
I have a house in the
shadows now and have
learned to eat minerals
straight from stone.

1985

---

# Carol Shields
## 1935–2003

---

Born in Oak Park, Illinois, outside Chicago, Carol Warner earned a BA at Hanover College, Indiana. In 1956, while on a student exchange visit to Scotland, she met Donald Shields, an engineering student from Canada; they married shortly after their return to North America, settling initially in Ottawa. Although Shields devoted much of the early years of her marriage to raising children (one son and four daughters), she found a way to begin her career as a writer at the same time by setting aside one hour each morning for her work. She initially thought of herself as a poet, publishing two collections: *Others* in 1972, and *Intersect* in 1974. In 1975, after taking an M.A. in English at the University of Ottawa (a revision of her master's thesis was published in 1976 as *Susanna Moodie: Voice and Vision*), she began to teach literature and writing at the University of Ottawa and then at the University of British Columbia. Deciding her creative instincts were better served by fiction, Shields produced in quick succession four novels: *Small Ceremonies* (1976), *The Box Garden* (1977), *Happenstance* (1980), and *A Fairly Conventional Woman* (1982). Responding to her sense that, for all their gains, women were still not sufficiently visible in our culture, she initiated, in these books, her lifelong project of investigating everyday women's lives and friendships.

In the 1980s, after Shields and her husband moved to Winnipeg to take up teaching positions at the University of Manitoba, her fiction began to change. Her 1985 collection of short stories, *Various Miracles* (1985)—small, intense explorations of individual perspectives—shows her widening her range. Describing her early work as 'quite traditional', Shields showed how 'elastic' and 'commodious' the novel's structure could be in *Swann: A Mystery* (1987). There, four voices come together in their attempts to hear a fifth one, the silent voice of Mary Swann, a murdered Canadian poet. The first four chapters of the novel, spoken by a literary critic, a biographer, a librarian, and a newspaper editor—each trying to understand Swann's life and work—are parodies of four different kinds of scholarship. The last chapter, a symposium in the form of a screenplay, not only identifies all the previous characters as fictions but also calls attention to the weakness in traditional narrative: its inability to explain life fully through linear structure and a unifying point of view.

While this novel brought Shields critical recognition, the short story as a form remained important to her, as can be seen in her second collection, *The Orange Fish* (1989). In it, she portrays characters who—like the widow trying to find her way in life in 'Hazel' (reprinted below)—seem outwardly unremarkable but reveal surprising depths. After her next novel, *The Republic of Love* (1992)—a succinct examination of two individuals both in need of love and in need of an understanding of what love is—Shields returned to poetry with *Coming to Canada* (1992). Published the year after she became a Canadian citizen, it contains new poems as well as selections from her two earlier collections.

In 1991, Shields and Canadian playwright Blanche Howard collaborated on an innovative work of fiction, *A Celibate Season*. Reinventing the epistolary novel by telling the story of a husband and wife who, during a work-necessitated separation, decide to communicate only by letters, the authors wrote back and forth to one another in the role of one of the novel's two I-narrators. In addition to being a prolific writer of fiction, Shields also wrote several dramas. *Thirteen Hands* (originally published in 1993), the best known of her plays, captures the relationship between life and the game of bridge. It was collected, with other of her dramas, in *Thirteen Hands and Other Plays* (2002).

Shields's next novel, *The Stone Diaries* (1993), gained international praise, winning a Governor General's Award in Canada and a Pulitzer Prize in the United States. Never a stereotype, its protagonist Daisy Goodwill fulfils the traditional roles of women—daughter, lover, wife, mother, and grandmother—in an arc of experience marked by her constant physical and spiritual need to discover an inherent self. While *The Stone Diaries* continues the examination begun in *Swann* of multiple voices and viewpoints, its perspectives are filtered through Daisy's consciousness. The inclusion of a group of photographs that are ostensibly pictures of its characters (from which Daisy is missing) gives additional verisimilitude to the deeply human portraiture of the book.

Published the year after Shields became chancellor of the University of Winnipeg, *Larry's Party* (1997) also garnered laurels (and in 2001, it was adapted as a musical for the Canadian Stage Company). Another extended examination of the forces shaping an individual life, this novel complements *The Stone Diaries*, with its focus is on a male protagonist, Larry Weller. Not attempting to plumb a man's experience the way *The Stone Diaries* does a woman's, it examines Larry's longing for order in a world that seems to be nothing but a series of accidents—a longing reflected in his preoccupation with mazes. Just as mazes 'make perfect sense when you look down on them from above', Larry discovers that lives can best be understood with perspective and distance.

After learning, in 1998, that she had cancer, Shields and her husband retired from teaching and moved to Victoria, where she continued writing. Her third book of stories, *Dressing Up for the Carnival*, came out in 2000; *Jane Austen: A Life* appeared the following year as a volume in the Penguin Lives series. Shields felt a deep affinity with Austen, perhaps because both can be described as miniaturists—that is, writers of domestic fiction who probe small moments of human interaction to produce revelations. During this period, she edited, with Marjorie Anderson, *Dropped Threads* (2001) and *Dropped Threads 2* (2003), two volumes of stories and essays by women dealing with topics so emotionally charged that they had previously kept them hidden. Her final novel, *Unless* (2002), published when Shields's death was imminent, is like *The Stone Diaries* and *Larry's Party*, an extended examination of the psychology of a particular character and the way social, geographical, and historical contexts influence the formation of a personality. It tells the story of a woman in her forties—a fiction writer (who 'wanted to write about the overheard and the glimpsed') alienated from one of her daughters—who reflects on her own life as if it were constructed as a novel.

The year after her death in 2003, all of Shields's short fiction (along with a fragment of an unfinished novel) was drawn together in a single volume, *The Collected Stories of Carol Shields*. In 2007, *Random Illuminations: Conversations with Carol Shields* was published by the arts journalist, Eleanor Wachtel. That same year, *A Memoir of Friendship: The Letters Between Carol Shields & Blanche Howard* appeared.

Shields's writing received an unusually large number of nominations and prizes: in addition to the honours she received for *The Stone Diaries*, *Larry's Party* garnered the US National Book Critics Circle Award, France's Prix de Livre, and the Orange Prize for Fiction; her *Jane Austen: A Life* won the 2002 Charles Taylor Prize for Literary Non-fiction. Her books have been nominated for the Giller Prize, the Booker Prize, and the Commonwealth Writers Prize. She received honorary doctorates from universities in Canada and the United States, was a fellow of the Royal Society of Canada and a member of the Order of Manitoba, and, in 2002, was elevated to the rank of Companion of the Order of Canada. In 2000, the government of France appointed her as a Chevalier de l'Ordre des Arts et des Lettres.

## Hazel

After a man has mistreated a woman he feels a need to do something nice which she must accept.

In line with this way of thinking, Hazel has accepted from her husband, Brian, sprays of flowers, trips to Hawaii, extravagant compliments on her rather ordinary cooking, bracelets of dull-coloured silver and copper, a dressing gown in green tartan wool, a second dressing gown with maribou trim around the hem and sleeves, dinners in expensive revolving restaurants and, once, a tender kiss, tenderly delivered, on the instep of her right foot.

But there will be no more such compensatory gifts, for Brian died last December of heart failure.

*The* heart failure, as Hazel, even after all these years, continues to think of it. In her family, the family of her girlhood that is, a time of gulped confusion in a place called Porcupine Falls, all familiar diseases were preceded by the horrific article: *the* measles, *the* polio, *the* rheumatism, *the* cancer, and—to come down to her husband Brian and his final thrashing with life—*the* heart failure.

He was only fifty-five. He combed his uncoloured hair smooth and wore clothes made of gabardinelike materials, a silky exterior covering a complex core. It took him ten days to die after the initial attack, and during the time he lay there, all his minor wounds healed. He was a careless man who bumped into things, shrubbery, table legs, lighted cigarettes, simple curbstones. Even the making of love seemed to him a labour and a recovery, attended by scratches, bites, effort, exhaustion and, once or twice, a mild but humiliating infection. Nevertheless, women found him attractive. He had an unhurried, good-humoured persistence about him and could be kind when he chose to be.

The night he died Hazel came home from the hospital and sat propped up in bed till four in the morning, reading a trashy, fast-moving New York novel about wives who lived in spacious duplexes overlooking Central Park, too alienated to carry on properly with their lives. They made salads with rare kinds of lettuce and sent their apparel to the dry cleaners, but they were bitter and helpless. Frequently they used the expression 'fucked up' to describe their malaise. Their mothers or their fathers had fucked them up, or jealous sisters or bad-hearted nuns, but mainly they had been fucked up by men who no longer cared about them. These women were immobilized by the lack of love and kept alive only by a reflexive bounce between new ways of arranging salad greens and fantasies of suicide. Hazel wondered as she read how long it took for the remembered past to sink from view. A few miserable tears crept into her eyes, her first tears since Brian's initial attack, that shrill telephone call, that unearthly hour. Impetuously she wrote on the book's flyleaf the melodramatic words 'I am alone and suffering unbearably.' Not her best handwriting, not her usual floating morning-glory tendrils. Her fingers cramped at this hour. The cheap ball-point pen held back its ink, and the result was a barely legible scrawl that she nevertheless underlined twice.

By mid-January she had taken a job demonstrating kitchenware in department stores. The ad in the newspaper promised on-the-job training, opportunities for advancement, and contact with the public. Hazel submitted to a short, vague, surprisingly painless interview, and was rewarded the following morning by a telephone call telling her she was to start immediately. She suspected she was the sole applicant, but nevertheless went numb with shock. Shock and also pleasure. She hugged the elbows of her dressing gown and smoothed the sleeves flat. She was fifty years old and without skills, a woman who had managed to avoid most of the arguments and issues of the world. Asked a direct question, her voice wavered. She understood nothing of the national debt or the situation in Nicaragua, nothing. At ten-thirty most mornings she was still in her dressing gown and had the sense to know this was shameful. She possessed a softened, tired body and rubbed-looking eyes. Her posture was only moderately good. She often touched her mouth with the back of her hand. Yet someone, some person with a downtown commercial address and an official letterhead and a firm telephone manner had seen fit to offer her a job.

Only Hazel, however, thought the job a good idea.

Brian's mother, a woman in her eighties living in a suburban retirement centre called Silver Oaks, said, 'Really, there is no need, Hazel. There's plenty of money if you live reasonably. You have your condo paid for, your car, a good fur coat that'll last for years. Then there's the insurance and Brian's pension, and when you're sixty-five—now don't laugh, sixty-five will come, it's not that far off—you'll have your social security. You have a first-rate lawyer to look after your investments. There's no need.'

Hazel's closest friend, Maxine Forestadt, a woman of her own age, a demon bridge player, a divorcée, a woman with a pinkish powdery face loosened by too many evenings of soft drinks and potato chips and too much cigarette smoke flowing up toward her eyes, said, 'Look. You're not the type, Hazel. Period. I know the type and you're not it. Believe me. All right, so you feel this urge to assert yourself, to try to prove something. I know, I went through it myself, wanting to show the world I wasn't just this dipsy pushover and hanger-oner. But this isn't for you, Haze, this eight-to-five purgatory, standing on your feet, and especially *your* feet, your arches act up just shopping. I know what you're trying to do, but in the long run, what's the point?'

Hazel's older daughter, Marilyn, a pathologist, and possibly a lesbian, living in a women's co-op in the east end of the city, phoned and, drawing on the sort of recollection that Hazel already had sutured, said, 'Dad would not have approved. I know it, you know it. I mean, Christ, flogging pots and pans, it's so public. People crowding around. Idle curiosity and greed, a free show, just hanging in for a teaspoon of bloody quiche lorraine or whatever's going. Freebies. People off the street, bums, anybody. Christ. Another thing, you'll have to get a whole new wardrobe for a job like that. Eye shadow so thick it's like someone's given you a punch. Just ask yourself what Dad would have said. I know what he would have said, he would have said thumbs down, nix on it.'

Hazel's other daughter, Rosie, living in British Columbia, married to a journalist, wrote: 'Dear Mom, I absolutely respect what you're doing and admire your courage. But Robin and I can't help wondering if you've given this decision enough thought. You remember how after the funeral, back at your place with Grandma and Auntie Maxine and Marilyn, we had that long talk about the need to lie fallow for a bit and not rush headlong into things and making major decisions, just letting the grieving process take its natural course. Now here it is, a mere six weeks later, and you've got yourself involved with these cookware people. I just hope you haven't signed anything. Robin says he never heard of Kitchen Kult and it certainly isn't listed on the boards. We're just anxious about you, that's all. And this business of working on commission is exploitative to say the least. Ask Marilyn. You've still got your shorthand and typing and, with a refresher course, you probably could find something, maybe Office Overload would give you a sense of your own independence and some spending money besides. We just don't want to see you hurt, that's all.'

At first, Hazel's working day went more or less like this: at seven-thirty her alarm went off; the first five minutes were the worst; such a steamroller of sorrow passed over her that she was left as flat and lifeless as the queen-size mattress that supported her. Her squashed limbs felt emptied of blood, her breath came out thin and cool and quiet as ether. What was she to do? How was she to live her life? She mouthed these questions to the silky blanket binding, rubbing her lips frantically back and forth across the stitching. Then she got up, showered, did her hair, made coffee and toast, took a vitamin pill, brushed her teeth, made up her face (going easy on the eye shadow), and put on her coat. By eight-thirty she was in her car and checking her city map.

Reading maps, the tiny print, the confusion, caused her headaches. And she had trouble with orientation, turning the map first this way, then that, never willing to believe that north must lie at the top. North's natural place should be toward the bottom, past the Armoury and stockyards where a large cold lake bathed the city edges. Once on a car trip to the Indian River country early in their married life, Brian had joked about her lack of map sense. He spoke happily of this failing, proudly, giving her arm a squeeze, and then had thumped the cushioned steering wheel. Hazel, thinking about the plushy thump, wished she hadn't. To recall something once was to remember it forever; this was something she had only recently discovered, and she felt that the discovery might be turned to use.

The Kitchen Kult demonstrations took her on a revolving cycle of twelve stores, some of them in corners of the city where she'd seldom ventured. The Italian district. The Portuguese area. Chinatown. A young Kitchen Kult salesman named Peter Lemmon broke her in, *familiarizing* her as he put it with the Kitchen Kult product. He taught her the spiel, the patter, the importance of keeping eye contact with customers at all times, how to draw on the mood and size of the crowd and play, if possible, to its ethnic character, how to make Kitchen Kult products seem like large beautiful toys, easily mastered and guaranteed to win the love and admiration of friends and family.

'That's what people out there really want,' Peter Lemmon told Hazel, who was surprised to hear this view put forward so undisguisedly. 'Lots of love and truckloads of admiration. Keep that in mind. People can't get enough.'

He had an aggressive pointed chin and ferocious red sideburns, and when he talked he held his lips together so that the words came out with a soft zitherlike slur. Hazel noticed his teeth were discoloured and badly crowded, and she guessed that this accounted for his guarded way of talking. Either that or a nervous disposition. Early on, to put him at his ease, she told him of her small-town upbringing in Porcupine Falls, how her elderly parents had never quite recovered from the surprise of having a child. How at eighteen she came to Toronto to study stenography. That she was now a widow with two daughters, one of whom she suspected of being unhappily married and one who was undergoing a gender crisis. She told Peter Lemmon that this was her first real job, that at the age of fifty she was out working for the first time. She talked too much, babbled in fact—why? She didn't know. Later she was sorry.

In return he confided, opening his mouth a little wider, that he was planning to have extensive dental work in the future if he could scrape the money together. More than nine thousand dollars had been quoted. A quality job cost quality cash, that was the long and short of it, so why not take the plunge. He hoped to go right to the top with Kitchen Kult. Not just sales, but the real top, and that meant management. It was a company, he told her, with a forward-looking sales policy and sound product.

It disconcerted Hazel at first to hear Peter Lemmon speak of the Kitchen Kult product without its grammatical article, and she was jolted into the remembrance of how she had had to learn to suppress the article that attached to bodily ailments. When demonstrating product, Peter counselled, keep it well in view, repeating product's name frequently and withholding product's retail price until the actual demo and tasting has been concluded.

After two weeks Hazel was on her own, although Peter Lemmon continued to meet her at the appointed 'sales venue' each morning, bringing with him in a company van the equipment to be demonstrated and helping her 'set up' for the day. She slipped into her white smock, the same one every day, a smooth permapress blend with grommets down the front and Kitchen Kult in red script across the pocket, and stowed her pumps in a plastic bag, putting on the white crepe-soled shoes Peter Lemmon had recommended. 'Your feet, Hazel, are your capital.' He also produced, of his own volition, a tall collapsible stool on which she could perch in such a way that she appeared from across the counter to be standing unsupported.

She started each morning with a demonstration of the Jiffy-Sure-Slicer, Kitchen Kult's top seller, accounting for some sixty per cent of total sales. For an hour or more, talking to herself, or rather to the empty air, she shaved hillocks of carrots, beets, parsnips and rutabagas into baroque curls or else she transformed them into little star-shaped discs or elegant matchsticks. The use of cheap root vegetables kept the demo costs down, Peter Lemmon said, and presented a less threatening challenge to the average shopper, Mrs Peas and Carrots, Mrs Corn Niblets.

As Hazel warmed up, one or two shoppers drifted toward her, keeping her company—she learned she could count on these one or two who were elderly women for the most part, puffy of face and bulgy of eye. Widows, Hazel decided. The draggy-hemmed coats and beige tote bags gave them away. Like herself, though perhaps a few years older, these women had taken their toast and coffee early and had been driven out into the cold in search of diversion. 'Just set the dial, ladies and gentlemen,' Hazel told the discomfited two or three voyeurs, 'and press gently on the Jiffy lever. Never requires sharpening, never rusts.'

By mid-morning she generally had fifteen people gathered about her, by noon as many as forty. No one interrupted her, and why should they? She was free entertainment. They listened, they exchanged looks, they paid attention, they formed a miniature, temporary colony of good will and consumer seriousness waiting to be instructed, initiated into Hazel's rituals and promises.

At the beginning of her third week, going solo for the first time, she looked up to see Maxine in her long beaver coat, gawking. 'Now this is just what you need, madam,' Hazel sang out, not missing a beat, an uncontrollable smile on her face. 'In no time you'll be making more nutritious, appealing salads for your family and friends and for those bridge club get-togethers.'

Maxine had been offended. She complained afterward to Hazel that she found it embarrassing being picked out in a crowd like that. It was insulting, especially to mention the bridge club as if she did nothing all day long but shuffle cards. 'It's a bit thick, Hazel, especially when you used to enjoy a good rubber yourself. And you know I only play cards as a form of social relaxation. You used to enjoy it, and don't try to tell me otherwise because I won't buy it. We miss you, we really do. I know perfectly well it's not easy for you facing Francine. She was always a bit of a you-know-what, and Brian was, God knows, susceptible, though I have to say you've put a dignified face on the whole thing. I don't think I could have done it, I don't have your knack for looking the other way, never have had, which is why I'm where I'm at, I suppose. But who are you really cheating, dropping out of the bridge club like this? I think, just between the two of us, that Francine's a bit hurt, she thinks you hold her responsible for Brian's attack, even though we all know that when our time's up, it's up. And besides, it takes two.'

In the afternoon, after a quick pick-up lunch (leftover grated raw vegetables usually or a hardboiled egg), Hazel demonstrated Kitchen Kult's all-purpose non-stick fry pan. The same crowds that admired her julienne carrots seemed ready to be mesmerized by the absolute roundness of her crepes and omelets, their uniform gold edges and the ease with which they came pulling away at a touch of her spatula. During the early months, January, February, Hazel learned just how easily people could be hypnotized, how easily, in fact, they could be put to sleep. Their mouths sagged. They grew dull-eyed and immobile. Their hands went hard into their pockets. They hugged their purses tight.

Then one afternoon a small fortuitous accident occurred: a crepe, zealously flipped, landed on the floor. Because of the accident, Hazel discovered how a rupture in routine could be turned to her advantage. 'Whoops-a-daisy,' she said that first day, stooping to recover the crepe. People laughed out loud. It was as though Hazel's mild exclamation had a forgotten period fragrance to it. 'I guess I don't know my own strength,' she said, shaking her curls and earning a second ripple of laughter.

After that she began, at least once or twice a day, to misdirect a crepe. Or over-cook an omelet. Or bring herself to a state of comic tears over her plate of chopped onions. 'Not my day,' she would croon. Or 'good grief' or 'sacred ratttlesnakes' or a shrugging, cheerful, 'who ever promised perfection on the first try'. Some of the phrases that came out of her mouth reminded her of the way people talked in Porcupine Falls back in a time she could not possibly have remembered. Gentle, unalarming expletives calling up wells of good nature and neighbourliness. She wouldn't have guessed she had this quality of rubbery humour inside her.

After a while she felt she could get away with anything as long as she kept up her line of chatter. That was the secret, she saw—never to stop talking. That was why these crowds gave her their attention: she could perform miracles (with occasional calculated human lapses) and keep right on talking at the same time. Words, a river of words. She had never before talked at such length, as though she were driving a wedge of air ahead of her. It was easy, easy. She dealt out repetitions, little punchy pushes of emphasis, and an ever growing inventory of affectionate declarations directed toward her vegetable friends. 'What a devil!' she said, holding aloft a head of bulky cauliflower. 'You darling radish, you!' She felt foolish at times, but often exuberant, like a semi-retired, slightly eccentric actress. And she felt, oddly, that she was exactly as strong and clever as she need be.

But the work was exhausting. She admitted it. Every day the crowds had to be wooed afresh. By five-thirty she was too tired to do anything more than drive home, make a sandwich, read the paper, rinse out her Kitchen Kult smock and hang it over the shower rail, then get into bed with a thick paperback. Propped up in bed reading, her book like a wimple at her chin, she seemed to have flames on her feet and on the tips of her fingers, as though she'd burned her way through a long blur of a day and now would burn the night behind her too. January, February, the first three weeks of March. So this was what work was: a two-way bargain people made with the world, a way to reduce time to rubble.

The books she read worked braids of panic into her consciousness. She'd drifted toward historical fiction, away from Central Park and into the Regency courts of England. But were the queens and courtesans any happier than the frustrated New York wives? Were they less lonely, less adrift? So far she had found no evidence of it. They wanted the same things more or less: abiding affection, attention paid to their moods and passing thoughts, their backs rubbed and, now and then, the tender grate-ful application of hands and lips. She remembered Brian's back turned toward her in sleep, well covered with flesh in his middle years. He had never been one for pyjamas, and she had often been moved to reach out and stroke the smooth mound of flesh. She had not found his extra weight disagreeable, far from it.

In Brian's place there remained now only the rectangular softness of his allergy-free pillow. Its smooth casing, faintly puckered at the corners, had the feel of myste-rious absence.

'But why does it always have to be one of my *friends!*' she had cried out at him once at the end of a long quarrel. 'Don't you see how humiliating it is for me?'

He had seemed genuinely taken aback, and she saw in a flash it was only laziness on his part, not express cruelty. She recalled his solemn promises, his wet eyes, new beginnings. She fondly recalled, too, the resonant pulmonary sounds of his night breathing, the steep climb to the top of each inhalation and the tottery stillness before the descent. How he used to lull her to sleep with this nightly music! Compensations. But she had not asked for enough, hadn't known what to ask for, what was owed her.

It was because of the books she read, their dense complications and sharp surprises, that she had applied for a job in the first place. She had a sense of her own life turning over page by page, first a girl, then a young woman, then married with two young daughters, then a member of a bridge club and a quilting club, and now, too soon for symmetry, a widow. All of it fell into small childish paragraphs, the print over-large and blocky like a school reader. She had tried to imagine various new endings or turnings for herself—she might take a trip around the world or sign up for a course in ceramics—but could think of nothing big enough to fill the vacant time left to her—except perhaps an actual job. This was what other people did, tucking in around the edges those little routines—laundry, meals, errands—that had made up her whole existence.

'You're wearing yourself out,' Brian's mother said when Hazel arrived for an Easter Sunday visit, bringing with her a double-layered box of chocolate almond bark and a bouquet of tulips. 'Tearing all over town every day, on your feet, no proper lunch arrangements. You'd think they'd give you a good hour off and maybe a lunch voucher, give you a chance to catch your breath. It's hard on the back, standing. I always feel my tension in my back. These are delicious, Hazel, not that I'll eat half of them, not with my appetite, but it'll be something to pass round to the other ladies. Everyone shares here, that's one thing. And the flowers, tulips! One or the other would have more than sufficed, Hazel, you've been extravagant. I suppose now that you're actually earning, it makes a difference. You feel differently, I suppose, when it's your own money. Brian's father always saw that I had everything I needed, wanted for nothing, but I wouldn't have minded a little money of my own, though I never said so, not in so many words.'

One morning Peter Lemmon surprised Hazel, and frightened her too, by saying, 'Mr Cortland wants to see you. The big boss himself. Tomorrow at ten-thirty. Downtown office. Headquarters. I'll cover the venue for you.'

Mr Cortland was the age of Hazel's son-in-law, Robin. She couldn't have said why, but she had expected someone theatrical and rude, not this handsome curly-haired man unwinding himself from behind a desk that was not really a desk but a gate-legged table, shaking her hand respectfully and leading her toward a soft brown easy chair. There was genuine solemnity to his jutting chin and a thick brush of hair across his quizzing brow. He offered her a cup of coffee. 'Or perhaps you would prefer tea,' he said, very politely, with a shock of inspiration.

She looked up from her shoes, her good polished pumps, not her nurse shoes, and saw a pink conch shell on Mr Cortland's desk. It occurred to her it must be one of the things that made him happy. Other people were made happy by music or flowers or bowls of ice cream—enchanted, familiar things. Some people collected china, and when they found a long-sought piece, *that* made them happy. What made *her* happy was the obliteration of time, burning it away so cleanly she hardly noticed it. Not that she said so to Mr Cortland. She said, in fact, very little, though some dragging filament of intuition urged her to accept tea rather than coffee, to forgo milk, to shake her head sadly over the proffered sugar.

'We are more delighted than I can say with your sales performance,' Mr Cortland said. 'We are a small but growing firm and, as you know'—Hazel did not know, how could she?—'we are a family concern. My maternal grandfather studied commerce at McGill and started this business as a kind of hobby. Our aim, the family's aim, is a reliable product, but not a hard sell. I can't stress this enough to our sales people. We are anxious to avoid a crude hectoring approach or tactics that are in any way manipulative, and we are in the process of developing a quality sales force that matches the quality of our product line. This may surprise you, but it is difficult to find people like yourself who possess, if I may say so, your gentleness of manner. People like yourself transmit a sense of trust to the consumer. We've heard very fine things about you, and we have decided, Hazel—I do hope I may call you Hazel—to put you on regular salary, in addition of course to an adjusted commission. And I would like also to present you with this small brooch, a glazed ceramic K for Kitchen Kult, which we give each quarter to our top sales person.'

'Do you realize what this means?' Peter Lemmon asked later that afternoon over a celebratory drink at Mr Duck's Happy Hour. 'Salary means you're on the team, you're a Kitchen Kult player. Salary equals professional, Hazel. You've arrived, and I don't think you even realize it.'

Hazel thought she saw flickering across Peter's guarded, eager face, like a blade of sunlight through a thick curtain, the suggestion that some privilege had been carelessly allocated. She pinned the brooch on the lapel of her good spring coat with an air of bafflement. Beyond the simple smoothness of her pay cheque, she perceived dark squadrons of planners and decision makers who had brought this teasing irony forward. She was being rewarded—a bewildering turn of events—for her timidity, her self-effacement, for what Maxine called her knack for looking the other way. She was a shy, ineffectual, untrained, neutral looking woman, and for this she was being kicked upstairs, or at least this was how Peter translated her move from commission to salary. He scratched his neck, took a long drink of his beer, and said it a third time, with a touch of belligerence it seemed to Hazel, 'a kick upstairs'. He insisted on paying for the drinks, even though Hazel pressed a ten-dollar bill into his hand. He shook it off.

'This place is bargain city,' he assured her, opening the orange cave of his mouth, then closing it quickly. He came here often after work, he said, taking advantage of the two-for-one happy hour policy. Not that he was tight with his money, just the opposite, but he was setting aside a few dollars a week for his dental work in the summer. The work was mostly cosmetic, caps and spacers, and therefore not covered by Kitchen Kult's insurance scheme. The way he saw it, though, was as an investment in the future. If you were going to go to the top, you had to be able to open your mouth and project. 'Like this brooch, Hazel, it's a way of projecting. Wearing the company logo means you're one of the family and that you don't mind shouting it out.'

That night, when she whitened her shoes, she felt a sort of love for them. And she loved, too, suddenly, her other small tasks, rinsing out her smock, setting her alarm, settling into bed with her book, resting her head against Brian's little fiber-filled pillow with its stitched remnant of erotic privilege and reading herself out of her own life, leaving behind her cut-out shape, so bulky, rounded and unimaginably mute, a woman who swallowed her tongue, got it jammed down her throat and couldn't make a sound.

Marilyn gave a shout of derision on seeing the company brooch pinned to her mother's raincoat. 'The old butter-up trick. A stroke here, a stroke there, just enough to keep you going and keep you grateful. But at least they had the decency to get you off straight commission, for that I have to give them some credit.'

'Dear Mother,' Rosie wrote from British Columbia. 'Many thanks for the water-less veg cooker which is surprisingly well made and really very attractive too, and Robin feels that it fulfills a real need, nutritionally speaking, and also aesthetically.'

'You're looking better,' Maxine said. 'You look as though you've dropped a few pounds, have you? All those grated carrots. But do you ever get a minute to yourself? Eight hours on the job plus commuting. I don't suppose they even pay for your gas, which adds up, and your parking. You want to think about a holiday, people can't be buying pots and pans three hundred and sixty-five days a year. JoAnn and Francine and I are thinking seriously of getting a cottage in Nova Scotia for two weeks. Let me know if you're interested, just tell those Kitchen Kult moguls you owe yourself a little peace and quiet by the seaside, ha! Though you do look more relaxed than the last time I saw you, you looked wrung out, completely.'

In early May Hazel had an accident. She and Peter were setting up one morning, arranging a new demonstration, employing the usual cabbage, beets and onions, but adding a few spears of spring asparagus and a scatter of chopped chives. In the inter-est of economy she'd decided to split the asparagus length-wise, bringing her knife first through the tender tapered head and down the woody stem. Peter was talking away about a new suit he was thinking of buying, asking Hazel's advice—should he go all out for a fine summer wool or compromise on wool and viscose? The knife slipped and entered the web of flesh between Hazel's thumb and forefinger. It sliced further into the flesh than she would have believed possible, so quickly, so lightly that she could only gaze at the spreading blood and grieve about the way it stained and spoiled her perfect circle of cucumber slices.

She required twelve stitches and, at Peter's urging, took the rest of the day off. Mr Cortland's secretary telephoned and told her to take the whole week off if necessary. There were insurance forms to sign, but those could wait. The important thing was—but Hazel couldn't remember what the important thing was; she had been given some painkillers at the hospital and was having difficulty staying awake. She slept the after-noon away, dreaming of green fields and a yellow sun, and would have slept all evening too if she hadn't been wakened around eight o'clock by the faint buzz of her doorbell. She pulled on a dressing gown, a new one in flowered seersucker, and went to the door. It was Peter Lemmon with a clutch of flowers in his hand. 'Why Peter,' she said, and could think of nothing else.

The pain had left her hand and moved to the thin skin of her scalp. Its remoteness as much as its taut bright shine left her confused. She managed to take Peter's light jacket—though he protested, saying he had only come for a moment—and steered him toward a comfortable chair by the window. She listened as the cushions subsided under him, and hurried to put the flowers, already a little limp, into water, and to offer a drink—but what did she have on hand? No beer, no gin, and she knew better than to suggest sherry. Then the thought came: what about a glass of red wine?

He accepted twitchily. He said, 'You don't have to twist my arm.'

'You'll have to uncork it,' Hazel said, gesturing at her bandaged hand. She felt she could see straight into his brain where there was nothing but rags and old plastic. But where had *this* come from, this sly, unpardonable superiority of hers?

He lurched forward, nearly falling. 'Always happy to do the honours.' He seemed afraid of her, of her apartment with its settled furniture, lamps and end tables and china cabinet, regarding these things first with a strict, dry, inquiring look. After a few minutes, he resettled in the soft chair with exaggerated respect.

'To your career,' Peter said, raising his glass, appearing not to notice how the word career entered Hazel's consciousness, waking her up from her haze of painkillers and making her want to laugh.

'To the glory of Kitchen Kult,' she said, suddenly reckless. She watched him, or part of herself watched him, as he twirled the glass and sniffed its contents. She braced herself for what would surely come.

'An excellent vin—' he started to say, but was interrupted by the doorbell.

It was only Marilyn, dropping in as she sometimes did after her self-defense course. 'Already I can break a collarbone,' she told Peter after a flustered introduction, 'and next week we're going to learn how to go for the groin.'

She looked surprisingly pretty with her pensive, wet, youthful eyes and dusty lashes. She accepted some wine and listened intently to the story of Hazel's accident, then said, 'Now listen, Mother, don't sign a release with Kitchen Kult until I have Edna look at it. You remember Edna, she's the lawyer. She's sharp as a knife; she's the one who did our lease for us, and it's airtight. You could develop blood poisoning or an infection, you can't tell at this point. You can't trust these corporate entities when it comes to—'

'Kitchen Kult', Peter said, twirling his glass in a manner Hazel found silly, 'is more like a family.'

'Balls.'

'We've decided', Maxine told Hazel a few weeks later, 'against the cottage in Nova Scotia. It's too risky, and the weather's only so-so according to Francine. And the cost of air fare and then renting a car, we just figured it's too expensive. My rent's going up starting in July and, well, I took a look at my bank balance and said, Maxine kid, you've got to tighten the old belt. As a matter of fact, I thought—now this may surprise you—I'm thinking of looking for a job.'

Hazel set up an interview for Maxine through Personnel, and in a week's time Maxine did her first demonstration. Hazel helped break her in. As a result of a dimly perceived office shuffle, she had been promoted to Assistant Area Manager, freeing

Peter Lemmon for what was described as 'Creative Sales Outreach'. The promotion worried her slightly and she wondered if she were being compensated for the nerve damage in her hand, which was beginning to look more or less permanent. 'Thank God you didn't sign the release,' was all Marilyn said.

'Congrats,' Rosie wired from British Columbia after hearing about the promotion. Hazel had not received a telegram for some years. She was surprised that this austere printed sheet went by the name of telegram. Where was the rough gray paper and the little pasted together words? She wondered who had composed the message, Robin or Rosie, and whose idea it had been to abbreviate the single word and if thrift were involved. *Congrats*. What a hard little hurting pellet to find in the middle of a smooth sheet of paper.

'Gorgeous,' Brian's mother said of Hazel's opal-toned silk suit with its scarf of muted pink pearl and lemon. Her lips moved appreciatively. 'Ah, gorgeous.'

'A helluva improvement over a bloody smock,' Maxine sniffed, looking sideways.

'Most elegant!' said Mr Cortland, who had called Hazel into his office to discuss her future with Kitchen Kult. 'The sort of image we hope and try to project. Elegance and understatement.' He presented her with a small box in which rested, on a square of textured cotton, a pair of enameled earrings with the flying letter K for Kitchen Kult.

'Beautiful,' said Hazel, who never wore earrings. The clip-on sort hurt her, and she had never got around to piercing her ears. 'For my sake,' Brian had begged her when he was twenty-five and she was twenty and about to become his wife, 'don't ever do it. I can't bear to lose a single bit of you.'

Remembering this, the tone of Brian's voice, its rushing, foolish sincerity, Hazel felt her eyes tingle. 'My handbag,' she said, groping blindly.

Mr Cortland misunderstood. He leaped up, touched by his own generosity, a Kleenex in hand. 'We simply wanted to show our appreciation,' he said, or rather sang.

Hazel sniffed, more loudly than she intended, and Mr Cortland pretended not to hear. 'We especially appreciate your filling in for Peter Lemmon during his leave of absence.'

At this Hazel nodded. Poor Peter. She must phone tonight. He was finding the aftermath of his dental surgery painful and prolonged, and she had been looking, every chance she had, for a suitable convalescent card, something not too effusive and not too mocking—Peter took his teeth far too seriously. Perhaps she would just send one of her blurry impressionistic hasty notes, or better yet, a jaunty postcard saying she hoped he'd be back soon.

Mr Cortland fingered the pink conch shell on his desk. He picked it up between his two hands and rocked it gently to and fro, then said, 'Mr Lemmon will not be returning. We have already sent him a letter of termination and, of course, a generous severance settlement. It was decided that his particular kind of personality, though admirable, was not quite in line with the Kitchen Kult approach, and we feel that you yourself have already demonstrated your ability to take over his work and perhaps even extend the scope of it.'

'I don't believe you're doing this,' Marilyn shouted over the phone to Hazel. 'And Peter doesn't believe it either.'

'How do you know what Peter thinks?'

'I saw him this afternoon. I saw him yesterday afternoon. I see him rather often if you want to know the truth.'

Hazel offered the Kitchen Kult earrings to Maxine who snorted and said, 'Come off it, Hazel.'

Rosie in Vancouver sent a short note saying, 'Marilyn phoned about your new position, which is really marvelous, though Robin and I are wondering if you aren't getting in deeper than you really want to at this time.'

Brian's mother said nothing. A series of small strokes had taken her speech away and also her ability to leave her bed. Nothing Hazel brought her aroused her interest, not chocolates, not flowers, not even the fashion magazines she used to love.

Hazel phoned and made an appointment to see Mr Cortland. She invented a pretext, one or two ideas she and Maxine had worked out to tighten up the demonstrations. Mr Cortland listened to her and nodded approvingly. Then she sprang. She had been thinking about Peter Lemmon, she said, how much the sales force missed him, missed his resourcefulness and his attention to details. He had a certain imaginative flair, a peculiar usefulness. Some people had a way of giving energy to others, it was uncanny, it was a rare gift. She didn't mention Peter's dental work; she had some sense.

Mr Cortland sent her a shrewd look, a look she would not have believed he had in his repertoire. 'Well, Hazel,' he said at last, 'in business we deal in hard bargains. Maybe you and I can come to some sort of bargain.'

'Bargain?'

'That insurance form, the release. The one you haven't got round to signing yet. How would it be if you signed it right now on the promise that I find some slot or other for Peter Lemmon by the end of the week? You are quite right about his positive attributes, quite astute of you, really, to point them out. I can't promise anything in sales though. The absolute bottom end of management might be the best we can do.'

Hazel considered. She stared at the conch shell for a full ten seconds. The office lighting coated it with a pink, even light, making it look like a piece of unglazed pottery. She liked the idea of bargains. She felt she understood them. 'I'll sign,' she said. She had her pen in her hand, poised.

On Sunday, a Sunday at the height of the summer in early July, Hazel drives out to Silver Oaks to visit her ailing mother-in-law. All she can do for her now is sit by her side for an hour and hold her hand, and sometimes she wonders what the point is of these visits. Her mother-in-law's face is impassive and silken, and occasionally driblets of spittle, thin and clear as tears, run from the corners of her mouth. It used to be such a strong, organized face with its firm mouth and steady eyes. But now she doesn't recognize anyone, with the possible exception of Hazel.

Some benefit appears to derive from these handholding sessions, or so the nurses tell Hazel. 'She's calmer after your visits,' they say. 'She struggles less.'

Hazel is calm too. She likes sitting here and feeling the hour unwind like thread from a spindle. She wishes it would go on and on. A week ago she had come away from Mr Cortland's office irradiated with the conviction that her life was going to be possible after all. All she had to do was bear in mind the bargains she made. This was an obscene revelation, but Hazel was excited by it. Everything could be made accountable, added up and balanced and fairly, evenly, shared. You only had to pay attention and ask for what was yours by right. You could be clever, dealing in sly acts of surrender, but holding fast at the same time, negotiating and measuring and tying up your life in useful bundles.

But she was wrong. It wasn't true. Her pride had misled her. No one has that kind of power, no one.

She looks around the little hospital room and marvels at the accident of its contents, its bureau and tumbler and toothbrush and folded towel. The open window looks out on to a parking lot filled with rows of cars, all their shining roofs baking in the light. Next year there will be different cars, differently ordered. The shrubs and trees, weighed down with their millions of new leaves, will form a new dark backdrop.

It is an accident that she should be sitting in this room, holding the hand of an old, unblinking, unresisting woman who had once been sternly disapproving of her, thinking her countrified and clumsy. 'Hazel!' she had sometimes whispered in the early days. 'Your slip strap! Your salad fork!' Now she lacks even the power to wet her lips with her tongue; it is Hazel who touches the lips with a damp towel from time to time, or applies a bit of Vaseline to keep them from cracking. But she can feel the old woman's dim pulse, and imagines that it forms a code of acknowledgment or faintly telegraphs certain perplexing final questions—how did all this happen? How did we get here?

Everything is an accident, Hazel would be willing to say if asked. Her whole life is an accident, and by accident she has blundered into the heart of it.

1989

---

# Alistair MacLeod
## b. 1936

Born in North Battleford, Saskatchewan, Alistair MacLeod lived in various small Prairie settlements in Saskatchewan and Alberta until 1946, when his parents moved back to the family farm in Cape Breton. After graduating from high school, MacLeod worked to support himself in a variety of jobs (salesman, editor, logger, truck driver, public-relations man, miner, and teacher). He put himself through Nova Scotia Teachers' College and, during the 1960s, while working as a teacher, he earned degrees at St Francis Xavier University (BA, BEd), the University of New Brunswick (MA), and the University of Notre Dame (PhD, 1968). MacLeod taught at the University of Indiana for three years before taking a position at the University of Windsor in 1969, where he taught courses in nineteenth-century British literature and creative writing until his retirement in 2000. In 2007, he was named an Officer of the Order of Canada.

MacLeod began to publish his short fiction in literary magazines in Canada and the United States while he was still a graduate student. His output has been small—he has written one novel and two collections of short stories, *The Lost Salt Gift of Blood* (1976) and *As Birds Bring Forth the Sun* (1986), which, along with two additional stories, are contained in the just over 400 pages of *Island: The Collected Stories* (2000)—but he has gained a considerable reputation as a meticulous craftsman, one whose accounts have great resonance and enduring power. In his writing, the traditional life of the small Maritime communities, though austere and even dangerous, provides a sense of stability and tradition that seems to be vanishing elsewhere.

MacLeod's novel *No Great Mischief* (1999; IMPAC Dublin Award) is the product of more than ten years of careful writing. Through reminiscences and anecdotes, this moving book chronicles the family history of the Cape Breton MacDonalds from 1779—when the first of the clan came to Cape Breton from Scotland following the defeat, at Culloden, of the Highlanders supporting Bonny Prince Charlie—to the present era. Out of these chronicles emerges a presiding narrative that blends stories from a mythic and heroic past with the theme of loss, often violent or tragic, both of individual family members and of their Gaelic heritage.

MacLeod has remarked: 'I'm one of those writers who believes storytelling is older than literacy and I think of myself as a storyteller.' Certainly, 'As Birds Bring Forth the Sun'—which is most often MacLeod's choice when he reads aloud from his work—feels oral as much as written, as the narrator tells of how he and his family have been haunted by a spectre from their past. Like all of his fiction, it speaks of a Celtic inheritance and of a world rich in memory, one still alive in tales that, however old, retain their pertinence and immediacy. For MacLeod, as for many contemporary Canadian writers, narrative is a meeting place where the everyday world and the mythic realm of the fable or folktale come together.

In 2004, 'To Every Thing There Is a Season', from *As Birds Bring Forth the Sun*, was printed separately in an illustrated edition as *To Every Thing There Is a Season: A Cape Breton Christmas Story*. It ends with an idea that runs through MacLeod's fiction: 'Every man moves on . . . but there is no need to grieve. He leaves good things behind.'

## As Birds Bring Forth the Sun

Once there was a family with a Highland name who lived beside the sea. And the man had a dog of which he was very fond. She was large and grey, a sort of staghound from another time. And if she jumped up to lick his face, which she loved to do, her paws would jolt against his shoulders with such force that she would come close to knocking him down and he would be forced to take two or three backward steps before he could regain his balance. And he himself was not a small man, being slightly over six feet and perhaps one hundred and eighty pounds.

She had been left, when a pup, at the family's gate in a small handmade box and no one knew where she had come from or that she would eventually grow to such a size. Once, while still a small pup, she had been run over by the steel wheel of a horse-drawn cart which was hauling kelp from the shore to be used as fertilizer. It was in October and the rain had been falling for some weeks and the ground was soft. When the wheel of the cart passed over her, it sunk her body into the wet earth as well as crushing some of her ribs; and apparently the silhouette of her small crushed body was visible in the earth after the man lifted her to his chest while she yelped and screamed. He ran his fingers along her broken bones, ignoring the blood and urine which fell upon his shirt, trying to soothe her bulging eyes and her scrabbling front paws and her desperately licking tongue.

The more practical members of his family, who had seen run-over dogs before, suggested that her neck be broken by his strong hands or that he grasp her by the hind legs and swing her head against a rock, thus putting an end to her misery. But he would not do it.

Instead, he fashioned a small box and lined it with woollen remnants from a sheep's fleece and one of his old and frayed shirts. He placed her within the box and placed the box behind the stove and then he warmed some milk in a small saucepan and sweetened it with sugar. And he held open her small and trembling jaws with his left hand while spooning in the sweetened milk with his right, ignoring the needle-like sharpness of her small teeth. She lay in the box most of the remaining fall and into the early winter, watching everything with her large brown eyes.

Although some members of the family complained about her presence and the odour from the box and the waste of time she involved, they gradually adjusted to her; and as the weeks passed by, it became evident that her ribs were knitting together in some form or other and that she was recovering with the resilience of the young. It also became evident that she would grow to a tremendous size, as she outgrew one box and then another and the grey hair began to feather from her huge front paws. In the spring she was outside almost all of the time and followed the man everywhere; and when she came inside during the following months, she had grown so large that she would no longer fit into her accustomed place behind the stove and was forced to lie beside it. She was never given a name but was referred to in Gaelic as *cù mòr glas*, the big grey dog.

By the time she came into her first heat, she had grown to a tremendous height, and although her signs and her odour attracted many panting and highly aroused suitors, none was big enough to mount her and the frenzy of their disappointment and the longing of her unfulfilment were more than the man could stand. He went, so the story goes, to a place where he knew there was a big dog. A dog not as big as she was, but still a big dog, and he brought him home with him. And at the proper time he took the *cù mòr glas* and the big dog down to the sea where he knew there was a hollow in the rock which appeared only at low tide. He took some sacking to provide footing for the male dog and he placed the *cù mòr glas* in the hollow of the rock and knelt beside her and steadied her with his left arm under her throat and helped position the male dog above her and guided his blood-engorged penis. He was a man used to working with the breeding of animals, with the guiding of rams and bulls and stallions and often with the funky smell of animal semen heavy on his large and gentle hands.

The winter that followed was a cold one and ice formed on the sea and frequent squalls and blizzards obliterated the offshore islands and caused the people to stay near their fires much of the time, mending clothes and nets and harness and waiting for the change in season. The *cù mòr glas* grew heavier and even more large until there was hardly room for her around the stove or even under the table. And then one morning, when it seemed that spring was about to break, she was gone.

The man and even his family, who had become more involved than they cared to admit, waited for her but she did not come. And as the frenzy of spring wore on, they busied themselves with readying their land and their fishing gear and all of the things that so desperately required their attention. And then they were into summer and fall and winter and another spring which saw the birth of the man and his wife's twelfth child. And then it was summer again.

That summer the man and two of his teenaged sons were pulling their herring nets about two miles offshore when the wind began to blow off the land and the water began to roughen. They became afraid that they could not make it safely back to shore, so they pulled in behind one of the offshore islands, knowing that they would be sheltered there and planning to outwait the storm. As the prow of their boat approached the gravely shore, they heard a sound above them, and looking up they saw the *cù mòr glas* silhouetted on the brow of the hill which was the small island's highest point.

'*M'eudal cù mòr glas*' shouted the man in his happiness—*m'eudal* meaning something like dear or darling; and as he shouted, he jumped over the side of his boat into the waist-deep water, struggling for footing on the rolling gravel as he waded eagerly and awkwardly towards her and the shore. At the same time, the *cù mòr glas* came hurtling down towards him in a shower of small rocks dislodged by her feet; and just as he was emerging from the water, she met him as she used to, rearing up on her hind legs and placing her huge front paws on his shoulders while extending her eager tongue.

The weight and speed of her momentum met him as he tried to hold his balance on the sloping angle and the water rolling gravel beneath his feet, and he staggered backwards and lost his footing and fell beneath her force. And in that instant again, as the story goes, there appeared over the brow of the hill six more huge grey dogs hurtling down towards the gravelled strand. They had never seen him before; and seeing him stretched prone beneath their mother, they misunderstood, like so many armies, the intention of their leader.

They fell upon him in a fury, slashing his face and tearing aside his lower jaw and ripping out his throat, crazed with blood-lust or duty or perhaps starvation. The *cù mòr glas* turned on them in her own savagery, slashing and snarling and, it seemed, crazed by their mistake; driving them bloodied and yelping before her, back over the brow of the hill where they vanished from sight but could still be heard screaming in the distance. It all took perhaps little more than a minute.

The man's two sons, who were still in the boat and had witnessed it all, ran sobbing through the salt water to where their mauled and mangled father lay; but there was little they could do other than hold his warm and bloodied hands for a few brief moments. Although his eyes 'lived' for a small fraction of time, he could not speak to them because his face and throat had been torn away, and of course there was nothing they could do except to hold and be held tightly until that too slipped away and his eyes glazed over and they could no longer feel his hands holding theirs. The storm increased and they could not get home and so they were forced to spend the night huddled beside their father's body. They were afraid to try to carry the body to the rocking boat because he was so heavy and they were afraid that they might lose even what little of him remained and they were afraid also, huddled on the rocks, that the dogs might return. But they did not return at all and there was no sound from them, no sound at all, only the moaning of the wind and the washing of the water on the rocks.

In the morning they debated whether they should try to take his body with them or whether they should leave it and return in the company of older and wiser men. But they were afraid to leave it unattended and felt that the time needed to cover it with protective rocks would be better spent in trying to get across to their home shore. For a while they debated as to whether one should go in the boat and the other remain on the island, but each was afraid to be alone and so in the end they managed to drag and carry and almost float him towards the bobbing boat. They lay him facedown and covered him with what clothes there were and set off across the still-rolling sea. Those who waited on the shore missed the large presence of the man within the boat and some of them waded into the water and others rowed out in skiffs, attempting to hear the tearful message called out across the rolling waves.

The *cù mòr glas* and her six young dogs were never seen again, or perhaps I should say they were never seen again in the same way. After some weeks, a group of men circled the island tentatively in their boats but they saw no sign. They went again and again but found nothing. A year later, and grown much braver, they beached their boats and walked the island carefully, looking into the small sea caves and hollows at the base of the wind-ripped trees, thinking perhaps that if they did not find the dogs, they might at least find their whitened bones; but again they discovered nothing.

The *cù mòr glas*, though, was supposed to be sighted here and there for a number of years. Seen on a hill in one region or silhouetted on a ridge in another or loping across the valleys or glens in the early morning or the shadowy evening. Always in the area of the half perceived. For a while she became rather like the Loch Ness Monster or the Sasquatch on a smaller scale. Seen but not recorded. Seen when there were no cameras. Seen but never taken.

The mystery of where she went became entangled with the mystery of whence she came. There was increased speculation about the handmade box in which she had been found and much theorizing as to the individual or individuals who might have left it. People went to look for the box but could not find it. It was felt she might have been part of a *buidseachd* or evil spell cast on the man by some mysterious enemy. But no one could go much farther than that. All of his caring for her was recounted over and over again and nobody missed any of the ironies.

What seemed literally known was that she had crossed the winter ice to have her pups and had been unable to get back. No one could remember ever seeing her swim; and in the early months at least, she could not have taken her young pups with her.

The large and gentle man with the smell of animal semen often heavy on his hands was my great-great-great-grandfather, and it may be argued that he died because he was too good at breeding animals or that he cared too much about their fulfilment and well-being. He was no longer there for his own child of the spring who, in turn, became my great-great-grandfather, and he was perhaps too much there in the memory of his older sons who saw him fall beneath the ambiguous force of the *cù mòr glas*. The youngest boy in the boat was haunted and tormented by the awfulness of what he had seen. He would wake at night screaming that he had seen the *cù mòr glas a'bhàis*, the big grey dog of death, and his screams filled the house and the ears and minds of the listeners, bringing home again and again the consequences of their loss. One morning, after a night in which he saw the *cù mòr glas a'bhàis* so vividly that his sheets were drenched with sweat, he walked to the high cliff which faced the island and there he cut his throat with a fish knife and fell into the sea.

The other brother lived to be forty, but, again so the story goes, he found himself in a Glasgow pub one night, perhaps looking for answers, deep and sodden with the whiskey which had become his anaesthetic. In the half darkness he saw a large, grey-haired man sitting by himself against the wall and mumbled something to him. Some say he saw the *cù mòr glas a'bhàis* or uttered the name. And perhaps the man heard the phrase through ears equally affected by drink and felt he was being called a dog or a son of a bitch or something of that nature. They rose to meet one another and struggled outside into the cobblestoned passageway behind the pub where, most improbably, there were supposed to be six other large, grey-haired men who beat him to death on the cobblestones, smashing his bloodied head into the stone again and again before vanishing and leaving him to die with his face turned to the sky. The *cù mòr glas a'bhàis* had come again, said his family, as they tried to piece the tale together.

This is how the *cù mòr glas a'bhàis* came into our lives, and it is obvious that all of this happened a long, long time ago. Yet with succeeding generations it seemed the spectre had somehow come to stay and that it had become *ours*—not in the manner of an unwanted skeleton in the closet from a family's ancient past but more in the manner of something close to a genetic possibility. In the deaths of each generation, the grey dog was seen by some—by women who were to die in childbirth; by soldiers who went forth to the many wars but did not return; by those who went forth to feuds or dangerous love affairs; by those who answered mysterious midnight messages; by those who swerved on the highway to avoid the real or imagined grey dog and ended in masses of crumpled steel. And by one professional athlete who, in addition to his ritualized athletic superstitions, carried another fear or belief as well. Many of the man's descendants moved like careful hemophiliacs, fearing that they carried unwanted possibilities deep within them. And others, while they laughed, were like members of families in which there is a recurrence over the generations of repeated cancer or the diabetes which comes to those beyond middle age. The feeling of those who may say little to others but who may say often and quietly to themselves, 'It has not happened to me,' while adding always the cautionary '*yet.*'

I am thinking all of this now as the October rain falls on the city of Toronto and the pleasant, white-clad nurses pad confidently in and out of my father's room. He lies quietly amidst the whiteness, his head and shoulders elevated so that he is in that hospital position of being neither quite prone nor yet sitting. His hair is white upon his pillow and he breathes softly and sometimes unevenly, although it is difficult ever to be sure.

My five grey-haired brothers and I take turns beside his bedside, holding his heavy hands in ours and feeling their response, hoping ambiguously that he will speak to us, although we know it may tire him. And trying to read his life and ours into his eyes when they are open. He has been with us for a long time, well into our middle age.

Unlike those boys in that boat of so long ago, we did not see him taken from us in our youth. And unlike their youngest brother who, in turn, became our great-great-grand-father, we did not grow into a world in which there was no father's touch. We have been lucky to have this large and gentle man so deep into our lives.

No one in this hospital has mentioned the *cù mòr glas a'bhàis*. Yet as my mother said ten years ago, before slipping into her own death as quietly as a grownup child who leaves or enters her parents' house in the early hours, 'It is hard to not know what you do know.'

Even those who are most skeptical, like my oldest brother who has driven here from Montreal, betray themselves by their nervous actions. 'I avoided the Greyhound bus stations in both Montreal and Toronto,' he smiled upon his arrival, and then added, 'Just in case.'

He did not realize how ill our father was and has smiled little since then. I watch him turning the diamond ring upon his finger, knowing that he hopes he will not hear the Gaelic phrase he knows too well. Not having the luxury, as he once said, of some who live in Montreal and are able to pretend they do not understand the 'other' language. You cannot not know what you do know.

Sitting here, taking turns holding the hands of the man who gave us life, we are afraid for him and for ourselves. We are afraid of what he may see and we are afraid to hear the phrase born of the vision. We are aware that it may become confused with what the doctors call 'the will to live' and we are aware that some beliefs are what others would dismiss as 'garbage'. We are aware that there are men who believe the earth is flat and that the birds bring forth the sun.

Bound here in our own peculiar mortality, we do not wish to see or see others see that which signifies life's demise. We do not want to hear the voice of our father, as did those other sons, calling down his own particular death upon him.

We would shut our eyes and plug our ears, even as we know such actions to be of no avail. Open still and fearful to the grey hair rising on our necks if and when we hear the scrabble of the paws and the scratching at the door.

1986

# Claire Harris

## b. 1937

Claire Harris moves across boundaries of all kinds, playing freely with both language and form. Author of a body of work concerned with social justice for women and for minorities, she writes primarily as a poet, but is drawn to narrative and has described two of her books, *Drawing Down a Daughter* (1992) and *She* (2000), as 'novels in poetry'. Born in Port of Spain, Trinidad, in 1937, Harris was the second of six children. Her father, an inspector of schools, and her mother, a teacher, home-schooled her until age seven. She then attended St. Joseph's Convent School, receiving what she has described as a classic British education: it 'concentrated on what the Europeans had done, the good things they had done. There was no discussion at all—ever—of slavery . . . and certainly no discussion of the Great Wars and the devastation of the last century.' Nevertheless, she has also said that her convent-school experience gave her 'an indelible sense of great beauty, of possibility in language, even as it provided a theatre to observe human nature' struggling with 'worldly social and cultural attitudes and evils'. After graduation, she travelled to Ireland to attend University College Dublin, where she received an honours BA in English in 1961. She returned to the Caribbean and earned a teacher's diploma at the University of West Indies in Jamaica in 1963; from 1963 to 1966, she taught at her old school and at Catholic Women's Teachers Training College. In 1966, Harris moved to Canada, where she taught English in Calgary's Catholic schools until her retirement in 1994.

In 1975, a year's leave allowed her to travel to Africa, where she earned a diploma in mass media and communications at the University of Lagos in Nigeria. She found the experience renewed her lifelong interest in writing. When she returned to Canada, Harris involved herself in literary publishing. From 1976 to 1979, she worked on Poetry Goes Public, a group project that put up posters of poems in Calgary as a way

of bringing poetry to a wider readership; from 1981 to 1989, she served as poetry editor for the literary magazine *Dandelion*; and in 1983, she helped found the magazine *blue buffalo* as an outlet for Alberta writers. She has said that, though being a visible minority in Canada was never easy, she found the Alberta writing community very supportive.

Harris identifies her decision to move to Canada as crucial in her career because it provided her with the 'space to write without the self-censorship necessary in a small society. Here I was anonymous, I could afford to fail.' In 1984, she published her first two books of poetry: *Translation into Fiction*, in which she records her feelings of exile in poems such as 'August', and *Fables from the Women's Quarters*, which won a Commonwealth Award. The latter intersperses long poems with brief moments of haiku and is notable for the formal experimentation that has come to characterize Harris's work—including close attention to the way the poem looks on the page. Made up of long poems that respond to injustices in the world, the book opens with 'Where the Sky Is a Painful Tent', in which she interweaves her own poetry with passages extracted from the work of Guatemalan writer Rigoberta Menchú running across the bottom of the page.

She followed these books with *Travelling to Find a Remedy* (1986) and *The Conception of Winter* (1989). The latter book, which turns around oppositions between summer and winter, warmth and cold, and life and death, opens with 'Towards the Color of Summer', a poetry sequence about three women travelling from Calgary to Barcelona—from which the poems 'To Dissipate Grief' and 'Conception of Winter', reprinted below, come—and ends with a long poem about the death of the poet's mother. Harris again uses the delicate Japanese form of the haiku to separate longer sections, such as with this poem:

*beyond the school door*
*a butterfly free of bells*
*slides on wind*

A book-length work that mixes poetry and prose, *Drawing Down a Daughter* (1996) explores the mother–daughter relationship and dramatizes the links that join one mother and daughter. (Her explorations of women's roles can also be seen in *Kitchen Talk*, the anthology she edited in 1992 with Edna Alford.)

Dipped in Shadows (1996), which collects five long poems, continues her investigation of forms and the use of space on the page, while expanding her social criticism. Her most recent book, *She*, is a tour de force that explores the voices of a woman with multiple personalities.

Believing that, because 'art is *meant* to shake people', it must keep renewing itself,

Harris has said of her writing, 'My work refuses the mind-quieting romanticism of regular rhythm, which conveys an aura of inevitability to work in the Western tradition, regardless of content.' Her poetry is sometimes dense and demands several rereadings—but, as the poem 'A Grammar of the Heart' reminds us, communication is of paramount importance to her. She is one who has

*lived language      at first she examined each word*
*skin peeled back      green flesh squeezed between*
*thumb and                  till she tasted sentences*
*   forefinger*
*rolled them in her                  swirled them*
*   curious mouth*
*around the sides and back                  waited*
*   of her tongue*
*for the aftertaste*

# August

Noon and the August haze veils gentle eastern hills the prim modest houses      along the Bow[1] poplars grow yellow stranded on the deck of this ship perched on cliffs edge I watch the steel city flaring in high noon      so bright I must look away      here where no one walks the traffic strung out at the lights like coils of a python tightens around the city endlessly      in the median men on huge earth movers go busily about their work cocooned in their own noise CP air[2] drones through the pale blue      I imagine passengers settling back before long suspension      and home      So distant from my own rainforested mountains      mountains rounded like whales stranded against the dawn      light lapping their ridges tiny shacks like barnacles riding their flanks      palms burst into green spume against the sky      I remember dark faces streaming out of the valleys      black women flowing currents & waves      their feet solid on earth      their unreasoned unhurried grace      this forever and indelible on the inner eye      This summer shades into the sixteenth autumn      I grow yellow in exile

1984

1  The Bow River, which runs through Calgary.
2  Canadian Pacific Airlines, which went out of business a few years after this poem was written.

# Black Sisyphus[1]

To propitiate the dreaming god at his centre
for months my father drove down green uneven

roads to the capital where tar flowed under
noonday heat in daily manoeuvres around new obstacles

to take form again in cold pale morning
he drove those roads in mutters searching through

the crumpled pathways of his brain while his
voice rose and stumbled in the sibilant argument

he enjoyed with life     he could not be
convinced that being human was not enough                    10

that there was no bridge he could cross
he would not 'forget de man' nor 'leave

him to God'     these were his sky/trees/
his streets to name     was he not greeted

by all be passed     naming     from a wilderness
of loss his fathers created this island garden

he would not be cast out again     he
rode his right to words     pointed and named

*the road from one way of life to another is hard*
*those who are ahead have a long way to go*[2]                 20

missionary zeal could not stomach such clarity
they damned him     thundered fire     brimstone     the sin

of pride     thus my father and his letters
raced weekly to the centre     the apology

won     he stood     nodded     bowed     strode in his own
echoing silence     out of lowered eyes/bells/incense

---

1 In Greek myth, Sisyphus was punished in the afterlife by having to roll a boulder up a hill, only to watch it roll
  down again. In *The Myth of Sisyphus* (1945), the French existentialist Albert Camus takes Sisyphus as a symbol
  for the absurd life of all humanity, doomed to futile tasks.
2 Lines from the 1963 poetry sequence 'From an African Diary' by the Swedish poet Tomas Tranströmer (b. 1931),
  describing his visit to Africa.

the worn organ's cough      out of village voices
wheeling in cracked Kyries[3]

to stand on the church steps muttering:
*it is enough to be a man      today*                                    30

his finger kneading my six year old hands
as if they would refashion them

1986

3  *Kyrie eléison* (Greek for 'Lord have mercy'), a phrase often used in the celebration of the Roman Catholic
   communion service.


## Conception of Winter

Sometimes in summer rain falls in great drops
heavy as loss      today
we see it black on ragged faces
on gypsy urchins crouched at the foot of columns
in this café      Not here spring's succulent promise
life like a peach
or even the thin stretched certitudes of winter
which we imagine as life      skin tight
drying on a frame nailed against a barn
in hot prairie summer                                                  10
Only this rain stirring clichés      it dulls
the cold incurious eyes on bowed men sitting
under arches we have discovered
sailing behind the rundown façades
and unfashionable shops
searching a way east      it stains rusty mirrors
where our faces shift      and what is new and strange
quickens for a moment      We find a table settle parcels
guidebooks      order drinks      wait for the sun
But some gesture which haunts this place      something          20
in these women carrying trays of beer      and pregnant
with old age      reminds us of ourselves
We become sad      we walk apart in the wet aftergloom
of rain      know ourselves already seeded
And this is not the voluptuous sadness in great love
or even grief at our friend's dying
Just that here in this place      in our determined joy

we find ourselves fearing the birth of winter
We resolve to invent passion     imagine it as beyond
the circling of tongues    As the cold rage          30
which changes something

1989

## To Dissipate Grief

| | |
|---|---|
| we hustle in & out of shops | *and this is what happens* |
| bustling to buy | *when you die* |
| everything | *first    you uncoil* |
| we say    'it | *the guts of pain* |
| is cheaper here' | *then you climb* |
| we point at things | *where it leads* |
| weigh values | *you gather yourself* |
| nudge each other | *pull yourself* |
| as goods are taken down | *out of nails* |
| from shelves | *out of split ends*    10 |
| or barstools | *gather your self* |
| spread over counters | *into the mouth* |
| so we can finger them | *a breath* |
| dream their effect | *that labours* |
| tallying silently the cost | *a sigh that goes* |
| in dollars | *on and on* |
| we buy shoes & bags | *because    this* |
| belts    wallets    luggage | *is    it* |
| clothes with french seams | *your last taste* |
| accents | *of earth*    20 |
| dresses    shirts | *you want to remember it* |
| suits    gowns | *suddenly    you are* |
| hotel rooms | *and all out* |
| a great shawl | *to your amazement* |
| we see our selves | *intact* |
| transformed | *blue inside* |
| strutting down closed | *outside    shimmering* |
| avenues    expensive | *made iridescent* |
| polished skins | *by peace* |
| on our arms | *even a species*    30 |
| draped over shoulders | *of joy* |
| we buy ropes | *but eye hath not seen* |
| of pearls    stones | *nor ear heard* |

twisted modern chains
a watch     a pen
is cheaper here
saying it
we buy elegant meals
we argue for hours
over packaging
then buy gifts
prints     glass
friendships
bottles of volcanic
sand     cards
plays     figures
sculpted from
flesh
lava
dreams
we buy writing
paper by
picasso
records
T shirts     stamped
with the faces
of cities
and tangles
of shells worked
by primitive fingers
we use cards
tongues     whatever
coin is necessary
we keep lists
balancing bills
and friends
against ourselves
here where we
are free
and the dollar
strong
we luxuriate
buying everything
we choose
it is cheaper here

*words lose their potency*
*and you begin to live*
*circling above*
*the final visibility*
*of your death*
*you remember*
*the cliches of a life*                                    40
*rendered remarkable*
*by dreams     by circumstance*
*and now     you*
*are free*
*of love     its tugs*
*its insensitivites*
*wild peculiar joy*
*of bodies*
*the landscapes*
*of childhood*                                             50
*slip from you*
*that clump of trees*
*that slight rise in the earth*
*those seas*
*that new land you chose*
*its particular weave*
*gone like mists*
*ghosts in this*
*brighter sun*
*this air*                                                 60
*filled with being*
*you*
*now     one*
*with time*
*space*
*whatever there is*
*of law*
*settle in*
*and through you*
*no wonder*                                                70
*(we think everything*
*is cheaper here*
*all things*
*considered)*
*you know who you are*

1989

# No God Waits on Incense

while babies bleed this is not the poem i wanted
it is the poem i could      though it is not that insistent
worm      it will not burrow through deaf ears
lay its eggs in your brain      yet it is all
for change
and it is not that beautiful weapon
it will not explode in the gut
despite your need      this poem is not that gift
it brings you nothing      you who insist on drinking
let your buckets into green and ruined wells      haul                    10
in darkness      village women will lead you smiling
step back polite in the face of skulls
this poem will not catch you as you fall
not a net      no      it is nothing      this poem
not a key      not a charm      not chicken soup
and it is no use at all      at all
nothing at all
it won't beat a drum      it can't dance      it can't
even claim to be written in dust if this morning
the Bow sky-sheeted in light      the silver air is bright      20
with balloons      yet it talks from a dark bed
this poem      though no
woman can lie curled beneath its covers
can hide before boots
can hope to be taken for bundles of clothes      can hope
not to cry out when the knife probes
pray her blood not betray her      nor the tiny sigh
no      this poem      not even a place where anyone is safe
it can nothing      still nothing      still nothing at all
at all      in the night and disinterested air this poem leaves no wound      30

1989

# Jack Hodgins

## b. 1938

Jack Hodgins was raised in the farming and logging town of Merville, British Columbia, on Vancouver Island—a town he has described as so small that everyone in it was either a relative or a friend. He attended the University of British Columbia, where he studied creative writing under Earle Birney. After completing his BEd in 1961, he took a job teaching high-school English in Nanaimo. In the late 1960s, he began to publish short stories set in the Comox Valley where he grew up: these were collected in 1976 as *Spit Delaney's Island*. The communities in Hodgins's fiction are on northern Vancouver Island, but they also exist in an alternate imaginative continuum in which some of the eccentric characters from that first collection reappear in later work.

The following year saw the publication of Hodgins's first novel, *The Invention of the World* (1977), a hyperbolic account of Vancouver Island life that blends local tales he heard growing up with broader history and legend. Following its publication, he became writer-in-residence at Simon Fraser University (1977–8). When his second novel, *The Resurrection of Joseph Bourne* (1979), won a Governor General's Award, he resigned from teaching high school to become a full-time writer. From 1979 to 1983, Hodgins was writer-in-residence and creative writing instructor at the University of Ottawa, while completing a collection of stories, *The Barclay Family Theatre* (1981). He then returned to Vancouver Island to teach creative writing at the University of Victoria (with the exception of 1986, which he spent in Australia as a result of winning the Canada–Australia Literary Prize). Hodgins continues to write and edit since his retirement from teaching in 2002.

In his early work, Hodgins established a characteristic way of telling stories that have the anecdotal feeling of a back-country yarn delivered with an extravagance that gives them the magical quality of myth. His utilization of the power of the tall tale associates him with the western Canadian tradition of W.O. Mitchell and Robert Kroetsch, but his fictional landscape differs from those Prairie novelists. Where their landscapes are wide and empty, his are often filled and lush—and confined. 'Islanded' is a word Hodgins likes to use for the geographically limited world of characters (an example being Leanne Collins in 'The Crossing', reprinted below) and for the way their physical state is reflected in their psyches.

His narratives are often flamboyant and fantastic; his communities innocently corrupt. Unlike the planned settlements of the mainland, these island Edens gone to seed have evolved haphazardly: one has been founded by a madman (*The Invention of the World*), while another is restored by a dead man (*The Resurrection of Joseph Bourne*). In the islands's ingrown states, normality and eccentricity exist in comfortable symbiosis—but they are regularly disturbed, as by a homecomer who has spent much of his life abroad (*The Honorary Patron*, 1987), or, more often, by the arrival of an outsider, like the mysterious girl from a Peruvian freighter who sets the narrative in motion in *The Resurrection of Joseph Bourne*. In *Innocent Cities* (1990), the protagonist, a nineteenth-century architect who wants to transform Victoria, finds the city altered by the arrival of a widow from Australia, while in *The Macken Charm*, Rusty Macken, who intends to leave Vancouver Island for an exciting cosmopolitan world, has his plans preempted by the funeral of a glamorous city girl, Glory. Hodgins's 1998 children's book, *Left Behind in Squabble Bay*, is told from the point of view of one of these outsiders: when an artistic boy from Eastern Canada is left by his father in a British Columbia island community, his caricatures of those around him attract their ire.

*Broken Ground* (1998) is a departure from Hodgins's extravagant and comedic style. Set on the 'soldier's settlement' of Portuguese Creek on Vancouver Island in 1922, this dark novel portrays a community struggling to recover from the tragic personal losses suffered in the First World War. Compounding—and echoing—war's devastating horrors, a forest fire threatens to sweep down upon the tiny settlement. In *Distance* (2003), a father approaching his death makes a journey with his son through the Australian outback, showing how islanders carry their place with them (Hodgins had previously described his own colourful journey through Australia in a 1992 travel narrative, *Over 40 in Broken Hill*).

Hodgins's most recent collection of short stories, *Damage Done by the Storm* (2004), combines the small, realistic details of daily lives with the surprising things that can suddenly transform them. In 'The Crossing', the middle-aged woman, exceptional only in how ordinary she is, who rides a ferry from Victoria to Vancouver, arrives at a moment that leaves behind the ordinary.

Hodgins's commitment as a teacher of creative writing—he has conducted workshops around the world—can be seen in his *Passion for Narrative: A Guide for Writing Fiction* (1993; expanded and with a new afterword in 2001), a valuable guide for apprentice writers. He begins it by quoting the Russian-American novelist Vladimir Nabokov: 'A major writer combines . . . storyteller, teacher, enchanter—but it is the enchanter in him that predominates and makes him a major writer.' It is clear that Hodgins has aspired to be such an enchanter.

# The Crossing

Sitting just inside the great slanting windows at the front of the observation lounge, Leanne Collins could almost believe this ferry was ploughing through the choppy waves just for her—rushing her toward those steep forested mountains, and all the mainland world. This could be a private run, a special mission. No one else's journey would have such urgency.

Of course she was not alone on the ferry. There could be hundreds, unseen, behind her. A woman who'd been sitting against a side window came over to stand nearby, perhaps to see what had caught Leanne's attention. The highway was a deep scar scraped cleanly along the side of the nearest mountain, suggesting a sort of waist-line. Winter sunlight flashed off fleeing vehicles. Below this road, houses clung to the rocky slopes, some of them propped up by posts that looked, from this distance, no more substantial than Popsicle sticks. And off to the right, beyond a series of stubby peninsulas, the crowded and shining white pillars of the city seemed to grow up at the water's edge as if on a tethered raft. The woman sighed. 'They'll be opening the big doors any minute now,' she said. 'Down below.'

Leanne knew this already. The two great doors of the car deck would part, and roll inward, opening up a gap large enough for coachline buses and transport trucks and rows of ordinary cars to drive through. There was a time when foot passengers disembarked down there as well—pressing against the rope until it was removed, then rushing up the ramp ahead of the vehicles, with impatient motorcyclists revving engines at their heels.

This woman was someone Leanne knew, or thought she knew, though the name did not come immediately. A pleasant face, someone seen here and there in her small island town. A little older than herself, perhaps fifty, with deep laugh lines out from her eyes. One of the Sawchuks, she thought. Angela Sawchuk's aunt? All the family had that unruly hair. 'They used to leave the doors open right across,' the woman said, 'but people started disappearing.'

There were very few others in the lounge, winter travellers scattered here and there in the rows of thinly padded seats, backpacks and newspapers spread out beside them. Someone had left a newspaper on the front-row seat next to Leanne. 'Ambassador Recalled', one headline shouted. Another began, 'Prominent City Financier Questioned In—' His crime was lost in the fold.

'One day this fellow went down and got into his car and drove off,' the woman said. She could be Angela Sawchuk's mother. She spoke with her eyes on the world they were rushing toward but at the same time moved over closer to Leanne. 'This was halfway across the strait. You must have heard about it.' She tossed the newspaper onto a nearby seat and sat. 'Sank straight to the bottom, of course.' She paused, perhaps to allow Leanne time to imagine a car and driver sinking down through fish and seaweed toward the mysterious floor of the sea. 'I knew someone else—got on at Departure Bay and didn't get off at the other end. They never found a trace. Just disappeared!'

Leanne was used to people disappearing. In fact, she was very nearly the only person in her family who had *not* disappeared. Of course she wasn't about to tell the woman this. If she'd recognized Leanne Collins she would already know this fact about her. Otherwise, it wasn't any of her business. Not today, anyway.

Her older sister, Rose, went off into the Cascade Mountains of Washington State several years ago in order to rendezvous with a space ship she claimed had been sending her messages. That was the kind of family she came from. No one had ever found a trace of Rose. No one had ever found their father, either, who had waited until his seventieth year to decide he would really rather be a Tahitian fisherman. He pushed off from shore in a stolen sailboat and that was the last of him. A cousin had simply not been there one morning: his bed had been slept in but his slippers and all his clothes still waited beside it. Either he had been atomized in his sleep or he was off and wandering naked in the world.

They were a queer lot. Even her mother was a bit strange, but in quite the opposite way. She appeared in your kitchen when she was least expected or most unwanted and stayed, smoking, talking, until you had to push her out the door.

Because Leanne considered herself the only sane one in the family, she had always expected to be around when she was ninety-five, still picking up after Ron. She had imagined making her exit in some conventional way, with forty grandchildren gathered around her bed. Perhaps they would even applaud, and pin a homemade medal on her chest for sticking it out to the end. But that was a long way down the road yet. She had only just started her forties.

Where had her relatives gone? That was what kept you thinking about them. Rose could be a New York model by now, or a bounty hunter in New Mexico, unless of course her space ship had actually shown up. She might have walked right down the back of that mountain and taken up with a band of terrorists.

Leanne's father had probably drowned, since he knew nothing about the sea, but you simply could not be sure. She found herself imagining him in a grass hut somewhere, a family of little natives playing with his toes. You could make up anything you wanted about any of them, and believe it true, while almost certainly no one ever made up a single thing about Leanne Collins.

She was *here*—that was why. You could see her, you could drive past her sprawling country house of cedar and brick and glass any time you liked, along the river's edge; you could see her husband driving to his architectural firm in town, you could see her boys walking down the gravel shoulder toward the high school every weekday morning.

Sometimes acquaintances, after a long absence, discovered they had to search their memories for her name. Yet these same people might confess to having had this great long vivid dream about Rose, who had just been named ambassador to Peru. 'I could tell you exactly what she was wearing. That Rose!'

If Leanne herself had been wearing snakeskin head to toe, they would not have noticed. Well, they might have noticed but afterwards they would not remember. It seemed that only the disappeared could be said to really exist. You had to be *gone*, in fact, before they credited you with a life worth thinking about.

Even her mother was guilty of this. When she dropped in uninvited she would sit smoking one cigarette after another at the kitchen table and talk about Rose's imaginary accomplishments as if Rose had actually sent home proof that she'd lived up to all her ambitions. 'I bet that little devil's living with some rich stockbroker somewhere,' her mother would say. 'She doesn't write because she's scared we'll all rush down and try to sponge off of her.'

'Rose doesn't write because she's ashamed,' was Ron's response to that. It was his belief that everything the members of Leanne's family did was meant to embarrass him in the eyes of the community. He came from a large family that never moved farther than a few miles from one another and believed he had married into a tribe of lunatics, though he considered Leanne to be all that they were not: the salt of the earth. 'Rose would probably like to come home but knows we'd laugh in her face!'

This woman who could be Angela Sawchuk's aunt or mother hummed to herself in the seat next to Leanne. Of course she might not be a Sawchuk at all. Leanne could be thinking of someone else altogether, a clerk in one of the shops.

What if a person refused? What if a person changed her mind and decided to stay on the ferry? 'If closing the doors is their way of making sure you don't get off before you're supposed to,' Leanne said, 'what if you changed your mind and refused to get off at all? What if you decided you just wanted to go back home?'

Obviously the woman had never considered this before. She looked around the lounge, perhaps hoping that someone in a uniform would have an answer. Finding no one, she attempted an answer herself. 'I suppose if they caught you hiding in the washroom they'd march you off and make you buy a ticket and then let you on again.' Looking rather pleased with herself, she added, 'If anyone was going to change their mind it would be me. The city scares me half to death. Such terrible things happen.' She gestured toward the waiting skyscrapers, half an hour's drive along the coastline. 'Muggings. Drugs. Awful murders.' Even so, she forced herself to go over once a year, she said. 'To do my Christmas shopping. I take the local bus straight to the Pacific Centre and plunge into the crowds. I hold my breath till it's over.'

'I shopped in August,' Leanne said. Was this a competition? 'I wrapped everything and hid them on a bedroom closet shelf.'

But she had forgotten to turn on the dishwasher this morning, before leaving the house. And had rushed out without making the beds or phoning Ron at work. She had even forgotten to let the dog out. He was in her kitchen now, wondering where he should lift his leg.

A young man in a turtleneck sweater appeared at the far side of the lounge, crushing a paper coffee cup in his hand before tossing it into the waste bin. Then, holding a striped gym bag, he stood at the window to watch the mainland sliding closer. Houses with plenty of glass. Trees clinging to an almost vertical slope. When he leaned forward to look up toward the snowy mountain peaks, the fingers of his left hand played with the hairs below his Adam's apple. He wore a wedding ring.

Perhaps he was one of those men who married young and then went off to have a good time while their wives stayed at home. She had seen him at the Drop-off Zone, saying goodbye to a friend. They'd laughed, recalling moments from a happy weekend together. They could be part of some athletic team a wife would just as soon avoid. Ron, she thought, did not have friends he could laugh with, though she wished that he had. He discussed laminated beams, vaulted ceilings, and leaky condos with fellow architects, and told Leanne that she was the only real friend he needed.

Of course the young man could have been staying with the friend in order to meet with someone his wife did not know about. A young beauty who'd waited after a game to congratulate him, a childhood classmate suddenly reappearing in his life. He glanced at Leanne without betraying any sign of a guilty conscience, or any flicker of interest either, and then sat at the far end of the front row, with his knees wide apart and his two hands shifting his gym bag back and forth. She had seen her son Cody toss a basketball back and forth between his hands like that while he tried to make up his mind which way to throw.

They were coming up to the familiar tiny island, no larger than a city lot. It was Leanne's habit to wait until the ferry was abreast—where she could see the bare rocks and the twisted trees with their exposed roots—before getting ready to disembark. *Disembark* was the term used by the smarmy actor's voice while giving instructions over the public-address system. Bus people were to head downstairs. Then, after a few minutes, vehicle passengers. Foot passengers would *disembark* from the forward lounge. She thought of herself as simply getting off the boat. *Disembark* made her think of other, similar words. Disembowel. Disembody. Disencumber. Disengage.

'You go over often?' the woman asked.

Leanne thought for a moment. How often was *often*? 'Once a month,' she said. 'To get out of the house for a few days.'

'My family would never let me get away with that.' This was said with considerable pride.

'Oh, mine doesn't mind.' A protest from the witness box. And it was true that Cody didn't mind. But Bert had threatened to take off himself if she kept this up. And would not speak to her for several hours when she returned. Ron took advantage of her absence to work late in his study, poring over blueprints. 'They're happy enough when my mother drops in and takes over.'

Her mother was only too glad to move in and pamper Leanne's husband and children, her own having escaped her influence long ago.

This wasn't one of the Sawchuks. Leanne remembered seeing her behind the counter at Tim Hortons. She was the manager, accustomed to being friendly to strangers. In fact, she was paid to be friendly to people she didn't know. She would see it as an off-duty part of her job to be pleasant to people she recognized as regular customers, even on the B.C. Ferries, to make sure they kept coming back. Leanne had never noticed her name tag, though of course she must wear one at work. In return, all she knew about Leanne Collins was that she was one of those women who dropped in once a week for a coffee and doughnut before starting her grocery shopping down the street.

'Ron hates the city—like you,' Leanne said. 'I spent part of my childhood in Winnipeg, and find small-town life a little stifling now and then.' She was saying this, she realized, to explain herself to someone who wasn't likely to care. 'I have a friend over here that I visit.'

The woman picked lint from the front of her heavy coat and said, 'Monday morning is a funny time to visit friends.'

Leanne might have explained that today's was an emergency trip, but did not. Derek would be racing along the Upper Levels Highway now, in his white BMW. Passing everyone. Swooping down the long slope cut into the mountain and across the curved canyon bridge and up the sharp incline toward the sign that warned you if the ferry lineup was congested. She imagined the two deep vertical creases between his eyes: he would make that little car fly if he could.

He drove with only his right hand, kept the other down on the seat between his long narrow thighs. He would stay in the inside lane until he caught up to someone, then he would gear down, switch lanes, roar past, and swerve back to his lane again. Anxious, he would periodically knead the back of his neck, and frown impatiently at the indirect and indifferent mountain road.

'I'll be there,' he'd said on the phone. 'If I'm not there when you get off, you won't have to wait very long.'

'Yes,' she'd said. She had not even got around to dressing when he called. The breakfast dishes were still on the table.

'And, Lee—don't talk to anyone about this. Okay?'

'I'm buying everyone sweaters this year,' the woman said. 'I'm tired of putting a lot of thought into my gifts. Racing all over the place to make sure I get exactly the right thing. And they never care about them anyway. I'll get a nice sweater for everyone and catch the first ferry home.'

Cody had recently decided he wanted a whole new sound system for Christmas. Bert wanted DVDs and a leather coat. By the time they made their demands she had already done her shopping: books and CDs, floor hockey sticks. All summer she wrote down things she'd overheard them saying they wanted, and bought them in August. Too early, it seemed, this year.

Ron insisted that this practice made no sense. They would now have to buy these new things as well. 'I can wait for next year,' Cody said. A good boy—she supposed she ought to start thinking of him as a young man. It was almost creepy the way he could guess what it was like to be a parent. Bert, however, said that if he didn't get what he wanted he would apply for a job on a cruise ship.

They were passing the tiny island now—mostly rock, some moss, a straggly tree bent from years of wind. Leanne checked her overnight bag. There was little inside except her makeup and a change of underwear, things she had grabbed on the fly. Curling iron. Nightgown. Her passport. All the cash she could find in the house. The young man in the turtleneck had already left his seat to start ambling toward the exit door to the outer deck. Eventually they would all step onto a little bridge—a modern gang-plank with railings—and for an uneasy moment could look down into that narrow gap you were passing over, of cold oily water far below.

'One weekend a month is better than nothing at all,' Derek had once agreed. 'So long as we don't do anything stupid to get our names in the papers.' At the time this was meant as a joke.

The ferry swept around the headland and entered the little bay. A smaller ferry had just pulled out from the slip. The large doors would certainly be open by now on the car deck—great curved slabs folded in against the side walls—yet there was probably a rope stretched across the enormous open front end of the ferry, to discourage the cyclists from standing too close to the edge, and foot passengers with dogs. An employee stood watch, alert for those who might be tempted to tarnish the company's safety record.

Leanne remained sitting while others stood with feet apart, braced for the lurch and the sideways swing when they struck the squealing, creosoted wood.

She had left her dishwasher loaded but not activated. Why did that bother her now? Perhaps because she could guess who would have to turn it on. And who would have to make the beds. The boys would come home after soccer practice and eat the cheese sandwiches she had hastily slapped together, and would find the note that suggested they call their grandmother.

'Today?' she'd said to Derek on the phone. 'Now?'

'Now! Catch one of those little float planes.'

'You know how scared I am of those things.'

'Then hurry, hurry. There'll be a ferry at nine. I'll have my lawyer with me when I pick you up, we can talk in the car.' He spoke to her, she thought, as he must speak to his secretary when things were not going well.

'Is it really so bad? Is there no way this can be avoided?'

'Can't you *hear* me?' he said.

He'd tried to restrain the sense of urgency in his voice, tried to maintain at least a hint of his customary kindness. 'My wife is going crazy. Not even my lawyer is sure he wants to believe me. If they put together the case he thinks they are trying to—my God! Think! When the treasurer of a company under investigation dies in suspicious circumstances—well, you can see. I'll be lucky if they even let me have bail.'

She made an effort to imagine his usually amused eyes, his quizzical brows, but discovered no hint of them in his tone.

'God knows what will be in the papers tonight, after this morning's sneering innu-
endoes. There could be anything, they'll be so glad to have an excuse to spread me
across the front page again. Do you understand?'

He'd said this as if to an inadequate employee, but he hadn't needed to spell it out.
She was his alibi for that certain weekend. A hotel clerk, she supposed, would be asked
to recall that he had been accompanied by 'an unnamed woman, a tall brunette in her
forties.'

But that would not be enough. She would be asked to speak to his lawyer, then to
the police. She would be in the papers herself, if he had his way. Her pale alarmed face
beside his sidelong contempt for the cameras.

And then?

'We can talk about afterwards once we've got this cleared up,' he'd said. 'Can you
imagine how frantic I am?'

The amazing thing was that she was not frantic herself. When she'd put down the
phone it was with a feeling that she had merely come to a moment she had known
about for a long time. She did not want to believe there was relief in what she felt, and
yet this seemed to be one of those situations where there was nothing you could do
except go along. The only urgency, at that moment, had been to catch the ferry.

The Tim Hortons woman was already lined up with others waiting on the outer
deck. She glanced back at Leanne, who was taking her time to join the others, and
rolled her eyes in a manner Leanne assumed was self-mockery—woman anxious to
grab an armload of sweaters and run. The young man, on the other hand, seemed
unaware of anyone around him. Rehearsing his story, perhaps—a convincing tale of
games played, of goals or points won or lost.

From below there came the squealing of metal against wood and the whirr of electric motors lowering the vehicle ramp. When the short passenger bridge had been slid
into place across the gap between ferry and the fixed ramp, they hurried forward past
a young man in uniform who stood back to observe—to supervise, she supposed. To
Leanne he looked as though he wished his job came with a cattle prod.

And it did seem as though they were all rushing in order to avoid something
unpleasant. Strangers impatient to shake off strangers. The Tim Hortons woman was
already far ahead, racing for the bus and the underground shopping malls, despite her
fear. The young man no doubt expected to be met by his wife, and to go home, perhaps to change clothes for an afternoon's work at the office. And Leanne Collins, eyes
searching the world ahead for that white BMW, hurried, hurried, rushed along the
sloped ramp from the ferry to join Rose and their father and all the others who lived
in the world of the disappeared.

2004

# John Newlove

## 1938–2003

Moving frequently during his childhood, John Herbert Newlove grew up in a number of farming communities in his native Saskatchewan. He continued to live a nomadic life after he left the Prairies in 1960, residing for short periods in California, British Columbia, Ontario, Quebec, and the Maritimes, before returning to the West in 1979, first to Regina (his birthplace), and then to Nelson, BC. In 1986, he moved once more, to Ottawa, where he remained—except for brief periods as a writer-in-residence—until his death.

A poet since his late teens, Newlove wrote (in the preface to his 1993 volume of selected poems) of his continued recourse to poetry:

*I don't know how I came to write. I don't know. One day, it seemed, I was, desperately, as if I were trying to explain the world, or bits of it, to myself. And to others eventually. This is what I thought.*

*Now I think that I am only trying to model tiny bits of a world too wide and too various and too frightening to be comprehended by anything but lies.*

*. . . I wish I could offer consolation, if not to others at least to myself. I am trying to hold the world together.* ('Being Caught')

Supporting himself primarily as an editor and writer, he also worked as a high-school teacher (in Birtle, Manitoba), taught writing for a year at David Thompson University Centre (in Nelson, BC), was a social worker (in Yorkton, Saskatchewan), and served as an announcer, news editor, and copywriter for radio stations in Weyburn, Regina, and Swift Current, Saskatchewan. In Ottawa, he worked as a civil servant for the federal government. Beginning with the appearance of the privately printed *Grave Sirs* (1962), he published eight full-length collections, as well as several chapbooks: *Moving in Alone* (1965); *Black Night Window* (1968); *The Cave* (1970); *Lies* (1972;

Governor General's Award); *The Fat Man: Selected Poems, 1962–1972* (1977), *The Night the Dog Smiled* (1986), and *Apology for Absence: Selected Poems, 1962–1992* (1993). In 1977, he also edited, while working for McClelland & Stewart, the anthology *Canadian Poetry: The Modern Era*.

Early in his career, Newlove developed his distinctive Prairie voice—spare, and free of complex imagery and metaphor. Its influence can be seen in the poetry of later Western Canadian writers such as Patrick Lane and Lorna Crozier, as well as in the work of writers such as Michael Ondaatje, who said that he 'devoured and loved his work'. Well-suited to his generally harsh vision of the world, Newlove's clipped syntax and austere diction give an ironic edge to his natural lyricism, expressing a psychic dissonance in which an unrelenting melancholy is occasionally eased by the natural wonder of the world. At times, a sense of the sublime emerges in his poems (as when he writes that beauty 'makes the adrenalin run'), but more frequent are the moments of despair, as in the concluding lines of 'By the Church Wall' (1965):

*I lie alone in the shadowed grass,*
*fond only, incapable of love or truth,*
*caught in all I have done, afraid*
*and unable to escape, formulating*
*one more ruinous way to safety.*

Confounded by his sense that humanity lacks control over its fate and is searching fruitlessly for meaning, Newlove was tempted by nihilism—though he sometimes leavened his dark vision with a wry ironic humour, as when he writes that 'it's hard, living without hopelessness'. He shows us figures from the past (such as Louis Riel, Samuel Hearne, and the nomadic Natives of the west) achieving the wrenching and harrowing integration with the landscape that he longed for—but he also suggests that defeat is the usual destiny for contemporary individuals in a world that they themselves have corrupted. 'I am a technician of the absurd, / I am a comedian of death', Newlove wrote, and in the face of this disturbing vision, he found solace in alcohol. In one of his late poems, 'Such Fun, Such Fun', he speaks frankly, if self-mockingly, about his drinking and the poetry that seemed to him its reward: 'the sheer pleasure of the gift, of a few gloomy words'.

*The Green Plain*, the long poem Newlove published as a chapbook in 1981, is an exception—in its recognition that 'once in a while . . . poets / must / speak // of Spring!' and its concluding images of cosmic profundity. In a preface to the poem, entitled 'An Accidental Life', the poet describes how, when he was young, he had had 'a tangible vision of paradise', but that—out of 'a child's misunderstanding of the world'—he had ruined it, 'not as Adam ruined Eden, but as Cain the spoiler'. He does not explain further, but he adds,

*Most of what I write seems to me to go back to that day: to the real knowledge of a veritable paradise and the real knowledge of the tiny monster, the ogre, lurking like a shadow in the greenness.*

The final books published during Newlove's life—*The Night the Dog Smiled*, which contains new poems and revisions of earlier unpublished work, and *Apology for Absence*, which, as well as reprinting a selection of his earlier poems, contains new poems that are more frankly personal than any before—return to his bleak vision of humanity as a degraded inhabitant of an indifferent universe. *A Long Continual Argument* (2007), a posthumous selection edited by Robert McTavish, reflects the overall shape of Newlove's career. In the afterword, Jeff Derksen describes his body of work as one 'rippling with friction and discontent', mixed with moments of 'clarity, joy, disappointment, and resignation'.

## Four Small Scars

This scar beneath my lip
is symbol of a friend's rough love
though some would call it anger,
mistakenly. This scar

crescent on my wrist
is symbol of a woman's delicate anger
though some would call it love,
mistakenly. My belly's scar

is symbol of a surgical precision:
no anger, no love. The small
fading mark on my hand

is a token of my imprecision,
of my own carving, my anger and my love.

1965

# The Double-Headed Snake

Not to lose the feel of the mountains
while still retaining the prairies
is a difficult thing. What's lovely
is whatever makes the adrenalin run;
therefore I count terror and fear among
the greatest beauty. The greatest
beauty is to be alive, forgetting nothing,
although remembrance hurts
like a foolish act, is a foolish act.

Beauty's whatever                                                    10
makes the adrenalin run. Fear
in the mountains at night-time's
not tenuous, it is not the cold
that makes me shiver, civilized man,
white, I remember
the stories of the Indians,
Sis-i-utl, the double-headed snake.[1]

Beauty's what makes
the adrenalin run. Fear at night
on the level plains, with no horizon                                 20
and the stars too bright, wind bitter
even in June, in winter
the snow harsh and blowing,
is what makes me
shiver, not the cold air alone.

And one beauty cancels another. The plains
seem secure and comfortable
at Crow's Nest Pass;[2] in Saskatchewan
the mountains are comforting
to think of; among                                                   30
the eastwardly diminishing hills
both the flatland and the ridge
seem easy to endure.

---

1 According to West Coast Native mythology, the sight of a Sisiutl—a monstrous snake with a head at each end
   of its body—can turn one to stone.
2 A pass in the Rocky Mountains between Alberta and British Columbia through which a Canadian Pacific
   Railway branch-line was built in 1898.

As one beauty
cancels another, remembrance
is a foolish act, a double-headed snake
striking in both directions, but I
remember plains and mountains, places
I come from, places I adhere and live in.

1968

## Samuel Hearne[1] in Wintertime

I

In this cold room
I remember the smell of manure
on men's heavy clothes as good,
the smell of horses.

It is a romantic world
to readers of journeys
to the Northern Ocean—

especially if their houses are heated
to some degree, Samuel.

Hearne, your camp must have smelled                          10
like hell whenever you settled down
for a few days of rest and journal-work:

hell smeared with human manure,
hell half-full of raw hides,
hell of sweat, Indians, stale fat,
meat-hell, fear-hell, hell of cold.

---

1  Samuel Hearne (1745–92), an early Canadian explorer and author of a classic travel narrative, *A Journey from Prince of Wales's Fort in Hudson's Bay to the Northern Ocean* (1795), about his explorations in the north (see pp. 29–36). The conclusion of Newlove's poem alludes to a famous passage in that book recounting Hearne's accompanying a band of Cree in their massacre of an Inuit village; in it, Hearne describes the death of an eighteen-year-old girl who, when struck by a spear, twisted herself about his legs and—as Hearne pleaded for mercy for her—was dispatched by two more Indians, her body 'twining round their spears like an eel!' (The full account can be found on p. 36.)

2

One child is back from the doctor's while
the other one wanders about in dirty pants
and I think of Samuel Hearne and the land—

puffy children coughing as I think,                                     20
crying, sick-faced,
vomit stirring in grey blankets
from room to room.

It is Christmastime
the cold flesh shines.
No praise in merely enduring.


3

Samuel Hearne did more
in the land (like all the rest

full of rocks and hilly country,
many very extensive tracts of land,                                     30
tittimeg, pike and barble,[2]

and the islands:
the islands, many
of them abound

as well as the main
land does
with dwarf woods,

chiefly pine
in some parts intermixed
with larch and birch) than endure.                                      40

The Indians killed twelve deer.
It was impossible to describe
the intenseness of the cold.

2  Three types of fish that Hearne found in the north.

4

And, Samuel Hearne,
I have almost begun to talk

as if you wanted to be
gallant, as if you went
through that land for a book—

as if you were not SAM, wanting
to know, to do a job.                                    50


5

There was that Eskimo girl
at Bloody Falls, at your feet,

Samuel Hearne, with two spears in her,
you helpless before your helpers,

and she twisted about them like
an eel, dying, never to know.

1968


# Ride Off Any Horizon

Ride off any horizon
and let the measure fall
where it may—

on the hot wheat,
on the dark yellow fields
of wild mustard, the fields

of bad farmers, on the river,
on the dirty river full
of boys and on the throbbing

powerhouse and the low dam                          10
of cheap cement and rocks
boiling with white water,

and on the cows and their powerful
bulls, the heavy tracks
filling with liquid at the edge

of the narrow prairie
river running steadily away.

      *    *    *

Ride off any horizon
and let the measure fall
where it may—                                20

among the piles of bones
that dot the prairie

in vision and history
(the buffalo and deer,

dead indians, dead settlers
the frames of lost houses

left behind in the dust
of the depression,

dry and profound, that
will come again in the land                30

and in the spirit, the land
shifting and the minds

blown dry and empty—
I have not seen it! except

in pictures and talk—
but there is the fence

covered with dust, laden,
the wrecked house stupidly empty)—

here is a picture for your wallet,
of the beaten farmer and his wife            40
leaning toward each other—

sadly smiling, and emptied of desire.

\*   \*   \*

Ride off any horizon
and let the measure fall
where it may—

off the edge
of the black prairie

as you thought you could fall,
a boy at sunset

not watching the sun             50
set but watching the black earth,

never-ending they said in school,
round: but you saw it ending,

finished, definite, precise—
visible only miles away.

       \*   \*   \*

Ride off any horizon
and let the measure fall
where it may—

on a hot night the town
is in the streets—             60

the boys and girls
are practising against

each other, the men
talk and eye the girls—

the women talk and
eye each other, the indians
play pool: eye on the ball.

       \*   \*   \*

Ride off any horizon
and let the measure fall
where it may—             70

and damn the troops, the horsemen
are wheeling in the sunshine,
the cree, practising

for their deaths: mr poundmaker,
gentle sweet mr bigbear,
it is not unfortunately

quite enough to be innocent,
it is not enough merely
not to offend—

at times to be born                                    80
is enough, to be
in the way is too much—

some colonel otter,[1] some
major-general middleton will
get you, you—

indian. It is no good to say,
I would rather die
at once than be in that place—

though you love that land more,
you will go where they take you.                       90


                *    *    *


Ride of any horizon
and let the measure fall—

where it may;
it doesn't have to be

the prairie. It could be
the cold soul of the cities
blown empty by commerce

---

1  Sir William Dillon Otter (1834–1929), Canadian colonel in command of the militia that relieved the settlers
   under attack at Fort Battleford; he was defeated by Poundmaker at Cut Knife Hill. 'Major-General Middleton':
   Sir Frederick Dobson Middleton (1825–98), British commander of the Canadian militia during the suppression
   of the Northwest Rebellion.

and desiring commerce
to fill up emptiness.

The streets are full of people.                    100

It is night, the lights
are on; the wind

blows as far as it may. The streets
are dark and full of people.

Their eyes are fixed as far as
they can see beyond each other—

to the concrete horizon, definite,
tall against the mountains,
stopping vision visibly.

1968

# The Green Plain

Small human figures and fanciful monsters
abound. Dreams surround us,
preserve us. We praise constancy as brave,
but variation's lovelier.

Rain surrounds us, arguments and dreams, there are
forests between us, there are
too many of us for comfort, always were.

                              Is civilization
only lack of room, only
an ant-heap at last?—the strutting cities                    10
of the East, battered gold,
the crammed walls of India,
humanity swarming, indistinguishable
                    from the earth?

Even the nomads roaming the green plain, for them
at last no land was ever enough.

Spreading—but now we can go anywhere
                        and we are afraid
and talk of small farms instead of the stars
                          and all the places we go       20
space is distorted.

How shall we save the symmetry of the universe?—
or our own symmetry, which is the same.

                                 Which myths
should capture us, since we do not wish
to be opened, to be complete?—
or are they the same, all of them?

Now a dream involves me, of a giant sprawled among stars,
face to the dark, his eyes closed.
                          Common.            30

Only he is not breathing, he does not heave,
Is it Gulliver?—huge, image of us, tied, webbed in,
and never learning anything,

                              always ignorant,
Always amazed, always capable of delight,
and giving it, though ending in hatred, but
an image only. Of disaster. But there is no disaster.
It is just that we lose joy and die.

But is there a symmetry?
                        Is there reason       40
in the galaxies—Or is this all glass,
a block bubbled in a fire, accident only,
prettiness fused without care, pettiness,
though some logic, alien but understandable,
in the ruined crystal?

              The forests, the forests, swaying,
there is no reason why they should be beautiful.
They live for their own reasons, not ours.
But they are.

It is not time that flows but the world.                 50

And the world flows,
still flows. Even in these worn-out days,
worn-out terms,
once in a while our poets
must
speak

of Spring! Of all things! The flowers
blow in their faces too, and they smell perfumes,
and they are seduced
by colour—rural as the hair crocus or urban as a waxy tulip.                    60

                    But confusion. The world
flows past. It is hard to remember age. Does
this always world flow? Does it? Please say it does,
not time.
           Do not say time flows.
Say: We do. Say: We live.

Fly-speck, fly-speck. In this ever island Earth
we are the tiny giants, swaggering
behind the dinosaurs, lovely,
tame brontosaurus, sweet cows lumbering                    70
among the coal trees, fronds offering
shade and future fuel.

And the land around us green and happy,
waiting as you wait for a killer to spring,
a full-sized blur,
waiting like a tree in southern Saskatchewan,
remarked on, lonely and famous as a saint.

The mechanisms by which the stars generate invention
live all over and around us
and yet we refine machines, defer                    80
to tricks as discovery. Everything is always here,
and burning.

There are no surprises, there is only
what is left. We live
inside the stars,

burning, burning,
the mechanisms.

Stars, rain, forests.
Stars rain forests.
Sew up the lives together. There is                                                    90
this only world. Thank God: this World
and its wrapped variations
spreading around and happy, flowing,
flowing through the climate of intelligence,
beautiful confusion looking around,
seeing the mechanics and the clouds
and marvelling, O Memory . . .

1981

# Margaret Atwood
## b. 1939

Since winning a Governor General's Award for her first full-length book, *The Circle Game* (1966), Margaret Atwood has created a body of poetry, short stories, novels, and non-fiction that has gained her a significant international reputation. Early in her career, she was also, as an editor for the House of Anansi Press with Dennis Lee, James Polk, and others, part of the energetic small press scene that played a vital role in the flowering of Canadian literature in the 1960s and 1970s. Atwood subsequently served as a member of Anansi's board of directors and edited several anthologies, including *The New Oxford Book of Canadian Verse* (1982) and two versions of *The Oxford Book of Canadian Short Stories* (with Robert Weaver in 1986 and 1995). She has been president of the Writers' Union of Canada (1982–3) and of PEN Canada (1984–6), and is currently Vice-President of PEN International. As a tireless promoter of Canadian literature, she has lectured about Canadian writers and culture—and discussed and read from her own work—in Canada, the United States, Europe, Asia, and Australia. As well as being a Fellow in the Royal Society of Canada, her many honours include the Norwegian Order of Literary Merit and the Prince of Asturias Prize (Spain's highest literary award).

Born in Ottawa, the daughter of an entomologist who took his family with him during his extended stretches of research in the northern Ontario and Quebec bush, Atwood did not attend a full year of formal school until grade 8, when her family moved to Toronto. After graduating from high school in 1957, she entered Victoria College, University of Toronto. Her teachers there included literary theorist Northrop Frye, poet Jay Macpherson, and poet-playwright James Reaney, all three of whom were formative influences on Atwood, particularly in their shared belief that myth was an important resource for literature. Around this time, she also became acquainted with Gwendolyn MacEwen. (After MacEwen's death, Atwood co-edited her collected poems with Barry Callaghan.)

Atwood completed her BA in 1961, publishing a slim poetry chapbook, *Double Persephone*, that year. Enrolling in graduate studies at Radcliffe College, she took a master's degree in 1962 and began a doctoral thesis at Harvard, on the 'English metaphysical romances' of George MacDonald and H. Rider Haggard. She left Harvard to work briefly as a market researcher in Toronto; between 1964 and 1973, she taught English or was writer-in-residence at Sir George Williams University (now part of Concordia), the University of Alberta, York University, and the University of Toronto. Except for some additional short residencies, she has been a full-time writer since 1973, living on a farm near Alliston, Ontario, and, since 1980, in Toronto.

Atwood began her career writing in a stark, unemotional style that often made readers uneasy. She demanded new ways of perceiving in the poetry collected in *The Circle Game*, *The Animals in That Country* (1968), *Procedures for Underground* (1970), and *You Are Happy* (1974), as well as those in the book-length sequences *The Journals of Susanna Moodie* (1970) and *Power Politics* (1973)—which opens with this very short piece:

> You fit into me
> like a hook into an eye
>
> a fish hook
> an open eye.

Her novels of this period (*The Edible Woman*, 1969; *Surfacing*, 1972; and *Lady Oracle*, 1976) share the tone and interests of her poems. Frequently told from the point of view of alienated individuals (sometimes people on the verge of breakdown), they express a distrust of the socially constructed world as a place of deceptive appearances and emotional shallowness. In both poetry and fiction Atwood indicts contemporary society as driven by commercial interests, mass media, and consumerism and affirms the benefits to be gained through

contact with nature, as well as the power of dreams, myth, and visions.

Atwood's nationalism and feminism complement one another in her approach to these questions. She looks at the problem of inequality for women in works such as *Power Politics* and *The Edible Woman*, and for Canadians in works such as *Surfacing* and *The Journals of Susanna Moodie*. In the afterword to that sequence of poems, she writes,

*If the national mental illness of the United States is megalomania, that of Canada is paranoid schizophrenia. Mrs Moodie is divided down the middle: she praises the Canadian landscape but accuses it of destroying her; she dislikes the people already in Canada but finds in people her only refuge from the land itself; she preaches progress and the march of civilization while brooding elegiacally upon the destruction of the wilderness. . . . She claims to be an ardent Canadian patriot while all the time she is standing back from the country and criticizing it as though she were a detached observer, a stranger. Perhaps that is the way we still live. We are all immigrants to this place even if we were born here: the country is too big for anyone to inhabit completely, and in the parts unknown to us we move in fear, exiles and invaders. This country is something that must be chosen—it is so easy to leave—and if we do choose it we are still choosing a violent duality.*

Atwood associated this condition with the idea that Canada was suffering from a lack of national identity because of a colonial mentality, a problem she addressed in *Survival: A Thematic Guide to Canadian Literature* (1972). A polemical work of criticism that uses literature to diagnose cultural ills, *Survival* synthesized ideas then current: not only that Canadian culture was inhibited by its colonial relationships to Britain and to the United States, but also that Canada's creative expression had been stifled by its harsh wintry environment, its historic patterns of settlement (in isolated garrison communities rather than by individuals moving along an advancing western frontier), and its religious inheritance of Scots-Calvinism. Atwood concluded that Canadian literature was, in consequence, filled with stories of victims. Although some writers and critics (especially those in the west) protested this reading of Canada's literary tradition as one-sided and subjective, this book and other works of cultural thematic criticism reflected the powerful new wave of cultural nationalism then taking place and its eagerness to define a national literary tradition. (*Survival* also sheds light on Atwood's early fiction and poetry: the most important lesson learned by the protagonist of *Surfacing* is 'this above all, to refuse to be a victim.')

The publication in 1976 and 1977 of two compilations, *Selected Poems* and *Dancing Girls* (her first collection of short stories), marked the end of the first phase of Atwood's writing career. Although her early writing is powerful, there is more range and depth in the work that follows—which includes the stories in *Bluebeard's Egg* (1983) and *Wilderness Tips* (1991) and in the short-story sequence, *Moral Disorder* (2006); the short prose pieces in *Murder in the Dark* (1983), *Good Bones* (1992), and *The Tent* (2006); and nine more novels: *Life Before Man* (1979), *Bodily Harm* (1981), *The Handmaid's Tale* (1985; Governor General's Award; the basis of a 1990 film and, in 2000, of an opera by Denmark's Poul Ruders and Paul Bentley), *Cat's Eye* (1988), *The Robber Bride* (1993), *Alias Grace* (1996; Giller Prize), *The Blind Assassin* (2000; Booker Prize), *Oryx and Crake* (2003), and *The Year of the Flood* (2009). In this later fiction, Atwood broadens her satirical and political targets and also begins to publish work that is more self-revealing and personal (*Moral Disorder* is a semi-fictional memoir). Characters in the novels are more fully drawn and varied (in *Life Before Man*, she uses a male viewpoint for the first time), and she shows the potential in human relationships for comfort as well as for conflict.

As the political level of her work shifts focus, Atwood's concerns about the effects on the world of imperialism and other forms of hegemony intensify, and she becomes more engaged with specific issues. *Bodily Harm*, a tale of a Canadian travel writer's naive involvement in a political coup in the Caribbean, makes it plain that Canada must now look beyond its own borders, as does *The Handmaid's Tale*, a dystopian fable about a repressive American society governed by male right-wing religious fundamentalists. From the multiple viewpoints of *The Robber Bride*, to the layered narrative structure of *The Blind Assassin*, which features excerpts from a science-fiction novella within the novel; to the historical setting of *Alias Grace*, about the mid-nineteenth century murder case of Grace Marks; through *The Penelopiad* (2005), with its retelling of the *Odyssey* from the point of view of Odysseus's wife, Atwood's later fiction demonstrates a virtuosic mastery of genres as well as a wide range of topics and narrative techniques, often moving across historical eras and even into the future.

In her post-apocalyptic novels *Oryx and Crake* and *The Year of the Flood*, Atwood shows an intensified focus on environmental and ecological issues. (She is at work on a third volume that will conclude this trilogy.) 'The Age of Lead', the story reprinted here (from *Wilderness Tips*), is also an ecological fable—developed through counterpoint between the narrator's growing understanding of the past, which comes to her in the form of a television show about the fate of the last Franklin expedition (for more details, see the headnote about John Franklin and Dr John Richardson on pages 65–7) and of her own social relationships. The explorations led by Franklin correspond to a larger drive in the Canadian psyche to go north, 'somewhere mapless, off into the unknown'; however, the mapless future the narrator finds herself venturing into holds unexpected terrors: 'People were dying. They were dying too early.'

Atwood has continued to write poetry: she published *Two-Headed Poems* in 1978, *True Stories* in 1981, and *Interlunar* in 1984. Since publishing a new *Selected Poems* in 1986, she has added only two further books: *Morning in the Burned House* (1995) and *The Door* (2007). Like her fiction, her later poetry has become more expressly political. *Two-Headed Poems* takes its title from a sequence about Canada's division between two cultures (the title also recalls the preoccupation with doubleness and duality that runs through Atwood's work). In that book, and in the work that follows, Atwood protests political oppression, adopting a global perspective that reflects her associations with Amnesty International and PEN Canada. At the same time, in books such as *True Stories*, she portrays family relationships for the first time (as in 'Spelling' and in the elegiac meditations on the death of her father in *Morning in the Burned House*), and is more introspective than she was in her earlier work. In a poem such as 'Variation on the Word *Sleep*', she can now write without irony of a woman's love for a man.

In the title poem of *The Door* Atwood confronts her own mortality as a door that opens into an unknowable darkness. Elsewhere, 'The Line: Five Variations' shows Atwood reflecting on the craft of writing. Offering five different perspectives and layered with allusions, the poem is indeed a series of variations, its five parts suggesting different ways of thinking about literature (I and II, for example, oppose archetypal and imagistic writing) and echoing different writers (the opening of Part IV recasts Jay Macpherson's famous poem 'The Fisherman', while Part V sounds like something out of Thomas King's coyote tales in *One Good Story, That One*). The whole poem suggests that, for better *and* for worse, poetry and narrative have been forces that have changed the world.

While creating a large corpus of poetry and fiction, Atwood has written non-fiction as well. *Second Words* (1982) and *Moving Targets: Writing with Intent, 1982-2004* (2004) gather reviews, lectures, and essays, some of which complement or comment on *Survival*. In 1995, Atwood published *Strange Things: The Malevolent North in Canadian Literature*, based on a series of lectures she gave at Oxford University. In it, she discusses the way the mystique of the North has played an important role in Canadian cultural mythology, discussing it under four rubrics: the ill-fated Franklin expedition and the fascination it has exerted; the idea of turning oneself into a northern Native (as Archie Belaney transformed himself into Grey Owl); the Wendigo (a monster in North American Native myth that 'has been seen as the personification of winter, or hunger, or spiritual selfishness'), and the changing roles of women in the North. Atwood's other non-fiction books include *Two Solicitudes: Conversations*, with Victor-Lévy Beaulieu (1998); *Negotiating with the Dead: A Writer on Writing* (2002), a moving set of meditations about the role of the writer, based on the Empson Lectures she delivered at the University of Cambridge in 2000; and *Payback: Debt and the Shadow Side of Wealth* (2008), a discussion of the meaning of debt in myth, literature, and the Bible, based on the Massey Lectures she delivered across Canada in the fall of 2008.

Given Atwood's critical awareness, it is not surprising that her fiction often makes use of metafictional and self-reflexive mirroring and frequently contains portraits of writers. In all her work—fiction, non-fiction, and poetry—Atwood takes very seriously the artist's duty to society and the power of the written word. As a passage in *Murder in the Dark* suggests, writing is an act of great import and so, therefore, is reading:

. . . *Beneath the page is a story. Beneath the page is everything that has ever happened, most of which you would rather not hear about.*

*Touch the page at your peril: it is you who are blank and innocent, not the page. Nevertheless you want to know, nothing will stop you. You touch the page, it's as if you've drawn a knife across it, the page has been hurt now, a sinuous wound opens, a thin incision. Darkness wells through.* ('The Page', 1983)

# This is a Photograph of Me

It was taken some time ago.
At first it seems to be
a smeared
print: blurred lines and grey flecks
blended with the paper;

then, as you scan
it, you see in the left-hand corner
a thing that is like a branch: part of a tree
(balsam or spruce) emerging
and, to the right, halfway up                                    10
what ought to be a gentle
slope, a small frame house.

In the background there is a lake,
and beyond that, some low hills.

(The photograph was taken
the day after I drowned.

I am in the lake, in the center
of the picture, just under the surface.

It is difficult to say where
precisely, or to say                                             20
how large or small I am:
the effect of water
on light is a distortion

but if you look long enough,
eventually
you will be able to see me.)

1966

# Progressive Insanities of a Pioneer

i

*verticality*

He stood, a point
on a sheet of green paper
proclaiming himself the centre,

with no walls, no borders
anywhere; the sky no height
above him, totally un-
enclosed
and shouted:

Let me out!

ii

He dug the soil in rows,                                        10
imposed himself with shovels.
He asserted
into the furrows, I
am not random.

The ground
replied with aphorisms:

a tree-sprout, a nameless
weed, words
he couldn't understand.

iii

The house pitched                                        20
the plot staked
in the middle of nowhere

At night the mind
inside, in the middle
of nowhere

The idea of an animal
patters across the roof.

In the darkness the fields
defend themselves with fences
in vain:
       everything
       is getting in.

          iv

By daylight he resisted.
He said, disgusted
with the swamp's clamourings and the outbursts
of rocks.
       This is not order
       but the absence
       of order

He was wrong, the unanswering
forest implied:

       It was
       an ordered absence

          v

For many years
he fished for a great vision,
dangling the hooks of sown
roots under the surface
of the shallow earth.

It was like
enticing whales with a bent
pin. Besides he thought

in that country
only the worms were biting.

30

40

50

vi

If he had known unstructured
space is a deluge
and stocked his log house-
boat with all the animals

even the wolves,

he might have floated.

But obstinate he                                              60
stated, The land is solid
and stamped,

watching his foot sink
down through stone
up to the knee.


vii

Things
refused to name themselves; refused
to let him name them.

The wolves hunted
outside.                                                      70

On his beaches, his clearings,
by the surf of under-
growth breaking
at his feet, he foresaw
disintegration
                and in the end
through eyes
made ragged by his
effort, the tension
between subject and object,                                   80

the green
vision, the unnamed
whale invaded.

1968

# From *The Journals of Susanna Moodie*[1]

## FROM JOURNAL 1, 1832–1840

## Disembarking at Quebec

Is it my clothes, my way of walking,
the things I carry in my hand
—a book, a bag with knitting—
the incongruous pink of my shawl

this space cannot hear

or is it my own lack
of conviction which makes
these vistas of desolation,
long hills, the swamps, the barren sand, the glare
of sun on the bone-white                                     10
driftlogs, omens of winter,
the moon alien in day-
time a thin refusal

The others leap, shout

      Freedom![2]

The moving water will not show me
my reflection.

The rocks ignore.

I am a word
in a foreign language.                                       20

---

1  In this book Atwood uses the historical Susanna Moodie (1803–85) as the speaker in poems inspired by her two
   narratives of settlement, *Roughing It in the Bush* (1852) and *Life in the Clearings* (1853). Most of the people and
   events alluded to in the poems reprinted here may be found in the selections from *Roughing It in the Bush*,
   pp. 110–39.
2  In Chapter 2 of *Roughing It*, Moodie says she was 'not a little amused at the extravagant expectations entertained
   by some of our steerage passengers. . . . In spite of the remonstrances of the captain and the dread of the cholera,
   they all rushed on shore to inspect the land of Goshen, and to endeavour to realize their absurd anticipations.'

# Further Arrivals

After we had crossed the long illness
that was the ocean, we sailed up-river

On the first island
the immigrants threw off their clothes
and danced like sandflies[1]

We left behind one by one
the cities rotting with cholera,
one by one our civilized
distinctions

and entered a large darkness.                    10

It was our own
ignorance we entered.

I have not come out yet

My brain gropes nervous
tentacles in the night, sends out
fears hairy as bears,
demands lamps; or waiting

for my shadowy husband, hears
malice in the trees' whispers.

I need wolf's eyes to see                          20
the truth.

I refuse to look in a mirror.

Whether the wilderness is
real or not
depends on who lives there.

1 In the first chapter of *Roughing It* the Moodies visited Grosse Isle for an afternoon while their ship stood off shore following an inspection by health officers (Quebec was then experiencing a cholera epidemic): 'Never shall I forget the extraordinary spectacle that met our sight. . . . A crowd of many hundred Irish emigrants had been landed . . . and all this motley crew—men, women, and children— . . . were employed in washing clothes. . . . The men and boys were in the water, while the women, with their scanty garments tucked above their knees, were tramping their bedding in tubs or in holes in the rocks. Those [not washing] were running to and fro, screaming and scolding in no measured terms . . . all accompanying their vociferations with violent and extraordinary gestures, quite incomprehensible to the uninitiated.'

## FROM JOURNAL II, 1840–1871

# Death of a Young Son by Drowning

He, who navigated with success
the dangerous river of his own birth
once more set forth

on a voyage of discovery
into the land I floated on
but could not touch to claim.

His feet slid on the bank,
the currents took him;
he swirled with ice and trees in the swollen water

and plunged into distant regions,                    10
his head a bathysphere;
through his eyes' thin glass bubbles

he looked out, reckless adventurer
on a landscape stranger than Uranus
we have all been to and some remember.

There was an accident; the air locked,
he was hung in the river like a heart.
They retrieved the swamped body,

cairn of my plans and future charts,
with poles and hooks                                  20
from among the nudging logs.

It was spring, the sun kept shining, the new grass
lept to solidity;
my hands glistened with details.

After the long trip I was tired of waves.
My foot hit rock. The dreamed sails
collapsed, ragged.

      I planted him in this country
      like a flag.

# Dream 2: Brian the Still-Hunter[1]

The man I saw in the forest
used to come to our house
every morning, never said anything;
I learned from the neighbours later
he once tried to cut his throat.

I found him at the end of the path
sitting on a fallen tree
cleaning his gun.

There was no wind;
around us the leaves rustled.                              10

He said to me:
I kill because I have to

but every time I aim, I feel
my skin grow fur
my head heavy with antlers
and during the stretched instant
the bullet glides on its thread of speed
my soul runs innocent as hooves.

Is God just to his creatures?

I die more often than many.                                20

He looked up and I saw
the white scar made by the hunting knife
around his neck.

When I woke
I remembered: he has been gone
twenty years and not heard from.

1 A 'still-hunter' is one who hunts stealthily on foot. In Chapter 10 of *Roughing It* Moodie describes her friendship with Brian, a man once subject to such fits of depression that he had tried to commit suicide. Brian tells
  her a vivid story of watching a 'noble deer' pulled down by a pack of wolves, concluding:
> At that moment he seemed more unfortunate even than myself, for I could not see in what manner he had deserved
> his fate. All his speed and energy, his courage and fortitude, had been exerted in vain. I had tried to destroy myself;
> but he, with every effort vigorously made for self-preservation, was doomed to meet the fate he dreaded! Is God just
> to his creatures?

Moodie ends the chapter by saying:
> We parted with the hunter as an old friend; and we never met again. His fate was a sad one. After we left that
> part of the country, he fell into a moping melancholy, which ended in self-destruction.

## FROM JOURNAL III, 1871–1969

# Thoughts from Underground[1]

When I first reached this country
I hated it
and I hated it more each year:

in summer the light a
violent blur, the heat
thick as a swamp,
the green things fiercely
shoving themselves upwards, the
eyelids bitten by insects

In winter our teeth were brittle                    10
with cold. We fed on squirrels.
At night the house cracked.
In the mornings, we thawed
the bad bread over the stove.

Then we were made successful
and I felt I ought to love
this country.
　　　　　I said I loved it
and my mind saw double.

I began to forget myself                             20
in the middle
of sentences. Events
were split apart

I fought. I constructed
desperate paragraphs of praise, everyone
ought to love it because

and set them up at intervals

　　　due to natural resources, native industry, superior
　　　penitentiaries
　　　we will all be rich and powerful                30

1 This poem is spoken by Moodie after her death.

flat as highway billboards

who can doubt it, look how
fast Belleville is growing

(though it is still no place for an english gentleman)

1970

## Tricks with Mirrors

i

It's no coincidence
this is a used
furniture warehouse.

I enter with you
and become a mirror.

Mirrors
are the perfect lovers,

that's it, carry me up the stairs
by the edges, don't drop me,

that would be bad luck,                    10
throw me on the bed

reflecting side up,
fall into me,

it will be your own
mouth you hit, firm and glassy,

your own eyes you find you
are up against    closed    closed

ii

There is more to a mirror
than you looking at

your full-length body
flawless but reversed, 20

there is more than this dead blue
oblong eye turned outwards to you.

Think about the frame.
The frame is carved, it is important,

it exists, it does not reflect you,
it does not recede and recede, it has limits

and reflections of its own.
There's a nail in the back

to hang it with; there are several nails, 30
think about the nails,

pay attention to the nail
marks in the wood,

they are important too.


      iii

Don't assume it is passive
or easy, this clarity

with which I give you yourself.
Consider what restraint it

takes: breath withheld, no anger
or joy disturbing the surface 40

of the ice.
You are suspended in me

beautiful and frozen, I
preserve you, in me you are safe.

It is not a trick either.
it is a craft:

mirrors are crafty.

iv

I wanted to stop this,
this life flattened against the wall,

mute and devoid of colour,
built of pure light,

this life of vision only, split
and remote, a lucid impasse.

I confess: this is not a mirror,
it is a door

I am trapped behind.
I wanted you to see me here,

say the releasing word, whatever
that may be, open the wall.

Instead you stand in front of me
combing your hair.


v

You don't like these metaphors.
All right:

Perhaps I am not a mirror.
Perhaps I am a pool.

Think about pools.

1974

## Siren Song[1]

This is the one song everyone
would like to learn: the song
that is irresistible:

the song that forces men
to leap overboard in squadrons
even though they see the beached skulls

the song nobody knows
because anyone who has heard it
is dead, and the others can't remember.

Shall I tell you the secret                                          10
and if I do, will you get me
out of this bird suit?

I don't enjoy it here
squatting on this island
looking picturesque and mythical

with these two feathery maniacs,
I don't enjoy singing
this trio, fatal and valuable.

I will tell the secret to you,
to you, only to you.                                                 20
Come closer. This song

is a cry for help: Help me!
Only you, only you can,
you are unique

at last. Alas
it is a boring song
but it works every time.

1974

---

1  In Greek mythology three sirens, half-women and half-birds, used their enchanting songs to lure sailors to their
   island in the Mediterranean Sea where, deprived of their will-power, they wasted away, leaving the beach strewn
   with their whitening bones.

# Spelling

My daughter plays on the floor
with plastic letters,
red, blue & hard yellow,
learning how to spell,
spelling,
how to make spells

      *

and I wonder how many women
denied themselves daughters,
closed themselves in rooms,
drew the curtains                                    10
so they could mainline words.

      *

A child is not a poem,
a poem is not a child.
There is no either/or.
However.

      *

I return to the story
of the woman caught in the war
& in labour, her thighs tied
together by the enemy
so she could not give birth.                         20

Ancestress: the burning witch,
her mouth covered by leather
to strangle words.

A word after a word
after a word is power.

      *

At the point where language falls away
from the hot bones, at the point
where the rock breaks open and darkness

flows out of it like blood, at
the melting point of granite                    30
when the bones know
they are hollow & the word
splits & doubles & speaks
the truth & the body
itself becomes a mouth.

This is a metaphor.

*

How do you learn to spell?
Blood, sky & the sun,
your own name first,
your first naming, your first name,          40
your first word.

1981

# Orpheus (2)[1]

Whether he will go on singing
or not, knowing what he knows
of the horror of this world:

He was not wandering among meadows
all this time. He was down there
among the mouthless ones, among
those with no fingers, those
whose names are forbidden,
those washed up eaten into

---

1 The entrancing singer from Greek myth, Orpheus travelled into Hades, the underworld of the dead, to rescue his wife Eurydice and through his own error lost her as he was bringing her back to Earth. Afterwards, he sang laments in the woods, away from other human beings, until a group of Thracian Maenads—female followers of Dionysus, the god of wine—found him and insisted that he celebrate with them in their frenzied revelries. When he refused, they tore him to pieces. His head, thrown into the Hebrus River, lived on, still singing; it was eventually found near the island of Lesbos and buried. In *Margaret Atwood's Fairy-Tale Sexual Politics* (1993), Sharon Rose Wilson finds in the details of Atwood's retelling of this story an allusion to the fate of Víctor Jara (1932–73), Chilean teacher, singer, director, and political activist, who became a symbol of resistance against General Augusto Pinochet and the military coup he led against the president of Chile, Salvador Allende. Jara, along with thousands of other Chileans, was taken by Pinochet's followers to Estadio Chile (now known as Estadio Victor Jara), where he and many of the other detainees were tortured and then killed. To make a specific example of Jara, the bones of his hands, which, with his voice, were the source of his music, were broken (some say cut off). Jara continued to sing until he was beaten and then machine-gunned to death.

among the grey stones                                    10
of the shore where nobody goes
through fear. Those with silence.

He has been trying to sing
love into existence again
and he has failed.

Yet he will continue
to sing, in the stadium
crowded with the already dead
who raise their eyeless faces
to listen to him; while the red flowers        20
grow up and splatter open
against the walls.

They have cut off both his hands
and soon they will tear
his head from his body in one burst
of furious refusal.
He foresees this. Yet he will go on
singing, and in praise.
To sing is either praise
or defiance. Praise is defiance.              30

1984

# The Line: Five Variations

I

The line is a white thread,
or so we're told.[1] You fasten
one end of it to a tree or bed

---

1 Although this phrase suggests a source outside the poem, it is not clear by whom 'we're told' about a white thread. One possible allusion (especially given the black thread that appears in Part III) is to an often-cited passage from the Koran about how to identify the beginning of a new day: when 'the white thread of dawn appears to you distinct from the black thread.' As well, in a frequently quoted passage from *The Golden Bough* (rev. ed. 1922)—a book read by all those of Atwood's generation interested in myth—Sir James Frazer advances his theory of the evolution of human thought by using threads as a metaphor: 'We may illustrate the course which thought has hitherto run by likening it to a web of three different threads—the black thread of magic, the red thread of religion, and the white thread of science.' (Frazer's colour choices are significant: 'red' because he thought the essence of religion was sacrifice; 'white' because he thought science brought enlightenment.)

or threshold,[2] and footfall
by footfall, you unscroll
this line behind you

as you step into the cave to meet
whatever's in there—

the ill will of the universe,
a shucked lover,                                          10
the core of your own head—
compacted fire,
monstrous, horned, sacred.

You hold your breath,
one heartbite
after another.
Tastes familiar.


II

The line is a lifeline,
it leads you out again
to the profane. To vegetables                             20
and sex, and eggs
and bacon. Fodder. Wallow. Time
as generally understood.
Breakfast, lunch, dinner,
architecture,
all those things
that won't miss you
when you're elsewhere.
There. Feel better?


III

Reverse the field and the line is black,                  30
the cavern a whiteout.
A blank, a snow.

---

2 In Greek legend, before entering the labyrinth to encounter the Minotaur (the offspring of the goddess Pasiphaë
  and a bull), the hero Theseus ties a thread—given to him by the Minotaur's half-sister Ariadne—to a doorpost
  so he can find his way out again.

The monster not a burning coal,[3]
but ice-furred shadow.[4]

Where does that get you?
Out of the body, onto the page,
the line the net
in which you tangle God—[5]
O, paper wendigo—

in the midst of his blizzard,                                    40
in the midst of his avalanche
of *nihilo*,[6]
going about his business,
wringing stars out of zero.


IV


The line's for fishing.

You hook the big one, haul him in.
You net his flounderings.
You write him down, the Word
made word.[7] You've earthed him,
all his acts and sufferings. He seeps                           50
out of your fingers now, like wine-dark blood[8]
set free.

3  Likely an allusion to the biblical story in which Hebrew prophet Isaiah, having seen God upon his throne, fears
   for his life. When Isaiah cries out, 'Woe is me! for I am undone; because I am a man of unclean lips, and I dwell
   in the midst of a people of unclean lips: for mine eyes have seen the King, the LORD of hosts' (Isaiah 6.5), one
   of the angels takes a piece of burning coal from the altar and places it on his lips, saying 'thine iniquity is taken
   away, and thy sin purged' (Isaiah 6.7). After this act of purification is completed, God, angry at his people, com-
   missions Isaiah as his prophet: 'Go, and tell this people, Hear ye indeed, but understand not; and see ye indeed,
   but perceive not.' When Isaiah asks, 'Lord, how long?' God answers, 'Until the cities be wasted without inhabitant, and the houses without man, and the land be utterly desolate.'
4  The fur-covered monster, the Wendigo (identified a few lines later). In her discussion of this creature in *Strange
   Things*, Atwood quotes from George Bowering's poem 'Windigo', which calls the creature 'a long shadow / on
   the ice.'
5  To use a net to 'tangle God' may allude to the Greek myth of Hephaestus, the betrayed husband of Aphrodite,
   who uses a net to trap her with her lover, the god Ares, in adulterous union; it may also allude to the myth of
   Proteus, the wise old man of the sea who can transform himself into any shape, even into water (note Atwood's
   use of 'seeps' in line 50); Proteus knows everything about the past, the present, and the future but will not reveal
   his knowledge unless captured, bound, and held until he tires of changing shape.
6  'Nothing' (Latin). The doctrine of *creatio ex nihilo* is the religious belief that God created the universe from
   nothing.
7  An allusion to John 1:1–14 on the coming of Jesus into the world: 'In the beginning was the Word, and the Word
   was with God, and the Word was God. . . . And the Word was made flesh and dwelt among us.'
8  A turn on Homer's description of the ocean ('the wine-dark sea') to suggest the Communion service—the com-
   memoration of the last supper before Jesus's crucifixion—in which the bread and wine represent the flesh and
   blood of Jesus.

Oh oh. You've cut his noose,
you've let him loose. He's gone
with the spiralling wind, he's roaring
from the mountaintop:[9]
*Here comes Time!*
*Yum! Yum! Yum! Yum!*

Now we'll have massacres.


V

That was some line                                          60
you fed us! What a bad story!

Keep your hands to yourself
next time! Don't touch that paper!
We don't need no war-surplus history
tall tales around this place. We don't
need more *And then.*

But you never would listen.
Think you're some kind of poet.
Now look what you've done,
you and your damn line—                                     70
mucking around with creation.

You just had to fool with it.
You just can't leave it alone.

2007

9  In the story of Elijah on the mountaintop (1 Kings 19): the mighty Hebrew prophet, threatened by the corrupt
   Queen Jezebel, retreats to a cave on Mount Horeb, where he endures a whirlwind before hearing the 'still small
   voice' of God. God tells him of the violence that will 'come to pass, that him that escapeth the sword of Hazael
   shall Jehu slay: and him that escapeth from the sword of Jehu shall Elisha slay.'


# The Age of Lead

The man has been buried for a hundred and fifty years. They dug a hole in the frozen
gravel, deep into the permafrost, and put him down there so the wolves couldn't get to
him. Or that is the speculation.

   When they dug the hole the permafrost was exposed to the air, which was warmer.
This made the permafrost melt. But it froze again after the man was covered up, so

that when he was brought to the surface he was completely enclosed in ice. They took the lid off the coffin and it was like those maraschino cherries you used to freeze in ice-cube trays for fancy tropical drinks: a vague shape, looming through a solid cloud.

Then they melted the ice and he came to light. He is almost the same as when he was buried. The freezing water has pushed his lips away from his teeth into an astonished snarl, and he's a beige colour, like a gravy stain on linen, instead of pink, but everything is still there. He even has eyeballs, except that they aren't white but the light brown of milky tea. With these tea-stained eyes he regards Jane: an indecipherable gaze, innocent, ferocious, amazed, but contemplative, like a werewolf meditating, caught in a flash of lightning at the exact split second of his tumultuous change.

Jane doesn't watch very much television. She used to watch it more. She used to watch comedy series, in the evenings, and when she was a student at university she would watch afternoon soaps about hospitals and rich people, as a way of procrastinating. For a while, not so long ago, she would watch the evening news, taking in the disasters with her feet tucked up on the chesterfield, a throw rug over her legs, drinking a hot milk and rum to relax before bed. It was all a form of escape.

But what you can see on the television, at whatever time of day, is edging too close to her own life; though in her life, nothing stays put in those tidy compartments, comedy here, seedy romance and sentimental tears there, accidents and violent deaths in thirty-second clips they call *bites*, as if they were chocolate bars. In her life, everything is mixed together. *Laugh, I thought I'd die,* Vincent used to say, a very long time ago, in a voice imitating the banality of mothers; and that's how it's getting to be. So when she flicks on the television these days, she flicks it off again soon enough. Even the commercials, with their surreal dailiness, are beginning to look sinister, to suggest meanings behind themselves, behind their façade of cleanliness, lusciousness, health, power, and speed.

Tonight she leaves the television on, because what she is seeing is so unlike what she usually sees. There is nothing sinister behind this image of the frozen man. It is entirely itself. *What you sees is what you gets,* as Vincent also used to say, crossing his eyes, baring his teeth at one side, pushing his nose into a horror-movie snout. Although it never was, with him.

The man they've dug up and melted was a young man. Or still is: it's difficult to know what tense should be applied to him, he is so insistently present. Despite the distortions caused by the ice and the emaciation of his illness, you can see his youthfulness, the absence of toughening, of wear. According to the dates painted carefully onto his nameplate, he was only twenty years old. His name was John Torrington. He was, or is, a sailor, a seaman. He wasn't an able-bodied seaman though; he was a petty officer, one of those marginally in command. Being in command has little to do with the ableness of the body.

He was one of the first to die. This is why he got a coffin and a metal nameplate, and a deep hole in the permafrost—because they still had the energy, and the piety, for such things, that early. There would have been a burial service read over him, and prayers. As time went on and became nebulous and things did not get better, they must have kept the energy for themselves; and also the prayers. The prayers would have ceased to be routine and become desperate, and then hopeless. The later dead ones got cairns of piled stones, and the much later ones not even that. They ended up as bones, and as the soles of boots and the occasional button, sprinkled over the frozen stony treeless relentless ground in a trail heading south. It was like the trails in fairy tales, of bread crumbs or seeds or white stones. But in this case nothing had sprouted or lit up in the moonlight, forming a miraculous pathway to life; no rescuers had followed. It took ten years before anyone knew even the barest beginnings of what had been happening to them.

All of them together were the Franklin Expedition. Jane has seldom paid much attention to history except when it has overlapped with her knowledge of antique furniture and real estate—'19th c. pine harvest table', or 'Prime location Georgian centre hall, impeccable reno'—but she knows what the Franklin Expedition was. The two ships with their bad-luck names have been on stamps—the *Terror*, the *Erebus*. Also she took it in school, along with a lot of other doomed expeditions. Not many of those explorers seemed to have come out of it very well. They were always getting scurvy, or lost.

What the Franklin Expedition was looking for was the Northwest Passage, an open seaway across the top of the Arctic, so people, merchants, could get to India from England without going all the way around South America. They wanted to go that way because it would cost less and increase their profits. This was much less exotic than Marco Polo or the headwaters of the Nile;[1] nevertheless, the idea of exploration appealed to her then: to get onto a boat and just go somewhere, somewhere mapless, off into the unknown. To launch yourself into fright; to find things out. There was something daring and noble about it, despite all of the losses and failures, or perhaps because of them. It was like having sex, in high school, in those days before the Pill, even if you took precautions. If you were a girl, that is. If you were a boy, for whom such a risk was fairly minimal, you had to do other things: things with weapons or large amounts of alcohol, or high-speed vehicles, which at her suburban Toronto high school, back then at the beginning of the sixties, meant switchblades, beer, and drag races down the main streets on Saturday nights.

Now, gazing at the television as the lozenge of ice gradually melts and the outline of the young sailor's body clears and sharpens, Jane remembers Vincent, sixteen and with more hair then, quirking one eyebrow and lifting his lip in a mock sneer and saying, 'Franklin, my dear, I don't give a damn.' He said it loud enough to be heard, but the history teacher ignored him, not knowing what else to do. It was hard for the teachers to keep Vincent in line, because he never seemed to be afraid of anything that might happen to him.

1 Marco Polo (*c.* 1254–*c.* 1324): Italian traveller whose book recounting his travels to China and the court of Kublai Khan via central Asia gave considerable impetus to the European quest to discover the riches of the East. The source of the Nile was a mystery and the subject of fascinated debate and speculation for centuries, and attracted considerable attention among explorers in the eighteenth and nineteenth centuries. The Scottish explorer James Bruce eventually identified Lake Tana as the source of the Blue Nile (1770); the English explorer John Speke is credited with identifying Lake Victoria and Ripon Falls as the source of the White Nile (1861–2).

He was hollow-eyed even then; he frequently looked as if he'd been up all night. Even then he resembled a very young old man, or else a dissipated child. The dark circles under his eyes were the ancient part, but when he smiled he had lovely small white teeth, like the magazine ads for baby foods. He made fun of everything, and was adored. He wasn't adored the way other boys were adored, those boys with surly lower lips and greased hair and a studied air of smouldering menace. He was adored like a pet. Not a dog, but a cat. He went where he liked, and nobody owned him. Nobody called him Vince.

Strangely enough, Jane's mother approved of him. She didn't usually approve of the boys Jane went out with. Maybe she approved of him because it was obvious to her that no bad results would follow from Jane's going out with him: no heartaches, no heaviness, nothing burdensome. None of what she called *consequences*. Consequences: the weightiness of the body, the growing flesh hauled around like a bundle, the tiny frill-framed goblin head in the carriage. Babies and marriage, in that order. This was how she understood men and their furtive, fumbling, threatening desires, because Jane herself had been a consequence. She had been a mistake, she had been a war baby. She had been a crime that had needed to be paid for, over and over.

By the time she was sixteen, Jane had heard enough about this to last her several lifetimes. In her mother's account of the way things were, you were young briefly and then you fell. You plummeted downwards like an overripe apple and hit the ground with a squash; you fell, and everything about you fell too. You got fallen arches and a fallen womb, and you hair and teeth fell out. That's what having a baby did to you. It subjected you to the force of gravity.

This is how she remembers her mother, still: in terms of a pendulous, drooping, wilting motion. Her sagging breasts, the downturned lines around her mouth. Jane conjures her up: there she is, as usual, sitting at the kitchen table with a cup of cooling tea, exhausted after her job clerking at Eaton's department store, standing all day behind the jewellery counter with her bum stuffed into a girdle and her swelling feet crammed into the mandatory medium-heeled shoes, smiling her envious, disapproving smile at the spoiled customers who turned up their noses at pieces of glittering junk she herself could never afford to buy. Jane's mother sighs, picks at the canned spaghetti Jane has heated up for her. Silent worlds waft out of her like stale talcum powder: *What can you expect*, always a statement, never a question. Jane tries at this distance for pity, but comes up with none.

As for Jane's father, he'd run away from home when Jane was five, leaving her mother in the lurch. That's what her mother called it—'running away from home'—as if he'd been an irresponsible child. Money arrived from time to time, but that was the sum total of his contribution to family life. Jane resented him for it, but she didn't blame him. Her mother inspired in almost everyone who encountered her a vicious desire for escape.

Jane and Vincent would sit out in the cramped backyard of Jane's house, which was one of the squinty-windowed little stuccoed wartime bungalows at the bottom of the hill. At the top of the hill were the richer houses, and the richer people: the girls who owned cashmere sweaters, at least one of them, instead of the Orlon and lambswool so familiar to Jane. Vincent lived about halfway up the hill. He still had a father, in theory.

They would sit against the back fence, near the spindly cosmos flowers that passed for a garden, as far away from the house itself as they could get. They would drink gin, decanted by Vincent from his father's liquor hoard and smuggled in an old military pocket flask he'd picked up somewhere. They would imitate their mothers.

'I pinch and scrape and I work my fingers to the bone, and what thanks do I get?' Vincent would say peevishly. 'No help from you, Sonny Boy. You're just like your father. Free as the birds, out all night, do as you like and you don't care one pin about anyone else's feelings. Now take out that garbage.'

'It's love that does it to you,' Jane would reply, in the resigned, ponderous voice of her mother. 'You wait and see, my girl. One of these days you'll come down off your devil-may-care high horse.' As Jane said this, and even though she was making fun, she could picture love, with a capital L, descending out of the sky towards her like a huge foot. Her mother's life had been a disaster, but in her own view an inevitable disaster, as in songs and movies. It was Love that was responsible, and in the face of Love, what could be done? Love was like a steamroller. There was no avoiding it, it went over you and you came out flat.

Jane's mother waited, fearfully and uttering warnings, but with a sort of gloating relish, for the same thing to happen to Jane. Every time Jane went out with a new boy her mother inspected him as a potential agent of downfall. She distrusted most of these boys; she distrusted their sulky, pulpy mouths, their eyes half-closed in the up-drifting smoke of their cigarettes, their slow, sauntering manner of walking, their clothing that was too tight, too full: too full of their bodies. They looked this way even when they weren't putting on the sulks and swaggers, when they were trying to appear bright-eyed and industrious and polite for Jane's mother's benefit, saying goodbye at the front door, dressed in their shirts and ties and their pressed heavy-date suits. They couldn't help the way they looked, the way they were. They were helpless; one kiss in a dark corner would reduce them to speechlessness; they were sleepwalkers in their own liquid bodies. Jane, on the other hand, was wide awake.

Jane and Vincent did not exactly go out together. Instead they made fun of going out. When the coast was clear and Jane's mother wasn't home, Vincent would appear at the door with his face painted bright yellow, and Jane would put her bathrobe on back to front and they would order Chinese food and alarm the delivery boy and eat sitting cross-legged on the floor, clumsily, with chopsticks. Or Vincent would turn up in a threadbare 30-year-old suit and a bowler hat and a cane, and Jane would rummage around in the cupboard for a discarded church-going hat of her mother's, with smashed cloth violets and a veil, and they would go downtown and walk around, making loud remarks about the passers-by, pretending to be old, or poor, or crazy. It was thoughtless and in bad taste, which was what they both liked about it.

Vincent took Jane to the graduation formal, and they picked out her dress together at one of the second-hand clothing shops Vincent frequented, giggling at the shock and admiration they hoped to cause. They hesitated between a flame-red with falling-off sequins and a backless hip-hugging black with a plunge front, and chose the black, to go with Jane's hair. Vincent sent a poisonous-looking lime-green orchid, the colour of her eyes, he said, and Jane painted her eyelids and fingernails to match. Vincent wore white tie and tails, and a top hat, all frayed Sally-Ann issue and ludicrously too large for him. They tangoed around the gymnasium, even though the music was not a tango, under the tissue-paper flowers, cutting a black swath through the sea of pastel tulle, unsmiling, projecting a corny sexual menace, Vincent with Jane's long pearl necklace clenched between his teeth.

The applause was mostly for him, because of the way he was adored. Though mostly by the girls, thinks Jane. But he seemed to be popular enough among the boys as well. Probably he told them dirty jokes, in the proverbial locker room. He knew enough of them.

As he dipped Jane backwards, he dropped the pearls and whispered into her ear, 'No belts, no pins, no pads, no chafing.' It was from an ad for tampons, but it was also their leitmotif. It was what they both wanted: freedom from the world of mothers, the world of precautions, the world of burdens and fate and heavy female constraints upon the flesh. They wanted a life without consequences. Until recently, they'd managed it.

The scientists have melted the entire length of the young sailor now, at least the upper layer of him. They've been pouring warm water over him, gently and patiently; they don't want to thaw him too abruptly. It's as if John Torrington is asleep and they don't want to startle him.

Now his feet have been revealed. They're bare, and white rather then beige; they look like the feet of someone who's been walking on a cold floor, on a winter day. That is the quality of the light that they reflect: winter sunlight, in early morning. There is something intensely painful to Jane about the absence of socks. They could have left him his socks. But maybe the others needed them. His big toes are tied together with a strip of cloth; the man talking says this was to keep the body tidily packaged for burial, but Jane is not convinced. His arms are tied to his body, his ankles are tied together. You do that when you don't want a person walking around.

This part is almost too much for Jane; it is too reminiscent. She reaches for the channel switcher, but luckily the show (it is only a show, it's only another show) changes to two of the historical experts, analyzing the clothing. There's a close-up of John Torrington's shirt, a simple, high-collared, pin-striped white-and-blue cotton, with mother-of-pearl buttons. The stripes are a printed pattern, rather than a woven one; woven would have been more expensive. The trousers are grey linen. Ah, thinks Jane. Wardrobe. She feels better: this is something she knows about. She loves the solemnity, the reverence, with which the stripes and buttons are discussed. An interest in the clothing of the present is frivolity, an interest in the clothing of the past is archaeology; a point Vincent would have appreciated.

After high school, Jane and Vincent both got scholarships to university, although Vincent had appeared to study less, and did better. That summer they did everything together. They got summer jobs at the same hamburger heaven, they went to movies together after work, although Vincent never paid for Jane. They still occasionally dressed up in old clothes and pretended to be a weird couple, but it no longer felt careless and filled with absurd invention. It was beginning to occur to them that they might conceivably end up looking like that.

In her first year at university Jane stopped going out with other boys: she needed a part-time job to help pay her way, and that and the schoolwork and Vincent took up all her time. She thought she might be in love with Vincent. She though that maybe they should make love, to find out. She had never done such a thing, entirely; she had been too afraid of the untrustworthiness of men, of the gravity of love, too afraid of consequences. She thought, however, that she might trust Vincent.

But things didn't go that way. They held hands, but they didn't hug; they hugged, but they didn't pet; they kissed, but they didn't neck. Vincent liked looking at her, but he liked it so much he would never close his eyes. She would close hers and then open them, and there would be Vincent, his own eyes shining in the light from the street-lamp or the moon, peering at her inquisitively as if waiting to see what odd female thing she would do next, for his delighted amusement. Making love with Vincent did not seem altogether possible.

(Later, after she had flung herself into the current of opinion that had swollen to a river by the late sixties, she no longer said 'making love'; she said 'having sex'. But it amounted to the same thing. You had sex, and love got made out of it whether you liked it or not. You woke up in a bed or more likely on a mattress, with an arm around you, and found yourself wondering what it might be like to keep on doing it. At that point Jane would start looking at her watch. She had no intention of being left in any lurches. She would do the leaving herself. And she did.)

Jane and Vincent wandered off to different cities. They wrote each other postcards. Jane did this and that. She ran a co-op food store in Vancouver, did the financial stuff for a diminutive theatre in Montreal, acted as managing editor for a small publisher, ran the publicity for a dance company. She had a head for details and for adding up small sums—having to scrape her way through university had been instructive—and such jobs were often available if you didn't demand much money for doing them. Jane could see no reason to tie herself down, to make any sort of soul-stunting commitment, to anything or anyone. It was the early seventies; the old heavy women's world of girdles and precautions and consequences had been swept away. There were a lot of windows opening, a lot of doors: you could look in, then you could go in, then you could come out again.

She lived with several men, but in each of the apartments there were always card-board boxes, belonging to her, that she never got around to unpacking; just as well, because it was that much easier to move out. When she got past thirty she decided it might be nice to have a child, some time, later. She tried to figure out a way of doing this without becoming a mother. Her own mother had moved to Florida, and sent rambling, grumbling letters, to which Jane did not often reply.

Jane moved back to Toronto, and found it ten times more interesting than when she'd left it. Vincent was already there. He'd come back from Europe, where he'd been studying film; he'd opened a design studio. He and Jane met for lunch, and it was the same: the same air of conspiracy between them, the same sense of their own potential for outrageousness. They might still have been sitting in Jane's garden, beside the cosmos flowers, drinking forbidden gin and making fun.

Jane found herself moving in Vincent's circles, or were they orbits? Vincent knew a great many people, people of all kinds; some were artists and some wanted to be, and some wanted to know the ones who were. Some had money to begin with, some made money; they all spent it. There was a lot more talk about money, these days, or among these people. Few of them knew how to manage it, and Jane found herself helping them out. She developed a small business among them, handling their money. She would gather it in, put it away safely for them, tell them what they could spend, dole out an allowance. She would note with interest the things they bought, filing their receipted bills: what furniture, what clothing, which *objets*. They were delighted with their money, enchanted with it. It was like milk and cookies for them, after school. Watching them play with their money, Jane felt responsible and indulgent, and a little matronly. She stored her own money carefully away, and eventually bought a town-house with it.

All this time she was with Vincent, more or less. They'd tried being lovers but had not made a success of it. Vincent had gone along with this scheme because Jane had wanted it, but he was elusive, he would no make declarations. What worked with other men did not work with him: appeals to his protective instincts, pretences at jealously, requests to remove stuck lids from jars. Sex with him was more like a musical work-out. He couldn't take it seriously, and accused her of being too solemn about it. She thought he might be gay, but was afraid to ask him; she dreaded feeling irrelevant to him, excluded. It took them months to get back to normal.

He was older now, they both were. He had thinning temples and a widow's peak, and his bright inquisitive eyes had receded even further into his head. What went on between them continued to look like a courtship, but was not one. He was always bringing her things: a new, peculiar food to eat, a new grotesquerie to see, a new piece of gossip, which he would present to her with a sense of occasion, like a flower. She in her turn appreciated him. It was like a yogic exercise, appreciating Vincent; it was like appreciating an anchovy, or a stone. He was not everyone's taste.

There's a black-and-white print on the television, then another: the nineteenth century's version of itself, in etchings. Sir John Franklin, older and fatter than Jane had supposed; the *Terror* and the *Erebus*, locked fast in the crush of the ice. In the high Arctic, a hundred and fifty years ago, it's the dead of winter. There is no sun at all, no moon; only the rustling northern lights, like electronic music, and the hard little stars.

What did they do for love, on such a ship, at such a time? Furtive solitary grop-ings, confused and mournful dreams, the sublimation of novels. The usual, among those who have become solitary.

Down in the hold, surrounded by the creaking of the wooden hull and the stale odours of men far too long enclosed, John Torrington lies dying. He must have known it; you can see it on his face. He turns towards Jane his tea-coloured look of puzzled reproach.

Who held his hand, who read to him, who brought him water? Who, if anyone, loved him? And what did they tell him about whatever it was that was killing him? Consumption, brain fever, Original Sin. All those Victorian reasons, which meant nothing and were the wrong ones. But they must have been comforting. If you are dying, you want to know why.

In the eighties, things started to slide. Toronto was not so much fun anymore. There were too many people, too many poor people. You could see them begging on the streets, which were clogged with fumes and cars. The cheap artists' studios were torn down or converted to coy and upscale office space; the artists had migrated elsewhere. Whole streets were torn up or knocked down. The air was full of windblown grit.

People were dying. They were dying too early. One of Jane's clients, a man who owned an antique store, died almost overnight of bone cancer. Another, a woman who was an entertainment lawyer, was trying on a dress in a boutique and had a heart attack. She fell over and they called the ambulance, and she was dead on arrival. A theatrical producer died of AIDS, and a photographer; the lover of the photographer shot himself, either out of grief or because he knew he was next. A friend of a friend died of emphysema, another of viral pneumonia, another of hepatitis picked up on a tropical vacation, another of spinal meningitis. It was as if they had been weakened by some mysterious agent, a thing like a colourless gas, scentless and invisible, so that any germ that happened along could invade their bodies, take them over.

Jane began to notice news items of the kind she'd once skimmed over. Maple groves dying of acid rain, hormones in the beef, mercury in the fish, pesticides in the vegetables, poison sprayed on the fruit, God knows what in the drinking water. She subscribed to a bottled spring-water service and felt better for a few weeks, then read in the paper that it wouldn't do her much good, because whatever it was had been seeping into everything. Each time you took a breath, you breathed some of it in. She thought about moving out of the city, then read about toxic dumps, radioactive waste, concealed here and there in the countryside and masked by the lush, deceitful green of waving trees.

Vincent has been dead for less than a year. He was not put into the permafrost or frozen in ice. He went into the Necropolis, the only Toronto cemetery of whose general ambience he approved; he got flower bulbs planted on top of him, by Jane and others. Mostly by Jane. Right now John Torrington, recently thawed after a hundred and fifty years, probably looks better than Vincent.

A week before Vincent's forty-third birthday, Jane went to see him in the hospital. He was in for tests. Like fun he was. He was in for the unspeakable, the unknown. He was in for a mutated virus that didn't even have a name yet. It was creeping up his spine, and when it reached his brain it would kill him. It was not, as they said, responding to treatment. He was in for the duration.

It was white in his room, wintry. He lay packed in ice, for the pain. A white sheet wrapped him, his white thin feet poked out the bottom of it. They were so pale and cold. Jane took one look at him, laid out on ice like a salmon, and began to cry.

'Oh Vincent,' she said. 'What will I do without you?' This sounded awful. It sounded like Jane and Vincent making fun, of obsolete books, obsolete movies, their obsolete mothers. It also sounded selfish: here she was, worrying about herself and her future, when Vincent was the one who was sick. But it was true. There would be a lot less to do, altogether, without Vincent.

Vincent gazed up at her; the shadows under his eyes were cavernous. 'Lighten up,' he said, not very loudly, because he could not speak very loudly now. By this time she was sitting down, leaning forward; she was holding one of his hands. It was thin as the claw of a bird. 'Who says I'm going to die?' He spent a moment considering this, revised it. 'You're right,' he said, 'They got me. It was the Pod People from outer space. They said, "All I want is your poddy."'

Jane cried more. It was worse because he was trying to be funny. 'But what *is* it?' she said. 'Have they found out yet?'

Vincent smiled his ancient, jaunty smile, his smile of detachment, of amusement. There were his beautiful teeth, juvenile as ever. 'Who knows?' he said. 'It must have been something I ate.'

Jane sat with the tears running down her face. She felt desolate: left behind, stranded. Their mothers had finally caught up to them and been proven right. There were consequences after all; but they were the consequences to things you didn't even know you'd done.

The scientists are back on the screen. They are excited, their earnest mouths are twitching, you could almost call them joyful. They know why John Torrington died; they know, at last, why the Franklin Expedition went so terribly wrong. They've snipped off pieces of John Torrington, a fingernail, a lock of hair, they've run them through machines and come out with the answers.

There is a shot of an old tin can, pulled open to show the seam. It looks like a bomb casing. A finger points: it was the tin cans that did it, a new invention back then, a new technology, the ultimate defence against starvation and scurvy. The Franklin Expedition was excellently provisioned with tin cans, stuffed full of meat and soup and soldered together with lead. The whole expedition got lead-poisoning. Nobody knew it. Nobody could taste it. It invaded their bones, their lungs, their brains, weakening them and confusing their thinking, so that at the end those that had not yet died in the ships set out in an idiotic trek across the stony, icy ground, pulling a lifeboat laden down with toothbrushes, soap, handkerchiefs, and slippers, useless pieces of junk. When they were found ten years later, they were skeletons in tattered coats, lying where they'd collapsed. They'd been heading back towards the ships. It was what they'd been eating that had killed them.

Jane switches off the television and goes into her kitchen—all white, done over the year before last, the outmoded butcher-block counters from the seventies torn out and carted away—to make herself some hot milk and rum. Then she decides against it; she won't sleep anyway. Everything in here looks ownerless. Her toaster oven, so perfect for solo dining, her microwave for the vegetables, her espresso maker—they're sitting around waiting for her departure, for this evening or forever, in order to assume their final, real appearances of purposeless objects adrift in the physical world. They might as well be pieces of an exploded spaceship orbiting the moon.

She thinks about Vincent's apartment, so carefully arranged, filled with the beautiful or deliberately ugly possessions he once loved. She thinks about his closet, with its quirky particular outfits, empty now of his arms and legs. It has all been broken up now, sold, given away.

Increasingly the sidewalk that runs past her house is cluttered with plastic drinking cups, crumpled soft-drink cans, used take-out plates. She picks them up, clears them away, but they appear again overnight, like a trail left by an army on the march or by the fleeing residents of a city under bombardment, discarding the objects that were once thought essential but are now too heavy to carry.

1991

# Patrick Lane
## b. 1939

Born in Nelson, British Columbia, Patrick Lane grew up near Vernon, in the BC Interior. Although he has travelled extensively—as a young man, he wandered through North and South America, working at manual jobs such as logger and miner—he has been based in Western Canada for most of his life. Like his older brother Red Lane, whose life was cut short by a cerebral hemorrhage in 1964, he began to write poetry in his early twenties. In 1966, he founded, with poets bill bissett and Seymour Mayne, Very Stone House, a small press that published a number of important poetry books, including Lane's *Letters from the Savage Mind* (1966) and his edition of *The Collected Poems of Red Lane* (1968). (From 1971 to 1980, the press was called Very Stone House in Transit, an allusion to Lane's constant movement from place to place.)

Over the course of a long career, Lane has produced broadsheets, pamphlets, and a substantial number of full-length books of poetry, among them *Beware the Months of Fire* (1974);

*Unborn Things* (1975); *Albino Pheasant* (1977); *Poems New and Selected* (1978; Governor General's Award); *The Measure* (1980); *Old Mother* (1982); *A Linen Crow, a Caftan Magpie* (1984); *Selected Poems* (1987), which contains a section of new work; *Mortal Remains* (1991); *The Bare Plum of Winter Rain* (2000); *Go Leaving Strange* (2004); and *Last Water Song* (2007), containing elegiac poems written in memory of fellow writers such as Adele Wiseman, Al Purdy, Earle Birney, and Irving Layton.

Although primarily a poet, Lane has, in recent years, increasingly turned to prose. After writing a children's book, *Milford and Me* (1989), he gathered twenty of his stories in *How Do You Spell Beautiful?* (1992). His first novel, *Red Dog, Red Dog* (2008), is the story of a family appropriately named Stark, living in

*a stone country where a bone cage could last a thousand years under the moon, its ribs a perch for Vesper sparrows, its skull a home for Harvest mice. The hills rose parched from the still lakes,*

*the mountains beyond them faded to a mauve*
*so pale they seemed stones under the ice.*

Set in British Columbia's Okanagan Valley in 1958, it tells of two brothers struggling against the toxic bonds of a warped family and a savage community.

In 2004, Lane published a memoir, *There Is a Season*, which is a beautiful and painful account that blends harrowing memories of his childhood with the story of his recovery from alcoholism by aid of a disciplined year he spent shaping his garden and tending its plants. In it, Lane talks frankly about the failure of his early marriage and about the difficulty he has had maintaining human bonds.

That changed in 1978, when he began a relationship with the poet Lorna Crozier—which they celebrated in the book *No Longer Two People* (1979), a series of poems set in dialogue. Among their several other joint projects, the two wrote the radio script 'Chile', which won the US National Radio Award's Best Public Radio Program for 1987, and edited *Breathing Fire: Canada's New Poets* (1995; with Al Purdy) and *Breathing Fire 2: Canada's New Poets* (2004). From 1986 to 1991, they shared an appointment in the English Department at the University of Saskatchewan and a writer-in-residence post at the University of Toronto. As well, Lane has taught creative writing or been writer in residence at Concordia University, the University of Notre Dame of Nelson, and the universities of Manitoba, Ottawa, Alberta, and Victoria.

Lane's characteristic style is suggested in the title of *Too Spare, Too Fierce*. His is a poetry of anecdotal narrative, frequently with violence at its centre—the result of casual acts of brutality or of his own reckless self-destructiveness—that is expressed, in poems such as 'Because I Never Learned' and 'The Far Field', in a haunting, stripped lyricism. These tough-minded investigations of the male ethos are coupled with an awareness of the world's pain, an intense response to nature, and an attachment to the land.

The shaping force of the environment is an extended subject in *Winter* (1990), a sequence of poems about the season sometimes thought to define what it is to be a Canadian. In the afterword, Lane writes: 'Winter is at once both symbol and metaphor, unique and ubiquitous. Alden Nowlan said once [in 'Canadian January Night'] that we live in country where simply to go outside is to die. I agree.' Describing Albert Johnson as an individual who has gone into the 'heart of winter', Lane closes *Winter* by retelling the story of the infamous 'mad trapper' whose ability to elude the Mounties by fleeing through incredibly harsh northern conditions became legendary.

Even though nature's predatory aspects (as embodied by the weasel in the poem about that 'thin as death' hunter) are prominent in Lane's work, the healing power of nature is also visible, as in 'The Sooke Potholes', where 'a tree frog's creak and croak are all that beauty is.' In both poetry and prose, Lane has written of the dangers of self-annihilation through addiction. In 2001, he and Crozier co-edited *Addicted: Notes from the Belly of the Beast*, to which a number of prominent figures from Canadian cultural life (including poet John Newlove, novelist David Adams Richards, and CBC radio personality Peter Gzowski—who died of emphysema soon after) contributed essays about their own experiences. In it, Lane's 'Counting the Bones' reflects on his mistaken belief that 'in order to achieve wisdom you must live with complete abandon' and on the way that belief led to his debilitating dependence on alcohol and harder drugs. His afterword to the book was written from the treatment centre in which he spent Christmas, 2000. He remains sober.

# Because I Never Learned

Because I never learned how
to be gentle and the country
I lived in was hard with dead
animals and men I didn't question
my father when he told me
to step on the kitten's head
after the bus had run over
its hind quarters.

Now, twenty years later,
I remember only:                                    10
the silence of the dying
when the fragile skull collapsed
under my hard bare heel,
the curved tongue in the dust
that would never cry again
and the small of my father's back
as he walked tall away.

1974

# Stigmata[1]

*for Irving Layton*[2]

What if there wasn't a metaphor
and the bodies were only bodies
bones pushed out in awkward fingers?
Waves come to the seawall, fall away,
children bounce mouths against the stones
man has carved to keep the sea at bay
and women walk with empty wombs
proclaiming freedom to the night.
Through barroom windows rotten with light
eyes of men open and close like fists.          10

I bend beside a tidal pool and take a crab from the sea.
His small green life twists helpless in my hand
the living bars of bone and flesh

1  Marks corresponding to the crucifixion wounds of Christ.
2  See pp. 504–15; compare particularly 'Butterfly on Rock' (where the poet crushes the butterfly under his hand)
   with the conclusion of this poem.

a cage made by the animal I am.
This thing, the beat, the beat of life
now captured in the darkness of my flesh
struggling with claws as if it could tear its way
through my body back to the sea.
What do I know of the inexorable beauty,
the unrelenting turning of the wheel I am inside me?                    20
Stigmata. I hold a web of blood.

I dream of the scrimshawed[3] teeth of endless whales,
the oceans it took to carve them. Drifting ships
echo in fog the wounds of Leviathan[4]
great grey voices giving cadence to their loss.
The men are gone
who scratched upon white bones their destiny.
Who will speak of the albatross in the shroud of the man,
the sailor who sinks forever in the Mindanao Deep?[5]
I open my hand. The life leaps out.                    30

1977

3 Intricately carved; scrimshaw is usually made from whale ivory, bone, or shells.
4 Biblical sea monster; a whale.
5 Deepest point in oceans.

# The Long Coyote Line

*for Andy Suknaski*

The long coyote line crosses the pure
white and the prairie is divided
again by hunger. The snowshoe hare
thin as January creates a running
circle encompassing a moon of snow
as the lean lope of the coyote
cuts in a curving radius
bringing escape down to a single terror.
It is the long line, coyote, and the man
who stands in your small disturbance                    10
counting the crystals of blood and bone:
three by three, coyote, hare and the howl
where the true prairie begins.

1980

# CPR Station—Winnipeg

You sit and your hands are folded in
upon you. The coffee is bleak, black. This
catacomb is lighted with the pale death
our fathers called marble in their pride.
This is an old song. This country.

This country was still a hope.
It is the CPR Station in Winnipeg,
11:30 and no one is leaving again.
The trains are late. The passengers wait
for the passing freight of the nation.                    10

The people have turned to stone, cannot be
moved. The coffee is black. The night is far
above us. Steel passes over in the rumbling
called destinations. The gates are dark.
There is no passing here.

There is no desire to pass. Someone with
a lantern hesitates and moves on.
The river of white marble swirls cold
beneath us. It is worn, worn by the feet
of a nation. Your heavy hands. Your                      20

fingers are huge, swollen with the
freight of years. This country has
travelled through you. The man with the
lantern sits in the far corner, waiting,
If you could lift your head I could go

out into the night with grace. O hell,
you are old. Winter is above us. Steel
wheels. If you could lift your head.
Bleak black. White marble.
And the trains, the trains pass over.                     30

1980

# Weasel

Thin as death,
the dark brown weasel slides
like smoke through night's hard silence.
The worlds of the small are still. He glides
beneath the chicken house. Bird life
above him sleeps in feathers as he creeps
among the stones, small nose testing every board
for opening, a hole small as an eye, a fallen knot,
a crack where time has broken through.
His sharp teeth chatter.                                    10
Again and again he quests the darkness
below the sleeping birds. A mouse freezes,
small mouth caught by silence in the wood.
His life is quick. He slips into his hole.
Thin as death, the dark brown weasel slides
like smoke. His needles worry wood.
The night is long.
Above him bird blood beats.

1982


# From *Winter*

# Winter I

The generosity of snow, the way it forgives
transgression, filling in the many betrayals
and leaving the world
exactly as it was. Imagine a man
walking endlessly and finding his tracks,
knowing he has gone in a circle. Imagine
his disappointment. See how he strikes out again
in a new direction, hoping this way
will lead him out. Imagine how much
happier he will be this time with the wind                 10
all around him, the wind filling in his tracks.

He is thinking of that man,
of what keeps him going.
The thought of snow,
small white grains sifting
into the holes where his feet went,
filling things in,
leaving no room for despair.


## Winter 4

He is thinking of the end of Oedipus,
not the beginning, not the part
where Oedipus chooses by giving the answer
to the beast at the Gate of Thebes.
No, it is the end he likes. The part
just after he puts out his eyes
and stands, suddenly
in that certain darkness, decided.[1]

It is not a story of winter
but of the sun, the ceaseless                                    10
perfection of the desert in Africa.

How different it would be
had it taken place here, he thinks.
Here the critical moment
would be putting the eyes back
in their sockets, that first shock
exactly the same as in the other story
only the beginning would have
to be different, all the roles
reversed.                                                        20

---

1  In the Greek myth, Oedipus, who, because of an oracle, was abandoned on a hillside and raised in a distant land,
   establishes his powers when, as a young man on the way to Thebes, he gives the correct solution to a riddle posed
   by the Sphinx (a winged monster with the body of a lioness and the head of a woman). Oedipus later fails, however, to use his mental powers to realize that the stranger he has killed on the way was his father and that the
   woman he meets and marries is his mother. In Sophocles' famous tragedy *Oedipus Rex*, once all has been revealed
   to him, Oedipus puts out his eyes.

# Winter 22

There is almost no air left
in the white balloon blowing across the snow.
It is wrinkled and barely lifts from the drifts.
If you could read the crinkled writing on its side
it would say: *Save the Whales,*
a temporary greed he loves,
the wish to preserve without regret.
He loves it in the way he loves
all those old poems about Byzantium,
cages full of gilded mechanical birds,                               10
that impossible dream of beauty
while everything blows away.[1]

---

1 The Irish poet William Butler Yeats (1865–1939) wrote two poems, 'Sailing to Byzantium' and 'Byzantium',
expressing his ideas about the immortality of art. In the first of these, to suggest the way poems outlive the poet,
he uses the metaphor of mechanical birds made 'of hammered gold', which go on singing long after their creators
have died.

# Winter 33

The brightness which is the light seen from a tomb
and which is what the dead see when they gaze
with their marble eyes from the dark rooms they are
laid in. This is a whole city this snow.

# Winter 35

One is about the man who walks out into the storm
and is never seen again. We all know that one.
It is the story about grief and music,
where all the dancing is an escape
from virtue, everyone shaken by a higher crime,
the emptiness that follows completion,
the one the body knows
in the formal gentleness of suffering, everything gone,
everything forgiven in the land East of Eden.[1]

---

1 According to the account in Genesis, for their disobedience, Adam and Eve are banished from the garden to the
land East of Eden.

Then there is the other story, the one                                    10
where the man enters out of the storm,
ice melting from his beard, his huge hands
moving over the fire, the fear of what will follow,
the women quiet, filling his cup and bowl
with all the food there is in hope it will be
enough, in hope he will be satisfied only with that,
and knowing he won't, knowing
this is the part of the story the reader will call
the middle, and hoping for an alternative, another
beginning, and ending it                                                  20
before the mind reaches the end
with everyone crying out, everyone
saying things like: *Lie down in sorrow!*
or: *This is the burden of Babylon!*[2]

There is another story, there always is.
The one about . . .
of course, of course.
How cold it is with only a lamp in this small room.

2  Two allusions to the Book of Isaiah. The first is to the warning for sinners found in Isaiah 50:11: 'Behold, all ye
   that kindle a fire, that compass yourselves about with sparks: walk in the light of your fire, and in the sparks
   that ye have kindled. This shall ye have of mine hand; ye shall lie down in sorrow.' The second is an allusion to
   Isaiah 13:1 ('The burden of Babylon, which Isaiah the son of Amoz did see'), which begins a passage foretelling
   an apocalyptic vengeance that will free the Israelites from Babylonian captivity.

# Winter 40

She is a northern woman, barely more
than a child, one who has walked through the drifts
to find her dream vision. Her eyes are
covered by a blade of bone, a thin slit
cut in it so the light does not blind her.
The man she has found is not one of the four
possibilities: father, brother, lover, son.
He is the dream man, given to her by the snow.

He has wandered far from the sea,
his crew dead, his ship broken in the ice.                                10
If there were someone there to translate his song
it would start with the words: *At last.*
But only she is there.

As he sings she cuts off his fingers,
only these small bones and the twenty-six
teeth for her necklace.

They will be her medicine, something
to shake over the bellies of women
in childbirth, the heads of men
who have returned empty from hunting,                    20
their minds become snow.

How like a real man he is, she thinks.
How real this dream, the blood on the ice.
How thin he is, how much like the snow is his flesh.

## Winter 42

It comes after the return, after
everything has been won and the body
feasts. It comes just after that.
That is what the story is all about,
the crashing through the door,
the shouts, the lamentation after
when the hero leaves all his dead behind
to find anything that terrible.

1990

## The Far Field

We drove for more than an hour, my father's hands
on the truck's wheel, taking us farther and farther
into the hills, both of us watching
the sagebrush and spare pines drift
past, both of us silent. He did not know
what to do with me. I think he thought of
my death, as a man will whose son has chosen
to destroy. I think that's why he drove
so long, afraid to stop for fear
of what he'd do. My mother had cried                    10
when we left, her hands over her mouth,

saying through her splayed fingers
my father's name, speaking
that word as if it were a question. I
sat there peaceful with him,
knowing for these hours he was wholly mine.

He stripped me naked in the last hour of day
and made me stand with my back to him, my bare
feet in the dust, my back and buttocks to him,
a naked body, hands braced upon the hood,                    20
staring across the metal at the hills.

I remember the limb of the tree falling
upon me, the sound of the white wood crying
as it hurt the air, and the flesh of my body
rising to him as I fell to the ground and rose
only to fall again. I don't remember pain,
remember only what a body feels
when it is beaten, the way it resists
and fails, and the sound of my flesh.

I rose a last time, my father dropping                       30
the last limb of the tree beside me.
I stood there in my bones wanting it not to be
over, wanting what had happened to continue, to go
on and on forever, my father's hands on me.

It was as if to be broken was love, as if
the beating was a kind of holding, a man
lifting a child in his huge hands and throwing him
high in the air, the child's wild laughter
as he fell a question spoken into both their lives,
the blood they shared pounding in their chests.             40

1991

# Cut-throat

A creek, brown water thick with spring run-off, and the trout
in the riffles come up out of the deep waters to feed. Cut-throat,
that red comma of blood, and the curl of thin water,
the elemental body, eating the eggs and larvae of insects
swept down from the banks high in the hills behind him.
When he was young he had read of a golden ring
found in the belly of a fish and standing there, so many years
later, remembering how he had thrown his wedding ring
into the same lake, he thought . . . *what?* That happiness eludes us
when we apprehend it, that the fallen world is the peculiar dialect          10
of the heart, that a ring flung out upon the waters will return
wearing the blood of angels in a choir of water? He
had fished there, long ago, with his young wife and
their first child. He had turned only once and saw her
pick up the baby and walk away into the willows,
her body and the body of his child
going away from him into the shade.
It is how the high waters talk to us in spring, how we cast out
with every hope imaginable, catching nothing, and casting again,
the line falling upon the waters and everything below the surface          20
sinking deeper, a silence waiting beyond the riffles of the creek
where it meets the lake, the good food come down from the hills.

2004

# The Spoon

He has picked up the spoon from among all the small things
on the table, the knife and fork, the salt shaker you don't shake
but turn and grind, the bowl with its applesauce, the glass of milk,
and how he hesitated between the glass and the spoon, but chose
the spoon, and his daughter's voice going on
in a low and steady murmur, her blonde hair cut short
and the bit of gray at her temples,
and how he remembers his old mother hating flowers
after his father's funeral, how she would never have any
in the house, and his daughter still talking to him          10
in her quiet steady voice about things he already knows,
but knowing it is important for her to say them,
important for her to make some kind of order

out of what must seem to her the chaos of what will be
his life now, and the dog barking outside, and the light
on the table, and the spoon in his hands, and he turns it
over among his fingers and marvels at how his hands
have been holding spoons all his life, and he holds it
by the end of the handle and looks carefully into the shallow
bowl polished so carefully by his wife and sees there                                    20
his face upside down, and how if he could understand
the spoon everything would become clear to him, if he
could understand something this simple, something
so small and ordinary that he has used every day of his life
and never paid attention to until now, something very small,
and very simple, and not a glass, not a flower, just a spoon,
and that without it everything in his life
would have been different if there had never been spoons, this spoon,
and he feels a sense of wonder at what he holds, and he reaches out
and takes a spoonful of applesauce from the bowl in front of him                        30
and gently, and very carefully lifts it not to his mouth,
but to his daughter's mouth, and he touches it against her lips
and she opens her mouth and it is very quiet now and the only thing
he knows he can do is in this moment, and that is what he does.

2004

# For Gwendolyn MacEwen

I was teaching 'Dark Pines under Water' today[1] and now it's almost too late to wonder what anything means. I used to think I understood, but everything's imperfect, mostly us. Isn't that what you taught us? A *close reading* is what this teaching's called, students lowering their hands up to their wrists in your dark imagined lake, the numbness that comes so quickly in February, the ice broken and the body learning what cold can do the mind. To them they were only words, to me too, without the *lonely*. Remember the time we sat in your apartment drinking scotch and talking about the poets and their poems? You kept brushing a lock of hair away from your eyes. I loved your laughter. Me? I had nowhere to go again, slept on your floor. It was Toronto, back in the day. I loved that you let me sleep alone. I paid for my beds back then, that one you gave me free. Later, we talked about Lawrence and his *Seven Pillars of Wisdom*,[2] his years in

---

1  See MacEwen's poem on p. 900.
2  Archaeologist, then British soldier during the First World War, T.E. Lawrence (1888–1935), known as Lawrence of Arabia, played a leading role in the Arab Revolt (1916–18), which he detailed in his autobiographical *Seven Pillars of Wisdom* (1926). MacEwen's *The T.E. Lawrence Poems* (1982) retells these events in a book-length sequence written from Lawrence's point of view.

the desert, his sordid soul in ruins. Your 'Manzini.'[3] I kept going back to him. Like all good poems he offers no escape beyond the listening, beyond that circle your words draw around me still. This computer keeps telling me I'm doing things wrong. It draws coloured lines under the fragments, tells me there's no *u* in colour, no structure to my lines. It says there's no Manzini. Perhaps there isn't except in poems, circuses and sideshows, the tattooed man, the bearded lady, the dwarf, the albino, the freaks I loved when I was a boy. You loved them too. How you laughed when I told you the story of the lady with the goiter I followed when I was a child and how she stopped and let me reach up to touch that growth that hung from her, that pendulant bag of flesh. I was seven years old and thought beauty was the suffering you gave to little boys. I think you wanted Lawrence to be simply a man.[4] How strange a woman's thinking is. When I was in my last room trying to swallow a mouthful of blood I thought of you, the bottle of vodka almost gone,[5] morning coming on, sleep the only thing I could imagine, the kind of sleep only the dead drunk know, the dreaming so terrible there is nothing to remember no matter how far down you reach. The closer I get to your poems the worse I feel. My students try, but there's no telling them they have to go deeper than their wrists in dark water. I remember so little now, Gwen. *Listen, there was this boy* . . .

2007; rev. 2010

3  See 'Manzini: Escape Artist' on p. 898.
4  Lane has said he is responding to 'Gwen's desire to see Lawrence as real, even as she idealizes him as a mythic character.' Of his use of the word 'man' in this line, Lane says he wanted to emphasize Lawrence's 'mortal being. That, and the ambiguity of his sexuality, his maleness self-destructive, his desire shameful in his own eyes. (Though what is it we know other than the fictions of himself in his book and the many books written about him, the unreality of it all?) In *The T.E. Lawrence Poems*, Gwen keeps insisting on the simple truth of his being a suffering man, even while she too makes him into a myth.'
5  MacEwen's death in 1987 came as a result of her long history of alcohol abuse; vodka was her drink of choice.

# The Sooke Potholes[1]

A tree frog's creak and croak are all that beauty is
when we're alone. Sometimes a song is all we have.
And the water swirls in the potholes down in the canyon.
The people are gone home to bed and I'm sitting on a stone
at the forest's edge listening to a tree frog's only song.
Out here in the dark alone I think of my woman.
A saw-whet owl calls from the other side of the canyon.
The frog answers back, happy there's someone he can talk to.
Above me the moon holds onto her bright daughter.
She wants to fly away from here, her curved arms wings of light.                10

1  Natural deep rock pools on the Sooke River (inside a forested regional park near Victoria, BC), created by erosion from the water.

I came to hold what is left of the wild and found
a blouse, a running shoe, and a torn cover of a book called
*Natural History*. But there's nothing natural about history.
I listen to the waters.
They say they've travelled far to find this place.
I say little, having little to say.
The waters go on to the ocean, busy,
happy to find the place where it all began. I think water
knows more than I of love. Old Hugh Latimer[2] back in 1549
told his king, *The drop of rain maketh a hole in the stone,*                    20
*not by violence, but by oft falling.*
Sometimes a gentle soul is what we want.
What can be saved, I ask, but the moon and the stars,
the owl and the frog tell me nothing of salvation.
If my woman were here she'd say all will be well,[3]
knowing I need love at times a little.
Her song saves me tonight, no matter love.
She tells me there are living things.
I listen to the waters far below, the scour of stone on stone.
Like the tree frog's song, I think the earth is singing.                    30
The owl knows he will starve if he waits for the mouse
to crawl under his talon, and the tree frog knows
no lovely frog will come without a song.
Nor pray for tree nor frog nor man,
but praise that *we* are a living place,
the whisper of these waters ours to hold,
however brief our stay.

2007

---

2  Hugh Latimer (c. 1485–1555); a Roman Catholic priest who became an important member of the new Church
   of England clergy under Henry VIII and a Protestant martyr during the reign of Queen Mary I. The king
   Latimer would have addressed was Edward VI.
3  Lorna Crozier, drawing on her reading of Julian of Norwich (1342–c.1416), an English mystic and visionary
   whose book *Revelations of Divine Love* taught the possibility of universal salvation and whose famous saying is,
   'All shall be well, and all shall be well, and all manner of thing shall be well' (Ch. 17).

# Dennis Lee

## b. 1939

In all his writing—his adult poetry, his children's poetry, his essays, and his book-length treatise on the effects of the contemporary world on our lives—Dennis Lee has wrestled with the question of how to live authentically when the world seems inauthentic. He has taken on a variety of roles in confronting this problem and has drawn on many strengths.

Grounded in place, Lee has been shaped by a lifetime in Toronto: he was born there and raised in suburban Etobicoke, was educated at the University of Toronto Schools and Victoria College at the University of Toronto (BA, 1962; MA, 1965), and participated in civic activism, such as the Stop Spadina movement that changed the direction of urban planning in the 1970s. Coming of age in the 1960s, with its growing Canadian cultural nationalism, Lee concluded that, to escape a colonial relationship with the United States and Britain, Canadian writers needed control over their means of production. In 1967, he co-founded (with Dave Godfrey) the House of Anansi Press, which became an outlet for a group of emerging young writers that included Margaret Atwood, Graeme Gibson, Roch Carrier, and Michael Ondaatje. (It also published important new books by established thinkers such as Northrop Frye and George Grant.) Famous for nurturing writers at Anansi, Lee continued literary editing after leaving the directorship of the press in 1972 and worked with some of Canada's best writers at Canadian publishers such as Macmillan and McClelland & Stewart. While at Anansi, Lee also was one of the founders of Rochdale College (a short-lived educational collective in downtown Toronto), and he taught there and also at York University.

A full-time writer since the 1980s, Lee has established two reputations—one as the author of a richly textured poetry for adults and another as Canada's best-loved author of children's verse. Both bodies of work share a common goal (poems such as 'The Coat' and 'When I Went Up to Rosedale' have appeared in both children's and adult collections), which is to respond to the lived experience of being Canadian. He served as writer-in-residence at Trent University, the University of Toronto, and the University of Edinburgh.

While the title of Lee's first book, *Kingdom of Absence* (1967), announced his lifelong sense that something is missing from modern life, it was the book that followed, *Civil Elegies* (1968), that established his reputation and his unique voice. A meditative sequence of poems inspired by philosopher George Grant's *Lament for a Nation* (1965), *Civil Elegies* reflects Lee's intense feelings about the public responsibilities of the individual within the body politic. Published in revised form as *Civil Elegies and Other Poems*, it won a Governor General's Award in 1972. The speaker of these elegies, 'one for whom the world is constantly proving too much,' is trying to find 'a civil habitation that is human / and our own.' He longs for a more immediate relationship with the public and private civic space he inhabits, a time when 'the poets spoke of earth and heaven. There were no symbols.'

The books that follow continue Lee's search for how to live meaningfully. In three long poems—*Not Abstract Harmonies But* (1974), *The Death of Harold Ladoo* (1976), and *The Gods* (1978)—this quest takes the form of a longing for visionary transcendence. These poems (substantially revised and published in a single volume entitled *The Gods*, 1979) are evidence of a religious and even mystic impulse that has manifested itself throughout Lee's work, an urge to edit the messy stuff of life into a cosmological vision of what lies beyond.

Lee came to see the individual's pursuit of authentic being as also Canada's. In his influential 1972 essay 'Cadence, Country, Silence: Writing in Colonial Space' (published in revised form in his collected essays, *Body Music*, 1998) and in his critical and philosophical book on the fiction of Michael Ondaatje and Leonard

Cohen, *Savage Fields* (1977), he delineates the factors that fill Canadians with a sense of self-alienation and irrevocable loss. Viewing Canada as disenfranchised both by modernity and by its colonial history, Lee describes, in 'Cadence, Country, Silence' the cultural void that existed when he was beginning to write,

*Canadians were by definition people who looked over the fence at America, unself-consciously learning from its comics, pop music, and television how to go about being alive. The disdainful amusement I and thousands like me felt for Canadian achievement in any field, especially those of the imagination, was a direct reflection of our sense of inferiority.*

Thus *Civil Elegies* and the poems that follow explore ways to reclaim a local existence and to define a national one. Lee desires, both for the individual and for the larger culture, an experience of intensity and presence in which separate concepts such as form and content, or writer and reader, are replaced by an intuitive wholeness.

Believing that Canadian children also needed an indigenous and living poetry, Lee began writing his 'kids' stuff'. His whimsical, zany children's verse has become widely popular since the appearance of *Wiggle to the Laundromat* (1970), and the title poem of *Alligator Pie* (1974) is so well known that it has been called Canada's unofficial national anthem. These collections were followed by several more volumes, including *Nicholas Knock and Other People* (1974), *Garbage Delight* (1977), *Jelly Belly* (1983), *The Ice Cream Store* (1991), and *So Cool* (2004). From 1983 to 1986, he wrote song lyrics (with Phil Balsam) for *Fraggle Rock*, a television show featuring Jim Henson's Muppets, an association that led to work on scripts for the Henson films *The Dark Crystal* (1983) and *Labyrinth* (1986). Lee also wrote the songs for two musical dramas based on Mordecai Richler's Jacob Two-Two books. In 1987, he turned his exuberant playfulness to rhymed comic poems he describes as 'kid's stuff for adults', *The Difficulty of Living on Other Planets*.

An inveterate reviser, Lee also worked for a long time on a sequence about a love affair gone wrong—told in the literary equivalent of jazz variations on a theme. An early version of this work appeared in *Tasks of Passion* (1982), a book of essays by and about Lee; the final version was published in 1993 as *Riffs*. In 1998, Lee brought that poem together with much of his other adult poetry in *Nightwatch: New & Selected Poems, 1968–1996*. The final third of that book, 'Nightwatch', is a new sequence of poems in which a speaker, having arrived at 'the wreck of my fortieth year,' finds himself alone in 'Dark house. Dark night', seeking to come to terms with the life he has so far lived ('Hunger', below, is a poem from that sequence). His most recent adult works, *UN* (2003) and *Yesno* (2007) are paired books that together form a ten-part sequence. In these, Lee takes his fondness for linguistic play to new lengths in his attempts to find words for a crisis that challenges articulation: the degradation of the planet.

Because Lee is a writer of process (as his many revisions—some long after a work's first publication—suggest), his poetry and essays are best viewed not as discrete units but as part of a single work in progress, one always subject to further refinement, always in development, always aspiring to understand what lies beyond. At the centre of Lee's work—as a poet, children's writer, lyricist, essayist, educator, and editor—is his struggle with the modern condition. Equally concerned with the ecological, the ontological, and the technological developments that have radically altered our existence in the twentieth and twenty-first centuries, he thinks about these things not as so much as a philosopher would but as a poet must. In the essay entitled 'Grant's Impasse', he writes (characteristically coining new words when he needs them): 'the way the world makes sense is not primarily conceptual; the coherence of things comes through as a cadence of being, a cosmophony.' In general, Lee laments a lost past when individuals had a sense of belonging and when ethics and belief seemed indivisible: he draws back from his own era with its loss of faith both in the autonomous self and in anything greater than the self. In his poetry and prose he suggests that we may confront an irresolvable problem: the thoughtful individual can neither accept today's milieu as 'real' nor define what would make it authentic—because defining falsifies a thing by restricting it to a limited idea.

# Sibelius Park[1]

I

Walking north from his other lives in a fine rain
          through the high-rise pavilion on Walmer
   lost in the vague turbulence he harbours
          Rochdale    Anansi    how many
   routine wipeouts has he performed since he was born?
                    and mostly himself;
           drifting north to the three-storey
       turrets & gables, the squiggles and arches and
 baleful asymmetric glare of the houses he loves
          Toronto gothic                    10
walking north in the fine rain, trudging home through the
late afternoon, he  comes to Sibelius Park.
Across that green expanse he sees
   the cars parked close, every second licence yankee, he thinks of
   the war and the young men dodging, his wife inside
        with her counsel    her second thoughts
         and the children, needing more than they can give.
And behind him, five blocks south, his other lives
    in rainy limbo till tomorrow:
        Rochdale, yes    Anansi                  20
          the fine iconic books, sheepish errata
            shitwork in a cold basement, moody
          triumphs of the mind
             hassling printers    hassling banks
         and the grim dudgeon with friends—men with
deep combative egos, driven men, they cannot sit still, they go on
       brooding on Mao    on Gandhi
and they cannot resolve their lives but together they make up
            emblems of a unified civilization,
        the fine iconic books;                   30
                he is rooted in books and in
  that other place, where icons come alive among the faulty
        heroes & copouts, groping for some new tension of
     mind and life, casting the type in their own
       warm flesh
            hassling builders      hassling banks

---

1 Sibelius Park (officially Jean Sibelius Square) is a small park in Toronto's Annex area, a short walk from the sites
  of Rochdale College and House of Anansi Press. (The park is named after the Finnish symphonic composer and
  nature lover, Johan 'Jean' Sibelius.) Walmer Road is nearby.

and he is constantly coming and going away,
appalled by the power of wishful affirmations, he thinks of the war,
he hears himself 10 years ago affirming his faith in Christ
    in the lockers, still half-clasped in pads & a furtive        40
            virgin still, flailing the
lukewarm school with rumours of God,
        gunning for psychic opponents
though he could not hit his father and what broke at last was the
        holiness; and he can't go back there any more
   without hearing the livelong flourish
         of Christ in his mouth, always he tasted His funny
   taste in every arraignment but it was himself he was burying.
And the same struggle goes on and when
          he drinks too much, or cannot sleep for his body's    50
    jaundiced repose he can scarcely read a word he's written,
      though the words are just but his life has the
funny taste, and the work pulls back and snickers when he begins.

And then Sibelius Park!
      The grass is wet, it
gleams, across the park's wide
     vista the lanes of ornamental
shrub comes breathing and the sun has filled the
    rinsed air till the green goes luminous and it does it
               does, it comes clear!    60

II

Supper is over, I sit
      holed up in my study, I have
no answers again, and I do not trust the
     simplicities, nor Sibelius Park;
        I am not to be trusted with them.

But I rest in one thing. The play of
      dusk and atmospherics, the beautiful rites of
synaesthesia, are not to be believed;
     but that grisly counter-presence, the warfare in the lockers,
myself against myself, the years of desperate affirmation and the    70
    dank manholes of ego which stank when they
come free at last—
        the seamy underside of every stiff
  iconic self—which are hard        which are welcome

are no more real than that unreal man who stood and took them in;
      are no more real than the glib epiphanies,
                though they ache to bring them down.

For they are all given, they are not
      to be believed but constantly
they are being
      given, moment by moment, the icons and what they
suppress, here and
      here and though they are not real they have their own real
presence, like a mirror in the grass and in the
      bodies we live in we are
acceptable.                                                              80

There is nothing to be afraid of.

1972


# The Coat

I patched my coat with sunlight.
It lasted for a day.
I patched my coat with moonlight,
But the lining came away.
I patched my coat with lightning
And it blew off in the storm.
I patched my coat with darkness:
That coat has kept me warm.

1974


# When I Went Up to Rosedale[1]

When I went up to Rosedale
I thought of kingdom come
Persistent in the city
Like a totem in a slum.

1 An old area of Toronto known for its concentration of wealthy and powerful residents.

The ladies off across the lawns
Revolved like haughty birds.
They made an antique metaphor.
I didn't know the words.

Patrician diocese! the streets
Beguiled me as I went                                    10
Until the tory founders seemed
Immortal government—

For how could mediocrities
Have fashioned such repose?
And yet those men were pygmies,
As any schoolboy knows.

For Head[2] reduced the rule of law
To frippery and push.
Tradition-conscious Pellatt[3] built
A drawbridge in the bush.                                20

And Bishop Strachan[4] gave witness, by
The death behind his eyes,
That all he knew of Eden
Was the property franchise.

And those were our conservatives!—
A claque[5] of little men
Who took the worst from history
And made it worse again.

The dream of tory origins
Is full of lies and blanks,                              30

To prove that we're not Yanks?

Nothing but the elegant
For Sale signs on the lawn,
And roads that wind their stately way
To dead ends, and are gone.

2  Sir Francis Bond Head (1793–1875), whose handling of the Rebellions of 1837 was so capricious and unreasoned that it led to his early resignation from public office.
3  Sir Henry Mill Pellatt (1860–1939), financier and soldier, who built Casa Loma, a palatial residence that is now a public landmark.
4  John Strachan (1778–1867), first Anglican bishop of Toronto and one of the leaders of the Family Compact. Bishop Strachan argued that the Church of England should have exclusive rights to the revenues from the Clergy Reserves (Crown lands set aside for the maintenance of the Protestant clergy).
5  Originally, an audience hired to applaud a performance; now also any group of fawning admirers (here, a self-admiring group).

When I came down from Rosedale
I could not school my mind
To the manic streets before me
Nor the courtly ones behind.

1979

# The Gods

I

Who, now, can speak of gods—

their strokes and carnal voltage,
old ripples of presence          a space ago
archaic eddies of being?

Perhaps a saint could speak their names.
Or maybe some
noble claustrophobic spirit,
crazed by the flash and
vacuum of modernity,
could reach back, ripe for</div>                                    10
gods and a hot lobotomy.
But being none of these, I sit
bemused by the sound of the word.
For a man no longer moves
through coiled ejaculations of meaning;
we live within
equations, models, paradigms
which deaden the world, and now in our
heads, though less in our inconsistent lives,
the tickle of cosmos is gone.                                    20
Though what would a god be *like*?
Would he know about DNA molecules? and
keep little haloes, for when they behaved? . . .
It is not from simple derision
that the imagination snickers;
but faced with an alien reality it
stammers, it races & churns for
want of a common syntax and,
lacking a possible language,

who now can speak of gods? for random example          30
a bear to our ancestors, and even to
grope in a pristine hunch back to that way of being on earth
is nearly beyond me.


II

And yet—
in the middle of one more day, in a clearing maybe          sheer
godforce
calm on the lope of its pads
furred          hot-breathing          erect, at ease, catastrophic
harsh waves of stink, the
dense air clogged with its roaring and          40
ripples of power fork through us:
hair gone electric          quick
pricklish glissando, the
skin          mind skidding, balking is
HAIL
and it rears foursquare and we are jerked and owned and
forgive us          and
brought to a welter, old
force & destroyer and
do not destroy us!          50
or if it seems good,
destroy us.

Thus, the god against us in clear air.
And there are gentle gods—
as plain as
light that
rises from lake-face,
melding with light
that steps like a skipping-stone spatter
down to          60
evoke it,
till blue embraces blue, and lake and sky
are miles of indigenous climax—
such grace in the shining air.

All gods, all gods and none of them
domesticated angels, chic of spat & wing,
on ten-day tours of earth. And if

to speak of "gods" recalls those antique
wind-up toys, forget the gods as well:
*tremendum*[1] rather,                                                    70
dimension of otherness, come clear
in each familiar thing—in
outcrop, harvest, hammer, beast and
caught in that web of otherness
we too endure & we
worship.
We lived among that force, a space ago.

Or,
whirling it reins into phase through us, good god it can
*use* us, power in palpable                                              80
dollops invading the roots of the
hair, the gap behind the neck,
power to snag, coax bully exalt into presence
clean gestures of meaning among the traffic of earth,
and until it lobs us aside, pale snot poor
rags we
also can channel the godforce.
Yet still not
abjcct: not
heaven & wistful hankering—I mean                                        90
the living power, insidc
and, that sudden that
plumb!
We lived in such a space.

III

I do say gods.
But that was time ago, technology
happened and what has been withdrawn
I do not understand, the absent ones,
though many then too were bright & malevolent and
crushed things that mattered,                                           100
and where they have since been loitering I scarcely comprehend,
and least of all can I fathom, you powers I
seek and no doubt cheaply arouse and
who are you?

---

1  i.e., *mysterium tremendum*: according to Rudolph Otto, in *The Idea of the Holy* (1923), the sense of awe inspired by our awareness of a numinous, or metaphysical, dimension of existence—said by to be central to all religious experience.

how I am to salute you, nor how contend with your being
for I do not aim to make prize-hungry words (and
stay back!), I want
the world to be real and
it will not;
for to secular men there is not given the glory of tongues, yet it is          110
better to speak in silence than squeak in the gab of the age,
and if I cannot tell your terrifying
praise, now Hallmark gabble and chintz nor least of all
what time and dimensions your naked incursions
announced, you scurrilous powers yet
still I stand against this bitch of a shrunken time
in semi-faithfulness,
and whether you are godhead or zilch or daily ones like before
you strike our measure still and still you
endure as my murderous fate, though I          120
do not know you.

1978; rev. 1979

## Hunger

Looking back—what made me run? What pushed me
year by year by year
through all those loves and jobs and drafts and last-ditch causes?
It was hunger. Hunger. And, deeper than every
nerve-end purr in the pleasure machines of the *polis*, it was
unfilled hunger. Though for what, I can't tell.
Outside the museums, the names of the sacred no longer work.
They say too much, they say nothing at all and
though it seems strange to me,
I cannot find words to declare what my heart was hungering for.          10

For the old ones grew exotic.
Marduk, Loki, Vishnu—
amen of dispersal;
Manitou, Ishtar, Zeus—
rustle of silent goodbye.
They have become a rare, achieved, and
dangerous hole in the species, residual nothing,
the space a passing makes—
Yü-huang, Utnapishtim, Quetzalcoatl;
Persephone, Yahweh, God.          20

For we rose. And thought. And trashed our sacramental
birthright.
But I have lived 45 years, and never once
have I inched beyond the safety of lament ...
But that's not what I *feel*. It's a playful itch,
a volt of desire, which
hankers towards what
*God* was a blasphemy of—never yet
have I danced full-tilt with my secret appetite:
to live in awe.                                                      30

To live, at last, in awe.
And I know, many reclaim that
sanity at the margins, where our bodies still sense
the tang of indigenous meaning. Returning to
granite, to cedar and loon—old
amniotic siblings.
Or, catgut hosannas; held in that burnished ache of sound, how the
soulmeat champs and respires!
Even graft and torture provoke it, the outraged
sense of a justice we half belong to, half can't find.             40

But now we live
closer to zero noon, and what I know best
is the simple need.
To flare in the wordless dimension. To hunch in my
other name, that doesn't have
*I* all over it.        Almost it hurts to relax.
But in that arterial stammer, my back to words,
the yen just breathes.
No storms of presence. My mind still yacks and fidgets.
But hunger hungers, and                                             50
sometimes I am permitted to mooch in the nearness.

1996

## Hiatus

And the unredeemable names
devolve in their
liminal slouch to abyss.
I gather the crumbs of hiatus.

The blank where *evil* held.
The hole called *beholden*.

That phantom glyphs[1] resound, that
lacunae be burnished.
That it not be leached from memory: once,
earth meant otherly.                                                    10

2003

1  Non-verbal symbols (for example, ➔); often symbolic figures that have been engraved in stone.

# Desaparecidos[1]

Through
glittery templates of e-
merce, say cheese.
Peekaboo in the
global lobophony.
Locked pocks in the heyday of value-free, I
shush to their witness:
that evil is real.
Unassimilable. Inexpungeable. Undisownable.                            10

2003

1  Spanish for 'the disappeared', a a way of referring to those who have been abducted or killed as an act of state-enforced terror.

# Wordly[1]

If inly, if only, if
unly: heart-
iculate improv,
sussing the emes[2] of what is.

Nor hunker in losslore, nor
kneejerk abracadaver.

1  This and the following poem come from the tenth and concluding section of *Un*; 'Tale' concludes the sequence.
2  '-eme' is a suffix indicating a distinct unit of linguistic structure, as in *phoneme, morpheme*, etc.

Cripcryptic rejuice! Ec-
statisyllabic largesse—
rekenning,[3] rekeening, re-
meaning our wordly demesne.[4]                    10

2007

3  A kenning is a compound metaphor, found in Anglo-Saxon verse (e.g., 'whaleroad' for sea); with a play on
   *reckoning*.
4  Estate; home.

## Tale

Tell me, tall-
tell me a tale. The one about
starless & steerless & pinch-me, the
one about unnable now—which they did-did-
did in the plume of our pride, and
could not find the way home.
Little perps lost.

Yet a rescue appeared, in the
story a saviour arose. Called
limits. Called                                    10
duedate, called countdown ex-
tinction/collide. Called, eyeball to ego:
hubris agonistcs.[1]

Bad abba the endgame. In-
seminal doomdom alert:
pueblo naturans,[2] or
else. But the breadcrumbs are gone, and the
story goes on, and how
haply an ending no
nextwise has shown us, nor known.              20

2007

# Fred Wah

## b. 1939

Born in Swift Current, Saskatchewan, Fred Wah grew up in Trail and in Nelson, British Columbia. He left the Kootenay region in 1959 to pursue his interest in music at the University of British Columbia. Once there, he also began to study poetry. In 1961, he helped found the poetry newsletter *Tish*, from which the *Tish* group took its name—the first of his many associations with literary publishing.

After completing a BA in music and English literature at UBC, Wah began graduate studies with the poet Robert Creeley at the University of New Mexico; he then followed Creeley when he moved to the State University of New York at Buffalo. There, he also studied with Charles Olson, the major theorist of Black Mountain poetics. The Black Mountain emphasis on a poetry of simple syntax, concreteness, a spontaneous-sounding poetic line felt to be an expression of the poet's breath, and organic literary forms were ideas already important to the *Tish* poets and became central to Wah's poetry.

In 1965, Wah joined George Bowering, Frank Davey, and David Dawson in founding *Open Letter*: this journal, which grew out of *Tish*, became an important forum for discussions in Canada of new writers and experimental poetics. That same year, he published his first book of poetry, *Lardeau*, following it, in 1967, with *Mountain*. Completing his MA that year, he returned to the Kootenays to teach at Selkirk College in Castlegar. When the short-lived David Thomson University Centre was created in Nelson in 1978, he became head of its creative-writing program and co-founded *Writing Magazine* there in 1980. After David Thompson closed in 1984, Wah and other instructors began the Kootenay School of Writing in Vancouver.

Wah published four books of poetry during the 1970s, including *Among* (1972), which contains work from earlier books, and *Pictograms from the Interior of B.C.* (1975). His 1980 volume of selected poems, *Loki Is Buried at Smoky Creek*, edited by Bowering, shows him working in a spare imagistic style to create short poems reflecting the experiences of everyday life. The book he published the following year, *Breathin' My Name with a Sigh* (1981), evinces Wah's continuing love of music in the way it explores sound as well as imagery as a resource for the poet. The playful connection he makes between the sound of his name and the sound of air being exhaled recalls the Black Mountain focus on breath as an element of poetry. Among his several books from the 1980s, *Waiting for Saskatchewan* (1985; Governor General's Award) includes selections from *Breathin' My Name with a Sigh* and from *Grasp the Sparrow's Tail* (1982). *Music at the Heart of Thinking* (1987), made up of responses to contemporary texts, is continued with *Alley Alley Home Free* in 1992.

Continuing his editorial commitment to Canadian writing, Wah edited *Net Work*, a selection of Daphne Marlatt's poetry, in 1980; in 1984, he founded, with Frank Davey, *SwiftCurrent*, the world's first electronic literary magazine, which continued until 1990. In 1989, Wah accepted an appointment at the University of Calgary. In 2003, he retired, moving with his wife, the poet Pauline Butling, to Vancouver. He was writer-in-residence at Simon Fraser University in 2006–7.

In the concluding statement in *Loki*, Wah emphasizes his sense that writing 'has a lot to do with "place", the spiritual and spatial localities of the writer.' In *Waiting for Saskatchewan*, he investigates both how personal history is grounded in place and how genealogy transcends place. It contains a sequence of prose poems, 'Elite'—which takes its name from the family café in Swift Current—that deals with a return Wah made to the Prairies and with his desire to understand the influence of his father, whose presence dominates the book. This direction in his work toward what he calls, following Bowering, 'biotexts', culminates in

*Diamond Grill* (1996), and in a series of essays (collected in 2000 as *Faking It—Poetics and Hybridity: Critical Writing, 1984–1999*) in which he examines his mixed heritage and the questions arising from it—such as how 'ethnic writing' is perceived in Canada.

In one of those essays, entitled 'Half-Bred Poetics', Wah writes that *Diamond Grill* is 'a text that interrogates the roots of my own anger as racial—genetically and culturally.'

*It's only one of a number of diatribes against the assumptions and confusions of identity. . . . The site of this poetics for me, and many other multi-racial and multi-cultural writers, is the hyphen, that marked (or unmarked) space that both binds and divides. . . . Though the hyphen is in the middle it is not in the centre. It is a property marker, a boundary post, a borderland, a bastard, a railroad, a last spike, a stain, a cipher, a rope, a knot, a chain (link), a foreign word, a warning sign, a head tax, a bridge, a no-man's land, a nomadic, floating magic carpet, now you see it now you don't.*

Like its author, *Diamond Grill* is a complex mixture: Wah began the book as a series of personal narratives in 1988 after bpNichol challenged him to enter Canada's annual 3-Day Novel Contest; he put away what he had written but came back to it from time to time until he felt—with the help of the novelist Aritha van Herk—he had found the right form. A sequence of short pieces that have the qualities of prose poetry, it reads like a memoir, has footnotes that recall the academic essay, and has won an award for short fiction. The work as a whole is a reflection of the dynamics and difficulties of self-identification and self-representation that arise when the heritage and experience of being 'Canadian' is inherently multiple, a self-portrait of a man born in Canada to a Swedish mother and a half-Chinese, half-Scots-Irish father, as he traces the way he was asked to choose between a single 'non-white' identity or a life lived 'in the hyphen'.

Examining the limitations of hyphenated representation in *Diamond Grill*, partly by using food imagery and its preparation in his family restaurant as a metaphor for questions of ethnic identity, Wah recognizes that, though he *does* strongly identify with his Chinese background, he has never been entirely comfortable in the Chinese community—in part because members of that group do not see him as one of them. The fact that English is his first language is a barrier, yet the influence of the Chinese language has affected Wah's way of speaking that English and has given him a sense of language distinct from that of other English Canadians with whom he comes into contact. In that mixture lies the history of Wah's family and of his nations, both old and new. *Diamond Grill* makes us aware of just how mixed language can be: one word in particular, *muckamuck*, comes to represent this complexity. Associating the word with his paternal grandfather, Wah assumes it is Chinese in origin until he learns about the confusions caused by mixtures of genealogies and languages.

In 2008, Wah published *Sentenced to Light*, a work that blends his interest in poetry and the visual arts (which can also be seen in his having served as editor of the journal *West Coast Line*). This book, Wah's response to a mixed-media installation by the artists Michelle Perron and Paul Woodrow, juxtaposes poetry with photographs and drawings (including cartoons) to produce the effect of *bavardage*—that is, small talk among friends.

# Waiting for saskatchewan

Waiting for saskatchewan
and the origins grandparents countries places converged
europe asia railroads carpenters nailed grain elevators
Swift Current my grandmother in her house
he built on the street

and him his cafes namely the 'Elite'[1] on Center
looked straight ahead Saskatchewan points to it
Erickson Wah Trimble houses train station tracks
arrowed into downtown fine clay dirt prairies wind waiting
for Saskatchewan to appear for me again over the edge          10
horses led to the huge sky the weight and colour of it
over the mountains as if the mass owed me such appearance
against the hard edge of it sits on my forehead
as the most political place I know these places these strips
laid beyond horizon for eyesight the city so I won't have to go
near it as origin town flatness appears later in my stomach why
why on earth would they land in such a place
mass of pleistocene
sediment plate wedge
arrow sky beak horizon still waiting for that                  20
I want it back, wait in this snowblown winter night
for that latitude of itself its own largeness
my body to get complete
it still owes me, it does

1981; rev. 1985

1 Wah has indicated that in his community the word was pronounced with a long *i*.

# From *Diamond Grill*

IN THE DIAMOND, AT THE END OF A

long green vinyl aisle between booths of chrome, Naugahyde, and Formica, are two large swinging wooden doors, each with a round hatch of face-sized window. Those kitchen doors can be kicked with such a slap they're heard all the way up to the soda fountain. One the other side of the doors, hardly audible to the customers, echoes a jargon of curses, jokes, and cryptic orders. Stack a hots! Half a dozen fry! Hot beef san! Fingers and tongues all over the place jibe and swear You mucka high!—Thloong you! And outside, running through and around the town, the creeks flow down to the lake with, maybe, a spring thaw. And the prairie sun over the mountains to the east, over my family's shoulders. The journal journey tilts tight-fisted through the gutter of the book, avoiding a place to start—or end. Maps don't have beginnings, just edges. Some frayed and hazy margin of possibility, absence, gap. Shouts in the kitchen. Fish an! Side a fries! Over easy! On brown! I pick up an order and turn, back through the doors, whap! My foot registers more than its own imprint, starts to read the stain of memory.

Thus: a kind of heterocellular recovery reverberates through the busy body, from the foot against the kitchen door on up the leg into the torso and hands, eyes thinking straight ahead, looking through doors and languages, skin recalling its own reconnaissance, cooked into the steamy food, replayed in the folds of elsewhere, always far away, tunneling through the centre of the earth, mouth saying can't forget, mouth saying what I want to know can feed me, what I don't can bleed me.

## MIXED GRILL IS AN ENTRÉE
### AT THE DIAMOND

and, as in most Chinese-Canadian restaurants in western Canada, is your typical improvised imitation of Empire cuisine. No kippers or kidney for the Chinese cafe cooks, though. They know the authentic mixed grill alright. It is part of their colonial cook's training, learning to serve the superior race in Hong Kong and Victoria properly, mostly as chefs in private elite clubs and homes. But, as the original lamb chop, split lamb kidney, and pork sausage edges its way onto every town cafe menu, its ruddy countenance has mutated into something quick and dirty, not grilled at all, but fried.

Shu composes his mixed grill on top of the stove. He throws on a veal chop, a ribeye, a couple of pork sausages, bacon, and maybe a little piece of liver or a few breaded sweetbreads if he has those left over from the special. While the meat's sizzling he adds a handful of sliced mushrooms and a few slices of tomato to sauté alongside. He shovels it all, including the browned grease, onto the large oblong platters used only for this dish and steak dinners, wraps the bacon around the sausages, nudges on a scoop of mashed potatoes, a ladle of mixed steamed (actually canned and boiled) vegetables, a stick of celery, and sometimes a couple of flowered radishes. As he lifts the finished dish onto the pickup counter he wraps the corner of his apron around his thumb and wipes the edge of the platter clean, pushes a button that rings a small chime out front, and shouts loudly into the din of the kitchen, whether there's anyone there or not, *mixee grill*!

*   *   *

## YET LANGUAGELESS. MOUTH ALWAYS
### A GAUZE, WORDS LOCKED

behind tongue, stopped in and out, what's she saying, what's she want, why's she mad, this woman-silence stuck, struck, stopped—there and back, English and Chinese churning ocean, her languages caught in that loving angry rip tide of children and coercive tradition and authority. Yet.

Grampa Wah's marriage to Florence Trimble is a surprise to most of the other Chinamen in the cafes around southern Saskatchewan, but not to his wife back in China. Kwan Chung-keong comes to Canada in 1892, returns to his small village in Hoiping County in 1900, and stays just long enough to marry a girl from his village and father two daughters and a son. When he returns to Canada in 1904 he has to leave his family behind because the head tax has, in his absence, been raised to five hundred dollars (two years' Canadian wages).[1] He realized he'll never be able to get his family over here so, against the grain for Chinamen, he marries a white woman (Scots-Irish from Trafalgar, Ontario), the cashier in his cafe. They have three boys and four girls and he never goes back to China again.

I don't know how Grampa Wah talks her into it (maybe he doesn't) but somehow Florence lets two of her children be sent off to China as recompense in some patriarchal deal her husband has with his Chinese wife. He rationalizes to her the Confucian idea that a tree may grow as tall as it likes but its leaves will always return to the ground. Harumph, she thinks, but to no avail.

Fred and his older sister are suddenly one day in July 1916 taken to the train station in Swift Current, their train and boat tickets and identities pinned to their coats in an envelope. My grandfather had intended to send number one son but when departure day arrives Uncle Buster goes into hiding. Grampa grabs the next male in line, four-year-old Fred, and, because he is so young, nineteen-year-old Ethel as well, to look after him. He has the word of the conductor that the children will be delivered safely to the boat in Vancouver and from there the connections all the way to Canton have been arranged. Fred, Kwan Foo-Lee, and Ethel, Kwan An-wa, spend the next eighteen years, before returning to Canada, being raised by their Chinese step-mother alongside two half-sisters and a half-brother.

Yet, in the face of this patrimonial horse-trading it is the women who turn it around for my father and Aunty Ethel. Back in Canada my grandmother, a deeply religious lady, applies years of Salvation Army morality to her heathen husband to bring her children home. But he is a gambler and, despite his wife's sadness and Christian outrage, he keeps gambling away the money that she scrapes aside for the kids' return passage.

Meanwhile, the remittance money being sent from Canada to the Chinese wife starts to dwindle when the depression hits. She feels the pinch of supporting these two half-ghosts and, besides, she reasons with my grandfather, young Foo-lee is getting dangerously attracted to the opium crowd. As a small landholder she sells some land to help buy his way back to Canada.

Aunty Ethel's situation is different. She is forced to wait while, back in Canada, Fred convinces his father to arrange a marriage for her with a Chinaman in Moose Jaw. She doesn't get back to Canada until a year later, 1935.

Yet the oceans of women migrant-tongued words in a double-bind of bossy love and wary double-talk forced to ride the waves of rebellion and obedience through a silence that shutters numb the traffic between eye and mouth and slaps across the face of family, yet these women forced to spit, out of bound-up feet and torsoed hips made-up yarns and foreign scripts unlucky colours zippered lips—yet, to spit, when possible, in the face of the father the son the holy ticket safety-pinned to his lapel—the pileup of twisted curtains intimate ink pious pages partial pronouns translated letters shore-to-shore Pacific jetsam pretending love forgotten history braided gender half-breed loneliness naive voices degraded miscourse racist myths talking gods fact and fiction

---

1 In 1885 the Act to Restrict and Regulate Chinese Immigration into Canada was passed, requiring that all Chinese immigrants entering Canada pay a 'head tax' (originally $50 per person). In 1903 the amount was raised to $500.

remembered faced different brothers sisters misery tucked margins whisper zero criss-cross noisy mothers absent fathers high muckamuck husbands competing wives bilingual I's their unheard sighs, their yet still-floating lives.

## Dirty heathens, Granny Erickson
### thinks of the Chinese,

the whole bunch of them, in their filthy cafes downtown. Just because that boy dresses up and has a little money, she throws herself at him. She and those other girls, they're always horsing around, looking for fun, running off to Gull Lake for a basketball game, a bunch of little liars, messing around in those cars, I know, not getting home until late at night, all fun and no work. I know what they're doing, they can't fool me, oof dah, that Coreen, she'll ruin herself, you wait and see, she'll be back here for help soon enough. Well she can look out for herself, she's not going to get any more of my money, she can just take her medicine, now that she's living with that Chinaman, nobody'll speak to her, the little hussy.

\* \* \*

## His mother's family are stern and
### religious Scots/Irish

railroad people from Ontario. His in-laws, when he marries Coreen Erickson in 1938, are post-WWI economic refugees from Sweden. While he and Ethel have been in China, their brothers and sisters have negotiated particular identities for themselves through the familiarity of a white European small prairie town commonality (albeit colonial democracy). Though he arrives back to everyone struggling through the thirties, they all have their place. They're part of the reputed latest Pleistocene migration staged to the middle of Canada. And they are, then, him and then his and her, and then me and so on, given the impediment, authority and, above all, the possibility of place. He thinks, after he and Ethel's intimidation as half-ghosts in China, that this Petri dish of hope and plenty is a great opportunity through which (and with which) he and his kind can go on, away from, hopefully, the fragmented diaspora, but always with some tag of chance that will continually fire a brand-spanking new trajectory into what has been, after all, an unrelentingly foreign world. Hybridize or disappear; family *in* place.

\* \* \*

## Famous Chinese Restaurant
### is the name of a

small, strip-mall Chinese cafe a friend of mine eats at once in awhile. We laugh at the innocent pretentiousness of the name, Famous.

But then I think of the pride with which my father names the Diamond Grill. For him, the name is neither innocent nor pretentious. The Diamond, he proudly regales the banquet at the grand opening, is the most modern, up-to-date restaurant in the interior of BC. The angled design of the booths matches the angles of a diamond and the diamond itself stands for good luck. We hope this new restaurant will bring good luck for all our families and for this town. Eat! Drink! Have a good time!

Almost anything in Chinese stands for good luck, it seems. You're not supposed to use words that might bring bad luck. Aunty Ethel is very upset when we choose a white casket for my father's funeral. She says, that no good! White mean death, bad luck!

So I understand something of the dynamics of naming and desire when I think of the names of some Chinese cafes in my family's history. The big one, of course, is the Elite, which we, with no disrespect for the Queen's English, always pronounce the eee-light. In fact, everyone in town pronounces it that way. My dad works in an Elite in Swift Current and that's what he names his cafe in Trail when we move out to BC. Elite is a fairly common Chinese cafe name in the early fifties, but not any more. I see one still on Edmonton Trail in Calgary and I know of one in Revelstoke. I like the reso-nant undertone in the word *élite*: the privilege to choose. In the face of being denied the right to vote up until 1949,[2] I smile a little at the recognition by the Chinese that choice is, indeed, a privilege.

Other names also play on the margins of fantasy and longing. Grampa Wah owns the Regal in Swift Current and just around the corner are the Venice and the Paris. Just as Chiang escapes to Taiwan my father gets into the New Star in Nelson.[3]

During the fifties and sixties, coincidental with the rise of Canadian nationalism, we find small-town cafes with names like the Canadian, Canada Chinese Take-Out, and, in respect of Hockey Night in Canada, the All Star. Along the border: American-Canadian Cafe and the Ambassador.

One could read more recent trends such as Bamboo Terrace, Heaven's Gate, Pearl Seafood Restaurant, and the Mandarin as indicative of both the recognized exoticiza-tion in orientalism as well as, possibly, a slight turn, a deference, pride and longing for the homeland.

Perhaps we might regard more concretely what resonates for us when we walk into places like White Dove Cafe and Hotel in Mossbank Saskatchewan or the even-now famous Disappearing Moon Cafe, 50 East Pender Street, Vancouver, BC.[4]

\* \* \*

THE RACE TRACK? SWEDISH, CHINESE,
    SCOTTISH, IRISH, CANADIAN.

You bet. But somewhere in that stable the purebreds dissolve into paints. The starting gate opens as my father's face implanted on my scowly brow, body rigid. Parts folding into body after body. His father Lucky Jim on the porch singing old Chinese nursery rhymes, tears but a gold-toothed smile always. My mother a smiler too, then her father

2 Prior to 1949 the British Columbia Qualifications of Voters Act of 1872 denied the Chinese and First Nations peoples the right to vote in provincial elections.
3 After the Nationalist government, which took a blue and white star design as its emblem, was defeated by the communists in China in 1949, Chiang Kai-shek fled the mainland with more than one million followers and established a government in exile on Taiwan.
4 Famous because of Sky Lee's novel, *Disappearing Moon Cafe* (1990).

sour, her mother more sour yet. Temper. The Teacher telling us who we get to be, to write down what our fathers are. Race, race, race. English, German, Doukhobor, Italian. But not Canadian, there's a difference between a race and a country. No matter what, you're what your father is, was, forever. After school. Chink, Limy, Kraut, Wop, Spik. The whole town. Better than the Baker street nickel millionaires[5] my dad calls them. Race makes you different, nationality makes you the same. Sameness is purity. Not the same anything when you're half Swede, quarter Chinese, and quarter Ontario Wasp. The Salvation Army my granny marches with, into the parade of other grannies, uncles, aunts, cousins, half quarter full and distant, all waiting for Saskatchewan to appear for them. Stuttered inventive, invective process. The domain of this track is an ordered fiction, a serious intervention. Until we now know the only fiction here has to be the reader. You know, relative.

\* \* \*

BETTER WATCH OUT FOR THE
     CRAW, BETTER WATCH

out for the goat. That's the mix, the breed, the half-breed, metis, quarter-breed, trace-of-a-breed true demi-semi-ethnic polluted rootless living technicolour snarl to complicate the underbelly panavision of racism and bigotry across this country. I know, you're going to say, that's just being Canadian. The only people who call themselves Canadian live in Ontario and have national sea-to-shining-sea twenty-twenty CPR vision.

When I was in elementary school we had to fill out a form at the beginning of each year. The first couple of years I was really confused. The problem was the blank after Racial Origin. I thought, well, this is Canada, I'll put down Canadian. But the teacher said no Freddy, you're Chinese, your racial origin is Chinese, that's what your father is. Canadian isn't a racial identity. That's turned out to be true. But I'm not really Chinese either. Nor were some of the other kids in my class *real* Italian, Doukhobor, or British.

Quite a soup. Heinz 57 Varieties. There's a whole bunch of us who've grown up as resident aliens, living in the hyphen. Like the Chinese kids who came over after 1949 couldn't take me into their confidence. I always ended up playing on the other team, against them, because they were foreign and I was white enough to be on the winning team. When I visited China and I told the guide of our tour group that I was Chinese he just laughed at me. I don't blame him. He, for all his racial purity so characteristic of mainland Chinese, was much happier thinking of me as a Canadian, something over there, white, Euro. But not Chinese.

That could be the answer in this country. If you're pure anything you can't be Canadian. We'll save that name for all the mixed bloods in this country and when the cities have Heritage Days and ethnic festivals there'll be a group that I can identify with, the Canadians. When the government gives out money for cultural centres we'll get ours too. These real Canadians could gain a legitimate marginalized position. The

---

5  That is, those who act as if they have a million dollars but really only have a million nickels.

French-Canadians would have to be Québécois, the Mennonites Mennonite, Brits Brit. And if you're a Scot from Hamilton or a Jew from Winnipeg, then be that; I don't care.

But stop telling me what I'm not, what I can't join, what I can't feel or understand. And don't whine to me about maintaining your ethnic ties to the old country, don't explain the concept of time in terms of a place called Greenwich, don't complain about not being able to find Tootsie Rolls or authentic Mexican food north of the 49th.

Sometimes I'd rather be left alone.

\* \* \*

SITKUM DOLLAH GRAMPA WAH
    LAUGHS AS HE FLIPS

a shiny half-dollar coin into the air. I say tails and he laughs too bad Freddy and shows me the head of King George the sixth. Then he puts a quarter into my hand, closes his brown and bony hand over mine, pinches my cheek while he says you good boy Freddy, buy some candy!

Whenever I hear grampa talk like that, high muckamuck, sitkum dollah, I think he's sliding Chinese words into English words just to have a little fun. He has fun alright, but I now realize he also enjoys mouthing the dissonance of encounter, the resonance of clashing tongues, his own membership in the diasporic and nomadic intersections that have occurred in northwest North America over the past one hundred and fifty years.

I don't know, then, that he's using Chinook jargon, the pidgin vocabulary of colonial interaction, the code-switching talkee-talkee of the contact zone.[6]

The term grampa uses most is high muckamuck (from *hyu muckamuck*, originally among First Nations meaning plenty to eat and then transformed, through the contact zone, into big shot, big-time operator). He exclaims high muckamuck whenever

6 'Mary Louise Pratt describes this as the practice of

*code-switching*, in which speakers switch spontaneously and fluidly between two languages. . . . In the context of fiercely monolingual dominant cultures like that of the United States, code-switching lays claim to a form of cultural power: the power to own but not be owned by the dominant language. Aesthetically, code-switching can be a source of great verbal subtlety and grace as speech dances fluidly and strategically back and forth between two languages and two cultural systems. Code-switching is a rich source of wit, humour, puns, word play, and games of rhythm and rhyme. ' "Yo soy la Malinche" ', in *Twentieth Century Poetry: From Text to Context*, edited by Peter Verdonk, London: Routledge, 1993: 177.

'Pratt's description of the 'contact zone' is equally useful in considering the dynamics of foreignicity:

The space of colonial encounters, the space in which peoples geographically and historically separated come into contact with each other and establish ongoing relations, usually involving conditions of coercion, radical inequality, and intractable conflict. . . . 'Contact zone' . . . is often synonymous with 'colonial frontier'. But while the latter term is grounded within a European expansionist perspective (the frontier is a frontier only with respect to Europe), 'contact zone' is an attempt to invoke the spatial and temporal copresence of subjects previously separated by geographic and historical disjunctures, and whose trajectories now intersect. By using the term 'contact', I aim to foreground the interactive, improvisational dimensions of colonial encounters so easily ignored or suppressed by diffusionist accounts of conquest and domination. A 'contact' perspective emphasizes how subjects are constituted in and by their relations among colonizers and colonized . . . not in terms of separateness or apartheid, but in terms of copresence, interaction, interlocking understandings and practices, often within radically asymmetrical relations of power. *Imperial Eyes: Travel Writing and Transculturation*. London: Routledge, 1992: 6–7.

he sees us get into our best clothes for Sunday school. Or, even sometimes when he gets all spiffed up, arranging his hanky to pouf out of the breast pocket of his suit, angling his tie into a full Windsor, fixing his diamond cuff-links and shaking his arms so the shirt-sleeves will fill out smooth, sticking the gold nugget tie pin through the layers of tie and shirt, brushing some lint off of his trouser leg as he stands to reach up for his best felt hat, and then walking out the door with a twinkle in his eyes chuckling high muckamuck.

Though my grandfather seems to say the phrase with a kind of humorous and testy tone, my father translates high muckamuck into a term of class derision. He doesn't like pretension and, though he certainly works hard to raise our family up a middle-class notch, he'll sideswipe anyone he sees putting on airs or using class advantage.

Don't think you're such a high muckamuck, my dad said to me after my brother Ernie ratted on my driving down Baker Street in Dad's Monarch with my right arm around a girl. It's not class itself, really, but how you use it.

For example, he tears into one of the Baker Street nickel millionaires who picks up a tip from a booth that hasn't been cleaned yet. We all know the tip's there; it's at least a bill because you can see it sticking out from under the plate. As the guy's looking through the menu my dad goes up to him and says jesus christ Murphy what do you think you're doing lifting the girls' tips. They work hard for that money and you got more'n you know what to do with. You think you're such a high muckamuck. You never leave tips yourself and here you are stealing small change. I want you to get out of here and don't come into this cafe again. The guy leaves, cursing at my dad, saying he doesn't know why anyone'd wanna eat this Chink food anyway. He never does come back. A pipsqueak trying to be high muckamuck.

And I only realize, right here on this page, when the cooks in the kitchen swear You mucka high! at me, they've transed the phrase out of their own history here. I thought they were swearing in Chinese.

Whenever my mother uses the term she adds a syllable by saying high muckety-muck.

\* \* \*

I'M JUST A BABY, MAYBE
    SIX MONTHS (.5%)

old. One of my aunts is holding me on her knee. Sitting on the ground in front of us are her two daughters, 50% Scottish. Another aunt, the one who grew up in China

---

'See also Monica Kin Gagnon's catalogue essay on Henry Tsang's installation 'Utter Jargon':

Chinook Jargon was developed initially as a pidgin language amongst west coast First Nations peoples. Used primarily for trade purposes, Chinook Jargon's (roughly) five-hundred word vocabulary can be more specifically traced to the dialect of the Columbia River Chinook with further influences from English, French, and Nuu-chah-nulth (a language group located predominantly on the west coast of Vancouver Island). At the height of its usage, Chinook Jargon had an estimated one hundred thousand speakers throughout a region stretching from northern California to Alaska, and from the Rockies to the Pacific Ocean. As Tsang notes, the jargon was unable to resist the dominance of English, and fell out of use during the first half of the 1900s. *Dual Cultures*, Kamloops Art Gallery: Kamloops, 1993: 9' [Wah's note].

with my father, sits on the step with her first two children around her. They are 75% Chinese. There is another little 75% girl cousin, the daughter of another 50% aunt who married a 100% full-blooded Chinaman (full-blooded, from China even). At the back of the black-and-white photograph is my oldest boy cousin; he's 25% Chinese. His mother married a Scot from North Battleford and his sisters married Italians from Trail. So there, spread out on the stoop of a house in Swift Current, Saskatchewan, we have our own little western Canadian multicultural stock exchange.

We all grew up together, in Swift Current, Calgary, Trail, Nelson and Vancouver (27% of John A.'s nation) and only get together now every three years (33%) for a family reunion, to which between 70% and 80% of us show up. Out of fifteen cousins only one (6.6%) married a 100% pure Chinese.

The return on these racialized investments has produced colourful dividends and yielded an annual growth rate that now parallels blue-chip stocks like Kodak and Fuji, though current global market forces indicate that such stocks, by their volatile nature, will be highly speculative and risky. Unexpected developments (like Immigration Acts) could knock estimates for a loop. Always take future projections with either a grain of salt or better still a dash of soy.

* * *

ON THE EDGE OF CENTRE.
        JUST OFF MAIN.

Chinatown. The cafes, yes, but further back, almost hidden, the ubiquitous Chinese store—an unmoving stratus of smoke, dusky and quiet, clock ticking. Dark brown wood paneling, some porcelain planters on the windowsill, maybe some goldfish. Goldfish for Gold Mountain men.[7] Not so far, then, from the red carp of their childhood ponds. Brown skin stringy salt-and-pepper beard polished bent knuckles and at least one super-long fingernail for picking. Alone and on the edge of their world, far from the centre, no women, no family. This kind of edge in race we only half suspect as edge. A gap, really. Hollow.

I wander to it, tagging along with my father or with a cousin, sent there to get a jar of some strange herb or balm from an old man who forces salted candies on us or digs for a piece of licorice dirtied with grains of tobacco from his pocket, the background of old men's voices sure and argumentative within this grotto. Dominoes clacking. This store, part of a geography, mysterious to most, a migrant haven edge of outpost, of gossip, bavardage,[8] foreign tenacity. But always in itself, on the edge of some great fold.

In a room at the back of the Chinese store, or above, like a room fifteen feet over the street din in Vancouver Chinatown, you can hear, amplified through the window, the click-clacking of mah-jong pieces being shuffled over the table tops. The voices

7 Because emigration from China in the second half of the nineteenth century was largely in response to gold rushes in California, British Columbia, and the Yukon, North America came to be referred to as Gold Mountain.
8 French term for 'prattle' or 'chatter'.

from up there or behind the curtain are hot-tempered, powerful, challenging, aggressive, bickering, accusatory, demeaning, bravado, superstitious, bluffing, gossipy, serious, goading, letting off steam, ticked off, fed up, hot under the collar, hungry for company, hungry for language, hungry for luck, edgy.

\* \* \*

AND YOU, OLD, MUMBLING TO
    YOURSELF SWEDISH GRAMPA,

what madnesses of northern Europe in 1922 drove you across an ocean to Saskatchewan? Uprooted, lost or new? What are you doing up there, silent on a wooden height in the sun and wind, nailing grain elevator after grain elevator. What sour images immigrated with you to that horizon, that languagelessness? His answer full of angst and sadness.

No. They weren't sour. Up here nailing nailing, the pictures of Uppsala and Vastmanland, my father cutting cordwood in the forest, the old city, streets and friends, this is erased slowly and softly, empty prairie wind whipped into the corners of my eyes, my mind, memory hammered into, day after day on the scaffold. But to hell with it, it's work.

This sky is the world now.

I know no one except for a few others on this job. On Saturday we'll have a few beers, relax a bit. Not like back home. Too much church.

After the war, lots of work. My brother got a good job in Göteborg, in the shipyards. He suggested we move there, he could get me on easily he said. But really, it was the same old thing. I wanted something different.

This sky is different: larger, bluer, farther. Maybe it will be different here. Maybe I will be different.

Smell this pine we're working with, still wet and bleeding pitch, turpentine. They say all our wood here comes from the mountains to the west. I believe it. You can smell that hot summer wind blowing pine bite through the forests anywhere, everywhere, over this prairie, over this ocean.

\* \* \*

ANOTHER CHIP ON MY SHOULDER
    IS THE APPROPRIATION

of the immigrant identity. I see it all over the place. Even one of the country's best-known writers has said We are all immigrants to this place even if we were born here.[9] Can't these people from *central* leave anything to itself? Why deny the immigrant his or her real world? Why be in such a rush to dilute? Those of us who have already been genetically diluted need our own space to figure it out. I don't want to be inducted into someone else's story, or project. Particularly one that would reduce and usurp my family's residue of ghost values to another status quo. Sorry, but I'm just not

9 See Margaret Atwood, page 811.

interested in this collective enterprise erected from the sacrosanct great railway imagination dedicated to harvesting a dominant white cultural landscape. There's a whole forest of us out here who don't like clear-cut, suspect the mechanical purity of righteous, clear, shining, Homelite Americas, chainsaws whining, just across the valley.

No way I'll let these chips fall where they may.

\* \* \*

## I HARDLY EVER GO INTO KING'S FAMILY RESTAURANT

because, when it comes to Chinese cafes and Chinatowns, I'd rather be transparent. Camouflaged enough so they know I'm there but can't see me, can't get to me. It's not safe. I need a clear coast for a getaway. Invisible. I don't know who I am in this territory and maybe don't want to. Yet I love to wander into Toronto's Chinatown and eat tofu and vegetables at my favourite barbecue joint and then meander indolently through the crowds listening to the tones and watching the dark eyes, the black hair. Sometimes in a store, say, I'm picking up a pair of new Kung-fu sandals and the guy checks my Mastercard as I sign and he says Wah! You Chinese? heh heh heh! because he knows I'm not. Physically, I'm racially transpicuous and I've come to prefer that mode.

I want to be there but don't want to be seen being there. By the time I'm ten I'm only white. Until 1949 the only Chinese in my life are relatives and old men. Very few Chinese kids my age. After '49, when the Canadian government rescinds its Chinese Exclusion Act, a wave of young Chinese immigrate to Canada. Nelson's Chinese population visibly changes in the early fifties. In a few years there are enough teenage Chinese kids around to not only form an association, the Nelson Chinese Youth Association, but also a basketball team. And they're good, too. Fast, smart. I play on the junior high school team and when the NYCA team comes to play us, I know a lot of the Chinese guys. But my buddies at school call them Chinks and geeks and I feel a little embarrassed and don't talk much with the Chinese kids. I'm white enough to get away with it and that's what I do.

But downtown, working in the cafe, things are different. Some of the young guys start working at our cafe and my dad's very involved with helping them all settle into their new circumstances. He acts as an interpreter for a lot of the legal negotiations. Everyone's trying to reunite with long-lost relatives. Anyway, I work alongside some of these new Chinese and become friends.

Shu brings his son over around 1953 and Lawrence is in the cafe business for the rest of his working life. Lawrence and I work together in the Diamond until I leave small-town Nelson for university at the coast. We're good friends. Even today, as ageing men, we always exchange greetings whenever we meet on the street. But I hardly ever go into his cafe.

So now, standing across the street from King's Family Restaurant, I know I'd love to go in there and have a dish of beef and greens, but he would know me, he would have me clear in his sights, not Chinese but stained enough by genealogy to make a difference. When Lawrence and I work together, him just over from China, he's a boss's son and I'm a boss's son. His pure Chineseness and my impure Chineseness don't make any difference to us in the cafe. But I've assumed a dull and ambiguous edge of difference in myself; the hyphen always seems to demand negotiation.

I decide, finally, to cross the street. I push myself through the door and his wife, Fay, catches me with the corner of her eye. She doesn't say anything and I wonder if she recognizes me. The white waitress takes my order and I ask if Lawrence is in the kitchen. He is, she says.

I go through Lawrence's kitchen door like I work there. I relish the little kick the door is built to take. He's happy to see me and stops slicing chicken on the chopping block, wipes his hands on his apron and shakes my hand. How's your mother? Whatchyou doing here? How's Ernie and Donnie? Family, that's what it is. The politics of the family.

He says something to the cook, a young guy. Then he turns to me and says hey Freddy, did you know this is your cousin? He's from the same area near Canton. His name is Quong. Then in Chinese, he gives a quick explanation to Quong; no doubt my entire Chinese family history. Lawrence smiles at me like he used to when were kids: he knows something I don't. I suffer the negative capability[10] of camouflage.

How many cousins do I have, I wonder. Thousands maybe. How could we recognize one another? Names.

The food, the names, the geography, the family history—the filiated dendrita[11] of myself displayed before me. I can't escape, and I don't want to, for a moment. Being there, in Lawrence's kitchen, seems one of the surest places I know. But then after we've exchanged our mutual family news and I've eaten a wonderful dish of tofu and vegetables, back outside, on the street, all my ambivalence gets covered over, camouflaged by a safety net of class and colourlessness—the racism within me that makes and consumes that neutral (white) version of myself, that allows me the sad privilege of being, in this white white world, not the target but the gun.

* * *

## I'M NOT AWARE IT'S CALLED
### TOFU UNTIL AFTER

I leave home. It's one of those ingredients that are transparent to me in the multitude of Cantonese dishes I grow up eating. So, until my dad tells me what that white stuff is called, I'm unable to order it during my forays into Vancouver Chinatown. Even when I first try it out on a waitress, she looks puzzled and says something in Chinese to her father who's hanging out by the till. She comes back to my booth and says o.k., you mean dow-uw foo, bean curd!

But over the past forty years, tofu has come into its own in North America, taking a choice place among the burgeoning macrobiotic and cholesterol-conscious diet

10 A term coined by the English Romantic poet John Keats (1795–1821); he defined it as the ability to entertain 'uncertainties, Mysteries, doubts, without any irritable reaching after fact and reason'.
11 That is, the related threads of Wah's inheritance that he sees before him; the phrase 'filiated dendrita' combines the idea of familial relationships (specifically, paternal acknowledgement of a son) with the image of treelike branches of mineral crystals or nerve cells.

fads. Available at any supermarket. If I'd been smart in the sixties I would have invested in soybean futures. There's even a little hippie tofu industry that has sprung up to supply the organic craze marketed through local co-ops. I wear my Kootenay Tofu T-shirt with pride.

This is all to my delight because tofu is, after rice, basic to my culinary needs. I've rendered this custard-like cake from pureed soybeans; I've pressed it, frozen it, mashed it, and cubed it; I've boiled, steamed, fried and maintained it; I even use Tofunaise as a substitute for mayonnaise. One summer I planted soybeans with some improbably fantasy of building my own tofu from the ground up. My attraction to this food is more than belief; it's a deep need, obsessive.

My basic all-time favourite dish is braised bean curd with vegetables. Cut each cake of tofu into one-inch cubes and very gently stir-fry along with some chopped green onion until the outer surface is lightly browned and the cake holds together without crumbling. Add some sliced vegetables: bok choy, carrots, green or red pepper, whatever you have around. Black Chinese mushrooms and water chestnuts are a nice option. As the dish is finishing, stir in a couple tablespoons of soy sauce and then some cornstarch mixed in water for thickening. This tasty and nutritious melange is spooned over steamed rice and washed down with oolong tea. There. That's a lunch.

\*    \*    \*

JUST ANOTHER TIGHT LIPPED HIGH
    MUCKAMUCK RECEPTION LISTENING

to the whining groans of an old-fart pink-faced investor worried about the Hong Kong real estate takeover, a wincing glance as he moans that UBC has become the University of a Billion Chinks, tense shoulder scrunch as I'm introduced, with emphasis on the Wah, to his built-and-fought-for-inheritor-of-the-country arrogant, raised-eyebrow, senior executive entrepreneur boss pig business associate—so that sometimes my cast of frown-furled brow looks right on past a bent nail, eyes screwed over the lake, into some trees, the tangle of bush impenetrable before they clear cut birch bark pocked crop settin' chokers'd break yer ass so fast you wouldn't even wanna look at a goddamned tree let alone cut through the crap backoff this Havoc old Hav Ok will stuff it in your cry this magic leaping tree will never be the apple of anyone else's eye because this is the last stand which for you is just a weekend pick-em-up truck so fuck the Husky Tower hustle and the Sleepy R train games this rusty nail has been here forever in fact the real last spike is yet to be driven.

\*    \*    \*

HIS HALF-DREAM IN THE STILL-
    DARK BREATHING SILENCE IS

the translation from the bitter-green cloudiness of the winter melon soup in his dream to the sweet-brown lotus root soup he knows Shu will prepare later this morning for the Chinese staff in the cafe. He moves the taste of the delicate nut-like lotus seeds through minor degrees of pungency and smokiness to the crunchy slices of lotus root suspended in the salty-sweet beef broth. This silent rehearsal of the memory of taste moves into his mind so that the first language behind his closed eyes is a dreamy play-by-play about making beef and lotus root soup. Simple: a pound of short ribs and a pound of lotus root in a small pot of water with some soy sauce and salt, a little sliced ginger, maybe a few red Chinese dates. Shu will surely touch it with a piece of dried tangerine peel because it's close to Christmas. He feels his tongue start to move as his mouth waters at the palpable flavour of words.

\*    \*    \*

HE USUALLY PARKS BEHIND THE
    CAFE. COMING DOWN

the hill he crosses Baker street, turns left behind Wood Vallance Hardware, drives halfway down the alley, manoeuvres around some garbage cans, and noses into his parking spot by a loading dock.

> *Fred Wah*
> *Diamond Grill*
> *Private*

is painted on the dirty cement wall. He climbs the wooden steps to the back door of the cafe and holds open the spring-hinged screen door with his left foot while he unlocks both the dead bolt and a padlock. The smoky glass in the top half of this door is covered by a heavy metal grill and, as he jars it open with a slight body-check, the door clangs and rattles a noisy hyphen between the muffled winter outside and the silence of the warm and waiting kitchen inside.

1996

# Maria Campbell
## b. 1940

Métis writer Maria Campbell was born in northern Saskatchewan and raised in one of its 'road-allowance' communities—that is, settlements that were built on public rights-of-way set aside for the construction of roads. In *Halfbreed* (1973), her autobiographical account of growing up the eldest child in a large Métis family, Campbell explains that the Métis—after the defeat in the North-West Rebellion that lost them their lands and after their once-abundant game was no longer available—settled illegally on such road allowances, each generation more defeated and poorer than the last.

Though the Métis culture out of which Campbell comes is warm and close-knit, the stability of her own family was disrupted by her mother's early death. At the age of fifteen, trying to find some way to keep her siblings from being dispersed by social agencies, Campbell made a disastrous marriage that eventually left her—in Vancouver with no secondary education and no job—the single mother of an infant. Placing her child in the care of nuns, she became a prostitute, an alcoholic, a drug addict, and a mule for cross-border smugglers. Although she tried to break free from her addictions in Vancouver and, later, in Calgary, she was not able to stay sober until after she joined Alcoholics Anonymous and began writing *Halfbreed*.

Campbell's subsequent life has been one of success: she has worked as an activist in Métis, Native, and women's affairs; as an educator; and in many capacities in the arts. She has been writer-in-residence at the universities of Alberta and Saskatchewan and at public libraries in Whitehorse, Prince Albert, and Regina; she was playwright-in-residence at the Persephone Theatre in Saskatoon. She taught literature, Native studies, and drama at Athabasca University, the University of Saskatchewan, and Brandon University, as well as at the Banff School of Fine Arts. She has served as an Elder for the Saskatchewan Aboriginal Justice Commission. Her numerous honours include the Molson Prize for distinguished accomplishments in the arts, the National Aboriginal Achievement Award, the Gabriel Dumont Medal of Merit, the Dora Mavor Moore Award, and the Chief Crowfoot Award, as well as honorary degrees from York University and the universities of Athabasca and Regina.

*Halfbreed* was among the first books in the wave of Native writing that emerged in North America in the late 1960s and early 1970s. Though Campbell said she began it only as a letter to herself, after its publication, it became a bestseller in Canada and made its way onto school and university reading lists. She has since written three children's books, all of them aimed at preserving aspects of Métis culture and heritage. Two of these, *People of the Buffalo* (1975) and *Riel's People* (1978), describe a variety of aspects of the culture of the Canadian Plains people and tell how the arrival of European settlers adversely affected traditional life in the Prairies. *Little Badger and the Fire Spirit* (1977) is a literary folktale set within a contemporary framework—the story of a blind boy who attempts a perilous journey to acquire fire for his people.

Campbell is also active in theatre and has written four plays, the best known of which is *Jessica*, a semi-autobiographical story of a Métis woman's journey of self-discovery, co-authored with Linda Griffiths. It opened in 1986 in Toronto and won the Dora Mavor Moore Award for outstanding new play that year. The play is reprinted in *The Book of Jessica: A Theatrical Transformation* (1989), where it is framed by an interwoven dialogue between Campbell and Griffiths that describes the story of the play's creation and documents the tensions that surfaced in this cross-cultural project.

*Stories of the Road-Allowance People* (1995), illustrated by Sherry Farrell Racette, is a collection of eight stories by Campbell based on tales she remembers being told in the Cree-Mitchif language spoken by the Plains Métis. In order to tell these stories of 'dem peoples dat belong in dah old days' and how 'dere starting to come back again / tank dah God for dat,' she cast them in the English spoken by the Métis of her community and set them in lines, like verse, to reflect the rhythms of this dialect.

The extent of Campbell's impact is suggested in the jury's citation that accompanied the Molson Prize: 'The brilliance of her break-through memoir, *Halfbreed*, which changed perceptions of the Métis experience forever, has been followed by other significant work, making a profound contribution to Canadian theatre, film, television, and radio. Her status as a teacher, mentor, and inspiration to Aboriginal people and all Canadians is unparalleled.'

# Jacob

Mistupuch he was my granmudder.
He come from Muskeg
dat was before he was a reservation.
My granmudder he was about twenty-eight when he
marry my granfawder.
Dat was real ole for a woman to marry in dem days
But he was an Indian doctor
I guess dats why he wait so long.

Ooh he was a good doctor too
All the peoples dey say dat about him.                                   10
He doctor everybody dat come to him
an he birt all dah babies too.
Jus about everybody my age
my granmudder he birt dem.

He marry my granfawder around 1890.
Dat old man he come to him for doctoring
and when he get better
he never leave him again.

Dey get married dah Indian way
an after dat my granfawder                                               20
he help him with all hees doctoring.
Dats dah way he use to be a long time ago.
If dah woman he work
den dah man he help him an if dah man he work
dah woman he help.
You never heerd peoples fighting over whose job he was
dey all know what dey got to do to stay alive.

My granfawder his name he was Kannap
but dah whitemans dey call him Jim Boy
so hees Indian name he gets los.                                30
Dats why we don know who his peoples dey are.
We los lots of our relations like dat.
Dey get dah whitemans name
den no body
he knows who his peoples dey are anymore.

Sometimes me
I tink dats dah reason why we have such a hard time
us peoples.
Our roots dey gets broken so many times.
Hees hard to be strong you know                                40
when you don got far to look back for help.

Dah whitemans
he can look back tousands of years
cause him
he write everything down.
But us peoples
we use dah membering
an we pass it on by telling stories an singing songs.
Sometimes we even dance dah membering.

But all dis trouble you know                                   50
he start after we get dah new names
cause wit dah new names
he come a new language an a new way of living.
Once a long time ago
I could 'ave told you dah story of my granfawder Kannap
an all his peoples but no more.
All I can tell you now
is about Jim Boy
an hees story hees not very ole.

Well my granmudder Mistupuch                                   60
he never gets a whitemans name an him
he knowed lots of stories.
Dat ole lady
he even knowed dah songs.
He always use to tell me
one about an ole man call Jacob.

Dat old man you know
he don live to far from here.
Well hees gone now
but dis story he was about him when he was alive.　70

Jacob him
he gets one of dem new names when dey put him in dah
residential school.
He was jus a small boy when he go
an he don come home for twelve years.

Twelve years!
Dats a long time to be gone from your peoples.
He can come home you know
cause dah school he was damn near two hundred miles
away.　80
His Mommy and Daddy dey can go and see him
cause deres no road in dem days
an dah Indians dey don gots many horses
'specially to travel dat far.

Dats true you know
not many peoples in dem days dey have horses.
Its only in dah comic books an dah picture shows dey
gots lots of horses.
He was never like dat in dah real life.

Well Jacob him　90
he stay in dat school all dem years an when he come
home he was a man.
While he was gone
his Mommy and Daddy dey die so he gots nobody.
And on top of dat
nobody he knowed him cause he gots a new name.
My granmudder
he say dat ole man he have a hell of time.
No body he can understand dat
unless he happen to him.　100

Dem peoples dat go away to dem schools
an come back you know dey really suffer.
No matter how many stories we tell
we'll never be able to tell
what dem schools dey done to dah peoples
an all dere relations.

Well anyways
Jacob he was jus plain pitiful
He can talk his own language
He don know how to live in dah bush.            110
It's a good ting da peoples dey was kine
cause dey help him dah very bes dey can.
Well a couple of summers later
he meet dis girl
an·dey gets married.

Dat girl he was kine
an real smart too.
He teach Jacob how to make an Indian living.

Dey have a good life togedder an after a few years
dey have a boy.            120
Not long after dat
dey raise two little girls dat was orphans.

Jacob and his wife dey was good peoples
Boat of dem dey was hard working
an all dah peoples
dey respec dem an dey come to Jacob for advice.

But dah good times dey was too good to las
cause one day
dah Preeses
dey comes to dah village with dah policemans.       130
Dey come to take dah kids to dah school.

When dey get to Jacob hees house
he tell dem dey can take his kids.

Dah Prees he tell him
he have to lets dem go cause dats the law.
Well dah Prees
he have a big book
an dat book he gots dah names
of all dah kids
an who dey belongs to.          140

He open dat book an ask Jacob for his name
an den he look it up.
'Jacob' he say
'you know better you went to dah school an you know
dah edjication hees important.'

My granmudder Mistupuch
he say Jacob he tell that Prees
'Yes I go to dah school
an dats why I don wan my kids to go.
All dere is in dat place is suffering.'                    150

Dah Prees he wasn happy about dat
an he say to Jacob
'But the peoples dey have to suffer Jacob
cause dah Jesus he suffer.'

'But dah Jesus he never lose his language an
hees peoples' Jacob tell him.
'He stay home in hees own land and he do hees
suffering.'

Well da Prees him
he gets mad                                                160
an he tell him its a sin to tink like dat
an hees gonna end up in purgatory for dem kind of
words.

But Jacob he don care
cause far as hees concern
purgatory
he can be worse den the hell he live with trying to
learn hees language and hees Indian ways.

He tell dat Prees
he don even know who his people dey are.            170
'Dah Jesus he knowed his Mommy and Daddy'
Jacob he tell him
'and he always knowed who his people dey are.'

Well
dah Prees he tell him
if he wans to know who hees people dey are
he can tell him dat
an he open in dah book again.

'Your Dad hees Indian name he was Awchak'
dah prees he say                                              180
'I tink dat means Star in your language.
He never gets a new name cause he never become a
Christian.'


Jacob he tell my granmudder
dat when da Prees he say hees Dad hees name
his wife he start to cry real hard.


'Jacob someday you'll tank the God we done dis.'
dah Prees he tell him
an dey start loading up dah kids on dah big wagons.
All dah kids dey was crying an screaming                     190
An dah mudders
dey was chasing dah wagons.


Dah ole womans
dey was all singing dah det song
an none of the mans
dey can do anyting.
Dey can
cause the policemans dey gots guns.


When dah wagons dey was all gone
Jacob he look for hees wife but he can find him no           200
place.
An ole woman he see him an he call to him
'Pay api noosim'
'Come an sit down my granchild I mus talk to you.
Hees hard for me to tell you dis but dat Prees
hees book he bring us bad news today.
He tell you dat Awchak he was your Daddy.
My granchild
Awchak he was your wife's Daddy too.'


Jacob he tell my granmudder                                  210
he can cry when he hear dat.
He can even hurt inside.
Dat night he go looking
an he fine hees wife in dah bush
Dat woman he kill hisself.

Jacob he say
dah ole womans
dey stay wit him for a long time
an dey sing healing songs an dey try to help him
But he say he can feel nutting.                               220
Maybe if he did
he would have done dah same ting.

For many years Jacob he was like dat
just dead inside.

Dah peoples dey try to talk wit him
but it was no use.
Hees kids dey growed up
an dey come home an live wit him.
'I made dem suffer' he tell my granmudder.
'Dem kids dey try so hard to help me.'            230

Den one day
his daughter he get married an he have a baby.
He bring it to Jacob to see.
Jacob he say
he look at dat lil baby
an he start to cry and he can stop.
He say he cry for himself an his wife
an den he cry for his Mommy and Daddy.
When he was done
he sing dah healing songs dah ole womans      240
dey sing to him a long time ago.

Well you know
Jacob he die when he was an ole ole man.
An all hees life
he write in a big book
dah Indian names of all dah Mommies and Daddies.
An beside dem
he write dah old names and
dah new names of all dere kids.

An for dah res of hees life                               250
he fight dah government to build schools on the
reservation.
'The good God he wouldn of make babies come
from Mommies and Daddies'

he use to say
'if he didn want dem to stay home
an learn dere language
an dere Indian ways.'

You know
dat ole man was right.                                          260
No body he can do dat.
Take all dah babies away. Hees jus not right.
Long time ago
dah old peoples dey use to do dah naming
an dey do dah teaching too.

If dah parents dey have troubles
den dah aunties and dah uncles
or somebody in dah family
he help out till dah parents dey gets dere life work
out.                                                            270
But no one
no one
he ever take dah babies away from dere peoples.

You know my ole granmudder
Mistupuch
he have lots of stories about people like Jacob.
Good ole peoples
dat work hard so tings will be better for us.
We should never forget dem ole peoples.

1995

# Gwendolyn MacEwen

## 1941–1987

Born in Toronto and raised there and in Winnipeg, Gwendolyn MacEwen published her first poem at seventeen in the *Canadian Forum* and left school a year later to become a writer. Interested in esoteric wisdom and myth, she read voraciously and began to frequent The Bohemian Embassy, a literary and folk-music coffee shop that served as a meeting place for Toronto's poets. As Rosemary Sullivan writes in *Shadow Maker: The Life of Gwendolyn MacEwen* (1995), 'mythology . . . was a topic of endless discussion at The Embassy, having filtered down from Robert Graves and from Northrop Frye's lectures at the University of Toronto; everyone had read Leonard Cohen's *Let Us Compare Mythologies* and Jay Macpherson's *The Boatman*.' She met many of Canada's poets there, including Milton Acorn, with whom she fell in love despite the generational difference in their ages. She lived with Acorn in Montreal for a while in the early 1960s, where she helped him edit the literary magazine *Moment*. They married in 1962—Al Purdy was their best man—but the marriage was brief and unhappy.

By the time she was twenty, MacEwen had produced two privately printed chapbooks, *Selah* (1961) and *The Drunken Clock* (1961). Two years later, Contact Press published her third book, *The Rising Fire*. She subsequently produced five more poetry collections: *A Breakfast for Barbarians* (1966); *The Shadow-Maker* (1969); *The Armies of the Moon* (1972); *The Fire Eaters* (1976); *The T.E. Lawrence Poems* (1982), a sequence about Lawrence of Arabia; and *Afterworlds* (1987), which—like *The Shadow-Maker*—received a Governor General's Award. In addition, there were two volumes of selected poetry in her lifetime: *Magic Animals* (1975), which contained some new poems; and *Earthlight* (1982). After MacEwen's death, her collected poems, *The Poetry of Gwendolyn MacEwen*, was published in two volumes: *The Early Years* (1993) and *The Later Years* (1994).

MacEwen also wrote plays and dramatic documentaries for CBC radio; one of these, *Terror and Erebus*—a drama in free verse about the last Franklin expedition—is reprinted in *Afterworlds*. Her two novels, *Julian the Magician* (1963) and *King of Egypt, King of Dreams* (1971), and her two collections of short stories, *Noman* (1972) and *Noman's Land* (1985), exhibit her predisposition for the foreign and the fantastic, as do her children's books—*The Chocolate Moose* (1979) and *Dragon Sandwiches* (1987).

The Mediterranean and western Asia were of particular interest to her and she travelled extensively in those areas. *Mermaids and Ikons: A Greek Summer* (1978) is a memoir of one of these journeys. She created a new version of Euripides' play *The Trojan Women*, and, with Greek singer Nikos Tsingos (to whom she was married for six years), she translated two long poems by the Greek poet Yannis Ritsos. The play and translations appear in *Trojan Women* (1981). Her modern adaptation of Aristophanes' ancient comedy *The Birds* appeared in 1983. She taught herself Arabic and published *The Honeydrum: Seven Tales from Arab Lands* (1983), which includes two original tales along with retellings of five folk tales. *The Selected Gwendolyn MacEwen*, edited by Meaghan Strimas (2007), contains samples from all of her writing along with a brief 'scrapbook' of archival material, providing an overview of her career.

A dark romantic, MacEwen blended mythologies from many sources to heighten commonplace Canadian experience (as in 'The Portage'). She was drawn to the great adventurers (as in *The T.E. Lawrence Poems*) and frequently investigated the mysteries of the ancient past (as in *King of Egypt, King of Dreams*). Deeply influenced by Carl Jung's ideas about archetypes, she had frequent recourse to paired oppositions such as spirit and flesh. As the poet-critic D.G. Jones observed (in his introduction to *Earthlight*), MacEwen was someone who could say 'what most will not, that we are ambiguous, that our exorbitant hungers and satisfactions are both erotic and holy.' Inhabiting both realms is the powerful figure that Margaret Atwood identified (in *Second Words*) as MacEwen's male muse. Sometimes semi-divine, sometimes a man struggling toward understanding, this figure can ascend to universal levels or find himself among the specifics of life and death. In MacEwen's poetry and fiction, he appears in many forms: Icarus, Manzini, Julian the magician, Noman, the Egyptian pharaoh Akhenaton, and T.E. Lawrence. Julian is particularly fascinating for the way he anticipates Magnus Eisengrim, the conjuror at the centre of Robertson Davies' Deptford trilogy:

*The people watch the magician and he pleases them. No, he does not please them—he frightens them. A soft quiet fright, fright of kittens in a blizzard. Julian employs mirrors, boxes, screens, veils. And the people believe, because Julian . . . does not force, suggest, tease, prod—he lets them believe, he draws margins over which he knows their minds can jump, he unscrews hinges on all doors. The magician feels his power growing like a live foetus in his skull.*

Though MacEwen's fantasy world was unusually rich, her reality proved difficult. Her life was brief and marked by struggles with alcohol, poverty, and the men she loved.

# Icarus[1]


Feather and wax, the artful wings
bridge a blue gulf between
the stiff stone tower
and its languid god, fat sky.

The boy, bent to the whim of wind,
the blue, and the snarling sun
form a brief triumvirate
—flesh, feather, light—
locked in the jaws of the noon
they rule with fleeting liberty.                          10

    These are the wings, then,
    a legacy of hollow light—
    feathers, a quill to write
    white poetry across the sky.

Through the mouth of the air, the boy
sees his far father, whose muscled flight
is somehow severed from his own.
Two blinking worlds, and Daedalus'
unbound self is a thing apart.

---

1 Character from Greek mythology who with his father, Daedalus (the master craftsman and inventor), escaped the island of Crete by means of wings made of wax and feathers. Forgetful of Daedalus's warning not to fly close to the sun, which might melt the wax, Icarus soared too high and fell to his death.

You, bound for that other area                20
know that this legacy of mindflight
is all you have to leave me.

The boy, Icarus, twists the threads of his throat
and his eyes argue with the sun
on a flimsy parallel, and
the mouth of the sun eager, eager,
smuggles a hot word to the boy's ear.

    But flying, locked in dark dream,
    I see Queen Dream, Queen Flight,
    the last station of the poet             30
    years above my brow, and

Something, something in the air,
in the light's flight, in the vaguely
voluptuous arc of the wings
drives a foreign rhythm into his arms
his arms which are lean, white willows.

Icarus feels his blood race to his wrist
in a marathon of red light. Swifter,
swift, he tears away the slow veil
from his tendons; the playful biceps           40
sing; they wish new power to the beautiful
false wings
and the boy loops up into tall cobalt.
His hair is a swirl of drunken light,
his arms are wet blades; wings wed with arms.

    You knew
    I would get drunk on beauty.
    The famous phantom quill
    would write me, pull me
    through the eye             50
    of needle noon.

Crete is a huge hump of a black whore beneath him.
Her breasts, two wretched mountains
tremble under his eye.
All is black, except the sun in slow explosion;
a great war strangles his vision
and knots his flying nerve.
Black, and fire, and the boy.

You and your legacy!
You knew I would try to                                          60
slay the sunlight.

Look, Icarus has kissed the sun
and it sucks the wax,
feathers and wax.
The wings are melting!

The boy Icarus is lean and beautiful.
His body grows limp and falls.
It is cruel poetry set
to the tempo of lightning; it is too swift,
this thin descent.                                               70

On the lips of the Aegean:
globules of wax,
strands of wet light,

    the lean poem's flesh
    tattered and torn
    by a hook
    of vengeful fire . . .

Combustion of brief feathers

1961


# Manzini:[1] Escape Artist

*now there are no bonds except the flesh;* listen—
there was this boy, Manzini, stubborn with
gut stood with black tights and a turquoise
leaf across his sex

and smirking while the big
brute tied his neck arms legs, Manzini
naked waist up and white with sweat

---

1 Manzini was an American magician whom MacEwen met in the 1960s. As an escape artist, he worked in the tradition of the famous early twentieth-century magician Harry Houdini (born Ehrich Weiss, 1874–1926), who was known for the rapidity of his dramatic escapes from chains, ropes, jail cells, and straitjackets.

struggled. Silent, delinquent, he
was suddenly all teeth and knee, straining slack
and excellent with sweat, inwardly          10

wondering if Houdini would take as long
as he; fighting time and the drenched
muscular ropes, as though his tendons were worn
on the outside—

as though his own guts were the ropes
encircling him; it was beautiful; it was thursday; listen—
there was this boy, Manzini

finally free, slid as snake from
his own sweet agonized skin, to throw his entrails
white upon the floor          20
with a cry of victory—

*now there are no bonds except the flesh,*
but listen, it was thursday, there was this boy,
Manzini—

1966


# The Portage

We have travelled far with ourselves
and our names have lengthened;
    we have carried ourselves
on our backs, like canoes
in a strange portage, over trails,
insinuating leaves
and trees dethroned like kings,
     from water-route to
     water-route
seeking the edge, the end,          10
the coastlines of this land.


On earlier journeys we
were master ocean-goers
going out, and evening always found us
spooning the ocean from our boat,

and gulls, undiplomatic
    couriers brought us
cryptic messages from shore
till finally we sealords vowed
we'd sail no more.                                   20


Now under a numb sky, sombre
cumuli weigh us down;
the trees are combed for winter
and bears' tongues have melted
all the honey;
    there is a lourd[1]
suggestion of thunder;
subtle drums under
the candid hands of Indians
are trying to tell us                                30
why we have come.


But now we fear movement
and now we dread stillness;
we suspect it was the land
that always moved, not our ships;
we are in sympathy with the fallen
trees; we cannot relate
    the causes of our grief.
We can no more carry
our boats our selves                                 40
over these insinuating trails.

1969

1 Sluggish, dull.


# Dark Pines under Water

This land like a mirror turns you inward
And you become a forest in a furtive lake;
The dark pines of your mind reach downward,
You dream in the green of your time,
Your memory is a row of sinking pines.

Explorer, you tell yourself this is not what you came for
Although it is good here, and green;
You had meant to move with a kind of largeness,
You had planned a heavy grace, an anguished dream.

But the dark pines of your mind dip deeper                                  10
And you are sinking, sinking, sleeper
In an elementary world;
There is something down there and you want it told.

1969


# The Real Enemies[1]

In that land where the soul aged long before the body,
My nameless men, my glamorous bodyguards,
                                        died for me.
My deadly friends with their rouged lips and pretty eyes
        died for me; *my bed of tulips* I called them,
        who wore every color but the white
        that was mine alone to wear.

But they could not guard me against the real enemies—
Omnipotence, and the Infinite—
                        those beasts the soul invents               10
        and then bows down before.
The real enemies were not the men of Fakhri Pasha,[2] nor
Were they even of this world.
                        One could never conquer them,
Never. Hope was another of them. Hope, most brutal of all.

For those who thought clearly, failure was the only goal.
Only failure could redeem you, there where the soul aged
        long before the body.
You failed at last, you fell into the delicious light
        and were free.                                             20

1  The narrative voice of this poem, and of the other poems in *The T.E. Lawrence Poems* is that of Thomas Edward
   Lawrence (1888–1935), known as Lawrence of Arabia. Author, archaeologist, and soldier, Lawrence led a successful rebellion of the Arabs against the Turks during the First World War and became a near-legendary figure.
   He subsequently assumed the name T.E. Shaw and retired to self-imposed obscurity to write *The Seven Pillars
   of Wisdom* (1926), his account of his Arabian adventure.
2  The leader of the Turkish forces.

And there was much honor in this;
                              it was a worthy defeat.
Islam is surrender—the passionate surrender of the self,
          the puny self, to God.
We declared a Holy War upon Him and were victors as He won.

1982


## The Death of the Loch Ness Monster

Consider that the thing has died before we proved it ever lived
          and that it died of loneliness, dark lord of the loch,
fathomless Worm, great Orm,[1] this last of our mysteries—
          *haifend ane meikill fin on ilk syde*
          *with ane taill and ane terribill heid—*
and that it had no tales to tell us, only that it lived there,
          lake-locked, lost in its own coils,
waiting to be found; in the black light of midnight
          surfacing, its whole elastic length unwound,
and the sound it made as it broke the water                          10
was the single plucked string of a harp—
this newt or salamander, graceful as a swan,
          this water-snake, this water-horse, this water-dancer.

Consider him tired of pondering the possible existence of man
          whom he thinks he has sighted sometimes on the shore,
and rearing up from the purple churning water,
          weird little worm head swaying from side to side,
he denies the vision before his eyes;
          his long neck, swan of Hell, a silhouette against the moon,
his green heart beating its last,                                    20
          his noble, sordid soul in ruins.

Now the mist is a blanket of doom, and we pluck from the depths
          a prize of primordial slime—
the beast who was born from some terrible ancient kiss,
          lovechild of unspeakable histories,
this ugly slug, half blind no doubt, and very cold,

---

1  Dragon, serpent, worm (Middle English). The italicized passage that follows is an account, from around 1500, of killing a lake creature 'having many fins on each side with a tail and a terrible head'.

      his head which is horror to behold
no bigger than our own;
      whom we loathe, for his kind ruled the earth before us,
who died of loneliness in a small lake in Scotland,                  30
      and in his mind's dark land,
where he dreamed up his luminous myths, the last of which was man.

1987


# Polaris
## or, Gulag Nightscapes[1]

At midnight in this foreign country
in the vivid snow as cold as vodka
you stand watching constellations which are ever
      so slowly turning
and the great bear of Russia is ever so slowly turning
round and round in the forest behind you.

You ask yourself are you
      the fixed centre of this scene
and you will stand here forever witnessing
the movement of stars, politics of the northern sky,           10
kinesis of snow?

You begin with freedom as a word,
freedom in its bleakest, purest form
and proceed through crazy stations of the compass
to this kingdom of snow where
      freedom is a prison; it is
Russia or America or the republic of your mind
where governments and constellations are endlessly rotating
and everything is a lie; there is no governing body,
there is nothing to direct you              20
      on your course, there
is no right course, there is no guiding star.

1 The Gulag was the system of forced labour camps under the Soviet regime in Russia from 1919, made infamous in Alexander Solzhenitsyn's memoirs of his imprisonment, which were published in English in the 1970s. This poem, responding to enduring Cold War tensions, plays with the fact that 'Polaris' was—as well as the name of the North Star, the fixed point by which mariners once found their way—the name given to one of the first of the ballistic missiles, deployed by the US via submarines and targeted at the USSR in the event of nuclear war.

Yet

*Everything points to Polaris—*
endlessly still star, endlessly unturning,
Alpha in Ursa Minor,
first letter in the alphabet of midnight, and
         America like a giant crystal
is ever so slowly turning, deflecting starlight,
the real and imagined missiles of real and imagined enemies.     30

If you consult the polestar for the truth
of your present position, you will learn that you have no
         position, position is illusion (consider this
endlessly still self, endlessly turning);
this prison is actually your freedom, and
         it is you, it is you, you
are the only thing in this frozen night which is really moving.

1987

---

# Don McKay
## b. 1942

---

Born in Owen Sound, Ontario, Don McKay grew up in Cornwall, Ontario. He attended Bishop's University for two years, then continued his education at the University of Western Ontario (MA, 1966). He taught for two years in Saskatchewan before travelling to Wales to complete a PhD at the University College of Swansea. He then taught at Western for several years (while there, he co-founded Brick Books, a publishing house devoted entirely to poetry) and at the University of New Brunswick (where, from 1991 to 1996, he edited *The Fiddlehead*, Canada's longest-lived literary magazine). He retired in 2002.

    McKay's books of poetry include *Moccasins on Concrete* (1972); the long poem *Long Sault* (1975); *Lependu* (1978); *Birding, or Desire* (1983); *Sanding Down This Rocking Chair on a Windy Night* (1987); *Night Field* (1991, Governor General's Award); *Apparatus* (1997); and *Another Gravity* (2000, Governor General's Award). *Camber* (2004) selects from those books, as does *Field Marks: The Poetry of Don McKay* (2006). He subsequently published *Strike/Slip* (2006; winner of the 2007 Griffin Poetry Prize) and *The Muskwa Assemblage* (2009). In addition to these, *Deactivated West 100* (2005), is a book of prose and poetic meditations that attempts to define *place* 'without using the usual humanistic terms—not home and native land, not little house on the prairie, not even the founding principle of our sense of beauty—but as a function of wilderness'.

His intense responses to the natural world have earned him a reputation as an ecological poet, but there is more than just appreciation for nature that gives power to his writing. In one of the delicately crafted essays published in *Vis à Vis: Fieldnotes on Poetry and Wilderness* (2001), he writes,

*By 'wilderness' I want to mean, not just a set of endangered spaces, but the capacity of all things to elude the mind's appropriations. . . . To what degree do we own our houses, hammers, dogs? Beyond that line lies wilderness. We probably experience its presence most often in the negative as dry rot in the basement, a splintered handle, or shit on the carpet. But there is also the sudden angle of perception, the phenomenal surprise which constitutes the sharpened moments of* haiku *and imagism. The coat hanger asks a question; the armchair is suddenly crouched: in such defamiliarizations, often arranged by art, we encounter the momentary circumvention of the mind's categories to glimpse something's autonomy its rawness, its* duende [magnetism], *its alien being.* ('Baler Twine: Thoughts on Ravens, Home, and Nature Poetry')

This drive toward visionary moments means that MacKay's interest in nature extends both to and beyond such things as the literal birds and the attention to flight found in so many of his poems: their occurrences constitute an urge to understand the meanings those birds convey, the mysterious significance flight holds for the human mind—seen not only in the arc of a bird's wing gracefully moving on a thermal draft or in the retelling of the mythic tale of Icarus, but also in the metaphorical flights of a hockey skate cutting the ice, of a musical sound entering the ear, and of the precise descent of the blade that the sushi chef swings to slice a morsel of fish.

*Birding, or Desire* is the book that established McKay's reputation as a poet's poet. One lyric in particular from that book, 'Kestrels'—it became a signature poem for McKay—provides a good example of how he finds art embedded in the external world. There, the vigorous beat of the kestrel's strong wings can be heard in musical terms, 'con brio' (an instruction to play 'with spirit'); its pulsing movements reminding the speaker of the 'sprung rhythm' in Gerard Manley Hopkins's poetry. That nod to Hopkins is more than casual, because 'Kestrels' is responsive to literature as well as to nature: McKay knows that Hopkins's 'The Windhover' is about the kestrel under another of its names, and the resonances he establishes with one of the most famous poems in the language gives additional depth to his own observations of the bird. Moreover, as is so often the case in McKay's writing, 'Kestrels' reaches beyond both nature and art toward a visionary realm, the 'frontier of nothing' that appears in its closing lines.

The richness of 'Kestrels' is characteristic of McKay's poetry. His writing is filled with finely drawn pictures and elegant lines that emerge from an informed mind, one in which the close observations of a naturalist and the wealth of tradition created by his precursors (his 'Icarus', for example, invites one to keep in mind W.H. Auden's 'Musée des Beaux Arts', along with the many other retellings of that Greek myth) are brought together by a probing curiosity that seeks to know more about the things we can know—and the things we cannot. In this ongoing project to return to our sense of wonder in the natural world, McKay utilizes, in *Strike/Slip*, the precise language of geology, with its enormous time spans and its consideration of our sedimented past beneath the 'all-dissolving ocean.' In the paired poems that open *Strike/Slip*, 'Astonished—' and 'Petrified—', he calls our attention to the duality of nature, its ability to inspire awe, with fossils that glow like gems, and to bring terror, in a literally petrifying lava flow.

# Kestrels

> 'The name "Sparrow hawk" is unfair to this handsome
> and beneficial little falcon.'
>
> —*The Birds of Canada*

### 1.

unfurl from the hydro wire, beat
con brio out across the field and
hover, marshalling the moment, these
gestures of our slender hostess,
ushering her guests into the dining room

### 2.

sprung rhythm[1] and
surprises, enharmonic change directions simply
step outside and let the earth turn
underneath, trapdoors, new lungs, missing bits
of time, plump familiar pods go                                                10
pop in your mind you learn not
principles of flight but how to fall, you learn
pity for that paraplegic bird, the heart

### 3.

to watch by the roadside singing *killy killy killy*,
plumaged like a tasteful parrot,
to have a repertoire of moves so clean their edge is
                                        the frontier of nothing
to be sudden        to send
postcards of distance which arrive in nicks of time

to open letters with a knife                                                    20

1983

---

1 Gerard Manley Hopkins's term for a poetic rhythm based on stresses in the line without regard for syllable
count. 'Enharmonic' designates notes such as C-sharp and D-flat that, while designated differently, are played
by the same key on the keyboard.

# Twinflower

What do you call
the muscle we long with? Spirit?
I don't think so. Spirit is a far cry. This
is a casting outward which
unwinds inside the chest. A hole
which complements the heart.
The ghost of a chance.

*

Then God said, ok let's get this show
on the road, boy, get some names
stuck on these critters, and Adam,                                    10
his head on the ground in a patch of tiny
pink-white flowers, said
mmn, just a sec.
He was, let's say,
engrossed in their gesture,
the two stalks rising, branching, falling back
into nodding bells, the fading arc
that would entrance Pre-Raphaelites[1] and basketball.
Maybe he browsed among the possibilities of elves.
Maybe he was blowing on the blossoms,                                 20
whispering whatever came into his head, I have
no way of knowing what transpired
as Adam paused, testing his parent's
limit, but I know
it matters.

*

Through the cool woods of the lower
slopes, where the tall
Lodgepole Pine point
into the wild blue while they supervise
the shaded space below, I walk,                                       30
accompanied by my binoculars and field guides.
I am working on the same old problem,

---

1 Among the aims of the Pre-Raphaelite Brotherhood—a group of English artists, poets, and critics who banded
  together in 1848 in reaction against what they considered the unimaginative, overly sentimental, and artificial
  historical painting of the Royal Society and who sought to express a new moral sincerity and simplicity in their
  works—was fidelity to nature, manifested in detailed first-hand observation of flora.

how to be both
knife and spoon, when there they are, and maybe have been
all along, covering the forest floor: a creeper, a shy
hoister of flags, a tiny lamp to read by, one
word at a time.
              Of course, having found them, I'm about
to find them in the field guide, and the bright
reticulated snaps of system will occur                    40
as the plant is placed, so, among the honeysuckles,
in cool dry northern woods from June to August.
But this is not, despite the note of certainty,
the end. Hold the book open,
leaf to leaf. Listen now,
*Linnaea Borealis*, while I read of how
you have been loved—
with keys and adjectives and numbers, all the teeth
the mind can muster. How your namer,
Carolus Linnaeus, gave you his[2]                    50
to live by in the system he devised.
How later, it was you,
of all the plants he knew and named,
he asked to join him in his portrait.
To rise in your tininess,
to branch and nod beside him
as he placed himself in that important
airless room.

1997

2  Carolus Linnaeus is the Latinized name of Swedish botanist Carl von Linné (1707–78), who devised an author-
itative classification system for flowering plants utilizing binomial Latin names—the 'reticulated' (networked)
system used by field guides referred to in lines 39–40. Linnaeus, who often named new genera after his friends
and colleagues, used his own name in choosing the taxonomic name of his favourite flower, *Linnaea Borealis*,
an evergreen trailing plant with small trumpet-shaped pink flowers, commonly known as the twinflower. In portraits, Linnaeus is often holding this flower.

# Short Fat Flicks

(i) *He rides into town*

already perfect, already filled with nothing. His music is a hawk scream which has been
crossed with a machine, perhaps eternity's lathe, and fashioned into a horse. His hat-
brim is horizon. It is all over. Only the unspeakable trauma which erased his name concerns him. Now it concerns the townsfolk as they scuttle, gutless, behind shopfronts.

Two minutes ago their houses were three-dimensional and contained kitchens, not to mention closets. Now the houses, the general store, livery, and sheriff's office are so obviously props that the townsfolk have stopped believing in them before the curtains twitch back into place. Now they are cover awaiting shootout, and the townsfolk are extras waiting to fall, aaargh, from their roofs, and crash, spratinkle tinkle tinkle, through their windows. He rides into town from another genre, from the black star that sucks the depth from everything, a soundless bell tolling. *You should have changed your life*, it says, *done, done, done.* Doesn't even consider that you fixed up the den and took that night class in creative writing.

(ii) *Their eyes meet*

ah, and there is a satisfying drag on the sprockets, as though the celluloid were suddenly too heavy to turn, as though the projector were sleepy. One violin has been stricken and starts, legato, a drugged smoke alarm, to troll the theme, which the camera catches, tracking left (always left) to take in a quiver of lips. Close-up, close-up, two-shot, their four eyes have begun to unbutton and bud, the strings now ahum, vibrato, zoom zoom zoom they shed the depth of field. Who needs it? The darkness is inhabited, the popcorn is buttered. Their lips approach like shy cats. Her eyes have decided to skinny-dip in his and his in hers: one more microzoom and they dive, leaving the rest of their faces behind to nuzzle and rub, attempting to smudge the irregular line between them. And the eyes? Are swimming with us, dolphins, in the darkness, which is rich and viscous, the lake of tears we've been waiting for.

(iii) *We take our seats*

and settle into our bodies, waiting for the lights to dim so we can feel ourselves falling, this is the best part, feel ourselves falling into a safer kind of sleep, an elaborate parkland of carefully prepared surprises. As the curtains begin to part, *lingerie*, we can see through them to the screen, which has begun to flicker into being. Will the plot matter? Of course not. Movies have been sent to us to make up for the bathroom mirror, with its rigid notion of representation, and the family, with its chain-link semantic net. Here we feel ideas wriggle into costume and images reach toward us out of light. Soon their logos will appear—the winged horse in the symmetrical cosmos, perhaps, or shifting constellations that swirl into an O. Everything will be incarnate, *in camera*,[1] anything can be a star.

1997

1 In private (Latin).

# To Danceland

'No one is ever happier than when they're dancing.'

—Margaret McKay

South through bumper crops we are driving to Danceland,
       barley
oats, canola, wheat, thick as a beaver pelt, but late, she said,
late, since June had been so cold already we were deep
in August and still mostly green so it was nip
and tuck with frost and somewhere between Nipawin and
         Tisdale finally
I found the way to say, um, I can't dance
you know, I can't dance don't ask me
why I am driving like a fool to Danceland having flunked it    10
twenty-seven years ago in the kitchen where my mother,
bless her, tried to teach me while I passively resisted,
doing the jerk-step while she tried to slow, slow, quick quick
slow between the table and the fridge, her face fading
like someone trying to start a cranky Lawnboy
          nevertheless,
     step by sidestep
we are driving down the grid, Swainson's hawks occurring
         every
thirty hydro poles, on average    20
     to Danceland
where the dancefloor floats on rolled horsehair
and the farmers dance with their wives even though it is
        not Chicago
where the mirror ball blesses everyone with flecks from
     another, less rigorous, dimension
where the Westeel granary dances with the weathervane,
the parent with the child, the John Deere with the mortgage
where you may glimpse occasional coyote lopes and
      gopher hops    30
where the dark may become curious and curl one long arm
       around us
as we pause for a moment, and I think about my mother
       and her
wishes in that kitchen, then
we feed ourselves to the world's most amiable animal,
in Danceland.

1997

# Homing

That things should happen
twice, and place
share the burden of remembering. Home,
the first cliché. We say it
with aspiration as the breath
opens to a room of its own (a bed,
a closet for the secret self), then closes
on a hum. Home. Which is the sound of time
braking a little, growing slow and thick as the soup
that simmers on the stove. Abide,                                    10
abode. Pass me that plate,
the one with the hand-painted *habitant*[1]
sitting on a log. My parents bought it
on their honeymoon—see? Dated on the bottom,
1937. He has paused to smoke his pipe, the tree
half cut and leaning. Is he thinking where
to build his cabin or just idling his mind
while his pipe smoke mingles with the air? A bird,
or something (it is hard to tell), hangs overhead.
Now it's covered by your grilled cheese sandwich.              20

Part two, my interpretation. The leaning tree
points home, then
past home into real estate and its innumerable
Kodak moments: kittens, uncles,
barbecues. And behind those scenes the heavy
footstep on the stair, the face locked
in the window frame, things that happen
and keep happening, reruns
of family romance. And the smudged bird? I say it's
a Yellow Warbler who has flown                                     30
from winter habitat in South America to nest here
in the clearing. If we catch it, band it,
let it go a thousand miles away it will be back
within a week. How?
Home is what we know
and know we know, the intricately
feathered nest. Homing
asks the question.

2000

1  An early French-Canadian settler, often depicted on tourist items as quaint and folksy.

# Icarus[1]

isn't sorry. We do not find him
doing penance, writing out the golden mean for all
eternity, or touring its high schools to tell student bodies
not to do what he done
done. Over and over he rehearses flight
and fall, tuning his moves, entering
with fresh rush into the mingling of the air
with spirit. This is his practice
and his prayer: to be translated into air, as air
with each breath enters lungs,                                    10
then blood. He feels resistance gather in his stiff
strange wings, angles his arms to shuck the sweet lift
from the drag, runs the full length
of a nameless corridor, his feet striking the paving stones
less and less heavily, then
they're bicycling above the ground,
a few shallow beats and he's up,
he's out of the story and into the song.

At the melting point of wax, which now he knows
the way Doug Harvey knows the blue line,[2]                       20
he will back-beat to create a pause, hover for maybe fifty
hummingbird heartbeats and then
lose it, tumbling into freefall, shedding feathers
like a lover shedding clothes. He may glide
in the long arc of a Tundra Swan or pull up sharp
to Kingfisher into the sea which bears his name.[3] Then,
giving it the full Ophelia, drown.

On the shore
the farmer ploughs his field, the dull ship
sails away, the poets moralize about our                          30
unsignificance. But Icarus is thinking tremolo and
backflip, is thinking
next time with a half-twist
and a tuck and isn't
sorry.

---

1  See p. 896, note 1.
2  Doug Harvey (1924–89), who played hockey for the Montreal Canadiens from 1947–61, is generally considered the best defenceman of his time.
3  The Icarian Sea, an ancient name for the southern part of the Aegean Sea around the island of Ikaria, between the Cyclades and Turkey, where Icarus is said to have fallen.

\*

Repertoire, technique. The beautiful contraptions bred from ingenuity and practice, and the names by which he claims them, into which—lift-off, loop-the-loop—they seem to bloom. Icarus could write a book. Instead he will stand for hours in that musing half-abstracted space, watching. During fall migrations he will often climb to the edge of a north-south running ridge where the soaring hawks find thermals like naturally occurring laughter, drawing his eyebeam up an unseen winding stair until they nearly vanish in the depth of sky. Lower down, Merlins[4] slice the air with wings that say crisp crisp, precise as sushi chefs, while Sharp-shins alternately glide and flap, hunting as they go, each line break poised, ready to pivot like a point guard or Robert Creeley.[5] Icarus notices how the Red-tails and Broadwings separate their primaries[6] to spill a little air, giving up just enough lift to break their drag up into smaller trailing vortices. What does this remind him of? He thinks of the kind of gentle teasing that can dissipate a dark mood so it slips off as a bunch of skirmishes and quirks. Maybe that. Some little gift to acknowledge the many claims of drag and keep its big imperative at bay. Icarus knows all about that one too.

In the spring he heads for a slough and makes himself a blind out of wolf willow and aspen, then climbs inside to let the marsh-mind claim his thinking. The soft splashdowns of Scaup and Bufflehead, the dives which are simple shrugs and vanishings; the Loon's wing, thin and sharp for flying in the underwater world, and the broad wing of the Mallard, powerful enough to break the water's grip with one sweep, a guffaw which lifts it straight up into the air. Icarus has already made the mistake of trying this at home, standing on a balustrade in the labyrinth and fanning like a manic punkah,[7] the effort throwing him backward off his perch and into a mock urn which the Minotaur[8] had, more than once, used as a pisspot. Another gift of failure. Now his watching is humbler, less appropriative, a thoughtless thinking amid fly drone and dragonfly dart. Icarus will stay in the blind until his legs cramp up so badly that he has to move. He is really too large to be a foetus for more than an hour. He unbends creakily, stretches, and walks home, feeling gravity's pull upon him as a kind of wealth.

---

4 A type of small falcon; Sharp-shins, Red-tails, and Broadwings are all varieties of hawk. The flight patterns of these birds—graceful, protracted sailing and circling with the ability to change direction suddenly and break into sharp descent— is contrasted with the deft diving and powerful swimming abilities of the water birds mentioned later in this section—the scaup, bufflehead, mallard, and loon.

5 That is, the agility of the birds recalls that of a point guard—usually the quickest and most skilled player on a basketball team—or of the American poet Robert Creeley, known for his facility of expression and technical precision.

6 The main flight feathers projecting along the outer edge of the bird's wing.

7 A fan, usually a large cloth fan on a frame suspended from the ceiling, moved backwards and forwards by pulling on a cord.

8 A creature, half-man and half-bull, who was the offspring of Pasiphaë and a bull with whom she fell in love. King Minos of Crete, Pasiphaë's husband, commissioned Daedalus to build the labyrinth to confine the beast, and fed it children sent from Athens as part of an annual tribute. Learning that Daedalus had helped Pasiphaë in her amours, Minos imprisoned him in the labyrinth with his son Icarus. Pasiphaë released them from it; Daedalus then devised wings for himself and his son when they still found it difficult to escape the Island of Crete.

*

Sometimes Icarus dreams back into his early days with Daedalus in the labyrinth. Then he reflects upon the Minotaur, how seldom they saw him—did they ever?—while they shifted constantly from no-place to no-place, setting up false campsites and leaving decoy models of themselves. Sometimes they would come upon these replicas in strange postures, holding their heads in their laps or pointing to their private parts. Once they discovered two sticks stuck like horns in a decoy's head, which Daedalus took to be the worst of omens. Icarus was not so sure.

For today's replay he imagines himself sitting in a corridor reflecting on life as a Minotaur (*The* Minotaur) while waiting for his alter ego to come bumbling by. They were, he realizes, both children of technology—one its *enfant terrible*, the other the rash adolescent who, they will always say, should never have been given a pilot's licence in the first place. What will happen when they finally meet? Icarus imagines dodging like a Barn Swallow, throwing out enough quick banter to deflect his rival's famous rage and pique his interest. How many Minotaurs does it take to screw in a light bulb? What did the queen say to the machine?

Should he wear two sticks on his head, or save that for later? He leaps ahead to scenes out of the Hardy Boys and Tom Sawyer. They will chaff and boast and punch each other on the arm. They will ridicule the weird obsessions of their parents. As they ramble, cul-de-sacs turn into secret hideouts and the institutional corridors take on the names of birds and athletes. They discover some imperfections in the rock face, nicks and juts which Daedalus neglected to chisel off, and which they will use to climb, boosting and balancing each other until they fall off. Together they will scheme and imagine. Somehow they will find a way to put their brute heads in the clouds.

2000

# Astonished—

astounded, astonied, astunned, stopped short
and turned toward stone, the moment
filling with its slow
stratified time. Standing there, your face
cratered by its gawk,
you might be the symbol signifying eon.[1]
What are you, empty or pregnant? Somewhere

---

1 As well as being a long period of time, in early use, *eon* could mean eternity, its symbol the serpent that devours its own tail. In geology, eon has a precise meaning: it is the longest division of geologic time, containing two or more eras (which contain two or more periods).

sediments accumulate on seabeds, seabeds
rear up into mountains, ammonites[2]
fossilize into gems. Are you thinking                10
or being thought? Cities
as sand dunes, epics
as e-mail. Astonished
you are famous and anonymous, the border
washed out by so soft a thing as weather. Someone
inside you steps from the forest and across the beach
toward the nameless all-dissolving ocean.

2006

2  Ammonites, an extinct group of marine animals; their fossils are used by geologists to identify the geological
   time periods of strata. Once their fossilized shells lose external layers and the iridescence of the inner shell is
   exposed, they can be polished and used as gems.

# Petrified—

your heart's tongue seized
mid-syllable, caught by the lava flow
you fled. Fixed,
you stiffen in the arms of wonder's dark
undomesticated sister. Can't you name her
and escape? You are the statue
that has lost the entrance into art,
wild and incompetent,
you have no house. Who are you?
You are the crystal that picks up                10
its many deaths.
You are the momentary mind of rock.

2006

# Pond

Eventually water,
having been possessed by every verb—
been rush been drip been
geyser eddy fountain rapid drunk
evaporated frozen pissed

transpired—will fall
into itself and sit.
                Pond. Things touch
or splash down and it
takes them in—pollen, heron, leaves, larvae, greater          10
and lesser scaup[1]—nothing declined,
nothing carried briskly off to form
alluvium[2] somewhere else. Pond gazes
into sky religiously but also
gathers in its edge, reflecting cattails, alders,
reed beds and behind them, ranged
like taller children in the grade four photo,
conifers and birch. All of them inverted, carried
deeper into sepia, we might as well say
pondered. For pond is not pool,                  20
whose clarity is edgeless and whose emptiness,
beloved by poets and the moon, permits us
to imagine life without the accident-
prone plumbing of its ecosystems. No,
the pause of pond is gravid and its wealth
a naturally occurring soup. It thickens up
with spawn and algae, while,
on its surface, stirred by every
whim of wind, it translates air as texture—
mottled, moiré, pleated, shirred or              30
seersuckered in that momentary ecstasy from which
impressionism, like a bridesmaid, steps. When it rains
it winks, then puckers up all over, then,
moving two more inches into metamorphosis,
shudders into pelt.
                Suppose Narcissus
were to find a nice brown pond
to gaze in: would the course of self-love
run so smooth with that exquisite face
rendered in bruin undertone,               40
shaken, and floated in the murk
between the deep sky and the ooze?

2006

---

1  The greater and lesser scaup are two species of ducks.
2  Sediment deposited by flowing water.

# Varves[1]

As I approach the high sandstone cliff with its stacked, individual, terribly numerable varves, I think of George from group, who was unable either to stop collecting newspapers or to throw them out. He would describe—not without some pride or at least amazement at his own extremity—how his basement, then living room, then bedroom had over the year become filled in with stacks of the *Globe and Mail,* the *Sun,* and the *Glengarry News,* all layered sequentially, until he was reduced to living in middle parts of his hallway and kitchen, his life all but occluded by sedimented public time. Unlike George's collection (which of course I saw only in my mind's eye), the cliff's is open to the eroding elements, so that bits have fallen off to form a talus slope[2] of flat, waferlike platelets at its base. This one in my hand has been clearly imprinted by a leaf—simple, lanceolate, probably an ancestor of our ash or elder. Published but vestigial, gone like an anonymous oriental poet, its image still floating on the coarse grains of summer.

On the flip side, winter. Under the eyelid of the ice. How often I thought of writing you, but the pen hung over the page. All the details on the desk too shy to be inscribed. To settle, to hesitate exquisitely, at last to lie, zero among zeroes. Much listening then, but no audience. Rhetoric elsewhere. Language itself has long since backed out of the room on tiptoe.

Sometimes we believe that we must diagnose the perils of the winter varve, and so do our talk-show hosts and shrinks, who number its shades and phases as though it were pregnancy *renversé*, with suicide at the end instead of a baby. As though death were really death. As though the unspoken were failure. Having misread even the newspapers. Having been deaf to the music of the beech leaves, who will cling to their branches until spring, their copper fading to transparency, making a faint metallic clatter.

---

1  'Alternating layers of coarse and fine sediment that have accumulated in an ancient lake and subsequently hardened into rock. The coarse layers accumulated during the summer months when streams carried silt and sand into the lake; the fine layers formed each winter when the surface was covered with ice, so that only slim grains of clay could settle to the bottom' [McKay's note].
2  A concave slope formed by the accretion of talus (fallen rock fragments, at the bottom of a cliff); 'lanceolate': in botany, having long, pointed leaves.

# Gneiss[1]

*On the Isle of Lewis, be sure to stop at Callanish and spend some time at the circle of standing stones erected by our neolithic ancestors.*
                    —Touring Scotland by Automobile

There is not much raw rock in that sentence, with its persuasive sibilants, not much scarp or grunt to remember the penalties paid—the load of it, the drag, the strained backs, smashed hands, and other proto-industrial injuries. It was not so long before this, not one whole afternoon as measured in the lifetimes of those upright slabs, that our

---

1  Metamorphic rock with vivid bands that result from the intense heat and pressure during its formation.

ancestors had themselves achieved the perpendicular. Now they required that some of the rocks that comprised their island should stand up with them against the levelling wind and eroding rain. And further, that they should form lines leading to the most common and hopeful of human signs—the circle of connection, of return. They insisted that rock be stone.

From across the heath it appears—and perhaps this testifies to the brilliance of our ancestors as landscape artists—that the amiable rocks have taken this on themselves, getting up as you or I might do, as a sign of respect. By presenting themselves in a rough circle they are simply performing a courtesy, like ships flying the flag of a country they are passing through. They arrange themselves into an image of the eternity we crave rather than the brute infinity we fear.

But close up it is more likely to be the commotion of stress lines swirling within each slab that clutches at the heart—each stone a pent rage, an agon.[2] None of the uniform grey of limestone, that prehistoric version of ready-mix concrete, in which each laid-down layer adds to the accumulated weight that homogenizes its predecessors. Think instead of Münch's *The Scream* with its contour lines of terror; then subtract the face. Or you could turn on the weather channel to observe those irresponsible isobars scrawling across the planet. Imagine our ancestors tracing these surfaces, whorled fingertip to gnarled rock, reading the earth-energy they had levered into the air. They had locked the fury into the fugue and the car crash into the high-school prom. They engineered this dangerous dance. Better stop here. Better spend some time.

2  That is, the lines recall the two competitors in an agon. (Agons are fierce struggles, such as the wrestling contests in ancient public games.)

## Some Last Requests

Of stone:

> That oblivion be tempered
> with remembrance and the limestone step be worn,
>
> be softened by our ins and outs.
> That swart chunks of granite
>
> hold our tent down tight
> when the wind blows all our tools away. That,
>
> after I'm over,
> you carry my name a little further on

till it gets past missing me. And if,
being fearful,

it still declines to fade, feed it,
phoneme by phoneme,

to the hawk scream it so badly mimicked
with its last long I.

Or winter.

Of rock:

That you teach me, as they say,
(insincerely) in the love songs,

to forget.
That my words should kiss

their complex personalities goodbye and sink
into Loss Creek, into

Ink Lake, into Black
Duck Brook, seeking the coarse

democracy of till.
That you instruct my bones in the art

of living rough and allow my thoughts
to fray into the weathers they have long

loved from afar.
As to my pain, that fine

pre-echo of the infinite:
keep it.

Keep it safe.

2006

# Daphne Marlatt
## b. 1942

Daphne Buckle was born in Melbourne, Australia, to English parents evacuated from the British colony of Malaya during the Second World War. After spending her early childhood in Penang, a northern Malayan island, she moved with her family to Vancouver in 1951. In 1960, she entered the University of British Columbia, where she studied with Warren Tallman, Robert Creeley, and Earle Birney. She also became involved with the *Tish* group (which included George Bowering and Fred Wah) and served as an editor of their newsletter. She was particularly inspired by the three-week-long Vancouver Poetry Conference organized by Tallman around a 1963 summer-school course. Roy Miki later described the readers and speakers who came that summer—mostly from the United States—as some of 'the most influential voices of the generation': they included Charles Olson, the chief theorist of Black Mountain poetics; Robert Duncan; Robert Creeley; Denise Levertov; Philip Whalen; Bobbie Louise Hawkins; Allen Ginsberg, the leading beat poet; and Donald Allen, editor of the touchstone anthology, *The New American Poetry, 1945–1960*. They were joined by Canadian poets Phyllis Webb and Margaret Avison. Marlatt, in an interview with Roseanne Harvey, described the whole group as writers 'whose work openly addressed the spiritual component in being human.' For her, this summer-school experience created a place 'where language, psyche and political consciousness came together in a large vision of what it means to be awake and alive in the world' and 'shaped me as a writer.'

In 1963, she married Gordon Marlatt. They moved, after she graduated in 1964, to Bloomington, Indiana, where she took an MA in comparative literature at the University of Indiana. Marlatt then began, in the poetry collected in *Frames of a Story* (1968) and *leaf leaf/s* (1969), to explore the possibilities of the Black Mountain–*Tish* tradition, while also looking

back to their sources in William Carlos Williams. In 1970, after separating from her husband, Marlatt returned to British Columbia with her son and began to teach at Capilano College and to edit *The Capilano Review*.

In the decade after her return to Canada, Marlatt published several books of poetry, including *Rings* (1971), *Our Lives* (1975), *The Story, She Said* (1977), and *What Matters* (1980)—as well as *Zócalo* (1977), a prose account of a visit to the Yucatán. Reflecting the *Tish* emphasis on writing about one's immediate environment, four of her books of that decade focus on the Vancouver area. Two are poetry: *Vancouver Poems* (1972) and *Steveston* (1974; with photographs by Robert Minden; reissued in 2001 with additional photos and one new poem). *Steveston*, which helped establish Marlatt's reputation as major figure, is a long poem about the fishing village at the mouth of the Fraser River.

> *Steveston: delta mouth of the Fraser where*
> *the river empties, sandbank after*
> *sandbank, into a muddy Gulf.*
> *Steveston: onetime cannery boomtown:*
> *'salmon capital of the world': fortunes*
> *made & lost on the homing instinct*
> *of salmon.*
> *Steveston: home to 2,000 Japanese, 'slaves*
> *of the company': stript of all their*
> *belongings, sent to camps in the interior*
> *away from the sea, wartime, who*
> *gradually drift back in the '40's . . .*
> *Steveston: hometown still for some, a story:*
> *of belonging (or is it continuing? lost,*
> *over & over . . .*

Marlatt's poem serves as a documentary while at the same time insisting—as is suggested in the title of its opening poem, 'Imagine: a town'—that the external world can only be brought into being by its subjective perception.

The two non-fiction books that Marlatt wrote during the 1970s are *Steveston Recollected: A Japanese-Canadian History* (1975) and *Opening Doors: Vancouver's East End* (1980)—oral histories that Marlatt constructed with the help of the BC Provincial Archives. (Marlatt's 1991 *Salvage*, a collection drawn from her previously unpublished work, contains several poems originally written for *Steveston*.)

In her essay 'The Measure of the Sentence', Marlatt says that in poems of this period—such as 'or there is love' (the concluding poem of *Steveston*)—she abandoned both 'the textbook notion of sentence as the container for a completed thought,' and the idea that the poetic line was a 'box for a certain measure of words.' Embracing what Charles Olson called 'proprioceptive' writing, she took a phenomenological approach to poetry. As Fred Wah points out in his introduction to Marlatt's *Selected Writing: Net Work* (1980), she sought to 'accurately reflect the condition of the writer at the moment of the writing.' Employing Olson's idea of 'open form', she thinks of each line as 'a moving step in the process of thought.' Thus, each line adds something to the preceding one—questioning, qualifying, or commenting upon it—without moving its statement to completion. Such poems invite readers to participate in the creation of meaning, not by thinking about the poem, but by hearing and feeling the poem's 'movement toward, and against, conclusion.' Marlatt's goal can be seen in the prose poem 'listen', which describes a man—reading to a woman—who is excited to find that an emotion has been 'named . . . at last'—or that it is being named 'even as he read, the shape of what he felt to be his own, recognized at last in words coming through him from the page, coming to her through his emphatic & stirred voice.'

In the decade that followed, Marlatt joined her art to political issues and played an important role in women's writing in Canada. She was a founding member of the Canadian feminist editorial collective that produced the journal *Tessera*. She also helped organize the important 1983 Women and Words/*Les femmes et les mots* conference. Her feminist perspective is evident throughout her creative work of this

period—*Here and There* (1981); *How Hug a Stone* (1983); and *Touch to My Tongue* (1984), which is a series of lyrical love poems addressed to poet Betsy Warland and a meditation on the feminist theories of Julia Kristeva and Mary Daly. Marlatt collaborated with Warland on *Double Negative* (1988), a long poem about two lesbians crossing the Australian desert; *Two Women in a Birth* (1994) gathers earlier work by both writers. In 1998, she published *Readings from the Labyrinth* (1998), a collection of new and previously published essays on subjects ranging from the immigrant imagination to women's autobiography and feminism. Marlatt's novel *Ana Historic* (1988) deals with the need to reject male-dominated historical accounts and to write women back into the historical record. These themes, which had earlier appeared in *Double Negative*, are expanded in *Ghost Works* (1993) and in *Taken* (1996), which is based on Marlatt's mother's life.

Marlatt has also worked as editor for the literary journals *Island* and *Periodics*; has served as writer-in-residence at the universities of Alberta and Western Ontario; and has taught in the creative-writing program at the University of Victoria. In 1989–90, she was the Ruth Wynn Woodward Professor in Women's Studies at Simon Fraser University. After the death of poet and artist Roy Kiyooka, who was her partner for some years, she gave final shape to his book, *Mothertalk: Life Stories of Mary Kiyoshi Kiyooka* (1997), which is based on his mother's conversations. It is Roy Kiyooka to whom the brief sequence of poems 'winter/rice/ tea strain' is addressed and who appears as the reader in 'listen'. These poems were published in Marlatt's 2001 broadside *winter/rice/tea* strain. Along with other revised and new poems, they then became part of her collection of love poems, *This Tremor Love Is* (2001). Similarly, the chapbook *Seven Glass Bowls* (2003) became the first part of *The Given* (2008), a long prose poem about Marlatt's mother's death that has the qualities of a novel. It complements *Taken*, which she originally conceived as a prose poem that turned into a novel.

Marlatt sees her own career as a series of transformative steps. Although most of her later work expresses deeply felt feminist concerns, her sexual identity has played an important role since 1990. Her interest in Buddhist philosophy and practice, begun in the early 1990s, also influenced her later writing: its emphasis on concrete details rather than abstractions and on the mind as a mirror of the world reinforces the principles she had already drawn from Black Mountain and *Tish* poetics.

In 2006, Marlatt became a Member of the Order of Canada.

# Imagine: a town

Imagine a town running
                    (smoothly?
a town running before a fire
canneries burning
                 (do you see the shadow of charred stilts
on cool water? do you see enigmatic chance standing
just under the beam?

                    He said they were playing cards in the
Chinese mess hall, he said it was dark (a hall? a shack.
they were all, crowded together on top of each other.                    10
He said somebody accidentally knocked the oil lamp over, off
the edge

    where stilts are standing, Over the edge of the
dyke a river pours, uncalled for, unending:

                        where chance lurks
fishlike, shadows the underside of pilings, calling up his hall
the bodies of men & fish corpse piled on top of each other (residue
time is, the delta) rot, an endless waste the trucks of production
grind to juice, driving through

                       smears, blood smears in the dark          20
dirt) this marshland silt no graveyard can exist in but water swills,
endlessly out of itself to the mouth

                    ringed with residue, where
chance flicks his tail & swims, through.

1974

# coming home

if it's to
get lost, lose
way as a wave
breaks

      'goodbye'

i am not speaking of
a path, the 'right'
road, no such
wonderlust

weigh all steps                                          10
shift weight
to left or right to

a place where one
steps thru all erratic
wanderings down to
touch:

i am here, feel
my weight on the wet
ground

1980


# winter/ rice/ tea strain

              ocha[1] words


—well into the winter,   we stir up out of what,   what dreams,   what
cause of communion,   names,   odd stirrings-up of the past as
honey pours,   *your dream was*   this & this reading, this poem
pouring this cup of tea   proposes (your favourite word)

---

1  Green tea.

days stream down any one of the window panes i press my nose against/
you—start & drop the book, your books, all over the floor  *so much*
*depends*  begin again, pressing these days into pages as if, paged
we could pull out any one to savour—this one so young, these

nouns i want to call out to you   winter/ rice/ tea strain, unlikely
sweet tongue, a green hope i bury my face into, steam's slip, & you                10
overheard, breathing yourself into sound


        touch


the music rice makes, rice on the tongue in our tea, tea & trout, while outside
rain's quintet batters our ears   hardly the bitterest month, sweet steep, sweet
infusion of green   tipping our lips at the smallest ordinary then   crescendo light
through dark your eye
                    stares i stare, in step, the skin of your foot so smooth it
startles, quick


      trout where the darkness lies


                          unformed its leap mere shine
ichthyic, from the base of the spinal column's chorded ascent (rippling                20
through the lines of what was planned, unplanned, undone—nothing
to catch our lines haphazard lie


          *gen mai cha*[2] grain
          between the teeth, still i see

you eye luminant, luminous wonder my eye wanders, amazed & touching
touched with *astony*, love, the thunder of it inflorescent you said   a downpour
trout weave through as you described yourself so slow to leap


                   out in what is


clearly the wonder of budding, leaves, scales of the old
miraculous, adart in the air as a friend would say *among*                30


---

2 Japanese green tea mixed with roasted rice. It has a mild nutty flavour with a sweet finish.

### bachi[3]

sea bush, 'small tree'  fruit-bearing, salt-sprung   fights your big wood
making a world—*poiein*[4]—to its own description   these drenched leaves
straining toward the light, spume, drift of repeated observation drawn
to shore

     you offer tea, wipe the wood of the table clearing sea wrack, surface
grit   we sip to a murmuring of visions, yours, mine, inter-inflected

                                    yet to break
our description of the world & thence to see   *the dreamer & the dreamed*  who's
dreaming who? you asked

wind buffets the windowpane   words incessant as rain fall   hear what slips     40
between   this tea we bring to our different lips, this space where nouns unfold

leaf
   by leaf

       bits on the floor of the pot we disappear

2000

3  Japanese, a basin or bowl.
4  Greek, 'to make'; the etymological root of the word poetry.

## listen

he was reading to her, standing on the other side of the kitchen counter where she was
making salad for supper, tender orange carrot in hand, almost transparent at its tip,
slender, & she was wondering where such carrots came from in winter.  he was standing in the light reading to her from a book he was holding, her son behind him at the
table where amber light streamed from under a glass shade she had bought for its
warm colour midwinter, though he had called it a cheap imitation of the real thing.

in its glow her son was drawing red Flash & blue Superman into a comic he was
making, painstakingly having stapled the pages together & now with his small &
definite hand trying to draw exact images of DC Superstars & Marvel heroes none of
them had ever seen except in coloured ink.

but he was reading to her about loss, excited, because someone had named it at last, was naming even as he read, the shape of what he felt to be his own, recognized at last in words coming through him from the page, coming to her through his emphatic & stirred voice stumbling over the rough edges of terms that weren't his, even as he embraced them. lost, how their dancing had lost touch with the ring dance which was a collective celebration, he said.

she was standing with the grater in one hand, carrot in the other, wondering if the grating sound would disturb him. she wanted to hear what had stirred him. she wanted to continue the movement of making salad which, in the light & the löwen-brau they shared, was for once coming so easily, almost was spring stirring around the corner of the house in a rhythm of rain outside she was moving in, had moved, barely knowing it was rain beyond the wetness of walking home—

hand in hand, he was saying, a great circle like the circle of the seasons, & now peo-ple barely touch, where at least with the waltz they used to dance in couples, then with rock apart but *to* each other, whereas now, he caught her eye, the dances we've been to you can see people dancing alone, completely alone with the sound.

lifting the carrot to the grater, pressing down, watching flakes of orange fall to the board, she felt accused in some obscure way, wanted to object (it was her generation after all), thought up an obscure argument about how quadrilles[1] could be called col-lective in ballrooms where privileged guests took their assigned places in the dance. but now, & she recalled the new year's eve party they'd been to, almost a hundred people, strangers, come together, & people don't know each other in the city the way they used to in a village. but that only glanced off what the book was saying about husbandry & caring for the soil as a collective endeavour.

the whole carrot was shrinking into a thousand flakes heaped & scattered at once, the whole carrot with its almost transparent sides shining in the light, had ground down to a stump her fingers clutched close to the jagged pockets of tin that scraped them, she saw her fingers, saw blood flying like carrot flakes, wondered why she imagined blood as part of the salad . . .

listen, he was saying, this is where he's really got it. & he read a long passage about their imprisonment in marriage, all the married ones with that impossible ideal of confining love to one—*one cannot love a particular woman unless one loves woman-kind*, he read. listen, he said, & he read her the passage about the ring dance, about the participation of couples in one great celebration, the *amorous feast that joins them to all living things*. he means fertility, she said, thinking, oh no, oh back to that, woman's one true function. he means the fertility of the earth, he said, he means our lives aware of seasonal growth & drawing nourishment from that instead of material

1 Square dances performed typically by four couples.

acquisition & exploitation.  listen, he read a passage about sexual capitalism, about the crazy images of romance that fill people's heads, sexual freedom & skill & the me-generation on all the racks of all the supermarket stores.

using her palms like two halves of a split spoon, she scooped up the heap of carrot flakes & dropped them onto a plate of lettuce, dark because it was romaine torn into pieces in the wooden bowl with other green things.  dance.  in & out.  she watched the orange flakes glisten in their oil of skin, touch the surface of green she tossed with real spoons, each flake dipping into the dark that lay at the heart of, what, their hearts, as they had, the other night, sunk into bed at the end of the party, drunk & floating, their laughter sifting in memory through conversations, wrapt in the warmth of what everyone had said & how they had moved away & toward each other & loved in very obscure ways, slowly they had made love to everyone they loved in each other, falling through & away from their separate bodies—listen, she said, as the rain came up & she set the salad on the wooden table underneath the lamp.

1980; rev. 2001


# (is love enough?)

*Salt through the earth conduct the sea*

— Olga Broumas


such green glistening, a sparrow preening a far-stretched wing, light full of pleasure-chirping, feathered bodies at home in earth's soft voltage & newness written over your face waking from dream, each blade, each leaf encased still in the wet from last night's rain

is love enough when the breast milk a mother jets in the urgent mouth of her baby is laced with PCBs?

hungry you said, for love, for light, armfulls of daffodils we refuse to gather standing luminous, pale ears listening, ochre trumpets at the heart darkness pools, & the radio, as we sit on a paint-blistered deck in brilliant sun reports that snow, whiter than chalk on the highest shelf of the Rockies is sedimented with toxins

the dead, the dying—we imprint our presence everywhere on every wall & rock

what is love in the face of such loss?

since dawn, *standing by my bed,* she wrote, *in gold sandals . . . that very/ moment* half-awake in a whisper of light her upturned face given to presence, a woman involved, a circle of women she taught how to love, how to pay a fine attention raising simply & correctly the fleeting phases of what is, arrives

we get these glimpses, you said, grizzlies begging at human doorways, two cubs & a mother so thin her ribs showed prominent under ratty fur, shot now that our salmon rivers run empty, rivers that were never ours to begin with—

& the sea, the sea goes out a long way in its unpublished killing ground

this webwork—what we don't know about the body, what we don't know may well be killing us—well  : spring : stream : river, these powerful points you set your fingers on, drawing current through blockages, moving inward, not out, to see

chi[1] equally in
*the salt sea and fields thick with bloom*
inner channels & rivers

a sea full of apparent islands, no jetting-off point, no airborne leap possible

without the body all these bodies
interlaced

2001

1 Circulating life force whose existence and properties are the basis of much Chinese philosophy and medicine.

# Michael Ondaatje
## b. 1943

The youngest of four siblings, Michael Ondaatje was born in Sri Lanka (then Ceylon) of Dutch, Sinhalese, and Tamil ancestry. When he was an infant, his parents separated and he went to live with relatives. (He saw little of the father he describes in 'Letters & Other Worlds', a poem he says was difficult to write.) In 1954, he joined his mother in England, where he received his secondary schooling at Dulwich College boarding school; then, in 1962, he followed his brother Christopher to Canada, which became his permanent home. After attending Bishop's University for three years, he took the fourth year of his BA at the University of Toronto in 1964–5. Completing an MA at Queen's University in 1967, he taught English at the University of Western Ontario until 1970, when he joined the faculty of Glendon College,

York University. He published *Leonard Cohen*, a brief study of Cohen's poetry and fiction that same year.

While Ondaatje was still an undergraduate at Bishop's, the poet-critic D.G. Jones recognized his talent and became his mentor. In 1966, Raymond Souster selected him as a young poet to watch in his anthology, *New Wave Canada*. Ondaatje's first book of poems, *The Dainty Monsters*, appeared the following year. Attracted to the 'documentary' mode that Dorothy Livesay has identified as important in Canadian poetry, he published *The Man with Seven Toes* in 1969, a unified sequence of poems based on the experience of a woman shipwrecked off the Queensland coast of Australia. His next book, *The Collected Works of Billy the Kid* (1970), makes use of the collage, joining his own prose and poetry to such things as a jailhouse interview with Billy, an excerpt from an old pulp novel, and historical photographs and period illustrations to fashion a chronicle of the legendary American outlaw and of Pat Garrett's pursuit of him. It won a Governor General's Award—but because separate prizes are normally given for novels, poetry, and non-fiction, the judges created, for that year only, an additional category of 'prose and poetry' to accommodate Ondaatje's book.

Ondaatje's interest in building narratives around historical events and individuals remains evident in his later works. His 1976 novel, *Coming through Slaughter*, set in the Storyville area of New Orleans, is based on the life of—and makes use of documents about—the influential early jazz musician Buddy Bolden. Like *Billy the Kid*, it is a portrait of an outsider driven to violence and self-destruction, both by society and by his own demons. Ondaatje's later blend of history and fiction in *In the Skin of a Lion* (1987) recalls the construction of two important edifices of twentieth-century Toronto: the Bloor Street Viaduct and the city's water-filtration plant. Two characters introduced in this novel— Hana, the step-daughter of the protagonist Patrick Lewis, and the thief Caravaggio—return in *The English Patient* (1992), which tells of a group of people brought together in Italy during the final days of the Second World War. A third character in that novel is Kip, a Sikh bomb-disposal expert, who comes to understand the British Empire and his place in it. The 'English patient' of the title is a man badly burned in a plane crash, whose mysterious identity and background are at the centre of the story. *The English Patient* earned Ondaatje a Governor General's Award and the Booker Prize (co-winner with Barry Unsworth), the first time the latter prize had been awarded to a Canadian. In 1996, the novel was made into a film, which won several Academy Awards, including best picture.

Although he is now best known for his fiction, Ondaatje has continued to write poetry throughout his career. His second book of short poems, *Rat Jelly* (1973) was followed by a book of selected and new poetry, *There's a Trick with a Knife I'm Learning to Do: Poems, 1963–1978* (1979; Governor General's Award). In contrast to his prose, Ondaatje's poems often draw on very personal material—such as the eccentric behaviour of his father, the old scars of 'A Time Around Scars', and his deep feelings for his growing child in 'To a Sad Daughter'.

In the 1980s, Ondaatje published two autobiographical works—*Running in the Family* (1982) and *Secular Love* (1984). *Running in the Family*, based on a trip Ondaatje made to Sri Lanka, combines prose sketches, poems, and photographs into a narrative of his family's history. *Secular Love* is a sequence of poems— including 'To a Sad Daughter'—that can be read in isolation but that together form a verse journal. With repetitions and echoes unifying the whole, it traces the poet's life from his near breakdown after the collapse of his first marriage through his recovery. A second book of selected poetry, *The Cinnamon Peeler*, appeared in 1992.

Ondaatje's exploration of autobiographical material coincides with a greater engagement in Sri Lanka. He used the money he received for the Booker Prize to inaugurate the Gratiaen Award—named in honour of his mother, Doris Gratiaen, and her family—as an annual literary prize for Sri Lankan writers and, in 1998, he published *Handwriting*, a book of poems focused chiefly on the country in which he was born. In 2000, he set a novel in Sri Lanka: *Anil's Ghost*. It won both a Governor General's Award and a Giller Prize. Set amid strife and civil war—like the poems in *Handwriting*—it tells the story of Anil Tissera, a forensic anthropologist, who returns to Sri Lanka to gather evidence about the campaigns of murder plaguing her homeland and asks whether international observers can play a role among people who have had to live amid unending terror.

The Governor General's Award that Ondaatje received for his most recent novel, *Divisadero* (2007), makes him one of only two Canadian writers ever to receive five such awards (the other is Hugh MacLennan). *Divisadero* is a lyric—yet at times a violent—narrative: set in San Francisco and then in France, it divides in two as it moves through time, forward from the 1970s, then back to the early twentieth century. Such disjunctions are common in Ondaatje's poems and prose. As a character in this novel observes, our minds refuse to

*move forward in linear development, circling instead . . . familiar moments of emotion* [because] *we live with those retrievals from childhood that coalesce and echo throughout our lives, the way shattered pieces of glass in a kaleidoscope reappear in new forms.*

Ondaatje has also been important in regard to Canadian small presses and has played a significant role in fostering new Canadian writing. From the 1970s until the early 90s, he was part of the Coach House Press editorial collective

and, from 1985, he served as one of the editors for the literary journal *Brick*. He edited *Personal Fictions* (1977) and the compendious gathering of Canadian short fiction, *From Ink Lake* (1992), as well as the *Long Poem Anthology* (1979), a collection that helped draw attention to the continuing importance of the long poem in Canada.

He has shown himself interested in forms of expression that go beyond the page. In the early 1970s, he made three movies, including one on bpNichol (*The Sons of Captain Poetry*, 1970). His interest in film is evident in *The Conversations: Walter Murch and the Art of Film Editing* (2002), a discussion about film editing and the writing of literature between Ondaatje and Murch, the master US film and sound editor, whom he met during the making of *The English Patient*. Ondaatje has also adapted three of his works—*The Man with Seven Toes*, *The Collected Works of Billy the Kid*, and *Coming through Slaughter*—for the stage.

Ondaatje's engagement in visual expression is not surprising. His work is filled with carefully realized physical images and actions. Though the contrast between the warmth and familiarity of these depictions of events and the cool objectivity of their rendering sometimes holds reader and characters at a distance, it also creates emotional intensity.

# The Time Around Scars

A girl whom I've not spoken to
or shared coffee with for several years
writes of an old scar.
On her wrist it sleeps, smooth and white,
the size of a leech.
I gave it to her
brandishing a new Italian penknife.
Look, I said turning,
and blood spat onto her shirt.

My wife has scars like spread raindrops
on knees and ankles,
she talks of broken greenhouse panes
and yet, apart from imagining red feet,

10

(a nymph out of Chagall[1])
I bring little to that scene.
We remember the time around scars,
they freeze irrelevant emotions
and divide us from present friends.
I remember this girl's face,
the widening rise of surprise.                    20

And would she
moving with lover or husband
conceal or flaunt it,
or keep it at her wrist
a mysterious watch.
And this scar I then remember
is medallion of no emotion.

I would meet you now
and I would wish this scar
to have been given with                            30
all the love
that never occurred between us.

1967

1 Marc Chagall (1887–1985), Russian-born French artist whose paintings often have a quality of fairytale fantasy.


# Letters & Other Worlds

*'for there was no more darkness for him and, no doubt
like Adam before the fall, he could see in the dark'*[1]

My father's body was a globe of fear
His body was a town we never knew
He hid that he had been where we were going
His letters were a room he seldom lived in
In them the logic of his love could grow

My father's body was a town of fear
He was the only witness to its fear dance
He hid where he had been that we might lose him
His letters were a room his body scared

1 Translation from Alfred Jarry's *La Dragonne* (1943), cited in *The Banquet Years* by Roger Shattuck (1955).

He came to death with his mind drowning.                              10
On the last day he enclosed himself
in a room with two bottles of gin, later
fell the length of his body
so that brain blood moved
to new compartments
that never knew the wash of fluid
and he died in minutes of a new equilibrium.

His early life was a terrifying comedy
and my mother divorced him again and again.
He would rush into tunnels magnetized                                 20
by the white eye of trains
and once, gaining instant fame,
managed to stop a Perahara² in Ceylon
—the whole procession of elephants dancers
local dignitaries—by falling
dead drunk onto the street.

As a semi-official, and semi-white at that,
the act was seen as a crucial
turning point in the Home Rule Movement
and led to Ceylon's independence in 1948.                             30

(My mother had done her share too—
her driving so bad
she was stoned by villagers
whenever her car was recognized)

For 14 years of marriage
each of them claimed he or she
was the injured party.
Once on the Colombo docks
saying goodbye to a recently married couple
my father, jealous                                                    40
at my mother's articulate emotion,
dove into the waters of the harbour
and swam after the ship waving farewell.
My mother pretending no affiliation
mingled with the crowd back to the hotel.

2  Religious ceremony celebrated by a parade.

Once again he made the papers
though this time my mother
with a note to the editor
corrected the report—saying he was drunk
rather than broken hearted at the parting of friends.          50
The married couple received both editions
of *The Ceylon Times* when their ship reached Aden.[3]

And then in his last years
he was the silent drinker,
the man who once a week
disappeared into his room with bottles
and stayed there until he was drunk
and until he was sober.

There speeches, head dreams, apologies,
the gentle letters, were composed.          60
With the clarity of architects
he would write of the row of blue flowers
his new wife had planted,
the plans for electricity in the house,
how my half-sister fell near a snake
and it had awakened and not touched her.
Letters in a clear hand of the most complete empathy
his heart widening and widening and widening
to all manner of change in his children and friends
while he himself edged          70
into the terrible acute hatred
of his own privacy
till he balanced and fell
the length of his body
the blood screaming in
the empty reservoir of bones
the blood searching in his head without metaphor

1973

---

3  International port in Yemen and a stop on the trip from Ceylon through the Suez Canal on the way to Europe.

# Pig Glass

Bonjour.    This is pig glass
a piece of cloudy sea


nosed out of the earth by swine
and smoothed into pebble
run it across your cheek
it will not cut you


and this is my hand a language
which was buried for years     touch it
against your stomach


                  The pig glass                         10
I thought
was the buried eye of Portland Township
slow faded history
waiting to be grunted up
There is no past until you breathe
on such green glass
                  rub it
over your stomach and cheek


The Meeks family used this section
years ago to bury tin                                  20
crockery forks dog tags
and each morning
pigs ease up that ocean
redeeming it again
into the possibilities of rust
one morning I found a whole axle
another day a hand crank
but this is pig glass
tested with narrow teeth
and let lie. The morning's . . . green present           30
Portland Township jewelry.


There is the band from the ankle of a pigeon
a weathered bill from the Bellrock Cheese Factory
letters in 1925 to a dead mother I
disturbed in the room above the tractor shed.
Journals of family love

servitude to farm weather
a work glove in a cardboard box
creased flat and hard like a flower.

A bottle thrown                                                              40
by loggers out of a wagon
past midnight
explodes against rock.
This green fragment has behind it
the *booomm* when glass
tears free of its smoothness

now once more smooth as knuckle
a tooth on my tongue.
Comfort that bites through skin
hides in the dark afternoon of my pocket.                                     50
Snake shade.
Determined histories of glass.

1979


# Light

*for Doris Gratiaen*

Midnight storm. Trees walking off across the fields in fury
naked in the spark of lightning.
I sit on the white porch on the brown hanging cane chair
coffee in my hand midnight storm midsummer night.
The past, friends and family, drift into the rain shower.
Those relatives in my favourite slides
re-shot from old minute photographs so they now stand
complex ambiguous grainy on my wall.

This is my Uncle who turned up to his marriage
on an elephant. He was a chaplain.                                           10
This shy looking man in the light jacket and tie was infamous,
when he went drinking he took the long blonde beautiful hair
of his wife and put one end in the cupboard and locked it
leaving her tethered in an armchair.
He was terrified of her possible adultery
and this way died peaceful happy to the end.

My Grandmother, who went to a dance in a muslin dress
with fireflies captured and embedded in the cloth, shining
and witty. This calm beautiful face
organised wild acts in the tropics.                                    20
She hid the mailman in her house
after he had committed murder and at the trial
was thrown out of the court for making jokes at the judge.
Her son became a Q.C.
This is my brother at 6. With his cousin and his sister
and Pam de Voss who fell on a pen-knife and lost her eye.
My Aunt Christie. She knew Harold Macmillan[1] was a spy
communicating with her through pictures in the newspapers.
Every picture she believed asked her to forgive him,
his hound eyes pleading.                                               30
Her husband Uncle Fitzroy, a doctor in Ceylon,
had a memory sharp as scalpels into his 80's
though I never bothered to ask him about anything
—interested then more in the latest recordings of Bobby Darin.[2]

And this is my Mother with her brother Noel in fancy dress.
They are 7 and 8 years old, a hand-coloured photograph,
it is the earliest picture I have. The one I love most.
A picture of my kids at Halloween
has the same contact and laughter.
My Uncle dying at 68, and my Mother a year later dying at 68.    40
She told me about his death and the day he died
his eyes clearing out of illness as if seeing
right through the room the hospital and she said
he saw something so clear and good his whole body
for a moment became youthful and she remembered
when she sewed badges on his trackshirts.
Her voice joyous in telling me this, her face light and clear.
(My firefly Grandmother also dying at 68.)

These are the fragments I have of them, tonight
in this storm, the dogs restless on the porch.                         50
They were all laughing, crazy, and vivid in their prime.
At a party my drunk Father
tried to explain a complex operation on chickens
and managed to kill them all in the process, the guests
having dinner an hour later while my Father slept

1  Harold Macmillan (b. 1894) was the prime minister of the United Kingdom from 1957 to 1963.
2  Bobby Darin was an American pop singer of the 1950s and 60s.

and the kids watched the servants clean up the litter
of beaks and feathers on the lawn.

These are their fragments, all I remember,
wanting more knowledge of them. In the mirror and in my kids
I see them in my flesh. Wherever we are                                    60
they parade in my brain and the expanding stories
connect to the grey grainy pictures on the wall,
as they hold their drinks or 20 years later
hold grandchildren, pose with favourite dogs,
coming through the light, the electricity, which the storm
destroyed an hour ago, a tree going down by the highway
so that now inside the kids play dominoes by candlelight
and out here the thick rain static the spark of my match to a cigarette
and the trees across the fields leaving me, distinct
lonely in their own knife scars and cow-chewed bark                      70
frozen in the jagged light as if snapped in their run
the branch arms waving to what was a second ago the dark sky
when in truth like me they haven't moved.
Haven't moved an inch from me.

1979


# Sallie Chisum/Last Words on Billy the Kid. 4 A.M.[1]

*for Nancy Beatty*

The moon hard and yellow where Billy's head is.
I have been moving in my room
these last 5 minutes. Looking for a cigarette.
That is a sin he taught me.
Showed me how to hold it and how to want it.

I had been looking and stepped forward
to feel along the windowsill
and there was the tanned moon head.
His body the shadow of the only tree on the property.

---

1 Billy the Kid achieved his notoriety while employed by the cattleman John Chisum in a range war; Sallie, Chisum's niece, met Billy while living with her uncle. Ondaatje makes her reminiscences an important feature in his retelling of Billy's story. This poem, written when *The Collected Works of Billy the Kid* was in production at the Stratford Festival, was added to a later production of the play. Ondaatje views it as a kind of postscript.

I am at the table.                                                    10
Billy's mouth is trying
to remove a splinter out of my foot.
Tough skin on the bottom of me.
Still. I can feel his teeth
bite precise. And then moving his face back,
holding something in his grin, says he's got it.


Where have you been I ask
Where have you been he replies


I have been into every room about 300 times
since you were here                                                   20
I have walked about 60 miles in this house
Where have you been I ask


Billy was a fool
he was like those reversible mirrors
you can pivot round and see yourself again
but there is something showing on the other side always.
Sunlight. The shade beside the cupboard


He fired two bullets into the dummy
on which I built dresses
where the nipples should have been.                                   30
That wasnt too funny, but we laughed a lot.


One morning he was still sleeping
I pushed the door and watched him from the hall
he looked like he was having a serious dream.
Concentrating. Angry. As if wallpaper
had been ripped off a wall.


Billy's mouth at my foot
removing the splinter.
Did I say that?


It was just before lunch one day.                                     40


I have been alive
37 years since I knew him. He was a fool.
He was like those mirrors I told you about.

I am leaning against the bed rail
I have finished my cigarette
now I cannot find the ashtray.
I put it out, squash it
against the window
where the moon is.
In his stupid eyes. 50

1979

## The Cinnamon Peeler

If I were a cinnamon peeler[1]
I would ride your bed
and leave the yellow bark dust
on your pillow.

Your breasts and shoulders would reek
you could never walk through markets
without the profession of my fingers
floating over you. The blind would
stumble certain of whom they approached
though you might bathe 10
under rain gutters, monsoon.

Here on the upper thigh
at this smooth pasture
neighbour to your hair
or the crease
that cuts your back. This ankle.
You will be known among strangers
as the cinnamon peeler's wife.

I could hardly glance at you
before marriage 20
never touch you
—your keen nosed mother, your rough brothers.
I buried my hands
in saffron, disguised them
over smoking tar,
helped the honey gatherers . . .

1  One who peels the cinnamon bark, the source of the spice, from the trees.

When we swam once
I touched you in water
and our bodies remained free,
you could hold me and be blind of smell.
You climbed on the bank and said
                    this is how you touch other women
the grass cutter's wife, the lime burner's daughter.
And you searched your arms
for the missing perfume
                            and knew

 

                    what good is it
to be the lime burner's daughter
left with no trace
as if not spoken to in the act of love                    40
as if wounded without the pleasure of a scar.

You touched
your belly to my hands
in the dry air and said
I am the cinnamon
peeler's wife. Smell me.

1982

# Lunch Conversation

Wait a minute, wait a minute! When did all this happen, I'm trying to get it
straight . . .

    Your mother was nine, Hilden was there, and your grandmother Lalla and David
Grenier and his wife Dickie.

    How old was Hilden?

    Oh, in his early twenties.

    But Hilden was having dinner with my mother and you.

    Yes, says Barbara. And Trevor de Saram. And Hilden and your mother and I were
quite drunk. It was a wedding lunch, Babette's I think, I can't remember all those
weddings. I know Hilden was moving with a rotten crowd of drinkers then so he was
drunk quite early and we were all laughing about the drowning of

David Grenier.

I didn't say a word.

Laughing at Lalla, because Lalla nearly drowned too. You see, she was caught in a current and instead of fighting it she just relaxed and went with it out to sea and eventually came back in a semi-circle. Claimed she passed ships.

And then Trevor got up in a temper and challenged Hilden to a duel. He couldn't *stand* everyone laughing, and Hilden and Doris (your mother) being drunk, two of them flirting away he thought.

But *why*?, your mother asked Trevor.

Because he is casting aspersions on you . . .

Nonsense, I love aspersions. And everyone laughed and Trevor stood there in a rage.

And then, said Barbara, I realized that Trevor had been in love with your mother, your father always *said* there was a secret admirer. Trevor couldn't stand Hilden and her having a good time in front of him.

Nonsense, said your mother. It would have been incest. And besides (watching Hilden and Trevor and aware of the fascinated dinner table audience), both these men are after my old age pension.

What happened, said Hilden, was that I drew a line around Doris in the sand. A circle. And threatened her, 'don't you dare step out of that circle or I'll thrash you.'

Wait a minute, wait a minute, *when* is this happening?

Your mother is nine years old, Hilden says. And out in the sea near Negombo David Grenier is drowning. I didn't want her to go out.

You were in love with a nine year old?

Neither Hilden nor Trevor were *ever* in love with our mother, Gillian whispers to me. People always get that way at weddings, always remembering the past in a sentimental way, pretending great secret passions which went unsaid . . .

No No No. Trevor *was* in love with your mother.

Rot!

I was in my twenties, Hilden chimes in. Your mother was nine. I simply didn't want her going into the water while we tried to rescue David Grenier. Dickie, his wife, had fainted. Lalla—your mother's mother—was caught in the current and out at sea, I was on the shore with Trevor.

Trevor was there too you see.

*Who* is Hilden? asks Tory.

*I* am Hilden . . . your host!

Oh.

Anyway . . . there seems to be three different stories that you're telling.

No, *one*, everybody says laughing.

One when your mother was nine. Then when she was sixty-five and drinking at the wedding lunch, and obviously there is a period of unrequited love suffered by the silent Trevor who never stated his love but always fought with anyone he thought was insulting your mother, even if in truth she was simply having a good time with them the way she was with Hilden, when she was sixty-five.

Good God, I was there with them both, says Barbara, and *I'm* married to Hilden.

So where is my grandmother?

She is now out at sea while Hilden dramatically draws a circle round your mother and says 'Don't you *dare* step out of that!' Your mother watches, David Grenier drowning. Grenier's wife—who is going to marry three more times including one man who went crazy—is lying in the sand having fainted. And your mother can see the bob of her mother's head in the waves now and then. Hilden and Trevor are trying to retrieve David Grenier's body, carefully, so as not to get caught in the current themselves.

My mother is nine.

Your mother is nine. And this takes place in Negombo.

OK

So an hour later my grandmother, Lalla, comes back and entertains everyone with stories of how she passed ships out there and they tell her David Grenier is dead. And nobody wants to break the news to his wife Dickie. Nobody could. And Lalla says, alright, she will, for Dickie is her sister. And she went and sat with Dickie who was still in a faint in the sand, and Lalla, wearing her elaborate bathing suit, held her hand. Don't shock her, says Trevor, whatever you do break it to her gently. My mother waves him away and for fifteen minutes she sits alone with her sister, waiting for her to waken. She doesn't know what to say. She is also suddenly very tired. She hates hurting anybody.

The two men, Hilden and Trevor, will walk with her daughter, my mother, about a hundred yards away down the beach, keeping their distance, waiting until they see Dickie sitting up. And then they will walk slowly back towards Dickie and my grandmother and give their sympathies.

Dickie stirs. Lalla is holding her hand. She looks up and the first words are, 'How is David? Is he all right?' 'Quite well, darling,' Lalla says. 'He is in the next room having a cup of tea.'

1982

## To a Sad Daughter

All night long the hockey pictures
gaze down at you
sleeping in your tracksuit.
Belligerent goalies are your ideal.
Threats of being traded
cuts and wounds
—all this pleases you.
*O my god!* you say at breakfast
reading the sports page over the Alpen
as another player breaks his ankle
or assaults the coach.     10

When I thought of daughters
I wasn't expecting this
but I like this more.
I like all your faults
even your purple moods
when you retreat from everyone
to sit in bed under a quilt.
And when I say 'like'
I mean of course 'love'
but that embarrasses you.     20
You who feel superior to black and white movies
(coaxed for hours to see *Casablanca*)
though you were moved
by *Creature from the Black Lagoon*.

One day I'll come swimming
beside your ship or someone will
and if you hear the siren
listen to it.[1] For if you close your ears
only nothing happens. You will never change.     30

1 For the myth of the sirens and their dangerous song, see page 826, note 1. Ondaatje's line here recalls the story of Odysseus, who, when he passed by the Sirens' island, had the ears of his crew stopped up to keep the ship safe but was himself lashed to the mast with his ears unstopped that he might hear their song.

I don't care if you risk
your life to angry goalies
creatures with webbed feet.
You can enter their caves and castles
their glass laboratories. Just
don't be fooled by anyone but yourself.

This is the first lecture I've given you.
You're 'sweet sixteen' you said.
I'd rather be your closest friend
than your father. I'm not good at advice                    40
you know that, but ride
the ceremonies
until they grow dark.

Sometimes you are so busy
discovering your friends
I ache with a loss
—but that is greed.
And sometimes I've gone
into *my* purple world
and lost you.                                               50

One afternoon I stepped
into your room. You were sitting
at the desk where I now write this.
Forsythia outside the window
and sun spilled over you
like a thick yellow miracle
as if another planet
was coaxing you out of the house
—all those possible worlds!—
and you, meanwhile, busy with mathematics.                 60

I cannot look at forsythia now
without loss, or joy for you.
You step delicately
into the wild world
and your real prize will be
the frantic search.
Want everything. If you break
break going out not in.
How you live your life I don't care
but I'll sell my arms for you,                              70
hold your secrets forever.

If I speak of death
which you fear now, greatly,
it is without answers,
except that each
one we know is
in our blood.
Don't recall graves.
Memory is permanent.
Remember the afternoon's      80
yellow suburban annunciation.
Your goalie
in his frightening mask
dreams perhaps
of gentleness.

1984


# The Medieval Coast

A village of stone-cutters. A village of soothsayers.
Men who burrow into the earth in search of gems.

Circus in-laws who pyramid themselves into trees.

Home life. A fear of distance along the southern coast.

Every stone-cutter has his secret mark, angle of his chisel.

In the village of soothsayers
bones of a familiar animal
guide interpretations.

This wisdom extends no more than thirty miles.

1998

# Wells

*i*

The rope jerked up
so the bucket flies
into your catch

pours over you

its moment
of encasement

standing in sunlight
wanting more,
another poem please

and each time                                              10
recognition and caress,
the repeated pleasure

of finite things.
Hypnotized by lyric.
This year's kisses

like diving a hundred times
from a moving train
into the harbour

like diving a hundred times
from a moving train                                          20
into the harbour


*ii*

The last Sinhala word I lost
was *vatura*.
The word for water.
Forest water. The water in a kiss. The tears
I gave to my ayah[1] Rosalin on leaving
the first home of my life.

---

1  Nursemaid.

More water for her than any other
that fled my eyes again
this year, remembering her,                              30
a lost almost-mother in those years
of thirsty love.

No photograph of her, no meeting
since the age of eleven,
not even knowledge of her grave.

Who abandoned who, I wonder now.


  *iii*


In the sunless forest
of Ritigala²

heat in the stone
heat in the airless black shadows                       40

nine soldiers on leave
strip uniforms off  ·
and dig a well

to give thanks
for surviving this war

A puja³ in an unnamed grove
the way someone you know
might lean forward
and mark the place
where your soul is                                       50
—always, they say,
near to a wound.

In the sunless forest
crouched by a forest well

pulling what was lost
out of the depth.

1998


2  Ancient city of Sri Lanka, site of a Buddhist monastery.
3  Ceremonial offering.

# Thomas King

## b. 1943

Thomas King, of Cherokee, German, and Greek descent, was born and raised in Roseville, California, near Sacramento. He dropped out after one year of university and took a series of jobs, first in the United States and then in New Zealand and Australia, where he worked as a photojournalist. In 1967, he returned to the US and enrolled at Chico State University (now California State University, Chico), completing his BA in 1970 and his MA two years later. King subsequently taught at the University of Minnesota, where he was chair of the American Indian Studies Program, before immigrating to Canada in 1980 to take a faculty position at the University of Lethbridge. While at Lethbridge, he undertook further graduate work, completing his PhD at the University of Utah in 1986 with a thesis called 'Inventing the Indian: White Images, Oral Literature, and Contemporary Native Writers'.

In his thesis, in his many essays, and in his Massey Lectures (collected as *The Truth about Stories: A Native Narrative*, 2003), King examines the role of narrative and the power of the oral tale. He is particularly critical, in 'Godzilla vs. Postcolonial', of the use of the postcolonial model in Aboriginal studies because it assumes that the European occupation of the Americas has been the single most important reference point for Native peoples. He does not argue that European contact should be ignored but insists that it is always important to 'cross the lines that definitions—no matter how loose—create.' King has also co-edited a collection of critical essays, *The Native in Literature: Canadian and Comparative Perspectives* (1987), as well as editing two anthologies of Native writing, *All My Relations: An Anthology of Contemporary Canadian Native Fiction* (1990) and *First Voices, First Words* (2001).

King's fiction has provided him with another avenue for his investigations of Native North American identity. His first novel, *Medicine River* (1989), is a humorous and ironic account of a Métis photographer's return to his hometown in the Prairies and to a nearby reservation. It was made into a 1993 CBC television movie, for which King wrote the teleplay. Although *Medicine River* is told in a traditional realist mode, King's discovery, early in 1990, of the work of Harry Robinson transformed his storytelling technique by revealing to him how oral ways of telling stories could be used in written fiction:

*I read those stories and they just sort of turned things around for me. I could see what he had done and how he worked it and I began to try to adapt it to my own fiction. It was inspirational. (Canadian Literature, pp. 161–2)*

This innovation in King's technique was first evident in a tale that originally appeared as a children's book, *A Coyote Columbus Story* in (1992). (King has written three more children's books: *Coyote Sings to the Moon*, 1998; *Coyote's Suit*, 1999; and *A Coyote Solstice Tale*, 2009). 'A Coyote Columbus Story' was reprinted, in revised form, along with a number of similarly told stories in his first short-story collection, *One Good Story, That One* (1993). There, King's use of an oral style ('You know, I hear this story up north') allows him to break free of established conventions. As well, he employs Coyote, the Native trickster figure, because 'trickster . . . allows us to create a particular kind of world in which the Judeo-Christian concern with good and evil and order and disorder is replaced with the more Native concern for balance and harmony.'

King extends Coyote's shape-shifting trickiness to his own handling of traditional narrative materials, changing the rules of the story as he goes along and challenging his reader to keep up. His Coyote is multiple, existing both in the age of pre-European contact and in the present of contemporary technology. A mercurial figure in a world that is itself unstable, he can, for example, change gender freely. Margaret Atwood has written of *One Good Story, That*

One, 'As narrations they are exquisitely timed. . . . They ambush the reader. They get the knife in, not by whacking you over the head with their own moral righteousness, but by being funny' (*Canadian Literature*, No. 124–5).

King's broadly comic second novel, *Green Grass, Running Water* (1993), combines the realism of *Medicine River* with these oral storytelling techniques and a world in which time, space, and matter are unstable to produce a fabulist and often surreal narrative. The novel further blends stories of the contemporary Native community, domestic life, and political activism with a range of allusions to the Bible, to both Native and non-Native myth, to Canadian and American literature and history, and to popular narratives and icons—all framed by stories about the creation of the world.

In 1995, King joined the Department of English at the University of Guelph, where he currently teaches Native literature and creative writing. His third novel, *Truth and Bright Water*, published in 1999, is about two neighbouring Native communities separated by the Canada–US border. Drawing on indigenous myths and narratives about the displacement of the Cherokee people after European settlement and the effects of that uprooting on the generations that followed, it is filled with doubles and doubling of all kinds and features the 'famous Indian artist' Monroe Swimmer, an enigmatic figure who, believing 'realism will only take you so far,' uses his art to restore what has been lost. In *A Short History of Indians in Canada* (2005), a second collection of stories, King employs his own brand of magic realism and makes playful use of the artifacts of popular culture to escape the postcolonial narrative of victimhood and despair.

King has also done extensive work for radio and television. He was story editor for *Four Directions*, a CBC television series by and about First Nations people and their storytelling traditions. He contributed several scripts for the CBC series *North of 60* in the early 1990s and adapted a number of the stories from *One Good Story, That One* for radio and television. He created, wrote, and co-starred in a series for CBC radio, *The Dead Dog Café Comedy Hour* (1997–2000), about Native peoples, government actions concerning Aboriginal affairs, and the folly of tourists searching for the 'last of the Indians and their way of life.' Told from a First Nations perspective, this series employed biting satire, gentled by comic stock characters. In 2007, King wrote and directed a short film, *I'm Not the Indian You Had in Mind*, another humorous meeting of cultures as seen through the Aboriginal eye.

In 2002, under the pseudonym Hartley GoodWeather, he began exploring a new genre, the comic mystery. The first of these, *DreadfulWater Shows Up*, introduced his detective, Thumps DreadfulWater, an ex-cop, now photographer, from California who is trying to fit into Chinook, a reservation on the Canadian border hoping to support itself with a tourist resort and casino. King continued the series with *The Red Power Murders* (2006). Under the guise of lightweight entertainment, these novels show King continuing to provoke and to raise serious issues. In many ways, King, who in 2004 was made a Member of the Order of Canada, is himself a Coyote, always at play, always having fun. 'What drives a writer to write novels is not money,' he observes. 'I suppose it's an addiction; maybe it's a desire to recreate the world.'

# A Coyote Columbus Story

You know, Coyote came by my place the other day. She was going to a party. She had her party hat and she had her party whistle and she had her party rattle.

I'm going to a party, she says.

Yes, I says, I can see that.

It is a party for Christopher Columbus, says Coyote. That is the one who found America. That is the one who found Indians.

Boy, that Coyote is one silly Coyote. You got to watch out for her. Some of Coyote's stories have got Coyote tails and some of Coyote's stories are covered with scraggy Coyote fur but all of Coyote's stories are bent.

Christopher Columbus didn't find America, I says. Christopher Columbus didn't find Indians, either. You got a tail on that story.

Oh no, says Coyote. I read it in a book.

Must have been a Coyote book, I says.

No, no, no, no, says Coyote. It was a history book. Big red one. All about how Christopher Columbus sailed the ocean blue looking for America and the Indians.

Sit down, I says. Have some tea. We're going to have to do this story right. We're going to have to do this story now.

It was all Old Coyote's fault, I tell Coyote, and here is how the story goes. Here is what really happened.

So.

Old Coyote loved to play ball, you know. She played ball all day and all night. She would throw the ball and she would hit the ball and she would run and catch the ball. But playing ball by herself was boring, so she sang a song and she danced a dance and she thought about playing ball and pretty soon along came some Indians. Old Coyote and the Indians became very good friends. You are sure a good friend, says those Indians. Yes, that's true, says Old Coyote.

But, you know, whenever Old Coyote and the Indians played ball, Old Coyote always won. She always won because she made up the rules. That sneaky one made up the rules and she always won because she could do that.

That's not fair, says the Indians. Friends don't do that.

That's the rules, says Old Coyote. Let's play some more. Maybe you will win the next time. But they don't.

You keep changing the rules, says those Indians.

No, no, no, no, says Old Coyote. You are mistaken. And then she changes the rules again.

So, after a while, those Indians find better things to do.

Some of them go fishing.

Some of them go shopping.

Some of them go to a movie.

Some of them go on a vacation.

Those Indians got better things to do than play ball with Old Coyote and those changing rules.

So, Old Coyote doesn't have anyone to play with.

So, she has to play by herself.

So, she gets bored.

When Old Coyote gets bored, anything can happen. Stick around. Big trouble is coming, I can tell you that.

Well. That silly one sings a song and she dances a dance and she thinks about playing ball. But she's thinking about changing those rules, too, and she doesn't watch what she is making up out of her head. So pretty soon, she makes three ships.

Hmmmm, says Old Coyote, where did those ships come from?

And pretty soon, she makes some people on the beach with flags and funny-looking clothes and stuff.

Hooray, says Old Coyote. You are just in time for the ball game.

Hello, says one of the men in silly clothes and red hair all over his head. I am Christopher Columbus. I am sailing the ocean blue looking for China. Have you seen it?

Forget China, says Old Coyote. Let's play ball.

It must be around here somewhere, says Christopher Columbus. I have a map.

Forget the map, says Old Coyote. I'll bat first and I'll tell you the rules as we go along.

But that Christopher Columbus and his friends don't want to play ball. We got work to do, he says. We got to find China. We got to find things we can sell.

Yes, says those Columbus people, where is the gold?

Yes, they says, where is that silk cloth?

Yes, they says, where are those portable colour televisions?

Yes, they says, where are those home computers?

Boy, says Old Coyote, and that one scratches her head. I must have sung that song wrong. Maybe I didn't do the right dance. Maybe I thought too hard. These people I made have no manners. They act as if they have no relations.

And she is right. Christopher Columbus and his friends start jumping up and down in their funny clothes and they shout so loud that Coyote's ears almost fall off.

Boy, what a bunch of noise, says Coyote. What bad manners. You guys got to stop jumping and shouting or my ears will fall off.

We got to find China, says Christopher Columbus. We got to become rich. We got to become famous. Do you think you can help us?

But all Old Coyote can think about is playing ball.

I'll let you bat first, says Old Coyote.

No time for games, says Christopher Columbus.

I'll let you make the rules, cries Old Coyote.

But those Columbus people don't listen. They are too busy running around, peeking under rocks, looking in caves, sailing all over the place. Looking for China. Looking for stuff they can sell.

I got a monkey, says one.

I got a parrot, says another.

I got a fish, says a third.

I got a coconut, says a fourth.

That stuff isn't worth poop, says Christopher Columbus. We can't sell those things in Spain. Look harder.

But all they find are monkeys and parrots and fish and coconuts. And when they tell Christopher Columbus, that one he squeezes his ears and he chews his nose and grinds his teeth. He grinds his teeth so hard, he gets a headache, and, then, he gets cranky.

And then he gets an idea.

Say, says Christopher Columbus. Maybe we could sell Indians.

Yes, says his friends, that's a good idea. We could sell Indians, and they throw away their monkeys and parrots and fish and coconuts.

Wait a minute, says the Indians, that is not a good idea. That is a bad idea. That is a bad idea full of bad manners.

When Old Coyote hears this bad idea, she starts to laugh. Who would buy Indians, she says, and she laughs some more. She laughs so hard, she has to hold her nose on her face with both her hands.

But while that Old Coyote is laughing, Christopher Columbus grabs a big bunch of Indian men and Indian women and Indian children and locks them up in his ships.

When Old Coyote stops laughing and looks around, she sees that some of the Indians are missing. Hey, she says, where are those Indians? Where are my friends?

I'm going to sell them in Spain, says Christopher Columbus. Somebody has to pay for this trip. Sailing over the ocean blue isn't cheap, you know.

But Old Coyote still thinks that Christopher Columbus is playing a trick. She thinks it is a joke. That is a good joke, she says, trying to make me think that you are going to sell my friends. And she starts to laugh again.

Grab some more Indians, says Christopher Columbus.

When Old Coyote sees Christopher Columbus grab some more Indians, she laughs even harder. What a good joke, she says. And she laughs some more. She does this four times and when she is done laughing, all the Indians are gone. And Christopher Columbus is gone and Christopher Columbus's friends are gone, too.

Wait a minute, says Old Coyote. What happened to my friends? Where are my Indians? You got to bring them back. Who's going to play ball with me?

But Christopher Columbus didn't bring the Indians back and Old Coyote was real sorry she thought him up. She tried to take him back. But, you know, once you think things like that, you can't take them back. So you have to be careful what you think.

So. That's the end of the story.

Boy, says Coyote. That is one sad story.

Yes, I says. It's sad alright. And things don't get any better, I can tell you that.

What a very sad story, says Coyote. Poor Old Coyote didn't have anyone to play ball with. That one must have been lonely. And Coyote begins to cry.

Stop crying, I says. Old Coyote is fine. Some blue jays come along after that and they play ball with her.

Oh, good, says Coyote. But what happened to the Indians? There was nothing in that red history book about Christopher Columbus and the Indians.

Christopher Columbus sold the Indians, I says, and that one became rich and famous.

Oh, good, says Coyote. I love a happy ending. And that one blows her party whistle and that one shakes her party rattle and that one puts her party hat back on her head. I better get going, she says, I'm going to be late for the party.

Okay, I says. Just remember how that story goes. Don't go messing it up again. Have you got it straight, now?

You bet, says Coyote. But if Christopher Columbus didn't find America and he didn't find Indians, who found these things?

Those things were never lost, I says. Those things were always here. Those things are still here today.

By golly, I think you are right, says Coyote.

Don't be thinking, I says. This world had enough problems already without a bunch of Coyote thoughts with tails and scraggy fur running around bumping into each other.

Boy, that's the truth. I can tell you that.

1993

---

# bpNichol
## 1944–1988

Born in Vancouver, Barrie Phillip Nichol was raised there and in Winnipeg and Port Arthur (now part of Thunder Bay). He styled himself 'B.P. Nichol', then 'bp Nichol', 'bpNICHOL', and 'bPNichol', before finally settling on 'bpNichol'. He began writing poetry in the early 1960s, and, while completing a teaching certificate in elementary education at the University of British Columbia (1962–3), he audited creative-writing courses and learned about the experimental work of Earle Birney, bill bissett, and the *Tish* poets. After teaching grade 4 (in Port Coquitlam, British Columbia) for part of the following year, he relocated to Toronto. While employed as a researcher at the University of Toronto library, he became friends with poets Margaret Avison and David Aylward and began to create his 'concrete' or visual poetry.

In 1964, Nichol started *Ganglia* magazine and Ganglia Press with Aylward; during the magazine's two-year existence, it served as an outlet for West Coast writers who did not have Toronto publishers. In 1967, he began *grOnk*, a newsletter devoted to visual poetry. Having met analyst Lea Hindley-Smith in 1963, Nichol also became deeply involved with the community she founded, Therafields, living there and working as a lay therapist from 1967 until 1982. Throughout the 1980s, he continued editing

(for Coach House Press, Underwhich Editions, and Frank Davey's *Open Letter* magazine) and taught creative writing at York University.

Nichol's creative work is notable for the freedom with which it crosses boundaries: it is very diverse and always formally innovative. Coining the word *borderblur* to convey his sense that contemporary art was no longer bounded by modes, forms, or genres, he wrote poetry, fiction, comic books, criticism, and literary theory, which was published as broadsides, pamphlets, chapbooks, and full-length books. He also worked in television (as well as contributing to Jim Henson's *Fraggle Rock* and other children's programs, he was the head writer for *Blizzard Island*, a twelve-episode fantasy for CBC) and as a visual artist in multiple forms (drawing, assemblage, collage). On stage as a sound poet, he chanted poems and improvised in wordless sounds that occupied a middle ground between jazz and Dada. In fashioning his concrete poems, he was fascinated by the technology of the typewriter—and no less fascinated by the computer when it emerged. His work is well represented on the Internet. See, especially, the archival site, www.bpnichol.ca; as well as vispo.com/bp, where some of Nichol's early experiments in animation can be viewed; and ubuweb (a site devoted to visual and concrete poetry), which has sound recordings of Nichol performing poems such as 'One Sing' and 'Dada Lama'.

Nichol's first 'book' of poems was *Journeying & the Returns* (1967; also entitled *bp*), a cardboard package that contains a phonograph record, a printed lyric sequence, an envelope containing visual poems, and a flip book. In 1970, he won a Governor General's Award for the four publications that appeared that year: *Still Water*, *The Cosmic Chef*, an anthology of concrete poetry in a box; *Beach Head*, a sequence of lyrics; and *The True Eventual Story of Billy the Kid*, a prose piece. In 1972, he formed, with poet and theorist Steve McCaffery, the Toronto Research Group (TRG). In statements appearing in *Open Letter*, TRG introduced new developments in European literary theory as a way of opposing the dominant focus in Canadian literary criticism of the time, which emphasized national identity. (McCaffery brought the project to an official close in 1992 with the publication of *Rational Geomancy: The Kids of the Book Machine: The Collected Research Reports of the Toronto Research Group, 1973–1982*.) Nichol's other critical statements have been collected by Roy Miki as *Meanwhile: The Critical Writings of bpNichol* (2002).

Nichol is best known for his work in concrete poetry (such as *ABC: The Aleph Beth Book*, 1971, and *LOVE: A Book of Remembrances*, 1974); for his multi-volume poem *The Martyrology* (nine books collected in six volumes, the first appearing in 1972, the most recent published posthumously, concluding with Book 9 in 1993); and for his involvement in the sound poetry movement. He co-edited, with Jack David, his *Selected Writing: As Elected* (1980), which includes previously unpublished work. *Zygal: A Book of Mysteries and Translations* (1985) shows Nichol's breadth: its poems range from the traditional, such as 'Lament', to experimental and Dadaist work, described in terms of what he and McCaffery called *'pataphysics*— a term coined by the nineteenth-century French proto-surrealist author Alfred Jarry. Nichol, following Jarry, defined 'pataphysics as 'the science of imaginary solutions' and his 'pataphysical playfulness is also visible in *Art Facts* (1990), in *Truth: A Book of Fictions* (1993), and throughout his critical essays. His experiments with unconventional prose forms include *Two*

*Novels* (1969); *Still*, which won the 3-Day Novel Contest in 1982; and the essay collection *Craft Dinner* (1978).

Experimenting with visual and sound poetry while maintaining an interest in traditional forms in which syntax continues to function as a carrier of meaning, Nichol sought to synthesize new modes of poetry and prose. For his first visual poems, he used the typewriter to produce concrete poetry out of letters and words arranged on a page pictorially rather than verbally or syntactically; later, he added graphics, freely combining drawings, letters, and words. After the mid-1970s, he often produced pure graphics, particularly cartoons.

In his sound poetry Nichol sought to recover the emotional possibilities of speech that were part of the oral tradition. Reducing language to phonemes, playing with homonyms, making use of unusual cadences and emphases, and (in group performance) overlaying one utterance upon another, his sound poems free the rich oral qualities of poetry from the silence of the page. Although he gave solo performances, Nichol was most often seen and recorded as a member of The Four Horsemen, a performance-poetry group whose 'readings' ranged from improvised pieces made entirely of non-verbal sounds to complicated contrapuntal verbal sequences. (Since Nichol's death, its remaining members—McCaffery, Paul Dutton, and Rafael Barreto-Rivera—have occasionally performed as The Horsemen.) Michael Ondaatje's film *The Sons of Captain Poetry* (1970) catches Nichol's dynamic presence as a performer, and he can be seen with The Four Horsemen in a brief appearance in Ron Mann's movie *Poetry in Motion* (1982).

*The Martyrology*, generally seen as Nichol's most ambitious and important work, unites the visual and oral aspects of his writing with narrative and personal dimensions, while showing his relationship to postmodernism and post-structuralism. Its volumes deconstruct literary forms and language, use parody both to criticize and to affirm, and work at several levels of intertextuality to invite many possible readings. The opening sections of this long poem build up a mythology that accounts for the structure of the universe through the existence of 'saints' hidden in words (so that, for example, 'storm' becomes

'St Orm' or 'saint orm'). Nichol's focus in later books turns from the saints' stories to a more general examination of language itself, and his taking apart of words yields to playful recombinations that combine sounds to form new words and discover new possibilities. In Book 5, Chain 8, for example, the neologism 'eyear' is both the union of 'eye' with 'ear' and the sound equivalent of 'a year'.

An H in the Heart: bp Nichol, a Reader (1994), edited by George Bowering and Michael Ondaatje, provides a good overview of Nichol's oeuvre, which can be seen as an ongoing effort to test all limits: at what point does the literary give way to other forms of art—or cease to be art at all? Can it inhabit many different media? Can it exist dispersed into pure play? By constantly reordering and reconstructing the relationships between image, sound, and form, he demanded that we reconsider not only the restrictions we tend to put on art but on all other forms of human expression.

# From *The Martyrology*

## FROM BOOK 1: 'THE SORROWS OF SAINT ORM'

my lady my lady

this is the day i want to cry for you
but my eyes are dry

somewhere i'm happy

not like the sky
outside this window
gone grey

this is the line between reality
when i hold your body
enter the only way i am                                    10

saint orm
keep her from harm

this ship journey safely

quick as it can

saint orm you were a stranger
came to me out of the dangerous alleys &
the streets

      lived in
that dirty room on
comox avenue

      me &                                    20
my friends
        playing what lives we had to
the end

     i want to tell you a story
in the old way
      i can't

haven't the words or
the hands to reach you

& this circus    this noise in                    30
my brain
      makes it hard to explain
my sorrow

you were THE DARK WALKER
stood by my side as a kid

i barely remember

except the heaven i dreamt of
was a land of clouds
you moved at your whim

knowing i walked
the bottom of a sea

40

that heaven was up there
on that world in the sky

that this was death

that i would go there
when i came to life

how do you tell a story?

saint orm you were the one

you saw the sun rise
knew the positions of the stars

how far we had to go
before the ultimate destruction

as it was prophesied in REVELATIONS[1]
nations would turn away from god & be destroyed

told me the difference between now & then
when i could no longer tell the beasts from men

50

---

1 See especially Revelation 11:18, 16. Revelation also predicts that before the final destruction of the world it will
be ruled by a man known as 'the beast' (13:11ff).

saint orm
grant me peace

days i grow sick of seeing

bring my lady                                    60
back from that sea she's crossed
tossed in a grey world of
her own

there is no beauty in madness

no sinlessness
in tossing the first stone

make her sea calm

bring her safe to
my arms

                    *    *    *

1972

## FROM BOOK 3, SECTION VIII.

\* \* \*

last take

late february 73                                                                 2070

dave & i look out towards the lion's gate[1]

years mass
             events
we made it out between the lion's paws
rear shocks gone
swerving to avoid the bumps
spell of spelling cast around us
tiny ripples in the blood stream the brain stem's rooted in
a body place &
           time                                                          2080
the lion's month before us the lamb's born in
the door
      you are not permitted to open again
enter thru the lion's mouth the man's root gets planted in
*not* to be consumed
                as tho the use of lips weren't speech
a doorway into the woman's soul intelligence comes out of
SCREAMING
        a complete thot
born from the dialogue between you                                2090

or what comes forth from my mouth
born from the woman in me
handed down thru my grandma ma & lea
is what marks me most a man
that i am finally this we
this one & simple thing
my father Leo
my mother Cancer
        she births herself
the twin mouths of women                                                3000
      w's omen
it turns over & reverses itself
the mirrors cannot trick us

---

1 The Lions Gate Bridge—connecting Vancouver with North and West Vancouver—is a mile-long suspension
bridge that is flanked by two stone lions at either end.

our words are spun within the signs our fathers left
the sibilance of s
                        the cross of t
there are finally no words for you father
too many letters multiply the signs
you are the one
                        the unifying                                          3010
no signifier when we cannot grasp the signified[2]
saints in between
                              the world of men
women
              the sign complete
the w & the circle     turning
add the E
              the three levels
linked by line
                        or the two fold vision                              3020
H to I
        the saints returned to this plane

the emblems were there when i began
seven years to understand
the first letter/level of
                              martyrdom

*CODA: Mid-Initial Sequence*

faint edge of sleep
a literal fuzzing in the mind
as tho the edge of
what was held clearly                                                      3030
became less defined
the penalty paid &
your father recognized
for what he is

for W

              HA!

the is

---

2 Structuralists divide the 'signs' we use to communicate—the most prominent of which are words—into 'signi-
  fiers' (the arbitrary conveyors of meaning, such as the combinations of letters or sounds) and 'signified' (the
  underlying sense, the meaning intended).

orange

the vague light
closing the eye

's lid

        home plate

the late P
      destroyed
leaving only b
& n

beginning again

b n a[3]

all history there

t  here

opposed against the suffering
we have yet to bear

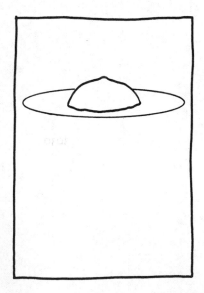

_____

3  The BNA Act, or British North America Act, is the name of the act passed by the British Parliament in 1867 to bring the Dominion of Canada into existence.

last note

no t
no e

I as no

I body
I where
I w here

no w
for w's sake

no is
    e
against the silent sleep

3060

bushes

dawn

the r rises
brushes drawn
the whole scene

the w hole
into which the world
disappears

d is a p
pear shaped

dear H
a p edges
into the sea

sun

the unenviable s

3070

there is no desire for speech 3080

there is no desire to spell

each gesture
against the chaos
must be made well

there is stillness in the heart of the power
as there is stillness in the heart of the storm

between the w & the d
the in side of
the mind /
     / 's a quiet place 3090
from which the power unwinds

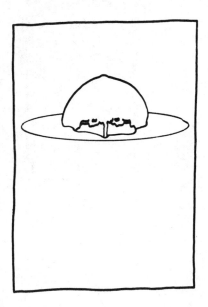

in vocation
i am
a singer

every letter
invokes a spell
ing is
the power
letters have
over me                                                           3100

word shaping

addition of the l

within the difference
if exists

tensions a
polarity

who is moved or moves
a distinction a disparity

a.d.          a.d.
history's spoken in                                               3110
the first four letters

all e to z
outside the head's
measure of our kind

man's time

1976

# FROM BOOK 5, CHAIN 8

out of the west the best rises
out of the east the beast
Leviathan[1]
        Utnapishtim's potential nemesis
a cloud of dust &
cliché in its sashay with the day-to-day
conversea in ation minor
variation
       recapitulation of
a to z themes                                        10

t hem e
   or e a
thrd yrs
     a vow the e makes with the l or a
capitulation
riddle read for writers:     cap it!
what?
   —ulation—
   ululation of its wake

roused from depths the deep                          20
double e threads our speech
full power of the beast noise
voice
we cling to     silence

Thunder Bay     roar & crash the storms made
echoed off the cliffs
so loud you thot the giant'd wake[2]
slept over the lake
millenia
    trees had covered him                        30
earth filled his pores
my mother'd hide in dread
took me to bed with her
protector from the storm

---

1 A mythical sea monster, sometimes identified with Satan (Isaiah 27:1), 'Utnapishtim': in Assyro-Babylonian mythology, the Noah-like figure (prominent in the *Epic of Gilgamesh, c.* 2000 BCE) who, as the only human to know of the impending worldwide deluge, built a boat to house his family and the earth's animal life. After the flood, Utnapishtim and his wife became·immortal.

2 The Sleeping Giant, a rock formation in Thunder Bay harbour, is identified in Ojibwa legend with Nanabozho, the famous trickster; he is expected to wake in the future and come to the aid of his people.

St Orm we've not forgotten you
you speak with voice of wind
power to bend the limbs of trees & man
blow down anything stands in the way of your word's truth
spoke with force
against the coarse lie we call our 'civilization'                              40

so i sing
stupefied by speech
brought under the spell eyear can bring
   ought          e    e              ing
thought         she sleeps         thing
emerges from the deep
the faceless dream
dreamt dreamer ter or
entered world of shifting imagery
we try to freeze                                                              50
make shiftless
because we feel less than
stored imagery's full weight

torn apart too often
that divisiveness
an isolation to protect the feared for work
valued as self is valued
defended as you would your life
'he laid it down for art'
does art thank us?                                                           60

Noel Coward[3] in the 1950's
'why must the show go on?'
the 'noble soul in torment' one does grow bored with
recognizing the romanticization
self-aggrandisement of one's own pain
we all fall prey to

you address the problems as they rise
prize what is most human as
worth the struggle
                    the will to better                                       70
your self & others
hate that poverty of spirit ignorance breeds

---

3 (1899–1973); English dramatist, actor, and composer. Noted for his sophisticated songs and plays that were wit-
   tily critical of society, Coward was less popular in the fifties when the theatre was dominated by realistic drama;
   during this period he became a commercially successful cabaret performer.

Hannah Arendt[4] speaking of Eichmann
'the face of evil is ordinary'

we build it up
look for it in cops & robbers morality plays
ignore its presence in the day-to-day
out of our own naivete

the distortion or ignoring of what is obvious
(that structural scale must remain human)                    80
leads to monumentalization
whatever the political belief
the ordinary man or woman is forgotten
because they are not known
sentimentalized or swept aside
noone takes the time to talk to them

noone t     t    t    t t    t t
seven crosses for our lack of humanity
        (akes)
seven crosses for our arrogance & pride                      90
             (he  ime)
seven crosses for our lack of humility
                  (o    alk o)
seven crosses for the people swept aside
                        (hem
'd in then

am id St Noise
the voices
ignorance
such lack of knowing                                         100
starts there

a beginning only
a tentative law or
exception
lets the self reveal itself
we claim despite our fear

                    *    *    *

1982

4 (1906–75), German-Jewish philosopher and political theorist who escaped the Nazis and settled in the United States; in *Eichmann in Jerusalem: A Report on the Banality of Evil* (1961) Arendt argues that Adolf Eichmann (1906–62), the Nazi leader who was in charge of the execution of the Jews, represents the modern figure of evil: the rational, pragmatic bureaucrat who accepts immoral commands as part of life's banal routine.

# landscape: I

alongthehorizongrewanunbrokenlineoftrees

1986

# lament[1]

cruelty     the land was
harsh     as is told you
a barren island marguerite de roberval was marooned on
in the mouth of the saint lawrence river
by her uncle
viceroy of canada
for having fallen in love with
a poor man
            he escaped the ship &
swam to join her                                                    10

this is the first european family we know of
one child is born to them
there on the isle of demons
so called because the wind howled over the rocks
drowned in sound the three of them

1  This poem retells the story of Marguerite de Roberval, the niece of French lieutenant-general Jean-Francois de La Rocque de Roberval (1500–60), viceroy of Canada, Newfoundland, and Labrador from 1540. Accompanying her uncle on his expedition to the colony in 1542–3, she incurred his wrath by becoming involved with a poor cavalier. The 'Isle of Demons' to which she was banished is thought to be Quirpon Island, off the coast of Labrador. Her lover, managing to escape his guards, jumped ship and swam ashore to join her.

later she is rescued
returned to france
her husband & her child dead of famine
rode out the storm her mind broken
by such cruelty as should never come again                    20
out of this land to haunt us


•


innocence
          in a sense
begins on   the outcrop

that we had it & lost it (maybe)
that we never had it (closer to the truth)
that we could all be to this day
marguerite de roberval's fantasy of company
alone on the isle of demons
dreaming of a country full of people                          30
a land you could grow food in
starving to death
human howling in the elemental grief

1986


# Bronwen Wallace
## 1945–1989

In her poetry and short stories, Bronwen Wallace traced out connections between the immediacies of her local region and the larger issues of her post-war generation. She was born in Kingston, Ontario, where her family had lived for more than 200 years, and she studied at Queen's University (BA, 1967; MA, 1969). Caught up in the political events and social ferment of the 1960s, she became a committed activist. In 1970, she moved with fellow activist Ron Baxter to a commune in British Columbia, and then to Windsor, where the two joined a commune dedicated to union reform. She gave birth to their son Jeremy, co-founded a women's bookstore, and worked on an oral history of the Windsor Union of Auto Workers before returning with Jeremy to Kingston in 1977. Remaining committed to social change through her work at Interval House, a shelter for abused women and children, she began to write poetry. She also taught at St Lawrence College and at Queen's and wrote a weekly column for the *Kingston Whig-Standard*. (A collection of these columns, and other essays and talks, was published posthumously as *Arguments with the World*, 1992.) In 1988, she was writer-in-residence at the University of Western Ontario.

Wallace's first book of poetry, *Marrying into the Family* (published in 1980 with Mary di Michele's first poetry book, *Bread and Chocolate*, then republished separately in 1994), explored the changing place of women in family structures. The collections that followed—*Signs of the Former Tenant* (1983), *Common Magic* (1985), *The Stubborn Particulars of Grace* (1987), and a posthumous collection of prose poems inspired by the country and western singer Emmylou Harris, *Keep That Candle Burning Bright and Other Poems* (1991)—continued Wallace's focus on women and their daily lives. With her partner, Chris Whynot, Wallace also made two films: *All You Have To Do* (1982), about a friend dying of cancer (an experience that also gave rise to the sequence 'Cancer Poems'), and *That's Why I'm Talking* (1984), about fellow poets di Michele, Pier Giorgio di Cicco, Carolyn Smart, and Robert Priest. A collection of short stories Wallace completed shortly before her death was published posthumously as *People You'd Trust Your Life To* (1990; a new edition appeared in 2001, adding a story that had previously remained in manuscript).

Wallace's poetry is often narrative, and it is always accessible, written in a colloquial manner that captures the rhythms of speech. In a fascinating exchange of letters with Erin Mouré—published in 1993 as *Two Women Talking: Correspondence, 1985–87*—Wallace demurs at Mouré's suggestion that poetry needs to be informed by deconstructionist theory if it is to resist patriarchal discourse:

*What matters to me in this whole language issue is that we remember that artists and intellectuals are not the only people who are going to change the language and that it is very important that we listen to and use the language of all sorts of people. Our language is being changed by women every day, by punks, by kids, by rock music, even by commercials, slang, and certainly gossip.* (26)

Wallace's easygoing style invites comparison with another eastern Ontario poet, Al Purdy. She was an avowed admirer of Purdy's work—though the voice in her poems is more introspective than Purdy's and less engaged in public history.

In an essay entitled 'The Contemplative Life: A Necessity as Well as a Limitation for the Writer', Wallace wrote that 'one of the challenges for me as a writer is to put some of what is missing, some of the messy details by which most of us live our lives, finally, on the page.' The deliberately rambling movement of her poems allowed her to gather and investigate these small elements and to suggest a mind in search of an elusive story that will explain the world or restore life's lost magnitude. For Wallace, stories are the currency of human exchange: 'My stories are my wealth' as the woman says in 'Testimonies': '. . . all I have to give / my children.' Memories, anecdotes, and inherited tales come together to illustrate the myriad roles women play and, more generally, to record the frailties of the human condition. Drawing on a welter of remembered details—from the first rainbow she saw as she walked home at the age of five to the small incidents that give meaning to a past relationship—Wallace engages the reader in the *process* of narratives.

Titles such as *Common Magic* and *The Stubborn Particulars of Grace* speak to the sense that from the often-overlooked minutiae of daily life the miraculous can emerge: events, perceptions, and ideas that seem banal give rise to intense experiences—bordering on the mystical. Wallace draws no easy conclusions but, as she depicts our fear of death and failure, our need for love and belonging, poems such as 'The Watermelon Incident' show the possibilities of what Wallace called 'grace'. The woman paralyzed in 'the middle of her spotless kitchen' (in 'The Woman in This Poem') is beset by anxieties: 'When we stop in the middle / of an ordinary day and / like the woman in this poem / begin to feel / our own deaths / rising slow within us.' In opposition to such fears, Wallace affirms, in poems such as 'Joseph MacLeod Daffodils', the heroism of going forward and accepting not only those around us, but ourselves.

When Wallace turned to short-story writing, she continued to investigate love, relationships, and female identity. *People You'd Trust Your Life To* is made up of portraits of individuals who seek to transcend the ordinary by discovering its miraculous qualities. 'An Easy Life' employs the clear, journalistic expression and attention to detail also found in 'The Woman in this Poem'. By the end of the story, we know that the woman in this scene of domestic order and contentment—with her gleaming kitchen and glowing crocuses—is feeling both 'anger and tenderness', and that her life is more complicated, and richer, than it at first appeared.

# The Woman in this Poem

The woman in this poem
lives in the suburbs
with her husband and two children
each day she waits for the mail and
once a week receives
a letter from her lover
who lives in another city
writes of roses     warm patches
of sunlight on his bed
*Come to me* he pleads       10
*I need you* and the woman
reaches for the phone
to dial the airport
she will leave this afternoon
her suitcase packed
with a few light clothes

But as she is dialing
the woman in this poem
remembers the pot-roast
and the fact that it is Thursday     20
she thinks of how her husband's face
will look when he reads her note
his body curling sadly toward
the empty side of the bed

She stops dialing and begins
to chop onions for the pot-roast
but behind her back the phone
shapes itself insistently
the number for airline reservations
chants in her head     30
in an hour her children will be
home from school and after that

her husband will arrive
to kiss the back of her neck
while she thickens the gravy
and she knows that
all through dinner
her mouth will laugh and chatter
while she walks with her lover
on a beach somewhere                                    40

She puts the onions in the pot
and turns toward the phone
but even as she reaches
she is thinking of
her daughter's piano lessons
her son's dental appointment

Her arms fall to her side
and as she stands there
in the middle of her spotless kitchen
we can see her growing                                   50
old like this
and wish for something      anything
to happen      we could have her go
mad perhaps and lock herself
in the closet      crouch there
for days her dresses withering
around her like cast off skins
or maybe she could take
to cruising the streets at night
in her husband's car                                     60
picking up teenage boys
and fucking them in the back seat
we can even imagine
finding her body
dumped in a ditch somewhere
on the edge of town

The woman in this poem offends us
with her useless phone and the persistent
smell of onions      we regard her as we do
the poorly calculated overdose                           70
who lies in a bed somewhere
not knowing how her life drips
through her drop by measured drop

we want to think of death
as something sudden
stroke or the leap
that carries us over the railing
of the bridge in one determined arc
the pistol aimed precisely
at the right part of the brain                                    80
we want to hate this woman

but mostly we hate knowing
that for us too it is
moments like this
our thoughts     stiff fingers
tear at again and again
when we stop in the middle
of an ordinary day and
like the woman in this poem
begin to feel                                                     90
our own deaths
rising slow within us

1987

# Joseph Macleod Daffodils

*for Isabel Huggan*[1]

'I'm planting perennials this year,' you tell me,
'because I'm scared and it's the only way I know
to tell myself I'm going to be here,
years from now, watching them come up.'
Maybe it's a phase we're going through,
since I'm at it too; lily of the valley,
under the back hedge, thinking *when Jeremy*
*is old enough to drive, I'll have to divide these,*
*put some under the cedars there; by the time*
*he leaves home, they'll be thick as grass,*                     10
and at the same time saying
'God, we're parodies of ourselves,
sixties children, still counting on flowers,
for chrissake, to get us through.'
Knowing you'll see it that way too,

1 Isabel Huggan's first book, *The Elizabeth Stories* (1984), was a linked sequence of short stories about a girl growing
up in small-town Ontario.

your snort of laughter
the index of my love and the wisdom
of George Eliot's[2] observation that
'a difference of taste in jokes
is a great strain on the affections.'
(Another thing we share, our delight
in quotations like that, exactly what you'd expect
from girls who grew up wearing glasses
into women who read everything;
your bathroom so much like mine,
a huge bin of books by the toilet
and on the shelves, all the bottles
turned label side out.
'The contents of somebody's bathroom',
Diane Arbus[3] said, 'is like reading their biography.')     30

This doesn't help much, does it?
You're laughing, but your hands stay
clenched in your lap, still forcing
the tight, dumb bulbs into the ground
as if you could force your life
to a pattern as serene as theirs,
a calm that flourishes in darkness
to the pull of the sun.
Still, I keep on talking.
It's the only wisdom that I've got.     40
How about this one: you know those
big, yellow daffodils—they're called
Joseph MacLeods—well, the way they got their name
was that the man who developed them
always kept a radio on in the greenhouse
and the day the first one bloomed, in 1942,
was the day he got the news
of the Allied victory, against Rommel,
at El Alamein, and the announcer who read the news
was Joseph MacLeod. Which shows a sense of history     50
I can appreciate; no *El Alamein Glorias* or
*Allied Victory Blooms* for this guy, you can be sure.
It's like the story my mother always tells
about joining the crowds on V-E day,[4] swollen with me,

---

2 Pseudonym of Mary Ann Evans (1819–80), a British novelist known for her depiction of provincial life.
3 American photographer (1923–71) known for her striking and bizarre pictures of people.
4 8 May 1945, the date of Germany's surrender to the Allied forces, which ended the Second World War. ('V-E' stands for 'victory in Europe'.)

but dancing all night, thinking *now*
*she can be born any time.*

What I love
is how these stories try to explain
the fit of things, though I can see
your mood's for something more sinister.                60
Like the reason Diane Arbus gave
for photographing freaks, maybe?
'Aristocrats,' she called them,
'they've already passed their test in life.'
Being born with their trauma, that is,
while the rest of us must sit around, dreading it.
Meaning you and me. *Normal.* Look at us,
practically wizened with worry, hunched
over coffee cups, whispering of cancer and divorce,
something happening to one of the kids, our lives          70
spread between us like those articles you read
about Mid-Life Crisis or Identity Anxiety,
Conflict of Role Expectations in Modern Marriages,
the kind that tell you you can fix all that
with less red meat and more exercise,
the ones that talk as if the future's
something you decide about,
though what it all comes down to, every time,
is making do. You can call it a choice
if you want, but that doesn't change                80
what we learn to rely on,
the smaller stratagems. Whatever works.
The socks in their neat balls, tucked on the right
side of the drawer, the iris coming up each summer
in the south bed. 'Be sincere and don't fuss.'
'Noble deeds and hot baths
are the best cures for depression.'

It's what I love in you, Isabel.
How you can stand here saying
'Brave and kind. I want to get through this          90
being brave and kind,' squaring your shoulders
like a heroine in those movies our mothers watched
where people knew their problems
didn't amount to a hill of beans
in this crazy world and let it go at that,
fitting themselves to the shape

a life makes for itself without meaning to.
I love your grin from the end of my sidewalk
as you head for home, posed like a photograph.
'Perfectly Ordinary Woman on Suburban Street.'          100
'A secret about a secret,' Arbus called this kind,
'the more it tells you,
the less you know.'

1987

# Testimonies

*for Julie Cruickshank*[1]

As the cadence in an old woman's voice
becomes the line that will lead others
into the territory her people saw,
you make me see
the importance of your work, the long hours
taping these languages which only a few
of the elders speak now. 'My stories are my wealth,'
one woman tells you, 'all I have to give
my children,' and you help create the alphabet
that takes them there. Linguistic anthropology,          10
the science of making language
into maps. The crazy detours
it can take you on, that story
of the parrot up in Carcross, NWT,
a bird someone brought over the pass
during the gold-rush and left at the Caribou Hotel
where it lived for another sixty years
entertaining customers by singing
nineteenth-century bar-room ballads
in a cockney accent. The voice of a dead miner          20
kept on in a brain the size of an acorn,
all the countries of his lifetime, contracted
to its bright, improbable presence
amid men who figure they've seen
just about everything now,
so that their sitting there, listening like that
becomes part of the story too,

---

1 Julie Cruickshank's *Stolen Women: Female Journeys in Tagish and Tutchone* (1983) is a study of narratives told by
  First Nations women in the Yukon.

just as I am added when I tell it,
as anyone will be, each version
a journey that carries us all along,                                      30
as the shards of pottery, carefully labelled
and carried up through layered villages
flesh out more hands
than the two that made them.

How can any of us know
what will speak for us or who
will be heard? We who are never
satisfied, eager for the evidence
no matter how it comes, slowing the car down
as we pass the accident, to see                                          40
what's pulled from the wreckage, crowding
the ones who were at the scene, the cop
or the ambulance driver, the survivors
stepping forward for their moment, blessed
by our terrible need to know everything.
Even those women we dread
sitting next to on buses or trains,
their bodies swelling with messy secrets,
the odour of complaint on their breath,
may be prophets. Whether we listen or not                                50
won't stop them from telling
our story in their own.

Not far from where I live, a man ploughs
someone's skull up in his cornfield
and the next spring, four more, a family maybe
though no one knows even that,
their being there at all,
and longer, the only claim that's offered.
Like the farms themselves, their few rich fields
the chance deposits of a glacier.                                        60
Even the ones that I keep looking for,
wading through goldenrod to a house
where just inside the door, the trunk of old clothes
or the chair that didn't make it
to the load on back of the truck
bears witness to those smaller choices
we all have to make
about the future
and what can be wisely carried into it.

What your work brings you to, I see now,
not the past. Each site, a threshold
into this slow discovery,
the random testimony gathered
as best we can, each of us down
to essentials, as the failed are
and the dead, who bear us forward
in their fine, accurate arms.

1987


## The Watermelon Incident

It was during this same summer,
in the back seat of another
speeding car, that I nearly
cut my finger off, slicing watermelon
with a jack-knife. We were all laughing
when the knife went in
to the bone, when it sucked out
one of those silences through which
blood spurted over my hand and onto the
watermelon, onto my other hand, my
knees, staining my new black and white
checked pedal-pushers which my mother said
were too tight anyway, made me look
cheap, like the peroxide streaks
Lorraine and I put in our hair when she
was babysitting at the Neilsons', onto
the grey plush seat and down to my
ankle socks, to my white sandals, onto
the floor, until Lorraine said 'Jesus
H. Christ,' and the car pulled over
rolled to a stop where we all got out
and stared. Two miles away,
the city bristled with hospitals,
antiseptic, doctors, cat-gut,
parents and tetanus shots, but we
were Beyond All That. Immortal.
And it's because I mean this
literally
that the bleeding stopped

that the end of my finger hung,                                          30
by a strand, from the rest of it
that Lorraine found some bandaids
she'd stuffed in her purse in case
her new shoes gave her blisters
that they held
that my mother was cooking dinner
when I got home
that my brother poked me in the ribs
and chewed with his mouth full
that nobody asked                                                       40
that it was after the sun went down
(and in that sudden way a sunburn
will) that the pain surfaced.
Through my sleep, my hand
the size of a boxing glove
as if all the blood still in my body
pushed to that spot
where the bandaids held me together
and on whatever cool square
of sheet or pillow                                                      50
I could find for it
kept it up: *pound-pound, pound-pound*
*pound-pound, pound-pound,*
until I knew for sure
it'd wake my parents
sleeping in the next room.

I'm one of those people
who believe that we remember
everything, though we may not know it.
Just the other day, in fact, I read                                     60
that even though we forget what we learn
when we're drunk, it'll all come back
sometime, when we're drunk again.
And that made me think
of the guy who lived in the apartment next
to the place I had before my son was born,
one of those buildings where so much
has passed from one room to another
that the walls thin out,
like those spots in an old shirt                                        70
where grease or sweat's been scrubbed at
so that the skin shines through,

so that every Friday night, when this guy
got drunk, I could hear the bottles
dropping, empty, to the table top
and by the tenth, maybe, the twelfth,
he'd be on to his mother, how he'd
disappointed her, he'd start wailing
and pounding the walls. Most of the time
I hated him, this old fart, sobbing                    80
in his beer for Mama. I'd turn
the TV up or go for a walk,
but other nights, I guess, he must have
got in with my own sounds, somehow,
like those bits of dreams you never
quite let go, until this thing
I read on drunkenness and memory
opens the door for him and he sings there,
fiercely, in the midst of all the other stuff
about the watermelon and the knife                    90
missing it, the blood and Lorraine's face,
the pain pounding out from my finger
to my wrist to my chest to my throat, my teeth
clenched over it, my parents
sleeping, soundly, on.

1983

# Songbirds and Hurtin' Songs

Of course, when I'm listening to Emmylou Harris,[1] I'm listening to a whole lot of
other people at the same time, like Gram Parsons, Rodney Crowell, Kitty Wells,
Chuck Berry, Merle Haggard, Dolly Parton and at least two busloads of church choirs.
All that proves is that nobody sings alone, though it's equally true that nobody, not
even Emmylou Harris, will ever sing 'Sweet Dreams of You' the way Patsy Cline[2] did
and that Jesse Winchester's rendition of 'Songbird' can't hold a candle to Emmylou's.
This is what I mean when I say that all lives weave that way, in and out, between all

1  This poem is part of a sequence for the American country singer and social activist Harris (b. 1947), initially
   inspired by her recording of the song 'Keep That Candle Burning Bright'. The list that immediately follows is
   of singers who influenced Harris. Gram Parsons (1946–73) rose to fame as a member of the Byrds and gave
   Harris her first musical break in 1972 when he asked her to sing harmony on his debut solo album.
2  Country singer Patsy Cline achieved wide success in the early 1960s with songs such as 'Sweet Dreams', 'Crazy',
   and 'Walkin' after Midnight'. The solo artist Jesse Winchester, who toured Canada with The Band in the 1970s,
   wrote the lyrics for, and made the original recording of, 'My Songbird' in 1977; Harris subsequently covered
   the song.

that we share and all that we don't, manners and mystery, History and the moment I get called on, as you do, to be nobody but me.

And since you already know all that, you'll also know what I mean when I say there's nothing like country for a hurtin' song, something to do with steel strings, I think, and the way a country voice isn't afraid to let you hear the places where it breaks, that twang it gets from carrying bluegrass and gospel a little further west.

A voice like that knows something about how to carry longing, too. I mean the hard, practical work of it, day to day. How Emmylou gets over it just long enough to let her heartache mend and then starts loving him again, her voice filling every note until it cracks and everything she's lost spills over, filling me up with all I have to lose, until I'm clumsy with the weight of it. How it's just that—in the voice—that shows me what I can't find by myself. How it sings on, using its breaking to do it.

1991

## An Easy Life

Right now, Marion is giving her kitchen its once-a-year major cleaning, right down to that little crack where the gunk builds up between the counter and the metal edge of the sink. She's going at it with Comet and an old toothbrush, singing along to the Talking Heads on her Walkman, having a great time. She smoked a joint with her coffee before she started this morning. It helps. She's already done the fridge, the stove, *and* the oven, wiped down the walls. Just the counters and drawers to go, really. Then the floor. Marion does a little dance over to the cupboard for the Lysol.

It's a beautiful day. The patio door is half open and the air that blows in is real spring air without that underscent of snow. Crocuses glow in creamy pools of purple and gold, all along the stone path to the garden. Soon, there'll be daffodils, tulips. And hyacinths, Marion's favourite, their sweet, heavy scent filling the kitchen, outrageous, it always seems to Marion, like the smell of sex.

Marion has thick auburn hair and the fine, almost translucent complexion that often goes with it. These days, she's got it cut short with longer wisps over her forehead and at the back of her neck. She has always been beautiful, not in any regular, classic way, certainly, but because she has the kind of bone structure that can give a face movement. At forty-two, her beauty seems deeper, more complex than it ever was, as if it's just beginning to discover all its possibilities. Everyone who knows Marion acknowledges how beautiful she is. The other thing they say is that she seems to have a very easy life.

She was born Marion Patterson, the youngest of three, the only daughter of a Home Economics teacher and a high school principal. Her health was always excellent, her teeth straight. She watched 'Howdy Doody' and 'Father Knows Best' and saw the first-time appearances on 'The Ed Sullivan Show' of both Elvis Presley and The

Beatles. In school she was one of those people who manage to get high marks without being a browner and at the same time is pretty, popular, and good at sports.

All of this had its predictable effect when she entered university. After her first class, English 101, Marion walked directly to the centre of the campus where a long-haired boy with deep-set, deep-brown eyes was handing out leaflets. END CANADIAN COMPLICITY IN VIETNAM, they said. Below that was the time and place of a meeting. Marion took a leaflet. She also went to the meeting.

By Christmas she was spending most of her time in the coffee shop reading *Ramparts* and *I.F. Stone's Biweekly,*[1] and talking to anyone who would listen about what she read. She wore short skirts, fishnet stockings, and turtleneck sweaters in dark colours. Her hair was long then, straight down her back, almost to her waist, and her face was sharper than it is now, vibrant in an almost aggressive way that some men found intimidating.

One man who was not intimidated was Carl Walker, a second-year art student who spent his afternoons in the coffee shop smoking and sketching. Marion had one of the strongest profiles he'd ever seen. In April, Carl and Marion were arrested at a demonstration outside the US Embassy in Toronto.

That summer they were married. Marion wore a long, red Indian cotton skirt, a tie-dyed T-shirt, and a crown of daisies and black-eyed Susans. Carl wore blue jeans, a loose white shirt, and a button that said, L.B.J. L.B.J. HOW MANY KIDS DID YOU KILL TODAY? Back at school, their tiny apartment was the favourite hangout of campus politicos. Carl made huge pots of chili, Marion rolled the joints, and everyone argued with their mouths full. Over the stereo was a poster showing the profiles of Karl Marx, Mao Tse Tung, and Ho Chi Minh. SOME PEOPLE TALK ABOUT THE WEATHER, it said above the profiles. And below, in larger letters, WE DON'T.

When Marion got pregnant, she and Carl decided to quit university and find a place in the country. They could grow their own food, Carl would continue painting, Marion would read.

'Who needs a degree?' Marion said.

'Just you wait,' replied Marion's women friends, among whom feminism (or Women's Lib as it was then called) was making rapid advances. 'Wait'll you have a colicky baby and it's thirty below outside. Carl'll go on painting the great male masterpiece and you'll be up to your elbows in shit.'

Not so, however. Jason Dylan Walker was rapidly followed by Benjamin Joplin and Joshua Guthrie. All of Marion's labours were short, the boys were born undrugged, screaming red and perfectly formed. Carl was always there. He was—and still is—an enthusiastic parent, willing to do his share. He also kept on painting and managed to mount two highly acclaimed shows in six years. His paintings began to sell for very respectable prices.

Both Marion and Carl took pride in their organic vegetable garden and were keenly involved in a protest that stopped Ontario Hydro from building transmitter towers through a strip of choice farmland in their community. Marion raised chickens, Carl baked bread, and they both spent hours taking the boys for walks in the woods around their farm. When Josh was five, Marion decided to go back to school. Carl's growing reputation got him an excellent faculty position in the art department of a small community college, they moved into the city, and Marion got her Masters in Psychology and Education. For the last five years, she has been a guidance counsellor at Centennial Secondary School. She is good at what she does. Not only do most of the kids like her, they sometimes listen to some of what she has to say. What's more, some of what she has to say is actually relevant to their lives as they see them.

Of course, Marion and Carl argue, who doesn't. And sometimes they both wonder what it would have been like if they'd waited a while, met other people, maybe travelled a little, if they hadn't been, well, so *young*. On the other hand, they also believe you have to go with what's happening at the time. Surprising as it may seem, this attitude still works for them.

Or so Marion says.

'Oh, Marion,' her friends reply, only half-laughing. 'Wake up. Look around. The sixties are over.'

Marion knows what they're getting at, of course. For every Marion Walker, married at eighteen and having three kids bang, bang, bang, who ends up cleaning her spacious kitchen in her tasteful house on her tasteful street, a little stoned and more beautiful than she was twenty years ago, there are thousands of others with their teeth rotted and their bodies gone to flab on Kraft Dinner and Wonder Bread, up to their eyeballs in shit. Women whose husbands left them (as, in fact, Marion's own brother, Jeff, left his first wife, Sandra, with a three year old and a set of twins, with no degree because she'd worked to put him through med school and with support payments based on his last year as a resident rather than his present salary as a pediatrician), or, worse yet, women whose husbands are still around, taking it out on them, women who are beaten, whose kids end up in jail or ruined by drugs or . . .

Or take Tracey Harper, for example. She's just come home from her Saturday afternoon shift at Harvey's. The kitchen is scrupulously clean, as it always is, and on the table, in exactly the same spot as last Saturday and the Saturday before and every day after school for as long as she can remember, is a note in her mother's thick, wavery writing: '*Your supper's in the fridge. Just heat and eat. Love, Leslie.*'

In the living room, the television is on full-blast, as always, 'Wheel of Fortune' is half over, and Leslie is sprawled on the couch, sound asleep, mouth open, snoring. On the table beside her, in a row, is a bottle of Maalox, a bottle of Coke, a bottle of rum, an empty glass, and an empty package of Export 'A's. If Leslie were still awake, which would be unusual, she would light a cigarette, take two drags, put it in the ashtray, take two sips of rum and Coke, a sip of Maalox, two more drags of her cigarette, and so on, never breaking her pattern until she ran out or passed out, whichever came first. It's by the same rigorous adherence to a system that she manages to keep her kitchen clean and food on the table for her daughter.

In so doing, she has done one helluva lot better—and she would be the first to tell you this—than her own mother. Like Tracey, Leslie came home to her mother passed out on the couch and the television blaring. Where Tracey stands in the doorway and watches men and women win glamorous merchandise and large sums of money on

'Wheel of Fortune', Leslie would stand and watch women's wildest dreams come true, right there, on 'Queen For a Day'. What's changed (besides the television shows, of course) is that Tracey comes home to a clean kitchen and a meal, whereas Leslie came home to a shithole and nothing to eat. The other thing that's changed is that she, Leslie, has managed to keep her boyfriends out of Tracey's bed, which is more than her mother ever did for her.

What hasn't changed (besides the idea that winning something will improve your life): Tracey's eyes and her way of standing in the doorway, both of which are exactly like her mother's. Already she has the look and posture of someone whose parents abandoned her early. It doesn't matter to what—drugs, alcohol, violence, madness, or death—she has that look. That particular sadness which starts in the eyes and goes bone-deep, displacing all traces of the child she was, leaving the shoulders stiff and thin, all their suppleness and softness gone for good. The softness that some of us are allowed to carry (that Marion Walker carries, for example) a good distance into our lives.

So Tracey is standing in the doorway of the living room, waiting for her supper to heat up, watching her mother sleep. Her mother is only seventeen years older than she is, which makes her thirty-four, but she looks about sixty. Her belly bloats out over the waistband of her jeans and the skin that shows, in the space between her jeans and her T-shirt, is grey and puckered. If statistics are anything to live by (and surely they're as reliable as game shows), Leslie will be dead in five to ten years. *How* is still being decided by her cells. Will it be her stomach, where the ulcer has already made its presence known? Her heart or her lungs, whose complaints she hears but manages to ignore? Right now, her cells are deciding her future.

As indeed Tracey's cells are deciding hers. If she goes back to her boyfriend Kevin's tonight after the movies, as she usually does, she will get pregnant. Everything in her body (the delicate balance of hormones controlled by her pituitary gland, the ripened ovum swimming in her right fallopian tube) is ready. In one sense, her pregnancy has already been decided. Statistically, it's almost inevitable. If it actually occurs, then, given that course of events which are so usual as to seem almost natural, Tracey may replace Leslie in a few years, exactly as she is—passed out, bloated on the couch.

Lately, though, Tracey is beginning to think that maybe it isn't such a great idea after all, dropping out of school and living together, which is what she and Kevin are planning to do as soon as he gets on at Petro-Can.

What she is hearing, under the chatter of the TV and her mother's snoring and the sausages hissing in the pan behind her and her own confused thoughts, is the voice of her guidance counsellor at school, Mrs Walker, who is one of the weirdest people Tracey has ever met. Sometimes they don't even talk, for fuck sake, they go to the mall and try on clothes. Seriously.

But what Mrs Walker is saying now inside Tracey's head is: *Well, really, Tracey, your marks aren't that bad, you know. And you've got more experience of life than most kids your age. What you've gotta decide is how you're going to use that to your advantage. Any ideas?*

And then Tracey is amazed to hear her own voice, there, inside her head. As amazed as she was last Wednesday, when she heard herself say: *Well, I always thought I might like to be a physiotherapist.*

Physiotherapist. Yeah, right. She'd just read it on one of those stupid pamphlets they have outside the guidance office.

*That's not a bad idea, Tracey,* Mrs Walker is saying now, *I think you'd be really good at that. In some ways working with people who've been injured might be a little like helping your mom. Now you'd have to go to university, so we're going to have to figure out some money schemes but I . . .*

And then she goes on, laying it all out like it's possible, and now Tracey sometimes thinks that maybe it just is. She walks over to the TV, turns it off, goes to the couch and picks up the empty glass and the cigarette pack, butts the last cigarette, which is stinking up the ashtray. She takes the glass, the full ashtray, and the empty pack to the kitchen counter, comes back and eases her mother's body gently along the couch a little ways so that her neck isn't cramped over the arm like that. Then she gets her sausages and macaroni from the stove and heads for her room.

Already, she's thinking she might tell Kevin she doesn't want to go out tonight, though it's hard to imagine having the nerve to actually say that to him. Right now, it's just sort of there, like a buzzy place, inside her head. Right now, she's just going to eat her supper and study for her math exam. Then she'll see.

Marion fills the sink with hot water, adds detergent and a few drops of Javex, and dumps in the contents of the left-hand middle drawer, the one where she keeps all the stuff she hardly ever uses. Tea strainers, pie servers, cookie cutters, two ice picks, and a couple of those things you use to make little scoops of melon for fruit salads.

'Melon ballers', the boys call them.

Outside, she can see Ben and Josh sorting stuff for a garage sale tomorrow, hauling everything into the driveway and organizing it into piles. Hockey sticks and skates, a huge box of Lego. Jason's old ten-speed, a bunch of flippers and some diving masks, tennis racquets, a badminton set, ski poles. They lift and carry the awkward bundles with ease, competent and serious. Even Josh is almost past the gangly stage, almost completely at home in the body he'll live in for the rest of his life.

A body that seems so much like a stranger's to Marion these days, even as she watches him, his every movement familiar. It's hard to believe she used to take it so for granted. All of it. The rooting motions their mouths made when she picked them up to nurse. The ease with which she oiled and powdered their bums, handling their penises as casually as she'd handle her own breasts, pushing back their foreskins to check for redness, helping them aim over the potty when she was training them. It doesn't seem possible.

Marion wipes out the drawer with a damp cloth, empties the sink, starts drying the stuff and putting it back, automatically, still watching the boys. Sometimes she doesn't know and it scares her. She can feel it, inside, what she doesn't know. It's like when she miscarried between Jason and Ben and how, even before the blood came, from the very beginning, she knew something was wrong, terribly wrong and there was nothing she could do about it even though it was there, right there, inside her own body. She can feel the cold sweat of it, the way she felt it then, all over her.

And no one else seems to notice, that's what really gets to her, they seem to see her as, well, *finished,* somehow. Carl and the boys. Or the kids she sees at work, other people's kids, as precious and impossible as her own. That she should be expected, should get *paid*, to sit in an office and tell other people's kids what to do with their lives seems crazy to her sometimes. Crazier that they listen.

Ben and Josh turn suddenly and see her in the window. They wave vigorously and Ben gets onto his old skateboard, mouthing something Marion can't hear with the Walkman on and the window between them. She shakes her head, but he keeps on, tilting the skateboard wildly, his arms waving a crazy semaphore, insisting on her attention. It reminds her of when they were little, all crowded around her, and she'd send them outside, just long enough for a coffee or to talk to Carl for a few minutes. How every two seconds they'd be at the door, wanting her to watch something or do something.

It used to drive her crazy sometimes. Still does. Even now as she waves, shaking her head again, vigorously this time, she can feel that familiar pulse of irritation at her temples, quick and absolute as the swell of love that comes with it.

Anger and tenderness. That she can feel so many conflicting things, that she can know so little about anything she feels and still manage to appear a competent adult. Sometimes it scares her. Knowing there's no end to feeling like this, ever.

The best Tracey Harper can do right now is to crouch behind the chest of drawers in her bedroom and listen as Kevin bangs and bangs and bangs on the door to the apartment. Before, it was the phone ringing and ringing and ringing. Her mother has slept through it all, which, even for her, is amazing.

'All right, bitch. I know you're in there.' Kevin gives the door a kick.

Silence.

Then Tracey hears him stomp down the stairs, she hears the outer door bang shut. In a few minutes his car squeals off down the street. Tracey can see it perfectly, the dark blue, rusted-out '78 Firebird and Kevin inside, his knuckles white around the steering wheel, really fuckin' pissed off.

For a minute she thinks of getting up, going out, trying to find him. It would be a lot easier than this is. She wishes she'd never met that fucking bitch Walker. Now she's going to have to spend her time avoiding Kevin, who will be on her ass every goddamn minute. Phoning her at all hours, following her to and from school. All she'll be able to do is ignore him and keep on walking.

Even when he grabs her arm, hard, next Friday afternoon and pulls her towards him. Even when she has to kick him, she won't speak, she'll just get the fuck out of there and keep on going. It's all she can do.

And it isn't Kevin's fault, either. Though he's acting like a jerk right now, he's an okay guy. Next week he'll get on at Petro-Can, and had he and Tracey gone through with their plan, everything might have worked out fine for them, statistics be damned.

As it is, Tracey will spend the next three weeks sitting silent in Marion Walker's office, not even looking at her, arms clamped around her chest as if it takes her whole strength to hold its contents in.

She will look a lot the way she looks now, crouching against the wall of her bedroom, hugging her knees to her chest as if the effort of keeping them from jumping up, running into the hallway and never stopping till she finds Kevin, wherever he is, takes everything she's got.

Which it does.

Drawers and counters done, Marion goes to the cupboard for the pail and sponge mop, but before she starts the floors, she fills the coffeemaker and turns it on so that it will be ready when she is. She puts a new tape—*Patsy Cline's Greatest Hits*—into the Walkman and gets down on her knees to do the tough spots near the sink and under the edge of the stove. A whiff of Lysol stings her nose. Once the hard stuff's loosened, she does the rest with the mop, singing again, having a great time.

Sometimes what Marion thinks is simply that she's lucky to have such an easy life. 'Karma' some of their friends used to call it, hanging out at the farm, smoking black hash, letting the boys run naked through the fields.

Other times she knows damn well it's because of Carl and their double income, her education, her parents' double income even, everything that's made her luck possible. Political, not spiritual, and she should damn well face up to what that means. Whatever that means.

Sometimes she just doesn't know, and it scares her.

Besides, who knows what will happen next, even in an easy life. In five minutes, for example, Jason will be driving in from the mall where he works part-time as a clerk at Music World, speeding, already late to pick up his girlfriend, Karen. While in an apartment nearby, someone else knocks back his last beer and climbs into his car to go get more before his friends show up. Two cars, both driven by teenage boys, hurtle towards each other, like sonar blips on a great map of possibilities, like cells gone haywire. Marion's own death ticks in her cells as it does in anybody's. Anything can happen, any time.

Still crouching behind her dresser, Tracey Harper has fallen asleep. She is dreaming. In the dream she is in a red Corvette convertible, moving very fast along a highway which is like a highway in a cartoon show, with flowers springing up on all sides, and birds and rainbows filling the sky. Mrs Walker is driving and the two of them are laughing and eating triple-scoop French chocolate ice-cream cones from Baskin-Robbins. The dream is so vivid that Tracey can taste the cold chocolate on her tongue and feel the wind in her hair. She can hear herself laughing and laughing, and in the dream she reaches over and puts her hand, just there, for a moment, on Mrs Walker's arm. In the dream, she has no idea where they are going.

Meanwhile, a few blocks away, Jason pulls up in front of Karen's place, gets out of the car and goes around to the back porch where she is waiting for him in brand-new acid-washed jeans and a yellow sweatshirt, one of her mother's daffodils stuck behind her ear.

Meanwhile, Marion's kitchen gleams, the sun shines through the window, the crocuses pulse and shimmer as the afternoon wanes. Marion pushes the mop and pail into the corner and tiptoes around the edge of the floor to the coffeemaker, pours herself a cup, and tiptoes back towards the patio door.

The breeze feels wonderful on her hot face. She wipes the sweat off her forehead with the back of her hand as she steps out, and that for some reason makes her think of the day she took Tracey Harper to the mall because she couldn't think of anything else to do and how they'd tried on clothes and makeup in The Bay. Tracey wanted to do Marion's face and she let her though she never wears makeup. Now, she can feel Tracey's fingertips again on her eyelids and her cheeks. They stick slightly, pulling at her skin, as if Tracey is pressing too hard, exasperated with something she sees there, something she can't erase or alter. And at the same time, they flutter and soothe, almost as a lover's would.

Anger and tenderness. From nowhere, Marion feels the tears start. On the Walkman Patsy Cline is singing one of those songs that someone sings when they've been ditched, trying to cram a lifetime of pain into every note.

And so Marion just stands there, on her patio, with a cup of coffee in her hand, crying like an idiot. Partly because of the song. Partly because it's finally spring and she's a little stoned. Because of her kids and her job. Because she's like that, Marion, soft and open, in her easy life.

But not only because.

1990

---

# Robert Bringhurst
## b. 1946

---

About his peripatetic background Robert Bringhurst once wrote that, before settling in British Columbia (he now lives on Quadra Island, in the Georgia Strait), he had lived

*Elsewhere, elsewhen. Born to migrant parents in the forties, nomadic without animals, and continued thoughtlessly but happily in the tradition for 25 years.*

He began his life in Los Angeles, California, the only child of Canadian parents. After the family returned to Canada in 1952, Bringhurst grew up in the Rockies, living chiefly in Alberta, but also in British Columbia, as well as in Montana, Utah, and Wyoming. As a young man, he held a variety of jobs, including one as a jazz drummer. He spent ten years off and on as an undergraduate, travelling restlessly and moving from one university to another, and began his studies at the Massachusetts Institute of Technology in 1963, where he studied architecture, physics, and linguistics. At the University of Utah, he took philosophy and Asian languages; at Indiana University, he completed his BA in 1973 in comparative literature. By the time he entered the writing program at the University of British Columbia, he had already published two books of poetry: *The Shipwright's Log* (1972) and *Cadastre* (1973). He received an MFA in creative writing from UBC in 1975, teaching there from 1975 to 1980 and then at Simon Fraser University for a year (1983–4). He has been poet-in-residence and writer-in-residence at several universities in North America and Europe, as well as a Guggenheim Fellow in poetry (1988–9) and the Philips Fund Resident Research Fellow at the American Philosophical Society Library in Philadelphia (2000).

A polymath who has studied and written on art history, Native history, and the history of the book, Bringhurst has travelled through and lived in Europe, Asia, and Latin America. Skilled in more than a dozen ancient and modern languages, he has published literary translations and commentaries on works in Arabic, Greek, French, Spanish, and Navajo. In 1985, he began an intensive study of the indigenous languages and cultures of British Columbia. He is also important as a typographer and press expert. In the 1970s, his small Kanchenjunga Press became well-known among poets and bibliophiles for its fine editions and chapbooks. His *Elements of Typographic Style* (1992; revised and expanded, 1997) is the premier work in the field, revered as the 'Bible' of typography and a beautiful book in its own right. In 1999, he revised and updated one of the classics in his field, Chappell's *A Short History of the Printed Word*. Bringhurst's *The Surface of Meaning: Books and Book Design in Canada*, published in 2008, celebrates the continuing significance of books as both artifacts and conveyors of meaning that make an 'intangible reality alive in the heart and mind.'

Bringhurst is the author of many chapbooks—several of which he designed and printed himself—as well as full-length books of poetry. His highly dramatic and informed poems draw on a variety of cultural sources ranging from the Italian Renaissance through Japanese Zen, the Bible, North American Aboriginal material and contemporary North American writing. Because he is fascinated by voice in all its manifestations, many of his works employ dramatic monologue (as in 'Deuteronomy'). In poems such as 'Conversations with a Toad', he experiments with polyphony to give the impression of 'several speakers [who] speak at the same time though they have different things to say'—a metaphor that expresses 'the cultural plurality of the world in which I live.' Using intricately layered voices, he takes this exploration of multiple speakers even further in *Blue Roofs of Japan* (1986), which won the CBC annual poetry competition; *Ursa Major* (2003), a polyphonic and polylinguistic masque juxtaposing Greek and Cree myths; and *New World Suite No. 3*

(2005). (Like several other of Bringhurst's books, *New World Suite No. 3* was first published as a fine example of the bookmaker's craft, issued in a very limited edition intended for collectors.) Other books of his poetry include *Bergschrund* (1975); *Tzuhalem's Mountain* (1982); *The Beauty of the Weapons: Selected Poems, 1972–82* (1982); *Pieces of Map, Pieces of Music* (1986), with an autobiographical 'meditation' and an interview on his working methods; and *The Calling: Selected Poems, 1970–1995* (1995). Using two, and at times three, colours to make the polyphonic poems easier to read, his more comprehensive *Selected Poems* (2009) gathers thirty-three years of work, including poems not previously published in book form.

Bringhurst frequently speaks of his dislike for the contemporary age, which he has characterized as dominated by a 'cult of personality and power, and the religion of money' and filled with 'ersatz information'. Never sentimental or confessional in his writing, he celebrates the entire body of history and knowledge that the twentieth and twenty-first centuries have inherited. Though his poems sometimes seem to indulge—readily and unfashionably—in high rhetoric (as in 'These Poems, She Said'), it is because he seeks 'to sing thought back into being, to personify it, state it, locate it, to clear the haze' ('Interview' in *Pieces of Map*). With Dennis Lee, Tim Lilburn, Don McKay, and Jan Zwicky, he is one of the contributors to the two influential essay collections edited by Lilburn: *Poetry and Knowing: Speculative Essays and Interviews* (1995) and *Thinking and Singing: Poetry and the Practice of Philosophy* (2002). There, he writes of the need to 'leave the conceptual jail where philosophy and poetry are confined to separate cells' because 'once outside that prison, we are . . . free to turn and find the poetry that exists, not on the surface but deep in the roots of the works of Aristotle, Descartes, Kant, and others.'

In poems such as 'Essay on Adam' and 'Leda and the Swan', Bringhurst makes use of this philosophical tradition to reconsider events from the mythic past—a recurring fascination for him, which has not only been one source of his engagement with the Greeks but also fuelled his interest in North American mythology. The author of several books on Aboriginal culture, he has published an illustrated collection of Haida trickster stories, *The Raven Steals the Light* (1984), an influential work produced in collaboration with his friend, the late Haida artist Bill Reid. Bringhurst has also published a study of Reid's work and its relationship to Haida art and culture, *The Black Canoe: Bill Reid and the Spirit of Haida Gwaii* (1991), with photographs by Ulli Steltzer—now considered one of the classics in the field of Native North American art history. His monumental *A Story as Sharp as a Knife: The Classical Haida Mythtellers and Their World* (1999) contains myths, stories, and songs in the Haida language (gathered from those recorded by American anthropologist and linguist John Swanton in 1901–2). In that book, he argues that

*A mythology is not a fixed body of stories; it is an open set. It is a narrative ecology, a watershed, a forest, a community of stories that are born and die and breed with one another and with stories from outside.*

*The mythteller's calling differs little from the scientist's. It is to elucidate the structure and workings of the world. . . . It is a kind of science in narrative form. . . . Both science and mythology aspire to be true, and both for that reason are perpetually under revision for as long as they are alive.*

Bringhurst followed *A Story as Sharp as a Knife*—which celebrated the nineteenth-century storytellers, Ghandl of the Qayahl Llaanas and Skaay of the Qquuna Qiighawaay—with his translations of nine of Ghandl's tales in *Nine Visits to the Mythworld* (2000) and of three of Skaay's stories in *Being in Being: The Collected Works of a Master Haida Mythteller* (2002). In all three volumes, Bringhurst's versions of these tales are cast in a spare free verse that owes as much to contemporary interpreters of Homer as to the Native mode of storytelling recorded in Swanton's or other transcriptions of Native tales

(such as Wendy Wickwire's rendering of Harry Robinson in this anthology).

These books aroused controversy among some of the Haida, who disputed Bringhurst's right (especially without permission of the Council of Haida Nations) to translate a literature they considered sacred. As well, some readers argued that Bringhurst distorted the Native texts by imposing on them a poetics alien to their original oral form. The issues arising from Bringhurst's treatment of these tales as works of individual genius comparable to Homer's *Odyssey* rather than as products of communal transmission are contentious. They involve the general problems of translation as well as very large questions about the nature of sacred texts and topics such as appropriation, exclusion and inclusion, and cross-cultural communication. While this debate is important, Bringhurst's versions of these Haida tales both serve as powerful evocations of a culture and a mythology and make an important argument for these works as profound poems. Added to these considerations is Bringhurst's belief that, to bring new readers into contact with unfamiliar but significant works, the translator must convey the energy and the artfulness, as well as the literal content, of the original.

*The Solid Form of Language* (2004), a long essay published on its own, shows Bringhurst's continuing fascination with the written language as artifact as well as medium. A number of Bringhurst's other essays have been collected in *The Tree of Meaning* (2006) and *Everywhere Being Is Dancing* (2007)—in them, he discusses poetry, oral literature, typography, mythology, and polyphony, and their interconnections. The latter volume also incorporates his translation from the Greek of the fragments of Parmenides, originally published separately as one of Bringhurst's limited-edition finely crafted books.

# Essay on Adam

There are five possibilities. One: Adam fell.
Two: he was pushed. Three: he jumped. Four:
he only looked over the edge, and one look silenced him.
Five: nothing worth mentioning happened to Adam.

The first, that he fell, is too simple. The fourth,
fear, we have tried and found useless. The fifth,
nothing happened, is dull. The choice is between:
he jumped or was pushed. And the difference between these

is only an issue of whether the demons
work from the inside out or from the outside                    10
in: the one
theological question.

1975

# Leda and the Swan[1]

Before the black beak reappeared
like a grin from in back of a drained cup,
letting her drop,
she fed at the sideboard of his thighs,
the lank air tightening in the sunrise,
yes. But no, she put on no knowledge

1  According to Greek myth, Zeus came to Leda in the form of a swan and mated with her; Leda also had sex with her husband that night. Four children were conceived from these unions: Helen, whose abduction was the cause of the Trojan War; Clytemnestra, whose husband, King Agamemnon, organized the Greeks to fight the war, and whom she killed on his return; and the twins Castor and Pollux, part of the Greek contingent that sacked Troy and rescued Helen. The Irish poet William Butler Yeats wrote a famous poem called 'Leda and the Swan' (1923), to which Bringhurst is here responding in detail. Yeats's poem concludes:

> How can those terrified vague fingers push
> The feathered glory from her loosening thighs?
> And how can body, laid in that white rush,
> But feel the strange heart beating where it lies?
>
> A shudder in the loins engenders there
> The broken wall, the burning roof and tower
> And Agamemnon dead.
>                 Being so caught up,
> So mastered by the brute blood of the air,
> Did she put on his knowledge with his power
> Before the indifferent beak could let her drop?

with his power. And it was his power alone
that she saved of him for her daughter.
Not his knowledge.
No.                                            10
He was the one who put on knowledge.
He was the one who looked down out of heaven
with a dark croak, knowing more
than he had ever known before,
and knowing he knew it:

knowing the xylophone of her bones,
the lute of her back and the harp of her belly,
the flute of her throat,
woodwinds and drums of her muscles,
knowing the organ pipes of her veins;                  20

knowing her as a man knows mountains he has hunted
naked and alone in—
knowing the fruits, the roots and the grasses,
the tastes of the streams
and the depths of the mosses,
knowing as he moves in the darkness he is also
resting at noon in the shade of her blood—
leaving behind him in the sheltered places
glyphs meaning mineral and moonlight and mind
and possession and memory,                         30
leaving on the outcrops signs meaning mountain
and sunlight and lust and rest and forgetting.

Yes. And the beak that opened to croak
of his knowing that morning creaked like a rehung
door and said nothing, felt nothing. The past
is past. What is known is as lean
as the day's edge and runs
one direction. The truth floats
down, out of fuel,
indigestible, like a feather. The lady                  40
herself, though—whether
or not she was truth or untruth, or both, or was neither—
she dropped through the air like a looped rope,
a necklace of meaning, remembering
everything forward and backward—
the middle, the end, the beginning—
and lit like a fishing skiff gliding aground.

That evening, of course, while her husband, to whom
she told nothing, strode like the king
of Lakonia through the orchestra                               50
pit of her body, touching
this key and that string in his passing,
she lay like so much
green kindling,
fouled tackle and horse harness under his hands
and said nothing, felt
nothing, but only
lay thinking
not flutes, lutes and xylophones,
no: thinking soldiers                                         60
and soldiers and soldiers and soldiers
and daughters,
the rustle of knives in his motionless wings.

1982


# These Poems, She Said

These poems, these poems,
these poems, she said, are poems
with no love in them. These are the poems of a man
who would leave his wife and child because
they made noise in his study. These are the poems
of a man who would murder his mother to claim
the inheritance. These are the poems of a man
like Plato, she said, meaning something I did not
comprehend but which nevertheless
offended me. These are the poems of a man                      10
who would rather sleep with himself than with women,
she said. These are the poems of a man
with eyes like a drawknife,[1] with hands like a pickpocket's
hands, woven of water and logic
and hunger, with no strand of love in them. These
poems are as heartless as birdsong, as unmeant
as elm leaves, which if they love love only
the wide blue sky and the air and the idea

---

1 Woodworker's tool with a handle at each end of the blade, used to shave off surfaces.

of elm leaves. Self-love is an ending, she said,
and not a beginning. Love means love                          20
of the thing sung and not of the song or the singing.
These poems, she said . . . .
                       You are, he said,
beautiful.
        That is not love, she said rightly.

1982


# The Reader

> . . . *der da mit seinem Schatten / getränktes liest*

> —Rainer Maria Rilke[1]

Who reads her while she reads? Her eyes slide
under the paper, into another world
while all we hear of it
or see is the slow surf of turning pages.

Her mother might not recognize her,
soaked to the skin as she is in her own shadow.
How could you then? You with your watch and tongue
still running, tell me: how much does she lose

when she looks up? When she lifts
the ladles of her eyes, how much                          10
flows back into the book, and how much
spills down the walls of the overflowing world?

Children, playing alone, will sometimes
come back suddenly, seeing what it is
to be here, and their eyes are altered. Hers too. Words
she's never said reshape her lips forever.

1986

---

1 From Rilke's '*Der Leser*' ('The Reader'), which Bringhurst is recasting here. The epigraph is from lines 5–6: 'immersed in his shadow / he reads'.

# Conversations with a Toad

I

*Not for the toad, no, but for us,*
                    In this poem a man talks
*as a prologue only: two*
                    to a toad. The toad may listen
*legends. One. That a three-legged*
                    or he may not. That, perhaps,
*crow with vermilion feathers*
                    is not the man's concern.
*nests in the sun; in the restless*
                    I suppose it is not the toad's concern          10
*moon, a rabbit, a willow tree, a toad.*
                    either. I am convinced, though,
*Two. Near water, a rock. Where a toad*
                    that the silences of the toad
*had been sitting, an old woman sits.*
                    are the most important—I mean
*She is deaf, dumb and blind. But she hears*
                    the most meaningful—parts of the poem,
*through the soles of her feet, speaks*
                    filling the dark shells                          20
*from under her skirt, and sees*
                    of the man's ears and the spaces
*through the holes in the palms of her hands.*
                    between his sentences,

*What do they mean, these*
                    filling his syllables, filling the wrinkled,
*images? I cannot tell you.*
                    stretched and invisible skins of his words,
*I learned them here and there*
                    filling his eyes wherever he looks              30
*among the Tsimshian[1] and the immigrants—*
                    and his lungs whenever he breathes.
*Celts and Chinese—who don't know*
                    So the silences of the toad would appear
*anything anymore except whatever it is*
                    to be nothing but empty space
*that everybody knows, and how*

---

1 A group of Native peoples living in coastal and interior northern BC. Remains of early Tsimshian villages date
    back as far as five thousand years, making theirs one of the oldest continuous cultural heritages in the New World.

if the poem were printed, but

*to keep silent—*

*who carry their other knowledge*                                          40
        the man in the poem would not know
*shrivelled into undeciphered images,*
        how to speak it without them.
*symbols, souvenirs. I lied then, didn't I,*
        In this poem a man talks
*when I said these legends were for us?*
        to a toad. He tries, at first,
*They don't have much to do*
        talking to us, but not very hard.
*with us, with me, with you. They are true*                              50
        It seems that he really wants
*stories. I should, instead,*
        to talk to the toad instead.
*have told them to the toad.*
        And so he does.


    II

So few bones, toad, you must know
how to count them and give them away.
You can swallow your own skin, and pluck dinner,
still living, out of the air without lifting a hand.
And you let in the weather, taking                                       60
your temperature from the world.

A toothless carnivore, an unarmed hunter. Your tongue
hinged at the lip like a swallowed reflection.
Like one who in preference to speaking
is spoken. Like one who *uneats*
bits of the world—or the whole world: whatever
is already eaten. Who unthinks what others have thought,
unreads what is read, unwrites what is written.

Nevertheless, toad, like us, you have traded
a tail for elbows and pelvis and fingers                                 70
and toes, and one mouth for another, the smooth
for the angular: traded the long
hug of the water for the abstemious,
pontifical kiss of the air.

### III

Behind you: the owl, whose eyes
have no corners: the owl with her quick
neck, who faces whatever she sees.
The raven, with voices like musselshell, wellwater, wood.
The dippers with voices like water on water.
The ruffed grouse drumming in the Douglas-fir.                    80
And the heron flying in whole notes,
the kingfisher crossing in dotted eighths
and in quarters—both silent; much later,
two voices like washboards:
one bass, coarser than gravel,
one mezzo, crushed gravel and sand.

Their beauty bites into the truth.
One way to fail to be is to be merely
pretty. But that beauty: it feeds on you; we
feed on it. As you feed on this                    90
moth, toad, or may: he met yet be
your dinner: his hazelnut tonsure,
the face like a goat's but clean,
and the mane like brown cornsilk.
Nerves spring from his forehead like fernfronds,
like feathers. He too is transformed.
*This is the last life*, toad.
Those who eat will be eaten. That
is the one resurrection.

We who kill not to eat but to mark                    100
our domain—to build and breed, in place
of what is, what we choose to create—
have reduced by that much the population of heaven.

### IV

The mind is the other. The mind
is a long complication of water. The mind
is time, space and all creatures. The mind
is the world. What we keep in the head,
with its dark facets, this jewel,
is a small, disproportional model.

What we are not is all we can think with.                          110
In the leaking cup of the skull
we dip up the other. Daily we trade it
for money, for comfort, for power. But what we are not
is all we can think with. To hold and let go
is all we can do with whatever we are.


            V


My people no longer stare into water
and fire for clues to the future. We no longer
read even the signs in our faces and hands.
Instead we grind lenses and mirrors
to sop up the spilled light of the stars. We decipher    120
the rocks that we walk on, too, while we loot them.

Toad, as we level the future we make
topographical maps of the past.

But the mirrors say at the edges
of what we can see, things are leaving
and taking their light with them, flying away
at six hundred million miles an hour—
or were when the light that is reaching us now
was just leaving them, ten billion years ago.

Ten billion years seems                                  130
long to us, toad, though to you
it is little: a few dozen times
the age of your ancestors' graves
in these rocks. Only two or three times
the age of the oldest rocks we have found.

What is is too quick for our fingers
and tongues to keep up with. The light
outmanoeuvres us. Time and space close over us, toad.
The lock of the sky will turn but not open.
We are where we are and have been here            140
forever. Longer, that is, than we can remember.

VI

Your ancestors, toad, were kings
in a world of trilobites, fish, bryozoans.[2]
Do you know any stories, toad, of a species
determined, as mine is, to cease to have meaning?
Is it really so onerous, toad, to live
and to die at less distance from being?

My people have named a million species of insects.
They tell me that millions more are unnamed—
tens of millions among the living                                    150
and hundreds of millions among the dead.

It is good news, toad: that no one can list
what exists in the world. But not good enough.
Named or unnamed, if it lives, we can kill it.
We owe to the stones
that many chances and that many means
to kill us.

In the blank rock of Precambrian time
the earliest creatures, too soft to leave fossils,
too light to leave footprints, have left us                          160
old proteins and sugars as signatures. We will leave
chronicles filled with our griefs and achievements,
a poetry spoken by locusts as they descend.

VII

Woodlice breed in the fallen alder.
Toad, the varied thrush is a beautiful bird.
And the red-shafted flickers, who feed there.
Uses will form for us too in the end.

What is is the truth. What precedes it
is meaning. We will not destroy
being, toad. We will not. But I think                                170
we will overreligiously clean it.

Yet the voices still seep through us too. Even
through us, who have long since forgotten:
to pray does not mean to send messages
to the gods; to pray means to listen.

2  Trilobites and bryozoans were early forms of marine life.

VIII

We have barely stopped binding the feet
of the women, toad. Is it true we ought to be binding
the hands of the men? Or weighting them
back into frequent touch with the ground?
Like eyes, the hands open and close, squeeze and release.          180
The feet, like the ears, are always wide open.

Toad, on the rocks near the stream
are the pictures of dreamers, and where the head
of the dreamer should be, there is a summary
of the dream. Close your eyes, say the rocks,
and dream of things seen in the darkness.
Open your eyes and dream of the sun.

The mind is a body, with shinbones and wrists
and roots, milkteeth and wings,
ankles and petals, fins,          190
feathers and dewclaws, leafstalks and lungs.
It is larva, pupa, imago, sea urchin,
tree. Ripening ideas drop from its limbs.

IX

Toad, all the roads from a man to a woman,
a man to a man, woman to man, woman to woman
lead through the nonhuman. This
is the reason, toad, for musicians.
                    *In this poem a man talks*
We speak to each other by means
                    *to a toad. The toad may listen*          200
of the bones and the horns and the bodies
                    *or he may not. That*
and bowels of dead animals, plucking
                    *is not the man's concern.*
their gutstrings, thumping their bellies, plinking
                    *I suppose it is not the toad's concern*
their evened teeth laid out in a row.
                    *either. I believe,*
The animals give us our speech and the means
                    *nevertheless, that the silences*          210
of our thinking, just as the dreamers'

> *of the toad are the most important—*
masks open the doors of our dreams.
>> *I mean the most meaningful—*
The voice is a face. The face is a vision.
>> *parts of the poem.*

>> *How could the man in the poem find*
>> *his own silence without them?*


X

In winter the mountain goats think.
In summer they gather. Thought                                    220
equals solitude. Toad, is there no other
answer? Thought is the mind walking
the ridges and edges of being, not
the tuned instruments crooning their perfect routines.

That smoothness is blasphemy. Thought
is the mute breaking through in the voice.
Like ice going out in the spring,
the voice giving way.
The language dug up by the roots
where thought has been speaking.                                  230

Leap, toad. Our invincible
greed, a dead silence, an absolute
absence of meaning, is closing.

1987


## Bone Flute Breathing

They say that a woman with steel-gray
eyes has lived for a thousand years
in these mountains. They say that the music
you almost hear in the level blue light
of morning and evening is music she played
in these mountains many years ago
on a flute she'd cut from the cannon bone

of a mule deer buck she'd tracked and wrestled
to the ground.
          They say that at the first few notes      10
she played, her sisters started giggling, because,
instead of listening, they were watching
the change that came over her face.
She stalked off in anger, and for years thereafter
only in darkness did anyone ever hear
the flute. Day after day
it lay silent on the mountain,
half hidden under a whitebark pine.
No one else was permitted to touch it,
much less to watch her while she played.      20

But a man came by one day from another
country, they say, who had never heard either
the flute or the story, and he found the flute
on the ground, under the pine tree, where it lay.
As soon as he put it to his lips, it played.
It breathed her music when he breathed,
and his hands began to find new
tunes between the tunes it played.

Angry once again at this intrusion,
the woman who lives in these mountains      30
complained about the stranger to her brother,
who lived on the other side of the world.
That very afternoon, her brother built
an elk's skull and antlers and a mountain cat's
intestines into a guitar, and as
he walked here, he taught himself to play.

Coming over the hills that way,
without a name, one stranger to another,
he challenged the stranger with the flute to a musical
duel to be judged by the woman who lives      40
in these mountains.
          It may be the stranger, as many people say,
was simply unwary. It may be
the sun slivered his eyes that day
in such a way that he could see only
one choice. In any case, everyone
says that he consented to the contest.

They played night and day, and the stranger,
while he listened, watched the eyes,
and when they wandered, watched the lips                                    50
of the woman who lives in these mountains.
*Sister*, said the eyes: *sister of the other*
*who is playing the guitar.* But the lips said, *Music*
*of the breath, music of the bone.* And the breath
of the woman, whether she willed it to or no,
kept moving in the flute whenever the stranger
played. After seven nights and days,
everyone knew the stranger was the winner.

That was when the man with the guitar said,
*Stranger, can you sing? Stranger, can you sing us*                          60
*a song along with the music you play?*
*Listen,* said the man with the guitar,
*and I will show you what I mean.*
And while the woman and the stranger watched
and listened, the man with the guitar stared
hard into the air, and his hands like water spiders
flickered over the guitar, and a song slid
out between his teeth and flowed
through the music he played.

The stranger in his turn stared                                             70
hard into the air and far into the eyes
of the woman who lives in these mountains.
And the eyes stared back, and the eyes said, *These*
*are the eyes of the sister of the other*, and the stranger
played and the stranger played, and no word
came. He stared long at her lips,
and the lips said, *Bone.* The lips said,
*Wordless breath in the bone.* And breathe
as he would, he could not
sing through the music he played.                                          80

So it was that the woman with the steel-gray
eyes, gazing into the whitebark
pine behind both of them, quietly declared
the man with the guitar to be the winner.

She reached for the flute,
but her brother stepped in front of her.
He picked up the flute and the guitar
and smacked them one against the other and against
the rocks until both of them shattered.

Then, taking the stranger by the throat,                     90
he threw him flat against the ground.
And taking a splinter from the flute,
and moving swiftly, like a crouching
dancer, he peeled the living flesh
away from the stranger's feet and hands.
He peeled his face and hips and ribs
and neatly filleted each of his limbs.

One by one he extracted the stranger's
bones, and one by one he replaced them
with the splinters of the deerbone flute                     100
and the shattered skull and antlers
that had been his own guitar.

He stitched the splinters into the stranger's
fingers, into his head and chest
and limbs with the mountain cat's intestines,
and set him on his feet, and propped the last splinter
of the bone flute upright in his hand,
and walked off, stopping to scrub
his own hands in a shrinking bank
of spring snow, never uttering a sound.                      110

The stranger stood there motionless
for years—but they say that the music you almost
hear in the level blue light of morning
and evening, now, is the sound of the stranger
moving, walking back toward his own country,
one step at a time.

1995

# Lorna Crozier
## b. 1948

Lorna Crozier was born and raised in Swift Current, Saskatchewan. She has said that she never dreamed of being a professional writer but that she always had a love of reading and writing—even though her family never had books around the house. She earned a BA in English and psychology at the University of Saskatchewan in 1969, and taught high-school English for ten years. Discovering her interest in and aptitude for poetry, she began attending the Saskatchewan Summer School of the Arts. Under what was then her married name, she published her first book of poems, *Inside the Sky*, in 1976, followed by Crow's *Black Joy* (1979) and *Humans and Other Beasts* (1980).

Crozier returned to university in 1978, taking an MA in 1980 at the University of Alberta, where she studied creative writing with Rudy Wiebe. In 1981, she co-authored *No Longer Two People* with Patrick Lane, a series of poems, set in dialogue, about the relationship they had begun three years before. (She says that it is Lane 'who always reads my new work before anyone else and who keeps me going.') In the decade that followed, Crozier's poems in *The Weather* (1983) and *The Garden Going on without Us* (new and selected work; 1985) gained a broad readership for the strength of feelings they communicate, for their intense response to the Prairie landscape, and for the way they address abuses of power in the contemporary milieu. Their vigorous style can be seen in witty and humorous meditations such as 'Poem about Nothing' and in feisty monologues like 'This One's for You'.

During this period, Crozier began teaching creative writing at the Saskatchewan Summer School of the Arts, the Banff School of Fine Arts, and elsewhere. From 1986 to 1991, she shared an appointment in the English Department at the University of Saskatchewan with Lane and fiction writer David Carpenter. During that time, she edited *A Sudden Radiance* (1987), an anthology of poetry by Saskatchewan

writers. In 1988, her *Angels of Flesh, Angels of Silence* won a Governor General's Award and solidified her reputation for frank and passionate writing. As well, the sequence in that book called 'The Penis Poems'—along with 'The Sex Lives of Vegetables' in the volume that preceded it—earned her a reputation for ribald humour.

In 1991, Crozier became a full-time member of the Department of Writing at the University of Victoria. The following year, she published *Inventing the Hawk*, a volume that draws on the stories she heard growing up, as do later poems such as 'The Old Order' in *Everything Arrives at the Light* (1995). In 1996, Crozier investigated another aspect of her Saskatchewan heritage in *A Saving Grace*, a sequence of poems written in the voice of Mrs Bentley, the protagonist of Sinclair Ross's classic novel set in the Prairies, *As for Me and My House*.

Crozier has always interwoven vignettes of daily life with myths as well as with old stories. She has returned many times to the imagery of her religious inheritance and the biblical texts she grew up hearing—with their garden of lost innocence, angels of various kinds, and a God who created the world out of nothing. Recalling 'Sunday school days in the United Church when we got rewards for memorizing [Bible] passages,' she once observed,

*I have gone back to those, in Psalms, Isaiah, and some of the prophetic books. A lot of this is very close to prairie experience—the droughts and barren wastes and the plagues of locusts.*

Her poems responding to this material frequently invoke a contemporary or a feminist revisionism (as in her poem describing Sarah's fury over her husband's intention to sacrifice their son Isaac). Sometimes, she employs gentle humour in these responses, as in her 1992 poem 'On the Seventh Day', in which she imagines that the large-sky prairie landscape is the result of an absent-minded God whose wife has to remind him to put some soil underneath all the light he is busily creating. Playing with the idea of the Apocrypha (sacred texts that were not accepted into the official canon of biblical books but that are often reprinted with them), Crozier fashions, in *Apocrypha of Light* (2002), an entire collection around her sometimes comic and sometimes profound reconsiderations of religious themes and biblical stories, of the human understanding of God, and of the need to praise.

In 2003, Crozier was appointed a distinguished professor and became the chair of the University of Victoria Writing Department. Along with a small book of ghazals, *Bones in Their Wings* (2006), Crozier's most recent collection of new poetry is *Whetstone* (2005). Dealing with aging, it has a darker tone than her earlier books. Her 2007 volume of selected poems, *The Blue Hour of the Day*, shows the consistency and excellence of a lifetime's achievement.

Crozier's zest, her willingness to write about her personal life, including her relationship with Patrick Lane, and her enjoyment in being provocative are all on display in 'My Last Erotic Poem'. She has also written two essays about her life with Lane: 'Changing into Fire' can be found in a book she edited, *Desire in Seven Voices* (1999), in which she and six other women writers talk frankly about how desire has played a role in their lives; 'Breathing under Ice', in *Addicted: Notes from the Belly of the Beast* (2001; co-edited with Lane), describes her experiences growing up as the daughter of an alcoholic father and reflects on the pain of living with Lane during his own struggles with alcoholism and addiction. Crozier and Lane also co-edited *Breathing Fire* (1995) and *Breathing Fire 2* (2004), anthologies that showcase poets born between the mid-1960s and 1980.

# This One's for You

Hey, big hummer,
who can strut like you?
Crotch-tight jeans, boots
shiny as pool balls, heels
pounding stars into pavement
you call sky.

Hey, big rooster,
who can cockadoodledo
like you do? You raise the
bloody sun from his corner          10
your voice, brass
bell in the ring.

Hey, prize fighter,
who can screw like you?
Women howl your name,
say no man will take
your place, buzz them
like an electric drill.
You spin the world
on the end of your cock.          20

Hey, big talker,
waited all my life
for a man like you.
Come my way, I'll blow
the fuses in your big machine,
short all your circuits.
I'll break the balls
you rack on the table,
I'll bust your pool cue.

1980

## Poem about Nothing

Zero is the one we didn't understand
at school. Multiplied by anything
it remains nothing.

When I ask my friend
the mathematician who studies rhetoric
if zero is a number, he says *yes*
and I feel great relief.

If it were a landscape
it would be a desert.
If it had anything to do                                    10
with anatomy, it would be
a mouth, a missing limb,
a lost organ.

                    Ø

Zero worms its way
                    between one and one
and changes everything.
It slips inside the alphabet.
It is the vowel on a mute tongue,
the pupil in a blind man's eye,
the image                                                   20
            of the face
he holds on his fingertips.

Ø

When you look up
from the bottom of a dry well
zero is what you see,
the terrible blue of it.

It is the rope
you knot around your throat
when your heels itch for wings.

Icarus[1] understood zero                                    30
as he caught the smell
of burning feathers
and fell into the sea.

Ø

If you roll zero down a hill
it will grow,
swallow the towns, the farms,
the people at their tables
playing tic-tac-toe.

Ø

When the Cree chiefs
signed the treaties on the plains                           40
they wrote $X$
beside their names.

In English, $X$ equals zero.

Ø

I ask my friend
the rhetorician who studies mathematics
*What does zero mean and keep it simple.*

He says *Zip.*

---

1  See page 896, note 1.

Ø

Zero is the pornographer's number.
He orders it through the mail
under a false name. It is the number                    50
of the last man on death row,
the number of the girl who jumps
three stories to abort.

Zero starts and ends
at the same place. Some compare it
to driving across the Prairies all day
and feeling you've gone nowhere.

Ø   Ø   Ø

In the beginning God made zero.

1985


## Forms of Innocence

The girl can tell you exactly
where and when her innocence
took flight,
how it soared from the window
beating its wings
high above the stubble field.

A strange shape for innocence
when you think of Leda[1]
but this girl insists
it was a swan, black
not white as you might expect.                          10
From its head no bigger than her fist
a beak blossomed red as if wings
pumped blood up the long neck
to where the bird split the sky.

_____

1  See p. 992, note 1.

She watched this through the windshield,
lying on her back, the boy's breath
breaking above her in waves, the swan's
dark flight across the snow so beautiful
she groaned and the boy groaned with her,                    20
not understanding the sound she made.

When she tells this story now, she says
though it was winter, she knows the swan
made it all the way to Stanley Park,[2]
a place she's never been, just seen
in the room where no one
ever touches anything
in the book her mother keeps
open on the coffee table,
one black swan swimming                                      30
endless circles among the white.

1985

2  A wilderness park in Vancouver.

## Getting Pregnant

You can't get pregnant
if it's your first time.

You can't get pregnant
if you do it standing up,
if you don't French kiss,
if you pretend
you won't let him
but just can't stop.

You can't get pregnant
if you go to the bathroom                                    10
right after,
if you ride a horse
bareback, if you jump
up and down on one leg,
if you lie in the snow
till your bum feels numb,

if you do it in the shower,
if you eat garlic,
if you wear a girdle,
if it's only your second time.                    20

You can't get pregnant
if he keeps his socks on,
if he's captain of the football team,
if he says he loves you,
if he comes quickly,
if you don't come at all,
if it's only your third time.

You can't get pregnant
if he tells you
you won't.                                        30

1992


# On the Seventh Day

On the first day God said
*Let there be light.*[1]
And there was light.
On the second day
God said, *Let there be light.*
and there was more light.

*What are you doing?* Asked God's wife,
Knowing he was the dreamy sort.
*You created light yesterday.*

---

1 This poem plays with the account found in the opening of the Bible of God's six days of creation, starting with light: 'In the beginning God created the heaven and the earth . . . and darkness was upon the face of the deep. . . . And God said, Let there be light: and there was light. And God saw the light, that it was good: and God divided the light from the darkness. And God called the light Day, and the darkness he called Night. And the evening and the morning were the first day' (Gen. 1:1–6). Crozier's having God create light more than once may have been suggested by the often remarked upon fact that the Genesis account has God create light a second time: 'And God said, Let there be lights in the firmament of the heaven to divide the day from the night; and let them be for signs, and for seasons, and for days, and years: And let them be for lights in the firmament of the heaven to give light upon the earth: and it was so. And God made two great lights; the greater light to rule the day, and the lesser light to rule the night: he made the stars also. And God set them in the firmament of the heaven to give light upon the earth, and to rule over the day and over the night, and to divide the light from the darkness: and God saw that it was good. And the evening and the morning were the fourth day' (Gen. 1:14–19).

*I forgot,* God said. *What can I do*                                    10
*about it now?*

*Nothing,* said his wife.
*But pay attention!*
And in a huff she left
to do the many chores
a wife must do in the vast
though dustless rooms of heaven.

On the third day God said
*Let there be light.* And
on the fourth and fifth                                    20
(his wife off visiting his mother).

When she returned there was only
the sixth day left. The light
was so blinding, so dazzling
God had to stretch and stretch the sky to hold it
and the sky took up all the room—
it was bigger than anything
even God could imagine,
*Quick,* his wife said,
*make something to stand on!*                                    30
God cried, *Let there be earth!*
and a thin line of soil
nudged against the sky like a run-over snake
bearing all the blue in the world on its back.

On the seventh day God rested
as he always did. Well, *rest*
wasn't exactly the right word,
his wife had to admit.
On the seventh day God
went into his study                                    40
and wrote in his journal
in huge curlicues and loops
and large crosses on the *t*'s,
changing all the facts, of course,
even creating Woman
from a Man's rib, imagine that!
But why be upset? she thought,
Who's going to believe it?

Anyway, she had her work to do.
Everything he'd forgotten 50
she had to create
with only a day left to do it.
Leaf by leaf,
paw by paw, two by two,
and now nothing
could be immortal
as in the original plan.

*Go out and multiply,* yes,[2]
she'd have to say it,
but there was too little room 60
for life without end,
forever and ever,
on that thin spit of earth
under that huge prairie sky.

1992

2  In the Genesis account, God created 'male and female' on the sixth day, and 'blessed them, and . . . said unto them, "Be fruitful, and multiply, and replenish the earth"' (1:27–28).

# The Old Order

A fear so huge
it pushed the girl from the window
three storeys up.

Thirteen years on earth
                and suddenly
she knew the air, a daring
graceful thing, then grass
hard as clay.

Her three older sisters
watched her jump without a sound 10
then picked her up
and carried her to bed.

They didn't call the doctor
until her cramps
and bleeding stopped,

what would have been a child
scooped into a bowl,
thrown in the furnace
in those days of coal and fire.

Imagine the afternoon they waited                    20
in that tall Victorian house
for their father to come home,
demanding reverence, embroidery and hours
of sitting, ankles crossed,
sips of lukewarm tea.

Every Sunday in the parlour
the dead Queen watched them
from above the mantle, beside her
the painting of the Morgan stud
their father broke in Tennessee.                    30
His eyes followed their skirts
whispering on dusty rugs,
their small buttoned shoes.

When their mother spoke
she called him *Sir*,
and sometimes stayed inside
her room for days, indisposed,
until her 'unnatural colour' went away.

The younger one
fell down the stairs,                                40
that's what her sisters said,
tripped on her skirts
(she always moved too fast),
leg snapping like willow sticks,
one, two, three.
                    Silly as any girls
dying to tell a story
yet her sisters kept the secret.

They didn't know
she could have bled to death                         50
or lay forever broken
like the thing inside their mother
that would not heal.

Two months later
she could run on crutches
beside them on the grass
and laugh like a child
at the tricks they played.

She was the one who came back
to nurse him
when their mother died,                                    60
twenty years since she'd leapt
from the window, belly
heavy as a stone.

In the room she'd never entered
as a child, she found his name
written in a young man's hand
across the first page of the Bible
that never left his bedside stand.
          A common name                                    70
she said out loud and it held
no fear

          imagine
the look on her face
as she changed him in that bed,
he who was so tall and fierce,
who begat and begat—
under her hands
                    his flesh
hot as a baby's                                            80
burned in coal.

1995

# At the Millstone

*Two women shall be grinding at the mill; the one shall be*
*taken, and the other left.*

—Matthew 24: 41[1]

She saw her sister spill her bowl,
then rise toward a cloud
as she'd seen her many times
stretch on tiptoes
to reach the hides of lambs
drying cleanly in the sun, morning
heavy with the scent of lanolin.

If the villagers had known their god
would choose between these two,
they could have guessed. The smaller                10
sister seemed all spirit, no rounded hips
or belly, no waxing breasts that made up
what a woman was. Hardly anything
to lift to heaven.

Not knowing what else to do,
the one left behind
began to grind the corn,
hands covered with golden dust
like pollen or what a soul might
leave when it ascends.                                20
She hoped there still was time
before the second coming,
the plagues and conflagration,
time to grind enough to make a loaf,
a last one for her lover.

She could see his shepherd's hands,
breaking the bread in half,
steam rising from its heart
like her body's heat
when they lay together in dirty straw         30
far from her father's terrible eyes,
he who loved her sister

1  One of the passages in the New Testament on which the concept of a 'secret rapture' is based—the idea that as the
   end of the world approaches, faithful Christians will be, without warning, taken up to Heaven and the unfaithful
   left behind to endure the 'tribulation' during the reign of the antichrist and prior to the second coming of Christ.

as fathers often loved the girl
but not the woman she'd become.

The last thing she saw of her,
rising out of sight,
was the bottom of her feet
which had never worn shoes,
suddenly unlined,
and from the cloud that seemed to carry her                    40
they wore the shine of flesh
lit up from loving.

The sister left on earth
couldn't help but think
she might be the chosen one,
her bare feet gripping the muscles
in his calves once more,
above her his belly rippling
like rows of ripened barley.

Even now as the sky darkened                                    50
over the houses of the village
was she not blessed? The millstone
turning one thing into another
before her eyes.

1995

# From *A Saving Grace: The Collected Poems of Mrs. Bentley*[1]

## Two Eternal Things

Early summer, the land wanting
colour—sienna, gamboge,
burnt umber—Philip[2] says,
making a joke of it,
he'll paint a thistle
against a rock.

---

1 'I met Mrs Bentley of Sinclair Ross's *As For Me and My House* when I was in my mid-twenties. She was the first literary character I'd encountered who inhabited the landscape where I was born. In some ways, I knew her instantly. Her ability to see the severe beauty of a countryside turned into desert was pure prairie; her sensibilities were shaped by wind, dust, and sky. One of the most enigmatic and controversial figures in Canadian literature, she has remained with me, particularly during the last ten years as I was writing these poems. The voice in her journals has been as hard to dispel from my imagination as a caragana rooted in soil' [from Crozier's afterword].
2 Mrs Bentley's withdrawing husband Philip is an amateur painter as well as the town minister. 'Gamboge' is a dark yellow or mustard-coloured pigment used by oil painters.

Two eternal things
in this godforsaken place:
rock—what the drought
cannot destroy,                                    10
thistle—what the grasshoppers
will not eat.

Call it *Hope*, I say.
*Despair*, he replies.


## Wilderness

Like Mrs Moodie I could say
the wilderness moved inside me[1]
but where there is no bush,
the wilderness is different.

It's really space that rushes at you
in spite of fences, the grid roads
laid in graphs across the earth.

A space not as empty as
you might imagine, it's a thing itself
minus details you can't separate                   10
the whole into any parts.
The worst is

        it doesn't need you.
It goes on and on whether the land
is broken or not, whether a town makes
its small exclamation mark or flattens out.

What's most like the prairie
is the mind of God, the huge way
he must have of looking at the world.
That's why I feel small and scared                 20
inside myself, and yet at times
full of wonder.

---

1 For Moodie, see pp. 108–139. This line also recalls Atwood's recreation of Moodie in *The Journals of Susanna Moodie*; compare her 'Departure from the Bush', in which Moodie says: 'In time the animals / arrived to inhabit me / . . . / I was not ready to be moved into'.

# The Sacrifice of Abraham[1]

Imagine the boy a goat,
pupils horizontal,
his laugh a bleating
wind shepherds through the grass.

I still count those seconds
when I raised the knife:

sunlight blinking
on his belly. God's terrible
desire to see the heart fly out.

Everything after                                          10
          comes from this.

2002

1 Abraham is, in the Hebrew Scriptures, the founding patriarch of Judaism, the man with whom, according to Genesis 12, God makes a covenant promising him a land of his own and the progeny to make 'a great nation'. Although Abraham eventually has one son by his wife's handmaid Hagar, the promise of offspring for him and his wife, Sarah, seems unfulfilled until, when he is a hundred years old and Sarah is ninety, God promises that they shall have a son, an idea that provokes Sarah to laughter. When Sarah does then bear a son to Abraham, she names him Isaac, which means 'he laughed'. This poem and the paired one that follows are based on Genesis 22, the famous trial of Abraham's faith, which begins: *'God did tempt [test] Abraham, and said unto him, Abraham . . . Take now thy son, thine only son Isaac, whom thou lovest, and get thee into the land of Moriah; and offer him there for a burnt offering. . . .'* Abraham makes all of the necessary preparations and is about to slay Isaac when the angel calls to him, saying: *'Lay not thine hand upon the lad, neither do thou any thing unto him: for now I know that thou fearest God, seeing thou hast not withheld thy son, thine only son from me. And Abraham lifted up his eyes, and looked, and behold behind him a ram caught in a thicket by his horns: and Abraham went and took the ram, and offered him up for a burnt offering in the stead of his son.'* Later interpreters have seen this event as a foundational story about perfect obedience to God, not only for Judaism but also for the two religions (Christianity and Islam) that descend from it.

# The Sacrifice of Isaac

I bind my breasts with hide. Eat a jackal's heart
and ride in dust to the mountains of Moriah.
Three nights I sit with what they cannot see
beyond their fires. Though I'm close enough
to touch his cheek, I will my hands to stillness.
Before dawn, our last day on the road, a caravan
stutters by, heavy with its load like something
from the past. I am too old for them to trouble me
though a boy rides up, tips his goatskin

and offers me a drink. He drops his eyes
when I unveil my mouth, the darkness there.
I swallow his breath with water from his father's well,
mumble a blessing though I do not know
his gods, their indifference or their lust.
When the groan of wheels fades, I hear
my child's laugh ringing through the grass
like bells tied to the morning wind.
He is climbing. Bent double under wood,
he bears his fire upon his back.
I wait by a thicket, tufts of ram's wool
on the brambles, knife cold against my thigh,
until the altar's built, Isaac asking,
*Father, where's the lamb?*
then I step into the open, fists on fire,
above my swinging arm
the bare throat of my husband's
Lord opening in a flood of crimson light.

2002

# Ice-fog

The air annunciates. It breathes a frosty haze
on my pants and jacket as if I'm growing fur.
Immeasurable, indifferent, now it can be touched
and tasted. It can be seen. Have I fallen through
to the other side of morning or risen above clouds?
This weight, this stillness: splendour thickening.
Down the road a dog barks. Someone walks toward me,
head and shoulders plumed with white. Father?
Lord of Winter? O Death! When his lips touch mine
they will be feathers. I don't know what to do.
I pray for wind, for sun, I pray for my father to speak
before he turns to crystals as he turned to ash.
In the visible around me hoarfrost
hallucinates a thousand shards of bone.

2005

## My Last Erotic Poem

Who wants to hear about
two old farts getting it on
in the back seat of a Buick,
in the garden shed among vermiculite,
in the kitchen where we should be drinking
ovaltine and saying no? Who wants to hear
about 26 years of screwing,
our once-not-unattractive flesh
now loose as unbaked pizza dough
hanging between two hands before it's tossed?            10

Who wants to hear about two old lovers
slapping together like water hitting mud,
hair where there shouldn't be
and little where there should,
my bunioned foot sliding
up your bony calf, your calloused hands
sinking in the quickslide of my belly,
our faithless bums crepey, collapsed?

We have to wear our glasses to see down there!

When you whisper what you want I can't hear,            20
but do it anyway, and somehow get it right. Face it,
some nights we'd rather eat a Häagen-Dazs ice cream bar
or watch a movie starring Nick Nolte who looks worse than us.
Some nights we'd rather stroke the cats.

Who wants to know when we get it going
we're revved up, like the first time—honest—
like the first time, if only we could remember it,
our old bodies doing what you know
bodies do, worn and beautiful and shameless.

2005[1]

1 Published in *The Literary Review of Canada* (revised slightly for republication here).

# Jane Urquhart
b. 1949

Jane Urquhart (née Carter) was born in the small mining community of Little Longlac, in northern Ontario. Though she moved with her family to Toronto when she was five, she spent her summers and holidays in Northumberland County where her grandparents and extended family had a number of farms. She still has property in the area and considers it her second home. While an undergraduate at the University of Guelph (BA in English literature, 1971), she met and, in 1968, married the artist Paul Keele. After he was killed in a car accident in 1973, she returned to Guelph for further study, completing the requirements for a BA in art history in 1976 and meeting the artist Tony Urquhart, whom she married that same year. They live in Wellesley, a small village outside Waterloo, Ontario.

Urquhart published three poetry collections in the early 1980s: *False Shuffles* (1982), *I Am Walking in the Garden of His Imaginary Palace* (1982; with illustrations by her husband), and *The Little Flowers of Madame de Montespan* (1983). These last two books were reissued, in one volume, as *Some Other Garden* (2000). In this poetry as well as in *Storm Glass* (a collection of short prose and prose poetry pieces that appeared in 1987) and in her novels, Urquhart shows her ability to render precise, emotionally evocative, scenes and images. The story printed here, 'The Drawing Master'—the last narrative in 'Five Wheelchairs', a sequence that opens *Storm Glass*—is about the nature and the importance of such images. Throughout this series of stories, wheelchairs are potential vehicles, literally or metaphorically, for individuals who seem immobile. 'The Drawing Master'— one of Urquhart's many works of fiction about artists and the making of art—suggests that the real importance of a work of art lies not in the subject matter but in the ability and vision of the maker of the image to make us see anew, an idea that recurs in Urquhart's later work.

The fact that the drawing master takes his students to a museum to draw objects from the past and that he himself makes sketches of Victorian artifacts is significant: Urquhart has returned, throughout her career, to the past. In an interview with *Books in Canada*, she said, 'I feel as if I grew up in the nineteenth century'—in part because 'the side of the family that I knew best as a child were mostly agricultural people . . . life had not changed that much,' and also because 'as a child I spent huge amounts of time reading nineteenth-century novels,' so much so that for her there were always 'two realities at work'.

Urquhart combines her image-rich writing with these historic settings in her first novel, *The Whirlpool* (1986; a French translation of that book won France's prestigious Prix du Meilleur Livre Étranger in 1992). Set in late nineteenth-century Niagara Falls, it makes the Niagara Gorge whirlpool a vivid image: symbolically rich, the whirlpool is parallel to a history that is 'moving nowhere and endlessly repeating itself'—its circular motion reiterated in the novel's three interconnected narrative lines.

In her second novel, *Changing Heaven* (1990), Urquhart extends her investigation of the nineteenth century as a period on which our own age has built its foundations: this tale marries fantasy and realism to show how the great Romantic and Victorian writers continue to haunt the contemporary imagination. Urquhart's third novel, *Away* (1993), which is also set in the nineteenth century, draws on oral history and Celtic and Native myth: in it, the novel's Irish-Canadian narrator, Esther O'Malley, recounts the story of her family's emigration during the Irish potato famine of the 1840s, and their settlement as pioneers in Ontario. *Away* received considerable acclaim, establishing Urquhart's critical reputation: it received the 1994 Trillium Award and was nominated for the IMPAC Dublin Literary Award.

Given the Marian Engel Award in 1994 for an outstanding body of prose written by a Canadian woman, Urquhart was named, in 1996, to France's Order of Arts and Letters. She has served as writer-in-residence at the universities of Ottawa and Toronto and at Memorial University in Newfoundland and Labrador. In 1997, she won a Governor General's Award for her fourth novel, *The Underpainter*, the story of Austin Fraser, a well-known landscape painter from upstate New York who has returned to Davenport, a town on the Canadian side of Lake Ontario where he spent his boyhood summers. Now in his eighties, Austin, a cold man who has lived a life of surfaces, thinks back over his life and its web of relationships but is unable to find a coherent pattern to give it meaning.

To her earlier considerations of literature and painting, Urquhart adds sculpture and architecture in *The Stone Carvers* (2001), which investigates the redemptive and memorial powers of art. The novel tells the story of three Canadians: Klara Becker, the inheritor of her grandfather's talent for sculpting; her brother Tilman, the inheritor of a Bavarian wanderlust; and Walter Allward, a historical figure who was a self-taught master architect and sculptor. Its central event is the construction, in France, of a memorial to the Battle of Vimy Ridge, which had been a successful but costly Canadian offensive in the First World War.

Published in 2006, Urquhart's sixth novel, *A Map of Glass*, again features characters who are artists. In the three parts of that novel, Urquhart frames a nineteenth-century narrative with one set in the present. Even more than in her previous fiction, this novel revolves around themes of change and loss, while asking new questions about the way art facilitates our understanding of the world. Urquhart returns to these ideas in her 2009 study, *L.M. Montgomery*, a response to an author she says shaped her mother's and, therefore, her own, love of reading. That book concludes with a chapter on the way reading Montgomery's fiction made her mother's own 'small community . . . become almost mythical,' giving 'added meaning and intensity to even to most arbitrary of its attributes'—and how, as a consequence, 'family tales have gained an added dimension':

*Because of her summer reading she has become enlightened to the fact that stories unfolding in the plain brick and clapboard houses of the Dominion of Canada can be just as riveting as those that take place in large, dark country houses set in sad, neglected grounds near glens and moors.*

# The Drawing Master

All but one of his students were drawing the canopied bed. Eleven of them were fixed, with furious attention, on the object, puzzling out the perspective and gritting their teeth over the intricate folds provided by the drapery of its rather dirty velvet curtains. Pencils in hand they twitched, scratched heads, scratched paper and erased. Individually, each studied his neighbour's work and vowed to give up drawing altogether. Collectively, they laboured with a singleness of purpose worthy of great frescoed ceilings and large blocks of marble. All for the rendering of a rather tatty piece of furniture where someone, long forgotten, had no doubt slept and maybe died.

He walked silently behind the group, noting how the object shrank, swelled, attained monumentality, or became deformed from notebook to notebook. What, he wondered, brought them to this? In a building full of displayed objects, why this automatic attraction to the funereal cast of velvet and dark wood? This must be the bed that the child in all of them longed to possess; to draw the dusty curtains round and suffocate in magic of contained privacy. It would be as cosy and frilly and mysterious as the darkened spaces underneath the fabric of their mother's skirts. The womb, he concluded, moves them like a magnet in all or any of its symbolic disguises.

The twelfth of the bunch was drawing a stuffed bird. Mottled by time and distorted by the glass bell that covered it, it pretended, without much credibility, to be singing its heart out perched on a dry twig. Its former colours, whatever they might have been, were now reduced to something approaching grey. The face of the young man who had chosen to reproduce this bundle of feathers was reflected once in the glass bell and again in the display case, and was also greyish. The drawing master glanced quickly over the young man's shoulder and discovered, as he had expected, a great deal of nothing. Fifteen years in the profession had taught him to read all signs with cynicism. A student who kept aloof from the crowd, or chose alternate subject matter: these, to his mind, were social rather than creative decisions.

'You must like birds, Roger,' he commented wryly, and then, 'There are some who seem to prefer beds.'

The young man's face acquired a spot of colour, but in no other way did he respond to the remark.

The drawing master moved on. At this point there was little he could do for them except leave them alone. This was usually the case once he had taught them the rules: he believed, through it all, that the rules were the bones of the work. Within the structure they provided, great experiments could be performed, giant steps could be taken. And so his students suffered through weeks of colour theory, months of perspective. They reduced great painting to the geometry of compositional analysis. Like kindergarten children, they arranged triangles and squares on construction paper. Then, after a written test, in which the acquired basics were transposed to paper, he hired a small bus and drove them to this old, provincial museum, where he allowed them to choose their own subject matter. Year after year, the drawing master searched in vain for the student who would make the giant step, who would perform the great experiment, just as year after year he looked for evidence of the same experiment, the same step, in his own work.

The drawing master moved on and now he was looking for his own subject matter. For he had brought with him a small bottle of ink and a tin box in which he kept his straight pen and his nibs. He could feel this paltry equipment weighing down his right-hand pocket, altering somewhat the drape of his jacket. Aware of this, he often rearranged the tools giving himself the look of a man with an abundance of coins that he liked to jingle. Then he shifted his shoulders back and mentally convinced himself that a slight bulge at the hip could not alter a look of dignity so long in the making. There were still, after all, the faultless cravat, the leather pants, and the well-trimmed beard speckled with grey.

And now he began to move past display cases; one filled with butter presses, another with spinning wheels, still another containing miniature interiors of pioneer dwellings, complete with tiny hooked rugs and patchwork quilts. He paused briefly before the collection of early Canadian cruets, interested in the delicate lines of twisted silver. But they turned to drawings so quickly in his mind that the actual execution on paper seemed futile and boring and he walked away from them. Past blacksmith's tools and tomahawks, past moccasins and arrowheads and beadwork, past churns and depressed glass, past century-old pottery from Quebec and early models of long-silent telephones, past ridiculously modern mannequins clothed in the nineteenth century, until he found himself looking through the glass of a window and out into the fields.

And then he thought of the drive through the countryside to this small county museum, which had been situated, with the intention of pleasing both, between the two major towns of the surrounding vicinity. The students, nervous and silent in such close quarters with their teacher, had offered little interference to the flow of his consciousness and he had almost become absorbed by the rush of the landscape as it flashed past the windows of the van. A strong wind had confused the angle of fields of tall grass and had set the normally well-organized trees lurching against the sky. Laundry had become desperate splashes of colour in farm-yards. Even the predictable black-and-white of docile cows seemed temporary, as if they might be sent spiralling towards fence wire like so much tumbleweed. The restlessness of this insistent motion, this constant churning hyperactivity, had distracted the drawing master, but he had felt the strong, hard-edged responsibility of the highway to such an extent that even now, when he observed the landscape through the safe, confining frame of the window, he was somehow unable to grasp it. And he turned back towards the interior of the museum.

Here he sketched, for his own amusement and possibly for the amusement of his children at home, two or three elderly puppets that hung dejectedly from strings attached to flat wooden crosses. Completing, with a few well-executed strokes, the moronic wide-eyed stare of the last one, he cleaned the nib of his pen with a rag that he carried with him for that purpose, and prepared to return to his class. Then his eye was caught by a large white partition set back against the left-hand corner of the room. He walked over to it with a kind of idle curiosity and peered around its edge.

There, awaiting either repair or display case, and hopelessly stacked together like tumbling hydro towers, were five Victorian wicker wheelchairs. A few had lost, either through overuse or neglect, the acceptable curve of their shape and sagged over their wheels like fat women. One had retained its shape but the woven grid of its back was interrupted by large gaping holes. The small front wheels of another had become permanently locked into a pigeon-toed position through decades of lack of oil. All in all they appeared to be at least as crippled as their absent occupants must have been—as if by some magic process each individual's handicap had been mysteriously transferred to his chair. The drawing master was fascinated. He had found his subject matter.

An hour later he had completed five small drawings. They were, as he knew, his best. The crazy twisted personality of each chair distributed itself with ease across the surface of the paper. Expressed in his fine line their abandoned condition became wistfully personal, as sad as forsaken toys in the attic or tricycles in the basement, childless for years. Vacant coffins, open graves, funeral wreaths—they were all there, competing with go-carts and red wagons. The drawing master carefully placed his precious drawings in his jacket pocket. When he arrived home that evening he would mat and frame them and put them under glass. But now he would stroll casually over to his pupils, who had dispersed and were wandering around the room gazing absently into display cases.

Except for the one young man who seemed still to be involved in the rendering of the dead bird. The drawing master approached him and bent over his shoulder to offer his usual words of quiet criticism—perhaps a few words about light and shade, or something about texture. He drew back, however, astonished. There before him on the paper was a perfectly drawn skeleton of a bird, and surrounding that and sometimes covering it or being covered by it, in a kind of crazy spatial ambiguity, drawn in by the student with the blunt ends of a pocketful of crayons, was the mad, turbulent landscape. It shuddered and heaved and appeared to be germinating from the motionless structure of the bird whose bones the young man had sensed beneath dust and feathers. It needed no glass to protect it, no frame to confine it. And it was as confused and disordered and wonderful as everything the drawing master had chosen to ignore.

1987

# Anne Carson
## b. 1950

Anne Carson began life in Toronto and grew up in several small Ontario towns before entering the University of Toronto. After interrupting her studies to pursue an interest in graphic art, she completed her BA in 1974, and went on to take an MA (1975) and PhD (1980) in classics. She taught at the University of Calgary and, from 1988 to 2001, in the Department of Classics at McGill University. When McGill decided to close the department at the end of the 1990s, Carson began to teach as a visiting professor at American universities (including Princeton and Berkeley) and eventually left McGill to take a faculty position at the University of Michigan, where she is cross-appointed to the departments of Classics, English, and Comparative Literature.

Carson's writing is known for being challenging and—like Carson herself—hard to categorize. She initially established her reputation as a classicist, publishing a study of erotic love in the writing of Sappho and Plato, *Eros the Bittersweet* (1986). However, this book is not typical of academic writing: instead, like her later classical study, *Economy of the Unlost: (Reading Simonides of Keos with Paul Celan)* (1999)—which makes connections between the ancient Greek poet and the twentieth-century French writer—it works more like poetry than like traditional scholarship. Conversely, her books of poems draw from a wide range of sources, making use of prose forms (as in her first book, *Short Talks*, 1992) and sometimes including scholarly essays as well as translations from classical texts. Carson sees this scholarship as an integral part of the creative act. In her introduction to the sequence 'The Life of Towns' (*Plainwater*, 1995), she writes,

To explain what I do is simple enough. A scholar is someone who takes a position. From which position, certain lines become visible. You will at first think I am painting the lines myself; it's not so. I merely know where to stand to see the lines that are there. And the mysterious thing, it is a very mysterious thing, is how these lines do paint themselves. Before there were any edges or angles or virtue—who was there to ask the questions?

Though fiercely intellectual, Carson is also drawn to the metaphysical, and in the poem 'God's Work' (from a sequence entitled 'The Truth about God', in *Glass, Irony, and God*, 1995), she shows herself attracted to the Buddhist doctrine of 'no-mind'. At the same time, even though her writing seems reticent and impersonal, it often focuses on erotic desire in a way that registers as immediate and the personal. It challenges assumptions about gender definitions and sexual roles—as can be seen in the dynamics between young males in *Autobiography of Red: A Novel in Verse* (1998), as well as in 'Irony Is Not Enough: Essay on My Life as Catherine Deneuve (2nd Draft)', her later tale of attraction between two women: a classics professor and a student (in *Men in the Off Hours*, 2000; it was later integrated into a dance piece by Ballett Frankfurt). In tension with the erotic dimensions of her writing is an undercurrent of violence, including natural violence: Carson is fascinated by volcanoes (*Autobiography of Red* speaks of 'people who saw the inside of the volcano. / And came back' with 'all their weaknesses burned away') and is said to seek them out in order to paint them while they are erupting. (One of these paintings appears on the cover of *Glass, Irony, and God*.)

Carson's movement across boundaries is apparent even within single works. Her best-known book, *Autobiography of Red* (which recasts the Greek myth of the winged monster Geryon as a contemporary story of spurned

love), has a title that suggests a work of self-narrated non-fiction, followed by a subtitle that describes the book as a novel—but it is neither: it comprises a poetic sequence preceded by an essay, a translation, and three appendices, and followed by a fictional interview. Elsewhere, Carson has invited connections between her poetry and musical forms: *The Beauty of the Husband* (2001) is subtitled *A Fictional Essay in 29 Tangos*. The tango (it appears elsewhere in her work) undoubtedly interests Carson because it is a difficult dance with a set of highly formal conventions that must be mastered, yet—almost the opposite of the essay, with which it is linked in her subtitle—its extraordinary technique expresses desire in a frenzy of motion.

In 2001, Carson published a new translation of Sophocles' *Electra*. Along with her versions of Aeschylus's *Agamemnon* and Euripides' *Orestes*, it was staged in 2009 by New York City's Classic Stage Company and the three plays were published together that year as *An Oresteia*. Her 2006 book, *Grief Lessons*, brings together translations of four of Euripides' lesser-known plays (*Alkestis, Herakles, Hekabe*, and *Hippolytos*), with an afterward by Carson written in Euripides' voice.

The fact that translation is an important part of the activity of a classicist (Carson describes translating as the 'mutual undoing of each language into the other') seems to have made her especially aware of the way language governs what can—and what cannot—be said. Because she wants to honour the gaps and fragments found in ancient manuscripts, *If Not, Winter: Fragments of Sappho* (2002), her translations of the ancient Greek poet to whom she has often turned, record the lacuna in ancient text with pages dominated by white space broken only by occasional words. Her poetry also sometimes calls attention to the etymologies and histories of the words she uses to remind her readers of what is lost in translation. For example, in *Glass, Irony, and God*, she concludes 'The Book of Isaiah' (reprinted here) by drawing attention to the puzzling fact that there are two Hebrew words for *righteousness*, one masculine and one feminine.

Because her profession as a teacher and a scholar brings her into constant contact with what she calls the 'haunted old phrases', Carson is aware of how those classical texts go on speaking in the works of later writers and of how the concerns and preoccupations of the ancient world illuminate our own. She responds by conjoining historical with contemporary events and technology, as in as 'TV Men', where various characters from the past—including Sappho, Lazarus, Antigone, and Tolstoy—make surprising appearances in the contemporary era. In the poem found here, the tale of Hektor becomes newly relevant and the familiar elements of the present become strange, as if they, rather than the ancient world, were archaic.

Carson also makes connections between a wide variety of artists. Allusions to Seurat, Prokofiev, Kafka, Ovid, Van Gogh, Rembrandt, Sylvia Plath, the Brontës, and others are scattered through *Short Talks*, and many of these figures reappear and join still others in her later work. Kafka is mentioned several times, suggesting that Carson feels a special affinity with that early-twentieth-century writer who treated dream and reality as indistinguishable.

Carson's *Decreation: Poetry, Essays, Opera* (2005) again displays her range and eclecticism.

It contains brief versions of operas, an oratorio, and a screenplay, as well as short poems, and essays: these deal with such figures and topics as Simone Weil, the medieval heretic Marguerite Porete, Samuel Beckett, the painter Betty Goodwin, Gnosticism, and sleep. Carson also participated in conceptual artist Roni Horn's *Wonderwater (Alice Offshore)*, a 2004 collaboration that brought her together with three other artists (sculptor Louise Bourgeois; philosopher-theorist Hélène Cixous; and film director and photographer John Waters), which was published as four short books, along with an envelope containing Carson's drawings. Her newest work, *NOX: An Epitaph for My Brother*, is scheduled for publication in 2010.

For this wide-ranging body of work, Carson has received numerous honours and prizes, including a Guggenheim Fellowship (1998), the Griffin Poetry Prize (2001), the T.S. Eliot Prize (2001), and the prestigious MacArthur Foundation 'genius' grant in 2000, which provided her with $500,000 over five years in support of any projects she wanted to pursue. She is currently the distinguished poet-in-residence at New York University.

# Short Talk on Rectification

Kafka[1] liked to have his watch an hour and a half fast. Felice kept setting it right. Nonetheless for five years they almost married. He made a list of arguments for and against marriage, including inability to bear the assault of his own life (for) and the sight of the nightshirts laid out on his parents' beds at 10:30 (against). Hemorrhage saved him. When advised not to speak by doctors in the sanatorium, he left glass sentences all over the floor. Felice, says one of them, had too much nakedness left in her.

1992

---

1 The Prague-born Jewish fiction writer Franz Kafka (1883–1924), whose work portrays an enigmatic and nightmarish reality about lonely, perplexed, and threatened individuals. Kafka met Felice Bauer (1887–1960) in 1912, and the two became engaged to be married; each was filled with doubts, and they broke it off, then became engaged again. After writing up his list of reasons for and against marriage in 1916, Kafka separated from Felice permanently in 1917. In that same year he was diagnosed with tuberculosis after a hemorrhage and began spending long periods of time in sanatoriums.

## Short Talk on Who You Are

I want to know who you are. People talk about a voice calling in the wilderness.[1] All through the Old Testament a voice, which is not the voice of God but which knows what is on God's mind, is crying out. While I am waiting, you could do me a favour. Who are you?

1992

1 In the Gospels, John the Baptist is described as 'he that was spoken of by the prophet Esaias [Isaiah], saying, The voice of one crying in the wilderness, Prepare ye the way of the Lord, make his paths straight' (Matthew 3:3; also Mark 1:3; Luke 3:4; John 1:23). The reference is to the verse in the Book of Isaiah (in the Old Testament), which describes the speaker as hearing 'The voice of him that crieth in the wilderness, Prepare ye the way of the LORD, make straight in the desert a highway for our God' (40:3).

## Book of Isaiah[1]

### I.

Isaiah awoke angry.
Lapping at Isaiah's ears black birdsong no it was anger.
God had filled Isaiah's ears with stingers.
Once God and Isaiah were friends.
God and Isaiah used to converse nightly, Isaiah would rush into the
   garden.
They conversed under the Branch,[2] night streamed down.
From the sole of the foot to the head God would make Isaiah ring.
Isaiah had loved God and now his love was turned to pain.
Isaiah wanted a name for the pain, he called it sin.                    10
Now Isaiah was a man who believed he was a nation.[3]
Isaiah called the nation Judah and the sin Judah's condition.
Inside Isaiah God saw the worldsheet burning.
Isaiah and God saw things differently, I can only tell you their
   actions.

1 The Book of Isaiah, attributed to an eighth-century-BCE prophet, begins: 'The vision of Isaiah the son of Amoz, which he saw concerning Judah and Jerusalem. . . . Ah sinful nation, a people laden with iniquity, a seed of evil-doers, children that are corrupters: they have forsaken the LORD, they have provoked the Holy One of Israel unto anger, they are gone away backward.' The most cited of the prophetic books in the Hebrew Scriptures (or Old Testament), in it, Isaiah like the other Hebrew prophets, sternly rebukes the Jews for their unrighteous behaviour. In the last part of the Book of Isaiah there are promises of redemption and restoration for the nation following reform.
2 Although the line suggests a literal 'branch', Carson is responding to a metaphor in the Book of Isaiah in which 'branch' refers to the restored community of Israel (Isaiah 4:2), and particularly to the descendants of the house of King David (Isaiah 11:1).
3 See Isaiah 65:1: 'Behold me, behold me, unto a nation that was not called by my name.'

Isaiah addressed the nation.

Man's brittleness! cried Isaiah.

The nation stirred in its husk and slept again.

Two slabs of bloody meat lay folded on its eyes[4] like wings.

Like a hard glossy painting the nation slept.     20

Who can invent a new fear?

Yet I have invented sin, thought Isaiah, running his hand over the
    knobs.

And then, because of a great attraction between them—

which Isaiah fought (for and against) for the rest of his life—

God shattered Isaiah's indifference.

God washed Isaiah's hair in fire.

God took the stay.[5]

From beneath its meat wings the nation listened.

You, said Isaiah.     30

No answer.

I cannot hear you, Isaiah spoke again under the Branch.

Light bleached open the night camera.

God arrived.

God smashed Isaiah like glass through every socket of his nation.

Liar! said God.

Isaiah put his hands on his coat, he put his hand on his face.

Isaiah is a small man, said Isaiah, but no liar.

God paused.

And so that was their contract.     40

Brittle on both sides, no lying.

Isaiah's wife came to the doorway, the doorposts had moved.[6]

What's that sound? said Isaiah's wife.

The fear of the Lord, said Isaiah.

He grinned in the dark, she went back inside.

---

4  Various images of blindness—in particular that of a nation that has shut or covered its eyes—run through the
Book of Isaiah. Regarding the nation's hands as 'bloody slabs of meat', see Isaiah 1:15: 'And when ye spread forth
your hands, I will hide mine eyes from you: yea, when ye make many prayers, I will not hear: your hands are
full of blood.' That the nation's eyes are covered by something like 'wings' gives it an ironic resemblance to the
seraphim described in Isaiah (see note 6).

5  See Isaiah 3:1: 'For, behold, the Lord, the LORD of hosts, doth take away from Jerusalem and from Judah the
stay and the staff, the whole stay of bread, and the whole stay of water.'

6  In Chapter 6, Isaiah describes a vision in which he saw 'the LORD sitting upon a throne, high and lifted up, and
his train filled the temple. Above it stood the seraphims: each one had six wings; with twain he covered his face,
and with twain he covered his feet, and with twain he did fly. And one cried unto another, and said, Holy, holy,
holy, is the LORD of hosts: the whole earth is full of his glory. And the posts of the door moved at the voice of
him that cried, and the house was filled with smoke.'

II.

There is a kind of pressure in humans to take whatever is most
    beloved by them
and smash it.
Religion calls the pressure *piety* and the smashed thing *a sacrifice to
    God.*
Prophets question these names.
What is an idol?
An idol is a useless sacrifice, said Isaiah.
But how do you know which ones are useless? asked the nation in its
    genius.                                                                    10
Isaiah pondered the various ways he could answer this.
Immense chunks of natural reality fell out of a blue sky
    and showers of light upon his mind.
Isaiah chose the way of metaphor.
Our life is a *camera obscura*, said Isaiah, do you know what that is?[7]
Never heard of it, said the nation.
Imagine yourself in a darkened room, Isaiah instructed.
Okay, said the nation.
The doors are closed, there is a pinhole in the black wall.
A pinhole, the nation repeated.                                               20
Light shoots through the pinhole and strikes the opposite wall.
The nation was watching Isaiah, bored and fascinated at once.
You can hold up anything you like in front of that pinhole, said
    Isaiah,
and worship it on the opposite wall.
Why worship an image? asked the nation.
Exactly, said Isaiah.
The nation chewed on that for a moment.
Then its genius spoke up.
So what about Isaiah's pinhole?                                               30
Ah, said Isaiah.
A memory fell through him as clear heat falls on herbs.
Isaiah remembered the old days, conversing with God under the
    Branch
and like an old butler waking in an abandoned house the day the
    revolution began,
Isaiah bent his head.

---

7  Isaiah's metaphor of the *camera obscura* is not Biblical but it does owe a great deal to Plato's allegory of the cave,
found in Book IV of *The Republic.* There Plato suggests that most people mistakenly believe the everyday world
is real when reality lies on a higher plane; he compares that situation to the kind of error that would be made
by individuals in a fire-lit cave if they were unable to turn their heads to see the real world and could only judge
it by the flickering shadows real things cast on the cave wall.

A burden[8] was upon Isaiah.
Isaiah opened his mouth.
A sigh came from Isaiah's mouth, the sigh grew into a howl.[9]                40
The howl ran along the brooks to the mouth of the brooks
and tore the nets of the fishers who cast angle into the brooks
and confounded the workers in fine flax who weave networks
and broke their purpose.
The howl rolled like a rolling thing past slain men and harvests and
    spoils
and stopped in a ditch between two walls.[10]
Then Isaiah unclamped his mouth from the howl.
Isaiah let his mouth go from the teat.
Isaiah turned, Isaiah walked away.                                        50
Isaiah walked for three years naked and barefoot with buttocks
    uncovered
to the shame of the nation.
All night you could see the Branch roaming against the sky like a
    soul.


                III.


Isaiah walked for three years in the valley of vision.
In his jacket of glass he crossed deserts and black winter mornings.
The icy sun lowered its eyelids against the glare of him.
God stayed back.
Now Isaiah had a hole in the place where his howl had broken off.
All the while Isaiah walked, Isaiah's heart was pouring out the hole.
One day Isaiah stopped.
Isaiah put his hand on the amputated place.
Isaiah's heart is small but in a way sacred, said Isaiah, I will save it.
Isaiah plugged the hole with millet and dung.                            10
God watched Isaiah's saving action.

8  This and the lines that follow are indebted to Isaiah's prophecy in 19:1–9: 'The burden [a prophecy] of Egypt.
   Behold, the LORD rideth upon a swift cloud, . . . and they shall seek to the idols, and to the charmers, and to
   them that have familiar spirits, and to the wizards. . . . And they shall turn the rivers far away; and the brooks
   of defence shall be emptied and dried up: the reeds and flags shall wither. The paper reeds by the brooks, by
   the mouth of the brooks, and every thing sown by the brooks, shall wither, be driven away, and be no more.
   The fishers also shall mourn, and all they that cast angle into the brooks shall lament, and they that spread nets
   upon the waters shall languish. Moreover they that work in fine flax, and they that weave networks, shall be
   confounded.'
9  Compare Isaiah 65:13–14: 'Therefore thus saith the LORD God, Behold, my servants shall eat, but ye shall be
   hungry: behold, my servants shall drink, but ye shall be thirsty: behold, my servants shall rejoice, but ye shall
   be ashamed: Behold, my servants shall sing for joy of heart, but ye shall cry for sorrow of heart, and shall howl
   for vexation of spirit.'
10 Recalling Isaiah 22:11: 'Ye made also a ditch between the two walls for the water of the old pool: but ye have
   not looked unto the maker thereof, neither had respect unto him that fashioned it long ago.'

God was shaking like an olive tree.[11]
Now or never, whispered God.
God reached down and drew a line on the floor of the desert in front
    of Isaiah's feet.
Silence began.
Silence roared down the canals of Isaiah's ears into his brain.
Isaiah was listening to the silence.
Deep under it was another sound Isaiah could hear miles down.
A sort of ringing.        20
Wake up Isaiah! said God from behind Isaiah's back.[12]
Isaiah jumped and spun around.
Wake up and praise God! said God smiling palely.
Isaiah spat.
God thought fast.
The nation is burning![13] God cried pointing across the desert.
Isaiah looked.
All the windows of the world stood open and blowing.
In each window Isaiah saw a motion like flames.
Behind the flames he saw a steel fence lock down.        30
Caught between the flames and the fence was a deer.
Isaiah saw the deer of the nation burning all along its back.
In its amazement the deer turned and turned and turned
until its own shadow lay tangled around its feet like melted wings.
Isaiah reached out both his hands, they flared in the dawn.
Poor flesh! said Isaiah.
Your nation needs you Isaiah, said God.
Flesh breaks, Isaiah answered. Everyone's will break. There is
    nothing we can do.
I tell you Isaiah you can save the nation.        40
The wind was rising, God was shouting.
You can strip it down, start over at the wires, use lions! use thunder!
    *use what you see—*
Isaiah was watching sweat and tears run down God's face.
Okay, said Isaiah, so I save the nation. What do *you* do?

11 An echo of a stern warning found in Isaiah 24, telling how 'the LORD maketh the earth empty, and maketh it
    waste, and turneth it upside down, and scattereth abroad the inhabitants thereof. . . . In the city is left desola-
    tion, and the gate is smitten with destruction. When thus it shall be in the midst of the land among the people,
    there shall be as the shaking of an olive tree, and as the gleaning grapes when the vintage is done. They shall lift
    up their voice, they shall sing for the majesty of the LORD, they shall cry aloud from the sea. Wherefore glorify
    ye the LORD in the fires, even the name of the LORD God of Israel in the isles of the sea.'
12 The Book of Isaiah ends with several injunctions for the people to awake: see, for example, 51:9: 'Awake, awake,
    put on strength, O arm of the LORD.'
13 See, for example, Isaiah 10:16–18: 'Therefore shall the Lord, the Lord of hosts, send among his fat ones lean-
    ness; and under his glory he shall kindle a burning like the burning of a fire. And the light of Israel shall be for
    a fire, and his Holy One for a flame: and it shall burn and devour his thorns and his briers in one day; And
    shall consume the glory of his forest, and of his fruitful field, both soul and body: and they shall be as when a
    standard-bearer fainteth.'

God exhaled roughly.
I save the fire, said God.
Thus their contract continued.


IV.

When Isaiah came back in from the desert centuries had passed.
There was nothing left of Isaiah but a big forehead.
The forehead went rolling around the nation and spoke to people
    who leapt to their feet
and fled.
If the nation had taken Isaiah to court he could have proven his
    righteousness.
But they met in secret and voted to cut him off.
Shepherds! Chosen ones! Skinny dogs! Blood of a dog! Watchmen
    all! said Isaiah.          10
Isaiah withdrew to the Branch.
It was a blue winter evening, the cold bit like a wire.
Isaiah laid his forehead on the ground.
God arrived.
Why do the righteous suffer? said Isaiah.
Bellings of cold washed down the Branch.
Notice whenever God addresses Isaiah in a feminine singular verb
    something dazzling is
about to happen.
Isaiah what do you know about women? asked God.        20
Down Isaiah's nostrils bounced woman words:
Blush. Stink. Wife. Fig. Sorceress—
God nodded.
Isaiah go home and get some sleep, said God.
Isaiah went home, slept, woke again.
Isaiah felt sensation below the neck, it was a silk and bitter sensation.
Isaiah looked down.
It was milk forcing the nipples open.
Isaiah was more than whole.
I am not with you I am *in* you, said the muffled white voice of God.    30
Isaiah sank to a kneeling position.
New pain! said Isaiah.
New contract! said God.
Isaiah lifted his arms, milk poured out his breasts.
Isaiah watched the milk pour like strings.
It poured up the Branch and across history and down into people's
    lives and time.

The milk made Isaiah forget about righteousness.
As he fed the milk to small birds and animals Isaiah thought only
    about their little lips.                                   40
God meanwhile continued to think about male and female.
After all there are two words for righteousness, Isaiah could not be
    expected to untie this
hard knot himself.
First the masculine word TSDQ, a bolt of justice that splits the oak in
    two.
Then in the empty muscle of the wood, mushrooms and maggots and
    monkeys set up a
livelihood:
here is (the feminine word) TSDQH.                                50
God grave the two words on Isaiah's palms.
God left it at that.
And although it is true Isaiah's prophecies continued to feature
    *eunuch cylinders* and
*clickfoot woman shame.*
And although it is true Isaiah himself knew several wives and begot a
    bastard son.
Still some nights through his dreams slipped a river of milk.
A river of silver, a river of pity.
He slept, the asters in the garden unloaded their red thunder into the     60
    dark.

1995

# TV Men: Hektor[1]

### I.

TV is hardhearted, like Lenin.[2]
TV is rational, like mowing.
TV is wrong, often, a worry.
TV is ugly, like the future.
TV is a classic example.

---

1  This poem responds to Homer's *Iliad* (Carson has called it the one work she would take to a desert island),
  which tells the story of the Greek siege of Troy during the Trojan War. Hektor, the eldest son of King Priam and
  Queen Hekabe, is the commander of the Trojan army, his prowess in battle second only to that of Achilles, the
  hero of the Greek army. Much of the poem focuses on Book 22 of the *Iliad*, in which the two meet in a climactic battle that ends with Hektor's defeat.
2  Vladimir Ilyich Lenin (1870–1924), the founder of Marxism-Leninism, was the principal figure in the Russian
  Revolution and, from 1918 to 1924, the first premier of the Soviet Union. By 1922 (six years after the rise of
  Communism in Russia), five million people had perished through famine; in response to strikes and uprisings
  against the Communist regime, Lenin began show trials with executions of dissidents.

Hektor's family members found themselves engaged in exciting acts,
and using excited language, which they knew derived from TV.

A classic example of what.

A classic example of a strain of cruelty.


II.

Hektor was born to be a prince of Troy not a man of TV,                    10
hence his success.
Wrong people look good on TV, they are so obviously
*a soul divided*[3]

and we all enjoy the pathos of that.
Let us join Hektor
on the eve of the Death Valley shoot.[4]
Hektor lies

on the motel bed in his armour observing himself and his red lips
high overhead.
The ceiling is mirrored in divine fire.                                    20
*Your Law has got hold*

*of my entrails,*[5] he murmurs. His lipstick grins at him
upside down.
Out the window he can see a horizon of low brown mountains
laid end to end.

They make a hissing sound. O prince of Troy!
Butter and honey
shall you eat, that you may know to refuse the evil
and choose the good.[6]

TV is inherently cynical. It speaks to the eye, but the mind has no eye.    30

3  Perhaps an allusion to Plato's theory that the soul is divided into three components — reason, will, and appetite—and
   that in some individuals the lack of balance among the parts of the soul is apparent as they clash with one another.
4  Carson playfully imagines this scene for television as being shot on location in Death Valley, California—where
   many Hollywood westerns were made—probably for the associations the name evokes, including that of the
   Greek underworld, to which Hektor is said to depart after his death in the *Iliad*.
5  This line may allude to the fate that those killed in battle may face, as when Achilles spears Hektor's younger
   brother Polydorus, and Hektor watches him die holding his entrails; or it may reflect the fear, expressed by Hektor
   as he dies at Achilles' hands, of the dishonour of being left after death for dogs and vultures to devour. As well,
   this line may also be intended to echo the phrase 'the law on entrails', as old laws governing the earth's resources
   (or 'entrails') are called. For the connection Carson makes between Hektor's name and 'hold', see note 7.
6  See Isaiah 7:14–16: 'Therefore the Lord himself shall give you a sign; Behold, a virgin shall conceive, and bear a
   son, and shall call his name Immanuel. Butter and honey shall he eat, that he may know to refuse the evil, and
   choose the good. For before the child shall know to refuse the evil, and choose the good, the land that thou
   abhorrest shall be forsaken of both her kings.'

III.

Hektor's name is from the ancient verb 'to hold'.[7]
Hold.
Hold on.
Hold out.
Hold up.
Hold off.
Hold in.
Hold together.
Hektor's name is the antithesis
of those temporary constructions on the shore                    40
(Greek army)
that
stood—
from opening kills to the day Troy was razed—
a mere ten years.

Head down against a thin winter wind
Hektor paces the floor of Death Valley,
repeating his line.
*I have learned to be brave.*[8]
The light-hole pulls away on every side.                          50

TV is dull, like the block of self in each of us.


IV.

Salt particle by salt particle the desert grows luminous at dawn.
It is the second day of the Death Valley shoot.
Hektor is alone in the light-hole.

The walkie-talkie taped to the small of his back is cold as a slab of
    meat.
It crackles alive and the director's voice
crawls up his spine like a bee.

7 Although the etymology of the Greek *Hektōr* is uncertain, Carson here accepts the possibility that it may derive from the Greek verb *echō*, to hold, making 'Hektor' the equivalent of 'holder'—and she calls attention to the implied contrast, in the *Iliad*, between Hektor's firm 'hold', as a bulwark protecting his city, with what she describes as the 'temporary constructions' of the Greeks—i.e. the tents and huts in which the Greek army has continued to live during their years of besieging Troy.
8 An allusion to a speech Hektor makes at the beginning of Book 22 to his wife, Andromache, after she tries to persuade him to remain within the walls of the city: 'My heart bids me not to [stay inside], since I have learned to be brave always and to fight among the front lines of the Trojans, winning great glory for my father and for myself there.'

*Places please! Helicopter five minutes away!*
Hektor hunkers down close to the sand.                                    60
The eunuch winter sun

stains him in a blind place. Cracks appear. And the silence—
a silence that starts so deep
under the rock

he can hear it ringing. Man is a slave and a sombre being.
Who does not know enough to lick the salt
off the low bushes at dawn.

TV is loud, yet we do not awake.


                    V.

TV wastes nothing, like a wife.

While Hektor was out making war, his wife heated water on the fire        70
for a bath when he returned wearied of killing.
Later that night

they brought news of his death. She puts away the water
and uses the fire to burn all his clothes.
*Since they will be no benefit to you,*

*nor will you wear them,* she says. Looking out over the parapet
to the arc-lit battlefield where men
with string

were measuring the distance from Hektor's darkening nipple
to the camera's eye.                                                      80
She saw men on their knees.


                    VI.

From the helicopter Death Valley looks like an entrail.
Vast coiling cracks of gold and grey lunge endlessly across it—
*Run Hektor!* [9]

---

9 Hektor runs away from Achilles in their final encounter, though he had resolved to stand to meet him. Achilles
  chases him three times around the city walls.

rasps the director from the walkie-talkie
as the helicopter goes squalling past Hektor's head
and the downdraft

knocks him flat. Plunged into the depths of encircling walls
an animal will lose its tuning knob.
Hektor was                                                                                      90

for Troy a source of food, a cause for exultation in prayer[10]
a likeness of God,
a human glory.

He had constructed throughout Troy a system of gutters,
which ran along both sides of every street,
squared with stone

in alternating blocks of polished and unpolished agate.
Waters ran quietly out of Troy.
Now Hektor worries

that stains on the back of his clothing will be visible                                          100
from the helicopter as he turns
to run.

TV is made of light, like shame.[11]


      VII.

As the bottom of a sea, which it once was, Death Valley is perpetually
   in motion.
A thin
silver
pressure rakes the dunes from north to west forming parallel grooves
miles

---

10 Carson is here reworking Hekabe's lament for Hektor after his death:
    *My child, ah woe is me! How shall I live in my sore anguish, now thou art dead?—thou that wast my boast night and day in the city, and a blessing to all, both to the men and women of Troy throughout the town, who ever greeted thee as a god; for verily thou wast to them a glory exceeding great, while yet thou livedst; but now death and fate are come upon thee.* (Trans. A.T. Murray)
    In referring to Hektor here as a 'source of food', Carson is playing with the Greek word *oneiar*, translated above as 'blessing'. (In its plural, *oneiata*, the word can mean good things to eat.) Her phrase 'Cause for exultation in prayer' is an exact translation of the Greek *euchōlē*, translated above as 'boast'.
11 Carson is apparently playing with the fact that the Greek word for shame, *aidōs*, contains -*id*-, the root of various words for 'see' and 'know'. (In Book 22 of the *Iliad*, being seen and being shamed are connected for Hektor—who doesn't want his reputation to be stained by being seen to be a coward.)

wide                                                                                           110
that vanish in half an hour and vanish again, tarrying and driving on,
marking,
blanking.
As the kings of Troy comb out their hair before battle
into
patterns
no one can remember after, Hektor is running
the
length
of a gravel groove heading straight for Troy.                                                  120

He
can
just see his wife on the parapet waving a piece of clothing.[12]
He
waves
too. He will never reach her. Under his feet the sand is shifting,
its
slight
incomprehensible ball bearings carrying him ever more west
and                                                                                            130
south
toward the unclocked clarity of his last and inland sea.

TV is a condition of weightless balance, like a game.
But TV is not a game.[13]


      VIII.


TV comes out of the dark, like Hektor's prayer verbs.

To blue.
To tear from the midpoint.
To lay bare crystals.
To lay bare a sky.
To ash.                                                                                        140
To put silence over it.

12 After Achilles' victory over Hektor, Andromache rushes from her house to the walls to find out why everyone
   is screaming: seeing Hektor's slain body being dragged behind Achilles' chariot, she grows faint and tears off
   her veil.
13 An echo of a passage in Book 22 that notes the way Hektor's attempt to escape resembles a sporting competition: 'They were running very quickly, since they were not competing for a sacrificial animal or an ox-hide
   shield, the kinds of things that are prizes for men's feet, but they were running for the life of Hektor.'

To not desist.
To inmost.
To mount smoke (of a soul).


## IX.


TV has a glare to it, like Hektor's prayer.

YOU PART. ENDANGERED WE.
HANG.
PERSONS OF ASH.


ASHED.


## X.


Late each night in his motel room Hektor puts on a headset                    150
to shut out the noise of the keno lounge next door
and sits down to write a postcard to his wife.

VERY COLD IN THE DESERT WE SHOOT FROM DAWN TO DUSK
MILITARY JETS CAVORTING OVERHEAD THE DIRECTOR RED
WITH RAGE NO TIME FOR LUNCH *THE LIGHT IS GOING!* YOU
WOULD LIKE MY COSTUME IT IS SILK THANK YOU FOR THE
*T*EARS THEY TASTE LIKE HOME
P

Then he takes out a big red notebook from the desk drawer
and puts on a sweater and sits again. Staring hard.                           160
DIARY FOR MYSELF ALONE says the cover.

> *Today Hektor fought like a boulder going downhill.*[14]
> *Torn from the rockface it bounds and flies, treetops*
> *roar past underneath,*
> *nothing can stop it—*
> *hits the plain!*
> *There he was stabbing away at a wall of skirmishers.*
> *Like a flashing snowpeak he moved,*
> *like a wave exploding foam, like a giant breaker*
> *boiling toward the beach—*                                                 170

---

14 Here Hektor's 'diary' entries assimilate and recast various passages and similes from the *Iliad*.

By now morning fires are being kindled throughout the motel.
Dawn pots are banging.
Hektor works on,

while behind him, the long blades of his spars and harpoons
stand propped on the wall
beside the TV—

> *there he was*
> *testing the enemy line at every point*
> *to see where it would give!*
> *The deaf day moved toward ox-time.*[15]
> *Truth*
> *rolled away from him*
> *under the cannon-bones of the night.*

180

TV uses for 'grave' the word 'sign', like Homer.[16]


### XI.

TV is presocial, like Man.

On the last day of the Death Valley shoot
driving through huge slow brown streaks of mountain
towards the light-hole,

Hektor feels his pits go dry.

Clouds drop their lines down the faces of the rock
as if marking out a hunting ground.
Hektor, whose heart

190

walked ahead of him always,

ran ahead like a drunk creature
to lick salt particles off the low bushes
as if they were butter or silver honey,

whose heart Homer compared to a lion

---

15 As can be seen in Book 23 of the *Iliad* (when Achilles' friend Patroclus is being buried while Hektor lies dead and dishonoured), ancient funerals featured the ritual slaughter of oxen.

16 The Greek word *sēma* can mean grave or tomb (in Book 24 it is used to refer to the tomb of Hektor), but it also has the more general meaning of 'sign'.

turning in a net of dogs and men and
whichever way the lion lunges the men and dogs give way
yet the net keeps contracting—                                                    200

Hektor trembles.

The human way includes two kinds of knowledge.
Fire and Night. Hektor has been to the Fire
in conditions of experimental purity.

It is 6:53 AM when his Night unhoods itself.

Hektor sees that he is lying at the centre of a vast metal disc.
A dawn clot of moon dangles oddly above
and this realization comes coldly through him:

the disc is tilting.

Very slowly the disc attains an angle of thirty degrees.                         210
Dark blue signal is flowing steadily
from the centre to the edge

as Hektor starts to slide.

It takes but an instant to realize you are mortal.
Troy reared up on its hind legs
and a darkness of life flowed through the town

from purple cup to purple cup.

*Toes to the line please*, says the assistant camera man,
slapping two pieces of yellow tape
on the surface of the disc                                                        220

just in front of Hektor's feet.

Dashing back to the camera he raises his slate.
*Places everyone*, calls the director as a thousand wasps
come stinging out of the arc lamp[17]

and the camera is pouring its black butter,

---

17 In Book 16, when the forces of Achilles, the Myrmidons, rush into battle behind Patroclus, they are compared
  to wasps pouring out to attack someone who has disturbed them.

its bitter honey,
straight into Hektor's eye.
Hektor steps to the line.

*War has always interested me,*[18] he begins.

1995

18 An echo of a passage in Book 6: before Hektor leaves Andromache to return to battle, he tells her, 'war will be a concern to all of the men, but especially to me.'

# Barbara Gowdy
## b. 1950

Born in Windsor, Ontario, Barbara Gowdy was raised in Don Mills, Ontario (a community then lying just outside Toronto—built in the 1950s as a completely planned 'new town' and based on modernist ideas about what would make an ideal suburb). The Gowdys, with a breadwinning father and a stay-at-home mother of three girls and a boy, were representative of what was then thought of as the perfect suburban family in this highly conformist and role-defined era. Despite growing up in this idyllic domestic milieu, Gowdy has become known for her creations of disconcerting fictional worlds populated by misfits. Her writing is sometimes identified with the Ontario Gothic tradition associated with James Reaney and Alice Munro and also resembles the contemporary American Gothicism of David Lynch's films and Stephen King's novels. However, though Gowdy's work does call attention to the overlooked dark corners in an apparently normal existence, it differs from these precursors in that it frequently *begins* with what seems odd or repellent in order to reveal that it can also be part of everyday life. In doing so, it shows the depths of feeling that can inform even the most unsympathetic of individuals, inviting us to respond to the unloved and the unlovable. As Gowdy observed in a 2006 interview with Stephen Heighton (in *Descant*

132, a special issue on her fiction): 'I'm not happy with euphemisms or half-truths. . . . Like it or not, fish do feel the hook. . . . How can you develop sympathy unless you perceive the suffering of others?'

Gowdy's first book was a traditional historical novel, *Through the Green Valley* (1988), about a family that fled the eighteenth-century Irish famine by emigrating to North America. It was her 1989 novel, *Falling Angels* (it had its origin in a short story selected for *Best American Short Stories*) that established the dialectic of normal versus abnormal that runs through the rest of her work. In *Falling Angels*, a suburban family takes a two-week vacation—not to Disneyland as originally planned, but inside the family fallout shelter, one of those underground bunkers that some Cold War–era families built in their backyards in the hope that it would protect them from a nuclear attack.

It was the short-story collection entitled *We So Seldom Look on Love* (1992) that showed the range of Gowdy's macabre imagination as well as the whimsy, and sometimes humour, that accompanies it (the title story, about a young necrophiliac woman, was the basis for Lynne Stopkewich's acclaimed 1996 film *Kissed*). Each of the stories portrays some transgression of the social norm—including voyeurism, exhibitionism, and transsexuality. But this collection also shows us the way every individual in it longs for love and affection—though suggesting that death and love are sometimes conflated (death is, for example, a source of energy to the corpse-embracing protagonist of 'We So Seldom Look on Love'). In 'Presbyterian Crosswalk', the story reprinted here, impending death is a lens through which Gowdy examines faith, family, and the difficulties of communication to suggest that, in our longing to go beyond our human limitations, we create rituals and fashion beliefs.

Gowdy's fourth book, *Mister Sandman* (1995), through its focus on the strange family of a brain-damaged savant—a girl who is a musical prodigy—asks the reader to consider who or what is 'normal'. *The White Bone* (1999), the novel that followed, goes beyond her previous narratives in its tragic story of a matriarch who attempts to find a land of peace and well-being—because its protagonist is an elephant named Mud. Unlike most fiction that uses the point of view of animals, *The White Bone* is successful in leaving its readers with a sense that its characters, while they may reason and feel strong emotions and form intention, do not think like people but in a way characteristic of their own species.

Gowdy's most recent novels—*The Romantic* (2003) and *Helpless* (2007; Trillium Award winner)—are about the shape obsessive love can take. In the first of these, a woman cannot stop herself from dwelling on her unrequited love for a man she has known from childhood but who is now dead. In the second, Gowdy accomplishes the difficult feat of drawing us into the consciousness of a man who abducts a nine-year-old girl. Though many found *Helpless*'s subject matter disturbing, Gowdy, in a conversation with T.F. Rigelhof (in *Books in Canada*), remarked, 'What I think I've been questioning all these years in my writing is, who is it we find worthy, what kind of human being? What are our yardsticks, and how qualified are we to judge? I am unswervingly on the side of giving the individual the benefit of the doubt.'

# Presbyterian Crosswalk

Sometimes Beth floated. Two or three feet off the ground, and not for very long, ten seconds or so. She wasn't aware of floating when she was actually doing it, however. She had to land and feel a glowing sensation before she realized that she had just been up in the air.

The first time it happened she was on the church steps. She looked back down the walk and knew that she had floated up it. A couple of days later she floated down the outside cellar stairs of her house. She ran inside and told her grandmother, who whipped out the pen and the little pad she carried in her skirt pocket and drew a circle with a hooked nose.

Beth looked at it. 'Has Aunt Cora floated, too?' she asked.

Her grandmother nodded.

'When?'

Her grandmother held up six fingers.

'Six years ago?'

Shaking her head, her grandmother held her hand at thigh level.

'Oh,' Beth said, 'when she was six.'

When Beth was six, five years ago, her mother ran off with a man down the street who wore a toupee that curled up in humid weather. Beth's grandmother, her father's mother, came to live with her and her father. Thirty years before that, Beth's grandmother had had her tonsils taken out by a quack who ripped out her vocal chords and the underside of her tongue.

It was a tragedy, because she and her twin sister, Cora, had been on the verge of stardom (or so Cora said) as a professional singing team. They had made two long-play records: 'The Carlisle Sisters, Sea to Sea' and 'Christmas with the Carlisle Sisters'. Beth's grandmother liked to play the records at high volume and to mouth the words. 'My prairie home is beautiful, but oh . . .' If Beth sang along, her grandmother might stand next to her and sway and swish her skirt as though Beth were Cora and the two of them were back on stage.

The cover of the 'Sea to Sea' album had a photograph of Beth's grandmother and Aunt Cora wearing middies and sailor hats and shielding their eyes with one hand as they peered off in different directions. Their hair, blond and billowing out from under their hats, was glamorous, but Beth secretly felt that even if her grandmother hadn't lost her voice she and Cora would never have been big stars because they had hooked noses, what Cora called Roman noses. Beth was relieved that she hadn't inherited their noses, although she regretted not having got their soft, wavy hair, which they both still wore long, in a braid or falling in silvery drifts down their backs. Beth's grandmother still put on blue eye shadow and red lipstick, too, every morning. And around the house she wore her old, flashy, full-length stage skirts, faded now—red, orange or yellow, or flowered, or with swirls of broken-off sequins. Beth's grandmother didn't care about sloppiness or dirt. With the important exception of Beth's father's den, the house was a mess—Beth was just beginning to realize and be faintly ashamed of this.

On each of Beth's grandmother's skirts was a sewed-on pocket for her pencil and pad. Due to arthritis in her thumb she held the pencil between her middle finger and forefinger, but she still drew faster than anyone Beth had ever seen. She always drew people instead of writing out their name or their initials. Beth, for instance, was a circle with tight, curly hair. Beth's friend Amy was an exclamation mark. If the phone rang and nobody was home, her grandmother answered it and tapped her pencil three times on the receiver to let whoever was on the other end know that it was her and that they should leave a message. 'Call', she would write, and then do a drawing.

A drawing of a man's hat was Beth's father. He was a hard-working lawyer who stayed late at the office. Beth had a hazy memory of him giving her a bath once, it must have been before her mother ran off. The memory embarrassed her. She wondered if he wished that she had gone with her mother, if, in fact, she was supposed to have gone, because when he came home from work and she was still there, he seemed surprised. 'Who do we have here?' he might say. He wanted peace and quiet. When Beth got rambunctious, he narrowed his eyes as though she gave off a bright, painful light.

Beth knew that he still loved her mother. In the top drawer of his dresser, in an old wallet he never used, he had a snapshot of her mother wearing only a black slip. Beth remembered that slip, and her mother's tight black dress with the zipper down the back. And her long red fingernails that she clicked on tables. 'Your mother was too young to marry,' was her father's sole disclosure. Her grandmother disclosed nothing, pretending to be deaf if Beth asked about her mother. Beth remembered how her mother used to phone her father for money and how, if her grandmother answered and took the message, she would draw a big dollar sign and then an upside-down v sitting in the middle of a line—a witch's hat.

A drawing of an upside-down v without a line was church. When a Presbyterian church was built within walking distance, Beth and her grandmother started going to it, and her grandmother began reading the Bible and counselling Beth by way of biblical quotations. A few months later a crosswalk appeared at the end of the street, and for several years Beth thought that it was a 'Presbyterian' instead of a 'Pedestrian' crosswalk and that the sign above it said Watch for Presbyterians.

Her Sunday school teacher was an old, teary-eyed woman who started every class by singing 'When Mothers of Salem',[1] while the children hung up their coats and sat down cross-legged on the floor in front of her. That hymn, specifically the part about Jesus wanting to hold children to His 'bosom', made Beth feel that there was something not right about Jesus, and consequently it was responsible for her six months of anxiety that she would end up in hell. Every night, after saying her prayers, she would spend a few minutes chanting, 'I love Jesus, I love Jesus, I love Jesus', the idea being that she could talk herself into it. She didn't expect to feel earthly love; she awaited the unknown feeling called glory.

When she began to float, she said to herself, 'This is glory.'

She floated once, sometimes twice a week. Around Christmas it began to happen less often—every ten days to two weeks. Then it dwindled down to only about once a month. She started to chant 'I love Jesus' again, not because she was worried any more about going to hell, she just wanted to float.

By the beginning of the summer holidays she hadn't floated in almost seven weeks. She phoned her Aunt Cora who said that, yes, floating was glory all right, but that Beth should consider herself lucky it had happened even once. 'Nothing that good lasts long,' she sighed. Beth couldn't stop hoping, though. She went to the park and climbed a tree. Her plan was to jump and have Jesus float her to the ground. But as she stood on a limb, working up her courage, she remembered God seeing the little sparrow fall and letting it fall anyway, and she climbed down.

She felt that she had just had a close call. She lay on her back on the picnic table, gazing up in wonder at how high up she had been. It was a hot, still day. She heard heat bugs and an ambulance. Presently she went over to the swings and took a turn on each one, since there was nobody else in the park.

She was on the last swing when Helen McCormack came waddling across the lawn, calling that a boy had just been run over by a car. Beth slid off the swing. 'He's almost dead!' Helen called.

'Who?' Beth asked.

---

1  A nineteenth-century hymn that begins, 'When mothers of Salem their children brought to Jesus, / the stern disciples drove them back and bade them to depart: / but Jesus saw them ere they fled and sweetly smiled and kindly said, / "Suffer little children to come unto me. / For I will receive them and fold them to My bosom."'

'I don't know his name. Nobody did. He's about eight. He's got red hair. The car ran over his leg *and* his back.'

'Where?'

Helen was panting. 'I shouldn't have walked so fast,' she said, holding her hands on either side of her enormous head. 'My cranium veins are throbbing.' Little spikes of her wispy blond hair stood out between her fingers.

'Where did it happen?' Beth said.

'On Glenmore. In front of the post office.'

Beth started running toward Glenmore, but Helen called, 'There's nothing there now, everything's gone!' so Beth stopped and turned, and for a moment Helen and the swings seemed to continue turning, coming round and round like Helen's voice saying, 'You missed the whole thing. You missed it. You missed the whole thing.'

'He was on his bike,' Helen said, dropping onto a swing, 'and an eyewitness said that the car skidded on water and knocked him down, then ran over him twice, once with a front tire and once with a back one. I got there before the ambulance. He probably won't live. You could tell by his eyes. His eyes were glazed.' Helen's eyes, blue, huge because of her glasses, didn't blink.

'That's awful,' Beth said.

'Yes, it really was,' Helen said, matter-of-factly. 'He's not the first person I've seen who nearly died, though. My aunt nearly drowned in the bathtub when we were staying at her house. She became a human vegetable.'

'Was the boy bleeding?' Beth asked.

'Yes, there was blood everywhere.'

Beth covered her mouth with both hands.

Helen looked thoughtful. 'I think he'll probably die,' she said. She pumped her fat legs but without enough energy to get the swing going. 'I'm going to die soon,' she said.

'You are?'

'You probably know that I have water on the brain,' Helen said.

'Yes, I know that,' Beth said. Everyone knew. It was why Helen wasn't supposed to run. It was why her head was so big.

'Well, more and more water keeps dripping in all the time, and one day there will so much that my brain will literally drown in it.'

'Who said?'

'The doctors, who else?'

'They said, "You're going to die"?'

Helen threw her an ironic look. 'Not exactly. What they tell you is, you're not going to live.' She squinted up at a plane going by. 'The boy, he had . . . I think it was a rib, sticking out of his back.'

'Really?'

'I *think* it was a rib. It was hard to tell because of all the blood.' With the toe of her shoe, Helen began to jab a hole in the sand under her swing. 'A man from the post office hosed the blood down the sewer, but some of it was already caked from the sun.'

Beth walked toward the shade of the picnic table. The air was so thick and still. Her arms and legs, cutting through it, seemed to produce a thousand soft clashes.

'The driver was an old man,' Helen said, 'and he was crying uncontrollably.'

'Anybody would cry,' Beth said hotly. Her eyes filled with tears.

Helen squirmed off her swing and came over to the table. Grunting with effort, she climbed onto the seat across from Beth and began to roll her head. 'At least I'll die in one piece,' she said.

'Are you really going to?' Beth asked.

'Yep.' Helen rotated her head three times one way, then three times the other. Then she propped it up with her hands cupped under her chin.

'But can't they do anything to stop the water dripping in?' Beth asked.

'Nope,' Helen said distantly, as if she were thinking about something more interesting.

'You know what?' Beth said, swiping at her tears. 'If every night, you closed your eyes and chanted over and over, "Water go away, water go away, water go away," maybe it would start to, and then your head would shrink down.'

Helen smirked. 'Somehow,' she said, 'I doubt it.'

From the edge of the picnic table Beth tore a long sliver of wood like the boy's rib. She pictured the boy riding his bike no-hands, zigzagging down the street the way boys did. She imagined bursting Helen's head with the splinter to let the water gush out.

'I'm thirsty,' Helen sighed. 'I've had a big shock today. I'm going home for some lemonade.'

Beth went with her. It was like walking with her grandmother, who, because of arthritis in her hips, also rocked from side to side and took up the whole sidewalk. Beth asked Helen where she lived.

'I can't talk,' Helen panted. 'I'm trying to breathe.'

Beth thought that Helen lived in the apartments where the immigrants, crazy people and bums were, but Helen went past those apartments and up the hill to the new Regal Heights subdivision, which had once been a landfill site. Her house was a split-level with a little turret above the garage. On the door was an engraved wooden sign, the kind that Beth had seen nailed to posts in front of cottages. No Solicitors, it said.

'My father is a solicitor,' Beth said.

Helen was concentrating on opening the door. 'Darn thing's always stuck,' she muttered as she shoved it open with her shoulder. 'I'm home!' she hollered, then sat heavily on a small mauve suitcase next to the door.

Across the hallway a beautiful woman was dusting the ceiling with a mop. She had dark, curly hair tied up in a red ribbon, and long, slim legs in white short shorts.

To Beth's amazement she was Helen's mother. 'You can call me Joyce,' she said, smiling at Beth as though she loved her. 'Who's this lump of potatoes,' she laughed, pointing the mop at Helen.

Helen stood up. 'A boy got run over on Glenmore,' she said.

Joyce's eyes widened, and she looked at Beth.

'I didn't see it,' Beth told her.

'We're dying of thirst,' Helen said. 'We want lemonade in my room.'

While Joyce made lemonade from a can, Helen sat at the kitchen table, resting her head on her folded arms. Joyce's questions about the accident seemed to bore her. 'We don't need ice,' she said impatiently when Joyce went to open the freezer. She demanded cookies, and Joyce poured some Oreos onto the tray with their coffee mugs of lemonade, then handed the tray to Beth, saying with a little laugh that, sure as shooting, Helen would tip it over.

'I'm always spilling things,' Helen agreed.

Beth carried the tray through the kitchen to the hallway. 'Why is that there?' she asked, nodding at the suitcase beside the front door.

'That's my hospital suitcase,' Helen said. 'It's all packed for an emergency.' She pushed open her bedroom door so that it banged against the wall. The walls were the same mauve as the suitcase, and there was a smell of paint. Everything was put away—no clothes lying around, no games or toys on the floor. The dolls and books, lined up on white bookshelves, looked as if they were for sale. Beth thought contritely of her own dolls, their tangled hair and dirty dresses, half of them naked, some of them missing legs and hands, she could never remember why, she could never figure out how a hand got in with her Scrabble letters.

She set the tray down on Helen's desk. Above the desk was a chart that said 'Heart Rate', 'Blood Pressure' and 'Bowel Movements' down the side. 'What's that?' she asked.

'My bodily functions chart.' Helen grabbed a handful of cookies. 'We're keeping track every week to see how much things change before they completely stop. We're conducting an experiment.'

Beth stared at the neatly stencilled numbers and the gently waving red lines. She had the feeling that she was missing something as stunning and obvious as the fact that her mother was gone for good. For years after her mother left she asked her father, 'When is she coming back?' Her father, looking confused, always answered, 'Never,' but Beth just couldn't understand what he meant by that, not until she finally thought to ask, 'When is she coming back for the rest of her life?'

She turned to Helen. 'When are you going to die?'

Helen shrugged. 'There's no exact date,' she said with her mouth full.

'Aren't you afraid?'

'Why should I be? Dying the way I'm going to doesn't hurt, you know.'

Beth sat on the bed. There was the hard feel of plastic under the spread and blankets. She recognized it from when she'd had her tonsils out and they'd put plastic under her sheets then. 'I hope that boy hasn't died,' she said, suddenly thinking of him again.

'He probably has,' Helen said, running a finger along the lowest line in the chart.

The lines were one above the other, not intersecting. When Beth's grandmother drew one wavy line, that was water. Beth closed her eyes. Water go away, she said to herself. Water go away, water go away . . .

'What are you doing?' The bed bounced, splashing lemonade out of Beth's mug as Helen sat down.

'I was conducting an experiment,' Beth said

'What experiment?'

More lemonade, this time from Helen's mug, poured onto Beth's leg and her shorts. 'Look what you're doing!' Beth cried. She used the corner of the bedspread to dry herself. 'You're so stupid sometimes,' she muttered.

Helen drank down what was left in her mug. 'For your information,' she said, wiping her mouth on her arm, 'it's not stupidity. It's deterioration of the part of my brain lobe that tells my muscles what to do.'

Beth looked up at her. 'Oh, from the water,' she said softly.

'Water is one of the most destructive forces known to mankind,' Helen said.

'I'm sorry,' Beth murmured. 'I didn't mean it.'

'So what did you mean you were conducting an experiment?' Helen asked, pushing her glasses up on her nose.

'You know what?' Beth said. 'We could both do it.' She felt a thrill of virtuous resolve. 'Remember what I said about chanting "water go away, water go away"? We could both chant it and see what happens.'

'Brother,' Helen sighed.

Beth put her lemonade on the table and jumped off the bed. 'We'll make a chart,' she said, fishing around in the drawer of Helen's desk for a pen and some paper. She found a red pencil. 'Do you have any paper?' she asked. 'We need paper and a measuring tape.'

'Brother,' Helen said again, but she left the room and came back a few minutes later with a pad of foolscap and her mother's sewing basket.

Beth wrote 'Date' and 'Size' at the top of the page and underlined it twice. Under 'Date' she wrote 'June 30', then she unwound the measuring tape and measured Helen's head—the circumference above her eyebrows—and wrote '27 1/2'. Then she and Helen sat cross-legged on the floor, closed their eyes, held each other's hands and said, 'Water go away,' starting out in almost a whisper, but Helen kept speeding up, and Beth had to raise her voice to slow her down. After a few moments both of them were shouting, and Helen was digging her nails into Beth's fingers.

'Stop!' Beth cried. She yanked her hands free. 'It's supposed to be slow and quiet!' she cried. 'Like praying!'

'We don't go to church,' Helen said, pressing her hands on either side of her head. 'Whew,' she breathed. 'For a minute there I thought that my cranium veins were throbbing again.'

'We did it wrong,' Beth said crossly. Helen leaned over to get the measuring tape. 'You should chant tonight before you go to bed,' Beth said, watching as Helen pulled on the bedpost to hoist herself to her feet. 'Chant slowly and softly. I'll come back tomorrow after lunch and we'll do it together again. We'll just keep doing it every afternoon for the whole summer, if that's what it takes. Okay?'

Helen was measuring her hips, her wide, womanly hips in their dark green Bermuda shorts.

'*Okay?*' Beth repeated.

Helen bent over to read the tape. 'Sure,' she said indifferently.

When Beth got back to her own place, her grandmother was playing her 'Sea to Sea' record and making black bean soup and dinner rolls. Talking loudly to be heard over the music, Beth told her about the car accident and Helen. Her grandmother knew about Helen's condition but thought that she was retarded—in the flour sprinkled on the table she traced a circle with a triangle sitting on it, which was 'dunce', and a question mark.

'No,' Beth said, surprised. 'She gets all A's.'

Her grandmother pulled out her pad and pencil and wrote, 'Don't get her hopes up.'

'But when you *pray*, that's getting your hopes up,' Beth argued.

Her grandmother looked impressed. 'We walk by faith,' she wrote.

There was a sudden silence. 'Do you want to hear side two?' Beth asked. Her grandmother made a cross with her fingers. 'Oh, okay,' Beth said and went into the living room and put on her grandmother's other record, the Christmas one. The first song was 'Hark! the Herald Angels Sing'. Beth's father's name was Harold. The black bean soup, his favourite, meant he'd be home for supper. Beth wandered down the hall to his den and sat in his green leather chair and swivelled for a moment to the music. 'Offspring of a Virgin's womb . . .'

After a few minutes she got off the chair and began searching through his wastepaper basket. Whenever she was in here and noticed that the basket hadn't been emptied, she looked at what was in it. Usually just pencil shavings and long handwritten business letters with lots of crossed-out sentences and notes in the margins. Sometimes there were phone messages from his office, where he was called Hal, by Sue, the woman who wrote the messages out.

'PDQ!' Sue wrote. 'ASAP!'

Today there were several envelopes addressed to her father, a couple of flyers, an empty cigarette package, and a crumpled pink note from her grandmother's pad. Beth opened the note up.

'Call', it said, and then there was an upside-down v. Underneath that was a telephone number.

Beth thought it was a message for her father to call the church. Her mother hadn't called in over four years, so it took a moment of wondering why the phone number didn't start with two fives like every other phone number in the neighbourhood did, and why her father, who didn't go to church, should get a message from the church, before Beth remembered that an upside-down v meant not 'church' but 'witch's hat'.

In the kitchen Beth's grandmother was shaking the bean jars to 'Here We Come a-Wassailing'. Beth felt the rhythm as a pounding between her ears. 'My cranium veins are throbbing,' she thought in revelation, and putting down the message she pressed her palms to her temples and remembered when her mother used to phone for money. Because of those phone calls Beth had always pictured her mother and the man with the toupee living in some poor place, a rundown apartment, or one of the insulbrick bungalows north of the city. 'I'll bet they're broke again,' Beth told herself, working up scorn. 'I'll bet they're down to their last penny.' She picked up the message and crumpled it back into a ball, then opened it up again, folded it in half and slipped it into the pocket of her shorts.

Sticking to her promise, she went over to Helen's every afternoon. It took her twenty minutes, a little longer than that if she left the road to go through the park, which she often did out of a superstitious feeling that the next time she floated, it would be there. The park made her think of the boy who was run over. On the radio it said that his foot had been amputated and that he was in desperate need of a liver transplant. 'Remember him in your prayers,' the announcer said, and Beth and her grandmother did. The boy's name was Kevin Legg.

'Kevin *Legg* and he lost his *foot!*' Beth pointed out to Joyce.

Joyce laughed, although Beth hadn't meant it as a joke. A few minutes later, in the bedroom, Beth asked Helen, 'Why isn't your mother worried about us getting your hopes up?'

'She's just glad that I finally have a friend,' Helen answered. 'When I'm by myself, I get in the way of her cleaning.'

Beth looked out the window. It hadn't occurred to her that she and Helen were friends.

Beth's best friend, Christine, was at a cottage for the summer. Amy, her other friend, she played with in the mornings and when she returned from Helen's. Amy was half Chinese, small and thin. She was on pills for hyperactivity. 'Just think what I'd be like if I *wasn't* on them!' she cried, spinning around and slamming into the wall. Amy was the friend that Beth's grandmother represented with an exclamation mark. Whatever they were playing, Amy got tired of after five minutes, but she usually had another idea. She was fun, although not very nice. When Beth told her about Helen dying, she cried, 'That's a lie!'

'Ask her mother,' Beth said.

'No way I'm going to that fat-head's place!' Amy cried.

Amy didn't believe the story about the doctor ripping out Beth's grandmother's tonsils, either, not even after Beth's grandmother opened her mouth and showed her her mutilated tongue.

So Beth knew better than to confide in Amy about floating. She knew better than to confide in anybody, aside from her grandmother and her Aunt Cora, since it wasn't something she could prove and since she found it hard to believe herself. At the same time she was passionately certain that she *had* floated, and might again if she kept up her nightly 'I love Jesus' chants.

She confided in Helen about floating, though, on the fifteenth day of *their* chanting, because that day, instead of sitting on the floor and holding Beth's hands, Helen curled up on her side facing the wall and said, 'I wish we were playing checkers,' and Beth thought how trusting Helen had been so far, chanting twice a day without any reason to believe that it worked.

The next day, the sixteenth day, Helen's head measured twenty-seven inches.

'Are you sure you aren't pulling the tape tighter?' Helen asked.

'No,' Beth said. 'I always pull it this tight.'

Helen pushed the tape off her head and waddled to the bedroom door. 'Twenty-seven inches!' she called.

'Let's go show her,' Beth said, and they hurried to the living room, where Joyce was using a nail to clean between the floorboards.

'Aren't you guys smart!' Joyce said, sitting back on her heels and wiping specks of dirt from her slim legs and little pink shorts.

'Come on,' Helen said, tugging Beth back to the bedroom.

Breathlessly she went to the desk and wrote the measurement on the chart.

Beth sat on the bed. 'I can't believe it,' she said, falling onto her back. 'It's working. I mean I *thought* it would, I *hoped* it would, but I wasn't absolutely, positively, one hundred per cent sure.'

Helen sat beside her and began to roll her head. Beth pictured the water sloshing from side to side. 'Why do you do that?' she asked.

'I get neck cramps,' Helen said. 'One thing I won't miss are these darn neck cramps.'

The next day her head lost another half inch. The day after that it lost an entire inch, so that it was now down to twenty-five and a half inches. Beth and Helen demonstrated the measurements to Joyce, who acted amazed, but Beth could tell that for some reason she really wasn't.

'We're not making it up,' Beth told her.

'Well, who said you were?' Joyce asked, pretending to be insulted.

'Don't you think her head *looks* smaller?' Beth said, and both she and Joyce considered Helen's head, which *had* looked smaller in the bedroom, but now Beth wasn't so sure. In fact, she was impressed, the way she used to be when she saw Helen only once in a while, by just how big Helen's head was. And by her lumpy, grown-up woman's body, which at this moment was collapsing onto a kitchen chair.

'You know, I think maybe it *does* look smaller,' Joyce said brightly.

'Wait'll Dr. Dobbs sees me,' Helen said in a tired voice, folding her arms on the table and laying her head down.

Joyce gave Helen's shoulder a little punch. 'You all right, kiddo?'

Helen ignored her. 'I'll show him our chart,' she said to Beth.

'Hey,' Joyce said. 'You all right?'

Helen closed her eyes. 'I need a nap,' she murmured.

When Beth returned home there was another message from her mother in her father's wastepaper basket.

This time, before she could help herself, she thought, 'She wants to come back, she's left that man,' and she instantly believed it with righteous certainty. 'I *told* you,' she said out loud, addressing her father. Her eyes burned with righteousness. She threw the message back in the wastepaper basket and went out to the back yard, where her grandmother was tying up the tomato plants. Her grandmother had on her red blouse with the short, puffy sleeves and her blue skirt that was splattered with what had once been red music notes but which were now faded and broken pink sticks. Her braid was wrapped around her head. 'She looks like an immigrant,' Beth thought coldly, comparing her to Joyce. For several moments Beth stood there looking at her grandmother and feeling entitled to a few answers.

The instant her grandmother glanced up, however, she didn't want to know. If, right at that moment, her grandmother had decided to tell her what the messages were about, Beth would have run away. As it was, she ran around to the front of the house and down the street. 'I love Jesus, I love Jesus,' she said, holding her arms out. She was so light on her feet! Any day now she was going to float, she could feel it.

Her father came home early that evening. It seemed significant to Beth that he did not change into casual pants and a sports shirt *before* supper, as he normally did. Other than that, however, nothing out of the ordinary happened. Her father talked about work, her grandmother nodded and signalled and wrote out a few conversational notes, which Beth leaned over to read.

After supper her father got around to changing his clothes, then went outside to cut the grass while Beth and her grandmother did the dishes. Beth, carrying too many dishes to the sink, dropped and smashed a saucer and a dinner plate. Her grandmother waved her hands—'Don't worry, it doesn't matter!'—and to prove it she got the Sears catalogue out of the cupboard and showed Beth the new set of dinnerware she intended to buy anyway.

It wasn't until Beth was eating breakfast the next morning that it dawned on her that if her mother was coming back, her grandmother would be leaving, and if her grandmother was leaving, she wouldn't be buying new dinnerware. This thought left Beth feeling as if she had just woken up with no idea yet what day it was or what she'd just been dreaming. Then the radio blared '. . . Liver . . .' and she jumped and turned to see her grandmother with one hand on the volume knob, and the other hand held up for silence. 'Doctors report that the transplant was a success,' the announcer said, 'and that Kevin is in serious but stable condition.'

'Did they find a donor?' Beth cried as the announcer said, 'The donor, an eleven-year-old girl, died in St. Andrew's hospital late last night. Her name is being withheld at her family's request.'

Her grandmother turned the volume back down.

'Gee, that's great,' Beth said. 'Everybody was praying for him.'

Her grandmother tore a note off her pad. 'Ask and it shall be given you,' she wrote.

'I know!' Beth said exultantly. 'I know!'

Nobody was home at Helen's that afternoon. Peering in the window beside the door, Beth saw that the mauve suitcase was gone, and the next thing she knew, she floated from Helen's door to the end of her driveway. Or at least she thought she floated, because she couldn't remember how she got from the house to the road, but the strange thing was, she didn't have the glowing sensation, the feeling of glory. She drifted home, holding herself as if she were a soap bubble.

At her house there was a note on the kitchen counter: a drawing of an apple, which meant that her grandmother was out grocery shopping. The phone rang, but when Beth said hello, the person hung up. She went into her bedroom, opened the drawer of her bedside table and took out the message with her mother's phone number on it. She returned to the kitchen and dialled. After four rings, an impatient-sounding woman said, 'Hello?' Beth said nothing. 'Yes, hello?' the woman said. 'Who's calling?'

Beth hung up. She dialled Helen's number and immediately hung up.

She stood there for a few minutes, biting her knuckles.

She wandered down to her bedroom and looked out the window. Two back yards away, Amy was jumping off her porch. She was climbing onto the porch railing, leaping like a broad jumper, tumbling on the grass, springing to her feet, running up the stairs and doing it again. It made Beth's head spin.

About a quarter of an hour later her grandmother returned. She dropped the groceries against a cupboard door that slammed shut. She opened and shut the fridge. Turned on the tap. Beth, now lying on the bed, didn't move. She sat bolt upright when the phone rang, though. Five rings before her grandmother answered it.

Beth got up and went over to the window again. Amy was throwing a ball up into the air. Through the closed window Beth couldn't hear a thing, but she knew from the way Amy clapped and twirled her hands between catches that she was singing, 'Ordinary moving, laughing, talking . . .'

She knew from hearing the chair scrape that her grandmother was pulling it back to sit down. She knew from hearing the faucet still run that her grandmother was caught up in what the caller was saying. Several times her grandmother tapped her pencil on the mouthpiece to say to the caller, 'I'm still listening. I'm taking it all down.'

1992

# M. G. Vassanji
## b. 1950

Multilingual and identifying with three continents, Moyez Gulamhussein Vassanji is both a Canadian writer and a global one. He has created a body of fiction that seeks to record the history of the Khoja, a small cultural group that originated in the Sindh and Gujarat regions of what was northwest India (after the Partition, Sindh became part of Pakistan). Traditionally, the Khoja were rich Hindu landowners who, while keeping some Hindu cultural practices, were converted to Islam six centuries ago by Pir Sadruddin, a Persian missionary. In the last two centuries, they have a history of emigration. Some travelled to East Africa as sailors and stayed to become merchants and administrators to colonial overlords; many of these left Africa after decolonization, settling in North America, among other places.

Born in Kenya to parents of Gujarati descent, Vassanji lost his father when he was five years old. He and his siblings were raised by his mother, who returned with them to her birth country of Tanzania. As a student at the Aga Khan Schools in Dar es Salaam, he had an opportunity to meet—and was impressed by—the Nigerian novelist Chinua Achebe, one of the first African writers to gain international readership. At nineteen, while at the University of Nairobi, Vassanji won a scholarship to the Massachusetts Institute of Technology, where he studied nuclear physics. He went on to complete a PhD in that field at the University of Pennsylvania. Vassanji immigrated to Canada in 1978 when he accepted a job in theoretical physics at the Chalk River Laboratories in Chalk River, Ontario.

During the 1980s, he worked at the University of Toronto as a lecturer and research associate. Around this time, he grew interested in medieval Indian literature and culture. He began to write and—becoming aware of the lack of outlets in Canada for writing by South Asians—he founded, with his wife Nurjehan Aziz, *The Toronto South Asian Review* in 1981. Broadening the journal's focus, they renamed it *The Toronto Review of Contemporary Writing Abroad* (in this incarnation, it lasted from 1993 to 2002). In 1995, they began TSAR Publications, a small press that has been important for its promotion of diasporan authors.

Vassanji's first novel, *The Gunny Sack*, appeared in 1989. It tells the story of a man who, having inherited a gunny sack containing trinkets from the past, reconstructs the stories of his South Asian family in their migrations from India to Kenya and Tanzania, and then to North America. *The Gunny Sack* won a Commonwealth Writers Prize in 1990 and gained Vassanji an invitation to spend a term at the University of Iowa's International Writing Program. As a result of that success, and feeling that writing was his real mission in life, he ended his career as a physicist. The following year he published *Uhuru Street*, a linked group of short stories about growing up in Dar es Salaam. He then turned to his experiences as an immigrant in Canada in *No New Land* (1991), a novel, in the form of a story sequence, about a high-rise apartment building in the Toronto suburb of Don Mills—one that is home to so many immigrants from Tanzania that it becomes a high-rise village within the larger city.

Vassanji gained broad recognition in Canada with his 1994 novel, *The Book of Secrets*, which won the inaugural Giller Prize. That novel deepens his considerations of the way stories from the past can be recovered and drawn together in a larger narrative: a man living in contemporary Dar es Salaam who comes into possession of the diary of a British colonial administrator from seventy-five years earlier feels compelled to 'follow the threads . . . in all their connections and possibilities' and 'weave them together.' 'Like a bloodhound I will follow the trail the diary leaves. Much of it is bloody; it's blood that endures.' His investigation leads him,

and the reader, to a deeper understanding of the the South Asian communities of East Africa.

The novel *Amriika* (1999) provides further expansion of Vassanji's examinations of border-crossing and the intersections of cultures: it tells of the confused feelings of a South Asian student who arrives in the United States during the turmoil of the 1960s and recounts his experiences there in the two decades that follow. As in his previous novels, Vassanji works with a broad canvas and a large cast of secondary characters, depicting the past as a heavy weight on the present. The way this kind of culture-crossing leads to the divided consciousness of the immigrant is emphasized throughout Vassanji's fiction and can be seen in the title of his 2003 novel *The In-Between World of Vikram Lall* (which was nominated for several awards and won Vassanji a second Giller Prize). Growing up in mid-twentieth-century Kenya in a family of Indian immigrants, its protagonist had occupied an ambiguous middle ground between the English colonizers and those around him of African descent. Now, living in Canada, he cannot adjust to his present because he cannot free himself from—or even fully understand—that troubled past.

The portrait of the woman in 'Her Two Husbands', the story reprinted here, which comes from the short-story collection *When She Was Queen* (2005), shows how gender also becomes a factor in these divisions. Yasmin finds that her two marriages to South Asian immigrants—the first to a man who 'had given up on Indian–Pakistani culture as of no significance to his life in the West' and who embraced instead 'what's authentic and around us'; the second to a man who remains a member of his diasporic community, which maintains the religion and values and the arts and culture of the old world they left behind—have given her two different ways of seeing the world. With her first husband, she travelled to Mexico and Europe, but with the second, she visits Pakistan; with the first, she went to see historic sites of Islamic rule in Spain—the Great Mosque in Cordoba and the palace of Alhambra—but with the second, she visits a living Islamic community in Pakistan and finds 'such warmth in the people she met; she had never experienced anything like it in Canada. You knew these were your people, in spite of the differences; and all the history of the country, going back two thousand years, was part of your history, too.' However, while Yasmin initially feels she has found a world that is more 'authentic and real', she soon learns that it also has its drawbacks.

The Assassin's Song (2007), which earned Vassanji a third Giller nomination, extends these considerations of the double-edged nature of mixed inheritances. Its central character—who has moved from a pre-modern village boyhood in India to twentieth-century Cambridge, and from there to a life as an English professor in British Columbia—is called back to India and to a world of violence he thought he had escaped. Vassanji plays this story off against that of Nur Fazal, a thirteenth-century Indian mystic who sought a middle way between Hinduism and Islam.

When Vassanji finally travelled to India to see the homeland of his grandparents in 1993, he says that it

seemed at once so startlingly familiar and yet so alien; so frustrating and yet so enlightening and humbling; so warm and friendly and yet so inhumanly cruel and callous. But above all it . . . was as if a part of me which had lain dormant all the while had awakened and reclaimed me.

That journey and subsequent trips, undertaken as research for the writing of The Assassin's Song, served as the basis of A Place Within: Rediscovering India (2008), which blends anecdotes about Vassanji's own experiences of return with a retelling of Indian history and myth.

Though the effects of immigration, of being a member of a subculture, and of negotiating the intersections of conflicting values are important elements in his fiction, Vassanji resists being pigeonholed. In an essay entitled 'Am I a Canadian Writer?' he writes, 'I am no more ethnic than you are; I am not a professional multiculturalist, a specimen demonstrating this country's political or social reality, justifying its place on some UN list of wonderful places just behind Switzerland and ahead of Belgium.' To Vassanji, being defined in essentialist terms such as religion (he is a non-believer who nonetheless sees himself as immersed in a religious culture), or 'roots' (he writes about and is often identified with the Indian diaspora, though neither he nor his parents were born in India), or—even though he feels deeply about the African environment in which he grew up—place of origin, or even immigrant status, is reductive. In Robin Benger's documentary film The In-Between World of M.G. Vassanji (2006) he remarks,

I tell people Margaret Atwood is not a Christian writer, so why on earth should someone put a religious or common label on me. It is insulting, it is offensive. It is racist. You only pick a few people and . . . say you're an immigrant writer or you're an Islamic writer. When everyone else is just a writer. It's the worst thing you can do to a creative person.

In 2009, Vassanji published a study of the Canadian writer for whom he seems to feel greatest affinity, one who, like Vassanji, found that standing to one side of the mainstream allowed him to observe it with a critical detachment: Mordecai Richler.

# Her Two Husbands

How ironic for him, she thought, that it began with a phone call, the unravelling of his presence in her life. He had said to her once, 'Yasmin, if someone were to sweet-talk to you on the phone and convinced you to do it, you would smother one of your own children.' Not fair, that taunt, it stung. But it was true that she was easy to take advantage of sometimes, because she found it hard to be abrupt with people, was loath to seem cold and rude to them. Once or twice something *had* got burnt on the stove because of the phone; and how many times had she been wheedled into a purchase or a donation she regretted as soon as she put the receiver down. But now he was dead and it was precisely the phone which had brought to her her new husband, and a new, more love-filled life.

It was almost a year since Aseema at the office had cornered her one day with an invitation, saying, 'There's a mushaira this weekend at Abid Bhai's—why don't you come, yaar, it should be a lot of fun.' Yasmin, smiles and apologies, had declined, but Aseema persisted: 'Step out of your weeds,[1] sweetheart, come and meet the world; you do have a life to lead, you know.' Yasmin said she would think about it, and Aseema had gone away looking pleased with herself.

Yasmin had no intention of going to the function. It was all right to go unescorted where people knew you well, or even sometimes where they were completely alien. But Pakistanis, Aseema's people, seemed familiar and yet also alien, and always so very formal and conservative . . . she would not at all feel comfortable among them.

Aseema herself was far from conservative in her manner; she made herself up with dabs of mascara and other eye stuff and dark purple lipstick spread thickly on her wide lips, and with her open-mouthed smile and half-closed eyes she could turn on a lascivious look to excite even the younger men who worked with her and Yasmin. But she was an exception. She had been to exclusive private schools in Pakistan, with American teachers and all that, a fact she never failed to stress if there was ever the slightest chance of her being taken for a regular 'Paki'. The invitation she had brought Yasmin was to a private Urdu poetry recital at her brother Abid's house. Over the years Aseema had extended several such invitations to Yasmin and Karim; and over the years Karim had pooh-poohed the very idea of an Urdu mushaira in Toronto, and put his wife off it too.

Yasmin had married a grim-natured man. Loving, yes, and passionate, too; but opinionated, for he was a widely read professor, and dark in outlook. *Dark* was the word; she had gotten used to watching ruefully as that telltale shadow came over his face, from its first appearance as a blank look in the eyes to the flush spreading across the cheeks, when some particularly sensitive issue, political or moral, came up. Regardless of the occasion, you only had to wait for the eruption—the barely controlled statement of opinion, and then gradually the furious torrent. He'd grown darker and angrier with age as he saw the world slip away from him, and himself become an old fogey to a new generation of young professors at work, to the young people he met, to the young women he saw.

What Urdu culture, he'd say scornfully. Do their children even *speak* Urdu anymore, let alone read or write Urdu poetry? Inviting an Urdu-wallah[2] from Pakistan or India to give a mushaira does not make the growth of Urdu literature in Canada. And how long can one go on hearing about the moth consumed in the flame of love, and the tender-cheeked rose weeping dewdrops at dawn. . . .

He was exaggerating, of course, even as he made flowing gestures with his right hand in imitation of Urdu poets, and he knew it. He had perfected damning scorn to a fine art. He was too learned for his own good. The truth was that he had given up

1 That is, 'widow's weeds', an old phrase for the black mourning clothes worn by a woman for a period following her husband's death.
2 An expert in Urdu culture.

on Indian-Pakistani culture as of no significance to his life in the West; to him it was the transplanted variety we had here, superficial and mediocre. Why not give up the game, he would say, and pay attention to what's authentic and around us?

A day or two after Aseema's invitation, her brother Abid had called.

'Yasmin,' he said, 'you know why I am calling.'

'No . . . well . . .' and she gave a little laugh. She had met Abid once when he came to see his sister at work, and she remembered him as an excessively polite and quite handsome man.

'What a pleasant laugh,' he said. 'Seriously, you've made my day already. Listen, Yasmin, aren't you interested even a little in Urdu poetry? It's our culture, after all—'

'I am,' she said hesitantly. Like many people, she enjoyed listening occasionally to ghazals sung to music, she even had a collection on a CD somewhere. But she didn't know much else about Urdu poetry, except the name of the most famous poet Ghalib, about whom she'd seen a popular Indian film. Aseema had told her about the others, but she couldn't quite remember their names. Iqbal? Faiz?

'I am calling to invite you personally, Yasmin. Gharib Ferangi—yes, his name rhymes with *Ghalib*, isn't that funny? And Gharib—yes, that name means 'poor'!— Ferangi is *the* most important poet in Urdu today. . . .'

Important according to whom?—she heard her dead husband's voice at the back of her head, imagined that scornful face behind her, as usual to the point and giving no quarter.

Abid's voice on the phone was melodious, respectful, and full of humility. If the consensus had ruled that Gharib Ferangi was the most important Urdu or Pakistani poet alive, he wouldn't be the one to argue the point.

'Only the most select people will be there, I assure you,' he went on, 'sophisticated people, not intrusive and not religious—I know that worries you. We all are not fundamentalists, and if you read some of Ferangi's poetry it will make you blush. He has even had some fatwas issued against him!'

She was trapped, what could she do? As Karim would say, The house may burn down, but you couldn't say to the person at the other end: lay off; no, I can't do it; I'm not buying; whatever.

'I really am not sure,' she replied, to Abid.

'It's only a cultural evening,' Abid insisted, 'a party, and we want the most diverse and enlightened group, Yasmin. . . .'

The critical voice in her mind she managed to squeeze out, and she said, 'Let me call you back. I'll have to check with the children and their plans.'

'Please do so,' Abid said. 'Of course you should, you are a mother. And thank you. I know you will enjoy yourself.'

You did it again, the voice said. She had tears in her eyes.

*

Abid was right. When she went to the mushaira-party at his house in Mississauga, she enjoyed herself thoroughly. The poet Ferangi was a short, balding man, wearing white kurta-pyjama and black waistcoat, and what a voice! He was given the place of honour, the wide sofa in the living room, his adulating audience gathered before him on the broadloomed floor. They were all familiar with his works, having studied them in college back in Pakistan. He would recite from their requests, and frequently they would spontaneously join in, in a happy chorus, and finish the last lines of a poem with him. He was a charming man, funny and profound; at times he stood up to recite, at times he sang, in the traditional posture, his left arm at his waist and his right arm before him performing for the audience. There would be back-and-forth banter, and behind every poem would be a spellbinding story. There was a break for dinner, which was a buffet with an immense variety of meat dishes. The poet was indulged with a glass and a bottle of Glenfiddich placed before him reverently where he sat. No one else drank alcohol. Yasmin was disappointed that Aseema had not come, but she was treated with a lot of respect and affection. The women, mostly sitting close together intimately, were warm in their manner, and looked lovely in saris and shalwar kameez. They listened to Ferangi's sometimes risqué pronouncements, casually delivered, about his or other poets' affairs, about genitalia or excrement, with the utmost composure. The poet had apparently picked his themes from his memories of life in the small town in India in which he had grown up. Yasmin made that observation to him and he expounded upon it. I was right to have come, she said both to herself and to the absent Karim. And all Urdu poetry is not about candles and moths, the rose and the early-morning dew, and 'gham'.[3]

And where does Ferangi live now? he retorted. England. And was there anyone under forty at the meeting? QED.

But no, QED or not, she had won the day. She had started to go out, and that was good.

*

Abid called her to thank her for coming—'for condescending to grace us with your presence,' was how he put it.

'What do you mean, "condescending"? It was such a wonderful opportunity to meet a genuine, living Urdu poet! Thank *you* for inviting me.'

'You are most welcome,' he told her. 'You were truly a blessing there.'

Typical Urdu flattery, said that voice in her mind, typical India-Pakistan—even when a dagger is being thrust at your back, in front is all honeyed talk, You first, *aap pahele*, please, there's no one such as your gracious self, all 'umble Uriah Heep[4]—

You're jealous! she retorted.

A couple of weeks later Aseema said to Yasmin, in her usual manner, 'You know, sweetie pie, I believe brother Abid is smitten with you—don't tell me I haven't warned you, kiddo.'

For the next few days Yasmin's nerves were on tenterhooks. What to do? What to think? This was totally unexpected, she was completely unprepared for it. Then Abid called.

---

3 Pain; sadness.
4 Uriah Heep is a character from Charles Dickens' 1850 novel *David Copperfield*. Heep exemplifies unctuous displays of false humility.

'How are you?'

'Fine', she answered, 'but don't tell me another Urdu event is coming up so soon!'

'No . . . well there is, but that's not why I called. I would like to take you to a concert, of the Toronto Symphony—you do like Western classical?'

'Yes, up to a point, I'm not really an expert—'

'Neither am I—'

'And I can't stand the modern stuff.'

Which Karim would sometimes take her to, saying, Listen with the mind sometimes, Yas, these days even the hip-hoppers are humming Beethoven's Ninth—

'Neither can I,' Abid told her. 'This is an all-Beethoven concert, with the Ninth Symphony, and it is my favourite!'

She hesitated. Was it right? Was this a date? What did Abid expect of her? There was a moment's silence while she quickly reflected and he let her.

Then he said, 'I had two tickets given me by a client and I thought you might like to come. It's discreet, our people don't usually go to these events—though I believe your late husband did. You know he was highly respected in our Asian communities, though I didn't quite agree with some of his comments—he struck me as . . . angry.' He caught himself and said, 'Come on, Yasmin, I'm quite harmless, really—'

She laughed, and she agreed to go.

\*

And so eventually she agreed to marry him; and the ghost of Karim, if there was one, became a glowering bitter face in the background, occasionally erupting but more often silent.

What she liked about Abid's people, his community—which consisted of friends and some near and distant relatives—was their gentility, the grace and respect they showed to each other. Of course this was only external form and etiquette; nevertheless, she realized that she had never been accorded such treatment before. In return she lived up to the expectations implicitly demanded of her. She now wore the sari or shalwar kameez, attires which she liked very much, with all their colour and grace, though there was the odd occasion when she sensed a qualm within herself and wished she had the pluck to look different—come out for instance in a khaki skirt and red tank top, or (God forbid) shorts, during summer. At parties she was pulled toward the women, away from the men. She had already learned to defer to the elders of her new community in the formal, elaborate, and quite charming ways expected, which reminded her of the Indian movies of her childhood. She felt a bit hypocritical after such displays. Abid himself was a soft-hearted, genial sort who rarely raised his voice, which was strange for her because she had been used to shows of excitement or anger from a husband. The whole tenor of her life had become orderly and calm, if a little constrained.

You've sunk, said that voice once. Don't you have an iota of a sense of who you were, who you really are?

What was I? she retorted. *You* made me!

She and Karim had met twenty years ago when she was a new assistant librarian in the history department of the University of Toronto and he a quiet professor. Even then he exuded that darkness of soul, though she saw it only as a romantic, somewhat Keatsian trait. They got to talking once about a journal recently discontinued by the library, then about other excellent journals guillotined by university cutbacks, and over the weeks gradually became intimate. She had no doubts when she accepted to marry him. He was charming and easy to be with, vastly educated, and slightly mysterious. She liked the fact that he was westernized, refreshingly different in his thinking from what she was used to seeing in men from their background. He took her to a whole new world of the opera, music concerts, book readings and museums, the thrill of living in the city, away from the suburban developments filling up with immigrants. The kids came and put a new twist on their existence. He spurned religious education for them as a regimen cooked up by a bunch of ignorant, uncultured managers to keep their people in line. She more or less agreed, but (as she sometimes argued) what was wrong with the kids spending time with their own kind? Her reservations arose mainly because she was losing friends. They were all professionals, married to other professionals or businessmen, and all observant community members—a class Karim had contemptuously dismissed as the 'Markhamites' and the 'Scarberians',[5] suburbanites spending their nonworking hours on the highways and in mosque. He was so passionate in his beliefs, she simply went along with them because ultimately she didn't quite care as much, and she wanted him happy. But she had her qualms and she had her guilt. She needed her God in small doses, like normal people.

He was, of course, a professed agnostic—all that meant was that he battled against God all the time, worried about all the problems ailing the world. What had seemed like a darkly romantic trait, a soulful detail in his character, had grown into a hopeless view of the world and an anger simmering beneath his surface. Deep in his heart, she believed, he missed being a suburbanite, happy with his people and happy in his simple, blind faith.

He always thought he would die young, and when he finally did so, in his fifties of stroke, it was almost with relief in his eyes, in all his demeanour—the world had been too much for him; and she too felt a semblance of relief, for he had made her so conscious of his impending death. But then, after he died, he started to haunt her—or, what was the same thing, she began to recall his presence. She heard his voice in her mind, felt his presence looming behind her, whenever she felt she was straying from the path the two of them had followed together.

Of their three children, the two eldest were on their own, the first, a son, working at a downtown brokerage firm, and the second, a daughter, in university in the States. The youngest, a son, was eleven and had come with her to her new life; he was reserved but polite with Uncle Abid. Her husband's attempts to teach him Urdu or interest him in the tenets of Islam had been to no avail.

Yasmin felt loved—by Abid; by his friends and their wives; by her stepdaughter Rabbia, who occasionally came to visit them with her young family and had taken an immense liking to Yasmin.

---

5 Residents of Markham, a northeastern suburb of Toronto, and of Scarborough (before amalgamation, an eastern suburb of Toronto), which is sometimes jokingly referred to as 'Scarberia'.

'Amma,' Rabbia said, 'you are an angel, you've come like a farishta[6] into my father's life. He gave up so many years of his life out of respect for my mother, worrying about me—but you know what, the wait was worth it. I've never known him happier—*never*, if you get my meaning.'

'I get your meaning, thank you', Yasmin replied, with a smile. 'And I've also . . . never been happier. . . .'

Never? And that pregnant pause, that sharp breath you took there for a moment before that glib remark . . . *never*? Not when the first child, Emil, was born? Not on that trip to Acapulco, or Spain—in Andalusia, in Cordoba—that second honeymoon?

I am happy as I've never been in a long time. I am respected as a woman and a wife, not as a mere companion and sex partner. I am the lady of the house and a lady in a community. My husband is calm and gentle; he rarely gets annoyed, and I have yet to see him at full boil. He is not at war with the world, he is a meditative, a spiritual man.

\*

Visiting Pakistan was the most wonderful event of her life. Yes, it eclipsed all those memories of Andalusia, strolling with Karim through fields of orange and bougainvillea, hand in hand staring up at the awesome ceiling of the Great Mosque in Cordoba or at the palace of Alhambra, the two of them picking up their lives again when the kids were older. Of course on this trip there was no dearth of the frustrations typical of the Third World—long waits at the airport, people jumping queues, dimwitted or sleazy officials, murderous traffic. But there was such warmth in the people she met; she had never experienced anything like it in Canada. You knew these were your people, in spite of the differences; and all the history of the country, going back two thousand years, was part of your history, too. They spent most of their time in Lahore, which was Abid's hometown. To his family, Yasmin was royalty; she was greeted by them with embraces and tears of joy, with gifts of clothing and jewellery. There were elaborate family feasts in her honour, she went shopping and sightseeing, was invited to private music parties with blood-curdling qawalis by the best singers—that makes you envious, doesn't it, Karim, all *authentic* and *real*, the way you wanted everything. Young women, older ones, confided in her, their new bhabhi or bahu from Canada, young men called her Auntie and teased her.

Abid had two brothers and a sister in Lahore. He also had Aseema in Toronto and another sister in Chicago. The family's business in Lahore was transportation. They also owned land. Abid's father was dead—Yasmin was taken to pay her respects at the grave—and his mother, tall and bony with grey eyes and a wonderful smile, was the matriarch to whom all paid respect. Nothing was done without consulting her. The family had a spiritual adviser, Sheikh Murad Ali, who also advised in worldly matters.

When the family took her to see the Sheikh, Yasmin had to tie a plain black scarf around her head—the Sheikh was insistent, they told her with a twinkle in their eyes, he had to be humoured. A loose dupatta,[7] with wisps of hair blowing at the forehead,

6 Angel.
7 A long scarf.

just wouldn't do in his presence. He was liable to produce a rough cloth himself and tie it firmly around your head if he didn't like your covering. He didn't care for jeans either, even on men.

He turned out to be a small-statured man with a radiant pink face and a long white beard, attired in a shimmering silk kurta of a pale colour and an embroidered cap. His cold grey eyes made her look away the first time he laid eyes on her. The walls in his study, where he received them, opening the double doors himself to let them in, were lined with books and bound manuscripts and hung in places with framed Arabic calligraphy. There was an odour of faint perfume and recent incense in the air. He bade them sit on the carpeted floor, from which a small prayer mat was first rolled away, and a large silver tray of offerings was placed before him, piled with presents—a pen and a Palm Pilot, some dried fruit, and cash in dollars—which he received without much ado. The talk soon turned to serious matters, and as his guidance to them the Sheikh warned them about Western materialism, which people everywhere in the world were blindly emulating while losing their own spiritual values. The men enjoyed discussing world politics with him, but they did this with due deference to his views. The women listened silently to this discussion or spoke to each other in whispers.

To Yasmin, the Sheikh's beliefs seemed narrow and rigid, and it was a trial of patience to keep sitting there on the floor meekly listening to them. She lost her control finally and sprung to the defence of her gender, saying, 'But women are not men's property, and they are not half the worth of men.' The Sheikh, at first startled into a pause, gave a look of amusement and replied, 'They are worth *more* than men, Béta, that's why Murshid-ul-kameel has given us all these elaborate laws regarding men and women.' Her in-laws explained to her what was meant, and Yasmin dutifully said, 'Oh.' But that fooled nobody.

'That's one side of Pakistan I will never accept', she said to Abid later, 'this treatment of women,' having told him first that she didn't think she cared too much for Sheikh Murad Ali.

That pleased Karim. Told you so, the voice said. Pakistan, he had always said, was a tragedy on the Indian subcontinent, a non-country that had never worked, never been really independent, never been democratic, was an embarrassment. He could go on and on, making judgments so sweeping, so cruel and unfair—the kinds of generalizations he would swiftly decry in others. Look what you got yourself into, he now gloated, an orthodox soup!

You are jealous, only, she replied. I have a people, a place to belong to, a culture and a faith—and you, you had zip, nothing, and that's why all your anger at the world. I have your number, Karim Bharwani, finally; I know where you came from, in spite of your Wagner and Beethoven, Marx and Freud—from nowhere, and how you longed for the certainty I've achieved. Even now, in death, what do you have? Have you found peace at last? No, you flit round the globe, from one disaster area to another, seeing only famine and genocide, car bombs and smart weapons, raging at the injustice and inhumanity all over. Not satisfied, you return to torment me.

\*

It was only Karim and the Sheikh in Lahore who were the spoilers in her new life. Karim she could manage. She knew him, and he was dead, after all. But the Sheikh?

'He's an old man, Yasu,' Abid assured her. 'He'll soon be gone—how long do you think he will live? And his heir Salamat Ali is not so old-fashioned.'

'Not so orthodox, you mean. Fundamentalist.'

He laughed. 'That's just a word.'

'Anyway, Murad Ali looked quite healthy to me. People like that take good care of themselves, they don't die easily. And his son could turn out even worse.'

'Don't *worry*,' Abid said. 'It's temporary, this edict. In time, Murad Ali will relent. Remember, he has our good at heart—he is our interpreter of the faith and our agent with God.'

Not two months had passed since their visit to Pakistan, when the Sheikh sent the edict that came like a rock thrown at the boat that was her life. Abid was told about it by his sister, who called late one night from Lahore. He was so stunned he forgot to hide his reaction from Yasmin, who was listening and watching from the bed.

'*What?* Are you sure . . . *every* woman? Even in Canada and US? Think of public relations. He won't relent? Arré what's come over him . . . thik hé, then. But try. Soften him up a bit. . . .'

The Sheikh had pronounced that the moral order in the world continued to decline. It pained him to see that even decent people had begun to deviate from the path of the righteous, dazzled by the attractions conjured up by wily Azazel, beguiled by honeyed words from the forked tongue of Satan. He, Sheikh Murad Ali of Lahore, was exhorting his followers to rectify their habits and come back to the path. Rules regarding halal were to be followed strictly. Personal hygiene was to be observed according to Islamic tradition. And women had to cover their heads with a black or white chador that reached at least to their shoulders.

Yasmin, shocked beyond belief, had little doubt that this edict from afar was the real answer to her outburst in the Sheikh's study in Lahore. She recalled the old man's initial reaction when she spoke up—that pause, the stillness that momentarily overcame him before he recovered with the smile and the patronizing comment. His eyes had grazed her neck, met hers, before he lightly dismissed her objection. She had met his eyes again on the way out. She felt humbled and defeated by his power over her now.

'You've betrayed me,' she said tearfully to her husband. 'You misled me—'

'Yasmin, my life, how can you say that?'

'You expect me to wear that . . . that tent over my head?'

'Not a *tent*—' he laughed—'it's supposed to come only to the shoulders. He's our Sheikh, my love, he stands between us and God. And it's only temporary. '

*My foot*, she wanted to blurt out, but held her peace.

She sulked and wept intermittently all that day, and the next.

The following evening a potluck dinner was arranged at a friend's house to discuss this new edict of Sheikh Murad Ali, their leader. Ten couples were present, and to Yasmin's surprise nobody showed any concern about the ruling. A few people even poked a little fun at it and at some of the Sheikh's ways (for example, he burped loudly and with relish). What could have set him off? the question was raised. Perhaps Benazir Bhutto's recent antics. Or the recent performance of the Pakistan cricket team. Or the jokes that were made even there about President Clinton's affair with that girl Monica Lewinsky, a name familiar in every village now, following the recent TV crash course on sex. They discussed ways of bending the new rule: the Sheikh had ordered white or black chador to be worn, but he didn't specify what material, and hadn't placed any injunctions on the designs printed or embroidered on it; and surely, they agreed, black meant simply dark, therefore blue would be acceptable; the chador should reach the shoulders, but even a dupatta did that. . . . There were of course arguments among the men, as there usually were, when the subject veered off toward world politics. There was plenty of food to eat. Poetry was recited, songs were sung. Yasmin was reminded sharply of the sense of community among these people, of their common struggles against life's crazy contradictions, and the sense of humour they could always call upon to cope with them. She went home immensely relieved.

That night she and Abid spent many tender moments together. At length, when they were ready to go to sleep, he asked, 'Is it too late for you to have a child?'

'I think so. Why, you want one? I could ask the doctor.'

'No. . . . We are both done with that. We need all the time to be with each other and enjoy life.'

'I agree.'

And so, said that voice in her head, as she lay on her back, wide awake but eyes gently shut, happy, listening to her own breathing, and that of the man beside her. And so, said that voice, a smidgin of sex, a bit of *meri jaan*,[8] and you'll go out tomorrow wearing a tent on the head—

Stop it! He loves me, and it's not a tent. You know that. . . . And what do you mean by 'a smidgin of sex' anyway? He's better at it than you were by a long shot—

Oh yeah, I didn't see you exactly moaning with helpless pleasure now or screaming for more—

It's not just the moaning and screaming, you insensitive man, it's also the gentleness, the love you feel inside every pore of your entire body, the—

I see.

That takes care of him, she thought, regaining her breath. Finally. She sensed him receding from her mind . . . he would go away for ever now, truly dead. She realized all of a sudden that she didn't quite want that to happen. She began to miss him.

Karim? she called.

Yes? Sullen, and distant, as if from the door.

But I do need you . . . stay . . .

Aw, he said.

It was almost a year since Abid had come into her life.

2005

8 My darling.

# Guy Vanderhaeghe

## b. 1951

Born in Esterhazy, Saskatchewan, in 1951, Guy Vanderhaeghe studied history at the University of Saskatchewan (BA, 1972; MA, 1975). After taking a B.Ed at the University of Regina in 1978, he taught high school and worked as an archivist and researcher. He served as writer-in-residence at the University of Ottawa (1985) and at the Saskatoon Public Library (1993–4). Since 1993, he has been associated with Saint Thomas More College, University of Saskatchewan, where he is now the St. Thomas More Scholar. Among his many honours, he has received Toronto's Harbourfront Literary Prize and the Timothy Findley Prize (for a body of work) and has been made an Officer of the Order of Canada and a Fellow of the Royal Society of Canada.

The short stories Vanderhaeghe began publishing in journals in the late 1970s were brought together in *Man Descending* (1982)—which established his reputation as a major writer of short fiction, winning him the Faber Prize and the first of his Governor General's Awards—and in *The Trouble with Heroes and Other Stories* (1983). A third collection of his short stories, *Things as They Are* (from which 'Man on Horseback', reprinted here, is drawn), appeared in 1992. Vanderhaeghe's novels—*My Present Age* (1984), *Homesick* (1989), *The Englishman's Boy* (1996; Governor General's Award), and *The Last Crossing* (2002)—further advanced his reputation. He is also the author of two plays: *I Had a Job I Liked. Once.* (1992) and *Dancock's Dance* (1996).

Vanderhaeghe's fiction can be seen as a series of responses to the western narratives he had inherited. Like Frederick Philip Grove and Sinclair Ross, Vanderhaeghe rejected the American 'myth of the Old West' to tell stories of an unromanticized Canadian west. However, his Prairie realism differs from that of his precursors: in place of details about the physical environment, he pays careful attention to the way individuals live and the culture they create, suggesting that region (not just landscape) shapes

lives. In his later work, Vanderhaeghe reacts to newer, revisionist perspectives on the west—in particular, the anti-romantic retelling of the American western in Larry McMurtry's *Lonesome Dove* (1985) and its highly ironic recasting in Cormac McCarthy's *Blood Meridian* (1985).

In developing his particularly Canadian version of the revisionist western, Vanderhaeghe expands his canvas, creates complex characters, and makes use of intricate narratives that are grounded in history. In 'Man on Horseback', with its protagonist who feels overshadowed by the vanishing heroic world of his father, Vanderhaeghe makes the figure of the horseman central in order to investigate its attraction and latent power. As a historian, the story's protagonist is acutely aware of the significance and symbolism of the horse in the past. This enrichment of meaning that historical consciousness brings is also at the centre of Vanderhaeghe's 1996 novel, *The Englishman's Boy*, which marked a new level of achievement in his career.

Vanderhaeghe himself sees his play *Dancock's Dance* as permitting this development. He has said that because this play (based on an actual event in which the inmates of a Saskatchewan mental hospital kept the institution running during the deadly Spanish influenza epidemic of 1918) allowed him to identify the problems inherent in historical fiction, he was able to write both *The Englishman's Boy* and *The Last Crossing*. He conceives of these novels as the first two books of a trilogy about the 1870s in Western Canada—a time and place of redefinitions of boundaries and nationality, of social order, and even of human relationships.

*The Englishman's Boy* is a doubled narrative that sets the event known in Canadian history as the Cypress Hills Massacre against the story of a filmmaker in the early days of Hollywood trying to make a movie about that occurrence—but distorting it to serve his own ends. In a 2003 interview with Jeremy Mouat, Vanderhaeghe observes that 'the real topic of the book' is 'the way history is used politically.' *The Last Crossing* has a picaresque narrative—two brothers from Victorian England search, with the assistance of a Métis guide, for a third brother, who preceded them—that portrays individuals moving through the 1870s Canadian west, while also showing how their previous lives in England and the United States continue to shape their experiences in Canada.

In raising questions about its myth and history, Vanderhaeghe explores the idea of the west as a powerful force in the construction of manhood. In all his fiction, the masculine ethos affects relationships—whether between men and women, or fathers and sons, or man and horse. It alienates father from son in 'Man on Horseback', but in an earlier story of Vanderhaeghe's, 'The Trouble with Heroes', the main character fears that today's men can no longer play heroic roles, and wonders: 'Without a belief in the possibility of heroism and endurance, what is left?' That question continues to occupy Vanderhaeghe in 'Man on Horseback' and throughout his work.

# Man on Horseback

Following his father's death, Joseph Kelsey discovered, in his bereavement, a passion for horses. Joseph's passion for horses was not of the same character as the old man's had been; Joseph's was searching, secretive, concerned with lore, confined to books. It was not love. When his wife asked him what he was doing, staying up so late night after night, he said he was working on an article. Joseph was a professor of history.

The article was a lie. He was reading about horses.

*A good horse sholde have three propyrtees of a man, three of a woman, three of a foxe, three of a hare, and three of an asse.*[1]

Joseph was born in a poor, backward town to a couple reckoned to be one of the poorest and most backward. It was a world of outhouses, chicken coops in backyards, eyeglasses purchased from Woolworth's, bad teeth that never got fixed. On the afternoon of October 29, 1949, when his mother's water broke his father ran down the lane to get Pepper Carmichael to drive them to the hospital. Rupert Kelsey didn't own an automobile, not even a rusted collection of rattles like Pepper's.

What Rupert Kelsey owned was seven horses. Horses slipped and slid through his fingers like quicksilver. When he was flush he bought more, when funds ran low he sold off one or two. Horses came and horses went in a continual parade, bays and sorrels, blacks and greys, chestnuts and roans, pintos and piebalds. His wife was jealous of them.

There was trouble with Joseph's birth right from the start. The hospital, staffed mostly by nuns, was tiny and antiquated, as backward as the town. Rupert Kelsey sat

1 A fifteenth-century definition found in *Brewer's Dictionary of Phrase and Fable*. The other passages in italics that appear throughout have been created by Vanderhaeghe from several different sources.

in the waiting room for an hour, and then a sister came out and told him they had telephoned everywhere but the doctor couldn't be found. It was understood what that meant. The doctor was either drunk—not an uncommon occurrence—or was off playing poker somewhere without having left a number where he could be reached. Rupert nodded solemnly and the nun left, face as starchy as her wimple.

The duty nurse behind the reception desk, a gossip, watched him closely, intrigued to see how he would take the news. He could sense her curiosity clear across the room and he was careful not to give away anything he was feeling. He had a country boy's wilful, adamant sense of what was private, the conviction that people in towns had no notion of what was their business and what wasn't.

Because this was his wife's first baby he knew that labour would likely be prolonged and hard. For three hours he sat, alternately studying the scuffed toes of his boots and the clock on the wall, his face held gravely polite against the duty nurse's inspection. The nurse was working a double shift because the woman who was to relieve her had called in at the last minute sick. She was bored and Rupert Kelsey was the only item of even mild interest in what was going to be a very long night. To the nurse he looked thirty, but seemed much older. Maybe it was the old-fashioned haircut which made his ears stand out like jug handles, maybe it was the way he shyly hid his dirty hands and cracked nails underneath the cap lying in his lap, maybe it was the bleak rawness of a face shaved with a blade sharpened that morning in a water glass, maybe it was the sum of all of these things or maybe it was none of these things which lent him that air of steadfast dignity she associated with men her father's age. He appeared to have nothing to do with her generation.

No one came out from the ward to tell Rupert Kelsey how matters stood. The Kelseys were not the sort of people that those in authority felt it necessary to make reports and explanations to. When the hands of the clock swung around to eleven he found it impossible to sustain a pose of calm any longer. Rupert got abruptly to his feet and started for the entrance.

The young nurse behind the desk spoke sharply to him. 'Mr Kelsey, Mr Kelsey, where are you going?' In her opinion this was not the way a father-to-be with a wife in the pangs of childbirth ought to behave.

'I'll be back,' he said, shouldering through the door.

It was cold, unusually cold for the end of October. The little town was dark, only its main street boasted streetlamps. Scarcely a window showed a light at this hour; in the days before television arrived, people here retired early, to sleep or entertain themselves in bed.

The barn where Kelsey stabled his horses was on the other side of town, but the other side of town was less than a ten-minute walk away. Just stepping into the heavy, crowded warmth of jostling bodies and freshly dropped dung, the ammoniac reek of horse piss, the dusty smell of hay and oats, the tang of sweat-drenched leather, made him hate that lifeless, sinister waiting room all the more.

He saddled the mare, led her into the yard, swung up on her back, and trotted through the town. The dirt roads were dry and packed and thudded crisply under the iron shoes. Like strings of firecrackers, dogs began to go off, one after another, along the streets he and his horse travelled. The mare carried her head high, neck twisted to the dogs howling out of the blackness, answering them with startled, fearful snorts. Easy and straight as a chair on a front porch, Rupert Kelsey rode her through the uproar and beyond the town limits.

It was a clear night, the sky pitilessly high, strewn faintly with bright sugary stars. Where the curtain of sky brushed the line of the horizon, poplar bluffs bristled. Beneath this cold sky Rupert Kelsey released his horse, let her fear of dogs and night bear human fear wild down the empty road, reins slack along her neck, hands knotted in the mane, braced for the headlong crash, the capsize into darkness. Her belly groaned hollowly between his legs, her breath tore in her chest. For three miles she fled, a runaway panicked.

At the bridge, the sudden glide of water, the broken shimmer unexpectedly intersecting the road caused the mare to shy, and as she broke stride he fought to turn her, striking back ruthlessly on the left rein, dragging her around open-mouthed like a hooked fish, swinging her back in the direction from which she had come, his heels drumming her through the turn, urging her, stretching her out flat down the road, back to the hospital.

By the time they reached the town the mare galloped on her last legs. On the planked railway crossing she stumbled, plunged, but kept her feet. Rupert whipped her the last five hundred yards to the hospital, reining her back on her haunches before the glass doors through which he could see the nurse as he had left her, at the desk. The nurse looked at him from where she sat and he looked at her. The mare trembled with exhaustion, a faint steam rising from wet flanks and neck. The nurse, finally realizing he was not about to dismount, got to her feet, came to the door, and pushed out into the night.

'Anything yet?' he asked.

She shook her head.

'The doctor come?'

She shook her head again.

He wheeled the horse around and was gone. For several moments the nurse stood straining for a glimpse of him, pink sweater draped over her shoulders, arms wrapped around herself against the piercing cold. Everything was swallowed up in darkness but the tattoo of hooves. She turned and went inside.

Back at the barn Kelsey pulled the bridle, blanket, and saddle off the mare and flung them on a four-year-old gelding, leaving the winded horse where she stood. Once again unseen dogs gave tongue, their wavering voices lifting along the streets. He rode hard into the countryside, the taste of a cold dark wind in his mouth.

The story was a favourite of the nurse's for a long time. 'Three times he rode up to the hospital and asked after his wife and then rode away again. Different horse every time. Looked drunker every time too. They usually are. Last time it was just after the sun came up, around eight in the morning that I told him she had finally delivered a boy. You know what he said? Said, "Tell the wife I'll be up to see her as soon as I can. I got some horses to look after." Imagine. And that woman came near dying too. It was a near thing if she'd lost any more blood.'

Joseph's mother always said to him. 'You, you little bastard, you wore out three horses and one woman getting born. It's got to be a record.'

*Wolf Calf of the Blackfoot first received horse medicine. It was given to him in a dream by a favourite horse which he had always treated respectfully and kindly. This horse appeared to him and said, 'Father, I am grateful for your kindness to me. Now I give you the sacred dance of the horses which will be your secret. I give you the power to heal horses and to heal people. In times of trouble I will always be near you.'*

*Horse Medicine Men could accomplish miracles. Not only could they cure sick horses and sick people, they could influence the outcome of races, causing horses to leave the course, buck, or refuse to run. Pursued by enemies, they would rub horse medicine on a quirt, point it at the pursuer and drop the quirt in the path of the foe's horse, causing the animal to falter.*

*All Horse Medicine Men recognized taboos. Rib bones and shin bones were not to be broken in the lodge of a Horse Medicine Man. No child should ride a wooden stick horse in a lodge in the presence of a Horse Medicine Man. If he did, misfortune and bad luck would befall that child.*

Before a vet arrived in the district, if a horse was sick or badly injured, its owner summoned Rupert Kelsey. Usually his father took Joseph along on these visits, although the boy wished he wouldn't. When Joseph was four a stud bit him on the shoulder. His mother told him that he had screamed bloody blue murder, screamed like a stuck pig. The purple, apple-green bruise lasted for weeks and if he hadn't been wearing a heavy parka, which had blunted the horse's teeth, the damage could have been a lot more severe. Years later Joseph would suppose that the sudden crushing pain, the breath hot on his neck and face, the mad glare of the eyes must have been the root of what, in a son of his father's, was an unnatural, shameful fear of horses. But he couldn't be sure. He had no memory of the incident. Envying his father's courage, he did all he could to conceal and dissemble his cowardice.

Once, when Joseph was eleven, a woman telephoned his father with horse trouble. Her husband was away from home working on the rigs[2] and his horse had hurt itself. The woman said she was afraid her husband would blame her for what had happened to the horse, accuse her of carelessness and neglect as he had a habit of doing whenever anything went wrong. This man was infamous for his hot, ungovernable temper. His wife had been seen in the grocery store, eyes blackened, looking like a racoon. Rupert agreed to come at once to see what he could do to help the horse and, by implication, her.

---

2  That is, working in the oil fields as wells are being dug. (A rig is the tall apparatus used for drilling oil wells.)

He and Joseph drove out to her place and found the horse pacing a corral, a long jagged gash on its chest dangling a piece of hide shaped like an envelope flap, an animal tormented, driven half-mad by pain and relentless clouds of flies. Joseph was ready to bet his father was going to get killed trying to catch this crazy horse. To start with, it tried to escape, clambered up six feet of fence rails, grunting and pawing, toppled over on its hind quarters, and collapsed in a whirl of slashing legs. Then it scrambled to its feet and came straight at his father, squealing, wriggling, kicking, teeth bared. His father broke the charge, made the horse veer away at the last possible second by flogging it across the face and eyes with the stock whip he carried. Joseph, clinging to the fence, begged and shouted at his father to come out of there, leave that horse be, but he wouldn't listen. Around and around the corral the two went, horse and man. The dust hung in the lowering evening light like a fine, golden powder. As it settled on his father's clothes and hair it turned from gold to grey, turning him into a ghost.

At last his father lassoed the horse and snubbed him down[3] as tight as he could to a post. Next he fashioned himself a makeshift twitch out of a bit of rope and stick and performed the dangerous sleight of hand of slipping the loop on the horse's nose and cranking it up like a tourniquet. The horse braced itself on widely splayed legs, mad eyes rolling, strong yellow teeth bared, slobber slopping off its bottom lip. But now his father had the son of a bitch, had him good. When he called Joseph to come and take the twitch, the boy came with no more protest than if God Almighty himself had ordered him out from behind the fence of poplar poles to keep a jug-headed man-killer squeezed into submission with a twist of hemp and dry wood. He was safe because his father was near, patiently sponging Creolin[4] into the raw mouth of the laceration, painstakingly picking slivers and dirt from the butcher-flesh. His father was there talking quietly and matter-of-factly to both horse and boy. 'Now when I pull this splinter loose, look out. Get set. He's going to breathe fire. Aren't you going to breathe fire, you no-nuts son of a bitch?' Nothing could go amiss or awry with his father there, speaking so calmly.

The wound was clean, there was nothing left to do but stitch the cut. Fishing through shirt pockets his father began to swear. Somehow his needle and thread had gone missing and he would have to borrow what he needed from the woman. Joseph was to hold the horse until he got back. 'He won't be going anywhere on you if you keep that twitch tight. Just keep the twitch tight,' his father reiterated and was gone before the boy could manufacture an excuse why he shouldn't leave him.

Over his shoulder, Joseph watched his father amble to the house, knock and disappear into the porch when the door was answered. He turned back to the horse. The wound was bleeding, dripping slow, fat drops of blood into the dust. It was like watching the second hand of a clock. He counted the drops, watched three hundred fall. Three hundred drops equalled five minutes. Five minutes ought to be enough time to scare up a needle and thread. He glanced nervously toward the house to see if his father

3 That is, severely restricted the horse's movement by wrapping the rope around its neck and then around a corral post. This horse is further restricted by the twitch—a cord looped around a stick and then the horse's mouth and upper lip—that can be tightened by twisting the stick.
4 A brand name for a disinfectant.

was returning. There was no sign of him. The boy swayed with panic. What was keeping him? Where was his father? How long was he supposed to stand holding this horse? He imagined the sun setting, his father still missing and night falling, alone with this glassy-eyed, devil horse, both rooted to this spot of ground by a twitch. Joseph's palms were slick with sweat. He thought of the stick slipping in his hands, the sudden blur of unwinding. The unwinding and springing of the fear twisted up inside him and the fear twisted up on a stick.

He began to count the drops of blood again. He would count another three hundred before he permitted himself to look again to see if his father was coming. Five minutes more. There were flies gathering at the growing puddle of black blood thickening on the ground. There were flies on Joseph. He could feel them crawling in his ears and at the corners of his eyes. He didn't dare swat them, he might lose his grip on the stick. One slip and that crazy horse might get him.

'Hurry up,' he said aloud and the horse laid back its ears at the sound of his voice, changing the shape of its head, giving it a snake's sleekness. 'Hurry up, please,' he said. He was still counting in his head, the numbers very loud. He got mixed up. Started counting flies, not tears of blood. He began over. Once again three hundred. He looked back at the dead calm of the yard soaked in evening light; everything motionless except for the swallows swooping and flitting above the peaked roof of the house. In the final flight of these birds before the coming darkness he experienced his own desertion. There was no logic to it, except the logic of association. Somehow he understood he would never be his father. It was that simple. He could never be a man like his father. The realization left him bereft, made him cry.

He was still crying when he heard the scrape of boots on the fence rails. His father wanted to know what had happened. Joseph couldn't explain. When his father came nearer and repeated the question, Joseph smelled the whisky on his breath. Now he felt entitled to his anger at his father's failure to understand.

'You been drinking!' he said. The shrillness of his voice was a clue, if not an explanation.

'She gave me a drink,' his father said. 'I had to have a drink for coming out. She wouldn't have it any other way.' He couldn't figure what was behind this. 'I was only gone fifteen minutes,' he said. 'Did he come at you? Take a jump? Scare you? Is that it? I told you to hold tight.'

'Tell me another one. Fifteen minutes,' Joseph said sullenly, trying to rub the tears on his cheek into the shoulder of his shirt.

'Okay, twenty minutes,' said his father. 'At the outside.' He threaded the needle and set about stitching the wound. The light was failing, he didn't have much time. Each time the needle penetrated the skin, the horse shivered, its hide rippled with a life of its own.

'You ought to think,' said Joseph.

'Think about what?' said his father. 'You tell me what to think about and I'll think about it.'

'Just think.' *Think about me*, he meant.

'Wait until you're my age,' his father said. 'Then you'll know what thinking is.'

*Think about what'd happen if I let go of this stick.* Joseph watched the poised needle. *You'd be sorry then.*

His father tied the thread in a neat surgical knot. He had a book of knots at home, there wasn't one he didn't know.

'Turn him loose,' he said to the boy. His father was getting angry. What was he supposed to apologize for? 'And another thing,' he added, 'just so you know who calls the shots in this outfit—get yourself ready for another fifteen-minute wait because the lady asked me in for another drink and I'm going to have it.'

Joseph refused to go into the house with his father.

'Pout if you want,' his father said. 'It's no skin off my ass.'

Joseph prowled around the house, chucking handfuls of gravel up under the eaves to drive the swallows out of their nests and into bursts of edgy flight to test the truth of his earlier feeling. He continued doing this until his father came roaring and raving outside, shouting enough was enough, he'd had all he could stand of this carry-on. Show some respect for other people's property or he'd get the worst jeezly licking of his life.

Another taboo broken.

*After France's defeat at the hands of the Prussians in 1870 and the annexation of Alsace-Lorraine, the humiliated nation cried out for revenge, for a saviour. The eyes of Frenchmen turned to the handsome General Georges Boulanger, The Man on Horseback. No one knew that The Man on Horseback had only learned to ride, to cut such a captivating figure, by the most diligent application. Boulanger after all was an infantry man, not a cavalry officer full of careless dash and daring. His riding school was an abandoned chapel which stood beside his house. Each morning at six o'clock the General would spur his horse through the doorway of the chapel and commence bouncing about in the sacral, coloured morning light falling through the stained-glass windows. The General was not a stupid man. Although he frequently toppled off his horse and took many embarrassing tumbles, he was careful to see to it that there were no witnesses to his hilarious accidents. His mistakes were made in private.*

*General Boulanger had an infallible sense of publicity. Everyone remembers the names of the horses of truly great generals. Alexander the Great and Bucephalus, Napoleon and the white stallion Marengo, General Lee and Traveller, Stonewall Jackson and Little Sorrel. But no general owed as much to a horse as General Boulanger did to Tunis. The General did not choose his horse himself, he left the choice of his mount to an expert, someone who knew his business. The man who picked Tunis for the General chose well. Tunis was a beautiful black which gleamed in the sunshine. Despite being a considerable age, the horse looked strong and had a striking carriage. He moved and pranced elegantly, with great elan, with great presence. Perhaps most important for a general who had only recently become an equestrian, sitting on Tunis was as comfortable as sitting in his own armchair beside his own fire. The horse's disposition was tested by trumpeting bugles in his ear and discharging rifle volleys under his nose. The animal didn't turn a hair, didn't startle. There would be no unfortunate and mortifying surprises for The Man on Horseback.*

*On July 14, 1886, the anniversary of the Fall of the Bastille, General Boulanger introduced Tunis to the public in a military review at Longchamps. By three o'clock in the* afternoon a crowd of one hundred thousand had gathered on the field to view the parade. Gunfire and military tunes announced the arrival of a squad of spahis[5] followed by fifteen generals, hundreds of officers and the military attachés of all the embassies. When they had passed, a solitary figure made his entrance on a black horse; General Boulanger garbed in turquoise dolman with gold epaulettes, pink trousers and black boots.

The crowd went wild. Cries of Vive Boulanger! drowned out the weak smattering of applause which greeted those dowdy, drab politicians, the Prime Minister and the President of France. While those two fussily took their seats in the presidential box, General Boulanger and Tunis capered about the field looking strenuously military, the eyes of the crowd fastened adoringly upon them.

When the review began, many of the common soldiers broke protocol by saluting General Boulanger rather than the President of the Republic. Thousands of voices thundered 'Vive Boulanger!' again and again. As the last troops departed, the hysterical crowd burst through the police and onto the field, men shouting frantically, women weeping. Only with the greatest reluctance did the overwhelming mob permit their darling to canter off on his beautiful black horse. For hours, like jilted brides and forsaken bridegrooms, they wandered about Longchamps, disconsolate. That night every restaurant and café in Paris was full, the streets were jammed with people shouting for Boulanger.

The striking figure he had cut on Tunis insured Boulanger's popularity and led to a ubiquitous celebrity. Over three hundred popular songs were composed in his honour. Photographs of his striking features sold out issues of eight hundred thousand. There were pottery statuettes of the General and cheap clay pipes with their bowls fashioned in the like- ness of The Man on Horseback. You could scrub yourself with Boulanger soap and eat your dinner from a Boulanger plate. His office in the Ministry of War was flooded with letters from the women of France offering their bodies to him with fervent, erotic patriotism. France gave its heart to Boulanger, but Boulanger's was pledged to his mistress, the Vicomtesse Marguerite de Bonnemains, lover, advisor, and administerer of ever increasing doses of morphine to alleviate the pain of an old war wound of the General's.

On January 27, 1887, General Boulanger was elected to the constituency of the Seine by a stunning majority of 80,000 votes. That night France was his for the taking, virtually without opposition he could have established his dictatorship. In the Restaurant Durand, where he awaited election results throughout the evening, an enthusiastic mob was kept at bay with the iron shutters closed over the windows. Admirers urged him to act, to seize the government. Workingmen, students from Montmartre, aristocrats chanted 'A l'Elysée! A l'Elysée!' in the streets. Boulanger withdrew to a private room in the restaurant and con- sulted Marguerite. When he returned he issued orders that nothing was to be done.

Sensing indecision and weakness on his part, the government set in train steps to arrest The Man on Horseback and General Boulanger fled wife and France accompanied by his mistress. A brief period of fashionable acclaim in English society followed, but the General was a spent force, an article for the shelf. In exile on the isle of Jersey, Marguerite fell ill while the General sat in front of a large portrait of Tunis.

---

5 French army cavalry units, usually of Algerian and Senegalese riders (originally Ottoman troops, composed of Turkish and Arab soldiers).

*The unhappy couple removed themselves to Belgium. There Marguerite died on July 16, two days after the date of the General's greatest triumph on the field of Longchamps. Several months later The Man on Horseback shot himself on his lover's grave. A large photograph of Marguerite which he carried under his shirt was so firmly pasted to the skin of his chest with dried blood that it had be torn to be removed.*

*A horse can carry a man only so far and no farther.*

Joseph Kelsey left home at the age of seventeen. For four years he attended the University of Saskatchewan, supporting himself with part-time jobs and scholarships. A Woodrow Wilson Fellowship took him to the University of Wisconsin. From there he went on to the University of Chicago and a PhD in modern French history. While in Chicago, he met and married Catherine Bringhurst, a medical student and a native of the Windy City. In 1974 Catherine completed her medical degree, Joseph took a job teaching history at Carleton, and they moved to Ottawa.

Each of these steps removed Joseph Kelsey a little further from his father, geographically and emotionally. Distance made visits more expensive and more infrequent. The world he lived and worked in now made the one he had departed seem impossible, at the very least improbable. Whenever he told Catherine stories of his childhood, of life in a shacky house, of a father and mother who never read a book, he felt self-dramatizing and false. The stories were true but in the alchemy of Catherine's imagination they were transformed and he became located in an unreal world of glamorous destitution. In rare moments of self-knowledge, Joseph Kelsey knew that this had always been his intention—to make his origins as romantic to her as hers were to him. His goal was a reciprocity of envy, something conceivable, given the mood of the sixties. Raised in an affluent suburb of Chicago by a doctor father and a psychiatrist mother, whom she addressed as Claude and Amelia, Catherine seemed inconceivably exotic to her young husband.

Joseph and his new wife made trips back to Sastatchewan twice in the years between 1974 and 1977. On both occasions they stayed in the local hotel at Catherine's insistence. Because Joseph's parents' house was so small, she didn't want Rupert and Mary disturbed by Andrew, a fussing baby on their first visit and, on their second, a small child in the throes of the terrible twos. Joseph didn't tell his wife that her middle-class consideration was interpreted by his parents as high and mightiness, a distaste for ordinary people and plain living. Overhearing his mother refer to Catherine as 'Dr Bringhurst' confirmed for her son that it was a sore point with his mother that his spouse had retained her maiden name.

How Catherine reacts to this, or doesn't react to this—she is oblivious in the way the protected, privileged so often are, they cannot conceive of opinions except the proper ones, *theirs*—makes Joseph swell with a mild, chafing contempt. *She has no idea.* For her the man with the prematurely, fiercely lined face and the woman with the home permanent and tough, callused hands are salt of the earth idealizations; honest, kindly peasants like the ones first encountered in a suburban fairy tale, Chicago-style. Deep in her heart she assumes that they must admire her because that is what peasants do with princesses. (Catherine would be shocked and hurt if Joseph accused her of such an attitude.) But Joseph knows what his parents think of women who give their boy child a doll to play with, or hang on to their maiden names, or put up in hotels on family visits. Hoity-toity bitch, is what they think. So his son turns five before Joseph can bring himself to pay another visit home, before he and Catherine, his mother and Andrew find themselves standing in the IGA parking lot, watching the local Canada Day parade assemble. This year, like each of the fifteen before, his father, on horseback, is going to lead the parade and bear the flag.

It is not a good day for a parade. The morning is woolly and grey with a fine, misty rain, which recalls for Joseph the barely perceptible spray suspended in the air above the observation railings at Niagara Falls. He wishes it would piss or get off the pot. The day has the feel of a sodden Kleenex about to shred in his hands. He doesn't know why he should feel this, but he does. Maybe it's because Andrew, holding Catherine's hand and delightedly awaiting the commencement of the parade in a brilliantly yellow rain-coat and sou'wester, seems to his father the only genuine patch of brightness on the scene, a patch of brightness soon to be eclipsed by disappointment. It's Joseph's guess that the boy expects a parade of pomp and magnitude, an Ottawa parade like he's used to. Andrew doesn't understand that all he is going to get is what is already collected in the parking lot.

That's the local high-school band whose uniform consists of the high-school jacket, nothing splashier, showier, or more elaborate. Also the local Credit Union, which has resurrected its perennial float, a six-foot-high papier mâché globe spotted with cardboard Credit Union flags to illustrate the international nature of credit unionism. The owner and parts man of the John Deere dealership are drunk and in clown costumes. The owner will drive a John Deere riding mower pulling a child's wagon in which the two-hundred-and-fifty-pound parts man will hunker, honking a horn and tossing wrapped candies to the children. The few remaining parade entries are of a similar calibre. Meanwhile the hapless drizzle continues, making everything fuzzier and murkier, wilting the pastel tissue paper flowers on the floats, frizzing the hair of the high-school queen and her attendants, painting a pearly film of moisture on the hoods, roofs, fenders of parked cars.

Buried in Joseph is the nagging realization that it is wrong to assign the feel of the day, the foreboding that it is about to fall apart in his hands, to any possible disappointment on Andrew's part. The real problem is his, adult disappointment. Because, ever since they arrived, grandson and grandfather have been stuck to one another like a new wooden rung glued into an old wooden chair. Joseph knows it is the horses. How can he compete with horses? Despite Catherine anxiously forbidding her father-in-law to carry Andrew wedged between his belly and the pommel of the saddle the way he once carried Joseph as a toddler, Joseph knows that hasn't stopped the old man when he's out of her sight: no woman is going to tell him what to do. And disobeying her has won him a friend for life.

Just now Andrew, all shining yellow, is standing riveted with admiration to the shining black asphalt of the parking lot, watching his grandfather show off for him on his horse.

There is no other word for what the old fool is doing but showing off and the performance leaves Joseph faintly disgusted. The pretence is that he is putting his mount through its paces, a sort of pre-parade disciplining, but in Joseph's books it is purely, simply, transparently, a pathetic ploy to impress a five year old.

The old man backs up the gelding across the parking lot, toes pointing outward in his stirrups, urging it backward with the pressure of his legs and firm tucks of the reins. Then he jumps it forward suddenly, swings it to the right in a tight, tail-chasing circle, the drooping standard shaking itself out from the flag pole in shuddering billows. Abruptly he throws the horse's head left, reversing the direction of the turn, rippling the flag with counter-spin. The slither of the gelding's hooves, the awkward, comic scramble of its back legs as they fight for purchase on the slippery pavement kick high-pitched laughter and skittish, excited hops out of Andrew. He's delighted with this cartoon.

Suddenly, in the midst of a spin, the horse's legs slip on the rain-slick pavement with a sound like a spoon scraping the bottom of a pot and shoot stiffly out, the horse going down, landing heavily on the old man's left leg, pinning him to the wet asphalt. For a moment, everyone except Andrew freezes. The boy, unable to judge the seriousness of the situation, continues laughing in shrill appreciation of the new trick until a squeal of terror from the fallen horse shocks him into silence.

Joseph runs through the rain. He sees the muscular arching of the horse's neck, the legs thrashing the air and pavement for a footing, his father clinging to the horn and heeling the horse hard with his free boot, urging it to its feet with shouts of 'Hup! Hup! Hup!', the horse whinnying, straining to rise with this dead weight, this sack of guts and bone unbalancing it.

As Joseph reaches out to seize the bridle and help lift the head, the horse heaves, heaves desperately again, scrambles to its feet snorting and jerking, the old man sticking on for dear life, slung precariously from the saddle like a sidecar, bouncing and pitching with each convulsion of the powerful body, fighting to pull himself upright. Which he does, the horse dancing a nervous side-step across the parking lot, one rein dragging, the old man leaning forward, snatching for it and calling out, 'Whoa! Whoa! Whoa, you son of a bitch!'

At last he grabs the rein and regains some control of the horse which stands blowing, snuffling, trembling, cornered eyes wary. People begin to crowd near, now that the danger is over. 'I'm going to walk him out', says the old man to Joseph, ignoring the others, 'to see he didn't bugger his legs.' Horse and rider slowly circle the parking lot. Andrew leans against his father, bumps his head on Joseph's hip, and cries. Now that it is over, now that he has absorbed what has happened, the boy is finally frightened. As the old man passes them on his second circuit he calls out to his grandson, 'Grandpa's okay, see? Look, Andy, Grandpa's okay.' He grins hugely and strikes his chest dramatically with his fist to demonstrate his soundness. Grandpa making a joke on himself,

Grandpa beating his chest wildly in this funny way, pitches the boy into no man's land, leaves him gulping tears, sucking back snot but also smiling with relief. Grandpa's all right. Grandpa's okay. He says so. However, a certain grim tightening about the mouth, the way the old man gingerly shifts his seat in the saddle contradict Grandpa's claim.

Reassured as to the horse's fitness, the old man asks Joseph to hand him the flag he dropped in the wreck. His son tries to talk him out of continuing but he'll hear none of that. Joseph knows it's injured pride, the shame of the apple cart upset in front of witnesses which prevents his father from withdrawing from the parade. Long ago he had said to Joseph, 'Just like a box of Crackerjacks, there's a surprise in every horse.' What went without saying was that Rupert Kelsey could handle any of those surprises. Now he is not going to let this surprise get the better of him, not with his grandson, his son, his daughter-in-law as onlookers.

Catherine is incredulous that Joseph won't stop him. 'He ought to have medical attention! He's sixty-five,' she says.

'You tell him he's sixty-five. You tell him he ought to have medical attention. You're the doctor, not me,' says Joseph and walks away from her.

His father troops the parade all around the town with a grinning face as grey and wan as the day itself, then leads it back again to the parking lot. When he tries to dismount he discovers his left leg, the one crushed under the horse, can't bear his weight and he has to suffer the indignity of having Joseph support him while he bails out on the right side of the horse, the wrong side, like some know-nothing dude ranch cowboy. The left leg is, of course, broken and has swollen to fill his riding boot like sausage meat stuffed tight in its casing. When they cut the cowboy boot off him in the hospital he keeps sadly remarking, 'Those are my show boots. Lizard skin. Expensive as all get out.'

Joseph knows the difficulty of unlearning the things you were taught as a kid—he's been trying to do it for nearly twenty years. Still he backslides, caught in the current of his father's assumptions like a rudderless boat. Take the question of toughness, grit, physical courage. Joseph Kelsey's colleagues condescend to any such notions as the last refuge of the pitiably stupid and primitive, the resort of macho Neanderthals with brains the size of peas and exaggerated testosterone levels—football players or men like Oliver North and Gordon Liddy.[6] They prefer moral courage, the variety of bravery on which intellectuals have a corner of the market.

Joseph has to concede that physical courage *is* inferior to moral courage. Nevertheless he often feels the need to play the devil's advocate, the devil prompting this reaction being his rooster-tough old man. Joseph wants to argue: But isn't physical courage sometimes a precondition of moral courage? Was moral courage in Hitler's Germany or Stalin's Russia possible without physical courage, without the guts to face the piano

6 Two individuals who refused to give evidence against their leader when called before US congressional hearings and questioned about their roles in aiding US presidents in breaking the law: Lt. Col. Oliver North was connected to Ronald Reagan's 'Iran-Contra' activities (which involved the covert sale of US armaments to Iran); G. Gordon Liddy, known for aggressive and belligerent behaviour, was a leader in the criminal activities associated with the Watergate break-in and the subsequent scandal that drove Richard Nixon from office.

wire, the fist in the face, the boot in the groin, worse? When smug self-congratulation is in full spate in the faculty club lounge he is tempted to say, 'Let's remember that it wasn't Heidegger who tried to blow up Adolf Hitler, it was army officers.'[7]

*Nineteenth-century explorers reported of the bare-back riding Ankwe of the Kwalla district of northern Nigeria that they ensured themselves a sticky, adhesive seat on their horses by cutting a strip of hide out of the centre of the animal's back approximately eight inches long and several inches wide. On this raw, bloody surface the rider settled, gluing himself to his beast. The scab was scraped off and the sore freshened up with a knife whenever the horse's owner intended to go for a gallop.*

Life went on. Joseph and Andrew paid annual visits to Saskatchewan; sometimes Catherine accompanied them, more frequently she did not. Her family medicine practice had grown to such an extent that it was difficult for her to get away. When she took time off, it was to see her own parents, both now retired and living in Florida. It was no secret that she wasn't missed by her in-laws.

The summer he turned fifteen Andrew trotted out a typical teenager's complaint. It was cruel and unusual punishment to be separated from his girlfriend and his buddies, trapped for ten days in a boring, geeky town where he didn't know a soul. Could he stay home this year? Joseph didn't put any pressure on Andrew to visit his grandparents because secretly he was glad that his son had proved to be as inconstant and disloyal as he had himself.

This was the August Joseph came home to find that his father had cancer. His mother was the one who broke the news to him, not the old man. That night, after supper was finished, the two men sat alone at the kitchen table with a bottle of rye between them while Mary Kelsey watched television in the living room. His father was not a drinking man, it was unusual for him to get drunk, but that night he did. For a long time neither Rupert Kelsey nor his son said anything. Joseph held himself sober, expecting the old man to raise the topic present in both their minds, but when his father did finally speak, it was to claim his innocence of crimes with which he had never been charged.

'One goddamn thing nobody could ever say about me was that I mistreated a horse,' he suddenly said. 'I never mistreated a horse. Am I right or am I wrong?'

Joseph looked at him with surprise. He said he was right. Nobody could ever accuse him of cruelty to a horse.

His father nodded to himself. 'Every horse I ever owned was fat and happy. Nobody can say otherwise. I had horses that died of old age on this place because I wouldn't sell them to the likes of those that wanted to buy them. Died, mind you, *of old age and natural causes.*'

7 Despite being one of the most profound philosophers of his day, Martin Heidegger supported Hitler. There were at least four attempts by German Army officers to assassinate Hitler.

'Yes,' said Joseph quietly.

'So, nobody, *nobody*', the old man repeated with stark emphasis, as if challenging his son to dare deny it, 'can say that Rupert Kelsey didn't do right by any goddamn horse he ever owned. And if they say he did—why they're goddamn liars. When there was money for nothing else around here, I saw to it my horses had oats. And nobody can say different. I never neglected a horse in my life!'

He continued on in a similar vein, justifying himself, offering evidence of his goodness, his kindness, his concern. Joseph wanted him to stop. It made painful listening. It put an ache in Joseph's chest, the kind that managed at one and the same time to feel heavy and sharp, the kind he hadn't carried around in him since he was a boy. It made him want to cry, the most inappropriate thing he could do in front of his father.

'Who's saying you did?' said Joseph. 'Nobody's saying you did.'

Rupert Kelsey picked up his glass with the calculated steadiness of the far gone in drink. 'There's some,' he said, 'who I won't name, who would like to paint me in a certain light. They're wrong. I was never cruel. I never mistreated a horse in my life.'

Joseph could not fathom what any of this struggled to express.

The following morning Joseph's father invited him to come for a ride. Because of the circumstances, Joseph couldn't see how he could refuse. It had been more than a dozen years since he had sat a horse and he felt ridiculous dragging himself aboard, feeling his ligaments tighten and burn alarmingly, his joints creak dryly as the horse plodded along.

His father led him down a little-travelled country lane, which was no more than the scar of old tire tracks. On either side of them the black poplars swirled masses of glittering leaves in the early morning breeze as birds hopped and sang noisily in the branches. A number of wrecked cars had been towed here to rust into the margins of the bush, shards of broken windshield grinning in the jaws of the frames with savage glass teeth. A woodpecker slashed by their horses' noses in the level, swift flight plan of its kind.

His father began to talk, not about his cancer, but in a different fashion from the night before.

He said, 'You won't believe it but I had the same idea as you once—about getting out of here. I thought about going to South America, one of those countries there. Argentina. I saw this book with pictures, all open country, no fences, lots of cattle. Lots of horses. They live on the backs of horses there. I was twenty-one. I thought about going. But then the war came along.' He paused. Joseph saw that in the morning light his father's face looked drawn, that in the light of day he looked sicker than he had in the electric light of the night before. 'Who knows?' his father said to himself. 'It doesn't matter. I likely wouldn't have gone. What do they speak there anyway? Mexican?'

'Yes,' said Joseph, restraining pedantry.

'I wouldn't have been one for learning Mexican,' said his father. 'I didn't learn nothing much in my time.'

They went along a little further in silence. The trail had dwindled away from lack of use. Chokecherry, pincherry, cranberry, and saskatoon bushes crowded in upon them. Tall grass, which had overgrown the tracks, feather-dusted their horses' bellies. The men were constantly fending off branches that threatened their faces, only a narrow channel of washed blue sky snaked above them. It felt to Joseph as if he were being swallowed up in a green dream.

His father said, 'I had another chance to get away when you were about ten—you wouldn't know this. A fellow who was up here from Texas buying horses said I should come down to Houston and break horses for him. He had this operation outside the city where he sold saddle horses to doctors and lawyers and businessmen, rich people. Then he stabled the horses for them, got them coming and going, got them twice. He said to me, "You can't live in Texas unless you own a horse. I got Jew dentists, come down from up north, never seen a horse in their lives, and even they end up owning horses. If they don't have to have one, their kids do. It's a fucking gold mine. You ought to throw in with me." I ought to have. He needed a horse-breaker. He was offering good wages.'

'And why didn't you?'

'Your mother didn't want to go some place strange.' His father laughed. 'You could have grown up a Texan.'

'Just in time for Vietnam,' said Joseph.

The grove of poplar was thinning, they came out into an opening in the bush, into the garish glare of prairie light unsifted by leaves overhead, rousting two large, rusty-brown hawks off the ground where they were tearing at a rabbit. The birds flapped into the air with harsh, indignant screams, inched up the sky steadily, one wing beat at a time, and disappeared from sight.

'I think we better turn back,' said his father.

'You don't have to go back for me,' said Joseph. 'I'll pay for it in stiffness later, but I'm okay for now. You want to go on, go on.'

'I ain't comfortable on a horse much any more,' his father said. 'I got this thing in my belly, after twenty or thirty minutes up on a horse, it hurts like a fucker. I been twenty minutes here. I got twenty minutes back. I don't have another twenty minutes in me.'

To Joseph this was the only direct reference his father made to his cancer. Ever.

It takes him two more years to die. There are inexorable advances of the disease and inexplicable remissions. Joseph is there for the last and final stage, by his bedside. His father is unrecognizable, all the deft grace and assured power of the horseman has been wasted, worn away against the grindstone of illness.

His father has a recurring dream that he recounts to Joseph repeatedly. In the dream it is spring, early April by the look of it, patches of melting snow on bare ground, water running in the gutters, a persistent, pushing spring wind. He is enjoying the warmth, the returning sap of life, when a nagging disquiet surfaces to spoil his pleasure. There is something important he meant to do, has forgotten. Then he remembers. Last fall he'd failed to bring the horses in from the pasture, they have spent the entire winter out, endured blizzards and bitter cold without food and shelter.

The horses are waiting for him at the gate, where they have waited all winter. Skeletons with ribs like barrel hoops under the long matted hair of their winter coats, feeble legs with swollen knees bulging like coconuts, cracked hooves planted in the cold trampled mud, pleading necks stretched across the barbed wire, dull eyes staring.

Joseph tells his father that dreams like this are common, mean nothing. Yet in the last hours of semi-consciousness, in the delirious prelude to death, his father makes him promise, again and again, that he will save the winter horses. 'Save the winter horses,' is his last appeal, to anyone. 'Save the winter horses,' he beseeches.

Nine months after his father's death when it is late at night, very late at night, and Joseph is sitting in his study supposedly working on his fictitious article about Charles Maurras and the Action Française[8] but really reading books on horses, he locates a memory, or a memory locates him. The yellow lamplight loses its harshness, softens and deepens, signalling this is a memory situated in late afternoon, sometime around the supper hour. He is a small boy riding with his father, tucked behind the saddle horn in the way not so long ago his father used to carry Andrew, half-hypnotized by the horse's head nodding up and down against the sky in the regular rhythm of a metronome, tick tock, tick tock, lulled by the rolling gait. Full of a child's floating torpor, he is adrift, the tired, fumble-footed shamble of the horse rocking him, rocking him, his heavy-lidded eyes blearing the long grass rippling around him in a vibrant smear of endless green. The heat of the sun burns on his face and chest, the horse burns beneath him, the curve of his father's belly burns on his back. Golden, burning, he is carried off in what direction, where, he doesn't know. In his child's heart this journey is forever, this hour is a day, this day a week, this week a month, this is infinite, this is everything. He falls back against his father and he sleeps.

*In Christian art the horse is held to represent courage and generosity. It is the companion of St Martin, St Maurice, St George, and St Victor, all of whom are pictured on horseback. In the catacombs it was, with the fish and the cross, a common symbol. No one is absolutely certain what its meaning was, although it is assumed it represents the swift, fleeting, and transitory character of life.*

1992

---

8 A radical right-wing party in France, the Action Française, founded by Charles Maurras, promoted violent anti-Semitic and anti-Republican views.

# Rohinton Mistry

## b. 1952

Born in Bombay (in 1995 the city's name officially became Mumbai), India, Rohinton Mistry took a degree in mathematics and economics at the University of Bombay before immigrating to Toronto in 1975. While supporting himself by working in a bank, he took night courses in English and philosophy at the University of Toronto. When the university instituted an annual short-story contest in 1983, he entered and won. The following year, he won the contest again (one of the judges was Mavis Gallant, who singled out his story for its excellence) and also received a *Canadian Fiction Magazine* contributor's prize for a third story. In 1987, these stories became part of *Tales from Firozsha Baag*.

In this short-story sequence, as in the fiction that followed, Mistry portrays the Bombay Parsi community from which he himself emerged. Parsis are those Zoroastrians who, centuries ago, emigrated from Persia (now Iran) to India to escape persecution. (Zoroastrians worship Ahura Mazda, the Creator of the universe out of chaos, and believe that the duty of all sentient beings is to strive for good deeds, good thoughts, and other manifestations of truth and order as a way of keeping chaos at bay until the final perfection of the world.) Though well-established in Bombay since the seventeenth century, Parsis are now a very small part of that population; many, like Mistry, have moved abroad. *Tales from Firozsha Baag*, set mostly in a Parsi-occupied apartment complex in Bombay, deals with life in that community and also with the possibility and difficulties of leaving it behind. Like M.G. Vassanji, Mistry documents the divided consciousnesses of those who choose to leave, showing them (as he describes the central character in 'Lend Me Your Light') split 'between two lives, the one in Bombay and the one to come in Toronto.'

The last story in the collection, 'Swimming Lessons' (anthologized here), serves as a coda. A self-reflexive narrative, it is told by an I-narrator who has written a book of stories corresponding to the one we are reading. When he sends that book to his parents in Firozsha Baag, we share our reading experience with them and are invited to speculate with them on the relationship between the writer's life and the art he makes from it.

A nuanced story, 'Swimming Lessons' is, in part, about the 'lessons' one needs to stay afloat in an unfamiliar culture—lessons that enable one to identify objects in a new environment (here, for example, the narrator learns to recognize the maple leaf) and that instruct one in the rules of daily life (such as the protocol of using shared washing machines). The story also suggests that while the generalizing involved in this kind of learning can have its ugly side—because generalizations are also the basis of stereotypes that lead to racism and sexism—it cannot be avoided. Moreover, as a writer, the narrator reads his own life for its possible symbolism and allegorical implications and wonders about its larger narrative shape—a reminder that the move from the specific to the general is the basic technique of literature, with its use of concrete details to get at larger truths.

Mistry's skill in these stories—particularly visible in the way he brings individuals to life and shows how they are defined by their relationships to others—serves him well in the novels that followed. *Such a Long Journey* (1991), which won both a Governor General's Award and a Commonwealth Writers' Prize, is set in Bombay in 1971 against the chaotic political backdrop of India's military intervention in the Bangladesh War. It is the account of the hapless Gustad Noble, whose misfortunes are both entangled with and paralleled by the volatile politics of Indira Gandhi's India.

Mistry's Giller Prize–winning second novel, *A Fine Balance* (1995), is similarly set amid the turmoil of India in the mid-1970s, with backward glances to the monumental events surrounding India's 1947 gaining of independence. It is about the bonds that develop, in defiance of class and religious barriers, between four unlikely people brought together in a small apartment: Dina, a middle-aged Parsi widow forced to work as a seamstress to maintain her independence; two tailors (whom Dina at first considers 'untouchable') seeking refuge from caste-based government violence that has destroyed their village home; and a young Parsi student exiled from his childhood home and alienated from his family. Their hardships, humiliations, and disillusionment play out in sharply drawn detail against the larger background of religious and ethnic violence, government-declared state of emergency, and political assassination. The 'balance' to which the title alludes is one that weighs resignation against fortitude, prejudice against acceptance, fear of weakness against the need for compassion, and the corrosive effects of atrocity against the restorative power of the world's beauty.

The dynamics and meaning of family, present in all of Mistry's fiction, are made central in *Family Matters* (2002). Again set in Bombay, it focuses on the seventy-nine-year-old Nariman Vakeel, who tests the limits of filial devotion after he breaks his leg in a fall and becomes dependent on his overburdened daughter, Roxana. Nariman's decline and the strain it puts on Roxana's family suggests parallels with India and its people, and raises questions about the resiliency of personal identity and the role of emigration. In *The Scream* (a short-story published as a book in 2008 in support of World Literacy of Canada; illustrated by Tony Urquhart), Mistry continues his consideration of the difficulties that come with aging. It is of an affecting monologue delivered by an old man living with his family in a Bombay apartment, distressed by a scream that only he can hear.

A writer who builds up textured worlds in the tradition of the great nineteenth-century novelists, Mistry has created narratives of humane social realism that, in their depiction of Indian life, make visible the interplay of the personal with the national and the universal. His craft, precision, and tenderness give significance to all of his characters, no matter how poor or weak.

# Swimming Lessons

The old man's wheelchair is audible today as he creaks by in the hallway: on some days it's just a smooth whirr. Maybe the way he slumps in it, or the way his weight rests has something to do with it. Down to the lobby he goes, and sits there most of the time, talking to people on their way out or in. That's where he first spoke to me a few days ago. I was waiting for the elevator, back from Eaton's with my new pair of swimming trunks.

'Hullo,' he said. I nodded, smiled.

'Beautiful summer day we've got.'

'Yes,' I said, 'it's lovely outside.'

He shifted the wheelchair to face me squarely. 'How old do you think I am?'

I looked at him blankly, and he said, 'Go on, take a guess.'

I understood the game; he seemed about seventy-five although the hair was still black, so I said, 'Sixty-five?' He made a sound between a chuckle and a wheeze: 'I'll be seventy-seven next month.' Close enough.

I've heard him ask that question several times since, and everyone plays by the rules. Their faked guesses range from sixty to seventy. They pick a lower number when he's more depressed than usual. He reminds me of Grandpa as he sits on the sofa in the lobby, staring out vacantly at the parking lot. Only difference is, he sits with the stillness of stroke victims, while Grandpa's Parkinson's disease would bounce his thighs and legs and arms all over the place. When he could no longer hold the *Bombay Samachar* steady enough to read, Grandpa took to sitting on the veranda and staring emptily at the traffic passing outside Firozsha Baag. Or waving to anyone who went by in the compound: Rustomji, Nariman Hansotia in his 1932 Mercedes-Benz, the fat ayah Jaakaylee with her shopping-bag, the kuchrawalli[1] with her basket and long bamboo broom.

The Portuguese woman across the hall has told me a little about the old man. She is the communicator for the apartment building. To gather and disseminate information, she takes the liberty of unabashedly throwing open the door when newsworthy events transpire. Not for Portuguese Woman the furtive peerings from thin cracks or spyholes. She reminds me of a character in a movie, *Barefoot in The Park* I think it was, who left empty beer cans by the landing for anyone passing to stumble and give her the signal. But PW does not need beer cans. The gutang-khutang of the elevator opening and closing is enough.

The old man's daughter looks after him. He was living alone till his stroke, which coincided with his youngest daughter's divorce in Vancouver. She returned to him and they moved into this low-rise in Don Mills. PW says the daughter talks to no one in the building but takes good care of her father.

Mummy used to take good care of Grandpa, too, till things became complicated and he was moved to the Parsi General Hospital. Parkinsonism and osteoporosis laid him low. The doctor explained that Grandpa's hip did not break because he fell, but he fell because the hip, gradually growing brittle, snapped on that fatal day. That's what osteoporosis does, hollows out the bones and turns effect into cause. It has an unusually high incidence in the Parsi community, he said, but did not say why. Just one of those mysterious things. We are the chosen people where osteoporosis is concerned. And divorce. The Parsi community has the highest divorce rate in India. It also claims to be the most westernized community in India. Which is the result of the other? Confusion again, of cause and effect.

The hip was put in traction. Single-handed, Mummy struggled valiantly with bedpans and dressings for bedsores which soon appeared like grim spectres on his back. *Mamaiji,* bent double with her weak back, could give no assistance. My help would be enlisted to roll him over on his side while Mummy changed the dressing. But after three months, the doctor pronounced a patch upon Grandpa's lungs, and the male ward of Parsi General swallowed him up. There was no money for a private nursing home. I went to see him once, at Mummy's insistence. She used to say that the blessings of an old person were the most valuable and potent of all, they would last my whole life long. The ward had rows and rows of beds; the din was enormous, the smells nauseating, and it was just as well that Grandpa passed most of his time in a less than conscious state.

But I should have gone to see him more often. Whenever Grandpa went out, while he still could in the days before parkinsonism, he would bring back pink and white sugar-coated almonds for Percy and me. Every time I remember Grandpa, I remember that; and then I think: I should have gone to see him more often. That's what I also thought when our telephone-owning neighbour, esteemed by all for that reason, sent his son to tell us the hospital had phoned that Grandpa died an hour ago.

---

1 Trash collector.

*The postman rang the doorbell the way he always did, long and continuous; Mother went to open it, wanting to give him a piece of her mind but thought better of it, she did not want to risk the vengeance of postmen, it was so easy for them to destroy letters; workers nowadays thought no end of themselves, strutting around like peacocks, ever since all this Shiv Sena agitation about Maharashtra for Maharashtrians,[2] threatening strikes and Bombay bundh all the time, with no respect for the public; bus drivers and conductors were the worst, behaving as if they owned the buses and were doing favours to commuters, pulling the bell before you were in the bus, the driver purposely braking and moving with big jerks to make the standees lose their balance, the conductor so rude if you did not have the right change.*

*But when she saw the airmail envelope with a Canadian stamp her face lit up, she said wait to the postman, and went in for a fifty paisa piece, a little* baksheesh[3] *for you, she told him, then shut the door and kissed the envelope, went in running, saying my son has written, my son has sent a letter, and Father looked up from the newspaper and said, don't get too excited, first read it, you know what kind of letters he writes, a few lines of empty words, I'm fine, hope you are all right, your loving son—that kind of writing I don't call letter-writing.*

*Then Mother opened the envelope and took out one small page and began to read silently, and the joy brought to her face by the letter's arrival began to ebb; Father saw it happening and knew he was right, he said read aloud, let me also hear what our son is writing this time, so Mother read: My dear Mummy and Daddy, Last winter was terrible, we had record-breaking low temperatures all through February and March, and the first official day of spring was colder than the first official day of winter had been, but it's getting warmer now. Looks like it will be a nice warm summer. You asked about my new apartment. It's small, but not bad at all. This is just a quick note to let you know I'm fine, so you won't worry about me. Hope everything is okay at home.*

*After Mother put it back in the envelope, Father said everything about his life is locked in silence and secrecy, I still don't understand why he bothered to visit us last year if he had nothing to say; every letter of his has been a quick note so we won't worry   what does he think we worry about, his health, in that country everyone eats well whether they work or not, he should be worrying about us with all the black market and rationing, has he forgotten already how he used to go to the ration-shop and wait in line every week; and what kind of apartment description is that, not bad at all; and if it is a Canadian weather report I need from him, I can go with Nariman Hansotia from A Block to the Cawasji Framji Memorial Library and read all about it, there they get newspapers from all over the world.*

The sun is hot today. Two women are sunbathing on the stretch of patchy lawn at the periphery of the parking lot. I can see them clearly from my kitchen. They're wearing bikinis and I'd love to take a closer look. But I have no binoculars. Nor do I have a car to saunter out to and pretend to look under the hood. They're both luscious and gleaming. From time to time they smear lotion over their skin, on the bellies, on the inside of the thighs, on the shoulders. Then one of them gets the other to undo the string of her top and spread some there. She lies on her stomach with the straps

---

2  Maharashtra is the state of which Bombay is the capital. Shiv Sena (the 'Army of Shiva') is a political party that expresses opposition to those from elsewhere in India taking jobs in their state. A bundh is a short general strike.
3  A gratuity.

undone. I wait. I pray that the heat and haze make her forget, when it's time to turn over, that the straps are undone.

But the sun is not hot enough to work this magic for me. When it's time to come in, she flips over, deftly holding up the cups, and reties the top. They arise, pick up towels, lotions, and magazines, and return to the building.

This is my chance to see them closer. I race down the stairs to the lobby. The old man says hullo. 'Down again?'

'My mailbox,' I mumble.

'It's Saturday,' he chortles. For some reason he finds it extremely funny. My eye is on the door leading in from the parking lot.

Through the glass panel I see them approaching. I hurry to the elevator and wait. In the dimly lit lobby I can see their eyes are having trouble adjusting after the bright sun. They don't seem as attractive as they did from the kitchen window. The elevator arrives and I hold it open, inviting them in with what I think is a gallant flourish. Under the fluorescent glare in the elevator I see their wrinkled skin, aging hands, sagging bottoms, varicose veins. The lustrous trick of sun and lotion and distance has ended.

I step out and they continue to the third floor. I have Monday night to look forward to, my first swimming lesson. The high school behind the apartment building is offering, among its usual assortment of macramé and ceramics and pottery classes, a class for non-swimming adults.

The woman at the registration desk is quite friendly. She even gives me the opening to satisfy the compulsion I have about explaining my non-swimming status.

'Are you from India?' she asks. I nod. 'I hope you don't mind my asking, but I was curious because an Indian couple, husband and wife, also registered a few minutes ago. Is swimming not encouraged in India?'

'On the contrary,' I say. 'Most Indians swim like fish. I'm an exception to the rule. My house was five minutes walking distance from Chaupatty beach in Bombay. It's one of the most beautiful beaches in Bombay, or was, before the filth took over. Anyway, even though we lived so close to it, I never learned to swim. It's just one of those things.'

'Well,' says the woman, 'that happens sometimes. Take me, for instance. I never learned to ride a bicycle. It was the mounting that used to scare me, I was afraid of falling.' People have lined up behind me. 'It's been very nice talking to you,' she says, 'hope you enjoy the course.'

The art of swimming had been trapped between the devil and the deep blue sea. The devil was money, always scarce, and kept the private swimming clubs out of reach; the deep blue sea of Chaupatty beach was grey and murky with garbage, too filthy to swim in. Every so often we would muster our courage and Mummy would take me there to try and teach me. But a few minutes of paddling was all we could endure. Sooner or later something would float up against our legs or thighs or waists, depending on how deep we'd gone in, and we'd be revulsed and stride out to the sand.

Water imagery in my life is recurring. Chaupatty beach, now the high-school swimming pool. The universal symbol of life and regeneration did nothing but frustrate me. Perhaps the swimming pool will overturn that failure.

When images and symbols abound in this manner, sprawling or rolling across the page without guile or artifice, one is prone to say, how obvious, how skilless; symbols, after all, should be still and gentle as dewdrops, tiny, yet shining with a world of meaning. But what happens when, on the page of life itself, one encounters the ever-moving, all-engirdling sprawl of the filthy sea? Dewdrops and oceans both have their rightful places; Nariman Hansotia certainly knew that when he told his stories to the boys of Firozsha Baag.

The sea of Chaupatty was fated to endure the finales of life's everyday functions. It seemed that the dirtier it became, the more crowds it attracted: street urchins and beggars and beachcombers, looking through the junk that washed up. (Or was it the crowds that made it dirtier?—another instance of cause and effect blurring and evading identification.)

Too many religious festivals also used the sea as repository for their finales. Its use should have been rationed, like rice and kerosene. On Ganesh Chaturthi,[4] clay idols of the god Ganesh, adorned with garlands and all manner of finery, were carried in processions to the accompaniment of drums and a variety of wind instruments. The music got more frenzied the closer the procession got to Chaupatty and to the moment of immersion.

Then there was Coconut Day, which was never as popular as Ganesh Chaturthi. From a bystander's viewpoint, coconuts chucked into the sea do not provide as much of a spectacle. We used the sea, too, to deposit the leftovers from Parsi religious ceremonies, things such as flowers, or the ashes of the sacred sandalwood fire, which just could not be dumped with the regular garbage but had to be entrusted to the care of Avan Yazad, the guardian of the sea. And things which were of no use but which no one had the heart to destroy were also given to Avan Yazad. Such as old photographs.

After Grandpa died, some of his things were flung out to sea. It was high tide; we always checked the newspaper when going to perform these disposals; an ebb would mean a long walk in squelchy sand before finding water. Most of the things were probably washed up on shore. But we tried to throw them as far out as possible, then waited a few minutes; if they did not float back right away we would pretend they were in the permanent safekeeping of Avan Yazad, which was a comforting thought. I can't remember everything we sent out to sea, but his brush and comb were in the parcel, his *kusti*,[5] and some Kemadrin pills, which he used to take to keep the parkinsonism under control.

Our paddling sessions stopped for lack of enthusiasm on my part. Mummy wasn't too keen either, because of the filth. But my main concern was the little guttersnipes, like naked fish with little buoyant penises, taunting me with their skills, swimming underwater and emerging unexpectedly all around me, or pretending to masturbate—I think they were too young to achieve ejaculation. It was embarrassing. When I look back, I'm surprised that Mummy and I kept going as long as we did.

I examine the swimming-trunks I bought last week. Surf King, says the label, Made in Canada–Fabriqué Au Canada. I've been learning bits and pieces of French

---

4 The Hindu festival celebrating the birth of Lord Ganesha, the elephant-headed son of Shiva and Parvati. 'Coconut Day' is an annual festival in which fishermen offer coconuts to the Hindu sea-god Varuna to solicit his protection. Avan Yazad is a Zoroastrian sea deity.

5 Zoroastrian sacred girdle (a sash woven from seventy-two threads), which is ritually tied and untied during the day.

from bilingual labels at the supermarket too. These trunks are extremely sleek and streamlined hipsters, the distance from waistband to pouch tip the barest minimum. I wonder how everything will stay in place, not that I'm boastful about my endowments. I try them on, and feel the tip of my member lingers perilously close to the exit. Too close, in fact, to conceal the exigencies of my swimming lesson fantasy: a gorgeous woman in the class for non-swimmers, at whose sight I will be instantly aroused, and she, spying the shape of my desire, will look me straight in the eye with her intentions; she will come home with me, to taste the pleasures of my delectable Asian brown body whose strangeness has intrigued her and unleashed uncontrollable surges of passion inside her throughout the duration of the swimming lesson.

I drop the Eaton's bag and wrapper in the garbage can. The swimming-trunks cost fifteen dollars, same as the fee for the ten weekly lessons. The garbage bag is almost full. I tie it up and take it outside. There is a medicinal smell in the hallway; the old man must have just returned to his apartment.

PW opens her door and says, 'Two ladies from the third floor were lying in the sun this morning. In bikinis.'

'That's nice,' I say, and walk to the incinerator chute. She reminds me of Najamai in Firozsha Baag, except that Najamai employed a bit more subtlety while going about her life's chosen work.

PW withdraws and shuts her door.

*Mother had to reply because Father said he did not want to write to his son till his son had something sensible to write to him, his questions had been ignored long enough, and if he wanted to keep his life a secret, fine, he would get no letters from his father.*

*But after Mother started the letter he went and looked over her shoulder, telling her what to ask him, because if they kept on writing the same questions, maybe he would under-stand how interested they were in knowing about things over there; Father said go on, ask him what his work is at the insurance company, tell him to take some courses at night school, that's how everyone moves ahead over there, tell him not to be discouraged if his job is just clerical right now, hard work will get him ahead, remind him he is a Zoroastrian: manashni, gavashni, kunashni, better write the translation also: good thoughts, good words, good deeds—he must have forgotten what it means, and tell him to say prayers and do* kusti *at least twice a day.*

*Writing it all down sadly, Mother did not believe he wore his* sudra[6] *and kusti any-more, she would be very surprised if he remembered any of the prayers; when she had asked him if he needed new* sudras *he said not to take any trouble because the Zoroastrian Society of Ontario imported them from Bombay for their members, and this sounded like a story he was making up, but she was leaving it in the hands of God, ten thousand miles away there was nothing she could do but write a letter and hope for the best.*

*Then she sealed it, and Father wrote the address on it as usual because his writing was much neater than hers, handwriting was important in the address and she did not want the postman in Canada to make any mistake; she took it off to the post office herself, it was*

---

6 A white shirt worn by Parsis that symbolizes purity; it is given in a ceremony (with the kusti) marking the move from childhood to the age of moral choice.

*impossible to trust anyone to mail it ever since the postage rates went up because people just tore off the stamps for their own use and threw away the letter, the only safe way was to hand it over the counter and make the clerk cancel the stamp before your own eyes.*

Berthe, the building superintendent, is yelling at her son in the parking lot. He tinkers away with his van. This happens every fine-weathered Sunday. It must be the van that Berthe dislikes because I've seen mother and son together in other quite amicable situations.

Berthe is a big Yugoslavian with high cheekbones. Her nationality was disclosed to me by PW. Berthe speaks a very rough-hewn English, I've overheard her in the lobby scolding tenants for late rents and leaving dirty lint screens in the dryers. It's exciting to listen to her, her words fall like rocks and boulders, and one can never tell where or how the next few will drop. But her Slavic yells at her son are a different matter, the words fly swift and true, well-aimed missiles that never miss. Finally, the son slams down the hood in disgust, wipes his hands on a rag, accompanies mother Berthe inside.

Berthe's husband has a job in a factory. But he loses several days of work every month when he succumbs to the booze, a word Berthe uses often in her Slavic tirades on those days, the only one I can understand, as it clunks down heavily out of the tight-flying formation of Yugoslavian sentences. He lolls around in the lobby, submitting passively to his wife's tongue-lashings. The bags under his bloodshot eyes, his stringy moustache, stubbled chin, dirty hair are so vulnerable to the poison-laden barbs (poison works the same way in any language) emanating from deep within the powerful watermelon bosom. No one's presence can embarrass or dignify her into silence.

No one except the old man who arrives now. 'Good morning,' he says, and Berthe turns, stops yelling, and smiles. Her husband rises, positions the wheelchair at the favourite angle. The lobby will be peaceful as long as the old man is there.

It was hopeless. My first swimming lesson. The water terrified me. When did that happen, I wonder, I used to love splashing at Chaupatty, carried about by the waves. And this was only a swimming pool. Where did all that terror come from? I'm trying to remember.

Armed with my Surf King I enter the high school and go to the pool area. A sheet with instructions for the new class is pinned to the bulletin board. All students must shower and then assemble at eight by the shallow end. As I enter the showers three young boys, probably from a previous class, emerge. One of them holds his nose. The second begins to hum, under his breath: Paki Paki, smell like curry. The third says to the first two: pretty soon all the water's going to taste of curry. They leave.

It's a mixed class, but the gorgeous woman of my fantasy is missing. I have to settle for another, in a pink one-piece suit, with brown hair and a bit of a stomach. She must be about thirty-five. Plain-looking.

The instructor is called Ron. He gives us a pep talk, sensing some nervousness in the group. We're finally all in the water, in the shallow end. He demonstrates floating on the back, then asks for a volunteer. The pink one-piece suit wades forward. He supports her, tells her to lean back and let her head drop in the water.

She does very well. And as we all regard her floating body, I see what was not visible outside the pool: her bush, curly bits of it, straying out at the pink Spandex V. Tongues of water lapping against her delta, as if caressing it teasingly, make the brown hair come alive in a most tantalizing manner. The crests and troughs of little waves, set off by the movement of our bodies in a circle around her, dutifully irrigate her; the curls alternately wave free inside the crest, then adhere to her wet thighs, beached by the inevitable trough. I could watch this forever, and I wish the floating demonstration would never end.

Next we are shown how to grasp the rail and paddle, face down in the water. Between practising floating and paddling, the hour is almost gone. I have been trying to observe the pink one-piece suit, getting glimpses of her straying pubic hair from various angles. Finally, Ron wants a volunteer for the last demonstration, and I go forward. To my horror he leads the class to the deep end. Fifteen feet of water. It is so blue, and I can see the bottom. He picks up a metal hoop attached to a long wooden stick. He wants me to grasp the hoop, jump in the water, and paddle, while he guides me by the stick. Perfectly safe, he tells me. A demonstration of how paddling propels the body.

It's too late to back out; besides, I'm so terrified I couldn't find the words to do so even if I wanted to. Everything he says I do as if in a trance. I don't remember the moment of jumping. The next thing I know is, I'm swallowing water and floundering, hanging on to the hoop for dear life. Ron draws me to the rails and helps me out. The class applauds.

We disperse and one thought is on my mind: what if I'd lost my grip? Fifteen feet of water under me. I shudder and take deep breaths. That is it. I'm not coming next week. This instructor is an irresponsible person. Or he does not value the lives of non-white immigrants. I remember the three teenagers. Maybe the swimming pool is the hangout of some racist group, bent on eliminating all non-white swimmers, to keep their waters pure and their white sisters unogled.

The elevator takes me upstairs. Then gutang-khutang. PW opens her door as I turn the corridor of medicinal smells. 'Berthe was screaming loudly at her husband tonight,' she tells me.

'Good for her', I say, and she frowns indignantly at me.

The old man is in the lobby. He's wearing thick wool gloves. He wants to know how the swimming was, must have seen me leaving with my towel yesterday. Not bad, I say.

'I used to swim a lot. Very good for the circulation.' He wheezes. 'My feet are cold all the time. Cold as ice. Hands too.'

Summer is winding down, so I say stupidly, 'Yes, it's not so warm any more.'

The thought of the next swimming lesson sickens me. But as I comb through the memories of that terrifying Monday, I come upon the straying curls of brown pubic hair. Inexorably drawn by them, I decide to go.

It's a mistake, of course. This time I'm scared even to venture in the shallow end. When everyone has entered the water and I'm the only one outside, I feel a little foolish and slide in.

Instructor Ron says we should start by reviewing the floating technique. I'm in no hurry. I watch the pink one-piece pull the swim-suit down around her cheeks and flip back to achieve perfect flotation. And then reap disappointment. The pink Spandex triangle is perfectly streamlined today, nothing strays, not a trace of fuzz, not one filament, not even a sign of post-depilation irritation. Like the airbrushed parts of glamour magazine models. The barrenness of her impeccably packaged apex is a betrayal. Now she is shorn like the other women in the class. Why did she have to do it?

The weight of this disappointment makes the water less manageable, more lung-penetrating. With trepidation, I float and paddle my way through the remainder of the hour, jerking my head out every two seconds and breathing deeply, to continually shore up a supply of precious, precious air without, at the same time, seeming too anxious and losing my dignity.

I don't attend the remaining classes. After I've missed three, Ron the instructor telephones. I tell him I've had the flu and am still feeling poorly, but I'll try to be there the following week.

He does not call again. My Surf King is relegated to an unused drawer. Total losses: one fantasy plus thirty dollars. And no watery rebirth. The swimming pool, like Chaupatty beach, has produced a stillbirth. But there is a difference. Water means regeneration only if it is pure and cleansing. Chaupatty was filthy, the pool was not. Failure to swim through filth must mean something other than failure of rebirth—failure of symbolic death? Does that equal success of symbolic life? death of a symbolic failure? death of a symbol? What is the equation?

*The postman did not bring a letter but a parcel, he was smiling because he knew that every time something came from Canada his baksheesh was guaranteed, and this time because it was a parcel Mother gave him a whole rupee, she was quite excited, there were so many stickers on it besides the stamps, one for Small Parcel, another Printed Papers, a red sticker saying Insured; she showed it to Father, and opened it, then put both hands on her cheeks, not able to speak because the surprise and happiness was so great, tears came to her eyes and she could not stop smiling, till Father became impatient to know and finally got up and came to the table.*

*When he saw it he was surprised and happy too, he began to grin, then hugged Mother saying our son is a writer, and we didn't even know it, he never told us a thing, here we are thinking he is still clerking away at the insurance company, and he has written a book of stories, all these years in school and college he kept his talent hidden, making us think he was just like one of the boys in the Baag, shouting and playing the fool in the compound, and now what a surprise; then Father opened the book and began reading it, heading back to the easy chair, and Mother so excited, still holding his arm, walked with him, saying it was not fair him reading it first, she wanted to read it too, and they agreed that he would read the first story, then give it to her so she could also read it, and they would take turns in that manner.*

*Mother removed the staples from the padded envelope in which he had mailed the book, and threw them away, then straightened the folded edges of the envelope and put it away safely with the other envelopes and letters she had collected since he left.*

The leaves are beginning to fall. The only ones I can identify are maple. The days are dwindling like the leaves. I've started a habit of taking long walks every evening. The old man is in the lobby when I leave, he waves as I go by. By the time I'm back, the lobby is usually empty.

Today I was woken up by a grating sound outside that made my flesh crawl. I went to the window and saw Berthe raking the leaves in the parking lot. Not in the expanse of patchy lawn on the periphery, but in the parking lot proper. She was raking the black tarred surface. I went back to bed and dragged a pillow over my head, not releasing it till noon.

When I return from my walk in the evening, PW, summoned by the elevator's gutang-khutang, says, 'Berthe filled six big black garbage bags with leaves today.'

'Six bags!' I say. 'Wow!'

Since the weather turned cold, Berthe's son does not tinker with his van on Sundays under my window. I'm able to sleep late.

Around eleven, there's a commotion outside. I reach out and switch on the clock radio. It's a sunny day, the window curtains are bright. I get up, curious, and see a black Olds Ninety-Eight in the parking lot, by the entrance to the building. The old man is in his wheelchair, bundled up, with a scarf wound several times round his neck as though to immobilize it, like a surgical collar. His daughter and another man, the car-owner, are helping him from the wheelchair into the front seat, encouraging him with words like: that's it, easy does it, attaboy. From the open door of the lobby, Berthe is shouting encouragement too, but hers is confined to one word: yah, repeated at different levels of pitch and volume, with variations on vowel-length. The stranger could be the old man's son, he has the same jet black hair and piercing eyes.

Maybe the old man is not well, it's an emergency. But I quickly scrap that thought—this isn't Bombay, an ambulance would have arrived. They're probably taking him out for a ride. If he is his son, where has he been all this time, I wonder.

The old man finally settles in the front seat, the wheelchair goes in the trunk, and they're off. The one I think is the son looks up and catches me at the window before I can move away, so I wave, and he waves back.

In the afternoon I take down a load of clothes to the laundry room. Both machines have completed their cycles, the clothes inside are waiting to be transferred to dryers. Should I remove them and place them on top of a dryer, or wait? I decide to wait. After a few minutes, two women arrive, they are in bathrobes, and smoking. It takes me a while to realize that these are the two disappointments who were sunbathing in bikinis last summer.

'You didn't have to wait, you could have removed the clothes and carried on, dear,' says one. She has a Scottish accent. It's one of the few I've learned to identify. Like maple leaves.

'Well,' I say, 'some people might not like strangers touching their clothes.'

'You're not a stranger, dear,' she says, 'you live in this building, we've seen you before.'

'Besides, your hands are clean,' the other one pipes in. 'You can touch my things any time you like.'

Horny old cow. I wonder what they've got on under their bathrobes. Not much, I find, as they bend over to place their clothes in the dryers.

'See you soon,' they say, and exit, leaving me behind in an erotic wake of smoke and perfume and deep images of cleavages. I start the washers and depart, and when I come back later, the dryers are empty.

PW tells me, 'The old man's son took him out for a drive today. He has a big beautiful black car.'

I see my chance, and shoot back: 'Olds Ninety-Eight.'

'What?'

'The car,' I explain, 'it's an Oldsmobile Ninety-Eight.'

She does not like this at all, my giving her information. She is visibly nettled, and retreats with a sour face.

*Mother and Father read the first five stories, and she was very sad after reading some of them, she said he must be so unhappy there, all his stories are about Bombay, he remembers every little thing about his childhood, he is thinking about it all the time even though he is ten thousand miles away, my poor son, I think he misses his home and us and everything he left behind, because if he likes it over there why would he not write stories about that, there must be so many new ideas that his new life could give him.*

*But Father did not agree with this, he said it did not mean that he was unhappy, all writers worked in the same way, they used their memories and experiences and made stories out of them, changing some things, adding some, imagining some, all writers were very good at remembering details of their lives.*

*Mother said, how can you be sure that he is remembering because he's a writer, or whether he started to write because he is unhappy and thinks of his past, and wants to save it all by making stories of it; and Father said that is not a sensible question, anyway, it is now my turn to read the next story.*

The first snow has fallen, and the air is crisp. It's not very deep, about two inches, just right to go for a walk in. I've been told that immigrants from hot countries always enjoy the snow the first year, maybe for a couple of years more, then inevitably the dread sets in, and the approach of winter gets them fretting and moping. On the other hand, if it hadn't been for my conversation with the woman at the swimming registration desk, they might now be saying that India is a nation of non-swimmers.

Berthe is outside, shovelling the snow off the walkway in the parking lot. She has a heavy, wide pusher which she wields expertly.

The old radiators in the apartment alarm me incessantly. They continue to broadcast a series of variations on death throes, and go from hot to cold and cold to hot at will, there's no controlling their temperature. I speak to Berthe about it in the lobby. The old man is there too, his chin seems to have sunk deeper into his chest, and his face is a yellowish grey.

'Nothing, not to worry about anything,' says Berthe, dropping rough-hewn chunks of language around me. 'Radiator no work, you tell me. You feel cold, you come to me, I keep you warm,' and she opens her arms wide, laughing. I step back, and she advances, her breasts preceding her like the gallant prows of two ice-breakers. She looks at the old man to see if he is appreciating the act: 'You no feel scared, I keep you safe and warm.'

But the old man is staring outside, at the flakes of falling snow. What thoughts is he thinking as he watches them? Of childhood days, perhaps, and snowmen with hats and pipes, and snowball fights, and white Christmases, and Christmas trees? What will I think of, old in this country, when I sit and watch the snow come down? For me, it is already too late for snowmen and snowball fights, and all I will have is thoughts about childhood thoughts and dreams, built around snowscapes and winter-wonder-lands on the Christmas cards so popular in Bombay; my snowmen and snowball fights and Christmas trees are in the pages of Enid Blyton's books, dispersed amidst the adventures of the Famous Five, and the Five Find-Outers, and the Secret Seven[7]. My snowflakes are even less forgettable than the old man's, for they never melt.

It finally happened. The heat went. Not the usual intermittent coming and going, but out completely. Stone cold. The radiators are like ice. And so is everything else. There's no hot water. Naturally. It's the hot water that goes through the rads and heats them. Or is it the other way around? Is there no hot water because the rads have stopped cir-culating it? I don't care, I'm too cold to sort out the cause and effect relationship. Maybe there is no connection at all.

I dress quickly, put on my winter jacket, and go down to the lobby. The elevator is not working because the power is out, so I take the stairs. Several people are gath-ered, and Berthe has announced that she has telephoned the office, they are sending a man. I go back up the stairs. It's only one floor, the elevator is just a bad habit. Back in Firozsha Baag they were broken most of the time. The stairway enters the corridor outside the old man's apartment, and I think of his cold feet and hands. Poor man, it must be horrible for him without heat.

As I walk down the long hallway, I feel there's something different but can't pin it down. I look at the carpet, the ceiling, the wallpaper: it all seems the same. Maybe it's the freezing cold that imparts a feeling of difference.

PW opens her door: 'The old man had another stroke yesterday. They took him to the hospital.'

The medicinal smell. That's it. It's not in the hallway any more.

*In the stories that he'd read so far Father said that all the Parsi families were poor or middle-class, but that was okay; nor did he mind that the seeds for the stories were picked from the sufferings of their own lives; but there should also have been something positive about Parsis, there was so much to be proud of: the great Tatas and their contribution to the steel industry, or Sir Dinshaw Petit in the textile industry who made Bombay the Manchester of the East,*

7  Enid Blyton (1897–1968) was a popular and prolific British children's author of adventure series (such as the Famous Five, the Five Find-Outers, and the Secret Seven) in which groups of children investigate mysteries.

*or Dadabhai Naoroji in the freedom movement, where he was the first to use the word swaraj[8], and the first to be elected to the British Parliament where he carried on his campaign; he should have found some way to bring some of these wonderful facts into his stories, what would people reading these stories think, those who did not know about Parsis—that the whole community was full of cranky, bigoted people; and in reality it was the richest, most advanced and philanthropic community in India, and he did not need to tell his own son that Parsis had a reputation for being generous and family-oriented. And he could have written something also about the historic background, how Parsis came to India from Persia because of Islamic persecution in the seventh century, and were the descendants of Cyrus the Great and the magnificent Persian Empire. He could have made a story of all this, couldn't he?*

*Mother said what she liked best was his remembering everything so well, how beautifully he wrote about it all, even the sad things, and though he changed some of it, and used his imagination, there was truth in it.*

*My hope is, Father said, that there will be some story based on his Canadian experience, that way we will know something about our son's life there, if not through his letters then in his stories; so far they are all about Parsis and Bombay, and the one with a little bit about Toronto, where a man perches on top of the toilet, is shameful and disgusting although it is funny at times and did make me laugh, I have to admit, but where does he get such an imagination from, what is the point of such a fantasy; and Mother said that she would also enjoy some stories about Toronto and the people there; it puzzles me, she said, why he writes nothing about it, especially since you say that writers use their own experience to make stories out of.*

*Then Father said this is true, but he is probably not using his Toronto experience because it is too early; what do you mean, too early, asked Mother and Father explained it takes a writer about ten years time after an experience before he is able to use it in his writing, it takes that long to be absorbed internally and understood, thought out and thought about, over and over again, he haunts it and it haunts him if it is valuable enough, till the writer is comfortable with it to be able to use it as he wants; but this is only one theory I read somewhere, it may or may not be true.*

*That means, said Mother, that his childhood in Bombay and our home here is the most valuable thing in his life just now, because he is able to remember it all to write about it, and you were so bitterly saying he is forgetting where he came from; and that may be true, said Father, but that is not what the theory means, according to the theory he is writing of these things because they are far enough in the past for him to deal with objectively, he is able to achieve what critics call artistic distance, without emotions interfering; and what do you mean emotions, said Mother, you are saying he does not feel anything for his characters, how can he write so beautifully about so many sad things without any feelings in his heart?*

*But before Father could explain more, about beauty and emotion and inspiration and imagination, Mother took the book and said it was her turn now and too much theory she did not want to listen to, it was confusing and did not make as much sense as reading the stories, she would read them her way and Father could read them his.*

---

8  Dadabhai Naoroji (1825–1917): a political leader who, concerned about the negative economic effects on India of British imperialism, was among the first to argue for swaraj (self-rule).

My books on the windowsill have been damaged. Ice has been forming on the inside ledge, which I did not notice, and melting when the sun shines in. I spread them in a corner of the living room to dry out.

The winter drags on. Berthe wields her snow pusher as expertly as ever, but there are signs of weariness in her performance. Neither husband nor son is ever seen outside with a shovel. Or anywhere else, for that matter. It occurs to me that the son's van is missing, too.

The medicinal smell is in the hall again, I sniff happily and look forward to seeing the old man in the lobby. I go downstairs and peer into the mailbox, see the blue and magenta of an Indian aerogramme with Don Mills, Ontario, Canada in Father's flawless hand through the slot.

I pocket the letter and enter the main lobby. The old man is there, but not in his usual place. He is not looking out through the glass door. His wheelchair is facing a bare wall where the wallpaper is torn in places. As though he is not interested in the outside world any more, having finished with all that, and now it's time to see inside. What does he see inside, I wonder? I go up to him and say hullo. He says hullo without raising his sunken chin. After a few seconds his grey countenance faces me. 'How old do you think I am?' His eyes are dull and glazed; he is looking even further inside than I first presumed.

'Well, let's see, you're probably close to sixty-four.'

'I'll be seventy-eight next August.' But he does not chuckle or wheeze. Instead, he continues softly, 'I wish my feet did not feel so cold all the time. And my hands.' He lets his chin fall again.

In the elevator I start opening the aerogramme, a tricky business because a crooked tear means lost words. Absorbed in this while emerging, I don't notice PW occupying the centre of the hallway, arms folded across her chest: 'They had a big fight. Both of them have left.'

I don't immediately understand her agitation. 'What . . . who?'

'Berthe. Husband and son both left her. Now she is all alone.'

Her tone and stance suggest that we should not be standing here talking but do something to bring Berthe's family back. 'That's very sad,' I say, and go in. I picture father and son in the van, driving away, driving across the snow-covered country, in the dead of winter, away from wife and mother; away to where? how far will they go? Not son's van nor father's booze can take them far enough. And the further they go, the more they'll remember, they can take it from me.

*All the stories were read by Father and Mother, and they were sorry when the book was finished, they felt they had come to know their son better now, yet there was much more to know, they wished there were many more stories; and this is what they mean, said Father, when they say that the whole story can never be told, the whole truth can never be known; what do you mean, they say, asked Mother, who they, and Father said writers, poets, philosophers. I don't care what they say, said Mother, my son will write as much or as little as he wants to, and if I can read it I will be happy.*

*The last story they liked the best of all because it had the most in it about Canada, and now they felt they knew at least a little bit, even if it was a very little bit, about his day-to-day life in his apartment; and Father said if he continues to write about such things he will become popular because I am sure they are interested there in reading about life through the eyes of an immigrant, it provides a different viewpoint; the only danger is if he changes and becomes so much like them that he will write like one of them and lose the important difference.*

The bathroom needs cleaning. I open a new can of Ajax and scour the tub. Sloshing with mug from bucket was standard bathing procedure in the bathrooms of Firozsha Baag, so my preference now is always for a shower. I've never used the tub as yet; besides, it would be too much like Chaupatty or the swimming pool, wallowing in my own dirt. Still, it must be cleaned.

When I've finished, I prepare for a shower. But the clean gleaming tub and the nearness of the vernal equinox give me the urge to do something different today. I find the drain plug in the bathroom cabinet, and run the bath.

I've spoken so often to the old man, but I don't know his name. I should have asked him the last time I saw him, when his wheelchair was facing the bare wall because he had seen all there was to see outside and it was time to see what was inside. Well, tomorrow. Or better yet, I can look it up in the directory in the lobby. Why didn't I think of that before? It will only have an initial and a last name, but then I can surprise him with: hullo Mr Wilson, or whatever it is.

The bath is full. Water imagery is recurring in my life: Chaupatty beach, swimming pool, bathtub. I step in and immerse myself up to the neck. It feels good. The hot water loses its opacity when the chlorine, or whatever it is, has cleared. My hair is still dry. I close my eyes, hold my breath, and dunk my head. Fighting the panic, I stay under and count to thirty. I come out, clear my lungs and breathe deeply.

I do it again. This time I open my eyes under water, and stare blindly without seeing, it takes all my will to keep the lids from closing. Then I am slowly able to discern the underwater objects. The drain plug looks different, slightly distorted; there is a hair trapped between the hole and the plug, it waves and dances with the movement of the water. I come up, refresh my lungs, examine quickly the overwater world of the washroom, and go in again. I do it several times, over and over. The world outside the water I have seen a lot of, it is now time to see what is inside.

The spring session for adult non-swimmers will begin in a few days at the high school. I must not forget the registration date.

The dwindled days of winter are now all but forgotten; they have grown and attained a respectable span. I resume my evening walks, it's spring, and a vigorous thaw is on. The snowbanks are melting, the sound of water on its gushing, gurgling journey to the drains is beautiful. I plan to buy a book of trees, so I can identify more than the maple as they begin to bloom.

When I return to the building, I wipe my feet energetically on the mat because some people are entering behind me, and I want to set a good example. Then I go to the board with its little plastic letters and numbers. The old man's apartment is the one on the corner by the stairway, that makes it number 201. I run down the list, come to

201, but there are no little white plastic letters beside it. Just the empty black rectangle with holes where the letters would be squeezed in. That's strange. Well, I can introduce myself to him, then ask his name.

However, the lobby was empty. I take the elevator, exit at the second floor, wait for the gutang-khutang. It does not come, the door closes noiselessly, smoothly. Berthe has been at work, or has made sure someone else has. PW's cue has been lubricated out of existence.

But she must have the ears of a cockroach. She is waiting for me. I whistle my way down the corridor. She fixes me with an accusing look. She waits till I stop whistling, then says: 'You know the old man died last night.'

I cease groping for my key. She turns to go and I take a step towards her, my hand still in my trouser pocket. 'Did you know his name?' I ask, but she leaves without answering.

*Then Mother said, the part I like best in the last story is about Grandpa, where he wonders if Grandpa's spirit is really watching him and blessing him, because you know I really told him that, I told him helping an old suffering person who is near death is the most blessed thing to do, because that person will ever after watch over you from heaven, I told him this when he was disgusted with Grandpa's urine-bottle and would not touch it, would not hand it to him even when I was not at home.*

*Are you sure, said Father, that you really told him this, or you believe you told him because you like the sound of it, you said yourself the other day that he changes and adds and alters things in the stories but he writes it all so beautifully that it seems true, so how can you be sure; this sounds like another theory, said Mother, but I don't care, he says I told him and I believe now I told him, so even if I did not tell him then it does not matter now.*

*Don't you see, said Father, that you are confusing fiction with facts, fiction does not create facts, fiction can come from facts, it can grow out of facts by compounding, transposing, augmenting, diminishing, or altering them in any way; but you must not confuse cause and effect, you must not confuse what really happened with what the story says happened, you must not loose your grasp on reality, that way madness lies.*

*Then Mother stopped listening because, as she told Father so often, she was not very fond of theories, and she took out her writing pad and started a letter to her son; Father looked over her shoulder, telling her to say how proud they were of him and were waiting for his next book, he also said, leave a little space for me at the end, I want to write a few lines when I put the address on the envelope.*

1987

# Dionne Brand

## b. 1953

In the anthology *A Caribbean Dozen* (1996), Dionne Brand writes,

*I was born deep in the south of Trinidad in a village called Guayguayare. . . . It is the place I remember and love the most. I now live in Toronto, Canada, but each time I go back to Trinidad I always go to Guayguayare just to see the ocean there, to breathe in the smell of copra drying and wood burning and fish frying. In the Sixties when I was in elementary and high schools, none of the books we studied were about Black people's lives; they were about Europeans, mostly the British. But I felt that Black people's experiences were as important and as valuable, and needed to be written down and read about. This is why I became a writer. . . . I went to a girls' high school where I was taught that girls could use their intellect to live a full life. My teachers and friends there helped me to see that women should enjoy the same rights and freedoms as men. When I moved to Canada in 1970 I joined the civil rights, feminist and socialist movements. I was only seventeen but I already knew that to live freely in the world as a Black woman I would have to involve myself in political action as well as writing.*

After coming to Canada, Brand attended the University of Toronto, where she earned a BA (1975) in English and philosophy and an MA in the philosophy of education (1988). She began a PhD in women's history while employed in community social work in such capacities as counsellor for the Immigrant Women's Centre and the Black Youth Hotline; facilitator for the Ontario Federation of Labour Women's Committee and the Metro Labour Council Anti-Racism Conference; and board member of a Toronto shelter for battered immigrant women. She was an information officer in Grenada in 1983 when the United States invaded that island nation, an experience that had a powerful effect on her. After her return, she put together two books of oral histories about the effects of race: *Rivers Have Sources, Trees Have Roots: Speaking of Racism* (1985; with Krisantha Sri Bhaggiyadatta) and *No Burden To Carry: Narratives of Black Working Women in Ontario, 1920s–1950s* (1991). She has taught in universities in Ontario and British Columbia, and has held the Ruth Wynn Woodward Chair in Women's Studies at Simon Fraser University (2000–2). She now holds a Canada Research Chair in creative writing at the University of Guelph and lives in Toronto.

In everything she writes, Brand returns to the damaging effects of discrimination and the repression that she finds in Canada—despite the country's reputation for tolerance. Poet, fiction writer, essayist, and social historian, she has produced a significant body of work intensely grounded in her own personal experience—as an immigrant, as a racial minority, as a woman, and as a lesbian. Her vision may be a harrowing one, but her language and imagery can be intoxicating.

Her 1990 book of poems, *No Language is Neutral*, portrays the divided experience of the immigrant as a result of the dislocation that produces an imagined and nostalgic life lived 'in another place not here': at first, the speaker tells us, 'Dumbfounded I walk as if these sidewalks are a place I'm visiting'; after a time, she says that 'I became more secretive, language seemed to split in two, one branch fell silent, the other argued hotly for going home.' Brand further documents this immigrant alienation in her first novel, *In Another Place, Not Here* (1996), where 'everyone is from someplace else but this city does not give them a chance to say this; it pushes their confusion underground.' In the collection of poems published a year later, *Land to Light On* (1997), which won both a Governor General's Award and a Trillium Award, she writes about her despair of finding any refuge in a world dominated by brutal global politics and crushing multinational capitalism.

Recognizing that those like her from the Caribbean are part of a larger black diaspora that searches for home throughout the world, Brand knows that the immigrant condition cannot be separated from the sickness that is racism. In the short fiction in *Sans Souci and Other Stories* (1988) and elsewhere, she finds that the experience of racism and the violence stemming from it is not limited to the immigrant. Her female protagonists discover that they are 'in enemy territory' whether they remain in the Caribbean (where sexism often leads to violence against women) or dwell in transplanted homes in Canada. In Brand's second novel, *At the Full and Change of the Moon* (1999), the descendants of Bola—a young girl who was the only survivor of a mass suicide, a protest against slavery led by her mother, Marie Ursule, in Trinidad in 1824—are traced through several generations as they move out through the Americas and Europe. As the characters spread across a globe filled with tragedy and suffering, the novel becomes an epic affirmation of the strength and endurance of a family, and, thus, of a people.

In spite of—or because of—her deep knowledge of the city's limitations, Brand has become an important chronicler of contemporary Toronto. The thirty-three parts of the long poem *thirsty* (2002) acutely dramatize the paradox of coming to a big city in a new country. Describing the city as a place where one may at first find 'beauty / unbreakable and amorphous as eyelids' and showing how one can experience its intensity as a 'polychromatic murmur, the dizzying / waves, the noise of it', she unveils its shadowy side, and its potential for tragic consequences.

*All the hope gone hard. That is a city.*
*The blind houses, the cramped dirt, the broken*
*air, the sweet ugliness, the blissful and tortured*
*flowers, the misguided clothing, the bricked lies*
*the steel lies, all the lies seeping from flesh*
*falling in rain and snow, the weeping buses,*
*the plastic throats, the perfumed garbage, the*
*needled sky, the smogged oxygen, the deathly clerical*
*gentlemen cleaning their fingernails at the stock*
*exchange, the dingy hearts in the newsrooms, that is*
*a city, the feral amnesia of us all.*

Toronto is again important in Brand's 2004 novel, *What We All Long For*, which looks at the next generation, the adult children of immigrants, showing them cut off from their parents, their parents' hopes, and their larger environment. The main characters face discrimination far more subtle than that their parents ever experienced. They find that Toronto is a city in which the majority is made up of minorities, a city in which blended identity may mean belonging to nothing but to the city itself. The problems of these young adults turn out to arise out of economic status as much as from race, while subgroups define themselves within the city as much by their relationship to a faraway lost homeland as by any shared ethnicity. In 2009, Brand was honoured for the attention she has paid to her adopted city by being named poet laureate of Toronto.

Brand's attention is global as often as it is local. In the poetry collected in *Inventory* (2005), she catalogues the horrifying events that have dominated the world in the early years of this century. A lamentation, *Inventory* is also a record of an individual caught between the numbness and denial that comes from traumatic shock and the need to remain sensitive in a world where 'the news was advertisement for movies / the movies were the real killings.'

Brand's most recent collection, *Ossuaries* (2010), takes its name from the receptacles (often portable boxes or urns) used to store the disconnected bones of the dead after they have been disinterred, a rich image—suggesting loss in preservation—that unifies this book about how forced immigration and slavery erased a culture's past. In her two books of essays, *Bread out of Stone* (1994) and *A Map to the Door of No Return: Notes to Belonging* (2001), Brand discusses, in personal and autobiographical terms, this deracinated condition, showing how it is the source of forgetfulness and loss. Linking this disruption of history to her grandfather's inability to say 'what people we came from', she argues that these losses matter to the individual:

*Having no name to call on was having no past;*
*having no past pointed to the fissure between the*
*past and the present. That fissure is represented in*
*the Door of No Return: that place where our*
*ancestors departed one world for another; the Old*
*World for the New. The place where all names*
*were forgotten and all beginnings recast. In some*

desolate sense it was the creation place of Blacks in the New World Diaspora at the same time that it signified the end of traceable beginnings. Beginnings that can be noted through a name or a set of family stories that extend farther into the past than five hundred or so years, or the kinds of beginnings that can be expressed in a name which in turn marked out territory or occupation.

She adds that, 'I am interested in exploring this creation place—the Door of No Return, a place emptied of beginnings—as a site of belonging or unbelonging.'

The naming that language does is an important topic in other ways to Brand. She has returned several times to the insight expressed in the title of *No Language is Neutral*—a phrase from Derek Walcott that speaks to her awareness of all communication as inherently political. Because language must always be examined skeptically for its ideological baggage and can fail one entirely, she suggests that the individual's body must be allowed to speak in its own way. In 'This Body for Itself', Brand writes of attending a symposium of Caribbean women writers and feeling that 'what is missing' from their discussions is 'the sexual body':

In a world where Black women's bodies are so sexualised, avoiding the body as sexual is a strategy. . . . I know that not talking about the sexual Black female self at all is as much an anti-colonial strategy as armed struggle. But what a trap. Often when we talk about the wonderful Black women in our lives, their valour, their emotional strength, their psychic endurance overwhelm our texts so much that we forget that apart from learning the elegant art of survival from them, we also learn in their gestures the art of sensuality, the fleshy art of pleasure and desire.

Having experienced discrimination based on sexual orientation as well as race, Brand must speak a language that is unconstrained, as in the sequence of poems entitled 'hard against the soul'. Throughout her work, she draws on her African background, her childhood experiences in the Caribbean, and her travels across the Canadian physical and cultural landscapes to meditate on the nature of identity in a culturally diverse society, observing, 'It is not the job of writers to lift our spirits. Books simply do what they do. . . . When you think you are in the grace of a dance, you come upon something hard.'

# From *No Language Is Neutral*

## hard against the soul

X

Then it is this simple. I felt the unordinary romance of
women who love women for the first time. It burst in
my mouth. Someone said this is your first lover, you
will never want to leave her. I had it in mind that I
would be an old woman with you. But perhaps I
always had it in mind simply to be an old woman,
darkening, somewhere with another old woman,
then, I decided it was you when you found me in that
apartment drinking whisky for breakfast. When I came
back from Grenada and went crazy for two years, that
time when I could hear anything and my skin was
flaming like a nerve and the walls were like paper
and my eyes could not close. I suddenly sensed you

10

at the end of my room waiting. I saw your back arched
against this city we inhabit like guerillas, I brushed my
hand, conscious, against your soft belly, waking up.

I saw this woman once in another poem, sitting,
throwing water over her head on the rind of a country
beach as she turned toward her century. Seeing her
no part of me was comfortable with itself. I envied her,          20
so old and set aside, a certain habit washed from her
eyes. I must have recognized her. I know I watched
her along the rim of the surf promising myself, an old
woman is free. In my nerves something there
unravelling, and she was a place to go, believe me,
against gales of masculinity but in that then, she was
masculine, old woman, old bird squinting at the
water's wing above her head, swearing under her
breath. I had a mind that she would be graceful in me
and she might have been if I had not heard you                    30
laughing in another tense and lifted my head from her
dry charm.

You ripped the world open for me. Someone said this
is your first lover you will never want to leave her. My
lips cannot say old woman darkening anymore, she
is the peace of another life that didn't happen and
couldn't happen in my flesh and wasn't peace but
flight into old woman, prayer, to the saints of my
ancestry, the gourd and bucket carrying women who
stroke their breasts into stone shedding offspring and                40
smile. I know since that an old woman, darkening,
cuts herself away limb from limb, sucks herself white,
running, skin torn and raw like a ball of bright light,
flying, into old woman. I only know now that my
longing for this old woman was longing to leave the
prisoned gaze of men.

It's true, you spend the years after thirty turning over
the suggestion that you have been an imbecile,
hearing finally all the words that passed you like air,
like so much fun, or all the words that must have                    50
existed while you were listening to others. What
would I want with this sentence you say flinging it
aside . . . and then again sometimes you were duped,
poems placed deliberately in your way. At eleven, the

strophe[1] of a yellow dress sat me crosslegged in my
sex. It was a boy's abrupt birthday party. A yellow
dress for a tomboy, the ritual stab of womanly gathers
at the waist. *She look like a boy in a dress*, my big
sister say, a lyric and feminine correction from a
watchful aunt, *don't say that, she look nice and pretty.* 60
Nice and pretty, laid out to splinter you, so that never,
until it is almost so late as not to matter do you grasp
some part, something missing like a wing, some
fragment of your real self.

Old woman, that was the fragment that I caught in
your eye, that was the look I fell in love with, the piece
of you that you kept, the piece of you left, the lesbian,
the inviolable, sitting on a beach in a time that did not
hear your name or else it would have thrown you into
the sea, or you, hear that name yourself and walked 70
willingly into the muting blue. Instead you sat and I
saw your look and pursued one eye until it came to
the end of itself and then I saw the other,
the blazing fragment.

Someone said this is your first lover, you will never
want to leave her. There are saints of this ancestry
too who laugh themselves like jamettes[2] in the
pleasure of their legs and caress their sex in mirrors.
I have become myself. A woman who looks
at a woman and says, here, I have found you, 80
in this, I am blackening in my way. You ripped the
world raw. It was as if another life exploded in my
face, brightening, so easily the brow of a wing
touching the surf, so easily I saw my own body, that
is, my eyes followed me to myself, touched myself
as a place, another life, terra. They say this place
does not exist, then, my tongue is mythic. I was here
before.

1990

---

1 In ancient Greek drama, the strophe was a turn in dancing; hence, a reversal of one's direction.
2 Prostitutes; by extension women of loose morals, living in a slum area (Caribbean English).

# I Have Been Losing Roads

### I i

Out here I am like someone without a sheet
without a branch but not even safe as the sea,
without the relief of the sky or good graces of a door.
If I am peaceful in this discomfort, is not peace,
is getting used to harm. Is giving up, or misplacing
surfaces, the seam in grain, so standing
in a doorway I cannot summon up the yard,
familiar broken chair or rag of cloth on a blowing line,
I cannot smell smoke, something burning in a pit,
or gather air from far off or hear anyone calling.                    10
The doorway cannot bell a sound, cannot repeat
what is outside. My eyes is not a mirror.

### I ii

If you come out and you see nothing recognizable,
if the stars stark and brazen like glass,
already done decide you cannot read them.
If the trees don't flower and colour refuse to limn
when a white man in a red truck on a rural road
jumps out at you, screaming his exact hatred
of the world, his faith extravagant and earnest
and he threatens, something about your cunt,                    20
you do not recover, you think of Malcolm[1]
on this snow drifted road, you think,
'Is really so evil they is then
that one of them in a red truck can split your heart
open, crush a day in fog?'

### I iii

I lift my head in the cold and I get confuse.
It quiet here when is night, and is only me
and the quiet. I try to say a word but it fall. Fall

---

1  Malcolm X (1925–65), American black activist, noted for his opposition to white racism. He rose to prominence
as the leading advocate of the American Black Muslim movement but grew unhappy with its leader, Elijah
Muhammad, and his restrictive views. After he broke with the Black Muslims in 1964, he was assassinated by
members of the group.

like the stony air. I stand up there but nothing
happen, just a bank of air like a wall. I could swear 30
my face was touching stone. I stand up but
nothing happen, nothing happen or I shouldn't say
nothing. I was embarrassed, standing like a fool,
the pine burdened in snow, the air fresh, fresh
and foreign and the sky so black and wide I did not
know which way to turn except to try again, to find
some word that could be heard by the something
waiting. My mouth could not find a language.
I find myself instead, useless as that. I sorry.
I stop by the mailbox and I give up. 40


    I iv


I look at that road a long time.
It seem to close.
Yes, is here I reach
framed and frozen on a shivered
country road instead of where I thought
I'd be in the blood
red flame of a revolution.
I couldn't be farther away.
And none of these thoughts
disturb the stars or the pine 50
or the road or the red truck
screeching cunt along it.


    I v


All I could do was turn and go back to the house
and the door that I can't see out of.
My life was supposed to be wider, not so forlorn
and not standing out in this north country bled
like maple. I did not want to write poems
about stacking cords of wood, as if the world
is that simple, that quiet is not simple or content
but finally cornered and killed. I still need the revolution 60
bright as the blaze of the wood stove in the window
when I shut the light and mount the stairs to bed.

### II i

Out here, you can smell indifference driving
along, the harsh harsh happiness of winter
roads, all these roads heading nowhere, all
these roads heading their own unknowing way,
all these roads into smoke, and hoarfrost, friezed
and scrambling off in drifts, where is this
that they must go anytime, now, soon, immediately
and gasping and ending and opening in snow dust.                    70
Quiet, quiet, earfuls, brittle, brittle ribs of ice
and the road heaving under and the day lighting up,
going on any way.

### II ii

I have to think again what it means that I am here,
what it means that this, harsh as it is and without
a name, can swallow me up. I have to think how I
am here, so eaten up and frayed, a life that I was
supposed to finish by making something of it
not regularly made, where I am not this woman
fastened to this ugly and disappointing world.                      80
I wanted it for me, to burst my brain and leap a distance
and all I have are these hoarse words that still owe
this life and all I'll be is tied to this century and waiting
without a knife or courage and still these same words
strapped to my back

### II iii

I know as this thing happens, a woman
sucks her teeth, walks into a shop on an island
over there to stretch a few pennies across another
day, brushes a hand over her forehead and leaves,
going into the street empty-handed. Her certainty                   90
frighten me. 'Is so things is,' she muse, reading
the shopkeeper's guiltless eyes, this hot hope the skin
tames to brooding, that particular advice, don't expect
nothing good. Quite here you reach and you forget.

## II iv

no wonder I could get lost here, no wonder
in this set of trees I lose my way, counting
on living long and not noticing a closing,
no wonder a red truck could surprise me
and every night shape me into a crouch
with the telephone close by and the doors                          100
checked and checked, all night. I can hear
everything and I can hear birds waking up
by four a.m. and the hours between three
and five last a whole day. I can hear wood
breathe and stars crackle on the galvanized
steel, I can hear smoke turn solid and this
house is only as safe as flesh. I can hear the
gate slam, I can hear wasps in my doorway,
and foraging mice, there's an old tree next
to my car and I can hear it fall, I can hear            ·              110
the road sigh and the trees shift. I can
hear them far away from this house late, late
waiting for what this country is to happen,
I listen for the crunch of a car on ice or gravel,
the crush of boots and something coming

## II v

A comet, slow and magnificent, drapes the north sky
but I cannot see it, cannot allow it, that would be
allowing another sign. And songs, songs to follow.
What songs can sing this anyway, what humming
and what phrase will now abandon me, what woman                     120
with a gun and her fingers to her lips draw us to another
territory further north, further cold, further on,
into the mouth of the Arctic.
I'm heading to frost, to freezing,
how perhaps returning south heads to fever,
and what I'm saving for another time is all our good,
good will, so not listening, not listening
to any dangling voice or low, lifting whistle.
All the sounds gone out, all the wind died away,
I won't look, won't look at the tail of lighted dust.              130

III i

In the middle of afternoons driving north
on 35, stopping for a paper and a coffee,
I read the terrifying poetry of newspapers. I
notice vowels have suddenly stopped their
routine, their alarming rooms are shut,
their burning light collapsed

*the wave of takeovers, mergers and restructuring*
*. . . swept the world's . . . blue chips rally in New York*
*. . . Bundesbank² looms . . . Imperial Oil increases dividends*
*. . . tough cutbacks build confidence*                                    140

Your mouth never opens to say all this.
The breathful air of words are taken. Swept, yes.
You feel your coffee turn asphalt, you look around
and your eyes hit the dirty corners of the windy store,
stray paper, stray cups, stray oil, stray fumes of gas.
Your mouth never opens, your keys look unfamiliar.

*is Microsoft a rapacious plunderer . . . or a benign*
*benevolent giant . . . rough road ahead*

Rough road ahead they say so I leave the gas
station, leaving the paper on the counter,                                  150
not listening to the woman calling me back,
my mouth full and tasteless


III ii

Where is this. Your tongue, gone cold, gone
heavy in this winter light.
On a highway burrowing north don't waste your breath.
This winter road cannot hear it and will swallow it
whole. Don't move.
This detail then, when grass leans in certain light.
In other days, blue. This, every week no matter what grows
worse you cannot say you are on the same road, green darkens    160
or yellows or snows or disappears. Leave me there then,
at 2 p.m. rounding 35 to the 121 hoping
never to return here.

2  The central bank of the Federal Republic of Germany and an integral component of the European system of
   the central banks.

I should have passed, gone my way.

You come to think
the next house one kilometre away might as well
be ten, it so far from love, and shouting would produce
no blood. If I believe anything it will not matter though.
Life is porous, unimaginable in the end, only substance
burning in itself, lit by the heat of touching. It's good          170
how we melt back into nothing.


### III iii

Look, let me be specific. I have been losing roads
and tracks and air and rivers and little thoughts
and smells and incidents and a sense of myself
and fights I used to be passionate about
and don't remember. And once I lost the mechanics, no,
the meaning of dancing, and
I have been forgetting everything, friends, and pain.
The body bleeds only water and fear when you survive
the death of your politics, but why don't I forget.          180
That island with an explosive at the beginning of its name[3]
keeps tripping me and why don't I recall my life
in detail because I was always going somewhere else
and what I was living was unimportant for the while


*Rough Road Ahead*

let me say that all the classrooms should be burned
and all this paper abandoned like dancing and the gas
stations heading north, and all the independents
who wasted time arguing and being superior, pulling out
dictionaries and refereed journals,[4] new marxists, neo-marxists,
independent marxists, all of us loving our smartness, oh jeez,          190
the arguments filling auditoriums and town halls with
smartness, taking our time with smartness for serious study,
committing suicide blowing saxophones of smartness, going
home, which windy night on Bloor Street knowing full well and
waking up shaky until smartness rings the telephone with
another invitation and postmortem about last night's meeting.
Then I lost, well, gave up the wherewithal

---

3  Grenada, which, because it is pronounced with a long a, sounds like 'grenade'.
4  Journals in which scholarly essays are published are said to be 'refereed' because each submission is sent out to
   two or three experts in the field for review and suggestions before it can be accepted.

III iv

One gleeful headline drives me to the floor, kneeling,
and all paint turns to gazette paper and all memory
collides into photographs we could not say happened,                    200
that is us, that's what we did. When you lose you become
ancient but this time no one will rake over those bodies
gently collecting their valuables, their pots, their hearts
and intestines, their papers and what they could bury.
This civilization will be dug up to burn all its manifestos.
No tender archaeologist will mend our furious writings
concluding, 'They wanted sweat to taste sweet, that is all,
some of them played music for nothing, some of them
wrote poems to tractors, rough hands, and rough roads,
some sang for no reason at all to judge by their condition.'            210


III v

After everything I rely on confusion. I listen for
disaster, a storm in the Gulf of Mexico, arctic air
wreathing the whole of this unblessed continent,
mud slides burying the rich in California and the
devil turned in on himself in Oklahoma.[5] And others,
and more than my desire reminding me that someone
used to say when I was a child don't wish for bad
you might get it, your own face might be destroyed,
you will call trouble on yourself and on your own house.
How I watch, like someone without a being, the whole                    10
enterprise come to zero and my skin not even able
to count on itself. Still, with snow coming, counting
by the slate sky, I hope for cars and hands to freeze,
lines and light to fall, since what I've learned,
the lie of it, is no amount of will can change it. There
are whole countries exhausted for it, whole villages,
whole arms, whole mornings and whole hearts burning.
And what I wish for is natural and accidental

5 A reference to the bombing of the Murrah Federal Building in Oklahoma City in 1995, an act of domestic
  terrorism.

# Land to Light On

V i

Maybe this wide country just stretches your life to a thinness
just trying to take it in, trying to calculate in it what you must
do, the airy bay at its head scatters your thoughts like someone
going mad from science and birds pulling your hair, ice invades
your nostrils in chunks, land fills your throat, you are so busy
with collecting the north, scrambling to the Arctic so wilfully, so
busy getting a handle to steady you to this place you get blown
into bays and lakes and fissures you have yet to see, except
on a map in a schoolroom long ago but you have a sense that
whole parts of you are floating in heavy lake water heading for                    10
what you suspect is some other life that lives there, and you, you
only trust moving water and water that reveals itself in colour. It
always takes long to come to what you have to say, you have to
sweep this stretch of land up around your feet and point to the
signs, pleat whole histories with pins in your mouth and guess
at the fall of words


V ii

But the sight of land has always baffled you,
there is dirt somewhere older than any exile
and try as you might, your eyes only compose
the muddy drain in front of the humid almond                    20
tree, the unsettling concrete sprawl of the housing
scheme, the stone your uncle used to smash his name
into another uncle's face, your planet is your hands,
your house behind your eyebrows and the tracing
paper over the bead of islands of indifferent and
reversible shapes, now Guadeloupe is a crab pinched
at the waist, now Nevis' borders change by mistake
and the carelessness of history, now sitting in Standard
Five,[1] the paper shifting papery in the sweat of your
fingers you come to be convinced that these lines will                    30
not matter, your land is a forced march on the bottom
of the Sargasso,[2] your way tangled in life

1 That is, the speaker is recalling sitting in class at school ('Standard Five' is a grade level in the Caribbean), tracing out the shapes of the islands as an exercise.
2 The Sargasso Sea is a region of the western Atlantic Ocean between the Azores and the Caribbean, so called because of the prevalence in it of floating and thickly matted sargasso seaweed. This sea was seen, in the days of sailing, as a danger to ships, which could become trapped in the massed vegetation.

V iii

I am giving up on land to light on, it's only true, it is only
something someone tells you, someone you should not trust
anyway. Days away, years before, a beer at your lips and the view
from Castara,[3] the ocean as always pulling you towards its bone
and much later, in between, learning to drive the long drive
to Burnt River, where the land is not beautiful, braised
like the back of an animal, burnt in coolness, but the sky is,
like the ocean pulling you toward its bone, skin falling away                40
from your eyes, you see it without its history of harm, without
its damage, or everywhere you walk on the earth there's harm,
everywhere resounds. This is the only way you will know
the names of cities, not charmed or overwhelmed, all you see is
museums of harm and metros full, in Paris, walls inspected
crudely for dates, and Amsterdam, street corners full of
druggists, ashen with it, all the way from Suriname, Curaçao,
Dutch and German inking their lips, pen nibs of harm blued in
the mouth, not to say London's squares, blackened in statues,
Zeebrugge,[4] searching the belly of fish, Kinshasa, through an                50
airplane window the dictator cutting up bodies grips the plane
to the tarmac and I can't get out to kiss the ground


V iv

This those slaves must have known who were my mothers, skin
falling from their eyes, they moving toward their own bone,
'so thank god for the ocean and the sky all implicated, all
unconcerned,' they must have said, 'or there'd be nothing to
love.' How they spent a whole lifetime undoing the knot
of a word and as fast it would twirl up again, spent
whole minutes inching their eyes above sea level only
for latitude to shift, only for a horrible horizon to list, thank god                60
for the degrees of the chin, the fooling plane of a doorway, only
the mind, the not just simple business of return and turning,
that is for scholars and indecisive frigates, circling and circling,
stripped in their life, naked as seaweed, they would have sat
and sunk but no, the sky was a doorway, a famine and a jacket,
the sea a definite post

3  A fishing village situated on the northwestern coast of Tobago.
4  A seaport on the coast of Belgium; 'Kinshasa': the capital of the Democratic Republic of Congo (Zaire), which
   was ruled by the dictator Mobutu from 1965 to 1997.

### V v

I'm giving up on land to light on, slowly, it isn't land,
it is the same as fog and mist and figures and lines
and erasable thoughts, it is buildings and governments
and toilets and front door mats and typewriter shops,                    70
cards with your name and clothing that comes undone,
skin that doesn't fasten and spills and shoes. It's paper,
paper, maps. Maps that get wet and rinse out, in my hand
anyway. I'm giving up what was always shifting, mutable
cities' fluorescences, limbs, chalk curdled blackboards
and carbon copies, wretching water, cunning walls. Books
to set it right. Look. What I know is this. I'm giving up.
No offence. I was never committed. Not ever, to offices
or islands, continents, graphs, whole cloth, these sequences
or even footsteps                                                        80


### V vi

Light passes through me lightless, sound soundless,
smoking nowhere, groaning with sudden birds. Paper
dies, flesh melts, leaving stockings and their useless vanity
in graves, bodies lie still across foolish borders.
I'm going my way, going my way gleaning shade, burnt
meridians, dropping carets,[5] flung latitudes, inattention,
screeching looks. I'm trying to put my tongue on dawns
now, I'm busy licking dusk away, tracking deep twittering
silences. You come to this, here's the marrow of it, not
moving, not standing, it's too much to hold up, what I                   90
really want to say is, I don't want no fucking country, here
or there and all the way back, I don't like it, none of it,
easy as that. I'm giving up on land to light on, and why not,
I can't perfect my own shadow, my violent sorrow, my
individual wrists.

1997

---

5  A caret is a mark [^] used by writers and proofreaders to indicate that something is inserted; on maps a line of
   carets is sometimes used to indicate routes. In this section, as in V iv, the instability of these carets, as of latitudes,
   meridians, and horizon, recalls the difficult shipboard journeys of 'those slaves . . . who were my mothers' and
   who were taken across the Atlantic, away from their homes and homelands—a historical context that reminds
   the reader that their 'land to light on' would be one of brutal servitude.

## From *thirsty*

I

This city is beauty
unbreakable and amorous as eyelids,
in the streets, pressed with fierce departures,
submerged landings,
I am innocent as thresholds
and smashed night birds, lovesick,
as empty elevators

let me declare doorways,
corners, pursuit, let me say
standing here in eyelashes, in                    10
invisible breasts, in the shrinking lake
in the tiny shops of untrue recollections,
the brittle, gnawed life we live,
I am held, and held

the touch of everything blushes me,
pigeons and wrecked boys,
half-dead hours, blind musicians,
inconclusive women in bruised dresses
even the habitual grey-suited men with terrible
briefcases, how come, how come                    20
I anticipate nothing as intimate as history

would I have had a different life
failing this embrace with broken things,
iridescent veins, ecstatic bullets, small cracks
in the brain, would I know these particular facts,
how a phrase scars a cheek, how water
dries love out, this, a thought as casual
as any second eviscerates a breath

and this, we meet in careless intervals,
in coffee bars, gas stations, in prosthetic         30
conversations, lotteries, untranslatable
mouths, in versions of what we may be,
a tremor of the hand in the realization
of endings, a glancing blow of tears
on skin, the keen dismissal in speed

### III

That north burnt country[1] ran me down
to the city, mordant as it is, the whole
terror of nights with yourself and what
will happen, animus, loose like that, sweeps
you to embrace its urban meter,                                    40
the caustic piss of streets,
you surrender your heart to a numb symmetry
of procedures, you study the metaphysics of
corporate instructions and not just,
besieged by now, the ragged, serrated theories
of dreams walking by, banked in sleep

that wild waiting at traffic lights off
the end of the world, where nothing is simple,
nothing, in the city there is no simple love
or simple fidelity, the heart is slippery,                         50
the body convulsive with disguises
abandonments, everything is emptied,
wrappers, coffee cups, discarded shoes,
trucks, street corners, shop windows, cigarette
ends, lungs, ribs, eyes, love,
the exquisite rush of nothing,
the damaged horizon of skyscraping walls,
nights insomniac with pinholes of light

### XXVIII

Anyone, anyone can find themselves on a street corner
eclipsed, as they, by what deserted them                           60
volumes of blue skirt with lace eyelets
a dance stroke you might have trimmed
the way a day can slip out of your hand,
your senses spill like water,
the tremolos of Leroy Jenkins' violin exiting
the Horseshoe Tavern,[2] the accumulation of tender

---

1  'Burnt Country', also alluded to in Part XX of *thirsty*, is a famous work by the Canadian painter Tom Thomson
   (1877–1917), who was associated with, though not a member of, the Group of Seven—one of a number of his
   paintings of forest areas after a wildfire had passed through.
2  A Toronto club since 1947, renowned for its live music: at first a country venue, it has also presented indie, alternative, and other forms of music. Leroy Jenkins (1932–2007) was a jazz composer, violinist, and violist, noted
   for his encyclopedic blending of black and European sounds and styles and for his virtuoso improvisation.

seconds you should have noticed, as mercy,
even these confessions of failure so unreliable,
hardly matter


### XXX

Spring darkness is forgiving. It doesn't descend          70
abruptly before you have finished work,
it approaches palely waiting for you
to get outside to witness another illumined hour

you feel someone brush against you,
on the street, you smell leather, the lake,
the coming leaves, the rain's immortality
pierces you, but you will be asleep when it arrives

you will lie in the groove of a lover's neck
unconscious, translucent, tendons singing,
and that should be enough, the circumference          80
of the world narrowed to your simple dreams

Days are perfect, that's the thing about them,
standing here in half darkness, I think this.
It's difficult to rise to that, but I expect it
I expect each molecule of my substance to imitate that

I can't of course, I can't touch syllables
tenderness, throats.
Look it's like this, I'm just like the rest,
limping across the city, flying when I can


### XXXIII

From time to time . . . frequently, always          90
there is the arcing wail of a siren, as seas
hidden in the ordinariness of the city
the stream and crash of things lived
if it is late at night and quiet, as quiet
as a city can get, as still as its murmurous genealogy
you can hear someone's life falling apart

Most people can sleep through a siren. I can't.
It isn't the proximity of it that wakes me, as shores,
it is its emotion. Its prophecy. Even at a great distance
you sense its mortal discoveries                                    100
whoever it is calling for, whoever is caught
human, you can hear their gnawed substance in its song

In a siren, the individual muscles of a life collapsing,
as waves, stuttering on some harm,
your fingers may flutter in the viscera of an utter stranger
I wake up to it, open as doorways,
breathless as a coming hour, and undone

2002

# Erin Mouré
## b. 1955

Born and raised in Calgary, Erin Mouré began her post-secondary education at the University of Calgary and continued it at the University of British Columbia before leaving school to go to work for the Canadian National Railway. (She became the first woman in CN's history to manage their trains.) During this period, she wrote and produced her first collections of poetry: *Empire, York Street* (1979); the chapbook *The Whisky Vigil* (1981); *Wanted Alive* (1983); and *Domestic Fuel* (1985).

Influenced, in her early writing, by the 'work poetry' movement, Mouré sought to integrate her work with her writing life; she became an active member of the Vancouver Industrial Writers' Union, a group formed in 1979 to support and promote creative writing about the workplace. At this point in her career, she thought of the artist as serving as a 'focal point' for the thoughts, feelings, and concerns of ordinary people, as can be seen in the poetry of *Wanted Alive*, with its lines about daily life ('the end of a city is still / a field, ordinary persons live there, a frame house, & occasionally— / a woman comes out to hang the washing') and the place of work in that life ('workers awake half the night / in the closed kitchens drinking beer / Sliding arms around each other / Lovers of humans, of steel diesel trains').

Mouré took a job with VIA Rail in 1984 and transferred to their Montreal offices in 1985. There, she focused on language, communication, and writing: she rewrote VIA Rail's handbooks to make them clearer and more effective and wrote the monthly newsletter. Her move to Montreal brought her into contact with writers such as novelist-critic Gail Scott and poet-theorist Nicole Brassard, encounters that profoundly changed the direction of Mouré's poetry because they led her to read the psychoanalytic, gender, and cultural theory then emanating from France. As is evident in the letters that she and Bronwen Wallace exchanged (published in 1994 as *Two Women Talking: Correspondence 1985–87*), as well as in her poetry of this period, including *Furious* (1988; Governor General's Award); *WSW (West South West)* (1989); *Sheepish Beauty, Civilian Love* (1992), and the poems in *The*

*Green World: Selected Poems, 1973–1992* (1994), Mouré was deeply affected by the idea that language internalized and obscured the patriarchal biases of society and, therefore, limited women's expressions and longings. In 'Blindness', for example, Mouré examines how a woman can bring long-hidden desires to the surface, while 'Miss Chatelaine' suggests that the act of representation can be dangerous and rejects the images of women created by the media. Becoming increasingly disturbed by the way communication can be manipulated to affect our perceptions and alter our understanding of reality, she comments in *Sudden Miracles* (a 1991 anthology of women poets edited by Rhea Tregebov): 'Sounds and words attract each other, and ideas, and worries. And dreams.' Mouré adds: 'The world is imbued with language and linguistic possibility, with bad and good expression, with hopefulness, with manipulation and trickery as well, with rationalizations and silence and gaps that alter, slowly, the structures of thought.' In 'Seebe', Mouré confronts the problems this recognition creates for the poet: how can she represent anything in language when she mistrusts language and when she fears the distortions inherent in such representation? That poem's conclusion—with the poet calling into question her own 'arrogance' in thinking that the writer can be an honest witness—suggests a crisis for Mouré's understanding of her role, one that shaped the direction her poetry took thereafter.

In 1996, Mouré gave up her position with VIA Rail to become a full-time poet, freelance writer, translator, and communications specialist. She has conducted poetry workshops across North America and in Europe and has been writer-in-residence at Concordia University, the University of Calgary, the University of Toronto, and the University of Ottawa. Since the early 1990s, her poetry has become increasingly freer and more focused on language itself. While retaining her earlier interests, the books that make up the trilogy formed by *Search Procedures* (1996); *Frame of the Book* (1999); and *O Cidadán* (2002) abandon the traditional conventions and forms of poetry. Though the line remains important as a unit of thought, she employs prose, charts, drawings and other graphic devices, and unusual page layouts; repeats forms,

words, and phrases; and moves into and out of different languages. While the short poems in these books can stand alone, their boundaries are blurred so that together they form three book-length long poems, which in turn can be read as one three-volume long poem.

A good example of Mouré's newer way of working can be seen in 'Dream of the Towns': although this poem about her experience of surgery resembles the traditional lyric more than many of her later poems, it is not a formally bounded set of lines that tell the reader about a feeling or an event. Mouré appends, to the lines of the 'poem' per se, a sketch of her post-operative scar; following that, she adds footnotes—taking on the role of scholar-critic of her own poem before others can do that job. These notes are not simply added information or explanation: they invite us to make connections between the highly personal 'lyric' experience that the poem seems to be about and the historical events they evoke.

In her subsequent books, which include *Pillage Laud* (1999), *Sheep's Vigil by a Fervent Person* (2001), *Little Theatres* (2005), and *O Cadoiro* (2007), Mouré continues to move away from the traditional poetics of lyrical representation—that of felt personal experience made available to the reader through aestheticized formal expression—and also beyond the activist feminism that she adopted in her first years in Montreal. These later works reflect the growth of interest among many Canadian poets in a poetry that draws on and extends *Tish* poetics, while also responding to the influences of the American L=A=N=G=U=A=G=E school. In these later books, Mouré extends her critique of the hidden biases of language into a challenge to language itself: by creating texts with disrupted narrative and syntax, poems that are non-linear and deliberately disjunctive, she casts doubt on language's ability to be transparent, neutral, or innocent. Her later poems are self-consciously experimental: some are mysterious, as in *Pillage Laud*, which is subtitled *Cauterizations, Vocabularies, Cantigas, Topiary, Prose* and which was created by selecting 'from pages of computer-generated word sequences' words that are used in a poem (written with a lesbian focus) and attached to a list of found words, placed at the bottom of the page. Passages in some later works, like *Little Theatres*, fascinate the reader *because* of their resistance to meaning:

> Did I have seized ruckus
> Job's weir
> > catching (outcome) these fishes
> > and old leaves
> me in the mill house at La Chaux
> it all broken down, stone pushed into
> auga agua eaux
> Writing's 'succumb' with great
> > > happiness

In the last few years, Mouré has concentrated on translation—translating other writers and also intermixing their work, untranslated, with her own. She has, as well, created ever-shifting representations of herself in these books, signalled by various changes in the spelling of her name. Since the publication of *Little Theatres*, Mouré has been known in part by her heteronym Elisa Sampedrín, the imagined Galician co-writer of that book. As the writer of *O Cidadán*, she signed herself Erín Moure, and she is Eirin Moure as the writer of *Sheep's Vigil by a Fervent Person*, an extremely free 'translation'—she calls it a 'transelation'—of *O Guardador de Rebanhos*, a poem by the Portuguese poet Fernando Pessoa (1888–1935), published under the name Alberto Caeiro, one of *his* many heteronyms. In what looks like bilingual translation with facing English pages, Pessoa's original text is transformed into a narrative about Mouré's term as the writer-in-residence for the University of Toronto. (These are among the most accessible of her recent poems.) Other works she has translated include *Charenton* (2007) by Galician poet Chus Pato and Nicole Brossard's *Notebook of Roses and Civilization* (2007; with Robert Majzels).

In 2008, Mouré was awarded an honorary PhD by Brandon University in recognition of her contributions to poetry. Even more recently, she co-authored, with Vancouver poet-translator Oana Avasilichioaei, *Expeditions of a Chimæra* (2009), in which the polyphony of two voices challenge monologic poetry. Here, Mouré continues her investigations of boundaries by employing techniques such as mistranslation and the use of aleatory lines. Her newest book of poetry is *O Resplandor* (2010). *My Beloved Wager* (2009) collects twenty-five years of her essays and shows her in thoughtful and informed engagements with post-structural theory, as well as offering commentaries on the writers she has translated, reflecting on poetry as a way of life, and making playful excursions into concrete expression.

# Blindness

Some of our desires are known only on the floor
of oceans, the nets dragged thru,
a light beyond colour we can't imagine, where we live now,
people of the surface,
whose foetuses still bear gills for a few days
& lose them, our kinship,
the water inside women,
water where we form & grow.

The halibut frozen whole, a sheet of memory,
held up, thawed, cut into slices
across the body, the central location of the spine,
our shared spine,
small bone hands of its vertebrae,
evolved away from us.

10

To feed us, first & lastly, taste
of white flakes upon the tongue,
soft resistance to the teeth & jaw;
our body is water &
the fish burn in it like fuel.

The flatfish that begins like any other,                    20
swims upright
buoyant in the water, one eye on each side
of the head.
Then adolescent, feeling the body stagger
& list, gone sideways, one eye
*migrates across the forehead or*
*thru the skull*
to the right or left side, depending on the species.

Some of our desires are known only here,
are only now being let loose & admitted,                    30
have only this moment stopped being
ashamed,
ashamed of the shape our bodies took & stayed on land
when the fish said No & went back
into the water,
mistake, mistake, fuck the lungs, some of our desires
are known only on the ocean floor, in the head

of the flatfish, halibut lying on its left side,
the eye that migrated across its skull
staring upward with the other.                              40
At rest with it, patient.
Some of us have lungs that suffocate in the air.
The human body, two eyes fixed in the skull,
a third eye that presses on the forehead
& gets nowhere, presses & lives,
its silence the silence under oceans,
in the deep water of the body,
its blind side facing the brain

1985

# Miss Chatelaine

In the movie, the horse almost dies.
A classic for children, where the small girl pushes a thin
knife into the horse's side.
Later I am sitting in brightness with the women
I went to high school with in Calgary,
fifteen years later we are all feminist, talking of the girl
in the film.
The horse who has some parasite & is afraid of the storm,
& the girl who goes out to save him.
We are in a baggage car on VIA Rail around a huge table,          10
its varnish light & cold,
as if inside the board rooms of the corporation;
the baggage door is open
to the smell of dark prairie,
we are fifteen years older, serious
about women, these images:
the girl running at night between the house & the barn,
& the noise of the horse's fear mixed in with the rain.

Finally there are no men between us.
Finally none of use are passing or failing according to          20
*Miss Chatelaine.*
I wish I could tell you how much I love you,
my friends with your odd looks, our odd looks,
our nervousness with each other,
the girl crying out as she runs in the darkness,
our decoration we wore, so many years ago, high school
boys watching from another table.

Finally I can love you.
Wherever you have gone to, in your secret marriages.
When the knife goes so deeply into the horse's side, a          30
few seconds & the rush of air.
In the morning, the rain is over.
The space between the house & barn is just a space again.
Finally I can meet with you & talk this over.
Finally I can see us meeting, & our true tenderness, emerge.

1988

# Seebe[1]

The mind's assumptive[2] power
The assumptive power of the mind over the mind
The carrying of spit upward to the mouth on the end of a knife
this incredible spillage,

release of the river behind the dam at Seebe, recoil of water
rushing the gorge, where we have stood, our lines
taut connection between us & the water's surface, our blastular[3] memory,
(t)autological[4]

who we are, now, the spaces between words where time leaks out
& we are finished, finished, gone old;                                          10
the table of food finished & the guests left, & the spillage of glasses, &
our shirts empty, empty,

---

1 Seebe (a Cree word for river, pronounced as if it were the letters *c, b*) is a town on the Bow River in southwestern Alberta.
2 'Assumptive' has several relevant meanings: 1) that which is taken up or adopted; 2) that which is taken for granted, rather than consciously examined; 2) of those rights, powers, etc., that are appropriated to an individual or group; 4) arrogant. In psychological theory, the 'assumptive world' is everything the individual doesn't need to consciously examine in order to negotiate daily life (i.e., everything about individual experience that is normal and predictable)—a cognitive process that can be detrimentally disrupted by traumatic experience. Feminist (and other) theorists have argued that this assumptive world may include normalized expectations that need to be consciously and critically examined. As well, given the events and language later in the poem, Mouré may be playing with a secondary meaning of 'assumption'—as an act of elevation, particularly an ascending to heaven.
3 Of the blastula (a very early stage in the development of the embryo).
4 A blend of *tautological*, describing a statement that is circular and therefore redundant (such as 'Death is the end of life'), and *autological*—a word that describes itself or has the qualities it describes (such as *polysyllabic* or *word*).

They say what saves the bones is weight-bearing exercise
except for the carrying of children
Which is our namesake,
which is what we do, naming

children,
taking their torsos in & out of the uterine wall
then carrying them, lifting
the weight of the small boy up from the side of the rails                    20
& running forward to the train, stopped for us, his leg soft with blood
spattered my uniform, his leg not broken, just torn a bit at the skin,

This spillage, rusted gates pulled upward
to release the downstream blood
The mind's assumptive power of the Bow at Seebe
Carrying the boy to the conductor & then running back for the
kit, sunlit, 'we hit a cow' they said in the lounge car afterward,
& me lifting the boy up from the dam where he was fishing,
the bridge where the whitefish run among the planted trout at Seebe

lifting him upward, his Stoney Indian face & bone weariness, watching me        30
white woman from the train taking him upward
into the vast, vast emptiness

Actually he was in the weeds
Actually he was nested hurt leg red in the weeds beside the train
so as not to be found again, got that?
All the tourists on the dam fishing sunlit maybe first hot weekend of
summer, delirium, delirium, trout dreams of the uterine memory,
pulled upward on the thin lines, water running high into the reservoir,
oh Bow, oh hotness,

we hit a cow, they said                                                         40

The sudden yet soft emergency braking, pulling the cars up expert not too hard, we hit a cow they said in the carved light of the lounge at the end of it, & breaking out the side door lifting the green box, knowing nothing, knowing the sunlit heat on the back of the blue uniform, running down the right of way, the body not used to it yet, this gravelled running, the hot smell of spruce & light air of curious voices, the boys on the bridge having run, then; not knowing what would be found there, thinking of what to do in the bright run in the sun,

1) check breathing if you can find the mouth,
2) stop the bleeding,                                                          50
3) immobilize fractures,

thinking the second step, going over it in the mind, so that when you look at someone completely bloody you see blood only where it moving, it is the assumptive power of the mind, the mind over the mind, the deconstructive power of the human body, to take this, outward

He was in the weeds. & scared. He looked up soft at me. Hey, I say. You're okay. He was hiding there from me. I could see him. & ignored his hiding. Dropped the kit & bent over the torn leg. Bloody, that's all. Only one leg The foot aligned well with the rest, okay, feeling up &            60 down the bone, no, okay, just torn up & bleeding where? Here. Bleeding here. Okay. Lifting him up then & running carrying him back up to the train, the blue cars creaking, conductor, wait

give him up

& run back, the green kit just sitting tipped on the right of way, based those weeds, grab it & run back, daring to look around at the trees & warm smell forest finally, jump back into the cars, we're off then

The poem has fallen apart into mere description.
It is years later, thinking of the mind's assumptive power & remembering
the train hitting the boy at Seebe, Alberta & how I went out                    70
to get him. Here we have only my assumptions, only the arrogance of
Erin Mouré made into the poem; in the course of history, which is
description, the boy is mute. We have no way of entering into his images
now. The description itself, even if questioned, portrays the arrogance
of the author. In all claims to the story, there is a muteness. The writer as
witness, speaking the stories, is a lie, a liberal bourgeois lie. Because the
speech is the writer's speech, and each word of the writer robs the
witnessed of their own voice, muting them.

*Lifting him up, bone weary, taking him*
*into the vast, vast emptiness.*                                               80

1989


# Dream of the Towns

I've been getting over a shaved pudenda
I've been playing the bagpipe of the intestines
& what have I learned
apocrypha

Then, I was in a hospital window high over Montréal
I called it my penthouse & lay in the horizon six days, for six days
they helped me rise up
& commit to memory my vital signs

Now I am just left of the alley where the weedy tree blooms its blossomy
leaves, sleeping face-down in shadowy afternoons                               10
I thank you everyone for your dream of the towns
where you saw me, running wildly

*Valença do Minho, Chlebowicz, Duga Res*

As for me I am abstinent awhile yet

The tremour still here

(the slice in me

---

Notes:
1) Valença do Minho is a northern Portuguese border town, directly across the Minho (Miño) from Tuy, in Pontevedra province, Galicia, España.
2) Chlebowicz is the birthplace in Poland, now in the Ukraine, of the author's mother. It may have a different name now.
3) The residents of the town of Duga Res in Croatia in 1992 or 1993 cut down a wood of 88 trees they themselves had planted to honour Marshall Tito's 88th birthday, saying they were removing 'the last remnants of the communist regime'

May 17, 1994

1996


# Amygdala[1]

> *For Gail*

> *To say what I am thinking . . .*


1

I am thinking of a beautiful almond in the brain.
My thought has to do with being a person.

Outside me the cat looks out on the ice-fallen snow.
B,i,r,d.s w:i;l,l c-o,m:e.

In my childhood, blue smoke rises slowly off of my father.
Those days I wanted him to come home & be

in the air force again, wearing the colour of smoke
that rose from him.

I am going to speak slowly & gently.
I am untying the rowboat of truth from the doorknob          10

---

1 Part of the limbic system, the amygdala is an almond-shaped region of the brain associated with innate behaviours; emotional processing, 'emotional memory', and the regulation of emotions, as well as with cognitive functions such as memory, attention, and perception. Research on the amygdala has focused on its role in emotional conditioning and the incitement of emotions, particularly fear and the 'fight or flight' response. Neuroscientists such as Gerald Edelman and Israel Rosenfield, whom Mouré mentions having read (in an interview in *Poets Talk*, 2004), see the limbic system as the source of the individual's construction of self-identity.

& closing the door.
& if I close the door fast enough, my tooth will rise up

from its harbour & depart on a trajectory of absence
the space between us increasing

a parabolic splendour


2

There is a strophe[2] we have all dreamed of.
There are metaphors for love
that the alphabet calibrates with its letters

There is a path thru rough weeds down to the river,
thru the weeds or dry grasses,                                    20
the gulch or arroyo,
the dry path that rages in one season only

I am carrying the tooth down to the river.
My back is wet.

All this is true,
'imaginary'.


3

Shimmer with me a few moments.
Light will take our faces upward.
The cars are blank & silent in the snowy road.                    30
We are weeding a rough patch here.

Our hoes are us.
Our pitted shovels are yammering, we know them, we have
no patience.

Smoke rises off the fathers but they never do burn, do they.
Smoke rises into the drapes.
Smoke curls.

Attend to this.

---

2  Literally, 'a turn'. In ancient Greece, a strophe was originally the turning movement of the chorus, in a poetic
drama, as it reached the end of its dance across the stage (followed by the antistrophe, or return); from that,
strophe came to designate a set of lines that form a structural unit, comparable to the later word *stanza*.

4

There are days we will wake up with our mouths dry
& our skin will be the borders of Croatia.[3]                                    40

One faces the warm sea.
Another faces the ornate brocade wall of the Vatican.
Another the inner furrowed plain.

Tracer lights. Curfew.


5

I am trying to think of the meaning of 'incitement'
There is no dawn light yet

Coffee stains my cheek, my jaw
An age creeps up on me thru the windows

I am trying to draw the line between cruelty & gentleness
What is inflicted on the self by the self                                    50

Personhood[4]

Where are we, the coves here are full of panicked horses


6

The name you give me is a rose.
An honest parabola born of the stars,
A few lights are shining here & there on the mountain.
We have seen no birch light.
A possible is given, given, given.

---

3  As well as being bounded by the Adriatic Sea (and facing Italy and the Vatican at a distance across that sea),
   Croatia has multiple borders that have often been under attack. (The references to 'tracer lights' and 'curfew'
   suggest ongoing warfare.)
4  *Personhood* is a concept important to Mouré in her poetry around this time, perhaps in part as a result of her
   reading of Edelman, who argues that personhood is not innate but constructed through symbolic interaction,
   thus a 'linguistic personhood'. In an interview with Mouré in *Mosaic* (36.4, 2003), Dawn McCance spoke to her
   about the importance of 'the between-ness of the self—the person, the citizen' in her poetry, adding, 'I find the
   notion of personhood [in your poetry] as between-ness very significant, and not at all in keeping with the Anglo-
   American legal-ethical-political definition of persons as bounded rational entities, minds and not bodies, private
   and not connected.' Mouré responded, 'Exactly!'

Orthograph[5] is ever waiting.
Your head & shoulders in the taxi at 6 a.m., the dome light
shining down on you.                                                60

I am thinking of the almond light inside the brain.
As you leave, I see it rise from you.

It is purpose.
It is beautiful.

*(yours truly, Erin)*

1996

5  An orthographic projection is a two-dimensional representation of three-dimensions (such as a brain scan). As
   well, the word *orthograph* can refer to handwriting and is the stem of *orthography*, the system or rules of writing
   that includes spelling, punctuation, hyphenization, etc.

# 14 Descriptions of Trees

1

My old habit attenuates an inner liquor or sigh.

Description sets up a distribution of effect
animals' furred ruffs may also cherish
Description demands its transformation to the letters,
the world did not conform to description
with immediacy

as light is solved. *'When I wake up, you are still
sleeping.'* The present tense herein invests

a simultaneity of affect
Ameliorates an absence                                             10

2

But the problems of description continue
The various sub-scopes of envision forest an extreme,
or obligation

3

Largely a travesty can possess,

or murmur

A night with no brink

trope assignation making us plural

who 'us' are

willed places destine

We hesitant before longing                                           20

4

Now someone has uttered the word 'Boltanski' in a yellow kitchen
Is this the form our grief has taken

A wide memory is ours, is ours
A terrace *trés jaune* to be traversed before waking

Sirop of such trees, a clamber out
of sleep or waking

A far journey is ours, is ours

this much is clear from the terrible story

5

Their leaves red words for
Impediment a hoarse or cry                                           30
An imagine does indicate or where
False gestures submerge us

6

Astonish me a core of blood

Trying to stick in this course to the 'believable'

our ephemeron does so compel me

The present tense is my imbroglio

my nymphic ore

dilatory or sonorous

a mediate or

7

Writing the lines call *Grief, or Sweetness*          40
& wanting your green-hazed name

1999

## From *Sheep's Vigil by a Fervent Person*

## VII From Garrison Creek I see the earth to the antipodes of the Universe . . .

From Garrison Creek I see the earth to the antipodes of the Universe
In this, my street is as big as any planet
Because I am the same size as what I see
And not the size of my height ever . . .

Downtown, life's so much smaller
Than here in my house at the creek bottom where they paved it.
Downtown, huge mansions lock sight away
Obscure the horizon, flatten sight and wrench us far from the sky,
torment us smaller because they can't stand our eyes' lovely capacity,
torment us poor because our rich sight was once tremendous . . .          10

## XX The Humber is pretty fabulous, really

The Humber is more fabulous than the creek under my avenue.
And the Humber is no more fab than the creek under my avenue.
You can't mix up the two when on my avenue;
For that matter neither of them are very big . . .

The Humber is too small for ships
Yet on its waters they still ply
For those who see the 'not there' in all things:
The memory of canoes.

The Humber descends from up north
And the Humber enters Lake Ontario.                              10
You always hear people say this on buses in the afternoon.
But few know the creek that races under Winnett
And where it heads
And where it came from.
And, as such, because fewer people claim it,
The creek of my avenue is more grand and free.

You can take the Humber out almost to Niagara Falls;
Beyond the Humber is America
Where fortunes are made.
No one ever thinks about what's beyond                           20
the creek under Winnett Avenue.

The creek under my avenue makes no one think of anything.
Whoever goes to the edge of it has only reached the curb.

## XXXI If at times I claim flowers smile and rivers sing

If at times I claim flowers smile and rivers sing
It's not from thinking there are smiles in flowers
And songs in fast currents . . .
I'm out on Vaughan Road where Taddle Creek runs under me
Duped men drive past me honking, I want to show them
The small buds just now in leaf alongside rivers,
and they want to get fast to Bathurst and St. Clair.

Who can blame them.

So I write, as if they'll read me, and even I fall at times
In love with their stupid feelings . . .                                    10
I'm against it but I forgive myself
Because all I am is Nature's guidepost, and if I don't get
Their attention, they won't see Nature's language
For Nature has no language ever,
Except maybe  a e i o                  *ssssshh* .

2001

# Jan Zwicky
## b. 1955

Born in Calgary, Jan Zwicky grew up in the Prairies. Having spent extended periods of her life in other regions of Canada, she now lives on Quadra Island in British Columbia with Robert Bringhurst. After completing her BA at the University of Calgary (1976), she took an MA (1977) and PhD (1981) in philosophy from the University of Toronto. Her doctoral thesis considered the concept of ineffability, arguing that language is limited in what it can express. Before joining the philosophy department at the University of Victoria in 1996, she taught philosophy—and, on occasion, creative writing, English, and the humanities—at Princeton University, the University of Waterloo, and the University of New Brunswick.

In addition to writing scholarly essays as a philosopher, Zwicky has published two books—*Lyric Philosophy* (1992) and *Wisdom and Metaphor* (2003)—that unite her academic and poetic careers. As a way of advancing her argument 'that lyric poetry and philosophy are not mutually exclusive,' each of these juxtaposes her own ideas with passages on facing pages drawn from a wide variety of texts. Her recent monograph on Plato's *Meno* (*Plato as Artist*, 2009) furthers her uniting of philosophy with literature by arguing that Plato is best understood as a dramatist.

Zwicky's own interest in creating a poetry of ideas, one that makes use of her academic background, is clear in *Wittgenstein Elegies* (1986), the second book of poems she published. It contains five polyphonic sequences that respond to the life and the teachings of the Austrian-born philosopher of language, Cambridge don Ludwig Wittgenstein (1889–1951). Her other books of poetry include *Where Have We Been* (1982); *The New Room* (1989); *Songs for Relinquishing the Earth* (1998); *21 Small Songs* (2000); *Robinson's Crossing* (2004); and *Thirty-Seven Small Songs and Thirteen Silences* (2005). Zwicky has also published *Contemplation and Resistance* (2003), which takes the form of a conversation with the poet Tim Lilburn.

Zwicky is, in addition to her career as an academic and a poet, a concert violinist who has performed with the Victoria-based Continuum Consort. Many of her poems take music as their subject; in some, she shows us how music serves as another language (as in 'String Practice' and 'Night Song'). In 'Bill Evans: "Here's That Rainy Day"' (reprinted here), jazz can be heard telling its own story to the listener at the end of a long day. Her interest in music has also led to several poetic collaborations with musicians and to an anthology (edited with Brad Cran) of blues poems by Canadian and American poets:

*Why I Sing the Blues* (2001; accompanied by a 13-song CD).

In her third collection of poetry, *The New Room*, Zwicky shows another side of her writing. Its personal lyrics deal with the details of memory and daily life as a way of investigating exile and home, as in its title poem about an empty room, soon to be furnished and occupied. *Songs for Relinquishing the Earth*, the book that followed, won a Governor General's Award for work that the jury described as a masterful blend of 'narrative and association, the colloquial and the elegant, metaphor and discourse, the conceptual and the sensuous.' It began life in 1996 as a handmade book, 'each copy individually sewn for its reader in response to a request'—Zwicky's way of affirming the close personal connection that she feels exists between poet and reader. When she couldn't keep pace with demand, Brick Books published a trade edition. The desire to draw meaningful connections among individuals, places, and ways of thinking is apparent throughout that collection in poems that Zwicky describes as 'meditations' ranging 'in

subject matter from Kant, Hegel, and Pythagoras to Beethoven, Bruckner, and Hindemith, unified by questions about the nature of home and our responsibilities to it.' For Zwicky, 'home' expands to take in the whole environment, the whole phenomenological world of visible details, even, in the poem 'Driving Northwest', the light that makes these visible.

Her desire to look at how human beings are shaped by, and become part of, their physical environment—while also changing that environment—is evident in poems like 'Robinson's Crossing' (from the book by that title). There, what initially seems the story of Zwicky's family homesteading becomes that of the land itself. Reflecting her idea in *Wisdom and Metaphor* that the 'shape of metaphorical thought is also the shape of wisdom,' 'Robinson's Crossing' and (from Zwicky's most recent book of poems) 'Study: North' look at how a core concept or story influences the way we experience and understand life. To read Zwicky is to experience Horace's ideal: hers is a poetry that both teaches and delights.

## The New Room

Find we don't notice
seams where we pieced, bubbles
subsiding like lymph pockets
over rotten plaster. (Christ,
not one square corner in the place.)
Wallpaper repeats
       repeats
that faded denim stripe
forever to the ceiling. Space is
vertical, smooth                  10
as the touch of sun through glass,
the beds of women
past the reach of love.

Empty now. A last skiff
of light drifts in across
flat seas of corn. Lines of loss
simple as a window.

We will fill this room
as if we owned them: bleached armchair,
the gouge-topped desk, those objects                              20
waiting outside, motionless.

      Their essence
is their loyalty. Their lives
are the accumulations
of our absence, bounded
by the moments when we draw them
into time. Their surfaces, defenceless
against incursions of our whimsy are
displaced, abandoned, taken
for granted. Here, we can                                        30
see them for an instant as they are,
all the mute axes of our lives
stretched behind them, racing away from us
row on row on row.

1978


# Bill Evans[1]: 'Here's That Rainy Day'

On a bad day, you come in from the weather
and lean your back against the door.
This time of year it's dark by five.
Your armchair, empty in its pool of light.

That arpeggio[2] lifts, like warmth, from the fifth of B minor,
offers its hand—*let me*
*tell you a story* . . . But in the same breath,
semitones falling to the tonic:
you must believe and not believe;
that door you came in                                            10
you must go out again.

---

1 (1929–80), solo jazz pianist, who also played with Miles Davis; his innovations in playing and composition
  influenced the shape of jazz. The song 'Here's That Rainy Day' appeared on his 1968 album *Bill Evans Alone*.
2 An arpeggio is a chord in which the notes are played separately in rapid succession. Here the notes of the
  B-minor chord (i.e. BDF#) are played ascending, beginning with the chord's 'fifth' (F#), while Evans also plays
  semitones (black and white keys on the piano such as C and C# are one semitone apart in the standard scale)
  that descend to the tonic or keynote of the scale, B.

In the forest, the woodcutter's son
sets the stone down from his sack and speaks to it.
And from nothing, a spring wells
falling as it rises, spilling out
across the dark green moss.
There is sadness in the world, it says,
past telling. Learn stillness
if you would run clear.

1998

## Transparence

> *Do not drink*
> *the darkness,* said Pythagoras,
> *the soul cannot become pure darkness.*
>
> —Robert Bringhurst

I would reply to Pythagoras[1]
nor can the soul
become pure light.

Or if it does, the experience,
unless you are freakishly lucky—like
that woman, thrown from her car, her car
rolling and bouncing up one side of the embankment and then
back down, to land on top of her, except
the roof had been dented by the guardrail
and it came down with the hollow                                    10
over her and she escaped
unscathed—will kill you.

So we are caught stumbling
in between, longing for home.

---

1 (*c.* 569–*c.* 475 BCE), pre-Socratic mathematician, philosopher, and mystic, who saw the world in terms of
numbers and sought out balances of qualities including darkness and light.

\*

Things we leave behind: the belief
that nothing else will matter as much again,
and this: if we could learn
to let go without leaving then
our real lives might begin.


Where do we hang our hats? Up the long slope                    20
we are always running to in dreams?

Or here, in the confused kitchen of paychecks
and good intentions, one black one
double-double, make that to go? Meaning
is a measure of resistance: to that hand
shoving you out over the cliff of your future,
to the thought of your own hands
gulping for the substance of the familiar. And
nothing *will* matter as much
as those back stairs, that red bench,                           30
the Matisse drawing cut from a calendar
years ago, left curling on the garage wall
after the yard sale, remembered suddenly
with vividness just west of Oshawa.
Something not a bone
but like a bone—just here, behind the clutter
in your chest—broken so many times
it's ground to dust; and you bend, resistless,
to shoulder every absence.

          \*


Light lives                                                     40
everywhere: no legs, no breath,
no need for shoes. Its unmoorings
effortless, nothing
in tow. No need
for hands: it does not take itself
to be responsible. Light
carries nothing, and the place
it thinks, it is.

*

Morning after rain, the mind wakes
dewy, tender—bad news, miscalculations                                    50
piled behind it like a shelf of badly-folded blankets.
Only in fairy tales,
or given freakish luck, does the wind
rise suddenly and set you down where everything
is safe and loved and in its place. The mind
does not expect it. But the heart,
                              the heart—
the heart keeps looking for itself.
It knows and does not know
where it belongs. It quivers                                              60
like a compass, taut with anticipation,
the sweep thump
of arrival. The heart,
a solid thing, is dark
like turf, and it believes
luck is a talent, or a form of light—
at least, its due for service—
and refuses to be schooled.


                *


Dust from the eighteen-wheeler
whipping in to the Dryden Husky as we                                     70
step out of the restaurant—it looks like fog—
and I'm reminded of the morning river-mists
in the scrub parkland where I grew up,
walking through them how they'd swirl,
evaporate, the dampness on the grass
sighed into sky. Here in August,
northern Ontario, evening,
grit sticks to my face and neck, sits in my lungs.
Out of sight, the rig door slams and someone laughs.
I spill my coffee as I struggle with the lid.                            80
As we pull away
the dust's still there, sun
catching it, and being caught,
exactly: a lightness you can see
right through, suspended
in the night-blue air.

1998

# Driving Northwest

Driving Northwest in July before
the long twilight that stretches into
the short summer dark, despite the sun
the temperature is dropping, air
slips by the truck, like diving,
diving,
　　　and you are almost blind
with light: on either side of you
it floats across the fields, young barley
picking up the gold, oats white,                                    10
the cloudy bruise of alfalfa
along the fencelines, the air itself
tawny with haydust, and the shadows of the willows
in the draw miles long, oh it is lovely
as a myth, the touch of a hand on your hair,
and you need, like sleep, to lie down now
and rest, but you are almost
blind with light, the highway
stretched across the continent
straight at the sun: visor,                                         20
dark glasses, useless against its gonging,
the cab drowns in it, shuddering, you cannot tell,
you might be bleeding or suffocating, shapes
fly out of it so fast there's no time to swerve:
but there is no other path, there is no other bed,
it is the only way home you know.

1998


# String Practice

The fingers of the left hand
are the chambers of the heart.
The thumb is character.
The heart alone
is voiceless. By itself, it knows
but cannot think, and so
it cannot close the door to fear.

Thought is the right arm
and it moves like breath.
The fingers of the right hand               10
are thought's tendons, which,
with practice, will take root along
the bone of breath. Breathe
from the shoulder. It is thought
that pulls the bright gut of the heart
to speech.

      Breathe also
from the knees, which tune
the ear to earth, its turning,
and the double-handed movement           20
of the day and night.
If the knees are locked
the mind is deaf:
it fills the house with clamour, then,
but never music.

The collarbone
is the lintel of the voice,
and the breastbone
bears its weight.
In their house, the heart lives            30
and the breath that is not bone
until thought touches it.

These are the elements,
which is to say,
the difficulty.
When we lack experience,
it is the motions of the heart
that most perplex us.
But of all these things
thought is the hardest,                     40
though its beauty is a distant river
in its plain of light.

2004

# Robinson's Crossing

       They say
the dog was crazy that whole evening:
whining at the door, tearing
around the yard in circles,
standing stock still in the cart track,
head cocked, whimpering.
They'd left him out and gone to bed, but he
kept barking until after midnight
when they finally heard him take off
down the railbed, east,                   10
toward the river. Next morning
Ernest said he'd met him
a half-mile from the house. The train
had got in late but he'd
been eager to get home, so walked
the eight miles from the crossing
at the steel's end. They had finished
with the harvest down south, he had money
in his pocket. He was
two days early,                          20
but the dog had known.

       My great-
grandmother slept
in a boxcar on the night
before she made the crossing. The steel
ended in Sangudo then, there was
no trestle on the Pembina, no siding
on the other side. They crossed
by ferry, and went on by cart through bush,
the same eight miles. Another          30
family legend has it that she stood there
in the open doorway of the shack
and said, 'You told me, Ernest,
it had windows and a floor.'

       The museum
has a picture of the Crocketts—
later first family of Mayerthorpe—
loading at the Narrows
on the trail through Lac Ste. Anne.
Much what you'd expect:          40

a wagon, crudely covered,
woman in a bonnet on the box seat,
man in shirt sleeves
by the horses' heads, a dog.
But what draws the eye, almost
a double-take, are the tipis
in the distance, three of them,
white, smudged—a view the lens
could not pull into focus.
And another photo,                                                    50
taken in the '30's maybe,
of a summer camp down on the river flats
between our quarter and the town.
At least a dozen tipis; horses, smoke.
By the time I was a kid,
they'd put the town dump there;
but I remember we picked arrowheads
out of the west field every spring
when it was turned. And a memory
of my uncle, sharp, impatient with                                    60
my grandfather for lending out
his .22 to Indians:
last time, didn't he remember?,
he never got it back.


            Robinson's Crossing
is how you come in to this country, still—
though it's not been on a map
since 1920, and the highway
takes a different route. You come in,
on the backs of slightly crazy Europeans, every time          70
you lift your eyes across a field of swath
and feel your throat catch
on the west horizon. It's the northern edge
of aspen parkland, here—
another ten miles down the track,
the muskeg's getting serious.
But my great-grandfather was right:
cleared, seeded, fenced,
trees left for windbreaks and along
the river's edge, it looks                                            80
a lot like England.
You could file
on a quarter section for ten dollars;

all you had to do to keep it
was break thirty acres in three years.
The homestead map shows
maybe two in three men
made it. Several of their wives
jumped from the bridge.

     There's no mention     90
in the local history book
of how the crossing got its name.
I found a picture of an Ernie
Robinson—part of a road gang
in the '20's—and of an old guy,
Ed, at some town function
later on. There's also
a photo of a sign, undated, shot
from an extreme low angle, as though
whoever took it had been standing    100
in the ditch beside the grade. I'll show you
where it was: just go out
the old road from the RV park, west,
about two miles. Nothing there now
but a farmer's crossing and a stretch
of old rail in the ditch. I'm guessing
that they closed it
when the steel moved on
after the war.

     A few years back     110
I was out behind the old house
picking twigs. (TransAlta
had come in and taken out
a poplar—it had left
enough junk in the grass
my mother couldn't mow.)
The rake had clawed
the grass out, more than
it had piled up twigs,
so I was squatting, sorting     120
dirt and grass by hand. The smell
was mesmerizing: musty, sweet,
dank, clay-ey; green—
and with a shock I realized
what it was: the same smell

as my family. Not because
our boots and gloves
were covered in it, nothing
you could shower off—it was
the body's scent, the one 130
that's on the inside
of your clothes, the one a dog
picks up. Our cells were
made of it: the garden, and the root
cellar, the oats
that fed the chickens, and the hay
the steers.
These days

the line north of the farmhouse
carries only freight, 140
infrequently; the highway's
being twinned; Monsanto
just released another herbicide-resistant
seed. Before the drought,
the river flooded every time it rained—
no trees upstream; this year
it's lower than it's been
since someone started
keeping records. The wooden
elevators, gone or going; ranks 150
of concrete silos that read
*Agricore* in flowing nineteenth-century
script—it's why

the story matters, why it
puzzles me. Here comes
my great-grandfather, he has made
Robinson's Crossing, he is walking
toward us, bone-tired
but whistling, it's a fine night, he has
money in his pocket, 160
and the dog, the family dog,
is going out to meet him.

2004

## Study: North

Down the dirt lane you have been
afraid to walk, back to the garden in its
loveliness, the scent of meadows stretching north
behind the barn, back to the sad ache
in the shadows, a lame thing, ugly,
but so small: you could cup it in the hollow of two hands.

It rises like a grey moon, like
the blue grave of your sister's heart.
Light of your father's bones.

Who will be waiting there?
No one.
Nothing that can say your name.

2004

10

---

# Anne Michaels
## b. 1958

Anne Michaels was born in Toronto, where her father, who had immigrated to Canada from Poland, ran a small record store. She and her three brothers grew up with books, classical music, and parents who loved discussions. She studied piano and violin and became interested in poetry as a teenager. After receiving her BA in English from the University of Toronto in 1980, she taught creative writing and worked as an arts administrator, a freelance writer, an editor, and a composer of music for theatre.

Michaels had already established herself as a poet—with *The Weight of Oranges* (1986; Commonwealth Prize) and *Miner's Pond* (1991)—before gaining international prominence when her first novel, *Fugitive Pieces* (1996), won a number of awards, including the

*Books in Canada* First Novel Award, the Trillium Award, the Guardian Fiction Award, the Lannan Literary Award for Fiction, and the Orange Prize for Fiction. The praise *Fugitive Pieces* received is due not only to the touching story it tells, but also to Michaels' ability to write about the Holocaust and its aftermath. After the Second World War ended, many writers found it impossible to respond adequately to its horrors. Primo Levi, a survivor of Auschwitz, used memoir to chronicle his experiences and also wrote fiction and poetry; Eli Wiesel wrote novels about his imprisonment in Nazi concentration camps; Nelly Sachs, who lost her entire family to the Holocaust, wrote poetry and drama about what had befallen Europe's Jews; and Paul Celan, who lost his parents, wrote poems. The philosopher Theodore Adorno, in contrast, opposed any aesthetic representation of the Holocaust, declaring, 'It is impossible to write poetry after Auschwitz.' Born long after the Second World War and its atrocities, Michaels—who wrote in her 1991 long poem 'What the Light Teaches' that 'language remembers, / … Even a word so simple / it's translatable. Number. Oven'—worked for many years on her novel to find a poetic-prose voice that would allow someone of her time and place to bear witness to this event.

Michaels published one further book of poems, *Skin Divers*, in 1999. In 2000, all three of her poetry books were reissued in a single volume, simply titled *Poems*. Her poetry, while personal and immediate, often turns, like her novel, around large questions about the nature of memory and the relationship of the past to the present. The long poem reprinted here, 'Lake of Two Rivers', states that 'we do not descend, but rise from our histories.' In it, the speaker recalls travelling with her family, as a child of six, to the Two Rivers campground in Ontario's Algonquin Park. This memory then blends with the stories her father told on those trips about the discovery of the wonderful land of Shangri-La (as depicted in the movie version of *Lost Horizon*) and about his terrifying flight across Poland as a teenager in 1931—and how all this is modulated by what she read 'when I was twenty-five.'

Other poems use the form of the dramatic monologue to deal with a more distant time. Historical figures turn their vision inward to examine the complexities of their own lives and strive to make the connection between language and experience. Michaels provides fresh perspectives on famous stories in poems such as 'Ice House', in which she dramatizes the voice of sculptor Kathleen Scott, the wife of explorer Robert F. Scott—whose final trip to the Antarctic to make scientific observations and to travel by land to the South Pole ended disastrously. Her newest poem, 'Repairing the Octave' (she was commissioned, along with Lorna Crozier and Jan Zwicky, by the Toronto-based Tafelmusik Baroque Orchestra and Chamber Choir to write something for a performance of J.S. Bach's music), looks at the way individuals and their experiences transcend time and space: in this poem, she brings together Bach and the speaker's father in their old age and shows how each is comforted and touched by music and by love when death is imminent.

Michaels' most recent book, the novel *The Winter Vault* (2009), again shows how moments in time interact and suggests that, while the past is important, 'the future casts its shadow on the past.' Its narrative connects the disruption associated with the building of the St Lawrence Seaway with the later need to take apart and relocate an Egyptian temple. This task, which will permit the construction of the Aswan Dam, speaks to the loss of sacred space and leads one of the characters to despair over what 'the built world had created' in its place: 'Waste space too narrow for anything but litter, dark walkways from carparks to the street; the endless dead space of underground garages; the corridors between skyscrapers, the space surrounding industrial rubbish bins and ventilator shafts … the space we have imprisoned between what we have built, like seeds of futility, small pockets on the earth where no one is meant to be alive.'

While the movement of time and the losses it brings is a recurrent theme in Michaels' work, as one of the narrators in *Fugitive Pieces* tells us, it is how we respond to our loss that is important: 'History is amoral: events occurred. But memory is moral; what we consciously remember is what our conscience remembers.' In *The Winter Vault*, the narrator adds, 'The past does not change, nor our need for it. What must change is the way of telling.'

# Lake of Two Rivers

### I

Pull water, unhook its seam.

Lie down in the lake room,
in the smell of leaves still sticky from their birth.

Fall to sleep the way the moon falls
from earth: perfect lethargy of orbit.

### 2

Six years old, half asleep,
a traveller. The night car mysterious
as we droned past uneasy twisting fields.

My father told two stories on these drives.
One was the plot of 'Lost Horizon',                                    10
the other: his life.
This speeding room, dim in the dashboard's green emission,
became the hijacked plane carrying Ronald Colman to Tibet,
or the train carrying my father across Poland in 1931.

Spirit faces crowded the windows of a '64 Buick.
Unknown cousins surrounded us, arms around each other,
a shawl of sleeves.

The moon fell into our car from Grodno.
It fell from Chaya-Elke's village,
where they stopped to say goodbye.                                     20
His cousin Mashka sat up with them
in the barn, while her face
floated down the River Neman in my father's guitar.
He watched to remember
in the embalming moonlight.

3

Sensate weather, we are your body,
your memory. Like a template,
branch defines sky, leaves
bleed their gritty boundaries,
corrosive with nostalgia.                                                30

Each year we go outside to pin it down,
light limited, light specific,
light like a name.

                    *

For years my parents fled at night,
loaded their children in the back seat,
a tangle of pyjamas anxious to learn the stars.

I watched the backs of their heads
until I was asleep, and when I woke
it was day, and we were in Algonquin.

I've always known this place,                                            40
familiar as a room in our house.

The photo of my mother, legs locked in water,
looking into the hills where you and I stand—

only now do I realize
it was taken before I was born.

                    *

Purple mist, indefinite hills.

At Two Rivers, close as branches.
Fish scatter, silver pulses with their own electric logic.

Milky spill of moon over the restless lake,
seen through a sieve of foliage.                                         50

In fields to the south
vegetables radiate underground,
displace the earth.
While we sit, linked by firelight.

4

The longer you look at a thing
the more it transforms.

My mother's story is tangled,
overgrown with lives of parents and grandparents
because they lived in one house and among them
remembered hundreds of years of history.                    60

This domestic love is plain, hurts
the way light balancing objects in a still life hurts.

The heart keeps body and spirit in suspension,
until density pulls them apart.
When she was my age
her mother had already fallen through.

Pregnant, androgynous with man,
she was afraid. When life goes out,
loss gets in, wedging a new place.

Under dark lanes of the night sky                           70
the eyes of our skin won't close,
we dream in desire.

Love wails from womb, caldera,[1] home.
Like any sound, it goes on forever.

                    *


The dissolving sun turns Two Rivers into skin.
Our pink arms, slightly fluorescent,
hiss in the dusky room, neon tubes bending
in the accumulated dark.

Night transforms the lake into a murmuring solid.
Naked in the eerie tremor of leaves rubbing stars,          80
in the shivering fermata[2] of summer,

---

1  A crater formed by a volcanic explosion or collapse.
2  The prolongation of a note or chord beyond its marked time value. 'Moebius ribbon': a band fastened into a
   loop after being twisted once, causing what seem opposing sides of its flat surface to double-back on themselves
   and become continuous; it is an unusual physical object in that it has both two-dimensional and three-
   dimensional properties.

in the energy of stones made powerful by gravity,
desire made powerful by the seam between starlight and skin,
we join, moebius ribbon in the night room.


        5

We do not descend, but rise from our histories.
If cut open memory would resemble
a cross-section of the earth's core,
a table of geographical time.
Faces press the transparent membrane
between conscious and genetic knowledge.                                    90
A name, a word, triggers the dilatation.
Motive is uncovered, sharp overburden in a shifting field.


        *


When I was twenty-five I drowned in the River Neman,
fell through when I read that bone-black from the ovens
was discarded there.[3]


Like a face pressed against a window,
part of you waits up for them,
like a parent, you wait up.


        *


A family now, we live each other's life
without the details.                                                        100


The forest flies apart, trees are shaken loose
by my tears,


by love that doesn't fall to earth
but bursts up from the ground, fully formed.

1985

---

3 The River Neman is the main river in Lithuania; when the Axis powers overran the area (Lithuania was then part of the Soviet Union), its banks were home to many Jewish families and settlements; more than 10,000 were killed by the Nazis, many cremated alive in the ovens of Axis concentration camps.

# Flowers

There's another skin inside my skin
that gathers to your touch, a lake to the light;
that looses its memory, its lost language
into your tongue,
erasing me into newness.

Just when the body thinks it knows
the ways of knowing itself,
this second skin continues to answer.

In the street—café chairs abandoned
on terraces; market stalls emptied                                    10
of their solid light,
though pavement still breathes
summer grapes and peaches.
Like the light of anything that grows
from this newly-turned earth,
every tip of me gathers under your touch,
wind wrapping my dress around our legs,
your shirt twisting to flowers in my fists.

1991

# There Is No City That Does Not Dream

There is no city that does not dream
from its foundations. The lost lake
crumbling in the hands of brickmakers,
the floor of the ravine where light lies broken
with the memory of rivers. All the winters
stored in that geologic
garden. Dinosaurs sleep in the subway
at Bloor and Shaw, a bed of bones
under the rumbling track. The storm
that lit the city with the voltage                                    10
of spring, when we were eighteen
on the clean earth. The ferry ride in the rain,
wind wet with wedding music and everything that
sings in the carbon of stone and bone
like a page of love, wind-lost from a hand, unread.

1999

# Ice House[1]

> 'I regret nothing but his suffering.'
>
> —Kathleen Scott

Wherever we cry,
it's far from home.

\*

At Sandwich, our son pointed
persistently to sea.
I followed his infant gaze,
expecting a bird or a boat
but there was nothing.
How unnerving,
as if he could see you
on the horizon,                                          10
knew where you were
exactly:
at the edge of the world.

\*

You unloaded the ship at Lyttleton[2]
and repacked her:

'thirty-five dogs
five tons of dog food
fifteen ponies
thirty-two tons of pony fodder
three motor-sledges                                      20
four hundred and sixty tons of coal
collapsible huts
an acetylene plant
thirty-five thousand cigars
one guinea pig
one fantail pigeon

---

1 'Kathleen Scott was a sculptor, and the wife of the Antarctic explorer Robert Falcon Scott. They had been married two years, with an eleven-month-old son, when Scott went south to the Pole. Upon parting in New
Zealand, they made a pact to keep a daily journal for each other. Scott perished on the return journey from the
Pole, and when his body and the bodies of his companions were found in the spring, his diary was brought back
to England. On the inside cover, Scott had written "Send this diary to my wife." Then Scott drew a line through
the word "wife" and wrote instead, "widow" ' [Michaels' note]. Scott died in 1912.
2 Kathleen recalls their trip to New Zealand, where they stayed in Lyttleton with friends (the Kinseys, mentioned
later in the poem).

three rabbits
one cat with its own hammock, blanket and pillow
one hundred and sixty-two carcasses of mutton and
an ice house'                                                    30

     *

Men returned from war
without faces, with noses lost
discretely as antique statues,
accurately as if eaten
by frostbite.
In clay I shaped their
flesh, sometimes
retrieving a likeness
from photographs.
Then the surgeons copied                                         40
nose, ears, jaw
with molten wax and metal plates
and horsehair stitches;
with borrowed cartilage,
from the soldiers' own ribs,
leftovers stored under the skin
of the abdomen. I held the men down
until the morphia
slid into them.
I was only sick                                                  50
afterwards.

Working the clay, I remembered
mornings in Rodin's studio,[3]
his drawerfuls of tiny hands and feet,
like a mechanic's tool box.
I imagined my mother in her blindness
before she died, touching my face,
as if still she could
build me with her body.

At night, in the studio                                          60
I took your face in my hands and your fine
arms and long legs, your small waist,
and loved you into stone.

---

3  As a young woman, Kathleen worked in the studio of the sculptor Auguste Rodin (1840–1917), who was famous
   for his evocative portrayals of the human figure.

The men returned from France
to Ellerman's Hospital.
Their courage
was beautiful.
I understood the work at once:
To use scar tissue to advantage.
To construct through art,                                    70
one's face to the world.
Sculpt what's missing.

                    *

You reached furthest south,
then you went further.

In neither of those forsaken places
did you forsake us.

                    *

At Lyttleton the hills unrolled,
a Japanese scroll painting;
we opened the landscape with our bare feet.
So much learned by observation.                              80
We took in brainfuls of New Zealand air
on the blue climb over the falls.

Our last night together we slept
not in the big house but
in the Kinseys' garden.
Belonging only
to each other.
Guests of the earth.

                    *

Mid-sea, a month out of range
of the wireless;                                             90
on my way to you. Floating
between landfalls,
between one hemisphere and another.
Between the words
'wife' and 'widow'.

*

Newspapers, politicians
scavenged your journals.

But your words
never lost their way.

*

We mourn in a place no one knows;                    100
it's right that our grief be unseen.

I love you as if you'll return
after years of absence.
As if we'd invented
moonlight.

*

Still I dream
of your arrival.

1999


# Repairing the Octave[1]

In order for the octave to sing true,
each third is stretched to dissonance:
thus is the keyboard mended
with discord.[2]

---

1  Published in the University of Toronto magazine *Idea&s*.
2  An octave can be formed from three major thirds, one on top of the other—e.g., C to E; E to G-sharp/A-flat; G-sharp/A-flat to C). In the 'natural' scale, however, G-sharp and A-flat are two different pitches. As keyboard instruments became more popular, ways of tuning, or tempering, the musical intervals in each octave were found to create dissonances relative to the natural harmonic series or intervals to prevent beating between harmonics and to make it possible for pieces written in more than one musical key to be played without interruption for retuning the instrument. At the beginning of the eighteenth century, J.S. Bach refined and popularized the system called 'well tempering', which caused the pure or 'just' major or minor thirds of each octave to be tuned slightly sharp ('stretched') so they would sound true in multiple keys. Michaels is responding, in this poem, to Bach's influential composition *The Well-Tempered Clavier*, which, with its twenty-four pairs of preludes and fugues in each of the twelve major and twelve minor classical keys, was written to demonstrate how well this tuning worked.

For there cannot be consonance
without dissonance,
birth without sufferance,
flesh without loneliness,

grief without desire.

Running through everything he wrote                                    10
were children, twenty in
twenty-seven years.[3] Running through
fugues, climbing the drapery
of chorales, hiding under tables
of hymns. Just as he came
from generations of musicians, so his sons
would compose. And when he was blind,
write down for him his last cantata
'When in my hour of greatest need'—
the father's sight restored                                           20
in the hand of the son.[4]

Handel was thirty miles away
in Halle, and Bach's most esteemed Prince Leopold
lent his horse.[5] Bach rode all night
but, unknowing, Handel had left
for England. In his youth
Bach rode 250 miles to hear Buxtehude
leap across the pedals
of the organ at Lubeck, but Handel—
only the distance from Eisenach to Halle!—                            30
was gone.

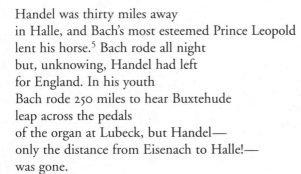

---

3  Bach was married twice. With his first wife, he had seven children, four of whom survived to adulthood; with
   his second wife, who survived him, he fathered thirteen more, seven of whom died in childhood. Four of Bach's
   sons became famous as composers in their own right.
4  His vision having failed toward the end of his life, Bach is said to have dictated 'When in the hour of greatest
   need' a few months before his death.
5  Of Bach's several employers, Leopold, Prince of Anhalt-Köthen (1694 O.S.–1728 N.S.) was a musician himself
   and treated Bach well. Bach travelled from Köthen to try to meet George Frideric Handel (1685–1759), the other
   great composer of his time, but was unable to do so. Dieterich Buxtehude (1637–1707) was a composer and great
   organist of the prior generation.

Yes, Bach would write his regret to him.
What is thirty miles, or thirty years,
between one voice and another?

It is dusk; he can tell by the coolness
of the breeze through the open window and
he imagines the white curtains
floating into the dark room.
He hears the papers on his desk moving,
answering the wind. 40
They bring in the chairs and Anna Magdalena[6]
takes his hand. Now she sings
when she is in another room,
to let him know she's near.
She sings or takes his hand—never both
at once, as if there were no difference
between her voice and her touch.

Who could guess she would die alone,
an almswoman, ten years from that moment?
But for now, they listen to their fine sons play. 50
All his life he has made an argument
for this sound, this tempered keyboard their hands sing.

There is a woman with a child, an infant,
who sits with him, and it is good
to be near her. It is familiar,
the feel of the music in his body;
each note sings inside him,
though his hands lie still in his lap.
Perhaps only he can hear it, though when he looks 60
in the woman's face, she seems to hear it too,
as if there might be flesh without loneliness.

6  Anna Magdalena Wilcke (1701–60) was Bach's second wife and a professional singer before their marriage. Her
   sons left home after their father's death, and she remained in Leipzig, with her two youngest daughters and a
   step-daughter, dependent on charity and dying in poverty.

If one could write to the dead
the woman would, to say how her father
seems to remember when he listens,
how the keyboard seems to remember him,
how the keyboard seems to remember
for him.
She would tell Sebastian Bach
that his keyboard contained a thousand                          70
consolations, a thousand mistakes,
each tone a thousand reparations;
separations. She remembers
sitting in the car with her father,
his cherry pipe smoke and
the white noise of the heater
against the clear precision of the fugue
on the car radio.

Now she slips off his watch
and leaves it beside the bed for him.                            80
He remembers a cardboard keyboard.
how it unfolded, how he used to lay it down
the length of the dining room table.
He knew it even then:
the notes in his head were the same pitch
as the paper. He remembers
the colours of the wood of the table-top,
the smell of the wood polish, he remembers
the first time he heard those sounds
from a phonograph in another room                                90
on a Sunday morning, how the voices of the fugue
entered each other like needle and thread
through cloth. It would be years before he could play
those notes himself
but he could sing them if he wanted to,
and he wanted to. For a long time
he stepped aside and let the sound pass through him,
but then, one mid-winter afternoon
with snow falling silently into the trees,
he understood he was meant to make each note                     100
unrepentantly
personal. The voices of the fugue
answer each other,
like the joy of an embrace
before you know you need it.

The woman will come before sleep
to slip the watch
from his wrist, though later it will seem
no one had come.
No one thinks of him.                                          110
No one remembers his childhood
but that woman—if he could remember
the word 'daughter' it would make
everything clear.

Now Anna Magdalena takes his hand.
Johann Sebastian Bach listens to his sons
and thinks of the kindnesses by which
a whole life can be set right,
the one note
that changes everything.                                      120

The white curtains touch the silence.
The keyboard is made of a thousand flaws,
a thousand consolations.
Each breath digs deep into silence.
Happiness can be lost in a moment.
The whole keyboard repents a mistake
for which we wish to be forgiven.

He thinks of all the ways we are shaped by another
and set right, the cup of tea brought in the evening,
the story in the middle of the night.                         130

The two men sit in the dark.

What is 300 years
between one voice
and another?

2007

# George Elliott Clarke
## b. 1960

George Elliott Clarke comes from what he calls 'Africadia', a word he coined for the culture of the 'several dozen Black Loyalist–and Black Refugee–settled communities' in what had once been the French colony of Acadia. Born just outside one of these—Three Mile Plains (near Windsor, Nova Scotia)—he is a seventh-generation descendant of the black Loyalists who immigrated to Nova Scotia after the American Revolution. Growing up in Halifax, in a household he has described as filled with 'television, radio, magazines, art and music,' he aspired to write song lyrics like those in the top-40 hits he was hearing on the radio in the early 1970s. He began studying marine topology at the University of Waterloo (BA 1984), but an intensified interest in poetry and in blues music led to his first book, *Saltwater Spirituals and Deeper Blues* (1983). He has described it as a 'verse collection inspired by assassinations, civil wars, insurrections, and the other blood-stained bric-à-brac of our century'. Returning to the Annapolis Valley as a community-development worker, he realized that the language of his own region was innately poetic. Deciding to give more attention to his writing, he took an MA in English at Dalhousie University; his thesis dealt with performance in Michael Ondaatje's poems.

In 1987, Clarke moved to Ottawa, where he worked as a parliamentary aide. While there, he completed *Whylah Falls* (1990), a 'poem-novel' about an imagined black community in Nova Scotia that is, according to the preface, a 'snowy, northern Mississippi, with blood spattered, not on magnolias, but on pines, lilacs, and wild roses.' *Whylah Falls* mixes poetry and prose with archival photographs of the region and clippings from a fictional newspaper (*The Whylah Moon*) to create portraits of its inhabitants as a group of vital people living in difficult circumstances. Clarke marries the sounds of black music with verse forms and rhythms drawn from the whole tradition of English literature to create a free-flowing fusion of the idiomatic and the formal. In the introduction to the book's tenth-anniversary edition, Clarke, describing *Whylah Falls* as 'born in the blues, the philosophy of the cry,' explains: 'It is a response to the call of popular angst in radio and folklore. You have to appreciate call-and-response, the antiphonal impulse.' He also emphasizes his debt to local oral heritage: 'I sought to restore the verbal magic of African United Baptist Association sermons. Shouts, hollers, coos, cries, screams—the jazz of life.'

In 1993, Clarke completed a PhD at Queen's University with a thesis comparing English-Canadian and African-American poetry and poetics. The following year, he published *Lush Dreams, Blue Exile* (1994), in which he declares, 'I yearn to be Ulyssean, to roam / foaming oceans or wrest / a wage from tough, mad adventure. / For now, I labour language'. While this volume of poems continues his exploration of black Nova Scotian experience, it also engages with history on a larger scale. (The use of the word *lush* in the title showed Clarke's break with the stripped, spare style of poetry favoured by many of his contemporaries.)

Clarke joined the faculty of Duke University in 1994, but he came to feel he would be happier back in Canada. In 1998, he spent a year as the Seagram Visiting Chair in Canadian Studies at McGill University; and in 1999, he joined the Department of English at the University of Toronto, where he is now the E.J. Pratt Professor of Canadian literature. In 2009, he received an honorary doctorate from the Royal Military College of Canada.

Beginning in 1999, Clarke created works that were notable for their performative aspects. That year saw the publication of the verse-play *Beatrice Chancy*, which recasts Percy Bysshe Shelley's 1819 lyric drama *The Cenci* as a tragedy of slavery in Canada, set in the Annapolis Valley in 1801. Clarke adapted the play as a libretto for an opera by James Rolfe, which has been performed in Toronto, Halifax, and elsewhere, and broadcast on CBC television. He turned *Whylah Falls* into a play (published in 1999) that was performed on CBC radio and then on stage; and he wrote a teleplay, *One Heart Broken into Song*, that was made into a film for CBC TV.

Trying to understand an event from his family history—the execution in 1949 of two of his cousins, George and Rufus Hamilton, for their murder of Nacre Pearly Burgundy, a Fredericton, New Brunswick, taxi driver—Clarke wrote *Execution Poems* (2000; Governor General's Award), and then told their story in a novel, *George and Rue* (2005). In 2001, he published *Blue*, a book of poems that expands his investigation of contemporary black identity—as in the poem addressed to Derek Walcott: 'Composing lines blustery, yet tender / your voice your own (Auden in the margins, / Eliot, Yeats, and Pound in the dungeon / . . . / extracting black blues from a yellowed Oxford).' That book was later complemented by *Black* (2006), which opens with 'George & Rue: Coda', a recapitulation of the story of the Hamilton brothers. (Like *Illuminated Verse*, published the year before, *Black* juxtaposes poems with photographs.) In 2009, Clarke published *I & I*, an illustrated verse novel that he describes as gothic, grotesque, and gaudy. Set in the 1970s, it has the qualities of a roman noir as it follows a man and a woman on a journey that carries them between two North American ports—from Halifax to Corpus Christi, Texas, and back.

His continuing interest in the interaction of words and music led Clarke to create *Québécité*, a jazz opera produced and published in 2003 for the Guelph Jazz Festival, with music composed by D.D. Jackson. It focuses on love and racial mixing as two couples wrestle with their desires and the demands of society. A third libretto, *Trudeau: Long March, Shining Path* (2007), also scored by Jackson, was performed in Toronto in 2007. It is a playful response to history that shows Trudeau—whom Clarke sees as a symbol for a dynamic, progressive, and inclusive Canada—in dialogue with other leaders who changed society in the twentieth century, including John F. Kennedy, Fidel Castro, and Nelson Mandela. Clarke has described this work as paying homage to one of his seven heroes from when he was a teenager:

*Seven artist-intellectuals—or poet-politicos—helped me to conceive my voice. They were jazz trumpeter Miles Davis, troubadour-bard Bob Dylan, libertine lyricist Irving Layton, guerrilla leader and poet Mao Zedong, reactionary modernist Ezra Pound, Black Power orator Malcolm X and the Right Honourable Pierre Elliott Trudeau. . . . I find their blunt talk, suave styles, acerbic independence, raunchy macho, feisty lyricism, singing heroics and scarf-and-beret chivalry quite, well, liberating.*

In an afterword to the small volume of his selected verse that appeared in 2008 as *Blues and Bliss*, Clarke says, 'When all's said and done, I remain, fundamentally, a songwriter.'

Clarke has edited two anthologies: *Fire on the Water: An Anthology of Black Nova Scotian Writing* (2 vols.; 1991–2) and *Eyeing the North Star: Directions in African-Canadian Literature* (1997). In 2002, he published *Odysseys Home: Mapping African-Canadian Literature*, a collection of critical essays that offer thoughtful examinations of African-Canadian writing in the contexts of the African diaspora and of Canadian culture. Rejecting those in Canada who may think 'whiteness is equal to Canadianness' and those US reviewers who speak of him as an 'African-American writer', Clarke sees the goal of all of his work as calling attention to a neglected history:

*As a writer of African descent who's also Canadian, I have this need to continue to reach out to my fellow and sister Canadians and educate them at the same time that I also need to speak to members of my own racial and regional community or communities.*

# From The Adoration of Shelley,[1] Whylah Falls

## The Argument

Crows trumpet indigo dawn. The rose sun blossoms. A paddlewheel steamer, spilling blues, country, and flamenco guitar, churns the still Sixhiboux River. Simultaneously, a dark blue engine steams into Whylah station—a white marble phantasm. Garbed in baroque motley, a theatre troupe disembarks. One actor, blurred completely in white, brandishes an oily shotgun. Another player, a poet, bears a satchel full of letters and seven books of the elegant verse that perished in the slaughter of The Great War. His black suit, tie, shirt, shoes, melt into the dark dawn. A comet streak of rose flames on one lapel. Thin as any dreamer, this Mandinga-M'ikmaq[2] wears circle lenses on his earthen face. A slow clock, Xavier Zachary turns, his hands crying rose petals, and wheels upward into the high, blue hills above Whylah.

*Wooooooo!* The train howls into steam and vanishes.

Shelley Adah Clemence, eighteen Aprils old, awakens, stretches in her brass bed. The train moans. She wonders, 'Is this trouble?' Small, slender, she rises, tossing back the covers like a spurned wave. She resembles Rousseau's Yadwigha.[3] Same almond-shaped eyes, same sloe-coloured hair. She peers into her diary, a garden of immortelles[4] and printed sunflowers. Then, Shelley opens her warm Bible and copies verses from The Song of Solomon[5] into her own book. A radio awakens, croons a Ma Rainey song rich with regretful guitars, and she crafts a song with Hebrew lyrics and a Coptic melody:

> *Snow softly, silently, settles*
> *White petals upon white petals.*

She buttons her long, ivory nightdress down to her thin, brown ankles and angles carefully down steep steps to the kitchen, a bath of yellow light. Her ma, Cora, is pulling fire from the woodstove. Othello, her brother, rests his guitar-troubled fingers on a mug of coffee. They suspect that X will arrive shortly, after five years of exile, to court Shelley with words that she will know have been pilfered from literature. Smooth lines come from Castiglione.[6] Shelley vows she'll not be tricked. She be wisdom.

Outside, Whylah shimmers. Sunshine illumines the mirage of literature, how everyone uses words to create a truth he or she can trust and live within.

---

1 The title of the first (and, later in the volume, of the seventh) of the seven parts of the book; the phrase 'The Adoration of Shelley' echoes the title of several famous religious paintings from the middle ages and the Renaissance (*The Adoration of the Magi*, *The Adoration of the Shepherds*), all of which emphasize the manifestation of a divine presence in the world.

2 That is, descended from both the West African Mandinga tribe and the M'ikmaqs, a Native people of eastern Canada.

3 In the painting *Le Rêve* (1910) by Henri Rousseau (1844–1910)—originally known as *Yadwigha's Dream*—a nude woman reclines on a red couch in the middle of a surreal jungle.

4 Dried flowers.

5 The Song of Solomon is unusual among the books of the Bible in that it is a work of love poetry without religious content. Its recurrent imagery of a woman within a walled garden has influenced the tradition of secular love poetry. 'Ma Rainey' (1889–1939): black American singer (born Gertrude Pridgett), known as the Mother of the Blues.

6 That is, from *The Courtier* (1528), the famous Renaissance treatise on courtly behaviour and Neo-Platonic theories of love by Baldassare Castiglione (1478–1529).

# The River Pilgrim: A Letter

At eighteen, I thought the Sixhiboux wept.
Five years younger, you were lush, beautiful
Mystery; your limbs—scrolls of deep water.
Before your home, lost in roses, I swooned,
Drunken in the village of Whylah Falls,
And brought you apple blossoms you refused,
Wanting Hank Snow[1] woodsmoke blues and dried smelts,
Wanting some milljerk's dumb, unlettered love.
    That May, freights chimed xylophone tracks that rang
To Montréal. I scribbled postcard odes,          10
Painted *le fleuve Saint-Laurent comme la Seine*—
Sad watercolours for Negro exiles
In France, and dreamt Paris white with lepers,
Soft cripples who finger pawns under elms,
Drink blurry into young debauchery,
Their glasses clear with Cointreau, rain, and tears.
    You hung the moon backwards, crooned crooked poems
That no voice could straighten, not even O
Who stroked guitars because he was going
To die with a bullet through his stomach.          20
Innocent, you curled among notes—petals
That scaled glissando from windows agape,
And remained in southwest Nova Scotia,
While I drifted, sad and tired, in the east.
    I have been gone four springs. This April, pale
Apple blossoms blizzard. The garden flutes
*E*-flats of lilacs, *G*-sharps of lilies.
Too many years, too many years, are past . . .
    Past the marble and pale flowers of Paris,
Past the broken, Cubist guitars of Arles,[2]         30
Shelley, I am coming down through the narrows
Of the Sixhiboux River. I will write
Beforehand. Please, please come out to meet me
               As far as Beulah Beach.

---

1 (1914–99); white Nova Scotian country music singer.
2 Arles was the base for the painters Pablo Picasso and Braque while they were creating many of their early cubist
  paintings, several of which feature cubist representations of guitars.

## Rose Vinegar

In his indefatigable delirium of love, Xavier wires rugosa rose blossoms to Shelley. Deluded by his quixotic romanticism, he cannot yet appreciate the practical necessities of friendship. But, Shelley trusts in reason; thus, though she admires the blossoms for their truthfulness to themselves, she does not hesitate to distill a delicate and immortal vinegar from what she considers the ephemeral petals of X's desire. An ornament becomes an investment. She fills a cup with the fresh rose petals; then, stripping off their heels (the white part), she pours the petals into a quart sealer and adds two cups of white vinegar. Then, she seals the jar and places it on the sunny livingroom windowsill for sixteen days, seven hours, and nine minutes. When the vinegar is ready, she strains it through a sieve and then pours it back into the bottle.

Rose vinegar. It's especially good on salads.

## Bees' Wings

This washed-out morning, April rain descants,
Weeps over gravity, the broken bones
Of gravel and graveyards, and Cora puts
Away gold dandelions to sugar
And skew into gold wine, then discloses
That Pablo gutted his engine last night
Speeding to Beulah Beach under a moon
As pocked and yellowed as aged newsprint.
Now, Othello, famed guitarist, heated
By rain-clear rum, voices transparent notes          10
Of sad, anonymous heroes who hooked
Mackerel and slept in love-pried-open thighs
And gave out booze in vain crusades to end
Twenty centuries of Christianity.
    His voice is simple, sung air: without notes,
There's nothing. His unknown, imminent death
(The feel of iambs ending as trochees
In a slow, decasyllabic death-waltz;
His vertebrae trellised on his stripped spine
Like a xylophone or keyboard of nerves)          20
Will also be nothing: the sun pours gold
Upon Shelley, his sis', light as bees' wings,
Who roams a garden sprung from rotten wood
And words, picking green nouns and fresh, bright verbs,

For there's nothing I will not force language
To do to make us one—whether water
Hurts like whisky or the sun burns like oil
Or love declines to weathered names on stone.


## Blank Sonnet

The air smells of rhubarb, occasional
Roses, or first birth of blossoms, a fresh,
Undulant hurt, so body snaps and curls
Like flower. I step through snow as thin as script,
Watch white stars spin dizzy as drunks, and yearn
To sleep beneath a patchwork quilt of rum.
I want the slow, sure collapse of language
Washed out by alcohol. Lovely Shelley,
I have no use for measured, cadenced verse
If you won't read. Icarus-like,[1] I'll fall                    10
Against this page of snow, tumble blackly
Across vision to drown in the white sea
That closes every poem—the white reverse
That cancels the blackness of each image.

1 See page 896, note 1.


## The Wisdom of Shelley

You come down, after
five winters, X,
bristlin' with roses
and words words words,
brazen as brass.
Like a late blizzard,
You bust in our door,
talkin' April and snow and rain,
litterin' the table
with poems—                                                    10
as if we could trust them!

I can't.
I heard pa tell ma
how much and much he
loved loved loved her
and I saw his fist
fall so gracefully
against her cheek,
she swooned.

Roses                                                                              20
got thorns.
And words
do lie.

I've seen love
die.

## Each Moment Is Magnificent

Othello practises *White Rum*, his scale of just music, and clears the love song of mud-
dying his morals. He sets his glass down lovingly, a whole chorus of molecules sloshing
in harmony. He vows he will not, he will not be a dead hero, no way, suffering a beautiful sleep, trimmed with ochre, hazelnut, dressed in mahogany, smelling of last-minute
honey and tears, regrets rained upon him too late in the guise of wilted, frail flowers.
Instead, he will sleep right now, while he still can, up to his thighs in thighs, gnaw dried,
salty smelts, and water song with rum. *Sweet Sixhiboux, run softly till I end my song.*

   Wearing the lineaments of ungratified desire, Selah sashays from the livingroom,
watches dusk bask in the River Sixhiboux. She tells Othello to shut up because
Jericho's where she's gonna go[1] when she falls in love. Yep, when that someday man
come out the blue to Whylah Falls, Beauty Town, to serenade her and close his wings
around her, she'll be in Jericho at last like the fortune-teller says. She'll jump the
broom[2] and cross the Nile.

   I stroll outside with strange music in my skull. Here's the Sixhiboux River, tossed
tinfoil, crinkling along the ground, undistracted by all the grave lovers it attracts, all
those late Romantics who spout Lake Poet Wordsworth, 'The world is too much with
us, late and soon,' and brood upon the river's shimmering bliss before tossing themselves within, pretending to be Percy Bysshe Shelley at Lerici.[3] I've thought of the
Sixhiboux in those erotic ways, dreamt it as being midnight-thick, voluptuous,
folding—like a million moths, furry with a dry raininess—over one. No matter where

1  In the Book of Joshua, the conquest of Jericho permits the Israelites to gain possession of the Promised Land.
2  Get married without a minister or priest.
3  The Romantic poet Shelley died on 8 July 1822, when his schooner sank on his return voyage from Livorno to
   Lerici, where he was staying in Italy.

you are in Sunflower County, you can hear it pooling, milling in a rainstorm, or thundering over a hapless town. Even now, I can hear its shining roar pouring over Shelley's house, polishing the roses that nod, drunken, or spring—petalled crude—from earth. All I hear is an old song, her voice, lilting, 'Lover Man.'

She's absent, far from here. My blood moves angry through its rooms; rain washes all my tears to the sea. My pain will never end unless I can sleep beside my love, pluck the ripe moon, halve it, and share its sweet milk between us: *Hear me, oh moon, hear my song:*

> *I am like that road that slinks to your door*
> *Like a married lover, sneaking around*
> *To curve his ribaldry about your form.*
> *Shelley, that's how much, that's how much, I feel.*

1990


# Primitivism

He could not escape
the wilderness. Bark
encrusted his wine bottles.
His pencils grew fur
and howled. Sentences
became wild eagles
that flew predatory patterns,
swooping out of a white sky-
page to tear apart field
mice-images, scurrying                                    10
for meaning. A carcass-
manuscript rotted on a shelf
or a hillside. He could
not tell the difference.
A bear-trap of ideas
snared him: he could
not poeticize
the country
and not become it;
his poems filling                                         20
with neanderthal nudes,
prowling punctuation,
snarling sounds, guttural.

1994

## From *Execution Poems*

## The Killing

*Rue:* I ingratiated the grinning hammer
with Silver's not friendless, not unfriendly skull.
Behind him like a piece of storm, I unleashed a frozen glinting—
a lethal gash of lightning.
His soul leaked from him in a Red Sea, a Dead Sea,
churning his clothes to lava.

*Geo:* No, it didn't look like real blood,
but something more like coal, that inched from his mouth.

*Rue:* It was a cold hit in the head. A hurt unmassageable.
Car seat left stinking of gas and metal and blood.                    10
And reddening violently.
A rhymeless poetry scrawled his obituary.

*Geo:* It was comin on us for awhile, this here misery.
We'd all split a beer before iron split Silver's skull.
Silver's muscles still soft and tender. That liquor killed him.
The blood like shadow on his face, his caved-in face.
Smell of his blood over everything.

*Rue:* Iron smell of the hammer mingled with iron smell of blood
and chrome smell of snow and moonlight.

*Geo:* He had two hundred dollars on him; bootleg in him.        20
We had a hammer on us, a spoonful of cold beer in us.

The taxi-driver lies red in the alabaster snow.
His skeleton has taken sick and must be placed in the ground.

This murder is 100 per cent dirt of our hands.

*Rue:* Twitchy, my hand was twitchy, inside my jacket.
The hammer was gravity: everything else was jumpy.
I wondered if Silver could hear his own blood thundering,
vermilion, in his temples, quickened, twitchy, because of beer;
jumpy molecules infecting his corpuscles, already nervous.

The hammer went in so far that there was no sound—              30
just the slight mushy squeak of bone.

Silver swooned like the leaden Titanic.
Blood screamed down his *petit-bourgeois* clothes.

*Geo:* Can we cover up a murder with snow?
With white, frosty roses?

*Rue:* Here's how I justify my error:
The blow that slew Silver came from two centuries back.
It took that much time and agony to turn a white man's whip
into a black man's hammer.

*Geo:* No, we needed money,                                    40
so you hit the So-and-So,
only much too hard.
Now what?

*Rue:* So what?

2000

# Nu(is)ance

*for Wayde Compton*

Jabbering double-crossing doubletalk,
Pale-assed poetasters void my 'blues-caucused,
Raucous lyrics'—too Negroid and rowdy,
While sable, sassy poets preach I ink
Too blankly, *comme les blancs,* my bleached-out verse
Bleating too whitey-like—worse—in they ears.
*What can I say?*
                    All this blather about
'Black' and 'white' verse is blackmail and white noise.
Cripes! English—fallacious—be finished here!                  10
    I'd rather stutter a bastard's language
Only spoken in gutters, a broken,
Vulgar, Creole screech, loud with bawling, slurring,
Balderdash, cussing, and caterwauling,
A corrupt palaver that bankrupts all meeching speech
Because it be literal, guttural *Poetry,*
I.e. *Hubbub.*

2001

# George & Rue: Coda

*I – January 7, 1949*

Near midnight, Rufus slammed the hammer
Down, down—bam!—into Burgundy's head—

Like a bullet bashing the skull.
The night heard a man halloo, 'Oh!'

At that stabbing noise, George whipped around.
The hurt cab bled as black as a hearse.

The moon that night: a white man's face.
Winds flickered black, slick, in the pines.

When Georgie sidled down the hill, glidin
Back to the car, Br'er[1] Rudy already had                    10

Burgundy's wallet tugged out his pocket.
Blood hugged Rue's body, snuggled up

His face. Giorgio shoved Burgundy aside,
So he could fist cash, watch, rosary, coins.

Later, George stove the taxi, a cadaver
Fluffed in the trunk, in Fredericton's snow,

And slinked off, whistling, to drink, drink, drink.
Snow cleansed everything, but memory.

The taxicab leaked a smoke-trail of blood,
Just because.                                                  20

Georgie weren't chilled; he waltzed back where
Rue be guzzlin blackberry wine in brand-new clothes.

Rue ain't feel nothing bad or wrong or upset.
A white man was dead, yes; but they had booze and cash.

---

1  Brother (dialect).

*II – Trials & Convictions*

Geo:    Everyone says
The noose is soon.

Rue:    What they mean is,
Life's meaning's gone.

Geo:    After I die, let my words be rain, grass:
I don't mind, in April, in Three Mile Plains.

Rue:    Gravediggers got job security,
And murderers got no reason to be jealous.

Justice:    It will be a crisply, British-accented lynching.
To exterminate two germs.             10

Narrator: The hanging? Will be disgusting.
Of two pterodactyls. Very disgusting.

The Edvard Munch moon screams like Pound
In night's icebox, while Van Gogh stars go mad.[2]


*III – The Hangings*

The gallows is carpentered so passionately,
Love itself seems engrained in the pine.

The pale, soft, easily worked pine
Transforms the gallows into a guillotine.

The two young Negro men, unhinged,
Swing lazily to a bluegrass, Dixieland tune.

A murmur of light, eh?
Then stars expire in dew.

---

2  A conflated allusion: *The Scream* and *Moon Light* are two of the most famous paintings by the Norwegian symbolist painter, Edvard Munch (1863–1944). Munch described *The Scream* as reflecting his nearly mad state of mind. Ezra Pound (1885–1972), one of the most important modernist poets, broadcast shrill propaganda from Italy in support of Fascism during the Second World War; he was subsequently tried for treason and—found not guilty by reason of insanity—incarcerated for twelve years in St Elizabeth's Hospital in Washington, DC. *The Starry Night* is among the best-known paintings of Vincent van Gogh (1853–90), the Dutch post-impressionist painter whose struggles with mental illness ended in suicide; in it, stars seem to swirl wildly through the night sky.

That repugnant civil servant, the hangman,
After this Sadean[3] idyll, will cultivate brambles.                    10

10,000 mad dogs bay and wolf-whistle
The outfoxed boys' falls.

The clangour of two hangings:
Those dangling feet, pealing.

2006

3  Cruel, sadistic. An allusion to the infamous Marquis de Sade, whose books contain extensive depictions of violence and perversion. He was imprisoned and later committed to an insane asylum.

## Mortality Sonnet

How the columns of the body
Corrode and collapse,
Despite girdings of cotton and silk,
Or buttresses of expensive ointments.

How *Death* camps out in the body
To seize it by surprise.

How it charges, then, through veins
And arteries, or along nerves and muscle,
Discharging tissue and organs,
So that the heart calcifies to bone.                    10

The issue is to sing until breath is gone.

Flagging, I hurl these words
To shout down *Time*
Just as it becomes *Eternity*.

2006

# Lisa Moore

## b. 1964

Lisa Doreen Moore is one of a number of new writers to emerge from Newfoundland and Labrador since the mid-1980s. Born in St John's, she grew up on the outskirts of that city. An inveterate reader as a child ('Books could take me over then, bodily, as if I were possessed'), she also showed early artistic interests. Encouraged by her parents, she took classes in visual art, from age ten, at 77 Bond Street (a community art school, affiliated with Memorial University in St John's). She describes, in her 2003 essay 'Kernels' (in *Writers Talking*), how these classes taught her to be 'astonished unexpectedly by ordinary things.' Moore later remarked, in an interview with Herb Wyile, that art school was also important because she learned about the Newfoundland painter Gerry Squires: 'Having landscapes that you were familiar with and that were particular to your experience celebrated all over Canada made it possible to think about being an artist' (*The Antigonish Review*). She went on to attend Nova Scotia College of Art and Design in Halifax, where she earned a BFA in 1988.

Moore has said that she began to write fiction after she grasped 'the parallels between visual composition and the composition of a piece of writing.' She took courses in creative writing at Memorial University, where she met Michael Winter, Claire Wilkshire, and Ramona Dearing, with whom she founded the Burning Rock Collective—a loosely defined writers' group that read and commented on one another's work in progress. Although they published two anthologies gathering their work, the Burning Rock Collective has never attempted to articulate a set of aesthetic principles. Its members all moved away from the 'traditional' rural material previously associated with Newfoundland writing to narratives about the meaningful small details of contemporary city life—the kind of fiction in which computer or television screens are as likely to make up the background as scenes of nature or of fisheries.

Moore's two collections of short fiction, *Degrees of Nakedness* (1995) and *Open* (2002), are urbane, fast-paced, and anxious. Her narratives frankly depict female desire in a time when the old rules for relationships have broken down. Although she employs a terse style that shows she has learned from reading Canadian short-story writer Norman Levine (she credits him in 'Kernels' with having shown her that 'the less a writer gives the reader the better'), she says that her 'contrary impulses' keep her from being simply a minimalist: 'I want to be hot, tell all, gab, gossip, narrate.'

Like Alice Munro, Moore constructs narratives that move freely through time. 'Craving' (reprinted here) makes us aware of the tension between two moments, the present of a dinner party, in which three couples have fallen into two gendered groups, and the remembered past of the women, who first met twenty years ago when they were all three on the cusp of puberty. Moore uses multi levelled dialogue to convey her characters' states of mind, while embedding carefully realized images—such as the stray plastic bag with 'meat juice coursing in the wrinkles' in the story's opening that reflect her training as a visual artist. The impact of her stories does not depend on how they end: they need to be understood backwards in terms of how each part modifies our understanding of the others. In an interview, Moore said of this way of writing,

*I want to break the parameters of what the reader expects is coming. So, if we're talking about any given sentence, I want the sentence to end in a way that the reader is not expecting. I want the paragraph to end and begin and be something the reader is not expecting. But also be inevitable. If there is a golden rule, that's it. If the reader knows where you're going, there's no point in reading that sentence. . . . It's not for the sake of being avant-garde that I want it to be unexpected. It's because I think a real engagement with a book means that the reader has to chase after the story. Their imagination has to be working, and it's the energy that's expended by the imagination at work that is the pleasure of reading.*

In 2005, Moore published *Alligator*. This first novel similarly takes the reader in unexpected directions in a series of vivid moments built around a variety of characters. The world they inhabit is a threatening one: the book opens with an alligator's jaws closing on a man's head and ends with moths descending like a plague: 'The city is covered . . . Moths on their hands, on their arms, on their upturned faces.'

Moore's second novel, *February* (2009), responds to the 1982 sinking of the oil rig *Ocean Ranger* and the deaths of the eighty-four men aboard. In asking how a woman deals with a catastrophic loss that takes away someone she loves, *February* suggests that the world can be both consuming and consoling. Near the end of the story, the central character looks out from her kitchen window at the snowstorm that has taken her husband from her:

*The blanket of white was aglitter out there. Magnificent and frigid and light-spangled. As long as she lives Helen will never forget how beautiful the snow was, and the sky, and how it flooded her and she couldn't tell the beauty apart from the panic. She decided then, and still believes that beauty and panic are one and the same. . . . Panic and beauty are inside each other, all the time, copulating in an effort to create more beauty and panic. . . . It is a demonic, angelic coupling.*

Moore has also written for television, radio, magazines, and newspapers and has edited *The Penguin Book of Contemporary Short Stories by Canadian Women* (2006). When she's not writing—or teaching creative-writing workshops in St John's and elsewhere—she spends her time in her home in St John's, where she lives with her husband, a sociology professor at Memorial University, and her two children.

# Craving

Jessica laughs very loud and the candle flames lie down stretched and flat. She moves the candelabra in front of her husband.

She says, I like aggressive men.

I say, I like aggressive women.

She dips her spoon into the mushroom soup.

But this is delicious, she says.

Vermouth, I say. On the way back from the liquor store a plastic bag of fierce yellow slapped against my shin. I peeled it away, meat juice coursing in the wrinkles like a living beast. It clung just as viciously to a telephone pole when I let it go. There was a poster on the pole just above the bag, Jessica Connolly at Fat Cat's. A band of men behind her. She looked resolute and charged, just like twenty years ago when the three of us would crush ourselves into a change room in the mall, forcing our bodies into the smallest-sized jeans we could find—she and Louise and I, twisting on the balls of our feet to see how our bums looked.

I like aggressive women too, she says.

That's because we're both aggressive.

I put my arm around Louise and squeeze her. I like you anyway, Lou, I say.

Jessica says, Oh, she's passive aggressive.

She isn't though, I say. Jessica pouts her lower lip, contemplating. We both concentrate on Louise's sweetness for a moment. Louise reaches for the bread, her brow furrowed. She's trying to think of something bad.

Lou's so wonderful, though, Jessica says, giving up. I glance at my husband. The men don't know each other. I should be drawing them into the conversation, but this is too heady. Jessica's so thoroughly herself, the genuine article.

Louise says, Do you remember when our class used to go to church? I loved the feeling of the sleeve of someone's blouse touching my arm. If they were unaware of it. Just brushing against my arm. Someone else's sleeve.

Jessica says, I love my daughter.

She's holding her spoon in the air. Jessica is far away, her eyes full of her daughter. She's in the park or the delivery room—somewhere with a lot of light—and the child is vigorous, screaming or running. Jessica sent a picture at Christmas of the four of them. The boy resting his cheek on her bare shoulder. Her daughter trying to tear off a white sunhat.

I love my son too, she says, and dips the spoon. But my daughter is going to do things. She'll get into a lot of trouble too. Jessica grins at her soup, proud and grim about the trouble her daughter's going to cause.

I tell them a story about a Bulgarian woman that ends with the shout, No matter, I must have it!

I say, This should be our motto. We clink our wine glasses and shout, No matter, I must have it! But the men go on with their conversation at the other end of the table. They are talking music, the different qualities a variety of sound systems offer.

Then Jessica says, I'm going through flux right now. Her eyes flit to her husband. I slam my hand flat on the table, the wine glasses jiggle.

Stop it, I say.

Stop what? The flux?

I won't have flux at the dinner table, I say.

Okay, she says, and she laughs, but it's more of a sly chuckle. We are twelve again, in the bloating, compressed heat of the canvas camper in her parents' driveway. She and Louise are trying to convince me I have to come out now. One of her brothers noticed my new bra and made some remark. Sitting alone in the trailer, with my arms crossed so tight over my chest that the next morning my arm muscles are stiff and it hurts to pull a sweater over my head. Jessica full of worldly disgust. Louise obstinately refusing to make Jessica relent, which she could do with a single tilt of her chin. They are united in the desire to punish my vanity. They don't have bras, but they have braces on their teeth, and that makes them a club.

Jessica says, Fine, if that's the way you want it.

I start to cry, knowing it's a gamble. Louise wavers but Jessica's scorn fulminates into a full-blown denouncement. She won't let me ruin all the fun. It's sunny outside and the camper smells of her brother's sports socks.

They wander off, their voices fading, Jessica's ringing laugh the last sound, not a forced laugh, they have forgotten me. Then I listen to the wind through the maples, straining to hear my parents' car coming for me.

Jessica admired the characters of her Siamese cats, haughty and lascivious. She could suss out the swift-forming passions of the gang of boys we knew, and make them heel. She knew the circuit of their collective synaptic skittering and played it like pinball. She couldn't be trusted with secrets, and we couldn't keep them from her.

I ask her husband if he wants more soup. I won't play a part in excluding him, though I'm sure everything is his fault.

He says, I don't know what else is coming.

There's dessert, says Louise. Lou wants to save him from the flux too. Save us all, because it's a big wave that could make the panes in the French door explode and we'd be up to our necks with the soup bowls floating.

Then Louise's boyfriend says, But pollution is a by-product of industry and we all want industry, so. He shrugs.

Lou catches my eye. She's thinking, Remember the guy on the surfboard in Hawaii? I felt total abandon. An evanescing of self, my zest uncorked.

Yes, but if you had kept going, it wouldn't have been abandon. He wouldn't be a man swathed in the nimbus of an incandescent wave, muzzling the snarling lip of that bone-crushing maw of ocean with a flexed calf muscle. He would be one of these guys at the table, half drunk and full of mild love.

There's my husband, heavy-lidded, flushed. The first time I saw him my skin tingled with the nascent what-would-come. Shane Walker. Red suspenders tugging at his faded jeans. The best way to make a thing happen is to not want it. I didn't want him so bad that he strode right over to the table and dropped down his books, *Mexico in Crisis* and *The Marxist Revolution*. He rubs his hands down the front of his faded jeans.

I read your sexy poem, he says.

A sheet of water falling from a canoe paddle like a torn wing. That's the only line of the poem I remember. So much bald longing in a paddle stroke. A torn wing, big deal, yet Shane Walker is blushing. Then I decided—No matter, I must have it.

Jessica taps her spoon on the edge of her cup. She's furious—why won't I have flux at the dinner table? It's only emotion, everything blows over. What am I afraid of? Let Louise have her beach boy.

I think, What if it wasn't abandon? What if some part of Louise stays on a surfboard in Hawaii forever when this guy, who considers the politics of pollution, wants her. Would Jessica have Louise long eternally for something that never existed? It's perverted. And what about Jessica? How long can this last, this brave refusal to compromise? There's redemption in submission. If Jessica wants to strut her charisma I'll stand aside, but in the end she's wrong and I'm right.

Why does the end matter, shrieks Jessica, there is no end. She doesn't say anything, of course, she's gone to the bathroom. We're only on the soup, there are several courses, whose idea was this, the plastic bag on my shin, her poster. Wouldn't it be fun? How have we changed? I think, This may be the end.

She says, I'd rather die ignited than sated.

I realize now, totally zonked—Jessica has rolled three joints since she got here, I haven't been stoned in years, it's so pleasurable, so good, I can hardly collect the plates— that I have always believed the flaws of men are born of a stupidity for which they, men, can't be held accountable. I recognize in a flash—I have balanced the sixth soup bowl, a spoon spins across the floor—that all my relations with men have been guided by this generous and condescending premise. I see now that the theory comes from the lack of courage required to face the truth, which is that men are pricks. They're aware women like me exist, women who believe they have been shafted in terms of a moral spine, and these men welcome these women's low estimation of themselves, and capitalize on it.

My neighbour, Allan, in the kitchen this afternoon while I was preparing for the dinner party. He was dropping off the flyers for the parent/teachers' auction. It disturbs me that Allan has never flirted with me. He flings himself onto a kitchen chair, spoons white sugar over a piece of bread, which he folds and eats in three bites.

He says, Aren't we all hungry?

I thought, Hungry for what? But I could remember a keening, an imminence. At certain hours it was strongest, at dawn riding my bike downhill, walking home from a bar at four in the morning.

I know I am, says Allan. I'm hungry.

I used to crave something, but what was it? Approval? It was bigger than the whole world approving, bigger than anything language could hog-tie. It compelled my every action, even eating a bran muffin I could tremble with excitement, thinking something might happen now, right now.

Allan certainly looks hungry, all shoulders and elbows splayed over the table.

I say, I can't help you, Allan.

I wasn't certain I'd spoken out loud. When I said *I can't help you*, I meant, I wish you wanted me, and even, I'd like to climb on the kitchen table with you—but I didn't say that, thankfully. What I said was terrible enough, *I can't help you*. I had been unaware, until that moment, that I wished to be desired by Allan.

He says, But I don't want you to help me.

Why wouldn't he want me too? If he is so damn hungry?

Louise: Why don't we unleash a primal battle screech, our friend is in flux for fuck's sake.

I think, Oh yes, it would be great to be Jessica. Let's all be Jessica, ready to burst into flame over an unpaid parking ticket. Ready, anyway, to sleep with the window washer who lowers himself to her office window on rope and pulley, blue overalls and cap, his powerful arms cutting slices of clarity through the soapy blur.

Fabulous, says Jessica.

We are very drunk now, it seems. Or I am, not used to smoking, but Jessica has a bristling fixity. She flicks her wrist to look at her watch. I have to go downtown, she says.

But it's our dinner party. We haven't seen each other. We don't know how we've changed.

Her husband says, I'll come with you.

Jessica says, You have to relieve the babysitter.

I think, It's too late. I didn't do my part. I have forsaken the promises of our ado-lescence; hiding near the warm tires of parked cars while playing spotlight at dusk, holding still while curling irons burn our scalps, splashes of silver raining from the disco balls in the parish hall, mashed banana emollients, face scrubs with twigs and bits of apricot, ears pierced with an ice cube and sewing needle, and the disquieting loss of a belief in God. The saturated aura, a kinetic field of blue light, that surrounded a silent phone while we willed it to ring. Our periods. Dusk, all by itself, dusk, walking home from school after a volleyball game and the light withdrawing from the pavement. I look at my husband, I try to feel dissatisfied but I can't, he's a beautiful man.

Jessica's husband wants her to give him money for the babysitter but she won't. She's angry he didn't take care of it himself. The chink of a wine glass on the marble fireplace. Louise's boyfriend rises from his chair and sways a little, he moves across the room and pats Jessica on the head.

Patronizing bitch, he says.

Jessica grins. She unfurls a peel of giggles tinny as a dropped roll of tinfoil bouncing across the kitchen tiles. She picks up her leather jacket and fires up the zipper. She grabs me by the shoulders, presses me into her big breasts. Then she holds me at arm's length.

You, she says, haven't changed a bit.

She moves to Louise, lifts her from the couch also by the shoulders, gives her a big hug.

She kisses her husband on both cheeks and hands him forty bucks.

She says, I love you, even at this moment.

She says to Louise's boyfriend, You, I'm not hugging.

She opens the French door and the window panes rattle.

Thank you so much, it was lovely.

The front door slams behind her. We each sit up a little, adjusting our posture, the draft from the front door sobering. Outside the dining-room window, we can hear her platform heels slapping the sidewalk, she has broken into a trot.

# Christian Bök
## b. 1966

Before he began publishing, Christian Book changed the spelling—but not the pronunciation—of his last name because, he says, he didn't want to publish a book written by 'Book'. He grew up in Toronto and, after five years in Ottawa attending Carleton University (BA, 1989; MA, 1990), he returned to pursue a PhD at York University, which he completed in 1998. There, he met the writers Christopher Dewdney, Darren Wershler-Henry, and Steve McCaffery. The latter was particularly important to him, Bök has said, because he had been initially influenced by Gwendolyn MacEwen,

Leonard Cohen, and Michael Ondaatje, but he wasn't happy with the 'emotive, lyrical anecdotes' he was writing as a consequence:

*I decided to become more experimental in my practice only after I encountered the work of Steve McCaffery during my graduate studies . . . [and* learned about] *the 'secret history' of the avant-garde (what with its wonderful zoo of conceptual novelties and linguistic anomalies). . . . I decided then that I would dedicate my complete, literary practice to nothing but a whole array of formalistic innovations.*

As well as drawing on the experimental and intensely theoretical poetics of McCaffery, Bök locates his writing in the Canadian traditions of *Tish* poetics and bpNichol's visual and sound poetry. In an essay entitled 'TISH and KOOT' (*Open Letter* 2006), Bök also identifies with the Kootenay School of Writing that emerged in the 1980s around David Thompson University Centre and Fred Wah, and sees Koot as extending and broadening the aims of the *Tish* movement.

Bök more generally places himself within an international avant-garde. He applies the term *avant-garde* (which originally described a movement associated with early French modernism and is now generally used to refer to experimental artists who, positioning themselves outside the artistic mainstream, seek to extend existing boundaries) to art that is anti-realist and anti-mimetic. Bök became particularly interested in the work of the French proto-surrealist Alfred Jarry (1873–1907), whose playful invention of the pseudoscience *'pataphysics* had already been taken up by bpNichol and McCaffery in their Toronto Research Group collaborations. In 1997, Bök co-edited (with Wershler-Henry) a special issue of *Open Letter* on 'millennial 'pataphysics'; and he subsequently published a revised version of his PhD thesis as *'Pataphysics: The Poetics of an Imaginary Science* (2002).

In his first collection of poetry, *Crystallography* (1994; revised and expanded, 2003), Bök, as well as including the kind of concrete poems that were Nichol's hallmark, showed that he shared Dewdney's interest in finding poetry in the language of science:

*chemosynthetic bacteria*
*feed upon sulphur manganese in limestone.*
*micro-organisms sculpt*
*crystal growth into bioengineered gardens:*

*aragonite dandelions . . .* ('Geodes')

His work on Jarry made Bök aware of the mid-twentieth century French group of writers and mathematicians influenced by 'pataphysics who called themselves *Ouvroir de littérature potentielle*, or Oulipo for short. They embraced the idea of writers taking on highly arbitrary formal constraints—setting themselves problems to solve or using artificial formulas to disrupt traditional forms or normal expressions—as a way of stimulating their creativity and of providing novelty for themselves and their readers. Perhaps the most noted of these Oulipians has been Georges Perec, whose *La Disparitions* (1969) is a novel written without using the letter E. (Such writing is called a lipogram, from the Greek *lippagramatos*, or 'missing letter'.) In response to Perec, Bök started work on a five-part poetic sequence in which each section would use only a single vowel, omitting the other four. He says that he had to read through the *Third Webster's International Dictionary* a total of five times, transcribing all of the single-vowelled words and arranging them into lists according to parts of speech and topics 'in an effort to determine what stories the vowels might actually permit.' He introduced several other constraints (each chapter had to allude to writing and to describe 'a culinary banquet, a prurient debauch, a pastoral tableau and a nautical voyage') and called the whole sequence 'Eunoia', a word he found in medical dictionaries. (It literally means 'well mind'; that is, the normal state of a healthy mind. Bök, pointing to its Greek etymology, defines it as 'beautiful thinking'.) Eunoia is also the shortest English word using all five vowels.

It took Bök over seven years to complete the sequence, which he published in 2001 as part of *Eunoia*. That book contains a second and complementary sequence called 'Oiseau' (the shortest French word that uses all five vowels), with more poems that play with words and the letters that compose them, including 'And Sometimes'—a poem made up of every English word that does not contain *a, e, i, o,* or *u*—and the playful anagrams of 'Vowels' (reprinted here).

In an afterword called 'The New Ennui', Bök says of the composition of 'Eunoia': 'The text makes a Sisyphean spectacle of its labour, wilfully crippling its language in order to show that, even under such improbable conditions of duress, language can still express an uncanny, if not sublime, thought.' Despite the difficulties inherent in its formal experimental nature, *Eunoia* became the best-selling book of poetry in Canadian literary history and received considerable praise from the literary establishment, winning a Griffin Prize for Poetry. (A new edition of *Eunoia*, with additional poems, appeared in 2009.)

Bök sees it as his duty to challenge the Canadian literary and poetic establishment. Attracted to experimental fiction, as well as to experimental poetry and critical writing, he edited an anthology entitled *Ground Works: Avant-Garde for Thee* in 2003 (Margaret Atwood provided an introduction), which traces Canadian avant-garde fiction and poetry from Leonard Cohen's *Beautiful Losers* and Michael Ondaatje's *The Collected Works of Billy the Kid.*

Bök has been part of the creative-writing faculty at the University of Calgary since 2005. His continuing interest in sound poetry is evident in his work-in-progress, *The Cyborg Opera*, which he describes as 'a kind of "spoken techno" that emulates the robotic pulses heard everywhere in our daily lives.' (Performances of this and other of Bök's sound poems can be viewed on YouTube.) He has also created artificial languages for the television series *Earth: Final Conflict* and *Peter Benchley's Amazon*. His visual art makes use of 'found' objects such as Rubik's cubes and Lego blocks. One of these, *Ten Maps of Sardonic Wit*, is a book created—spine, cover, pages, and words—from thousands of Lego bricks, with each page displaying, in mosaic, a line of poetry. Each of these lines is anagrammatically derived from the letters in the title of the work. In addition, Bök says he is now attempting to genetically encode a poem into an extremophile (a micro-organism adapted to living under extreme conditions), remarking, 'Because of the microbe's endurance, the poem may well outlast humanity—and perhaps even the planet itself. . . . Poetry, in one form or another, will go on forever.'

# Crystals

A crystal is an atomic tessellation, a tridimensional
jigsaw puzzle in which every piece is the same shape.

A crystal assembles itself out of its own constituent
disarray: the puzzle puts itself together, each piece
falling as though by chance into its correct location.

A crystal is nothing more
than a breeze blowing sand
into the form of a castle
or a film played backwards
of a window being smashed.

A compound (word) dissolved in a liquid
supercooled under microgravitational
conditions precipitates out of solution
in (alphabetical) order to form crystals
whose structuralistic perfection rivals
the beauty of machine-tooled objects.

An archaeologist without any mineralogical
experience
might easily mistake a crystal
for the artificial product of a precision
technology.

A word is a bit of crystal in formation

c r y s t a l s

                a
            s
        r
                a
                    l


                    s
                a
                    l
                t



        c
                a
            s
                t



                    a
                s
                t
            r
                    a
        y

1994; rev. 2003

# From *Eunoia*

## Chapter O

*for Yoko Ono*

Loops on bold fonts now form lots of words for books. Books form cocoons of comfort—tombs to hold bookworms. Profs from Oxford show frosh who do post-docs how to gloss works of Wordsworth. Dons who work for proctors or provosts do not fob off school to work on crosswords, nor do dons go off to dorm rooms to loll on cots. Dons go crosstown to look for bookshops known to stock lots of top-notch goods: cookbooks, workbooks—room on room of how-to books for jocks (how to jog, how to box), books on pro sports: golf or polo. Old colophons on schoolbooks from schoolrooms sport two sorts of logo: oblong whorls, rococo scrolls—both on worn morocco.

10

Monks who vow to do God's work go forth from donjons of monkhood to show flocks lost to God how God's word brooks no crooks who plot to do wrong. Folks who go to Sodom kowtow to Moloch, so God drops H-bombs of horror onto poor townsfolk, most of whom mock Mormon proofs of godhood. Folks who do not follow God's norms word for word woo God's scorn, for God frowns on fools who do not conform to orthodox protocol. Whoso honors no cross of dolors nor crown of thorns doth go on, forsooth, to sow worlds of sorrow. Lo! No Song of Solomon comforts Job or Lot, both of whom know for whom gongs of doom doth toll. Oh, *mondo doloroso.*

20

Porno shows folks lots of sordor—zoom-shots of Bjorn
Borg's bottom or Snoop Dogg's crotch. Johns who don
condoms for blowjobs go downtown to Soho to look for
pornshops known to stock lots of lowbrow schlock—                    30
off-color porn for old boors who long to drool onto
color photos of cocks, boobs, dorks or dongs. Homos
shoot photos of footlong schlongs. Blond trollops who
don go-go boots flop pompoms nonstop to do promos
for floorshows. Wow! Hot blonds who doff cotton
frocks show off soft bosoms. Hot to trot, two blonds
who smooch now romp on cold wood floors for crowds
of morons, most of whom hoot or howl: *whoop, whoop.*

Blond showfolk who do soft porn go to boomtowns to
look for work on photo shoots. Molls who hobnob from               40
mob boss to mob boss croon solos from old torchsongs.
Molls who do so do so *molto sordo*—too slow for most
crowds to follow, so most crowds scoff: *boo, boo.* Folks
who do not know how to plot common chords for rock
songs or folk songs soon look for good songbooks on
how to do so. Folks too cool to go to sock hops go to
Woodstock rock shows to do pot, not to foxtrot to
Motown rondos of pop, bop or doo-wop. Congo bongos
throb to voodoo hoodoo; tom-toms for powwows go
*boom, boom.* Gongs go *bong.* Kotos go *bonk.* Horns          50
honk: *toot, toot.*

Folks from Kokomo do lots of shrooms (not snow, not
blow—no form of hops). Folks who long to prolong
moods of torpor do Zoloft or nod off on two drops of
chloroform. Goofs who goof off go off to poolrooms to
jolt down lots of good strong bock from Coors or Stroh.
Most tosspots who toss down jolts of Grolsch do so to
drown sorrows. Poor sots, blotto on two shots of scotch,
go loco for old port or hot grog. Lots of hobos who do
odd jobs for food go off to work to work on jobs no             60
boss stoops to do—jog brooms of soot, mop floors of
loos. Old coots, known to go to grogshops for snorts of
wormwood hooch, go on to mooch dogfood from dogs.

Snobs who go to Bonn for bonbons know how to shop
for good food: go to Moncton for cod, go to Concord
for lox. Cooks who know how to cook *coq d'or* cook
*cochon d'Ormont* or *cochon d'Orloff,* not pork chops
or pork hocks. Cooks who do not know how to cook
posh food do not opt to shop for lots of tools: no
woks, spoons or forks, no pots, crocks or bowls.                    70
Cooks from Foochow or Soochow chow down on two
sorts of broth: oolong or wonton. Folks from
Stockholm scoff down bowls of borscht. Folks too
poor to chow down on *bon porc* or *coq gros* wolf
down corncobs or corndogs. Moms cook hotdogs for
tots who chomp on orts of popcorn.

Scows from London go to Moscow, not to Boston,
to drop off bolts of mothproof cloth: wool for long
johns, wool for work socks. Moors from Morocco,
not from Kowloon, go to Oporto to drop off two                     80
sorts of orlon floss (both sold to commonfolk, most
of whom know how to do clothwork on looms):
spools of cord (for hooks to hook), spools of woof
(for combs to comb). Folks who work on looms
knot knots to form cloth goods for showrooms to
show: cotton shorts or cotton smocks—lots of togs
for fops who go from shop to shop to look for
thong gowns, now worn to proms. Folks who don
ponchos for comfort don boots or clogs to go for
strolls on downtown docks.                                         90

Brown logbooks show how scows from Norfolk go
from port to port to stow on docks tons of hotchpotch
goods: tools from workrooms, props from workshops
(cogs for motors, rods for rotors)—box on box of
foolproof clocks, row on row of clockwork robots.
Scows from Toronto tow lots of logs thrown onto
pontoons: tons of softwood, tons of cordwood—block
on block of wood good for woodwork: boxwood,
bowwood, dogwood, logwood (most sorts of wood sold
to workfolks who work for old woodshops). Holds hold            100
loot from Hong Kong or gold from Fort Knox. Old
stockrooms stock lots of shopworn dross: doorknobs for
doors, lockworks for locks.

Dhows from Colombo confront monsoons—strong storms known to slosh spoom onto prows of sloops. Folks who row old scows to cross floods of froth do not row scows worn down from wood rot (for most dolts who do so go forth, shorn of control, to rock, to roll, on storm-blown bobs of cork—now blown to or fro, now blown on or off, most known plots to known ports): *whoosh, whoosh.* Moms who sob for lost sons blow conch horns to honor poor fools who, thrown from port bows, go down, down, down (*oh no*) to drown—lost for good, now food for worms. Pods of octopods swoop down onto schools of cod to look for food: *swoosh, swoosh.*

110

Cold stormfronts from snowstorms blow snow onto fjords north of Oslo. Most storms howl for months: frost snows onto woods; froth blows onto rocks. From now on, snowplows plow snow. Cool brooks flow from grottos, down oxbows, to form pools or ponds. Long fronds of moonwort, known to grow from offshoot growths of rootstock, grow on moss bogs of sod. Soft blossoms of snowdrop now bloom on moors. Soon fog, not smog, rolls off old lochs onto boondocks of phlox. Lots of frogs hop from rock to rock: 'frog, pond, plop'. Cows *moo-moo* to foghorns. Dogs *bow-wow* to moonglow. Most loons coo soft coos: *coo, coo.* Hoot owls hoot: *hoo, hoo.*

120

Brown storks flock to brooks to look for schools of smolt or schools of snook. Wolf dogs (*los lobos*) prowl woods or moors to look for spoor of woodfowl or moorfowl. Most sorts of fox go off to snoop for coops known to hold woodcocks or moorcocks. Zoos known to stock zoomorphs (crocs or komodos, coons or bonobos) show off odd fowl: condors, hoopoos, flocks of owls or loons (not flocks of rocs or dodos). Most sloths, too slow to scoot from log to log, loll on mossgrown knolls of cottonwood to chomp on bollworms. Most worms molt from soft pods of cocoons to form broods of moths (two sorts: wood moth or moon moth): *shoo, moth, shoo.*

130

140

Scots from hogtowns or cowtowns work from cock-crow to moondown—to chop down woodlots, to plow down cornrows. Folks who work from morn to noon throw down slop to hogs or corn to sows. Most workfolk who sow crops of broomcorn grow corn crops sown from lots of cowflop compost (blobs of poo or globs of goo). From two o'clock on, workfolk groom colts born of broncos. Most cowfolk who hold onto cowprods to prod two sorts of ox (shorthorn or pronghorn) flog no shod ox sold to tow oxplows. Most honchos who own lots of longhorns on hoof shoot cows known to host cowpox. Dogs growl. Hogs snort. Most rooks or crows roost on rooftops.

150

Crooks who con folks go door to door to show folks lots of books on how to boost longshot growth of hot-shot stocks or low-cost bonds. Crooks who do so fob off fool's gold onto fools. Crowds of droogs, who don workboots to stomp on downtrod hobos, go on to rob old folks, most of whom own posh co-op condos. Goons who shoot folks knock down doors, storm control rooms. Bronx cops do crowd control. Corps of shock-troops cordon off two blocks of shops to look for kooks who concoct knockoff bombs. Corps of storm-troops confront mobs of lowborn hoods, most of whom lob Molotov bombs to bomb pollbooths or tollbooths: *pow, pow—boom.*

160

170

Crowds of Ostrogoths who howl for blood go off on foot—to storm forts, to torch towns. Mongol troops, grown strong from bloodsport, loot strongholds of lords known to own tons of gold. Goths who lop off locks on doors of tombs spot no strongbox of loot—no gold, no boon—for Goths confront horrors too gross for words: gorgons from Mordor, kobolds from Chthon. Bold sons of Thor, god of storms, hold off, sword for sword, mobs of Morlocks—trolls who flood forth from bottommost worlds of rockbottom gloom. Orcs shoot bolts from crossbows. Lots of potshots, shot off from bows, mow down throngs of cohorts, most of whom swoon from loss of blood.

180

Goths who rob tombs confront old ghosts (most of whom prowl from ghost town to ghost town to spook poltroons). Lots of ghosts, who brood, forlorn, on moods of loss, howl for long-lost consorts—blond frows, sworn to honor fond vows of forsworn troth (now long forgot). Most consorts, too forlorn to long for comfort from sorrow, sob: *boohoo, boohoo*—so bozo clowns, who know not how to frown, don coxcombs, for pomp, for show, to spoof droll plots from books. Most fools who josh lords or mock snobs don hoods or cowls to do so (for wroth lords who scowl oft long to shoot folks who honor no form of snobdom). Most fools go: 'oops, ow—oh, bollocks: *ho, ho*'.

190

Troop doctors who stop blood loss from torn colons or shot torsos go to Kosovo to work pro bono for poor commonfolk, most of whom confront horrors born of long pogroms. Good doctors who go to post-op to comfort folks look for sponsors to sponsor downtrod POWs from Lvov or Brno. Good doctors do months of work on blood flow to show how no form of pox (no protozoon, no sporozoon) clots blood from blood donors. Most Dogon, voodoo doctors, who splosh oxblood onto voodoo dolls, know how to concoct good mojo for octoroons from Togo. Folk doctors cook pots of bromo from roots of bloodwort or toothwort—common worts for common colds.

200

Profs who work for Komsomol go to Novgorod to work on robot bombs: H-bombs or N-bombs (two sorts of bloodshot horror for worlds of tomorrow). Most profs who know how to work control knobs on chronotrons shoot protons from cosmotrons to clock how long two photons glow. Orbs of phosphor throw off bolts of hot volts (googols of bosons from photoprotons of thoron). Lots of robots mold strong forms of boron for hot-rod motors (most sold to Ford, not to Volvo): *zoom, zoom—vroom*. Poof! Dots of color, blown off from blow-torch torchglow, scorch lots of moths (for moths oft bob from torch to torch). Most glowworms glow.

210

220

Profs who go to Knossos to look for books on Phobos
or Kronos go on to jot down monophthongs (*kof* or
*rho*) from two monoglot scrolls on Thoth, old god of
Copts—both scrolls torn from hornbooks, now grown
brown from mold. Profs who gloss works of Woolf,
Gogol, Frost or Corot look for books from Knopf:
*Oroonoko* or *Nostromo*—not *Hopscotch* (nor *Tlooth*).    230
Profs who do schoolwork on Pollock look for
photobooks on Orozco or Rothko (two tomfools who
throw bold colors, blotch on blotch, onto tondos of
dropcloth). Log onto Hotbot dotcom to look for
books on who's who or wot's wot (for books of *bons
mots* show folks lots of mottos to follow). How now
brown cow.

## Vowels

loveless vessels

we vow
solo love

we see
love solve loss

else we see
love sow woe

selves we woo
we lose

losses we levee                    10
we owe

we sell
loose vows

so we love
less well

so low
so level

wolves evolve

2001

# Michael Redhill

## b. 1966

Highly versatile, Michael Redhill is a successful poet, playwright, novelist, short-story writer, editor, blogger, and occasional journalist. Born of a Canadian mother and British father, he moved to Canada as an infant after his physician father completed his residency at a hospital in Baltimore, Maryland. He grew up in Toronto, and attended Indiana University in 1985–6, before moving to York University to study film. He eventually took a BA in English at the University of Toronto in 1992. From 1993 to 1996, he served on the editorial board of Coach House Books. In 1998, he became co-editor, with Michael Ondaatje, Linda Spalding, and Esta Spalding, of the literary magazine *Brick*; since 2003, he has also been the magazine's publisher. From 2005 to 2007, he taught creative writing at the University of Toronto's Scarborough campus. He spent the next two years writing in France, returning to Canada in 2009 with his wife and two children. In 2010 he was writer-in-residence at the University of Toronto.

Redhill is the author of six books of poetry. He self-published the first of these, *Music for Silence*, in 1985, while still an undergraduate. His later poetry books include *Lake Nora Arms* (1993; it was also performed on stage in 1996), *Asphodel* (1997), and *Light-Crossing* (2001). In 1991, he co-edited, with Stephen Heighton and Peter Ormshaw, *A Discord of Flags*, an anthology of Canadian poets protesting the first Persian Gulf War. He is also the editor of *Blues & True Concussions: Six New Toronto Poets* (1996).

Beginning with a one-act play at the Toronto Fringe Festival in 1991, Redhill has written a number of dramatic works—four have been published. One of these, *Building Jerusalem* (produced in 1996; published in 2001), won both Dora and Chalmers Awards. Taking place on New Year's Eve, 1899, it invites us to consider the future of Toronto from the perspective of the past. His most recent play, *Goodness*, is a moving treatment of genocide in the modern world. First produced and published in 2005, it won the Carol Tambor Prize as the best play at the Edinburgh Festival in Scotland and was performed in Rwanda in 2009.

Redhill has shown himself no less skilled in his fiction, which has been highly praised. His first novel, *Martin Sloane* (2001), told from a woman's point of view, turns around the enigmatic figure of an artist with whom the narrator begins a love affair. Martin Sloane makes art by assembling object-filled boxes that, while drawing on events from his personal life, have the aesthetic power to suggest larger meanings. His abrupt and troubling disappearance from the narrator's life shows us how one person can be powerfully attracted to another without understanding that individual's inner life.

The relationship between art and life is again important in Redhill's second novel, *Consolation* (2006). This novel comprises two intertwined stories, one that takes place in contemporary Toronto in the wake of a suicide and one that unfolds in the nineteenth century. The older story, we discover, can, in its narrative ordering, give meaning to that lost life in the contemporary world and offer consolation to those who remain.

The title of Redhill's collection of short fiction, *Fidelity* (2003), suggests that the stories are in some way about faithfulness—but it might be more accurate to say they show fidelity as a difficult virtue. 'The Flesh Collectors', reprinted here, also offers a commentary on the meaning of religious faithfulness and the role belief plays in the life of the individual. This comic and sometimes bawdy story (which, as the name of the central character suggests, is in part an homage to the American writer, Philip Roth, and, thus, to the North American Jewish tradition) traces out the tensions between the ancient rules of orthodoxy and the compromises that the contemporary world demands. Are the customary beliefs of one's religion meant to be taken literally—or, as Roth's rabbi suggests, can they be understood as metaphors?

# The Flesh Collectors

By forty-eight, Roth had had his midlife crisis, four children, and three wives, the last of whom was still interested in sex, but not in having babies, and who had developed a serious allergy to latex. It was bad enough that they were still using condoms at their ages (although, granted, Sybil was eight years younger than he and could still, theoretically, reproduce), but his wife had ruled out having any part of her body removed for the purposes of pleasure, since she believed, like most Jews, that it was crucial to go to the grave whole, or else when the Messiah came you might be walking around for eternity lacking a crucial component. A missing appendix was forgivable, and certainly anything that had to be shed for life-saving reasons was as well, just as it was not a sin to drink water on Yom Kippur if you had to take medication. 'Doctor's orders,' you'd hear someone saying in the synagogue hallway, pushing some capsule to the back of their throat and drinking long and deep from the fountain between the bathrooms.

The pill was absolutely out as well for Sybil, not because it was forbidden, but rather because it was apt to make her behave like a drugged monkey. Roth had often argued that some discomfort in the service of a happy marriage was an obligation to a good husband or wife, but Sybil had turned this argument against him. This was why Roth was staring down the possibility that he would soon have to submit a tender part of himself to a surgeon's knife. Such an operation would leave him whole—it was more a sundering than a deletion—and so, in the sense intended by the ancients, his options were considerably less fraught than hers.

His GP, Arnold Gravesend, told him that vasectomies, in this day and age, were twenty-minute affairs and didn't even have to be done by scalpel. Still, the prospect of having this part of his body interfered with made Roth woozy. He'd been delaying for months now, and Sybil was withholding connubially and building a wifely case against him. 'I don't feel like breaking out into a yeast infection every time, Nathan. We're not newlyweds anymore. If you care about our marriage, you'll do what you have to do.'

In principle, Roth agreed. To his own thinking, condoms provided biblical loopholes for people who were otherwise happy to follow the laws. His rabbi, Stern of Beth Israel, said that condoms did not release their users from the burden of sin. It was still spilling semen in vain,[1] said Rabbi Stern. The good Jewish couple knows when the woman is in season and takes advantage accordingly.

Roth had relaxed his own strictures as he'd got older. With Adele, his first wife, he didn't even sleep in the bed with her when she was in cycle (a holdover of custom from his orthodox upbringing, even though he considered himself conservative now), but after they'd divorced he decided to be more 'humane', as the therapist had put it to him, back when there was a chance to save the marriage. There was no sense in treat-

---

1 This story turns around two beliefs associated with Orthodox Judaism. The first, alluded to here, is based on Genesis 38, which tells the story of how Onan is punished by God because—unwilling to perform what was then the custom of fathering a child with his deceased brother's widow—he practises withdrawal to prevent conception. This passage has been interpreted as meaning that God will punish a man for 'spilling the seed' and, thus, as forbidding both male masturbation and any form of barrier contraception. The second belief, referred to in the opening paragraph, is that, in preparation for the physical resurrection of the body anticipated when the messiah comes, 'it was crucial to go to the grave whole'—meaning that even amputated parts should be preserved for burial.

ing the person you loved as an opportunity *not* to sin if it meant hurting their feelings for one week out of every four. This was excellent advice, and his second marriage, to a dark-eyed beauty named Lila he'd met at a bazaar, would have lasted for life if she hadn't died. 'The Cancer', Lila's mother had called it, as if there had been only one cancer in the whole world and it struck her daughter. At the funeral, she'd keened over and over again, *Why did we name her for the night?* 'Lila' was Hebrew for night, a time when Roth's soul was always calm.

Sybil was a North Toronto woman. Not exotic, and street- rather than booksmart, but for Roth, it was time to slow down anyway and to lead a simpler life. Everything but his sexual urges, which frequently troubled him, had come to a better balance. He'd blown his relationships with his first two children, from Adele, but the last two, with Lila, were still growing up and hadn't yet learned to view him as an old fool. (That he wasn't old, not really, was of no consequence to the first two, to whom he suspected he'd been old since he was thirty.) As time went on, Roth seemed to fill with more love for his own children than he'd ever thought he could feel, and there was still a chance to hold Lila's and his children in the goodness of this love. These two still lived with him, ten-year-old Mitchell and his younger sister Sarah. Roth was all they had of their mother. They treated Sybil like an intruder and took his side in everything.

'Are you going to your doctor?' Sybil had asked at breakfast.

'Are you sick, Daddy?'

He was going to reply to his son, but Sybil turned her moisturized face toward the child and said, 'There is nothing wrong with your father that can't be fixed in ten minutes.'

'Is this the snip-snip?'

His sister, her spoon dripping with milk coloured by her cereal, looked up with her eyes creased. 'What's the snip-snip?' she asked.

'I'm perfectly healthy, you guys,' Roth said. 'There's nothing wrong with me. And we don't use words like "snip-snip" at the kitchen table.'

'I can't remember the real word,' said the boy.

Sybil collected her and Roth's plates and lay them in the sink. She didn't do dishes. The girl did the dishes. Roth hated having a maid, especially one that didn't live with them. It seemed to strip the position of any residual dignity it may have had, by forcing her to show up every morning to sweep through the house, and return every evening to whatever cramped squalor she no doubt lived in. 'Vasectomy', said Sybil. The word caused a metallic wave of energy to run down Roth's spine, as if every bone in his body had been rubbed with aluminum foil.

'What is *that*?' said Sarah with disgust.

'It means Daddy won't be able to make a baby anymore,' he said.

'Why?'

Sybil ruffled the little girl's thin black hair. 'Because step-mummy doesn't want any kids.'

'Oh,' said his daughter. He'd already told her and Mitchell how reproduction worked. Rabbi Stern said it was all right to be explicit with children, as long as they were aware that the mysteries of sex were more important than its mechanics. Always foreground the wonders of the great fabric of life, said Stern. Roth had sought his advice less and less in recent years. *I've had divorce and death*, he thought. *It sounds like God's already made up his vast mind about me.*

When he'd sat down to talk with the children, he did so without the aid of a book or pen and paper. He simply told them the raw facts. What happened in the man's body, in the woman's. How it actually worked, sex. And after. The baby, inside, growing. They were fascinated. This was when Lila was still alive. It was the four of them, inviolate. The children got used to the fact that their parents had touched in that way. It made them all magical.

Now they considered that their father did much the same thing with their stepmother. Mitchell had some sense that it was not just for making children, and the snip-snip confirmed this. Their father wanted to stop having children for good, but he still wanted to put his penis inside their stepmother's vagina. Something else must be going on, thought the boy, like a hidden level in a video game.

Roth and Sybil got the children ready for the bus and saw them off up at the corner. She linked her arm in his. 'I'm sorry,' she said.

'What for.'

'This whole operation thing makes you uncomfortable, and I'm being pushy. Forgive me. If you do it, you'll do it when you're ready, and from now on, I'll be *schtum*.'[2]

'*Schtum* and you have never been that close, Sybil. But thank you. I am going to do it, though. I will.'

'I know you will,' she said, and she squeezed his arm tight to her body. 'Then you can have me at the drop of a hat, Mr. Roth.'

He had to admit, there was an imperishable upside to the whole thing, and that was the thought of the entire garden of Sybil's body, open at all hours. He'd always been able to admit to himself that where his relationships were concerned, lust had always been a factor. Even the dourest rabbis of history would have told you no man or woman marries for the mere sake of a likeness of mind or spirit. How else to make you 'as numerous as the stars in the heavens'?[3] Such a covenant could not be accomplished without giving men and women the benefit of appetites. Roth had never had it in short supply. For a man whose external life had been as dull as the need for money can make it (he operated a company called Storage Solutions), his true life, his inner life, was lush. With Adele it had perhaps been wasted a little: the impatience and artlessness of youth. But with Lila. They'd worn the hinges off each other. Unlike many of the women he'd known then, she didn't care for the strictest of the laws, and she wore jeans and T-shirts. She dressed for comfort. Seeing her walking around the house in the uniform of the pagan world inflamed Roth terribly. He thought it was pathetic that something as banal as blue-jeans could do this to him, but desire blossoms in forbidden soil.

---

2 Yiddish: 'quiet'.

3 In Genesis 15 and 17, God's promises the then-childless Abraham that he will have descendants as numerous as the stars; in Deuteronomy 1:10, Moses tells his followers that the fulfilment of this promise is one of the several blessings God has bestowed upon them. As Roth later observes, Judaism regards having children as a *mitzvah*, a blessing.

He imagined that the sight of the tip of a woman's nose would have a similar effect on his Moslem brethren. As long as husband and wife could be kind to each other, the prohibited was the seedbed of passion.

Roth's uncertainty about his options (he would never have used the word *bewilderment*) brought him to Beth Israel, to see Rabbi Stern. Roth had long since given up on making sense of the many laws that were to govern his life and his behaviour. These things had been drummed into him as a child, which was part of the reason he had strayed, although straying from orthodoxy to conservativism was a deviation on the order of dark rye to light. In any case, much of what he once thought he knew was now so much clutter in his mind. Stern had admonished him about his confusion many times: Roth was dangerously close to leading an unguided—and therefore impious—life.

Stern's study at the temple was cluttered and dark. Only a fish tank that took up one whole wall provided a useful light. Going into the Rabbi's office was like descending into an underground exhibit, with its blue glow and its undulating creatures moving back and forth behind glass.

'Sybil wants me to have a vasectomy,' said Roth once he'd sat down.

'You have a problem with this?'

'No, not really.' The rabbi unwrapped a candy and left the silvery paper on the tabletop. He waited for Roth. 'My problem is that I've had three wives. How do I know this is the last one? What if I need—?'

'What if you need your *sperm*?'

'Yes.'

'Mmm,' said Stern. 'You love Sybil?'

'Yes.'

'So? Have a vasectomy. You're almost fifty, Nathan; Sybil's almost forty. It's over for children.'

Roth nodded. It wasn't really about loving Sybil, though. It was about the future, and what it might want from him. What if, one day, it wanted him to start over, not as a husband, but as a father? What if he blew it this time too, with Mitchell and Sarah? 'What if I *want* more children, though?' he said.

The rabbi leaned forward. He regarded Roth as one would look into a cloudy puddle, to judge its depth. 'What are you thinking, Nathan?'

'I want to save some of my sperm. In case.'

'You can't do that.'

'Why.'

Stern lifted his large hands off the table and let them drop back down. The noise startled Roth; they made a sound like two mallets falling. 'Either you commit the sin of Onan, or you commit adultery—and not just a garden variety adultery my friend—one you're *planning*. This is like the same difference between first- and second-degree murder.'

'I thought it was a *mitzvah* to have children, Rabbi. To repopulate the land.'

Stern extended a hand toward Roth as if it held an offering. 'Here, Nathan. You go to some place that will freeze your sperm, and if that sperm is not used to make a baby, then you've spilled it in vain. *But*—' and here he held out the other hand '—let's say you *intend* to make a baby with that sperm. We already know it's not going any-where near Sybil. Correct?'

'Yes.'

'*So*, this sperm is intended for *another* woman. That's your premeditated sin, Roth. This is not good.'

Roth stood up then, irritated enough to raise his voice. 'Look—'

'—sit down,' said the rabbi.

'Can't you just advise me as a man? Either I do this thing that makes me a bad per-son, or I go crazy. You tell me.'

'Don't do it, Nathan,' said Stern. 'It's not for me to tell you to go flush your soul down the toilet so you can have your cake and eat it too.' He stared at Roth a moment, blinking. 'You know what I mean.'

Sweat slicked Roth's back. What had he thought the man was going to tell him, anyway? He shook the rabbi's hand.

'You've made up your mind?'

'I don't know,' said Roth.

Is there much difference, Roth wondered, between a person who is interested in your money and one who is interested in your soul? Should you automatically assume that the second person is looking out for you? From his years of working in a retail envi-ronment, Roth was sure he knew a great many more fulfilled people among those who had placed their faith in business, rather than in God. Money had a reassuring finite-ness to it; money didn't get ambiguous or allegorical on you. And although he under-stood, abstractly, that money was a metaphor, it was still true that if something cost ten dollars and you had ten dollars, you could have it. It didn't seem to work that way in the Kingdom of Heaven. The news from up there was that through hard work and application you could ruin your first marriage, but then you could have a second chance, and you could even have two more lovely children and do it right this time. But then you could lose it all over again. If you invested your soul at ten per cent com-pounded over fifty years, you could still have nothing in the end.

Roth knew that this kind of talk was just some bitter kind of Hebraic stand-up routine that looped through the mind of anyone who'd lost something or someone important to them. It went all the way back to the Tribes of Israel in the desert outside of Egypt, when God said, *Guess what? You're not slaves no more. Congratulations. Oh, by the way, did I mention the desert? Forty years only, without nothing to eat except crackers and scorpions? I thought maybe I didn't say the desert part.*[4] No doubt that when they finally got there—the Land of Milk and Honey—half got diarrhea from the milk, and the other half went into anaphylactic shock from the honey. No, blind faith was a bad thing, and perhaps the elders were just elders, a little confused from centuries of try-ing to figure out the worth of an oxen. Roth was smart to go it alone.

4 In his comic retelling of Exodus, Roth freely paraphrases the story by calling the unleavened bread that the Jews took with them when they fled into the desert 'crackers' and by describing the journey through 'that great and terrible wilderness, wherein were fiery serpents, and scorpions, and drought' (Deuteronomy 8:1) as if the Jews had been forced to eat the scorpions.

As it was, he'd already had the advice of the vasectomist. He'd made and actually kept an appointment some weeks earlier. He'd gone to the doctor's office, out in the east end, and kept his eyes down in the waiting room filled with other men. There was a receptionist whose hair was the only thing that showed over the countertop. The sound of unread pages being turned was the only noise in the place, except for the occasional invitation to someone to go see the doctor. Then they'd come out and huddle over the desk with the secretary, and most of them, at one point, would offer a nervous laugh, then take their coat and leave.

When it was his turn, Roth went in and sat in the doctor's private office. It had all the soothing ornaments a doctor's office is supposed to have: the signed documents, the wood panelling, the framed pictures with their backs turned like embarrassed party guests. The only thing out of place was the big plastic testicle on the doctor's desk. This he used to demonstrate the brief, painless procedure with the brief, only slightly uncomfortable recovery period. Roth tried to pay attention to the big nut with its removable layers and tubes, but all he could hear the doctor say, at least three times, was, 'Then we make a very small incision here.'

'I thought there was a method that didn't require an incision,' said Roth.

'Well, some doctors use a puncture method that's more like making a little hole through which the vas deferens is extracted, but it's essentially the same thing, Mr. Roth. You have to get into the scrotum somehow, and from there it's a cruel cut no matter how you look at it.' He'd taken the top layer off to show the blue vas deferens beneath, and now he pulled the vas apart in the middle. It split into two with a neat little *click*.

Roth nodded. 'I see.'

'Do you have any more questions?'

'Can it be reversed?'

The doctor sighed dramatically and looked away from Roth, tapping the denuded testicle with the tip of his pen. Roth saw now that the top of the plastic model was stippled with pen marks. 'If you are concerned with reversal, Mr. Roth, you may want to think harder about your reasons for seeking vasectomy. Are you sure they're *your* reasons? The point of a vasectomy is to take the bullets out of the chambers, so to speak. If you think you're going to want to use live ammo again, then maybe this isn't for you.'

'I just want to know what my options are.'

'Some doctors undo it,' he said curtly. 'I don't. It's not *meant* to be undone.' He brusquely reassembled the model, snapping the two ends of the vas deferens back together and covering it with the scrotal sac. 'And it's not this easy, either,' he said.

Back out at the reception, the woman gave him a nice smile and stood up.

'Will you be making an appointment, Mr. Roth?'

'Yes,' he said quietly. She looked down behind her desk and removed two sheets of paper, which she spun toward him so that he could read them. She pointed out what he needed to know with the tip of a pencil.

'No anti-inflammatories for ten days before the procedure,' she said, 'so no Aspirin or Advil, you know. Tylenol is okay.' He nodded dumbly. 'Make sure there's someone here to pick you up afterwards, and remember to bring this form—' here she brought out the second sheet '—which is a consent form you have to sign saying you understand the risks and that we don't guarantee sterility.'

'It's not guaranteed?'

'Well, it is,' she said, 'but by law we have to put that. And will you be paying for prep or would you like to prep yourself?'

'I'm sorry?' Roth said.

'Someone here can shave the area for you, at a nominal cost, or you can do it yourself.'

His mouth was dry. 'I'll do it myself.'

'Very good,' said the receptionist, folding his information and slipping it into an envelope. 'Just make sure you don't do the whole operation by accident.'

Roth laughed nervously.

It seemed to him that in all the years he'd been seeing doctors the luxury of a bedside manner was one rarely found. If you weren't really that sick, it was a quick scribble on a piece of paper and out you went, there were sicker people than you. But if you *were* truly ill, if there was no hope for you, it was worse. Dead customers are no good for any business. When Lila had taken ill, he'd been amazed at the clinical distance they encountered at their various stops on the road to her death. It had got so bad that Roth wanted to strangle some of them. *What would it cost for a little comfort?* But Lila kept herself in check. She wanted to save her strength.

Little bits of her went off regularly to be tested. Cell counts and biopsies. The children didn't understand why their mother was losing weight. She told them she was tired from the sickness and didn't need as much to eat as she did before, but Roth knew it was because they were taking her away, biopsy by biopsy. Stern had been cold comfort here as well.

'She'll go to her death half the woman she once was,' he'd complained to the rabbi. 'And you tell me it's still kosher with the *meshiach*?'[5]

'God's not going to keep Lila out of the Promised Land because she had a few operations. It doesn't work that way.'

'Then how *does* it work?'

Stern stood up then, his face dark with worry. 'Nathan, you need to go and be with her and with your children and stop worrying about the next life. She needs you.'

He was shaking. 'Do I keep everything they take out of her, Rabbi? Does it all get buried with her?'

'The cancer isn't *her*. And it's not the point, Nathan. It's a metaphor, this whole thing. You want to present yourself to God as an *entire* human being, not just a complete body. Think about it like that.'

This was what was in Roth's mind as he drove north through midtown to the clinic he'd found in the Yellow Pages. The clinic was beyond where he'd grown up, clear beyond all the Reform synagogues with their big lawns and *goyish*-looking stained-glass

---

5 Kosher refers to the preparation of foods in accord with the dietary laws, but the word is often used casually, as here, to mean anything that does not violate one's rules; '*meshiach*': messiah.

windows. It was in a strip of offices beside a tennis club, a non-descript building with a sign on the door that said simply, FDS Technologies.

There was no one in this waiting room, and the secretary sat at a desk, where it was easy to make eye contact.

'Mr. Roth,' she said. He was right on time. She stood up and came around the desk to shake his hand. 'Why don't I take your jacket and you can fill out a few forms. Then we'll go in.'

He took the forms from her and sat. He couldn't imagine how he was going to provide a sample; there was nothing about the place that made it likely. The lady took the clipboard back from him after she saw him sign it.

'It's two hundred dollars the first year and seventy-five for every year afterwards. That's for one vial. It's half-price for every vial after that.'

'How many vials do most people give?'

'Oh, that's a personal decision, Mr. Roth. Some people give two or three, and some even come back after that and give a few more. It's whatever you think you'll need, and whatever you're comfortable with.'

The image of the back rooms behind her desk filled with men on return visits filled Roth with disgust. Did some people treat this as a hobby? This last-ditch, strip-mall, storage facility? At least the place he ran had pretty signage and he could look his customers in the eye. 'I think I'll just be doing the one.'

'All right then.'

'It's in case of . . .' He hunted in his wallet for a credit card. 'I probably won't ever need it.'

'If you ever get to the point where you want us to dispose of the vial, we do that at no extra charge.'

'Can somebody else use it?'

'I'm not sure what you mean, Mr. Roth.'

'Maybe for medical research. Or for a couple who can't have one on their own.'

'We can't pass along unwanted specimens, I'm sorry. You can have it back if you choose, but otherwise we destroy it.'

This information sent Roth into a strange revery, this notion that he could have his own sperm back. He imagined himself, perhaps twenty years down the road, a vasectomized man about sixteen hundred dollars out-of-pocket, finally returning to FDS Technologies to reclaim his specimen, and then onward to one of the doctors in town who actually did reversals, where he'd have his tubes reconnected and his own sperm put back into his own testicles. How he'd laugh at the rabbi then. *Who's a sinner now, Stern?*

'Mr. Roth,' the receptionist repeated. 'If you'll come with me?'

He followed the woman down a hall of doorways. To the clinic's credit, they had not decorated the walls with pictures. What do you put on a wall in such a place? Everything could be taken the wrong way.

The woman was approaching a door with a blue plastic tag on it. She turned it around on its hook to its red side and opened the door with a key. 'For your privacy, Mr. Roth, the lock on the other side of this door, once you turn it, locks the room from the inside. So you can relax knowing there is no way that anyone can enter.'

She pushed the door open and they went inside. There was a single bed and a La-Z-Boy chair, in a space that looked like a very nice bachelor apartment. There was a bookshelf with a few books on it (no erotic masterpieces, noted Roth, seeing the names Deighton and King), and there were a couple of cabinets and a television hanging from a steel pole in the ceiling. The receptionist put a glass vial down on a desk beside the door.

'Now, this room is yours, Mr. Roth, for as long as you like. In that cabinet over there—' she pointed to the space below the television '—are some items you may feel you need, and many men do use them, so please feel free. Don't be embarrassed. This is the business we're in and the thing we really want is a good, healthy specimen to be put aside and kept for future use, so it's important to relax and let your body do what it knows how to do. That's the way you get your money's worth. Now, some men prefer to take a nap and take advantage of one of those wonderful things about their physiology, and just do what they need to do as soon as they wake up. This is why we ask you to come in when you've got at least five free hours—that way you can nap if you like.'

Roth listened carefully, nodding as if someone were telling him how to operate a new and interesting machine. He felt curiously empty, as though he'd somehow signed away all his worldly possessions and he was the only thing that remained of his life. The receptionist was explaining that there were normal television channels and normal books, everything you might need to feel that you're on a little vacation. She held out her hand and Roth took it with a fixed smile.

'Most men laugh when I say good luck, but good luck.' Roth broadened his smile. 'To get to the last thing, the actual placement of the specimen, we really do recommend that you use one of the sterilized condoms that you'll find in the drawer beside the bed and only worry about getting the specimen into the bottle once you've got it. So don't get all knotted up over the mechanics of aiming or anything like that. All right, then?'

Roth was still holding the woman's hand. 'All right,' he said, and she went out and he turned the big silver lock to the left and stood alone in the quaint, anonymous room.

A half-hour later, Roth lay under the covers in the little bed, thinking maybe he'd drowse. He'd told Rachel, his manager, that he was not going to be available all afternoon owing to the fact that he was having minor day surgery, something to do with his dermatologist and some liquid nitrogen. Sybil never called him at work, so there was little worry that he'd later have to square anything with her. At the very least, he wouldn't have to square the details, since Rachel hadn't asked for any, dermatological procedures being the kind of thing people were not so naturally curious about.

He had spent the better part of twenty minutes utterly failing to accomplish something he'd been doing successfully since before his bar mitzvah. The banal fantasies he'd called to action lacked any erotic dimension, and he'd lain in the bed feeling squalidly lonesome. His imaginings had segued within five minutes to a fantasy in which he was in front of a Russian firing squad, his pants around his ankles, and he would be shot if he did not bring himself to orgasm. This was an involving fantasy, but it had no power to bring about the required reaction, so he'd stopped altogether. So far his experience at FDS Technologies (*A Public Company*, he'd noted on the form he had to fill out) had veered between horror and despair.

Beside the bed was an array of switches, and he experimented with them until one dropped the room into darkness. Being less aware of where he was might help, he thought, and he settled himself down into the bed again. In the jet darkness, he couldn't see anything at all, but he was suddenly more aware of the workings of the building: the air being shuttled from one space to the next, overhead lights somewhere near, coolly buzzing, and even conversation, distant and with a hollow bass-line, maybe even in the restaurant three doors down from where he was. Nevertheless, he closed his eyes and focused, and began to build himself an imaginary woman. She was wearing a one-piece red bathing suit and her legs were oiled with lotion. The straps coming off her shoulders barely contained her breasts. She was darkly tanned, and her hair was raven black. Roth had her slip the bathing suit off, one shoulder at a time, peeling it over her chest and down her belly. She gracefully brought out one foot and then the other, gestures that he found stirring. Then she stood there naked in front of him, her legs open a little, one fist on a cocked hip, a sun-kissed Amazon.

She was beginning to work for him; Roth kept his eyes squeezed shut and moved a hand into place. But the moment he made contact with himself, the Amazon's breasts began to sag and the nut-brown nipples enlarged and became uneven. Her hair went sandy blonde, and dark lines appeared below her navel, rivulets of flesh that swam down toward her pubic hair. The long, thin legs thickened, and puckered flesh popped out on her thighs. Roth tracked his gaze up her body—the loved, imperfect body—and reached Lila's sad face. She was smiling at him, the smile meant to reassure him. She put her hands on his chest, spreading her fingers so that his hair sprouted between them, a forest of grey in the interstices of her long brown fingers. And she put her mouth to him, taking him in, enclosing and containing him, and he died there. She could not contain him, he could not allow that, although he had wished the best of him, the most vital parts of himself, could have done that for her.

He opened his eyes on the darkness again and fumbled for the light. The room blinked into existence around him, the sterile replica of a warm and homey space. What kind of sin was it that not only was he about to spill his seed in vain (with his luck), but that he appeared to want to commit the infidelity that Rabbi Stern had spoken of with his dead wife?

He pushed the covers back with his feet, shoving them off the bed. He was not tired enough to nap and had no faith, anyway, that he'd wake up in a state of physiological readiness, as the receptionist had so admiringly suggested.

Roth went into the bathroom and splashed some water on his face. He was surprised to see how red his cheeks were. Then he went back out and, without a pause in his step, he strode over to the cabinet under the hanging television. The items the receptionist had referred to were here, magazines printed on a paper stock much glossier than in any of the magazines he read. He dared not touch them, sharply aware of the duties they'd been pressed into by other clients of FDS Technologies. Despite their glossiness, he was not sure how easily such things wiped clean. On top of the magazines was the television converter; a thin strip of paper taped to the bottom of it said, simply, 'Channel 55'. Roth switched on the television and found it was tuned to Channel 11. Haltingly, he went up the dial, station by station, pausing on all the soap operas and the home shopping and the midday movies. He passed all the cable stations he and Sybil watched in the evenings and was surprised to see that their midday programming was just as interesting. They showed yet more of the dangerous car chases and explorations of distant ecologies that were their night-time specialties.

When he got to 54 (a channel that specialized in foreign sports), Roth paused, his eyes feeling heavy and his breathing tight, then he switched to 55. There, a bright pink surface moved rhythmically to a musical score that might have been written for a bad spy film. He knew he was looking at a body, or bodies, and after a moment he made out that the largest object on the screen was the back of a woman's leg, which she herself was holding up (he could make out her forearm at the top of the screen, tucked under the back of her knee), and therefore, following down, the expected anatomies came into view.

The camera changed angle, and now it was clear what Roth was looking at. Neither performer wore anything, although the woman still had on a pair of socks. He stared at the image, under which he could make out the repetitive sounds of the man's effort and the woman's apparent pleasure, and felt his body respond. Now he could probably do it, as long as he was quick about it and didn't think too much and didn't take his eyes off the television. This was why the La-Z-Boy was positioned the way it was, about six feet from the cabinet, since you could tilt it back and be right in the eyeline of the television. But whereas Roth could count on the bedsheets having been changed, the chair was upholstered, and nothing could compel him to sit down on it. Instead, he gingerly lowered his pants, put the converter on the floor, took a deep breath, and the man on the television withdrew himself from his partner and spilled himself in vain all over her face.

'For Christ's sake!' shouted Roth, completing some kind of sin circuit, and he reached down violently for the remote as the woman on the screen began massaging the vainly spilled fluids into her chest and neck. 'Lord, Lord,' Roth groaned, pushing the buttons to switch the images off. He pressed the power button, but nothing happened. He whacked the device against his leg in fury, stumbling backwards and wrenching his pants up. But this somehow turned up the volume so that the murmured sounds of approval coming from the woman filled the room with a low, wet growling. Roth's arms and legs went cold and he was afraid he might black out. He went right up under the television and jumped up to hit the power switch on the console, and on his second try, the converter slipped from his hand and hit the floor and the batteries spilled out. At the same moment, the channel changed as well, and Roth was looking at a news report from the Middle East.

He let his shoulders drop and he exhaled, his heart still squeezing madly inside his chest. He would not do this; he knew it now. This last moment in his life when his body might have had some role in the future had passed. He got down on the floor and started to look for the batteries, then had to sit up on his haunches to collect his air again. The sound from the television was encompassing; he was sure they could hear it three doors down. Instead of a hyperventilating woman, it was now an American newscaster's voice filling the room.

Someone had blown up a bus in Haifa. Above Roth's head, yellow tape flapped in close-up at the perimeter of the scene. The newscaster's voice numbered the casualties and reported that the work of the police had just begun. The camera closed in on the cramped space of the disaster, the shattered form of the bus at its centre, bits of red steel pointing up nakedly. The police stood outside the tape while men in green and white uniforms wandered the site, their hands protected by surgical gloves. The voice swarmed the air around Roth with its urgency, identifying the men as orthodox Jews appointed as representatives of the community, there to gather anything that looked like human remains for the sake of religious burial. They were allowed access to such disasters to do holy duty, combing with their bodies bent double the dark little spaces where someone's hand might have come to rest, where a strip of flesh might be clinging to a shard of glass like a flag. All of this went into their bags, to be blessed and returned to the earth where, at some longed-for moment in the future, the Angel of Mercy would open the graves and gather the assembly of the chosen, recreating their shattered bodies from remains.

Roth watched the scene numbly, his hands limp at his sides, his ears pulsing with the sounds of the ruined street. And as the men continued their terrible work, moving slowly back and forth over the smoking street, he realized they were calling his name, they were saying, *Roth, Roth*, over and over. They believed he was there. He was the only survivor and they were calling for him. *Roth!* they were calling. Hearing his name spoken like that made a strange kind of sense to him, and it filled his head with brightness, it made him feel like he was carrying a charge.

'I'm here,' he said quietly, standing and stepping back so they could see him. He raised his arms; the men were frantically searching for him now, shouting *Roth, can you hear us?* His face lit up with hope, it glistened, he could hear them, they must be close now. He called out to them: 'Here I am! I'm here!'

But despite answering them, they continued to look. What if they did not find him? What if he perished here, despite their efforts, what if he died under this great weight and he never again saw the children who still loved him? He would never fix then what was wrong in his life; his love would never grow to gather in his other children, the ones he'd lost, or grow to tie Sybil to him more perfectly. He would never have the chance to accept that he would grow older now, his strength would wane; here he would die at an age people would say was too young, and he didn't want that—he *was* too young, he still had much of his old vitality, he could have been a father again at this age if he'd wanted! All of this would fade from him, and he from it if the men gave up, and he cried out in desperation now, 'HERE I AM!' until finally the door behind him was forced open and a security guard stood in the verge with the woman from the reception and they called out to him over the din. But Roth could not hear them; his attention was fastened to the flesh collectors. He was waiting until one of them turned and finally saw him there and reached out a gloved hand to deliver him to safety.

2003

# Eden Robinson

## b. 1968

Born of a Haisla father and a Heiltsuk mother in the northern interior of British Columbia at the Haisla Nation Kitamaat Reserve, Victoria Lena Robinson—she changed her name to Eden when she entered university—is not the only member of her family committed to communication. Her uncle, Gordon Robinson, whose *Tales of the Kitamaat* (1956) recorded the oral stories of his people, was the first Haisla writer to be published, and her sister, Carla Robinson, is a CBC News Network host. After her BFA at the University of Victoria in 1992, Eden Robinson completed an MFA in creative writing at the University of British Columbia in 1995. The material she worked on for her master's thesis served as the starting point for her published fiction.

Robinson is drawn to both popular and literary writing. Before encountering Michael Ondaatje's *The Collected Works of Billy the Kid*, which she calls the book that most affected her life ('I've never looked at language the same way again'), her early influences were Stephen King's fiction and the nineteenth-century gothic tales of Edgar Allan Poe (whose birthday she shares). She tried to write a Harlequin romance at the beginning of her career, but realized she was working in the wrong genre when her main character 'developed an obsession with power tools and self-mutilation.' Her subsequent fiction reflects her sense that, in a world filled with the 'many horrible, horrible things that we see every day around us and on the news,' we are close to the 'darker aspects of ourselves than we'd like to think.'

Written in a plain style, the short fiction collected in *Traplines* (1996) established Robinson's reputation as a writer with a tough and powerful voice. The book, which describes young people living on the edges of both urban and rural society, opens with an image of being caught in a snare ('Dad takes the white marten from the trap') that thematically unifies the collection. In all four stories, characters face abuse and violence arising from their economic class and milieu and exacerbated by dysfunctional families and the failures of male–female relationships. In the last story ('Queen of the North', reprinted here), the protagonist's marginalized existence as a Native living on a northern reservation also contributes to her difficulties. Her nickname, 'Karaoke' (which she gained the night she drunkenly took over a karaoke machine) is more than a detail of characterization. The pop songs she sings, like the references in the story to Barbie Dolls and their accessories, Bugs Bunny, and *Star Trek*, suggests something about the way today's commercialized and corporatized society has displaced a more authentic culture, disrupting communication and distorting individual development. How to confront and convey the truth of her situation is a problem Karaoke eventually solves by creating her own displacements. *Traplines* won the Winifred Holtby Prize for the best first work of fiction in the Commonwealth.

Robinson develops the characters and relationships of 'Queen of the North' further in the novel *Monkey Beach* (2000). The short story closes when Karaoke's lover, Jimmy, and her Uncle Josh depart together on a fishing boat; the novel opens with that boat reported missing. (Because the novel is not told from Karaoke's point of view, but from that of Jimmy's sister, Lisa, readers encounter many of the same events from a different point of view. Until the end of the novel, Lisa remains ignorant of Karaoke's secret, which is gradually revealed to readers in 'Queen of the North'.) In this coming-of-age novel, Lisa recalls the events of her past—many of them traumatic. Once she realizes that she has inherited her grandmother's shamanistic powers, she understands that the red-haired 'leprechaun' that has been appearing to her is a Haisla tree spirit. (Karaoke's memory, in 'Queen of the North', of how she 'used to see leprechauns' suggests that she also has shamanistic potential.) By allowing for the possibility that such spirits may exist, along with other figures from Native beliefs—such as the trickster Raven and b'gwus (the Haisla word for the Sasquatch)—the novel portrays North American Aboriginal culture as still enduring, though obscured by contemporary trivialities such as soap operas and reality TV. *Monkey Beach* won the Ethel Wilson Fiction Prize for the best book of the year by a British Columbia resident.

In 2003, Robinson moved back to the Haisla reservation to be near her parents. Although she left the urban environment behind, she set her second novel, *Blood Sports* (2006), in Vancouver's tough and dangerous Downtown Eastside neighbourhood, a place where no redeeming culture seems available. She again returns to characters from *Traplines*—this time developing the relationship between the cousins Tom and Jeremy, who first appeared in the novella, 'Contact Sports'. In *Blood Sports*, which she characterizes as a 'dark fantasy' that, nevertheless, uses the 'stylistic conventions of social realism,' Robinson describes in detail the brutal suffering that Tom endures as a consequence of a past he cannot escape. This novel is more grim, violent, and pessimistic than *Monkey Beach*, and offers much less hope in its conclusion. Robinson, who tends to work on several projects at once, has written a draft of a sequel, while also writing short stories and poetry.

# Queen of the North

## FROG SONG

Whenever I see abandoned buildings, I think of our old house in the village, a rickety shack by the swamp where the frogs used to live. It's gone now. The council covered the whole area with rocks and gravel.

In my memory, the sun is setting and the frogs begin to sing. As the light shifts from yellow to orange to red, I walk down the path to the beach. The wind blows in from the channel, making the grass hiss and shiver around my legs. The tide is low and there's a strong rotting smell from the beach. Tree stumps that have been washed down the channel from the logged areas loom ahead—black, twisted silhouettes against the darkening sky.

The seiner[1] coming down the channel is the *Queen of the North*, pale yellow with blue trim, Uncle Josh's boat. I wait on the beach. The water laps my ankles. The sound of the old diesel engine grows louder as the boat gets closer.

Usually I can will myself to move, but sometimes I'm frozen where I stand, waiting for the crew to come ashore.

The only thing my cousin Ronny didn't own was a Barbie Doll speedboat. She had the swimming pool, she had the Barbie-Goes-to-Paris carrying case, but she didn't have the boat. There was one left in Northern Drugs, nestling between the puzzles and the stuffed Garfields, but it cost sixty bucks and we were broke. I knew Ronny was going to get it. She'd already saved twenty bucks out of her allowance. Anyway, she always got everything she wanted because she was an only child and both her parents worked at the aluminum smelter. Mom knew how much I wanted it, but she said it was a toss-up

---

1 A small boat in which fish are caught in a seine, a flat net hung vertically in the water behind the boat.

between school supplies and paying bills, or wasting our money on something I'd get sick of in a few weeks.

We had a small Christmas tree. I got socks and underwear and forced a cry of surprise when I opened the package. Uncle Josh came in just as Mom was carving the turkey. He pushed a big box in my direction.

'Go on,' Mom said, smiling. 'It's for you.'

Uncle Josh looked like a young Elvis. He had the soulful brown eyes and the thick black hair. He dressed his long, thin body in clothes with expensive labels—no Sears or Kmart for him. He smiled at me with his perfect pouty lips and bleached white teeth.

'Here you go, sweetheart,' Uncle Josh said.

I didn't want it. Whatever it was, I didn't want it. He put it down in front of me. Mom must have wrapped it. She was never any good at wrapping presents. You'd think with two kids and a million Christmases behind her she'd know how to wrap a present.

'Come on, open it,' Mom said.

I unwrapped it slowly, my skin crawling. Yes, it was the Barbie Doll speedboat.

My mouth smiled. We all had dinner and I pulled the wishbone with my little sister, Alice. I got the bigger piece and made a wish. Uncle Josh kissed me. Alice sulked. Uncle Josh never got her anything, and later that afternoon she screamed about it. I put the boat in my closet and didn't touch it for days.

Until Ronny came over to play. She was showing off her new set of Barbie-in-the-Ice-Capades clothes. Then I pulled out the speedboat and the look on her face was almost worth it.

My sister hated me for weeks. When I was off at soccer practice, Alice took the boat and threw it in the river. To this day, Alice doesn't know how grateful I was.

There's a dream I have sometimes. Ronny comes to visit. We go down the hallway to my room. She goes in first. I point to the closet and she eagerly opens the door. She thinks I've been lying, that I don't really have a boat. She wants proof.

When she turns to me, she looks horrified, pale and shocked. I laugh, triumphant. I reach in and stop, seeing Uncle Josh's head, arms, and legs squashed inside, severed from the rest of his body. My clothes are soaked dark red with his blood.

'Well, what do you know,' I say. 'Wishes do come true.'

Me and five chug buddies are in the Tamitik arena, in the girls' locker room under the bleachers. The hockey game is in the third period and the score is tied. The yells and shouting of the fans drown out the girl's swearing. There are four of us against her. It doesn't take long before she's on the floor trying to crawl away. I want to say I'm not part of it, but that's my foot hooking her ankle and tripping her while Ronny takes her down with a blow to the temple. She grunts. Her head makes a hollow sound when it bounces off the sink. The lights make us all look green. A cheer explodes from inside the arena. Our team has scored. The girl's now curled up under the sink and I punch her and kick her and smash her face into the floor.

My cuz Ronny had great connections. She could get hold of almost any drug you wanted. This was during her biker chick phase, when she wore tight leather skirts, teeny weeny tops, and many silver bracelets, rings, and studs. Her parents started coming down really hard on her then. I went over to her house to get high. It was okay to do it there, as long as we sprayed the living room with Lysol and opened the windows before her parents came home.

We toked up and decided to go back to my house to get some munchies. Ronny tagged along when I went up to my bedroom to get the bottle of Visine. There was an envelope on my dresser. Even before I opened it I knew it would be money. I knew who it was from.

I pulled the bills out. Ronny squealed.

'Holy sheep shit, how much is there?'

I spread the fifties out on the dresser. Two hundred and fifty dollars. I could get some flashy clothes or nice earrings with that money, if I could bring myself to touch it. Anything I bought would remind me of him.

'You want to have a party?' I said to Ronny.

'Are you serious?' she said, going bug-eyed.

I gave her the money and said make it happen. She asked who it came from, but she didn't really care. She was already making phone calls.

That weekend we had a house party in town. The house belonged to one of Ronny's biker buddies and was filled with people I knew by sight from school. As the night wore on, they came up and told me what a generous person I was. Yeah, that's me, I thought, Saint Karaoke of Good Times.

I took Ronny aside when she was drunk enough. 'Ronny, I got to tell you something.'

'What?' she said, blinking too fast, like she had something in her eye.

'You know where I got the money?'

She shook her head, lost her balance, blearily put her hand on my shoulder, and barfed out the window.

As I listened to her heave out her guts, I decided I didn't want to tell her after all. What was the point? She had a big mouth, and anything I told her I might as well stand on a street corner and shout to the world. What I really wanted was to have a good time and forget about the money, and after beating everyone hands down at tequila shots that's exactly what I did.

'Moooo.' I copy the two aliens on *Sesame Street* mooing to a telephone. Me and Uncle Josh are watching television together. He smells faintly of the halibut he cooked for dinner. Uncle Josh undoes his pants. 'Moo.' I keep my eyes on the TV and say nothing as he moves toward me. I'm not a baby like Alice, who runs to Mommy about everything. When it's over he'll have treats for me. It's like when the dentist gives me extra suckers for not crying, not even when it really hurts.

I could have got my scorpion tattoo at The Body Hole, where my friends went. A perfectly groomed beautician would sit me in a black-leather dentist's chair and the tattoo artist would show me the tiny diagram on tracing paper. We'd choose the exact spot on my neck where the scorpion would go, just below the hairline where my hair comes to a point. Techno, maybe some funky remix of ABBA, would blare through the speakers as he whirred the tattoo needle's motor.

But Ronny had done her own tattoo, casually standing in front of the bathroom mirror with a short needle and permanent blue ink from a pen. She simply poked the needle in and out, added the ink, and that was that. No fuss, no muss.

So I asked her to do it for me. After all, I thought, if she could brand six marks of Satan on her own breast, she could certainly do my scorpion.

Ronny led me into the kitchen and cleared off a chair. I twisted my hair up into a bun and held it in place. She showed me the needle, then dropped it into a pot of boiling water. She was wearing a crop top and I could see her navel ring, glowing bright gold in the slanting light of the setting sun. She was prone to lifting her shirt in front of complete strangers and telling them she'd pierced herself.

Ronny emptied the water into the sink and lifted the needle in gloved hands. I bent my head and looked down at the floor as she traced the drawing on my skin.

The needle was hot. It hurt more than I expected, a deep ache, a throbbing. I breathed through my mouth. I fought not to cry. I concentrated fiercely on not crying in front of her, and when she finished I lay very still.

'See?' Ronny said. 'Nothing to it, you big baby.'

When I opened my eyes and raised my head, she held one small mirror to my face and another behind me so I could see her work. I frowned at my reflection. The scorpion looked like a smear.

'It'll look better when the swelling goes down,' she said, handing me the two mirrors.

As Ronny went to start the kettle for tea, she looked out the window over the sink. 'Star light, star bright, first star—'

I glanced out the window. 'That's Venus.'

'Like you'd know the difference.'

I didn't want to argue. The skin on the back of my neck ached like it was sunburned.

I am singing Janis Joplin songs, my arms wrapped around the karaoke machine. I fend people off with a stolen switchblade. No one can get near until some kid from school has the bright idea of giving me drinks until I pass out.

Someone else videotapes me so my one night as a rock star is recorded forever. She tries to send it to *America's Funniest Home Videos*, but they reject it as unsuitable for family viewing. I remember nothing else about that night after I got my first hit of acid. My real name is Adelaine, but the next day a girl from school sees me coming and yells, 'Hey, look, it's Karaoke!'

The morning after my sixteenth birthday I woke up looking down into Jimmy Hill's face. We were squashed together in the backseat of a car and I thought, God, I didn't.

I crawled around and found my shirt and then spent the next half hour vomiting beside the car. I vaguely remembered the night before, leaving the party with Jimmy. I remembered being afraid of bears.

Jimmy stayed passed out in the backseat, naked except for his socks. We were somewhere up in the mountains, just off a logging road. The sky was misty and gray. As I stood up and stretched, the car headlights went out.

Dead battery. That's just fucking perfect, I thought.

I checked the trunk and found an emergency kit. I got out one of those blankets that look like a large sheet of aluminum and wrapped it around myself. I searched the car until I found my jeans. I threw Jimmy's shirt over him. His jeans were hanging off the car's antenna. When I took them down, the antenna wouldn't straighten up.

I sat in the front seat. I had just slept with Jimmy Hill. Christ, he was practically a Boy Scout. I saw his picture in the local newspaper all the time, with these medals for swimming. Other than that, I never really noticed him. We went to different parties.

About midmorning, the sun broke through the mist and streamed to the ground in fingers of light, just like in the movies when God is talking to someone. The sun hit my face and I closed my eyes.

I heard the seat shift and turned. Jimmy smiled at me and I knew why I'd slept with him. He leaned forward and we kissed. His lips were soft and the kiss was gentle. He put his hand on the back of my neck. 'You're beautiful.'

I thought it was just a line, the polite thing to say after a one-night stand, so I didn't answer.

'Did you get any?' Jimmy said.

'What?' I said.

'Blueberries.' He grinned. 'Don't you remember?'

I stared at him.

His grin faded. 'Do you remember anything?'

I shrugged.

'Well. We left the party, I dunno, around two, I guess. You said you wanted blueberries. We came out here—' He cleared his throat.

'Then we fucked, passed out, and now we're stranded.' I finished the sentence. The sun was getting uncomfortable. I took off the emergency blanket. I had no idea what to say next. 'Battery's dead.'

He swore and leaned over me to try the ignition.

I got out of his way by stepping out of the car. Hastily he put his shirt on, not looking up at me. He had a nice chest, buff and tan. He blushed and I wondered if he had done this before.

'You cool with this?' I said.

He immediately became macho. 'Yeah.'

I felt really shitty then. God, I thought, he's going to be a bragger.

I went and sat on the hood. It was hot. I was thirsty and had a killer headache. Jimmy got out and sat beside me.

'You know where we are?' Jimmy said.

'Not a fucking clue.'

He looked at me and we both started laughing.

'You were navigating last night,' he said, nudging me.

'You always listen to pissed women?'

'Yeah,' he said, looking sheepish. 'Well. You hungry?'

I shook my head. 'Thirsty.'

Jimmy hopped off the car and came back with a warm Coke from under the driver's seat. We drank it in silence.

'You in any rush to get back?' he asked.

We started laughing again and then went hunting for blueberries. Jimmy found a patch not far from the car and we picked the bushes clean. I'd forgotten how tart wild blueberries are. They're smaller than store-bought berries, but their flavor is much more intense.

'My sister's the wilderness freak,' Jimmy said. 'She'd be able to get us out of this. Or at least she'd know where we are.'

We were perched on a log. 'You gotta promise me something.'

'What?'

'If I pop off before you, you aren't going to eat me.'

'What?'

'I'm serious,' I said. 'And I'm not eating any bugs.'

'If you don't try them, you'll never know what you're missing.' Jimmy looked at the road. 'You want to pick a direction?'

The thought of trekking down the dusty logging road in the wrong direction held no appeal to me. I must have made a face because Jimmy said, 'Me neither.'

After the sun set, Jimmy made a fire in front of the car. We put the aluminum blanket under us and lay down. Jimmy pointed at the sky. 'That's the Big Dipper.'

'Ursa Major,' I said. 'Mother of all bears. There's Ursa Minor, Cassiopeia . . .' I stopped.

'I didn't know you liked astronomy.'

'It's pretty nerdy.'

He kissed me. 'Only if you think it is.' He put his arm around me and I put my head on his chest and listened to his heart. It was a nice way to fall asleep.

Jimmy shook me awake. 'Car's coming.' He pulled me to my feet. 'It's my sister.'

'Mmm.' Blurrily I focused on the road. I could hear birds and, in the distance, the rumble of an engine.

'My sister could find me in hell,' he said.

When they dropped me off at home, my mom went ballistic. 'Where the hell were you?'

'Out.' I stopped at the door. I hadn't expected her to be there when I came in.

Her chest was heaving. I thought she'd start yelling, but she said very calmly, 'You've been gone for two days.'

You noticed? I didn't say it. I felt ill and I didn't want a fight. 'Sorry. Should've called.'

I pushed past her, kicked off my shoes, and went upstairs.

Still wearing my smelly jeans and shirt I lay down on the bed. Mom followed me to my room and shook my shoulder.

'Tell me where you've been.'

'At Ronny's.'

'Don't lie to me. What is wrong with you?'

God. Just get lost. I wondered what she'd do if I came out and said what we both knew. Probably have a heart attack. Or call me a liar.

'You figure it out,' I said. 'I'm going to sleep.' I expected her to give me a lecture or something, but she just left.

Sometimes, when friends were over, she'd point to Alice and say, 'This is my good kid.' Then she'd point to me and say, 'This is my rotten kid, nothing but trouble. She steals, she lies, she sleeps around. She's just no damn good.'

Alice knocked on my door later.

'Fuck off,' I said.

'You've got a phone call.'

'Take a message. I'm sleeping.'

Alice opened the door and poked her head in. 'You want me to tell Jimmy anything else?'

I scrambled down the hallway and grabbed the receiver. I took a couple of deep breaths so it wouldn't sound like I'd rushed to the phone. 'Hi.'

'Hi,' Jimmy said. 'We just replaced the battery on the car. You want to go for a ride?'

'Aren't you grounded?'

He laughed. 'So?'

I thought he just wanted to get lucky again, and then I thought, What the hell, at least this time I'll remember it.

'Pick me up in five minutes.'

I'm getting my ass kicked by two sisters. They're really good. They hit solidly and back off quickly. I don't even see them coming anymore. I get mad enough to kick out. By sheer luck, the kick connects. One of the sisters shrieks and goes down. She's on the ground, her leg at an odd angle. The other one loses it and swings. The bouncer steps in and the crowd around us boos.

'My cousins'll be at a biker party. You want to go?'

Jimmy looked at me like he wasn't sure if I was serious.

'I'll be good,' I said, crossing my heart then holding up my fingers in a scout salute.

'What fun would that be?' he said, revving the car's engine.

I gave him directions. The car roared away from our house, skidding a bit. Jimmy didn't say anything. I found it unnerving. He looked over at me, smiled, then turned back to face the road. I was used to yappy guys, but this was nice. I leaned my head back into the seat. The leather creaked.

Ronny's newest party house didn't look too bad, which could have meant it was going to be dead in there. It's hard to get down and dirty when you're worried you'll stain the carpet. You couldn't hear anything until someone opened the door and the music throbbed out. They did a good job with the soundproofing. We went up the steps just as my cousin Frank came out with some bar buddies.

Jimmy stopped when he saw Frank and I guess I could see why. Frank is on the large side, six-foot-four and scarred up from his days as a hard-core Bruce Lee fan, when he felt compelled to fight Evil in street bars. He looked down at Jimmy.

'Hey, Jimbo,' Frank said. 'Heard you quit the swim team.'

'You betcha,' Jimmy said.

'Fucking right!' Frank body-slammed him. He tended to be more enthusiastic than most people could handle, but Jimmy looked okay with it. 'More time to party,' he said. Now they were going to gossip forever so I went inside.

The place was half-empty. I recognized some people and nodded. They nodded back. The music was too loud for conversation.

'You want a drink?' Frank yelled, touching my arm.

I jumped. He quickly took his hand back. 'Where's Jimmy?'

'Ronny gave him a hoot and now he's hacking up his lungs out back.' Frank took off his jacket, closed his eyes, and shuffled back and forth. All he knew was the reservation two-step and I wasn't in the mood. I moved toward the porch but Frank grabbed my hand. 'You two doing the wild thing?'

'He's all yours,' I said.

'Fuck you,' Frank called after me.

Jimmy was leaning against the railing, his back toward me, his hands jammed into his pockets. I watched him. His hair was dark and shiny, brushing his shoulders. I liked the way he moved, easily, like he was in no hurry to get anywhere. His eyes were light brown with gold flecks. I knew that in a moment he would turn and smile at me and it would be like stepping into sunlight.

In my dream Jimmy's casting a fishing rod. I'm afraid of getting hooked, so I sit at the bow of the skiff. The ocean is mildly choppy, the sky is hard blue, the air is cool. Jimmy reaches over to kiss me, but now he is soaking wet. His hands and lips are cold, his eyes are sunken and dull. Something moves in his mouth. It isn't his tongue. When I pull away, a crab drops from his lips and Jimmy laughs. 'Miss me?'

I feel a scream in my throat but nothing comes out.

'What's the matter?' Jimmy tilts his head. Water runs off his hair and drips into the boat. 'Crab got your tongue?'

This one's outside Hanky Panky's. The woman is so totally bigger than me it isn't funny. Still, she doesn't like getting hurt. She's afraid of the pain but can't back down because she started it. She's grabbing my hair, yanking it hard. I pull hers. We get stuck there, bent over, trying to kick each other, neither one of us willing to let go. My friends are laughing their heads off. I'm pissed at that but I'm too sloshed to let go. In the morning my scalp will throb and be so tender I won't be able to comb my hair. At that moment, a bouncer comes over and splits us apart. The woman tries to kick me but kicks him instead and he knocks her down. My friends grab my arm and steer me to the bus stop.

Jimmy and I lay down together on a sleeping bag in a field of fireweed. The forest fire the year before had razed the place and the weeds had only sprouted back up about a month earlier. With the spring sun and just the right sprinkling of rain, they were as tall as sunflowers, as dark pink as prize roses, swaying around us in the night breeze.

Jimmy popped open a bottle of Baby Duck. 'May I?' he said, reaching down to untie my sneaker.

'You may,' I said.

He carefully lifted the sneaker and poured in some Baby Duck. Then he raised it to my lips and I drank. We lay down, flattening fireweed and knocking over the bottle. Jimmy nibbled my ear. I drew circles in the bend of his arm. Headlights came up fast, then disappeared down the highway. We watched the fireweed shimmer and wave in the wind.

'You're quiet tonight,' Jimmy said. 'What're you thinking?'

I almost told him then. I wanted to tell him. I wanted someone else to know and not have it locked inside me. I kept starting and then chickening out. What was the point? He'd probably pull away from me in horror, disgusted, revolted.

'I want to ask you something,' Jimmy whispered. I closed my eyes, feeling my chest tighten. 'You hungry? I've got a monster craving for chicken wings.'

## BLOODY VANCOUVER

When I got to Aunt Erma's the light in the hallway was going spastic, flickering like a strobe, little bright flashes then darkness so deep I had to feel my way along the wall. I stopped in front of the door, sweating, smelling myself through the thick layer of deodorant. I felt my stomach go queasy and wondered if I was going to throw up after all. I hadn't eaten and was still bleeding heavily.

Aunt Erma lived in east Van in a low-income government housing unit. Light showed under the door. I knocked. I could hear the familiar opening of *Star Trek*, the old version, with the trumpets blaring. I knocked again.

The door swung open and a girl with a purple Mohawk and Cleopatra eyeliner thrust money at me.

'Shit,' she said. She looked me up and down, pulling the money back. 'Where's the pizza?'

'I'm sorry,' I said. 'I think I have the wrong house.'

'Pizza, pizza, pizza!' teenaged voices inside screamed. Someone was banging the floor in time to the chant.

'You with Cola?' she asked me.

I shook my head. 'No. I'm here to see Erma Williamson. Is she in?'

'In? I guess. Mom?' she screamed. 'Mom? It's for you!'

A whoop rose up. 'Erma and Marley sittin' in a tree, k-i-s-s-i-n-g. First comes lust—'

'Shut up, you social rejects!'

'—then comes humping, then comes a baby after all that bumping!'

'How many times did they boink last night!' a single voice yelled over the laughter.

'Ten!' the voices chorused enthusiastically. 'Twenty! Thirty! Forty!'

'Hey! Who's buying the pizza, eh? No respect! I get no respect!'

Aunt Erma came to the door. She didn't look much different from her pictures, except she wasn't wearing her cat-eye glasses.

She stared at me, puzzled. Then she spread open her arms.

'Adelaine, baby! I wasn't expecting you! Hey, come on in and say hi to your cousins. Pepsi! Cola! Look who came by for your birthday!'

She gave me a tight bear hug and I wanted to cry.

Two girls stood at the entrance to the living room, identical right down to their lip rings. They had different colored Mohawks though—one pink, one purple.

'Erica?' I said, peering. I vaguely remembered them as having pigtails and making fun of Mr. Rogers. 'Heather?'

'It's Pepsi,' the purple Mohawk said. 'Not, n-o-t, Erica.'

'Oh,' I said.

'Cola,' the pink-Mohawked girl said, turning around and ignoring me to watch TV.

'What'd you bring us?' Pepsi said matter-of-factly.

'Excuse the fruit of my loins,' Aunt Erma said, leading me into the living room and sitting me between two guys who were glued to the TV. 'They've temporarily lost their manners. I'm putting it down to hormones and hoping the birth control pills turn them back into normal human beings.'

Aunt Erma introduced me to everyone in the room, but their names went in one ear and out the other. I was so relieved just to be there and out of the clinic I couldn't concentrate on much else.

'How is he, Bones?' the guy on my right said, exactly in synch with Captain Kirk on TV. Captain Kirk was standing over McCoy and a prone security guard with large purple circles all over his face.

'He's dead, Jim,' the guy on my left said.

'I wanna watch something else,' Pepsi said. 'This sucks.'

She was booed.

'Hey, it's my birthday. I can watch what I want.'

'Siddown,' Cola said. 'You're out-voted.'

'You guys have no taste at all. This is crap. I just can't believe you guys are watching this—this cultural pabulum. I—'

A pair of panties hit her in the face. The doorbell rang and the pink-haired girl held the pizza boxes over her head and yelled, 'Dinner's ready!'

'Eat in the kitchen,' Aunt Erma said. 'All of youse. I ain't scraping your cheese out of my carpet.'

Everyone left except me and Pepsi. She grabbed the remote control and flipped through a bunch of channels until we arrived at one where an announcer for the World Wrestling Federation screamed that the ref was blind.

'Now this,' Pepsi said, 'is entertainment.'

By the time the party ended, I was snoring on the couch. Pepsi shook my shoulder. She and Cola were watching Bugs Bunny and Tweety.

'If we're bothering you,' Cola said. 'You can go crash in my room.'

'Thanks,' I said. I rolled off the couch, grabbed my backpack, and found the bathroom on the second floor. I made it just in time to throw up in the sink. The cramps didn't come back as badly as on the bus, but I took three Extra-Strength Tylenols anyway. My pad had soaked right through and leaked all over my underwear. I put on clean clothes and crashed in one of the beds. I wanted a black hole to open up and suck me out of the universe.

When I woke, I discovered I should have put on a diaper. It looked like something had been hideously murdered on the mattress.

'God,' I said just as Pepsi walked in. I snatched up the blanket and tried to cover the mess.

'Man,' Pepsi said. 'Who are you? Carrie?'

'Freaky,' Cola said, coming in behind her. 'You okay?'

I nodded. I wished I'd never been born.

Pepsi hit my hand when I touched the sheets. 'You're not the only one with killer periods.' She pushed me out of the bedroom. In the bathroom she started water going in the tub for me, poured some Mr. Bubble in, and left without saying anything. I stripped off my blood-soaked underwear and hid them in the bottom of the garbage. There would be no saving them. I lay back. The bubbles popped and gradually the water became cool. I was smelly and gross. I scrubbed hard but the smell wouldn't go away.

'You still alive in there?' Pepsi said, opening the door.

I jumped up and whisked the shower curtain shut.

'Jesus, don't you knock?'

'Well, excuuuse me. I brought you a bathrobe. Good thing you finally crawled out of bed. Mom told us to make you eat something before we left. We got Ichiban, Kraft, or hot dogs. You want anything else, you gotta make it yourself. What do you want?'

'Privacy.'

'We got Ichiban, Kraft, or hot dogs. What do you want?'

'The noodles,' I said, more to get her out than because I was hungry.

She left and I tried to lock the door. It wouldn't lock so I scrubbed myself off quickly. I stopped when I saw the bathwater. It was dark pink with blood.

I crashed on the couch and woke when I heard sirens. I hobbled to the front window in time to see an ambulance pull into the parking lot. The attendants wheeled a man bound to a stretcher across the lot. He was screaming about the eyes in the walls that were watching him, waiting for him to fall asleep so they could come peel his skin from his body.

Aunt Erma, the twins, and I drove to the powwow at the Trout Lake community center in East Vancouver. I was still bleeding a little and felt pretty lousy, but Aunt Erma was doing fundraising for the Helping Hands Society and had asked me to work her bannock booth. I wanted to help her out.

Pepsi had come along just to meet guys, dressed up in her flashiest bracelets and most conservatively ripped jeans. Aunt Erma enlisted her too, when she found out that none of her other volunteers had showed up. Pepsi was disgusted.

Cola got out of working at the booth because she was one of the jingle dancers. Aunt Erma had made her outfit, a form-fitting red dress with silver jingles that flashed and twinkled as she walked. Cola wore a bobbed wig to cover her pink Mohawk. Pepsi bugged her about it, but Cola airily waved good-bye and said, 'Have fun.'

I hadn't made fry bread in a long time. The first three batches were already mixed. I just added water and kneaded them into shapes roughly the size of a large doughnut, then threw them in the electric frying pan. The oil spattered and crackled and steamed because I'd turned the heat up too high. Pepsi wasn't much better. She burned her first batch and then had to leave so she could watch Cola dance.

'Be right back,' she said. She gave me a thumbs-up sign and disappeared into the crowd.

The heat from the frying pan and the sun was fierce. I wished I'd thought to bring an umbrella. One of the organizers gave me her baseball cap. Someone else brought me a glass of water. I wondered how much longer Pepsi was going to be. My arms were starting to hurt.

I flattened six more pieces of bread into shape and threw them in the pan, beyond caring anymore that none of them were symmetrical. I could feel the sun sizzling my forearms, my hands, my neck, my legs. A headache throbbed at the base of my skull.

The people came in swarms, buzzing groups of tourists, conventioneers on a break, families, and assorted browsers. Six women wearing HI! MY NAME is tags stopped and bought all the fry bread I had. Another horde came and a line started at my end of the table.

'Last batch!' I shouted to the cashiers. They waved at me.

'What are you making?' someone asked.

I looked up. A middle-aged red-headed man in a business suit stared at me. At the beginning, when we were still feeling spunky, Pepsi and I had had fun with that question. We said, Oh, this is fish-head bread. Or fried beer foam. But bullshitting took energy.

'Fry bread,' I said. 'This is my last batch.'

'Is it good?'

'I don't think you'll find out,' I said. 'It's all gone.'

The man looked at my tray. 'There seems to be more than enough. Do I buy it from you?'

'No, the cashier, but you're out of luck, it's all sold.' I pointed to the line of people.

'Do you do this for a living?' the man said.

'Volunteer work. Raising money for the Helping Hands,' I said.

'Are you Indian then?'

A hundred stupid answers came to my head but like I said, bullshit is work. 'Haisla. And you?'

He blinked. 'Is that a tribe?'

'Excuse me,' I said, taking the fry bread out of the pan and passing it down to the cashier.

The man slapped a twenty-dollar bill on the table. 'Make another batch.'

'I'm tired,' I said.

He put down another twenty.

'You don't understand. I've been doing this since this morning. You could put a million bucks on the table and I wouldn't change my mind.'

He put five twenty-dollar bills on the table.

It was all for the Helping Hands, I figured, and he wasn't going to budge. I emptied the flour bag into the bowl. I measured out a handful of baking powder, a few fingers of salt, a thumb of lard. Sweat dribbled over my face, down the tip of my nose, and into the mix as I kneaded the dough until it was very soft but hard to shape. For a hundred bucks I made sure the pieces of fry bread were roughly the same shape.

'You have strong hands,' the man said.

'I'm selling fry bread.'

'Of course.'

I could feel him watching me, was suddenly aware of how far my shirt dipped and how short my cutoffs were. In the heat, they were necessary. I was sweating too much to wear anything more.

'My name is Arnold,' he said.

'Pleased to meet you, Arnold,' I said. 'Scuse me if I don't shake hands. You with the convention?'

'No. I'm here on vacation.'

He had teeth so perfect I wondered if they were dentures. No, probably caps. I bet he took exquisite care of his teeth.

We said nothing more until I'd fried the last piece of bread. I handed him the plate and bowed. I expected him to leave then, but he bowed back and said, 'Thank you.'

'No,' I said. 'Thank you. The money's going to a good cause. It'll—'

'How should I eat these?' he interrupted me.

With your mouth, asshole. 'Put some syrup on them, or jam, or honey. Anything you want.'

'Anything?' he said, staring deep into my eyes.

Oh, barf. 'Whatever.'

I wiped sweat off my forehead with the back of my hand, reached down and unplugged the frying pan. I began to clean up, knowing that he was still standing there, watching.

'What's your name?' he said.

'Suzy,' I lied.

'Why're you so pale?'

I didn't answer. He blushed suddenly and cleared his throat. 'Would you do me a favor?'

'Depends.'

'Would you—' he blushed harder, 'shake your hair out of that baseball cap?'

I shrugged, pulled the cap off, and let my hair loose. It hung limply down to my waist. My scalp felt like it was oozing enough oil to cause environmental damage.

'You should keep it down at all times,' he said.

'Good-bye, Arnold,' I said, picking up the money and starting toward the cashiers. He said something else but I kept on walking until I reached Pepsi.

I heard the buzz of an electric razor. Aunt Erma hated it when Pepsi shaved her head in the bedroom. She came out of her room, crossed the landing, and banged on the door. 'In the bathroom!' she shouted. 'You want to get hair all over the rug?'

The razor stopped. Pepsi ripped the door open and stomped down the hall. She kicked the bathroom door shut and the buzz started again.

I went into the kitchen and popped myself another Jolt. Sweat trickled down my pits, down my back, ran along my jaw and dripped off my chin.

'Karaoke?' Pepsi said. Then louder. 'Hey! Are you deaf?'

'What?' I said.

'Get me my cell phone.'

'Why don't you get it?'

'I'm on the can.'

'So?' Personally, I hate it when you're talking on the phone with someone and then you hear the toilet flush.

Pepsi banged about in the bathroom and came out with her freshly coiffed Mohawk and her backpack slung over her shoulder. 'What's up your butt?' she said.

'Do you want me to leave? Is that it?'

'Do what you want. This place is like an oven,' Pepsi said. 'Who can deal with this bullshit?' She slammed the front door behind her.

The apartment was quiet now, except for the chirpy weatherman on the TV promising another week of record highs. I moved out to the balcony. The headlights from the traffic cut into my eyes, bright and painful. Cola and Aunt Erma bumped around upstairs, then their bedroom doors squeaked shut and I was alone. I had a severe caffeine buzz. Shaky hands, fluttery heart, mild headache. It was still warm outside, heat rising from the concrete, stored up during the last four weeks of weather straight from hell. I could feel my eyes itching. This was the third night I was having trouble getting to sleep.

Tired and wired. I used to be able to party for days and days. You start to hallucinate badly after the fifth day without sleep. I don't know why, but I used to see leprechauns. These waist-high men would come and sit beside me, smiling with their brown wrinkled faces, brown eyes, brown teeth. When I tried to shoo them away, they'd leap straight up into the air, ten or twelve feet, their green clothes and long red hair flapping around them.

A low, gray haze hung over Vancouver, fuzzing the street lights. Air-quality bulletins on the TV were warning the elderly and those with breathing problems to stay indoors. There were mostly semis on the roads this late. Their engines rumbled down the street, creating minor earthquakes. Pictures trembled on the wall. I took a sip of warm, flat Jolt, let it slide over my tongue, sweet and harsh. It had a metallic twang, which meant I'd drunk too much, my stomach wanted to heave.

I went back inside and started to pack.

## HOME AGAIN, HOME AGAIN, JIGGITY-JIG

Jimmy and I lay in the graveyard, on one of my cousin's graves. We should have been creeped out, but we were both tipsy.

'I'm never going to leave the village,' Jimmy said. His voice buzzed in my ears.

'Mmm.'

'Did you hear me?' Jimmy said.

'Mmm.'

'Don't you care?' Jimmy said, sounding like I should.

'This is what we've got, and it's not that bad.'

He closed his eyes. 'No, it's not bad.'

I poured myself some cereal. Mom turned the radio up. She glared at me as if it were my fault the Rice Crispies were loud. I opened my mouth and kept chewing.

The radio announcer had a thick Nisga'a accent. Most of the news was about the latest soccer tournament. I thought, that's northern native broadcasting: sports or bingo.

'Who's this?' I said to Mom. I'd been rummaging through the drawer, hunting for spare change.

'What?'

It was the first thing she'd said to me since I'd come back. I'd heard that she'd cried to practically everyone in the village, saying I'd gone to Vancouver to become a hooker.

I held up a picture of a priest with his hand on a little boy's shoulder. The boy looked happy.

'Oh, that,' Mom said. 'I forgot I had it. He was Uncle Josh's teacher.'

I turned it over. *Dear Joshua, it read. How are you? I miss you terribly. Please write. Your friend in Christ, Archibald.*

'Looks like he taught him more than just prayers.'

'What are you talking about? Your Uncle Josh was a bright student. They were fond of each other.'

'I bet,' I said, vaguely remembering that famous priest who got eleven years in jail. He'd molested twenty-three boys while they were in residential school.

Uncle Josh was home from fishing for only two more days. As he was opening my bedroom door, I said, 'Father Archibald?'

He stopped. I couldn't see his face because of the way the light was shining through the door. He stayed there a long time.

'I've said my prayers,' I said.

He backed away and closed the door.

In the kitchen the next morning he wouldn't look at me. I felt light and giddy, not believing it could end so easily. Before I ate breakfast I closed my eyes and said grace out loud. I had hardly begun when I heard Uncle Josh's chair scrape the floor as he pushed it back.

I opened my eyes. Mom was staring at me. From her expression I knew that she knew. I thought she'd say something then, but we ate breakfast in silence.

'Don't forget your lunch,' she said.

She handed me my lunch bag and went up to her bedroom.

I use a recent picture of Uncle Josh that I raided from Mom's album. I paste his face onto the body of Father Archibald and my face onto the boy. The montage looks real enough. Uncle Josh is smiling down at a younger version of me.

My period is vicious this month. I've got clots the size and texture of liver. I put one of them in a Ziploc bag. I put the picture and the bag in a hatbox. I tie it up with a bright red ribbon. I place it on the kitchen table and go upstairs to get a jacket. I think nothing of leaving it there because there's no one else at home. The note inside the box reads, 'It was yours so I killed it.'

'Yowtz!' Jimmy called out as he opened the front door. He came to my house while I was upstairs getting my jacket. He was going to surprise me and take me to the hot springs. I stopped at the top of the landing. Jimmy was sitting at the kitchen table with the present that I'd meant for Uncle Josh, looking at the note. Without seeing me, he closed the box, neatly folded the note, and walked out the door.

He wouldn't take my calls. After two days, I went over to Jimmy's house, my heart hammering so hard I could feel it in my temples. Michelle answered the door.
'Karaoke!' she said, smiling. Then she frowned. 'He's not here. Didn't he tell you?'
'Tell me what?'
'He got the job,' Michelle said.
My relief was so strong I almost passed out. 'A job.'
'I know. I couldn't believe it either. It's hard to believe he's going fishing, he's so spoiled. I think he'll last a week. Thanks for putting in a good word, anyways.' She kept talking, kept saying things about the boat.
My tongue stuck in my mouth. My feet felt like two slabs of stone. 'So he's on *Queen of the North*?'
'Of course, silly,' Michelle said. 'We know you pulled strings. How else could Jimmy get on with your uncle?'

The lunchtime buzzer rings as I smash this girl's face. Her front teeth crack. She screams, holding her mouth as blood spurts from her split lips. The other two twist my arms back and hold me still while the fourth one starts smacking my face, girl hits, movie hits. I aim a kick at her crotch. The kids around us cheer enthusiastically. She rams into me and I go down as someone else boots me in the kidneys.

I hide in the bushes near the docks and wait all night. Near sunrise, the crew starts to make their way to the boat. Uncle Josh arrives first, throwing his gear onto the deck, then dragging it inside the cabin. I see Jimmy carrying two heavy bags. As he walks down the gangplank, his footsteps make hollow thumping noises that echo off the mountains. The docks creak, seagulls circle overhead in the soft morning light, and the smell of the beach at low tide is carried on the breeze that ruffles the water. When the seiner's engines start, Jimmy passes his bags to Uncle Josh, then unties the rope and casts off. Uncle Josh holds out his hand, Jimmy takes it and is pulled on board. The boat chugs out of the bay and rounds the point. I come out of the bushes and stand on the dock, watching the *Queen of the North* disappear.

1996

# Ken Babstock

## b. 1970

Born in Burin, Newfoundland, Ken Babstock moved to Ontario with his family when he was two, growing up in the tiny village of South Woodslee (near Windsor), then in Stratford, and, as a teenager, in Pembroke (in the Ottawa Valley). Having begun to write poems while in high school, he enrolled in a creative writing course taught by Irving Layton when he entered Concordia University in 1989. Encouraged by his encounter with a living Canadian poet and excited by his discovery of contemporary philosophers in another of his courses, Babstock quit school to devote himself to reading and to writing poetry, while he worked and lived in various cities, including Dublin, Vancouver, and Kingston. In 1999, he settled in Toronto, where he now lives with his partner and their young child.

Influenced at the beginning of his career by writers such as Al Purdy, Don McKay, and Seamus Heaney, Babstock says he was 'drawn toward compression and the . . . clanging of consonants and vowels.' For him 'language itself is its own generator of meaning, of significance and importance. Language is like a big mountain and the author is this small thing crawling around on the outside.' Since 2003, he has been the poetry editor at House of Anansi Press. He taught creative writing courses as an adjunct faculty member in the University of Guelph–Humber College program and, since 2006, has been teaching creative writing at the University of Toronto.

Babstock published his first collection, *Mean*, in 1999. Highly praised by reviewers, it won the Atlantic Poetry Prize and the Milton Acorn People's Poetry Award. In it, he responds to the natural world with striking metaphors in precisely chosen language—as in 'Montana Nocturne', reprinted here, and as in the following image, which opens a poem called 'Crow, for the Time Being':

> Out of the weed-lunged ditch,
> tapered, phlegmatic—

> a wet-knot—crow gun-struts
> gunless, an umbilical
> of cack-brown, lamentable
> sluice

In his second poetry collection, *Days into Flatspin* (2001), Babstock suggests something of his poetic principles when he writes, 'We're here to be emptied under the emptying sky / eyes cast outward, trolling for the extraordinary.' Babstock's tone is more varied in this second book: there is, for example, a newly playful note in 'The 7-Eleven Formerly Known as Rx' (in which the speaker is the store itself). His formal range is also broader, expanding on the lyric poems built around vivid images and metaphors that constituted *Mean*. *Days into Flatspin* contains a dramatic monologue ('Firewatch'), for example, that is spoken by someone atop a wilderness fire tower (it was made into a five-minute film by Anthony Wong, which is available online). As well, there are powerful brief narratives such as 'Regenerative' (reprinted here). 'Regenerative' develops by moving from the speaker's experience of an event into his mind for a series of enigmatic associations provoked by the traumatic effects of that event (Babstock describes the second half of this poem as 'oneiric').

In *Airstream Land Yacht* (2006), which won a Trillium Book Award for Poetry, Babstock explores voices and perspectives—as in 'The World's Hub', the dramatic monologue seen below. He includes love poetry that brings new emotional depth to his writing. In several poems, including 'Essentialist', which opens the book, and 'Compatibilist', which closes it, he addresses philosophical questions. Three other poems in the book—'Pragmatist', 'Materialist', and 'Verifcationist'—complement these (all five use the same shaped stanzas: for details see the footnote to 'Compatibilist'). Drawing on his wide-ranging reading, which includes literary, Marxist, and psychoanalytic theory, Babstock has said (in a CBC radio interview) that he wanted the poems in *Airstream Land Yacht* 'to try everything from song, to murmur, to whimper, to wander, to arguments and evasions' in order to gain 'a playful raggedness and tone of self-invention that wasn't there in the earlier books'.

The reception for *Airstream* was enthusiastic. In a review for *The Globe and Mail*, Todd Swift observed, 'As Auden was to the English 1930s, so too is Ken Babstock to the Canadian 2000s—the key figure of the under-40s generation, around which other younger poets circle.' When Babstock made the short list for the Griffin Poetry Prize, the nominating committee described him as a 'poet who can do almost anything, both formally and in his exploration of . . . the sensory details of a world full of marvels and riddles.'

Babstock has long been a fan of contemporary music, counting Joe Strummer, Michael Stipe, and Nick Cave among his early influences. (When he lived in Vancouver, he shared a house with Dan Bejar of the musical groups Destroyer and The New Pornographers.) His poems have been used in recordings by the Deadly Snakes, the Rheostatics (in the middle of one of their songs he can be heard reading his poem 'The Expected'), Ron Hawkins, and Jim Bryson. Because he 'grew up, like every other young person, loving music', he says that 'finding out that some of these bands that you're listening to are reading poetry is fantastic. It's wonderful because when you start writing poetry, this party line is drummed into you that only other poets, and possibly students, read poetry. And that's just bull.'

# In Brendan's Boat[1]

*—a letter from Ireland*

Frail as ash in a bowl, perhaps
Brendan did make it; faith-sailor.
A voyage that snipped nautical law
like new paper, landing his cloaked
and salted body quivering on the edge
of this country's dirt. Perhaps
he did 'predate the Norse' and
glimpsed Labrador's black breathing
arc like the sleek back of a whale
shining through maritime weather                    10
and thought of his brothers,
                          as I do,
in a squirrelly huddle
in their stone church hovel,
as I was in Glendalough, Ireland,
God fading as fast as Brendan, yet

---

1 St. Brendan of Ireland made a legendary sixth-century journey in search of the Isle of the Blessed (the earthly paradise), during which he is said to have encountered many marvels and to have landed on and explored an island across the ocean. This legend may be based on an actual voyage and Brendan and his party (or other Irish monks, who were known to be making extended sea-voyages at this time) may have been the first Europeans to visit the New World—arriving earlier than the Viking raiding parties that crossed from Norway to Newfoundland-Labrador in the eighth century. To demonstrate that such a journey was possible, a leather-hulled boat of the kind used by early Irish sailors was built in Ireland in the 1970s and sailed across the Atlantic to Labrador; this boat is on display at Glendalough.

believing his breath woven in wind
combing the backlit hills of heather,
and believing I'll make it back
to spit myself onto the guttural                                    20
green rock of Newfoundland's south
shore, where I was born, scouting
the Atlantic depth, the sea floor's crag
and canyon. Skimming the swell, the spray
and wave, bread-crumbing
the journey in gull squawks.

1999

# Montana Nocturne

Monstrous night, great wing of no
weight. These stars slotted in chinks
between dark and dark, sequestered,

numb, and undone in the racket of ever . . .

Tent flap. Plains breeze. Pre-sleep's
a cattle guard my mind's caught

its hoof in; here and not
here, how hard I want
not to be isolate—embryonic on

a sage-powdered bleakness where borders                             10
fall back and swarm in in sickening waves and
something like yearning Catherine-wheels[1] out

from its hub under ribs, mouthing
drowsed list of false stops: Heart
Butte, Dupuyer, Troy, and on where

prairie dogs are nervous clerics at prayer
on their haunches, eyeing us
sideways. Soaked in candescent blue

---

1 A Catherine wheel is a kind of firework that spins, like a pinwheel, emitting sparks.

off Dead Man's Basin, we watch frantic
silhouettes on our tent's dim                                    20
screen, hear tiny burr-like claws

scritching in grit and this fussing's
a mother's blessing our fevered
fall into sleep where our bodies make

covenants and trade heat with the earth.

1999


## Marsh Theatre

Reeds like violin bows quiver in the pit, glinting
in low, angled light. They point to grey
weather, an incoming chill curdling beyond
the porticoes of stripped willow.
A thousand exclamation marks in dun-coloured
felt are skewered on wands, on flagpoles driven
into the murk, where NASA turtles
mime zero-gravity walk, knocking
up silt clouds that roll like mushrooms
of cream in black tea. Walnut skulls adrift                      10
in a dark they've yawned into being—
a backstage of jostle and bump and *so what*,
a barbiturate calm in the brain stem—
blinking leather change-purse lids, wondering
at nothing but what it might be to wonder.
A frigid gel cataracts the one floodlight.
Their sky freezes solid; a stage, a mirror in front
of which they suck in arrogant underbites, hook
horned thumbs into waistcoat folds and
audition for the only role going: stone—                        20
stone for a run of months,
to mild applause from mallards who missed
a cue, who stand and sit down and stand and
sit down. Delicate ankles shackled in the cold snap.

2001

# Regenerative

That dog padded home wearing a rip
in his back, clicked onto the kitchen linoleum
with a five-inch smile down his saddling spine.

Where pebbles and dark grit stuck to the wound's
lips, vertebrae like molars grinned through
in an anemic bluish white. The dumb grey

meat of his tongue like a sodden flag waiting
for breeze in the post-storm still of that house—
how he lashed the plucked chicken length of it,

then lapped at the seepage that hung from black                    10
flews. He turned, and turned, and in turning sparks
of shock shot from his eyes as his chances of seeing

pain dimmed, coiled to a brute whine in his chest. I
pictured a bald nest of lab mice pulsing in there
crying its cancer away; pictured a shed door, askew

on its hinges, mowing thick weeds as it swung; even
pictured a field in that dog, where choirs of crickets
sawed through the night with the ache in their legs.

I could smell the top-heavy cattails' thinning brown
felt as it burst, breathing commas on parachutes              20
into the world; heard the travelling *s*'s of garter snakes

playing wet grass blades with cadmium scales as
they passed through invisible shivers. A lost leather
sneaker shone near a stump, like a child's plug-in

night-light, or a chipped-off sample of moon. Blue
shell casings coughed funnelled web from the throats
where their packed shot had been, and bleached-out

pages of porn doubled as mainsails, fitted to masts
of wild rose. Dew, meltwater cold, slid down my calves
like wet wrists unburdening jewels in my boots. Then no one      30

I knew approached through the dark, swinging a carved
column of light,[1] prodding the bramble and weeds with
this staff that worked like a blind man's stick in reverse.

1  A beam of light, as from a flashlight.

The mauve starbursts of thistles passed through it, casting
peaked shadows like crowns. Bugs strafed the beam, reared
from the black, threading it again, and again. He didn't

call out or raise his free hand or even target his lamp
on my head, just kept cresting the weeds with the twin
prows of his knees while scanning the foreground

for snags. Whether it was that he couldn't imagine me                          40
there, and therefore I wasn't, or that my body actually
weighed in at nothing, doused as it was in that field's

feral moulting, bucking, breathing—its bull-stubborn
morphing of intrauterine moments—I couldn't decide.
There wasn't time. He passed on the left, dragged by

his light as if some shadowy, leashed mastiff tractored
him on, plunging through weed. Solid black silhouette, receding,
until distance undermined outline, form bled into field.

2001

## To Willow

1.

Your sorrow—
          feelers, antennae—
                    your sorrow.

2.

In winter's throat, this light like a grey film of greyer film
from the thirties, there's that much smoke: a great rigging
of cloud stalled in doldrums like a drugged armada,
the plume from the pipe where the dryer's at work
and my own exhaling and the dog exhaling and
every chimney visible from this suburban breezeway—

3.

I'm out of work. Willow, I'm broke.                          10

4.

One arrives at a bad time yet wants, simply, to be,

5.

meaning during any nut shortage each spiral
of squirrel inside you spirals tighter, stays
out of it longer, tugging the quilted dark in
its fingers, gnawing on nothing, dreaming
plenitude with its teeth.

6.

Every D string ever snapped
by Joe Strummer.[1] Marcus
Aurelius growing his hair out.
René Lévesque's lung in negative,                      20
or that unforgettable comb-over
again, and again, and again . . .

7.

How one day last week a Cooper's hawk lit in a low elbow
of yours, a thick crook only feet from the earth, and it gripped
in its talon what looked like a pigeon, the soft boneless flop
of its form onto bark, its near-weightless skull striking wood
like a mid-range xylophone note. Its black eye a full stop
in a language all verb.

8.

The feeding.
And in the eaves other pigeons rehearsing short speeches, sounding    30
vaguely impressed.

1  Born John Graham Mellor (1952–2002); lead singer, lyricist, and guitar player for the English punk-rock band
The Clash. Marcus Aurelius (121–180 ce; r. 161–180 CE), stoic philosopher and Roman emperor, is convention-
ally depicted as having short curly hair. René Lévesque (1922–87), founder of the Parti Québécois and the
twenty-third premier of Quebec (1976–85), was well-known for his chain smoking and, in later life, for a hair
style arranged to cover his increasing baldness.

The drama
you're centre stage for, the drama you're the black backdrop for,
and the drama you watch.

9.

I remember as a child each spring being ordered
to stay clear of the mudflats and each spring
venturing down to those mudflats where the river
had bloated, flooded the trunks of six willows,
then receded again to a manageable brown gush.
Drawn by the deep sucking pits each step left                                    40
behind as we struggled—the flatulent, choked
mud, its stink of rain-barrel bottoms, of hot
attic wood—we couldn't resist, and our goal was
the willows: to grab three or four wind-braided
lifelines then watch ourselves sink waiting for help.

10.

Hearing: *Find me*
        *find me*
           *don't find me.*

11.

How your insistent, years-long stooping could
be taken for the weight and waiting                                              50
that will come with age; that downcast
gaze toward comforts cradled
in seed, but as easily seen
as disposition. Strategy of flux. Thin
whips of unhurried reach, like the makeshift
fishing rods that allowed us brown-rivered
afternoons filled with confronting
precisely nothing,
and all that nothing had to teach.

2001

# Essentialist[1]

Snug underground in the civic worm burrowing
   west, I was headed to class when a cadet
      in full combat dress got on my train.

      But for a pompom sprucing up the beret,
   his age, the fact he was alone, and here,
this boy could've been boarding amphibious

landing craft. I checked for guns, grew pious
   of this spinning orb's hotter spots. He
      was all camo, enactment-of-shrubbery, semblance

      of flora in varying shades, hues, mottlements   10
   of green. A helmet dangled on his back, a hillock
in spring, sprouting a version of verdant grasses

in plastic. I got past enjoying a civilian's recoil
   from things military, brutal, conformist, and took
      a peek at what my soldier was so engrossed in—

      Thoreau's *Walden*[2]—imagine him, rubbing oil
   into a Sten gun's[3] springed bolts, working through
his chances at a life away from men: berries

plumping in among their thorns, night's
   curtain drawn across the window of the lake . . .   20
      *We must reconcile the contradictions as we*

      *can, but their discord and their concord*
   *introduce wild absurdities into our thinking*
*and speech. No sentence will hold the whole*

---

1 An essentialist is a person who believes that the essence (the intrinsic nature or Platonic Ideal) of a thing is manifest in its characteristics. As a philosophical position, essentialism holds that if two things have the same characteristics, then they share the same essence.
2 In *Walden* (first published in 1854 as *Walden Pond; or, Life in the Woods*), Henry David Thoreau describes his
 desire to escape from the routine lives lived by his companions in town for a retreat into nature ('While my
 acquaintances went unhesitatingly into trade or the professions, I contemplated . . . ranging the hills all summer to pick the berries which came in my way')—a desire that led him to retreat to an isolated cabin on Walden
 Pond, near Concord, Massachusetts. His nearly hermit-like existence there lasted over two years, during which
 Thoreau put into practice his philosophy of economy—that of living simply and self-sufficiently and thereby
 being able to give up many things regarded as necessities. (For example, he writes that in the wilderness he had
 no need for curtains beyond that 'which nature has provided'.)
3 A kind of submachine gun.

*truth, and the only way in which we can be just*
       *is by giving ourselves the lie; speech is better*
              *than silence; silence is better than speech;—*

       *All things are in contact; every atom has*
    *a sphere of repulsion;—Things are, and are*
*not, at the same time;—and the like.*[4] There are other          30

minds. Surfacing at St. George,[5] I cupped my hands
       and blew—bodies scattering among museums,
              bank towers, campus rooms, and shops, each

              to where they're thinking of or not, seemed
       to prove a law we're locked into, demonstrable
with iron filings, magnets, and clean tabletop.

I can watch their faces go away. The singing's not
       to record experience, but to build one viable
              armature of feeling sustainable over time.

              The stadium's lit, empty, and hash-marked         40
       for measuring the forward push. On the surface
of the earth are us, who look in error, and only seem.

2006

---

4 From 'Nominalist and Realist', an essay by Ralph Waldo Emerson (1803–82). Emerson's ideas on nature were an important influence on Thoreau. The paragraph from which this passage comes begins, 'The end and the means, the gamester and the game,—life is made up of the intermixture and reaction of these two amicable powers, whose marriage appears beforehand monstrous, as each denies and tends to abolish the other'; and continues: 'All the universe over, there is but one thing, this old Two-Face, creator-creature, mind-matter, right-wrong, of which any proposition may be affirmed or denied. Very fitly, therefore, I assert, that every man is a partialist, that nature secures him as an instrument by self-conceit, preventing the tendencies to religion and science; and now further assert, that, each man's genius being nearly and affectionately explored, he is justified in his individuality, as his nature is found to be immense; and now I add, that every man is a universalist also, and, as our earth, whilst it spins on its own axis, spins all the time around the sun through the celestial spaces, so the least of its rational children, the most dedicated to his private affair, works out, though as it were under a disguise, the universal problem. We fancy men are individuals; so are pumpkins; but every pumpkin in the field, goes through every point of pumpkin history.' Elsewhere in this essay, Emerson addresses the question of essentialism: 'General ideas are essences. They are our gods: they round and ennoble the most partial and sordid way of living. Our proclivity to details cannot quite degrade our life, and divest it of poetry.'
5 The speaker comes out (at the Bedford exit) of the Toronto subway station named for St. George Street; Varsity Stadium and the University of Toronto lie ahead.

# The World's Hub

*After Pier Paolo Pasolini*[1]

Not poor, but adjacent to that, I lived
in an outer suburb, undistinguished but
for the mauve-blue mirrored panels of glass

alongside the feeder lanes. Not country
and no sort of city. Everyone drove, to all points
within the limits of nowhere; the rest

incarcerated on public transit: packed
in the high-wattage strip light
sat the poor, the mad, the adolescent

and license-suspended, the daylight                          10
drunk, and Malton's[2] newly arrived.
Hours-long treks through air-quality

alerts, fingering vials of hash oil and
transfers back. Or earlier, at the thin edge
of long dusks, the Bookmobile

dripping grease on clean tarmac
nudging the lower leaves of young maples,
I kissed a Jamaican boy with three

names, his loose jheri curls[3]
looked wet and right, black helices                          20
in the bay windows' blue glow.

And something inside me took root;
a thing mine that I didn't own, but cared
for, as I had for a pink-eyed rabbit,

---

1  Pier Paolo Pasolini (1922–1975), Italian poet and film director. In this poem, Babstock has recast Pasolini's poem 'Il Centro del Mondo', with suburban Toronto replacing the outskirts of Rome. Babstock's note says, 'I am entirely indebted to Martin Bennett's beautiful translation from the Italian as published in *The Faber Book of 20th Century Italian Poems*. . . . My transplanted version also contains lyrics by Joel Gibb of The Hidden Cameras—possibly misheard.'
2  The former municipality of Malton is a neighbourhood in Mississauga, northwest of Toronto, near Pearson International Airport. It has, since the end of the Second World War, been one of the principal destinations for new immigrants.
3  A hairstyle popular in the late 1970s and 80s in the North American black community; its tight spiralling curl is, in the next line, compared to a helix.

loved without reason and was returned
nothing in kind, and so what? The flurry
of rose-brick façades being raised

on cul de sacs without sidewalks, outlets
and outlets, the sameness, and grimmer storeys
of the projects beyond the ballpark                              30

were a weird history I was casting love
upon even as I wanted to leave it. I worked
retail, weekends, from within an awareness

of myself as Self; the brown carpeted tiers
of the library, ravine parties, parading
my young body through malls. The world's

hub, improbably, here, under untranslatable
verses of powerlines, kestrels
frozen above vast grassland of what used

to be farm. November like a tin sheet                            40
blown up from the lake over Mimico,[4] with
garbage and refuse I'd build

a hilltop to the moon over Mississauga—
chip bags, flattened foil wrappers, shopping
carts growing a fur of frost, the shocking

volume and echo of squat women's voices,
here from blasted South Balkan huts
via Budapest; Filipinos, Croatians

with income come to make good
and did, dressed us in suede pantsuits                           50
at ten, or terry summer halters, confident

with adults, curious, clean. Damp
electrical storms, bloated purgings
of rain turning the avenues to linked lakes.

---

4 Another former municipality, Mimico is a Toronto community to the south of Malton, on the shore of Lake
  Ontario. The thirteen words that follow are the passage Babstock sampled from the song 'Mississauga Goddam'
  by Joel Gibb.

The low slung buses veering. Albion-bound[5]
But stalled in a monoxide cloud
Somewhere on the usual grid . . .

it was the world's hub.
If you feel otherwise, that it constituted negative
space, I can only say it's a postulate                                        60

without need of proof but for the love
I had for it. I knew before I could speak
of it—that great, horrible sprawl

folded under airport turbulence, advancing inland
each year, breeding signposts, arteries, housing—
it was life as it was lived. Raspberries. The smell of gas.

2006

5 Albion is a township north of Toronto. (Its name is taken from an early name for Great Britain, which in turn
  may have derived from a Celtic word meaning *world* or—because of the white cliffs of Dover—from an Indo-
  European root for *white*.)

# Compatibilist[1]

Awareness was intermittent. It sputtered.
          And some of the time you were seen
                    asleep. So trying to appear whole

                    you asked of the morning: Is he free
          who is not free from pain? It started to rain
a particulate alloy of flecked grey; the dogs[2]

1 In philosophy, a compatibilist believes that free will and determinism are not logically disjunctive and that individuals must therefore take responsibility for their actions. In science, compatibilists argue against the view that
  immutable laws determine everything that happens in the physical world on the grounds that the indetermin-
  ism introduced by quantum physics allows room for free will. In theology, the compatibilist position considers
  the question of whether human decisions are freely made or predetermined by God. (The two moments in the
  Christian narrative that are particularly intertwined with questions of free will and determinism are the stories
  of Adam and Eve's fall from God's grace through disobedience and the story of Jesus's free acceptance of his crucifixion as redemption for humankind's fallen state.)
2 The line arrangement of the stanzas in this poem (like the stanzas in 'Essentialist') are modelled on the two
  shaped stanzas of 'Easter Wings' (1633), a poem by the metaphysical poet and Christian mystic, George Herbert.
  In 'Easter Wings', Herbert argues that the fallen human condition is a necessary precondition for divine
  redemption. Herbert's poem is part of a long dialogue within Christianity around the idea of 'felix culpa' ('the
  happy fault'; or 'fortunate fall')—a doctrine suggesting that Adam's fall was both freely chosen and necessary.

wanted out into their atlas of smells; to pee
        where before they had peed, and might
            well pee again—though it isn't

            a certainty. What is? In the set,            10
        called Phi, of all possible physical worlds[3]
resembling this one, in which, at time $t$,

was written 'Is he free who is not free—'
        and comes the cramp. Do you want
            to be singular, onstage, praised.

            or blamed? I watched a field of sun-
        flowers dial their ruddy faces toward
what they needed and was good. At noon

they were chalices upturned, gilt-edged,
        and I lived in that same light but felt           20
            alone. I chose to phone my brother,

            over whom I worried, and say so.
        He whispered, lacked affect. He'd lost
my record collection to looming debt. I

forgave him—through weak connections,
        through buzz and oceanic crackle—
            immediately, without choosing to,

            because it was him I hadn't lost; and
        later cried myself to sleep. In that village
near Dijon, called Valley of Peace,           30

a pond reflected its dragonflies
        over a black surface at night, and
            the nuclear reactor's far-off halo

            of green light changed the night sky
        to the west. A pony brayed, stamping
a hoof on inlaid stone. The river's reeds

---

3 The idea of other possible worlds has been discussed since Gottfried Leibniz postulated that ours was 'the best of all possible worlds' in 1710. Since the 1950s, the idea of possible worlds that are a series of alternatives to our own has been used in philosophy as a way of discussing ideas of freedom and necessity. In a set that contains all possible worlds, one can argue for freedom and necessity coexisting—because if an individual is free to perform an act in one of those worlds, for the set to contain all possible worlds, there must exist a counterpart to that individual who, by logical necessity, must act in the opposite way.

lovely, but unswimmable. World death
        on the event horizon;[4] vigils with candles
             in cups. I've mostly replaced my records,

            and acted in ways I can't account for.         40
        Cannot account for what you're about
to do. We should be held and forgiven.

2006

4  The term *event horizon* usually refers to the boundary of a black hole. Matter and energy crossing an event horizon will become trapped within the black hole.

---

# Wayde Compton
## b. 1972

Wayde Compton says his 'strange background' motivated 'the search for recognizable social roots that you see in all my writing.' Born in Vancouver of a white mother and a black father who gave him up for adoption at birth, he was, by coincidence, adopted by a white Canadian mother and a black father who, after growing up in Texas, had immigrated to Vancouver. As an adult, Compton tracked down his birth mother and discovered that, in addition to the adopted brother he grew up with, he had a sister he hadn't previously known about. (He has never met his biological father.) A man for whom things are never simply black and white, Compton identifies himself as 'Halfrican'.

In his formative years, Compton found that, except for the music in his parents' record collection and stories told by his father and his father's friends, there was little in his British Columbia experience that reflected his black heritage. In a 2002 interview with Myler Wilkinson and David Stouck for *West Coast Line*, he describes how as a young man:

*I was finding it impossible to write without some sense of what my culture is, and there weren't many sources that I could go to and use as cues. The experience of people who are ethnically and culturally my combination of things—Canadian, west coast, mulatto—is scarcely ever referred to in canonical literature or popular culture, and at the point that I started getting serious about writing, I realized that I needed to know a bunch of things about my own circumstances in order to do something artistic that felt honest and important.*

As an undergraduate in English at Simon Fraser University (BA, 1997), Compton encountered George Elliott Clarke's first book, *Saltwater Spirituals and Deeper Blues* (1983). Struck by the way Clarke had constructed a history of blackness for Nova Scotia, he searched for something similar for his own province. Discovering that nothing existed, he wrote the poems and prose pieces that make up his first book, *49th Parallel Psalm* (1999) as a way of 'creating a context, or mapping out a context, uncovering what the conditions are here that I could write from.' Then, as a research project for his 2001 Simon Fraser MA, he located and collected the work of black writers from British Columbia. Along with those from the past who had been ignored and forgotten, Compton included contemporaries, and also represented his own work with selections from his *49th Parallel Psalm*. The result was *Bluesprint: Black British Columbian Literature and Orature* (2001).

He says these two books allowed him to address important questions: 'Is blackness here different from other places? If so, how? What is the history of black people here in BC? How does it change things if I know that there is a black tradition here? How does being mixed-race shape the things that happen to me and how I move through the world?' Working on these projects led him to articulate the aesthetic principles with which he opens his introduction to *Bluesprint*:

*The Barbadian poet and theorist Kamau Braithwaite coined the term tidalectics to describe an Africanist model for thinking about history. In contrast to Hegel's dialectics . . . tidalectics describes a way of seeing history as a palimpsest, where generations overlap generations, and eras wash over eras like a tide on a stretch of beach. There is change, but the changes arise out of slight misduplications of the pattern rather than from essential antagonisms. Repetition, whether in the form of ancestor worship or the poem-histories of the* griot, *informs black ontologies more than does the Europeanist drive for perpetual innovation, with its concomitant disavowals of the past. . . . in tidalectics, we do* not *improve upon* the past, *but are ourselves* versions *of the past.*

In *49th Parallel Psalm*, Compton takes as one of the important figures of British Columbia's past the first governor of the Pacific colonies, James Douglas—a mixed-race man of whom he writes,

*O James Douglas*
*our own quadroon Moses,*
*should I place a violet on your grave*
*or hawk a little spit*
*for your betraying ways.*

Douglas's history, Compton observes, 'shows us how both race and culture are unstable concepts subject to shifting social trends. Douglas's race, during his life and long after, has altered countless times, depending on who is doing the

looking, what political points need to be made, and what the viewer can lose or gain by calling him white or black.'

In 'The Cover', a sequence of poems at the centre of *49th Parallel Psalm*, Compton imagines black men of his father's generation coming across the 'strait razorous border' into Canada. It begins,

> *he crossed. the border*
> *line in a northern corner.*
>
> > > *four*
> > *cardinal* *points*
> > > *for*
>
> *a better over there. created a here*
>
> *one foot in A* *one in a*
> *merica.* *Canada.*
>
> > *one Negro,*
> > *liminal.*
>
> ('Legba Landed', 1999)

Compton describes the central figure in this sequence as 'a representation of the loneliness that first confronted the blacks who came here around that time,' loneliness that arose because of 'how few black people there were in the city and how strange that would have been for an African-American coming from the American South and suddenly realizing that there was hardly anybody around, and there's no real substantial black church, or where the community is sort of a black community, but not quite—it's where the blacks live, but it's also where the Italians and Chinese and a whole bunch of other people live.'

These themes of border crossing and community are central in 'The Blue Road'. A humorous and whimsical fable from *49th Parallel Psalm* about a young man's quest for a home, it is also an allegory about divided consciousness and about the way the margins and centres of culture are defined. The central character of the tale, Lacuna, has always wanted to leave home, so when a powerful entity decides to exclude him, he goes in search of the Northern Kingdom. After he successfully passes through a disorienting environment and thinks of a trick that will allow him to cross a difficult border, he finds that, on the other side, he is bound by rules that make immigrants visibly distinct from native-born citizens. His ingenious response speaks to all who are not part of the majority culture.

In 2004, Compton published *Performance Bond*, a collection that mixes poetry, prose, and photographs and that—by including both a print version of his long turntablist poem 'The Reinventing Wheel' (reprinted here) and a CD of that work—joins poetry on the page with poetry as music in performance. In 2006, Compton founded Commodore Books, a publishing house with a mandate to provide an outlet for black writers from Western Canada. He has been writer-in-residence at Green College (the graduate college at UBC) and at Simon Fraser University, where he is now part of The Writer's Studio. He also teaches at the Emily Carr University of Art and Design and at Coquitlam College.

## The Reinventing Wheel

Compton wants to understand his inheritance in relation to attempts to recover and renew North America's 'black Englishes'. In the last decades the forces of *mediation* (in the sense of experiences being filtered through various mass media) and its flattening of difference have worked against Braithwaite's *tidalectics*, in which change comes from the slow accretion of 'misduplications' for each generation. Globalized circulation of culture reduces nuanced cultural distinctions, perhaps particularly among diasporic black cultures. Compton does not reject such transculturalism nor think we can avoid the global media or ignore their impact. But because context is important to him, he wants to find an identity appropriate to his specific time and place, one that, by restoring local variations to global forms and languages, resists the homogenization of mediated experience.

Compton has turned to the American musical genre of hip hop to develop this transcultural expression while making something uniquely personal out of the conventions and forms of that genre. The performance-poem that resulted is 'The Reinventing Wheel'. In an accompanying essay, 'The Reinventing Wheel: On Blending the Poetry of Cultures through Hip Hop Turntablism' (2003), he writes,

*Hip hop has changed the world. Black American culture has been flung around the globe before, due to the position of American power in world cultural trade. But hip hop is the conduit of a new kind of black American voice, and therefore a new globally known black voice. I believe that hip hop's forms are reflective of (to name a few important things) the failure of the American Black Power movement, the marginal success of the American Civil Rights movement, and the*

*near totalization of electronic media in black expressive life in the first world. Hip hop's trademark vocal tone is a sort of seething aggravation. This vocal trope is loaded with history, namely the dashed promises of utopian black nationalisms. But at the same time, this voice exhibits an uncoded starkness that is distanced far enough from the furtive, masked complaints of the blues to show the gulf between then and now, in terms of collective self-confidence. The contradictory space between these facts accounts for a creeping nihilism in black expressive culture, as well as an unprecedented degree of freedom-of-speech presently being seized upon by black speakers, and the passing of communal renewals of black languages in favour of a standardizing dialect disseminated worldwide through the media.*

Even while celebrating its oral quality, Compton is aware of the ironic fact that hip hop 'is a type of music that is never quite completely live, but is plugged into a vast media machine that extends into every home and every ear individually more than communally.' Pursuing the artistic questions implicit in this interlinking of art as performance with its means of mass reproduction and reduplication, he has become increasingly interested in 'the manipulation of received sound and received culture' that is part of *turntablism*. This term was coined in the 1990s as a way of pointing to the creative role of the individual who makes new music from old by manipulating two turntables at once, blending, mixing, and remixing; sampling, overdubbing, scratching, and otherwise distorting the sounds of the vinyl records being played. Describing turntablism as 'a black postmodern form, in that it creates a secondary art out of black canons of music,' Compton found in 'the dualism of the turntables' a metaphor for what he is trying to accomplish in his written work.

Compton regularly recreates his poem 'The Reinventing Wheel' as performance art when he presents it live as a turntablist (originally in what he called the 'Cargo Cult Mix'). The CD included with *Performance Bond* is the 'Ouroboros Mix'; still another version, the 'Rolling Wave Mix' (performed by The Contact Zone Crew, which is Compton and Jason de Couto, using four turntables) can be found in the online journal *HorizonZero*.

Compton's essay on 'The Reinventing Wheel' is also available on this site. In it, he describes how he wanted 'to make poetry on the turntables' so that

*elements of ancient, non-literate, vestigial African culture could be blended directly into textual poetry, and both could be blended back into hip hop. The back-and-forth reflection of forms and conditions seems evident in the very imagery of the 'ones and twos': the cornerstones of hip hop, the DJ's materials—the left and the right turntable, two halves of a dichotomy. The poetry would arise through the cultural 'feedback' these loops would spark.*

The written version of 'The Reinventing Wheel' is itself a work of intricate richness.

Using sampling and overdubbing as models for his own poetics, Compton layers his work with numerous brief quotations, echoes, and allusions that draw the past into a contemporary context. Mixing biblical stories (in particular, the Moses narrative, which has long been important for North American black culture) with references to black history, music, and religion, he also interweaves voodoo—the syncretic belief system that emerged out of Haiti and New Orleans as an amalgam of West African religion, Roman Catholicism, and Aboriginal beliefs. Voodoo serves Compton

*as a cosmological source culture—for the way that it features possession, the idea of spirits speaking through a person using one's voice and body from a position far away in the spirit realm. It was a good formal metaphor for the historical recovery I was practising in my poems.*

Central to the poem, the figure of the revolving wheel—which is physically embodied in the discs played and manipulated by the turntablist—suggests the cultural flow that has taken place, from Africa to the West and back. Recreating art through its endless revolutions, the record's centre hole is a significant absence that permits its endless turning.

# The Blue Road: A Fairy Tale

*The wind bloweth where it listeth, and thou hearest the sound thereof, but canst not tell whence it cometh, and whither it goeth: so is every one that is born of the Spirit.*

—John 3:8

## HOW THE MAN ESCAPED THE GREAT SWAMP OF INK

The man had lived in the Great Swamp of Ink for as long as he could remember, and for as long as he could remember, he had always lived there alone. The swamp was made of the deepest and bluest ink in the world. The man's name was Lacuna.[1]

One night, just before dawn, Lacuna tossed and turned, unable to sleep. He sat up against a tree and wept. He was hungry and thirsty, but all there ever was to eat in the Great Swamp of Ink were bulrushes, and he was forced to drink the bitter-tasting ink to survive. He dreamed, as always, of leaving the terrible swamp. As he cried, he noticed the swamp brightening. Lacuna looked up to see a large glowing ball of light

---

1 A gap, missing piece, or empty space; especially a lost portion of a manuscript; a missing word in a language causing translation problems; or a period of silence in a musical composition.

as bright as a sky full of full moons. He stood up rubbing the tears from his eyes, and stared at the ball of light that hovered above the blue marsh.

It spoke.

'My name is Polaris,'[2] said the ball in a bottomless voice. 'I live in this swamp, but I have never seen you here before. What are you doing in my home?'

'I beg your pardon,' Lacuna replied, barely keeping his composure in the face of this very remarkable event. 'I don't mean to trespass. Are you a ghost?' He was terribly afraid of this talking ball of light.

'I am Polaris!' the ball shouted. 'I am a will-o'-the-wisp,[3] the spirit of this bog. And I ask you again, what are you doing in my home?'

Lacuna was very frightened, but he was also very clever, and he saw an opportunity to escape the swamp.

'I'd gladly leave your home, Mr Polaris, sir,' he said carefully, 'but I'm afraid I've lost my way. Since I can't remember which direction is home, I guess I'm just going to have to stay here.'

The will-o'-the-wisp grew larger and pulsated.

'You can't live here!' Polaris roared. 'This is my home. You must leave immediately or I will shine brighter and brighter and blind you with the light of a thousand suns!'

'Now look here, Mr Polaris, there's no need to get angry.' Lacuna spoke soothingly. 'If you'll tell me the direction that I need to go to get home, and lead me to the edge of the swamp, I'll get out of here forever and let you be.'

'And you'll tell all the others like you to stay out of my home?' the will-o'-the-wisp persisted.

Lacuna, who was very clever, realized that other people may some day find themselves here in the Great Swamp of Ink. He thought very quickly of an answer that would not get them into trouble with the will-o'-the-wisp because he was not a selfish man, and he did not want others to be blinded.

'I'll be sure to tell people to stay clear of your swamp,' he said sincerely, 'but when I tell them about how big and shiny and pretty you are, I'm sure some of them will want to come and see you for themselves.'

Polaris' glow softened.

'Really?' he said wonderingly. 'You think they might come into the swamp just to see me?'

'Oh, of course they will! When I tell them how bright and sparkly you look, just like a star fallen loose from the sky, a few of the brave ones are bound to come just to catch a sight. They won't be wanting to stay, though—just to catch a sight and be on their way. I'm sure you can understand that?'

The will-o'-the-wisp was quiet for a moment, and Lacuna held his breath waiting for his answer.

2  The North Star (also known as the Pole Star), the brightest star in the constellation Ursa Minor (i.e., the star at the end of the Little Dipper). The stable point in the sky around which all the other stars seem to revolve, it was used by navigators and others to guide themselves at night.

3  A ghostly flickering light (probably caused by the natural oxidation of a naturally produced flammable gas), sometimes seen on the horizon of swamps and bogs at twilight. Figuratively used for something elusive and possibly deceptive.

'Well,' the will-o'-the-wisp said slowly, 'I can understand how some of your people might want to come and see me. I *am* rather dazzling, especially on clear nights like tonight. But if they come, they cannot stay! They can only catch a quick glimpse and then I will escort them immediately to the edge of the swamp! This is *my* home and no one else's. Surely you can understand the sanctity of one's home?'

Lacuna nodded gravely.

'And now it's time for you to leave. You have witnessed my beauty for long enough. Now tell me: which direction is your home?'

Lacuna had successfully tricked the will-o'-the-wisp into leading him out of the swamp, but now he was faced with a question that confused and confounded him more than any other: which way *was* his home? He didn't know. He visualized the four directions in his mind as if they were on a wheel, and in his mind he spun that wheel; the point was chosen.

'North.'

'North,' the spirit repeated. 'I'll take you to the northernmost margin of the Great Swamp of Ink.'

The will-o'-the-wisp picked up Lacuna and flew into the sky in a grand and luminous arc.

### THE THICKET OF TICKETS

Polaris gently set Lacuna down at the edge of the swamp, at the bottom of a steep grassy hill.

'Here is where we part,' the will-o'-the-wisp said. 'At the top of that hill you will find a vast briar called the Thicket of Tickets. If you can find your way through the thicket, they say there is a Blue Road that leads to the Northern Kingdom. There you will find others like yourself, and you will certainly live a better life than living in my swamp. Good luck.'

'Goodbye,' Lacuna said as he watched Polaris float back into the murk of the Great Swamp of Ink.

Lacuna climbed to the top of the hill and looked back in the direction he now knew was south: the vast swamp stretched out as far as he could see. He jumped up and clapped his hands together, then he did a little dance, because he realized that he was out of the inky wilderness forever. He looked at it and laughed out loud before turning northward, forever turning his back on the horrible swamp. He then noticed what faced him.

The Thicket of Tickets, as Polaris had called it, was the most dense briar[4] he had ever seen. It stretched out to his left and right all the way beyond each horizon. There was no way to go but through it or back into the swamp. He walked up to the thicket and examined its tangled mass.

The thicket consisted of coil upon coil of paper tickets, little squares of every colour, each with the words

# Admit One

---

4 A collection of briar-like or thorny plants; here, the thicket itself.

stamped on its surface in a stern black font. The coils were so tangled they reminded him of his hair when he did not comb it for several days; to pry it apart became a painful and daunting task. He reached his left arm in and found he could push the paper aside quite easily, however, so he stepped into the thicket with his entire body.

Lacuna soon found that he could walk through the Thicket of Tickets if he ripped the paper coils whenever he got too tangled. The only problem was that he could not see where he was going. He could not even see beyond his next footstep. He kept walking in faith but worried that at any moment he would step off a cliff, or into a tree or a rock. He stopped and pondered his situation after he had gone a dozen or so steps into the thicket.

'I can't go any farther,' he thought, 'because I don't know if I'm walking in a safe path or a dangerous one. I also can't be sure if I'm even heading north or not.' He thought and thought, because he was a clever man and he knew all sorts of tricks that had helped him survive worse situations than this.

Finally an answer came to him.

'I'll go back to the edge of the thicket and make a fire. Since this is only a paper briar, it will burn easily and quickly, and when all the tickets are burned up, I'll be able to see and walk all the way to the Blue Road and on to the Northern Kingdom!'

Lacuna started to walk back in the direction he had first come. After he had walked for what seemed like the same amount of time it took him to get this far into the thicket, he realized that he was not yet out. A wave of panic swept over him; he could not tell if he was actually walking in the same direction he had come because he could not see where he was going! He started to run, frantically ripping through the tickets, but by the time he ran out of breath, he was still nowhere near the edge. Or perhaps the edge was but a few steps away—he couldn't tell! For all his cleverness, the Thicket of Tickets had swallowed him up and he realized that he would just have to take a guess and walk in some random direction.

He walked for what seemed like days. He was hungry and thirsty and he even missed the horrible swamp because at least there were bulrushes and ink that he could eat and drink. He walked and walked, and his legs were painfully tired, but he knew he had no choice but to continue. Lacuna lost all track of time; he didn't know whether it was day or night. He could only hope that he was heading north, and in his desperate state he began to wonder if north was even the best way to go anyway. Lacuna began to miss the old swamp desperately, and cursed himself for leaving it in the first place.

'Surely I could have tricked Polaris into letting me stay,' he thought. Lacuna wanted to cry, but he was so thirsty and dry no tears would come, which made him even sadder. His feet and legs ached. The edges of the tickets cut his skin in a thousand tiny slices. He was tortured.

Just when he had resigned himself to the idea that he would soon die, but at least he would die walking until he collapsed of exhaustion, the coils of tickets got thinner and thinner until suddenly he found himself in the open air.

He emerged from the thicket at the top of a grassy hill. It was sunny and bright, and his vision was blurry from spending so long in darkness, and he tried wearily to focus. At the bottom of the hill, he could make out what looked like trees. Weakened and half-blinded by the full light of day, Lacuna started down the hill. His aching legs gave out, and he fell, tumbling down the slope in a jumble of arms and legs and bruises.

When he finally stopped rolling, Lacuna's cheek was resting on the cold, hard ground. He realized it was not grass, but stone. He sat up slowly and stiffly and found himself on a dark blue cobblestone road that ran from the bottom of the hill off into a dense forest. The faint sound of running water could be heard from beyond the trees, and he knew he had come out on the far side of the terrible thicket. Perhaps there would be fish in that stream, he thought.

The bricks of the road were a beautiful sight, bright and rich, though they were startlingly close to the colour of the ink in the Great Swamp of Ink. Although Lacuna was very happy to have found this Blue Road to the Northern Kingdom, he couldn't help but wish it were a different colour.

After a day of resting and regaining his strength, he turned his thoughts to the Thicket of Tickets.

'If people find themselves trying to cross the thicket like me, they won't realize how easy it is to get lost in there. I was lucky to survive, let alone make it to the right destination. I had a good idea to burn it, but I thought it too late.' Because he was not a selfish man, but one who often thought of others, he decided to go back and set fire to the dangerous thicket.

Lacuna took a burning stick from his campfire and proceeded up the hill. He cast the stick into the tangled mass of tickets. As he had suspected, the paper caught fire instantly and burned fiercely. He had to retreat down the hill to avoid the intense heat of the fire. From the edge of the forest, he watched the entire Thicket of Tickets burn to a pile of ashes. For a moment, he felt a strange sadness seeing such a curious thicket destroyed by his own hand, but he knew it was for the best.

'Now,' he thought, 'no one will face the troubles I had to face if they make it this far.'

Satisfied, he set out on the Blue Road.

The way through the forest was long but pleasant. The road was well-kept and food was more plentiful and infinitely more nourishing here than in the Great Swamp of Ink. On his journey, he picked fruit from wild trees, fished in streams, and gathered dark berries. Lacuna was still lonely, but he consoled himself with the knowledge that the Northern Kingdom was at the end of this road, and even if it were far, the travelling was easy. He sang songs to himself as he walked, to make himself feel less lonely; he sang songs about his loneliness. He dreamed of a place where he could settle down. He tried to imagine what the Northern Kingdom would be like, but the thought of it frightened him a little. Lacuna was very clever, and he knew that kingdoms were not always good. 'The Northern Kingdom' *sounded* wonderful; the words felt good on his tongue. But what did he really know of this place he was seeking?

Up until now, Lacuna had drunk water straight out of the stream, but he decided to fill his canteen so he could sip the river water while he walked. When he pulled the canteen from his back pocket and opened it, he realized it was full of the ink that he used to drink when he had lived in the swamp. He smiled, thinking about how he would never have to drink ink again, but he decided he would keep the canteen full of it as a souvenir and a reminder of where he had come from. This way, he would never forget his past.

Finding the canteen full of ink caused Lacuna's thoughts to drift to the swamp. He thought about Polaris and how he had tricked that old will-o'-the-wisp. Although he had flattered Polaris to trick him, he now realized for the first time that Polaris really was pretty. His brightness *was* dazzling and beautiful, but somehow, in the telling of his trick, Lacuna had not even realized the truth of this.

## THE RAINBOW BORDER

As he walked and thought, Lacuna noticed a small booth beside the road up ahead in the distance. When he got closer to the booth, he also noticed a strip of seven colours painted across the Blue Road; it looked like a rainbow cutting across his path. An old man in a blue suit and a blue hat sat next to the booth on a wobbly two-legged stool. The old-timer only had one leg. A strange-looking crutch leaned against the wall of the booth next to him.

'Hello,' said Lacuna to the old man. 'I'm on my way to the Northern Kingdom. Are you from there?'

'Am I *from* there?' the old man snapped in an angry voice. 'No, I'm not *from* there. You don't know much, do you?' He stared at Lacuna without a trace of humour in his eyes.

Lacuna felt annoyed at this unprovoked attack. He quickly decided that since this old man was not from the Northern Kingdom, and was not very friendly, he would just be on his way.

'I have to be going,' he said curtly, and started down the Blue Road once more.

'Hey, wait a minute, wait a minute!' the old man shouted frantically, jumping up out of his seat, which promptly fell over. Lacuna stopped still, startled by the man's sudden outburst. The old-timer limped onto the road with the aid of his strange-looking crutch.

'Don't you see what's right in front of your eyes, boy?' He was pointing at the rainbow painted across the Blue Road.

'Yeah, so?' Lacuna said indifferently. He wanted to get going.

'That's the *border*. You can't just up and cross the border like that. What's the matter, have you lost your mind?'

'So what am I supposed to do?' Lacuna said impatiently. He began to wonder if the old man was insane. He wanted to be on his way northward.

'Listen to me, boy, because obviously there's a whole lot you don't know about this world. *That* is the *border*,' he said, pointing again at the rainbow painted on the road, 'and I'm the Border *Guard*. You can't cross the border until *I* say so.' He shifted his weight from his good leg to his crutch. Lacuna, now that he was up close to the Border Guard, could see that his crutch was actually a huge skeleton key.

'There are rules involved,' the Border Guard added cryptically. 'I'll need your ticket,' he said, holding out his hand.

Lacuna immediately remembered the Thicket of Tickets he had burned to the ground. He felt a sinking feeling in the pit of his stomach.

'I don't have a ticket,' he said quietly.

'You don't have a ticket?' the Border Guard snapped. 'Then you can't pass. That's the rules: no ticket, no road.'

'But I have to go to the Northern Kingdom,' Lacuna said, trying to keep the sound of desperation out of his voice. 'How am I supposed to get there if I don't keep following the road?' He was angry and frustrated, and wondered if he should even listen to this strange Border Guard with his crazy skeleton key crutch. After all, how did he know that the Border Guard had any real authority over the Blue Road? Polaris hadn't told him anything about this. But then again, perhaps Polaris didn't know about the border. Lacuna considered crossing it without the Border Guard's permission; he was only an old man with one leg, and he wouldn't be able to stop a young man like himself. However, perhaps the Border Guard worked for the Northern Kingdom, and not following these rules would get him into trouble when he finally got there.

'Isn't there some way of continuing on the Blue Road, Mr Border Guard?' he asked politely. 'I really desperately need to go to the Northern Kingdom. I have nowhere else to go.'

'Well,' the Border Guard said slowly, 'according to the rules, there *is* a way for people who don't have a ticket. But it isn't easy.' He grinned enigmatically. 'Have you ever seen a dance called "the limbo"? Two people hold a stick a few feet off the ground and the dancer leans way back and shuffles underneath the stick.'

Lacuna nodded. He knew the dance.

'Well, if you can limbo under the border, you may pass freely. That's all I can do for you.'

Lacuna looked at the border again: it was painted onto the road. There was no way anyone could limbo beneath a painted border.

'Oh, and you can't dig underneath it,' the Border Guard added, 'you have to dance under it, you have to limbo underneath the border. It's nothing personal, son. I'm just following the rules.'

Lacuna could barely contain his anger, but he knew he needed to remain calm and think of some way out of this situation. He carefully considered his circumstances. He knew that no one can limbo beneath a painted border. He thought and thought but could see no way out of his predicament.

There was nothing else to do but set up a camp beside the Border Guard's booth and wait until an idea came to him.

## HOW THE MAN LIMBO DANCED BENEATH A PAINTED BORDER

For four days, Lacuna camped beside the Border Guard's booth. During these days he passed the time by playing cards with the Border Guard. Once, while they were playing cards, he noticed a tiny starling flying low to the ground; it was heading north towards the border. Just as the little bird was about to cross the place where the border was, the Border Guard leapt from his two-legged stool (which promptly fell over), hopped on his good leg towards the bird, and chopped the bird in half in mid-flight with the edge of his skeleton key crutch. He did this all in one dazzlingly swift motion, whereupon he returned to his two-legged stool to continue their card game. Lacuna was dumbfounded at the unlikely speed and agility that the Border Guard showed, not to mention the horror of seeing the tiny bird sliced in half.

'Sorry about the interruption,' the Border Guard said, 'but no one can cross the border without properly observing the rules.'

'Not even birds?' Lacuna asked incredulously.

'Nobody at all,' the Border Guard answered firmly. He went on to explain that his skeleton key crutch also doubled as an axe. In fact, according the Border Guard, it was the sharpest axe in the world, capable of slicing easily through any material. Lacuna realized that now, more than ever, he had to think of a way to limbo beneath the painted border.

On the fourth night of camping, while he tossed and turned unable to sleep, he finally came up with a plan.

When he awoke in the morning, Lacuna stretched for a while, then stood pondering the sky. He carefully studied the clouds and the horizon. He then breakfasted with the Border Guard.

That afternoon, while they were playing cards over lunch, Lacuna periodically looked up and observed the sky. When night fell, he bedded down and slept soundly until the morning.

This pattern continued for three more days. On the third day after Lacuna had had his idea, the Border Guard finally asked him what he was going to do. It had been raining all morning, and the two of them sat at the table inside the booth playing their afternoon game of cheat.[5] The sun was just beginning to emerge from behind the coal-coloured clouds.

'So what are you going to do, boy?' the Border Guard asked him. 'You can't stay camped here forever, although I suppose there's no rule against it. I don't mind the company, but I just don't think you're ever going to be able to limbo underneath that painted border. It just can't be done.'

While he talked, Lacuna was staring out the window and into the sky.

'Are you a betting man, Mr Border Guard?'

The Border Guard eyed him cautiously. 'Well, that depends on what the bet is, doesn't it?'

'Yes, it does,' Lacuna said seriously. He thought about how he had burnt the Thicket of Tickets to help the people that might follow him, without knowing that they would need those tickets to get across this border. Now he would make up for his mistake.

'I'll bet you your skeleton key crutch that I'll limbo beneath the border today. If I don't succeed, I'll give you all of what little money I have.'

The Border Guard shook his head.

'That's a stupid bet to make, boy. It can't be done. I'd be taking your money, as sure as you're born.'

Lacuna held his gaze steadily. 'Will you bet me or not?'

The Border Guard scratched his head and wondered at the younger man's stupidity.

5  That is, the card game also known as I Doubt It.

'Why not? If you want to give your money away, I'll take it. Sure. Why not? But if you walk down that road without limbo dancing beneath the border like I said, I'll have to cut you in half just like I did that bird. I hope you understand that.'

Lacuna nodded.

'I'm going to go pack up my campsite. When I'm finished, you'll watch me limbo beneath the border.'

The Border Guard shook his head in disbelief as Lacuna left the booth to pack up his gear.

While he was outside of the booth, Lacuna examined the sky once more. Satisfied, he went to his campsite and rummaged around in his knapsack until he found the canteen filled with ink from the Great Swamp of Ink. He then went to the Blue Road and poured the ink over the painted rainbow border. Since the ink was the exact colour of the Blue Road, the painted border was completely blotted out. He finished packing up his things and returned to the Border Guard's booth.

'Well, I'm ready to limbo beneath the border. And remember: if I succeed, you have to give me your skeleton key crutch.'

'And *when* you fail, you'll have to give me all your money. And I'll most likely have to chop you in half.'

The two of them went to the spot on the Blue Road where the border had been, but the border was nowhere to be seen. The Border Guard was panic-stricken.

'But where is it?' he shouted. 'The border's gone!'

Lacuna smiled and pointed into the sky.

Both men looked up to see an arcing rainbow far above them among the shifting clouds and sunlight.

'There it is,' Lacuna said sharply.

The Border Guard stared silently at the rainbow, completely baffled by this unthinkable turn of events. He looked back at Lacuna, utterly perplexed, but could not think of a single thing to say.

Lacuna slung his pack over his shoulder, bent backwards ever-so-slightly, and limbo danced a few steps down the Blue Road, beneath the rainbow that hung fast in the sky above them. He then turned around and held his hand toward the Border Guard.

'I did it. Now give me your skeleton key crutch.'

The Border Guard's mouth hung open. He still could say nothing, but he looked at his crutch. Without it, he would no longer be able to properly guard the border.

'Give me the crutch,' Lacuna persisted. He thought for a moment about something the Border Guard had said to him. 'Listen: we made a deal. I'm just following the rules.'

The Border Guard reluctantly handed him the skeleton key crutch, which Lacuna snatched out of his hand. He immediately turned his back on the Border Guard, laughed, and headed down the Blue Road, and on towards the Northern Kingdom.

If he had turned around to look, which he didn't, he would have seen the Border Guard balancing on his one leg, with his mouth still open in disbelief. The Border Guard stared first down at the road, then up at the rainbow, then down at the road again. He continued to do this until long after Lacuna had dropped out of sight in the distance.

## THE GATES OF THE NORTHERN KINGDOM

Once past the border, Lacuna's journey was easy. He reflected upon the incident with the Border Guard and felt confident he had done the right thing. He used the skeleton key crutch-axe as a walking stick, and cheerfully sang to himself as he walked the Blue Road.

After several days of uneventful travel, Lacuna at last saw a great city looming on the horizon. As he got closer he could see that the Blue Road led straight to its gates, through a high alabaster-coloured wall that surrounded the city. Lacuna knew from its magnificence that this had to be the Northern Kingdom itself.

As he approached the gates, Lacuna passed several people, some going in or coming out of the city, others selling goods by the side of the road. He marvelled that the people looked just like he did, but were all shapes, sizes, and ages. He was overwhelmed at seeing so many people in one place after seeing so few for so long—and this was only the outskirts of town. His mind boggled when he thought about how many more people there would be inside the vast metropolis.

He noticed several Gate Keepers checking people's bags and letting them through the massive portcullis. When it was Lacuna's turn to enter the city, a Gate Keeper stopped him.

'Your papers,' the Gate Keeper said tersely.

Lacuna wasn't sure what to do. He remembered the Border Guard; perhaps he was supposed to have gotten papers that would allow him passage into the Kingdom from the Border Guard.

'I don't have any papers, sir,' he said to the Gate Keeper. 'I'm not from here. I come from the, uh, south.' He had begun to say that he was from the Great Swamp of Ink, but decided that it might not make a very good impression; he wanted to erase his past forever and start again as a northern person, so he decided right there that he would mention the swamp as little as possible from now on.

'Go over there,' the Gate Keeper said, pointing to a small stone gatehouse. He proceeded to inspect the next person's papers.

Lacuna approached the gatehouse and knocked on the door. Another Gate Keeper opened it and let him in.

'What can I do for you?'

'Well, sir, the man at the gate asked me for my papers and I told him I don't have any papers. See, I'm not from here, I'm from the south. Was I supposed to get my papers at the border?'

'The border?' the Gate Keeper said with a frown. 'I don't know what you're talking about. He was asking you for your papers of citizenship. You have to have papers to prove that you are a citizen of the Northern Kingdom to enter, of course.'

Lacuna felt despair welling in his chest. He had come so far, only to be denied.

'What am I going to do?' he asked desperately.

'Don't worry,' the Gate Keeper said, beginning to grasp Lacuna's situation. He shook his head and moved his hand as if to wave away Lacuna's worries like so much smoke.

'Have a seat. Listen, I have the authority to issue you papers immediately. All you have to do is register here, and sign some forms.'

The Gate Keeper pushed a stack of papers towards Lacuna.

'It's just so we know who you are. If you sign the papers and become a citizen, you can come and go as you please. You can leave the Kingdom and return any time you want. We welcome new subjects. All you have to do is fill out the forms and sign on the dotted line, and you'll be an instant citizen.'

He passed a quill pen and a small pot of blue ink across his desk to where Lacuna sat listening intently.

'There's only one rule that I have to inform you of before you sign.'

As he spoke, the Gate Keeper's eyes strayed absent-mindedly to the wall of his office. Lacuna followed the man's gaze to a portrait that hung there depicting a stern-looking man wearing a crown full of enormous sapphires. The Gate Keeper cleared his throat and continued without taking his eyes off the portrait.

'Citizens like yourself are required to take possession of a special mirror, which they are to carry on their person at all times. Now listen carefully: *as long as you are within the gates of the city you must never take your eyes off this mirror.* The mirror is magical, and if you look away from it for even a second, you will feel a sharp pain that will grow in intensity until it eventually kills you; all this will only take a matter of minutes. However, if you close your eyes entirely, you will not feel any pain. But as long as your eyes are open, you must be gazing into the mirror. That way, you may sleep at night quite normally, provided you do not open your eyes until the mirror is in front of you when you wake up.'

Lacuna could not believe what he was hearing. A magical mirror from which he wasn't allowed to break his gaze?

'This is insane,' he protested. 'How will I get around? How will I hold a job or even walk down the street if I always have to look into this magical mirror? Does everyone in the Northern Kingdom have to do this?'

The Gate Keeper sighed as if he had explained this far too many times to feel altogether sympathetic.

'Only people who were not born in the city are assigned mirrors. Those who were born here do not need them. As for getting around, I assure you that the Mirror People—as we call citizens like yourself—do just fine. They manage to hold down jobs and raise families, and they get around the best they can. Believe me, it may seem strange now, but you'll adjust in no time. And if you can't, well, you can always go back where you came from.'

Lacuna felt a horrid mixture of disappointment, anger, and frustration. He wished he had gone west or east or south: anywhere but here. But he had come so far that he was determined at least to see this great city with all its people. He reached for the papers, dipped the quill pen in the pot of deep blue ink, and signed on the dotted line. Immediately afterward, the Gate Keeper brought forth a large golden-framed mirror from beneath his desk and handed it to him. It was heavy and unwieldy, as wide as Lacuna's shoulders, and square. He took it grudgingly and returned to the gates with his freshly validated papers.

## THE MIRROR PEOPLE AND THE MIRRORLESS PEOPLE

Once inside the city, the first thing Lacuna noticed was that he had to strap everything onto his back, including his skeleton key crutch-axe, because it took both of his hands to hold the magical mirror in front of his face. He also noticed that the Gate Keeper was not lying about the intense pain that came to him when he glanced away for merely a moment to take in the city; the pain shot like lightning through his temples, and out of necessity he quickly returned his gaze to the mirror. He noticed, however, that there were several people on the streets who held mirrors up to their faces, although the majority of the people in the city did not. He saw that the Mirror People walked backwards, using their mirrors to see over their shoulders which direction they were going. It looked like many of these people had been doing this for years because they seemed very skilled at walking backwards, talking to each other, and even reading words in books or newspapers backwards, all by angling the mirror in the right direction. They looked awkward, but managed as best they could.

He spent his first day walking around the city, trying to get used to walking backwards and with his mirror as his guide, looking for somewhere to stay and places that might hire him for work. He felt foolish with his mirror, especially when he was around people who did not need mirrors.

At one point, he had to ask directions of a man who also carried a mirror, and for the first time realized that such a conversation meant that they had to stand back to back, each holding his mirror so as to see over his shoulder into the other person's mirror. He did not actually get to look directly into the man's face, but rather he was seeing a reflection of a reflection of the man talking to him.

After several days of orienting himself, Lacuna started working shining mirrors on a street corner for pocket change. He polished mirrors for the Mirror People who were busily going to and fro in the great city. He also found a cheap rooming house that he could afford, and spent his days working hard and wondering what his future would bring.

'I'm happy to be here,' he thought to himself as he shined an old woman's mirror, 'and I know this is better than the Great Swamp of Ink, but it isn't what I expected at all.' His thoughts circled around in his mind like seagulls over a low tide, but they would not perch at a conclusion. He was not happy, nor was he entirely sad; he was puzzled.

'You're awfully quiet there, young man.'

The old woman's voice caught Lacuna's attention. He looked up at her: she was a dignified-looking woman, and she sat in the little chair he had set up for customers, her eyes closed as he was busy polishing her mirror.

'I was just thinking about the Kingdom,' he said to the woman. 'I'm still trying to get used to these mirrors, to tell you the truth, ma'am.'

'Don't you worry about it, youngster,' she said kindly. He could hear in her voice that she cared and understood how he felt. 'It might take a while, but you'll get the hang of it. Soon you'll barely notice that you have that mirror. It becomes like a friend after awhile.'

'I still don't understand why we have to have them at all,' he said.

'Now, that kind of talk is foolishness,' the old woman retorted. 'It's just the way things are. The King wants it that way, and this is the Northern Kingdom, right? There's no point in not understanding something as simple as that.'

When he finished polishing her mirror, Lacuna put it into her hands. She opened her eyes and examined how well he had cleaned the glass and, satisfied, reached into her purse to pay him. Her eyes, in the angle of her mirror, fixed on the skeleton key crutch-axe which lay at Lacuna's side. He had gotten into the habit of carrying it around with him wherever he went.

'What's that?' she asked.

'It's a crutch. And an axe, sort of.' He realized that he wasn't very sure what to call it. 'It's mine,' he offered finally.

'It's pretty,' said the old woman. 'I've never seen anything like it. It's unusual. I bet you could make an interesting costume for the Festival around something that unusual.'

'What festival?' Lacuna asked.

'What do you mean, "What festival?" *The* Festival. Only the biggest event of the year. You really must not be from around here. Once a year we have a celebration called the Festival of the Aurora Borealis. The great Aurora Borealis comes out and lights up the whole sky above the Kingdom. It's an unbelievably dazzling light show, and everyone wears strange and unique costumes for the occasion. We all look up into the sky and at midnight the Aurora Borealis arrives in all its glory. The Festival is only a month and a half away. You watch, business will pick up around the time before the Festival. Everyone will be getting their mirrors polished so they can see the lights best.'

With that, the woman paid Lacuna, thanked him, and went on her way.

For the next few nights, he found it difficult to sleep. Thoughts circled in his head like his hand circled with its cloth when he polished someone's mirror. He realized that since he had come to the Northern Kingdom he had barely spoken to a Mirrorless Person, and the only Mirror People he knew were those he met as he worked. Amazingly, he still felt lonely even though he was surrounded by people. He hated carrying his mirror around all day, and it took all his patience to keep from smashing it every time he thought about how foolish it all seemed. He wondered if he would go on forever at this job, living in a tiny room, and feeling alone. But the Festival of the Aurora Borealis was something to look forward to. Surely the Aurora Borealis would be at least as beautiful as Polaris. Lacuna wondered if he should really make a costume using the skeleton key crutch-axe as the old woman had suggested. Perhaps he would dress up as the Border Guard. He thought that it would be such a pity that he and all the Mirror People would have to watch the Aurora Borealis through these stupid mirrors. He had had the experience of witnessing Polaris up close with his own eyes, and he didn't realize what a privilege that had been until this moment.

With these disjointed thoughts spinning in his head, Lacuna drifted off to sleep.

## THE FESTIVALS OF THE AURORA BOREALIS

He woke abruptly out of a startling dream, and immediately opened his eyes by reflex; instantly, the pain rushed in. He groped for his mirror, which lay beside the bed, and looked into it. By the time the mirror was safely in front of his eyes, he realized that he had already forgotten his dream.

Later in the day, while polishing an accountant's mirror, Lacuna suddenly remembered what his dream had been about.

He had dreamt of a vast sheet of ice. Lacuna wore a pair of skates and glided effortlessly across the ice. He felt as if he were flying; he felt just as he did when Polaris carried him through the air out of the Great Swamp of Ink. Lacuna skated in large figure-eights, looping a broad curve, then arcing back across his previous path. His skates cut a massive figure into the ice that looked like this:

He skated and skated around and around on the ice. That was all.

When he remembered this dream, Lacuna stopped still in his polishing. An idea had finally come to him.

With his mirror, he looked up at the accountant sitting in the customer's chair; the accountant wore a pair of wire-rim glasses. Lacuna quickly checked his pockets to see how much money he had on him. He handed the accountant back his mirror, so that they could see each other.

'Listen, sir,' Lacuna said, 'can I buy those glasses from you? I'll give you this.' He held out a week's earnings to the accountant.

The accountant frowned and looked at the money, then back at Lacuna.

'That's a lot of money. Why would you want to buy my glasses? If your eyesight is bothering you, you ought to go to the optometrist. You need to get glasses that work for you specifically. They're unique that way, you know.'

Lacuna shook his head and thrust the money at the accountant.

'No, no, I don't need them for that. Please take my money, it's more than enough to buy a new pair. I just need your glasses right now.'

'Are you feeling alright?' the accountant said suspiciously. None of this made sense to him, and, after all, he had only wanted his mirror shined.

Lacuna was getting impatient and blurted out, 'Look, I'm fine, I'm fine. Will you please sell me your glasses right away? Please? I mean, if you don't want the money, I'll find someone else.'

The accountant was reluctant, but he knew that the money was enough to buy a newer and better pair, and he really didn't care much if a crazy mirror polisher wanted to throw his money away on foolish things. He took the money, and gave Lacuna his glasses, but waited around to see what this crazy mirror polisher was going to do with them.

Lacuna took the accountant's glasses and immediately smashed the lenses out of them. The accountant shook his head, certain now that the poor boy had lost his mind. But then Lacuna carefully picked all the glass out of the frames of the spectacles until there was nothing but the wire rims. He laid his own mirror on the ground and picked up the skeleton key crutch-axe, which was at his side as always. He paused for a moment, remembering that the Border Guard had said the skeleton key crutch-axe was the sharpest blade in the whole world. He carefully pressed the blade of the axe against the glass of his mirror and cut out a small circle. The blade sliced easily through the glass, as easily as if he were dipping it into water. He gently lifted up the small circle of mirror and fitted it into one of the frames of the wire rims. The accountant watched speechlessly, and a small crowd began to gather. Lacuna put the small circle of mirror into the frame so that the mirror faced inward. Then he put on the glasses. His left eye stared directly into the mirror, while his right eye scanned the crowd, the buildings, and the sky directly; there was no pain because he had not broken eye contact with the piece of mirror with one eye, while his other eye was free to see the world plain.

The crowd grew until the whole corner was buzzing with people. The ones who had been there to witness the event were telling the newcomers, and people were talking to one another excitedly. Everyone was visibly awed, and some actually gasped when they heard the news that this young mirror polisher had figured out a way to see with one eye on and one eye off his cursed mirror.

The accountant, who had watched the whole spectacle, said, 'Boy, will you make me a pair of glasses like that? I'll give you double your money back.'

Suddenly, everyone pushed forward, some waving money at Lacuna, dozens of Mirror People asking him to make them a pair of the miraculous glasses. Right there on the street, he set about to making dozens of pairs of glasses for those who had the money and the frames. In less than an hour, he had made more money than he had ever dreamed of. The accountant offered Lacuna his financial services, which he accepted because he was too busy making glasses to handle the great crowd. The accountant organized the excited Mirror People into a line-up. By the end of the day, Lacuna had made enough money to live in leisure for years.

In the next few weeks, Lacuna opened up a shop and hired the accountant as his personal assistant. He used his idea and his skeleton key crutch-axe-glasscutter to accumulate for himself a small fortune. In the days leading up to the Festival of the Aurora Borealis, business, as the old woman had predicted, boomed. Everyone wanted the new glasses; everyone wanted to see the world directly with at least one eye, and without the medium of their cursed mirror. In time, he knew, other people would take his idea and start their own businesses with ordinary glasscutters, but he had already firmly established himself.

On the eve of the Festival of the Aurora Borealis, Lacuna and the accountant dressed up for the event, the accountant in a dazzling rented costume of silver and gold, Lacuna in a tailored blue approximation of the Border Guard's uniform. The two partners strutted out into the night to join the greatest celebration of the year in the Northern Kingdom. As they walked through the crowd, Lacuna thought about how fortunate he had been. Many of the Mirror People walked around in the glasses that he had made for them, excited to see their first Festival inside the city with one good eye. It was true that there were Mirror People who still held the old, large mirrors—those who couldn't afford to buy his new innovation—but he generally avoided looking at them. There were also the ones outside the walls of the city. He had learned that it was a tradition for many Mirror People to leave the city on this night to watch the Aurora Borealis from the countryside where they didn't need their cursed mirrors. There, some Mirror People had always gathered together to create their own Festival.

He wondered about them, and he wondered about the ones who still held their large, cumbersome mirrors. He even wondered what the Mirrorless People thought about all the recent changes he had sparked. He wondered about these things, but his thoughts just circled in his head, round and round like the alabaster walls of the city.

At midnight, the Aurora Borealis arrived. It was beautiful, and everyone in the crowd gasped and cheered at its wavering colours. The lights danced and weaved across the sky, and everyone, in their brilliant and bizarre costumes, began the traditional dances that imitated the vacillations and the shimmer of the Aurora Borealis itself.

Lacuna stood still, among his people, looking up, gaping at the motion of the lights with one half of his vision, staring at his own open eye with the other.

2004

# The Reinventing Wheel

The reading of the Red Sea[1] bleeds into me
as parable. The parabola[2]
of the word crossing water,
*Kamby Bolongo*.[3] The perambulation
of call and response,
the word made vinyl.[4] The Nile,
like the culture,
overflows,[5] the line secedes. Jordan,[6]
like papyrus,
tears or folds.                                        10

---

1  This reference to the Red Sea (many biblical scholars believe this name is a mistranslation for 'Reed Sea') begins a series of allusions to the story of Moses. According to the Book of Exodus, Moses was adopted as an infant by the Egyptian Pharaoh's daughter, raised as an Egyptian, and became an advisor to the Pharaoh. After a divine revelation, he embraced his Israelite heritage and led his people out of their bondage as Egyptian slaves to a land of their own, promised them by God. When the Pharaoh's army pursued them, God caused the Red Sea to part, allowing Moses and the Israelites to cross; the pursuing Egyptians were destroyed when the water returned.

2  As well as having its broad contemporary meaning here of an arc or curving trajectory, in earlier use, *parabola*— etymologically related to parable, an allegorical fable—formerly designated a figure of speech involving comparison. (Both meanings derive from a common etymology of *a throw across*.)

3  In *Roots: The Saga of an American Family* (1976), Alex Haley tells how these two words, passed down in his family, probably referred, in the Mandinka language, to the 'Gambia River', their African place of origin. His Pulitzer Prize–winning narrative, along with the immensely popular twelve-hour television mini-series made from it, spurred interest among African-Americans in recovering their African ancestry.

4  A play on the opening of the Gospel of John, which describes the incarnation of the Son of God as 'the Word made flesh.' *Call and response* is a musical device, used extensively in African-American music, in which a phrase sung by one singer is responded to by a second.

5  The annual flooding of the Nile, the river that flows through Egypt into the Mediterranean Sea, turns dry land into fertile ground.

6  The Jordan River, the dividing line between Jordan and Israel, was crossed by the Israelites when they arrived in the Promised Land. Symbolically, crossing the Jordan is to achieve freedom and salvation.

'Snatch It Back and Hold
It,' Junior Wells told us,[7]
and Arrested Development sampled
it. The passage is collapsing
and Moses' magic for passing as African
is the fashion
among blacks.
The lighter skinned, the damned-
near-white among us blush
with pride when called 'nigga', flushed                                    20
out. Snatched back and held. Elemental.
And all there is to say to that is,

> It be's like that sometimes
> cause I can't control the rhyme.
>
> (Keith Murray)[8]

Or that's the way the wave breaks, homes.

Moses, says the speaker, can you take us to the bridge?
Can you hit it and quit? Can you shake your meaning maker,[9]
old restless spook? Speak us
out of this mess, this unpassable test, this pattern.                      30
Hold it back and snatch it.
Fix that word, cause the shit is broke.
Write it in stone.

---

7  Junior Wells (1934–98), né Amos Blackmore, was a Chicago-based singer and harmonica player who recorded
   'Snatch It Back and Hold It' on the album *Hoodoo Man Blues* (1965). This song was sampled by the alternative
   hip hop group Arrested Development in 'Mama's Always On Stage' (1992). *Passage* in the following line can refer
   to the original passage being sampled, but it also evokes the idea of both the Israelites' passage across the Red
   Sea and its subsequent 'collapsing' and 'the Middle Passage'—the ocean-crossing that brought slaves from Africa
   to the Americas. As well, it resonates with 'passing' in the next line, in the sense of individuals representing
   themselves as a member of a race that has attempted to exclude them (historically, there was a great deal of anxiety among whites in the American South about light-skinned African-Americans 'passing as white'). *Elemental*
   (below) may be a reference to the Croatian hip hop band by that name; to the Atlanta, Georgia, rapper
   'Elemental Emcee'; or the Brighton, England, hip hop MC and dub artist (though specializing in African-
   American music, none of three are of African descent).
8  Keith Murray (b. 1974): MC and later rapper and member of the rap trio Def Squad, known for the complexity of his lyrics; this passage is from 'The Rhyme', a song on Murray's album *Enigma* (1996).
9  American singer-songwriter James Brown (1933–2006) would improvise his songs in performance, calling out
   instructions to his band; one phrase for which he was particularly well known was 'Take me to the [musical]
   bridge.' He can be heard shouting this on his 1970 hit 'Get Up (I Feel Like Being a) Sex Machine'. He brings
   that song to a conclusion by telling the band to 'hit it and quit' and also uses the traditional blues line, 'Shake
   your money maker.' Brown was an important figure in the transition from gospel and early rhythm and blues
   to soul and funk. As well as slang for 'ghost', *spook* is a derogatory racist term for African-American men.

Xerox the tablets.[10]
Cause Lord knows the author
got to get over.
Take us home. Keep it real. Word is bond. The age

demands bling bling not Mau Mau,[11] but I'm still down
with ID. I'm out of sync
with the attrition. Perpetually                                    40
beat juggling history and ethnicity.
From Hegel[12] to turntablism,
revolution to fusion,
the fall of the Soviet Union
is what really blew up Chuck D's spot.[13]

Hip hop is black Canada's CNN [sic].
Talk stops for no border cop. Black
slang is the new cash crop. One drop[14]
half-castes can't cope with that.
Forget about Ebonics,[15]                                          50
I'm reverting to scat.

Translation live on location.
Sounding for the *griot*[16] in my bloodstream.

10  During the Israelites' time in the desert before arriving at the Promised Land, God called Moses to the top of
Mount Sinai and gave him two stone tablets on which were written the Ten Commandments. When Moses came
down from the mountain, he saw that his people had begun to worship an idol and, in anger, threw the tablets
down, breaking them. He therefore had to return to God on Mount Sinai for a second copy (which Compton
jokingly calls a 'Xerox') of the commandments.

11  A turn on 'The age demanded an image'—a famous line from Ezra Pound's long poem 'Hugh Selwyn Mauberly'
(1920). The Mau Mau Rebellion was a militant nationalist movement in Kenya, 1952–60, opposing British colonial rule. In US urban slang, 'Mau Mau' can be used as a verb (to coerce; to commit violence on) or as a noun
(a member of a black street-gang).

12  Georg Wilhelm Friedrich Hegel (1770–1831), influential German philosopher; his theory of historical progress
(often summed up as 'thesis, antithesis, synthesis') is one in which opposing forces create a dialectic that is
resolved into a third new element. (Although Hegel thought art was the highest expression of this resolution
of opposites, his dialectics were appropriated into Karl Marx's materialist theories of revolution.) Perhaps the
most influential feature of Hegel's theory is his discussion of the master–slave dialectic, in which a contest for
dominance resolves into mutual recognition and co-operation.

13  Carlton Douglas Ridenhour (b. 1960), a politically active rapper and writer, whose group Public Enemy made
sampling central to rap while creating socially conscious music that attacked capitalist social structures in the
United States and elsewhere as manifestations of a master–slave relationship. In a 2000 interview with *Time*
magazine, he said 'hip-hop has always been Black America's CNN.'

14  White American racism has historically identified anyone with 'one drop' of African blood as black.

15  A term coined in the 1970s to collectively describe African-American dialects. 'Scat' is jazz singing as vocal
improvisation without words, the equivalent of an instrumental solo (it was introduced in the 1920s by African-
American singers).

16  A West-African term for a travelling poet, musician, and singer who passes down history and traditional stories
through songs.

Jazz as
evisceration.
The mulatto will not be metaphorized,
but will a word be live?
Is the hole in the machine ghostly,[17]
the lapse in the record? Is there breath in its backmask?[18]
Schroedinger's cat[19] cast out                                        60
in this infinitive synthesis.[20] The drum

has gotten ghost.[21] But where was the death? No throat
was cut or hide disrupted
from blood. No body was hided, no matter,
no breathing was skinned in the making of this. The drum
is the black pole[22] of this constellation,
the collapsed lung of this breath line, the fissure,
the shape-shifter. Osiris.[23] The delayed
decay.

The line between                                                       70
us and I swells
like the Nile swells,

---

17 Gilbert Ryle (1900–76) used the phrase 'ghost in the machine' as a critical evaluation of the division between mind and body in René Descartes' philosophy.

18 To backmask (or backward mask) is to record sound or words in reverse.

19 'Schroedinger's cat' is shorthand for a 1935 thought experiment by the Austrian physicist Erwin Schrödinger to demonstrate the apparent absurdity of applying the indeterminacy of quantum mechanics to the experiential world. He predicated that a live cat had been placed in a sealed container for an hour with a radioactive isotope trigger that equally might or might not release a lethal poison. In terms of quantum physics, the cat would be 'entangled' in its own life–death probability and would, thus, be quantumly both alive and dead until the box was opened and an observation made.

20 Compton identifies this phrase as a jocular antonym to 'split infinitive'—and as part of the poem's theme of 'not split, but kept together'. It also recalls the use of the synthesizer in music.

21 'Ghost drums' is a term used to describe the addition of a secondary, softer drum track to fill in the main drum beat on a recording, or the addition by a drummer of soft beats to fill in what would otherwise be a silent moment in a drum rhythm. In the lines that follow, there has been no death connected to the drum because, where drum heads were once made of animal hides (for which reason drums are still sometimes referred to as 'skins'), they are now made of plastic, while on recordings the sound of drums is often produced by synthesizers. Compton writes that, in composing this poem, he saw himself 'in conversation with "The Making of the Drum" by Kamau Brathwaite—from his book *Masks*, part of his trilogy *The Arrivants*. He writes there about the Akan tradition of killing a goat to make a drum, and their spiritual system's concept that the soul of the animal continues to speak through the playing of the instrument for musical and ceremonial purposes; Brathwaite's exploration of the connection between sacrifice, identity and voice. I was trying to "translate" some of Brathwaite's thinking—which seems, to me, to be a kind of black existentialism—into the contemporary experience of hip hop and electronic music.'

22 The pole star, or North Star, traditionally used by navigators to orient themselves, is, here, blended with a black hole—believed to lie at the centre of every large galaxy. 'Breath line' was a term used by the US poet Charles Olson to suggest a way of thinking about the length of a line of poetry as an oral form and without reference to metre.

23 The Egyptian god of regeneration and rebirth: after being killed and dismembered by his brother, Set, he is reassembled by his wife, Isis. As fertility god, Osiris is, in his death and rebirth, symbolically identified with the annual seasonal cycle from infertility to fertility—particularly with the yearly drought and flooding of the Nile.

as the Afrocentripetalists[24] have it.
Everything this side two founding nations
is yours to dwell
in.

The rupture is the inscription, the brokenness the tradition,
the repetition the affliction, the body the preserved fiction.
The script the friction.

It's Xango[25] who performs in RCA the peristyle,                               80
his arms reaching, pointing: *Remember.* It's Damballah too,
dialing, fixing me, (604)-specific. Matsushita crossed the Pacific,[26]
and that's where we're taking it. You can blame
all ignorance on the failure to feed
the ghosts in these Technics. There is immortality
in the track. A snake
chasing its tail.[27] The groove
moving the text. The descendant's speak
unsheathing the record. The beat
of skin remembered. The donning                                                90
of masks we become, membered.

Legba's rood[28] cock-rockism,
forever coming. We are conscious now, aroused, the noise gates

24 A coinage combining *Afrocentric* with *centripetal* (i.e., moving to the centre): thus, those who see everything as
   both centring on and returning to Africa as the hub.
25 Xango is the Voodoo god of thunder and lightning (who serves in this poem, Compton has observed, as 'a
   black embodiment of electricity'); he is also the god of music and dance, and possessor of the *Bata*, three double-headed drums. Here, his reaching arms recall the tone arm of the turntable. (*RCA* refers to the plugs and
   cables.) *Damballah* is the creator god in Voodoo (frequently identified with Moses): a serpent god ('coiled, like
   the spiral groove' of vinyl records, Compton has remarked), he embodies the spirits of the ancestors (hence,
   like the phonograph record, he allows access to the past as an archive). *Peristyle*: the Voodoo temple; in its centre is a pole (the poto mitan) around which dancing revolves and which represents the centre of the universe—
   thus analogous here to the spindle in the centre of the turntable. The priest occupies the peristyle during rituals
   and is possessed by a spirit. '604': is Vancouver's area code.
26 Japan's Matsushita Electric Industrial Company, which became Panasonic. 'Technics': a brand of audio equipment made by Panasonic and especially known for high quality turntables.
27 An allusion to the ouroboros, a self-devouring snake—a symbol of infinity and of self-renewing cycles—which
   Compton here compares to the apparently endless cycles of a record's grooves.
28 In Voodoo, Papa Legba is a master linguist who serves as the translator and intermediary between human
   beings and the spirit world; he opens the gate of the temple and is the guardian of the poto mitan. He is
   depicted as an old man with a crutch, cane, or rod. Compton discusses (in the *West Coast Line* interview) the
   importance of Legba in his work as 'a god of indeterminacy, the crossroads, and chance.' A rood is a cross.
   (Compton is probably aware of Jimi Hendrix's belief that the Christian cross and the Voodoo poto mitan were
   both symbols of an axis that links heaven and earth.) Given the context, there also may be a pun here on 'rude',
   since cock rock is music, typically heavy metal or hard rock, that is ostentatious in its celebration of male sexuality or macho behaviour.

blown down.[29] Now we got beautiful monuments to our pronouns,
carved from rock. We are awake. We have archived ourselves.
The ancestors we have honoured
will be born as our descendants
to remember us. We are conscious
as we speak our names.
So we live. We don't sleep. We drop silence.                                  100
The cock has crowed, the chickens are home
to roost under eves. We are awake
as surely as we speak our names.

The speakers are feeding back; Jimi played *that*,[30]
the backtalk, the lip. His hymn was tradition
and ignition,[31] following the pillar
of an inner immolition.

Back Homeists want to bring it on,
want the Black Star Line,[32] every ear here,[33]
a siding God,[34] and a line-in, line-out[35]                                 110
I. I

---

29 Perhaps an allusion to the story of Joshua's conquest of the city of Jericho: he caused its walls and gates to fall
 by sounding a ram's horn and a trumpet and giving 'a great shout' (Joshua 6:5). 'Noise gates' are used to control the volume or threshold of audio signals and to suppress noise.
30 Rock guitarist and singer Jimi Hendrix (1942–70), whose innovations on the guitar included using feedback
 from the speakers as part of the performance, as in his famous rendition of 'The Star-Spangled Banner' at
 Woodstock in 1969.
31 Hendrix famously set his guitar on fire at the 1967 Monterrey Pop Festival. *Immolition*: a variant spelling of
 'immolation', sacrifice, often by fire and associated with self-sacrifice; 'pillar' recalls the pillar of fire God
 provided as a guide for Moses and the Israelites in the wilderness.
32 A shipping line (1919–22) started by Marcus Garvey (1887–1940) as a way of promoting worldwide commerce
 among black communities; Garvey, a black organizer (sometimes known as the 'Black Moses'), was the founder
 of the first important black nationalist movement in the United States and one of the first to articulate the idea
 of black pride; his ideas on racial separatism led him to become a promoter of a controversial Back-to-Africa
 movement (thus, an example of what Compton calls 'Back Homeists'), arguing that Africans in the Western
 World had been, like the Jews taken to Babylon in the sixth century BCE, abducted into an alien, unjust, and
 materialistic culture.
33 A punning rephrasing (repeated later in the poem) of sermon rhetoric, 'Let those with ears hear', based on
 statements in the Bible such as Matthew 11:15: 'He that hath ears to hear, let him hear.'
34 That is, a God who takes sides in an argument.
35 As well as a reference to the shipping line making a round trip, connectors in an audio set-up for carrying the
 signal in and out.

am plugged into my mixer, lashed, with wax
stopping my ears.[36] Tacking
into Tradition,
taking it all in:
the phones, the speakers,
the way it was is and ever shall be,[37]
the intractable track
of the word.

Lyrical / prosaic,                                                      120
settler / native,
American / North American,
nationalism / segregation,
gold / pyrite,
familiarity / contempt,
ocean / border,
sub / urban,
dispersal / determinacy,
mulatto,
mestizo,                                                                 130
métis,
cabra,[38]
Eurasian,
creole,
coloured,
colored,
split.

Those who have no history are doomed.[39]

36 An allusion to the story, in Homer's *Odyssey*, of Odysseus and the sirens. Journeying on his ship, Odysseus had
   his men stop up their ears with wax so they would not hear the sirens' dangerously tempting song; leaving his
   own ears unstopped, he had them lash him to the mast so he could hear but not yield to their call. In
   Compton's poem, 'wax' has a punning reference, as slang for vinyl records. *Tacking* is a nautical term for making progress when sailing into the wind by running an oblique course, or series of courses, rather than moving
   directly forward; hence, zigzagging.
37 An allusion to the short Christian praise-hymn known as the Doxology: 'Glory be to the Father, and to the
   Son, and to the Holy Ghost. As it was in the beginning, is now and ever shall be.'
38 One of the many gradations of mixed race in Brazil.
39 A recasting of George Santayana's famous epigram: 'Those who cannot learn from history are doomed to
   repeat it.'

I am plugged into the tradition
to stop my ears against the temptation.                                    140
I can't get next to you. The drum
is the black hole. Shango is the breath
into coal, into diamond.
Without the drum's death,
we have to watch ourselves, stop our ears
against the soundlessness. The sacredness
in the wax, the gris-gris, the ju-ju,[40] the repeat. The sacredness
is the popular. The ventriloquist act. The limbo. Zombification.
Dancing in the low-ceilinged cargo hold.

The author was born in 1972.                                               150
In 1972 the Matsushita Electric Industrial Company
introduced the Technics SL1200 turntable.
They did not pay respects to Xango or Raiju,[41]
and that is the source of the wow and flutter of our souls.

The word is the body
of Osiris, it's spliced. A communion
is happening worldwide, a whirlwind
of performances, black English, black expropriation
scattered to the four corners. Every ear shall here.
The words of the prophets are written in graf.[42]                         160
James Brown never said, 'Say it loud,
I'm mixed-race in a satellite of the U.S. and proud.'[43]
There's no echo, but there is culture
falling from the firmament like virga,[44]
and I'm an instrument of the verge,[45]
cupping the snail shell to my ear, hearing
and placing the phrases brought forth from rock by Thoth,[46]

40  Ju-ju is the magical power of an object; or an object imbued with magic. Gris-gris is usually an amulet or small
    bag (containing such things as herbs, oils, hair, and stones) whose magical properties protect its wearer from
    evil or bring luck.
41  A god of thunder, lightning, and fire from Japanese mythology; 'wow and flutter' are terms describing playback
    distortions caused by a turntable not maintaining an even speed.
42  A turn on a line from Simon and Garfunkel's 1965 song 'The Sounds of Silence': 'The words of the prophets
    are written on the subway walls / And tenement halls.' Graph: graffiti.
43  James Brown's song 'Say It Loud—I'm Black and I'm Proud' (1968) became identified with the American black
    power and black pride movements of the 1960s and 70s.
44  A streak of precipitation that falls from a cloud, evaporating before it hits the earth. Such phenomena appear
    as slightly diagonal shafts of light extending down from a cloud.
45  Rod, staff (especially of authority); also, boundary, edge.
46  The Greek name of the ibis-headed Egyptian god, who is the voice of the supreme Egyptian god Ra; as an inter-
    mediary between human beings, a judge, and arbitrator, he is sometimes associated with Moses; he resembles
    both Legba and Moses in that he carries a staff associated with magical or divine powers. As the source of human
    knowledge and the inventor of writing in the form of pictograms, Thoth could be said to have brought forth
    phrases from rock (i.e., stone—but with the obvious pun on the musical form), just as Moses brought forth water
    from a rock. His name is a palindrome if the phoneme 'th' at the beginning and end is treated as a graphic unit.

the living palindrome and magician.
Transcription is the fixing of fiction as history
and speaking is the encryption of the world as euphony.                    170
Every ear shall here. Every eye shall sea.
We ain't maintaining,[47] yet we be
defamiliar.
My family history is fractured, impure,
history imported with deft warp and weft.
You don't know your past, you don't know your future.
History imperative.
You don't maintain,
yet it gets told.

Up from my vestigial vinyl lobe, Blow[48]                                  180
at the conch shell goes, 'These are the breaks.'
But these are the bends,[49] on the real. Those gold
chains at his throat—a rope alchemical and atrophied.
When you were new school, we didn't know
we would come to plunder your phatic calls[50] to 'Throw your hands in
the air,'
Kurtis. It is ridiculous to see this as anything but the down
hill slope, sugar. My main
man, my partner, my old school Prometheus,[51]
give me some skin in                                                       190
membrance. Finally

---

47  'Maintaining': Staying in control; remaining composed. 'Defamiliar': In literary theory, *defamiliarization* has
    been described as one of the chief functions of art: that is, art allows us to perceive familiar things freshly by
    making them appear unfamiliar.
48  Kurtis Blow (né Curtis Walker, b. 1959), who began as a breakdancer and DJ while a student at City College,
    became the first rapper to record with a major label (Mercury). The line, 'throw your hands in the air' (from his
    first single, 'Christmas Rappin') became a signature element in Blow's performances. His second hit, 'The
    Breaks' (with the lines 'I'm Kurtis Blow and I want you to know / that these are the breaks!'), went gold in 1980.
    Although he is usually considered old school—that is, in the early rap style, which featured DJs rapping while
    scratching vinyl records and overdubbing drum loops—Blow's activity as a DJ-performer and producer in New
    York made him a transitional figure between rap and hip hop. His first releases came shortly after 'Rapper's
    Delight' by the Sugarhill Gang (alluded to a few lines later in the phrase, 'the down hill / slope, sugar') became
    the first commercially successful rap record.
49  There may be a playful echo here of John Donne's Holy Sonnet 74, with its request to God 'that I may rise,
    and stand, o'erthrow me, and bend / your force, to break, blow, burn and make me new.'
50  Phatic utterances (such as 'How are you?') have a social function rather than being primarily communicative.
51  The Greek god who brought fire to humankind when the other gods preserved it for themselves—thus, a fig-
    ure who is both culture bringer and rebel. He was punished by being chained to a mountain peak for eternity
    and visited each night by an eagle that ripped into his body and devoured his liver. *Give me some skin*: to touch
    hands in greeting; this has at times referred to handshakes and high fives but has most often been used for a
    greeting (associated with mid-twentieth-century jazz musicians) in which one person's open hand slides gently
    across the other person's, without grasping it.

it really is, we really are, I really am
wavering
like I just don't care.

> *Some wise people say that stories never end. Stories are open like doors,*
> *and no one can ever shut them. Stories stay open for hundred of years,*
> *and grandchildren stand in front of an open door, learning to tell.*
> *But maybe stories end more than once. End, again and again.*

> (George Bowering)

Where my unreal niggas at? Accented evaporation. Virtuosos       200
of the used record. In the out there, somewhere,
drifting,
dreaming,
backcueing,[52]
hacking
the jingle of this Germanic chain.[53] It's a thin lane
between Hogan's Alley[54] and self-hatred.
My ghosthood,
those old standards.

> *How doth the city sit solitary, that was full of people!*      210

> *Turn thou us unto thee, O Lord, and we shall be turned;*
> *renew our days as of old.*

> (Lamentations 1:1; 5:21)[55]

Act like you know.
I take my cue out of crates and boxes,
speak by outfoxing rock. That's hip hop
in the boondocks,
the relief package
drop zone. I echo New York back
like a code-cracker.       220
Reality hacker. A Crusoe.

52 To back cue is to return to a point on a record in order to play a passage again.
53 That is, the chain of languages, including English, German, Swedish, etc., that are descended from primitive German.
54 From 1910 until the 1960s, the only black neighbourhood in Vancouver; it was destroyed to make room for more freeway space. Compton is a co-founder of the Hogan's Alley Memorial Project, an effort to commemorate this place and its history.
55 The Book of Lamentations, attributed to the prophet Jeremiah, is traditionally understood as a response by those Jews in captivity to the conquest and destruction of Jerusalem by Babylon.

Cuts cued.
I intervene
by plugging in
code, tapping
Babylonian routes. My cuneiform.

*Starting all over again*
*Is gonna be rough*

(Mel and Tim)[56]

when there's no glossary for the wicked,                                    230
no rest for the ibid. No justice, no peace.
No misprision,[57] no progress.

Just the ether[58]
of 'Other: _____,' the either
and neither, the nether-centre
of miscellany culture. Done time
Mahalia[59] gutterally tol us, in tongues, po
ssessed, how I, how we,
you and me, got over

run. River                                                                 240
Jordon. This side the speaking. This side
being undone.

It's the white page
versus black finality, vinyl
versus anthropology,
bangin on wax. Auto-ventriloquism
and tribalism gone Osirian. The importation
of broken English, open, north.
Griftin.

---

56 American soul music duo Mel Hardin and Tim McPherson recorded 'Starting Over' in 1972.
57 A wrongful act. More especially, in Harold Bloom's literary theory—as laid out in *Anxiety of Influence: A Theory of Poetry* (1973) and developed in *A Map of Misreading* (1975)—the creative process by which writers misread and misinterpret their precursors, which allows them to find room in their inherited tradition to create new work. Here, perhaps a reference to the way 'No Justice, No Peace' (the title of a 1990 song by Famous Hoodlum) recasts Martin Luther King's statement: 'Without justice, there can be no peace.' In 1992, 'No justice, no peace' became a rallying cry in Los Angeles for the violent black protests that followed the acquittal of four police officers accused of beating Rodney King.
58 Because of the success of 'Ether'—a track on Nas's *Stillmatic* album (2001) responding to Jay-Z's earlier attack in 'Takeover'—the word has come to mean a devastating 'diss' or an irreversible loss in a rivalry between hip hop artists or MCs.
59 The African-American Mahalia Jackson (1911–72), one of the most influential singers of the twentieth century; considered the world's greatest gospel singer. To speak in tongues is to be given, like the apostles in the Book of Acts on the day of Pentecost, divinely inspired ability to speak many languages.

And no trade tariff on riffin.                                                                            250
No law against trafficking tradition,
or trading on insider's nihilism,
or bullets-to-water crypticism.[60] All this and still
riven. Translation:
His master's voice[61]
biting the air.

Here in the hole
of a dug up mine,
objects pan for distinction. Somethin glitterin,
centre of the world or presence,                                                                          260
Prester John in the mirror.[62] Analogous
hands, digital
countenances.

I shake my rattle to the global click track:[63] product/product/metronomic
ethnic nationalist manna crackles
out of satellites like
prestidigitation. All my fellow postsufferers
at sea in the new lingua franca, the stutter: we are a cargo cult[64]
of reception. A buffer
between selves. Come again?                                                                               270
The packaging of our trauma, blood,
our bastardizing of the scripts from the metropole, the black ones:
these are the ready-made blues in the backwoods, backwards.
A spiral lineage. A root through.

2004

60 Early in the nineteenth century, after a sorcerer promised to turn the bullets of the British soldiers into water,
the Xhosan tribes revolted against British rule in the African cape—with disastrous results; in fomenting the
Maji-Maji rebellion against German colonizers, a spirit medium made a similar promise early in the twentieth
century, with a similar outcome.
61 A reference to an early ad or trademark (used by HMV and RCA) that depicted a fox terrier listening to a
recording of its master's voice on a gramophone.
62 A figure from medieval legend, Prester John was a Christian king said to rule over a lost kingdom in Asia or
Africa that had within it many wondrous creatures and things, including a mirror through which he could keep
track of events in his kingdom.
63 A click track is a regular series of audio cues, like a metronome, that can be used to keep the tempo of multiple musical tracks synchronized. (Compton's use of 'global' here plays on the fact that the mixer used by a
turntablist has a 'global' setting.) Manna: the miraculous food that God provided Moses and his followers in
the wilderness.
64 A cult within an indigenous culture and religion operating in the belief that the 'cargo' or belongings of an outside culture with which it has come into contact are actually intended by their indigenous gods to be theirs.
Such groups enact rituals to ensure that their own gods will recognize them and will in the future bring them
their rightful cargo (usually technologically advanced goods).

# Madeleine Thien

## b. 1974

Born in Vancouver to Chinese-Malaysian parents a year after they and her two older siblings emigrated from Malaysia, Madeleine Thien trained as a dancer before becoming interested in literature and in writing during her undergraduate years. She received her bachelor's degree at the University of British Columbia in 1997 and began publishing short stories while waiting for two years to gain admission to the very selective UBC graduate creative-writing program. In 2001, she completed her MFA; in the same year she published her short-story collection *Simple Recipes* (it won the Ethel Wilson Fiction Prize)—along with a children's book, *The Chinese Violin*. In 2001, she also received the Canadian Authors Association Air Canada Award for the most promising writer under the age of 30. (Thien is one of several UBC creative-writing students of her generation who have gone on to success; Eden Robinson is another.)

While still enrolled in the graduate program, Thien began research for a novel, travelling to Malaysia and Thailand for a few months. That novel, *Certainty,* was published in 2006 (it won the Amazon.ca/*Books in Canada* First Novel Award). In recent years she has lived in the Netherlands, Quebec City, and Montreal. In 2009, she spent three months as the first writer-in-residence at the Historic Joy Kogawa House in Vancouver.

Alice Munro professed herself 'astonished by the clarity and ease of the writing' in *Simple Recipes,* finding there 'a kind of emotional purity.' Although the stories are not autobiographical, Thien does draw on her observations of the neighbourhoods around her: 'It seemed to me there were so many things going on inside each of these households and families that were . . . mysterious to the outsider. There really was that facade of house where you can't see past the surface. You really want to get inside.'

The story printed here, 'Dispatch', dramatizes the narrator's own desire to get inside the life of another, a woman she has never met but who has, unexpectedly, altered the way she views her own life. Because this story unfolds slowly, the reader's understanding of the central character's life and situation changes in the process of reading.

Like 'Dispatch', *Certainty* weaves a narrative across time and space. It focuses on the lives of four characters, two of whom live (as did Thien's parents) in Malaysia before and during the period of the Second World War and Japanese occupation. Although the novel's characters have their own imaginative integrity, they came into existence because Thien wanted to write about her own family, beginning with her grandfather's death (he was killed by the Japanese) and her parents' experiences around the time of the war. The novel both explores events from the past and asks about the function of recalling them. (One the characters asks, 'What good did it do, after all, to remember . . . to hold on the past, if the most crucial events in life could not be changed? What good did memory do if one could never make amends?')

Thien makes states of mind as important as events both in her short stories and in *Certainty*. This emphasis is consistent with other features of her writing: she has a tendency, she remarks, 'to leave off physical descriptions.' She also notes that her work often lacks any 'sense of writing from a specific ethnicity.' Instead, she offers her readers a more ambiguous perspective, one similar to her own background:

*I'm sort of existing between . . . worlds and trying to find a way to tell a story that encompasses those worlds and has a sort of give-and-take between both. Maybe this is because I was the only one in my family born in Canada. My brother and sister were born in Malaysia. I occupy a different kind of place. . . . I'm the child of immigrants without being an immigrant. I am the sister of immigrants without being an immigrant. It's a sense of occupying a new world, feeling I could embrace a new place right away, without hesitation, unlike my parents and siblings, but still feeling I was close to them.*

While Thien was working on *Certainty* and only months before she was to make, with her mother, her first trip to Hong Kong, her mother died. This personal loss reinforced the sense of grief that pervades the novel, and it may also have underlined its ironic title. The novel's epigraph reminds us that we can never renounce our desire for certainty, but all of Thien's fiction tells us that it can never really be attained—and that what is not known can never be completely discovered.

# Dispatch

The way you imagine it, the car is speeding on the highway. Over Confederation Bridge,[1] streetlamps flashing by. It's early spring and the water below, still partially frozen, shines like a clouded mirror. You saw this bridge on a postage stamp once. It is thirteen kilometres, made of concrete, and it is not straight. It curves right and left so that no one will fall asleep at the wheel. In the morning sunshine, the concrete is blindingly white.

'Here we go,' Heather, the driver, says. She has a calm, collected voice.

Charlotte—you saw a picture of her once, dark-brown hair tied in a low ponytail—has her feet propped up against the dashboard. Her toenails are lacquered a deep sea blue. In the back seat, Jean leans forward, nodding appreciatively at the coastal landscape. The earth is red, the way they imagined it would be. It is rolling and the colours segue together, red and coffee brown and deep green. A flower garden on a hill shapes the words *Welcome to New Brunswick*.

Beside the road there are cows standing in a circle, heads together, like football players in a huddle. Charlotte points through the windshield at them. 'Strange sight,' she says. Her words get lost under the radio and the engine accelerating, but the other two nod and laugh. They wave to the cows. The car is shooting down the highway, trailing over the yellow line and back again, down to a curve in the stretch of road where they slip out of sight.

This country is a mystery to you. The farthest east you have been is Banff, Alberta. To imagine these three women then, Charlotte and Heather and Jean, you have to make everything up as you go. Take Atlantic Canada, for instance. You remember postcards of white clapboard churches, high steeples glinting in the sun. You've never met Charlotte, but you picture yourself with the three of them, driving by, snapping pictures. Along winding dirt roads, they chance upon coastal towns, lobster boats bobbing on the water. Or else abandoned canneries, paint bleached and peeling, the wood still smelling like the sea.

Instead of working, you daydream or sit cross-legged on the couch roaming the television channels. For you, news is a staple food. There's a story about a freighter that sprang a leak crossing the Atlantic Ocean. Thousands of boxes fell into the water. Months later, the cargo—a load of bathtub toys—washes up on the shoreline. Children

1 The bridge that joins Prince Edward Island and New Brunswick.

and adults comb the beach. 'I am six and three-quarters years old,' one boy tells the cameras proudly. 'I have collected fifty-three rubber ducks.' He smiles, his pockets and hands overflowing with yellow.

You're writing a book about glass, the millions of glass fishing floats that are travelling across the Pacific Ocean. They come in all shapes, rolling pins, Easter eggs, perfect spheres. And the colours, cranberry, emerald, cobalt blue. In North America, these glass floats wash up in the hundreds. Decades ago, boys and girls ran to gather them in, the buoys shimmering at their feet. They sold them for pocket money. Now, the floats are harder to come by. In the wake of storms, collectors pace the beach. Every so often, a rare one appears. Recently, on Christmas morning, a man and his granddaughter came across a solid black orb. Shine it as he did, the glass float remained dark as a bowling ball. The float has no special markings and, to date, its origins are unknown.

For hours, you stare at the computer screen thinking about the load of bathtub toys. You have far too much time on your hands. Sometimes a thought settles in your mind like a stray hair and refuses to leave. Like now, you remember your husband coming in after a jog in the rain. He went straight into the bathroom. When you heard the sound of water drumming against the bathtub, you snuck inside, steam and hot air hitting your lungs. For a full minute, you watched your husband shower, his back to you. The skin on your face broke into a sweat. You watched his body, the runner's muscles, the tendons. You reached your hand out and placed it flat against his spine, where the vertebrae curved into sacrum. He didn't even startle.

You think now that he always knew you were there. You think of the million ways he could have read this gesture. But what did you mean, putting your hand out? Perhaps you only wanted to surprise him. Perhaps you only wanted to see if through the steam and heat he was truly there, or just a figment of your imagination.

Sometimes when they're driving, no one wants to stop. Like they're married to the highway, the exit signs flashing past. They're thousands of exits away from Vancouver.

It's food that lures them off the road. A Tim Hortons at the side of the highway, beckoning. You watch them giggle into a booth, Styrofoam cups of coffee balanced in their trembling, stir-crazy fingers. The first half-dozen doughnuts go just like that. Heather lines up for more. 'Get the fritters,' Jean says, laughing, her voice shrill in the doughnut shop. 'I just *love* those fritters.' Heather buys a dozen. They're sugar-crazed by the end of it, strung out on the sidewalk in front, their legs stretched in front of them.

At night, the three of them pile into a double bed. 'I've forgotten what the rest of my life is like,' Heather says. They've each written up a handful of postcards, but have yet to send them off.

Charlotte lies back on her pillow. Her hair has come loose from its elastic band and it floats down beside her. 'Don't you ever wonder what it would be like *not* to go back?'

'If I had a million dollars,' Heather says.

'Don't you ever think, though, overland, we could drive to Chile. If we just started going in a different direction. Instead of going west, we could be in Chile.'

The next morning they continue west and no one complains. Outside Thunder Bay, they pull over at the statue of Terry Fox.[2] Charlotte sits down on the stone steps and cries. She can't stop. 'It's the fatigue,' she tells them, struggling to catch her breath. 'God, I'm tired of sleeping in motel rooms every night. Let's pull out the tents and camp. To hell with indoor plumbing. Can't we do that?' The tears are streaming down her face, mascara thick on her cheeks.

Later on, in the dark of their tent, she tells them how she remembers the day he died. When she describes it—how she stood at her elementary school in a jogging suit, listening to the announcement on the radio, watching the flag lowered to half-mast—she feels her life coming back to her. Bits and pieces she thought were long forgotten. Before that moment, she was too young to fully understand that death could happen. But then the young man on the television, the one with the curly hair and the grimace, he died and it broke her heart.

Your husband has the body and soul of a long-distance runner. He is a long-haul kind of man. Even asleep, he has that tenacity. At a moment's notice, he'll be up again, stretched and ready. Unlike you. When you lie down, you doubt your ability to up yourself again. You are the Sloppy Joe of women. You watch TV lying on the couch, you read in bed, curled up on one side. Sometimes, when the lights are out, you drag your computer into bed with you. While your husband snores, you write about the woman who owned four thousand glass floats. An arsonist torched the building she lived in. The apartment collapsed but, miraculously, no one was killed. The morning after, passers-by came and picked the surviving balls from the rubble—black and ashy and melted down.

At night, in the glow of the screen, you type to the up, down of your husband's breathing. It's difficult to look at him in these moments. His face is so open, so slack-jawed, vulnerable and alone. Both of you have always been solitary people. Like big cedars, your husband says, bulky and thick, growing wider year by year. You are charmed by your husband's metaphors, the quiet simplicity of them.

Your husband has never been unfaithful to you. But only a few months ago, you found the letter he had written to Charlotte. They had grown up together and, in the letter, he confessed that he loved her. Your husband left the letter, and her reply, face up on the kitchen table. You imagine the instant he realized, standing on the warehouse floor, broom in one hand. He tried to call you, but you just stood there, letting the telephone ring and ring. When you read his confession on that piece of looseleaf, your husband's perfect script stunned you. You thought of his face, his brown eyes and the receding slope of his hairline, the way he sat at the kitchen table reading the paper, frowning, his lips moving silently to read the words.

The woman, Charlotte, had written back. She had told him to pull himself together. She'd returned his letter, telling him that their friendship would never recover. And then he left both letters on the kitchen table. Not maliciously. You refuse

---

2 A statue memorializing the young athlete, Terry Fox (1958–81), who, after he lost a leg to cancer, embarked on a cross-country run ('the Marathon of Hope') to raise money for cancer research. He began it in St John's, Newfoundland, with the intention of completing it in Victoria, British Columbia. After covering nearly 5400 km in 143 days, he became too ill to continue and had to give up just outside Thunder Bay. When he died the following year, he was honoured as a national hero.

to believe he did it maliciously. Your husband is not that kind of man. He is the kind of person who honours privacy, who can carry a secret until the end. Shell-shocked and hurt, he must have forgotten everything.

You've imagined it perfectly. Before he left for work, he took both letters and laid them on the kitchen table. He read them over and over. He'd offered to leave his marriage for her, but she had turned him down flat. *Pull yourself together.* He made a pot of coffee and poured himself a cup. He put on his shoes, then his jacket. The envelope was on the counter. He folded it up and tucked it in his pocket. Hours later, while his mind wandered back and forth, he pulled it out, only to discover the envelope was empty. The letters were still face up on the kitchen table, where his wife, sleep-creased and hungry, had found them. He called, but the phone just rang and rang.

That night, you went out and didn't come home. You climbed on a bus and crossed the city, crying intermittently into the sleeve of your coat. At a twenty-four-hour diner, you ordered a hamburger and fries and sat there until dawn, when the early risers started showing up for breakfast. You read the paper from the night before, and then the paper from that day, cover to cover, and then you walked home, through the tree-lined streets and the slow muscle of traffic heading downtown. At home, your husband was already gone. You turned on the TV, then you lay down in bed and slept for hours.

You've pictured it from beginning to end, upside and down, in every direction. You've pictured it until it's made you sick and dizzy. Your husband has never been unfaithful to you, but something in your life is loose now. A pin is undone. When he came home and lay down beside you, you told him, 'We'll work things out,' and he, ashen-faced, nodded.

His skin was pale in the white sheets and you hovered above him, kissing his skin, trying not to miss anything. You have never been unfaithful. That's what you were thinking every time you kissed him. Look at me, you thought. I have never been unfaithful, and here I am, kissing you. You looked straight at him. Your husband's heart was broken and it wasn't you who did it. That's what you thought, when he pushed his face against your chest, his body taut and grieving.

There's a memory in your mind that you can't get rid of. The two of you in bed, lying next to one another like fish on the shore, watching images of Angola.[3] Out on Oak Street there's the white noise of traffic, endlessly coming. Catastrophe. Your husband said that line again, 'Too many cameras and not enough food,' and the two of you watched a woman weep. She wiped her eyes in her dirty handkerchief. And you, on the other side of the world, on another planet, watched soundlessly.

Instead of writing your book, you are watching the midday news. Like some kind of teenage kid, you're lying on the couch, the remote cradled on your stomach, hand in the popcorn. The world is going to hell in a handbasket. You think this but never say it aloud because it's terrible to be so cynical. But look at the world. While your city works its nine-to-five, bombs detonate, planes crash, accidents happen. You sound like your mother. While your marriage stutters on, revolutions rise and fall, blooming on the

---

3 The Angolan Civil War (1975–2002) was one of the longest and most devastating wars in modern history; intentional disruption of Angola's farm culture by both sides culminated in a severe famine.

midday news like some kind of summer flower. There's dinner to be made. Lately you have discovered your weak heart. Instead of sitting at the kitchen table writing your book, you're watching flood waters in Central America, you're watching Dili,[4] people in trucks with rifles strung on their arms. You've never even heard a shot fired. You know you think about your marriage far too much. You know that, given the chance, you will sit all day on your couch like this, watch what happens in another country. There is a woman clinging to a rooftop. A flood in Mozambique. A lack of supplies, everything coming too late. By morning, the water may rise over the spot where she sits. You want to get on a plane. You who have always wanted to please people, you want to sandbag and work. You know what you think of this woman on the rooftop—she did nothing to deserve this. But what would she think of you? She would look at you with dis-believing eyes. She would look at you with only the faintest expression of pity.

Through small-town Ontario, the three women snap photos of water towers. While you watch from the background, Charlotte climbs through the passenger window, her body swaying recklessly out. When she ducks back in, her hair is wild, blown frizzy around her head. She smiles a lopsided grin.

Past hockey arenas and high-steepled churches, blue sky over dry fields, they're singing along to the radio. Looking forward to night, when they will pitch their tent under cover of stars, break out the beer bottles which clank in the trunk. They can see themselves dancing carelessly in the hot evening. Charlotte, drunk and spinning, saying, 'Girls, I've known you all my life. What would I do without you, girls?' How bittersweet it is, when she says that. How she wonders what it would be like to be nineteen again, or twenty-one. But she'll settle for this, curled up with her friends in front of the fire. When they arrive in Vancouver, her life will return to normal. Heading home to Saskatoon again, catching up on all the time she's missed.

You're afraid of why it comes to you, clear as a picture. You tell yourself you're bound to Charlotte, but what you're afraid of is this: instead of getting on with your life, you're following her. To make sure that she's gone. To chase her out of your life. In all these vivid imaginings, you are the spectator, the watcher, the one who refuses to leave until the last act. You move through your emotions, anger settling on you like some forgotten weight. It makes you watch until the end.

So badly, you want to be the person who grieves for her. Not the envious one, the one whose heart has toughened up. You're standing on the road. There's even a space for you. A bus stop, of sorts, lit up with harsh fluorescent lights. You never stray from it. No matter what, come hell or high water, come death or disease, you'll stand there watching it all unfold.

When you see the accident, you know it must have happened a hundred times before. The stretch of highway heading to Lloydminster, straight as an arrow. Wide open, it tricks the driver into believing she's awake.

---

4 The capital of East Timor, which, after it declared itself independent in 1975, was invaded and, until 1999, occupied by Indonesia, whose brutal rule was marked by a 1991 massacre.

You almost convince yourself you're there, that it's you, semi-conscious in the driver's seat: exactly when you realize that the car is out of control, that it cannot be undone, exactly when, you're not sure. Even the impact seems part of your dream. It knocks you out. But not before you see Charlotte, sitting beside you, the slow-motion crumbling of the passenger side. Her sleeping body, belted in, thrown sideways. She's in your lap, slouched awkwardly against your body. You know you're going under. The car. You have the sensation the car is closing in. Then you don't even know it, you're under, the three of you in your seats.

Later on, Heather can only say, *We were speeding and the car slipped out of control.* Hundred and forty kilometres on a flat stretch of highway. Over the ditch and straight for a tree on the border of a farmhouse.

When the crash comes, this is what you see: lights flashing on all around. Houses you couldn't see for the dark. Snapping to life. Hurrying out into road, all these people, half-dressed. Running in the dewy grass.

The car is wrapped around the tree, the interior light miraculously blinking.

You don't want to be lovesick. You dream yourself sitting in an orange rocking chair, a steaming cup of coffee resting on the arm, the chair tipping back and forth and nothing spills. As if you could do that. Keep moving and the tiny thing you balance, the thing that threatens, stays secure. You love your husband, love him in a way that makes you heartsick. You think it is irrational to feel this way, to be so overwhelmed by the small tragedies of your life when all around you, there are images of men and women and children, in Dili there are the ones who never ran away to hide in the mountains. You pray for them in the best way you know how. You picture them standing on the street on a summer day, dust against their feet. You picture them safe. Before you know it, your hands are clasped in front of your face. It takes you aback, the way you sit there, shocked and unhappy.

Hardly a month passed between the time you found the letters and the night the accident happened. In the morning, your husband heard the news by phone. He stayed on the phone all morning, calling one person then another. He knew them all, Jean and Heather and Charlotte, childhood friends from Saskatoon. You learned that after the car hit the tree, Jean and Heather stood up and walked away. In shock, Heather started running, straight down the road. An elderly man, still dressed in pyjamas, guided her gently back to the site.

It was Heather who called your husband. 'Charlotte was asleep the whole time,' she told him. 'She never felt a thing.'

If your husband grieved, he did the gracious thing and refused to show it. When you asked him how he felt, he held himself together. 'I don't know,' he said. 'It's over.'

The expression on his face was closed and you knew better than to push. You left him alone in the apartment. It's space that he needs and that's what you give him. No confrontation or rehashing of that small betrayal, though each day you tilt between anger and sorrow. You expect his grief, are willing to understand it even. Still, he refuses to part with it—his private sorrow is not on display for you. It belongs to him alone.

These days, he spends hours reading the paper. But you can tell that it's only a cover. Like you, he's thinking. Your house is a silent place. The two of you, solicitous but lost in thought, the radio constantly murmuring in the living room. And because you believe in protocol, in politeness and respect, you don't ask him and you never mention her name. When you dropped those letters into the trash, you were telling him the terms of your agreement. Don't mention it, you were saying. Pretend it never happened. Both of you like two cedars, side by side and solitary.

You'd never met Charlotte. You worry that it's sick, this fascination with her life. But in the middle of the day, your hands poised over the keyboard, you have a vivid image of her in the passenger seat, asleep and dreaming. Something in you wants to reach your hand out, the way children lay their fingers on the television screen. When the car leaves the road, you want to nudge it back. Point it back on course. Let it not end like this.

Really, you are just a bystander. It's your husband who should be there, standing in the road. You in the background, curious. It's your husband whose emotions run deep, who weeps the way he never did in real life. If this were a picture, you would be a blur in the background.

Saskatchewan is a photo to you, a duotone of blue and gold. Wheat fields bent against the wind or motionless in the heat, a freeze frame. There's a picture of Charlotte when she was sixteen, a lovely girl standing outside of a barn laughing, dark hair shaking against the blue sky. You have never been to Saskatchewan. Imagine a sky so huge it overwhelms you. Wheat vast as the desert. You picture Charlotte on a dirt road somewhere, a road that cuts through a field. This is the way that you remember her, because between you and your husband, she will always have a kind of immortality.

For a long time you think of her as the kind of person you would like to be. She is a farmer's daughter, a one-time schoolteacher, a bus driver. You think of her as a dreamer. People are drawn to her. They say, *She really knows how to live.* Even you, in your make-believe world, are drawn to her. You watch the way her hands move, not gingerly, not tentatively. You hear her voice. It booms through space.

You play a game with her. The kind of game friends play to pass the time. *If I was an animal, what kind of animal would I be?* You tell her she is an elephant, a tiger, a gazelle. Your husband, she says, is a camel. He is a long-haul kind of man. But what are you? A tern, she says. You do not know what this is. A bird, she says. It flies over the sea. It is swift in flight. You imagine it is the kind of bird that could fly forever. Given the choice, it would never land. You say this is a fault and she laughs. She says you see the negative in everything. She has a smile that fills the room. What kind of person are you? There's some part of you that's glad she's gone. Glad that all those qualities, that smile, that confidence, couldn't save her.

You make a list of all the things you're afraid of: Nuclear catastrophe. Childbirth. War. A failed marriage. As if there is any equality between these things. You know that writing them out will not make them go away. But the list worries you. You don't want to be selfish. Walking along your Vancouver street, you press a blueberry muffin into the hand of a young man sitting on the sidewalk beside his dog. There's an apple in your coat pocket you're saving for someone else.

At home, you and your husband lie beside each other in bed, sunlight streaking through the blinds. You lie motionless like people in shock. A part of you knows that you're doing everything wrong. You know it, but still, you're sitting at the kitchen table each day, working hard. While researching Japanese glass floats, you come across the *ama*—divers in Japan's coral reefs who, with neither wetsuits nor oxygen masks, search the water for abalone. For up to two minutes at a time, these women hold their breath underwater. Their lung capacity astonishes you. Some of the *ama* are as old as sixty. Imagine them dotting the water, chests bursting for air, going on about their daily work.

One night, when neither of you can sleep, you take a late-night walk together. Through sidewalks coated with autumn leaves, you walk hand-in-hand. It is three in the morning and the streets are empty. A car turning the corner sweeps its lights across you, then disappears. You can hear it travelling away from you, you listen until the sound evaporates. At one point, in a gesture that reminds you of children, your husband swings your hand back and forth, and your joined arms move lightly between you.

The road you are following goes uphill, ending in a circle of mansions. There is a small green park in the centre and this is where you and your husband stop, turning slowly, examining the houses, trying to guess if the mansions are really abandoned as they appear. Nothing stirs. Out here, in this dark patch of land, it's easy to believe that only you and he exist. In the quiet, your husband hums softly, a tune you can't identify. He catches your eye and stops abruptly. You look at him with so much grief and anger, it surprises you both, what you can no longer withhold.

He tells you that it is unforgivable, what he has done. But he cannot go back and he does not know how to change it.

Something in your body collapses. It just gives way. Maybe it is the expression on your husband's face, telling you that there is no longer any way out. You tell your husband you've been seeing strange things, imagining cities you've never visited, people you've never met. You say, 'I cannot go on like this any more,' and your own words surprise you, the sad certainty of them.

He paces behind you, nodding his head, then begins walking the perimeter of the park. As he walks away from you, your husband raises his voice, as if he believes that no one can hear him. Perhaps he no longer cares if anyone does. He tells you more than you can bear to hear. He says that when he read Charlotte's letter, he was devastated. He wished her so far away that he would never see her again. He talks and he cannot stop. He says he is afraid of being alone, afraid of making terrible mistakes. He is ashamed of being afraid.

This is what you wanted, finally. Here is his private grief, laid out in view of the world. But your chest is bursting with sadness. You are not the only ones affected. There is still that woman who haunts you. What will she think of all your efforts, your tossing, your fear and guilt? How long will she remain with you?

Out front, the houses are still. You stand on your side of the park, watching for signs of movement, expecting the lights to come on, expecting people to come hurrying into the road.

In the end, you know that the two of you will pick yourselves up, you will walk home together not because it is expected or even because it is right. But because you are both asking to do this, in your own ways, because you have come this far together.

For a long time you stand this way, the two of you hunched in the grass. In your mind's eye there are people all around the world turning, diving, coming up for air. Your husband and you in this quiet circle. He crouches down to the ground, face in his hands. There is Charlotte, asleep and dreaming in a car moving through the Prairies. Your husband comes to his feet and looks for you, through the dark and the trees. One perilous crossing after another.

2001

# Acknowledgements

MARGARET ATWOOD. 'This is a Photograph of Me' from *The Circle Game* © 1967 by Margaret Atwood. Reprinted by permission of House of Anansi Press. • 'Progressive Insanities of a Pioneer', 'Disembarking at Quebec', 'Further Arrivals', 'Death of a Young Son by Drowning', 'Dream 2: Brian the Still-Hunter, and 'Thoughts from Underground', from *Selected Poems 1966–1984* by Margaret Atwood. Copyright © Oxford University Press Canada 1990. Reprinted by permission of the publisher. • 'Tricks with Mirrors', 'Siren Song', and 'Spelling', from *Selected Poems 1966–1984* by Margaret Atwood. Copyright © Margaret Atwood 1990. Reproduced by permission of Oxford University Press Canada. • 'Strawberries' from *Murder in the Dark* by Margaret Atwood © 1997. 'The Age of Lead' from *Wilderness Tips* by Margaret Atwood © 1991. 'The Line' from *The Door* by Margaret Atwood © 2007. Published by McClelland & Stewart Ltd. Used with permission of the publisher.

MARGARET AVISON. 'Neverness', 'Perspective', 'Snow', and 'Light (I)', from *Selected Poems*. 'The Swimmer's Moment', from *Always Now Vol 1*. 'Job: Word and Action', from *Always Now Vol 3*. 'Tennis', from *Winter Sun/The Dumbfounding Poems 1940–66*. 'We the poor who are always with us' and 'Just Left *or* The Night Margaret Laurence Left', from *Always Now Vol 2*. From *Always Now: The Collected Poems* (in three volumes) by Margaret Avison by permission of the Porcupine's Quill. Copyright © Margaret Avison, 2003. • 'Poetry Is', from *Momentary Dark* by Margaret Avison © 2006. Published by McClelland & Stewart Ltd. Used with permission of the publisher.

KEN BABSTOCK. 'Brendan's Boat' and 'Montana Nocturne', from *Mean* © 1999 by Ken Babstock. 'Marsh Theatre', 'Regenerative', and 'To the Willow' from *Days in Flatspin* © 2001 by Ken Babstock. 'Compatibilist', 'The World's Hub', and 'Essentialist' from *Airstream Land Yacht* © 2006 by Ken Babstock. Reprinted by permission of House of Anansi Press.

EARLE BIRNEY. 'Vancouver Lights', 'The Ebb Begins from Dream', 'Pacific Door', 'Bushed', 'Can Lit', 'El Greco: *Espolio*', from *One Muddy Hand: Selected Poems of Earle Birney*, Harbour Publishing 2006. Used by permission. 'Buildings II', from *Ghost in the Wheels,* used by permission.

CHRISTIAN BÖK. 'Chapter O' and 'Vowels', from *Eunoia* by Christian Bök (Coach House Books, 2001). 'Crystals', from *Crystallography* (Coach House Press, 1994).

GEORGE BOWERING. 'Grandfather', from *Points on the Grid*. Reprinted by permission of the author. • 'Elegy Two', from *Kerrisdale Elegies*. 'The Great Local Poem' and 'Prodigal', from *Blonds on Bikes*. Full acknowledgement and Reprinted by permission of Talon Books Ltd.

DIONNE BRAND. 'Hard Against the Soul' from *No Language is Neutral* by Dionne Brand © 1990. 'i', 'iii', 'xxviii', 'xxx', and 'xxxiii' from *Thirsty* by Dionne Brand © 2002. 'I Have Been Losing Roads' and 'Land to Light On' from *Land to Light On* by Dionne Brand © 1997. Published by McClelland & Stewart Ltd. Used with permission of the publisher.

ROBERT BRINGHURST. 'Essay on Adam' and 'These Poems, She Said', from *The Beauty of Weapons: Selected Poems*. 'Conversations with a Toad', 'Leda and the Swan', 'Bone Flute Breathing', and 'The Reader', from *The Calling: Selected Poems 1970–1995*. Copyright © Robert Bringhurst. Reprinted with the permission of Gaspereau Press.

MORLEY CALLAGHAN. 'Watching and Waiting', from *The Complete Stories, Volume One*, by Morley Callaghan, pages 77–85, published by Exile Editions, © 2003.

MARIA CAMPBELL. 'Jacob', from *Stories of the Road Allowance People*. (Theytus Books, 1995).

ANNE CARSON. 'Book of Isaiah' and 'TV Men: Hektor', from *Glass, Irony, and God* by Anne Carson, Copyright © 1995 by Anne Carson. Reprinted by permission of New Directions Publishing Corp. • 'Short talk on Rectification' and 'Short talk on Who you Are', from *Short Talks* by Anne Carson, originally published in Canada by Brick Books. Copyright Anne Carson, 1992. All rights reserved. Reproduced by permission of Lippincott Massie McQuilkin.

GEORGE ELLIOTT CLARKE. 'The Argument', 'The River Pilgrim: A Letter', 'Rose Vinegar', 'Bees' Wings', 'Blank Sonnet', 'The Wisdom of Shelley', and 'Each Moment is Magnificent', from *Whylah Falls*. 'Nu(is)ance', from *Blue*. 'George and Rue: Coda' and 'Mortality Sonnet', from *Black*. Reprinted by permission of Raincoast. • 'Primitivism', from *Lush Dreams, Blue Exile: Fugitive Poems, 1978–93* (Lawrencetown Beath, NS: Potersfield Press, 1994). Reprinted by permission of the author. • 'The Killing' from *Execution Poems*. Copyright © George Elliott Clarke, 2001. Reproduced with the permission of Gaspereau Press.

LEONARD COHEN. 'You Have the Lovers', 'Suzanne', 'Everybody Knows', and 'Closing Time', from *Stranger Music* Copyright © 1993 by Leonard Cohen and Leonard Cohen Stranger Music, Inc. 'In the Eyes of Men', 'It Is All Around Me', 'Holy Is Your Name', from *Book of Mercy* Copyright © 1984 by Leonard Cohen. 'Thousand Kisses Deep', 'the truth of the line' (including the line drawing), and 'Looking Through My Dreams', from *Book of Longing* Copyright © 2006 by Leonard Cohen, Drawings and decorations Copyright © 2006 by Leonard Cohen. Published by McClelland & Stewart. Used with permission of the publishers.

WAYDE COMPTON. Reprinted by permission of the publisher: 'The Blue Road: A Fairy Tale' from *49th Parallel Psalm* (Arsenal Pulp Press, 1999) and 'The Reinventing Wheel', reprinted from *Performance Bond* by Wayde Compton (Arsenal Pulp Press, 2004).

LORNA CROZIER. 'Poem about Nothing' and 'Forms of Innocence', from *The Garden Going on Without Us* by Lorna Crozier © 1985. 'Getting Pregnant' and 'On the Seventh Day', from *Inventing the Hawk* by Lorna Crozier © 1992. 'Two Eternal Things', from *A Saving Grace* by Lorna Crozier © 1996. 'The Sacrifice of Issac', from *Apocrypha of Light* by Lorna Crozier © 2002. 'Ice Fog', from *Whetstone* by Lorna Crozier © 2005. Published by McClelland & Stewart Ltd. Used with permission of the publishers. • 'My Last Erotic Poem', Copyright © Lorna Crozier. Reprinted by permission of the author. • 'This One's for You', from *The Garden Going on Without Us*. 'The Old Order' and 'At the Millstone', from *Everything Arrives at the Light*. 'Wilderness', from *A Saving Grace*. 'The Sacrifice of Abraham', from *Apocrypha of Light*. Scholarly citation and Copyright © Lorna Crozier. Reprinted by permission of the author.

TIMOTHY FINDLEY. 'Dreams', from *Stones* by Timothy Findley. Copyright © Pebble Productions Inc., 1988. Reprinted by permission of Penguin Group (Canada), a Division of Pearson Canada Inc.

MAVIS GALLANT. 'Varieties of Exile', by Mavis Gallant. Copyright © 2003 by Mavis Gallant. Originally appeared in *The New Yorker*. Reprinted by permission of Georges Borchardt, Inc., on behalf of the author.

BARBARA GOWDY. 'Presbyterian Crosswalk', from *We So Seldom Look on Love* by Barbara Gowdy (Somerville House Publishing, 1992). Copyright © 1992 Barbara Gowdy. With permission of the author.

CLAIRE HARRIS. 'August' was originally published in *Translation into Fiction*. Copyright © 1984 by Claire Harris. 'Black Sisyphus' was originally published in *Travelling to Find a Remedy*. Copyright © 1986 by Claire Harris. 'Death in Summer', 'To Dissipate Grief', and 'No God Waits for Incense' was originally published in *The Conception of Winter*. Copyright © 1995 by Claire Harris. Reprinted by permission of Goose Lane Editions.

JACK HODGINS. 'The Crossing', from *Damage Done by the Storm* by Jack Hodgins © 2004. Published by McClelland & Stewart Ltd. Used with permission of the publisher.

THOMAS KING. 'A Coyote Columbus Story', from *A Coyote Columbus Story* by Thomas King (Groundwood Books, 1992). Copyright © 1992 Thomas King. With permission of the author.

A.M. KLEIN. 'Reb Levi Yitzhok Talks to God', 'Heirloom', 'The Rocking Chair', 'Political Meeting', 'Portrait of the Poet as Landscape', and 'Autobiographical', from *A.M. Klein: Complete Poems*. Copyright © University of Toronto Press Inc., 1990, reprinted with permission of the publisher.

JOY KOGAWA. 'Obasan', a short story by Joy Kogawa, is reprinted with the permission of the author. First published by *Canadian Forum* in 1980 and subsequently adapted and incorporated into the novel *Obasan* published in 1981 by Lester & Orpen Dennys and by Penguin Canada in 1983. • 'Where There's a Wall', 'Road Building by Pick Axe', and 'Minerals from Stone', from *Woman in the Woods*. Full acknowledgement. Reprinted by permission of the publisher.

ROBERT KROETSCH. 'F.P. Grove: The Finding' from *Stone Hammer Poems 1960–1975* by Robert Kroetsch (Oolichan Books, 1975). Copyright © 1975 Robert Kroetsch. With permission of the author. • 'Seed Catalogue' from *Completed Field Notes: The Long Poems of Robert Kroetsch* by Robert Kroetsch (McClelland & Stewart Ltd., 1989). Copyright © 1989 Robert Kroetsch. With permission of the author.

PATRICK LANE. 'Because I Never Learned', 'Stigmata', and 'The Long Coyote Line', from *How Do You Spell Beautiful?* 'CPR Station—Winnipeg', 'The Weasel', 'Winter 1', 'Winter 4', 'Winter 22', 'Winter 33', 'Winter 35', 'Winter 40', 'Winter 42', and 'The Far Field', from *Selected Poems 1977–1997*. Reprinted by permission of the author. • 'The Spoon', by Patrick Lane, *Go Leaving Strange*, Harbour Publishing, 2004. 'The Sooke Potholes', by Patrick Lane, *Last Water Song*, Harbour Publishing, 2007. 'For Gwendolyn MacEwan', by Patrick Lane, revised from original version published in *Last Water Song*, Harbour Publishing, 2007. Reprinted by permission of the publisher.

MARGARET LAURENCE. 'To Set Our House in Order' from *A Bird in the House* by Margaret Laurence. © 1963, 1964, 1965, 1966, 1967, 1970. Published by McClelland & Stewart Ltd. Used with permission of the publisher.

IRVING LAYTON. 'The Birth of Tragedy', 'The Cold Green Element', 'The Fertile Muck', 'Whatever Else, Poetry is Freedom', 'Keine Lazarovitch 1870–1959', 'Butterfly on Rock', and 'A Tall Man Executes a Jig', from *A Wild Peculiar Joy: The Selected Poems of Irving Layton* Copyright © 1982, 2004 by Irving Layton. Published by McClelland @ Stewart Ltd. Used with permission of the publisher.

DENNIS LEE. 'Sibelius Park' from *Civil Elegies and Other Poems* © 1972 by Dennis Lee. 'Hiatus' and 'Desaparecidos' from *UN* © 2003 by Dennis Lee. 'Wordly' and 'Tale' from *Yesno* © 2007 by Dennis Lee. Reprinted by permission of House of Anansi Press. • 'When I Went Up to Rosedale' and 'The Gods', from *The Gods* © 1979 by Dennis Lee. 'The Coat', 'Summer Song', and 'Hunger', from *Nightwatch: New and Selected Poems 1968–1996* © 1996 by Dennis Lee. Published by McClelland & Stewart Ltd. Used with permission of the publishers.

DOROTHY LIVESAY. 'Green Rain', 'The Difference', 'Day and Night', 'Bartok and the Geranium', 'The Secret Doctrine of Women', and 'The Artefacts: West Coast'. Reprinted by permission of Jay Stewart, literary executrix for the Estate of Dorothy Livesay.

GWENDOLYN MACEWEN. 'Icarus', 'Manzini: Escape Artists', 'The Portage', and 'Dark Pines under Water', from *Magic Animals: Selected Poetry of Gwendolyn MacEwen*. 'The Death of the Loch Ness Monster' and 'Polaris', from *Afterworlds*. Permission for use granted by the author's family. • 'The Real Enemies', from *The T.E. Lawrence Poems*. Full acknowledgement. Reprinted by permission of the publisher.

DON MCKAY. 'Kestrels', from *Birding, or Desire*. Permission for use granted by Don McKay. • 'Twinflower', 'Short Fat Flicks', and 'to Danceland' from *Apparatus* by Don McKay © 1997. 'Homing' and 'Icarus' from *Another Gravity* by Don McKay © 2000. 'Astonished', 'Petrified', 'Varves', 'Gneiss', and 'Some Last Requests' from *Strike/Slip* by Don McKay © 2006. Published by McClelland & Stewart Ltd. Used with permission of the publisher.

ALISTAIR MACLEOD. 'As Birds Bring Forth the Sun' from *Island: The Collected Stories of Alistair MacLeod* by Alistair MacLeod © 2000. Published by McClelland & Stewart Ltd. Used with permission of the publisher.

DAPHNE MARLATT. 'Imagine a Town', from *Steveston*. Reprinted by permission of Ronsdale Press. • 'Coming Home'. Reprinted by permission of the author. 'Coming Home' first appeared in *What Matters: Writing 1968–70*, a 1980 collection of Daphne Marlatt's poetry published by Coach House Press. • 'winter/rice/tea strain', 'listen' (2001), and '(is love enough)', from *This Tremor Love Is*. Full acknowledgement and reprinted by permission of Talon Books Ltd.

ANNE MICHAELS. 'There is No City That Does Not Dream' and 'Ice House' from *Skin Divers* by Anne Michaels © 1999. 'Lake of Two Rivers' and 'Flowers' from *The Weight of Oranges/Miner's Pond* by Anne Michaels © 1997. Published by McClelland & Stewart Ltd. Used by permission of the publisher. • 'Repairing the Octave', from *Bach and the Muses* (Tafelmusik, 2007).

ROHINTON MISTRY. 'Swimming Lessons' from *Tales from Firozsha Baag* by Rohinton Mistry © 1987. Published by McClelland & Stewart Ltd. Used with permission of the publisher.

LISA MOORE. 'Craving' from *Open* © 2002 by Lisa Moore. Reprinted by permission of House of Anansi Press.

ERIN MOURÉ. 'Blindness' from *Domestic Fuel* © 1985 by Erin Mouré. • 'Miss Chatelaine' from *Furious* © 1992 by Erin Mouré. 'Dream of the Towns' and 'Amygdala' from *Search Procedures* © 1996 by Erin Mouré. 'From Garrison Creek I see the earth to the antipodes of the Universe', 'The Humber is pretty fabulous, really', and 'If at times I claim flowers smile and rivers sing' from *Sheeps' Vigil by a Fervent Person* © 2001 by Erin Mouré. Reprinted by permission of House of Anansi Press. • 'Seebe', from *West South West*. Reprinted by permission of the publisher.

ALICE MUNRO. 'The Progress of Love' from *Selected Stories* by Alice Munro © 1996. Published by McClelland & Stewart Ltd. Used with permission of the publisher.

JOHN NEWLOVE. 'Four Small Scars', 'The Double-Headed Snake', and 'Samuel Hearne in Wintertime', from *The Fat Man*. 'Ride Off any Horizon', from *Black Night Window*. 'The green plain', from *The Green Plain*. 'Like an eel', from *The Tasmanian Devil and Other Poems*. From A Long Continued Argument: The Selected Poems of John Newlove, Ottawa ON: Chaudiere Books, 2007.

bpNICHOL. 'The Sorrows of Saint Orm', from *The Martyrology Books 1&2* (Coach House Books, 1972). 'Section VIII', from *The Martyrology Books 3&4* (Coach House Books, 1976). 'Chain 8', from *The Martyrology Book 5* (Coach House Books, 1982). 'landscape: I' and 'lament', from *Zygal: A Book of Mysteries and Translations* (Coach House Books, 1985).

ALDEN NOWLAN. 'Temptation' from *Bread, Wine, and Salt*. Reprinted by permission of Claudine Nowlan. • 'Country Full of Christmas' from *The Mysterious Naked Man* © 1969 by Alden Nowlan. 'Canadian January Night' from *Between Tears and Laughter* © 1971 by Alden Nowlan. 'The Broadcaster's Poem' from *I'm a Stranger Here Myself* © 1974 by Alden Nowlan. 'On the Barrens' from *Smoked Glass* © 1997 by Alden Nowlan. Reprinted by permission of Anansi Press.

MICHAEL ONDAATJE. 'The Time Around Scars', 'Letters & Other Worlds', 'Pig Glass', 'Light', and 'Sally Chisum/Last Words on Billy the Kid, 4 A.M.', from *There's a Trick with a Knife I'm Learning to Do*. 'The Cinnamon Peeler', 'Lunch Conversations', from *Running in the Family*. 'To a Sad Daughter' from *Secular Love*. 'The Medieval Coast' and 'Wells' from *Handwriting*. By permission of the author.

P.K. PAGE. 'Stories of Snow', 'Photos of a Salt Mine', 'Arras', 'Cry Arrat!', 'Evening Dance of the Grey Flies', 'The Gold Sun', 'Poor Bird', 'Kaleidoscope', 'Unless the Eye Catch Fire . . . ', from *The Hidden Room* (in two volumes) by P.K. Page by permission of the Porcupine's Quill. Copyright © P.K. Page, 1997.

E.J. PRATT, 'The Shark', 'Newfoundland', 'Silences', 'Come Away, Death', 'The Truant', and from *Towards the Last Spike*; and 'The Prize Cat', from *Selected Poems of E.J. Pratt*. Copyright © University of Toronto Press Inc., 2000, reprinted with permission of the publisher.

AL PURDY. 'The Country North of Belleville', 'Tress at the Arctic Circle', 'Wilderness Gothic', 'Lament for the Dorsets', 'At the Quinte Hotel', 'Roblin's Mills (II)', 'Elegy for a Grandfather' [1986], 'For Steve McIntyre (1912–1984)', 'On the Flood Plain', 'Grosse Isle', 'Say the Names', 'A Handful of Earth', and 'The Dead Poet', by Al Purdy, *Beyond Remembering: The Collected Poems of Al Purdy*, Harbour Publishing, 2000. Reprinted by permission of the publisher.

JAMES REANEY. 'The School Globe', 'The Lost Child', 'The Alphabet', 'Starling with a Split Tongue', from *Poems*. Reprinted by permission of the Estate of James Reaney.

MICHAEL REDHILL. 'The Flesh Collectors', excerpted from *Fidelity* by Michael Redhill. Copyright © Caribou River Ltd. 2003. Reprinted by permission of Doubleday Canada.

MORDECAI RICHLER. 'Playing Ball on Hampstead Heath' from *St. Urbain's Horseman* by Mordecai Richler © 2001. Published by McClelland & Stewart Ltd. Used with permission of the publisher.

EDEN ROBINSON. 'Queen of the North', excerpted from *Traplines* by Eden Robinson. Copyright © 1996 by Eden Robinson. Reprinted by permission of Knopf Canada.

HARRY ROBINSON. 'Coyote Challenges God' and 'Indian Doctor', from *Write It On Your Heart*. Full acknowledgement and reprinted by permission of Talon Books Ltd.

SINCLAIR ROSS. 'The Runaway' from *The Lamp at Noon and Other Stories* by Sinclair Ross © 1968. Published by McClelland & Stewart Ltd. Used with permission of the publisher.

F.R. SCOTT. 'The Canadian Authors Meet', 'Trans Canada', 'Lakeshore', 'Poetry', 'W.L.M.K.', and 'All the Spikes But the Last'. Reprinted with the permission of William Toye, literary executor for the Estate of F.R. Scott.

CAROL SHIELDS. 'Hazel', excerpted from *The Orange Fish* by Carol Shields. Copyright © 1989 Carol Shields Literary Trust. Reprinted by permission of Random House Canada.

A.J.M. SMITH. 'The Lonely Land', 'On Reading an Anthology of Popular Poetry', 'Far West', 'Sea Cliff', 'The Wisdom of Old Jelly Roll', 'Business as Usual', and 'Fear as Normal'. Reprinted with the permission of William Toye, literary executor for the Estate of A.J.M. Smith.

RAYMOND SOUSTER. 'The Penny Flute', 'At Split Rock Falls', 'Get the Poem Outdoors', 'Queen Anne's Lace', 'Like the Last Patch of Snow', and 'Trying One On for Size' are reprinted from *Collected Poems of Raymond Souster* by permission of Oberon Press.

MADELEINE THIEN. 'Dispatch' from *Simple Recipes* by Madeleine Thien © 2001. Published by McClelland & Stewart Ltd. Used with permission of the publisher.

JANE URQUHART. 'The Drawing Master' from *Storm Glass* by Jane Urquhart © 1987. Published by McClelland & Stewart Ltd. Used with permission of the publisher.

GUY VANDERHAEGHE. 'Man on Horseback', from *Things As They Are?* by Guy Vanderhaeghe © 1992. Published by McClelland & Stewart Ltd. Used with permission of the publisher.

M.G. VASSANJI. 'Her Two Husbands', excerpted from *When She Was Queen* by M.G. Vassanji. Copyright © 2005 M.G. Vassanji. Reprinted by permission of Doubleday Canada.

FRED WAH. 'Waiting for Saskatchewan', from *Waiting for Saskatchewan* (Turnstone Press, 1985). • From *Diamond Grill*. Reprinted with permission from NeWest Press.

BRONWEN WALLACE. 'Songbirds and Hurtin' Songs', from *Keep that candle burning bright and other poems*. 'Joseph Macleod Daffodils', 'Testimonies', and 'The Watermelon Incident', from *The Stubborn Particulars of Grace*. Reprinted by permission of the Estate of Bronwen Wallace. • 'The Woman In This Poem' by Bronwen Wallace is reprinted from *Signs of the Former Tenant* by permission of Oberon Press. • 'An Easy Life' from *People You'd Trust Your Life To* by Bronwen Wallace © 1990. Published by McClelland & Stewart Ltd. Used with permission of the publisher.

SHEILA WATSON. 'And the Four Animals', from *A Father's Kingdom* © 2004 by Sheila Watson. Published by McClelland & Stewart Ltd. Used with permission of the publishers.

PHYLLIS WEBB. 'Marvell's Garden', 'Suite I', 'Suite II', from *Selected Poems: The Vision Tree*. 'The Making of a Japanese Print', from *Hanging Fire*. 'I Daniel', from *Water and Light: Ghazals and Anti Ghazals*. 'Spots of Blood', from *Wilson's Bowl*. Full acknowledgement and reprinted by permission of Talon Books Ltd.

RUDY WIEBE. 'Where Is the Voice Coming From?', excerpted from *River of Stone* by Rudy Wiebe. Copyright © 1995 Jackpine House Inc. Reprinted by permission of Knopf Canada.

ANNE WILKINSON. 'The Great Winds', 'Winter Sketch', 'Easter Sketches', 'In June and Gentle Oven', and 'Nature Be Damned', from *The Collected Poems of Anne Wilkinson*. Reprinted by permission of the publisher.

ETHEL WILSON. 'The Window', from *Mrs. Golightly and Other Stories* by Ethel Wilson. Copyright © Ethel Wilson, 1961. Reprinted by permission of The University of British Columbia.

JAN ZWICKY. 'The New Room' from *The New Room* (Coach House Press, 1989). 'Bill Evans: Here's That Rainy Day, Transparence', and 'Driving Northwest', from *Songs for Relinquishing the Earth* (Brick Books, 1998). 'String Practice' and 'Robinson's Crossing', from *Robinson's Crossing* (Brick Books, 2004). Reprinted by permission of Brick Books. • 'Study: North', from *Thirty-Seven Small Songs & Thirteen Silences*. Copyright © Jan Zwicky 2005. Reproduced with the permission of Gaspereau Press.

Every effort has been made to contact copyright owners. In the case of any omissions, the publisher will be pleased to make suitable acknowledgment in future editions.

# Index

Age of Lead, The (Atwood), 832–42
All the Spikes But the Last (Scott), 413
Alphabet, The (Reaney), 624–6
Amygdala (Mouré), 1130–3
And the Four Animals (Watson), 480–1
Anglosaxon Street (Birney), 441
Arras (Page), 525–6
Artefacts, The (Livesay), 492–4
As Birds Bring Forth the Sun (MacLeod), 777–82
As Down the Woodland Ways (Roberts), 199
Astonished— (McKay), 914–15
At Split Rock Falls (Souster), 589
At the Cedars (Scott), 251–2
At the Long Sault (Lampman), 246–9
At the Millstone (Crozier), 1017–18
At the Quinte Hotel (Purdy), 576–7
Atwood, Margaret, 810–13
    Age of Lead, The, 832–42
    From *The Journals of Susanna Moodie*, 818–23
    Line, The, 829–32
    Orpheus (2), 828–9
    Progressive Insanities of a Pioneer, 815–17
    Siren Song, 826
    Spelling, 827–8
    This Is a Photograph of Me, 814
    Tricks with Mirrors, 823–5
August (Harris), 784
Autobiographical (Klein), 475–7
Avison, Margaret, 547–8
    Butterfly, The, 548
    Butterfly Bones; or Sonnet Against Sonnets, 553
    Job: Word and Action, 555–65
    Neverness, 549–51
    Perspective, 551–2
    Poetry Is, 565–6
    Snow, 552
    Swimmer's Moment, The, 554
    Tennis, 553
    We the Poor Who Are Always with Us, 554–5

Babstock, Ken, 1223–4
    Compatibilist, 1235–7
    Essentialist, 1231–2
        In Brendan's Boat, 1224–5
        Marsh Theatre, 1226
        Montana Nocturne, 1225–6
        Regenerative, 1227–8
        To Willow, 1228–30
        World's Hub, The, 1233–5
*Backwoods of Canada, The* (Traill), 102–8
Bartok and the Geranium (Livesay), 489–90
Battle of Lundy's Lane, The (Scott), 258–60
Because I Never Learned (Lane), 844
Bill Evans: 'Here's That Rainy Day' (Zwicky), 1139–40
Bird in the Room, The (Pickthall), 386
Birney, Earle, 439–40
    Anglosaxon Street, 441
    Bushed, 446–7
    Can. Lit., 447
    Ebb Begins from Dream, The, 443–4
    El Greco: *Espolio*, 448
    Newfoundland, 449
    Pacific Door, 445–6
    Vancouver Lights, 440–1
Birth of Tragedy, The (Layton), 506–7
Black Sisyphus (Harris), 785–6
Blindness (Mouré), 1123–4
Blue Road, The (Compton), 1240–55
Bök, Christian, 1182–4
    Crystals, 1184–5
    From *Eunoia*, 1186–92
    Vowels, 1192
Book of Isaiah (Carson), 1030–6
*Book of Mercy* (Cohen), 723–4
Bone Flute Breathing (Bringhurst), 1002–5
Bowering, Angela, 742
    From 'Pictures', 749–50
Bowering, George, 740–2
    Grandfather, 742–3
    Great Local Poem, The, 748
    From *Kerrisdale Elegies*, 744–8
    From 'Pictures', 749–50
Brand, Dionne, 1103–5
    I Have Been Losing Roads, 1108–14
    Land to Light On, 1115–17
    From *No Language Is Neutral*, 1105–8
    From thirsty, 1118–21
Bringhurst, Robert, 989–91
    Bone Flute Breathing, 1002–5

Conversations with a Toad, 996–1002
Essay on Adam, 992
Leda and the Swan, 992–4
Reader, The, 995
These Poems, She Said, 994–5
Broadcaster's Poem, The (Nowlan), 715–16
Brooke, Francis, 10–11
    *Letters from The History of Emily Montague*,
      11–27
Bushed (Birney), 446–7
Business as Usual (Smith), 430
Butterfly, The (Avison), 548
Butterfly Bones; or Sonnet Against Sonnets
    (Avison), 553
Butterfly on Rock (Layton), 512

Callaghan, Morley, 432–4
    Watching and Waiting, 434–8
Canada to England (Crawford), 188–90
Canadian Authors Meet, The (Scott), 407–8
Canadian January Night (Nowlan), 714
Can. Lit. (Birney), 447
Campbell, Maria, 886–7
    Jacob, 887–94
Carman, Bliss, 206–7
    Eavesdropper, The, 207–8
    Lord of My Heart's Elation, 209–10
    Low Tied on Grand Pré, 108–9
    Morning in the Hills, 210–11
    World Voice, The, 211
Carson, Anne, 1027–9
    Book of Isaiah, 1030–6
    Short Talk on Rectification, 1029
    Short Talk on Who You Are, 1030
    TV Men: Hektor, 1036–45
Cinnamon Peeler, The (Ondaatje), 939–40
City of the End of Things, The (Lampman),
    242–4
Clarke, George Elliott, 1164–5
    From *Whylah Falls*, 1166–71
    From *Execution Poems*, 1172–3
    George & Rue: Coda, 1174–6
    Mortality Sonnet, 1176
    Nu(is)ance, 1173
    Primitivism, 1171
Clockmaker, The (Haliburton), 98–101
Closing Time (Cohen), 726–7
Coat, The (Lee), 861
Cohen, Leonard, 718–20
    From *Book of Mercy*, 723–4
    Closing Time, 726–7
    Everybody Knows, 724–6
    Looking Through My Dreams, 731

Suzanne, 722–3
Thousand Kisses Deep, 727–30
'truth of the line, the', 730
You Have the Lovers, 720–1
Cold Green Element, The (Layton), 507–8
Come Away, Death (Pratt), 349–50
coming home (Marlatt), 923
Compatibilist (Babstock), 1235–7
Compton, Wade, 1237–40
    Blue Road, The, 1240–55
    Reinventing Wheel, The, 1255–66
Conception of Winter (Harris), 786–7
Conversations with a Toad (Bringhurst),
    996–1002
Country Full of Christmas (Nowlan), 714
Country North of Belleville, The (Purdy),
    569–71
Coyote Challenges God (Robinson), 415–418
Coyote Columbus Story, A (King), 949–53
CPR Station—Winnipeg (Lane), 846
Craving (Moore), 1178–82
Crawford, Isabella Valancy, 146–7
    Canada to England, 188–90
    Esther, 187–8
    Malcolm's Katie, 149–86
    Said the Canoe, 190–2
Crossing, The (Hodgins), 791–7
Crozier, Lorna, 1006–7
    At the Millstone, 1017–18
    Forms of Innocence, 1010–11
    Getting Pregnant, 1011–12
    Ice-fog, 1021
    My Last Erotic Poem, 1022
    Old Order, The, 1014–16
    On the Seventh Day, 1012–1014
    Poem about Nothing, 1008–10
    Sacrifice of Abraham, The, 1020
    Sacrifice of Isaac, The, 1020–1
    From *A Saving Grace: The Collected Poems
      of Mrs. Bentley*, 1018–19
    This One's for You, 1007–8
Cry Ararat! (Page), 521–4
Cry from an Indian Wife, A (Johnson), 227–8
Crystals (Bök), 1184–5
Cut-throat (Lane), 853

Dark Pines under Water (MacEwen), 900–1
Day and Night (Livesay), 484–9
Death of the Loch Ness Monster, The
    (MacEwen), 902–3
Desaparecidos (Lee), 868
*Diamond Grill* (Wah), 872–85
Difference, The (Livesay), 483–4

Dispatch (Thien), 1268–76
Double-Headed Snake, The (Newlove), 800–1
Dream of the Towns (Mouré), 1129–30
Dreams (Findley), 667–81
Driving Northwest (Zwicky), 1143
Duncan, Sara Jeannette, 212–14
    From *The Imperialist*, 214–25

Easter Sketches, Montreal (Wilkinson), 498–500
Easy Life, An (Wallace), 982–9
Eavesdropper, The (Carman), 207–8
Ebb Begins from Dream, The (Birney), 443–4
Elegy for a Grandfather [1986] (Purdy), 580–1
El Greco: *Espolio* (Birney), 448
Elusive Vote, The (McClung), 285–92
Essay on Adam (Bringhurst), 992
Essentialist (Babstock), 1231–2
Esther (Crawford), 187–8
*Eunoia* (Bök), 1186–92
Evening Dance of the Grey Flies (Page), 524
Everybody Knows (Cohen), 724–6
*Execution Poems* (Clarke), 1172–3

Far Field, The (Lane), 851–2
Far West (Smith), 428–9
Fear as Normal (Smith), 430
Fertile Muck, The (Layton), 508–9
Findley, Timothy, 665–6
    Dreams, 667–81
Flesh Collectors, The (Redhill), 1194–1205
Flight of the Crows, The (Johnson), 228–9
Flight of the Geese, The (Roberts), 197
Flowers (Michaels), 1155
For Gwendolyn MacEwen (Lane), 854–5
Forms of Innocence (Crozier), 1010–11
Forsaken, The (Scott), 255–7
For Steve McIntyre (Purdy), 581–2
Four Small Scars (Newlove), 799
14 Descriptions of Trees (Mouré), 1133–5
F.P. Grove: The Finding (Kroetsch), 647–9
Franklin, John, and Dr. John Richardson, 65–7
    From *Narrative of a Journey to the Shores*
        *of the Polar Sea in the Years 1819,*
        *20, 21 and 22,* 67–83
Frogs, The (Lampman), 238–40

Gallant, Mavis, 593–4
    Varieties of Exile, 594–607
George & Rue: Coda (Clarke), 1174–6
Get the Poem Outdoors (Souster), 590
Getting Pregnant (Crozier), 1011–12
Gneiss (McKay), 917–18
Gods, The (Lee), 863–6

Going Over (Roberts), 198–9
Goldsmith, Oliver, 50
    The Rising Village, 51–64
Gold Sun, The (Page), 526–7
Gowdy, Barbara, 1045–6
    Presbyterian Crosswalk, 1046–57
Grandfather (Bowering), 742–3
Great Local Poem, The (Bowering), 748
Great Winds, The (Wilkinson), 496–7
Green Plain, The (Newlove), 807–10
Green Rain (Livesay), 483
Grosse Isle (Purdy), 584–5
Grove, Frederick Philip, 315–17
    Snow (1922), 317–34
    Snow (1932), 335–41

Haliburton, Thomas Chandler, 94–5
    Clockmaker, The, 98–101
    Trotting Horse, The, 96–8
Harris, Claire, 783–4
    August, 784
    Black Sisyphus, 785–6
    Conception of Winter, 786–7
    No God Waits on Incense, 789
    To Dissipate Grief, 787–8
Hazel (Shields), 764–76
Hearne, Samuel, 27–9
    From *A Journey from Prince of Wales's*
        *Fort in Hudson's Bay to the*
        *Northern Ocean*, 29–36
Heat (Lampman), 237–8
Height of Land, The (Scott), 260–4
Heirloom (Klein), 466–7
Her Two Husbands (Vassanji), 1059–68
Hiatus (Lee), 867–8
His Majesty the West Wind (Johnson), 226–7
*History of Emily Montague, The* (Brooke), 11–27
Hodgins, Jack, 790–1
    Crossing, The, 791–7
Homing (McKay), 911
How Betty Sherman Won a Husband
    (Montgomery), 309–14
Hunger (Lee), 866–7

Icarus (MacEwen), 896–8
Icarus (McKay), 912–14
Ice-fog (Crozier), 1021
Ice House (Michaels), 1156–9
I Daniel (Webb), 636–40
I Have Been Losing Roads (Brand), 1108–14
Imagine: a town (Marlatt), 922
*Imperialist, The* (Duncan), 214–25
In an Old Barn (Roberts), 196

In Brendan's Boat (Babstock), 1224–5
Indian Doctor (Robinson), 419–24
In June and Gentle Oven (Wilkinson), 500–1
In November (Lampman), 241–2
(is love enough?) (Marlatt), 927–8

Jacob (Campbell), 887–94
Jameson, Anna Brownell, 84–6
     From *Winter Studies and Summer Rambles*
          *in Canada*, 87–93
Job: Word and Action (Avison), 555–65
Johnson, E. Pauline, 225–6
     Cry from an Indian Wife, A, 228–30
     Flight of the Crows, The, 230–1
     His Majesty the West Wind, 228
     Lost Island, The, 233–5
     Silhouette, 231–2
     Song My Paddle Sings, The, 226–7
     'Through Time and Bitter Distance', 232–3
Joseph Macleod Daffodils (Wallace), 974–7
*Journals of Susanna Moodie, The* (Atwood),
     818–23
*Journey from Prince of Wales's Fort in Hudson's Bay*
     *to the Northern Ocean, A* (Hearne), 29–36

Kaleidoscope (Page), 529–31
Keine Lazarovitch 1870–1959 (Layton), 511
*Kerrisdale Elegies* (Bowering), 744–8
Kestrels (McKay), 906
King, Thomas, 948–9
     Coyote Columbus Story, A, 949–53
Klein, A.M., 462–3
     Autobiographical, 475  7
     Heirloom, 466–7
     Political Meeting, 468–9
     Portrait of the Poet as Landscape, 469–74
     Reb Levi Yitschok Talks to God, 464–6
     Rocking Chair, The, 467–8
Kogawa, Joy, 750–2
     Minerals from Stone, 761–2
     Obasan, 752–7
     Road Building by Pick Axe, 758–61
     Where There's a Wall, 758
Kroetsch, Robert, 645–7
     F.P. Grove: The Finding, 647–9
     Seed Catalogue, 649–65

Labrie's Wife (Scott), 266–77
Lake of Two Rivers (Michaels), 1151–4
Lakeshore (Scott), 409
Lament (Nichol), 969–70
Lament for the Dorsets (Purdy), 574–6

Lampman, Archibald, 235–6
     At the Long Sault, 246–9
     City of the End of Things, The, 243–5
     Frogs, The, 238–40
     Heat, 236–8
     In November, 241–2
     Railway Station, The, 240
     Summer Dream, A, 242
     To a Millionaire, 246
     Voices of Earth, 245
     Winter Evening, 245–6
landscape: I (Nichol), 969
Land to Light On (Brand), 1115–17
Lane, Patrick, 842–3
     Because I Never Learned, 844
     CPR Station—Winnipeg, 846
     Cut-throat, 853
     Far Field, The, 851–2
     For Gwendolyn MacEwen, 854–5
     Long Coyote Line, The, 845
     Sooke Potholes, The, 855–6
     Spoon, The, 853–4
     Stigmata, 844–5
     Weasel, 847
     From *Winter*, 847–51
Laurence, Margaret, 608–9
     To Set Our House in Order, 609–20
Layton, Irving, 504–6
     Birth of Tragedy, The, 506–7
     Butterfly on Rock, 512
     Cold Green Element, The, 507–8
     Fertile Muck, The, 508–9
     Keine Lazarovitch 1870–1959, 511
     Tall Man Executes a Jig, A, 512–15
     Whatever Else Poetry Is Freedom, 509–11
Leacock, Stephen, 293–4
     Marine Excursion of the Knights of
          Pythias, The, 294–307
Leda and the Swan (Bringhurst), 992–4
Lee, Dennis, 857–8
     Coat, The, 861
     Desaparecidos, 868
     Gods, The, 863–6
     Hiatus, 867–8
     Hunger, 866–7
     Sibelius Park, 859–61
     Tale, 869
     When I Went Up to Rosedale, 861–3
     Wordly, 868–9
Letters & Other Worlds (Ondaatje), 931–3
[Life among the Peigans] (Saukamapee), 2–10
Light (Ondaatje), 935–7
Like the Last Patch of Snow (Souster), 589–90

Line, The (Atwood), 829–32
listen (Marlatt), 925–7
Livesay, Dorothy, 481–3
    Artefacts, The, 492–4
    Bartok and the Geranium, 489–90
    Day and Night, 484–9
    Difference, The, 483–4
    Green Rain, 483
    Secret Doctrine of Women, The, 490–2
Lonely Land, The (Smith), 427–8
Long Coyote Line, The (Lane), 845
Looking Through My Dreams (Cohen), 731
Lord of My Heart's Elation (Carman), 209–10
Lost Child, The (Reaney), 623–4
Lost Island, The (Johnson), 233–5
Low Tied on Grand Pré (Carman), 108–9
Lunch Conversation, (Ondaatje) 940–3

McClung, Nellie, 283–4
    Elusive Vote, The, 285–92
MacEwen, Gwendolyn, 895–6
    Dark Pines under Water, 900–1
    Death of the Loch Ness Monster, The,
        902–3
    Icarus, 896–8
    Manzini: Escape Artist, 898–9
    Polaris, 903–4
    Portage, The, 899–900
    Real Enemies, The, 901–2
McKay, Don, 904–5
    Astonished—, 914–15
    Gneiss, 917–18
    Homing, 911
    Icarus, 912–14
    Kestrels, 906
    Petrified—, 915
    Pond, 915–16
    Short Fat Flicks, 908–9
    Some Last Requests, 918–19
    To Danceland, 910
    Twinflower, 907–8
    Varves, 917
MacLeod, Alistair, 776–7
    As Birds Bring Forth the Sun, 777–82
Made in His Image (Pickthall), 387
Making of a Japanese Print, The (Webb),
    640–4
Malcolm's Katie (Crawford), 149–86
Man on Horseback (Vanderhaeghe), 1070–85
Manzini: Escape Artist (MacEwen), 898–9
Marine Excursion of the Knights of Pythias,
    The (Leacock), 294–307

Marlatt, Daphne, 920–2
    coming home, 923
    Imagine: a town, 922
    (is love enough?), 927–8
    listen, 925–7
    winter/ rice/ tea strain, 923–5
Marsh Theatre (Babstock), 1226
Martyrology, The (Nichol), 955–68
Marvell's Garden (Webb), 629–31
Medieval Coast, The (Ondaatje), 945
Michaels, Anne, 1149–50
    Flowers, 1155
    Ice House, 1156–9
    Lake of Two Rivers, 1151–4
    Repairing the Octave, 1159–63
    There Is No City That Does Not Dream,
        1155
Minerals from Stone (Kogawa), 761–2
Miss Chatelaine (Mouré), 1125
Mistry, Rohinton, 1086–7
    Swimming Lessons, 1087–102
Montana Nocturne (Babstock), 1225–6
Montgomery, L.M., 307–9
    How Betty Sherman Won a Husband,
        309–14
Moodie, Susanna, 108–9
    From Roughing It in the Bush, 110–39
Moore, Lisa, 1177–8
    Craving, 1178–82
Morning in the Hills (Carman), 210–11
Mortality Sonnet (Clarke), 1176
Mouré, Erin, 1121–3
    Amygdala, 1130–3
    Blindness, 1123–4
    Dream of the Towns, 1129–30
    14 Descriptions of Trees, 1133–5
    Miss Chatelaine, 1125
    Seebe, 1126–9
    From Sheep's Vigil by a Fervent Person, 1135–7
Mowing, The (Roberts), 196
Munitions! (Sime), 278–82
Munro, Alice, 681–3
    Progress of Love, The, 683–701
My Last Erotic Poem (Crozier), 1022

Naked Poems (Webb), 631–4
Narrative of a Journey to the Shores of the Polar
    Sea in the Years 1819, 20, 21 and 22
    (Franklin and Richardson), 67–83
Narrative of His Explorations in Western North
    America (Thompson), 1784–1812, 38–49
Nature Be Damned (Wilkinson), 501–3

Neverness (Avison), 549–51
Newfoundland (Birney), 449
Newfoundland (Pratt), 344–6
Newlove, John, 798–9
    Double-Headed Snake, The, 800–1
    Four Small Scars, 799
    Green Plain, The, 807–10
    Ride Off Any Horizon, 803–7
    Samuel Hearne in Wintertime, 801–3
New Room, The (Zwicky), 1138–9
Nichol, bp, 953–5
    lament, 969–70
    landscape: I, 969
    From *The Martyrology*, 955–68
Night Hymns on Lake Nipigon (Scott), 254–5
No God Waits on Incense (Harris), 789
*No Language Is Neutral* (Brand), 1105–8
Nowlan, Alden, 712
    Broadcaster's Poem, The, 715–16
    Canadian January Night, 714
    Country Full of Christmas, 714
    On the Barrens, 716–18
    Temptation, 713
Nu(is)ance (Clarke), 1173

Obasan (Kogawa), 752–7
Old Order, The (Crozier), 1014–16
Ondaatje, Michael, 928–30
    Cinnamon Peeler, The, 939–40
    Letters & Other Worlds, 931–3
    Light, 935–7
    Lunch Conversation, 940–3
    Medieval Coast, The, 945
    Pig Glass, 934–5
    Sallie Chisum/Last Words on
        Billy the Kid. 4 A.M., 937–9
    Time Around Scars, The, 930–1
    To a Sad Daughter, 943–5
    Wells, 946–7
Onondaga Madonna, The (Scott), 253
On Reading an Anthology of Popular Poetry
    (Smith), 431
On the Barrens (Nowlan), 716–18
On the Flood Plain (Purdy), 582–4
On the Seventh Day (Crozier), 1012–1014
Orpheus (2) (Atwood), 828–9

Pacific Door (Birney), 445–6
Page, P.K., 516–18
    Arras, 525–6
    Cry Ararat!, 521–4
    Evening Dance of the Grey Flies, 524

    Gold Sun, The, 526–7
    Kaleidoscope, 529–31
    Photos of a Salt Mine, 519–20
    Poor Bird, 527–8
    Stories of Snow, 518–19
    Unless the Eye Catch Fire, 531–46
Penny Flute, The (Souster), 588–9
Perspective (Avison), 551–2
Petrified— (McKay), 915
Photos of a Salt Mine (Page), 519–20
Pickthall, Marjorie, 384–5
    Bird in the Room, The, 386
    Made in His Image, 387
    Sleep-Seekers, The, 385–6
    Third Generation, The, 387–95
'Pictures' (Bowering), 749–50
Pig Glass (Ondaatje), 934–5
Playing Ball on Hampstead Heath (Richler),
    704–11
Poem about Nothing (Crozier), 1008–10
Poetry (Scott), 411
Poetry Is (Avison), 565–6
Polaris (MacEwen), 903–4
Political Meeting (Klein), 468–9
Pond (McKay), 915–16
Poor Bird (Page), 527–8
Portage, The (MacEwen), 899–900
Portrait of the Poet as Landscape (Klein),
    469–74
Pratt, E.J., 341–3
    Come Away, Death, 349–50
    Newfoundland, 344–6
    Prize Cat, The, 348
    Shark, The, 343–4
    Silences, 346–7
    *Towards the Last Spike*, 356–83
    Truant, The, 351–6
Presbyterian Crosswalk (Gowdy), 1046–57
Primitivism (Clarke), 1171
Prize Cat, The (Pratt), 348
Progressive Insanities of a Pioneer (Atwood),
    815–17
Progress of Love, The (Munro), 683–701
Purdy, Al, 567–9
    At the Quinte Hotel, 576–7
    Country North of Belleville, The, 569–71
    Elegy for a Grandfather [1986], 580–1
    For Steve McIntyre, 581–2
    Grosse Isle, 584–5
    Lament for the Dorsets, 574–6
    On the Flood Plain, 582–4
    Roblin's Mills (2), 578–9

Say the Names, 585–6
Trees at the Arctic Circle, 571–2
Wilderness Gothic, 573–4

Queen Anne's Lace (Souster), 590–1
Queen of the North (Robinson), 1207–22

Railway Station, The (Lampman), 236–7
Reader, The (Bringhurst), 995
Real Enemies, The (MacEwen), 901–2
Reaney, James, 620–2
    Alphabet, The, 624–6
    Lost Child, The, 623–4
    School Globe, The, 622–3
    Starling with a Split Tongue, 626–7
Reb Levi Yitschok Talks to God (Klein), 464–6
Redhill, Michael, 1193
    Flesh Collectors, The, 1194–1205
Regenerative (Babstock), 1227–8
Reinventing Wheel, The (Compton), 1255–66
Repairing the Octave (Michaels), 1159–63
Richardson, Dr John, 65–7; see also Franklin,
    John, and Dr John Richardson
Richler, Mordecai, 702–4
    Playing Ball on Hampstead Heath, 704–11
Ride Off Any Horizon (Newlove), 803–7
Rising Village, The (Goldsmith), 51–64
Road Building by Pick Axe (Kogawa), 758–61
Roberts, Charles G.D., 192–4
    As Down the Woodland Ways, 199
    Flight of the Geese, The, 197
    Going Over, 198–9
    In an Old Barn, 196
    Mowing, The, 196
    Skater, The, 197–8
    Tantramar Revisited, 194–5
    Under the Ice-Roof, 200–5
Robinson, Eden, 1206–7
    Queen of the North, 1207–22
Robinson, Harry, 414–15
    Coyote Challenges God, 415–418
    Indian Doctor, 419–24
Robinson's Crossing (Zwicky), 1145–8
Roblin's Mills (2) (Purdy), 578–9
Rocking Chair, The (Klein), 467–8
Ross, Sinclair, 449–51
    Runaway, The, 451–61
Roughing It in the Bush (Moodie), 110–39
Runaway, The (Ross), 451–61

Sacrifice of Abraham, The (Crozier), 1020
Sacrifice of Isaac, The (Crozier), 1020–1

Said the Canoe (Crawford), 190–2
Sallie Chisum/Last Words on Billy the Kid.
    4 A.M. (Ondaatje), 937–9
Samuel Hearne in Wintertime (Newlove), 801–3
Sangster, Charles, 140–1
    From Sonnets Written in the Orillia Woods,
        145–6
    From The St Lawrence and the Saguenay,
        142–5
Saukamapee, 1
    [Life among the Peigans], 2–10
Saving Grace, A (Crozier), 1018–19
Say the Names (Purdy), 585–6
School Globe, The (Reaney), 622–3
Scott, Duncan Campbell, 249–50
    At the Cedars, 251–2
    Battle of Lundy's Lane, The, 258–60
    Forsaken, The, 255–7
    Height of Land, The, 260–4
    Labrie's Wife, 266–77
    Night Hymns on Lake Nipigon, 254–5
    Onondaga Madonna, The, 253
    To a Canadian Aviator Who Died for
        His Country in France, 265
    Watkwenies, 253
Scott, F.R., 406–7
    All the Spikes But the Last, 413
    Canadian Authors Meet, The, 407–8
    Lakeshore, 409
    Poetry, 411
    Trans Canada, 408
    W.L.M.K., 412–13
Sea Cliff (Smith), 429
Secret Doctrine of Women, The (Livesay),
    490–2
Seebe (Mouré), 1126–9
Seed Catalogue (Kroetsch), 649–65
Shark, The (Pratt), 343–4
Sheep's Vigil by a Fervent Person (Mouré), 1135–7
Shields, Carol, 762–4
    Hazel, 764–76
Short Fat Flicks (McKay), 908–9
Short Talk on Rectification (Carson), 1029
Short Talk on Who You Are (Carson), 1030
Sibelius Park (Lee), 859–61
Silences (Pratt), 346–7
Silhouette (Johnson), 231–2
Sime, Jessie Georgina, 276–8
    Munitions!, 278–82
Siren Song (Atwood), 826
Skater, The (Roberts), 197–8
Sleep-Seekers, The (Pickthall), 385–6

Smith, A.J.M., 425–7
    Business as Usual, 430
    Far West, 428–9
    Fear as Normal, 430
    Lonely Land, The, 427–8
    On Reading an Anthology of Popular
        Poetry, 431
    Sea Cliff, 429
    Wisdom of Old Jelly Roll, The, 432
Snow (Avison), 552
Snow (1922) (Grove), 317–34
Snow (1932) (Grove), 335–41
Some Last Requests (McKay), 918–19
Songbirds and Hurtin' Songs (Wallace), 981–2
Song My Paddle Sings, The (Johnson), 230–1
Sonnets Written in the Orillia Woods (Sangster),
    145–6
Sooke Potholes, The (Lane), 855–6
Souster, Raymond, 587–8
    At Split Rock Falls, 589
    Get the Poem Outdoors, 590
    Like the Last Patch of Snow, 589–90
    Penny Flute, The, 588–9
    Queen Anne's Lace, 590–1
    Trying One on for Size, 591–2
Spelling (Atwood), 827–8
Spoon, The (Lane), 853–4
Spots of Blood (Webb), 635–6
Starling with a Split Tongue (Reaney), 626–7
Stigmata (Lane), 844–5
St Lawrence and the Saguenay, The (Sangster),
    142–5
Stories of Snow (Page), 518–19
String Practice (Zwicky), 1143–4
Study: North (Zwicky), 1149
Summer Dream, A (Lampman), 244
Suzanne (Cohen), 722–3
Swimming Lessons (Mistry), 1087–102
Swimmer's Moment, The (Avison), 554

Tale (Lee), 869
Tall Man Executes a Jig, A (Layton), 512–15
Tantramar Revisited (Roberts), 194–5
Temptation (Nowlan), 713
Tennis (Avison), 553
Testimonies (Wallace), 977–9
There Is No City That Does Not Dream
    (Michaels), 1155
These Poems, She Said (Bringhurst), 994–5
Thien, Madeleine, 1267–8
    Dispatch, 1268–76
Third Generation, The (Pickthall), 387–95

thirsty (Brand), 1118–21
This Is a Photograph of Me (Atwood), 814
This One's for You (Crozier), 1007–8
Thompson, David, 37
    From Narrative of His Explorations in
        Western North America, 1784–1812,
        38–49
Thousand Kisses Deep (Cohen), 727–30
'Through Time and Bitter Distance' (Johnson),
    232–3
Time Around Scars, The (Ondaatje), 930–1
To a Canadian Aviator Who Died for His
    Country in France (Scott), 265
To a Millionaire (Lampman), 246
To a Sad Daughter (Ondaatje), 943–5
To Danceland (McKay), 910
To Dissipate Grief (Harris), 787–8
To Set Our House in Order (Laurence), 609–20
Towards the Last Spike (Pratt), 356–83
To Willow (Babstock), 1228–30
Traill, Catharine Parr, 101–2
    From The Backwoods of Canada, 102–8
Trans Canada (Scott), 408
Transparence (Zwicky), 1140–2
Trees at the Arctic Circle (Purdy), 571–2
Tricks with Mirrors (Atwood), 823–5
Trotting Horse, The (Haliburton), 96–8
Truant, The (Pratt), 351–6
'truth of the line, the' (Cohen), 730
Trying One on for Size (Souster), 591–2
TV Men: Hektor (Carson), 1036–45
Twinflower (McKay), 907–8

Under the Ice-Roof (Roberts), 200–5
Unless the Eye Catch Fire (Page), 531–46
Urquhart, Jane, 1023–4
    Drawing Master, The, 1024–7

Vancouver Lights (Birney), 440–1
Vanderhaeghe, Guy, 1069–70
    Man on Horseback, 1070–85
Varieties of Exile (Gallant), 594–607
Varves (McKay), 917
Vassanji, M.G., 1057–9
    Her Two Husbands, 1059–68
Voices of Earth (Lampman), 245
Vowels (Bök), 1192

Wah, Fred, 870–1
    From Diamond Grill, 872–85
    Waiting for saskatchewan, 871–2
Waiting for saskatchewan (Wah), 871–2

Wallace, Bronwen, 970–2
    Easy Life, An, 982–9
    Joseph Macleod Daffodils, 974–7
    Songbirds and Hurtin' Songs, 981–2
    Testimonies, 977–9
    Watermelon Incident, The, 979–81
    Woman in this Poem, The, 972–4
Watching and Waiting (Callaghan), 434–8
Watermelon Incident, The (Wallace), 979–81
Watkwenies (Scott), 253
Watson, Sheila, 478–9
    And the Four Animals, 480–1
Weasel (Lane), 847
Webb, Phyllis, 628–9
    I Daniel, 636–40
    Making of a Japanese Print, The, 640–4
    Marvell's Garden, 629–31
    From Naked Poems, 631–4
    Spots of Blood, 635–6
Wells (Ondaatje), 946–7
We the Poor Who Are Always with Us (Avison),
    554–5
Whatever Else Poetry Is Freedom (Layton),
    509–11
When I Went Up to Rosedale (Lee), 861–3
Where Is the Voice Coming From? (Wiebe),
    734–40
Where There's a Wall (Kogawa), 758
Whylah Falls (Clarke), 1166–71
Wiebe, Rudy, 732–3
    Where Is the Voice Coming From?,
        734–40
Wilderness Gothic (Purdy), 573–4

Wilkinson, Anne, 495–6
    Easter Sketches, Montreal, 498–500
    Great Winds, The, 496–7
    In June and Gentle Oven, 500–1
    Nature Be Damned, 501–3
    Winter Sketch, Rockcliffe, Ottawa, 497–8
Wilson, Ethel, 395–6
    Window, The, 396–405
Window, The (Wilson), 396–405
Winter (Lane), 847–51
Winter Evening (Lampman), 245–6
winter/ rice/ tea strain (Marlatt), 923–5
Winter Sketch, Rockcliffe, Ottawa (Wilkinson),
    497–8
Winter Studies and Summer Rambles in Canada
    (Jameson), 87–93
Wisdom of Old Jelly Roll, The (Smith), 432
W.L.M.K. (Scott), 412–13
Woman in this Poem, The (Wallace), 972–4
Wordly (Lee), 868–9
World's Hub, The (Babstock), 1233–5
World Voice, The (Carman), 211

You Have the Lovers (Cohen), 720–1

Zwicky, Jan, 1137–8
    Bill Evans: 'Here's That Rainy Day', 1139–40
    Driving Northwest, 1143
    New Room, The, 1138–9
    Robinson's Crossing, 1145–8
    String Practice, 1143–4
    Study: North, 1149
    Transparence, 1140–2